Dear Professor:

Special Education in Contemporary Society is first and foremost a textbook about people—individuals who, in many ways, are very similar to their peers without a disability. Second, this book serves as a comprehensive introduction to the dynamic field of special education and the children and young adults who benefit from receiving a special education.

My intention in writing this book is to provide you and your students with a readable, research-based text that also stresses learning in inclusive settings and classroom application. By blending theory with practice, my aim is to provide preservice educators and practicing professionals with the knowledge, skills, attitudes, and beliefs that are so crucial to constructing learning environments that allow *all* students to reach their full potential.

I also want to portray the "human" side of special education. The field of special education is about children and their families—their frustrations and fears—but perhaps more importantly, it is about their accomplishments, successes, and triumphs. To me, special education is real. I personally live with it on a daily basis—it is my passion.

As technology allows us new ways to reach students, we've incorporated a new chapter on assistive technology written by an expert in the field, Emily Bouck, an associate professor at Michigan State University. Today's teachers have the opportunity to embrace technology to create new learning opportunities for students, and the new chapter provides readers with the tools they need.

With my best regards,

Richard

Richard M. Gargiulo

A PEOPLE-FIRST APPROACH

Chapter-opening vignettes in the categorical chapters, primarily written by children with disabilities and their parents, offer personal stories on the exceptionality studied in a specific chapter. Through these vignettes, students gain a firsthand, vivid account of the parents' fears and frustrations, their accomplishments and triumphs, and the issues they face on a daily basis.

6 Individuals With Intellectual Disability

Lauren's Story

Our daughter, Lauren, is an extraordinary child. But she is certainly not an easy child. Sometimes people use the word *exceptional* to describe a child like Lauren, who has Down syndrome.

Jason and I were married when we were both 33 and were ready to have children. I was pregnant with Lauren by the time we celebrated our first anniversary. The delivery of our baby was long and difficult, with some concerns about an irregular heartbeat and a possible emergency cesarean section. Finally, she was born on a Monday afternoon around 5:00. As exhausted as I felt, I was excitedly anticipating holding my new baby. I noticed a nurse looking at the baby and whispering into the doctor's ear. My doctor looked at me and said, "We think the baby has Down's," as they passed Lauren to me. I was stunned for a moment and then asked, "Is it a boy or a girl?" I was only allowed to see my baby girl very briefly, before my husband and the nurse took her to the special care nursery. It was not the moment of joy we had been expecting at the birth of our child. Instead, we were both shocked and divided into our own private worlds of grief.

Even though I was familiar with Down syndrome (due to my training as a special educator), I suddenly felt that I knew nothing. I wanted to be able to hold Lauren because I felt it would help me to make a connection with her. Nothing about her delivery had gone the way we expected, and then I realized that in all the conversations we had before she was born, not one time had we discussed or considered the possibility of a birth defect or any problems.

Lauren's health was a critical issue as I began an endless series of doctor visits with her, making sure to check each possible health complication associated with Down syndrome. Our pediatrician saw Lauren frequently and guided us through the process step by step. Lauren had a very mild heart defect, but it did not require surgery or even medication. Her hearing and vision were normal, except for nystagmus—Lauren's eyes waver from side to side constantly as if she were reading. The ophthalmologist told us this would never go away but it would become less obvious and improve with time. We talked with a geneticist who explained the characteristics of Down syndrome, and we met

VIDEO
Intellectual Disability

LEARNING OBJECTIVES
After reading Chapter 6, you should be able to:

- **Summarize** the key elements of the AAIDD definitions of intellectual disability from 1961 to 2010.
- **Describe** the concepts of intellectual ability and adaptive behavior.
- **Explain** four ways of classifying individuals with intellectual disability.
- **Provide** examples of pre-, peri-, and postnatal causes of intellectual disability.
- **Outline** society's reaction to and treatment of individuals with intellectual disability.
- **Identify** representative learning and social/behavioral characteristics of persons with intellectual disability.
- **Define** *functional curriculum*, *functional academics*, and *community-based instruction*.
- **List** the key features of the following instructional strategies: task analysis, cooperative learning, and scaffolding.
- **Describe** the goals of early intervention for young children with intellectual disability.
- **Characterize** contemporary services for adults with intellectual disability.

Students get more out of first-person case studies and stories than they do out of "facts," so I appreciate the generous use of case studies throughout the text—they put a "face" on the information.

—Jenny Fererro, Palomar College

The **interactive e-book** and our new student and instructor website, **SAGE edge,** includes **video interviews with students, parents, and teachers, as well as video from real special education and inclusive classrooms** created specifically by SAGE for *Special Education in Contemporary Society* in each chapter.

VIDEO

Watch more about planning for transitions.

The **First Person** feature adds a human touch to the information students are learning. These stories, written by or about individuals with exceptionalities or their teachers, provide an up-close and personal encounter with children, adults, and families.

The First Person stories are fabulous ways to engage the students in their reading.

—Jenny Fererro, Palomar College

FIRST PERSON: MATTHEW

Teaching in the Age of Technology

Since graduating with my bachelor's degree in special education, I have worked at an alternative school. My school is a state-accredited residential and day school program that serves students between the ages of 6 and 21 who have learning disabilities and/or emotional behavior disorders and who struggle in a typical school setting, as well as students with intellectual disability, including students with autism spectrum disorder. Our students with learning disabilities and/or emotional behavior disorders are not reading or writing at grade level. For our older students who still struggle with handwriting, pencil grips or weighted

pencils are available. I do see pencil grips benefiting my students. For our younger students who struggle with reading, we take advantage of books on CD or electronic books played through an MP3 player. In my school, we have advanced technology to support students with more intense needs as well. Every classroom has an iPad, and we do use Proloquo2Go® for students with communication needs. Most of our assistive technology needs and decisions for individual students are determined by our occupational therapists or speech-language pathologists. ∎

–Matthew Wright
Program Coordinator
T. C. Harris School
Lafayette, Indiana

Author Richard M. Gargiulo **uses language that focuses on the abilities and assets** of students with exceptionalities throughout the book.

I appreciate the author's person-centered approach and his statement that it is a book about people.

—Douglas E. Carothers, Florida Gulf
Coast University

Students are provided context with **sections on the history of special education in the United States**. Understanding the historical conditions provides students with a foundation for understanding an ever changing and, hopefully, progressive field.

I like the book, especially the historical background, which is missing in so many special education textbooks (that is one of the two major reasons why I chose this textbook for my class).

—Johan W. van der Jagt, Bloomsburg
University of Pennsylvania

TOOLS FOR TODAY

The **Making Inclusion Work** feature highlights special and general educators, offering candid perspectives and practical advice about providing services to students with special needs in inclusive settings.

Suggestions for the Classroom boxes provide instructional strategies, tips, techniques, and other ideas.

*Overall, I like this entire text, but some of **my favorite features in the book are Insights, Suggestions for the Classroom, First Person, Making Inclusion Work, and Effective Instructional Practices.** I teach an Introduction to Special Education course and typically have 60+ students in each class. It can be difficult to create a classroom community and do activities with so many students. However, I find that I often use one of the features I mentioned above as the foundation for **small group discussions and activities**.*

—Penny Cantley, Oklahoma State University

The fifth edition includes **video examples** from inside **inclusive classrooms** so students can see inclusive education in action.

WHAT'S NEW?

A **new chapter on assistive technology** by Emily Bouck guides students through using assistive technology with students with exceptionalities.

Each chapter now utilizes the new **Council for Exceptional Children (CEC) initial level special educator preparation standards**.

This edition **includes the latest from the *Diagnostic and Statistical Manual of Mental Disorders* (DSM-5)** on attention deficit hyperactivity disorder and the new paradigm for classifying individuals with **autism spectrum disorders** as outlined in the DSM-5.

TOOLS YOU CAN USE

SAGE edge™

SAGE provides comprehensive multimedia online resources at **edge.sagepub.com/gargiulo5e**.

SAGE edge Instructor Teaching Site supports teachers by making it easy to integrate quality content and create a rich learning environment for students within a password-protected platform.

Comprehensive Instructor Resources (Password Protected)

- Test banks that provide a diverse range of prewritten options as well as the opportunity to edit any question and/or insert personalized questions to effectively assess students' progress and understanding

- Sample course syllabi for semester and quarter courses that provide suggested models for structuring one's course

- Editable, chapter-specific PowerPoint® slides that offer complete flexibility for creating a multimedia presentation for the course

- Exclusive! Access to full-text SAGE journal articles, including some from the Council for Exceptional Children (CEC) journals, that have been carefully selected to support and expand on the concepts presented in each chapter to encourage students to think critically

- Multimedia content that includes original SAGE videos that appeal to students with different learning styles; interviews with students, parents, and teachers; plus new footage inside inclusive classrooms

- Lecture notes that summarize key concepts by chapter to ease preparation for lectures and class discussions

- A course cartridge that provides easy learning management system (LMS) integration

I was impressed with the existing materials and how they can be used in a face-to-face format as well as online!

—Doug Eicher, Missouri Western State University

SAGE edge for Students provides a personalized approach to help students accomplish their coursework goals in an easy-to-use, open-access learning environment.

Personalized Student Study Site (Open Access)

- Mobile-friendly e-flashcards that strengthen understanding of key terms and concepts

- Mobile-friendly practice quizzes that allow for independent assessment by students of their mastery of course material

- An online action plan including tips and feedback on progress through the course and materials, which allows students to individualize their learning experience

- Chapter summaries with learning objectives that reinforce the most important material

- Web exercises and meaningful web links that facilitate students' use of Internet resources, further exploration of topics, and responses to critical thinking questions

- Exclusive! Access to full-text SAGE journal articles, including some from the Council for Exceptional Children (CEC) journals, that have been carefully selected to support and expand on the concepts presented in each chapter

- Multimedia content that includes original SAGE videos that appeal to students with different learning styles; interviews with students, parents, and teachers; and new footage inside inclusive classrooms

- A Spanish glossary, included as an additional resource to support students working in a Spanish-speaking community

SPECIAL EDUCATION TITLES FROM SAGE AND CORWIN

Richard M. Gargiulo
*Special Education in
Contemporary Society,*
Fifth Edition
978-1-4522-1677-5
©2015

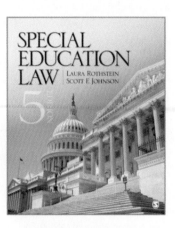

Rothstein/Johnson
Special Education Law,
Fifth Edition
978-1-4522-4109-8
©2014

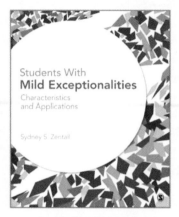

Sydney S. Zentall
*Students With Mild
Exceptionalities*
978-1-4129-7470-7
©2014

Daniels/Patterson/Dunston
*The Ultimate Student
Teaching Guide,*
Second Edition
978-1-4522-9982-2
©2015

Rohrer/Samson
*10 Critical Components for
Success in the Special
Education Classroom*
978-1-4833-3916-0
©2015

Osborne/Russo
*Special Education and
the Law,* Third Edition
978-1-4833-0314-7
©2015

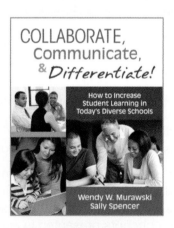

Murawski/Spencer
*Collaborate,
Communicate, and
Differentiate!*
978-1-4129-8184-2
©2011

Kaufman/Wandberg
*Powerful Practices for
High-Performing Special
Educators*
978-1-4129-6807-2
©2010

SPECIAL EDUCATION IN CONTEMPORARY SOCIETY 5e

This book is dedicated to my wife. Thank you for your love, support, and encouragement, and for always believing in me throughout the years. This one's for you, kid.

—RMG
May 2014

SPECIAL EDUCATION IN CONTEMPORARY SOCIETY 5e

AN INTRODUCTION TO EXCEPTIONALITY

RICHARD M. GARGIULO

University of Alabama at Birmingham

Los Angeles | London | New Delhi
Singapore | Washington DC

Los Angeles | London | New Delhi
Singapore | Washington DC

FOR INFORMATION:

SAGE Publications, Inc.
2455 Teller Road
Thousand Oaks, California 91320
E-mail: order@sagepub.com

SAGE Publications Ltd.
1 Oliver's Yard
55 City Road
London, EC1Y 1SP
United Kingdom

SAGE Publications India Pvt. Ltd.
B 1/I 1 Mohan Cooperative Industrial Area
Mathura Road, New Delhi 110 044
India

SAGE Publications Asia-Pacific Pte. Ltd.
3 Church Street
#10–04 Samsung Hub
Singapore 049483

Acquisitions Editor: Theresa Accomazzo
Associate Editor: Jessica Miller
Associate Digital
   Content Editor: Rachael Leblond
Editorial Assistant: Georgia McLaughlin
Production Editors: Brittany Bauhaus
                                 Amy Schroller
Copy Editor: Melinda Masson
Typesetter: C&M Digitals (P) LTD
Proofreaders: Caryne Brown
                         Dennis Webb
Indexer: Karen Wiley
Cover & Interior Designer: Gail Buschman
Marketing Manager: Terra Schultz

Printed in Canada

Library of Congress Cataloging-in-Publication Data

Gargiulo, Richard M.

Special education in contemporary society : an introduction to exceptionality / Richard M. Gargiulo, University of Alabama at Birmingham. — Fifth edition.

pages cm
Includes bibliographical references and index.

ISBN 978-1-4522-1677-5 (pbk. : alk. paper)

1. Special education—United States. I. Title.

LC3981.G37 2014
371.90973—dc23   2014018747

This book is printed on acid-free paper.

MIX
Paper from
responsible sources
FSC® C011825

15 16 17 18 10 9 8 7 6 5 4 3 2

Brief Contents

Detailed Contents

10. Individuals With Autism Spectrum Disorders   327

12. Individuals With Hearing Impairments 399

13. Individuals With Visual Impairments   445

14. Individuals With Physical Disabilities, Health Disabilities, and Related Low-Incidence Disabilities   485

Special Features

Making Inclusion Work

Suggestions for the Classroom

Preface

pecial Education in Contemporary Society is first and foremost a textbook about people—individuals who, in many ways, are very much just like you. Yet these individuals happen to be recognized as exceptional—either as someone with a disability or as someone with unique gifts and talents. Second, this book serves as a comprehensive introduction to the dynamic field of special education and the children and young adults who benefit from receiving a special education. My intention in writing *Special Education in Contemporary Society* was to provide you with a readable, research-based book that also stresses classroom application. By blending theory with practice, my aim was to provide teachers-in-training and practicing professionals with the knowledge, skills, attitudes, and beliefs that are crucial to constructing learning environments that enable all students to reach their potential. I also wanted to portray the "human" side of special education. The field of special education is much more than meetings, forms, legal issues, or specific instructional strategies; it is about children and their families—their frustrations and fears—but perhaps more important, it is also about their accomplishments and triumphs. As a father of four daughters, I have traveled this rocky road. Each of my girls is recognized as exceptional: Three are gifted, and one has a disability. To me, special education is real. I confront it on a daily basis—it is my passion. I hope that by studying this book you, too, will develop an appreciation for and an understanding of the children whose lives you will touch.

Audience

Special Education in Contemporary Society was written for two primary audiences. First are those individuals preparing to become teachers, either general educators or special educators. Second, because meeting the needs of students with exceptionalities is often a shared responsibility, this book is also appropriate for professionals who work with individuals who have special needs. Physical therapists, school psychologists, orientation and mobility specialists, and speech-language pathologists are only a few of the individuals who share in the responsibility of providing an appropriate education.

Organization of the Text

The first five chapters constitute Part I and focus on broad topics affecting all individuals with an exceptionality; these chapters are foundational for the remainder of the book. Chapter 1 introduces the field of special education, providing an overview of important terms, the prevalence of children and young adults with disabilities, and a framework for understanding exceptionality. An overview of important litigation and legislation, the identification and assessment of individual differences, the development of meaningful individualized instructional programs, and the issue of where students with exceptionalities are to be served are addressed in Chapter 2. In Chapter 3 we examine cultural and linguistic diversity and its relationship to exceptionality. Chapter

4 looks at issues confronting the parents and families of individuals with special needs. The final chapter of Part I explores the exciting field of assistive technology and the role it plays in the lives of individuals with exceptionalities.

Part II consists of ten chapters that thoroughly examine particular categories of exceptionality using a life span approach. We will talk about intellectual disability; learning disabilities; attention deficit/hyperactivity disorder (ADHD); emotional and behavioral disorders; autism spectrum disorders; speech and language impairments; hearing impairments; visual impairments; and physical disabilities, health disabilities, and related low-incidence disabilities; we conclude by looking at individuals who are gifted and talented. Despite the diversity of these topics, each chapter follows a fairly consistent format. You will learn definitions, historical information, prevalence, causes, characteristics, assessment techniques, educational considerations, services for young children as well as adults, family issues, diversity, the role of technology, and current trends and controversies. Each chapter in Part II begins with a vignette offering a personal perspective on the exceptionality you will be studying. These stories should remind you that you are learning about real people who confront myriad issues that most individuals will never have to deal with.

Key Features of the Text

In order to make this textbook meaningful, practical, and also enjoyable to read, I have incorporated several distinct features. These learning tools include the following:

- **Chapter-opening vignettes** in the categorical chapters, primarily written by parents of children with disabilities, offer personal stories on the exceptionality studied in a specific chapter. Through these vignettes, students gain a firsthand, vivid account of these parents, their fears and frustrations, their accomplishments and triumphs, and the issues they face on a daily basis.
- **Suggestions for the Classroom** boxes provide instructional strategies, tips, techniques, and other ideas.
- The **Insights** feature contains relevant information that adds depth and insight to particular discussion topics.
- The **First Person** feature adds a human touch to the information students are learning. These stories, written by or about individuals with exceptionalities, provide an up-close and personal encounter with children, adults, and families.
- The **Making Inclusion Work** feature highlights special and general educators offering candid perspectives and practical advice about providing services to students with special needs in inclusive settings.
- Each chapter concludes with **study questions** designed to help you focus on key chapter content and gauge your understanding of the material.
- A series of **learning activities** brings the content to life. Many of these suggested activities ask you to engage in a wide variety of meaningful and worthy tasks.
- Additionally, you will find a **list of professional organizations and associations** that you may wish to contact for additional information about a topic of particular interest.

New to This Edition

In addition to its key hallmarks, the fifth edition incorporates the following features and content:

Additions Found Throughout the Book

- References have been completely revised and updated to reflect the most current thinking in the field.
- Updated or new tables and figures portray current information.
- Learning Objectives at the beginning of each chapter guide the reader to the most important points to be gleaned from the chapter.
- End-of-chapter key terms include the page number where the term is initially introduced.
- Each chapter now utilizes the new Council for Exceptional Children (CEC) initial level special educator preparation standards.
- A glossary of key terms in Spanish is available on the website and in the e-book edition.

Chapter-Specific Additions

- Chapter 5, "Assistive Technology," is new to this edition and provides the most current ideas on using assistive technology with individuals with exceptionalities.
- Chapter 8 reflects the latest thinking found in the fifth edition of the *Diagnostic and Statistical Manual of Mental Disorders* (DSM-5) on ADHD.
- Chapter 10, "Individuals With Autism Spectrum Disorders," incorporates the new paradigm for classifying individuals on the spectrum as outlined in the DSM-5.
- Appendix B has been redesigned so that chapter content is aligned with the new CEC teacher preparation standards.

Ancillaries

SAGE edge offers a robust online environment featuring an impressive array of tools and resources for review, study, and further exploration, keeping both instructors and students on the cutting edge of teaching and learning. SAGE edge content is open access and available on demand. Learning and teaching have never been easier!

edge.sagepub.com/gargiulo5e

SAGE edge for Students provides a personalized approach to helping students accomplish their coursework goals in an easy-to-use learning environment.

- Mobile-friendly **e-flashcards** strengthen understanding of key terms and concepts.
- Mobile-friendly practice **quizzes** allow for independent assessment by students of their mastery of course material.
- A customized online **action plan** includes tips and feedback on progress through the course and materials, which enables students to individualize their learning experience.
- **Multimedia content** includes original SAGE videos that appeal to students with different learning styles.
- *Exclusive!* Full-text **SAGE journal, handbook, and encyclopedia articles** have been carefully selected to support and expand on the concepts presented in each chapter.
- Links to a sample **individualized education program (IEP)**, a sample **individualized family service plan (IFSP)**, and state-specific **special education standards** are provided for easy access.

SAGE edge for Instructors supports teaching by making it easy to integrate quality content and create a rich learning environment for students.

- **Microsoft Word and Diploma test banks** provide a diverse range of prewritten options as well as the opportunity to edit any question and/or insert personalized questions to effectively assess students' progress and understanding.
- **Sample course syllabi** for semester and quarter courses provide suggested models for structuring one's course.
- Editable, chapter-specific **PowerPoint® slides** offer complete flexibility for creating a multimedia presentation for the course.
- *Exclusive!* Full-text **SAGE journal, handbook, and encyclopedia articles** have been carefully selected to support and expand on the concepts presented in each chapter to encourage students to think critically.
- **Multimedia content** includes original SAGE videos that appeal to students with different learning styles.
- **Lecture notes** summarize key concepts by chapter to ease preparation for lectures and class discussions.
- Classroom activities and discussion questions reinforce active learning.
- A **course cartridge** provides easy learning management system (LMS) integration.

Acknowledgments

Writing a textbook is a team effort, and this one is no exception. I owe a huge debt of gratitude to several friends and colleagues who shared my vision for this book and were also gracious enough to contribute their talents and expertise by writing chapters. I wish to publicly thank them for their hard work, dedicated effort, and patience with my compulsive behavior and attention to detail.

- Emily Bouck, Michigan State University, "Assistive Technology"
- Betty Nelson, University of Alabama at Birmingham, "Individuals With Hearing Impairments"
- Carol Allison and Mary Jean Sanspree, previously affiliated with the University of Alabama at Birmingham, "Individuals With Visual Impairments"
- Kathy Wolff Heller, Georgia State University, "Individuals With Physical Disabilities, Health Disabilities, and Related Low-Incidence Disabilities"
- Julia Link Roberts, Western Kentucky University, "Individuals Who Are Gifted and Talented"

I am especially grateful to the following individuals who reviewed the fifth edition of this book. Their guidance and professional expertise, eye for accuracy, and thoughtful suggestions contributed immensely to making the fifth edition of *Special Education in Contemporary Society* a market leader. I applaud and deeply appreciate the generous assistance of the following individuals: Norma Blecker, Richard Stockton College of New Jersey; Penny Cantley, Oklahoma State University; Douglas E. Carothers, Florida Gulf Coast University; Doug Eicher, Missouri Western State University; Richard A. Evans Jr., Angelo State University; Jenny Fererro, Palomar College; and Leah M. Herner-Patnode, The Ohio State University at Lima.

I would also like to acknowledge the individuals who reviewed the fourth edition of the book: Julie R. Alexandrin, University of South Maine; Rahul Ganguly, Kent State University; Teresa Gardner, Jacksonville State University; Jennifer Lancaster, St. Francis College; and Karen A. Vuurens, South Texas College.

I would also like to thank those professionals who reviewed the third edition: J'Anne Affeld, Northern Arizona University; Mark Alter, New York University; Michele Augustin, Washington University in St. Louis; Emiliano C. Ayala, Sonoma State University; Pam Baker, George Mason University; Andrew Beigel, Keuka College; Kristin Bewick, Wilkes University; Cheryl Camenzuli, Molloy College; Domenico Cavaiuolo, East Stroudsburg University; Walter Cegelka, St. Thomas University; Patricia Morris Clark, University of Maine at Augusta; Jo Beth DeSoto, Wayland Baptist University; Beverly Doyle, Creighton University; Teresa Gardner, Jacksonville State University; Heather Garrison, East Stroudsburg University; Annette Gorton, Miles Community College; Janice Grskovic, Indiana University Northwest; Robert Harrington, University of Kansas; Thienhuong Hoang, California State Polytechnic University, Pomona; Jack Hourcade, Boise State University; Sheila Dove Jones, Bloomsburg University of Pennsylvania; Juanita Kasper, Edinboro University of Pennsylvania; Donna Kearns,

University of Central Oklahoma; Craig Kennedy, Vanderbilt University; Ava Kleinmann, Western New England College; Michelle LaRocque, Florida Atlantic University; Marcel Lebrun, Plymouth State University; DeAnn Lechtenberger, Texas Tech University; Diane K. Mann, Edinboro University of Pennsylvania; Maria L. Manning, James Madison University; Nancy Marchand-Martella, Eastern Washington University; Teresa Oettinger Montani, Fairleigh Dickinson University; Rita Mulholland, Richard Stockton College of New Jersey; Charolette Myles-Nixon, University of Central Oklahoma; Kimberely Fletcher Nettleton, Morehead State University; Ashley A. Northam, Chemeketa Community College; Holly Pae, University of South Carolina Upstate; Lee R. Pearce, Black Hills State University; Nicole Phillips, Daemen College and Frontier Central School District; Shaila Rao, Western Michigan University; Saleem Rasheed, Indiana University Northwest; Bruce A. Shields, Daemen College; Dale Smith, Alvernia College; Angela Snyder, Virginia Commonwealth University; Terry Spigner, University of Central Oklahoma; David W. Steitz, Nazareth College of Rochester; Suzanne Swift, Eastern New Mexico University; Ron Tinsley, Richard Stockton College of New Jersey; Sheila Marie Trzcinka, Indiana University Northwest; Tandra Tyler-Wood, University of North Texas; Linda B. Walker, Kent State University; Ronald P. Weitzner, Cleveland State University; Julia Wilkins, St. Cloud State University; Denise Winsor, University of Nevada, Las Vegas; Penelope Wong, Centre College; Ann K. Yehle, University of Wisconsin–Madison; and Cheryl Zaccagnini, Shippensburg University.

I had the privilege of working with an outstanding and very talented team of professionals at SAGE Publications, who took my jumbled ideas, poor sentence structure, and sometimes inaccurate references and turned them into a superb and scholarly book. Thank you for your support, enthusiasm, and confidence in me.

I will always be grateful for the encouragement, visionary leadership, professionalism, and good humor of my first editor, Diane McDaniel. Diane's enthusiasm for this project and her editorial creativity and competency are clearly evident throughout this book. A huge debt of gratitude is also due to Theresa Accomazzo, my acquisitions editor. Terri always made me feel as though no other book was more important than mine. Her insightful suggestions, attention to the smallest of details, "no problem" attitude, and ability to deal with my compulsiveness, along with her pleasant demeanor, made my job so much easier. Terri is priceless. Lucy Berbeo was another key member of "Team Gargiulo." Lucy served as my primary contact person throughout the evolution of this book. She saw that critical deadlines were met, responded to countless e-mails and telephone calls, helped secure permissions, and ensured that this textbook actually made it to print. I also wish to acknowledge the invaluable contribution of Melinda Masson, a copy editor par excellence. Thank you, Melinda, for noticing the slightest of inconsistencies, catching my grammatical errors and omissions, and helping to produce a stylistically accurate and reader-friendly book. It was a pleasure to work with someone with exceedingly high standards and a desire for perfection. Caryne Brown and Dennis Webb are proofreaders with the eyes of an eagle. I appreciate your attention to the smallest of details. The creativity and impressive artistic talents of Gail Buschman are clearly evident throughout the text. This book definitely "pops," it will be the envy of countless authors largely due to Gail's efforts. Finally, a huge thank you to Brittany Bauhaus and Amy Schroller for producing a well designed, engaging, and aesthetically attractive book. Your collective ability to beautifully integrate text, photos, tables, figures, and features is truly remarkable and deeply appreciated. I am very grateful to all of the players on "Team Gargiulo."

So many other individuals, many of whom labored behind the scenes, also contributed to the development of a book of which I am very proud to be the author. I deeply appreciate the dedicated efforts of those who created the supplemental materials for the SAGE edge site, including Abigail Baxter at University of South Alabama, Nancy Burton at Concord University, Laura Geraci at SUNY Fredonia, and Erika Diaz.

One other group of professionals whose contributions add a very practical perspective to this book are the educators who willingly shared their experiences and insights about working in inclusive settings: Susan Brennan, Brooke Bunn, Lisa Cranford, Catherine Davis, Erin de Haven, Astrid Freeman, Tonya Perry, Sarah Reynolds, Teresea Teaff, and Jennifer J. Tumlin. Thank you for sharing your expertise with the readers.

I would be remiss if I did not honor and praise those individuals who contributed to the First Person features and the chapter-opening vignettes. A very special thank-you for telling your story. The ability of each and every one of you to poignantly share an aspect of your lives added immensely to the "human side" of this text—a goal that I hope I achieved.

Finally, a very special acknowledgment is reserved for my family, who survived my 3 A.M. wake-up calls; struggled with my attempts at balancing the roles of husband, father, and author; and also understood why this book was personally so very important to me. Thank you. I love you dearly.

A Special Thank You to Our Filming Participants

We would like to express our gratitude to the teachers and administrators who graciously allowed us to film their schools and classrooms. The video footage includes instructional activities in inclusive and special education classrooms, as well as interviews with teachers.

CHIME Institute's Schwarzenegger Community School:

- Jennifer Hill, Director of Curriculum and Instruction
- Adie Buchinsky, Special Education Teacher, Kindergarten and 1st grade
- Jessica Leonard, General Education Teacher, 4th grade
- Katie Palacios, General Education Teacher, Kindergarten
- Angela Rinnert, General Education Teacher, 1st grade
- Aparna Tyagi, Special Education Teacher, Kindergarten
- Michael Young, Special Education Teacher, 4th grade
- Natalie Melanson, General Education Teacher, 4th grade

Triton Academy:

- Kristen Hardy, Principal
- Robert DeCandia, Special Education Teacher
- Nathan Dybvig, Special Education Teacher
- Denise Pannell, Special Education Teacher
- Adam Underberger, Special Education Teacher

Ventura High School:

- Brett Taylor, Principal, Ventura County Office of Education
- Beth Underberger, Special Education Teacher

The exciting footage from these classrooms, along with other exclusive SAGE content, and can be found at:

edge.sagepub.com/gargiulo/5e

Look for these icons throughout the text **VIDEO** to see when there is a video that corresponds with the text!

PART

I

Foundations of Special Education

> "We know that equality of individual ability has never existed and never will, but we do insist that equality of opportunity still must be sought."
>
> —Franklin D. Roosevelt
> Thirty-second President of the United States

Special Education in Context
People, Concepts, and Perspectives

We are all different. It is what makes us unique and interesting human beings. Some differences are obvious, such as our height, the color of our hair, or the size of our nose. Other features are not so readily discernible, such as our reading ability or political affiliation. Of course, some characteristics are more important than others. Greater significance is generally attached to intellectual ability than to shoe size. Fortunately, appreciation of individual differences is one of the cornerstones of contemporary American society.

Although most people would like to be thought of as "normal" or "typical" (however defined), for millions of children and young adults this is not possible. They have been identified and labeled by schools, social service agencies, and other organizations as exceptional, thus requiring special educational services. This textbook is about these individuals who are exceptional.

You are about to embark on the study of a vibrant and rapidly changing field. Special education is an evolving profession with a long and rich heritage. The past few decades in particular have been witness to remarkable events and changes. It is truly an exciting time to study human exceptionality. You will be challenged as you learn about laws and litigation affecting students with special needs, causes of disability, assessment techniques, and instructional strategies, to mention only a few of the topics we will present. But perhaps more important than any of these issues is our goal to help you develop an understanding and appreciation for a person with special needs. We suspect that you will discover, as we have, that individuals with disabilities are more like their typically developing peers than they are different from them. People with disabilities and those without disabilities share many similarities. In fact, we believe that special education could rightly be considered the study of similarities as well as differences.

Finally, we have adopted a people-first perspective when talking about individuals with disabilities. We have deliberately chosen to focus on the person, not the disability or specific impairment. Thus, instead of describing a child as "an autistic student," we say "a pupil with autism." This style reflects more than just a change in word order; it reflects an attitude and a belief in the dignity and potential of people with disabilities. The children and adults whom you will learn about are first and foremost people.

LEARNING OBJECTIVES

After reading Chapter 1, you should be able to:

- **Define** exceptional children, disability, handicapped, developmentally delayed, at risk, and special education.
- **Identify** the thirteen disability categories recognized by the federal government.
- **Distinguish** between prevalence and incidence.
- **Describe** the historical evolution of services for children and adults with disabilities.
- **List** the related services sometimes required by students with disabilities.
- **Outline** the differences between multi-, inter-, and transdisciplinary team models.
- **Describe** common instructional models of cooperative teaching.
- **Identify** key dimensions of universal design for learning.
- **Explain** the services typically available to infants/toddlers, preschoolers, adolescents, and adults with disabilities.

VIDEO
Changing Language

Definitions and Terminology

Teachers work with many different types of pupils. Let's take a look at some of the children in the fifth-grade class of Daniel Thompson, a first-year teacher. As in many other classrooms across the United States, most of his students are considered to be educationally typical; yet five youngsters exhibit special learning needs. Eleven-year-old Victoria, for instance, is a delightful young girl with a bubbly personality who is popular with most of her classmates. She has been blind since birth, however, as a result of a birth defect. Miguel is shy and timid. He doesn't voluntarily interact with many of his classmates. This is his first year at Jefferson Elementary. Miguel's family only recently moved into the community from their previous home in Mexico. Mr. Thompson tells us that one boy is particularly disliked by the majority of his classmates. Jerome is verbally abusive, is prone to temper tantrums, and on several occasions has been involved in fights on the playground, in the lunchroom, and even in Mr. Thompson's classroom despite the fact that his teacher is a former college football player. Mr. Thompson suspects that Jerome, who lives with his mother in a public housing apartment, might be a member of a local gang. Stephanie is teased by most of her peers. Although many of her classmates secretly admire her, Stephanie is occasionally called "a nerd," "a dork," or "Einstein." Despite this friendly teasing, Stephanie is always willing to help other students with their assignments and is sought after as a partner for group learning activities. The final student with special learning needs is Robert. Robert is also teased by his fellow pupils, but for reasons opposite to Stephanie. Robert was in a serious automobile accident when he was in kindergarten. He was identified as having cognitive delays in the second grade. Sometimes his classmates call him "a retard" or "Dumbo" because he asks silly questions, doesn't follow class rules, and on occasion makes animal noises that distract others. Yet Robert is an exceptional athlete. All his classmates want him on their team during gym class.

As future educators, you may have several questions about some of the students in Mr. Thompson's classroom:

- Why are these pupils in a general education classroom?
- Will I have students like this in my class? I'm going to be a high school biology teacher.
- Are these children called disabled, exceptional, or handicapped?
- What does *special education* mean?
- How will I know if some of my students have special learning needs?
- How can I help these pupils?

One of our goals in writing this textbook is to answer these questions as well as address other concerns you may have. Providing satisfactory answers to these queries is not an easy task. Even among special educators, confusion, controversy, and honest disagreement exist about certain issues. As you continue to read and learn, acquire knowledge and skill, and gain experience with individuals with disabilities, we hope you will develop your own personal views and meaningful answers.

Exceptional Children

Both general and special educators will frequently refer to their students as exceptional children. This inclusive term generally refers to individuals who differ from societal or community standards of normalcy. These differences may be due to significant physical, sensory, cognitive, or behavioral characteristics. Many

exceptional children: Children who deviate from the norm to such an extent that special educational services are required.

of these children may require educational programs customized to their unique needs. For instance, a youngster with superior intellectual ability may require services for students identified as gifted; a child with a visual impairment may require textbooks in large print or Braille. However, we need to make an important point. Just because a pupil is identified as exceptional does not automatically mean that he or she will require a special education. In some instances, the student's educational needs can be met in the general education classroom by altering the curriculum and/or instructional strategies.

Children with disabilities are first and foremost children.

We must remember that exceptionality is always relative to the social or cultural context in which it exists. As an illustration, the concept of normalcy, which forms an important part of our definition of exceptionality, depends on the reference group (society, peers, family) as well as the specific circumstances. Characteristics or behaviors that might be viewed as atypical or abnormal by a middle-aged school administrator might be considered fairly typical by a group of high school students. Normalcy is a relative concept that is interpreted or judged by others according to their values, attitudes, and perceptions. These variables, along with other factors such as the culture's interpretation of a person's actions, all help to shape our understanding of what it is to be normal. Is it normal:

- To use profanity in the classroom?
- For adolescent males to wear earrings or shave their head?
- To run a mile in less than four minutes?
- To study while listening your MP3 player?
- To always be late for a date?
- To stare at the floor when reprimanded by a teacher?
- To be disrespectful to authority figures?
- To wear overly large, yet stylish, clothes?

The answer, of course, is that it all depends.

Disability Versus Handicap

On many occasions, professionals, as well as the general public, will use the terms *disability* and *handicap* interchangeably. This is incorrect. These terms, contrary to popular opinion, are not synonymous but have distinct meanings. When talking about a child with a disability, teachers are referring to an inability or a reduced capacity to perform a task in a specific way. A disability is a limitation imposed on an individual by a loss or reduction of functioning, such as the paralysis of leg muscles, the absence of an arm, or the loss of sight. It can also refer to problems in learning. Stated another way, a disability might be thought of as an incapacity to perform as other children do because of some impairment in sensory, physical, cognitive, or other areas of functioning. These limitations become disabilities only when they interfere with a person's attainment of his or her educational, social, or vocational potential.

disability: An inability or incapacity to perform a task or activity in a normative fashion.

REFERENCE
Handicap Defined

The term handicap refers to the impact or consequence of a disability, not the condition itself. In other words, when we talk about handicaps, we mean the problems or difficulties that a person with a disability encounters as he or she attempts to function and interact with the environment. We would like to extend this definition and suggest that a handicap is more than just an environmental limitation; it also can reflect attitudinal limitations imposed on the person with the disability by people without disabilities.

Individuals with disabilities often encounter various forms of discrimination in their daily lives, which frequently limits their full participation in society. As a result, some would suggest that these citizens are "marginalized and excluded from mainstream society" (Kitchin, 1998, p. 343). Sadly, in some ways, this is an accurate portrayal of contemporary life in the United States despite the ongoing efforts of activists and the disability rights movement, which seeks to end discrimination on the basis of disabilities. In fact, the term handicapism was coined more than three decades ago to describe the unequal and differential treatment experienced by those with a disability (Bogdan & Biklen, 1977).

A disability may or may not be a handicap, depending on specific circumstances and how the individual adapts and adjusts. An example should help clarify the differences between these two concepts. Laura, a ninth grader who is mathematically precocious, uses a wheelchair because of a diving accident. Her inability to walk is not a problem in her calculus class. Architectural barriers at her school, however, do pose difficulties for her. She cannot access the water fountain, visit the computer lab on the second floor, or use the bathroom independently. When describing Laura in these situations, we would be correct in calling her handicapped. It is important that professionals separate the disability from the handicap.

Gargiulo and Kilgo (2014) remind us that an individual with a disability is first and foremost a person, a student more similar to than different from his or her typically developing classmates. The fact that a pupil has been identified as having a disability should never prevent us from realizing just how typical he or she is in many other ways. As teachers, we must focus on the child, not the impairment; separate the ability from the disability; and see the person's strengths rather than weaknesses. The accompanying First Person feature provides an example of this thinking. Also see Suggestions for the Classroom (page 9) when writing about or discussing individuals with disabilities.

Developmentally Delayed and At Risk

Before we can answer the question "What is special education?" we have two more terms to consider: *developmentally delayed* and *at risk*. These labels are incorporated in federal legislation (PL 99–457 and PL 108–446, discussed in Chapter 2) and are usually used when referring to infants and preschoolers with problems in development, learning, or other areas of functioning. Although these terms are incorporated into our national laws, Congress failed to define them, leaving this responsibility to the individual states. As you can imagine, a great deal of diversity can be found in the various interpretations, and no one definition is necessarily better than another. The result is the identification of a very heterogeneous group of youngsters.

Each state has developed specific criteria and measurement procedures for ascertaining what constitutes a developmental delay. Many states have chosen to define a developmental delay quantitatively, using a youngster's performance on standardized developmental assessments. In one state, a child might be described as being delayed if her performance on a standardized test is at least 25 percent below the

handicap: Difficulties imposed by the environment on a person with a disability.

handicapism: The unequal and differential treatment accorded individuals with a disability.

developmental delay: A term defined by individual states referring to children ages 3 to 9 who perform significantly below developmental norms.

FIRST PERSON: ELIZABETH

Perceptions and Impressions

As a woman in my early 40s with cerebral palsy, I can readily reflect on how I am perceived by those who are not disabled. I was born with cerebral palsy, which affects my motor skills. I contend that it is much easier to be born with a disability than to acquire one later in life—I don't know what it is like to be "normal."

I am very blessed in being more independent than I ever dreamed would be possible! I drive an unadapted car, work part-time for a law firm, and live alone with help from a wonderful outside support team. I'm active in my church and in community affairs, serving on the board of the Independent Living Center, as well as in other activities. I'm a member of a local United Cerebral Palsy sports team. As you can see, not much grass grows under my feet!

Throughout my life, I have encountered many and varied reactions to my disability. Some people see me as a person who happens to be disabled. It is wonderful to be around them. They accept me as "Elizabeth." Yes, my speech is, at times, difficult to understand. Yes, I'm in constant motion. But these people see me first and can look beyond my disability, many times forgetting it. I am able to be myself!

When I do need assistance, all I have to do is ask. I have a strong family pushing me to be as independent as possible. I'm grateful to my stepfather, who said, "You can do it!" My mother, afraid I might fall, was hesitant but supportive. My siblings have been great encouragers. I have many friends who are able to see beyond my disability.

I have also met people who have not been around individuals with physical disabilities. I can easily spot those who are uncomfortable around me. Sometimes, after being around me for a while, they may get used to me and then feel quite comfortable. In fact, when people ask me to say something again, rather than nodding their heads pretending to understand me, it shows that they care enough about what I said to get it right.

From those who feel uncomfortable around me, I usually get one of two reactions: "Oh, you poor thing!" or "You're such an inspiration—you're a saint to have overcome cerebral palsy!" I realize people mean well, but I see right through their insecurities. Think about some of their comments. I'm not a "thing," I'm an individual. I have the same thoughts, dreams, and feelings as anyone else.

Many times I am perceived as being mentally retarded, even though I have a college degree. When I'm in a restaurant, my friend may be asked, "What does she want?" One day I was getting into the driver's seat of my car, and a lady inquired, "Are you going to drive that car?" I kept quiet, but I thought, "No, it will drive itself!" Recently, while flying home from Salt Lake City, the flight attendant asked my friend if I understood how the oxygen worked. I chuckled to myself. I have been flying for over thirty years! Furthermore, my former roommate had lived with an oxygen tank for three years, and we were constantly checking the flow level. (In defense of airlines, I must say that I have been treated with great respect.)

For those who say I am an inspiration, I can respond in one of two ways. I can take the comment as a sincere compliment and genuinely say, "Thank you." On the other hand, I can see it as an off-the-cuff remark. Those who say that I inspire them may be thinking, "I'm glad I'm not like her" or "Boy, she goes through so much to be here." As I stated earlier, I do things differently, and it takes me longer. But I have learned to be patient and the importance of a sense of humor. I am very grateful to have accomplished as much as I have. ■

SOURCE: E. Ray, personal communication.

mean for children of similar chronological age in one or more developmental areas, such as motor, language, or cognitive ability. In another state, the determination is made when a preschooler's score on an assessment instrument is two or more standard deviations below the mean for youngsters of the same chronological age. Each approach has its advantages and disadvantages. What is really important, however, is that the pupil be identified and receive the appropriate services (Gargiulo & Kilgo, 2014).

Contemporary thinking suggests that students with disabilities should be educated in the most normalized environment.

The use of the broad term *developmentally delayed* is also in keeping with contemporary thinking regarding the identification of young children with disabilities. Because of the detrimental effects of early labeling, the Individuals with Disabilities Education Act (PL 101–476), commonly referred to as IDEA, permits states to use the term *developmentally delayed* when discussing young children with disabilities. In fact, PL 105–17, the 1997 reauthorization of this law, allows the use of this term, at the discretion of the state and local education agency, for children ages 3 through 9. We believe, as other professionals do, that the use of a specific disability label for young children is of questionable value. Many early childhood special education programs offer services without categorizing children on the basis of a disability. We believe this approach is correct.

When talking about children who are at risk, professionals generally mean individuals who, although not yet identified as having a disability, have a high probability of manifesting a disability because of harmful biological, environmental, or genetic conditions. Environmental and biological factors often work together to increase the likelihood of a child's exhibiting disabilities or developmental delays. Exposure to adverse circumstances *may* lead to future difficulties and delays in learning and development, but it is not guaranteed that such problems will present themselves. Many children are exposed to a wide range of risks, yet fail to evidence developmental problems. Possible risk conditions include low birth weight, exposure to toxins, child abuse or neglect, oxygen deprivation, and extreme poverty, as well as genetic disorders such as Down syndrome or PKU (phenylketonuria).

Special Education

When a student is identified as being exceptional, a special education is sometimes necessary. Recall that just because the student has a disability does *not* mean that a special education is automatically required. A special education is appropriate only when a pupil's needs are such that he or she cannot be accommodated in a general education program. Simply stated, a special education is a customized instructional program designed to meet the unique needs of an individual learner. It may necessitate the use of specialized materials, equipment, services, and/or teaching strategies. For example, an adolescent with a visual impairment may require books with larger print; a pupil with a physical disability may need specially designed chairs and work tables; a student with a learning disability may need extra time to complete an exam. In yet another instance, a young adult with cognitive impairments may benefit from a cooperative teaching arrangement involving one or more general educators along with a special education teacher. Special education is but one component of a complex service delivery system crafted to assist the individual in reaching his or her full potential.

A special education is not limited to a specific location. Contemporary thinking requires that services be provided in the most natural or normalized environment appropriate for the particular student. Such settings might include the local Head Start

at risk: An infant or child who has a high probability of exhibiting delays in development or developing a disability.

special education: Specially designed instruction to meet the unique needs of an individual recognized as exceptional.

VIDEO

Special Education

SUGGESTIONS FOR THE CLASSROOM

Suggestions for Communicating About Individuals With Disabilities

As a teacher, you are in a unique position to help shape and mold the attitudes and opinions of your students, their parents, and your colleagues about individuals with disabilities. Please consider the following points when writing about or discussing people with disabilities:

→ **Do not focus on a disability** unless it is crucial to a story. Avoid tear-jerking human interest stories about incurable diseases, congenital impairments, or severe injury. Focus instead on issues that affect the quality of life for those same individuals, such as accessible transportation, housing, affordable health care, employment opportunities, and discrimination.

→ **Do not portray successful people with disabilities as superhuman**. Even though the public may admire superachievers, portraying people with disabilities as superstars raises false expectations that all people with disabilities should achieve at this level.

→ **Do not sensationalize a disability** by saying "afflicted with," "crippled with," "suffers from," or "victim of." Instead, say "person who has multiple sclerosis" or "man who had polio."

→ **Put people first**, not their disability. Say "a youngster with autism," "the teenager who is deaf," or "people with disabilities." This puts the focus on the individual, not his or her particular functional limitation.

→ **Emphasize abilities**, not limitations. For example, say "uses a wheelchair/braces" or "walks with crutches," rather than "is confined to a wheelchair," "is wheelchair bound," or "is crippled." Similarly, do not use emotional descriptors such as *unfortunate* or *pitiful*.

→ **Avoid euphemisms** in describing disabilities. Some blind advocates dislike *partially sighted* because it implies avoiding acceptance of blindness. Terms such as *handicapable, mentally different, physically inconvenienced,* and *physically challenged* are considered condescending. They reinforce the idea that disabilities cannot be dealt with up front.

→ **Do not equate disability with illness**. People with disabilities can be healthy, though they may have chronic diseases such as arthritis, heart disease, and diabetes. People who had polio and experienced aftereffects have postpolio syndrome; they are not currently experiencing the active phase of the virus. Also, do not imply disease if a person's disability resulted from anatomical or physiological damage (for example, a person with spina bifida). Finally, do not refer to people with disabilities as patients unless their relationship with their doctor is under discussion, or if they are referenced in the context of a clinical setting.

→ **Show people with disabilities as active participants** in society. Portraying persons with disabilities interacting with nondisabled people in social and work environments helps break down barriers and open lines of communication.

SOURCE: Adapted from *Guidelines: How to Write and Report About People with Disabilities*, Research and Training Center on Independent Living, University of Kansas, Lawrence.

---

program for preschoolers with disabilities, a self-contained classroom in the neighborhood school for children with hearing impairments, or a special high school for students who are academically gifted or talented. Many times a special education can be delivered in a general education classroom.

Finally, if a special education is to be truly beneficial and meet the unique needs of students, teachers must collaborate with professionals from other disciplines who provide **related services**. Speech-language pathologists, social workers, and occupational therapists are only a few of the many professionals who complement the work of general and special educators. Related services are an integral part of a student's special education; they allow the learner to obtain benefit from his or her special education.

related services: Services defined by federal law whose purpose is to assist a student with exceptionalities in deriving benefit from a special education.

Before leaving this discussion of definitions and terminology, we believe it is important to reiterate a point we made earlier. Individuals with disabilities are more like their typical peers than they are different from them. Always remember to see the person, not the disability, and to focus on what people can do rather than what they can't do. It is our hope that as you learn about people with disabilities, you will develop a greater understanding of them, and from this understanding will come greater acceptance.

Categories and Labels

Earlier we defined a person with exceptionalities as someone who differs from a community's standard of normalcy. Students identified as exceptional may require a special education and/or related services. Many of these pupils are grouped or categorized according to specific disability categories. A category is nothing more than a label assigned to individuals who share common characteristics and features. Most states, in addition to the federal government, identify individuals receiving special education services according to discrete categories of exceptionality. Public Law (PL) 108–446 (the Individuals with Disabilities Education Improvement Act of 2004) identifies the following thirteen categories of disability:

- Autism
- Deaf-blindness
- Developmental delay
- Emotional disturbance
- Hearing impairments including deafness
- Intellectual disability
- Multiple disabilities
- Orthopedic impairments
- Other health impairments
- Specific learning disabilities
- Speech or language impairments
- Traumatic brain injury
- Visual impairments including blindness

The federal government's interpretation of these various disabilities is presented in Appendix A. Individual states frequently use these federal definitions to construct their own standards and policies as to who is eligible to receive a special education.

Notably absent from the preceding list are individuals described as gifted or talented. These students are correctly viewed as exceptional, although they are not considered individuals with disabilities; nevertheless, most states recognize the unique abilities of these pupils and provide a special education.

In the following chapters, we will explore and examine the many dimensions and educational significance of each of these categories. It is important to remember, however, that although students may be categorized as belonging to a particular group of individuals, each one is a unique person with varying needs and abilities.

category: Label assigned to individuals who share common characteristics and features.

Table 1.1 **The Advantages and Disadvantages of Labeling Individuals With Special Needs**

Advantages	Disadvantages
• Labels serve as a means for funding and administering education programs.	• Labels can be stigmatizing and may lead to stereotyping.
• Teacher certification programs and the credentialing process are frequently developed around specific disability categories (e.g., intellectual disabilities, hearing impairment).	• Labeling has the potential of focusing attention on limitations and what a person cannot do instead of on the individual's capabilities and strengths.
• Labels allow professionals to communicate efficiently in a meaningful fashion.	• Labels can sometimes be used as an excuse or a reason for delivering ineffective instruction (e.g., "Marvin can't learn his multiplication facts because he is intellectually disabled").
• Research efforts frequently focus on specific diagnostic categories.	
• Labels establish an individual's eligibility for services.	• Labels can contribute to a diminished self-concept, lower expectations, and poor self-esteem.
• Treatments, instruction, and support services are differentially provided on the basis of a label (e.g., sign language for a student who is deaf, an accelerated or enriched curriculum for pupils who are gifted and talented).	• Labels are typically inadequate for instructional purposes; they do not accurately reflect the educational or therapeutic needs of the individual student.
• Labels heighten the visibility of the unique needs of persons with disabilities.	• Labeling can lead to reduced opportunities for normalized experiences in school and community life.
• Labels serve as a basis for counting the number of individuals with disabilities and thus assist governments, schools, agencies, and other organizations in planning for the delivery of needed services.	• A label can give the false impression of the permanence of a disability; some labels evaporate upon leaving the school environment.
• Advocacy and special interest groups, such as the Autism Society of America or the National Federation of the Blind, typically have an interest in assisting particular groups of citizens with disabling conditions.	

The entire issue of categorizing, or labeling, individuals with disabilities has been the subject of controversy. Labeling, of course, is an almost inescapable fact of life. How would you label yourself? Do you consider yourself a Democrat or a Republican? Are you overweight or thin, Christian or non-Christian, and liberal or conservative? Depending on the context, some labels may be considered either positive or negative. Labels may be permanent, such as *cerebral palsy*, or temporary, such as *college sophomore*. Regardless, labels are powerful, biasing, and frequently filled with expectations about how people should behave and act.

Labels, whether formally imposed by psychologists or educators or casually applied by peers, are capable of stigmatizing and, in certain instances, penalizing children. Remember your earlier school days? Did you call any of your classmates "a retard," "Four-Eyes," "Fatso," "a geek," or "a nerd"? Were these labels truly valid? Did they give a complete and accurate picture of the person, or did the teasing and taunting focus only on a single characteristic? The labels we attach to people and the names we call them can significantly influence how individuals view themselves and how others in the environment relate to them.

Special educators have been examining the impact of labels on children for many years; unfortunately, the research evidence is not clear-cut, and it is difficult to draw consistent conclusions (Bicard & Heward, 2010; Ysseldyke, Algozzine, & Thurlow, 1992). The information gleaned from a variety of studies is frequently inconclusive, contradictory, and often subject to methodological flaws. Kliewer and Biklen (1996) perhaps best capture this state of affairs when they note that labeling or categorizing certain youngsters is a demeaning process frequently contributing to stigmatization

AUDIO
Labels

and leading to social and educational isolation; on the other hand, a label may result in a pupil's receiving extraordinary services and support.

Despite the advantages of labeling children (see Table 1.1), we, like many of our colleagues in the field of special education, are not ardent supporters of the labeling process. We find that labeling too often promotes stereotyping and discrimination and may be a contributing factor to exclusionary practices in the educational and social arenas. Hobbs (1975) commented, many years ago, that labeling erects artificial boundaries between children while masking their individual differences. Reynolds and his colleagues (Reynolds, Wang, & Walberg, 1987), who strongly oppose labeling pupils with special needs, astutely observe that "the boundaries of the categories [*intellectual disability* is a good illustration] have shifted so markedly in response to legal, economic, and political forces as to make diagnosis largely meaningless" (p. 396). Some professionals (Cook, 2001; Harry & Klingner, 2007) are of the opinion that labeling actually perpetuates a flawed system of identifying and classifying students in need of special educational services.

One of our biggest concerns is that the labels applied to children often lack educational relevance. Affixing a label to a child, even if accurate, is not a guarantee of better services. Rarely does a label provide instructional guidance or suggest effective management tactics. We are of the opinion that the delivery of instruction and services should be matched to the needs of the child rather than provided on the basis of the student's label. This thinking has led to calls for noncategorical programs constructed around student needs and common instructional requirements instead of categories of exceptionality. These programs focus on the similar instructional needs of the pupils rather than the etiology of the disability. Although noncategorical programs are gaining in popularity, it is still frequently necessary to classify students on the basis of the severity of their impairment—for example, mild/moderate or severe/profound.

Prevalence of Children and Young Adults With Disabilities

How many children and adolescents are identified as exceptional and have special needs? Before answering this question we must clarify two key terms frequently encountered when describing the number of individuals with disabilities.

Statisticians and researchers often talk about *incidence* and *prevalence*. Technically speaking, incidence refers to a rate of inception, or the number of *new* instances of a disability occurring within a given time frame, usually a year. As an illustration, it would be possible to calculate the number of infants born with Down syndrome between January 1 and December 31, 2015, in a particular state. This figure would typically be expressed as a percentage of the total number of babies born within the prescribed period of time; for example, 20 infants with Down syndrome out of 15,000 births would yield an incidence rate of .133 percent. Prevalence refers to the *total* number of individuals with a particular disability existing in the population at a given time. Prevalence is expressed as a percentage of the population exhibiting this specific exceptionality—for instance, the percentage of pupils with learning disabilities enrolled in special education programs during the current school year. If the prevalence of learning disabilities is estimated to be 5 percent of the school-age population, then we can reasonably expect about 50 out of every 1,000 students to evidence a learning disability. Throughout this text, we will report prevalence figures for each area of exceptionality that we study. Of course, establishing accurate estimates of prevalence is based on our ability to gather specific information about the number of individuals with disabilities across the United States. Obviously, this is not an easy job. Fortunately, the federal government has assumed this responsibility. Each year the

noncategorical: Programs developed based on student needs and common instructional requirements rather than on disability.

incidence: A rate of inception; number of new cases appearing in the population within a specific time period.

prevalence: The total number of individuals in a given category during a particular period of time.

Number of Students Ages 6–21 Receiving a Special Education During School Year 2011–2012

Disability	Number	Percent of Total
Specific learning disabilities	2,357,533	40.71%
Speech or language impairments	1,071,555	18.50%
Intellectual disability	431,152	7.44%
Emotional disturbance	371,600	6.41%
Multiple disabilities	125,150	2.16%
Hearing impairments	69,312	1.19%
Orthopedic impairments	54,410	0.93%
Other health impairments	734,348	12.68%
Visual impairments	25,704	0.44%
Autism	407,214	7.03%
Deaf-blindness	1,378	0.02%
Traumatic brain injury	24,886	0.42%
Developmental delay	115,642	1.99%
Total	5,789,884	100.00%

NOTE: Table based on data from the fifty states, Puerto Rico, the District of Columbia, and outlying areas.

SOURCE: U.S. Department of Education. (2013). *Historical state-level IDEA files*. Retrieved November 13, 2013, from http://tadnet.public.tadnet.org/pages/712

Department of Education issues a report (*Annual Report to Congress on the Implementation of the Individuals with Disabilities Education Act*) on the number of children receiving a special education. These data are based on information supplied by the individual states.

Number of Children and Young Adults Served

Approximately 5.8 million U.S. students (5,789,884) between the ages of 6 and 21 were receiving a special education during the 2011–2012 school year (U.S. Department of Education, 2013a). The number of students in each of the thirteen disability categories recognized by the federal government is recorded in Table 1.2 (see this page, above). Learning disabilities account for about four out of every ten pupils with disabilities (40.71%); students with dual sensory impairments (deaf-blindness) represent the smallest category of exceptionality (.02%). Figure 1.1 visually presents the percentages of students with various disabilities receiving a special education.

With the passage of PL 99–457 (the Education of the Handicapped Act Amendments of 1986, currently referred to as IDEA), services for infants, toddlers, and preschoolers with special needs have significantly increased. This first major amendment to PL 94–142 was enacted because more than half the states did not require special education services for preschoolers with disabilities (Koppelman, 1986). PL 99–457 remedied this situation by mandating that youngsters between 3 and 5 years of age receive the same educational services and legal protections as their school-age counterparts, or else states

REFERENCE
Youth and Disability

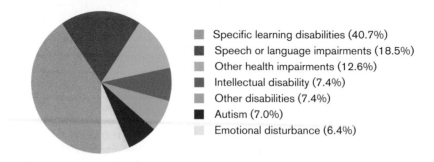

- Specific learning disabilities (40.7%)
- Speech or language impairments (18.5%)
- Other health impairments (12.6%)
- Intellectual disability (7.4%)
- Other disabilities (7.4%)
- Autism (7.0%)
- Emotional disturbance (6.4%)

NOTE: Percents based on data from the fifty states, Puerto Rico, the District of Columbia, and outlying areas.

Other disabilities include multiple disabilities, hearing impairments, orthopedic impairments, visual impairments, deaf-blindness, traumatic brain injury, and developmental delay.

SOURCE: U.S. Department of Education. (2013). *Historical state-level IDEA files.* Retrieved November 13, 2013, from http://tadnet. public.tadnet.org/pages/712

would risk the loss of significant federal financial support. Full compliance with this mandate was finally achieved during the 1992–1993 school year. During the 2011–2012 school year, approximately 746,000 preschoolers with special needs were receiving services under Part B of IDEA (U.S. Department of Education, 2013a). By way of comparison, approximately 399,000 youngsters were served during the 1990–1991 school year (U.S. Department of Education, 1992). This growth translates into an 87 percent increase in the number of preschoolers receiving a special education.

Infants and toddlers with disabilities—that is, youngsters from birth through age 2—also benefited from PL 99–457. Part C of IDEA, which addresses this population, does *not* require that early intervention services be provided. Instead, states were encouraged, via financial incentives, to develop comprehensive and coordinated programs for these youngsters and their families. All states have met this challenge, and almost 337,000 infants and toddlers were the recipients of services as of the fall of 2011 (U.S. Department of Education, 2013a).

You may have noticed that, throughout this discussion, we have failed to present any data concerning individuals who are gifted and talented. This was not an oversight. Federal legislation does *not* require that the states provide a special education for these students. Unfortunately, not all states mandate a special education for children identified as gifted and talented. As of the 2006 school year, almost 3.3 million children and young adults were identified as gifted and talented and receiving a special education (National Center for Education Statistics, 2011b). If these students were included in the overall federal calculation of pupils with exceptionalities, this group of learners would rank as the largest.

A Brief History of the Development of Special Education

The history of special education can perhaps best be characterized as one of evolving or changing perceptions and attitudes about individuals with disabilities. Generally speaking, at any given time, the programs, resources, and practices that affect citizens with disabilities are a reflection of the current social climate. As people's ideas and beliefs about exceptionality change, so do services and opportunities. A transformation in attitude is frequently a prerequisite to a change in the delivery of services.

Pioneers of Special Education

The foundation of contemporary U.S. societal attitudes toward individuals with disabilities can be traced to the efforts of various European philosophers, advocates, and humanitarians. These dedicated reformers and pioneering thinkers were catalysts for change. Educational historians typically trace the beginnings of special education to the late eighteenth and early nineteenth centuries.

One of the earliest documented attempts at providing a special education were the efforts of the French physician Jean-Marc Gaspard Itard (1774–1838) at educating 12-year-old Victor, the so-called "wild boy of Aveyron." According to folklore, Victor was discovered by a group of hunters in a forest near the town of Aveyron. When found, he was unclothed, was without language, ran but did not walk, and exhibited animal-like behavior (Lane, 1979). Itard, an authority on diseases of the ear and teaching youngsters with hearing impairments, endeavored in 1799 to "civilize" Victor. He attempted to teach Victor through a sensory training program and what today would be called behavior modification. Because this adolescent failed to fully develop language after five years of dedicated and painstaking instruction, and only mastered basic social and self-help skills, Itard considered his efforts a failure. Yet he successfully demonstrated that learning was possible even for an individual described by his contemporaries as a hopeless and incurable idiot. The title *Father of Special Education* is rightly bestowed on Itard because of his groundbreaking work 200 years ago.

Another influential pioneer was Itard's student Edouard Seguin (1812–1880). He developed instructional programs for youngsters whom many of his fellow professionals believed to be incapable of learning. Like his mentor Itard, Seguin was convinced of the importance of sensorimotor activities as an aid to learning. His methodology was based on a comprehensive assessment of the student's strengths and weaknesses coupled with a carefully constructed plan of sensorimotor exercises designed to remediate specific disabilities. Seguin also realized the value of early education; he is considered one of the first early interventionists. Seguin's ideas and theories, which he described in his book *Idiocy: And Its Treatment by the Physiological Method*, provided a basis for Maria Montessori's later work with the urban poor and children with intellectual disability.

The work of Itard, Seguin, and other innovators of their time helped to establish a foundation for many contemporary practices in special education. Examples of these contributions include individualized instruction, the use of positive reinforcement techniques, and a belief in the capability of all children to learn.

The Europe of the 1800s was a vibrant and exciting place, filled with idealism and fresh ideas about equality and freedom. It also gave birth to new concepts and approaches to educating individuals with disabilities, which eventually found their way to North America. In 1848, for example, Seguin immigrated to the United States, where in later years he helped establish an organization that was the forerunner of the American Association on Intellectual and Developmental Disabilities. American reverend Thomas Hopkins Gallaudet (1787–1851) traveled to Europe, where he studied the latest techniques and innovations for teaching children who were deaf. Upon his return, he was instrumental in helping establish the Connecticut Asylum for the Education and Instruction of Deaf and Dumb Persons in Hartford, Connecticut. This facility, founded in 1817, was the first residential school in the United States and is currently known as the American School for the Deaf. Gallaudet University, a liberal arts college devoted to the education of students with hearing impairments, is named in honor of his contributions.

VIDEO
**History of
Special Education**

REFERENCE
**History of
Special Education**

Table 1.3 summarizes the work of some of the progressive European and American thinkers and activists whose ideas and convictions have significantly influenced the development of special education in the United States.

The Establishment of Institutions

By the middle of the nineteenth century, several institutions—commonly referred to as asylums, or sometimes as "schools"—were established to benefit citizens with disabilities. These facilities provided primarily protective care and management rather than treatment and education (Gargiulo & Kilgo, 2014). Typically, these early efforts were established by enlightened individuals working in concert with concerned professionals. They were frequently supported financially by wealthy benefactors and philanthropists rather than state governments. Some states, however, mainly in the Northeast, began to support the development of institutions by the middle of the nineteenth century. Such efforts were seen as an indication of the state's progressive stature. At this time, there was no federal aid for individuals with disabilities.

By the end of the nineteenth century, residential institutions for persons with disabilities were a well-established part of the American social fabric. Initially established to provide training and some form of education in a protective and lifelong environment, they gradually deteriorated in the early decades of the twentieth century for a variety of reasons, including overcrowding and a lack of fiscal resources. The mission of institutions also changed from training to custodial care and isolation. The early optimism that had initially characterized the emerging field of special education was replaced by prejudice, unwarranted scientific views, and fears, slowly eroding these institutions into gloomy warehouses for the forgotten and neglected (Meisels & Shonkoff, 2000).

Special Education in the Public Schools

It was not until the second half of the nineteenth century and the early years of the twentieth century that special education classes began to appear in public schools. Services for children with exceptionalities began sporadically and slowly, serving only a very small number of individuals who needed services. Of course, during this era, even children without disabilities did not routinely attend school. An education at this time was a luxury; it was one of the benefits of being born into an affluent family. Many children, some as young as 5 or 6, were expected to contribute to their family's financial security by laboring in factories or working on farms. Being able to attend school was truly a privilege. It is against this backdrop that the first special education classes in public schools were established. Examples of these efforts are listed in Table 1.4.

The very first special education classrooms were **self-contained**; students were typically grouped together and segregated from the other pupils. The majority of their school day was spent with their teacher in a classroom isolated from the daily activities of the school. In some instances, even lunch and recess provided no opportunity for interacting with typical classmates. This type of arrangement characterized many special education classrooms for the next fifty years or so.

After World War II, the stage was set for the rapid expansion of special education. Litigation, legislation, and leadership at the federal level, coupled with political activism and parental advocacy, helped to fuel the movement. Significant benefits for children with exceptionalities resulted from these efforts. In 1948, only about 12 percent of children with disabilities were receiving an education appropriate to their needs (Ballard, Ramirez, & Weintraub, 1982). From 1947 to 1972, the number of pupils enrolled in special education programs increased by an astonishing 716 percent, compared with an 82 percent increase in total public school enrollment (Dunn, 1973).

self-contained: A separate classroom for children with disabilities, usually found in a public school.

The Individuals	Their Ideas
Jacob Rodrigues Pereire (1715–1780)	Introduced the idea that persons who were deaf could be taught to communicate. Developed an early form of sign language. Provided inspiration and encouragement for the work of Itard and Seguin.
Philippe Pinel (1745–1826)	A reform-minded French physician who was concerned with the humanitarian treatment of individuals with mental illness. Advocated releasing institutionalized patients from their chains. Pioneered the field of occupational therapy. Served as Itard's mentor.
Jean-Marc Gaspard Itard (1774–1838)	A French doctor who secured lasting fame because of his systematic efforts to educate an adolescent thought to have a severe intellectual disability. Recognized the importance of sensory stimulation.
Thomas Hopkins Gallaudet (1787–1851)	Taught children with hearing impairments to communicate through a system of manual signs and symbols. Established the first institution for individuals with hearing impairments in the United States.
Samuel Gridley Howe (1801–1876)	An American physician and educator accorded international fame because of his success in teaching individuals with visual and hearing impairments. Founded the first residential facility for individuals who are blind and was instrumental in inaugurating institutional care for children with intellectual disability.
Dorothea Lynde Dix (1802–1887)	A contemporary of S. G. Howe, Dix was one of the first Americans to champion better and more humane treatment of individuals who are mentally ill. Instigated the establishment of several institutions for individuals with mental disorders.
Louis Braille (1809–1852)	A French educator, himself blind, who developed a tactile system of reading and writing for people who were blind. His system, based on a cell of six embossed dots, is still used today. This standardized code is known as Standard English Braille.
Edouard Seguin (1812–1880)	A pupil of Itard, Seguin was a French physician responsible for developing teaching methods for children with intellectual disability. His training emphasized sensorimotor activities. After immigrating to the United States, he helped to found an organization that was the forerunner of the American Association on Intellectual and Developmental Disabilities.
Francis Galton (1822–1911)	A scientist concerned with individual differences. As a result of studying eminent persons, he believed that genius is solely the result of heredity. Those with superior abilities are born, not made.
Alexander Graham Bell (1847–1922)	A pioneering advocate of educating children with disabilities in public schools. As a teacher of students with hearing impairments, Bell promoted the use of residual hearing and developing the speaking skills of students who are deaf.
Alfred Binet (1857–1911)	A French psychologist who constructed the first standardized developmental assessment scale capable of quantifying intelligence. The original purpose of this test was to identify students who might profit from a special education and not to classify individuals on the basis of ability. Binet also originated the concept of mental age with his student Theodore Simon.
Maria Montessori (1870–1952)	Achieved worldwide recognition for her pioneering work with young children and youngsters with intellectual disability. First female to earn a medical degree in Italy. Expert in early childhood education. Demonstrated that children are capable of learning at a very early age when surrounded with manipulative materials in a rich and stimulating environment. Believed that children learn best by direct sensory experience.
Lewis Terman (1877–1956)	An American educator and psychologist who revised Binet's original assessment instrument. The result was the publication of the Stanford-Binet Scale of Intelligence in 1916. Terman developed the notion of intelligence quotient, or IQ. Also famous for lifelong study of gifted individuals. Considered the grandfather of gifted education.

Year	City	Disability Served
1869	Boston, MA	Deafness
1878	Cleveland, OH	Behavioral disorders
1896	Providence, RI	Intellectual disability
1898	New York, NY	Slow learners
1899	Chicago, IL	Physical impairments
1900	Chicago, IL	Blindness
1901	Worcester, MA	Giftedness
1910	Chicago, IL	Speech impairment

Beginning in the mid-1970s and continuing to the present time, children with disabilities have secured the right to receive a free and appropriate public education provided in the most normalized setting. An education for these students is no longer a privilege; it is a right guaranteed by both federal and state laws and reinforced by judicial interpretation. We will talk about some of these laws and court cases in the next chapter. Special education over the past thirty-five years can perhaps best be seen as a gradual movement from isolation to participation, one of steady and progressive inclusion. (See the accompanying Insights feature.)

Professionals Who Work With Individuals With Exceptionalities

It is very common for teachers to work with professionals from other disciplines. A special education may require the expertise of other individuals outside the field of education. Recall our earlier definition of a special education, which incorporates this idea and the concept of related services. IDEA, in fact, mandates that educational assessments of a student's strengths and needs be multidisciplinary and that related services be provided to meet the unique requirements of each learner. Examples of related services include:

- Audiology
- Interpreting services
- Medical services
- Nutrition
- Occupational therapy
- Orientation and mobility
- Parent counseling
- Physical therapy
- Psychology
- Recreational therapy
- Rehabilitation counseling
- School nurse services
- Speech and language

At one time education was a privilege, not a right.

- Social work
- Transportation
- Vocational education

Related services are neither complete nor exhaustive, and additional services—such as assistive technology devices or interpreters for pupils with hearing impairments—may be required if a student is to benefit from a special education. The issue of what constitutes a related service, however, has generated some controversy among educators and school administrators. Disagreements are also common as to what kinds of services should be provided by the public schools and which services are rightfully the responsibilities of the child's parent(s).

There is a growing recognition of the importance of professionals working together regardless of the different disciplines they may represent. No one discipline or profession possesses all of the resources or clinical skills needed to construct the appropriate interventions and educational programs for children and young adults with disabilities, a large number of whom have complex needs. Although the idea of professionals working together in a cooperative fashion has been part of special education since the enactment of PL 94–142 over thirty-five years ago, we have not always been successful in implementing this idea. Obstacles range from poor interpersonal dynamics, to concerns about professional turf, to the lack of planning time, to the absence of administrative

VIDEO

Advice for Future Teachers

A Timeline of Key Dates in the History of Special Education in the United States

1817   Rev. Thomas Hopkins Gallaudet becomes principal of the Connecticut Asylum for the Education and Instruction of Deaf and Dumb Persons, the first residential school in the United States.

1829   Samuel Gridley Howe establishes the New England Asylum for the Blind.

1834   Louis Braille publishes the Braille code.

1839   First teacher training program opens in Massachusetts.

1848   Samuel Gridley Howe establishes the Massachusetts School for Idiotic and Feeble Minded Children.

1848   Dorothea Lynde Dix calls attention to the shocking conditions of American asylums and prisons.

1869   First public school class for children with hearing impairments opens in Boston.

1876   Edouard Seguin helps organize the first professional association concerned with intellectual disability, a predecessor of today's American Association on Intellectual and Developmental Disabilities.

1897   National Education Association establishes a section for teachers of children with disabilities.

1898   Elizabeth Farrell, later to become the first president of the Council for Exceptional Children, begins a program for "backwards" or "slow learning" children in New York City.

1904   Vineland Training School in New Jersey inaugurates training programs for teachers of students with intellectual disability.

1916   Lewis Terman publishes the Stanford-Binet Scale of Intelligence.

1920   Teachers College, Columbia University, begins a training program for teachers of pupils who are gifted.

1922   Organization that later would become the Council for Exceptional Children is founded in New York City.

1928   Seeing Eye dogs for individuals with blindness are introduced in the United States.

1936   First compulsory law for testing the hearing of school-age children is enacted in New York.

1949   United Cerebral Palsy association is founded.

1950   National Association for Retarded Children is founded (known today as The Arc of the United States or simply The Arc).

1953   National Association for Gifted Children is founded.

1963   Association for Children with Learning Disabilities (forerunner to Learning Disabilities Association of America) is organized.

1972   Wolf Wolfensberger introduces the concept of normalization, initially coined by Bengt Nirje of Sweden, to the United States.

1973   Public Law 93–112, the Vocational Rehabilitation Act of 1973, is enacted; Section 504 prohibits discrimination against individuals with disabilities.

1975   Education for All Handicapped Children Act (PL 94–142) is passed; landmark legislation ensures, among other provisions, a free and appropriate public education for all children with disabilities.

1986   Education of the Handicapped Act Amendments of 1986 (PL 99–457) are enacted; mandate a special education for preschoolers with disabilities and incentives for providing early intervention services to infants and toddlers.

1990   Americans with Disabilities Act (PL 101–336) becomes law; prohibits discrimination on the basis of disability.

1990   PL 101–476, the Individuals with Disabilities Education Act (commonly known as IDEA), is passed; among other provisions, emphasizes transition planning for adolescents with disabilities.

1997   Individuals with Disabilities Education Act (PL 105–17) is reauthorized, providing a major retooling and expansion of services for students with disabilities and their families.

2001   No Child Left Behind Act of 2001 (PL 107–110) is enacted; a major educational reform effort focusing on academic achievement of students and qualifications of teachers.

2004   Individuals with Disabilities Education Improvement Act of 2004 (PL 108–446) is passed; aligns IDEA legislation with provisions of the No Child Left Behind Act; modifies the individualized education program process in addition to changes affecting school discipline, due process, and evaluation of students with disabilities.

2008   Americans with Disabilities Act Amendments of 2008 are enacted; expand statutory interpretation of a disability while affording individuals with disabilities greater protections.

SOURCE: Based on information from the 75th Anniversary Issue, *Teaching Exceptional Children, 29*(5), 1997, pp. 5–49.

support for this concept. However, we find that professionals are increasingly working together. Professional cooperation and partnership are the key to delivering services in an efficient and integrated manner. "Serving students with disabilities in inclusive settings depends greatly on effective collaboration among professionals" (Hobbs & Westling, 1998, p. 14). McLean, Wolery, and Bailey (2004) identify several reasons why collaboration is beneficial:

- Incorrect placement recommendations are likely to be reduced.
- There is a greater likelihood that assessments will be nondiscriminatory.
- More appropriate educational plans and goals are likely to result from professional teaming.

Effective programming for students with disabilities requires meaningful involvement of teachers, parents, and related service providers.

Collaboration is *how* people work together; it is a style of interaction that professionals choose to use in order to accomplish a shared goal (Friend & Cook, 2013). For collaboration to be effective, however, service providers must exhibit a high degree of cooperation, trust, and mutual respect and must share the decision-making process. Additional key attributes necessary for meaningful collaboration include voluntary participation and parity in the relationship, along with shared goals, accountability, and resources (Friend & Cook, 2013). A good example of the beneficial outcomes of these collaborative efforts can be found in the development of a student's individualized education program, or IEP, which necessitates a collaborative team process involving parents, teachers, and professionals.

Several models are available for building partnerships among related services personnel, general education teachers, and special educators. We have chosen to examine two different approaches: consultative services and service delivery teams.

Consultative Services

A growing number of school districts are developing strategies for assisting general educators in serving children with disabilities. This effort is part of a larger movement aimed at making the neighborhood school and general education classroom more inclusive. One effective support technique is to provide assistance to general educators through consultative services. Consultation is a focused, problem-solving process in which one individual offers expertise and assistance to another. The intent of this activity is to modify teaching tactics and/or the learning environment in order to accommodate the needs of the individual student with disabilities. Instructional planning and responsibility thus become a shared duty among various professionals. Assistance to the general education teacher may come from a special educator, the school psychologist, a physical therapist, or any other related services provider. A vision specialist, for example, may provide suggestions on how to use various pieces of mobility equipment needed by a student who is visually impaired; a school psychologist or behavior management specialist may offer suggestions for dealing with the aggressive, acting-out behaviors of a middle school student with emotional problems. Hourcade and Bauwens (2003) refer to this type of aid as indirect consultation. In

collaboration: How individuals work together; a style of interaction among professionals.

individualized education program (IEP): A written detailed plan developed by a team for each pupil ages 3–21 who receives a special education; a management tool.

consultation: A focused problem-solving process in which one individual offers support and expertise to another person.

VIDEO
Classroom
Suggestions

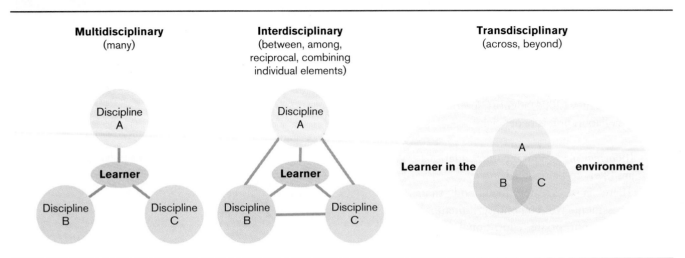

SOURCE: M. Giangreco, J. York, and B. Rainforth, "Providing Related Services to Learners with Severe Handicaps in Educational Settings: Pursuing the Least Restrictive Option," *Pediatric Physical Therapy, 1*(2), 1989, p. 57.

other instances, services are rendered directly to the student by professionals other than the classroom teacher. In this situation, specific areas of weakness or deficit are the target of remediation. Interventions are increasingly being provided by related services personnel in the general education classroom. The general educator also typically receives instructional tips on how to carry out the remediation efforts in the absence of the service provider.

We should also point out that consultative services are equally valuable for special educators. The diverse needs of pupils with disabilities frequently require that special education teachers seek programming suggestions and other types of assistance from various related services personnel. It should be obvious that no one discipline or professional possesses all of the answers. The complex demands of today's classrooms dictate that professionals work together in a cooperative fashion.

According to Pugach and Johnson (2002), consultative services are an appropriate and beneficial strategy, a means whereby all school personnel can collaboratively interact as part of their commitment to serving *all* children. Meaningful collaborative consultation requires mutual support, respect, flexibility, and a sharing of expertise. No one professional should consider himself or herself more of an expert than others. Each of the parties involved can learn and benefit from the others' expertise; of course, the ultimate beneficiary is the student. We believe that the keys to developing effective collaborative practices are good interpersonal skills coupled with professional competency and a willingness to assist in meeting the needs of all children.

Service Delivery Teams

Another way that professionals can work together is to construct a team. Special education teachers seldom work completely alone. Even those who teach in a self-contained classroom function, in some way, as part of a team (Crutchfield, 1997). Simply stated, a team consists of a group of individuals whose purpose and function are derived from a common philosophy and shared goals. Obviously, educational teams will differ in their membership; yet individual professionals, who typically represent various disciplines, appreciate their interdependence and sense of common ownership of their objective (Gargiulo & Metcalf, 2013).

Besides having members from different fields, teams will also differ according to their structure and function. Such teams are often used in evaluating, planning, and delivering services to individuals with disabilities, especially infants and toddlers. The three most common approaches identified in the professional literature (McDonnell, Hardman, & McDonnell, 2003) are multidisciplinary, interdisciplinary, and transdisciplinary teams. These approaches are interrelated and, according to Giangreco, York, and Rainforth (1989), represent a historical evolution of teamwork. This evolutionary process can be portrayed as concentric circles, with each model retaining some of the attributes of its predecessor. Figure 1.2 illustrates these various configurations.

Multidisciplinary Teams

The concept of a **multidisciplinary team** was originally mandated in PL 94–142 and was reiterated in the 2004 reauthorization of IDEA (PL 108–446). This approach utilizes the expertise of professionals from several disciplines, each of whom usually performs his or her assessments, interventions, and other tasks independent of the others. Individuals contribute according to their own specialty area with little regard for the actions of other professionals. There is a high degree of professional autonomy and minimal integration. A team exists only in the sense that each person shares a common goal. There is very little coordination or collaboration across discipline areas. Friend and Cook (2013) characterize this model as a patchwork quilt whereby different, and sometimes contrasting, information is integrated but not necessarily with a unified outcome.

Parents of children with disabilities typically meet with each team member individually. They are generally passive recipients of information about their son or daughter. Because information flows to them from several sources, some parents may have difficulty synthesizing all of the data and recommendations from the various experts. Gargiulo and Kilgo (2014) do not consider the multidisciplinary model to be especially "family friendly."

Interdisciplinary Teams

The **interdisciplinary team** model evolved from dissatisfaction with the fragmented services and lack of communication typically associated with the multidisciplinary team model (McCormick, 2003c). In this model of teaming, team members perform their evaluations independently, but program development and instructional recommendations are the result of information sharing and joint planning. Significant cooperation among the team members leads to an integrated plan of services and a holistic view of the student's strengths and needs. Greater communication, coordination, and collaboration are the distinctive trademarks of this model. Direct services such as physical therapy, however, are usually provided in isolation from one another. Families typically meet with the entire team or its representative; in many cases, a special educator performs this role.

Transdisciplinary Teams

The **transdisciplinary team** approach to providing services builds on the strengths of the interdisciplinary model. In this model, team members are committed to working collaboratively across individual discipline lines. The transdisciplinary model is distinguished by two additional and related features: role sharing and a primary therapist. Professionals from various disciplines conduct their initial evaluations and assessments, but they relinquish their role (role release) as service providers by teaching their skills to other team members, one of whom will serve as the primary interventionist. This

multidisciplinary team: A group of professionals from different disciplines who function as a team but perform their roles independent of one another.

interdisciplinary team: A group of professionals from different disciplines who function as a team but work independently; recommendations, however, are the result of sharing information and joint planning.

transdisciplinary team: A group of professionals from different disciplines who function as a team but work independently; however, they share roles, and a peer is identified as the primary interventionist.

Multidisciplinary teams	Interdisciplinary teams	Transdisciplinary teams

Least collaborative

Most collaborative

Least cooperative

Most cooperative

Least coordinated

Most coordinated

Least integrative

Most integrative

SOURCE: From R. Gargiulo and J. Kilgo, *An Introduction to Young Children with Special Needs,* 4th ed. ©2014. Wadsworth, a part of Cengage Learning, Inc. Reproduced by permission. www.cengage.com/permissions

person is regarded as the team leader. For many children and adolescents with special needs, this role is usually filled by an educator. This individual relies heavily on the support and consultation provided by his or her professional peers. Discipline-specific interventions are still available, although they occur less frequently.

"The primary purpose of this approach," according to Bruder (1994), "is to pool and integrate the expertise of team members so that more efficient and comprehensive assessment and intervention services may be provided" (p. 61). The aim of the transdisciplinary model is to avoid compartmentalization and fragmentation of services. It attempts to provide a more coordinated and unified approach to assessment and service delivery. Members of a transdisciplinary team see parents as full-fledged members of the group with a strong voice in the team's recommendations and decisions.

Figure 1.3 illustrates some of the characteristics of each team model as viewed by Gargiulo and Kilgo (2014).

Cooperative Teaching

Cooperative teaching, or co-teaching as it is sometimes called, is an increasingly popular approach for achieving inclusion (Gargiulo & Metcalf, 2013; Potts & Howard, 2011; Scruggs, Mastropieri, & McDuffie, 2007). With this strategy, general education teachers and special educators work together in a cooperative manner; each professional shares in the planning and delivery of instruction to a heterogeneous group of students. Hourcade and Bauwens (2003) define cooperative teaching as

> direct collaboration in which a general educator and one or more support service providers voluntarily agree to work together in a co-active and coordinated fashion in the general education classroom. These educators, who possess distinct and complementary sets of skills, share roles, resources, and responsibilities in a sustained effort while working toward the common goal of school success for all students. (p. 41)

More recently, Sileo (2011) characterized

> co-teaching as an instructional delivery model used to teach students with disabilities and those at risk for educational failure in the least restrictive, most productive, integrated classroom setting where both general and special educators share responsibility for planning, delivering, and evaluating instruction for all students. (p. 33)

cooperative teaching: An instructional approach in which a special education teacher and a general educator teach together in a general education classroom to a heterogeneous group of students.

The aim of cooperative teaching, which is analogous to a marriage (Murawski, 2012), is to create options for learning and to provide support to *all* students in the general education classroom by combining the content expertise of the general educator with the pedagogical skills of the special educator (Smith, Polloway, Patton, & Dowdy, 2012). General education teachers can be viewed as "masters of content" while their special education colleagues are considered "masters of access" (Sileo, 2011). Cooperative teaching can be implemented in several different ways. These approaches, as identified by Friend and Cook (2013), Murawski (2012), and Sileo (2010), typically occur for set periods of time each day or on certain days of the week. Some of the more common instructional models for co-teaching are depicted in Figure 1.4. The particular strategy chosen often depends on the needs and characteristics of the pupils, curricular demands, amount of professional experience, and teacher preference, as well as such practical matters as the amount of space available. Many experienced educators use a variety of arrangements depending on their specific circumstances.

One Teach, One Observe

In this version of cooperative teaching, one teacher presents the instruction to the entire class while the second educator circulates, gathering information (data) on a specific pupil, a small group of students, or targeted behaviors across the whole class such as productive use of free time. Although this model requires a minimal amount of joint planning, it is very important that teachers periodically exchange roles to avoid one professional being perceived as the "assistant teacher."

One Teach, One Support

Both individuals are present, but one teacher takes the instructional lead while the other provides support and assistance to the students. It is important that one professional (usually the special educator) is not always expected to function as the assistant; rotating roles can help alleviate this potential problem.

Station Teaching

In this type of cooperative teaching, the lesson is divided into two or more segments and presented in different locations in the classroom. One teacher presents one portion of the lesson while the other teacher provides a different portion. Then the groups rotate, and the teachers repeat their information to new groups of pupils. Depending on the class, a third station can be established where students work independently or with a "learning buddy" to review material. Station teaching is effective at all grade levels.

Parallel Teaching

This instructional arrangement lowers the teacher-pupil ratio. Instruction is planned jointly but is delivered by each teacher to one half of a heterogeneous group of learners. Coordination of efforts is crucial. This format lends itself to drill-and-practice activities or projects that require close teacher supervision. As with station teaching, noise and activity levels may pose problems.

Alternative Teaching

Some students benefit from small-group instruction; alternative teaching meets that need. With this model, one teacher provides instruction to the larger group while the other teacher interacts with a small group of pupils. Although commonly used for remediation purposes, alternative teaching is equally appropriate for enrichment activities and in-depth study. Teachers need to be cautious, however, that children with disabilities

VIDEO
Cooperative
Teaching

Figure 1.4 Cooperative Teaching Arrangements

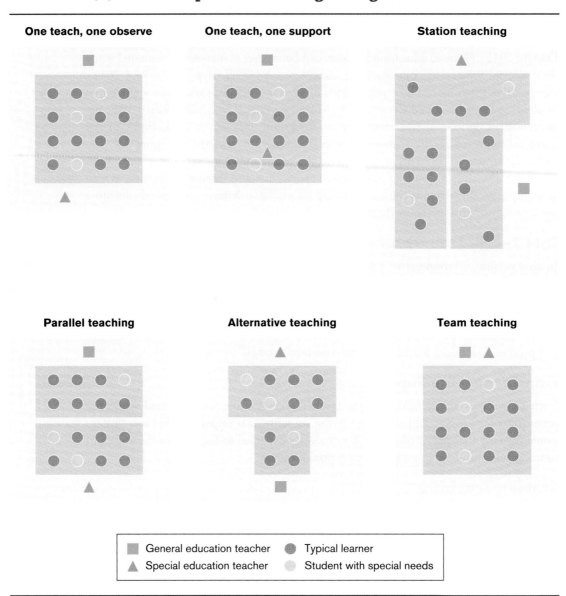

One teach, one observe	One teach, one support	Station teaching
Parallel teaching	**Alternative teaching**	**Team teaching**

■ General education teacher   ● Typical learner
▲ Special education teacher   ○ Student with special needs

SOURCE: Adapted from M. Friend and L. Cook, *Interactions: Collaboration Skills for School Professionals*, 7th ed. (Boston, MA: Pearson Education, 2013), p. 169.

are not exclusively and routinely assigned to the small group; all members of the class should participate periodically in the functions of the smaller group.

Team Teaching

In this type of cooperative teaching, both teachers share the instructional activities equally. Each teacher, for example, may take turns leading a discussion about the causes of World War II, or one teacher may talk about multiplication of fractions while the co-teacher gives several examples illustrating this concept. This form of cooperative teaching, sometimes called interactive teaching (Walther-Thomas, Korinek, McLaughlin, & Williams, 2000), requires a significant amount of professional trust and a high level of commitment.

Cooperative teaching should not be viewed as a panacea for meeting the multiple challenges frequently encountered when serving students with disabilities in general education classrooms; it is, however, one mechanism for facilitating successful inclusion. According to researchers (Potts & Howard, 2011; Rice, Drame, Owens, & Frattura, 2007; Scruggs et al., 2007; Sileo, 2011), some of the key ingredients required for successful cooperative teaching include the following:

- Adequate planning time
- Administrative support
- Communication skills
- Flexibility and creativity
- Mutual respect
- Personal and professional compatibility
- Shared instructional philosophy
- Voluntary participation

Today's classrooms serve all children.

Teachers also need to openly address potential obstacles, such as workload issues, classroom noise, daily chores, and time management, if co-teaching is to be successful (Sileo, 2011; Smith et al., 2012).

To ensure that co-teaching is efficient and effective, Reinhiller (1996) recommends that teachers address the following five questions:

- Why do we want to co-teach?
- How will we know whether our goals are being met?
- How will we communicate and document the collaboration?
- How will we share responsibility for the instruction of all students?
- How will we gain support from others? (p. 46)

Keefe, Moore, and Duff (2004) offer the following guidelines for creating and maintaining a successful co-teaching experience:

- *Know yourself*—recognize your strengths and weaknesses; acknowledge preconceived notions about teaching in an inclusive setting.
- *Know your partner*—foster a friendship; accept each other's idiosyncrasies; appreciate differences in teaching styles.
- *Know your students*—discover the students' interests; listen to their dreams; embrace acceptance.
- *Know your "stuff"*—share information and responsibility; jointly create IEPs; be knowledgeable about classroom routines.

Like Murawski and Dieker (2004), we believe that in the final analysis the key question that must be answered is, "Is what we are doing good for the both of us and good for our students?"

Advantages and disadvantages of cooperative teaching are summarized in Table 1.5. An award-winning teacher's recommendations for facilitating successful co-teaching experiences are offered in Table 1.6.

Universal Design for Learning

In today's climate of high-stakes testing and calls for greater student and teacher accountability, full access to the general education curriculum for students with disabilities

VIDEO

UDL

Table 1.5 Advantages and Disadvantages of Cooperative Teaching Arrangements

Instructional Model	Advantages	Disadvantages
Team Teaching	• Provides systematic observation/data collection • Promotes role/content sharing • Facilitates individual assistance • Models appropriate academic, social, and help-seeking behaviors • Teaches question asking • Provides clarification (e.g., concepts, rules, vocabulary)	• May be job sharing, not learning enriching • Requires considerable planning • Requires modeling and role-playing skills • Becomes easy to "typecast" specialist with this role
Station Teaching	• Provides active learning format • Increases small-group attention • Encourages cooperation and independence • Allows strategic grouping • Increases response rate	• Requires considerable planning and preparation • Increases noise level • Requires group and independent work skills • Is difficult to monitor
Parallel Teaching	• Provides effective review format • Encourages student responses • Reduces pupil-teacher ratio for group instruction or review	• Hard to achieve equal depth of content coverage • May be difficult to coordinate • Requires monitoring of partner pacing • Increases noise level • Encourages some teacher-student competition
Alternative Teaching	• Facilitates enrichment opportunities • Offers absent students "catch-up" time • Keeps individuals and class on pace • Offers time to develop missing skills	• May select same low-achieving students for help • Creates segregated learning environments • Is difficult to coordinate • May single out students

SOURCE: Walther-Thomas, C., Korinek, L., McLaughlin, V. L., Williams, B. T., *Collaboration for Inclusive Education: Developing Successful Programs,* 2000. Printed and Electronically reproduced by permission of Pearson Education, Inc., Upper Saddle River, New Jersey.

is receiving growing attention. One way of ensuring access to, along with participation and progress in, the general education curriculum, as required by PL 108–446, is via the concept of universal design. Originally an idea found in the field of architectural studies, **universal design for learning** (UDL) can be simply stated as "the design of instructional materials and activities that allows the learning goals to be achievable by individuals with wide differences in their abilities to see, hear, speak, move, read, write, understand English, attend, organize, engage, and remember" (Orkwis & McLane, 1998, p. 9). Universal design allows education professionals the flexibility necessary to design curriculum, instruction, and evaluation procedures capable of meeting the needs of *all* students (Hitchcock, Meyer, Rose, & Jackson, 2002). Universal design for learning is accomplished by means of flexible curricular materials and activities that offer alternatives to pupils with widely varying abilities and backgrounds. These adaptations are built into the instructional design rather than added on later as an afterthought. Universal design for learning provides equal access to learning, not simply equal access to information. It assumes that there is no one method of presentation or expression, which provides equal access for all learners. Learning activities and materials are purposely designed to allow for flexibility and offer various ways to learn (Scott, McGuire, & Shaw, 2003).

universal design for learning:
The design of curriculum materials, instructional activities, and evaluation procedures that can meet the needs of learners with widely varying abilities and backgrounds.

For working with children with disabilities:	For working with general education teachers:
• When you construct your plan, think about how you can make it visual, auditory, tactile, and kinesthetic. You'll have a better chance of meeting different learning styles.	• Find teachers who welcome your students and whom you enjoy working with if possible. It is helpful to find co-teachers who have different strengths so you can complement each other.
• Think about what is the most important thing all students need to learn and then think about how you can break the task into smaller parts for some students and make it more challenging for students who are ready to move ahead.	• Faithfully plan ahead with these teachers—at least a week ahead.
• Be keenly aware of student strengths, and plan to find a way for each student to be successful academically every day.	• Be willing to do more than your share at first if necessary to get a solid footing for the year. It will pay off.
• Working with a peer/buddy is often a helpful strategy.	• Keep communication open and frequent. Use positive language with each other as much as possible. Brainstorm solutions to challenges together, and try different solutions.
• Mix up your groups now and then. A student may need a different group for reading than for math. Try not to "label" anyone.	• Document the work you do with students. Help with assessment as much as possible.
• Children with disabilities (many children actually) need very clear, precise directions. Pair auditory with visual directions if possible. Students with more severe impairments may need to see objects.	• Attend open houses, parent conferences, and other similar meetings so the parents view you as part of the classroom community.
• It may be helpful to give only one direction at a time. This doesn't mean the pace has to be slow. In fact, a fast pace is often quite effective. Using signals (e.g., for getting attention, transitions) can also be very helpful.	• Look for the good in the teacher(s) and students, and tell them when you see a "best practice."
• Be consistent.	• If you don't know the answer to something, ask. If you don't know some of the content very well, study. Find out who does something well, and observe him or her if it is a skill you need to work on.
• Notice students being "good"—offer verbal praise or perhaps a small positive note.	• When you say you will do something, be sure you follow through.
• Have high expectations for *all* children.	

SOURCE: D. Metcalf, East Carolina University and Pitt Co. Schools. The Council for Exceptional Children (CEC) 2004 Clarissa Hug Teacher of the Year.

Table 1.7 presents some of the many different ways in which a teacher could present a lesson.

Universal design for learning is envisioned as an instructional resource, a vehicle for diversifying instruction in order to deliver the general education curriculum to each pupil. UDL does not remove academic challenges; it removes barriers to access. Simply stated, universal design for learning is just good teaching (Ohio State University Partnership Grant, 2013). UDL encourages teachers to design curriculum, learning environments, and assessment procedures that are "smart from the start" (Pisha & Coyne, 2001). By doing so, educators are able to significantly impact student learning.

According to Wehmeyer, Lance, and Bashinski (2002), "universally designed curriculum takes into account individual student interests and preferences and individualizes representation, presentation, and response aspects of the curriculum delivery accordingly" (p. 230). It offers the opportunity for creating a curriculum that is sufficiently flexible or tailored to meet the needs of the individual learner. Universal design provides a range of options for accessing, using, and engaging learning materials—explicitly acknowledging that no one option will work for all students (Gargiulo & Metcalf, 2013). Some of the beneficiaries of this strategy include, for example, individuals who speak English as a second language, pupils with disabilities, and students whose

Table 1.7 **Multiple Methods of Presenting Instructional Content**

Auditory	Visual	Tactile/Kinesthetic	Affective	Technology
Lecture	Video clips	Field trip	Small-group work	Digitized video Tablet iPad Videoconferencing
Discussion	Sign language Speech reading	Sign language Gestures	Cross-age tutoring Peer-mediated instruction	Electronic discussion boards Online chat rooms
Song	Watch a play	Drawing	Role play	
Read aloud	Books	Braille books		Tape recorder iPod
Questioning	Graph, table, chart Slide show Transparency Whiteboard	Demonstration Role play Dance Games Manipulatives Build an object		Spreadsheet PowerPoint Overhead data projector

NOTE: Not an exhaustive list; some methods may fit more than one category.

preferred learning style is inconsistent with the teacher's teaching style (Ohio State University Partnership Grant, 2013). There are three essential elements of universal design for learning that are often considered when developing curriculum for learners with diverse abilities. These components (see Figure 1.5) are multiple means of representation, engagement, and expression.

Exceptionality Across the Life Span

When we talk about special education, most people envision services for children of school age, yet the field embraces a wider range of individuals than students between the ages of 6 and 18. In recent years, professionals have begun to focus their attention on two distinct populations: infants/toddlers and preschoolers with special needs, and students with disabilities at the secondary level who are about to embark on adulthood. Meeting the needs of pupils at both ends of the spectrum presents myriad challenges for educators as well as related services personnel; however, professionals have a mandate to serve individuals across the life span.

Our purpose at this point is only to introduce some of the concepts and thinking about these two age groups. In later chapters, we will explore more fully many of the issues specific to young children with special needs as well as services for adults with disabilities.

Infants/Toddlers and Preschoolers With Special Needs

Prior to PL 94–142, services for infants, toddlers, and preschoolers with disabilities or delays were virtually unheard of. In many instances, parents had to seek out

Multiple Means of Representation Recognition Networks The "What" of Teaching and Learning	**Multiple Means of Engagement Affective Systems** The "Why" of Teaching and Learning	**Multiple Means of Expression Strategic Systems** The "How" of Teaching and Learning
Offers *flexibility in ways of* • . . . presenting, receiving, and interpreting information/content (to assess and build connections) • . . . adapting for different languages, learning styles, multiple intelligences, congnitive stages of development, sensory needs, perceptual differences, social needs • . . . adjusting the complexity of material presented (customizing content) • . . . adjusting environment so all can see, hear, and reach	Offers *flexibility in ways of* • . . . customizing the affective network systems in learning to increase participation • . . . adjusting for student interests and cultural backgrounds • . . . arranging the environment to allow for variety in grouping arrangements, individual work, and access technology and other materials • . . . using human resources in the classroom and school (collaboration)	Offers *flexibility in ways of* • . . . how students respond to information presented • . . . providing output formats that can be changed easily to accommodate preferred means of control (perceptual, sensory, motor control) • . . . using different cognitive strategic systems • . . . tracking progress of students • . . . identifying areas of strengths and needs • . . . assessing knowledge of content

SOURCE: From R. Gargiulo and D. Metcalf, *Teaching in Today's Inclusive Classrooms*, 2nd ed. © 2013. Wadsworth, a part of Cengage Learning, Inc. Reproduced by permission. www.cengage.com/permissions

assistance on their own; public schools did not routinely offer early intervention or other supports. As we noted earlier in this chapter, even with the enactment of the Education for All Handicapped Children Act, more than half the states did not provide a special education for preschoolers with special needs. Today, professionals realize the importance and value of intervening in the lives of young children. In fact, the earlier that intervention is begun, the better the outcomes (Bruder, 2010; Sandall, Hemmeter, McLean, & Smith, 2005). "Without early intervention many [young] children with disabilities fall further and further behind their nondisabled peers, and minor delays in development often become major delays by the time the child reaches school age" (Bicard & Heward, 2010, p. 331). Providing services to our youngest citizens with disabilities or delays has become a national priority. Presently, well over 1 million children from birth to age 5 receive some form of intervention or special education (U.S. Department of Education, 2013a).

The Education of the Handicapped Act Amendments of 1986 (PL 99–457) are largely responsible for the rapid development of services for youngsters with disabilities or delays and those children who are at risk for future problems in learning and development. PL 99–457 is concerned with the family of the youngster with special needs as well as the child. This law clearly promotes parent–professional collaboration and partnerships. Parents are empowered to become decision makers with regard to programs and services for their son or daughter. We can see this emphasis in the

REFERENCE

Early Intervention

Young children with special needs greatly benefit from early intervention.

individualized family service plan, or IFSP as it is commonly known. Similar to an IEP for older students with disabilities, the IFSP is much more family focused and reflective of the family's resources, priorities, and concerns. (Both of these documents will be fully discussed in Chapter 2.)

When professionals talk about providing services to very young children with disabilities or special needs, a distinction is generally made between two frequently used terms: *early intervention* and *early childhood special education*. Early intervention is typically used, according to Gargiulo and Kilgo (2014), to refer to the delivery of a coordinated and comprehensive package of specialized services to infants and toddlers (birth through age 2) with developmental delays or at-risk conditions and their families. Early childhood special education is used to describe the provision of customized services uniquely crafted to meet the individual needs of youngsters with disabilities between 3 and 5 years of age.

Early intervention represents a consortium of services, not just educational assistance but also health care, social services, family supports, and other benefits. The aim of early intervention is to affect positively the overall development of the child—his or her social, emotional, physical, and intellectual well-being. We believe that incorporating a "whole child" approach is necessary because all of these elements are interrelated and dependent on one another (Zigler, 2000).

Adolescents and Young Adults With Disabilities

Preparing our nation's young people for lives as independent adults has long been a goal of American secondary education. This objective typically includes the skills necessary for securing employment, pursuing postsecondary educational opportunities, participating in the community, living independently, and engaging in social/recreational activities, to mention only a few of the many facets of this multidimensional concept. Most young adults make this passage, or transition, from one phase of their life to the next without significant difficulty. Unfortunately, this statement is not necessarily true for many secondary students with disabilities. Full participation in adult life is a goal that is unattainable for a large number of citizens with disabilities. Consider the implications of the following facts gathered from various national surveys:

- Only 21 percent of adults with disabilities are employed on a full- or part-time basis, compared to 59 percent of adults without disabilities (Kessler Foundation/National Organization on Disability, 2010).
- Approximately one out of five adults with disabilities has less than a high school education; by way of comparison, only 11 percent of adults without disabilities lack a high school diploma (Kessler Foundation/National Organization on Disability, 2010).
- Only 57 percent of youths with disabilities are competitively employed after secondary school (National Longitudinal Transition Study 2, 2009).

individualized family service plan (IFSP): A written plan developed by a team that coordinates services for infants and toddlers and their families.

early intervention: The delivery of a coordinated and comprehensive package of specialized services to infants and toddlers with developmental delays or at-risk conditions and their families.

early childhood special education: Provision of customized services uniquely crafted to meet the individual needs of youngsters with disabilities ages 3 to 5.

transition: A broad term used to describe the movement of an individual from one educational environment to another, from one class to another, or from one phase of life (high school) to another (independent adulthood).

- More than twice as many individuals with disabilities live in poverty (incomes below $15,000) as compared to adults without disabilities (Kessler Foundation/ National Organization on Disability, 2010).
- Approximately one out of four adolescents with disabilities exits school by dropping out (U.S. Department of Education, 2011).
- About one out of three adults with disabilities is very satisfied with life in general compared to 61 percent of adults without disabilities (Kessler Foundation/ National Organization on Disability, 2010).

The picture that the preceding data paint is rather bleak. For many special educators this profile is totally unacceptable and unconscionable. What do these statistics say about the job professionals are doing in preparing adolescents with disabilities for the adult world? Can we do better? Obviously, we need to. It is abundantly clear that a large percentage of young people with disabilities have difficulty in making a smooth transition from adolescence to adulthood and from high school to adult life in their community. With more than 645,000 students with disabilities exiting the educational system annually (U.S. Department of Education, 2013a), what happens to them after they leave is a crucial question confronting professionals and parents alike. This issue of transition has become one of the dominant themes in contemporary special education. Rarely has one topic captured the attention of the field for such a sustained period of time. Transitioning from high school to the many dimensions of independent adulthood has become a national educational priority.

Transition Defined

Several different definitions or interpretations of transition can be found in the professional literature. One of the earliest definitions was offered by Madeleine Will (1984), Assistant Secretary of Education, Office of Special Education and Rehabilitative Services (OSERS). Will viewed transition as

> a period that includes high school, the point of graduation, additional postsecondary education or adult services, and the initial years in employment. Transition is a bridge between the security and structure offered by the school and the opportunities and risks of adult life. . . . The transition from school to work and adult life requires sound preparation in the secondary school, adequate support at the point of school leaving, and secure opportunities and services, if needed, in adult situations. (p. 3)

According to Will (1984), three levels of services are involved in providing for an individual to move successfully from school to adult employment. The top level, "no special services," refers to those generic services available to any citizen within the community, even if special accommodations may be necessary. An example of this form of support might be educational opportunities at a local community college or accessing state employment services. The middle rung of this model, "time-limited services," involves specialized, short-term services that are typically necessary because of a disability. Vocational rehabilitation services best illustrate this level of the model. "Ongoing services" constitute the third level of this early model. This type of ongoing employment support system was not widely available in the early 1980s. However, it represented an integral component of Will's paradigm, and these services were promoted through federally funded demonstration projects (Halpern, 1992).

Commonly referred to as the "bridges model," Will's (1984) proposal sparked almost immediate debate and controversy from professionals who considered the

AUDIO

After Transition

Figure 1.6 **Halpern's Model of Transition Goals**

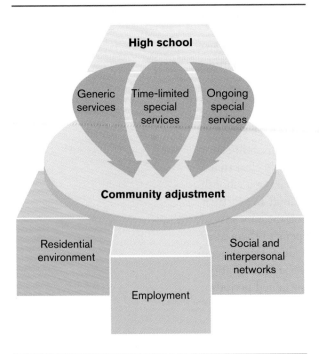

High school

Generic services | Time-limited special services | Ongoing special services

Community adjustment

Residential environment

Social and interpersonal networks

Employment

SOURCE: From "Transition: A Look at the Foundations" by A. Halpern, *Exceptional Children, 51*(6), 1985, p. 481. Copyright © 1985 by the Council for Exceptional Children. Reprinted with permission.

OSERS interpretation of transition too restrictive or narrow (Brown et al., 1988; Clark & Knowlton, 1988; Halpern, 1985). Adult adjustment, they argued, must be viewed as more than just employment. We agree with this point of view. Halpern (1985), for example, believes it is wrong to focus exclusively on employment. Instead, he proposes that the primary goal of transition be community adjustment, which includes "a person's residential environment and the adequacy of his or her social and interpersonal network. These two dimensions are viewed as being no less important than employment" (p. 480). Thus, living successfully in the community should be the ultimate goal of transition. Halpern's reconfiguration of the OSERS model is portrayed in Figure 1.6.

Today, transition is viewed in much broader terms than Will (1984) originally proposed. This concept presently includes many different aspects of adult adjustment and participation in community life. Employment, personal competence, independent living, social interaction, and community adjustment are just some of the factors associated with the successful passage from school to adult life for secondary special education students.

Federal Definition of Transition Services

PL 108–446 (IDEA 2004) stipulates that each student with a disability is to receive transition services, which are defined as a coordinated set of activities for a student with a disability that

A. is designed within a results-oriented process, focused on improving the academic and functional achievement of the child with a disability to facilitate the child's movement from school to postschool activities, including postsecondary education, vocational training, integrated employment (including supported employment), continuing and adult education, adult services, independent living, or community participation;

B. is based on the child's needs, taking into account the child's strengths, preferences, and interests; and

C. includes instruction, related services, community experiences, the development of employment and other postschool adult living objectives, and, when appropriate, acquisition of daily living skills and functional vocational evaluation. [20 U.S.C. § 1401 (34)]

transition services: Individualized and coordinated services that assist the adolescent with a disability to successfully move from school to postschool activities.

individualized transition plan (ITP): An individualized plan with identified goals and objectives used to prepare the student in making the transition from high school to work (or college).

Individualized Transition Plan

To ensure that the mandate for transition services is met, IDEA 2004 requires that each student, beginning no later than age 16 (and annually thereafter), have a statement of transition services incorporated into his or her IEP. Commonly referred to in education circles as an individualized transition plan (ITP), this document must include postsecondary goals as well as a statement of the linkages and/or responsibilities that various agencies such as employment services, vocational rehabilitation, and the school system will assume in order to move the individual smoothly from school to living and working in the community. The ITP must also include a statement of

VIDEO
Transition Planning

transition service needs and courses of study that are intended to enhance the student's postschool success. Simply stated, an ITP is an annually updated instrument of coordination and cooperation. It is a working document that identifies the range of services, resources, supports, and activities that each student may require during the transition process.

Transition Challenges

We conclude this introduction to transitioning adolescents from school to adult life by briefly examining two related areas of concern for professionals. The first issue is how to create a curriculum that prepares students to participate fully in all aspects of community life. Such a curriculum would need to address not only educational needs but also work behaviors, independent living skills, and recreational and leisure time activities. For some secondary students, the traditional high school curriculum is often inadequate for equipping them for life after school. As educators, we must increase the relevance of the curriculum. If we are to prepare students for successful postschool adjustment, then secondary programming for students with disabilities should reflect the basic functions of adult life—work, personal management, and leisure. The goal, according to McDonnell et al. (2003), is to link curricular content to the demands of living and working in the community as an independent adult. If we are to meet this challenge, our instructional strategies must change. Accompanying this shift from remedial academics to functional skills is the requirement that instruction occur in community-based settings—that is, in the natural environment where the skills are to be exhibited (Halpern, 1992). Research evidence (Hartman, 2009) sup-

Preparing young adults with disabilities to enter the workforce is an important role for schools.

ports the value and benefit of teaching skills in the actual environment in which they are to be performed.

The issue of curricular redesign must be balanced, however, by the increasing number of calls for greater emphasis on academic excellence. Thus, the second challenge for professionals is how to respond to the demands for higher standards while still preparing students for life after high school.

Beginning in the mid-1980s, various national reports strongly criticized the American educational system (Goodlad, 1984; National Commission on Excellence in Education, 1983). Major areas of concern included the declining academic achievement of U.S. students in comparison to youths from other industrialized nations, adult illiteracy, dropout rates, and readiness for school. These concerns were initially addressed in 1989 by the nation's governors, meeting at the first-ever Education Summit. Several broad national goals emerged from this historic conference, establishing a blueprint for educational progress. In March 1994, Congress enacted Goals 2000: Educate America Act (PL 103–227), which translated these reform efforts into law. Similarly, in 2001, Congress reauthorized the Elementary and Secondary Education Act, popularly known as the No Child Left Behind Act of 2001 (PL 107–110). This legislation (to be discussed in Chapter 2) reflects President George W. Bush's commitment to educational reform and greater accountability. This ambitious law requires that

REFERENCE
Postsecondary Education

AUDIO
Chapter 1 Summary

eventually all pupils, including those in special education, be expected to demonstrate proficiency in reading and mathematics, with science eventually being included.

Consequently, one question now confronting educators, parents, and even students is "What is an appropriate curriculum for students with disabilities at the secondary level, given this climate of tougher academic standards and greater educational accountability?" Should the curriculum reflect an academic emphasis, should it focus on preparation for adult life, or is it possible to merge these two potentially conflicting points of view? Obviously, these are difficult questions, with no easy solution. What is best for one student may not be appropriate for another. Transition programs must be customized to the individual needs and desired outcomes of each young adult.

We believe an argument can be made that transitioning is for *all* students, not just those with disabilities. Transitioning can play a role in the overall educational reform movement. Many students, with and without disabilities, will require support and assistance as they cross the bridge from school to adult life in the community. Our job as educators is to make this journey as successful as possible for each and every one of our pupils.

CHAPTER IN REVIEW

Definitions and Terminology

- Exceptional children are individuals who resemble other children in many ways but differ from societal standards of normalcy. These differences may be due to physical, sensory, cognitive, or behavioral characteristics.
- When educators talk about a student with a disability, they are referring to an inability or incapacity to perform a particular task or activity in a specific way because of sensory, physical, cognitive, or other forms of impairment.
- The term *handicap* should be restricted to describing the consequence or impact of the disability on the person, not the condition itself.
- A special education can be defined as a customized instructional program designed to meet the unique needs of the pupil. A special education may include the use of specialized materials, equipment, services, or instructional strategies.

Categories and Labels

- The Individuals with Disabilities Education Improvement Act (PL 108–446) identifies thirteen disability categories.
- Empirical investigations fail to provide clear-cut answers to questions about the effects of labels on children and young adults with disabilities.

Prevalence of Children and Young Adults With Disabilities

- At the present time, almost 5.8 million students between the ages of 6 and 21 are receiving a special education. Of this total, 40 percent are individuals with learning disabilities.
- Collectively, states are providing a special education to approximately 6.9 million individuals from birth through age 21.

A Brief History of the Development of Special Education

- Historically speaking, the foundation of contemporary societal attitudes can be traced to the contributions of various reform-minded eighteenth- and nineteenth-century European educators, philosophers, and humanitarians.
- By the middle of the nineteenth century, several specialized institutions were established in the United States.
- It was not until the latter part of the nineteenth century and early years of the twentieth century that special education classes began to appear in public schools.

Professionals Who Work With Individuals With Exceptionalities

- Educators frequently work with a variety of other professionals representing several distinct disciplines. These individuals provide a wide variety of related services, ranging from occupational therapy to therapeutic recreation to psychological services and even transportation to and from school.

- Providing consultative services to both general and special educators is one way that school districts are attempting to meet the increasingly complex demands of serving students with disabilities.
- The three teaming models most frequently mentioned in the professional literature are multidisciplinary, interdisciplinary, and transdisciplinary teams.

Cooperative Teaching

- Cooperative teaching, or co-teaching as it is sometimes called, is an increasingly popular approach for facilitating successful inclusion.
- Cooperative teaching is an instructional strategy designed to provide support to all students in the general education classroom.
- Teachers can choose from multiple models of cooperative teaching depending on their specific circumstances.

Universal Design for Learning

- Universal design for learning is an instructional resource designed to meet the needs of all students; it provides equal access to learning.
- Universal design for learning allows for multiple means of representation, engagement, and expression.

Exceptionality Across the Life Span

- Twenty-five years ago, services for children with disabilities younger than age 6 were virtually unheard of. Today, however, well over 1 million children younger than 6 receive some type of intervention or special education.
- The issue of transition has become one of the dominant themes in contemporary special education.
- Every high school student who is enrolled in a special education program is to have an individualized transition plan as part of his or her individualized education program.

STUDY QUESTIONS

1. How is the concept of normalcy related to the definition of children identified as exceptional?

2. Differentiate between the terms *disability* and *handicap*. Provide specific examples for each term.

3. What is a special education?

4. Name the thirteen categories of exceptionality presently recognized by the federal government.

5. Compare and contrast arguments for and against the practice of labeling pupils according to their disability.

6. How are the terms *prevalence* and *incidence* used when discussing individuals with disabilities?

7. Identify contributing factors to the growth of the field of special education.

8. Why do you think the federal government has not mandated special education for students who are gifted and talented?

9. What role did Europeans play in the development of special education in the United States?

10. What are related services, and why are they important for the delivery of a special education?

11. List the characteristics that distinguish multidisciplinary, interdisciplinary, and transdisciplinary educational teams. What are the advantages and disadvantages of each teaming model?

12. How can cooperative teaching benefit students with and without disabilities?

13. Explain how universal design for learning benefits all students.

14. Why is transitioning important for students with disabilities at the secondary level?

15. What challenges do professionals face as they prepare adolescents to move from school to adult life in the community?

KEY TERMS

exceptional children,   4

disability,   5

handicap,   6

handicapism,   6

developmental delay,   6

at risk,   8

special education,   8

related services,   9

category,   10

noncategorical,   12

incidence,   12

prevalence,   12

LEARNING ACTIVITIES

1. Keep a journal for at least four weeks in which you record how individuals with disabilities are represented in newspapers, magazines, television commercials, and other media outlets. Are they portrayed as people to be pitied, or as superheroes? Is "people-first" language used? Do your examples perpetuate stereotyping, or are they realistic representations of persons with disabilities? In what context was each individual shown? What conclusions might a layperson draw about people with disabilities?

2. Visit an elementary school and a high school in your community. Talk to several special educators at each location. Find out how students with disabilities are served. What related services do these pupils receive? Ask each teacher to define the term *special education*. How are regular and special educators collaborating to provide an appropriate education for each learner? What strategies and activities are secondary teachers incorporating to prepare their students for life after graduation?

3. Obtain prevalence figures for students enrolled in special education programs in your state. How do these data compare to national figures? Identify possible reasons for any discrepancies. Do the figures suggest any trends in enrollment? Which category of exceptionality is growing the fastest?

4. Interview a veteran special educator (someone who has been teaching since the early 1990s). Ask this person how the field of special education has changed over the past decades. In what ways are things still the same? What issues and challenges does this teacher confront in his or her career? What is this person's vision of the future of special education?

5. Contact the office of disability support at your college or university. What types of services does it provide to students with disabilities? Volunteer to serve in this program.

REFLECTING ON STANDARDS

The following exercises are designed to help you learn to apply the Council for Exceptional Children (CEC) standards to your teaching practice. Each of the reflection exercises below correlates with knowledge or a skill within the CEC standards. For the full text of each of the related CEC standards, please refer to the standards integration grid located in Appendix B.

Focus on Learning Environments (CEC Initial Preparation Standard 2.1)

Reflect on what you have learned about co-teaching in this chapter. If you were to have a student with special needs in your class, which of these models (team teaching, station teaching,

parallel teaching, or alternative teaching) would you want to integrate into your teaching? What would be the advantages and disadvantages to you and your class in incorporating these strategies?

Focus on Collaboration (CEC Initial Preparation Standard 7.1)

Reflect on what you have learned in this chapter about the importance of building partnerships to create students' individualized education programs. What collaborative skills do you have that will benefit you in this type of teamwork? What skills do you need to improve upon?

$\circledS$ SAGE edge™

Sharpen your skills with SAGE edge at **edge.sagepub.com/gargiulo5e. SAGE edge for students** provides a personalized approach to help you accomplish your coursework goals in an easy-to-use learning environment.

Policies, Practices, and Programs

Many of the policies, procedures, and practices that are common in special education today have resulted from the interaction of a variety of forces, situations, and events. One example is the role that litigation and legislation have played in the development of the field. Coupled with this activity was the gradual realization by professionals that many of our earlier educational customs and methods were ineffective in meeting the needs of individuals with disabilities and their families. Several currently accepted practices, such as nondiscriminatory assessment, placement in a least restrictive environment, and meaningful parent involvement, reflect this correction in thinking.

The purpose of this chapter is to review a variety of contributions that have helped to shape contemporary special education. Besides the impact of national legislation and the courts, we will examine the identification and assessment of individual differences, instructional programming, and models of service delivery.

- **Identify** the court cases that led to the enactment of Public Law 94–142.
- **Summarize** the key components of the Individuals with Disabilities Education Act from 1975 to 2004.
- **Describe** the legislative intent of Section 504 of the Rehabilitation Act of 1973 and the Americans with Disabilities Act.
- **Distinguish** between inter- and intraindividual differences.
- **Describe** the difference between norm- and criterion-referenced assessments.
- **Outline** the steps in the referral process for the delivery of special education services.
- **List** the key components of an individualized education program (IEP) and an individualized family service plan (IFSP).
- **Define** mainstreaming, least restrictive environment, regular education initiative, and full inclusion.

Litigation and Legislation Affecting Special Education

Over the past several decades, the field of special education has been gradually transformed and restructured, largely as a result of judicial action and legislative enactments. These two forces have been powerful tools in securing many of the benefits and rights presently enjoyed by more than 6.5 million pupils with disabilities.

Securing the opportunity for an education has been a slowly evolving process for students with disabilities. What is today seen as a fundamental right for these children was, at one time, viewed strictly as a privilege. Excluding students with disabilities from attending school was a routine practice of local boards of education in the 1890s and early 1900s. In 1893, local school officials in Cambridge, Massachusetts, denied an education to one individual because this student was thought to be too "weak minded" to profit from instruction. In 1919, in Antigo, Wisconsin, a student of normal intelligence but with a type of paralysis attended school through the fifth grade but was subsequently suspended because "his physical appearance nauseated teachers and other students, his disability required an undue amount of his teacher's time, and he had a negative impact on the discipline and progress of the

VIDEO
Legislation

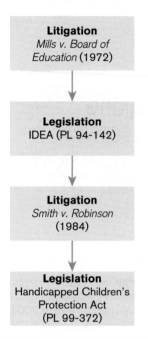

Figure 2.1

An Example of the Interrelationship Between Litigation and Legislation

Litigation
Mills v. Board of Education (1972)

↓

Legislation
IDEA (PL 94-142)

↓

Litigation
Smith v. Robinson
(1984)

↓

Legislation
Handicapped Children's
Protection Act
(PL 99-372)

SOURCE: Adapted from M. Yell, *The Law and Special Education*, 3rd ed. (Upper Saddle River, NJ: Pearson Education, 2012), p. 12.

school" (Osborne, 1996, p. 4). In both instances, state supreme courts upheld the decisions of the school boards. Today, these actions would be seen as clear violations of the pupils' rights and a flagrant disregard for the equal protection clause of the Fourteenth Amendment to the U.S. Constitution. Still, almost four decades passed before students with disabilities had a legal means for acquiring educational rights.

In the 1954 landmark school desegregation case, *Brown v. Board of Education of Topeka, Kansas* (347 U.S. 483), the U.S. Supreme Court reasoned that it was unlawful to discriminate against a group of individuals for arbitrary reasons. The Court specifically ruled that separate schools for black and white students were inherently unequal, contrary to the Fourteenth Amendment, and thus unconstitutional. Furthermore, education was characterized as a fundamental function of government that should be afforded to all citizens on an equal basis. Though primarily recognized as striking down racial segregation, the thinking articulated in *Brown* had major implications for children with disabilities. Much of contemporary litigation and legislation affecting special education is legally, as well as morally, grounded in the precedents established by *Brown*.

The movement to secure equal educational opportunity for children with disabilities was also aided by the U.S. civil rights movement of the 1960s. As Americans attempted to deal with issues of discrimination, inequality, and other social ills, advocates for individuals with disabilities also pushed for equal rights. Parental activism was ignited. Lawsuits were filed, and legislation was enacted primarily as a result of the untiring, vocal, collaborative efforts of parents and politically powerful advocacy groups. The success of these tactics was felt at the local, state, and eventually national level.

It is exceedingly difficult to say which came first, litigation or legislation. Both of these forces have played major roles in the development of state and federal policy concerning special education. They enjoy a unique and almost symbiotic relationship—one of mutual interdependence. Litigation frequently leads to legislation, which in turn spawns additional judicial action as the courts interpret and clarify the law, which often leads to further legislation (see Figure 2.1). Regardless of the progression, much of special education today has a legal foundation.

Key Judicial Decisions

Since the 1960s and early 1970s, a plethora of state and federal court decisions have helped shape and define a wide range of issues affecting contemporary special education policies and procedures. Although a thorough review of this litigation is beyond the scope of this chapter, Table 2.1 summarizes, in chronological order, some of the landmark cases affecting the field of special education. Several of the judicial remedies emanating from these lawsuits serve as cornerstones for both federal and state legislative enactments focusing on students with disabilities. Furthermore, many of today's accepted practices in special education, such as nondiscriminatory assessments and due process procedures, can trace their roots to various court decisions.

Individuals With Disabilities Education Act: 1975–1997

Federal legislative intervention in the lives of persons with disabilities is of relatively recent origin. Before the late 1950s and early 1960s, little federal attention was paid to citizens with special needs. When legislation was enacted, it primarily assisted specific groups of individuals, such as those who were deaf or people with intellectual disability. The past forty years or so, however, have witnessed a flurry of legislative activity that

REFERENCE
Litigation

Case	Year	Issue	Judicial Decision
Brown v. Board of Education of Topeka, Kansas	1954	Educational segregation	Segregation of students by race ruled unconstitutional; children deprived of equal educational opportunity. Effectively ended "separate but equal" schools for white and black pupils. Used as a precedent for arguing that children with disabilities cannot be excluded from a public education.
Diana v. State Board of Education	1970	Class placement	Linguistically different students must be tested in their primary language as well as English. Students cannot be placed in special education classes on the basis of IQ tests that are culturally biased. Verbal test items to be revised so as to reflect students' cultural heritage. Group-administered IQ tests cannot be used to place children in programs for individuals with intellectual disability.
Pennsylvania Association for Retarded Children v. Commonwealth of Pennsylvania	1972	Right to education	State must guarantee a free public education to all children with intellectual disability ages 6–21 regardless of degree of impairment or associated disabilities. Students to be placed in the most integrated environment. Definition of education expanded. Case established the right of parents to participate in educational decisions affecting their children. State to engage in extensive efforts to locate and serve ("child-find") all students with intellectual disability. Preschool services to be provided to youngsters with intellectual disability if local school district serves preschoolers who do not have intellectual disability.
Mills v. Board of Education, District of Columbia	1972	Right to education	Extended the *Pennsylvania* decision to include all children with disabilities. Specifically established the constitutional right of children with exceptionalities to a public education regardless of their functional level. Students have a right to a "constructive education" matched to their needs, including specialized instruction. Presumed absence of fiscal resources is not a valid reason for failing to provide appropriate educational services to students with disabilities. Elaborate due process safeguards established to protect the rights of the child, including parental notification of pending initial evaluation, reassignment, or planned termination of special services.
Larry P. v. Riles	1972, 1979	Class placement	A landmark case parallel to the *Diana* suit. African American students could not be placed in classes for children with mild intellectual disability solely on the basis of intellectual assessments found to be culturally and racially biased. The court instructed school officials to develop an assessment process that would not discriminate against minority children. Failure to comply with this order resulted in a 1979 ruling that completely prohibited the use of IQ tests for placing African American students in classes for children with mild intellectual disability. Ruling applies only to the state of California.
Lau v. Nichols	1974	Equal educational opportunity	A milestone case in the field of bilingual education. U.S. Supreme Court ruling noted that "there is not equality in treatment merely by providing students with the same facilities, textbooks, teachers, and curriculum; for students who do not understand English are effectively foreclosed from a meaningful education." Decision significantly affected the education of culturally and linguistically diverse learners. Schools required to offer special language programs to English language learners if the schools are to confer equal educational opportunity.
Armstrong v. Kline	1980	Extended school year	State's refusal to pay for schooling in excess of 180 days for pupils with severe disabilities is a violation of their rights to an appropriate education as required by PL 94–142. The court found that some children with disabilities will regress significantly during summer recess and have longer recoupment periods; thus, they are denied an appropriate education if not provided with a year-round education.

(Continued)

Case	Year	Issue	Judicial Decision
Tatro v. State of Texas	1980	Related services	U.S. Supreme Court held that catheterization qualified as a related service under PL 94–142. Catheterization was not considered an exempted medical procedure, as it could be performed by a health care aide or school nurse. Court further stipulated that only those services that allow a student to benefit from a special education qualify as related services.
Board of Education of the Hendrick Hudson Central School District v. Rowley	1982	Appropriate education	First U.S. Supreme Court interpretation of PL 94–142. Court addressed the issue of what constitutes an "appropriate" education for a student with a hearing impairment making satisfactory educational progress. Supreme Court ruled that an appropriate education does not necessarily mean an education that will allow for the maximum possible achievement; rather, students must be given a reasonable opportunity to learn. Parents' request for a sign language interpreter, therefore, was denied. An appropriate education is not synonymous with an optimal educational experience.
Daniel R.R. v. State Board of Education	1989	Class placement	Fifth Circuit Court of Appeals held that a segregated class was an appropriate placement for a student with Down syndrome. Preference for integrated placement viewed as secondary to the need for an appropriate education. Court established a two-prong test for determining compliance with the least restrictive environment (LRE) mandate for students with severe disabilities. First, it must be determined if a pupil can make satisfactory progress and achieve educational benefit in the general education classroom through curriculum modification and the use of supplementary aids and services. Second, it must be determined whether the pupil has been integrated to the maximum extent appropriate.

Successful compliance with both parts fulfills a school's obligation under federal law. Ruling affects LRE cases in Louisiana, Texas, and Mississippi, but has become a benchmark decision for other jurisdictions as well. |
Oberti v. Board of Education of the Borough of Clementon School District	1992	Least restrictive environment	Placement in a general education classroom with supplementary aids and services must be offered to a student with disabilities prior to considering more segregated placements. Pupil cannot be excluded from a general education classroom solely because curriculum, services, or other practices would require modification. A decision to exclude a learner from the general education classroom necessitates justification and documentation. Clear judicial preference for educational integration established.
Agostini v. Felton	1997	Provision of services	U.S. Supreme Court reversed a long-standing ruling banning the delivery of publicly funded educational services to students enrolled in private schools. Interpreted to mean that special educators can now provide services to children in parochial schools.
Cedar Rapids Community School District v. Garret F.	1999	Related services	U.S. Supreme Court expanded and clarified the concept of related services. Affirmed that intensive and continuous school health care services necessary for a student to attend school, if not performed by a physician, qualify as related services.

SOURCE: Adapted from R. Gargiulo and J. Kilgo, *An Introduction to Young Children with Special Needs*, 4th ed. (Belmont, CA: Wadsworth/Cengage Learning, 2014), pp. 29–30.

has aided the growth of special education and provided educational benefits and other opportunities and rights to children and adults with disabilities.

Given the multitude of public laws[1] affecting special education, we will focus our attention only on landmark legislation. Our initial review will examine PL 94–142, the Education for All Handicapped Children Act, or, as it came to be known, the Individuals with Disabilities Education Act (IDEA). This change in legislative titles resulted from the enactment on October 30, 1990, of PL 101–476, which will be addressed later in this chapter.

Public Law 94-142

IDEA is viewed as a "Bill of Rights" for children with exceptionalities and their families; it is the culmination of many years of dedicated effort by both parents and professionals. Like many other special educators, we consider this law to be one of the most important pieces, if not the most important piece, of federal legislation ever enacted on behalf of children with special needs. PL 94–142 may rightfully be thought of as the legislative heart of special education.

The purpose of this bill, which was signed into law by President Gerald Ford on November 29, 1975, is

> to assure that all handicapped children have available to them . . . a free appropriate public education which emphasizes special education and related services designed to meet their unique needs, to assure that the rights of handicapped children and their parents or guardians are protected, to assist States and localities to provide for the education of all handicapped children, and to assess and assure the effectiveness of efforts to educate handicapped children. [Section 601(c)]

In pursuing these four purposes, this legislation incorporates six major components and guarantees that have forever changed the landscape of education across the United States. Despite legislative and court challenges over the past four decades, the following principles have endured to the present day:

- **A free appropriate public education (FAPE).** All children, regardless of the severity of their disability (a "zero reject" philosophy), must be provided with an education appropriate to their unique needs at no cost to the parent(s)/guardian(s). Included in this principle is the concept of related services, which requires that children receive, for example, occupational therapy as well as other services as necessary in order to benefit from special education.
- **The least restrictive environment (LRE).** Children with disabilities are to be educated, to the maximum extent appropriate, with students without disabilities. Placements must be consistent with the pupil's educational needs.
- **An individualized education program (IEP).** This document, developed in conjunction with the parent(s)/guardian(s), is an individually tailored statement describing an educational plan for each learner with exceptionalities. The IEP, which will be fully discussed later in this chapter, is required to address (1) the present level of academic functioning (commonly referred to by school

---

[1]National legislation, or public law (PL), is codified according to a standardized format. Legislation is thus designated by the number of the session of Congress that enacted the law followed by the number of the particular bill. PL 94–142, for example, was enacted by the 94th session of Congress and was the 142nd piece of legislation passed.

REFERENCE

Special Education Law

personnel as present level of performance); (2) annual goals and accompanying instructional objectives; (3) educational services to be provided; (4) the degree to which the pupil will be able to participate in general education programs; (5) plans for initiating services and length of service delivery; and (6) an annual evaluation procedure specifying objective criteria to determine if instructional objectives are being met. Many teachers and school administrators refer to this as progress monitoring.

- **Procedural due process.** The act affords parent(s)/guardian(s) several safeguards as it pertains to their child's education. Briefly, parent(s)/guardian(s) have the right to confidentiality of records; to examine all records; to obtain an independent evaluation; to receive written notification (in parents' native language) of proposed changes to their child's educational classification or placement; and to an impartial hearing whenever disagreements arise regarding educational plans for their son/daughter. Furthermore, the student's parent(s)/guardian(s) have the right to representation by legal counsel.
- **Nondiscriminatory assessment.** Prior to placement, a child must be evaluated by a multidisciplinary team in all areas of suspected disability by tests that are not racially, culturally, or linguistically biased. Students are to receive several types of assessments, administered by trained personnel; a single evaluation procedure is not permitted for either planning or placement purposes.
- **Parental participation.** PL 94–142 mandates meaningful parent involvement. Sometimes referred to as the "Parents' Law," this legislation requires that parents participate fully in the decision-making process that affects their child's education.

Congress indicated its desire by September 1, 1980, to provide a free appropriate public education for all eligible children ages 3 through 21. The law, however, did not require services to preschool children with disabilities. Because many states were not providing preschool services to typical children, an education for young children with special needs, in most instances, was not mandated. Although this legislation failed to require an education for younger children, it clearly focused attention on the preschool population and recognized the value of early education.

PL 94–142 did contain some benefits for children under school age. It offered small financial grants (Preschool Incentive Grants) to the individual states as an incentive to serve young children with disabilities. It also carried a mandate for schools to identify and evaluate children from birth through age 21 suspected of evidencing a disability. Finally, PL 94–142 moved from a census count to a child count of the actual number of individuals with disabilities being served. The intent was to encourage the states to locate and serve children with disabilities.

Over the past several years Congress has reauthorized the Individuals with Disabilities Education Act. As a result of this legislative activity services for individuals with disabilities have been expanded, student and parental rights clarified, and discipline procedures articulated along with several other key provisions. Table 2.2 presents a brief overview of some of these revisions to IDEA.

Educational Reform: Standards-Based Education

Over the past two decades, there has been a growing movement toward greater educational accountability, with accompanying calls for educational reform or restructuring

Legislation has greatly benefited individuals with disabilities and their families.

resulting in enhanced academic excellence. (See, for example, President Clinton's Goals 2000: Educate America Act of 1994 [PL 103–227].) As a result of this trend, many states initiated challenging academic standards and more stringent graduation requirements for their students, while several professional organizations published performance indicators in various content areas, such as mathematics, language arts, and science. Likewise, many state departments of education are moving toward performance-based standards when establishing teacher licensure/certification requirements, thus linking student success with teacher qualifications. The overall focus of this movement, fueled by various political, social, and economic forces, was a concern over the learning outcomes of our students. It is equally concerned with establishing educational equity among all learners.

Educational standards, which are "general statements of what students should know or be able to do as a result of their public school education" (Nolet & McLaughlin, 2005, p. 5), are important for a couple of reasons. First, "they are intended," according to Nolet and McLaughlin (2005), "to create equity across schools and classrooms in that they define what all teachers should teach and . . . [they] also define the content that will be assessed and for which schools will be held accountable" (p. 5). Recent

VIDEO
Parents and Legislation

Table 2.2 Highlights of IDEA Reauthorizations: 1986–1997

Year	Public Law	Key Components
1986	PL 99–457	• Legislation viewed as a downward extension of PL 94–142 • Mandated services for preschoolers with disabilities, ages 3–5 • Permissive early intervention services for infants and toddlers, from birth through age 2, with developmental delays or disabilities • Individualized family service plan (IFSP) established for infants and toddlers • "Developmentally delayed" label created
1990	PL 101–476	• Name of legislation changed to Individuals with Disabilities Education Act (IDEA) • Autism and traumatic brain injury identified as discrete disability categories • Rehabilitation counseling and social work considered related services • Established the requirement of an individualized transition plan (ITP) by age 16 • States' immunity from lawsuits for violating IDEA repealed
1997	PL 105–17	• Students with disabilities required to participate in state- and districtwide assessments • Transition planning commences at age 14 • Orientation and mobility included as a related service • Discretionary use of "developmentally delayed" label for pupils ages 3–9 • General educators required to participate on IEP team • Students with disabilities are to be involved in and have access to general education curriculum • Mediation offered as a means of resolving disputes • Benchmarks and measurable annual goals emphasized • Pupils who violate student code of conduct may be removed from their current educational placement only after a due process hearing • Assistive technology needs of each learner must be assessed • Students expelled or suspended from school are still entitled to receive services in accordance with their IEP • Greater variety of assessment tools and strategies are permissible for initial evaluations and reevaluations

SOURCE: U. S. Department of Education.

federal legislation embraces this thinking. The importance attached to standards-driven reform is clearly evident in the No Child Left Behind Act of 2001.

No Child Left Behind Act of 2001

In 2001 Congress reauthorized the Elementary and Secondary Education Act, popularly known as the No Child Left Behind Act of 2001 (PL 107–110). This legislation reflects President Bush's commitment to educational reform and accountability. A brief synopsis of this ambitious law reveals that eventually all pupils, including those in special education, are expected to demonstrate proficiency in mathematics, reading, and science. Annual testing of children in Grades 3 through 8 is required, with students in Grades 10 through 12 assessed at least once. Schools were expected to show adequate yearly progress toward the goal of 100 percent proficiency by 2014. (A small percentage of students may be excused from participating in state- and districtwide achievement tests if their IEP provides for their exemption.) Because this law is concerned with the achievement of *all* students, test scores must be disaggregated according to the pupil's disability, socioeconomic status, race, ethnicity, and English language proficiency. The anticipated benefit of this requirement is that assessment results will directly translate into instructional accommodations, further aligning special education and general education into a unified delivery system responsible for serving all learners (Salend, 2011).

Many young children with developmental delays or disabilities have benefited from early intervention.

Schools that experience difficulty attaining the goal of adequate yearly progress will be provided with technical and financial assistance. If a school fails to demonstrate adequate yearly progress for three consecutive years, the local school district is required to offer supplemental instructional services such as tutoring, after-school classes, and summer programs (Council for Exceptional Children, 2003a). Parents of children in "failing" schools will be given the opportunity to transfer their children to other schools, including private and parochial schools.

In addition to stressing student educational accomplishment, other aspects of this law require that the public as well as parents be informed of individual school performance and the qualifications of teachers. All elementary and secondary school teachers were expected to be "highly qualified" by the end of the 2005–2006 school year according to state criteria. Rigorous standards are also being imposed on teacher aides.

What are the implications of this law for general as well as special educators? How competently will students with special needs perform in this age of educational reform and standards-based education? Obviously, PL 107–110 emphasizes academic achievement as measured by student performance on standardized tests. The expectation seems to be that effective instructional strategies can compensate for a student's disability. The enactment of this law has ushered in an era of what is now commonly referred to as "high-stakes testing" or "high-stakes assessment." Greater emphasis will most likely be placed on ensuring that pupils in special education are exposed to the general education curriculum. One can also anticipate that greater attention will be focused on aligning IEP goals with the content standards of the general education curriculum (Council for Exceptional Children, 2003a). Finally, how colleges and universities prepare future teachers will also likely undergo significant change in an effort to ensure that graduates are highly qualified professionals.

The current focus on exposing individuals with special needs to the general education curriculum is clearly seen in a recent initiative known as the Common Core State Standards (CCSS) (Common Core State Standards Initiative, 2012). Put forth by the National Governors Association and the Council of Chief State School Officers, the CCSS redefine the general education curriculum while outlining a set of grade-level expectations that describe what students should know in mathematics and English language arts in order to succeed in college and later careers. As of September 2012,

AUDIO

No Child Left Behind

forty-five states and the District of Columbia had adopted these standards (Common Core State Standards Initiative, 2012).

These standards apply to all students, including pupils receiving a special education. The work of aligning IEP goals to the Common Core State Standards will certainly challenge many special educators. How does one adapt instruction to meet the unique learning needs of a child with a disability while also addressing rigorous content standards? Teachers of students with disabilities will need to carefully consider how the students' disabilities impact their involvement with and progress in the general education curriculum (Constable, Grossi, Moniz, & Ryan, 2013). The reforming of the general education curriculum with its emphasis on academic achievement for all learners is certainly praiseworthy, yet we believe that it cannot—nor should it—replace an effective special education program that provides specialized, individually tailored, and intensive services to children with special needs (Zigmond & Kloo, 2011).

See the accompanying First Person feature (page 52) for one educator's perspective on teaching in the current era of heightened accountability.

Individuals With Disabilities Education Improvement Act of 2004

On November 19, 2004, Congress passed legislation reauthorizing the Individuals with Disabilities Education Act. The new version of this law is called the Individuals with Disabilities Education Improvement Act of 2004, commonly referred to as IDEA 2004. President George W. Bush signed this bill (PL 108–446) into law on December 3, 2004. Many of the provisions of this legislation became effective on July 1, 2005; some elements of the law became effective, however, on the date the president signed the bill. It is safe to say that IDEA 2004 will significantly affect the professional lives of both general education teachers and special educators. Parents of children with disabilities will also encounter new roles and responsibilities as a result of this law.

> The Individuals with Disabilities Education Improvement Act of 2004 (IDEA) [has] increased the focus of special education from simply ensuring access to education to improving the educational performance of students with disabilities and aligning special education services with the larger national school improvement efforts that include standards, assessments, and accountability [i.e., greater conformity with the No Child Left Behind Act]. (Nolet & McLaughlin, 2005, pp. 2–3)

Some of the significant issues addressed in this historic document are portrayed in Table 2.3

The coming years will be ones of exciting opportunities and challenges as the entire educational community responds to the mandates of PL 107–110 and PL 108–446. These laws, like PL 94–142 more than thirty-five years ago, will dramatically change the educational landscape for both general education and special education.

Civil Rights Legislation

Section 504 of the Rehabilitation Act of 1973

The pieces of legislation that we just examined are representative special education laws (the exception being PL 107–110). PL 93–112, the Rehabilitation Act of 1973,

- Modified criteria for identifying students with specific learning disabilities. Schools can now elect to use a process that determines whether the pupil responds to empirically validated, scientifically based interventions—commonly called response to intervention (RTI)

- Eliminates use of short-term objectives in IEPs except for students evaluated via alternate assessments that are aligned with alternate achievement standards

- IEPs must include a statement of the student's present level of academic achievement and functional performance; annual goals must be written in measurable terms

- Relaxes requirements for participation in IEP meetings

- Multiyear IEPs are permissible

- IEPs to incorporate research-based interventions

- Transition planning to begin with first IEP in effect once student reaches age 16

- Students with disabilities may be removed to an interim alternative educational setting for up to 45 school days for offenses involving weapons, drugs, or inflicting serious bodily injury

- *All* pupils are required to participate in all state- and districtwide assessments with accommodations or alternate assessments as stipulated in their IEP

- Special educators must be "highly qualified" according to individual state standards

- Resolution session required prior to a due process hearing

- Statute of limitations imposed on parents for filing due process complaints

- Modifies provision of student's native language and preferred mode of communication

SOURCE: U. S. Department of Education.

however, is a *civil rights* law. Section 504 of this enactment was the first public law specifically aimed at protecting children and adults against discrimination due to a disability. It said that no individual can be excluded, solely because of his or her disability, from participating in or benefiting from any program or activity receiving federal financial assistance, which includes schools (Council for Exceptional Children, 1997b).

Unlike IDEA, this act employs a functional rather than categorical model for determining a disability. According to this law, individuals are eligible for services if they

1. have a physical or mental impairment that substantially limits one or more major life activities;

2. have a record of such an impairment; or

3. are regarded as having such an impairment by others.

"Major life activities" are broadly defined and include, for example, walking, seeing, hearing, working, and learning.

To fulfill the requirements of Section 504, schools must make "reasonable accommodations" for pupils with disabilities so that they can participate in educational programs provided to other students. Reasonable accommodations might include modifications of the general education program, the assignment of an aide, a behavior management plan, or the provision of special study areas (Smith, 2002; Smith & Patton, 2007). Students may also receive related services such as occupational or physical therapy even if they are not receiving a special education through IDEA.

VIDEO

Special Education Law

FIRST PERSON: LISA

Teaching in the Age of Accountability

Having taught for almost ten years, I can safely say there is a definite need for accountability in education, but teaching in the twenty-first century presents some unique challenges. Everyone is accountable to someone for something. Teachers, for example, are accountable for teaching curriculum in preparation for high-stakes assessments, delivering data-driven instruction, using research-based strategies, and meeting the demands and deadlines imposed by administrators, while also communicating with parents. Students, on the other hand, are accountable for passing the high-stakes assessments and responding to the data-based instruction and research-based instructional strategies, while making adequate progress at increasingly higher levels of performance. Each year it almost seems as though we have to surpass what was accomplished the previous year. The accompanying paperwork to prove this accountability doesn't get any less cumbersome either.

All this accountability comes from increasing concerns about the quality of our education. Yet, even with all this accountability, we see many students transfer with gaps in learning from not having been taught to the same high expectations. There are disparities from school system to school system that make it difficult to reach these ever increasing levels of accountability. This "achievement gap" affects what we have to work with, yet we are still accountable for getting these pupils to the academic level they need to be at. If there is one thing you can count on in teaching, it is that change is constant.

Teaching is a balancing act, and educators have to be sure that they do not get lost in the "accountability jungle" or forget that one of the reasons we teach is to help our students become discoverers of their own learning, not simply to be able to pass a high-stakes assessment. As educators, our accountability goal should be how well our students apply and generalize the

knowledge and information that we share with them, not how well they can regurgitate facts in order to pass an isolated test that represents only a small sample of what they have learned.

The school days are getting longer, lunchtimes are getting shorter, and weekends are often spent in a quiet classroom in preparation for teaching in the coming week. It seems as though we are overly accountable to the point that we are losing valuable instructional time and focus. With all that said, accountability is important as long as we view it wisely.

General education teachers are now being required to prove that their students are being taught with research-based tools and that student performance is documented. No longer are student performance, methods of instruction, and teaching practices at the teacher's discretion. This new level of accountability for general education teachers is going to require them to rely more and more on the expertise of special education teachers not only for the students who have IEPs but also for all struggling learners. At the same time, the special educator is also held accountable for ensuring compliance with regulations, timelines, and mounting paperwork with increasingly larger caseloads. It is a constant battle to find the proper balance—the demands of paperwork, the needs of individual students, and communication with families and general education teachers are all under the accountability microscope. This balance is more difficult to find with each new law, mandate, and policy. Although I feel it is a privilege to work as a teacher, and more particularly as a special education teacher, working as an inclusive teacher in the age of accountability becomes increasingly difficult each year. ■

–Lisa Cranford
Instructional Support Teacher
Rocky Ridge Elementary, Hoover, Alabama

Because the protections afforded by this law are so broad, an individual who is ineligible for a special education under IDEA may qualify for special assistance or accommodations under Section 504. A student with severe allergies, for example, would be eligible for services via Section 504 although it is unlikely that he or she would be eligible to receive services under IDEA. All students who are eligible for a special education and related services under IDEA are also eligible for accommodations under Section 504; the converse, however, is *not* true.

Special educators are required to be highly qualified.

As with IDEA, there is a mandate contained within Section 504 to educate pupils with special needs with their typical peers to the maximum extent possible. In addition, schools are required to develop an accommodation plan (commonly called a "504 plan") customized to meet the unique needs of the individual. This document should include a statement of the pupil's strengths and weaknesses, a list of necessary accommodations, and the individual(s) responsible for ensuring implementation. The purpose of this plan is to enable the student to receive a free appropriate public education (Gargiulo & Metcalf, 2013).

Finally, unlike IDEA, which offers protections for students only between the ages of 3 and 21, Section 504 covers the individual's life span. See Table 2.4 for a comparison of some of the key provisions of IDEA and Section 504.

Public Law 101–336 (Americans With Disabilities Act)

Probably the most significant civil rights legislation affecting individuals with disabilities, the Americans with Disabilities Act (ADA) was signed into law on July 26, 1990, by President George H. W. Bush, who stated, "Today, America welcomes into the mainstream of life all people with disabilities. Let the shameful wall of exclusion finally come tumbling down." This far-reaching enactment, which parallels Section 504 of PL 93–112, forbids discrimination against persons with disabilities in both the public and private sectors. Its purpose, according to Turnbull (1993), is to "provide clear, strong, consistent, and enforceable standards prohibiting discrimination against individuals with disabilities without respect for their age, nature or extent of disability" (p. 23).

The ADA goes far beyond traditional thinking of who is disabled and embraces, for instance, people with AIDS, individuals who have successfully completed a substance abuse program, and persons with cosmetic disfigurements. In fact, any person with an impairment that substantially limits a major life activity is covered

Table 2.4 **A Comparison of Key Features of IDEA and Section 504**

Provision	IDEA	Section 504
Purpose	Provides a free appropriate public education to children and youth with specific disabilities.	Prohibits discrimination on the basis of a person's disability in all programs receiving federal funds.
Ages Covered	Individuals 3–21 years old.	No age restriction.
Definition of Disability	Twelve disabilities defined according to federal regulations plus state/local definition of *developmentally delayed.*	Broader interpretation of a disability than found in IDEA—a person with a physical or mental impairment that substantially limits a major life activity, who has a record of such impairment, or who is regarded as having such impairment.
Funding	States receive some federal dollars for excess cost of educating students with disabilities.	Because this is a civil rights law, no additional funding is provided.
Planning Documents	Individualized education program (IEP).	Accommodation plan (commonly referred to as a "504 plan").
Assessment Provisions	A comprehensive, nondiscriminatory eligibility evaluation in all areas of suspected disability conducted by a multidisciplinary team; reevaluations every three years unless waived.	Eligibility determination requires nondiscriminatory assessment procedures; requires reevaluation prior to a "significant change" in placement.
Due Process	Extensive rights and protections afforded to student and parents.	Affords parents impartial hearing, right to inspect records, and representation by counsel. Additional protections at discretion of local school district.
Coordination	No provision.	School district required to identify a 504 coordinator.
Enforcement	U.S. Department of Education, Office of Special Education Programs.	Office for Civil Rights, U.S. Department of Education.

by this legislation. It extends protections and guarantees of civil rights in such diverse arenas as private sector employment, transportation, telecommunications, public and privately owned accommodations, and the services of local and state government.

Examples of the impact of this landmark legislation include the following:

- Employers of fifteen or more workers must make "reasonable accommodations" so that an otherwise qualified individual with a disability is not discriminated against. Accommodations might include a Braille computer keyboard for a worker who is visually impaired or wider doorways to allow easy access for an employee who uses a wheelchair. Furthermore, hiring, termination, and promotion practices may not discriminate against an applicant or employee who has a disability.
- Mass transit systems, such as buses, trains, and subways, must be accessible to citizens with disabilities.
- Hotels, fast-food restaurants, theaters, hospitals, early childhood centers, banks, dentists' offices, retail stores, and the like may not discriminate against individuals with disabilities. These facilities must be accessible, or alternative means for providing services must be available.
- Companies that provide telephone service must offer relay services to individuals with hearing or speech impairments.

Think what this legislation means for the field of special education in general, and specifically for adolescents with disabilities as they prepare to leave high school and transition to the world of adulthood as independent citizens able to participate fully in all aspects of community life. Thanks to this enactment, the future of the almost 57 million Americans with disabilities is definitely brighter and more secure.

Public Law 110–325 (the Americans With Disabilities Act Amendments of 2008)

On September 25, 2008, President George W. Bush signed into law the

The Americans with Disabilities Act requires that mass transit systems be accessible to citizens with disabilities.

Americans with Disabilities Act Amendments. PL 110–325 became effective on January 1, 2009. Commonly called ADAA, this legislation revises the definition of a disability in favor of a broader interpretation, thereby extending protections to greater numbers of individuals. In fact, this law expressly overturns two Supreme Court decisions that had previously limited the meaning of the term *disability*. Additionally, ADAA expands the definition of "major life activities" by including two noninclusive lists, the first of which includes activities not expressly stipulated, such as reading, concentrating, and thinking. The second list includes major bodily functions—for example, functions of the immune system or neurological functioning (U.S. Equal Employment Opportunity Commission, 2013). The act also states that the interpretation of "substantial limitation" must be made without regard to the ameliorative effects of mitigating measures like medication or medical equipment. (The only stated exception is eyeglasses or contact lenses.)

Changes incorporated in this legislation also apply to students eligible for protections under Section 504 of PL 93–112. According to Zirkel (2009), "the overall effect is obviously to expand the number and range of students eligible under Section 504" (p. 69). A pupil, however, cannot be "regarded as" having a disability if his or her disability is minor or transitory (a duration of six months or less). It is anticipated that the new ADAA eligibility standards will have a significant impact on special education. "IDEA eligibility teams will need to closely coordinate with Section 504 eligibility teams not only when determining that a student is ineligible for initial services under IDEA but also upon exiting the student from an IEP" (Zirkel, 2009, p. 71).

We see the overall intent of this enactment as ensuring that individuals with disabilities receive the protections and services to which they are legally entitled.

Identification and Assessment of Individual Differences

One of the distinguishing characteristics of our field is the individuality and uniqueness of the students we serve. There is considerable wisdom in the maxim "No two children are alike." Experienced educators will quickly tell you that even though students may share a common disability label, such as *learning disabled* or *visually impaired*, that is where the similarity ends. These pupils are likely to be as different as day and night. Of course, the individuality of our students, both typical and atypical, has the potential for creating significant instructional and/or management concerns for the classroom teacher. Recall from Chapter 1 the types of youngsters enrolled in Mr. Thompson's fifth-grade classroom. Today's schools are serving an increasingly diverse student population. At the same time, there is greater cooperation and more shared responsibility between general and special educators as they collectively plan appropriate educational experiences for all learners.

When teachers talk about the individuality of their students, they often refer to interindividual differences. These differences are what distinguish each student from his or her classmates. Interindividual differences are differences *between* pupils. Examples might include distinctions based on height, reading ability, athletic prowess, or intellectual competency. Some interindividual differences are more obvious and of greater educational significance than others.

Interindividual differences are frequently the reason for entry into special education programs. One child might be significantly above (or below) average in intellectual ability; another might exhibit a significant degree of hearing loss. Categorization and placement decision making by school personnel revolve around interindividual differences. Stated another way, school authorities identify, label, and subsequently place a student in an instructional program on the basis of the student's interindividual differences.

However, not all pupils in a given program are alike. Children also exhibit intraindividual differences—a unique pattern of strengths and weaknesses. Intraindividual differences are differences *within* the child. Instead of looking at how students compare with their peers, teachers focus on the individual's abilities and limitations. We should point out that this is a characteristic of all pupils, not just those enrolled in special education programs. For example, Victoria, who is the best artist in her eighth-grade class, is equally well known for her inability to sing. One of her classmates, Melinda, has a learning disability. Her reading ability is almost three years below grade level, yet she consistently earns very high grades in math.

Intraindividual differences are obviously of importance to teachers. A student's IEP (individualized education program) reflects this concern. Assessment data, derived from a variety of sources, typically profile a pupil's strengths and needs. This information is then used in crafting a customized instructional plan tailored to meet the unique needs of the learner.

Referral and Assessment for Special Education

"Evaluation [assessment] is the gateway to special education but referral charts the course to the evaluation process" (Turnbull, Turnbull, Erwin, & Soodak, 2006, p. 232). Litigation, IDEA requirements, and today's best practices serve as our road map as we travel along the evaluation pathway to providing appropriate educational experiences for students with disabilities. This journey from referral to assessment to the development of an IEP and eventual placement in the most appropriate environment is a comprehensive process incorporating many different phases. Figure 2.2 illustrates this process. In the following sections, we examine several of the key elements involved in developing individualized program plans.

Prereferral

Although evaluation may be the gateway to special education, a great deal of activity occurs prior to a student's ever taking the first test. Careful scrutiny of our model

interindividual differences:
Differences between two or more persons in a particular area.

intraindividual differences:
Differences within the individual; unique patterns of strengths and weaknesses.

reveals an intervention strategy known as **prereferral intervention**, which occurs prior to initiating a referral for possible special education services. The purpose of this strategy is to reduce unwarranted referrals while providing individualized assistance to the student without the benefit of a special education. Although not mandated by IDEA, prereferral interventions have become increasingly common over the past two decades. In fact, IDEA 2004 permits the use of federal dollars to support these activities. Well over half of the states either require or recommend the use of this tactic with individuals suspected of having a disability (Buck, Polloway, Smith-Thomas, & Cook, 2003).

Prereferral interventions are preemptive by design. They call for collaboration between general educators and other professionals for the express purpose of developing creative, alternative instructional and/or management strategies designed to accommodate the particular needs of the learner. This process results in shared responsibility and joint decision making among general and special educators, related service providers, administrators, and other school personnel, all of whom possess specific expertise; the pupil's parents typically do not participate in this early phase. The child's success or failure in school no longer depends exclusively on the pedagogical skills of the general educator; rather, it is now the responsibility of the school-based intervention assistance team (also commonly known as teacher-assistance teams, instructional support teams, or child study teams) (Buck et al., 2003).

As beneficial as this strategy often is, it is not always successful. Detailed documentation of these intervention efforts provides a strong justification for the initiation of a formal referral.

Referral

A **referral** is the first step in a long journey toward receiving a special education. As we have just seen, a referral may start as a result of unsuccessful prereferral interventions, or it may be the outcome of **child-find** efforts (IDEA-mandated screening and identification of individuals suspected of needing special education).

Simply stated, a referral is a written request to evaluate a student to determine whether the child has a disability. Typically, a referral begins with a general educator; it may also be initiated by a school administrator, a related services provider, a concerned parent, or another individual. Referrals typically arise from a concern about the child's academic achievement and/or social/behavioral problems. In some instances, a referral may be initiated because of a pupil's cultural or linguistic background; it may even be the result of problems caused by inappropriate teacher expectations or poor instructional strategies. Thus, the reasons for the referral may not always lie within the student. This is one reason why prereferral intervention strategies are so important. Only about 75 percent of the referrals for special education services actually result in placement; the remaining children are found ineligible (Ysseldyke, 2001).

Referral forms vary in their format. Generally, in addition to student demographic information, a referral must contain detailed reasons as to why the request is being made. Teachers must clearly describe the pupil's academic and/or social performance. Documentation typically accompanies the referral and may include test scores, checklists, behavioral observation data, and actual samples of the student's work. Teachers need to paint as complete a picture as possible of their concern(s), as well as their efforts to rectify the situation.

In most schools, the information that has been gathered is then reviewed by a committee, often known as the child study committee, the special services team, or another such name. The composition of this group of professionals varies but typically includes an administrator, a school psychologist, and experienced teachers. Other

prereferral intervention: Instructional or behavioral strategies introduced by a general educator to assist students experiencing difficulty; designed to minimize inappropriate referrals for special education.

referral: A formal request by a teacher or parent that a student be evaluated for special education services.

child-find: A function of each state, mandated by federal law, to locate and refer individuals who might require special education.

REFERENCE
Referral

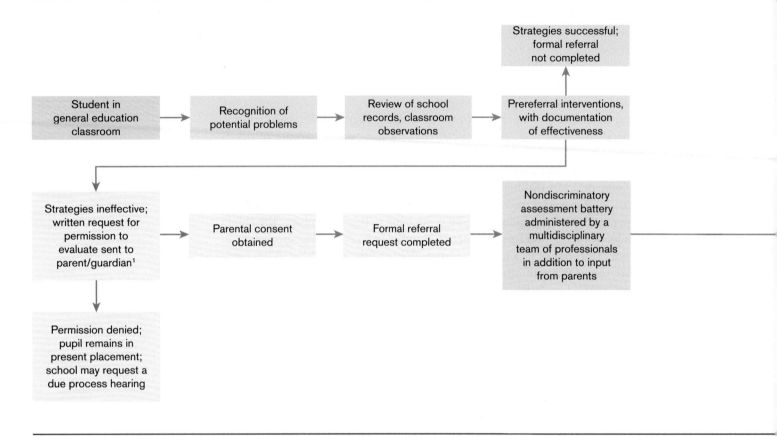

1. IDEA does not mandate parental consent for referral but does require consent for evaluation.

2. Eligibility determination must occur within sixty days of referral.

personnel may also be involved, depending on the nature of the referral. It is the job of this committee to review the available information and decide whether further assessment is warranted. If the team decides to proceed, a written request for permission to evaluate is sent to the child's parent(s). School authorities *must* obtain permission from the parent/guardian before proceeding with a formal evaluation. Interestingly, IDEA does not require parental consent for referrals. We believe, however, that it is wise to notify parents that a referral is being initiated, explain the reasons for the referral, and solicit their input and cooperation in the referral process.

Assessment

The first step in determining whether a student has a disability, and is in need of a special education, is securing the consent of the child's parent(s)/guardian(s) for the evaluation. As noted previously, this step is mandated by IDEA as part of the procedural safeguards protecting the legal rights of parent(s)/guardian(s). Under the provisions of IDEA, school officials must notify the pupil's parent(s)/guardian(s), in their native language, of the school's intent to evaluate (or refusal to evaluate) the student and the rationale for this decision; they must explain the assessment process and alternatives available to the parent(s)/guardian(s), such as the right to an independent evaluation of

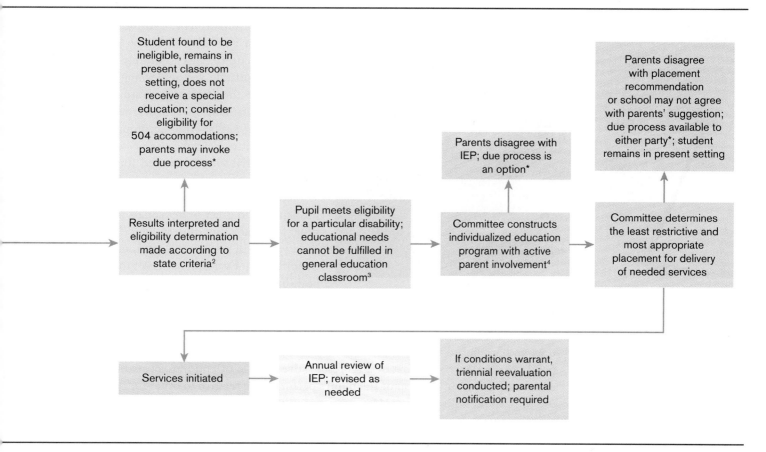

3. If parents refuse consent for a special education, the school district is not responsible for providing a free appropriate public education.

4. The IEP must be developed within thirty days of eligibility determination.

*Mandatory resolution session required prior to a due process hearing.

their son or daughter. Many schools automatically send parent(s)/guardian(s) a statement of their legal rights when initial permission to evaluate is sought.

Assessment, according to Gargiulo and Metcalf (2013), is a generic term that refers to the process of gathering information about a pupil's strengths and needs. Educational assessment can rightly be thought of as an information-gathering and decision-making process.

One of the goals of the assessment process is to obtain a complete profile of the student's abilities and his or her needs. By law (IDEA), this requires the use of a **multidisciplinary team** of professionals, of which one member must be a teacher. In practice, some school districts are fulfilling this mission by establishing inter- and transdisciplinary assessment teams. Regardless of the model adopted by the school district, the team is responsible for developing an individualized and comprehensive assessment package that evaluates broad developmental domains (cognitive, academic achievement) as well as the specific areas of concern noted on the referral, such as social/emotional problems or suspected visual impairments.

Successful accomplishment of this task dictates the use of both formal and informal assessment tools. Once again, IDEA is very clear about this issue: No one procedure may be used as the sole basis of evaluation; a multitude of tests is required. IDEA regulations further require that the evaluations be presented in the pupil's native

assessment: The process of gathering information and identifying a student's strengths and needs through a variety of instruments and products; data used in making decisions.

multidisciplinary team: A group of professionals from different disciplines who function as a team but perform their roles independent of one another.

Assessments can be conducted at a young age and must be individualized and comprehensive.

language or, when necessary, via other modes of communication such as sign language or Braille for students with a sensory impairment. Additionally, the selection and administration of the assessment battery must accurately reflect the child's aptitude and achievement and not penalize the student because of his or her impairment in sensory, manual, or speaking skills. The accompanying Insights feature describes some accommodations that may be needed for accurate assessment.

School psychologists, educational diagnosticians, and other professionals responsible for evaluating the student have a wide variety of assessment instruments at their disposal. Evaluators attempt to gauge both inter- and intraindividual differences by using both norm- and criterion-referenced assessments. Simply stated, **norm-referenced assessments** are standardized tests and are linked to interindividual differences. Norm-referenced tests compare a pupil's performance with that of a representative sample of children, providing the evaluator with an indication of the pupil's performance relative to other individuals of similar chronological age. Data are typically presented in terms of percentile ranks, stanines, or grade-equivalent scores. Data gleaned from norm-referenced tests provide limited instructional information. In contrast, **criterion-referenced assessments** are associated with intraindividual differences and can provide data that are useful for instructional planning. In this type of assessment procedure, a student's performance on a task is compared to a particular level of mastery. The criterion level is typically established by the classroom teacher. Criterion-referenced assessments are especially helpful, according to Gargiulo and Metcalf (2013), in pinpointing the specific skills that the pupil has mastered as well as determining what skills necessitate additional instruction. Teachers are concerned with the individual's pattern of strengths and needs rather than how the student compares with his or her classmates.

As mentioned earlier, evaluators must put together a complete educational portrait of the student's abilities. This frequently requires multiple sources of information, which typically include standardized tests, work samples, and observational data, among other forms of input. Table 2.5 summarizes some of the types of assessments increasingly being used by evaluation specialists to complement data derived from norm-referenced tests.

Instructional Programming and Appropriate Placement

When properly conducted, educational assessments lead to the development of meaningful IEPs and IFSPs. Measurable annual goals (and short-term objectives/benchmarks for pupils evaluated via alternate assessments) are crafted based on data gleaned from these evaluations. But first, the multidisciplinary team must determine whether the

norm-referenced assessments: Refers to standardized tests on which a pupil's performance is compared to that of his or her peers.

criterion-referenced assessment: An assessment procedure in which a student's performance is compared to a particular level of mastery.

REFERENCE

Assessment

INSIGHTS

Assessment Accommodations

In order to accurately portray a pupil's abilities and needs, assessment accommodations are sometimes necessary. Accommodations are changes in how students access and demonstrate learning without changing the standards they are working toward. Accommodations must be individualized; not all pupils require them, nor do students with the same disability require the same type of accommodations. The need for accommodations may change over time; some individuals may require fewer accommodations in one situation while in other situations additional support is required. Listed below are examples of accommodations that IEP teams may find beneficial.

Presentation accommodations let students access assignments, tests, and activities in ways other than reading standard print. Students with print disabilities (inability to visually decode standard print because of a physical, sensory, or cognitive disability) may require a combination of these accommodations:

- Visual: large print, magnification devices, sign language, visual cues
- Tactile: Braille, Nemeth code, tactile graphics
- Auditory: human reader, audio recording or CD, audio amplification device
- Visual and auditory: screen reader, video recording, descriptive video, talking materials

Response accommodations allow students to complete assignments, tests, and activities in different ways or solve or organize problems using an assistive device or organizer. Response accommodations include:

- Different ways to complete assignments, tests, and activities: expressing responses to a scribe through speech, sign language, pointing, or an assistive communication device; typing on or speaking to a word processor, Brailler, or audio recorder; writing in a test booklet instead of on an answer sheet
- Materials or devices to solve or organize responses: calculation devices; spelling and grammar assistive devices; visual or graphic organizers

Timing and scheduling accommodations give students the time and breaks they need to complete assignments, tests, and activities and may change the time of day, day of the week, or number of days over which an activity takes place. These include:

- Extended time
- Multiple or frequent breaks
- Changing the testing schedule or order of subtests
- Dividing long-term assignments

Setting accommodations change the location in which a student receives instruction or the conditions of the setting. Students may be allowed to sit in a different location than the majority of students to:

- Reduce distractions
- Receive accommodations
- Increase physical access
- Use special equipment

SOURCE: Adapted from S. Thompson, "Choosing and Using Accommodations on Assessments," *CEC Today, 10*(6), 2004, pp. 12, 18.

---

student is eligible to receive special education services according to specific state criteria. Eligibility standards differ from state to state, but most are framed around IDEA criteria.

If team members, working in concert with the child's parent(s), determine that the student fails to qualify for a special education, we suggest developing intervention strategies and recommendations for accommodations to address the referral concerns. We believe this is necessary because the pupil will remain in his or her present placement—the general education classroom. Additionally, the team may wish to consider the pupil for a 504 accommodation plan if the student is eligible for such services. Parent(s)/guardian(s) must be sent written notification summarizing the evaluation and stating why their son or daughter is ineligible to receive a special education. If, however, it is determined that the pupil is eligible for a special education, the multidisciplinary team is then confronted with two monumental tasks: constructing the IEP/IFSP and determining the most appropriate placement for the student.

VIDEO
Consulting Professionals

Table 25 **Emerging Sources of Assessment Information**

Source	Description
Naturalistic Observation	Documentation of qualitative as well as quantitative aspects of a youngster's behavior in the natural environment. Information may be recorded formally (rating scales, observational recording systems) or informally (anecdotal records, audio recordings). Data can be used to support or refute information gathered from other sources.
Interviews	Information obtained from significant individuals in a student's life—parents, teachers, older siblings, or the pupil him- or herself. Interviews are a planned and purposeful activity whose purpose is to gain insight or perspective on specific areas of interest, such as the child's background or possible reasons for behavioral problems. Formal may be formal (interviewer follows a predetermined set of questions) or informal (interview proceeds according to the individual's responses). Data may be gathered orally or in writing.
Work Samples	Evidence of a pupil's actual classroom performance, typically focused on particular skill development. Sometimes referred to as a permanent product. Spelling tests, arithmetic fact sheets, and handwriting samples are examples of this information source. Work samples are especially useful when planning instructional intervention and modification. Requires the teacher to think diagnostically and look, for example, at error patterns or clarity of directions.
Portfolios	A type of authentic assessment, portfolios are an outgrowth of the familiar work folder concept. They include a wide range of examples of a student's emerging abilities and accomplishments over time. Qualitative and quantitative indicators of performance might include writing samples, audio/video recordings, worksheets, drawings, photographs, or other forms of evidence. Useful for student self-assessment.

Designing Individualized Instructional Programs

According to IDEA, each student identified by a multidisciplinary child study team as having a disability and in need of special education must have an individualized program of specially designed instruction that addresses the unique needs of the child and, in the case of infants and toddlers, the needs of the family as well. IEPs and IFSPs are guides to the design and delivery of customized services and instruction. They also serve as vehicles for collaboration and cooperation between parents and professionals as they jointly devise appropriate educational experiences.

Individualized Education Program

An individualized education program (IEP) is part of an overall strategy designed to deliver services appropriate to the individual needs of pupils ages 3 and older. By the time we reach the IEP stage, the appropriate permissions have been gathered, assessments have been conducted, and a disability determination has been made. We are now at the point where the IEP is to be developed, followed by placement in the most appropriate and least restrictive setting. Bateman and Linden (2012) make a very important point about *when* the IEP is to be developed. They believe that IEPs are often written at the wrong time. Legally, the IEP is to be developed within thirty days following the evaluation and determination of the child's disability, but *before* a placement recommendation is formulated. Placement in the least restrictive and most normalized setting is based on a completed IEP, not the other way around. An IEP should not be limited by placement options or the availability of services. We believe it is best to see the IEP as a management tool or planning vehicle that ensures that children with disabilities receive an individualized education appropriate to their unique needs. It also guides the integration of the general and special education

VIDEO

IEPs

Elements of a Meaningful IEP

Current Performance. A statement of the student's present levels of educational and functional performance, including how the pupil's disability affects his or her involvement and progress in the general education curriculum, or, for preschoolers, how the disability affects participation in age-appropriate activities.

Goals. A statement of measurable annual goals (both functional and academic) that address the student's involvement and progress in the general education curriculum as well as the student's other education needs; short-term objectives or benchmarks are required for pupils who take alternate assessments aligned to alternate achievement standards.

Special Education and Related Services. A statement of special education, related services, and supplementary aids and services (based on peer-reviewed research) to be provided, including program modifications or supports necessary for the student to advance toward attainment of annual goals; to be involved and progress in the general education curriculum, extracurricular activities, and nonacademic activities; and to be educated and participate in activities with other children both with and without disabilities.

Participation With Typical Students. An explanation of the extent, if any, to which the student will *not* participate in the general education classroom.

Participation in State- and Districtwide Assessments. A statement of any individual modifications needed for the student to participate in a state- or districtwide assessment; if a student will not participate, a statement of why the assessment is inappropriate and how the pupil will be assessed.

Dates and Places. Projected date for initiation of services; expected location, duration, and frequency of such services.

Transition Services. Beginning at age 16, a statement of needed transition services identifying measurable postschool goals (training, education, employment, and, if appropriate, independent living skills), including a statement of interagency linkages and/or responsibilities.

Measuring Progress. A statement of how progress toward annual goals will be measured and how a student's parents (or guardians) will be regularly informed of such progress.

Age of Majority. Information provided at least one year before reaching the age of majority regarding transfer of rights to the student upon reaching the age of majority.

---

curriculum (Diliberto & Brewer, 2012). This focus is in concert with both the intent and the spirit of IDEA.

IEPs are written by a team. At a minimum, participation must include a parent/guardian; the child's teachers, including a general education teacher and a special educator; a representative from the school district; and an individual able to interpret the instructional implications of the evaluation. When appropriate, the student, as well as other professionals who possess pertinent information or whose expertise is desired, may participate at the discretion of the parent or school. Parents have a legal right to participate meaningfully in this planning and decision-making process; they serve as the child's advocate. Although IDEA mandates a collaborative role for parents, it does not stipulate the degree or extent of their participation.

IEPs will vary greatly in their format and degree of specificity. Government regulations do not specify the level of detail considered appropriate, nor do they stipulate how the IEP is to be constructed—only that it be a written document. What is specified are the components (see the accompanying Insights feature).

As stated previously, an IEP is, in essence, a management tool that stipulates *who* will be involved in providing a special education, *what* services will be offered, *where* they will be delivered, and for *how long*. In addition, an IEP gauges *how successfully* goals have been met. Although the IEP does contain a measure of accountability, it is not a legally binding contract; schools are not liable if goals are not achieved. Schools

> For an in-depth example of an IEP, visit the SAGE Study Site at edge.sagepub.com/gargiulo5e.

Parents play a crucial role in developing their child's individualized education program.

are liable, however, if they do not provide the services stipulated in the IEP. IEPs are to be reviewed annually, although parents may request an earlier review. A complete reevaluation of the pupil's eligibility for special education must occur every three years. PL 108–446 waives this requirement, however, if both the parents and school officials agree that such a review is not necessary.

IEPs are not meant to be so detailed or complete that they serve as the entire instructional agenda, nor are they intended to dictate what the individual is taught. They do have to be individualized, however, and address the unique learning and/ or behavioral requirements of the student. It is for this reason that we find fault with the growing reliance on computer-generated goals and objectives. Although computer-managed IEPs may serve as a useful logistical tool, like Bateman and Linden (2012), we have grave doubts as to the educational relevancy of this procedure and question its legality. We hope teachers will use this resource only as a starting point for designing customized and individually tailored plans.

One of the challenges confronting the IEP team is ensuring that students have access to the general education curriculum as stipulated in both the 1997 and 2004 reauthorizations of IDEA. But what is the general education curriculum? In most instances, it is the curriculum that typical learners are exposed to, which is often established by individual state boards of education. The IEP must address how the pupil's disability affects his or her involvement in and ability to progress in the general education curriculum. The underlying assumption seems to be that even if a child is receiving a special education, he or she should engage the general education curriculum. Documentation is required if the team believes that this curriculum is inappropriate for a particular student.

IDEA 2004 requires the IEP team to develop measurable annual goals while also emphasizing exposure to the general education curriculum. Goal statements are purposely broad. Their intent is to provide long-range direction to a student's educational program, not to define exact instructional tasks. Based on the pupil's current level of performance, goals are "written to reflect what a student needs in order to become involved in and to make progress in the general education curriculum" (Yell, 2012, p. 253). They represent reasonable projections or estimates of what the pupil should be able to accomplish within the academic year. They also answer the question "What should the student be doing?" Annual goals can reflect academic functioning, social behavior, adaptive behavior, or life skills. Regardless of their emphasis, goal statements should be positive, student oriented, and relevant (Polloway, Patton, Serna, & Bailey, 2012).

Measurable annual goals should include the following five components:

- The student (the who)
- Will do what (the behavior)

AUDIO
Student Involvement

SUGGESTIONS FOR THE CLASSROOM

Suggested Individualized Education Program Meeting Agenda

→ Welcome and introduction of participants and their respective roles

→ Statement of purpose

→ Review of previous year's IEP (except for initial placement) and accomplishments

→ Discussion of student's present level of performance and progress:
- Assessment information
- Strengths and emerging areas

→ Consideration of specific needs:
- Instructional modifications and accommodations
- Participation in state- and districtwide assessments
- Related services

- Assistive technology needs
- Transition goals
- Behavior intervention plan
- Language needs for student with limited English proficiency
- Braille instruction for student who is visually impaired

→ Development of annual goals (and benchmarks if appropriate)

→ Recommendations and justification for placement in least restrictive environment

→ Closing comments, securing of signatures

→ Copies of IEP to all team members

- To what level or degree (the criterion)
- Under what conditions (the conditions)
- In what length of time (the time frame)

Quality IEPs largely depend on having well-written and appropriate goals (and objectives) that address the unique needs of the individual. IEPs are the primary means of ensuring that a specially designed educational program is provided. The accompanying Suggestions for the Classroom feature provides a sample agenda for an IEP team meeting.

Individualized Family Service Plan

The individualized family service plan (IFSP) is the driving force behind the delivery of early intervention services to infants and toddlers who are at risk or have a disability. The IFSP was originally conceived to focus on children younger than age 3, but recent changes in thinking now allow this document to be used with preschoolers who require a special education. This change was initiated by the federal government in an effort to minimize the differences between early intervention and preschool special education services; the government is now encouraging states to establish "seamless systems" designed to serve youngsters from birth through age 5. As a result of this policy decision, states now have the authority to use IFSPs for preschoolers with special needs until the children enter kindergarten (Lipkin & Schertz, 2008).

Like an IEP, an IFSP is developed by a team consisting of professionals and the child's parents as key members. In addition, parents may invite other family members to participate, as well as an advocate. Typically, the service coordinator who has

For an in-depth example of an IFSP, visit the SAGE Study Site at edge.sagepub.com/gargiulo5e.

VIDEO
IEP Meetings

■ ■ ■ ■ ■ Table 2.6 **Comparable Components of an IEP and IFSP**

Individualized Education Program	Individualized Family Service Plan
A statement of the child's present levels of academic achievement and functional performance, including involvement and progress in the general education curriculum	A statement of the infant's or toddler's present levels of physical, cognitive, communication, social/emotional, and adaptive development
No comparable feature	A statement of the family's resources, priorities, and concerns
A statement of measurable annual goals, including benchmarks or short-term instructional objectives for children who take alternate assessments aligned to alternate achievement standards	A statement of measurable results or outcomes expected to be achieved for the infant or toddler and the family
A statement indicating progress toward annual goals and a mechanism for regularly informing parents/guardians of such progress	Criteria, procedures, and timelines used to determine the degree to which progress toward achieving the outcomes or results is being made
A statement of specific special education and related services and supplementary aids and services, based on peer-reviewed research, to be provided and any program modifications	A statement of specific early intervention services, based on peer-reviewed research, necessary to meet the unique needs of the infant or toddler and the family
An explanation of the extent to which the child will not participate in general education programs	A statement of the natural environments in which early intervention services will appropriately be provided, or justification, if not provided
Modifications needed to participate in state- or districtwide assessments	No comparable feature
The projected date for initiation of services and the anticipated duration, frequency, and location of services	The projected date for initiation of services and the anticipated duration of services
No comparable feature	The name of the service coordinator
At age 16, a statement of transition services needed, including courses of study in addition to measurable postsecondary goals	The steps to be taken to support the child's transition to other services at age 3

SOURCE: Adapted from Individuals with Disabilities Education Improvement Act of 2004, Title 20 U.S. Code (U.S.C.) 1400 *et seq*, Part B Section 614 (d) (1) (A), and Part C Section 636 (d).

been working with the family, the professionals involved in the assessment of the youngster, and the service providers constitute the remainder of the group charged with the responsibility of writing the IFSP. The elements required for an IFSP, as stipulated in PL 108–446, are summarized in Table 2.6.

The IFSP was intentionally designed to preserve the family's role as primary caregiver. Well-constructed IFSPs, which are reviewed every six months, fully support the family and encourage their active and meaningful involvement. This thinking is in keeping with an empowerment model (Turnbull, Turnbull, Erwin, Soodak, & Shogren, 2011) that views families as capable (with occasional assistance) of helping themselves. It allows parents to retain their decision-making role, establish goals, and assess their own needs. It is also in keeping with our support of an ecological perspective (Gargiulo & Kilgo, 2014), which argues that one cannot look at a child without considering the various systems and spheres of influence that provide support—in this instance, the infant's or toddler's family and community.

Information obtained from the assessment of the family and data about the infant's or toddler's developmental status are used to generate outcome statements or goals for the child and his or her family. Practitioners are increasingly emphasizing real-life or authentic goals for children with special needs (Pretti-Frontczak & Bricker, 2004). These goals, which are based on the priorities and concerns of the family, are

■ ■ ■ ■ ■ ■ *Table 2.7* **Definitions of Typical Educational Settings Serving School-Age Students With Disabilities**

Setting	Definition
Regular Classroom	Students who spend at least 80 percent of the school day in a regular or general education classroom.
Resource Room	Students who receive special education and related services in the regular classroom between 40 and 79 percent of the school day. Students are "pulled out" of the regular classroom and receive specialized instruction or services in a separate classroom for limited periods of time. Services may be individualized or offered in small groups.
Separate Class	Students who receive special education and related services in the regular classroom for less than 40 percent of the school day. Commonly known as a self-contained classroom wherein pupils, usually those with more severe disabilities, receive full-time instruction or, in a modified version, participate in nonacademic aspects of school activities. Classroom is located in typical school building.
Separate School	Students who receive special education and related services in a public or private separate day school for students with disabilities, at public expense, for more than 50 percent of the school day.
Residential Facility	Students who receive a special education in a public or private residential facility, at public expense, twenty-four hours a day.
Homebound/Hospital	Students placed in and receiving a special education in a hospital or homebound program.

SOURCE: Adapted from U.S. Department of Education. (2000). *Twenty-second Annual Report to Congress on the Implementation of the Individuals with Disabilities Education Act* (Washington, DC: U.S. Government Printing Office), p. II–14.

reflected in the IFSP's required outcome statements. Interventionists no longer teach skills in isolation; rather, goals are developed that are relevant to the daily activities of the youngsters and their families. These statements need to be practical and functional, reflecting real-life situations occurring in the natural environment.

Service Delivery Options: Where a Special Education Is Provided

Now that the IEP/IFSP team has decided *what* will be taught, it must decide *where* special education services will be provided. The issue of appropriate placement of children with disabilities has generated considerable controversy and debate. In fact, it has been a point of contention among special educators for almost forty years. IDEA mandates that services be provided to students in the least restrictive setting—or, as Henry and Flynt (1990) called it, the most productive environment. The question confronting the team is "What is the most appropriate placement for achieving the goals (outcomes) of the IEP (IFSP)?" The chosen setting must allow the pupil to reach his or her IEP (IFSP) goals and work toward his or her potential.

It is at this point in our decision-making model that school authorities, in collaboration with the child's parent(s)/guardian(s), attempt to reach agreement about where the student will be served. The principle guiding this decision is known as the **least restrictive environment (LRE)**. This is a relative concept; it must be determined individually for each pupil. We interpret this principle to mean that students with disabilities should be educated in a setting that most closely approximates the general education classroom *and* still meets the unique needs of the individual. As we will see shortly, for a growing number of students, this setting is the general education classroom. The concept of LRE calls for maximum opportunity for meaningful involvement and participation with classmates who are not disabled. One of its inherent difficulties

least restrictive environment (LRE): A relative concept individually determined for each student; principle that each pupil should be educated, to the maximum extent appropriate, with classmates who are typical.

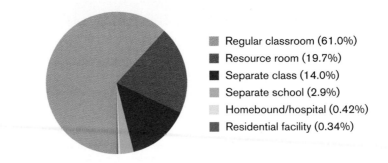

Legend:
- Regular classroom (61.0%)
- Resource room (19.7%)
- Separate class (14.0%)
- Separate school (2.9%)
- Homebound/hospital (0.42%)
- Residential facility (0.34%)

NOTE: Data are for students ages 6–21 enrolled in special education during the 2011–2012 school year.

Separate schools include both public and private facilities; residential settings include both public and private facilities.

Information based on data from the fifty states, the District of Columbia, Puerto Rico, and outlying areas.

SOURCE: U.S. Department of Education. (2013). *Historical state-level IDEA data files*. Retrieved November 13, 2013, from http://tadnet.public.tadnet.org/pages/712

is the required balancing of maximum integration with the delivery of an appropriate education.

Educational Placements

The federal government annually monitors the different settings in which pupils with disabilities receive a special education. Figure 2.3 illustrates the percentage of students in each of six environments recognized by the U.S. Department of Education. This figure does not include, however, the very small number of students (1.3%) served in correctional facilities or individuals placed in private schools by their parents. Table 2.7 describes the six typical school settings. We will report placement information in future chapters according to these six environments.

A Cascade of Service Delivery Options

As we have just seen, the federal government recognizes that no one educational setting is appropriate for meeting the needs of all children with disabilities. Effective delivery of a special education requires an array or continuum of placement possibilities customized to the individual requirements of each pupil. The concept of a continuum of educational services has been part of the fabric of American special education for over four decades. Reynolds (1962) originally described the concept of a range of placement options in 1962. His thinking was later elaborated on and expanded by Deno (1970), who constructed a model offering a "cascade" or continuum of settings. A traditional view of service delivery options is portrayed in Figure 2.4.

In this model, the general education classroom is viewed as the most normalized or typical setting; consequently, the greatest number of students are served in this environment. This placement would be considered the least restrictive option. Deviation from the general education classroom should occur only when it is educationally necessary for the pupil to receive an appropriate education. Each higher level depicted in Figure 2.4 represents a progressively more restrictive setting. Movement up the hierarchy generally leads to the delivery of more intensive services to children

AUDIO

Placement

Figure 2.4 **A Traditional View of Service Delivery Options**

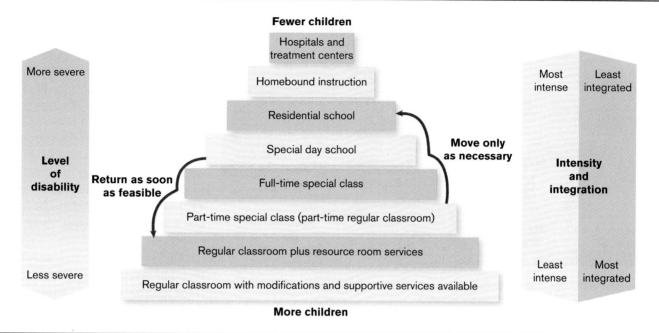

SOURCE: Adapted from S. Graves, R. Gargiulo, and L. Sluder, *Young Children: An Introduction to Early Childhood Education* (St. Paul, MN: West, 1996), p. 398.

with more severe disabilities, who are fewer in number. However, intensive supports are now being provided in general education classrooms with increasing frequency. Environments at the upper levels are considered to be the most restrictive and least normalized, yet, as we will see shortly, they may be the most appropriate placement for a particular individual.

As originally conceived, the natural flow of this cascade of service delivery options would be in a downward movement from more restrictive settings to those viewed as least restrictive, such as the general education classroom with or without support services. Contemporary thinking, however, suggests that pupils begin in the general education classroom and ascend the model, reaching a level that meets their unique needs. A key feature of this model, too often overlooked, is that a particular placement is only temporary; flexibility or freedom of movement is what makes this model work. The settings must be envisioned as fluid rather than rigid. As the needs of the pupil change, so should the environment; this is why there is an array of service delivery possibilities. In our opinion, there is no one best educational placement for each and every student with disabilities.

A Contemporary Challenge

At the present time, the field of special education is confronting the challenge of calls for greater inclusion of individuals with disabilities into all aspects of society, especially educational programs. Simply stated, some advocates for people with disabilities (and some parents as well) dismiss the long-standing concept of a continuum of service delivery possibilities and argue that *all* pupils with disabilities, regardless of the type or severity of their impairment, should be educated in general education classrooms at neighborhood schools. They argue further that students should be served on the basis of their chronological age rather than academic ability or mental age. This is truly

Inclusion

Federal law stipulates that, to the maximum extent appropriate, pupils with disabilities are to be educated with their typical classmates.

an explosive proposal. The debate surrounding this issue is an emotionally charged one with great potential for polarizing the field of special education, as other professionals, advocates, and parents argue fervently against this thinking. According to Gargiulo and Kilgo (2014), supporters of this movement see it as the next great revolution in special education, whereas opponents consider it the start of a return to the "dark ages" of special education—the era before PL 94–142. We suspect that the truth lies somewhere between these two extremes.

The intensity of this debate is fueled by several factors, one of which is the inconsistent use of terminology. As frequently happens in arguments, people are often saying the same thing but using different words. Therefore, we offer the following interpretations of key terms frequently encountered in describing this movement.

Mainstreaming

The first potentially confusing term is mainstreaming, which first appeared on the educational scene more than forty years ago. It evolved from an argument put forth by Dunn (1968), who, in a classic essay, questioned the pedagogical wisdom of serving children with mild intellectual disability in self-contained classrooms, which was then common practice. Other professionals soon joined with Dunn in his call for a more integrated service delivery model, resulting in the beginning of a movement away from isolated special classes as the placement of choice.

We define mainstreaming—or, in contemporary language, integration—as the social and instructional integration of students with disabilities into educational programs whose primary purpose is to serve typically developing individuals. It represents a common interpretation of the principle of educating children with disabilities in the least restrictive environment. Interestingly, the term *mainstreaming* itself never appears in any piece of federal legislation.

Parents no longer have to prove that their son or daughter should be mainstreamed; rather, schools must justify their position to exclude. They must prove that they have made a good-faith effort at integration or present strong evidence that an inclusionary setting is unsatisfactory (Yell, 2012). PL 108–446 currently supports this thinking.

Mainstreaming must provide the student with an appropriate education based on the unique needs of the child. It is our opinion that policymakers never envisioned that mainstreaming would be interpreted to mean that *all* children with special needs must be placed in integrated placements; to do so would mean abandoning the idea of determining the most appropriate placement for a particular child. IDEA clearly stipulates that, to the maximum extent appropriate, children with disabilities are to be educated with their typical peers. We interpret this provision to mean that, for

mainstreaming: An early term for the practice of integrating students with special needs into a general education classroom for all or part of the school day.

VIDEO
Staying Current

some individuals, an integrated setting, even with supplementary aids and services, might be an inappropriate placement in light of the child's unique characteristics. A least restrictive environment does not automatically mean placement with typical learners. As educators, we need to make the distinction between appropriateness and restrictiveness.

Least Restrictive Environment

Least restrictive environment (LRE) is a legal term often interpreted to say individuals with disabilities are to be educated in environments as close as possible to the general education classroom setting. An LRE is not a place but a concept.

Determination of the LRE is made individually for each child. An appropriate placement for one student could quite easily be inappropriate for another. The LRE is based on the pupil's educational needs, not on his or her disability. It applies equally to children of school age and to preschoolers. Even infants and toddlers with disabilities are required by law (PL 102–119) to have services delivered in normalized settings.

Inherent within the mandate of providing a special education and/or related services within the LRE is the notion of a continuum of service delivery possibilities. Figure 2.4 (page 69) reflects varying degrees of restrictiveness, or amount of available contact with typical learners. Being only with children with disabilities is considered restrictive; placement with peers without disabilities is viewed as least restrictive. As we ascend the continuum, the environments provide fewer and fewer opportunities for interaction with typically developing age-mates—hence the perception of greater restrictiveness. Despite a strong preference for association with students who are typical, this desire must be balanced by the requirement of providing an education appropriate to the unique needs of the individual. Consequently, an integrative environment may not always be the most appropriate placement option. Each situation must be individually assessed and decided on a case-by-case basis. The educational setting must meet the needs of the learner. The philosophy of the LRE guides rather than prescribes decision making (Meyen, 1995).

We recognize, as do many other special educators, that maximum integration with typically developing children is highly desirable and should be one of our major goals. The question is when, where, with whom, and to what extent individuals with disabilities are to be integrated.

Regular Education Initiative

The third concept that requires our attention is the regular education initiative, or, as it is commonly called, REI. REI is an important link in the evolution of the full inclusion movement. The term was introduced in 1986 by former Assistant Secretary of Education (Office of Special Education and Rehabilitative Services) Madeleine Will, who questioned the legitimacy of special education as a separate system of education and called for a restructuring of the relationship between general (regular) and special education. She endorsed the idea of shared responsibility—a partnership between general and special education resulting in a coordinated delivery system (Will, 1986b). Will recommended that general educators assume greater responsibility for students with disabilities. She envisioned a meaningful partnership whereby general and special educators would "cooperatively assess the educational needs of students with learning problems and cooperatively develop effective educational strategies for meeting those needs" (Will, 1986a, p. 415). Will (1986b) also believes that educators must "visualize

regular education initiative (REI): An approach that advocates that general educators assume greater responsibility for the education of students with disabilities.

REFERENCE
Least Restrictive Environment

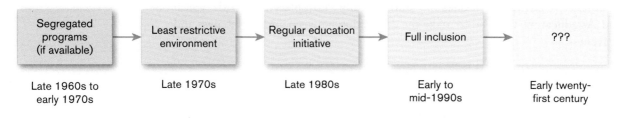

SOURCE: From R. Gargiulo and J. Kilgo, *An Introduction to Young Children With Special Needs*, 4th ed. ©2014 Wadsworth, a part of Cengage Learning, Inc. Reproduced by permission. www.cengage.com/permissions

a system that will bring the program to the child rather than one that brings the child to the program" (p. 21). As special educators, most of us can embrace this idea. Few professionals would dispute that the delivery of special education services would be significantly enhanced if there were greater coordination, cooperation, and collaboration between general and special educators.

Full Inclusion

We see the movement toward **full inclusion** as an extension of REI and earlier thinking about where children with disabilities should be educated. Full inclusion represents the latest trend in meeting the requirement of providing an education in the least restrictive environment (Bennett, DeLuca, & Bruns, 1997). Fox and Ysseldyke (1997) consider full inclusion as a further attempt at operationalizing the concept of LRE. Figure 2.5 illustrates the evolution of this thought process.

Full inclusion is a potentially explosive issue, with vocal supporters as well as detractors. It has emerged as one of the most controversial and complex subjects in the field of special education. As with other controversial topics, an agreed-upon definition is difficult to develop. We offer the following succinct interpretation: Full inclusion is a belief that *all* children with disabilities should be taught exclusively (with appropriate supports) in general education classrooms at neighborhood schools—that is, in the same school and age-/grade-appropriate classrooms they would attend if they were not disabled. Successful implementation will require new thinking about curriculum design along with increased collaboration between general and special educators (Noonan & McCormick, 2006). Recall that Will (1986b) originally proposed this type of partnership in her regular education initiative.

Although the trend in judicial interpretations is toward inclusionary placement (Yell, 2012), the LRE mandate does not require that all pupils be educated in general education classrooms or in their neighborhood schools. The framers of IDEA never pictured, according to Kauffman (1995), that the general education classroom located in the neighborhood school would be the least restrictive setting for all pupils. In fact, policymakers believed that a cascade of placement options would be required in order to provide an appropriate education for students with disabilities.

Advocates of full inclusion (Downing, 2008; Kennedy & Horn, 2004; Peterson & Hittie, 2010) argue that the present pullout system of serving students with special needs is ineffective. They contend that "the diagnostic and instructional models, practices, and tools associated with the EHA [PL 94–142] and mainstreaming are fundamentally flawed, particularly for students considered to have mild to

full inclusion: An interpretation of the principle of least restrictive environment advocating that all pupils with disabilities be educated in the general education classroom.

Full inclusion results in students with disabilities being seen as full-fledged members of the general education classroom.

moderate disabilities" (Skrtic, 1995, p. 625). Children are labeled and stigmatized, their programming is frequently fragmented, and general educators often assume little or no ownership for students in special education (a "your" kids versus "my" kids attitude). Placement in a general education classroom, with a working partnership between special education teachers and general educators, would result in a better education for all pupils, not just those with special needs, and would occur within the context of the least restrictive environment.

When correctly instituted, full inclusion is characterized by its virtual invisibility. Students with disabilities are not segregated but dispersed into classrooms they would normally attend if they were not disabled. They are seen as full-fledged members of, not merely visitors to, the general education classroom. Special educators provide an array of services and supports in the general education classroom alongside their general education colleagues, often using strategies such as cooperative teaching in an effort to meet the needs of the pupils. Table 2.8 summarizes the key components of most models of full inclusion.

Full inclusion is definitely a controversial topic; even professional organizations have opposing viewpoints. For instance, the Association for Persons with Severe Handicaps (TASH) has issued a statement fully supporting inclusion, which it considers to be a national moral imperative. However, the desirability of full inclusion is questioned in some

VIDEO

Inclusion

Table 2.8 Representative Elements of Full Inclusion Models

Model	Description
"Home school" attendance	Defined as the local school the child would attend if he or she did not have a disability.
Natural proportion at the school site	The percentage of children with special needs enrolled in a particular school is in proportion to the percentage of pupils with exceptionalities in the entire school district; in general education classes, this would mean approximately two to three students with disabilities.
Zero rejection	All students are accepted at the local school, including those with severe impairments; pupils are not screened out or grouped separately because of their disability.
Age-/grade-appropriate placement	A full inclusion model calls for serving children with special needs in general education classrooms according to their chronological age rather than basing services on the child's academic ability or mental age.

SOURCE: W. Sailor, M. Gerry, and W. Wilson, "Policy Implications for Emergent Full Inclusion Models for the Education of Students with Disabilities," in W. Wang, H. Wolberg, and M. Reynolds (Eds.), *Handbook of Special Education,* Vol. 4 (New York, NY: Pergamon Press, 1991), pp. 175–193; S. Stainback and W. Stainback, "Schools as Inclusive Communities," in W. Stainback and S. Stainback (Eds.), *Controversial Issues Confronting Special Education: Divergent Perspectives* (Boston, MA: Allyn & Bacon, 1992), pp. 29–43.

professional circles. The Council for Learning Disabilities, for example, endorses the continuation of service delivery options. The Council for Exceptional Children (CEC), the premier professional organization in the field of special education, has also taken a stand on this issue. Its policy statement on full inclusion, adopted in 1993, reads as follows:

> The Council for Exceptional Children (CEC) believes that all children, youth, and young adults with disabilities are entitled to a free and appropriate education and/or services that lead to an adult life characterized by satisfying relations with others, independent living, productive engagement in the community, and participation in society at large. To achieve such outcomes, there must exist for all children, youth, and young adults with disabilities a rich variety of early intervention, educational, and vocational program options with experiences. Access to these programs and experiences should be based on individual educational need and desired outcomes. Furthermore, students and their families or guardians, as members of the planning team, may recommend the placement, curriculum option, and the exit document to be pursued.
>
> CEC believes that a continuum of services must be available for all children, youth, and young adults. CEC also believes that the concept of inclusion is a meaningful goal to be pursued in our schools and communities. In addition, CEC believes children, youth, and young adults with disabilities should be served whenever possible in general education classrooms in inclusive neighborhood schools and community settings. Such settings should be strengthened and supported by an infusion of specially trained personnel and other appropriate supportive practices according to the individual needs of the child. (Council for Exceptional Children, 1994, pp. 5–6)

The argument, as we see it, is not about *what* is taught or the kinds of services to be provided to students with disabilities, but about *where* services are to be provided. We ought to be primarily concerned with how best to achieve the desired educational outcomes appropriate to the needs of the individual learner, rather than with the specific setting in which this occurs. Finally, there is one perplexing issue that still must be resolved. If we have accurately portrayed and interpreted full inclusion, then we believe

AUDIO
Chapter 2 Summary

it represents a radical departure from the concept of a cascade of placement options and, therefore, may well be a violation of current federal law. We suspect that, unfortunately, the resolution of this debate will rest with the courts.

Litigation and Legislation Affecting Special Education

- National and state laws, along with their subsequent interpretation by the courts, have certainly helped shape and define contemporary special education policy and procedures.

Educational Reform: Standards-Based Education

- The No Child Left Behind Act is an example of federal legislation that focuses on educational accountability. All students, including those with a disability, are expected to demonstrate proficiency in key academic subjects.
- The reauthorization of the Individuals with Disabilities Education Act in 2004 (PL 108–446) aligns this legislation with some of the provisions of the No Child Left Behind Act. In addition, substantial changes occurred in the following areas of the law: the IEP process, the identification of an individual for a possible learning disability, teacher qualifications, student discipline, due process procedures, the evaluation of pupils, and participation of individuals with disabilities in state- and districtwide assessments.

Civil Rights Legislation

- Section 504 of PL 93–112 is the first federal law specifically aimed at protecting children and adults against discrimination due to a disability.
- The Americans with Disabilities Act (PL 101–336), which parallels Section 504 of PL 93–112, forbids discrimination against individuals with disabilities in both the public and private sectors of society.

Identification and Assessment of Individual Differences

- Interindividual differences are those characteristics that distinguish each student from his or her classmates. Interindividual differences might include distinctions based on height, intelligence, or gross motor skills.
- Intraindividual differences are differences within a particular student—that child's unique profile of strengths and weaknesses.

Referral and Assessment for Special Education

- When properly conducted, educational assessments lead to the development of meaningful IEPs (individualized education programs) and IFSPs (individualized family service plans).
- Multidisciplinary teams use norm- and criterion-referenced tests to determine if a student is eligible to receive a special education and/or related services.

Designing Individualized Instructional Programs

- An individualized education program (IEP) is essentially a management tool that stipulates who will be involved in providing a special education, what services and instruction will be provided, where they will be delivered, and for how long. In addition, the IEP is designed to gauge whether or not goals are successfully achieved.
- The individualized family service plan (IFSP) is the driving force behind the delivery of early intervention services to infants and toddlers and their families.
- The IFSP is family focused and is designed to preserve the parent's role of primary caregiver and principal decision maker. It must address the concerns and priorities of the family while also acknowledging the resources and strengths of the family.

Service Delivery Options: Where a Special Education Is Provided

- According to the principle of least restrictive environment (LRE), services are to be provided in the setting that most closely approximates the general education classroom while still meeting the unique needs and requirements of the learner.
- Mainstreaming represents a popular interpretation of the principle of LRE.
- Implicit in the mandate of LRE is the notion of a continuum or cascade of service delivery options—a hierarchy of educational environments that allows for customized placement possibilities based on the needs of the individual pupil.
- Full inclusion seeks to place all students with disabilities, regardless of the type or severity of their impairment, in age-/grade-appropriate classrooms at neighborhood schools.
- The concept of full inclusion evolved from the regular education initiative, which sought a shared responsibility or partnership between general and special educators, resulting in greater collaboration and cooperation in meeting the needs of pupils with disabilities.

STUDY QUESTIONS

1. How have litigation and legislation influenced the field of special education?

2. What is the significance of the following cases?
   - Brown v. Board of Education of Topeka, Kansas
   - Pennsylvania Association for Retarded Children v. Commonwealth of Pennsylvania
   - Larry P. v. Riles
   - Board of Education of the Hendrick Hudson Central School District v. Rowley
   - Daniel R.R. v. State Board of Education

3. Name and describe the six major components and guarantees contained in PL 94–142.

4. What was the purpose of the Americans with Disabilities Act? List four areas where this law affects the lives of individuals who are disabled.

5. How did PL 108–446 modify PL 105–17?

6. Distinguish between interindividual and intraindividual differences.

7. How do prereferral interventions benefit the student suspected of requiring a special education?

8. How do norm-referenced and criterion-referenced tests differ?

9. List the key elements required of a meaningful IEP. Who is responsible for developing this document?

10. Compare the provisions and purpose of an IFSP with those of an IEP.

11. Define the following terms: mainstreaming, least restrictive environment, and regular education initiative. How are these terms related to the mandate of providing services in the LRE?

12. Distinguish between a cascade of services delivery model and the philosophy of full inclusion. What do you see as the advantages and disadvantages of full inclusion?

KEY TERMS

interindividual differences, 56

intraindividual differences, 56

prereferral intervention, 57

referral, 57

child-find, 67

assessment, 59

multidisciplinary team, 59

norm-referenced assessments, 60

criterion-referenced assessments, 60

least restrictive environment (LRE), 67

mainstreaming, 70

regular education initiative (REI), 71

full inclusion, 72

LEARNING ACTIVITIES

1. Interview an administrator of special education programs for your local school district. Find out how court decisions and legislative requirements have affected the delivery of special education services. Here are some suggested topics for discussion:
   - How has special education changed over the past several years as a result of judicial and legislative mandates?
   - What does the school district do to protect the rights of the students, involve parents, ensure due process, and assess in a nondiscriminatory manner?
   - How is the school district meeting the requirement of educating pupils with disabilities in the least restrictive environment?
   - What are the perceived advantages and disadvantages of IDEA at the local level?

2. Obtain a copy of your state's special education law. How do the requirements and provisions of the law compare with IDEA?

3. Obtain samples of several IEPs and IFSPs from different school districts in your vicinity. In what ways do the forms differ? How are they the same? Do they fulfill the requirements of the law as outlined in your textbook?

4. Visit several elementary and high schools in your area. What service delivery options are available for students with disabilities? Are children with different exceptionalities served in similar settings? Ask the teachers what they believe are the advantages and disadvantages of their particular environment.

The following exercises are designed to help you learn to apply the Council for Exceptional Children (CEC) standards to your teaching practice. Each of the reflection exercises below correlates with a knowledge or skill within the CEC standards. For the full text of each of the related CEC standards, please refer to the standards integration grid located in Appendix B.

Focus on Professional Learning and Ethical Practice (*CEC Initial Preparation Standard 6.2*)

Reflect on what you have learned in this chapter about the rights of individuals with disabilities. What measures would you take in your classroom to make sure that your students were educated in the least restrictive environment possible?

Focus on Learner Development and Individual Learning Differences (*CEC Initial Preparation Standard 1.2*)

Reflect on what you have learned in this chapter about understanding the uniqueness of each of your students. Pair up with another student and assess his or her intraindividual differences (unique patterns of strengths and weaknesses). If you were to create an individualized education program for this "student," what unique needs would he or she have?

Sharpen your skills with SAGE edge at **edge.sagepub.com/gargiulo5e. SAGE edge for students** provides a personalized approach to help you accomplish your coursework goals in an easy-to-use learning environment.

3 Cultural and Linguistic Diversity and Exceptionality

■■■■■■■■■■■■■■■■■■■■■■■

The United States is an enormously diverse and pluralistic society—an amalgamation of different races, languages, folkways, religious beliefs, traditions, values, and even foods and music. As a nation, we greatly benefit from this cultural mixture; it is a defining characteristic of the United States and one of its great strengths. Perhaps nowhere else is this diversity more noticeable than in our schools.

Although in many instances we value and celebrate the richness of American diversity, all too often cultural differences result in prejudice and stereotypes as well as outright discrimination and unequal opportunities. Unfortunately, this statement is a valid characterization of some U.S. schools. In the opinion of various business leaders, policymakers, and educators, the educational environment encountered by many students from culturally and linguistically diverse backgrounds is inadequate, damaging, and openly hostile (Quality Education for Minorities Project, 1990). In some of our public schools, children from minority groups are seen as less than capable and/or difficult to teach. To our way of thinking, this situation is unacceptable and inexcusable. As educators working in increasingly culturally diverse environments, we need to model respect for and sensitivity to the cultural and linguistic characteristics represented by our students and their families.

The goal of this chapter is to examine the link between cultural and linguistic diversity and exceptionality. We will explore the historical patterns of American reaction to and acceptance of people from other lands. We will discuss issues of multicultural and bilingual education and consider the multitude of challenges confronting teachers who work with students with special needs from culturally and linguistically diverse backgrounds (see the accompanying Insights feature).

Cultural Diversity: The Changing Face of a Nation

The United States is made up of people from many different lands; in fact, only about 1 percent of Americans are native (U.S. Census Bureau, 2011). A vast number of Americans are descended from the millions of immigrants who entered the United States through Ellis Island, located in lower New York Harbor, in the latter part of the nineteenth and the early decades of the twentieth century. Immigration to the United States has continued since then, but the countries of origin have shifted from Europe to Latin America

▶ **VIDEO**
Diversity.

INSIGHTS

Cultural and Linguistic Diversity Quiz

True or False?

1. Many teachers have little or no training in working with children from diverse cultural and linguistic backgrounds.

2. Multicultural education is for all students.

3. Cultural differences have little effect on the way students learn.

4. Immigrants are in the United States to stay. The best thing teachers can do is to help them assimilate.

5. Young children don't really notice differences, so why make a big deal of multicultural education? It is better to be color-blind.

6. Schools in which there are no minority groups don't need a multicultural perspective.

7. The great majority of general and special education teachers in the United States come from the dominant culture.

8. Older students from diverse backgrounds are more at risk for educational failure than are younger children.

9. Most of the concepts of multicultural education are simply too difficult for children with disabilities.

10. A school should reflect and sanction the range of languages and dialects spoken by the students.

11. Multicultural education is a total curricular and instructional approach.

12. Children from minority groups are overrepresented in special education and underrepresented in programs for the gifted and talented.

(Answers on page 103)

SOURCE: Adapted from M. Winzer and K. Mazurek, *Special Education in Multicultural Contexts* (Upper Saddle River, NJ: Prentice Hall, 1998), pp. 8, 45, 168.

and Asia (Lustig & Koester, 2013). Approximately 1.25 million people immigrate to the United States annually (Camarota, 2007).

What are the implications of the following estimates and projections for our schools and classroom practices?

- By the year 2020, students of color are projected to make up almost half of all school-age youth (Gollnick & Chinn, 2013).
- By the year 2050, the U.S. population is projected to be approximately 46 percent Anglo, 28 percent Latino, 13 percent black, 7 percent Asian, and 1 percent Native American with about 4 percent of citizens identifying themselves as belonging to two or more groups (U.S. Census Bureau, 2012b).
- About one in five residents, or approximately 20 percent of the U.S. population over the age of 5, speaks a language other than English at home (U.S. Census Bureau, 2012a).
- At the present time, children of color make up the majority of students in several states (for example, California, Texas, Mississippi) and many urban areas, including Detroit, Los Angeles, Atlanta, Miami, Baltimore, New York, Chicago, Birmingham, and Houston (Gollnick & Chinn, 2013; Lustig & Koester, 2013; National Center for Education Statistics, 2012a).
- Despite increasing cultural and linguistic diversity in our schools, the overwhelming majority (over 80%) of general and special education teachers are white (National Center for Education Statistics, 2012a).
- Children from minority groups are often disproportionately represented in special education programs. Enrollment patterns suggest, for instance, an

overrepresentation of African Americans in classes for students with intellectual disability or behavior disorders. Asian Americans are underrepresented in those programs but tend to be overrepresented in programs for individuals who are gifted and talented (Gollnick & Chinn, 2013; Sullivan, 2011; U.S. Department of Education, 2009; Waitoller, Artiles, & Cheney, 2010).

The reasons for these changing demographics are many and varied. They include shifting immigration patterns and varying birthrates among women of various ethnic groups as well as other factors.

It is abundantly clear that the ethnic makeup of the United States is changing. It is equally obvious that this diversity will be reflected in our schools. Classrooms in the coming years will evidence even greater diversity than we find today. Teachers will most likely encounter families whose beliefs and practices vary significantly in important ways from those of mainstream American families. The challenge confronting educators and other professionals is how best to meet the needs of this changing and expanding population of learners.

Cultural Diversity in the Teaching Profession

As the number of students from culturally and linguistically diverse backgrounds continues to grow, the diversity of our teaching workforce has failed to keep pace with this expansion. At the present time, there is a notable absence of racial diversity among educators; teachers do not reflect the diversity of students they teach (Ford, 2012). Approximately 83 percent of teachers are white, about 7 percent are African American, approximately 7 percent are Hispanic, and about 1 percent are Asian (National Center for Education Statistics, 2012a). A similar pattern is evident with special educators. About 84 percent of the members of the workforce are white, 11 percent are African American, and a scant 5 percent consider themselves Hispanic (Boyer & Mainzer, 2003). Overall, this situation is not expected to improve; in fact, it is projected that the teaching profession will become increasingly homogeneous in the coming years (National Education Association, 2013).

We do not wish to imply or suggest that students who are culturally and linguistically diverse should be taught exclusively by teachers from traditionally underrepresented groups. There is little empirical evidence to suggest that children "of color learn better when taught by teachers of color" (Ladson-Billings, 1994, p. 26). Such a proposal would be neither feasible nor desirable and, according to Voltz (1998), would be counter to the goal of achieving greater diversity in the teaching force.

Schools in the United States are grounded in white, middle-class values, a culture that may hold little meaning for vast numbers of children who are poor and/or from ethnically or culturally diverse backgrounds (Benner, 1998). Still, most teachers, regardless of their own cultural and ethnic heritage, belong to the middle class and subscribe to the values of this group. Teachers from minority groups play a critical role in the education of all children, but especially for pupils from minority populations. In addition to serving as role models, these professionals often act as "cultural translators" and "cultural mediators" (National Collaborative on Diversity in the Teaching Force, 2004; Smith, Smith-Davis, Clarke, & Mims, 2000) for these students, helping them function successfully in the dominant culture.

From Assimilation to Cultural Pluralism

Issues of multiculturalism and bilingualism have challenged educators for almost a century. In the early decades of the twentieth century, one aim of schools was to assimilate children of immigrants into American culture as quickly as possible. There was a widely held belief that public education could unite the population and instill the ideals of American society in diverse groups of people. The goal of this assimilation or homogenizing process was to "Americanize" vast numbers of new citizens. They were expected to abandon their native languages, cultural heritage, beliefs, and practices. In their place would emerge a common American culture—*E pluribus unum* ("Out of many, one")—with an allegiance to the "American way of doing things." Metaphorically speaking, the United States was seen as a huge melting pot—a cauldron into which diverse people were dumped to melt away their differences, thus creating a citizenry who were very much alike (Tiedt & Tiedt, 2010).

For a variety of political and social reasons, Americans in the 1960s slowly began to question the wisdom of a melting pot theory as the country struggled with issues of civil rights and equal opportunity. Schools were no longer seen as the primary vehicle for homogenizing new citizens; instead, a student's ethnic heritage was to be valued and prized. Interest in cultural pluralism and multicultural education was ignited. As a result, a new set of metaphors evolved to counter the philosophy of America as a melting pot. The United States is now likened to a patchwork quilt or a floral bouquet.

The notion of the United States as a melting pot society has gradually given way to cultural pluralism wherein cultural and ethnic differences are appreciated and respected. Cultural pluralism does *not* require cultural groups to relinquish or abandon their cultural heritage. Schools now value the richness that diversity brings to the classroom; diversity is seen as a strength rather than a weakness.

Terminology of Cultural Differences

Educators and other professionals in the field of education are confronted with a barrage of labels and terms used to describe the education of children from different cultural backgrounds. Sometimes this terminology contributes to inaccurate generalizations, stereotyping, and incorrect assumptions about certain individuals or groups of people. In some instances, it is even difficult to know how to correctly describe the youngsters themselves. Do we, for example, refer to some children as black or African American? Is it more appropriate to identify a student as Hispanic or Latino, and how about pupils from Asian cultures? Also, what is the difference between bilingual education and multicultural education? As you can see, the topic of cultural and linguistic diversity can easily become a source of confusion and controversy. Perhaps it is best to begin our discussion of key terminology by arriving at an understanding of what we mean by culture.

Culture

We define culture as the attitudes, values, belief systems, norms, and traditions shared by a particular group of people that collectively form their heritage. A culture is transmitted in various ways from one generation to another. It is typically reflected in language, religion, dress, diet, social customs, and other aspects of a particular lifestyle (Gargiulo & Kilgo, 2014). Siccone (1995) points out that culture also includes the way particular groups of people interpret the world; it provides individuals with a frame of reference or perspective for attaching meaning to specific events or situations, such as the value and purpose of education or the birth of a child with a disability.

Gargiulo and Kilgo (2014) caution educators to guard against generalizing and stereotyping when working with pupils from various cultural groups. Even within specific groups, each person is unique, even though all members of the group may share distinctively similar group characteristics. Two students from the same racial group will most likely perform quite differently in the classroom regardless of their shared cultural heritage.

melting pot: A metaphor describing the United States in the early decades of the twentieth century.

cultural pluralism: The practice of appreciating and respecting ethnic and cultural differences.

culture: The attitudes, values, belief systems, norms, and traditions shared by a particular group of people that collectively form their heritage.

Multiculturalism

We live in a multicultural society, yet **multiculturalism** is frequently a confusing and poorly understood concept. In its most basic interpretation, multiculturalism refers to more than one culture. It acknowledges basic commonalities among groups of people while appreciating their differences. Implicit within the concept of multiculturalism is the belief that an individual can function within more than one culture. Multiculturalism also provides us with a foundation for understanding multicultural education.

Because of the increasing diversity of our society, the United States is now often likened to a floral bouquet or patchwork quilt.

Multicultural Education

Multicultural education is an ambiguous and somewhat controversial concept. Sleeter and Grant (2009) characterize multicultural education as an umbrella concept involving issues of race, language, social class, and culture as well as disability and gender. Banks (2013) and Gollnick and Chinn (2013) portray multicultural education as an educational strategy wherein the cultural background of each pupil is valued, viewed positively, and used to develop effective instruction.

Bilingual Education

A term frequently associated with multicultural education is **bilingual education**, an equally controversial and somewhat confusing concept. The two are not synonymous, however. Multicultural education can be infused throughout the curriculum without the benefit of bilingual education. Simply defined, bilingual education is an educational strategy whereby students whose first language is not English are instructed primarily through their native language while developing their competency and proficiency in English. Teachers initially use the language that the child knows best (Baca & Baca, 2004b). Once a satisfactory command of English is achieved, it becomes the medium of instruction.

Describing Diversity

U.S. society is an amalgamation of many different cultures. The U.S. government, however, officially recognizes only a handful of distinct racial groups. The federal government uses this classification scheme when reporting, for example, Head Start enrollment, poverty figures, high school graduation rates, and other such statistics. Citizens of the United Sates are typically categorized as follows:

- *American Indian or Alaskan Native.* A person having origins in any of the original peoples of North and South America and who maintains cultural identification through tribal affiliation or community recognition.
- *Asian.* A person having origins in any of the original peoples of the Far East, Southeast Asia, and the Indian subcontinent. This area includes, for example, Cambodia, China, India, Japan, Korea, Malaysia, Pakistan, the Philippine Islands, Thailand, and Vietnam.

multiculturalism: Referring to more than one culture; acknowledges basic commonalities among groups of people while appreciating their differences.

multicultural education: An ambiguous concept that deals with issues of race, language, social class, and culture as well as disability and gender. Also viewed as an educational strategy wherein the cultural heritage of each pupil is valued.

bilingual education: An educational approach whereby students whose first language is not English are instructed primarily through their native language while developing competency and proficiency in English.

VIDEO

Cultural Attitudes

- *Black.* A person having origins in any of the black racial groups of Africa.
- *Hispanic.* A person of Mexican, Puerto Rican, Cuban, Central or South American, or other Spanish culture or origin regardless of race.
- *Native Hawaiian or Other Pacific Islander.* A person having origins in any of the original peoples of Hawaii, Guam, Samoa, or other Pacific Islands.
- *White.* A person having descended from any of the original peoples of Europe, North Africa, or the Middle East.
- *Two or more races.* An individual who selects two or more of the preceding categories when offered the option of indicating his or her racial designation (National Center for Education Statistics, 2010).

We should point out that the preceding descriptions are arbitrary and represent umbrella terms. This terminology camouflages immense cultural and racial variability while obscuring the richness of individual cultures. Regardless of how specific groups of people are described, the diversity and variation within each group are tremendous. Various cultural groups are anything but homogeneous; differences are likely to be found in language, ethnicity, social class, home country, and a host of other dimensions (Lustig & Koester, 2013). It is important for teachers to acknowledge and respect this heterogeneity. They must also guard against perpetuating ethnic and racial stereotypes. Educators frequently fail to use qualifiers such as *some*, *many*, or *most* when discussing various cultural groups. This insensitivity to individuality can easily result in students' receiving an erroneous, oversimplified, and possibly stereotypical impression of a particular racial group (Ryan, 1993).

Teachers must also guard against assuming that the behaviors, beliefs, and actions of their particular cultural group are the correct or only way of doing something. Such assumptions reflect ethnocentrism—viewing one's own cultural group characteristics as superior or correct and the ways of other groups as inferior or peculiar.

Multicultural Education, Bilingual Education, and Student Diversity

By now it should be apparent that multicultural education is closely intertwined with issues of student diversity. Because the clientele of American schools is rapidly changing, there has been much debate and controversy over how best to educate children with culturally and linguistically diverse backgrounds. It is axiomatic that all students are different and not all people learn in the same way; this is especially true for students who are culturally and linguistically diverse. It would be foolish for teachers to expect children (or adults, for that matter) to leave their values, traditions, beliefs, and even language at the schoolhouse door. Effective teachers are sensitive to the cultural heritage of each learner and attempt to provide educational experiences that are culturally relevant and culturally appropriate.

Multicultural Education: Concepts and Characteristics

Embedded within the concept of multicultural education is a belief that all students, regardless of their race, ethnicity, culture, and other characteristics, such as social class or disability, should experience equal educational opportunities. It is important for all teachers to remember that multicultural education is an orientation or a perspective and not a specific pedagogical technique or a subject to be taught.

Throughout this chapter, we have stressed the multicultural nature of U.S. society. At the heart of this society is a core national culture, identified as the macroculture, which

ethnocentrism: A perspective whereby a person views his or her cultural practices as correct and those of other groups as inferior, peculiar, or deviant.

macroculture: The shared or national culture of a society.

VIDEO

Multicultural Teaching

represents a shared culture. Traits such as individualism, independence, competitiveness, and ambition are characteristic of the American macroculture (Gollnick & Chinn, 2013), along with values such as equality and fair play. Within this larger culture are several distinct subcultures, or microcultures, which, while sharing attributes of the macroculture, maintain their own distinct values, norms, and behaviors. The United States is composed of many different microcultures, as illustrated in Figure 3.1. According to Banks (2013), the various microcultures to which a person belongs are interrelated and interact with one another to collectively influence the individual's behavior. Membership in a particular group does not define a person's behavior, but it does make certain types of behavior more likely.

Differences between the various microcultures and the macroculture are frequently a source of conflict and misunderstanding. A major goal of multicultural education, therefore, is for pupils to acquire the knowledge, attitudes, and skills needed to function effectively in each cultural setting

The clientele of U.S. schools is rapidly changing.

(Banks, 2013). Banks (2013) argues that students in contemporary society should be able to function in their own as well as other microcultures, the macroculture, and the global community.

Bilingual Education: Concepts and Characteristics

As noted previously, multicultural education and bilingual education are not the same thing. Multicultural education can exist independently of bilingual education, but bilingual education cannot exist without multicultural education because it emphasizes the student's culture as well as language. As we have seen, approximately one out of five Americans, or almost 20 percent of the population, speaks a language other than English. The U.S. government estimates that there are in excess of 11 million school-age children whose primary language is not English (National Center for Education Statistics, 2011a). Yet controversy and debate continue over how best to meet the needs of these students. In many school districts, bilingual education provides one possible answer. Not everyone, however, agrees with this strategy. Thirty-one states have enacted legislation or passed constitutional amendments establishing English as the "official" language of their state (U.S. English, 2014), and five states actually prohibit bilingual education in their schools (Baca & Baca, 2004a).

microcultures: Distinct subcultures within a larger culture; these groups maintain their own distinct values, norms, folkways, and identification.

REFERENCE
Optimizing Services

AUDIO
Equality in Education

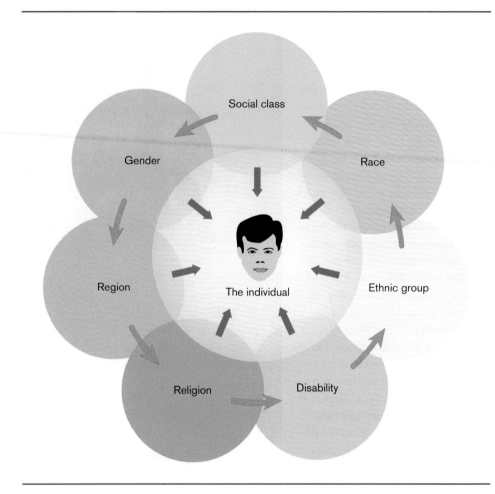

SOURCE: Adapted from J. Banks, *Cultural Diversity and Education,* 5th ed. (Needham Heights, MA: Allyn & Bacon, 2006), p. 77.

Students whose first language is not English represent a very heterogeneous group of individuals. Their competency in their primary language, as well as in English, may vary greatly. According to contemporary professional practice, these pupils are often identified as **English learners (ELs)**—individuals whose primary or home language is not English and who have yet to achieve proficiency in English. Consequently, these students are often unable to profit fully from instruction provided in English.

The primary purpose of bilingual education programs is to provide assistance to students with limited abilities in English so that they can "function effectively in both their native language and English. . . . The student's native language and culture are taught concurrently with English and the dominant culture" (Gollnick & Chinn, 2006, p. 299). The result is that the pupil becomes bilingual and bicultural in the process. Similarly, Baca and Baca (2004b), authorities in the field of bilingual education, see the primary mission of bilingual education as providing instruction to pupils using the language they know best and then reinforcing this information through English, while also promoting cognitive as well as affective development and cultural enrichment. Although it is not explicitly stated, we believe that one of the principal goals of bilingual education is to provide increased educational opportunities for students whose native language is not English. It is interesting to note that, contrary to popular belief, the original aim of

English learners (ELs): Students whose primary language is not English and who have yet to achieve proficiency in English.

bilingual education was not to advocate bilingualism but rather to promote the acquisition of English language skills. Bilingual education was thought to be the quickest way for a non-English-speaking person to become literate in English (Janzen, 1994).

The research evidence on the effectiveness of bilingual education strongly suggests that bilingual education is the most appropriate approach for working with students who are ELs. Greater academic gains and improved language skills can be directly attributed to bilingual education (Winzer & Mazurek, 1998). Of course, the key to effective bilingual education is to match the instructional strategy to the specific needs and background of the student. Depending on the child's proficiency in his or her native language and English, different instructional models are used. The accompanying Insights feature summarizes some of the approaches typically used with students who are bilingual while the First Person feature describes one teacher's experiences working with ELs.

Experts in the field of bilingual education disagree as to which pedagogical strategy is most effective for teaching students who are bilingual. There is general agreement, however, that the more opportunities individuals have to use their newly acquired language skills with classmates, friends, family members, and others, the more proficient they will become. In comparison to classroom settings, the natural environment seems to better facilitate language development.

Educators must consider carefully when they transition students with emerging proficiency in English to all-English classrooms. Many of these pupils' academic failures appear to be due to transitioning too quickly. Conversational fluency typically develops in children who are ELs after approximately two years of instruction. Teachers, therefore, assume that pupils are ready to move on because they appear to be proficient in English. However, according to investigators (Hoover, Klinger, Baca, & Patton, 2008; Salend & Salinas, 2003), the deeper and more complex language skills needed for academic success require an additional five to seven years of instruction. Movement to a monolingual English class setting should occur only if the teacher is certain that the student possesses the requisite language skills to compete in an academic environment.

Bilingual Special Education: Concepts and Characteristics

Students who are culturally and linguistically diverse *and* disabled present significant challenges for educators. How do we meet the needs of this growing population of pupils? What is the most normalized environment for students experiencing "double jeopardy"—that is, linguistic differences and disability? Which area should teachers primarily focus on—the problems posed by the disability or the lack of proficiency in English? These questions have no easy answers. One frequently mentioned solution is to place these pupils in classrooms with a special educator who is bilingual. In the majority of instances, however, this is not a feasible solution because of a severe shortage of qualified personnel (Council for Exceptional Children, 2013). What these students truly need is an instructional model known as bilingual special education. Baca, Baca, and de Valenzuela (2004) define this concept as

> the use of the home language and the home culture along with English in an individually designed program of special instruction for the student in an inclusive environment. Bilingual special education considers the child's language and culture as foundations upon which an appropriate education may be built. (p. 18)

The main goal of these efforts is to assist the pupil in reaching his or her maximum potential. The student's primary language and culture are the vehicles for accomplishing this task.

bilingual special education: Strategy whereby a pupil's home language and culture are used along with English in an individually designed program of special instruction.

INSIGHTS

Instructional Options for Students Who Are Bilingual

Approach	Strategies
1. Transitional programs	Students are instructed in academic content areas via their native language only until they are sufficiently competent in English, then transition to all-English classes. Primary goal of this program is to move students as quickly as possible to English-only classes. Many students exit after two to three years of instruction. Most common instructional model; bilingual education legislation favors this approach.
2. Maintenance (developmental) programs	Strong native language emphasis. Pupils maintain proficiency in first language while receiving instruction in English. A long-term approach with less emphasis on leaving program. Solid academic foundation is stressed.
3. Enrichment programs	Typically used with monolingual children, who are introduced to new language and culture.
4. Immersion programs	English language is the exclusive medium of instruction; first language and culture are not incorporated. A "sink or swim" philosophy.
5. English as a second language (ESL) programs	Not a true form of bilingual education. Children typically receive instruction in English outside the regular classroom. Goal is to quickly develop English proficiency in bilingual students. Exclusive emphasis on English for teaching and learning; native language not used in instruction. An assimilationist model with multiple variations.
6. Sheltered English	Students receive instruction in academic subjects exclusively in English; no effort is made to maintain or develop proficiency in first language. English instruction is continually monitored and modified to ensure pupil's comprehension. Simultaneous exposure to English language and subject content matter. Pupils who are culturally and linguistically diverse and disabled present unique challenges for teachers.

One of the critical issues confronting professionals is how to merge two different programs, bilingual education and special education, into one cogent paradigm. The integration of these two programs requires a focus not only on the acquisition of English language proficiency but also on the construction of individualized educational interventions. The goal is the development of both academic and English language skills, which often requires a team approach. Meaningful instruction for pupils who are culturally and linguistically diverse and disabled entails a coordinated effort involving general educators, special education teachers, and bilingual educators (Gollnick & Chinn, 2013; Salend & Salinas, 2003).

Attempts at providing a special education to pupils who are ELs have frequently encountered a number of problems, including challenges obtaining an accurate diagnosis coupled with assessment difficulties, which often lead to an inappropriate placement. These issues are intricately interrelated and complementary and must be considered within a broader context. Most educators recognize that disability and cultural and linguistic differences are related phenomena that play a significant role in a student's learning and development. Cultural and linguistic characteristics frequently coexist and interact with disability-related factors (Sullivan, 2011). Consider if you will Ramón, a 9-year-old boy identified as having an intellectual disability and limited English language skills. Ramón's parents are migrant workers. His family of six has an income below the federal poverty line. Ramón's special education program must address the

REFERENCE

Bilingual Special Education

Teaching English Learners

I began my teaching career as a French and English teacher in a large school system in an urban high school. The majority of the student population was African American. In my first year of teaching I had a couple of students in my French class from Vietnam who were English learners (ELs). Perhaps because I was a language teacher, I was very interested in learning what instructional techniques I could use to help them. At that time, the school only offered an immersion program. I was very frustrated by this policy and wished that I spoke Vietnamese so that I could better support my students. After three years, I moved and began teaching in a middle-class suburban high school in a small school district. This high school has increased in its cultural and economic diversity during my twenty years of teaching there.

In my first years there, I sought opportunities to work with the few ELs who were in the school. Initially, the ELs included a variety of European, Asian, and African students who were the children of professionals, such as researchers and college professors. I developed the first English as a second language (ESL) program classes at the school, using my knowledge as a language teacher. I provided support to students with their assignments in content classes and collaborated with their teachers regarding accommodations and assessments. After a couple of years, our ESL program began assessing the English proficiency of the students and creating instructional plans. I think that being both an ESL teacher and a general education teacher helped me to collaborate with other general education teachers—we spoke the same language, and I had to do what I suggested my colleagues do.

Gradually our high school EL population increased and changed. Currently, the majority of our students are Hispanic, and most of their parents are employed in the service industry. I went back to school and completed a master's degree in special education and certification as an ESL teacher. As a result of my training and the changes in our EL population, I coauthored curriculum for sheltered English courses to supplement our ESL classes. I also began to co-teach in some content-area classes. I still have the occasional opportunity to teach an English class, where I hone my skills at accommodation and have to practice what I ask other teachers to do. In addition, because of my degree in special education, I am a more effective advocate for the appropriate assessment of ELs who might be eligible for special education services.

One of the biggest challenges my students face is acquiring English proficiency while meeting requirements for graduation—both earning credits and passing graduation exams. As older learners, my pupils have less time to acquire English proficiency and greater course requirements to master. Other challenges may include differences in learning styles and educational expectations. In addition, teachers of ELs may have confusion about or resistance to differentiating instruction for ELs. Most teachers never expected to also have to teach their students to speak English. They may also have strong feelings about teaching students who might be undocumented immigrants.

Addressing the challenges ELs and their teachers face can be demanding, yet being an ESL teacher is a highly rewarding job. I get to work with students and their families over a period of several years and to learn from them about their cultures. I observe them sharing their culture with other students and becoming successful in academic and extracurricular activities. ■

—Jenny Harvey
ESL Teacher
Homewood High School, Homewood, Alabama

interaction of these confounding variables. Winzer and Mazurek (1998) caution teachers to remember that pupils who are ELs do not give up their right to bilingual education when found to be eligible for special education services.

PL 108–446 directly speaks to the issue of appropriate programming for these children. A student *cannot* be considered eligible for special education services under this law if his or her educational difficulties are primarily the result of limited proficiency in English or poor instruction.

REFERENCE
Instructional Strategies

Pupils who are culturally and linguistically diverse and disabled present unique challenges for teachers.

Disproportionate Representation of Minority Students in Special Education Programs

The disproportionate presence of pupils from minority groups in special education programs has been a pressing and volatile concern of educators for more than four decades (Ford, 2012). The fact that greater numbers of children from minority groups are placed in special education programs than would be anticipated based on their proportion of the general school population is commonly referred to as overrepresentation. At the same time, there is a long-standing pattern of underrepresentation (fewer students in a particular category than one might expect based on their numbers in the school population) of African Americans (blacks), American Indian/Alaskan Natives, and Hispanics/Latinos in programs for children and youth who are gifted and talented (Clark, 2013; Gollnick & Chinn, 2013). Generally speaking, Asian children and other Pacific Islanders are typically underrepresented in special education classes but tend to be overrepresented in classes for students who are gifted and talented (Donovan & Cross, 2002; Ford, 2012; Ford, Grantham, & Whiting, 2008; U.S. Department of Education, 2009).

The fact that a disproportionate number of students from minority groups are enrolled in special education classrooms is a stinging indictment of the efficacy of the professional practices of special educators and a challenge to the concept of honoring diversity—presumably the cornerstone of our field (Meyer, Bevan-Brown, Park, & Savage, 2013). At the heart of the discussion about disproportionate representation is the issue of

overrepresentation: A situation in which a greater number of students from minority groups are placed in special education programs than would be expected based on the proportion of pupils in the general school population.

underrepresentation: A situation in which fewer children from minority groups are placed in special education programs than would be expected based on the proportion of pupils in the general school population.

inappropriate placement in special education programs. The primary concern is with false positives—when a pupil from a cultural or linguistic minority is identified as disabled when, in fact, he or she is *not* disabled and is therefore inappropriately placed in a class for students with disabilities. To ignore the gifts and talents of children from diverse backgrounds is equally damaging and denies them the opportunity to reach their full potential (Artiles & Zamora-Durán, 1997). Many complex factors and circumstances influence student placement; however, for those racially and ethnically diverse students who are misclassified and inappropriately placed or denied access to appropriate services, the outcomes are often serious and enduring (U.S. Department of Education, 1997).

It should be noted that the problem of overrepresentation does not occur across all categories of disabilities. The disproportionate presence of students from minority groups typically occurs only in those disability categories in which professional judgment and opinion play a role in the decision-making process, such as mild intellectual disability or behavior disorders. Overrepresentation is not a problem in disability areas that have a clear biological basis. For instance, sensory or motor impairments do not yield dramatically different proportions than one would anticipate on the basis of the ethnic composition of the general school population (Artiles, Kozleski, Trent, Osher, & Ortiz, 2010; Harry, 2008; Harry & Klinger, 2007; Skiba et al., 2008).

The 1998–1999 school year was the first time that the states were required to report the race and ethnicity of students with disabilities served under the Individuals with Disabilities Education Act (IDEA). Table 3.1 presents recent information on the percentage and number of students receiving a special education in representative disability categories according to race. Although black students represent only about 19 percent of the total enrollment in special education programs, approximately 28 percent of the pupils in classes for students with intellectual disability are African American. Interestingly, fewer black children are enrolled in programs for pupils with hearing impairments than one might expect based on their contribution to the total special education population. Additional representative comparisons can be found in the table.

Bicard and Heward (2013) wisely note that

> the fact that culturally [and linguistically] diverse students are identified as having disabilities is not in itself a problem. . . . Disproportionate representation is problematic, however, if students have been wrongly placed in special education, are segregated and stigmatized, or are denied access to needed special education because their disabilities are overlooked as a result of their membership in a racial or ethnic minority group. (p. 261)

The entire issue of representational discrepancies is subject to debate and controversy. Harry (1992), for instance, does not believe that placement rates in special education programs for Native American and Hispanic students are suggestive of overrepresentation when examined nationally. At the individual state and local level, however, a different picture emerges. Like Benner (1998), Harry argues that placement statistics must be examined cautiously and kept in perspective. In the opinion of Benner and Harry, the larger the enrollment of pupils from minority groups within a school district, the greater their representation will be in special education classrooms. This is to be expected. Furthermore, the larger the education program, the greater the likelihood of disproportionate representation. Harry sees this phenomenon as a classic "chicken-and-egg" question. "While large numbers of minority children may lead to a perceived need for more special education programs, it may also be that the greater availability of programs encourages increased placement of minority children" (Harry, 1992, p. 66).

REFERENCE

Disproportionate Representation

Table 3.1 Number and Percentage of Students Ages 6–21 Receiving a Special Education for Select Disability Categories

Disability		American Indian/ Alaskan Native	Asian	Black	Hispanic/ Latino	Native Hawaiian/ Other Pacific Islander	Two or More Races	White	Total
Specific Learning Disabilities	N	36,952	34,027	463,474	650,353	8,045	48,979	1,112,960	2,354,790
	%	1.56%	1.44%	19.68%	27.61%	0.34%	2.07%	47.26%	
Speech or Language Impairments	N	12,890	34,421	151,978	258,071	2,086	25,718	586,036	1,071,200
	%	1.20%	3.21%	14.18%	24.09%	0.19%	2.40%	54.70%	
Intellectual Disability	N	5,577	9,531	118,656	89,107	1,211	8,278	198,459	430,819
	%	1.29%	2.21%	27.54%	20.68%	0.28%	1.92%	46.06%	
Emotional Disturbance	N	5,356	3,180	99,817	52,674	971	11,395	198,032	371,425
	%	1.44%	0.85%	26.87%	14.18%	0.26%	3.06%	53.31%	
Hearing Impairments	N	753	3,647	10,298	19,055	359	1,385	33,723	69,220
	%	1.08%	5.26%	14.87%	27.52%	0.51%	2.00%	48.71%	
Traumatic Brain Injury	N	318	589	3,877	4,041	74	616	15,363	24,878
	%	1.27%	2.36%	15.58%	16.24%	0.29%	2.47%	61.75%	
All Disabilities	N	79,993	124,727	1,093,674	1,308,211	17,057	134,325	3,027,216	5,785,203
	%	1.38%	2.15%	18.90%	22.61%	0.29%	2.32%	52.32%	

NOTE: Information is for the 2011 school year.

Based on data from the fifty states, Puerto Rico, and the District of Columbia. Outlying areas not included.

Due to rounding, percentages do not always add upto 100.

SOURCE: Adapted from U.S. Department of Education. (2012). *IDEA data*. Retrieved March 26, 2013, from http://www.ideadata.org/PartBChildCount.asp

These precautionary observations notwithstanding, the misclassification and/ or inappropriate placement of students from minority groups in special education programs frequently leads to stigmatization and lower expectations. This is especially true when a pupil is removed from the general education setting and consequently denied access to the general education curriculum, which often results in limited postsecondary educational and employment opportunities. In some school systems, the disproportionate representation of these students also results in significant racial separation.

Factors Contributing to Over- and Underrepresentation

A myriad of explanations have been put forth to explain the problem of over- and underrepresentation of culturally diverse students in some categories of special education. No one explanation fully accounts for this situation; the various reasons are complex and frequently intertwined. Scholars (Artiles et al., 2010; Harry & Klinger, 2006; Waitoller et al., 2010) often see this problem as deeply rooted in the commingling of socioeconomic, sociocultural, and sociopolitical forces.

The overrepresentation of children of color is perhaps best understood as a relationship between family socioeconomic status and disability rather than between disability and minority group status per se. Individuals from minority groups typically populate urban centers and tend to be poor. Poverty and ethnicity are inextricably interwoven variables in American society (Artiles & Bal, 2008; Artiles et al., 2010; Donovan & Cross, 2002). Report after report and survey after survey routinely indicate an overrepresentation of minority groups living in poverty. According to the Children's Defense Fund (2012), 39 percent of black children and 35 percent of Hispanic youngsters are considered poor.

Poverty often means limited access to health care (especially prenatal care), poor nutrition, and adverse living conditions. All of these variables increase the probability of a child being at risk for learning and developmental difficulties. Cultural and language differences only exacerbate the student's vulnerability, increasing the likelihood of educational failure and his or her need for special education services (Gargiulo & Kilgo, 2014).

The evidence strongly suggests that socioeconomic status rather than ethnicity is one of the primary reasons that students from racially and ethnically diverse populations encounter persistent academic problems in the public schools (MacMillan & Reschly, 1998). Poverty, however, is not the only culprit contributing to the disproportionate representation of minorities in some special education programs. Faulty identification procedures, ineffective prereferral strategies, test bias, and inappropriate assessment techniques may also account for some of the overrepresentation. The lack of standardized tests appropriate for use with students who have limited English language skills is another contributing factor (Coutinho & Oswald, 2000; Voltz, 1998). As Ford (2012), along with Winzer and Mazurek (1998), points out, although biased and discriminatory assessment instruments do play a role, these factors alone are insufficient to account for the misplacement and disproportionate representation of pupils from minority groups in special education classes. Other relevant variables include teacher bias, different behavioral and academic performance standards for students from minority populations, and incongruity or discrepancy between the child's home culture and school expectations. For example, behaviors considered adaptive in a student's home, such as nonassertiveness and cooperation, may conflict with expectations in the classroom, where independence and competition are valued.

Incongruity may also exist in instructional methodology. Research has demonstrated that children from minority groups learn differently than white youngsters. African American pupils, for example, tend to be *field dependent/sensitive* (relational, global) learners who approach learning intuitively rather than analytically and logically (Banks, 2013; Ford, 1998). These students perform better in social settings like those found in cooperative learning environments and group work (Gollnick & Chinn, 2013). In contrast, white students and Asian/Pacific Islanders are typically

---

Key Facts About Children in the United States

- Almost 22 percent of children in the United States live in poverty.
- Of all U.S. children, almost 27 percent (19.9 million) receive food stamps.
- Of U.S. children under the age of 6, 64.6 percent have both parents in the workforce.
- Approximately 9.4 percent of children (6.9 million) are without health insurance.
- Over two-thirds of fourth graders in public schools read below grade level.

SOURCE: Children's Defense Fund, Children in the United States, July 2013. Available at www.childrensdefense.org/

field dependent/sensitive: Students who approach learning intuitively rather than analytically and logically. These students tend to find success in cooperative learning situations and group work.

Poverty and ethnicity are inextricably interwoven aspects of American society.

field independent (detail-oriented and analytically inclined) learners who thrive in competitive settings where achievement and individual accomplishment are prized.

White teachers, as a whole, are typically field independent, whereas educators from minority populations are more likely to be field dependent. The lack of congruency between the cognitive style of many culturally diverse students and that of their teachers is another possible reason for disproportionate representation. Teachers often perceive pupils with cognitive styles different from their own in negative ways. This, of course, exacerbates the student's learning problems. This incongruity frequently causes teachers to overlook a youngster's strengths and abilities and increases the likelihood of a referral for special education services. By the same token, a teacher may fail to recognize the attributes of the brightest pupils and thus be less likely to refer them to programs for students with special gifts and talents.

The reasons for the underrepresentation of certain groups in programs for the gifted and talented are as varied as the explanations for overrepresentation in other programs. Benner (1998) suggests that relevant factors include the politics of race and social class, attitudinal bias, and pressure from peers not to excel academically. Ford (1998, 2012) cites problems related to screening and identification, low teacher expectations and negative perceptions of minority pupils, and a lack of teacher training in the area of gifted education.

Consequences of Disproportionate Representation

The over- and underenrollment of racial and ethnic minorities in some special education programs often leads to unequal educational opportunities. In many instances, removal from the general education classroom and assignment to a special education classroom results in an inferior and ineffective educational experience for these children (Donovan & Cross, 2002; Harry & Klinger, 2007; Jasper & Bouck, 2013). The educational experiences of racially, ethnically, and culturally diverse pupils often put them at risk for underachievement and dropping out of school. In comparison to their white peers, students from ethnically and racially diverse backgrounds drop out of school at a much higher rate. In the 2010 school year, the dropout rate for Hispanic youth (15%) was three times the rate for white pupils (5%). About 8 percent of African American students leave school before completing their education (National Center for Education Statistics, 2012a). Adolescents who fail to graduate are more likely to be unemployed and constitute a disproportionate percentage of the incarcerated population (Amos, 2008; Jasper & Bouck, 2013).

The disproportionately high representation of racial and ethnic minorities as well as culturally and linguistically diverse students in some special education classrooms is a problem that has plagued educators for more than forty years. Unfortunately, the debate over disproportionate representation, inappropriate placement, and misclassification of minority pupils is far from being resolved. However, advocates, policymakers, researchers, educators, and parents have moved beyond the mere condemnation of this long-standing and complex problem to seek solutions. Yet solutions to the issue of greater educational opportunity and quality of education remain elusive. A multifaceted, broad-based attack is necessary. Attention needs to be focused on the identification and referral process,

■ ■ ■ ■ ■ Table 3.2 **Assessment Outcomes for Culturally and Linguistically Diverse Students**

- An accurate appraisal of a child's level and mode of functioning within the context of the child's cultural experiences

- A focus on a child's strengths and abilities as a basis for the development of new skills

- Identification of a child's specific educational needs, including both first and second language acquisition

- Literacy and basic level skills evaluation, especially for students who lack educational experiences

- Identification of emotional difficulties

- Generation of data that may be used for placement decisions and the formulation of an individual education program, if necessary

SOURCE: M. Winzer and K. Mazurek, *Special Education in Multicultural Contexts* (Upper Saddle River, NJ: Prentice Hall, 1998), pp. 177–178.

assessment bias, instructional factors, and teacher attitudes, as well as environmental factors impinging on the student and the interrelationships among these variables.

Issues in Assessing Students From Culturally and Linguistically Diverse Groups

While the number of pupils from culturally and linguistically diverse backgrounds continues to grow, the percentage of students who are white is decreasing (National Center for Education Statistics, 2010). As a result, teachers can expect to encounter an especially challenging and difficult task—accurately assessing children from diverse cultures for disabilities. The appropriate assessment of all students has been a long-standing concern among special educators, but it is an especially critical issue for youngsters from minority populations. Assessment is the primary vehicle through which access to services is determined and progress is evaluated, using a variety of formal and informal means. We consider assessment to be a dynamic, multifaceted, multipurpose decision-making process whose primary goal is to evaluate the academic and behavioral progress of a student. Table 3.2 identifies some of the outcomes of this process for children from diverse cultural backgrounds.

Assessment of students from culturally and linguistically diverse backgrounds is both controversial and problematic (Utley & Obiakor, 2001). Because of the inherent difficulties, assessment of these learners has been characterized as "random chaos" (Figueroa, 1989). The absence of best practice guidelines for evaluating language minority and culturally diverse pupils results in a complicated and confusing assignment for teachers and other service providers.

Inappropriate assessment measures and evaluation procedures are thought to be one of the primary reasons for the disproportionate representation of culturally and linguistically diverse students in various special education programs. Concerns focus mainly on the use of standardized testing with this population, especially standardized tests of intelligence. Recall from Chapter 2 that the *Larry P.* and *Diana* lawsuits centered on claims that IQ tests were inherently unfair to students from minority groups and thus resulted in the misidentification and inaccurate labeling of these pupils, resulting in an inappropriate education.

Standardized testing has frequently been criticized for its failure to consider the cultural and experiential background of culturally and linguistically diverse students. A disregard for the life experiences of these students results in an unfair evaluation and a depressed portrayal of their ability. Remember, not all children approach a testing

SUGGESTIONS FOR THE CLASSROOM

Recommendations for Assessing Culturally and Linguistically Diverse Pupils

→ Assessment of an individual's language competency in both English and his or her native language should be completed before administering other tests.

→ In order to be eligible for a special education, a student must exhibit a disability when evaluated in his or her native language.

→ Schools should incorporate ecological assessments that include not only multiple evaluation tools familiar to the examiner but also information gathered from the student's teachers, the student's parents, and the student.

→ Evaluators should use evaluation techniques that are as unbiased as possible. For example, a bilingual professional, not an interpreter, should administer the test.

→ If a bilingual professional is unavailable, an interpreter may be used if he or she is first trained in assessment principles and terminology.

→ Parents and other stakeholders should be involved when developing alternate assessments.

situation with homogeneous backgrounds or a reservoir of similar life experiences. "A student who has no experience with an item presented on a test or has experienced it differently is apt to answer the question incorrectly" (Council for Exceptional Children, 1997a, p. 9). For instance, a 10-year-old from Hawaii, a state where there are no snakes, may have difficulty answering a question about rattlesnakes, whereas a youngster from New Mexico is very likely to be familiar with this creature. Likewise, an adolescent from rural Alabama who is asked about ice fishing is much less likely to answer the question correctly than his cousin from northern Wisconsin. Gollnick and Chinn (2013) believe that the use of standardized tests with children from minority groups measures only their degree of cultural assimilation, not their intelligence.

Assessment Challenges

There are several roadblocks to the goal of achieving meaningful and valid assessments of students who are culturally and linguistically diverse. Foremost is the lack of measurement tools that provide an accurate assessment of these students' abilities. Many standardized tests are simply not available in languages other than English or in appropriate dialects. Coupled with this problem is the issue of bias in the assessment process. All tests are biased to some degree; it is an unavoidable artifact of psychometric evaluation. Yet some of these unwanted influences are of greater concern than others. As a result of bias, test scores are frequently rendered suspect and may not reflect an accurate appraisal of the student's ability or skill. Linn, Miller, and Gronlund (2013) note that bias may involve extrinsic variables, such as the child's response style or the value attached to competitive behavior in the pupil's culture. Intrinsic bias factors are difficulties with the instruments themselves, such as culturally bound test items (recall our rattlesnake example) or normative sampling issues. Bias can also come from several other sources, some of which are external to the child and others internal, such as issues of test validity and reliability when tests are translated; a lack of test-taking skills such as performing under time constraints, motivation, and appropriate response selection strategies; and other issues in addition to the obvious concern of linguistic bias when the student's primary language is not English. Individually and collectively, these sources of

VIDEO

Assessment
Challenges

bias often result in incorrect assumptions about a student's abilities and may lead, in turn, to an inappropriate educational placement.

Assessment Safeguards

Professionals are fully aware of the importance of obtaining an accurate profile of an individual's strengths and weaknesses. To accomplish this goal and to minimize potential for abuses in the assessment process, PL 94–142 and its subsequent amendments contain several procedural safeguards. Realizing that nonbiased evaluations are crucial to special education, the framers of IDEA mandated nondiscriminatory testing. School districts are required to adopt

> procedures to assure that testing and evaluation materials and procedures utilized for the evaluation and placement of children with disabilities will be selected and administered so as not to be racially or culturally discriminatory. Such materials or procedures shall be provided and administered in the child's native language or mode of communication, unless it is clearly not feasible to do so, and no single procedure shall be the sole criterion for determining an appropriate educational program for a child. (20 U.S.C. § 1412 [5] [C])

In addition, students are to be assessed by trained personnel who are part of a multidisciplinary team that is responsible for the evaluation. Written communications with the pupil's parents are to be provided in the parents' native language.

Assessment Innovations

Professionals have long recognized that bias is a very real threat to the assessment process, especially for persons from culturally and linguistically diverse groups. Concern about this problem has resulted in efforts at minimizing test bias. Although a completely nonbiased or culture-fair assessment is unlikely, initial attempts at reducing bias focused on the instruments themselves. Many tests were revised in an effort to reduce the number of culturally specific test items (content bias) and the reliance on culturally specific language. Tests were also renormed, or restandardized, to reflect the growing diversity of American schoolchildren. Even the testing environment and the race of the examiner and his or her interactions with the student have come under scrutiny.

The primary purpose of these modifications has been to obtain a more accurate picture of a student's abilities, especially for pupils from culturally and linguistically diverse populations. The search for solutions to the problem of test bias has resulted in the development of pluralistic assessment techniques that are meant to be sensitive to the cultural and linguistic characteristics of children from minority groups. One example of this effort is the second edition of the Kaufman Assessment Battery for Children (KABC-II) designed by Kaufman and Kaufman (2004).

The KABC-II is used to assess children between 3 and 18 years of age. This instrument was normed on groups of white, Hispanic, African American, Native American, and Asian American children in addition to a population of individuals with disabilities. The KABC-II minimizes a student's verbal skills and abilities, thus enhancing its usefulness with children with limited proficiency in English. A Spanish version is also available.

Concern about test bias has also resulted in an expanded understanding of the concept of intelligence. IQ tests have traditionally looked at intelligence in a somewhat narrow and restricted fashion, limiting the performance of many students. For instance, success in the classroom often depends on linguistic intelligence, an area in which many students from culturally and linguistically diverse backgrounds are deficient. Gardner (1983/2011, 1993,

nondiscriminatory testing: Federal mandate that assessments be conducted in a culturally responsive fashion.

REFERENCE
Cross-Cultural Assessment

Because of bias, test scores may be suspect and may not reflect an accurate appraisal of a child's disability.

2006), however, argues for the concept of **multiple intelligences**. According to his theory, problem solving involves eight different, though somewhat related and interactive, intelligences:

- Bodily/kinesthetic
- Interpersonal
- Intrapersonal
- Logical/mathematical
- Musical/rhythmic
- Naturalist
- Verbal/linguistic
- Visual/spatial

His ideas have gained widespread acceptance among practitioners but, unfortunately, have received little attention from publishers of standardized tests (de Valenzuela & Baca, 2004). We believe that Gardner's theory has considerable merit. As educators, we need to stop thinking about how smart a student is and start asking, "*How* is the child smart?"

Contemporary Assessment Strategies

Many school districts are searching for better ways of assessing the growing population of students who are culturally and linguistically diverse. One particularly promising practice is the movement toward more authentic, performance-based assessment strategies such as **portfolio assessment** (Friend & Bursuck, 2012). This innovation could possibly help in resolving the problem of the over- and underrepresentation of language and ethnic minorities in some special education programs. This alternate assessment model is a relatively new idea for educators, although architects and graphic artists have been demonstrating their skills and competencies via work products for years.

Portfolio assessment is uniquely intriguing because it emphasizes the instructional environment and focuses on student performance and the outcomes of learning (McLoughlin & Lewis, 2008). Unlike infrequent or one-time standardized testing, performance-based assessment relies on the pupil's learning experiences and evaluates meaningful, real-world tasks using multiple performance indicators such as writing samples, speeches, artwork, videotapes, and work samples gathered over time and collected in a portfolio. Authentic assessments are relevant and culturally responsive assessments (Gargiulo & Metcalf, 2013).

Portfolios are able to document, in a tangible way, a student's developmental progress. They can pinpoint areas of strength and weakness, thus facilitating instructional intervention. It is our opinion that portfolio assessment has great potential for meeting the needs of students who are culturally and linguistically diverse, especially those with disabilities. Information gleaned from portfolios typically results in more numerous, more specific, and more detailed recommendations and judgments about a child than does information derived from traditional, standardized testing (Linn et al., 2013).

Portfolio assessment, of course, is not the complete solution to eliminating bias in the assessment of culturally and linguistically diverse children. Several questions and concerns about this performance-based measure remain unanswered. Does portfolio assessment result in a fairer and more accurate portrayal of students from minority

multiple intelligences: An alternative perspective on intelligence suggesting that there are many different kinds of intelligence.

portfolio assessment: A type of authentic assessment; samples of different work products gathered over time and across curriculum areas are evaluated.

groups? Do portfolio data generate decisions about these students that differ from those formulated around the results of traditional testing? What is the basis for our standards or benchmarks? Do teachers use individual standards, or are comparisons based on districtwide, statewide, or even national performance indicators? The answers to these and other questions await further research evidence.

We believe that portfolio assessment should be an integral component of the assessment process. It represents an exciting alternative to assessing learning and the funds of student knowledge.

Assessment Recommendations

Accurately assessing students from culturally and linguistically diverse backgrounds presents many challenges for professionals. Issues of language, test bias, and other such matters are of real concern because they affect assessment results, which in turn affect educational decision making. Completely fair and nonbiased assessments may not be possible, but professionals can at least minimize those variables that may influence performance outcomes. The recommendations in the accompanying Suggestions for the Classroom represent attempts at achieving authentic data and ensuring fairer, more accurate appraisals of culturally and linguistically diverse pupils and those with emerging English language skills.

Educational Programming for Students With Exceptionalities Who Are Culturally and Linguistically Diverse

Providing specific instructional strategies and tactics for students with disabilities who are culturally and linguistically diverse (and even pupils who are nondisabled) is an arduous, if not impossible, task. We can, however, offer some general suggestions for enhancing instructional effectiveness. Earlier we noted that effective teachers are sensitive to the cultural heritage of each student and attempt to provide educational experiences that are culturally relevant and appropriate. This is critically important. Our instructional practices must be culturally affirming, sensitive, and responsive. The pupil's cultural background should be seen as an instructional resource (Ford, 2012; Garcia & Ortiz, 2006; Shealey & Callins, 2007). A meaningful educational program must incorporate the individual's language and culture. The degree to which this integration occurs is a valid gauge of academic success.

A pupil's life experiences can be the building blocks or foundation for developing a curriculum that is authentic and culturally relevant. Programs and services for children who are culturally and linguistically diverse and exceptional should be crafted around the principles and purposes of multicultural education in an effort to create a supportive climate for learning (Gollnick & Chinn, 2013). Additionally, Hoover and Collier (2004) suggest that the instructional strategies identified in the individualized education program (IEP) "exhibit culturally appropriate cues and reinforcements as well as culturally appropriate motivation and relevance" (p. 285). While attention to instructional strategies is crucial, effective programs for culturally and linguistically diverse students with exceptionalities must also consider the content (needed academic skills and knowledge), the instructional environment, and student behaviors, and how these elements reciprocally interact and are influenced by the pupil's linguistic and cultural heritage (Hoover & Patton, 2005; Voltz, Sims, Nelson, & Bivens, 2005). Meaningful IEPs for pupils with disabilities who also exhibit cultural and/or linguistic diversity should reflect goals and instructional strategies that are appropriate to the student's disability while also reflecting his or her language status.

SUGGESTIONS FOR THE CLASSROOM

Guidelines for Selecting and Evaluating Instructional Materials

→ Are the perspectives and contributions of people from diverse cultural and linguistic groups—both men and women, as well as people with disabilities—included in the curriculum?

→ Are there activities in the curriculum that will assist students in analyzing the various forms of the mass media for ethnocentrism, sexism, "handicapism," and stereotyping?

→ Are men and women, diverse cultural/racial groups, and people with varying abilities shown in both active and passive roles?

→ Are men and women, diverse cultural/racial groups, and people with disabilities shown in positions of power (i.e., the materials do not rely on the mainstream culture's character to achieve goals)?

→ Do the materials identify strengths possessed by so-called underachieving diverse populations? Do they diminish the attention given to deficits, to reinforce positive behaviors that are desired and valued?

→ Are members of diverse racial/cultural groups, men and women, and people with disabilities shown engaged in a broad range of social and professional activities?

→ Are members of a particular culture or group depicted as having a range of physical features (e.g., hair color, hair texture, variations in facial characteristics and body build)?

→ Do the materials represent historical events from the perspectives of the various groups involved or solely from the male, middle-class, and/or Western European perspective?

→ Are the materials free of ethnocentric or sexist language patterns that may make implications about persons or groups based solely on their culture, race, gender, or disability?

→ Will students from different ethnic and cultural backgrounds find the materials personally meaningful to their life experiences?

→ Are a wide variety of culturally different examples, situations, scenarios, and anecdotes used throughout the curriculum design to illustrate major intellectual concepts and principles?

→ Are culturally diverse content, examples, and experiences comparable in kind, significance, magnitude, and function to those selected from mainstream culture?

SOURCE: S. Garcia and D. Malkin, "Toward Defining Programs and Services for Culturally and Linguistically Diverse Learners in Special Education," *Teaching Exceptional Children, 26*(1), 1993, p. 55.

Attainment of IEP goals depends, in part, on establishing a supportive learning environment. One way of enhancing the context in which teaching and learning occur is through the careful selection and evaluation of instructional materials. Materials that reflect the sociocultural, linguistic, and experiential backgrounds of the students increase the likelihood that children will respond to them in a positive manner (Gollnick & Chinn, 2013). The accompanying Suggestions for the Classroom feature presents several guidelines that educators should consider when evaluating materials for their classroom.

Effectively instructing students with exceptionalities who are also culturally and linguistically diverse requires that teachers provide experiences that are culturally appropriate and pertinent. Instructional success with children from diverse populations depends largely on the teacher's ability to construct meaningful pedagogical bridges that cross over different cultural systems (Garcia & Ortiz, 2006; Meyer et al., 2013). "When instruction and learning are compatible with a child's culture and when minority students' language and culture are incorporated into the school program, more effective learning takes place" (Winzer & Mazurek, 1998, p. vii).

AUDIO
Chapter 3 Summary

Cultural Diversity: The Changing Face of a Nation

- Although the population of culturally and linguistically diverse students continues to grow, the diversity of the teaching workforce has failed to keep pace. About 80 percent of U.S. teachers are white, and it is projected that the teaching profession will become increasingly homogeneous over the next few years.
- The task of assimilating or "Americanizing" the children of immigrants was metaphorically described as a melting pot, whereby the various languages, beliefs, and customs of immigrants were melted away and replaced with a common American culture.
- In the latter part of the twentieth century, interest in cultural pluralism and multicultural education was sparked. U.S. society is now characterized metaphorically as a floral bouquet or patchwork quilt; cultural and ethnic differences are valued and respected.

Multicultural Education, Bilingual Education, and Student Diversity

- Multicultural education addresses issues of race, language, social class, and culture as well as disability and gender.
- Bilingual education is an educational strategy whereby students whose first language is not English are instructed primarily through their native language while developing competency and proficiency in English.
- *English learners (ELs)* is a term used to describe individuals with reduced proficiency in reading, writing, or speaking English.
- Bilingual special education services embrace the use of the pupil's primary language and culture coupled with an individually tailored program of special instruction.

Disproportional Representation of Minority Students in Special Education Programs

- Historically, greater numbers of children from minority groups have been placed in special education classrooms

than would be anticipated based on their proportion of the school population. This situation is commonly referred to as overrepresentation. Underrepresentation in certain programs, or fewer students than one would anticipate based on their numbers in the school population, is also a problem.
- The overrepresentation of children of color is perhaps best understood as a relationship between socioeconomic status and disability rather than between minority group membership and disability.
- Test bias, teacher expectations and bias, and incongruity in instructional methodology and cognitive styles may also account for this phenomenon.

Issues in Assessing Students From Culturally and Linguistically Diverse Groups

- Some of the barriers to achieving meaningful and valid assessments of students from culturally and linguistically diverse backgrounds are the lack of appropriate measurement tools and bias in the assessment process.
- Federal law requires that professionals use nondiscriminatory testing practices when evaluating pupils for possible special education placement.
- Some professionals have expanded their understanding of the notion of intelligence and argue for the concept of multiple intelligences.
- Another attempt at meaningful assessment of students from culturally and linguistically diverse backgrounds is a movement toward authentic, performance-based assessment techniques, such as portfolio assessment.

Educational Programming for Students With Exceptionalities Who Are Culturally and Linguistically Diverse

- The child's cultural and linguistic heritage must be reflected in his or her individualized education program (IEP) if instructional strategies are to be effective. The instructional materials should also mirror the sociocultural, linguistic, and experiential backgrounds of the students.

1. What do the terms *culture* and *cultural diversity* mean to you?

2. At one time, the United States was described as a melting pot. Why? Metaphorically speaking, American society is now characterized as a floral bouquet or patchwork quilt. What factors contributed to this change in thinking?

3. Define the following terms: *cultural pluralism, multicultural education,* and *bilingual education.*

4. Why is bilingual education a controversial topic?

5. Compare and contrast the various instructional models used with students who are bilingual.

6. Explain why pupils from minority groups experience disproportionate representation in some special education programs.

7. What are the consequences of disproportionate representation?

8. Why is the assessment of culturally and linguistically diverse students perceived to be problematic? How might these difficulties be corrected?

9. Define portfolio assessment. Identify the advantages of this strategy for evaluating the performance of children who are culturally and linguistically diverse.

KEY TERMS ▪▪▪

melting pot, 82

cultural pluralism, 82

culture, 82

multiculturalism, 83

multicultural education, 83

bilingual education, 83

ethnocentrism, 84

macroculture, 84

microcultures, 85

English learners (ELs), 86

bilingual special education, 87

overrepresentation, 90

underrepresentation, 90

field dependent/sensitive, 93

field independent, 94

nondiscriminatory testing, 97

multiple intelligences, 98

portfolio assessment, 98

LEARNING ACTIVITIES ▪▪▪

1. Talk to a school psychologist, an educational diagnostician, or another assessment specialist about strategies and procedures used when evaluating students from a culturally or linguistically diverse background. What types of modifications, if any, does he or she use? Does he or she have any concerns about the validity of the assessment process? What is his or her opinion about alternate assessments, such as portfolios?

2. Visit several different schools in your area. Interview administrators or teachers about services available for pupils from culturally and linguistically diverse groups. Is there a problem of over- and underrepresentation in

special education classes? What types of modifications are available to meet the needs of these pupils? How are parents and other family members involved in the school? Is multicultural education reflected in the school environment?

3. Attend various functions sponsored by ethnic groups in your community. Activities may include musical programs, art exhibitions, festivals, religious celebrations, school functions, and other ceremonies. How did you feel about participating in these activities? What did you learn as a result of your involvement? Were your personal viewpoints and stereotypes challenged as a result of this experience?

REFLECTING ON STANDARDS ▪▪▪▪▪▪▪▪▪▪▪▪▪▪▪▪▪▪▪▪▪▪▪▪▪▪▪▪▪▪▪▪▪▪▪▪▪▪

The following exercises are designed to help you learn to apply the Council for Exceptional Children (CEC) standards to your teaching practice. Each of the reflection exercises below correlates with a knowledge or skill within the CEC standards. For the full text of each of the related CEC standards, please refer to the standards integration grid located in Appendix B.

Focus on Learner Development and Individual Learning Differences (*CEC Initial Preparation Standard 1.1*)

Reflect on your own culture and how you interact with people of other cultures. In what ways would you share your cultural

background with your students? What strategies would you use to help your students appreciate their own cultural background and value the cultural diversity of others?

Focus on Professional Learning and Ethical Practice (*CEC Initial Preparation Standard 6.3*)

Reflect on what personal cultural biases you have. How might these biases affect your teaching? If possible, find an assessment to help you understand what hidden cultural biases you might have. Talk to colleagues, family, and friends to try to understand what biases you have that might hinder your teaching.

$SAGE edge™

Sharpen your skills with SAGE edge at **edge.sagepub.com/gargiulo5e. SAGE edge for students** provides a personalized approach to help you accomplish your coursework goals in an easy-to-use learning environment.

Answer Key to Cultural and Linguistic Diversity Quiz on p. 80

1. True	4. False	7. True	10. True
2. True	5. False	8. True	11. True
3. False	6. False	9. False	12. True

Parents, Families, and Exceptionality

LEARNING OBJECTIVES

After reading Chapter 4, you should be able to:

- **Outline** the evolution of parent-professional partnerships.
- **Describe** the four key elements of a family systems model for understanding the impact of a disability on the family constellation.
- **List** the emotional responses associated with the stages of parents' reaction to their child's disability.
- **Summarize** the effects of an individual with a disability on family members.
- **Explain** how a family's cultural and linguistic background influences its reaction to a disability.

The family is our most fundamental social institution, the cornerstone of our society. It is also the primary arena in which an individual, whether disabled or not, is socialized, educated, and exposed to the beliefs and values of his or her culture. This crucial responsibility is generally assumed by the youngster's parents, who serve as principal caregivers and the child's first teachers. In this chapter, when we refer to a parent, we mean any adult who fulfills these essential caregiving duties and responsibilities for a particular child.

Being a parent of a child with a disability is not a role most parents willingly choose for themselves. Generally speaking, few individuals ever ask to be a parent of a person with special needs, and most parents are never fully prepared for this tremendous responsibility. Parenting a child with a disability can be a difficult, demanding, and confusing job, yet we believe it is a role that can also be filled with joy, triumphs, and satisfaction.

Although exceptionality can certainly change the ecology of the family and the interactions that occur within it, the role of the family, and of the parents in particular, remains essentially the same. Stated another way, although each family is unique, in the majority of instances professionals are primarily working with just another family—not a family that is dysfunctional. We believe it is important for teachers and other service providers to focus on the strengths and the resources of the family and not concentrate solely on the challenges and stresses that are sometimes experienced by families with a child who has a disability.

The purpose of this chapter is to more fully explore the issue of parent-professional partnerships and to examine the interactive relationship of exceptionality and its impact on the family. We have adopted a family systems approach to guide us on our journey. We will also explore the topic of cultural and linguistic diversity as it pertains to families and exceptionality. We conclude with suggestions for facilitating parent-professional partnerships.

Parent-Professional Relationships: Changing Roles

Many teachers believe that parental involvement is crucial to the success of the educational experience, especially for children with disabilities. Parents are a valuable resource for professionals; in comparison to teachers and other service providers, parents typically have a greater investment in their children,

VIDEO
Family

VIDEO
Parent Interview

not only of time but also of emotion. Generally, no one else will know the child as well as the parents do; their experiences predate and exceed those of the professional. Yet only recently have professionals realized the value of parents and sought to establish collaborative relationships with them.

The history of parent–professional relationships is generally one of gloomy and counterproductive activities on the part of professionals (Gallagher, Beckman, & Cross, 1983). Today, parents are seen as collaborators and equal partners with professionals, but this was not always the case. The contemporary role of parents and families in alliance with professionals has been an evolving one. Turnbull, Turnbull, Erwin, and Soodak (2006) have outlined the major roles that parents and families have played over time (see Figure 4.1). They characterize these shifting roles and responsibilities as a pendulum swinging back and forth across several dimensions:

- From regarding parents and other family members as part of the child's problem to regarding them as partners in addressing the challenges of exceptionality
- From insisting on passive roles for parents to expecting active partnership roles for families
- From regarding families as consisting only of a mother–child dyad to recognizing the preferences and needs of all members of a family
- From responding to family needs in a general way to individualizing for the family as a whole and for each member of the family (Turnbull et al., 2006, p. 110)

Not only have the roles of parents and families shifted, but relationships between parents and professionals have also changed over the years. We believe it is possible to describe three distinct periods in the history of parent–professional relationships:

1. Antagonistic and adversarial relationships

2. Working partnerships

3. Parent empowerment and family-centered relationships

Antagonistic and Adversarial Relationships

The eugenics movement represents an early and dismal period in the history of parent–professional relationships. This campaign sought to improve the quality of humankind through selective breeding. It resulted in laws forbidding marriage between individuals with intellectual disability and led to calls for their sterilization. The goal of the eugenicists was to reduce the number of "unfit" parents and thus, according to their faulty logic, the number of inferior offspring (Turnbull, Turnbull, Erwin, Soodak, & Shogren, 2011).

Although the eugenics movement gradually lost influence by the middle of the twentieth century, it provided the foundation for later thinking that parents were the cause of their child's disability. Perhaps nowhere else was this belief more prominent than in the work of Bettelheim (1950, 1967), who saw parents, especially mothers, as the primary reason that their son or daughter was autistic. Bettelheim coined the term *refrigerator moms,* viewing these mothers as cold, detached, uncaring, and rigid. He even went so far as to advocate that these youngsters be taken away from their natural parents and institutionalized so that they could receive loving and competent care.

This time period (mid-1940s to early 1970s) was characterized by professional dominance. Professionals frequently adopted an attitude of superiority and were clearly

eugenics movement: A campaign that sought to improve the quality of humankind through carefully controlled selective breeding.

VIDEO
Parent Involvement

AUDIO
Parent–Professional Relationships

seen as being in control. They were the exclusive source of knowledge and expertise. Doctors, teachers, psychologists, and other service providers automatically assumed that the parents would defer to their judgment and passively submit to their recommendations, advice, and suggestions. It is easy to see how this climate laid the groundwork for less than positive relationships. As a result of their treatment by professionals, parents often became angry, confused, frustrated, and distrustful. This "mishandling" by professionals (Roos, 1978) led many parents to become aggressive activists and advocates for change.

In all fairness, however, part of the reason for less than positive relationships may reside with the parents. In some situations, Gargiulo (1985) writes,

> part of the blame for less than positive interaction falls squarely on the shoulders of the parents. In some instances, parents have condemned the professional for not recognizing the disability sooner and occasionally have even accused the professional of causing the handicap [disability]. Some parents have inhibited the growth of the relationship with professionals by withdrawing. They have judged professionals to be insensitive, offensive, and incapable of understanding their situation because professionals themselves are rarely parents of an exceptional person. (p. 6)

Consequently, the actions and attitudes of both professionals and parents resulted in establishing barriers and an unfavorable atmosphere for working together.

Working Partnerships

For the better part of the twentieth century, the families of children with disabilities had to contend with schools, and on occasion with professionals, that were at best apathetic to their needs and the needs of their children (Berry & Hardman, 1998). This situation dramatically improved with the enactment of PL 94–142 in 1975. The Individuals with Disabilities Education Act, or IDEA, as it is presently known, requires that parents participate fully in education decisions affecting their son or daughter. Today, parents no longer speak of privileges; instead, they talk of rights.

IDEA ushered in a new era of parent–professional relationships. The status of parents has changed from that of passive recipients of services and advice to that of active participants—educational decision makers. These new roles and responsibilities for parents and families include active involvement in the identification and assessment process, program planning, and evaluation, as well as input on placement decisions. These roles are coupled with extensive due process and procedural safeguards. It is easy to see how PL 94–142 has come to be designated the "Parent's Law" (Gargiulo & Kilgo, 2014).

Table 4.1 illustrates how the attitudes and services of professionals have evolved over the past few decades. Notice the contemporary emphasis on families instead of just parents across each of the six areas.

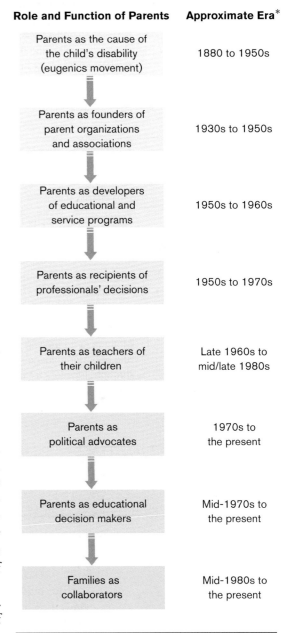

Figure 4.1 **A Timeline of the Changing Roles of Parents of Children With Disabilities**

Role and Function of Parents	Approximate Era*
Parents as the cause of the child's disability (eugenics movement)	1880 to 1950s
Parents as founders of parent organizations and associations	1930s to 1950s
Parents as developers of educational and service programs	1950s to 1960s
Parents as recipients of professionals' decisions	1950s to 1970s
Parents as teachers of their children	Late 1960s to mid/late 1980s
Parents as political advocates	1970s to the present
Parents as educational decision makers	Mid-1970s to the present
Families as collaborators	Mid-1980s to the present

*Eras do not represent discrete time periods; roles frequently overlap.

SOURCE: Adapted from A. Turnbull, R. Turnbull, E. Erwin, L. Soodak, & K. Shogren, *Families, Professionals, and Exceptionality*, 6th ed. (Upper Saddle River, NJ: Pearson Education, 2011), pp. 97–107.

Table 4.1 Changing Perspectives of Professionals Toward Families With a Child With a Disability

Issue	Traditional Attitude	Contemporary Attitude
1. "Vision"	Parents' greatest need (to which professional counseling and advice is geared) is to accept the burden of raising their child and to become realistic about his or her limitations and the fact that disability necessarily results in second-class citizenship.	Families need to be encouraged to dream about what they want for themselves and their son or daughter with a disability, and they need assistance in making those dreams come true. These dreams and future plans should lead to expectations that all members of the family are entitled to full citizenship. Vision replaces despair.
2. Support and assistance	Parents' difficulties in coping with the child are largely psychological or psychiatric in nature, and the proper interventions are psychiatric or psychological counseling.	Families can benefit from one another. One benefit that almost all families need is the emotional resiliency and information that other families have acquired about life with disabilities.
3. Socialization	Mothers need respite to alleviate the stress and burden of caring for their child.	Families need the child with disabilities to have friends and integrated recreational opportunities in order to respond to the child's needs for socialization, affection, and identity.
4. Hope for the future	Mothers need clinical information about disability.	Families need information about and inspiration from people with a disability who are successfully integrated into community life.
5. Instructional emphasis	Mothers need training related to skill development and behavior management so they can be "follow-through" teachers for their child and implement home-based lesson plans.	Families need encouragement and ways to ensure that the child has a functional education taught in natural environments. This encouragement and help should assist families to enlist the support of the natural helpers in those environments (e.g., family, friends, store clerks, bus drivers, scout leaders).
6. Social support	Many families are financially unable to meet their child's needs and should seek out-of-home placement.	Many families need new policies to provide, for example, direct subsidies and new tax credits to help meet the financial demands associated with disability in the home and family setting.

SOURCE: Adapted from A. Gartner, D. Lipsky, and A. Turnbull, *Supporting Families With a Child with a Disability* (Baltimore, MD: Paul H. Brookes, 1991), pp. 202–204.

The building of positive school–home partnerships requires that the family be viewed as a key partner in the education of the student with a disability. Parents are beneficial allies with professionals. Successful school experiences require the involvement of parents. Despite the importance of active and meaningful involvement, however, Turnbull et al. (2011) observe that many parents participate only passively in the educational decision-making process. These noted special educators speculate that some parents may not have the motivation to assume a more active role or may lack the requisite knowledge and skills to become active participants. In the vast number of cases, however, it is a lack of empowerment that limits or restricts their role as educational decision makers. It is this state of affairs that has led to the third stage of parent–professional interaction: parent empowerment and family-centered services. The current emphasis is on families as collaborators with professionals.

VIDEO

Parent Empowerment

Parent Empowerment and Family-Centered Relationships

The implementation of PL 99–457 and PL 101–476 signaled a change in the status of parent–professional relationships. With these enactments came the idea that families, not parents, should be the focal point of professionals' attention. One of the reasons for this shift was the evolving recognition that partnerships should not be limited exclusively to biological parents but can and should include other immediate and extended family members (Turnbull et al., 2011). Many professionals now operate under the assumption that the family serves as the primary decision maker in regard

Successful school experiences require the meaningful involvement of parents.

to setting goals and establishing priorities for the student with a disability. This change, of course, vastly extends the concept of parental involvement and significantly redefines the role of the special educator. Professionals no longer provide suggestions and services *to* families; rather, they work collaboratively *with* families, acting as coordinators and facilitators of service delivery (Blue-Banning, Summers, Frankland, Nelson, & Beegle, 2004; Gargiulo & Metcalf, 2013).

The contemporary emphasis on building family-professional partnerships implies that families are full and equal partners with professionals. It also strongly suggests a collaborative relationship. Collaboration involves the sharing of information and resources as well as expertise and a commitment to jointly reaching decisions. Implicit within the concept of collaboration is an ethic of mutual respect and shared responsibility. For professionals, collaboration also means that they no longer have power *over* families but rather achieve power *with* families. Families and professionals thus find themselves linked together in a mutually supportive and empowering alliance.

The idea of a collaborative partnership between home and school is in concert with the theorizing of Bronfenbrenner (1977, 1979), who argued that an individual cannot be viewed in isolation but can only be viewed as part of a larger social system. Professionals must have an appreciation of the social context in which the student develops and the interactions that occur among and between the various settings and individuals. Thus, we find that home, school, and community interact reciprocally, and the actions of parents, siblings, grandparents, teachers, and other professionals all influence one another. How a family relates to the other social systems is crucial to the overall functioning of the family. Finally, Bronfenbrenner's ecological thinking provides a foundation for family systems theory, which views the family as a social system. In this interactive system, whatever happens to one member affects the rest. We now turn our attention to examining this contemporary approach to working with families.

A Family Systems Approach

The fundamental belief underlying a family systems model is that a family is an interrelated social system with unique characteristics and needs. It operates as an interactive

family systems model: A model that considers a family as an interrelated social system with unique characteristics and needs.

Figure 4.2 **A Family Systems Framework**

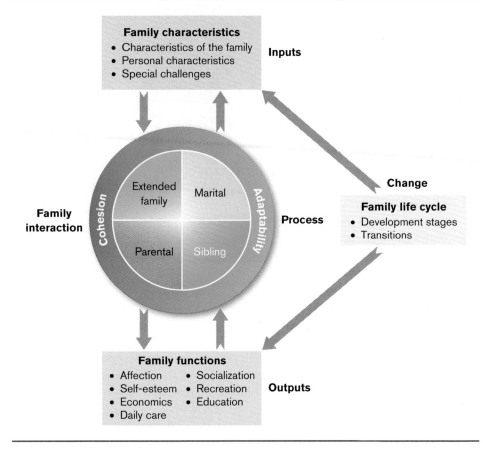

SOURCE: Adapted from A. Turnbull, J. Summers, and M. Brotherson, *Working with Families with Disabled Members: A Family Systems Approach* (Lawrence: Kansas Affiliated Facility, 1984), p. 60.

and interdependent unit. Events and experiences that affect a particular family member also affect the other members of the family. Because of this relationship, teachers and other service providers consider the entire family constellation as the appropriate focal point for professionals' attention.

Turnbull et al. (2011) have incorporated this thinking into a framework for applying family systems concepts to the study of families that have a child who is disabled. Their model (see Figure 4.2) contains four key elements, all of which are interrelated:

- Family characteristics
- Family interaction
- Family functions
- Family life cycle

Family characteristics are those features that make the family unique. "Inputs" include family size and form, cultural background, socioeconomic status, and geographic location. Additionally, each member's health status (both physical and mental), each member's individual coping style, and the nature and severity of each member's disability are included as personal characteristics. A final component includes special challenges facing the family, such as poverty, substance abuse, and parents who themselves may have a disability. Collectively, these variables provide each family with its own unique identity, influence interactional patterns among the members, and determine how the family responds to the individual's exceptionality. It is easy to understand how a large

family characteristics: One dimension of a family systems model; aspects include family size and form, cultural background, and socioeconomic status, as well as the type and severity of the disability.

A family can be viewed as an interrelated social system with its own unique characteristics.

family living in poverty in a rural location might differ in adaptation from an affluent suburban family with an only child who is disabled.

Family interactions comprise the relationships and interactions among and between the various family subsystems. How members of a particular family interact depends in part on their degree of cohesion and adaptability. These two factors affect the quality of interactions and can be interpreted only in light of the family's cultural heritage.

Simply defined, cohesion refers to the degree of freedom and independence experienced by each member of the family. Cohesion occurs along a continuum, with some families being overly cohesive. In this situation, the development of an individual's autonomy and independence may be impeded. Such families are viewed as being overly protective. Other families may have a low degree of cohesiveness. In this situation, families are depicted as being underinvolved, and the person with the disability fails to receive needed support. Well-functioning families aim to achieve a balance in cohesiveness.

Adaptability can be defined as the family's ability to change in response to a crisis or stressful event (Olson, 1988). Like cohesiveness, adaptability occurs along a continuum and is influenced by the family's cultural background. When a stressful event occurs, rigid families respond according to prescribed roles and responsibilities. They are unable to adapt to the demands of the new situation. This behavior places the family at risk for becoming isolated and dysfunctional (Seligman & Darling, 2007). For example, the introduction into a family of a youngster with multiple disabilities would very likely require some form of accommodation. Yet in a rigid family, with a clear hierarchy of power, the child care responsibilities would almost always fall on the mother. Such duties, according to the father's perception, are exclusively "women's work"; therefore, he

family interactions: One aspect of a family systems model; refers to the relationships and interactions occurring among and between various family subsystems.

cohesion: Within a family, the degree of freedom and independence experienced by each member.

adaptability: The ability of an individual or family to change in response to a crisis or stressful event.

has no obligation to assist. On the other hand, it is impossible to predict how a chaotic family would respond to this situation. Chaotic families are characterized by constant change and instability. There is often no family leader, and the few existing rules are often altered, creating significant confusion (Turnbull et al., 2011). The key for most families is to maintain a balance between the extremes of high and low adaptability.

Family functions are the seven interrelated activities listed in Figure 4.2, all of which are necessary to fulfill the individual and collective needs of the family:

- Affection—emotional commitments and display of affection
- Self-esteem—personal identity and self-worth, recognition of positive contributions
- Economics—production and utilization of family income
- Daily care—day-to-day survival needs (food, shelter, health care)
- Socialization—developing social skills, establishing interpersonal relationships
- Recreation—leisure time activities for both family and individuals
- Education—involvement in educational activities, career choices

Turnbull et al. (2011) identify these nonprioritized functions as "outputs" and remind us that it is impossible to discuss family functions without regard to the other three main dimensions of their framework. These tasks and activities are common to all families, but they are likely to be affected by the presence of a member with a disability (Berry & Hardman, 1998). The effect may be positive, negative, or neutral.

Individual families will establish their own priorities for each of these functions. In one family, meeting the daily needs of food and shelter is of utmost importance; another family may emphasize recreation and leisure. Berry and Hardman (1998) note that some families may require assistance in several areas, and others in only a few. Also, the amount of help from professionals will vary depending on specific circumstances.

Family life cycle is an important component of the Turnbull et al. (2011) framework. It refers to the developmental changes that occur in most families over time. These changes, though fairly predictable, may alter the structure of the family and in turn affect relationships, functions, and interactions.

The movement from one stage to another and the accompanying adjustment period are characterized as **transitions**. Transitions can be particularly stressful events for families, but especially for families with a member who is disabled. For many families, it is a time of challenge and uncertainty as to what the next stage holds for the family and the individual. For instance, when a toddler transitions from an early intervention program to Head Start or when a young adult leaves high school and secures employment, these events can be times of heightened anxiety and significant stress. Not all families successfully negotiate life cycle changes.

Life cycle functions, according to Seligman and Darling (2007), are highly age related. As a family moves through its life cycle and encounters new situations, its priorities shift. Turnbull et al. (2011) have identified four major life cycle stages and the accompanying issues that the parents and siblings of a child with a disability may encounter along the family's journey. Table 4.2 describes some of the developmental issues that an individual with an exceptionality presents to his or her family. We caution you, however, that how any particular family responds to a member with a disability is unique.

The Effects of a Child's Disability on Parents and the Family

It is important for teachers and other professionals to realize that the identification of an individual as disabled affects the entire family constellation and produces a wide

family functions: Interrelated activities found within a family systems model; functions range from affection to economics to socialization, among other variables.

family life cycle: Developmental changes occurring within a family over time.

transition: A broad term used to describe the movement of an individual from one educational environment to another, from one class to another, or from one phase of life (high school) to another (independent adulthood).

REFERENCE

Family
Management

■ ■■ ■ ■ Table 4.2 **Potential Family Life Cycle Issues**

Stage	Parental Issues	Sibling Issues
Early Childhood (Birth–Age 5)	• Obtaining an accurate diagnosis • Informing siblings and relatives • Locating services • Seeking to find meaning in the exceptionality • Clarifying a personal ideology to guide decisions • Addressing issues of stigma • Identifying positive contributions of exceptionality • Setting great expectations	• Less parental time and energy for sibling needs • Feelings of jealousy over less attention • Fears associated with misunderstandings of exceptionality
School Age (Ages 5–12)	• Establishing routines to carry out family functions • Adjusting emotionally to educational implications • Clarifying issues of mainstreaming [inclusion] vs. special class placement • Participating in IEP conferences • Locating community resources • Arranging for extracurricular activities	• Division of responsibility for any physical care needs • Oldest female sibling may be at risk • Limited family resources for recreation and leisure • Informing friends and teachers • Possible concern about younger sibling surpassing older • Issues of "mainstreaming" into same school • Need for basic information on exceptionality
Adolescence (Ages 12–21)	• Adjusting emotionally to possible chronicity of exceptionality • Identifying issues of emerging sexuality • Addressing possible peer isolation and rejection • Planning for career/vocational development • Arranging for leisure time activities • Dealing with physical and emotional changes of puberty • Planning for postsecondary education	• Overidentification with sibling • Greater understanding of differences in people • Influence of exceptionality on career choice • Dealing with possible stigma and embarrassment • Participation in sibling training programs • Opportunity for sibling support groups
Adulthood (Ages 21+)	• Planning for possible need for guardianship • Addressing the need for appropriate adult implications of dependency • Addressing the need for socialization opportunities outside the family for individuals with exceptionality • Initiating career choice or vocational program	• Possible issues of responsibility for financial support • Addressing concerns regarding genetic implications • Introducing new in-laws to exceptionality • Need for information on career/living options • Clarifying role of sibling advocacy • Possible issues of guardianship

SOURCE: Adapted from A. Turnbull and H. Turnbull, *Families, Professionals, and Exceptionality: A Special Partnership,* 2nd ed. (Columbus, OH: Merrill, 1990), pp. 134–135.

range of reactions, responses, and feelings. In some cases, the awareness comes shortly after the birth of the baby; in others, it may occur during the preschool years as a result of illness or accident; many times, parents are told that their son or daughter has a disability upon entering school.

The effect on the family of a child with a disability mainly involves perceptions and feelings that are highly subjective and personalized for each family member. How a

Parental reaction to the news of a disability typically results in a wide range of emotions.

mother responds will most likely differ from the response of her father-in-law, and an older sibling will very likely have a different point of view. Likewise, exceptionality is frequently interpreted differently by different families, even if the type of disability (such as blindness or intellectual disability) is the same. In some families, having a child with a disability is perceived as a tragedy; in others, it may be viewed as a crisis but one that can be managed; in still others, it is merely one more factor to be considered in a daily struggle to survive.

Stages of Parental Reaction to Disability

A number of writers in the field describe a stage theory approach when characterizing parental reactions to the diagnosis of a disability (Cook, Klein, & Tessier, 2013; Johnson, 2011; Lambie, 2008; Lerner & Johns, 2012; Zajicek-Farber, 2013). This popular interpretation suggests that some parents pass through a series of reactive stages to the news of their child's disability. Although no two families will respond identically, researchers have identified common transformative stages that many families exhibit as they adjust to a member with a disability (Cook et al., 2013).

Of course, it is impossible to predict how families, and parents in particular, will respond to a disability. Most stage theory models are constructed around the premise that families experience a grief or mourning cycle much like the developmental stages of reaction to the death of a loved one (Kubler-Ross, 1969). Some models are more elaborate than others, but most identify three distinct stages or phases of parental reaction. The classic work of Gargiulo (1985) provides a good example. Before examining this model, we should point out that the stage theory approach has been criticized as being unduly negative, overly rigid, and lacking in empirical evidence (Blacher, 1984). However, the writings of many parents of children with disabilities eloquently and poignantly attest to the validity of this approach (Hill-Patterson, 2011).

According to Gargiulo's (1985) model (see Figure 4.3), parental reaction to a disability includes three stages and encompasses a wide variety of feelings and reactions. This model is a generic one because parents of children with different disabilities frequently experience common feelings and react in similar fashion. Reactions differ more in degree than in kind. Gargiulo stresses the uniqueness and variability of the response pattern. He also emphasizes flexibility because of each family's unique situation and that feelings and emotions are likely to recur over the family life cycle. The order of parental response is not predictable, nor does movement completely depend on successful resolution of an earlier feeling. Gargiulo explains,

It should be noted that not all parents follow a sequential pattern of reaction according to a predetermined timetable. The stages should be viewed as fluid, with parents passing forward and backward as their individual adjustment process allows. Some individuals may never progress beyond hurt and anger; others may not experience denial; still others accept and adjust rather quickly

stage theory: A hypothesized pattern of parents' reaction to the news that their child has a disability.

AUDIO

Family Issues

■ ■ ■ ■ ■ *Figure 4.3* **A Stage Model of Parental Reaction to Disability**

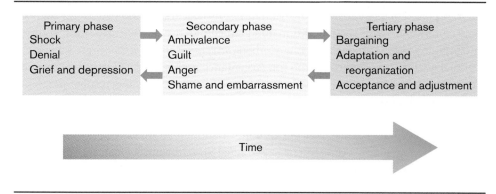

Primary phase	Secondary phase	Tertiary phase
Shock	Ambivalence	Bargaining
Denial	Guilt	Adaptation and reorganization
Grief and depression	Anger	
	Shame and embarrassment	Acceptance and adjustment

Time

SOURCE: R. Gargiulo, *Working with Parents of Exceptional Children: A Guide for Professionals* (Boston, MA: Houghton Mifflin, 1985), pp. 22–30.

to their child's abilities and disabilities. Also both parents do not necessarily go through these stages together. Each parent will react in his or her own unique way. (p. 21)

Figure 4.3 suggests the diverse emotional pattern that some parents experience. The initial response is often one of *shock* and disbelief; parents are poorly prepared, in most instances, for the news of their child's disability. Parents will sometimes evidence *denial* as a form of escape from the reality of the disability. The primary phase is also characterized by *grief,* as parents mourn the loss of their "ideal child" or "perfect baby." Depression and withdrawal are common consequences of the grieving process.

These initial reactions are followed by a secondary phase distinguished by what Blacher (1984) calls a period of emotional disorganization. It would not be uncommon during this stage for parents to vacillate between periods of total dedication and self-sacrifice (a martyr's posture) and rejection (in terms of affection and/or physical needs). Gargiulo (1985) identifies these behaviors as indicating *ambivalence.* One of the most common and difficult feelings for parents to deal with is *guilt*—that somehow they may have contributed to their son or daughter's disability. Guilt generally follows an "if only" thought pattern: "If only I hadn't had that drink while I was pregnant," "If only we had gone to the hospital sooner," "If only I kept the medicine cabinet locked." During this stage, overcompensation is common, as parents attempt to "make it up" to the child. This represents an effort to appease the parents' feelings of guilt. Equally common is a display of *anger* and hostility, frequently followed by the question "Why me?" for which no satisfactory answer exists. Finally, *shame and embarrassment* are also typical consequences that parents may experience as a result of having a child who is disabled. Some parents are fearful of how family, friends, and society in general will react to their son or daughter, and social withdrawal is not unusual. A parent's self-esteem may also be threatened. One parent writes:

> I felt I was a nobody. Any credits of self-worth that I could give myself from any of my personal endeavors meant nothing. Graduating from college and a first-rate medical school, surviving an internship, practicing medicine and having two beautiful sons and a good marriage counted for nil. All I knew at this point was that I was the mother of an abnormal and most likely retarded child. (Ziskin, 1978, p. 75)

VIDEO
Parental Reactions

Bargaining commences the tertiary phase, as parents seek to "strike a deal" with God, science, or anyone they believe might be able to help their child. Rarely seen by outsiders, it represents one of the final steps in a parent's ongoing process of adjustment. A period of *adaptation and reorganization* also occurs, as parents become increasingly comfortable with their situation and gain confidence in their parenting abilities. In Gargiulo's (1985) model, as in many others, *acceptance and adjustment* are seen as the eventual goal that most parents aim for. Acceptance is characterized as a state of mind whereby a deliberate effort is made to recognize, understand, and resolve problems. Parents also discover that acceptance involves not only accepting their son or daughter but also accepting themselves and acknowledging their strengths and weaknesses. Related to acceptance is the concept of adjustment, which implies both positive and forward-moving action. Adjustment is a gradual and, in some instances, difficult and lifelong process that demands a realignment of goals and ambitions. For many parents, it is an ongoing struggle.

Gargiulo (1985) and, more recently, Berry and Hardman (1998) believe that the preceding reactions and feelings are legitimate, automatic, understandable, and perfectly normal. Parents have a right to exhibit these emotions and to express their feelings. They are natural and necessary for adjustment. They do not represent reflections of pathology or maladjustment.

Knowledge of these stages and patterns of reaction can facilitate professionals' understanding of parental behavior and assist them in providing appropriate support when necessary. Sensitive and caring support from professionals can be very important for parents because typical sources of support, such as friends and other family members, may not be available (Berry & Hardman, 1998). Researchers believe that a family's adaptation to disability is closely linked to the level of support received from other family members as well as community resources (Blasco, Johnson, & Palomo-Gonzalez, 2008; D'Asaro, 1998). The availability and quality of social support are crucial to a family's ability to cope with and adjust to a child with a disability (Santelli, Turnbull, Marquis, & Lerner, 1997; Singer, 2002).

Disability and the Family

A family systems approach and the theorizing of Bronfenbrenner (1977, 1979) suggest that the entire family constellation is altered and affected in various ways by the presence of a child with an exceptionality. Contemporary thinking about families of children with disabilities has evolved from a dyadic focus on mother–child interactions to an exploration of family dynamics within an ecological framework. Because we consider a family to be an interdependent and interactive social system, when a situation arises such as a child's disability, this issue must be viewed and can only be fully understood within the context of the family unit. As one sibling of a child with a disability notes:

> All of the members of my family are disabled. But most people recognize only the disability of my deaf sister. They do not realize that the disability of one member affects the entire family. Parents realize this to some extent because they themselves are affected—their attitude, their priorities, their lifestyles. But sometimes they become so involved with the problems directly related to their disabled child that they lose sight of the effect upon the other children. (Hayden, 1974, p. 26)

There is no easy way to answer the question "How does a child with a disability affect his or her family?" How one family copes and adapts to a member's disability

REFERENCE

Family

will most likely be radically different from how another family does. Much depends on individual family factors such as the parents' marital integration, religious beliefs and values, financial resources, cultural heritage, and external support system. Additionally, child characteristics such as gender and the severity of the impairment also mediate the family's adaptation. In our view, all of these variables interact and commingle to produce overall family adaptation.

Marital Relationships

Being a parent of a child with a disability may contribute to marital tension and stress in some families. The research literature on divorce in families of children with disabilities is limited, however, and the findings are frequently contradictory. In some instances, divorce and marital difficulties are common adjustment problems (Banks, 2003; Hodapp & Krasner, 1995); in other situations, marriages are strengthened (Scorgie & Sobsey, 2000; Scorgie, Wilgosh, & McDonald, 1998). Investigators have also found no difference in divorce rates between families with and without children with disabilities (Seligman & Darling, 2007; Turnbull et al., 2011). Although being a parent of a child with disabilities may result in significantly greater stress for both mothers and fathers (Hutton & Caron, 2005; Olsson & Hwang, 2001), it would be false to conclude that marital deterioration is an automatic consequence (Blasco et al., 2008). It is simply unclear why some marriages remain intact and others disintegrate. We suspect that the answer lies in the mixture of parent and child characteristics interacting with specific ecological factors.

Mothers of Children With Disabilities

In many American households, women are primarily responsible for the raising of children, although more men are currently assuming greater child-rearing responsibilities. Still, in many families, mothers are particularly vulnerable to the stresses, strains, and added difficulties engendered by a child with a disability (Trachtenberg, Batshaw, & Batshaw, 2007). In some circumstances, these problems may be immediate, such as when a baby is born with Down syndrome or multiple disabilities; in other instances, mothers may encounter added stress when a disability is recognized after a son or daughter enters school. New roles, responsibilities, and routines for mothers are not uncommon when a youngster has a disability. The dynamics of the entire family relationship may also change.

A sense of feeling overwhelmed, concern about family finances, physical—and, in some instances, mental—exhaustion, impaired relationships with other family members, and the impact on employment are just some of the issues confronting mothers when their child has a disability. Of course, the type and severity of the disability, the time of its onset, and access to support systems often mediate the situation. Having a supportive husband or partner is crucial to helping mothers successfully cope with the stresses of raising their son or daughter with a disability (Power & Dell Orto, 2004). In some communities, support groups and respite care provide a valuable source of relief for mothers as well as other family members.

Fathers of Children With Disabilities

Fathers are beginning to receive more attention from professionals, who are becoming increasingly cognizant of the needs of fathers and urging their active involvement in intervention programs for children with disabilities (Flynn & Wilson, 1998; Rump, 2002).

respite care: Temporary or occasional care of an individual with disabilities by nonfamily members.

When researchers investigate the effect of a child with disabilities on fathers and mothers, discrepant findings are not unusual. Lamb and Meyer (1991) and, more recently, Trachtenberg et al. (2007) found, for example, that fathers and mothers react differently to the news of their child's disability. Fathers, in general, are less emotional in their reaction, tend to focus on the long-term consequences, and seem to be more affected by the visibility of the disability. Mothers are more expressive in their responses and are worried about the day-to-day burdens of child care.

The father's attitude toward his son or daughter who is disabled is very likely to influence the attitude of other family members (Flynn & Wilson, 1998; Seligman & Darling, 2007). A disability diagnosis can also affect how a father evaluates his family life, which can subsequently influence the perceptions of the entire family. These conclusions are in line with our family systems approach to understanding the effect of a disability. (See the accompanying First Person feature.)

Siblings of Children With Disabilities

Is having a sibling with a disability a positive or negative experience? The safest answer to this intriguing question is "It depends." The research evidence provides conflicting findings. The impact of a brother or sister with special needs seems to be mediated by a number of variables; and, of course, the child's needs can only be considered within the context of the entire family constellation. Siblings are likely to exhibit a wide range of adaptive responses that are affected by parental attitudes and expectations, family socioeconomic status, the severity and type of impairment, family size, sibling gender and age spacing, child-rearing practices, cultural heritage, and the availability of support systems (Gargiulo & Kilgo, 2014; Seligman & Darling, 2007). We must not forget, of course, that while a child with a disability affects his or her typical brother or sister, this sibling is also influencing, in both positive and negative ways, the sibling with an exceptionality.

Over the years, several investigators (Gallagher, Powell, & Rhodes, 2006; Hutton & Caron, 2005; Simpson & Mundschenk, 2010) have identified adverse outcomes in sibships involving an individual with a disability. Some of the frequently mentioned deleterious effects include depression or social withdrawal and anxiety, jealousy, and sadness, as well as lower self-esteem and poor peer relationships. In addition, excessive child care requirements placed on older siblings often result in feelings of anger and resentment (McHugh, 2003). Some brothers and sisters exhibit "survivor's guilt" due to the absence of illness or disability in their own lives (Russell, Russell, & Russell, 2003). Younger siblings who are typical are sometimes concerned about becoming disabled or ill themselves. Finally, when siblings lack adequate information about their brother's or sister's disability, they often become confused and concerned about their own identity (Seligman & Darling, 2007).

It would be totally incorrect, however, to portray sibships with a brother or sister with a disability as having exclusively negative outcomes (Simpson & Mundschenk, 2010). The research literature also provides a more optimistic outlook. As an example, Grossman's (1972) classic retrospective investigation of siblings of children with intellectual disability notes such benefits as greater tolerance toward others, increased compassion, and higher levels of empathy and altruism as a result of growing up with a brother or sister with a disability. Meyer's (2009) more recent work also poignantly validates the many positive aspects experienced by siblings of individuals with special needs.

Siblings typically exhibit a myriad of feelings toward a brother or sister with special needs. The accompanying First Person feature vividly captures some of these emotions. Table 4.3 gives examples of some of the reactions and feelings sustained by brothers and sisters of children with disabilities.

VIDEO

Goals

FIRST PERSON: KRISTINA

Day Dreams

More than once during the last twelve years since our daughter, Kristina, was born with cerebral palsy I have daydreamed wistfully about what she might have been like if only . . .

Would she run fast and jump high? Would she enjoy reading as much as her mom and I? Would she love to climb trees like her dad, or make crafts like her mom? How much different would she look, would her face change, how might she look if she could sit or stand straight? Would her voice be different? Would she like the same things she likes now: cards, telephones, swimming, speed? Would she have done well in school? Would she enjoy math or English? What kinds of friends would she have made? How would I have responded to her first boyfriend? What kind of nickname might she have been given? Could she have performed a solo in a choir or played an instrument? How would she look riding a bike or rollerblading down the hill? Would she like tennis? Would she have gotten the same thrill with horses as her grandmother?

At first, I daydreamed out of self-pity; later I felt ashamed but now I have grown to view it as an occasionally pleasant diversion. I realize now, it is only human nature to wonder and second guess about choices made and paths not taken. Once our lives have irrevocably gone in one direction, many look back and wonder what it might be like to live in another place or time, do another job, or live another life. It's harmless, it's healthy.

I guess I stopped feeling ashamed of my daydreams when I realized that I couldn't be happier than I am right now. I have a wonderful wife, three willful and happy children, and many things that others daydream about.

Despite human nature, down deep I do not want anything around me to change. While I might like to try on a different job much as I might like to try on a different style of clothes, I know it wouldn't be me. In the same way, I might like to meet a different Kristina, but she wouldn't have the same infectious laugh, the same genuine feelings, or the same love of life. I wouldn't like the impostor much and I know I couldn't love her. I've been blessed with the perfect one, and I could never have imagined anything better. ■

SOURCE: J. Cox, "Day Dreams," *Young Exceptional Children*, 1(1), 1997, p. 17.

Siblings can sometimes benefit from support groups or workshops such as Sibshops (Meyer & Vadasy, 2008) where brothers and sisters of siblings with special needs can share feelings and obtain peer support as well as information within a recreational environment. One valuable resource for siblings is the Sibling Support Project,[1] a national organization that focuses on the concerns of brothers and sisters of individuals with special needs.

Grandparents of Children With Disabilities

Professionals are becoming increasingly aware of the important role that grandparents play in contemporary family life. They are significant members of many family constellations. When a child with a disability enters the family unit, grandparents are affected just as parents and siblings are.

Just as parents exhibit a wide range of emotional responses to the news that their son or daughter has a disability, grandparents are not immune to feelings of grief, shock, depression, anger, and so forth (Zajicek-Farber, 2013). They, too, often go through stages of acceptance. Grandparents also experience a dual hurt: They are concerned and anxious not only about their grandchild but also about their own child, whom they may perceive as chronically burdened (Seligman, Goodwin, Paschal, Applegate, & Lehman, 1997).

How grandparents respond to a grandchild with a disability can be an additional stressor for the child's parents or a source of strength and support. Grandparents, in

VIDEO
Family Relationships

Emotion	Response
Resentment	Perhaps the most common reaction experienced by typical siblings is resentment. It is a natural by-product of being angry about having a brother or sister with a disability. Resentment may develop because the child with special needs may require a disproportionate amount of the parents' attention. This sibling may also prohibit the family from participating in certain experiences or excursions. Special treatments and/or therapy may contribute to family financial hardship. Older siblings may resent having to babysit, or having social constraints placed upon them by their younger brother or sister who is disabled.
Jealousy	Resentment can easily develop into jealousy, especially if the typical sibling perceives that he or she has lost "favor" with the parents. The brother or sister with a disability may become a rival or competitor for the parents' attention and affection. Often the typical sibling will engage in behaviors designed to secure parental attention, such as having academic or behavioral problems in school, telling lies, or exhibiting unusual mischievousness.
Hostility	From feelings of jealousy often comes hostility, which is a perfectly natural reaction. Unlike objective adults, children are subjective and consider events in terms of how they are personally affected. They may view their brother or sister with special needs, rather than the disability, as the source of all their problems. Therefore, feelings of hostility are usually aimed toward their sibling. These feelings may manifest themselves in physical aggression or verbal harassment and ridicule. In some instances, hostility is directed toward the parents through acts of disobedience or impertinence.
Guilt	Siblings without disabilities frequently evidence feelings of guilt; however, these reactions differ from the parents'. Their guilt may stem from the negative feelings they have about their brother or sister, or it may be a consequence of having mistreated their sibling. Furthermore, when viewing their sibling who has an impairment, some children experience guilt because of their own good fortune to be thought of as typical.
Grief	Siblings frequently grieve for their brother or sister who is disabled. Their grief is often a reflection of their parents' sorrow. They grieve not for what they have lost, but for what will possibly be denied to their sibling.
Fear	Typical siblings may also experience fear. They may be fearful of acquiring a disability or of their own future children being disabled. A further worry is that someday they may have to assume total responsibility for the care of their sibling.
Shame and embarrassment	Shame and embarrassment are common emotional responses of typical siblings. A child may be ashamed of his or her brother or sister who is intellectually disabled, embarrassed to have friends visit, or embarrassed to be seen in public with his or her sibling.
Rejection	In some families, siblings who are typical may reject their brother or sister with a disability. They may reject the reality of the impairment. More commonly, however, rejection is shown by withholding affection or ignoring the sibling's existence.

SOURCE: Adapted from R. Gargiulo, *Working with Parents of Exceptional Children: A Guide for Professionals* (Boston, MA: Houghton Mifflin, 1985), pp. 51–52.

the words of Gearheart, Mullen, and Gearheart (1993), can be "the glue that holds the family constellation together" (p. 493). They are capable of greatly contributing to the overall functioning and well-being of the family. Their contributions can range from serving as alternative caregivers, to providing sources of community support, to assisting in the daily chores of shopping or running errands, but perhaps the greatest area of assistance is providing emotional support (Seligman & Darling, 2007).

As we have just seen, a person with a disability affects his or her family in many ways—some positive and others negative. It is refreshing, however, to see researchers and other professionals acknowledging the positive effects that a child with a disability has on family life. No longer is a disability exclusively thought to be a burden for

---

[1]For additional information see www.siblingsupport.org/

FIRST PERSON: MINDY

The Other Children

I first remember having a sense of special responsibility for my deaf sister when I was 3. It was my duty to keep her out of danger and mischief—a seemingly normal responsibility for an older sister. But the responsibility has at times felt unbearably heavy. As a 2-year-old, Mindy was not only typically rambunctious, she lived in a bizarre and often dangerous world all her own—separated from the rest of us by her deafness and her inability to communicate. It was a world of fascinating objects to handle, of races with Mother, Daddy, and big sister—a world, even, of nocturnal romps in the street while the rest of the family slept. And once, it was a world of pretty colored pills in the bathroom medicine cabinet.

"Second Mother" to Mindy

When Daddy spent a year in Korea, I became Mother's sole helper. My role as a second mother to Mindy held some prestige and much responsibility. It took away from play time with children my own age. And, just as a mother serves as an example for her children, I was expected to be an exceptionally "good" little girl. The high standards my mother set for my behavior, though, had not only to do with my setting an example; her reasons were also practical. Mindy's impetuous behavior left her with little patience, energy, or time to put up with shenanigans from me. As I got older, problems resulting from my having a deaf sister increased. My mother began to attend college, and the new pressures and demands caused her to be demanding and dependent upon me. I did not understand why I would be severely chastised for the same behavior that Mindy, who embodied the behavior problems of three children, "couldn't help." My friends' parents seemed less critical of their children than my parents were of me. Mother and Daddy "expected more" from me, but it seemed to me that they gave me less. The responsibility I felt for Mindy was tremendous. One year, when my "baby-sitting" duties involved periodic checking on my sister, Mindy wandered away between checks. After a thorough but fruitless search of the neighborhood, my mother hysterically told me that if anything happened to Mindy I would be to blame. I felt terrified and guilty. I was 7.

Competition and Rivalry

Mindy's achievements always met with animated enthusiasm from our parents. In contrast, it seemed, Mother and Daddy's response to my accomplishments were on the pat-on-the-back level. I was expected to perform well in every circumstance. I wanted my parents to be enthusiastic about my accomplishments too. I didn't want to have to beg for praise. I didn't want to be taken for granted. I wanted to be noticed.

Babysitter and Manager

When I was not baby-sitting, there was my role of "fetch and carry"—sometimes literally. Mindy's deafness prevented my parents from calling to her so I was appointed official messenger. "Go tell Mindy to come to dinner." "Go tell Mindy to come inside." "Go tell Mindy to clean up her room." At first I probably gloried a bit in my "authority." But that soon grew stale. I was expected to stop whatever I was doing and bear some message to Mindy. And I discovered that like the royal messengers of old, bearers of orders or bad tidings are not cordially received. In retaliation against the inconvenience and hostile receptions, I made a point of being as bossy in my deliveries as possible—which resulted in acute mutual aggravation.

Love and Respect

In my junior year of high school, Mindy and I began to grow close as sisters. Our increased maturity and the circumstances of our father's being away in Vietnam caused us to turn to one another for companionship and comfort. In the process, we began to discover one another as individuals. We took time to understand our mutual antagonisms and to forgive each other a little. Mindy now understands that as a child my responsibility for her was immense and often intolerable, and that she thoughtlessly made it more difficult for me. She has forgiven me for the hurt and resentment I caused her. Differences between us will always exist, but Mindy and I now understand and respect each other's needs without resentment. The impact a disabled child has upon the other children in a family is tremendous—in both a positive and negative sense. Parents must not expect sainthood from their "other children." Most likely many years will pass before their nondisabled children fully understand why their sister or brother "couldn't help it," why they were expected to be model children, why attention from their parents was rationed, and why their parents sometimes seemed unduly critical and impatient. Until the "other children" do understand, their reactions may be "thoughtless" or "unfair." Before love can replace misunderstanding and intolerance, resentment must be recognized and accepted as a legitimate and even inevitable part of the struggle of growing up together. ■

SOURCE: V. Hayden, "The Other Children," *Exceptional Parent, 4*, 1974, pp. 26–29.

Siblings often exhibit myriad feelings toward a brother or sister with special needs.

the family. "There has been a growing recognition," Glidden and Floyd (1997) write, "of the rewards and benefits involved in rearing children with disabilities" (p. 250). It is primarily a matter of perspective.

Working With Families Who Are Culturally and Linguistically Diverse

As we discovered in Chapter 3, teachers are working with a growing population of pupils who are culturally and linguistically diverse, of which a disproportionate number are enrolled in special education programs. Effective teachers are sensitive to the needs of these children as well as the needs of their parents and extended family members. If the cultural and linguistic heritage of the parents is not respected, then the development of optimal relationships will likely be undermined (Gargiulo & Kilgo, 2014).

Many of the strategies and programs, however, that are designed to solicit parental involvement have been devised primarily to serve middle- and upper-income English-speaking families from the macroculture (Lynch & Hanson, 2004; Meyer, Bevan-Brown, Park, & Savage, 2013). Thus, it is highly probable that families from culturally and linguistically diverse backgrounds will fail to appreciate and respond to strategies designed to support home–school partnerships and enhance their role in the special education process.

Some of the roadblocks or obstacles that may impede the full and meaningful involvement of caregivers from outside the mainstream American culture include the parents' limited English proficiency, their previous negative experiences with schools, an unfamiliarity with their rights and responsibilities, a deference to teachers and other professionals as the decision makers ("teacher knows best"), and, in some instances, a lack of trust in the educational system (Lo, 2012; Matuszny, Banda, & Coleman, 2007; Meyer et al., 2013; Parette & Petch-Hogan, 2000). Establishing meaningful collaborative relationships with families from culturally and linguistically diverse backgrounds also requires that professionals respect the family's interpretation of the disability and its origin; the family's child-rearing beliefs, medical practices, and traditions; the family's structure and decision-making style; and the family's religious views and preferred manner of communication (Gargiulo & Kilgo, 2014). The best intentions of teachers can easily be misinterpreted if they fail to consider the family's value system and cultural traditions. For example, a Hispanic American family may be uncomfortable with and reluctant to agree to a recommendation that it consider placement in a group home for its daughter with an intellectual disability. To the transition specialist, this may appear to be a perfectly reasonable and appropriate suggestion. However, unlike Anglo Americans, who generally emphasize accomplishment, independence, and self-reliance, Hispanic Americans are more likely to value interdependence, cooperation, and familial cohesiveness. Because of these differences in values and beliefs, this recommendation will likely be inappropriate for this particular family.

It is very important that teachers exhibit cultural sensitivity when working with families with a cultural or linguistic heritage different from their own. Cultural sensitivity implies an awareness of, respect for, and appreciation of the many factors that influence and shape the values, priorities, and perspectives of both individuals and families (Hanson, 2004a). Educators need to be knowledgeable about different values, social customs, and traditions so that they can respond effectively to the needs of all their pupils while concurrently building partnerships with the students' families. By becoming informed about and sensitive to cultural differences, teachers are in a position to empower parents and create equitable relationships (Lustig

Teachers must exhibit cultural sensitivity when working with families whose cultural or linguistic heritage is different from theirs.

& Koester, 2013). We offer the following note of caution, however: Building effective alliances with families from different cultural groups demands that professionals refrain from generalizing about families. Although similarities may exist among families, such as a shared heritage or common language, assuming that a family will behave in a certain way simply because of membership in a particular group often leads to stereotyping, which only hinders the development of meaningful home–school partnerships. Remember, just as each student is unique, so is each family. Although families are influenced by their cultural background, they should not be defined by it. No list of ideas or suggestions can guarantee that services will be provided in a culturally sensitive fashion, but the accompanying Suggestions for the Classroom feature offers recommendations for building meaningful relationships with families who have culturally or linguistically diverse children.

Cultural Reactions to Disability

A family's cultural heritage shapes its reaction to and interpretation of disabilities. Because a disability is a socially and culturally constructed phenomenon (Gollnick & Chinn, 2013; Harry & Klinger, 2007), families from culturally diverse backgrounds may have differing perspectives on the meaning of exceptionality. These alternative views can easily affect the evaluation process, educational planning, life goals, and our attempts at establishing collaborative relationships (Turnbull et al., 2011).

A disability should always be considered within its cultural context. Each culture defines what it considers to be deviant as well as normal. "Aspects of human variance that are perceived as disabling conditions in one culture may not be perceived as such in another" (Voltz, 1998, p. 66). Harry's (1995) research with families who are culturally diverse seems to suggest that a disability is defined by the child's ability to function in the home environment coupled with the family's expectations for the child's future. Differences in interpretation can pose problems for professionals. For instance, some parents may not consider their child's variance to be severe enough to warrant the label *disabled*. Harry (1992) relates an account of a grandmother living in Puerto Rico

cultural sensitivity: A perspective adopted by professionals when working with families in which there is an awareness of and respect for the values, customs, and traditions of individuals and families.

SUGGESTIONS FOR THE CLASSROOM

Recommendations for Providing Families With Culturally Sensitive Services

→ Provide information using the family's desired language and preferred means of communication—written notes, telephone calls, informal meetings, or even audio recordings.

→ When appropriate, recognize that extended family members often play a key role in a child's educational development. Give deference to key decision makers in the family.

→ Use culturally competent interpreters who are not only familiar with the language but also knowledgeable about educational issues and the special education process.

→ Seek cultural informants from the local community who can assist teachers in understanding culturally relevant variables such as nonverbal communication patterns, child-rearing strategies, gender roles, academic expectations, medical practices, and specific folkways that might affect the family's relationships with professionals.

→ Attend social events and other functions held in the local community.

→ With the help of other parents or volunteers, develop a survival vocabulary of key words and phrases in the family's native language.

→ Address parents and other caregivers as "Mr.," "Ms.," or "Mrs.," rather than using first names. Formality and respect are essential, especially when speaking with older members of the family.

→ In arranging meetings, be sensitive to possible barriers such as time conflicts, transportation difficulties, and child care issues.

→ Conduct meetings, if necessary, in family-friendly settings such as local community centers or houses of worship.

→ Invite community volunteers to serve as cultural liaisons between the school and the pupil's family.

SOURCES: Graves, Gargiulo, & Sluder, 1996; Linan-Thompson & Jean, 1997; Lo, 2012; Misra, 1994; Parette & Petch-Hogan, 2000; Salend & Taylor, 1993.

---

whose daughter was labeled intellectually disabled; the process repeated itself with her granddaughter. This grandmother questions the wisdom involved in the identification of her granddaughter:

> Now they're saying the same thing about my granddaughter, but she has nothing wrong with her mind either. She behaves well and she speaks clearly in both Spanish and English. Why do they say she's retarded?
>
> Americans say that the word *handicap* [italics added] means a lot of things, it doesn't just mean that a person is crazy. But for us, Puerto Ricans, we still understand this word as "crazy." For me, a person who is handicapped is a person who is not of sound mind, or has problems in speech, or some problem of their hands or legs. But my children have nothing like that, thanks to God and the Virgin! (Harry, 1992, p. 147)

Just as the notion of disability is determined by society, the etiology or cause of a disability is a reflection of a family's cultural reference. Different cultures perceive the cause of disability differently. Generally speaking, in the United States, we believe that the cause of a disability can be identified and treated scientifically (Hanson, 2004b). Families from different cultures may express a belief in fate, spiritual reasons, violation of social taboos, or intergenerational reprisals as possible causes for the child's disability (Gannotti, Handwerker, Groce, & Cruz, 2001; Harry, 2002). At the risk of stereotyping, some Hispanic American families may attribute a youngster's disability to "God's will." In some Asian American families, a disability is thought to bring overwhelming shame upon the family, especially if the child is male; the etiology of the disability may be seen as punishment or retribution for past sins (Misra, 1994). Many Native American cultures have no word for *disability*. In these families a child with a disability is typically accepted and integrated into their community, fulfilling roles commensurate with his or her abilities (Lovern, 2008).

Different meanings of disability and its etiology can be a source of tension between professionals and families from diverse cultural backgrounds. Alternative perspectives on disability and its meaning can easily affect the type of services and interventions a family is willing to ask for and accept, the family's degree of involvement in educational planning, and attempts at establishing partnerships. We are in complete agreement with Salend and Taylor (1993), who urge educators to be cognizant of and sensitive to parents' belief systems and to adjust their services and practices as needed.

Suggestions for Facilitating Family and Professional Partnerships

What ingredients are needed to establish a meaningful and effective alliance between professionals and families with children who are disabled? The answer to this question has commanded a great deal of attention. We believe that an awareness of and sensitivity to the needs of the family are essential prerequisites for establishing cooperative relationships. These relationships must be built around trust, mutual understanding, and respect. Perl (1995) suggests that interactions between parents and professionals be facilitated when professionals are able to establish an atmosphere of genuine caring. The traits of honesty, empathy, and genuineness are also crucial to working effectively with families. Additionally, professionals must engage in active listening, which requires that service providers listen to parents and other significant persons and caregivers with understanding. Those who seek to establish meaningful partnerships with families must focus on the feelings and attitudes that accompany the words. They must be constantly aware of both verbal and nonverbal messages and their emotional significance. Listening demands the use of both the head and the heart.

As schools and other agencies continue to reach out to families and seek to build partnerships, it seems appropriate that the concept of *parent* involvement be broadened in favor of the term *family* involvement. In contemporary American life, many primary caregivers are adults other than the youngster's biological parents; grandparents, older siblings, foster parents, and extended family members often fill this vital role. The involvement of families can have a beneficial effect on many different dimensions of school life:

- Pupil achievement
- The student's educational aspirations
- The length of time individuals stay in school
- Teachers' perceived efficacy of their teaching abilities
- Teachers' perceptions of caregiver effectiveness
- Caregivers' ratings of schools (Matuszny et al., 2007)

active listening: A type of listening in which a person is attentive to the feelings as well as the verbal message that is being communicated.

VIDEO

Cultural Reactions

Today, parent (family) participation in the educational decision-making process is a right, not a privilege. Professionals can facilitate meaningful partnerships with families by their actions and attitudes. Being supportive of families and their unique circumstances, demonstrating concern and empathy, and acknowledging one's own limitations can go a long way toward building lasting partnerships with a student's family. Carefully consider the following statements. Do you think that caregivers would appreciate hearing these remarks from a professional?

- It's not your fault. You are not powerful enough to have caused the kinds of problems your child has.
- What do you need for yourself?
- I think your son could be a success story for our agency.
- I value your input.
- Under the circumstances, you are doing the best you can do. Frankly, I don't know what I would do or how I would be able to carry on.
- If you were a perfect parent, your son would still be in this condition.
- I agree with you.
- Your child has made progress, and I know he can do more, so we will continue to work with him.
- Why are you taking all of the blame? It takes two to make or break a relationship.
- I don't know. I can't tell you what's wrong with your child or what caused the problem.
- Your child knows right from wrong. She knows most of society's values, and that's because you taught them to her.
- There is a lot of love in your family.
- You know, it's okay to take care of yourself too.
- I don't know. I have to give that serious thought.
- I believe in your instincts. You're the expert on your child.
- You're being too hard on yourself.
- Our agency will take your case.
- Thanks so much for your participation in the group [parent support group]. Your intelligence and your calm reasonableness are important influences in the group. (*Family Support Bulletin*, 1991, p. 20)

We also believe that effective alliances with caregivers of children with special needs require that service providers attend to the following suggestions developed by Gargiulo and Graves (1991):

1. *Explain terminology.* Many parents [caregivers] have no previous experience with exceptionality. This may be their first exposure to a disability label. The parents' [caregivers'] conceptualization of cerebral palsy or intellectual disability is most likely very different from that of the professional.

2. *Acknowledge feelings.* Parents [caregivers] will frequently exhibit negative feelings when confronted with the news that their son or daughter is disabled. Professionals need to send a message that it is okay to have these feelings. They need to be acknowledged and then understood.

3. *Use a two-step process when initially informing parents [caregivers] that their child requires special educational services.* After sharing diagnostic information, it is strongly suggested that professionals allow parents [caregivers] time to comprehend and absorb what they have been told. The parents' [caregivers'] affective

VIDEO
Communication

AUDIO
Chapter 4 Summary

concerns must be dealt with before proceeding with matters such as intervention recommendations, treatment regimens and strategies, or duration of services. These issues should be addressed in a follow-up interview as the parents' [caregivers'] emotional state permits.

4. *Keep parents [caregivers] informed.* Use a variety of two-way communication techniques. Be as positive as possible when discussing a child's performance. Demonstrate respect, concern, and a sincere desire to cooperate.

5. *Be accountable.* If you agree to assume certain responsibilities or gather information for the parents [caregivers], be certain to follow through. Accountability demonstrates to the parents [caregivers] that they can depend on you. Trust, consistency, and dependability significantly increase the chances for an effective relationship. (p. 178)

Remember, being a parent of a child with disabilities is not a role that most parents freely choose for themselves. Yet it is within professionals' power to help make this a beneficial experience while promoting the development and effective functioning of the entire family unit.

Special attention is sometimes required when working with parents of students from culturally and linguistically diverse backgrounds. Like many other parents, these families are often an untapped resource for educators. As we have seen, effective involvement of these families in the educational lives of their children requires that teachers be sensitive to the cultural norms, values, and beliefs held by the family.

CHAPTER IN REVIEW

Parent–Professional Relationships: Changing Roles

- Three distinct periods characterize the history of parent–professional relationships: (1) antagonistic and adversarial relationships, (2) working partnerships, and (3) parent empowerment and family-centered relationships.
- The passage of IDEA changed the status of parents from passive recipients of services to active participants and allies with professionals.
- The focal point of professionals' attention is now the child's family rather than just the parents. The family is seen as the primary decision maker.

A Family Systems Approach

- A family systems model considers the family to be an interactive and interdependent unit; whatever affects one family member has repercussions for the other members of the unit.
- The Turnbull family systems model contains four interrelated components: family characteristics, family interactions, family functions, and family life cycle.

Stages of Parental Reaction to Disability

- A stage theory model for explaining parental reactions to the diagnosis of a disability is constructed around the premise that parents experience a grief cycle similar to the stages of reaction to the death of a loved one.

Disability and the Family

- The entire family constellation is affected by the presence of a child with a disability. The various subsystems and individual family members are uniquely impacted. No two families are likely to deal with an exceptionality in quite the same way.

Working With Families Who Are Culturally and Linguistically Diverse

- If the values, traditions, and beliefs of caregivers from culturally and linguistically diverse backgrounds are not addressed, then the development of optimal relationships will very likely be hindered.
- Teachers must exhibit culturally sensitive behavior when working with families whose backgrounds differ from their own.

Suggestions for Facilitating Family and Professional Partnerships

- In order to establish meaningful and effective alliances with families with children who are disabled, it is recommended that professionals create partnerships built around the principles of honesty, trust, and respect.
- Service providers must be genuine and exhibit a caring attitude, using active listening when communicating with family members and other significant adults.

STUDY QUESTIONS

1. How has the relationship between parents and professionals changed over the years? What circumstances have aided this process?

2. What was the purpose of the eugenics movement, and how did it affect relationships between professionals and parents?

3. Why do professionals currently believe that efforts should be directed toward working with families of children with special needs instead of just parents?

4. Define the term *collaboration* as it pertains to professionals and parents.

5. What is the rationale behind a family systems model?

6. Identify the four key components of the Turnbull family systems framework. Explain the characteristics of each of these elements.

7. How does the concept of cohesion differ from adaptability in the Turnbull model?

8. What are the stages of emotional response that many parents go through when informed that their child has a disability? Give examples of the types of behavior typically exhibited at each stage.

9. What cautions does Gargiulo stress when applying a stage theory model to parents of children with disabilities?

10. In what ways might a child with a disability affect his or her family?

11. What does the research literature suggest about the impact of childhood disability on marital relationships, mothers, fathers, siblings, and grandparents of children with special needs?

12. Name five emotional responses typically exhibited by siblings of children with disabilities.

13. Why are an awareness of and sensitivity to cultural and linguistic differences important for professionals when working with families of children with disabilities?

14. Describe what you believe to be key personal characteristics of professionals who work with families of individuals with disabilities.

KEY TERMS

eugenics movement, 106

family systems model, 109

family characteristics, 110

family interactions, 111

cohesion, 111

adaptability, 111

family functions, 112

family life cycle, 112

transition, 112

stage theory, 114

respite care, 117

cultural sensitivity, 123

active listening, 125

LEARNING ACTIVITIES

1. Talk to family members of a person with a disability. Learn how the family adapted to the person's exceptionality and how the family as a whole and individual members were or still are affected by the disability. Be certain to ask sensitive questions and ensure confidentiality.

2. Attend a support group meeting for family members of a person with a disability. What kinds of information were presented, and how was it delivered? In your opinion, did those in attendance benefit from the experience?

3. Develop a list of resources and supports in your community aimed at assisting individuals with disabilities and their families. Share your list with your classmates. Examples of resources and supports might include recreational opportunities, religious programs, support groups, respite care, local chapters of national parent/advocacy groups, and health care professionals who work with people with disabilities.

4. Discuss with two general educators and two special education teachers the strategies and techniques they use to establish parent-professional partnerships. What activities seem to be most effective for ensuring meaningful participation? How do these professionals ensure the involvement of parents from culturally and linguistically diverse backgrounds?

5. Volunteer to work for an organization that provides respite care for families of children with disabilities. Keep a journal about your experiences.

6. Interview parents or other family members from diverse cultural backgrounds as a means of learning about their perspectives on disabilities and the educational system, as well as any culturally specific behaviors and values such as child-rearing practices and communication styles.

REFLECTING ON STANDARDS

The following exercises are designed to help you learn to apply the Council for Exceptional Children (CEC) standards to your teaching practice. Each of the reflection exercises below correlates with knowledge or a skill within the CEC standards. For the full text of each of the related CEC standards, please refer to the standards integration grid located in Appendix B.

Focus on Learner Development and Individual Learning Differences (*CEC Initial Preparation Standard 1.1*)

Reflect on a time when you negatively stereotyped someone because of his or her culture, language, religion, gender, disability, socioeconomic status, or social orientation. How might stereotyping a student or his or her family negatively affect your teaching? What strategies might you want to put in place in your classroom to avoid stereotyping?

Focus on Collaboration (*CEC Initial Preparation Standard 7.3*)

Reflect on the various ways your family was involved in your education. What are the advantages to fostering meaningful partnerships with your students' families? How will you want to involve families in your classroom?

STUDENT STUDY SITE

Sharpen your skills with SAGE edge at **edge.sagepub.com/gargiulo5e. SAGE edge for students** provides a personalized approach to help you accomplish your coursework goals in an easy-to-use learning environment.

Assistive Technology

LEARNING OBJECTIVES

After reading Chapter 5, you should be able to:

Technology is now a part of the lives of *all* students inside and outside of school. In fact, recent statistics suggest students are increasingly spending their time outside of school with technology, resulting in some calling call today's students the iGeneration (Coldewey, 2010; Rosen, 2011). To illustrate the trend in technology use, surveys suggest the majority of school-aged children own their cell phones—increasingly smartphones—and MP3 players (Banks, 2008; Madden, Lenhart, Duggan, Cortesi, & Gasser, 2013; Rideout, Foehr, & Roberts, 2010). The majority of U.S. teenagers also report access to a computer at home (Madden et al., 2013).

- **Discuss** what makes a technology an assistive technology for students with disabilities.
- **Understand** the legal and legislative aspects of assistive technology.
- **Explain** how assistive technology can benefit students with disabilities.
- **Describe** the difference between low-tech, mid-tech, and high-tech assistive technology.
- **Describe** the different purposes of assistive technology.
- **Identify** assistive technology devices that support students with disabilities across content-area instruction.

Technology in Education

Educational technology is defined multiple ways, including the study and practice of facilitating learning and improving performance by creating, using, and managing technological processes and resources (Mishra, Koehler, & Kereluik, 2009). In other words, educational technologies are tools that address educational problems, for instance, issues of teaching and learning (Newby, Stepich, Lehman, & Russell, 2000). While some narrowly define educational technology as computers and computer-based applications, many define it in a broader sense and suggest educational technology has existed since the era of chalk and slate (Blackhurst, 2005a; Mishra & Koehler, 2009). Regardless of the concept of educational technology, one thing is consistent—the claim that use of a particular *technology* in education will revolutionize teaching and learning. Such claims were made for the talking picture (Deveraux, 1933; Mishra et al., 2009), the blackboard (Lewis, 1988), and cell phones (Kolb, 2008; Mishra et al., 2009), just to name a few.

Despite the term *educational technology*, Mishra and Koehler (2009) suggest the technologies teachers typically use in education are not designed for educational purposes; rather, teachers repurpose such technology to be educational. In other words, teachers often take a technology, regardless of its intended purpose, and use it to fit their needs in the classroom (Kereluik, Mishra, & Koehler, 2011; Mishra & Koehler, 2007). Repurposing can involve such common technologies as digital cameras and software (for example, Photoshop) for taking pictures of objects and then manipulating the images to demonstrate mathematical concepts such as transformations (Terry, Mishra, Henriksen, Wolf, & Kereluik, 2013), as well as social media like Facebook (Kereluik, Mishra, & Koehler, 2010).

educational technology:
Technology used for educational purposes such as teaching and learning.

Chapter contribution written by Emily Bouck, Michigan State University.

Table 5.1 **Examples of Six Distinct Types of Educational Technology**

Technology of Teaching	Medical Technology	Productivity Technology	Information Technology	Instructional Technology	Assistive Technology
• Direct instruction • Inquiry	• Cochlear implants • Feeding tubes	• Word processor • Presentation tools (e.g., PowerPoint)	• The Internet	• Computer-assisted instruction • Smartboards	• Text-to-speech • Wheelchair

SOURCE: Adapted from A. Blackhurst, "Perspectives on Applications of Technology in the Field of Learning Disabilities," *Learning Disability Quarterly, 28*(2), 2005, pp. 175–178.

Today's students use many different types of educational technology.

Within educational technology, pulling from a wide conceptualization, Blackhurst (2005a, 2005b) suggests the existence of six distinct types: technology of teaching, medical technology, productivity technology, information technology, instructional technology, and assistive technology (see Table 5.1). Technology of teaching is typically devoid of tools or devices, as it refers to instructional techniques. Medical technology involves devices used to support and monitor a medical condition or one's health. Tools that help educators and students create products efficiently and effectively are considered productivity technologies. Information technologies involve tools that provide resources and access to information. Instructional technology involves hardware and software designed to support effective instruction to increase student learning. Finally, assistive technologies are tools and devices that support students with disabilities to access materials, increase independence, and experience an improved quality of life (Blackhurst, 2005b).

Assistive Technology

assistive technology device: Any item, piece of equipment, or product system that increases, maintains, or improves functional capabilities of individuals with disabilities.

assistive technology service: Any service that directly assists an individual in the selection, acquisition, or use of an assistive technology device.

assistive technology specialist: A person trained to provide assistive technology services to individuals with disabilities.

Assistive technology actually refers to devices *and* services, although most commonly people associate the term *assistive technology* with the tools or devices. An **assistive technology device** refers to "any item, piece of equipment, or product system, whether acquired commercially off the shelf, modified, or customized, that is used to increase, maintain, or improve the functional capabilities of a child with a disability" (Individuals with Disabilities Education Improvement Act of 2004, Section 300.5). **Assistive technology services**, as defined in PL 100–407, include "any service that directly assists an individual in the selection, acquisition, or use of an assistive technology device." While devices are the tools and technologies that students use, assistive technology services are a necessary component and involve selecting (based on an evaluation of student's assistive technology needs), acquiring, implementing, and maintaining devices (Parette, Peterson-Karlan, & Wojcik, 2005). Assistive technology services can be provided by an **assistive technology specialist**; however, these individuals may be infrequent within a school system. In that case,

REFERENCE

Instructional Technology

special education teachers, speech-language pathologists, occupational therapists, and/or instructional technologists may be responsible for providing assistive technology services (Edyburn, 2004; Marino, Marino, & Shaw, 2006). See Figure 5.1 for a diagram of assistive technology services.

History and Legislation of Assistive Technology

The previous definitions of assistive technology devices and services are found in IDEA 2004 (the Individuals with Disabilities Education Improvement Act) and PL 100–407, the 1988 Technology-Related Assistance for Individuals with Disabilities Act (also known as the "Tech Act"). The Tech Act was reauthorized in 1998 and again in 2004 as the

Assistive technology services are multifaceted, including evaluating the needs of students with disabilities.

Assistive Technology Act. However, actual use and legislation pertaining to the idea of assistive technology far predate the 1988 Tech Act. For example, in 1832 Louis Braille published the Braille code (Blackhurst, 2005a). Since then we have seen the invention of electric amplifying devices for individuals with hearing impairments (1900), devices to magnify printed material (1953), and the talking calculator (1975), to name just a few (Blackhurst, 2005a; Nazzaro, 1977). In the 1970s, with the invention of the microcomputer, additional assistive technology became available to support students with disabilities, including text-to-speech (voice output of digital words so students can hear the text), **augmentative and alternative communication (AAC)** devices (low-tech, mid-tech, and high-tech communication tools that can replace, supplement, or enhance one's traditional means of communication), and speech-to-text (spoken words appearing as typed text on a computer-based technology) (Belson, 2003; Blackhurst, 2005a).

Legislation for assistive technology also predates the 1988 Tech Act. In 1879, following the invention of Braille, PL 45–186 was passed, which authorized funding for the production of Braille materials by the American Printing House for the Blind. In 1958, PL 85–905 provided funding to purchase and distribute closed-captioned films to state schools for the deaf. The Elementary and Secondary Education Amendments of 1968, PL 90–247, legislated the provision of educational technology for students with disabilities (Blackhurst, 2005a).

However, much of what guides assistive technology today for students with disabilities comes from reauthorizations of the Individuals with Disabilities Education Act (IDEA). Although IDEA was initially passed in 1975 (PL 94–142), it was not until the 1990 reauthorization (PL 101–476) that assistive technology was included. The 1990 IDEA included the Tech Act definition of assistive technology as well as provided for assistive technology if the Individualized Education Program (IEP) team determined it was needed (Smith & Jones, 1999). The 1997 reauthorization of IDEA mandated that IEP teams consider assistive technology for *all* students with disabilities, shifting the focus of assistive technology as primarily for students with more severe or low-incidence disabilities (for example, students with visual impairments or students with severe intellectual disability) to also include students with high-incidence disabilities, such as individuals with learning disabilities (Quinn et al., 2009; Smith & Jones, 1999).

augmentative and alternative communication (AAC): Symbols, aids, strategies, and techniques used as a supplement or alternative to oral language.

VIDEO
Assistive Technology

REFERENCE
Assistive Technology

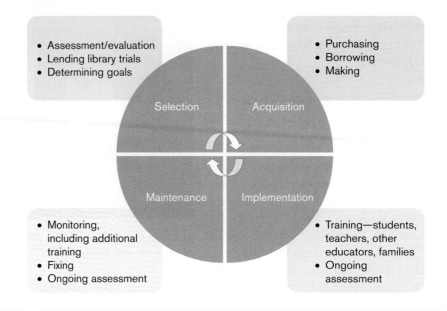

The latest reauthorization of IDEA in 2004 upheld the mandate that IEP teams *consider* assistive technology for all students with disabilities and that, pending determination by the IEP team, the assistive technology be provided at no cost to the student (Lee & Templeton, 2008). However, there was one exclusion in the 2004 IDEA; surgically implanted assistive technologies (cochlear implants) were omitted from the definition of assistive technology. Consequently, schools are not required to pay for such devices (Zirkel, 2007). Related to assistive technology, IDEA 2004 included the National Instructional Materials Accessibility Standard (NIMAS), which stipulated students with print disabilities, commonly considered students with visual impairments and reading-based learning disabilities, be provided with accessible instructional materials, such as large print, Braille, or digital text (National Center on Accessible Instructional Materials, 2011).

Assistive Technology Decision Making

As previously stated, assistive technology services provide for the consideration, selection, acquisition, and implementation of assistive technology devices and tools for students with disabilities. But how do IEP teams consider and select assistive technology for an individual student? While making an assistive technology decision can be challenging, given the range and types of tools and devices available, frameworks do exist to aid IEP teams in their decision-making progress. Perhaps the most well-known decision-making framework is the Student, Environments, Tasks, and Tools (SETT) framework by Joy Zabala (1995). (See Table 5.2 for assistive technology decision-making resources.) The SETT framework involves the identification and consideration of the student (for example, strengths, needs, preferences), the environments in which the student functions, and the tasks the student is expected to perform. In other words, the tools selected need to match with the pupil, work within various environments, and adequately and appropriately address the student's tasks.

print disabilities: A disability that prevents an individual from gaining information from printed material; requires the use of alternative methods to access the material.

AUDIO

General Assistive Technology

Resources for Assistive Technology Decision-Making Frameworks or Assessments

Decision-Making Framework/Assessment	Resources
Student, Environments, Tasks, and Tools (SETT)	http://www.joyzabala.com/Documents.html (Downloadable documents to assist in implementing the SETT framework)
Wisconsin Assistive Technology Initiative (WATI)	http://www.wati.org/?pageLoad=content/supports/free/index.php (Downloadable documents to assist in assistive technology decision making and assessments)
University of Kentucky Assistive Technology (UKAT) Toolkit	http://edsrc.coe.uky.edu/www/ukatii/ (Downloadable documents to assist in assistive technology decision making)
National Assistive Technology Research Institute (NATRI), Assistive Technology Planner	http://natri.uky.edu/atPlannermenu.html http://www.tamcec.org/publications/planning-tools/ (Downloadable kit and for-purchase documents to assist in assistive technology decision making)

The SETT framework is similar to the Matching Person and Technology (MPT) framework, which also suggests assistive technology devices or tools should match with the student (strengths, challenges, attitudes, and interests), work within the student's contexts, and fit the student's tasks (Bryant & Bryant, 2003; Raskind & Bryant, 2002; Scherer & Craddock, 2002).

Beyond the SETT and MPT, other grant-funded projects and initiatives created decision-making tool kits for IEP teams to use in considering and selecting assistive technology for individual students. For example, the Wisconsin Assistive Technology Initiative (WATI) created an assessment system to help IEP teams identify the types of technology that may benefit students with various disabilities, based on the students' abilities and challenges, environments, and tasks (Gierach, 2009). Lahm et al. (2002) developed the University of Kentucky Assistive Technology (UKAT) Toolkit, which provides resources in the form of worksheet-like pages to complete in order to guide an IEP team through assistive technology decision making. Lastly, the National Assistive Technology Research Institute (NATRI) developed an assistive technology planner for use by teachers, parents, and students to actively participate in assistive technology planning and decision making on an IEP team (Bausch & Ault, 2008; Bausch, Ault, & Hasselbring, 2006).

When IEP teams are making assistive technology decisions, they may opt for a student to try out an assistive technology device or tool before recommending that the pupil use such assistive technology. IEP teams can take advantage of state lending libraries. For example, in the state of Indiana, the Promoting Achievement through Technology and Instruction for all Students (PATINS) Project (www.patinsproject.com) serves as the statewide technical assistance network for assistive technology. PATINS not only lends assistive technology to schools to aid in decision making but also provides educators in the state with professional development related to assistive technology through face-to-face conferences as well as online tutorials or webinars. We recommend that IEP teams consult their state assistive technology project for resources as well as devices and tools available through their lending libraries. (See Table 5.3 for examples of state programs.)

VIDEO

Using Assistive Technology in the Classroom

■ ■ ■ ■ ■ Table 5.3 **Representative State Programs for Assistive Technology**

State	Statewide Assistive Technology Project
Alabama	STAR www.rehab.alabama.gov/individuals-and-families/star
Michigan	Michigan Integrated Technology Supports (MITS) http://mits.cenmi.org/Home.aspx
Minnesota	Minnesota STAR Program www.starprogram.state.mn.us/index.htm
Ohio	Ohio Center for Autism and Low Incidence (OCALI) www.ocali.org/center/at
Texas	Texas Assistive Technology Network (TATN) www.texasat.net

Assistive Technology and the IEP

As previously noted, IEP teams (and individualized family service plans teams for youngsters from birth to age 3) are required to consider assistive technology for all students with disabilities. Assistive technology is included within a student's IEP as appropriate. It can be represented in multiple ways—for instance, as a related service, as an accommodation, or as an annual goal or short-term objective, where appropriate (Netherton & Deal, 2006). Typically, however, assistive technology is selected and implemented to assist a student in meeting his or her goals. Hence, IEP teams may want to consider assistive technology toward the end of an IEP meeting (Beard, Carpenter, & Johnston, 2011). It is important for IEP teams to remember that if assistive technology devices or services are written into a student's IEP, it is the responsibility of the school to cover the costs. However, schools are not required to pay for all assistive technology (for example, surgically implanted assistive technology); hence, other outlets, such as private insurance, Medicare, Medicaid, or donations, are frequently used by families.

Assistive Technology Categorization

Assistive technology, by its definition in IDEA 2004, is vague and ambiguous. Broken down, assistive technology essentially is anything or can come from anywhere, as long as it helps or just maintains an individual's skills. Because assistive technology can be anything, it can be instructional technology (something that teachers use in the instruction of all students; for example, computer-based concept mapping and calculators), it can be everyday technology that is repurposed (for example, cell phones and iPads), and it can be specifically designed tools and devices (such as text-to-speech, speech-to-text, and AAC) (Bouck, Flanagan, Miller, & Bassette, 2012; Bouck, Shurr et al., 2012; Edyburn, 2004). In other words, the definition of assistive technology can leave one with two questions: "What isn't assistive technology?" and "When is something assistive technology?" (Edyburn, 2004).

instructional technology: Any apparatus or device that supports the teaching-learning process, such as computers or televisions; a tool for the delivery of instruction.

AUDIO

Examples of Assistive Technology

■ ■ ■ ■ ■ Table 5.4 **Examples of Assistive Technology Devices by Categorization**

No-Tech	Low-Tech	Mid-Tech	High-Tech
• Mnemonics (HOMES for remembering the names of the Great Lakes) • Graphic organizers	• Pencil grips • Raised lined paper • Highlighter strips • Braille playing cards	• Calculators • Audio recorder • Switches	• Speech-to-text • iPad • Word prediction

Given the questions surrounding what is and what is not assistive technology, a way to better understand assistive technology is through the different categorization schemes. One way in which assistive technology is often categorized is through the level of technology. While typically one conceptualizes assistive technology as low-tech (minimum technology) and high-tech (sophisticated technology), other conceptualizations also exist, including no-tech, low-tech, mid-tech, and high-tech as well as low-tech, moderate-tech (or mid-tech), and high-tech (Blackhurst, 1997; Edyburn, 2005; Johnson, Beard, & Carpenter, 2007; Vanderheiden, 1984). No-tech assistive technology most commonly refers to when no tool or device is actually used, but perhaps a teaching strategy is implemented, such as a mnemonic (Behrmann & Jerome, 2002; Blackhurst, 1997). Low-tech assistive technologies are generally tools or devices that are low in cost, require less training, and are typically not sophisicated (for example, pencil grips) (Behrmann & Schaff, 2001; Blackhurst, 1997). Moderate- or mid-tech assistive tchnologies are then typically tools or devices that are battery operated; the technology is more sophisticated, may require more training, and has a higher cost than low-tech assistive technology (for example, a calculator). Finally, high-tech assistive technologies are sophisticated devices and tools and are commonly associated with computer-based technology. High-tech assistive technology is considered to have a higher cost and require more training (for example, text-to-speech) (Blackhurst, 1997; Edyburn, 2005; Johnson et al., 2007; Vanderheiden, 1984). See Table 5.4 for examples of assistive technology devices according to categorization.

Another way assistive technology can be categorized is by purpose. Bryant and Bryant (2003) suggested seven purposes for assistive technology: positioning, mobility, augmentative and alternative communication, computer access, adaptive toys and games, adaptive environments, and instructional aids. Likewise, the WATI suggested 14 categories for assistive technology: seating, positioning and mobility, communication, computer access, recreation and leisure, activities of daily living, motor aspects of writing, composition of written material, reading, mathematics, organization, vision, hearing, and multiple challenges (Gierach, 2009). See Table 5.5 for examples of assistive technology devices by purpose. Overall, these categorizations suggest assistive technology can meet a wide range of needs for a diverse population of students with disabilities.

Devices and Tools

Assistive technology is central to the education of students with disabilities. Each chapter in Part II of this book examines assistive technology tools and devices that are unique or commonly used by individuals with a specific disability such as an

VIDEO
Using Assistive Technology in the Classroom

■ ■■ ■■ ■ Table 5.5 **Example Assistive Technology Devices by Purpose**

Bryant & Bryant (2003) Purpose	Wisconsin Assistive Technology Initiative (WATI) Categories	Examples
Positioning	Seating and positioning	• Adjustable-height desks • Custom wedges
Mobility	Mobility	• Wheelchair • Gait trainer
Augmentative and alternative communication	Communication	• Picture Exchange Communication System® • Proloquo2Go® for iPod, iPad
Computer access	Computer access	• Alternative keyboard • Speech/voice recognition
Adaptive toys and games	Recreation and leisure	• Switch-operated battery toys • Larger or Braille playing cards
Adaptive environments	Activities of daily living	• Adapted utensils, bowls, and cups • Motion-controlled lights
Instructional aids	Motor aspects of writing	• Speech-to-text • Pencil grips
	Composition of written material	• Word prediction • Portable spell checker
	Reading	• ReadingPen • E-text or supported e-text
	Mathematics	• Concrete or virtual manipulatives • Calculator
	Organization	• WatchMinder • Picture schedule
	Vision	• Text-to-speech • Screen magnification
	Hearing	• FM system • Hearing aid

SOURCE: AssistiveWare® http://www.assistiveware.com; E. Bouck and S. Flanagan, "Assistive Technology and Mathematics: What Is There and Where Can We Go," *Journal of Special Education Technology*, 24(2), 2009, pp. 17–30; D. Bryant and B. Bryant, *Assistive Technology for People with Disabilities* (Boston, MA: Allyn & Bacon, 2003); J. Gierach, *Assessing Students' Needs for Assistive Technology*, 5th ed. (Milton: Wisconsin Assistive Technology Initiative, 2009); L. Johnson, L. Beard, and L. Carpenter, *Assistive Technology: Access for All Students* (Upper Saddle River, NJ: Pearson Education, 2007).

AAC device for pupils with speech and language impairments or various sound amplification systems for students with hearing impairments. We now focus our attention on assistive technology within content-specific domains, as well as other organizational capabilities for students with high- and low-incidence disabilities. In addition, we touch upon assistive technology for young children with disabilities and the association between universal design for learning and assistive technology.

VIDEO

Assistive Technology for Communication

FIRST PERSON: MATTHEW

Teaching in the Age of Technology

Since graduating with my bachelor's degree in special education, I have worked at an alternative school. My school is a state-accredited residential and day school program that serves students between the ages of 6 and 21 who have learning disabilities and/or emotional behavior disorders and who struggle in a typical school setting, as well as students with intellectual disability, and students with autism spectrum disorder. Our students with learning disabilities and/or emotional behavior disorders are not reading or writing at grade level. For our older students who still struggle with handwriting, pencil grips or weighted pencils are available. I do see pencil grips benefiting my students. For our younger students who struggle with reading, we take advantage of books on CD or electronic books played through an MP3 player. In my school, we have advanced technology to support students with more intense needs as well. Every classroom has an iPad, and we do use Proloquo2Go® for students with communication needs. Most of our assistive technology needs and decisions for individual students are determined by our occupational therapists or speech-language pathologists. ∎

–Matthew Wright
Program Coordinator
T. C. Harris School
Lafayette, Indiana

Reading

Reading is a fundamental but complex skill and often considered the most critical academic skill (Strangman & Dalton, 2005). In 2000, the National Reading Panel suggested reading instruction should consist of five areas: phonemic awareness, phonics instruction, fluency, vocabulary, and reading comprehension. Despite its value, reading is an area of struggle for many students, with varying statistics presenting the frequency of struggling readers, let alone students with disabilities. The most recently available data from the National Assessment of Educational Progress (NAEP), which assesses reading at Grades 4 and 8, suggest that 33 percent of fourth graders and 24 percent of eighth graders scored below a basic level, which "denotes partial mastery of prerequisite knowledge and skills that are fundamental for proficient work at each grade" (National Center for Education Statistics, 2012e, p. 6). For students with disabilities, of which the majority who participated were provided with accommodations, 68 percent of fourth graders and 70 percent of eighth graders were assessed as below the basic level (National Center for Education Statistics, 2012e). Given the challenges reading can pose, it is important to consider how technology can support these students. See Suggestions for the Classroom for examples of assistive technology used for instruction in the various content areas.

Low-Tech Reading Assistive Technology. When deciding upon assistive technology, IEP teams should always first consider low-tech, of which there are a number of options for reading. There is not always a research base, however, on using the tools and devices for students with disabilities. Some common low-tech reading-based assistive technologies include highlighter pens, highlighter tape (nonpermanent), and highlighter strips—strips of colored, transparent film that students can use to guide their reading. Another low-tech means for providing support for reading is the placement of picture symbols in written text to provide additional support for comprehension (Shurr & Taber-Doughty, 2012).

VIDEO
**Assistive Technology
for Reading**

SUGGESTIONS FOR THE CLASSROOM

Assistive Technology Examples for Content-Area Instruction

	Low-Tech	Mid-Tech	High-Tech
Reading	• Highlighter strips or tape • Picture symbols	• ReadingPen • Books on CD	• Text-to-speech • E-readers or supported e-text
Writing	• Pencil grips • Raised lined paper	• Handheld spell checkers • Portable word processors	• Speech-to-text • Word prediction
Mathematics	• Concrete manipulatives • Number lines • Graph paper	• Calculators (e.g., four-function, graphing)	• Virtual manipulatives • Computer-assisted instruction

Mid- and High-Tech Reading Assistive Technology. Many mid-tech and high-tech assistive technology devices and tools exist. Perhaps one of the most common technologies to consider for students who struggle with reading is text-to-speech. Text-to-speech, known by different names depending on its application (for example, screen readers when accessing text on a computer, or e-text) (Anderson-Inman & Horney, 2007), is essentially printed or digital text spoken aloud to the reader; in other words, there is a voice output. Not only did the National Reading Panel (2000) suggest text-to-speech as a promising intervention, but researchers found use of text-to-speech positively influenced decoding, fluency, and comprehension skills (Hasselbring & Bausch, 2005; King-Sears, Swanson, & Mainzer, 2011). However, it should be noted that the research is also full of contradictions regarding the positive or neutral effect of text-to-speech (Strangman & Dalton, 2005).

Many different types of text-to-speech options exist. For example, there is the ReadingPen2, a handheld optical character recognition system that reads printed text as the device scans it (another example is Quicktionary2) (Higgins & Raskind, 2005; WizcomTech, 2012, 2013). A number of computer-based text-to-speech programs exist, including both free and for-purchase options. One free option, although one can also purchase its upgraded features, is NaturalReader (www.naturalreaders.com) (NaturalSoft Limited, 2013). NaturalReader is a downloadable option that provides natural-sounding voices and also highlights the text as it is read on word documents, websites, PDFs, and e-mails on both PCs and Mac computers. Students can adjust the volume and pace of a voice even with the free version. Other free text-to-speech programs include browser-specific options, such as SpeakIt! for Google Chrome (Petrov, 2013) and Click, Speak for Firefox (Chen, n.d.). For-purchase text-to-speech programs also exist, such as Read&Write Gold. Not only does the program provide auditory text with simultaneous text highlighting on a computer, but the company also recently released an iPad version (Texthelp, 2012).

Closely related to text-to-speech is e-text or supported e-text. E-text is electronic text, and supported e-text is enhanced e-text, which includes such additional features to benefit students as linked dictionaries (Anderson-Inman & Horney, 2007). Use of

e-text: An electronic presentation of a text, also known as a digital text, that can be read on a computer.

supported e-text: An e-text that allows for content to be presented in multiple modalities while providing additional supports.

VIDEO
Assistive Technology for School

e-text is related to the NIMAS, which mandated that students with print disabilities receive access to accessible text, including digital text (National Center on Accessible Instructional Materials, 2011). Several specifically designed e-text readers were developed following NIMAS, which supported a file format referred to as Digital Accessible Information System (DAISY) Digital Talking Books. ReadHear™, by gh, LLC, is one such technology. ReadHear™ offers many of the same features as text-to-speech programs, including synthesized speech and text highlighting. It also offers magnification and can be used through keyboard shortcuts for individuals with visual impairments. In addition, commercially available products, such as Kindle, Nook, and iPad, are becoming increasingly popular for providing e-text to students (Larson, 2010). However, not all e-readers meet the accessibility needs of all pupils, such as students with visual impairments. If a student does use an e-reader, he or she can acquire text from multiple places, including Amazon.com and other online sellers (for example, Barnes & Noble), as well as take advantage of free e-books, including those from iTunes, Bookshare (www.bookshare.org), and Project Gutenberg (www.gutenberg.org).

Writing

Writing is another critical skill, but it often gets less attention than reading (National Commission on Writing for America's Families, Schools, and Colleges, 2005). Writing is complex and multifaceted, involving not just technical elements like handwriting and spelling but also the processes of planning and organizing, generating and drafting text, and then editing and revising (Flower & Hayes, 1981). All of these components, from handwriting to planning to writing to revising, can cause challenges for students with disabilities (Mason, Harris, & Graham, 2011). Recent data from the NAEP writing assessment suggest students with and without disabilities struggle with writing (National Center for Education Statistics, 2012f). The 2011 assessment found only 27 percent of eighth- and twelfth-grade students were above a basic level (that is, proficient or advanced), meaning almost three-fourths of students in each grade were at a basic or below-basic level. The data were not disaggregated for students with disabilities.

No- and Low-Tech Writing Assistive Technology. Many low-tech assistive technologies exist to support students with writing (see Table 5.4, page 137). For example, pencil grips and adaptive pens can help students with handwriting issues. Teachers can also use raised lined paper (a student can feel the lines of the paper), whiteboards, gel boards, and even shaving cream. Outside of the technical elements, no- and low-tech strategies can assist with the writing process. Advanced organizers such as procedural facilitators, graphic organizers, concept maps, and think sheets have a strong research base in terms of helping students with and without disabilities plan and organize their writing (Englert, Zhao, Dunsmore, Collings, & Wolbers, 2007). Whether using the advanced organizer–based acronym POWER—planning, organizing, writing, editing, and revising (Mariage, Englert,

The Bunny

The bunny is in a car.
He likes his little car.
The car can go fast.

1. The _____ is in a car.
   A. dog
   B. cat
   C. bunny

2. He likes his _____.
   A. car
   B. bus
   C. van

3. The car is _____.
   A. big
   B. little
   C. a bus

Highlighter strips can serve as a low-tech assistive technology for students with reading difficulties.

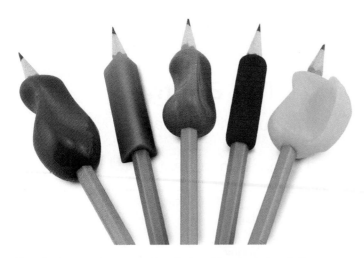

Pencil grips can serve as a low-tech writing-based assistive technology to support students with disabilities.

& Garmon, 2000)—or the hamburger paragraph organizer—in which the top bun serves as a topic or main sentence; the meat, lettuce, and tomato function as supporting sentences; and the bottom bun is a concluding sentence (Mariage & Bouck, 2004)—these tools help students to structure their writing for improvement in quality and quantity.

Mid- and High-Tech Writing Assistive Technology. A number of mid-tech and high-tech technologies exist to support the writing process as well as the technical components of handwriting and spelling. For the prewriting portion of the writing process, planning and organizing, students can use computer-based concept mapping programs, such as the for-purchase Inspiration and Kidspiration (Inspiration Software, 2012a, 2012b) or the free options Cmap-Tools (Institute for Human & Machine Cognition, n.d.) and Visual Understanding Environment (Tufts University, 2008). Computer-based concept maps are similar to paper-based concept maps, although students can edit more easily with the computer options. In addition, some computer-based concept mapping programs come equipped with pictures to help students represent their ideas with images as well as words, and others include such built-in assistive technologies as text-to-speech and speech-to-text.

When writing or drafting, students can use a range of assistive technology, including technology to actually get words on the paper as well as technology to select correct words. Speech-to-text—also known as speech or voice recognition—is a computer-based program that translates the words a user says to typed text (MacArthur, 2009). In other words, speech-to-text can create word documents, e-mails, and other digital documents from narrated speech rather than keystrokes. Common speech-to-text programs are associated with a fee, such as Dragon NaturallySpeaking (Nuance Communications, 2013) for PCs or Macs. However, some free options exist, such as Dictation Pro (DeskShare, 2012) for Windows-based operating systems. Windows operating systems also come standard with Windows Speech Recognition, which can recognize voices and translate narration into text in different programs (Microsoft Windows, 2011). Likewise, Mac computers with the Mountain Lion and later operating systems also come standard with an easy-to-use speech-to-text program known as Dictation (Apple, 2013b). Users should note that using speech-to-text programs may require training, and typically programs become better at recognizing one's speech the more they are used.

Aside from speech-to-text, word prediction is another computer-based program that supports students in writing text. Word prediction programs predict what word an individual is typing, based on the letters, and provide suggestions (for example, as one types *h-o*, a word prediction program might suggest "home," "house," and "hole") (MacArthur, 2009). A few free computer-based word prediction programs exist, such as eType (eType, 2012) and Turbo Type (Soft Grup Construct, 2012), which are both compatible with Windows-based operating systems. Both free options have drawbacks, including advertisements and needing to reboot after a length of time. For-purchase options include Co:Writer 7 (Don Johnston, n.d.), which is compatible with both PC and Mac computers; SoothSayer (Applied Human Factors, 2013), which is Windows based; and Typ-O (SecondGuess ApS, 2013), which works on Apple products including Mac computers as well as iPads and iPods.

In terms of postwriting, students can use text-to-speech to receive auditory feedback on their writing as well as spelling and grammar check programs. The text-to-speech program NaturalReader can be used to support a student's editing and revising through reading the text the student transcribed into the computer. Obviously, students can use the built-in spell-check programs with their word processing software, such as Microsoft Word. However, other free or for-purchase programs may provide additional support. For example, Ginger Software (n.d.) is a spelling and grammar check program that suggests different words when a word is grammatically correct and spelled correctly but out of context (for instance, with "I would like to meat her," Ginger would suggest "I would like to meet her").

Read&Write Gold is one example of a text-to-speech and speech-to-text word prediction program.

Several computer-based programs exist to support the writing process; however, having many separate programs to support a pupil across planning and organizing through editing and revising can be overwhelming to the student as well as the teacher. For-purchase options do exist to support multiple needs, such as speech recognition, word prediction, and grammar checking. Two such options include Read&Write Gold (Texthelp, 2012) and wordQ+speakQ (GoQ, 2011). Read&Write Gold provides reading as well as writing support, including word prediction, speech recognition, text-to-speech, and grammar assistance (for example, checking verb tenses and homophones). Read&Write Gold is available for Windows- and Mac-based operating systems, for Google Apps for Education, and through an app for iPads. In addition, one can purchase Read&Write Gold mobile, which contains all the software on a flash drive so it can be used with any computer rather than just one computer when the program is downloaded. The downloadable program wordQ+speakQ combines text-to-speech and word prediction (wordQ—Windows and Mac compatible) with speech-to-text (speakQ—Windows compatible).

Not all mid-tech and high-tech assistive technologies to support writing are computer based. Students can also benefit from portable word processors. Portable word processors are battery-powered tools that include standard keyboards but smaller screens and focus on word processing features or productivity tools like PowerPoint as opposed to accessing the Internet and running separate programs. Examples of portable word processors include Dana (NEO Direct, 2013), and such devices typically allow easy transfer of files to a standard computer as well as to a printer.

Mathematics

Mathematics can be a challenging content area for students with and without disabilities, although individuals with disabilities often lag behind their peers in terms of mathematics. The challenges students face range from fluency with basic facts to problem solving to fractions to algebra (Calhoon, Emerson, Flores, & Houchins, 2007). The most recently available NAEP mathematics assessment data support the challenge mathematics can pose to pupils with disabilities (National Center for Education

REFERENCE

Technology and Test Accommodations

Statistics, 2012d). While 85 percent of fourth graders without disabilities were at or above the basic level, only 55 percent of fourth-grade students with disabilities were at or above the basic level. In terms of being at or above proficient, 43 percent of pupils without disabilities qualified compared to 17 percent of students with disabilities. For eighth graders, the data are even less encouraging; only 35 percent of students with disabilities were at or above a basic level, with 9 percent at or above proficient compared to 77 percent of students without disabilities at a basic level and 36 percent at or above proficient.

No- and Low-Tech Mathematics AT. Although fewer specifically developed technology options exist to support students with disabilities in mathematics in comparison to reading and writing, a number of technologies are available (Edyburn, 2004). (See Table 5.4, page 137.) One of the most common low-tech assistive technologies for mathematics is concrete manipulatives. Concrete manipulatives are typically found in elementary and secondary classrooms and are considered an evidence-based practice for educating students with disabilities. Students with disabilities successfully solved a range of mathematics problems—algebra, integers, area and perimeter, and fractions—with concrete manipulatives (Cass, Cates, Smith, & Jackson, 2003; Jordan, Miller, & Mercer, 1998; Maccini & Hughes, 2000; Maccini & Ruhl, 2000).

Mid- and High-Tech Mathematics AT. In terms of mid-tech or high-tech assistive technology, common options include calculators, virtual manipulatives, anchored instruction, and computer-assisted instruction (Bouck & Flanagan, 2009). Research on these areas suggests technology benefits students with disabilities, although most of the research involved pupils with more high-incidence disabilities like individuals with learning disabilities (Bouck & Flanagan, 2009; Maccini & Gagnon, 2005). Calculators—four-function, scientific, and graphing—are one of the most common accommodations for students with disabilities on IEPs (Maccini & Gagnon, 2000, 2006). Calculators can help students with disabilities who struggle with basic facts or working memory challenges when solving word problems. Virtual manipulatives are similar to concrete manipulatives but available on a computer. In fact, almost every concrete manipulative is also available as a virtual manipulative that can do everything concrete manipulatives do but in a virtual space (that is, on a computer). The most well-known virtual manipulative website is the National Library of Virtual Manipulatives (Cannon, Dorward, Duffin, & Heal, 2004). However, other sites, such as Illuminations by the National Council of Teachers of Mathematics (n.d.) and Inter*activate* by the Shodor Education Foundation (n.d.), also exist (Bouck & Flanagan, 2010).

Anchored instruction and computer-assisted instruction (CAI) are less *assistive* and more *instructional* technologies that support students with and without disabilities in mathematics. Anchored instruction involves an alternative presentation (for example, CD-ROM) of a mathematics lesson or problems situated in real-world contexts. The majority of the work on anchored instruction for students with disabilities is led by Brian Bottge, and the research base supports the view that this technology helps students with disabilities in problem solving. In contrast to anchored instruction, the majority of CAI for students with disabilities in mathematics focuses more on basic facts than problem solving and is administered individually rather than in groups. However, the research on mathematics-based CAI is also generally positive (Bouck & Flanagan, 2009).

Other Academic and Functional Performance Areas

Outside of the two main content areas in which students with disabilities struggle, literacy and mathematics, other content domains and academic or functional performance

VIDEO

Assistive Technology
for Mathematics

Teaching in the Twenty-First-Century Classroom

I work in a secondary life skills classroom and have obtained my bachelor's degree in special education. I have technology available, including a smartboard in my classroom and two iPads to use at my discretion.

Individual students also have a range of assistive technology, including AAC devices. One technology I have increasingly incorporated into my life skills instruction is actually an audio recorder to provide audio prompts to students as they engage in life skills in the community independently, such as grocery shopping. I found an inexpensive audio recorder is more age-appropriate and promotes independence more than picture prompts. I—or the students—can record our grocery list, and then during our weekly outing to the local grocery store to purchase items we use in the classroom, such as for cleaning, hygiene, or cooking, students use the audio recorders to prompt them on the list. The audio recorders have increased my students' independence. ■

–Whitney Bartlett
Special Education Teacher
Lafayette, Indiana

areas can be supported through assistive technology. Although limited, some assistive technology exists in the areas of science and social studies; however, the majority of the assistive technology for these two content areas can be drawn from literacy and mathematics. Assistive technology can also benefit the instruction of life skills, and specific tools and devices exist that can increase, maintain, or improve the capabilities of students relative to study skills like note taking and organization.

Science and Social Studies. Although not exclusively, science and social studies instruction is often dominated by textbooks and other literacy-based activities, including reading and writing (Scruggs, Mastropieri, & Okolo, 2008). Hence, many of the assistive technologies discussed to support students with disabilities in reading and writing (such as text-to-speech and speech-to-text) are also applicable to support students with disabilities in engaging the content areas of science and social studies. One science assistive technology product to note is Science Writer by the Center for Applied Special Technology (2009). Science Writer supports secondary students as they construct science reports in terms of both writing and text-to-speech so pupils can listen to what they have written. Science Writer is offered online at no cost.

Life Skills. Assistive technology can also help students learn life skills such as grocery shopping and food preparation. One particular category of assistive technology, self-operating prompting devices, supports students with disabilities in the acquisition of life skills. Students with intellectual disability, autism spectrum disorders, and other disabilities use such technology (for example, picture prompts, audio recorders, video iPods, or iPads) to learn life skills (Ayres, Mechling, & Sansosti, 2013; Mechling, 2007).

Organization and Management Skills. Executive functions, such as organization and memory, as well as self-management skills, can be beneficial to students with disabilities, who often struggle with these areas. Teachers suggest a relationship between such executive functions (for instance, meeting deadlines, following directions, or being prepared) and academic performance (McMullen, Shippen, & Dangel, 2007).

REFERENCE

**Assistive Technology
in Postsecondary
Education**

WatchMinder is an assistive technology device that can provide prompts to students to assist with organization.

Multiple low-tech through high-tech options exist to support students with disabilities in organization and self-management. Students can use common technologies such as audio recorders and other handheld devices (smartphones) to record reminders for themselves or to serve as an alarm. Specifically designed technologies for these purposes also exist, such as the WatchMinder (2011), a programmable sports watch that can set 30 alarms (for example, "study for test" or "take medication") and has 65 preprogrammed messages.

Technology can also assist students with disabilities in note taking. One common technology marketed to support anyone with note taking is a Livescribe™ smartpen. With a Livescribe™ pen, when a student writes on the specifically designed paper, he or she is not only taking written notes but can also record the conversations or lectures occurring. If a student wants to go back to his or her notes, when the student taps on a specific place on the paper, the audio will actually play from that point. The Livescribe™ pen is also only slightly larger than a typical pen.

Assistive Technology and the Young Child

As previously noted, assistive technology considerations are mandated for children served under IDEA. Hence, assistive technology considerations also apply to children from birth until age 3 who are served via an individualized family service plan. While many of the assistive technology devices and tools discussed in the following chapters are applicable to young children, there are some unique assistive technology considerations. Adaptive toys and games represent one category of assistive technology (Bryant & Bryant, 2003). For example, battery-operated toys can easily be modified to work with a switch through acquisition of a copper wafer. In addition, companies are increasingly creating accessible or adaptive toys for young children, such as triangular crayons, crayon rocks, or crayons with knobs for better grasping. Young children can also take advantage of adaptive utensils or other dishes. In addition, young children are prime candidates for repurposing everyday technology and items to be assistive technology, such as a Hula-Hoop to keep objects within grasp or a cookie sheet with objects affixed with magnets.

Issues With Assistive Technology

Although assistive technology offers much potential for students with disabilities, there are challenges with assistive technology that educators need to take into consideration. Despite the benefits of assistive technology, the use of various tools and devices may stigmatize some pupils. This occurs when individuals use a technology in a general education classroom that makes them stand out or makes them feel as if they do (Parette & Scherer, 2004). For example, if a student struggles to read independently but is the only one in the class reading on a computer, he or she may feel that use of the technology is stigmatizing. Avoiding stigmatization in the selection of assistive technology is important, as feeling different can lead

stigmatization: To experience undesired negative attention due to using assistive technology.

REFERENCE

Assistive Technology and Young Children

to assistive technology abandonment, whereby the pupil quits using the tool. Hence, when the IEP team members consider the use of assistive technology, it is important that they also examine the student's interests, attitudes, and sense of self-confidence as well as the context in which the assistive technology will be used.

Another important issue for assistive technology is ensuring that all parties receive adequate training or possess sufficient knowledge to correctly implement the technology. The use of technology can be overwhelming to many individuals, including students, teachers, related service providers, and parents. To help ensure successful assistive technology implementation and minimize abandonment, students, teachers, other educators, *and* parents need to receive training on how to use the tool as well as how to support the individual in using the tool (Lee & Templeton, 2008). Some school districts may have assistive technology specialists to support the implementation and training of assistive technology devices; however, in other situations, professionals and parents may have to rely on instructional technologies, occupational therapists, or special education teachers for support and training (Bausch, Ault, Evmenova, & Behrmann, 2008).

Cost is another challenge with assistive technology, although cost cannot explicitly be a decision-making factor (Bryant & Bryant, 2003). Assistive technology devices can run the gamut in terms of cost from free to expensive. See Table 5.6 for examples of free or low-cost assistive technology software and apps. Another consideration besides cost, stigmatization, and training issues is to repurpose everyday technology, such as iPads or Livescribe™ pens, as assistive technology tools for students with disabilities (Bouck, Shurr et al., 2012).

Assistive technology allows children to engage with a variety of toys.

Assistive Technology Future Trends

Assistive technology represents an important component of the educational services received by individuals with disabilities. Assistive technology benefits the students who need it and can help them access and succeed in the general education curriculum as well as daily living skills (for example, communication and independent living). In addition, assistive technology is one aspect that can support the implementation of universal design for learning (UDL), introduced in Chapter 1. Assistive technology can support the multiple means of engagement and expression that are critical for UDL. Assistive technology also allows for the flexibility principle of UDL to occur in classrooms.

abandonment: When an individual stops using an assistive technology device.

universal design for learning: The design of curriculum materials, instructional activities, and evaluation procedures that can meet the needs of learners with widely varying abilities and backgrounds.

Table 5.6 Free Assistive Technology Examples: Software and Apps

	Literacy	Mathematics
Software/Internet-based	• NaturalReader (text-to-speech) • TalkTyper (speech-to-text)	• National Library of Virtual Manipulatives
Mobile technology apps	• NaturalReader (text-to-speech) • Spell Better (word prediction and text-to-speech)	• MyScript Calculator (calculator that recognizes handwriting) • MathSquared (logical thinking and reasoning)

Many assistive technologies can be used to support UDL. The Center for Applied Special Technology (CAST), for instance, has developed specific technologies in support of UDL (see www.cast.org/learningtools/index.html). For example, CAST offers the UDL Book Builder™, which allows educators to create digital or e-books to share with students. The digital books developed through this program can be embedded with characters that provide prompts and scaffolds to aid in comprehension. The digital books are also equipped with text-to-speech software. CAST also offers two mathematics-based apps to support students in mathematics reasoning: MathSquared and MathScaled (both available for download through iTunes). Aside from student-centered UDL products, CAST offers products geared toward teachers to support the implementation of UDL in classrooms, such as the UDL Exchange and the UDL Curriculum Self-Check.

In addition to even greater attention to assistive technology as a predicted future trend, assistive technology tools and devices are likely to follow the trend of all technology: mobile, personalized, smaller, and faster (Bolkan, 2012). In other words, mobile devices—such as iPods, iPads, and smartphones and their apps—will be increasingly used as assistive technology. Hence, students may increasingly use iPads and, for example, text-to-speech, speech-to-text, and AAC apps to participate in curriculum and everyday life activities. With the likely increase of mobile devices and apps to provide assistive technology, as well as instructional technology, teachers and other education professionals will need to become savvy consumers. In other words, educators need to think critically about apps and to validate their educational use, including those used for assistive technology purposes.

Although a standard rubric or model does not exist for evaluating apps for mobile devices for all students, let alone students with disabilities, some options do exist. For example, the website http://learninginhand.com/blog/ways-to-evaluate-education al-apps.html offers a variety of rubrics educators can use to make decisions about apps. Educators need to think critically about the apps they are using; for example, some apps are free while others are not. Prices can vary from $0.99 to $210. There is not necessarily a correlation between the cost of an app and its quality. Although the education and special education lists on iTunes offer educators one place to start, these lists should not be taken at face value. Nor should Internet-based lists of apps for particular topics in special education (for example, functional life skills) be used without scrutiny. Educators need to read each app's description as well as carefully consider the reviews. Although apps can benefit students with disabilities, as assistive and instructional technologies they can do so only if careful attention is given to their selection and implementation, which can be time-consuming.

Technology in Education

- Multiple types of educational technology exist, including assistive technology.

Assistive Technology

- Assistive technology devices are *anything* that can benefit a student with a disability.
- Assistive technology services are services that support the selection, acquisition, implementation, and maintenance of assistive technology tools and devices.
- Assistive technology can be categorized by levels of technology, including no-tech, low-tech, mid-tech, and high-tech.
- Assistive technology can also be categorized by purpose, such as positioning, mobility, augmentative and alternative communication, computer access, adaptive toys and games, adaptive environments, and instructional aids.

History and Legislation of Assistive technology

- Assistive technology was first included in the 1990 reauthorization of IDEA, although development and use of assistive technology by students with disabilities predate its inclusion in IDEA 1990 by more than a century.
- The 1997 reauthorization of IDEA mandated the consideration of assistive technology for *all* students with disabilities, including students with high-incidence disabilities.

Assistive Technology Decision Making

- Frameworks exist to support assistive technology decision making by IEP teams, including the SETT framework.

- Within an IEP, assistive technology supports goals and short-term objectives as a related service or accommodation.

Assistive Technology Devices

- Multiple low-tech (highlighter strips) and high-tech (text-to-speech) assistive technologies exist to support students in reading.
- Challenges with handwriting, spelling, and the writing process can be supported through low-tech (pencil grips) and high-tech (speech-to-text and word prediction) assistive technology.
- In mathematics, low-tech (concrete manipulatives), mid-tech (calculators), and high-tech (virtual manipulatives) technologies all can support students with disabilities.
- Assistive technology devices also support students in organization (Livescribe™ pens) as well as other executive functions, such as attention or memory (WatchMinder).

Assistive Technology Issues

- Assistive technology abandonment is a concern for students with disabilities.
- To minimize abandonment, IEP teams need to consider the potential stigmatization associated with use of of devices or tools and ensure that students, teachers, other educators, and parents all receive the training to use the technology.

Assistive Technology Future Trends

- Assistive technology represents one way to implement universal design for learning in practice.
- Mobile devices and their apps are increasingly used as assistive technology; educators need to critically evaluate apps for their educational value.

STUDY QUESTIONS

1. How does educational technology differ from assistive technology?

2. What is the difference between assistive technology devices and assistive technology services?

3. Who provides assistive technology services?

4. Describe the different levels of assistive technology and provide an example of each.

5. Identify the seven different purposes of assistive technology and give an example of each type.

6. What can IEP teams use to aid in assistive technology decision making?

7. What can schools and school personnel do to avoid assistive technology abandonment?

8. What is the relationship between assistive technology and universal design for learning?

educational technology, 131

assistive technology device, 132

assistive technology service, 132

assistive technology specialist, 132

augmentative and alternative communication (AAC), 133

print disabilities, 134

instructional technology, 136

e-text, 140

supported e-text, 140

stigmatization, 146

abandonment, 147

universal design for learning (UDL), 147

LEARNING ACTIVITIES

1. Search for your state's assistive technology program. Determine what assistive technology is available through the lending library and what other resources or supports the program offers.

2. Visit several elementary and secondary classrooms in your area. What assistive technology is being implemented to support students with disabilities in content-area learning? Ask the teachers about the perceived benefits and challenges of using the assistive technology devices.

3. Visit the college or university office on your campus that provides services to students with disabilities. Inquire about the assistive technology services that are offered

to students who qualify for such services. If possible, visit the area that provides assistive technology and explore the technology that is available to help students with disabilities achieve success in the classroom.

4. Search online for the free content-area assistive technology mentioned in this chapter. Explore the assistive technology online or by downloading it to a computer. Critically examine these assistive technology tools. Evaluate them for ease of use, challenges with implementation in a classroom, the benefits they may provide to a student with a disability, and if such assistive technology could be made available to all students.

REFLECTING ON STANDARDS

The following exercises were designed to help you learn to apply the Council for Exceptional Children (CEC) standards to your teaching practice. Each of the reflection exercises below correlates with knowledge or a skill within the CEC standards. For the full text of each of the related CEC standards, please refer to the standards integration grid located in Appendix B.

Focus on Curricular Content Knowledge (*CEC Initial Preparation Standard 3.1*)

Reflect on what you learned in this chapter about assistive technology to support content-area learning for students with disabilities. As a general or special education teacher, what assistive technology would you recommend considering or

discussing at the IEP team meeting if a student struggles with handwriting? Mathematical computation? Decoding words? Or staying organized and on task?

Focus on Instructional Planning and Strategies (*CEC Initial Preparation Standard 5.2*)

Reflect on how you use technology to support your own learning or daily living activities. How does using the technology make you feel? Does it allow you to complete your work or activities faster or easier? What if you were not allowed to use such technology—how would that impact your learning or daily life activities?

Assistive Technology Industry Association (ATIA)

info@ATIA.org

www.atia.org

Center for Applied Special Technologies (CAST)

cast@cast.org

www.cast.org

Rehabilitation Engineering and Assistive Technology Society of North America (RESNA)

www.resna.org

Technology and Media Division (TAM), Council for Exceptional Children (CEC)

contactus@tamcec.org

www.tamcec.org

STUDENT STUDY SITE

Sharpen your skills with SAGE edge at **edge.sagepub.com/gargiulo5e. SAGE edge for students** provides a personalized approach to help you accomplish your coursework goals in an easy-to-use learning environment.

56 57 58 59 60 61 62 63 64 65 66 67 68 69 70 71 72 73 74 75 76 77 78 79 80 81 82 83 84 85 86 87
AY'S LESSON:
MATH
3+3=
2+5=
3+2=
3+5=
3

PART

2

A Study of Individuals With Special Needs

" "It is not our disability that is the problem, but rather it is the way our disabilities are viewed by others." "

—Drexel Deal

President, Disabled Persons' Organization

6 Individuals With Intellectual Disability

Lauren's Story

Our daughter, Lauren, is an extraordinary child. But she is certainly not an easy child. Sometimes people use the word *exceptional* to describe a child like Lauren, who has Down syndrome.

Jason and I were married when we were both 33 and were ready to have children. I was pregnant with Lauren by the time we celebrated our first anniversary. The delivery of our baby was long and difficult, with some concerns about an irregular heartbeat and a possible emergency cesarean section. Finally, she was born on a Monday afternoon around 5:00. As exhausted as I felt, I was excitedly anticipating holding my new baby. I noticed a nurse looking at the baby and whispering into the doctor's ear. My doctor looked at me and said, "We think the baby has Down's," as they passed Lauren to me. I was stunned for a moment and then asked, "Is it a boy or a girl?" I was only allowed to see my baby girl very briefly, before my husband and the nurse took her to the special care nursery. It was not the moment of joy we had been expecting at the birth of our child. Instead, we were both shocked and divided into our own private worlds of grief.

Even though I was familiar with Down syndrome (due to my training as a special educator), I suddenly felt that I knew nothing. I wanted to be able to hold Lauren because I felt it would help me to make a connection with her. Nothing about her delivery had gone the way we expected, and then I realized that in all the conversations we had before she was born, not one time had we discussed or considered the possibility of a birth defect or any problems.

Lauren's health was a critical issue as I began an endless series of doctor visits with her, making sure to check each possible health complication associated with Down syndrome. Our pediatrician saw Lauren frequently and guided us through the process step by step. Lauren had a very mild heart defect, but it did not require surgery or even medication. Her hearing and vision were normal, except for nystagmus—Lauren's eyes waver from side to side constantly as if she were reading. The ophthalmologist told us this would never go away but it would become less obvious and improve with time. We talked with a geneticist who explained the characteristics of Down syndrome, and we met

- **Summarize** the key elements of the AAIDD definitions of intellectual disability from 1961 to 2010.
- **Describe** the concepts of intellectual ability and adaptive behavior.
- **Explain** four ways of classifying individuals with intellectual disability.
- **Provide** examples of pre-, peri-, and postnatal causes of intellectual disability.
- **Outline** society's reaction to and treatment of individuals with intellectual disability.
- **Identify** representative learning and social/behavioral characteristics of persons with intellectual disability.
- **Define** functional curriculum, functional academics, and community-based instruction.
- **List** the key features of the following instructional strategies: task analysis, cooperative learning, and scaffolding.
- **Describe** the goals of early intervention for young children with intellectual disability.
- **Characterize** contemporary services for adults with intellectual disability.

with a developmental pediatrician who assessed Lauren's development. We were grateful for their help and recommendations.

Soon after Lauren was home I began to call agencies in the area that assisted parents of children with special needs. We were directed to a federally funded agency that provides assistance to parents of children who are developmentally delayed from birth to 3 years of age. At 6 weeks old Lauren was the focus of a group assessment conducted in our home by a team of professionals, including a speech therapist, an occupational therapist, a physical therapist, a special education teacher, and a service coordinator, to assist with all the paperwork. Lauren was lying on the floor, the center of our attention. She was already smiling and holding her head up. We all identified goals for us to work on and set up regular visits by her teacher and therapist. I felt more confident that I was taking the right steps to help Lauren develop to her full potential. It seems incredible how many people were involved in our lives during those early years.

I will always remember Lauren learning to walk; it's one of my favorite memories. She has to work so hard to do things that can be so easy for other children. Our physical therapist would visit us once a month. She advised us not to encourage Lauren to walk because she was developing upper body strength by crawling. So that kind of relieved us of one more concern. By 13 or 14 months Lauren did start walking. And she loved it. You could see it in her facial expression just how exciting it must have felt; she was so proud of herself. I can still see her walking across the yard. She would take a few steps, fall down, and get up over and over again. You could hear her laughing the whole time. Lauren is certainly not a timid child; she does the things she enjoys with enthusiasm.

Because of Lauren's excellent motor development we expected her other milestones would continue to be close to a typical progression. Unfortunately, Lauren's speech progress was very slow. She said her first word around 15 months, which was *ba* for ball. She really didn't refer to Jason or me with any words, even though she was making the sounds *mama* and *dada*. We insisted she begin receiving speech therapy at 2 years old. Everything I read told me that children with Down syndrome have trouble developing language, and I was seeing it firsthand.

Currently I am enrolled in a sign language class because Lauren communicates better with signs and visual prompts. I am looking forward to the day she and I can have our first conversation. She communicates in any way that she is able, which is a combination of words, signs, and gestures. She and I deal with many frustrating moments struggling to understand each other. It may take some time, but I cannot wait to hear her express her thoughts and feelings to me with words.

Lauren is now in elementary school, where she participates in an inclusion class for most of the school day and attends a resource class for direct speech instruction and some academics for about one hour a day. We love having her included with her typical peers in a general education classroom.

Lauren's progress is exciting to witness. When we went to a local restaurant for lunch recently, the hostess looked at her and said, "How are you?" and Lauren looked at her and clearly responded "Good" with the sign. She loves greetings and will ask others, "How are you?" This is a welcome change from that awkward feeling you have as a parent when you feel as though you have to "talk" for your child.

Lauren's behavior is the biggest obstacle for our family. The days when we could scoop her up and move on as we managed to calm her down are over. She currently weighs 80 pounds, and she is next to impossible to move when she decides she isn't going anywhere. Transitions are difficult for her, and flexibility isn't Lauren's style.

Although it is helpful to have a routine to structure her day, it just isn't realistic to always follow routines, especially on weekends.

We feel fortunate that we have neighbors, teachers, friends, and family who accept and celebrate Lauren's accomplishments with us. They don't mind singing "Happy Birthday" and blowing out the candles just because there is a cake, even when it isn't anyone's birthday. My dream is for Lauren to form lasting friendships with peers, develop her own personal interests, and achieve her academic potential. I believe meeting these goals will help Lauren live a full and meaningful life.

—D. Shipman

Intellectual disability is a very powerful term. It is also an emotionally laden label, one that conjures up various images of people with intellectual disability. What do you think of when someone says "intellectual disability"? Do you immediately think of the character from the movie *Radio*, *The Other Sister*, or *I Am Sam*? Maybe you recall meeting a young girl with Down syndrome when you volunteered to help during last year's Special Olympics, or perhaps you recollect how you felt when a group of adults with intellectual disability sat by you in a restaurant. Often our images of individuals with an intellectual disability are based on stereotypes resulting from limited contact and exposure. Consequently, many of us are susceptible to inaccuracies, misconceptions, and erroneous beliefs about this population. As a result, people with intellectual disability frequently encounter prejudice, ignorance, and, in some instances, outright discrimination simply because society has identified them as being "different." Yet despite the diversity represented by this group, we firmly believe that children and adults with intellectual disability are first and foremost people who are more like their typically developing peers than they are different from them. In fact, very few ever fit the images and stereotypes commonly portrayed by the media.

Until very recently, individuals with an intellectual disability were often identified as *mentally retarded*—a pejorative, stigmatizing, and highly offensive label (commonly referred to in some circles as the "R" word). Today, the terminology of choice is *intellectual disability*. The acceptance of this new terminology has been championed by the premier professional organization in the field—the American Association on Intellectual and Developmental Disabilities.

The term *intellectual disability* is currently preferred by many policymakers, advocates, parents, service providers, teachers, and scholars. It is generally seen as less offensive to persons with this disability and is also consistent with contemporary Canadian and European terminology. The United Sates recently adopted this position. In October 2010, legislation was enacted (PL 111–256, Rosa's Law) that removed the terms *mental retardation* and *mentally retarded* from federal health, education, and labor statutes. In their place, we now find the designation *intellectual disability* to be the preferred language.

The goal of this chapter is to examine basic issues and concepts necessary for understanding the field of intellectual disability and individuals with this disability. In this chapter, we will look at historical foundations, evolving definitions and classification models, causes of intellectual disability, characteristics of persons with intellectual disability, contemporary educational practices, and trends in service delivery along with related concepts. We have adopted a life span perspective for exploring the concept of intellectual disability. This chapter, and those that follow, will therefore address topics and issues pertaining to infancy through adulthood.

Defining Intellectual Disability: An Evolving Process

Intellectual disability is a complex and multifaceted concept. Intellectual disability has been studied by psychologists, sociologists, educators, physicians, and many other professionals. This multidisciplinary interest in and investigation of intellectual disability, while beneficial, has significantly contributed to problems of conceptual and definitional clarity (Drew & Hardman, 2007). Yet by its very nature, intellectual disability cannot be studied independently of other disciplines. We fully agree with Drew and Hardman (2007) that there is considerable merit in a multidisciplinary approach; however, we must not lose sight of what should be our central focus, the individual with an intellectual disability.

Historical Interpretations

Over the years, the American Association on Intellectual and Developmental Disabilities (AAIDD) has put forth several different interpretations of intellectual disability. (In previous decades, the organization identified this disability as mental retardation.) We will briefly examine some of these early definitions to gain a better appreciation of how our understanding of this disability has evolved.

1961 AAIDD Definition. AAIDD's sixth definition appeared in 1961 and was widely accepted by professionals. At this point in time, intellectual disability was described as "subaverage general intellectual functioning which originates during the developmental period and is associated with impairments in adaptive behavior" (Heber, 1961, p. 3). Let us analyze the meaning of these phrases. *Subaverage general intellectual functioning* is defined as an intelligence quotient (IQ) greater than one standard deviation (SD) (a statistic describing variance from the mean or average score of a particular group) below the mean for a given age group. In 1961, this was interpreted to be an IQ below 85 or 84, depending on which standardized IQ test was used. The *developmental period* extended from birth to approximately age 16. The criterion of *impairments in adaptive behavior* is a critical and unique aspect of this definition. The inclusion of this factor establishes dual criteria for identifying someone as having an intellectual disability (Scheerenberger, 1987). Adaptive behavior, which Heber (1961) first introduced, refers to an individual's ability to meet the social requirements of his or her community that are appropriate for his or her chronological age; it is an indication of independence and social competency. Thus, according to Heber's definition, a person with an IQ of 79 who did not exhibit a significant impairment in adaptive behavior could not be identified as having an intellectual disability.

1973 AAIDD Definition. Herbert Grossman chaired a committee charged with revising the 1961 AAIDD definition. Grossman's (1973) definition viewed intellectual disability as "significantly subaverage general intellectual functioning existing concurrently with deficits in adaptive behavior, and manifested during the developmental period" (p. 11). Though paralleling its predecessor, the Grossman definition is conceptually distinct. First, the 1973 definition refers to significantly subaverage intellectual ability. Operationally, intellectual disability was psychometrically redefined as performance at least two standard deviations below the mean. This more conservative approach considered the upper IQ limit to be 70 or 68 (again, depending on whether the Stanford-Binet Intelligence Scale [SD = 16 points] or the Wechsler Intelligence Scale for Children [SD = 15 points] was used). Statistically speaking, this represents the lower 2.27 percent of the population instead of the approximately 16 percent included in the Heber (1961) definition. (See Figure 6.1.) Adopting this standard eliminated the classification of "borderline" intellectual disability incorporated in Heber's conceptual scheme.

standard deviation (SD): A descriptive statistic that expresses the variability and distribution of a set of scores relative to the mean.

adaptive behavior: The ability of an individual to meet the standards of personal independence as well as social responsibility appropriate for his or her chronological age and cultural group.

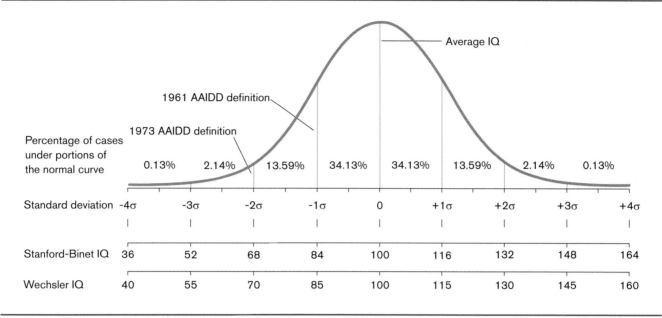

NOTE: The 1961 AAIDD definition defines intellectual disability as an IQ lower than 85 (84) on a standardized measure of intelligence. The 1973 AAIDD definition defines intellectual disability as an IQ lower than 70 (68). Later versions allow for professional judgment when considering intellectual performance.

The Grossman (1973) definition also sought to clarify the relationship between adaptive behavior and intellectual functioning. This definition attempted to focus greater attention on adaptive behavior and described it as the ability of an individual to meet "the standards of personal independence and social responsibility expected of his [or her] age and cultural group" (Grossman, 1973, p. 11). Adaptive behavior was to be considered within the context of the person's age and sociocultural group. Grossman's work attempted to strengthen the link between IQ and adaptive behavior in an effort to reduce the number of pupils identified with intellectual disability solely on the basis of their IQ. The 1973 definition also extended the concept of the developmental period to age 18 to more accurately reflect when most people complete their education. Although this definition forms the foundation for the IDEA 2004 (Individuals with Disabilities Education Improvement Act) definition of intellectual disability, some educators were concerned that lowering the IQ threshold to 68 (70) could possibly deny a special education to students who otherwise would have been eligible. It was feared that these children would be misclassified and inappropriately placed and thus "drown in the mainstream" (Scheerenberger, 1987).

1983 AAIDD Definition. In 1983, AAIDD published yet another revision to its manual on terminology and classification. Once again, Grossman led the organization's efforts. The eighth edition mirrors its 1973 predecessor. Though very similar in wording to the 1973 definition, this version contains some important changes. The 1983 Grossman edition suggests using a range of 70–75 when describing the upper limits of intellectual performance on a standardized measure of intelligence rather than a strict cutoff of 70. An IQ score of 70 is intended only as a guideline. Flexibility is the key to understanding the operation of this definition. The clinical judgment of the professional now plays an important role when making a diagnosis of intellectual disability.

1992 AAIDD Definition. In May 1992, Ruth Luckasson and her colleagues crafted a new definition of intellectual disability, which was published in *Mental Retardation:*

AUDIO
Labels and Definitions

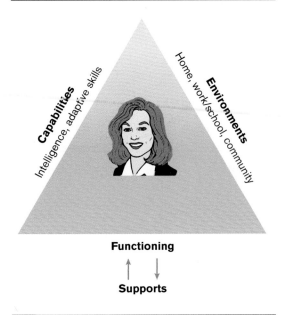

Figure 6.2 **General Structure of the 1992 AAIDD Definition of Intellectual Disability**

Functioning

↑   ↓

Supports

SOURCE: *Mental Retardation: Definition, Classification, and Systems of Supports,* 9th ed. (Washington, DC: American Association on Mental Retardation, 1992), p. 10. Reprinted with permission.

Definition, Classification, and Systems of Support. According to this manual,

> Mental retardation [intellectual disability] refers to substantial limitations in present functioning. It is characterized by significantly subaverage intellectual functioning, existing concurrently with related limitations in two or more of the following applicable adaptive skill areas: communication, self-care, home living, social skills, community use, self-direction, health and safety, functional academics, leisure, and work. Mental retardation [intellectual disability] manifests before age 18. (Luckasson et al., 1992, p. 5)

Application of this definition requires careful consideration of the following four essential assumptions:

1. Valid assessment considers cultural and linguistic diversity as well as differences in communication and behavioral factors.

2. The existence of limitations in adaptive skills occurs within the context of community environments typical of the individual's age peers and is indexed to the person's individualized needs for supports.

3. Specific adaptive limitations often coexist with strengths in other adaptive skills or other personal capabilities.

4. With appropriate supports over a sustained period, the life functioning of the person with mental retardation [intellectual disability] will generally improve. (Luckasson et al., 1992, p. 5)

The 1992 AAIDD definition is a highly functional definition. It portrays intellectual disability as a relationship among three key elements: the individual, the environment, and the type of support required for maximum functioning in various settings. It essentially reflects the "fit" between the person's capabilities and the structure and expectations of the environment. This ninth version also represents a conceptual shift away from viewing intellectual disability as an inherent trait to a perspective that considers the person's present level of functioning and the supports needed to improve it. The interaction among the individual, the environment, and support is depicted in Figure 6.2. The framers of the 1992 definition selected an equilateral triangle to represent their thinking because it shows the equality among the three elements.

The 1992 AAIDD description of intellectual disability stresses functioning in one's community rather than just focusing on the clinical aspect of the individual such as IQ or adaptive behavior (Smith, Polloway, Patton, & Dowdy, 2008). This definition is an optimistic one; it assumes that a person's performance will improve over time when appropriate supports are provided. Though certainly a unique portrayal of intellectual disability, this definition, like its predecessors, retains an emphasis on intellectual performance coupled with impairments in adaptive skills.

Contemporary Viewpoints

2002 AAIDD Definition. As times have changed, so has our understanding of the construct of intellectual disability. Because the 1992 AAIDD definition proved to be fairly controversial and not well accepted by professionals in the field, yet another definition was crafted a decade later. The 2002 AAIDD definition represents another effort in our evolving understanding of intellectual disability. The purpose of the tenth edition was to "create a contemporary system of diagnosis, classification, and systems of support for the disability currently known as mental retardation [intellectual disability]" (Luckasson et al., 2002, p. xii).

This definition states that "mental retardation [intellectual disability] is a disability characterized by significant limitations both in intellectual functioning and in adaptive behavior as expressed in conceptual, social, and practical adaptive skills. This disability originates before age 18" (Luckasson et al., 2002, p. 1).

Accompanying this description are five assumptions considered essential when applying this definition:

- Limitations in present functioning must be considered within the context of community environments typical of the individual's age, peers, and culture.
- Valid assessment considers cultural and linguistic diversity as well as differences in communication and sensory, motor, and behavioral factors.
- Within an individual, limitations often coexist with strengths.
- An important purpose of describing limitations is to develop a profile of needed supports.
- With appropriate personalized supports over a sustained period, the life functioning of the person with mental retardation [intellectual disability] will generally improve. (Luckasson et al., 2002, p. 1)

Like its predecessor, the 2002 AAIDD definition retains a positive perspective toward individuals with intellectual disability while continuing to acknowledge the significance of adaptive behavior and systems of support. It also preserves the idea that intellectual disability is a "function of the relationship among individual functioning, supports, and contexts" (Wehmeyer, 2003, p. 276). This conceptualization of intellectual disability, while not flawless, represents a logical step in the continuing challenge of advancing our understanding of the concept of intellectual disability.

2010 AAIDD Definition. The eleventh AAIDD definition (Schalock et al., 2010) both reiterates and strengthens key concepts found in the 2002 definition of intellectual disability. Developed by a committee of eighteen medical and legal scholars as well as policymakers, educators, and other professionals, the 2010 definition emphasizes the abilities and assets of individuals with intellectual disability rather than their deficits or limitations.

Intellectual disability is viewed as a state of functioning rather than an inherent trait. As in earlier definitions, one of the goals of the 2010 definition is to maximize support services so as to allow persons with intellectual disability to participate fully in all aspects of daily life.

The description of intellectual disability in the 2010 manual mirrors the wording found in the tenth edition, as do the five accompanying assumptions. The eleventh edition also retains the emphasis on adaptive behavior while stressing systems of support. The term *mental retardation*, however, is replaced by the more contemporary label, *intellectual disability*. This term is less pejorative while also reflecting a social-ecological understanding of disability (Schalock, 2013). The committee notes, however, that despite the change in terminology, the term *intellectual disability* refers to the same population of individuals who were recognized previously as being mentally retarded (Schalock et al., 2010).

VIDEO

AAIDD Definitions

Figure 6.3 **A Conceptual Framework of Human Functioning**

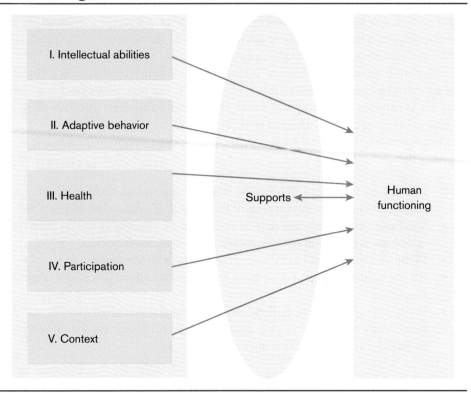

SOURCE: *Intellectual Disabilities: Definition, Classification, and Systems of Support,* 11th ed. (Washington, DC: American Association on Intellectual and Developmental Disabilities, 2010), p. 15.

The latest AAIDD definition reflects best practices and new thinking about classifying individuals with intellectual disability. Rather than using intellectual functioning as a basis for classifying persons with cognitive limitations, the 2010 definition encourages professionals and service providers to classify on the basis of various dimensions of human functioning—intellectual abilities, adaptive behavior, health, participation, and context (see Figure 6.3). *Human functioning* is essentially viewed as "an umbrella term for all life activities and encompasses body structures and functions, personal activities, and participation, which in turn are influenced by one's health and environmental or contextual factors" (Schalock et al., 2010, p. 15). This multidimensional perspective allows one to classify depending on the questions being asked (for example, "Is this person competent to be a self-advocate, maintain a bank account, or have sexual relations?") and the specific purpose of the classification system. Classification is then linked to personalized systems of support for that individual (Schalock, 2013).

Assessing Intellectual Ability and Adaptive Behavior

The constructs of intelligence and adaptive behavior play key roles in our understanding of the concept of intellectual disability. Yet both of these terms are somewhat difficult to define and assess. For the sake of clarity we will discuss each concept separately; but remember they are intricately interrelated and provide the foundation for contemporary thinking about intellectual disability.

Intellectual Ability

The question of what constitutes intelligence and how to describe it has challenged educators, psychologists, and thinkers throughout the years. Even today there is disagreement among professionals as to the meaning of this term and the best way of measuring intelligence. Intelligence is perhaps best thought of as a construct or theoretical abstraction; it is not a visible entity but rather a human trait whose existence is inferred based on a person's performance on certain types of cognitive tasks. Because no one has ever seen intelligence and we have only deduced its presence, professionals have come to the realization that they are "attempting to explain one of the most complex and elusive components of human functioning" (Beirne-Smith, Patton, & Kim, 2006, p. 95).

These difficulties notwithstanding, a great amount of effort has been expended on trying to accurately assess intellectual functioning. The most common way of determining an individual's cognitive ability is through an IQ or intelligence test. Two of the more widely used individually administered IQ measures are the Wechsler Intelligence Scale for Children (4th ed.), or WISC-IV (Wechsler, 2003), and the fifth edition of the original work of Binet and Simon from the early twentieth century, the Stanford-Binet Intelligence Scale (Roid, 2003). As noted in Chapter 3, some psychologists and psychometrists rely on the second edition of the Kaufman Assessment Battery for Children (Kaufman & Kaufman, 2004), especially when evaluating youngsters from culturally and linguistically diverse backgrounds.

Data gleaned from the WISC-IV, the Stanford-Binet V, and similar measures are thought to represent a sample of an individual's intellectual skills and abilities.

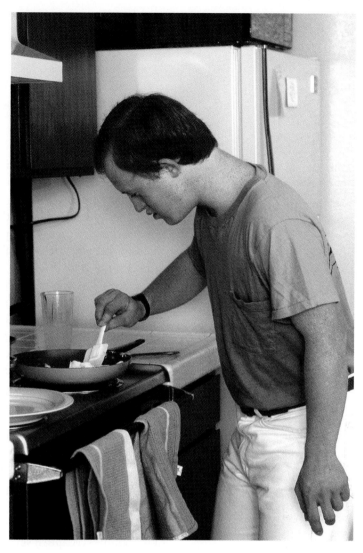

Persons with an intellectual disability can be taught how to live independently.

These data are usually summarized as an IQ score. Originally an IQ was defined as a ratio between the person's mental age (MA or developmental level) and chronological age (CA) multiplied by 100. For instance, a student whose chronological age is 10 but who performs on an IQ test like a typical 5-year-old would have an IQ of 50; if accompanied by deficits in adaptive behavior, this individual would very likely be identified as having an intellectual disability. Today, deviation IQs or standard scores have replaced intelligence quotients in most professional circles. A standard score is nothing more than an expression of how far a particular raw score deviates from a specific reference point such as the test mean. Standard scores are often expressed as standard deviations. One standard deviation on both the Stanford-Binet V and the WISC-IV is equivalent to 15 IQ points. Both tests have a mean IQ of 100.

Although IQ testing is very common in schools, the issue of assessing someone's intelligence, especially if a special education placement may result, is somewhat controversial. Cautionary flags and reasons for concern tend to focus on these issues:

- Potential for cultural bias. Intellectual assessments are often criticized because of their highly verbal nature and reflection of middle-class Anglo standards.

- Stability of IQ. An IQ test reports a person's performance only at a particular point in time; intelligence is not static but capable of changing, and in some cases, the change can be significant.
- Overemphasis on IQ scores. An IQ score is not the sole indicator of an individual's ability, nor is it a measure of the person's worth, yet IQ is often stressed at the expense of other factors, such as motivation or adaptive skills.

Adaptive Behavior

The notion of adaptive behavior was first introduced in the 1973 AAIDD definition of intellectual disability. It was retained in the 1983 description and is the underpinning of the most recent AAIDD definitions. Adaptive behavior is seen as "the degree to which, and the efficiency with which, the individual meets the standards of maturation, learning, personal independence, and/or social responsibility that are expected for his or her age level and cultural group" (Grossman, 1983, p. 11). In continuing this thinking, the 2002 AAIDD definition by Luckasson et al. describes adaptive behavior as "the collection of conceptual, social, and practical skills that have been learned by people in order to function in their everyday society" (p. 73). Stated another way, it is how well a person copes with the everyday demands and requirements of his or her environment. The idea of context is important for understanding the concept of adaptive behavior. Because behavior is strongly influenced by cultural factors, age and situation appropriateness must always be considered within the setting in which it occurs. For example, a teenage girl who uses her fingers while eating might be viewed as exhibiting inappropriate behavior; however, this behavior is maladaptive only when considered within the context of Western cultures.

The 1992, 2002, and 2010 AAIDD definitions, like earlier formulations, emphasize adaptive behavior, but now it is more clearly articulated. In earlier versions, adaptive behavior was described globally; in the Luckasson et al. (2002) configuration, it is seen as significant limitations in the expression or performance of conceptual (for example, reading and writing, money concepts), social (for example, obeying laws, following rules), and practical (for example, eating, dressing oneself, meal preparation, occupational abilities) adaptive skills.

It is not always easy to assess adaptive behavior. It is usually measured via direct observation, structured interviews, or standardized scales. Information may be obtained from family members, teachers, caregivers, or other professionals. AAIDD is currently developing the Diagnostic Adaptive Behavior Scale (DABS) as a standardized measure of adaptive behavior. Based on the three adaptive skill areas (conceptual, social, and practical), this new instrument is being normed on individuals in the chronological age range of 4–21 years old with and without intellectual disability. Designed as a diagnostic test, the DABS seeks to provide a precise cutoff point for persons deemed to have "significant limitations" in adaptive behavior (American Association on Intellectual and Developmental Disabilities, 2013). Recall that such limitations are one of the key components of the 2002 and 2010 AAIDD definitions of intellectual disability.

Classification of Individuals With Intellectual Disability

A classification system is a convenient way of differentiating among individuals who share a common characteristic—in this instance, intellectual disability. Of course, we must remember that there is a great degree of variability among members of this population despite the fact that they share a common label. Because intellectual disability

REFERENCE

Adaptive Behavior
Assessment

■ ■ ■ ■ Table 6.1 **Classification of Intellectual Disability According to Measured Intelligence**

Classification Level	Measured IQ	SD Below Mean
Mild intellectual disability	55–70	2 to 3
Moderate intellectual disability	40–55	3 to 4
Severe intellectual disability	25–40	4 to 5
Profound intellectual disability	Under 25	More than 5

NOTE: IQ scores are approximate.

SD = standard deviation.

exists along a continuum, there have been numerous proposals on how to classify people with this disability. Like definitions of intellectual disability, classification models tend to vary according to a particular focus. We will examine several systems—some vintage ones along with the most contemporary thinking in this area.

An Etiological Perspective

Traditionally, individuals with intellectual disability have been classified based on known or presumed medical/biological causes. This etiological orientation assumes that intellectual disability is a consequence of a disease process or biological defect. Examples include intellectual disability that is due to infections such as rubella (German measles) or maternal syphilis, chromosomal abnormalities such as Down syndrome, or metabolic disorders such as phenylketonuria (PKU). (These examples and others will be more fully explored in a later section of this chapter.) Although useful for physicians and other health care workers, this classification scheme has limited applicability for nonmedical practitioners.

Intellectual Deficits

A long-standing and popular classification scheme among psychologists and educators is one based on the severity of intellectual impairment as determined by an IQ test. This model is one of the most widely cited in the professional literature and, until recently, reflected the position of AAIDD dating back to the 1973 Grossman definition of intellectual disability. According to this system, deficits in intellectual functioning and related impairments in adaptive behavior result in individuals being classified into one of four levels of intellectual disability—mild, moderate, severe, or profound—with *mild* representing the highest level of performance for persons thought to have an intellectual disability and *profound* the lowest. Intellectual competency is often the primary variable used in constructing these discriminations; Table 6.1 presents the IQ ranges typically used.

An Educational Perspective

Another classification system popular with educators since the 1960s is to classify students with intellectual disability based on expected or anticipated educational accomplishments. Generally speaking, special education teachers classified children into one

Classification of Intellectual Disability According to Intensities of Support

Support Level	Description	Examples
Intermittent	Supports on an as-needed or episodic basis. Person does not always need the support(s), or person needs short-term supports during life span transitions. When provided, intermittent supports may be of high or low intensity.	• Loss of employment • Acute medical crisis
Limited	Supports characterized by consistency over time, time-limited but not intermittent; may require fewer staff and less cost than more intense levels of support.	• Job training • Transitioning from school to adult status
Extensive	Supports characterized by regular involvement (e.g., daily) in at least some environments (such as work or home) and not time-limited.	• Ongoing home living assistance
Pervasive	Supports characterized by their constancy and high intensity; provided across all environments, potential life-sustaining nature. Pervasive supports typically involve more staff and intrusiveness than extensive or time-limited supports.	• Chronic medical situation

SOURCE: Adapted from *Mental Retardation: Definition, Classification, and Systems of Supports,* 10th ed. (Washington, DC: American Association on Mental Retardation, 2002), p. 152.

of two groups: educable mentally retarded (EMR) or trainable mentally retarded (TMR). These designations are roughly equivalent to the AAIDD labels of *mild* and *moderate intellectual disability*, with IQs ranging from about 50–55 to 70–75 and 35–40 to 50–55, respectively. (Before the enactment of PL 94–142, public schools rarely served individuals with IQs lower than 35; therefore, these youngsters were not labeled according to this system.) As you might expect, the term *educable* implies that a youngster has some, albeit limited, academic potential; *trainable* implies that a child is incapable of learning but possibly could be trained in nonacademic areas. Over the years, professionals have learned that these prognostic labels, which represent an "educability quotient," are inaccurate and present a false dichotomy; we affirm that all children are capable of learning when presented with the appropriate circumstances. The notion of presumed academic achievement has slowly fallen out of favor in professional circles. These terms are currently considered pejorative and tend to perpetuate stereotypical and prejudicial attitudes.

Levels of Support

In the early nineties, AAIDD (Luckasson et al., 1992), in a dramatic and controversial maneuver, shifted from a classification model based on severity of intellectual impairment to one based on the type and extent of needed supports. This scheme, retained in the 2002 definition by Luckasson et al., classifies individuals with intellectual disability according to the level of support—intermittent, limited, extensive, or pervasive—needed to effectively function across adaptive skill areas in various natural settings, rather than according to their deficits. In fact, AAIDD recommends abandoning references to severity. Table 6.2 describes the four classification levels endorsed by AAIDD.

The aim of this approach is to explain an individual's functional (rather than intellectual) limitations in terms of the amount of support he or she requires to achieve optimal growth and development at home, at school, at the workplace, and in other community settings (Beirne-Smith et al., 2006). This model, which represents more than a mere substitution for the previous AAIDD IQ-based classification scheme,

educable mentally retarded (EMR): Classification of a person with mild intellectual disabilities who typically develops functional academic skills at a third- or fourth-grade level; IQ range generally between 50–55 and 70–75.

trainable mentally retarded (TMR): Classification of a person with moderate intellectual disabilities who is capable of learning self-care and social skills; IQ range generally between 35–40 and 50–55.

level of support: A classification scheme for individuals with intellectual disabilities that is based on the type and extent of assistance required to function in various areas.

extends the concept of support beyond the intensity of needed support to include the type of support system required. Natural supports typically include family members, friends, teachers, and coworkers. Formal supports are usually thought of as government-funded social programs like Social Security payments or health care programs, habilitation services, and even the efforts of groups like the Council for Exceptional Children or The Arc, a national advocacy organization on intellectual disability. It is probably too early to tell how professionals, school systems, and other groups will respond to this new way of thinking about classifying people with intellectual disability.

A Brief History of the Field

It is generally believed that individuals with intellectual disability have been present in all societies throughout the ages. Historically speaking, the field of intellectual disability resembles an ever-changing mosaic influenced by the sociopolitical and economic climate of the times. Attitudes toward and understanding of intellectual disability have also affected the treatment of people with intellectual disability. Intellectual disability is a field that is continually evolving—from the ignorance of antiquity to the highly scientific and legal foundations of the early twenty-first century. Along this pathway, people with intellectual disability have had to endure and battle myths, fear, superstition, attempts at extermination, and educational and social segregation before arriving at today's policy of normalization and inclusion.

Early Civilizations

Early written records from the era of the Greek and Roman empires make reference to citizens with intellectual disability. In some instances, these accounts date back to almost 1550 B.C. (Lindman & McIntyre, 1961). In many ways, the Greek and Roman societies were highly advanced and civilized, but the treatment of infants with disabilities would be judged cruel and barbaric by today's standards. Scheerenberger's (1983) detailed account of the history of intellectual disability reveals, for example, that in the city-state of Sparta, which placed a premium on physical strength and intellectual ability, eugenics and infanticide were common, everyday occurrences. Only the brightest and strongest of citizens were encouraged to have children. Newborns were examined by a council of inspectors, and babies thought to be defective or inferior were thrown from a cliff to die on the rocks below.

The early days of the Roman Republic mirrored the practices of the Greeks. Deformed infants were routinely allowed to perish—but only during the first eight days of life. Fathers held complete control over their children and could do whatever they wished, including selling or killing them. This doctrine of *patria potestas* is unparalleled in any other society.

The Middle Ages

From the fall of the Roman Empire in A.D. 476 to the beginning of the Renaissance in the 1300s, religion became a dominant social force, heralding a period of more humane treatment of individuals with disabilities. Churches established monasteries and asylums as sanctuaries for persons with intellectual disability. Children with intellectual disability were often called *les enfants du bon Dieu* ("the children of God"). Infanticide was rarely practiced because the largely agrarian societies required many workers in the fields. In some instances, individuals thought to have an intellectual disability found their way into castles where, though protected and shown favor, they served as buffoons and court jesters entertaining the nobility (Gargiulo, 1985). King Henry II of England

natural supports: Assistance rendered by family members, friends, teachers, and coworkers.

formal supports: Assistance provided by government social programs, habilitation services, or advocacy groups.

REFERENCE
History of the Field

enacted a policy in the twelfth century, *de praerogativa regis* ("of the king's prerogative"), whereby "natural fools" became the king's wards (Drew & Hardman, 2007).

At the same time, it was an era in which fear and superstition ran rampant. People with intellectual disability were frequently thought to be "filled with Satan" and to possess demonic powers, which often led to torture and death for practicing witchcraft. It was not uncommon for individuals with intellectual disability to be sent to prison and kept in chains because they were perceived to be a danger to society and their behavior was seen as unalterable.

Early Optimism

The "modern" period in the history of intellectual disability traces its roots to the early nineteenth century. It was during this period that the groundbreaking work of Jean-Marc Gaspard Itard (1774–1838) occurred. Recall from Chapter 1 that his pioneering efforts with Victor, the so-called "wild boy," earned him the title *Father of Special Education*. His systematic attempts at educating Victor, whom he believed to be a victim of social/educational deprivation, signals the start of the notion that individuals with intellectual disability are capable of learning—however limited it may be.

Edouard Seguin (1812–1880) was inspired by the work of his mentor, Itard. Based on his religious convictions, Seguin was a fervent advocate for the education of children with intellectual disability. In 1837, Seguin established the first school in Paris for the education of children with intellectual disability. Because of the political turmoil in France in the mid-1800s, Seguin immigrated in 1848 to the United States, where he played a principal role in helping to establish residential facilities for persons with intellectual disability in several states. In 1876, the Association of Medical Officers of American Institutions for Idiotic and Feebleminded Persons was established, with Seguin serving as its first president. This association was the forerunner of today's American Association on Intellectual and Developmental Disabilities.

Protection and Pessimism

The late nineteenth and early twentieth centuries witnessed the development of large, geographically isolated institutions for individuals with intellectual disability. The focus of these facilities changed as the invigorating optimism of the early 1800s generally gave way to disillusionment, fear, and pessimism (Morrison & Polloway, 1995). Institutions were overcrowded and understaffed. Their mission shifted from one of education and rehabilitation, as espoused by Seguin and others, to a new custodial role. Caring concern was slowly replaced by an unjustified concern with protecting society from individuals with intellectual disability.

One of the unfortunate consequences of this shift in societal attitude was that institutions became permanent residences for people with intellectual disability; thus, they were no longer prepared for their eventual return to society (Drew & Hardman, 2007). Education and training functions virtually disappeared, and only the most rudimentary care was provided. Over time, these institutions deteriorated, becoming warehouses for society's unwanted citizens. Living conditions were harsh and often deplorable. This situation was poignantly captured by Blatt and Kaplan (1966) in their classic photographic essay on institutional life, *Christmas in Purgatory*.

Beginning in the 1960s, a highly visible call for more humane and normalized living arrangements for people with intellectual disability was issued. Initiated in Sweden by Nirje (1969), the principle of **normalization** emphasizes "making available to the mentally retarded [intellectually disabled] patterns and conditions of everyday life which are as close as possible to the norms and patterns of the mainstream of

normalization: A principle advocating that individuals with disabilities should be integrated, to the maximum extent possible, into all aspects of everyday living.

society" (p. 181). In the United States, the idea that persons with intellectual disability have a right to culturally normative experiences was championed by Wolfensberger (1972). This concept, coupled with a renaissance of societal concern for individuals with intellectual disability, helped to facilitate a movement, beginning in the 1970s, toward deinstitutionalization and more community-based services for individuals with intellectual disability. Today, legislative as well as legal action has resulted in more normalized lifestyles and greater access to all aspects of society for our fellow citizens with intellectual disability.

The Emergence of Public Education for Students With Intellectual Disability

Although institutions were firmly established as part of the American social fabric in the late 1800s, public education for children with intellectual disability was virtually nonexistent. The first public school class for "slow learning" youngsters was formed in Providence, Rhode Island, at the very end of the nineteenth century. You might remember that these programs were largely segregated or self-contained classes and would remain so for the better part of the twentieth century. Classes for higher-functioning pupils with intellectual disability began to grow, in part as a result of the popularizing of IQ testing. Scheerenberger (1983) reports that by 1930, sixteen states had enacted either mandatory or permissive legislation regarding special classes for children with intellectual disability. By 1952, forty-six of the forty-eight states provided an education to children with intellectual disability. Youngsters with severe or profound intellectual disability, however, were largely excluded from public education.

The 1960s and 1970s marked the beginning of an era of national concern for the rights of individuals, a focus that continues today. People with intellectual disability would benefit from this attention. Aided by the actions of President Kennedy, who had a sister with intellectual disability, enlightened social policies, new educational programs, and a national research agenda were all forthcoming. At the same time, advances in the field of psychology and education demonstrated that, to some degree, all individuals with intellectual disability are capable of learning. Professionals also began a movement toward less restrictive and more integrated educational placements for students with intellectual disability—an emphasis with a very contemporary flavor. But perhaps the principal legacy of this era, which is foundational to today's educational programming, is a greater acceptance of persons with intellectual disability and their right, as fellow citizens, to live their lives in the most normalized fashion possible.

Prevalence of Intellectual Disability

How many students in the United States have an intellectual disability? According to data from the U.S. Department of Education (2013a), 431,152 children between the ages of 6 and 21 were identified as intellectually disabled and receiving a special education during the 2011–2012 school year. These students represent approximately 7.4 percent of all pupils with disabilities but less than 1 percent of the total school-age population. Although a figure of approximately 431,000 may seem large, over the years the number of students classified as having an intellectual disability has decreased significantly for a variety of reasons ranging from the benefits of prevention and early intervention, to changing definitions, to improved referral tactics.

The federal government, for the first time since the 1987–1988 school year, is now requiring states to report the number of preschoolers receiving a special education according to their disability label. This requirement represents a shift away from

deinstitutionalization: A movement whereby persons with intellectual disabilities are relocated from large institutions into smaller, community-based, group living settings.

allowing states to use the term *developmentally delayed* when reporting preschoolers with disabilities. According to the U.S. Department of Education (2013a), more than 12,200 preschoolers are recognized as intellectually disabled. This figure represents 1.6 percent of all youngsters with a disability.

Within the population of individuals identified as having an intellectual disability, persons with a mild intellectual disability, to use a familiar or common term, constitute the largest proportion. It is estimated that approximately 90 percent of people with intellectual disability function at the mild level (IQ 50–70/75). The remaining 10 percent are classified as exhibiting moderate, severe, or profound intellectual disability (Drew & Hardman, 2007).

Etiology of Intellectual Disability

Determining the cause, or etiology, of an intellectual disability is a difficult process. Multiple reasons are typically involved, and frequently the cause is unknown. In fact, in only about half of all cases of intellectual disability can a specific cause be cited (American Association on Intellectual and Developmental Disabilities, 2010). Generally speaking, the less severe the disability, the greater the likelihood that a particular cause cannot be determined.

Although scientists and other researchers are unable to determine the etiology of intellectual disability in every instance, we do know a great deal about what causes, or is at least implicated as, possible etiological factors. Investigators have designed several different schemes or models for classifying known and/or suspected causes of intellectual disability. For the purpose of this discussion, we have adopted the AAIDD (Luckasson et al., 2002) format for categorizing etiological factors typically associated with intellectual disability. The 2002 AAIDD model as well as the 2010 conceptualization designate three main sources of possible causes of intellectual disability that are based on the time of onset: prenatal (occurring before birth), perinatal (occurring around the time of birth), and postnatal (occurring after birth). Table 6.3 identifies some of the variables that could possibly lead to an intellectual disability.

Prenatal Contributions

Even a quick glance at Table 6.3 suggests that many different factors, of various origins, contribute to the possibility that a developing fetus may be at risk for intellectual disability. In some instances, intellectual disability will be an inescapable fact; in other cases, it is highly probable. Fortunately, researchers are making great strides in the areas of detection and prevention of certain types of intellectual disability.

Chromosomal Abnormalities

Down syndrome, the most common and perhaps best-known genetic disorder, was first described by Dr. John Langdon Down in 1866; however, it was not until 1959 that Down syndrome was linked to a chromosomal abnormality (Lejune, Gautier, & Turpin, 1959). Most people have forty-six chromosomes arranged in twenty-three pairs; people with Down syndrome have forty-seven. Chromosomes are rod- or threadlike bodies that carry the genes that provide the blueprint or building blocks for development. About 5 percent of all people with intellectual disability have Down syndrome (Beirne-Smith et al., 2006). The most common type of Down syndrome, accounting for approximately 90 percent of cases, is known as trisomy 21. In this instance, an extra chromosome becomes attached to the twenty-first pair, with the result that there are three (tri) chromosomes at this particular site.

etiology: A term frequently used when describing the cause of a disability.

prenatal: Events occurring before birth.

perinatal: Events occurring at or immediately after birth.

postnatal: Events occurring after birth.

Down syndrome: A chromosomal abnormality frequently resulting in intellectual disabilities with accompanying distinctive physical features.

VIDEO

Causes of
Intellectual Disability

Prenatal Factors	Examples	Perinatal Factors	Examples	Postnatal Factors	Examples
Chromosomal abnormalities	• Down syndrome • Fragile X syndrome • Turner syndrome	Gestational disorders	• Low birth weight • Prematurity	Infections and intoxicants	• Child abuse/neglect • Head trauma • Malnutrition • Environmental deprivation
Metabolic and nutritional disorders	• Phenylketonuria • Tay-Sachs disease • Galactosemia • Prader-Willi syndrome	Neonatal complications	• Hypoxia • Birth trauma • Seizures • Respiratory distress • Breech delivery • Prolonged delivery	Environmental factors	• Lead poisoning • Encephalitis • Meningitis • Reye's syndrome
Maternal infections	• Rubella • Syphilis • HIV (AIDS) • Cytomegalovirus • Rh incompatibility • Toxoplasmosis			Brain damage	• Neurofibromatosis • Tuberous sclerosis
Environmental conditions	• Fetal alcohol syndrome • Illicit drug use				
Unknown influences	• Anencephaly • Hydrocephalus • Microcephaly				

Scientists are uncertain as to exactly what causes Down syndrome. Thyroid problems, drugs, and exposure to radiation are all suspected, but there appears to be a strong link between maternal age and Down syndrome (Roizen, 2013). It is estimated that at age 25, the incidence of Down syndrome is about 1 out of 1,250 births; at age 30, it is 1 in 1,000 births; at age 35, it is 1 in 400 births; at age 40, it is 1 in 100 births; and at age 45, the risk is about 1 out of 30 births (March of Dimes, 2013b). It is important to note that age itself does *not* cause Down syndrome, only that there is a strong correlation. Down syndrome affects all racial and socioeconomic groups equally.

Physicians will frequently offer women who are age 35 or older on their due date or those whose blood screening is abnormal diagnostic testing procedures that are capable of detecting chromosomal abnormalities like Down syndrome. Chorionic villus sampling (CVS) is one example. It is typically performed at about ten to twelve weeks of gestation while amniocentesis is more common during the second trimester of pregnancy.

With CVS a small sample of chorionic villi (tiny fingerlike projections that make up the placenta) is removed from the placenta and analyzed for chromosomal or genetic birth defects with results typically available within a few days. Although CVS carries a higher risk for a miscarriage than amniocentesis, detection of

chorionic villus sampling (CVS): A diagnostic medical procedure used to detect a variety of chromosomal abnormalities, usually conducted in the first trimester of pregnancy.

amniocentesis: A diagnostic medical procedure performed to detect chromosomal and genetic abnormalities in a fetus.

Down syndrome most often results in mild to moderate intellectual disability.

problems occurs earlier in fetal development. It is considered the safest invasive diagnostic procedure prior to the fourteenth week of pregnancy (Schonberg, 2013). Amniocentesis, on the other hand, is usually done at about fifteen to eighteen weeks in the pregnancy. A small amount (1–2 ounces) of amniotic fluid is withdrawn via a needle from the sac surrounding the fetus. This fluid is then analyzed and a determination made, usually within ten to fourteen days, if the baby portrays atypical chromosomal development (Schonberg, 2013).

In the vast majority of instances, these prenatal biochemical analyses do not reveal the presence of a disorder or defect. When the results are positive, however, and indicate that the fetus has, for example, Down syndrome, parents are confronted with a decision as to whether to terminate the pregnancy (called an elective or therapeutic abortion) or to begin planning and preparation for an infant who will most likely have a disability. These are very difficult and often painful decisions involving a variety of moral and ethical dilemmas.

Down syndrome most often results in mild to moderate intellectual disability. In some instances, however, individuals may have a severe intellectual disability, and in other situations, near normal intelligence is possible. Besides intellectual disability, this chromosomal aberration frequently results in other health concerns, such as heart defects, hearing loss, intestinal malformations, vision problems, and an increased risk for thyroid difficulties and leukemia (March of Dimes, 2013b).

People with Down syndrome have distinctive physical characteristics. Among the most commonly observed features are an upper slant of the eyes, short stature, a flat nose, somewhat smaller ears and nose, an enlarged and sometimes protruding tongue, short fingers, reduced muscle tone, and a single crease (simian crease) across the palm of the hand (people without Down syndrome have parallel lines). Most individuals with Down syndrome will exhibit some, but not all, of these identifying characteristics.

Life expectancies for people with Down syndrome have increased dramatically. In the 1920s and 1930s, the life span for a child with Down syndrome was generally less than ten years; today, thanks to advances in medicine and health care, large numbers of individuals with Down syndrome are living to age 60 (Roizen, 2013). With advancing chronological age, however, individuals with Down syndrome face a greater risk for developing Alzheimer's disease (National Down Syndrome Society, 2013).

Fragile X syndrome is one of the more recently identified conditions linked to intellectual disability. This syndrome affects approximately 1 in 4,000 males and about 1 in 6,000 to 8,000 females, making it one of the leading inherited causes of intellectual disability (Batshaw, Gropman, & Lanpher, 2013; March of Dimes, 2013c). Because of the involvement of the X chromosome, this condition, which is caused by an abnormal or defective gene, predominantly affects males, although females can be carriers of the gene that causes it. Fragile X occurs in all racial and ethnic groups.

Individuals who have this disorder have a deficiency in the structure of the X chromosome of the twenty-third pair. Under a microscope, one of the "arms" of

therapeutic abortion: Elective termination of a pregnancy due to the presence of a birth defect.

fragile X syndrome: A chromosomal abnormality leading to intellectual disabilities along with physical anomalies; believed to be the most common form of inherited intellectual disabilities.

the X chromosome appears pinched or weakened and thus fragile. Females, who have two X chromosomes, are less susceptible to the defective gene; males, who have one X and one Y chromosome, are substantially at risk.

Typical characteristics associated with this syndrome include cognitive deficits of varying degrees, a long narrow face, large ears, a prominent forehead, and a large head circumference. At puberty, enlarged testicles are present (March of Dimes, 2013c; Meyer, 2007). Behaviorally, individuals with fragile X syndrome typically exhibit attention disorders, self-stimulatory behaviors, and speech and language problems. Meyer reports that about one third of girls with this disorder have mild intellectual disability or learning disabilities. The fragile X syndrome also appears to be associated with other disabilities such as autism and disorders of attention (Beirne-Smith et al., 2006).

Metabolic and Nutritional Disorders

Phenylketonuria, more commonly known by its acronym, PKU, is an example of an inborn error of metabolism. It is a recessive trait, meaning that both parents have to be carriers of the defective gene. When this occurs, there is a 25 percent chance that the infant will be born with PKU. There is an equal probability, however, that the baby will be healthy (and a 50 percent chance it will be an asymptomatic carrier) (March of Dimes, 2013d). In the United States, PKU appears in about 1 out of every 10,000 births and is more common among whites of European descent (Pellegrino, 2013).

PKU affects the way an infant's body processes or metabolizes protein. Affected babies lack the liver enzyme needed to process phenylalanine, which is common in many high-protein foods such as meat and dairy products. As a result of this deficiency, phenylalanine accumulates in the bloodstream and becomes toxic. This metabolic malfunction, if not promptly treated, leads to brain damage and intellectual disability, which is often severe.

Elevated levels of phenylalanine can be detected in the blood and urine of newborns within the first few days of life. All states now mandate screening for this disorder. If unusually high levels of phenylalanine are found, the infant is placed on a special diet, reducing the intake of protein. Researchers have found that if dietary restrictions are introduced shortly after birth, the devastating consequences of PKU are significantly minimized (Batshaw & Lanpher, 2013). It is unclear, however, how long the dietary restrictions must be maintained. As individuals with PKU get older, dietary control becomes more difficult. Of particular concern are women of childbearing age who have PKU. The metabolic imbalances within these women can cause serious consequences to the developing fetus. In more than 90 percent of these pregnancies, babies are born with intellectual disability and heart defects, and they are usually of low birth weight. However, returning to an individualized, restricted diet prior to pregnancy and maintaining it throughout pregnancy usually results in a healthy baby (Batshaw & Lanpher, 2013). Awareness of this concern has resulted in warning labels on many popular food items such as diet soft drinks and some low-fat foods ("Caution: product contains phenylalanine").

Galactosemia is another example of an inborn error of metabolism. In this disorder, infants are unable to process galactose, a form of sugar, typically found in milk and other food products. Manifestation of this condition in newborns typically includes jaundice, liver damage, heightened susceptibility to infections, failure to thrive, vomiting, and cataracts, along with impaired intellectual functioning (Drew & Hardman, 2007). If galactosemia is detected early, a milk-free diet can be started, which substantially reduces the potential for problems and delays.

phenylketonuria (PKU): An inherited metabolic disorder resulting from the inability of the body to convert phenylalanine to tyrosine; can be detected at birth and controlled by diet; left untreated, consequences are often severe.

galactosemia: An inborn error of metabolism that makes infants unable to process galactose, resulting in a variety of physical problems in addition to intellectual disabilities; dietary intervention reduces potential for problems.

Maternal Infections

Viruses and infections often cause intellectual disability and a host of other problems. While pregnant, a woman and her developing child are very susceptible to a wide variety of potentially damaging infections. Exposure during the first trimester of pregnancy usually results in severe consequences. Rubella (German measles) is a good example of this type of infection. This mild but highly contagious illness has been linked to intellectual disability, vision and hearing defects, heart problems, and low birth weight. Rubella is one of the leading causes of multiple impairments in children. With the introduction of a rubella vaccine in 1969, instances of rubella-related disabilities have substantially decreased.

Sexually transmitted diseases such as gonorrhea and syphilis are capable of crossing the placenta and attacking the central nervous system of the developing fetus. In contrast to rubella, the risk to the unborn child is greater at the later stages of fetal development.

Acquired immune deficiency syndrome (AIDS), which is attributed to the human immunodeficiency virus (HIV), is another probable cause of intellectual disability and other developmental delays. Generally transmitted via unprotected sexual intercourse with an infected person, exposure to contaminated blood or bodily fluids, or the sharing of hypodermic needles, HIV crosses the placenta and affects the central nervous system while also damaging the immune system, leaving the fetus substantially at risk for opportunistic infections. Pediatric AIDS is suspected of being a leading infectious cause of intellectual disability. At the same time, HIV is the single most preventable cause of infectious intellectual disability.

Maternal–fetal Rh incompatibility, although technically not an infection, is another potential cause of intellectual disability. At one time, this disease was a leading cause of intellectual disability; however, thanks to preventive efforts, this is no longer the case. Simply stated, Rh disease is a blood group incompatibility between a mother and her unborn child. This discrepancy is the result of the Rh factor, a protein found on the surface of red blood cells. Rh-positive blood contains this protein; Rh-negative blood cells do not (Beirne-Smith et al., 2006).

Rh incompatibility often leads to serious consequences such as intellectual disability, cerebral palsy, epilepsy, and other neonatal complications. The problem arises when an Rh-negative mother carries an Rh-positive baby, which causes her to produce antibodies against any future Rh-positive fetus. For this reason, Rh-negative women today generally receive an injection of Rh immunoglobulin (Rhlg) within 72 hours of delivering an Rh-positive baby. In the vast majority of cases, this procedure prevents the production of antibodies, thus preventing problems in any future pregnancies.

Toxoplasmosis is a further example of maternal infection that typically poses grave risks to an unborn child. Toxoplasmosis is contracted through exposure to cat fecal matter; it is also present in undercooked or raw meat and raw eggs. If the mother is exposed to this parasitic infection during pregnancy, especially in the third trimester, it is very likely that fetal infection will occur. Infected infants may be born with an intellectual disability, cerebral palsy, damaged retinas leading to blindness, microcephaly (unusually small head), enlarged liver and spleen, jaundice, and other very serious complications. Antibiotics seem to provide some defense for both mother and child.

Our final illustration of maternal infections is cytomegalovirus (CMV), an especially common virus that is part of the herpes group. Most women have been exposed to this virus at some time in their lives and thus develop immunity. If initial exposure occurs during pregnancy, however, the fetus may be severely affected. CMV often leads to brain damage and thus intellectual disability, blindness, and hearing impairments.

rubella: A viral disease also known as German measles; contact in first trimester of pregnancy often results in a variety of significant impairments.

syphilis: A venereal disease; infection of the mother in the last trimester of pregnancy can cause intellectual disabilities in the child.

acquired immune deficiency syndrome (AIDS): An infectious disease caused by HIV (human immunodeficiency virus) that destroys the immune system, leaving the person open to serious, life-threatening diseases.

Rh incompatibility: A condition that results when a woman who is Rh negative carries an Rh positive fetus. Mother's body will produce antibodies that can affect babies resulting from future pregnancies; often leads to intellectual disabilities and other impairments if mother does not receive an injection of Rho immune globulin.

toxoplasmosis: A maternal infection resulting from contact with parasites; especially devastating if exposure occurs during third trimester of pregnancy.

cytomegalovirus (CMV): A common virus that is part of the herpes group; if initial exposure occurs during pregnancy, severe damage to the fetus often results.

Environmental Contributions

Many unsafe maternal behaviors—among them, smoking, illicit drug use (for example, cocaine, heroin), and the consumption of alcohol before and during pregnancy—have been linked to impaired fetal development. The use of alcohol, in particular, has captured the attention of scientists and researchers for many years. In 1973, the term fetal alcohol syndrome, or FAS, was first coined (Jones, Smith, Ulleland, & Streissguth, 1973). FAS is one of the leading causes of intellectual disability in the United States (Davidson & Myers, 2007). Each year an estimated 40,000 babies are born with some degree of alcohol-associated damage or defect (March of Dimes, 2008). It is important to note that there is no known safe level of alcohol consumption during pregnancy (Paulson, 2013).

Alcohol can damage the central nervous system of the unborn child, and brain damage is not uncommon. FAS is characterized by a variety of physical deformities, including facial abnormalities, heart defects, low birth weight, and motor dysfunctions. In addition to mild to moderate intellectual disability, attention disorders and behavioral problems are usually present. Less severe and subtler forms of alcohol-related damage are recognized as fetal alcohol effect (FAE). The effects of excessive alcohol consumption last a lifetime, yet this condition is entirely preventable.

Unknown Influences

Several types of cranial malformations are the result of unknown prenatal factors. Anencephaly is but one illustration. In this condition, the entire brain or a large portion of it fails to develop properly, with devastating consequences for the infant. A more common condition is microcephaly, characterized by an unusually small head and severe intellectual disability. Hydrocephalus is a disorder associated with the interference or blockage of the flow of cerebrospinal fluid, resulting in an accumulation of excess fluid that typically leads to an enlarged cranial cavity and potentially damaging compression on the brain. Doctors can surgically implant shunts that remove the excess fluid, thereby minimizing the pressure on the infant's brain and consequently the severe effects of this condition.

Perinatal Conditions

Gestational Disorders

The two most common problems associated with gestational disorders are low birth weight and premature birth. Prematurity is generally defined as a birth that occurs prior to thirty-six weeks of gestation. Low birth weight is defined as less than 5 pounds, 8 ounces (2,500 grams), and very low birth weight as less than 3 pounds, 5 ounces (1,500 grams). In the majority of instances, but not all, infants with low birth weight are premature. Not all babies with gestational disorders will have a disability or encounter future difficulties in school. However, some of these children may develop subtle learning problems, some may have an intellectual disability, and still others may have sensory and motor impairments.

Neonatal Complications

Complications surrounding the birth process may cause intellectual disability and other developmental delays. One common example is anoxia (oxygen deprivation) or hypoxia (insufficient oxygen). Anoxia may occur because of damage to the umbilical cord or as a result of a prolonged and difficult delivery. Obstetrical or birth trauma, such as the improper use of forceps, may cause excessive pressure on the skull, which in

fetal alcohol syndrome (FAS): Results from mother's consumption of alcohol while pregnant; mild to moderate intellectual disabilities are common, along with physical deformities. A leading cause of intellectual disabilities, although completely preventable.

fetal alcohol effect (FAE): A less severe and more subtle form of fetal alcohol syndrome; caused by drinking alcohol while pregnant.

anencephaly: Cranial malformation; large part of the brain fails to develop.

microcephaly: A condition in which the head is unusually small, leading to inadequate development of the brain and resulting in intellectual disabilities.

hydrocephalus: A condition in which the head is unusually large due to accumulation of excessive cerebrospinal fluid; brain damage often minimized by surgically implanting a shunt to remove excess fluid.

low birth weight: A term frequently used to describe babies who are born weighing less than 2,500 grams (5 lbs., 8 oz.).

premature births: Babies born prior to 37 weeks of gestation age.

anoxia: Loss of or inadequate supply of oxygen associated with birth process and frequently resulting in brain damage.

hypoxia: Insufficient amount of oxygen to the brain; can result in brain damage.

birth trauma: Difficulties associated with the delivery of the fetus.

VIDEO
Genetic Causes

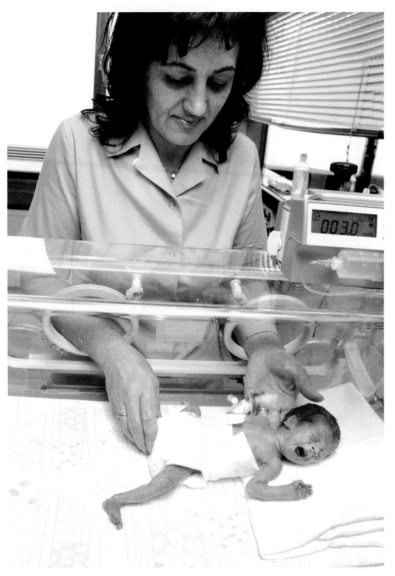

Complications surrounding the birth process may cause intellectual disability and other developmental delays.

breech presentation: Fetus exits the birth canal buttocks first rather than typical headfirst presentation.

precipitous birth: Birth that occurs in less than two hours.

lead poisoning: An environmental toxin used at one time in the manufacture of gasoline and paint; ingestion of lead can cause seizures, brain damage, and impaired central nervous system functioning.

meningitis: A viral or bacterial infection of the membranes covering the brain and spinal cord; associated with hearing loss and intellectual disabilities.

turn may damage a portion of the infant's brain. A breech presentation is another illustration of a neonatal problem. In a breech delivery, the infant exits the birth canal buttocks first instead of the more typical headfirst presentation. This fetal delivery position raises concerns about the possibility of damage to the umbilical cord and a heightened threat of injury to the baby's head because of the greater intensity and frequency of uterine contractions later in the birth process. Worries about the infant's skull also arise when a precipitous birth (one lasting less than two hours) occurs. The gentle molding of the skull may not take place during a precipitous birth, thus increasing the risk of tissue damage and intellectual disability (Drew & Hardman, 2007).

Postnatal Factors

Infections and Intoxicants

Lead and mercury are two examples of environmental toxins that can cause intellectual disability. Lead poisoning is a serious public health problem. Because of its highly toxic nature, lead is no longer used in the manufacturing of gasoline or paint. But even though it is no longer commercially available, some youngsters are still at risk for lead poisoning. Children who live in older homes or apartments may ingest lead by eating peeling paint chips containing lead. Lead poisoning can cause seizures, brain damage, and disorders of the central nervous system.

Infections represent another source of concern for young children. Meningitis, a viral infection, causes damage to the covering of the brain known as the meninges. Meningitis may result from complications associated with typical childhood diseases such as mumps, measles, or chicken pox. Because it is capable of causing brain damage, intellectual disability is a distinct possibility. Equally devastating is encephalitis, which is an inflammation of the brain tissue. Encephalitis may cause damage to the central nervous system and can result from complications of infections typically associated with childhood, such as mumps or measles.

Environmental Factors

A wide variety of environmental or psychosocial influences are often associated with intellectual disability, especially instances of mild intellectual disability. Debilitating factors may include nutritional problems, adverse living conditions, inadequate health care, and a lack of early cognitive stimulation. Many of these factors are associated with lower socioeconomic status. Child abuse and neglect along with head trauma resulting from automobile accidents or play-related injuries are also potential contributing factors. Of course, not all children exposed to these traumatic postnatal situations become intellectually disabled. These illustrations represent only evidence correlated with, but not necessarily causes of, intellectual disability. It is perhaps best to think of these variables as interacting risk factors, with some children being more vulnerable than others. Fortunately, most children exposed to these unfavorable circumstances develop normally.

Although a large portion of intellectual disability is attributed to environmental factors, contemporary thinking suggests that intellectual disability associated with psychosocial influences are the result of interaction between environmental and genetic or biological contributions.

Some students with intellectual disability experience difficulty learning because they fail to attend to the relevant attributes of the task.

Stated another way, a youngster's genetic endowment provides a range of intellectual opportunity that is then mediated by the environment to which that individual is exposed.

Characteristics of Individuals With Intellectual Disability

When discussing characteristics common to people with intellectual disability, it is important to remember that although, as a group, they may exhibit a particular feature, not all individuals identified as intellectually disabled will share this characteristic. Persons with intellectual disability are an especially heterogeneous population; interindividual differences are considerable. Many factors influence individual behavior and functioning, among them chronological age, the severity and etiology of the disability, and educational opportunities. We caution you to remember that the following descriptions represent generalizations and are useful only for framing this discussion. Finally, in several ways, individuals with intellectual disability are more like their typically developing counterparts than they are different from them, sharing many of the same social, emotional, and physical needs.

Learning Characteristics

The most common defining characteristic of someone identified as intellectually disabled is impaired cognitive functioning, which, you may recall, can vary greatly. Investigators are typically not concerned with the person's intellectual ability per se but rather are concerned with the impact that lower IQ has on the individual's ability to learn, acquire concepts, process information, and apply knowledge in various settings, such as school and community. Scientists do not yet fully understand the complexity of the learning process in human beings. Learning is a difficult concept to define—in many ways, it is unique to the individual—and is composed of many interrelated cognitive processes. Learning, then, is not a unitary variable. We have chosen, therefore, to briefly examine several of the characteristics that researchers believe influence learning.

encephalitis: An inflammation of the brain; may cause damage to the central nervous system.

Attention

Attention, which is a multidimensional concept, plays a key role in learning. Many of the learning difficulties of individuals with intellectual disability are thought to be due to attentional deficits. Before learning a task, a person must be able to attend to its relevant attributes. Individuals with an intellectual disability often experience difficulty focusing their attention, maintaining it, and selectively attending to relevant stimuli. They often ignore the salient attributes of a task but instead focus on its irrelevant features. It may well be that children with intellectual disability perform poorly on certain learning tasks because they do not know how to attend to the critical aspects or dimensions of the problem (Alevriadou & Grouios, 2007).

Memory

Memory, which is an important component of learning, is often impaired in children with intellectual disability. Generally speaking, the more severe the cognitive impairment, the greater the deficits in memory (Drew & Hardman, 2007; Owens, 2009). Short-term memory (information stored for a few seconds or hours) is especially problematic for individuals with intellectual disability; for example, they may have trouble following teacher directions given in sequence or sequential job tasks from an employer. Working memory, on the other hand, refers to the ability to retain information while simultaneously performing another cognitive task (Jarrold & Brock, 2012). Recalling an address while listening to directions illustrates this process.

Academic Performance

As you might anticipate, students with intellectual disability encounter difficulties in their academic work. Generally, this deficiency is seen across all subject areas, but reading appears to be the weakest area, especially reading comprehension (Katims, 2000). Pupils identified as intellectually disabled are also deficient in arithmetic, but their performance is more in line with their mental age (Drew & Hardman, 2007). Remember, just because a student is academically unsuccessful does not mean that he or she cannot excel in other school endeavors, such as athletics or the arts.

Motivation

Motivational factors are crucial for understanding the discrepancy that often exists between an individual's performance and his or her actual ability. It is not unusual for students with intellectual disability to approach a learning situation with heightened anxiety. A history of failure in earlier encounters contributes to this generalized feeling of apprehension; consequently, pupils seem to be less goal oriented and lacking in motivation.

Past experiences with failure typically lead individuals with intellectual disability to exhibit an external locus of control; that is, they are likely to believe that the consequences or outcomes of their behavior are the result of circumstances and events beyond their personal control, rather than their own efforts (Shogren, Bovaird, Palmer, & Wehmeyer, 2010). Repeated episodes of failure also give rise to a related concept, learned helplessness—the perception that no matter how much effort they put forth, failure is inevitable. ("No matter how hard I try, I won't be successful!") This expectancy of failure frequently causes students with intellectual disability to stop trying, even when the task is one they are capable of completing. Educators sometimes refer to this behavior as the "pencil down syndrome."

Accumulated experiences with failure also result in a style of learning and problem solving characterized as outer-directedness, or a loss of confidence and trust in one's

short-term memory: The recall of information after a brief period of time.

working memory: The ability to retain information while also engaging in another cognitive activity.

external locus of control: The belief that the consequences or outcomes of a person's actions are the result of circumstances and situations beyond one's control rather than a result of one's own efforts.

learned helplessness: A lack of persistence at tasks that can be mastered; a tendency to expect failure.

outer-directedness: A condition characterized by a loss of confidence in one's own capabilities and a reliance on others for cues and guidance.

own abilities and solutions and a reliance on others for cues and guidance (Bybee & Zigler, 1998). While not solely limited to individuals with intellectual disability, this overreliance on others contributes to a lack of motivation and increased dependence. Once again, the origin of this behavior can be traced to the debilitating effects of repeated failure.

Generalization

It is not unusual for individuals with intellectual disability to experience difficulty in transferring or generalizing knowledge acquired in one context to new or different settings. In a large number of instances, learning in someone with an intellectual disability is situation specific; that is, once a particular skill or behavior is mastered, the individual has difficulty duplicating the skill when confronted with novel circumstances—different cues, different people, or different environments (Taylor, Brady, & Richards, 2005). For example, an adolescent with intellectual disability who can successfully determine correct change from a purchase in the school cafeteria might experience difficulty when counting his or her change at a grocery store or a restaurant. Therefore, teachers must systematically plan for generalization; typically it does not occur automatically. Generalization of responses can be facilitated, for example, by using concrete materials rather than abstract representations, by providing instruction in various settings where the strategies or skill will typically be used, by incorporating a variety of examples and materials, or by simply informing the pupils of the multiple applications that are possible.

Language Development

Speech and language development are closely related to cognitive functioning. In fact, speech and language difficulties are more common among individuals with intellectual disability than in their typically developing counterparts (Gleason & Ratner, 2013). Given the association between intellectual ability and speech and language, it is not surprising that students with intellectual disability experience a great deal of difficulty with academic tasks, such as reading, that require verbal and language competency.

Speech disorders are common among individuals with intellectual disability. These may include errors of articulation such as additions or distortions, fluency disorders (stuttering), and voice disorders such as hypernasal speech or concerns about loudness. In fact, researchers have found that speech and language difficulties are a fairly common secondary disability among students with intellectual disability (Beirne-Smith et al., 2006).

Despite the prevalence of speech disorders, language problems are receiving increased attention from professionals because deficits in this arena are highly debilitating. There is a strong correlation between intellectual ability and language development—the higher the IQ, the less pervasive the language disorder. Although children with intellectual disability, especially those with higher IQs, acquire language in the same fashion as their typically developing peers, development occurs more slowly, their vocabulary is more limited, and grammatical structure and sentence complexity are often impaired (Owens, 2014). Yet language is crucial for the independent functioning of individuals with an intellectual disability. Deficits in this area can significantly impede social development and hinder peer relationships (Friend & Bursuck, 2012).

Social and Behavioral Characteristics

The ability to get along with other people is an important skill, and it is just as significant for individuals who are intellectually disabled as it is for those without an intellectual disability. In fact, in some situations, social adeptness or proficiency may be

generalizing: The ability to transfer previously learned knowledge or skills acquired in one setting to another set of circumstances or situation.

VIDEO

Instructional Strategies

as important as, if not more important than, intellectual ability. In the area of employment, for example, when workers with intellectual or other developmental disabilities experience difficulty on the job, it is frequently due to problems of social interactions with coworkers and supervisors rather than job performance per se (Hendricks & Wehman, 2009).

Individuals with intellectual disability often exhibit poor interpersonal skills and socially inappropriate or immature behavior; as a result, they frequently encounter rejection by peers and classmates. It is not unusual for individuals with intellectual disability to lack the social competency necessary to establish and maintain appropriate interpersonal relations (Vaughn, Bos, & Schumm, 2014). Friend and Bursuck (2012) note that the success or failure of students with intellectual disability who are placed in general education classrooms is often determined by their social skills. This lack of social ability can pose significant difficulties as increasing numbers of individuals with intellectual disability are seizing the opportunity to participate in more normalized environments. Direct social skill instruction is one way of enhancing the social development of persons with an intellectual disability. Behavior modification techniques can reduce inappropriate social behaviors while establishing more desirable and acceptable behaviors. The modeling of the appropriate behavior of classmates is another way that students with intellectual disability can acquire more socially attractive behaviors, which in turn can lead to greater peer acceptance.

Table 6.4 presents a summary of select learning and behavioral characteristics of individuals with intellectual disability.

Educational Considerations

Educators and other professionals no longer consider students with intellectual disability to be incapable of learning. To be successful, however, they require an instructional program that is individualized to meet their unique needs. Additionally, the instruction provided to these learners must be comprehensive and functional, equipping them, to the maximum extent possible, with the experiences they need to live and work in their respective communities, both now and in the future. As with other pupils, our goal as teachers should be one of developing independence and self-sufficiency. Obviously, for this population of children, this objective dictates that an education be interpreted broadly and not construed solely as academic learning. As we explore the issue of educational opportunities for individuals with intellectual disability, you will discover that the concepts of individualization and appropriateness are of paramount importance.

In this part of the chapter, we will explore the various educational options available to children who are intellectually disabled and where these services are delivered. Our focus here is on school-age individuals; preschool and adult programming will be addressed in later sections.

Where Are Students With Intellectual Disability Educated?

Despite the contemporary trend toward educating children with disabilities in more normalized settings, pupils with intellectual disability are more than three times as likely as other students with exceptionalities to be educated in a separate class. Only 14 percent of all individuals with disabilities were educated in self-contained classrooms during the 2011–2012 school year; however, almost half (48.7%) of youngsters with intellectual disability were placed in this environment during the 2011–2012 school year (U.S. Department of Education, 2013a). Historically speaking, this administrative

REFERENCE

Behavior Modifications

Representative Learning and Behavioral Characteristics of Individuals With Intellectual Disability

Dimension	Associated Attributes and Features
Attention	• Inability to attend to critical or relevant features of a task • Diminished attention span • Difficulty ignoring distracting stimuli
Memory	• Deficits in memory correlated with severity of intellectual disability • Limitations in ability to selectively process and store information • Inefficient rehearsal strategies • Difficulty with short-term memory is common—recalling directions in sequence presented seconds earlier • Long-term retrieval (recalling a telephone number) is similar to that of peers without intellectual disability
Motivation	• History of and a generalized expectancy for failure—learned helplessness—effort is unrewarded; failure is inevitable • Exhibit external locus of control—belief that outcomes of behavior are the result of circumstances (fate, chance) beyond personal control rather than own efforts • Evidence outer-directedness, a loss of confidence and a distrust of own abilities, reliance on others for cues and guidance
Generalization	• Difficulty applying knowledge or skill to new tasks, situations, or settings • Problem in using previous experience in novel situations • Teachers must explicitly plan for generalization; typically it does not automatically occur
Language Development	• Follow same sequence of language acquisition as typical individuals, albeit at a slower pace • Strong correlation between intellectual ability and language development—the higher the IQ, the less pervasive the language difficulty • Speech disorders (articulation errors, stuttering) more common than in peers without intellectual disability • Vocabulary is often limited • Grammatical structure and sentence complexity are often impaired
Academic Development	• Generally exhibit difficulties in all academic areas with reading being the weakest • Problem-solving difficulties in arithmetic
Social Development	• Typically lacking in social competence • Rejection by peers and classmates is common—poor interpersonal skills • Frequently exhibit socially inappropriate or immature behavior—difficulty establishing and maintaining friendships • Diminished self-esteem coupled with low self-concept

SOURCE: Adapted from R. Gargiulo and D. Metcalf, *Teaching in Today's Inclusive Classrooms*, 2nd ed. (Belmont, CA: Wadsworth/Cengage Learning, 2013), p. 88.

arrangement has characterized the delivery of educational services to pupils with an intellectual disability. Figure 6.4 portrays the educational settings where students with intellectual disability are typically served.

Educational Programming Options

Generally speaking, educational programming for pupils who are intellectually disabled reflects a marriage of various emphasis areas or focal points. Among these concentrations are functional academic skills, vocational training, community living,

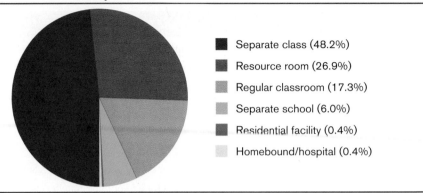

NOTE: Figure represents percentage of enrollment of students with intellectual disability during the 2011–2012 school year. Excludes pupils enrolled in parentally placed private schools and individuals in correctional facilities.

SOURCE: U.S. Department of Education. (2013). *Historical state-level IDEA data files.* Retrieved November 14, 2013, from http://tadnet.public.tadnet.org/pages/712

and self-help skills, along with a growing emphasis on exposure to the general education curriculum. Of course, the individual needs of the student must dictate how a specific educational program is constructed. Remember, children with an intellectual disability represent an especially heterogeneous population of learners with a wide range of skills and abilities. The curriculum designed for these pupils must be individualized, functional, and comprehensive (Beirne-Smith et al., 2006). In addition, instructional programming for individuals who are intellectually disabled must be forward looking, giving due consideration to these students' current needs and future life goals.

We cannot stress enough the importance of individually crafted instructional programs. A "one size fits all" approach for instructing individuals with intellectual disability is inappropriate. An effective curriculum must not only be individualized, emphasizing academic as well as adaptive skills; it must also be comprehensive (Drew & Hardman, 2007). A comprehensive curriculum for learners with cognitive limitations (Polloway, Patton, Serna, & Bailey, 2013) should, among other things,

- be responsive to the needs of the individual student at the current time;
- provide maximum interaction with peers who are not disabled and access to the general education curriculum, while also attending to specific curricular needs missing in the general education curriculum;
- be based on a realistic assessment of adult outcomes; and
- be sensitive to diploma requirements and graduation goals.

Functional Curriculum

functional curriculum: A curriculum that emphasizes practical life skills rather than academic skills.

functional academics: The application of life skills as a means of teaching academic tasks; core of many instructional programs for students with mild or moderate intellectual disabilities.

A **functional curriculum** is one that instructs pupils in the life skills they require for successful daily living and prepares them for those situations and environments they will encounter upon leaving school. In a functional curriculum, academic skills are applied to everyday, practical life situations—for example, calculating change, following directions in a cookbook, reading washing instructions, or completing a job application. Known as **functional academics**, these skills are often the core of instructional

VIDEO
Educational Considerations

A functional curriculum may be appropriate for some students with intellectual disability.

programs for some individuals with mild or moderate intellectual disability. Additionally, these students are exposed to curriculum content focusing on personal hygiene, independent living skills, community resources, and other issues that, collectively, are designed to enhance their current and future independence and successful adjustment (Johnson, 2005).

Several approaches are available for teaching functional academics. Two of the more commonly used strategies are functional, generalized skills useful for life routines and embedded academic skills appropriate to specific life situations. For some students, however, it may be necessary to simply bypass academic instruction (Browder & Snell, 2000). Browder and Snell (2000) recommend that the individualized education program (IEP) team consider the following six factors when selecting an instructional approach:

1. The student's preferences

2. The parents' preferences

3. The student's chronological age or number of years left in school

4. The student's current and future settings

5. The student's rate of learning academic skills

6. The student's other skill needs (p. 500)

Table 6.5 provides an example of the application of these instructional options.

A functional curriculum is concerned with the application of skills to real-life situations. This requires that instruction occur as much as possible in natural settings, using actual items rather than mere representations in simulated settings. This instructional technique, known as community-based instruction, is appropriate for individuals with intellectual disability. This strategy eliminates many of the difficulties these pupils encounter when attempting to transfer and generalize skills learned in the classroom to other settings in which the skill is to be used. Simulated experiences, though useful, are often ineffective with this population. For example, reading a menu or shopping for groceries can easily be simulated in the classroom; however, it is generally more effective when these particular skills occur in vivo, or in the actual environment. Research suggests that students with intellectual disability learn more efficiently and retain greater information if skill instruction occurs in a natural setting (Hartman, 2009; Walker, Uphold, Richter, & Test, 2010; Wehman & Scott, 2013).

Variations of a functional curriculum are also appropriate for individuals identified as moderately intellectually disabled and, in some cases, for students with severe intellectual impairments. As with their higher-functioning counterparts, areas of emphasis—or domains, as they are sometimes called—are individualized based on the current and future needs of the student. Typical domains include self-help skills, socialization, communication, and vocational training, along with using community resources and exposure to very basic or "survival" academics. An example of this last domain might include functional or environmental reading of survival words and phrases such as *danger, exit, on, off, gentlemen, detour, fire escape, don't walk, keep out, beware of dog,* and other key protective vocabulary. Equally useful are career and vocational terms identified by Schilit and Caldwell (1980). Their list of a hundred important terms includes words such as *boss, wages, tools, break,* and *first aid.* Arithmetic concepts might stress quantitative concepts such as big/little or more/less, telling time, learning telephone numbers and addresses, calendar activities, money recognition, and other types of functional numerical concepts. As noted previously, instruction should occur in the community using natural settings to maximize the meaningfulness and relevancy of the instruction and to allow for the integration of skills from other domains (Thoma, Bartholomew, & Scott, 2009). An illustration of this type of activity would be a trip to a local grocery store, where several different functional skills could be practiced. The goal of these activities, and others like them, is to decrease the students' dependence on others and to enhance their ability to live and work independently in their community.

Standards-Based Curriculum

In some instances, a functional curriculum approach may not be appropriate. The needs of some individuals with intellectual disability may best be served by exposure to both traditional academic subjects—in other words, the general education curriculum—and life skills, depending on the needs of the student and the wishes of the parents. As students get older and progress through school, however, there is sometimes a sense

community-based instruction:
A strategy for teaching functional skills in the environment in which they would naturally occur rather than in simulated settings.

VIDEO
Community-Based Instruction

■ ■ ■ ■ ■ Table 6.5 **Approaches for Teaching Functional Academics**

Academic Approach	Learning Outcomes	Examples
Functional, generalized skills usable across life routines	Student will learn some pivotal skills (e.g., useful word and number recognition and counting) and use them in home, school, and community activities.	Sharon is mastering generalized counting skills. She can count dollars to make a purchase, objects to do simple addition in math class, and ingredients when cooking with her mother. She not only learns sight words related to daily activities, such as following her schedule, but also learns high-frequency words that she uses in reading and other academic subjects.
Embedded academic skills usable in specific life routines	Student will acquire an academic response as part of a daily life routine (e.g., use money to buy school lunch; use time and word schedule to organize day).	Juan has a sight word vocabulary of five words. He uses each of these words in a specific way. For example, he finds his name on a set of job cards at his work site. He can select a sweatshirt that has the name of his school to wear on school spirit day.
Adaptations to bypass academic skills	Student will learn to use adaptations that avoid the need for an academic skill (e.g., money envelopes, bus passes).	Because it is difficult for Lauren to count money, her teacher helps her use a predetermined amount of money to make purchases (e.g., a dollar for a soda).

SOURCE: Adapted from M. Snell and F. Brown, *Instruction of Students with Severe Disabilities,* 5th ed. (Upper Saddle River, NJ: Prentice Hall, 2000), p. 498.

of urgency to incorporate a life skills curriculum in preparation for adulthood. Yet one perplexing challenge confronting both general and special educators is how to blend or integrate rigorous academic content standards with a life skills curriculum (Hoover & Patton, 2004; McDonnell & Copeland, 2011; Polloway et al., 2013). Recall that IDEA 2004 mandates that the IEP team consider how the student will participate and progress in the general education curriculum regardless of the severity of his or her disability.

In some ways, a functional curriculum runs counter to the basic tenets of the philosophy of full inclusion with its emphasis on age- and grade-appropriate placement and thereby exposure to the general education curriculum. Does this philosophy mean that a student with intellectual disability should enroll, for example, in a geometry or foreign language class? In some instances, the answer might be yes; in other cases, this would be an inappropriate recommendation. The IEP team must identify academic skills that are aligned with the state's academic content standards while ensuring that the skills selected for instruction also allow the pupil to participate successfully in school, home, and community settings (McDonnell & Copeland, 2011).

We believe that all students with intellectual disability should be integrated, to the maximum extent possible, in classrooms and activities with their same-age peers who are not disabled. The general education classroom with its focus on the general education curriculum, however, is not necessarily the appropriate learning environment for all pupils with an intellectual disability. Some pupils will achieve greater educational benefit from a functional curriculum taught in settings outside of school. The key to an appropriate education for students with intellectual disability is individualization. Just as all students in the general education classroom do not learn the same material, pupils with intellectual disability must have their instructional program developed around their unique characteristics and specific educational requirements.

Instructional Methodology

Once a decision is made about what to teach, educators are then confronted with the question of how best to instruct their students. These important issues are interrelated. Decisions that professionals make about what and how to teach pupils with intellectual disability are crucial for the students' success in school (Beirne-Smith et al., 2006). We will now briefly examine representative instructional strategies that have proven effective with individuals with intellectual disability.

Instructional methodologies and accommodations that are often used with pupils with intellectual disability are the same ones that make learning successful for all students (Friend & Bursuck, 2012). Friend and Bursuck (2012) believe that general educators are capable of reasonably accommodating in their classrooms most students with special needs, including pupils with intellectual disability. To accomplish this goal, they recommend the following seven steps, which they call INCLUDE:

- **I**dentify classroom demands.
- **N**ote student learning strengths and needs.
- **C**heck for potential areas of student success.
- **L**ook for potential problem areas.
- **U**se information to brainstorm ways to differentiate instruction.
- **D**ifferentiate instruction.
- **E**valuate student progress. (p. 132)

This generic model is applicable to a variety of classroom settings. It is based on the assumption that student performance is a result of the interaction between the learner's characteristics and the instructional environment. By skillfully analyzing the student's learning needs and the requirements of the classroom, teachers are often able to maximize student success and accomplishment.

Similarly, Smith, Polloway, Patton, and Dowdy (2012) recommend that teachers consider the following teaching and learning adaptations, which are designed to improve learning outcomes for students with intellectual disability:

- Ensure attention to relevant task demands.
- Teach ways to learn content while teaching content itself.
- Focus on content that is meaningful to the students, to promote learning as well as to facilitate application.
- Provide training that crosses multiple learning and environmental contexts.
- Offer opportunities for active involvement in the learning process. (p. 245)

In our opinion, these suggestions are applicable to all pupils, not just individuals with intellectual disability.

Task Analysis

We begin with an approach known as task analysis, which is often identified with a functional or life skills curriculum. A functional curriculum is a highly individualized, individually referenced model (Hickson, Blackman, & Reis, 1995) in which the teacher crafts each pupil's curriculum based on the skills and abilities that are part of the student's repertoire. In task analysis, which is part of a behavioral approach to instruction, a complex behavior or task is broken down and sequenced into its component parts (Alberto & Troutman, 2013). Task analysis, according to Alberto and Troutman

task analysis: An instructional methodology whereby complex tasks are analyzed and broken down into sequential component parts; each part is taught separately and then as a whole.

VIDEO

Assessment

(2013), is the foundation for teaching complex functional and vocational skills to individuals with disabilities.

Alberto and Troutman (2013) offer working guidelines that define the basic steps for conducting a task analysis:

- Define the target behavior or task.
- Identify the prerequisite skills for learning the task: "What does the student need to know?"
- Identify needed materials to perform the task.
- Observe a competent person performing the task, and list the steps necessary for successful task completion in sequential order.

Cooperative learning is a popular instructional strategy for teaching pupils with intellectual disability in inclusive settings.

We believe that an additional component is necessary. Teachers must take steps to ensure that the student is capable of generalizing the particular skill to other settings. Recall that this is part of the reasoning for teaching functional skills in the student's natural setting.

Over the years researchers have used task analysis to teach a wide variety of daily living and vocational skills to individuals with varying degrees of cognitive impairment. Examples of these successful efforts include teaching food preparation skills to elementary students with moderate to severe intellectual disability (Fiscus, Schuster, Morse, & Collins, 2002), teaching functional counting skills to young children with moderate to severe intellectual disability (Xin & Holmdal, 2003), teaching laundry skills to high school students with moderate intellectual disability (Taylor, Collins, Schuster, & Kleinert, 2002), and teaching leisure time activities to adults with intellectual disability (Jared, Frantino, & Sturmey, 2007).

Cooperative Learning

Cooperative learning is another instructional intervention that educators frequently employ, especially when teaching pupils with intellectual disability in inclusive or integrated settings. Unlike most of today's classrooms, which tend to emphasize competition among students, cooperative learning encourages pupils with varying strengths and abilities to work together toward achieving a common goal. Cooperative learning can be defined as an instructional technique in which small, heterogeneous groups of learners are actively involved in jointly accomplishing an activity or assignment. The teacher structures the task in such a fashion that each pupil significantly contributes to the completion of the activity according to his or her ability. Although recognition and rewards are based on group performance, the success of each individual directly affects the accomplishments of his or her classmates (Johnson, Johnson, & Holubec, 1998, 2002).

Cooperative learning, which can take many different forms and be used across multiple subject areas, requires careful planning and consideration of the needs and

cooperative learning: Instructional process whereby heterogeneous groups of students work together on an assignment.

VIDEO

Cooperative Learning

SUGGESTIONS FOR THE CLASSROOM

Using Scaffolding in the Classroom

→ **Introduce the concept**. List all of the steps in the strategy using concrete illustrations. Teacher then models the strategy.

→ **Regulate difficulty during guided practice**. Strategy is presented one step at a time using simplified situations. Pupils are guided through the process with the teacher providing assistance.

→ **Provide varying contexts for student practice**. Students initially practice the strategy using authentic problems under the guidance of their teacher. Pupils eventually conduct practice sessions in small-group settings.

→ **Provide feedback**. Instructor provides constructive feedback. Evaluative checklists are available so students can self-evaluate their performance.

→ **Increase student responsibility**. Students are required to use the strategies independently. As pupils become increasingly proficient, supports are gradually decreased. Teacher evaluates for student mastery.

→ **Provide independent practice**. Students are provided with extensive opportunities for practice and apply the steps to novel situations. (Friend & Bursuck, 2012)

abilities of each team member. Pupils with disabilities, for example, may require special preparation and support to ensure their maximum participation (Johnson et al., 1998). Teachers may need to review specific social skills with their students with intellectual disability in order for them to successfully participate and benefit from this experience.

Cooperative learning has been shown to increase the opportunities for students with disabilities to experience success in school (Lewis & Doorlag, 2011). Cooperative learning benefits all pupils, contributes significantly to student achievement, enhances the self-esteem of individuals with special needs, and increases the acceptance and understanding of children with disabilities (Smith et al., 2008).

Scaffolding

Our final example is a teaching strategy called scaffolding. This technique is especially applicable to students with intellectual disability, who are often characterized as "inactive" or "passive" learners. The aim of this approach is to help pupils become independent, proficient problem solvers. Scaffolding is a cognitive approach to instruction. In this teacher-directed strategy, various forms of support are provided to students as they initially engage in learning a new task or skill. As the student becomes increasingly competent, the supports or "scaffolds" are gradually removed.

Vaughn and Bos (2012) describe scaffolding as a way of

adjusting and extending instruction so that the student is challenged and able to develop new skills. The teacher can scaffold instruction to meet the needs of the students by manipulating the task, materials, group size, pace, presentation, and so on. The metaphor of a scaffold captures the idea of an adjustable and temporary support that can be removed when it is no longer needed. (p. 25)

scaffolding: A cognitive teaching strategy in which teacher provides temporary support to student who is learning a new task; supports are gradually removed as pupil becomes increasingly competent with the activity.

This instructional method begins with what the pupil already knows and attempts to connect new information with previously learned material. New information is presented in a logical sequence, building on the student's knowledge base. Pupils are then

REFERENCE
Scaffolding

Steps to Good Teaching

Students with intellectual disability, like other pupils, typically respond to well-planned instructional strategies. The following mnemonic (CLOCS-RAM) identifies eight steps that are characteristic of good teaching.

C = Clarity — The student must know exactly what to do (i.e., have no doubt about what is expected).

L = Level — The student must be able to do the task with a high degree of accuracy (i.e., be able to get at least 80% correct), but the task must be challenging (i.e., the student should not easily get 100% correct repeatedly).

O = Opportunities — The student must have frequent opportunities to respond (i.e., be actively engaged in the task a high percentage of the time).

C = Consequences — The student must receive a meaningful reward for correct performance (i.e., the consequences of correct performance must be frequent and perceived as desirable by the student).

S = Sequence — The tasks must be presented in logical sequence so that the student gets the big idea (i.e., steps must be presented and learned so that the knowledge or skill is built on a logical progression or framework of ideas, which is a systematic curriculum).

R = Relevance — The task must be relevant to the student's life and, if possible, the student understands how and why it is useful (i.e., the teacher attempts to help the student see why the task is important in the culture).

A = Application — The teacher helps the student learn how to learn and remember by teaching memory and learning strategies and applying knowledge and skills to everyday problems (i.e., teaches generalizations, not just isolated skills, and honors the student's culture).

M = Monitoring — The teacher continuously monitors student progress and always knows and can show what the student has mastered and the student's place or level in a curriculum or sequence of tasks.

SOURCE: J. Kauffman, P. Pullen, M. Mostert, and S. Trent, *Managing Classroom Behavior,* 5th ed. (Boston, MA: Allyn & Bacon, 2011), p. 25.

given the opportunity to apply and practice what they have learned. Suggestions for using this instructional technique can be found in the accompanying Suggestions for the Classroom (page 188).

These three examples are by no means the only instructional models appropriate for students with intellectual disability. Other approaches, such as direct instruction and learning strategies (discussed in Chapter 7), are also useful.

Services for Young Children With Intellectual Disability

The importance of early intervention for young children identified as, or suspected of being, intellectually disabled cannot be overestimated. Early intervention can be defined as the services and supports rendered to children age 3 and younger with disabilities, or those who evidence risk factors, and their families. Early intervention

As an eighth-grade English language arts teacher with over a decade of teaching experience, I find teaching to be a new adventure every day.

I strive to enhance the learning opportunities for all of my students. Many of my current students are struggling writers, as identified by teachers from previous years. Keeping these students involved, interested, and yearning to learn, but at the same time making sure that every child is challenged and thriving, can sometimes be a difficult task. But I have asked for this setting because I want to rise to the occasion and see my students succeed.

Inclusive Education Experience

Working in an inclusive classroom takes careful planning. First, I make sure that I know my students' abilities and needs. I make the classroom inclusive of all learners, which builds a positive community. I have had students in my regular English classes who are visually impaired, students who are in wheelchairs, and students who are self-contained in another teacher's room except for reading class. I have come to understand the importance of community and peer support. The teacher in any classroom, but especially the inclusive classroom, becomes the coach or facilitator of learning. Since the children come to school at multiple levels of learning, the teacher must meet the student where he or she is in the learning process and build from that point.

The challenge lies in assisting each child at his or her level and moving him or her along in the learning process. With one teacher and a class of twenty-five learners, moving around the class to help every child is difficult. The student–teacher ratio is high in the regular education class. Another challenge is keeping up with the paperwork that informs the teacher of the accommodations or modifications in the child's IEP. Third, a child who is too challenged or is not challenged enough can become frustrated, which may lead to other disruptive classroom issues. Finally, having all of the students involved in learning at the same time with material that everyone can understand is a challenge. Some students may feel comfortable reading lower-level books while others need more advanced materials. As their teacher, I am responsible for teaching them all.

I am constantly working on resolutions for my dilemmas, however, and I come closer to my answers every day. I rely on my colleagues for ideas that work in their classes. We have an idea exchange at team meetings as we discuss pedagogy and students. I learn from reading professional articles and books. I have always individualized my instruction, but I have learned to do it more effectively.

Strategies for Inclusive Classrooms

Collaboration with special education teachers is a must. They have teaching tips that work well with all students.

- Accommodate instruction and assignments as needed to ensure success for all students, not just those with IEPs; however, only modify assignments for those students who have IEPs. Simple accommodations include providing a word bank for vocabulary quizzes, a study guide before a test, rubrics before a project, a copy of class notes, a book on audiotape, and the use of a computer. Testing or quizzing accommodations include reading a quiz or test aloud to a student, allowing the student to read the quiz or test aloud, explaining directions or language, reducing the number of choices but covering the same objectives, extending the time permitted, allowing the student to dictate his or her answers, allowing mistakes to be corrected for extra points, or allowing a test to be retaken for an average of both scores.
- Understand the importance of presentation. Type assignment directions, activity sheets, quizzes, and tests in a larger font size such as 14 point to make the print easier to read. Be sure the print is clear and legible for the student. Allow students to use a note card to read line-by-line multiple-choice answers separately. Allow for white space around directions so the students will not confuse the directions with the actual test or quiz questions.
- Teach students that organization is pertinent to learning success. Allow a peer to help a student organize his or her notebook. Often a student has difficulty studying because he or she lacks the organizational skills needed to prepare for tests or quizzes.
- Realize that students are often embarrassed to ask for help during class. Periodically monitor students' progress throughout class by individually inquiring with each student about his or her progress. Be available before and

represents a consortium of services—not just educational assistance but also health care, social services, family supports, and other benefits. The aim of early intervention is to affect positively the overall development of the child—his or her social, emotional, physical, and intellectual well-being. Thanks to the work of social scientists from various

after school for study sessions and in between classes for additional assistance.

- Make sure students are on task by walking around their desks and prompting them to return to the task at hand if they are not working diligently.
- Elicit the aid of parents in a three-way partnership among student, parents, and teacher. Communicate the progress of the student through the student's daily assignment agenda. For example, have the student record any special assignments or daily homework in an agenda. This teaches the student the responsibility of finding out the daily requirements expected of him or her. As a teacher, read the student's agenda and clarify any mistakes or omissions the student may have made, record any newly earned grades, and comment on the student's progress. At night, parents also check the student's agenda and communicate any questions or comments by writing in the student's agenda for the teachers to read the following day.

Working With Parents and Families

Parents want to be informed. When a student does not do well on an assignment or seems to fall behind in class, contact the parents via e-mail, phone, or note or in person to inform them of their child's progress or any concerns. Parents also enjoy seeing samples of their child's classwork. For instance, sending home a portfolio during each grading period gives parents an opportunity to see growth in writing skills or progress in reading comprehension. A commentary sheet requesting parents and child to analyze the enclosed work is an excellent means of feedback for teachers. This process of commenting on favorite pieces of writing and selecting a writing piece for publication in a contest or school literary magazine also causes the child to reflect on his or her improvements.

Hosting parent seminars as a team of teachers once a semester on topics such as "Boosting Your Child's Study Habits," "Interpreting SAT-10 Scores" with an emphasis on building on strengths and improving weaknesses, and "Improving Reading Comprehension With Reading Strategies" provides an avenue for improving students' learning with the collaboration of students, parents, and teachers. Parents often desire to help their child at home but are not always equipped with the necessary tools to do so. Through parent seminars, parents learn strategies they can use at home to reinforce

the learning that takes place at school. Parents learn of these seminars and other events through team newsletters that are distributed with report cards or progress reports during each grading period.

Each effort at communication through phone calls, notes, person-to-person contact, or e-mail is recorded in my communication log, including the name of the person with whom I spoke, the means of communication, the time and date, and a brief description of the conversation. This helps me to remember the conversation's details in case I need to follow up with the student and parent in the future.

Advice for Making Inclusion and Collaboration Work

My advice to new teachers working in inclusive settings would be to learn as much as possible not only about a student's academic needs but also about the student as a person. Sometimes just knowing about a student's personal interests can be a catalyst to help him or her improve learning. Learn about the student's academic performance and needs by talking with the special education teacher and reviewing last year's report card, standardized test scores, and portfolio. Learn about the student's personal interests by having the student complete a reading and writing questionnaire, participate in book talks or reading/writing conferences, and observe the student interacting with other students. Use the knowledge that you have gained to improve students' learning progress.

Knowing a child's learning styles, needs, and strengths allows you to approach the child's difficulties and challenges with new insight. This also shows the student that you care about him or her as an individual and not just as a member of a class. Finally, do not be afraid to continue to elicit the help of parents, special education teachers, other team teachers, counselors, administrators, and other education professionals who work directly with the child. Sharing ideas and collaborating with others will greatly benefit all involved.

–**Tonya Perry**
Former middle school language arts teacher
Alabama State Teacher of the Year 2001
One of the four national finalists,
National Teacher of the Year 2001
Currently, Assistant Professor,
University of Alabama at Birmingham

disciplines, federally funded research projects, and the impact of legislation such as PL 99–457 (the Education of the Handicapped Act Amendments of 1986), significant advancements have occurred in this arena. As a result, the quality of life for countless youngsters with intellectual disability and other impairments has been improved.

VIDEO
Inclusion

Hickson et al. (1995) describe two main goals of early intervention for young children with intellectual disability. The focus of these efforts varies, depending on the severity of the impairment. For preschoolers considered to have moderate or greater degrees of intellectual disability, the main emphasis is on furthering their development by reducing delays in reaching significant developmental and cognitive milestones, such as walking or talking. (Similar programs that focus on infants with intellectual disability, such as babies with Down syndrome, are frequently identified as infant stimulation programs.) Some youngsters may also profit from programs that stress functional objectives centered on activities of daily living. Children thought to have a mild intellectual disability and those considered to be at risk will benefit from programs whose chief aim is to prepare these young students for successful academic experiences upon entering school. These experts go on to state that the primary objectives of early intervention for young children with less severe cognitive limitations are "(1) to minimize and, if possible, reverse the impact of delays or deficits in normal cognitive development on later school performance; and (2) to support family efforts to achieve desired intellectual, vocational, and social outcomes" (Hickson et al., 1995, p. 223). The second goal, in our opinion, seems to be appropriate for all individuals with intellectual disability regardless of their age or severity of impairment.

To these two laudable goals we would like to add a third objective: prevention of intellectual disability. You may remember that in Chapter 1 we reviewed the benefits of early intervention for young children who were at increased risk of delayed development and possible intellectual disability due to environmental factors such as poverty and related conditions. Gargiulo and Kilgo (2014) identify these children as being environmentally at risk. Children who are at risk or highly vulnerable for cognitive impairments include youngsters with established risk—that is, children with a diagnosed medical disorder of known etiology and a predictable outcome or prognosis, such as Down syndrome or fragile X syndrome. In other cases, infants, toddlers, and preschoolers who are biologically at risk for intellectual delays and deficits because of low birth weight, prematurity, fetal alcohol syndrome, or HIV infection often profit from involvement with early intervention activities.

It is important to keep in mind that early intervention programs for youngsters with intellectual disability, regardless of the severity of cognitive impairment, are not designed as "anti–intellectual disability vaccinations"; rather, they are a first step in a comprehensive, coordinated, and ongoing effort aimed at enhancing the child's potential in all areas of development. Combating the deleterious effects of intellectual disability will require a coordinated effort among parents, professionals, advocates, and government officials.

Today, many early intervention programs are structured around a concept known as family-centered early intervention. Although the needs of young children with disabilities are an important intervention focus, early interventionists and other service providers are becoming increasingly aware that the needs of youngsters are often inseparable from those of their family. Young children with special needs frequently require a constellation of services based not only on their specific needs but also on the differential needs of the family unit. Family-centered early intervention embraces a positive view of the youngster's family; professionals now talk about enabling and empowering families rather than viewing the child and his or her family as having deficits that necessitate intervention to "fix" the problem. This movement away from a deficit model reflects contemporary thinking (Gargiulo & Kilgo, 2014).

An emphasis on family-centered early intervention characterizes many early childhood special education programs, but it is important to remember that the delivery of services is customized to meet the unique needs of the child as well as the

infant stimulation: Programs for infants with disabilities or those experiencing delays; emphasis usually on achieving developmental or cognitive milestones.

environmentally at risk: Youngsters who are biologically typical yet encounter life experiences or environmental circumstances that are so limiting that there is the possibility of future delayed development.

established risk: Youngsters with a diagnosed medical disorder of known etiology and predictable prognosis or outcome.

biologically at risk: Young children with a history of pre-, peri-, or postnatal conditions and developmental events that heighten the potential for later atypical development.

family-centered early intervention: A philosophy of working with families that stresses family strengths and capabilities, the enhancement of skills, and the development of mutual partnerships between service providers and families.

family. Besides the importance attached to individualization, effective programs are comprehensive, normalized, and outcome based, and provide for interaction between disabled and nondisabled youngsters. These benchmarks are appropriate regardless of the curriculum orientation adopted. Typical approaches include a developmental model based largely on the theorizing of Jean Piaget, an operant or behavioral approach consistent with the work of B. F. Skinner, the Montessori method, and a functional curriculum representing a hybrid of the first two approaches. Beirne-Smith et al. (2006) note that no one approach has been shown to be clearly superior to the others and stress that "curriculum should be chosen based on the individual needs of the child and the family" (p. 340).

Transition Into Adulthood

Adolescence is a time of transition and, for individuals with intellectual disability, one that is often difficult and stressful. Edgar (1988) characterizes this period of movement from student to independent adulthood as one of "floundering." For many young adults with intellectual disability, this journey is not a successful one. Becoming a productive, self-sufficient, and independent adult frequently remains an elusive goal.

The graduates of special education programs, according to Drew and Hardman (2007), do not yet participate fully in the economic and social mainstream of their communities. Today, unfortunately, many individuals with intellectual disability either are underemployed or remain unemployed. Besides employment difficulties, researchers have found that for many citizens with intellectual disability, independent living is an objective not yet attained (Kessler Foundation/National Organization on Disability, 2010; National Longitudinal Transition Study 2, 2009). The preceding evidence suggests that professionals must do a better job of planning timely transitioning experiences for adolescents with intellectual disability if they are to reach their full potential as adults.

Transition planning is a shared responsibility of educators and other school personnel, adult service providers from the community, family members, and, perhaps most important, the student. It is a comprehensive and collaborative activity focusing on adult outcomes that are responsive to the adolescent's goals and vision for adulthood (Sitlington, Neubert, & Clark, 2009). Thoma (1999) believes that meaningful transition planning requires that adult team members listen to and respect the desires and preferences of the student for his or her own adult lifestyle. You may also remember that transition services are mandated by federal law.

Successful adjustment as an independent adult requires careful planning commencing long before graduation from high school. Public Law 108–446, which reauthorized IDEA, requires that transition services begin no later than the first IEP in effect when the student turns 16 (and be updated annually). This legislation also established a new requirement for postsecondary goals pertaining to appropriate education, training, employment, and independent living skills.

In earlier chapters, we reviewed the requirements for effective transition planning and the key elements of an individualized transition plan or ITP. Here we focus on the area that is probably preeminent in transition planning for adolescents with intellectual disability: employment.

For most individuals, with or without intellectual disability, work is an important part of daily life. Work is often used as a gauge of social status, financial success, and personal fulfillment, and is a vehicle for opportunities to participate in one's community. Oftentimes uninformed persons believe that individuals with intellectual disability are incapable of obtaining and holding a job. This is simply not true, even though

VIDEO

Transition Services

Many adults with intellectual disability are capable of working successfully in the community.

employment rates for adults with intellectual disability are dismal—especially for young women with intellectual disability (Kessler Foundation/National Organization on Disability, 2010; National Longitudinal Transition Study 2, 2009). Generally speaking, with appropriate training, individuals with intellectual disability are able to secure and maintain meaningful and gainful employment. Persons who are intellectually disabled make good employees. In those cases where they are unsuccessful on the job, it is frequently due not to their skill level or job performance but to a lack of interpersonal and social behaviors appropriate to the workplace.

Training is often the key to successful employment, and it begins during the transition period. Historically speaking, early job training programs centered on a model known as a **sheltered workshop**. At one time this was a very popular training option, particularly for individuals with moderate or severe intellectual disability, who typically require long-term and intense support. Sheltered workshops are generally large facilities that provide job training in a segregated environment. Clients, as the workers are called, typically work on contract jobs that are often repetitive in nature and require low skill level—for instance, sorting "junk mail" inserts. Typically, these jobs are of short duration and offer the clients minimal job training. Placement in a sheltered workshop may, in some cases, be transitional to obtaining employment in the community, but it is more likely to be a permanent position.

In recent years, sheltered workshops have come under fire. Critics (Migliore, Mank, Grossi, & Rogan, 2007; Murphy, Rogan, Handley, Kincaid, & Royce-Davis, 2002; Simmons & Flexer, 2013) have focused their attention on the low wages paid to workers, the segregated work setting, the absence of meaningful training, and the failure to move clients into competitive employment. This dissatisfaction, coupled with the contemporary movement toward more integrated and normalized experiences for individuals with intellectual disability, has given rise to the notion of **supported competitive employment**. In this model, which has proven effective in preparing adolescents for employment in community settings, an individual with intellectual disability is placed on a competitive job site alongside other workers who are not disabled. A **job coach** or employment specialist provides on-the-job assistance and support to the worker with intellectual disability. This person's role is to train the adolescent with intellectual disability on the specific job requirements and then, as everyone hopes, to decrease support services as the employee becomes more proficient. Job coaches are also usually responsible for locating the job and matching the needs of the employer to the abilities of the student (worker).

The use of a supported competitive employment model has grown significantly over the past decade; it has been shown to be a cost-effective strategy with benefits accruing to both employer and employee (Beirne-Smith et al., 2006; Simmons & Flexer, 2013). Researchers have found that individuals with intellectual disability who are prepared

sheltered workshop: A structured work environment for persons with disabilities in which vocational and social skills are often the focus of attention; may be a temporary or permanent placement.

supported competitive employment: At a work site for typical workers, individuals with disabilities are employed and work alongside their typical peers but receive ongoing assistance from a job coach.

job coach: An individual who supervises a person with a disability for all or part of the day to provide training, assistance, or support to maintain a job.

using this approach tend to function better in competitive employment settings than persons who have experience only in sheltered workshops (McDonnell, Hardman, & McDonnell, 2003), in addition to reporting higher job satisfaction (Test, Carver, Evers, Haddad, & Person, 2000). Employment opportunities typically range from entry-level custodial or food service positions to jobs in various high-technology industries.

Although this model is in keeping with contemporary thinking regarding self-determination (discussed in the next section of this chapter), supportive competitive employment has its limitations. Some of the drawbacks include excessive dependence on the job coach, disruption of the work environment by the presence of the job coach, and differential performance when the job coach is on-site (Simmons & Flexer, 2013). These disadvantages have contributed to the idea of using coworkers as natural supports (Mank, Cioffi, & Yovanoff, 2003). These individuals typically function as mentors and friends, offering valuable assistance and encouragement as needed to workers with intellectual disability.

For many young adults with intellectual disability, competitive employment is a realistic goal. By providing early and carefully crafted transitioning experiences, schools can maximize the probability that students with intellectual disability will have successful postschool adjustment, not only in the area of employment but in other domains as well.

Adults With Intellectual Disability

Over the past several years, professionals and advocates alike have devoted increased attention to the needs of adults with intellectual disability. For some of these individuals, successful adjustment to the community is an appropriate and achievable objective. For all intents and purposes, they are no different from most adults without disabilities, although at times they may require (as others sometimes do) support and assistance from family members, friends, coworkers, or social service agencies. Here we will focus on the community adjustment of adults with intellectual disability who require more intense and ongoing support.

Earlier in this chapter, we introduced the principle of normalization, defined as "making available to the mentally retarded [intellectually disabled] patterns and conditions of everyday life which are as close as possible to the norms and patterns of the mainstream of society" (Nirje, 1969, p. 181). The principle of normalization attempts "to establish and/or maintain personal behaviors which are as culturally normative as possible" (Wolfensberger, 1972, p. 28). The overarching philosophy is that individuals with intellectual disability (and other disabilities) should be integrated, to the greatest extent possible, into all aspects of daily life such as employment, recreation, living arrangements, and other areas of community life.

The principle of normalization has given rise to the belief that individuals with intellectual disability, especially those with more severe cognitive impairments, have a right to make their own choices and decisions in life and to become as independent as possible—in short, to have some degree of personal control over their own lives. These decisions may be as simple as what to watch on television, what time to go to bed, or which dress to wear, or they may involve more profound choices, such as where to live and with whom. This decision-making capacity is often referred to as **self-determination** or, to use AAIDD terminology, self-direction. Self-direction is often seen as a crucial component for success in later adult life for individuals with intellectual disability (Hughes, Washington, & Brown, 2008). Although self-determination is a critical adaptive skill, educators should bear in mind that self-determination reflects North American and Western European ideals and beliefs; other cultures may not value independence and personal decision making as highly as European Americans. Teachers,

self-determination: Self-advocacy efforts by an individual with a disability; expression of desire to live one's life according to one's own wishes; assuming personal control over one's life.

VIDEO

Adulthood

Persons with intellectual disability are seeking greater control over their lives and fuller participation in all aspects of society.

therefore, are strongly encouraged to consider the cultural preferences and heritage of their pupils when formulating instructional strategies for developing skills in self-determination (Turnbull, Turnbull, Erwin, Soodak, & Shogren, 2011).

Because free choice is typically a restricted activity for large numbers of adults with intellectual disability, self-advocacy is gaining in both popularity and importance. People with intellectual disability are encouraged, via self-help groups, to speak out on issues of personal importance, such as living arrangements and personal relationships. The purpose of self-advocacy is for individuals with intellectual disability to gain greater personal control over their lives and to foster their own independence. Self-advocacy empowers people and helps them to assertively state their needs, wants, and desires. Of course, successfully adjusting to life in one's community requires more than skills in self-determination and self-advocacy; it is also predicated of acceptance and support from the general public.

Family Issues

A child with intellectual disability (or any other disability) typically elicits a wide range of emotional responses, which can vary from anger and denial to awareness and acceptance. Additionally, parents may worry about financial obligations, educational concerns, the impact of the disability on siblings, long-term care requirements, and a host of other fears. These families often require understanding, assistance, and support. The importance of a natural support network, which may include coworkers, neighbors, friends, aunts and uncles, and other family members, should not be underestimated (McDonnell et al., 2003). For many parents of children with disabilities, these individuals, and not professionals, serve as the "first line of defense" in dealing with a child who is recognized as intellectually disabled. Other parents of youngsters with Down syndrome, for example, can often provide sensitive assistance and serve as a valuable resource on community services for infants with special needs. Long-term and mutually sustaining relationships are frequently established between parents of children with intellectual disability because of this common connection. Support is necessary because a child with intellectual disability may significantly affect the structure, function, and overall development of the entire family constellation (Gargiulo & Kilgo, 2014). In this case, valuable assistance is available from The Arc, a national organization on intellectual disability, which offers information and support not only to parents but also to siblings and other family members, such as grandparents.

It is impossible to predict how a family will respond to a child with intellectual disability. This term means different things to different families. As a society, we must value all families and should not overlook the potential benefits that an individual with intellectual disability brings to his or her family. See the accompanying First Person feature written by a young adult with Down syndrome.

self-advocacy: Speaking out for one's personal preferences; protecting one's own interests.

AUDIO
College

REFERENCE
Family

FIRST PERSON: MEREDITH

In Her Own Words

What can you tell us about yourself and your family?

I am Meredith, age 22, and I live with my parents in Alabama. I have a younger brother named Zach. One of my favorite childhood memories is dressing up at Halloween. Zach was Captain Hook, and I was Peter Pan, and another time he was a cowboy and I was an Indian. We also had fun at Christmas, which is my favorite holiday to celebrate. My family has many traditions I enjoy. One is getting an ornament each year to remind us of our interests, like my Barbie Doll collection, and my two former dogs, Scamper and Misha.

What do you like to do in your free time?

For fun, I go out with my boyfriend, Matthew, or my girlfriends. Matthew and I usually go out to dinner and a movie. We take turns having dinner at each other's house, and we love watching the Three Stooges videos. I'm also involved with People First, a self-advocacy group for people with disabilities. I am the chaplain and open the meeting with words of encouragement about having a positive attitude. At church I help out in the fourth-grade Religious Education classroom. I also volunteer for the North Shelby County Library and Alabama Wildlife Rehabilitation Center.

What can you tell us about your experience at school?

I graduated from Oak Mountain High School. During high school, I was nominated for the Homecoming Court, and was voted Best Choral Student. I really enjoyed high school because it had a great atmosphere and I had many friends. My favorite subjects were government, choir, and environmental science. I also liked our pep rallies and football games. My least favorite subject was math. My best high school memory is getting to be in the Macy's Thanksgiving Day parade. We walked three miles singing and dancing in New York City, where it was very cold. Some of the challenges were trying to be smart and independent. While in high school I joined the Special Olympics Rhythmic Gymnastics Team, and I still compete today. I also am on a Special Olympics bowling team.

What can you tell us about your work background?

During my senior year, I started to get work experience. I got to work at a video store, a card shop, a restaurant, and Jefferson State Community College. My first real job was at a department store, where I helped organize and fold clothes. I don't have a job right now, but I'm working with my job coach to find one. I'd like to work in an office or clothing store.

What do you see yourself doing in the future?

My dream for the future is to have a job, live in my own place, and maybe one day get married. My grandmother, who was very sweet, is my role model. She was a very strong woman and never complained even though she had diabetes for over fifty years. She always encouraged me to be healthy and take care of myself.

What is one thing you want people to remember about you?

I would like people to know that I love my life.

❖

When our daughter, Meredith, was born with Down syndrome, we faced numerous medical, social, and educational challenges. We had no way of knowing that very soon we would become partners with doctors; speech, physical, and occupational therapists; early interventionists; teachers; job coaches; and other advocates who value the rights and dignity of individuals with disabilities. This partnership has created lasting bonds of friendship, changed attitudes, strengthened inclusive educational practices, and allowed Meredith to achieve many goals.

Meredith's literary abilities have far exceeded our earliest expectations. She is an excellent reader with incredible spelling and comprehension skills. Her passion for learning and wanting to educate herself is remarkable. Meredith is a delightful, self-confident young woman with a sense of humor; knows no prejudice; and loves unconditionally. Meredith is an extraordinary person trying to live an ordinary life, and we are blessed to be her parents. ■

Issues of Diversity

A long-standing concern exists among special educators about the misclassification and/or inappropriate placement of students from culturally/linguistically diverse backgrounds in special education programs. All too often, diversity is incorrectly linked with disability. It is indeed unfortunate that children from minority groups are frequently seen as deviant or disabled.

The issue of cultural diversity is intricately interwoven into the fabric of American special education. It is related to discussions of identification, assessment procedures, etiology, educational placement, and intervention. The overrepresentation of children of color is particularly relevant to a discussion of intellectual disability. While African American youth, for example, constitute only 15 percent of public school enrollment (National Center for Education Statistics, 2012a), more than one out of every four pupils in classes for individuals with intellectual disability are from this group (U.S. Department of Education, 2012a). Drew and Hardman (2007) observe that individuals are often misdiagnosed as intellectually disabled when, in fact, their behavior is more a reflection of cultural differences than an indication of reduced or impaired functioning.

We know that the overrepresentation of minorities in special education classes, especially programs for children with intellectual disability, is a multifaceted problem. Contributing factors range from culturally biased assessment instruments to the insidious role of poverty to teacher bias and expectation. The challenge that continually confronts educators and other professionals is how to combat this problem. The answer to this perplexing issue has eluded special educators for much too long.

Technology and Individuals With Intellectual Disability

Students with intellectual disability, like all pupils with disabilities, use and benefit from a variety of technology, including low-tech (for example, picture symbols), mid-tech (for example, audio recorders), and high-tech (for example, iPads, computer-assisted instruction) assistive technology. From a survey, Wehmeyer, Palmer, Smith, Davies, and Stock (2008) suggested the top technology used by students with intellectual disability were computers; augmentative and alternative communication (AAC), which includes picture symbols and voice output devices in which words or phrases are prerecorded or digitally generated; and self-prompting devices (for example, audio recorders and mobile technologies). Self-operated prompting devices have a long and successful history in the field of educating students with intellectual disability. Self-operated prompting devices—devices individuals use independently that provide prompts in a particular format—have included picture prompts provided through picture symbols, oral prompts provided through audio recorders, and video prompts or video modeling (Mechling, 2007). These options, each with their own advantages and limitations, allow students to be more independent in completing daily activities, such as grocery shopping, vocational tasks/employment, and food preparation or cleaning. Recently prompting for pupils with intellectual disability increasingly involves popular mobile technologies, such as iPods, cell phones, and iPads (Ayres, Mechling, & Sansosti, 2013). Outside of these specific technologies, which are largely used to support daily living and life skills, students with intellectual disability can also benefit from the technologies to support students in the content-area domains of literacy and mathematics as well as organization. Recall that these technologies were discussed in depth in Chapter 5.

Trends, Issues, and Controversies

As we conclude this chapter, we hope that you have gained an understanding of and appreciation for the many complex and often related issues surrounding the subject of intellectual disability. Topics such as amniocentesis and the accompanying question of

augmentative and alternative communication (AAC): Symbols, aids, strategies, and techniques used as a supplement or alternative to oral language.

AUDIO

Chapter 6 Summary

abortion, test bias and the overrepresentation of children of color in programs for students with intellectual disability, concerns about appropriate placement, and thoughts about the quality of life of persons with intellectual disability are only some of the many issues that have captured the attention of parents, educators, policymakers, advocates, legislators, and a host of other concerned individuals.

Like others, we too are concerned about where we have been, where we are today, and what the future holds for the field of intellectual disability. Understanding the present state of affairs is often beneficial when contemplating where we might be headed. In fact, the past is often seen as a prologue to the future. With this in mind, we must point out that although individuals with intellectual disability will most likely benefit from advances in technology, medical breakthroughs, new legislation, and a host of other beneficial developments, attitudinal change is frequently the precursor of a change in the delivery of services and the recognition of the rights of our fellow citizens with disabilities.

Attempting to anticipate where the field of intellectual disability is going is perhaps best left to the futurist or the clairvoyant. This disclaimer notwithstanding, our vision of the future includes the following:

- More community-based activities will be available across several domains, including employment, education, and residential options.
- There will be a growing emphasis on the application of assistive technology to meet the needs of the person with intellectual disability; to varying degrees, individuals with intellectual disability will join the information age.
- Quality of life and normalization across the life span will become increasingly prominent national advocacy issues.
- Human services providers as well as communities will be confronted with a growing geriatric population with intellectual disability.
- Biomedical research and well-designed psychosocial interventions will lead to a reduction in the number of people identified as intellectually disabled.
- More inclusive educational placements will be the norm for students with significant cognitive impairments, requiring intensive supports.
- Greater attention will be paid across all age groups to fostering self-advocacy and self-determination, as persons with intellectual disability seek greater control over their lives and fuller participation in all aspects of society.

Overall, we foresee significant improvement in the coming years in both the quality and the quantity of programs and services for persons with intellectual disability.

CHAPTER IN REVIEW

Defining Intellectual Disability: An Evolving Process

- Contemporary practice considers intellectual disability to be the result of interactions among the person, the environment, and those supports required to maximize the individual's performance in particular settings or environments.

Assessing Intellectual Ability and Adaptive Behavior

- Intelligence is a theoretical construct whose existence can only be inferred on the basis of a person's performance on certain types of cognitive tests that represent only a sample of the person's intellectual skills and abilities.

Classification of Individuals With Intellectual Disability

- Some models group persons with intellectual disability according to the etiology or cause of the disability; others label persons according to the severity of their cognitive impairment, such as mildly or severely intellectually disabled.
- Educators sometimes identify students with intellectual disability as educable mentally retarded (EMR) or trainable mentally retarded (TMR), terms now considered pejorative.
- The 2002 AAIDD definition classifies individuals with intellectual disability on the basis of the extent or levels of support they require to function effectively across adaptive skill areas in various natural settings, such as home, school, or job.

Prevalence of Intellectual Disability

- Currently, approximately 7 percent of all students with disabilities, or about 1 percent of the total school-age population, are recognized as being intellectually disabled.
- The vast majority of persons with intellectual disability have an IQ between 50 and 70–75.

Etiology of Intellectual Disability

- One way of categorizing etiological factors is on the basis of time of onset: before birth (prenatal), around the time of birth (perinatal), or after birth (postnatal).

Characteristics of Individuals With Intellectual Disability

- Common behaviors of persons with intellectual disability include attention deficits, or difficulty focusing and attending to relevant stimuli, and memory problems.
- Past experiences with failure frequently lead individuals with intellectual disability to doubt their own abilities and thus exhibit an external locus of control.
- Recurring episodes of failure also give rise to learned helplessness. These accumulated instances of failure frequently result in a loss of confidence and trust in one's own problem-solving abilities and a reliance on others for direction and guidance. This behavior is identified as outer-directedness.

- Individuals with intellectual impairments also often exhibit poor interpersonal skills and socially inappropriate or immature behaviors.

Educational Considerations

- Students with intellectual disability are more than three times as likely as other children with disabilities to be educated in a self-contained classroom.
- Many students with intellectual disability are exposed to a functional curriculum, whose goal is to equip these children with the skills they require for successful daily living both now and in the future.
- Best practice dictates that instruction occur as much as possible in natural settings rather than simulated environments. This instructional concept is known as community-based instruction.
- Task analysis is frequently used with persons with intellectual disability.
- Cooperative learning is another instructional intervention that educators often employ. This strategy is especially useful when teaching pupils with intellectual disability in inclusive or integrated classrooms.
- Scaffolding, which is a cognitive approach to instruction, is a teacher-directed strategy in which various forms of support are provided to students as they engage in learning a new task or skill.

Adults With Intellectual Disability

- The principle of normalization currently guides the delivery of services to individuals with intellectual disability. This notion suggests that persons with intellectual disability should have a lifestyle that is as culturally normative as possible.
- The principle of normalization has also given rise to the belief that individuals who are intellectually disabled should have a right to make their own choices and decisions about various aspects of their lives. This decision-making capacity is often referred to as self-determination.

Technology and Individuals With Intellectual Disability

- Individuals with intellectual disability are increasingly using various formats of assistive technology in their daily lives.

STUDY QUESTIONS

1. How has the definition of intellectual disability changed over the past several decades?

2. Identify the three key elements of the 1992 AAIDD definition of intellectual disability. How are they conceptually interrelated?

3. Why is the assessment of intelligence such a controversial issue?

4. What is adaptive behavior, and how is it assessed?

5. List four different strategies for classifying individuals with intellectual disability.

6. How have society's view and understanding of persons who are intellectually disabled changed over the centuries?

7. What factors have contributed to the gradual reduction in the number of individuals classified as intellectually disabled?

8. Intellectual disability is often the result of various etiological factors. List seven possible causes of intellectual disability. Give an example of each.

9. How do learned helplessness, outer-directedness, and generalizing affect learning in students with intellectual disability?

10. Define the term *functional academics*. How are functional academics related to the concept of community-based instruction?

11. What is cooperative learning, and why is it a popular instructional technique?

12. List and describe the necessary steps for effectively using scaffolding with students with intellectual disability.

13. How has family-centered early intervention influenced programming activities for young children with intellectual disability?

14. Distinguish between a sheltered workshop for adults with intellectual disability and the contemporary practice of supported competitive employment.

15. How can assistive technology benefit individuals with intellectual disability?

KEY TERMS

standard deviation (SD),   158

adaptive behavior,   158

educable mentally retarded (EMR),   166

trainable mentally retarded (TMR),   166

level of support,   166

natural supports,   167

formal supports,   167

normalization,   168

deinstitutionalization,   169

etiology,   170

prenatal,   170

perinatal,   170

postnatal,   170

Down syndrome,   170

chorionic villus sampling (CVS),   171

amniocentesis,   171

therapeutic abortion,   172

fragile X syndrome,   172

phenylketonuria (PKU),   173

galactosemia,   173

rubella,   174

syphilis,   174

acquired immune deficiency syndrome (AIDS),   174

Rh incompatibility,   174

toxoplasmosis,   174

cytomegalovirus (CMV),   174

fetal alcohol syndrome (FAS),   175

fetal alcohol effect (FAE),   175

anencephaly,   175

microcephaly,   175

hydrocephalus,   175

low birth weight,   175

premature birth,   175

anoxia,   175

hypoxia,   175

birth trauma,   175

breech presentation,   176

precipitous birth,   176

lead poisoning,   176

meningitis,   176

encephalitis,   177

short-term memory,   178

working memory,   178

external locus of control,   178

learned helplessness,   178

outer-directedness,   178

generalizing,   179

functional curriculum,   182

functional academics,   182

community-based instruction,   184

task analysis,   186

cooperative learning,   187

scaffolding,   188

infant stimulation,   192

environmentally at risk,   192

established risk,   192

biologically at risk,   192

family-centered early intervention,   192

sheltered workshop,   194

supported competitive employment,   194

job coach,   194

self-determination,   195

self-advocacy,   196

augmentative and alternative communication (AAC),   198

LEARNING ACTIVITIES

1. Make arrangements to visit classrooms serving students with intellectual disability. What differences did you observe between elementary and secondary programs? Did the instructional program differ for students with severe or profound cognitive impairments in comparison to pupils with mild or moderate intellectual disability? What pedagogical techniques or teaching strategies did the teachers use? How did the other children interact with and relate to their classmates with intellectual disability? Was a particular curriculum incorporated? What was your overall impression of the program; what specific features stood out?

2. Visit several businesses in your community that employ individuals with intellectual disability. Interview the employer or supervisor. Find out how successful these individuals have been. What type of training do workers with intellectual disability require? How have customers and/or coworkers accepted these individuals? Why did the company hire people with an intellectual disability (financial reasons, corporate policy, public relations)? Are they good employees? Have the workers with intellectual disability posed any special challenges or problems for the employer?

3. Visit various residential facilities in your area that serve individuals with intellectual disability. Interview the caregivers. Discover what the daily routine is like for individuals with intellectual disability. Do the various facilities allow for different degrees of independence and decision making on the part of the residents? What is your

opinion of the quality of life of these individuals? How has the community accepted its neighbors with intellectual disability? What supports and services are made available to the residents? Do the individuals with intellectual disability participate in the life of the community—attend special events and festivities; utilize community recreational facilities such as parks, museums, or the zoo; or make purchases in local shops?

4. Involve yourself with various community agencies and organizations that focus on individuals with intellectual disability. Attend a meeting of The Arc or a parent support group. Volunteer to work at the Special Olympics, become a Best Buddy, or assist in programs offering respite care to parents of children with intellectual disability.

5. Prepare a multimedia presentation for your class on an aspect of intellectual disability that personally interests you. Here are some possible topics:

- Assessment of intelligence
- Assistive technology
- Causes and prevention of intellectual disability
- Early intervention
- Group homes
- Overrepresentation of children of color in classes for individuals with intellectual disability
- Prenatal diagnostic screening
- Supported competitive employment

REFLECTING ON STANDARDS

The following exercises are designed to help you learn to apply the Council for Exceptional Children (CEC) standards to your teaching practice. Each of the reflection exercises below correlates with knowledge or a skill within the CEC standards. For the full text of each of the related CEC standards, please refer to the standards integration grid located in Appendix B.

Focus on Learner Development and Individual Learning Differences (*CEC Initial Preparation Standard 1.2*)

Reflect on an individual with intellectual disability whom you have known. How has that individual made an impact on his or

her family, friends, teachers, and/or community? What struggles did that individual have as a result of his or her differences? What did you learn from this person about individuals with disabilities?

Focus on Instructional Planning and Strategies (*CEC Initial Preparation Standard 5.1*)

Reflect on what you have learned in this chapter about students with intellectual disability. If you were to have a student with Down syndrome in your class, how would you need to modify your teaching to integrate affective, social, and life skills within your day-to-day curriculum?

American Association on Intellectual and Developmental Disabilities

http://aaidd.org

The Arc (formerly the Association for Retarded Citizens of the United States)

www.thearc.org

National Down Syndrome Congress

www.ndsccenter.org

National Down Syndrome Society

http://www.ndss.org

STUDENT STUDY SITE

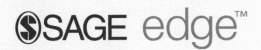

Sharpen your skills with SAGE edge at **edge.sagepub.com/gargiulo5e. SAGE edge for students** provides a personalized approach to help you accomplish your coursework goals in an easy-to-use learning environment.

Individuals With Learning Disabilities

What's a Mother To Do?

"What's a mother to do?" I moped silently. I knew that there was something slightly wrong. Was Ryan just lazy? His seventh-grade teachers had just told us so in the parent conference. As I painfully replayed the conference in my mind, I reflected on my son's school experiences.

Ryan had a very successful elementary school experience up until the fifth grade. In fifth grade things got a bit more difficult. His disorganization and his lack of ability to do written work began to destroy his confidence and academic success. Grades dropped from mostly As to Cs and Ds. Ryan's teacher and his classmates loved him; but he failed at least one subject each grading period—usually a different one each time. He never brought assignments home, frequently did the wrong homework—if he did it at all—and forgot to turn in finished homework. His teacher said that he had trouble getting his books, pen, and paper out at the beginning of class. She said that he was, therefore, behind before he even got started. His fifth-grade penmanship looked like that of a much younger child. He could not spell. His backpack was a mess of wadded-up papers. We all thought Ryan was just a typical boy. Neither we nor the teachers ever mentioned the possibility of a learning disability.

Then we were in middle school. Ryan was still one of the most popular kids in the class—sociable, handsome, and clearly the class "stud"—but his grades were gradually deteriorating. We asked for a parent–teacher conference. At the conference, my husband and I were attacked by his team of teachers. They seemed to think we were bad parents. "Why don't you make Ryan do his work?" they asked.

Ryan's seventh-grade test scores clearly showed a large discrepancy. Spelling was at the third-grade level while all other skills were at or above a twelfth-grade level. His reading comprehension was excellent, and his vocabulary was extensive; yet he did not read for pleasure. He passed most classes with only average grades. His teachers told us he was lazy. Once again, not one teacher mentioned the possibility of a learning disability.

I did not know what to do with this child who was smart yet obviously learning disabled. I finally asked for help when our son was in the eighth grade. I agree that being classified as a special education student gives a child a

LEARNING OBJECTIVES

After reading Chapter 7, you should be able to:

- **Summarize** the key components of the IDEA definition of learning disabilities.
- **Outline** the four phases in the development of the field of learning disabilities.
- **Identify** possible causes of learning disabilities.
- **List** representative learning and social/emotional characteristics of individuals with learning disabilities.
- **Explain** the concept of response to intervention.
- **Describe** the following instructional approaches: cognitive training, direct instruction, and learning strategies.
- **Summarize** educational services for persons with learning disabilities across the life span.

VIDEO

Learning Disabilities

certain unfavorable stigma; but I did not know any other way to help my child. Ryan somehow survived middle school, thanks largely to the efforts of his special education teacher.

That summer we moved to a larger city about two hours away. As a family, we decided not to seek special education services for Ryan as he began his freshman year in high school. We did not want him to carry the stigma of special education into this new environment. His grades always ranged from As to Fs. I had to constantly help him with his written work. He composed very well, but sometimes I had to type as he "wrote" his work orally. He had to go to summer school every summer to keep up, but somehow he managed to pass almost all of his classes and eventually graduate.

After a few years of successful employment Ryan was ready for college. He began by taking a history class at a nearby university and, with Mom's help on all papers, made a B in that class. He joined a fraternity. It was great fun. In the fall, he took a full load and quickly landed on academic probation. At that point I started looking for help from the university, only to find out that he could not get financial help until he got off academic probation. Ryan was still ambivalent about letting his professors know that he had a learning disability and would not ask the office of disability support services to contact his professors. So, again, he was in school depending on his mother to be his personal "special education" resource. He is now a third-semester freshman. He composes beautifully, but we are still writing orally while I or his girlfriend types his papers. He forgets to go to class sometimes and usually runs late to his part-time job or the pool where he coaches swim teams. His notebooks and his car are full of school supplies, athletic equipment, and miscellaneous stuff that is wildly disorganized.

I want my child to get a college degree and not have to work night shifts in the retail world for the rest of his life. We are now borrowing money to send him to school, hoping that he will pass every class, and worrying what will happen with his health insurance when he turns 26 and our policy no longer covers him. The financial burden is killing us, and I'm still in a quandary. What's a mother to do?

—Anonymous

Persons with learning disabilities are a very heterogeneous group. We will learn about children and adults who typically have normal intelligence but, for some reason, fail to learn as easily and efficiently as their classmates and peers. The idea that some individuals might possess a hidden or invisible disability is of relatively recent origin. The notion of learning disabilities is only about five decades old, but it has quickly grown and today represents the largest category of children and youth enrolled in special education.

The study of learning disabilities involves professionals from many different disciplines. Our knowledge base about this perplexing field has been greatly enriched by the contributions of investigators and practitioners from psychology, medicine, speech and language, and education, as well as other disciplines. Despite this solid multidisciplinary foundation, individuals with learning disabilities are often an enigma to their parents, teachers, and researchers, and the field itself has generated significant controversy, confusion, and debate.

In reality, most individuals have imperfections and, to some degree, experience difficulty in learning, but in some instances these problems are more pronounced than in others. For large numbers of people, these learning difficulties are chronic and will persist throughout life. It would be wrong to assume, however, that these individuals are incapable of accomplishments and a life of quality. Some of the most distinguished individuals and brightest minds the world has ever known had extreme difficulty in learning and could easily be considered learning disabled. These eminent people include Leonardo da Vinci, Auguste Rodin, Albert Einstein, Thomas Edison, Woodrow Wilson, Winston Churchill, and Ernest Hemingway. Other noted personalities include Walt Disney, George Patton, Nelson Rockefeller, Tom Cruise, Charles Schwab, and Bruce Jenner (Lerner & Johns, 2012; Smith, Polloway, Patton, & Dowdy, 2012). By all accounts, the preceding individuals are very successful persons, but they are exceptions. The vast majority of children and adults with learning disabilities will be frequently misunderstood and experience ongoing challenges and frustrations in their daily lives.

In this chapter, we will explore several issues and attempt to answer a number of questions related to learning disabilities. What is a learning disability? How many individuals are thought to be learning disabled? Can we cure it? What instructional strategies work best for students who are learning disabled? How do professionals determine if someone has a learning disability? Of course, there are many other questions about this puzzling field of study, and some for which we do not have complete answers. We begin our exploration of learning disabilities by examining various definitions.

Defining Learning Disabilities

Students with learning disabilities have always been in our classrooms, but professionals have often failed to identify these pupils and recognize their special needs. These children have been known by a variety of confusing and sometimes controversial labels, including *neurologically impaired*, *perceptually disordered*, *dyslexic*, *slow learner*, *remedial reader*, and *hyperactive*. Over forty years ago, Cruickshank (1972) published a list of some forty terms used to describe students known today as learning disabled. Deiner's (1993) more recent analysis found more than ninety terms used in the professional literature to characterize individuals with learning disabilities. It is easy to see why controversy and confusion surround this population of learners. Part of the problem is the many different disciplines involved in serving these students. Based on their professional training, physicians, speech-language pathologists, educators, and psychologists each describe persons with learning disabilities in their own unique way. Over the years, however, the various terms have been consolidated into the concept now known as learning disabilities. Today, this term enjoys wide acceptance among educators and the general public.

The term *learning disabilities* was initially used by Samuel Kirk in 1963 at a meeting of parents and professionals concerned about children with various learning difficulties. His proposed label was enthusiastically received and helped to unite the participants into an organization known as the Association for Children with Learning Disabilities, the forerunner of today's Learning Disabilities Association of America. Although the term was coined in 1963, Kirk had defined the concept a year earlier. His definition of learning disabilities was

> a retardation, disorder, or delayed development in one or more of the processes of speech, language, reading, writing, arithmetic, or other school subject resulting from a psychological handicap caused by a possible cerebral dysfunction and/or emotional or behavioral disturbances. It is not the result of mental retardation [intellectual disability], sensory deprivation, or cultural and instructional factors. (Kirk, 1962, p. 263)

As you will see, elements of this definition, which is an umbrella concept encompassing a multitude of educational "sins," appear in later definitions of learning disabilities, including subaverage academic performance, processing disorders, and the exclusion of certain etiological possibilities.

learning disability: A disability in which there is a discrepancy between a person's ability and academic achievement; individual possesses average intelligence.

A learning disability is an umbrella concept covering a wide range of difficulties.

Federal Definition of Learning Disabilities

After the Education for All Handicapped Children Act was enacted in 1975, the U.S. Office of Education spent two years developing the accompanying rules and regulations for identifying and defining individuals with learning disabilities. The following official federal definition of learning disabilities was published in the *Federal Register* in December 1977:

> "Specific learning disability" means a disorder in one or more of the basic psychological processes involved in understanding or in using language, spoken or written, which may manifest itself in an imperfect ability to listen, speak, read, write, spell, or to do mathematical calculations. The term includes such conditions as perceptual handicaps, brain injury, minimal brain dysfunction, dyslexia, and developmental aphasia. The term does not include children who have learning disabilities which are primarily the result of visual, hearing, or motor handicaps, or mental retardation, or emotional disturbance, or of environmental, cultural, or economic disadvantage. (U.S. Office of Education, 1977, p. 65083)

This definition was retained in the Individuals with Disabilities Education Act (PL 101–476), commonly called IDEA, and is incorporated, with a few word changes, in both the 1997 and 2004 reauthorizations of IDEA (PL 105–17, PL 108–446).

In the same issue of the *Federal Register,* the U.S. Office of Education issued the regulations and operational guidelines that were to be used by professionals as the criteria for identifying pupils suspected of being learning disabled. These regulations required that

(a) A team may determine that a child has a specific learning disability if:

   1. The child does not achieve commensurate with his or her age and ability levels in one or more of the areas listed in paragraph (a) (2) of this section, when provided with learning experiences appropriate for the child's age and ability levels; and

   2. The team finds that a child has a severe discrepancy between achievement and intellectual ability in one or more of the following areas:

      i. Oral expression;

      ii. Listening comprehension;

      iii. Written expression;

      iv. Basic reading skill;

      v. Reading comprehension;

      vi. Mathematics calculation; or

      vii. Mathematics reasoning. (U.S. Office of Education, 1977, p. 65083)

This definition of learning disabilities and its accompanying regulations describe a syndrome rather than a particular student. Like other definitions, the federal interpretation is useful for classifying children but provides little information on how to instruct these pupils.

The IDEA definition contains two key elements worthy of additional attention. One central component is the idea of a discrepancy between the student's academic performance and his or her estimated or assumed ability or potential. This discrepancy would not be anticipated on the basis of the pupil's overall intellectual ability—generally average to above-average IQ. This discrepancy factor is considered by many professionals to be the *sine qua non* of the definition of learning disabilities. It explains how, for instance, a 10-year-old with above-average intelligence reads at a level a year or more below expectations for his chronological age. Generally speaking, in most instances, a discrepancy of two years or more below expected performance levels in one academic area is necessary for a designation of learning disabilities. Unfortunately, the federal government failed to stipulate what was meant by "a severe discrepancy." Early on, it attempted to quantify the notion of a discrepancy by offering several formulas, but its efforts only led to criticism and confusion (Council for Learning Disabilities, 1986; Reynolds, 1992). Thus, the rules and regulations were published without a method for quantifying a severe discrepancy.

You may recall from Chapter 2 that IDEA 2004 removed this discrepancy provision. While PL 108–446 does not prohibit the use of a discrepancy approach for identifying pupils suspected of being learning disabled, it does give educators another way of discovering whether a student has a learning disability. School districts are now able, if they so choose, to use a process that determines if the pupil responds to empirically validated, scientifically based interventions—a procedure known as response to intervention, or RTI. We will have much more to say about this new way of thinking later in this chapter.

The 1977 federal interpretation also specifies that a learning disability cannot be due primarily to sensory impairments, intellectual disability, emotional problems, or environmental, cultural, or economic disadvantage. This language has come to be known as the exclusionary clause. This concept has generated considerable concern in

discrepancy: In regard to learning disabilities, the difference between the student's actual academic performance and his or her estimated ability.

response to intervention (RTI): A strategy used for determining whether a pupil has a learning disability. Student is exposed to increasing levels of validated instructional intervention; responsiveness to the instruction is assessed; a lack of adequate progress typically leads to a referral for possible special education services.

exclusionary clause: In regard to learning disabilities, the elimination of possible etiological factors to explain a pupil's difficulty in learning.

◼ ▪ ◼ ▪ ◼ ▪ Table 7.1 **Common Components of Definitions of Learning Disabilities**

• Intellectual functioning within normal range
• Significant gap or discrepancy between a student's assumed potential and actual achievement
• Cognitive processing deficits
• Inference that learning disabilities are not primarily caused by other disabilities or extrinsic factors
• Difficulty in learning in one or more academic areas
• Presumption of central nervous system dysfunction
• Lifelong condition

some circles because it seems to suggest that students with other impairments cannot be considered learning disabled as well. Mercer and Pullen (2009), however, believe that the word *primarily* suggests that a learning disability can coexist with other exceptionalities. We believe that what is important is that professionals recognize that a pupil is experiencing learning difficulties, regardless of their etiology, and thus is in need of some form of intervention.

Association for Children With Learning Disabilities

The federal definition of learning disabilities has had its share of criticism and accompanying controversy. As a result, in 1986 the Association for Children with Learning Disabilities (now known as the Learning Disabilities Association of America) proposed a definition that incorporates several key elements not found in the IDEA definition. This substitute definition stresses the lifelong aspect of learning disabilities, addresses issues of socialization and self-esteem, eliminates the exclusionary language, and suggests that adaptive behaviors (daily living skills) may also be compromised by this disability. This group's definition is as follows:

> Specific Learning Disabilities is a chronic condition of presumed neurological origin which selectively interferes with the development, integration, and/or demonstration of verbal and/or nonverbal abilities. Specific Learning Disabilities exists as a distinct handicapping condition and varies in its manifestations and in degree of severity. Throughout life, the condition can affect self-esteem, education, vocation, socialization, and/or daily living activities. (Association for Children with Learning Disabilities, 1986, p. 15)

The Continuing Debate

After reading these two definitions, you may believe that the field of learning disabilities is in a continual state of confusion and raucous debate over what a learning disability is. You may be partly correct. It is perhaps best to envision learning disabilities as a family or syndrome of disabilities affecting a wide range of academic and/or behavioral performance. The key elements of these definitions are summarized in Table 7.1.

A Brief History of the Field

Learning disabilities is an evolving and ever-changing field. Over the years, it has been influenced and significantly shaped by eminent individuals, various movements, governmental policies, research findings, and theoretical debates and has benefited from

VIDEO

Defining Learning Disabilities

the activities of various advocacy/interest groups. The collective outcome of these sometimes competing efforts has been the present-day concept of learning disabilities.

The origins of the field of learning disabilities are international, multicultural, and multidisciplinary (Hallahan, Kauffman, & Lloyd, 1999). In fact, according to Hallahan et al. (1999), over the past century several different groups and professions have been involved, to varying degrees, in influencing the growth of the field. These influences include medicine, law, education, psychology, and advocacy groups, among others.

Lerner and Johns (2012) divide the development of the field into four distinct historical periods spanning almost two hundred years. These phases, illustrated in Figure 7.1, are discussed in the following sections.

Foundation Phase

Although the modern-day concept of learning disabilities traces its origin to an address given by Samuel Kirk in 1963, the roots of this concept lie in the studies of brain functions conducted in the nineteenth and early twentieth centuries. Neurologists and other physicians of this era were interested in detecting which areas of the brain control specific activities such as speech or reading. By investigating adults with brain damage, these early pioneers were able to identify regions of the brain that appeared to be associated with particular cognitive impairments such as aphasia (inability to speak). James Hinshelwood, for example, was a Scottish medical researcher who was intrigued by a young boy's inability to learn to read. Despite apparently normal intelligence and vision, this child exhibited a severe reading disability that Hinshelwood called "word blindness." He attributed this problem to a defect in a specific area of the boy's brain.

These pioneering efforts paved the way for later scientists such as Kurt Goldstein, a physician who studied soldiers suffering from traumatic brain injuries acquired during World War I. He noticed that many of these young men exhibited perceptual impairments; they were highly distractible, unable to attend to relevant stimuli, and overly meticulous. He hypothesized that these behavioral and perceptual impairments were the consequence of damage to the brain. Goldstein's theorizing was later expanded on by Alfred Strauss, a neuropsychiatrist, and his colleague Heinz Werner, a developmental psychologist. Both men fled Nazi Germany and joined the research staff at the Wayne County Training School in Michigan, where they studied children thought to have brain injury and intellectual disability. Interestingly, they observed that these students exhibited characteristics similar to those identified by Goldstein, although they had not suffered any obvious head injuries. Werner and Strauss speculated that the pupils' intellectual disability could be attributed to brain damage resulting from nongenetic factors. They developed a list of behavioral characteristics that distinguished between individuals with and without brain injury and suggested instructional tactics that could benefit students with learning disabilities.

Transition Phase

Beginning in the 1930s, teachers, reading specialists, psychologists, and others began to apply the scientific research evidence to children with learning problems. During this period, various individuals from different professional backgrounds played key roles in developing assessment instruments and remediation strategies designed to ameliorate academic difficulties (Lerner, 2003). Among the important theorists and contributions of this period are the following:

- Samuel Orton, a specialist in neurology, hypothesized that language disorders in children were due to the absence of cerebral dominance. He also devoted

Figure 7.1 **Phases in the Development of the Field of Learning Disabilities**

Foundation phase	Transition phase	Integration phase	Current phase
1800–1930	1931–1960	1961–1980	1981 to present

Areas of emphasis

Brain research	Clinical study of the child	Implementation in the schools	New directions

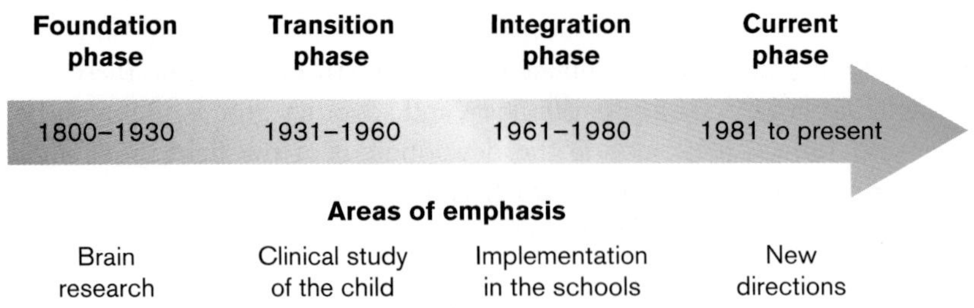

SOURCE: Adapted from J. Lerner and B. Johns, *Learning Disabilities and Mild Disabilities*, 12th ed. (Belmont, CA: Wadsworth/Cengage Learning, 2012), p. 30.

considerable energy to working with pupils with severe reading disorders, whom he called dyslexic. He speculated that their reading difficulties were due to neurological problems. The Orton Dyslexia Association, now the International Dyslexia Association, was named in honor of his contributions in this area.

- Grace Fernald, an educator who worked at the laboratory school at the University of California, Los Angeles, established a clinic for children who were experiencing significant learning difficulties despite their normal intellect. Over the years, she perfected various remedial reading and spelling programs. One of her tactics was a visual-auditory-kinesthetic-tactile (VAKT) approach to learning. This technique is the foundation of today's multisensory approach to instruction.
- Newell Kephart, a colleague of Strauss at the Wayne County Training School, pioneered a perceptual-motor development theory of learning. He advocated movement and physical exercises, among other corrective activities, as a means of remediating learning problems, which he attributed to deficiencies in perceptual-motor integration.
- Marianne Frostig was another early worker in the field of learning disabilities. She believed that a youngster's academic difficulties, especially poor reading, were a consequence of poorly developed visual perceptual skills. Assessment and remediation efforts, therefore, centered on specific aspects of visual perception. Frostig constructed her Developmental Test of Visual Perception as a means of pinpointing areas of weakness. Deficits were remediated by means of specially prepared exercises in hopes of improving visual perceptual abilities and thus the student's performance in reading. Her approach, like Kephart's, remained popular for many years but eventually fell out of favor among professionals for lack of empirical evidence documenting its effectiveness.

Integration Phase

In the latter part of the twentieth century, learning disabilities became an established disability area in schools across the United States (Lerner & Johns, 2012). As mentioned earlier, it was Samuel Kirk who initially popularized the term *learning disabilities*. This new term was welcomed by parents whose children had previously been identified as neurologically impaired, perceptually handicapped, brain damaged, and other pejorative labels. When schools elected to serve these students, many of whom were experiencing significant academic difficulties, they were often incorrectly placed in classes for pupils with intellectual disability or, in some instances, in settings for children with emotional problems; others received services from remedial reading specialists. Some pupils were denied help because school authorities were unable to classify them using the then current disabilities categories necessary for placement in a special education program.

The integration era witnessed the enactment of PL 91–230, the Specific Learning Disabilities Act of 1969, soon followed by the landmark "Bill of Rights" for children with disabilities, PL 94–142, now referred to as IDEA. Other milestones included the establishment of the Association for Children with Learning Disabilities in 1964, followed four years later by the birth of the Division for Children with Learning Disabilities (DCLD) as part of the Council for Exceptional Children (CEC). In 1982, a group of DCLD members withdrew from CEC over policy issues and created an independent association also concerned about individuals with learning disabilities, the Council for Learning Disabilities. Also in 1982, other former DCLD members began a new division under the auspices of CEC, the Division for Learning Disabilities.

Current Phase

It is hard to pinpoint the end of the integration phase and the beginning of the current phase. Beginning in the last decades of the twentieth century, however, the field of learning disabilities has been affected by several, sometimes controversial, forces. Some special educators believe that the field is embarking on a period of turbulent transition (Hallahan & Mercer, 2002). Mercer and Pullen (2009) predict that the field will be buffeted by a variety of social, political, economic, and professional forces. The question is "How will the field respond to these challenges?" Some of the emerging challenges or issues identified by Lerner and Johns (2012) include concerns about the movement toward full inclusion, how best to serve culturally and linguistically diverse learners, and the impact of assistive technology, along with issues of high-stakes assessment, response to intervention, and several other matters. Many of these topics will be addressed elsewhere in this chapter.

Prevalence of Learning Disabilities

Recent statistics compiled by the federal government suggest that approximately 2.35 million pupils ages 6 to 21 are identified as learning disabled (U.S. Department of Education, 2013a). Thus, learning disabilities is by far the largest category of special education, accounting for four out of every ten students (40.7%) receiving a special education in the 2011–2012 school year. This figure represents about 3.5 percent of the school-age population.

Over the past few years there has been a gradual, but steady, decrease in the number of students identified as learning disabled (McLeskey, Landers, Hoppey, & Williamson, 2011). In fact, between 2000 and 2009 the number of individuals identified as learning disabled declined by 14 percent (Cortiella, 2011). Possible reasons for this decrease include pupils being identified in other disabilities categories such as attention deficit hyperactivity disorder (ADHD); improvements in the quality of instruction in the general education classroom; better identification procedures; and the expansion of early childhood education programs (Lerner & Johns, 2012).

The number of pupils identified as learning disabled varies by both gender and age. Boys are two to four times more likely to be identified as learning disabled than girls (Cortiella, 2011; Lerner & Johns, 2012). Among school-age children, we find a steady increase in the number of pupils recognized as learning disabled between 6 and 9 years of age. The overwhelming majority of students, however, are in the age range 10–16, with a decreasing trend among older adolescents (U.S. Department of Education, 2013a).

Finally, the U.S. Department of Education (2013a) reports slightly more than 9,100 young children with a learning disability. This number represents 1.2 percent of all preschoolers with a disability.

Etiology of Learning Disabilities

Despite intense research activity over the years, pinpointing the precise cause or causes of learning disabilities has remained an elusive goal. Many of the proposed causal factors remain largely speculative. In the vast majority of instances, the cause of a person's learning disability remains unknown. Just as there are many different types of learning disabilities, there appear to be multiple etiological possibilities. We should point out that the cause of an individual's learning difficulties is often of little educational relevance. In other words, knowing why a particular pupil exhibits a learning disability does not necessarily translate into effective instructional strategies and practices. Nonetheless, investigators posit four basic categories for explaining the etiology of learning disabilities: acquired trauma, genetic/hereditary influences, biochemical abnormalities, and environmental possibilities (Mercer & Pullen, 2009).

Neurological dysfunction is a suspected cause of some learning disabilities.

Acquired Trauma

The medical literature uses the term *acquired trauma* when describing injury or damage to the central nervous system (CNS) that originates outside the person and results in learning disorders. Depending on when the damage occurs, the trauma is identified as prenatal (before birth), perinatal (during birth), or postnatal (after birth). These traumas, according to Mercer and Pullen (2009), have been linked to learning problems in children.

One example of an acquired trauma that may manifest itself pre-, peri-, or postnatally is brain injury, or, in contemporary terms, brain dysfunction. Historically speaking, professionals have long presumed CNS dysfunction as a probable cause of learning disabilities (Hallahan & Mercer, 2002; Rourke, 2005). Advances in neuroimaging techniques such as magnetic resonance imaging (MRI), positron emission tomography (PET), and other computerized neurological measures have now allowed researchers to establish the importance of neurological dysfunction as a possible cause of learning disabilities. Neuroimaging research suggests anatomical (structural) and functional differences in the brains of individuals with and without a learning disability (Gabrieli, 2009; Stasi & Tall, 2010).

CNS dysfunction is certainly one type of acquired trauma, but a number of other factors have also been implicated as possible causes of learning disabilities:

Prenatal Causes

- Illicit drugs
- Smoking
- Use of alcohol

Perinatal Causes

- Anoxia
- Prematurity/low birth weight
- Prolonged and difficult delivery
- Trauma caused by medical instruments such as forceps

Postnatal Causes

- Concussions
- Head injury resulting from falls or accidents
- High fever
- Meningitis/encephalitis
- Strokes (Mercer & Pullen, 2009)

Genetic/Hereditary Influences

Do learning disabilities "run" in families? Researchers investigating this question believe that some learning problems are indeed inherited; however, no single gene is believed to cause learning disabilities. Over the years, a fairly strong link has been established between heredity and some types of learning disabilities (Galaburda, 2005; Isles & Humby, 2006; Shapiro, Church, & Lewis, 2007). Raskind (2001) notes, for instance, that reading and spelling deficits are substantially inherited. Familiality studies, which examine the tendency of certain conditions to occur in a single family, suggest that some reading difficulties and certain types of math disorders are family related (Lewis, Shapiro, & Church, 2013). Familiality does not clearly prove heritability, however; learning problems may occur in certain families for environmental reasons, such as child-rearing practices.

Although it is difficult to control for the effect of environmental influences on learning, heritability studies enable investigators to more clearly answer the question "Are learning disabilities inherited?" In this investigative technique, scientists compare the school performance of monozygotic twins (identical twins, developing from the same egg with identical genetic characteristics) with that of dizygotic twins (fraternal twins, developing from two different eggs with different genetic makeup). The research evidence generally supports the hypothesis that certain types of learning problems, including reading and math disabilities, are more common among identical twins than fraternal twins (Cohen Kadosh & Walsh, 2007; Shalev, 2004; Wadsworth & DeFries, 2005; Wood & Grigorenko, 2001).

Biochemical Abnormalities

In some youngsters, biochemical conditions are suspected of causing learning disabilities. Over the years, several different theories have enjoyed varying degrees of popularity among parents and professionals. In the mid-1970s, Feingold (1975, 1976) championed the view that allergic reactions to certain artificial colorings, flavorings, and additives contained in many food products contribute to children's learning problems and hyperactive behavior. He recommends that parents restrict the consumption of foods containing natural salicylates, including apples, oranges, and some types of berries; ban products containing artificial colors and flavors; and limit the intake of certain other products such as toothpaste and compounds containing aspirin. The scientific community, however, has found little support for Feingold's theory (Kavale & Forness, 1983).

Another popular theory of this era was megavitamin therapy, whose chief advocate was psychiatrist Alan Cott. Cott (1972) theorizes that learning disabilities can be caused by the inability of a person's blood to synthesize a normal amount of vitamins. In an effort

familiality study: A method for assessing the degree to which a particular characteristic is inherited; the tendency for certain conditions to occur in a single family.

heritability studies: A method for assessing the degree to which a specific condition is inherited; a comparison of the prevalence of a characteristic in fraternal versus identical twins.

AUDIO
Potential Causes

to treat learning disabilities, large daily doses of certain vitamins are recommended to counteract the suspected vitamin deficiency. Again, scientific research (Arnold, Christopher, Huestis, & Smeltzer, 1978) has failed to substantiate the benefit of this treatment.

We suspect that, in some instances, an individual's biochemical makeup may affect his or her learning and behavior. The current research evidence, however, cannot definitively support this hypothesis.

Environmental Possibilities

Another school of thought attributes the etiology of learning disabilities to a host of environmental factors such as low socioeconomic status, malnutrition, lack of access to health care, and other variables that may contribute to neurological dysfunction (Hallahan, Lloyd, Kauffman, Weiss, & Martinez, 2005). Although the IDEA definition and others specifically exclude these conditions as etiological possibilities, many educators believe that these risk factors indirectly contribute to the learning and behavioral difficulties of some pupils.

Another variable implicated as causing learning disabilities is the quality of instruction that students receive. Simply stated, some children are identified as learning disabled as a result of poor teaching. Engelmann (1977) estimates that the vast majority of students labeled as learning disabled "have been seriously mistaught. Learning disabilities are made, not born" (p. 47). Recently, during a visit to a foreign country, your author was told by a veteran special educator of a slogan in her country that speaks directly to this issue: "There are no bad students, only poor teachers." Lyon et al. (2001) also contend that learning disabilities may result from poor teachers and inadequate or ineffective instruction. While implying that the quality of the learning environment contributes to learning disabilities, researchers also note that learning problems can often be remediated by exposure to individualized and high-quality instructional practices.

Characteristics of Individuals With Learning Disabilities

There is probably no such entity as a "typical" person with learning disabilities; no two students possess the identical profile of strengths and weaknesses. The concept of learning disabilities covers an extremely wide range of characteristics. One pupil may have deficits in just one area while another exhibits deficits in several areas; yet both will be labeled as learning disabled. Some children will experience cognitive difficulties, others may have problems with motor skills, and still others may exhibit social deficits.

Over the years, parents, educators, and other professionals have identified a wide range of characteristics often associated with learning disabilities. A typical profile may include elements of the following learning and behavioral characteristics:

- Disorders of attention
- Hyperactivity
- Information-processing problems
- Lack of cognitive strategies needed for efficient learning
- Memory difficulties
- Oral language difficulties
- Poor gross and fine motor skills
- Psychological processing deficits
- Quantitative disabilities

AUDIO
Identification

VIDEO
Individuals

- Reading disorders
- Social/emotional challenges
- Written language problems (Lerner & Johns, 2009; Mercer & Pullen, 2009)

Not all students with learning disabilities will exhibit these characteristics, and many pupils who demonstrate these same behaviors are quite successful in the classroom. It is often the frequency, intensity, and duration of the behaviors that lead to problems in school and elsewhere.

In the past, professionals typically focused on the elementary school–age child with a learning disability; in recent years, however, the field has adopted a life span approach. We now realize that learning disabilities can be a lifelong problem. Also, learning disabilities present themselves in different ways depending on the age of the individual. A language disorder, for instance, may exhibit itself as delayed speech in a preschooler, as a reading problem in the elementary grades, and as a writing difficulty at the secondary level (Lerner & Johns, 2012).

Learning Characteristics

Most professionals agree that the primary characteristics of students with learning disabilities are deficits in academic performance. A learning disability does not exist without significant impairments in academic achievement. These deficits may involve several different categories of school performance.

Reading

Well over half of all students identified as learning disabled exhibit problems with reading (Bender, 2008; Lerner & Johns, 2012). The difficulties experienced by these youngsters are as varied as the children themselves. Some pupils have trouble with reading comprehension; others evidence word recognition errors; still others lack word analysis skills or are deficient in oral reading. Table 7.2 lists several areas of reading difficulty common among students with learning disabilities. Deficits in reading are thought to be a primary reason for failure in school; they also contribute to a loss of self-esteem and self-confidence (Polloway, Patton, Serna, & Bailey, 2013).

One term frequently heard when discussing reading problems is dyslexia. Simply stated, dyslexia is a type of reading disorder in which the student fails to recognize and comprehend written words—a severe impairment in the ability to read. It is generally thought that this problem results from difficulties with phonological awareness—a lack of understanding of the rules that govern the correspondence between specific sounds and certain letters that make up words (Lyon, Shaywitz, & Shaywitz, 2003; Simmons, Kame'enui, Coyne, Chard, & Hairrell, 2011). In other words, letter-sound recognition is impaired.

Phonemic awareness, or understanding that words are constructed of small units of sounds known as phonemes, is another important element of learning to read. Some pupils, for example, may experience reading problems because they are unable to decode the word *cat* into three distinct phonemes—/c/ /a/ /t/—while other students might experience difficulty isolating beginning, middle, and ending sounds. For example, "What is the first sound in the word *rabbit*?" (Simmons et al., 2011).

Mathematics

Researchers estimate that about one out of every four pupils with learning disabilities receives assistance because of difficulties with mathematics (Lerner & Johns, 2012). Students who experience this problem are unique; not all children exhibit the same deficiency or impairment. In some instances, pupils may have difficulty with computational

dyslexia: A severe reading disability; difficulty in understanding the relationship between sounds and letters.

phonological awareness: Possible explanation for the reading problems of some students with learning disabilities; difficulty in recognizing the correspondence between specific sounds and certain letters that make up words.

phonemic awareness: The ability to recognize that words consist of different sounds or phonemes.

phoneme: Smallest unit of sound found in spoken language.

Table 7.2 Common Reading Problems of Students With Learning Disabilities

	Problem Areas	Observations
Reading Habits	Tension movements	Frowning, fidgeting, using a high-pitched voice, lip biting
	Insecurity	Refusing to read, crying, attempting to distract the teacher
	Loses place	Losing place frequently (often associated with repetitions)
	Lateral head movements	Jerking head
	Holds material close	Deviating extremely (from 15 to 18 inches)
Word Recognition Errors	Omissions	Omitting a word (e.g., *Tom saw [a] cat*)
	Insertions	Inserting words (e.g., *The dog ran [fast] after the cat*)
	Substitutions	Substituting one word for another (e.g., *The house horse was big*)
	Reversals	Reversing letters in a word (e.g., *no* for *on, was* for *saw*)
	Mispronunciations	Mispronouncing words (e.g., *mister* for *miser*)
	Transpositions	Reading words in the wrong order (e.g., *She away ran* for *She ran away*)
	Unknown words	Hesitating for 5 seconds at words they cannot pronounce
	Slow, choppy reading	Not recognizing words quickly enough (20 to 30 words per minute)
Comprehension Errors	Cannot recall basic facts	Unable to answer specific questions about a passage (e.g., *What was the dog's name?*)
	Cannot recall sequence	Unable to tell sequence of the story that was read
	Cannot recall main theme	Unable to recall the main topic of the story
Miscellaneous Symptoms	Word-by-word reading	Reading in a choppy, halting, and laborious manner (no attempt to group words into thought units)
	Strained, high-pitched voice	Reading in a pitch higher than conversational tone
	Inadequate phrasing	Inappropriately grouping words (e.g., *The dog ran into [pause] the woods*)
	Ignored or misinterpreted punctuation	Running together phrases, clauses, or sentences

SOURCE: C. Mercer and P. Pullen, *Students with Learning Disabilities,* 6th ed. (Upper Saddle River, NJ: Prentice Hall, 2005), p. 195. Reprinted by permission of Pearson Education, Inc., Upper Saddle River, NJ.

skills, word problems, spatial relationships, or writing numbers and copying shapes. Other classmates may have problems with telling time, understanding fractions and decimals, or measuring. Problems that begin in elementary school generally continue through high school and may have debilitating consequences in adulthood.

Written Language

Many individuals with learning disabilities exhibit deficits in written language, including spelling, handwriting, and composition (Vaughn, Bos, & Schumm, 2014). Researchers (Jennings, Caldwell, & Lerner, 2010) speculate that a link exists between these areas of deficiency and a person's reading ability. The association between reading and writing impairments should not be too surprising, as both may arise from a lack of phonological awareness.

Poor penmanship may be due to the absence of the requisite fine motor skills needed for legible handwriting and/or a lack of understanding of spatial relationships (for example, up, down, bottom), which may contribute to difficulties with letter formation and spacing between words and sentences (see Figure 7.2).

Children's writing changes as they mature. According to Hallahan et al. (1999), the focus of a youngster's writing "shifts from (1) the process of writing (handwriting and

Figure 7.2 **Writing Sample of a 10-Year-Old Girl**

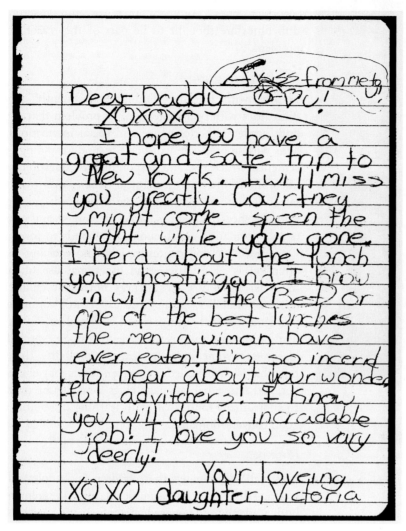

Dear Daddy

A kiss from me to you!

XOXOXO

I hope you have a great and safe trip to New York. I will miss you greatly. Courtney might come spend the night while you are gone. I heard about the lunch you are hosting and I know it will be the best or one of the best lunches the men and women have ever eaten! I'm so interested to hear about your wonderful adventures! I know you will do a incredible job! I love you so very dearly.

XOXO

Your loving daughter, Victoria

---

spelling) to (2) the written product (having written something) to (3) communication with readers (getting across one's message)" (p. 396). Early on, pupils focus on becoming competent in mastering the mechanical aspects of composition—spelling and handwriting; in later grades, they learn to organize and present their ideas in a lucid and logical fashion. Children who are learning disabled, however, lag behind their typical peers. Investigators have observed that individuals with learning disabilities use less complex sentence structure, incorporate fewer ideas, produce poorly organized paragraphs, and write less complex stories (Hallahan et al., 2005).

VIDEO
Teaching Strategies

Reading difficulties are very common among students with learning disabilities.

Spelling is another problem area for students with learning disabilities. They may omit certain letters or add incorrect ones. Auditory memory and discrimination difficulties are thought to be part of the reason for their problem.

Spoken Language

Persons with learning disabilities frequently experience difficulties with oral expression—a problem that can affect both academic performance and social interactions. Problems with appropriate word choice, understanding complex sentence structures, and responding to questions are not uncommon. Specific mechanical deficits may involve syntax (rule systems that determine how words are organized into sentences), semantics (word meanings), and phonology (sound formation and blending of sounds to form words). One aspect of oral expression that is receiving increased attention is pragmatics—the functional use of language in social situations. Researchers note that children with learning disabilities sometimes experience communication problems in social settings (Pearl & Donahue, 2004). Participating in conversations with friends can be especially troublesome for someone with a learning disability. The ebb and flow that is characteristic of conversations may elude him or her, and nonverbal language clues may also be overlooked. In short, many individuals with learning disabilities are not good conversationalists.

Memory

It is well documented that children and adolescents with learning disabilities have significant difficulties remembering both academic and nonacademic information, such as doctor appointments, homework assignments, multiplication facts, directions, and telephone numbers. Teachers frequently comment that, with these students, it seems to be "in one ear and out the other," which can be highly aggravating for teachers as well as parents.

Research evidence suggests that many students with learning disabilities have problems with short-term memory as well as working memory (Swanson, Cooney, & McNamara, 2004; Swanson & Jerman, 2007; Swanson, Zheng, & Jerman, 2009). Short-term memory tasks typically involve the recall, in correct order, of either aurally or visually presented information (such as lists of digits or pictures) shortly after hearing or seeing the items several times. Working memory requires that an individual retain information while simultaneously engaging in another cognitive activity. Working memory is involved, for example, when we try to remember a person's address while also listening to directions on how to arrive there.

Students with learning disabilities, in contrast to their typical peers, apparently do not spontaneously use effective learning strategies (such as rehearsal or categorizing of items) as an aid in recall. Deficits in memory, particularly working memory, often translate into difficulties in the classroom. Success with reading and math seems to depend more on working memory than on short-term memory (Council for Exceptional Children, 2003b). Working memory also appears to be crucial for word recognition and reading comprehension.

pragmatics: A sociolinguistic system involving the use of communication skills in social contexts.

short-term memory: The recall of information after a brief period of time.

working memory: The ability to retain information while also engaging in another cognitive activity.

metacognition: The ability to evaluate and monitor one's own performance.

Metacognition

It is not unusual for persons with learning disabilities to exhibit deficits in metacognition—the ability to evaluate and monitor one's own performance. Students who are learning disabled often lack an awareness of their own thinking process. Metacognitive skills typically consist of several key components: (1) a recognition of task requirements—that is, the strategies and resources needed to perform effectively; (2) implementation of the appropriate process; and (3) monitoring, evaluating, and adjusting one's performance to ensure successful task completion. Competency as a learner requires that students exhibit these metacognitive skills (Meltzer & Krishnan, 2007).

The reading problems of some children with learning disabilities may be due to deficiencies in metacognition. Reading comprehension difficulties, for example, may be due to deficits in the following skills:

- **Clarifying the purpose(s) of reading**: Pupils do not adjust their reading styles to accommodate the difficulty of the text.
- **Focusing attention on important goals**: Youngsters with reading problems experience difficulty in selecting the main ideas of a paragraph.
- **Monitoring one's level of comprehension**: Inefficient readers do not recognize that they are failing to understand what they are reading.
- **Rereading and scanning ahead**: Children with learning disabilities do not go back and reread portions of previously read text, nor do they scan upcoming material as an aid to comprehension.
- **Consulting external sources**: Ineffective readers do not utilize external sources like dictionaries and encyclopedias. (Hallahan et al., 2005)

Fortunately, as you will learn later, metacognitive skills can be taught.

Attributions

What individuals believe about what contributes to their success or failure on a task is known as *attribution*. Many students with learning disabilities attribute success not to their own efforts but to situations or events beyond their control, such as luck. These pupils are identified as exhibiting outer-directedness.

Chronic difficulties with academic assignments often lead children with learning disabilities to anticipate failure; success is seen as an unattainable goal no matter how hard they try. Youngsters who maintain this attitude frequently give up and will not even attempt to complete the task. Friend and Bursuck (2012) identify this outlook as learned helplessness. Loss of self-esteem and a lack of motivation are common consequences of this phenomenon.

Because of their propensity for academic failure, individuals with learning disabilities tend to be passive learners. They are not actively involved or engaged in their own learning and fail to demonstrate initiative in the learning process. These pupils are often characterized as inactive or inefficient learners (Hallahan et al., 2005). Some students with learning disabilities simply have not "discovered how to go about the business of learning" (Lerner & Johns, 2012, p. 162). These attributions can be altered, however, by teaching effective learning strategies (Lenz & Deshler, 2004).

Social and Emotional Problems

Research suggests that some students with learning disabilities, in comparison to their typical peers, have lower self-esteem (Manning, Bear, & Minke, 2006; Wiener &

outer-directedness: A condition characterized by a loss of confidence in one's own capabilities and a reliance on others for cues and guidance.

learned helplessness: A lack of persistence at tasks that can be mastered; a tendency to expect failure.

Learning Disabilities

Many individuals with learning disabilities believe that no matter how hard they try, they will still fail.

Timmermanis, 2012) and a poor self-concept, most likely due to frustration with their learning difficulties (Mercer & Pullen, 2009). Shapiro and his colleagues (2007) observe that "these individuals are less likely to take pride in their successes and more likely to be overcome by their failures" (p. 374).

Investigators are now beginning to realize that deficits in social skills are a common characteristic among many, but not all, individuals with learning disabilities (Wiener, 2004; Wiener & Timmermanis, 2012). Many of these students are deficient in social cognition; they are inept at understanding and interpreting social cues and social situations, which can easily lead to impaired interpersonal relationships. The social-emotional difficulties of persons with learning disabilities may be the result of social imperceptiveness—a lack of skill in detecting subtle affective cues. Students with learning disabilities often experience rejection by nondisabled peers and have difficulty making friends, possibly because they misinterpret the feelings and emotions of others (Lerner & Johns, 2012; Wiener & Timmermanis, 2012).

Attention Problems and Hyperactivity

Individuals who are learning disabled frequently experience difficulty attending to tasks, and some exhibit excess movement and activity, or hyperactive behavior. It is not unusual for educators to mention these characteristics when describing students with learning disabilities. Teachers note that some pupils have difficulty staying on task and completing assignments, following directions, or focusing their attention for a sustained period of time—they are easily distracted. In other instances, children are perceived to be overly active and fidgety, racing from one thing to another as if driven. Problems with inattention, distractibility, and hyperactivity can easily impair and impede an individual's successful performance in the classroom, at home, and in social situations.

The term usually heard when discussing this condition is **attention deficit hyperactivity disorder (ADHD)**, typical in the language of medical professionals and psychologists. This label is derived from the *Diagnostic and Statistical Manual of Mental Disorders* (American Psychiatric Association, 2013). Although hyperactivity and attention disorders are fairly common among persons with learning disabilities, with estimates ranging from about 25 to 40 percent of children with learning disabilities displaying characteristics of ADHD (Cortiella, 2011; Lerner & Johns, 2012), the terms are *not* synonymous—not all students with learning disabilities have ADHD, and vice versa. The exact relationship between learning disabilities and ADHD is not fully understood, but scientists and researchers are now beginning to unravel this complex phenomenon.

Assessment of Learning Disabilities

attention deficit hyperactivity disorder (ADHD): A disorder characterized by symptoms of inattention, hyperactivity, and/or impulsivity. Frequently observed in individuals with learning disabilities.

Federal law dictates that individuals being considered for possible placement in a program for children with learning disabilities receive a multidisciplinary evaluation that is conducted by a team of professionals in a nondiscriminatory fashion. Recall that this evaluation process will only occur if the recommended prereferral strategies have proven ineffective. IDEA requires, among other regulations, that

VIDEO

Attention Problems

- tests be administered by trained individuals;
- tests be reliable and valid and appropriate for the purpose for which they are being used;
- tests be neither racially nor culturally discriminatory;
- tests be administered in the student's native language or preferred means of communication; and
- no single measure be used as the basis for determining a pupil's eligibility.

Once the evaluation is completed, the team determines the student's eligibility for placement in a learning disabilities program in light of the state's definition of learning disabilities and federal guidelines.

Assessment Decisions

At the heart of assessing a student for possible placement in a program for individuals with learning disabilities is determining whether the pupil exhibits a severe discrepancy between assumed ability and actual educational achievement. This discrepancy is typically established by comparing a student's performance on a standardized achievement test with a measure of cognitive abilities or intelligence. Frequently used measures of intellectual performance (mentioned in Chapter 6) include the Wechsler Intelligence Scale for Children (4th ed.), the Stanford-Binet Intelligence Scale (5th ed.), and the more recently developed Kaufman Assessment Battery for Children (2nd ed.). A wide variety of achievement tests are available to educational diagnosticians. Comprehensive batteries designed to measure overall academic achievement include, for example, the well-known Iowa Test of Basic Skills, the Stanford Achievement Test (10th ed.), the Woodcock-Johnson III Tests of Achievement, and the Wechsler Individual Achievement Test III. Many other achievement tests assess a student's abilities in content areas such as math, reading, and language arts.

Several states use the concept of a severe discrepancy to identify individuals as learning disabled.

Unfortunately, there is no nationally agreed-upon mechanism for determining a discrepancy; different states use different formulas and even different tests in an effort to quantify the gap between potential and performance. As a result, a student identified as learning disabled in one state may be ineligible for services if the family relocates to another state.

Researchers, parents, and practitioners alike are now questioning the educational validity of identifying youngsters as learning disabled solely on the basis of a discrepancy formula and are calling for the use of alternative strategies such as relying on professionals' clinical judgment and experience in addition to assessing discrepancies among various cognitive and academic skills (Lerner & Johns, 2012).

Response to Intervention

With the reauthorization of IDEA in 2004, some of the preceding concerns were addressed. States and local school districts now have the option of choosing between the achievement-ability discrepancy model and making eligibility decisions on the basis of how a pupil responds to scientific, research-based educational interventions. This strategy is commonly referred to as response to intervention (RTI). While offered as an alternative way of identifying students with a possible learning disability, many schools are now using RTI as a prereferral strategy because *all* pupils are initially screened and provided with scientifically validated instruction (Gargiulo & Metcalf, 2013).

Figure 7.3 **A Response-to-Intervention Model**

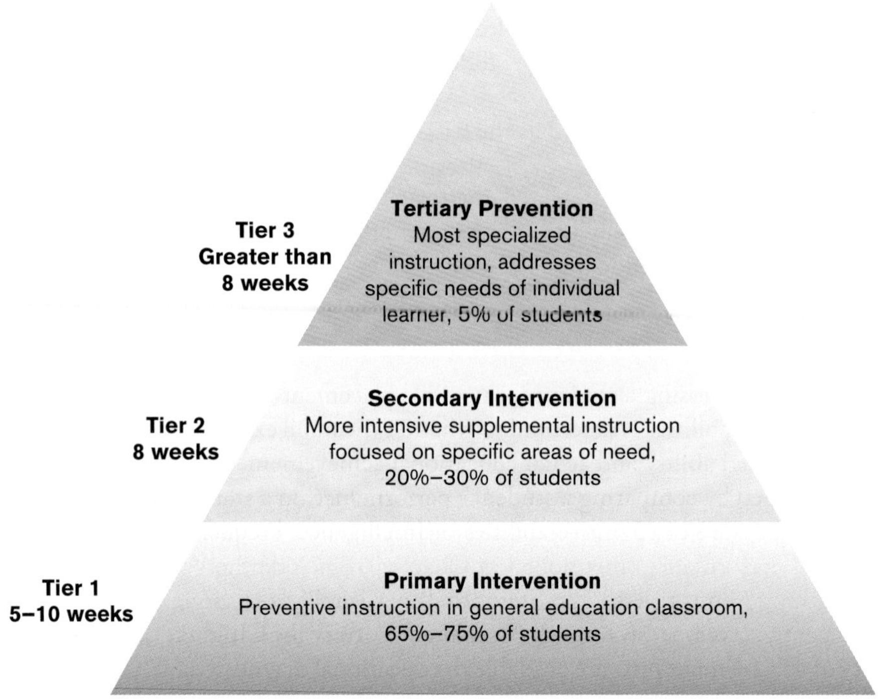

Tier 3
Greater than
8 weeks

Tertiary Prevention
Most specialized instruction, addresses specific needs of individual learner, 5% of students

Tier 2
8 weeks

Secondary Intervention
More intensive supplemental instruction focused on specific areas of need, 20%–30% of students

Tier 1
5–10 weeks

Primary Intervention
Preventive instruction in general education classroom, 65%–75% of students

NOTE: Percentage of students participating at each level is approximate.

Duration of intervention is approximate.

Students may move between tiers as individual needs dictate.

There is no formal definition of RTI, nor is there one model or strategy that is widely accepted (Berkley, Bender, Peaster, & Saunders, 2009; Vaughn & Bos, 2012). Generally speaking, RTI is a procedure whereby a pupil is exposed to increasingly intensive tiers or levels of instructional intervention with ongoing progress monitoring. The fidelity or integrity of RTI is predicated upon two crucial elements: (1) the use of evidence-based or scientifically validated instructional practices and (2) the frequent and systematic assessment of the individual's performance, known as progress monitoring. Essentially, RTI is an instructional and dynamic assessment process based on rigorous scientific research (Fletcher & Vaughn, 2009; Kame'enui, 2007) and is typically portrayed as a multitiered model of prevention generally consisting of three levels. One such conceptualization is illustrated in Figure 7.3. This configuration is thought to best serve the early intervention and identification aims of RTI (Fuchs, Fuchs, & Compton, 2012).

All students initially receive research-based instruction in the general education classroom. If a particular pupil fails to demonstrate "responsiveness" after receiving increasingly individualized and intensive instruction, a learning disability is presumed to be present, and a referral for special education services with a more comprehensive evaluation is usually initiated. Using reading instruction as an example, Table 7.3 highlights the differences, according to one RTI model, among primary, secondary, and tertiary interventions.

The RTI model represents a significant conceptual shift in thinking from a "wait to fail" approach to one that emphasizes early identification, intervention, and

progress monitoring: The frequent and systematic assessment of a pupil's academic progress.

Table 7.3 **A Response-to-Intervention Model: Tiers of Instruction**

	Tier 1 (Primary)	Tier 2 (Secondary)	Tier 3 (Tertiary)
Definition	Reading instruction and programs, including ongoing professional development and benchmark assessments (3 times per year)	Instructional intervention employed to supplement, enhance, and support Tier 1; takes place in small groups	Individualized reading instruction extended beyond the time allocated for Tier 1; groups of 1–3 students
Focus	All students	Students identified with reading difficulties who have not responded to Tier 1 efforts	Students with marked difficulties in reading or reading disabilities who have not responded adequately to Tier 1 and Tier 2 efforts
Program	Scientifically based reading instruction and curriculum emphasizing the critical elements	Specialized, scientifically based reading instruction and curriculum emphasizing the critical elements	Sustained, intensive, scientifically based reading instruction and curriculum highly responsive to students' needs
Instruction	Sufficient opportunities to practice throughout the school day	• Additional attention, focus, support • Additional opportunities to practice embedded throughout the day • Preteach, review skills; frequent opportunities to practice skills	Carefully designed and implemented, explicit, systematic instruction
Interventionist	General education teacher	Personnel determined by the school (classroom teacher, specialized reading teacher, other trained personnel)	Personnel determined by the school (e.g., specialized reading teacher, special education teacher)
Setting	General education classroom	Appropriate setting designated by the school	Appropriate setting designated by the school
Grouping	Flexible grouping	Homogeneous small-group instruction (e.g., 1:4, 1:5)	Homogeneous small-group instruction (1:2, 1:3)
Time	Minimum of 90 minutes per day	20–30 minutes per day in addition to Tier 1	50-minute sessions (or longer) per day depending upon appropriateness of Tier 1
Assessment	Benchmark assessments at beginning, middle, and end of academic year	Progress monitoring twice a month on target skill to ensure adequate progress and learning	Progress monitoring at least twice a month on target skill to ensure adequate progress and learning

SOURCE: Adapted from S. Vaughn and G. Roberts, "Secondary Interventions in Reading," *Teaching Exceptional Children, 39*(5), 2007, p. 41. Copyright © 2007. Reprinted with permission by the Council for Exceptional Children.

possible prevention (Fuchs et al., 2012; Vaughn & Bos, 2012; Vaughn et al., 2014). This approach to determining whether a pupil has a learning disability eliminates ineffective or inadequate instruction as a possible reason for low achievement. It also provides significant opportunities for general and special educators to work collaboratively (Cohen & Spenciner, 2011; Sileo, 2011).

While most of the early attention of RTI has focused on its application to reading, several benefits are recognized. Some of the advantages include a reduction in the number of inappropriate referrals for special education, including pupils from culturally and linguistically diverse backgrounds; interventions linked to ongoing assessment and learning outcomes; fewer students recognized as having a learning disability; and less stigma placed on the individual learner (Lerner & Johns, 2012).

Although support for RTI is growing in some educational circles, the research evidence is still somewhat limited. Some educators view RTI as a "promising practice" while acknowledging that several issues need to be addressed, for instance

- its application to other content areas such as mathematics;
- how responsiveness to intervention is determined;
- a lack of fidelity in delivering high-quality intensive instruction in the general education classroom;
- what the most effective duration of intervention is; and
- how many tiers or levels of intervention are required before a student is identified as learning disabled (Fuchs et al., 2012; Fuchs, Mock, Morgan, & Young, 2003; McLeskey & Waldron, 2011; O'Connor & Sanchez, 2011; Stecker, 2007; Vaughn & Fuchs, 2003).

We suspect that these and other issues will be successfully resolved in the coming years. It will be interesting to see how individual states and local school districts respond to the RTI option for identifying pupils suspected of having a learning disability. National surveys (Zirkel & Thomas, 2010a, 2010b) indicate significant variability in individual state practices regarding the adoption of RTI. In most instances, the choice is left up to the local school districts. It seems safe to say that RTI might best be viewed as a "work in progress."

Assessment Strategies

Traditionally, standardized tests have played a major role in the evaluation of students thought to have a learning disability. These instruments are also known as **norm-referenced assessments** because an individual's performance is compared to that of a normative group of peers (for example, all sixth graders in their state or a national sample of sixth graders) who have taken the same test. Standardized assessment requires rigid adherence to directions for administering, scoring, and interpreting the results. Teachers and psychologists rely heavily on standardized tests when assessing for learning disabilities. Norm-referenced tests provide a great deal of statistical information, allowing professionals to *compare* a particular student's performance with that of other pupils in the normative group. **Criterion-referenced assessments**, on the other hand, *describe* a youngster's performance. Criterion-referenced tests measure a student's abilities against a predetermined criterion or mastery level. In other words, the child's performance is compared with a standard expectation (100% knowledge of multiplication facts), not with the performance of others. Criterion-referenced tests, also commonly called teacher-made tests, offer a means of educational accountability, in that a teacher can demonstrate that a student has learned specific skills. It is a bit more difficult to show improvement in terms of percentile rankings or even grade-level scores (Lerner & Johns, 2012).

Although standardized testing is a useful component of a nondiscriminatory evaluation and provides meaningful information for identification purposes, norm-referenced tests are weak in providing instructional direction. Teacher-made tests are perhaps better suited for guiding instruction. One of the chief benefits of criterion-referenced tests is that they can help in instructional planning and decision making and in monitoring progress toward educational goals. Individualized education programs (IEPs) are often constructed around data gleaned from various types of criterion-referenced tests.

norm-referenced assessments: Refers to standardized tests on which a pupil's performance is compared to that of his or her peers.

criterion-referenced assessment: An assessment procedure in which a student's performance is compared to a particular level of mastery.

REFERENCE

Response to Intervention

Assessment strategies should always fit the question we are asking about a particular student. Professionals must also pay careful attention to the purpose of the assessment and how the data will be used (Aiken & Groth-Marnat, 2006).

Curriculum-Based Measurement

One frequently voiced concern about standardized testing is that the test items do not necessarily reflect or represent the content of the curriculum that a student has been exposed to. Curriculum-based measurement (CBM), on the other hand, is a form of criterion-referenced assessment in which test items are based on objectives found in the local school curriculum. In this model, a pupil's performance, usually in the areas of math, spelling, and reading, is evaluated several times a week with test items mirroring the daily instructional tasks. The student's performance is then charted or graphed so that his or her progress toward specific educational goals is easily recognized. The frequent and systematic sampling of a child's performance provides teachers with evidence of the effectiveness of their teaching tactics and may suggest the need for changes in instructional strategies. CBM is fairly common in special education and is often used with students with a learning disability because it reinforces the important link between assessment and instruction.

Portfolio Assessment

Disillusionment with traditional testing has contributed, in some educational circles, to a movement toward alternative assessment procedures. One form of alternative assessment is authentic assessment, which is believed to paint a more accurate or genuine picture of what a pupil can and cannot accomplish in real-life situations such as in the classroom or at home. An example of an authentic procedure is portfolio assessment. A portfolio is simply a collection of samples of a student's best work gathered over a period of time. According to Paulson, Paulson, and Meyer (1991), "a portfolio is a purposeful collection of student work that exhibits the student's effort, progress, and achievements in one or more areas" (p. 60). Mercer and Pullen (2009) see portfolio assessment as an attempt to improve the evaluation process and enhance instructional decision making.

One of the critical issues in portfolio assessment is knowing what to include in the portfolio and how to evaluate the person's efforts. A portfolio should have a specific purpose; without direction, it can easily become a mere collection of products.

A wide variety of student-generated products can be included in a portfolio. The teacher must first consider the goals of the instructional program and then select samples to match its intent. Using goals from the child's IEP is one strategy the teacher may wish to employ in determining what to include (Lerner & Johns, 2012). Examples of the diverse work products that might be part of a portfolio include audio recordings of oral reading samples, summaries of science experiments, poems, art projects, book reports, excerpts from journals, weekly quizzes, and math worksheets. Because portfolios reflect student progress, Salend (1998) recommends that they be used during parent–teacher conferences.

Educational Considerations

As noted elsewhere, individuals with learning disabilities are an especially heterogeneous population whose disabilities range from mild to severe. These students require a diversity of educational interventions and teaching strategies designed to meet their unique academic, social, and behavioral needs.

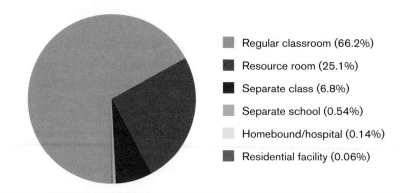

- Regular classroom (66.2%)
- Resource room (25.1%)
- Separate class (6.8%)
- Separate school (0.54%)
- Homebound/hospital (0.14%)
- Residential facility (0.06%)

NOTE: Figure represents percentage of enrollment of students with learning disabilities during the 2011–2012 school year. Excludes pupils enrolled in parentally placed private schools and individuals in correctional facilities.

SOURCE: U.S. Department of Education. (2013). *Historical state-level IDEA data files*. Retrieved November 14, 2013, from http://tadnet.public.tadnet.org/pages/712

Where Are Students With Learning Disabilities Educated?

The educational placement of children with special needs is currently one of the most controversial issues in the field of special education, and pupils with learning disabilities are not immune to this debate. Where students receive instruction can significantly affect their attitude, achievement, and social development (Mercer & Pullen, 2009).

From a historical perspective, the resource room has been one of the most common service delivery models for serving children with learning disabilities. Since the mid-1990s, however, there has been a subtle shift away from this option—most likely reflecting the trend toward more inclusive programs. Recent statistics indicate that the regular classroom is currently the most popular placement. During the 2011–2012 school year, two thirds (66.2%) of all students with learning disabilities were receiving services in the general education classroom while one in four students (25.1%) were assigned to a resource room (U.S. Department of Education, 2013a). This means that almost nine out of every ten individuals with learning disabilities spend some, most, or all of their school day in a regular classroom (see Figure 7.4).

The environment that is most appropriate for pupils with learning disabilities is the setting that is most enabling. Placement decisions must be individually determined based on the unique learning needs and characteristics of each student.

Instructional Approaches

There is no one "best" or "correct" way to teach individuals with learning disabilities. Individualization is the key to meeting the instructional needs of pupils with learning disabilities. Teachers often find that a wide variety of accommodations are necessary if the student is to experience success in the classroom. Some children will need additional time for testing or ask that a learning task be broken into smaller and more manageable segments; other pupils may require the privacy provided by a study carrel;

VIDEO
Educational Placement

Effective Instructional Practices
Teaching Reading

Phonic Analysis

Many students with learning disabilities experience difficulty with reading. A skill deficit often encountered is phonic analysis. Phonic analysis is a vital component of early reading instruction. Students must establish a strong understanding of letter-sound combinations and correspondence. They must also be able to recognize word parts. The following teaching strategies can help struggling readers learn to decode using phonic analysis skills.

- **Instructional content**: Teach letter-sound correspondence in a logical order. Most useful initially are the consonants *b, c, d, f, g, h, k, l, m, n, p, r, s,* and *t* and the vowels. Present continuous letter sounds (e.g., *s* and */sss/*, *m* and */mmm/*, *n* and */nnn/*) before stop letter sounds (*p* and /p/, *k* and /k/). Select letters that represent sounds found in decodable text that students will read.
- **Instructional content**: Introduce the most common sounds of the letters first. Lowercase letters should be taught before uppercase ones.
- **Instructional content**: Teach the letter combinations that most frequently occur in text.
- **Instructional content**: Avoid teaching letter-sound correspondence and letter combinations that sound similar and may confuse students. For instance, /m/ and /n/ and /sh/ and /ch/ should not be taught together. Letter combinations with the same sound, such as /ir/ and /ur/ and /ee/ and /ea/, can be taught at the same time.
- **Instructional content**: Teach phonograms containing letter-sound correspondences that have been introduced. Phonograms or rimes (which are parts of a word to which consonants or blends are added to make a word) such as *ap, at, ip, it, un,* and *et* paired with initial consonants or onsets provide opportunities to segment and blend sounds to make words. These words should be featured in the decodable text that students will read.
- **Instructional delivery**: Teach students to blend the letter sounds together in a seamless fashion. For instance, students should be taught to say *mmmaaannn* rather than separating the sounds /m/ /a/ /n/.
- **Instructional materials**: Have students read decodable texts—texts that contain words with the sounds and patterns you have previously taught and students have mastered.
- **Connections to spelling**: Have students spell the words so that their phonics instruction can be reinforced. Spelling and reading are closely related skills. Here are some examples of ways to make connections to spelling:
  - Introduce letter-sound correspondences for spelling as they are being introduced and taught in reading.
  - Have students sort words into spelling patterns.
  - Have students identify words from their text with patterns that match what they are learning in phonics.

SOURCE: D. Bryant, D. Smith, and B. Bryant, *Teaching Students with Special Needs* (Boston, MA: Allyn & Bacon, 2008), pp. 404–405.

---

some youngsters may need assistance in developing effective learning strategies; still others will benefit from additional drill and practice. What works for one student will not necessarily be appropriate for another pupil.

In this section, we look at some of the various pedagogical strategies for teaching students with learning disabilities. Educators have a broad array of instructional approaches and strategies at their disposal, some of them more effective than others. We recommend that teachers select their instructional tactics only after carefully considering the research evidence. The field of learning disabilities has a history of "jumping on the bandwagon" and vigorously advocating a particular instructional approach or strategy; unfortunately, in some cases, these procedures were lacking in empirical support. It is important, therefore, for teachers to validate the effectiveness of their interventions.

VIDEO
Instructional Approaches

We have chosen to examine three broad approaches to teaching academic skills: cognitive training, direct instruction, and learning strategies. Keep in mind that there is no "silver bullet" or magic formula for teaching students with learning disabilities; in most instances, it is a matter of matching the needs of the student to a particular instructional model.

Cognitive Training

Cognitive training is an umbrella approach covering a variety of educational procedures. It seeks to manipulate or modify a student's underlying thought patterns to effect observable changes in performance. Proponents of this approach believe that what occurs internally in the learner during the learning process is just as important as what happens externally. The pupil is seen as the critical agent in determining how information is processed—that is, identified, interpreted, organized, and utilized (Mercer & Pullen, 2009). Self-instruction and the use of mnemonic strategies are two instructional techniques frequently associated with cognitive training.

Developed by Meichenbaum (1977; Meichenbaum & Goodman, 1971), self-instruction is a strategy whereby students initially talk to themselves out loud while performing a task—children verbalize instructions necessary to complete the activity and then verbally reward themselves for success. Self-instruction makes the pupil aware of the various steps used in problem solving and then gradually brings these strategies under covert verbal control. According to Hallahan et al. (2005) and Lerner and Johns (2012), the following six steps are typically used during cognitive training:

1. Student observes the teacher perform a task while verbalizing aloud.
    a.   Questions about the activity
    b.   Instructions on how to perform the task
    c.   A self-evaluation of performance

2. Pupil performs the task with teacher providing verbal directions.

3. Child performs the activity while verbalizing aloud.

4. Student performs the task while whispering instructions.

5. Pupil performs the activity while using covert or inner speech.

6. Child monitors and self-evaluates own performance (for example, "I did a good job" or "I need to work faster").

The goal of cognitive training, considered by some authorities to be a form of cognitive behavior modification, is not only to modify the pupil's behavior but also to increase the learner's awareness of the behavior and the thinking process affiliated with it (Lerner & Johns, 2012). Cognitive training has proven to be a beneficial strategy for remediating a wide variety of academic difficulties typically encountered by individuals with learning disabilities (Hallahan et al., 2005). Table 7.4 provides a list of suggestions for teachers using cognitive training strategies.

Mnemonic strategies are memory tools for helping students recall facts and relationships. Teachers frequently help their students transform abstract material into a more concrete form by constructing personally meaningful representations of the information—that is, a picture or pattern of letters. For example, one popular trick frequently used by beginning music students to help recall the treble staff is the acrostic "**E**very **g**ood **b**oy **d**oes **f**ine," which represents the notes e, g, b, d, and f.

REFERENCE

Algebra and Learning
Disabilities

Principle	Example
Teach a few strategies at a time	Rather than bombard children with a number of strategies all at once, teach them just a few. In this way, there is a better chance that the students can learn the strategies in a comprehensive and not a superficial fashion.
Teach self-monitoring	It is helpful if students keep track of their own progress. When checking their own work, if they find an error, they should be encouraged to try to correct it on their own.
Teach them when and where to use the strategies	Many students with learning disabilities have problems with the metacognitive skill of knowing when and where they can use strategies that teachers have taught. Teachers must give them this information as well as extensive experience in using the strategies in a variety of settings.
Maintain the students' motivation	Students need to know that the strategies work. Teachers can help motivation by consistently pointing out the benefits of the strategies, explaining how they work, and charting students' progress.
Teach in context	Students should learn cognitive techniques as an integrated part of the curriculum. Rather than using cognitive training in an isolated manner, teachers should teach students to employ cognitive strategies during academic lessons.
Don't neglect a nonstrategic knowledge base	Sometimes those who use cognitive training become such avid proponents of it that they forget the importance of factual knowledge. The more facts children know about history, science, math, English, and so forth, the less they will need to rely on strategies.
Engage in direct teaching	Because the emphasis in cognitive training is on encouraging students to take more initiative in their own learning, teachers may feel that they are less necessary than is actually the case. Cognitive training does not give license to back off from directly teaching students. Students' reliance on teachers should gradually fade. In the early stages, teachers need to be directly in control of supervising the students' use of the cognitive strategies.
Regard cognitive training as long term	Because cognitive training often results in immediate improvement, there may be a temptation to view it as a panacea or a quick fix. To maintain improvements and have them generalize to other settings, however, students need extensive practice in applying the strategies they have learned.

SOURCE: Adapted from D. Hallahan, J. Lloyd, J. Kauffman, M. Weiss, and E. Martinez, *Learning Disabilities,* 3rd ed. (Needham Heights, MA: Allyn & Bacon, 2005), p. 239. Reprinted with permission.

Direct Instruction

Unlike cognitive training with its emphasis on the uniqueness of each learner, Direct Instruction (DI) focuses on the characteristics or components of the task or concept to be learned. The aim of DI is to produce gains in specific academic skills without worrying about possible processing deficits. "The key principle in Direct Instruction," Gersten, Carnine, and Woodward (1987) write, "is deceptively simple. For all students to learn, both the curriculum materials and teacher presentation of these materials must be clear and unambiguous" (pp. 48–49).

Based on the pioneering work of Bereiter and Engelmann (1966) in the 1960s, DI represents a highly organized instructional approach. Proponents of this model emphasize controlling details of instruction so as to actively engage students' involvement in learning. Drill and practice are stressed. DI lessons, which are teacher directed, are precisely scripted, fast paced, and typically presented to small groups of children, usually five to ten. Teachers lead their students using a "script" or precisely worded lesson in an effort to ensure consistency and quality of instruction. Teachers elicit student response via hand signals or cues (such as clapping or snapping the fingers), which results in choral or unison responding by the group. This technique is designed to maintain the pupils' attention. Correct answers are immediately praised, and incorrect responses receive corrective feedback.

Learning strategies help pupils become more actively engaged in their own learning.

According to Lerner and Johns (2012), qualities of DI include the following:

1. Academic skills directly taught

2. Teacher-controlled and -directed instruction

3. Carefully sequenced and structured materials

4. Clear student goals

5. Sufficient instructional time

6. Continuous monitoring of student performance

7. Immediate feedback to students

8. Continuous instruction until mastery is achieved

The effectiveness of this skills training instructional model is well documented. Students exposed to DI methods demonstrate significant gains in academic learning (Marchand-Martella, Slocum, & Martella, 2004; Vaughn & Linan-Thompson, 2003; Walker, Shippen, Alberto, Houchins, & Cihak, 2005). Several different types of commercial programs based on DI teaching principles are available in the areas of reading, language, mathematics, social studies, and science.

Learning Strategies

Some authorities believe it is not enough to teach specific academic skills to pupils with learning disabilities. Many of these students tend to be passive and inefficient learners because they often lack systematic strategies and plans for remembering, monitoring, and directing their own learning. In contrast to proficient learners, individuals with learning disabilities haven't learned the "tricks of the trade"—the secrets to being a successful student (Lerner & Johns, 2012). A learning strategies approach to instruction focuses on teaching students *how* to learn—how to become a more purposeful, active, and efficient learner.

Unlike other instructional methodologies, which focus on learning a particular task or academic content, learning strategies are seen as the "techniques, principles, or rules that facilitate the acquisition, manipulation, integration, storage, and retrieval of information across situations and settings" (Alley & Deshler, 1979, p. 13). In other words, learning strategies are the tools that individuals use to help themselves learn and recall new material. The goal of this approach is to help students become more actively engaged and involved in their own learning.

Learning strategies are skills for learning. Probably the most widely used model for teaching these skills, which has evolved after years of research, is the Strategies Intervention Model (SIM) developed by scholars at the University of Kansas (Deshler, Ellis, & Lenz, 1996; Lenz, Ellis, & Scanlon, 1996). Renamed the Strategic Instruction Model, this approach is one of the field's most comprehensive models for providing strategy instruction. It can, according to one authority, "be used to teach virtually any strategic intervention" (Sturomski, 1997, p. 7).

learning strategies: Instructional methodologies focusing on teaching students how to learn; designed to assist pupils in becoming more actively engaged and involved in their own learning.

SUGGESTIONS FOR THE CLASSROOM

Suggestions for Teaching Students With Learning Disabilities

→ Capitalize on the student's strengths.

→ Provide high structure and clear expectations.

→ Use short sentences and a simple vocabulary.

→ Provide opportunities for success in a supportive atmosphere to help build self-esteem.

→ Allow flexibility in classroom procedures (for example, allowing the use of audio recorders for note taking and

test taking when students have trouble with written language).

→ Make use of self-correcting materials that provide immediate feedback without embarrassment.

→ Use computers for drill and practice and teaching word processing.

→ Provide positive reinforcement of appropriate social skills at school and home.

SOURCE: Adapted from National Dissemination Center for Children with Disabilities, *Fact Sheet No. 7: Learning Disabilities* (Washington, DC: Author, 2004, 2011).

Most often used with adolescents who are learning disabled, the SIM can be applied to all areas of curriculum typically encountered by middle school and high school students. This pedagogical technique emphasizes the cognitive aspects of learning rather than focusing on mastering specific subject content (Lenz & Deshler, 2004).

Success has been demonstrated across a wide range of academic areas, including essay writing, study skills, reading comprehension, math problems, and science (Bender, 2008). A learning strategies approach is especially relevant for today's classroom. As more emphasis is placed on exposure to the general education curriculum, this model can assist students in meeting this demand. With its emphasis on mastering cognitive strategies and empowering the student, a learning strategies model is a natural complement to the general classroom curriculum.

We believe, as others do, that no one instructional approach can meet the vast and complex needs of all individuals with learning disabilities. Teachers need to have an array of interventions at their disposal. Success in the classroom often depends, in part, on the match between learner characteristics and the teaching techniques used.

The accompanying Suggestions for the Classroom feature offers instructional recommendations that have been found to be effective with some students who are learning disabled.

Services for Young Children With Learning Disabilities

Determining whether a young child is learning disabled, or at risk for learning disabilities, is a difficult task. Many professionals believe that the earlier we identify a child as such, the sooner intervention can be initiated; of course, prevention is always preferable

VIDEO
Instructional Strategies

REFERENCE
Vocabulary Instruction Strategies

My training in the field of special education began many years ago in South America where it was common practice to teach children with disabilities in self-contained classrooms. After I transferred to the United States and earned a degree in special education, the range of possibilities for educating children with disabilities was a welcomed change. Starting out as a resource room teacher and eventually becoming an inclusion specialist has been an interesting and rewarding educational experience.

Inclusive Education Experience

Evolving into an inclusion teacher from a resource room teacher has definitely been an interesting journey. In the beginning it was challenging, although I welcomed the opportunity to serve my students in their least restrictive environment. It was difficult, however, for some general education teachers. This was especially true of the veteran teachers who did not understand the purpose of having students with disabilities in their classroom as well as having another educator in "their room." When the time came to implement the accommodations stated in the students' IEPs, some teachers had difficulty understanding the need for the accommodations. A few made comments relating to the fact that the children should be able to do the work if they were being served in the regular classroom, while others alluded to the fairness to the other children. Working through this process was trying at times. This was especially true when working with students with learning disabilities—mainly because their disability is not readily obvious. Often, general educators could not figure out why these children were not performing like the rest of the class. Many times these children were labeled lazy, or they were simply misunderstood. It took the general education teachers some time to appreciate the benefits of inclusion for *all* students in the class. It took some convincing and collaboratively working with them on a daily basis to make it successful.

Through the years I have seen tremendous changes toward the acceptance of children with disabilities. General educators have become more knowledgeable about pupils with disabilities thanks, in part, to working collaboratively with special educators. Working together as a team has proven to be the most productive and effective way to teach students with special needs.

Strategies for Inclusive Classrooms

The support of the school administration is the backbone of any solid inclusion program. It takes a great deal of time to effectively plan for students in an inclusive class. I would say this is one of the most important aspects of an inclusion model. It is crucial that the general education teacher has time to meet

to remediation. Yet the notion of a preschool child having a learning disability is controversial. Testing at this age is mainly for purposes of prediction, not identification. The challenge confronting educators is determining which factors are truly indicative of future learning difficulties and which are simply manifestations of variation in growth and development. It is not uncommon for professionals to talk about a young child's being at risk for problems in learning and development. Because of their exposure to adverse circumstances, some youngsters experience greater vulnerability and have a heightened potential for future problems in the classroom. Factors that *may* place a child at risk (Gargiulo & Kilgo, 2014; National Joint Committee on Learning Disabilities, 2006) include the following:

- Accidents and head trauma
- Chronic poverty
- Home environment lacking adequate stimulation
- Inadequate maternal and infant nutrition
- Low birth weight
- Maternal alcohol and drug abuse
- Oxygen deprivation

and plan with the special education teacher. It is important to communicate openly about students' needs. It is necessary to evaluate the effectiveness of the various instructional strategies used in the classroom and to be sure that the needs of all learners are being met. It is vitally important that related service providers, paraprofessionals, and other individuals working with these students be informed of their progress or the problems that sometimes arise.

Successful Collaboration

Successful collaboration entails a wide variety of options. In my opinion, one of the most important things that special educators can do is to earn the trust of the teacher(s) they work with on a daily basis. When there is trust in the relationship, collaboration will naturally fall into place. It is important that the special educator and general education teacher share responsibilities for all students. Together they plan and implement strategies that will benefit not only students with IEPs, but all children in the class. Each teacher brings his or her own strengths, skills, and knowledge to the classroom in an effort to serve all students. It is important that if problems ever develop, both the special educator and the general education teacher support each other and work together in problem solving.

Working With Parents and Families

Parent and family involvement is crucial. Parents' input during the development of the individualized education program is extremely important since they work with the child on a daily basis outside of school. It is necessary that they share their concerns with the team in order to better serve their son or daughter. Parents need to become "educators" and help their child continue the learning process at home. Additionally, it is important that parents communicate openly with their child's teachers and provide feedback. Together parents and school personnel can provide an effective inclusive environment that meets the unique needs of the child.

Advice for Making Inclusion and Collaboration Work

Making inclusion and collaboration work entails a wide array of strategies. It is not an easy task and takes hours of planning to successfully implement, but the results are worth it. Yet, even when school personnel and parents have their hearts in the right place, difficulties may arise that make the process extremely frustrating. This is when all concerned need to focus on the common goal of what is best for the child. Administrative support, teachers working together for the good of all children, and active parent involvement often result in a successful inclusive environment benefiting all students.

–Astrid Freeman
Oak Mountain Middle School
Shelby County (Alabama) Schools

- Prematurity
- Prolonged or unusual delivery
- Rh incompatibility

Remember, these factors do not guarantee that problems will arise; they only set the stage. Many young children are subject to a wide variety of risks yet never evidence any problems in school.

A related controversy is the application of the *learning disability* label to preschoolers. The regulations accompanying the current federal definition of learning disabilities consider deficits in academic performance and a discrepancy between a child's ability and academic achievement when identifying a pupil as learning disabled. How appropriate is this label when most preschoolers have not been exposed to academic work? Academic tasks are typically not introduced until the first grade, although we recognize that a growing number of kindergartens and some preschools are stressing preacademic skills. Vaughn and Bos (2012) characterize the use of a discrepancy approach for identifying a learning disability in young children as a "wait to fail" method for ascertaining who may be eligible for special educational services. We believe that the needs of the young child are best served when professionals focus on possible antecedents of learning difficulties. Simply observing the child engaging in a variety of age-appropriate activities (for example, using scissors, coloring, skipping, following directions) and noting any difficulties in performing the tasks may suggest potential problems. Remember, these may simply be warnings; they do *not* mean that learning problems will inevitably appear later in school.

There is also a growing reluctance among some educators to label young children as having a learning disability. Instead, the more generic, and less stigmatizing, noncategorical label *developmentally delayed* is finding increasing favor in some professional circles. The reauthorization of IDEA in 1997 (PL 105–17) allowed states to use this descriptor for children ages 3 through 9 who require a special education and related services. Unfortunately, there is no federal definition of this term; each state is responsible for determining what the label means. Despite this drawback, this label suggests a developmental status and not a disability category, which hopefully will result in more inclusive models of service delivery (Gargiulo & Kilgo, 2014).

Transition Into Adulthood

Adolescence is a difficult period for many young persons, but especially for students with learning disabilities. These individuals frequently have a history of failure at academic tasks, a diminished self-concept, a lack of motivation, and some degree of social ineptness. The daily demands encountered in high school often make it extremely difficult for adolescents with learning disabilities to succeed. Mercer and Pullen (2009) identify some of the many challenges confronting these pupils:

- Demonstrating knowledge through tests
- Exhibiting motivation and sustained effort
- Gaining information from lectures and written materials
- Interacting appropriately
- Working independently with little feedback

Only recently have professionals become cognizant of the unique requirements facing students with learning disabilities in secondary schools. For many years, educators incorrectly assumed that children with learning disabilities would simply "outgrow" them. As a result, adolescents with learning disabilities have received less attention than their younger counterparts. What professionals failed to realize is that problems with attention and memory, deficits in planning and organizing, and difficulties with problem solving often continue well into adolescence and beyond (see the accompanying First Person feature).

One of the purposes of an education is to prepare individuals to lead independent and productive lives as adults—to become contributing members of society. Unfortunately, our educational system has a less than stellar record of success with secondary students who are learning disabled. Recent statistics compiled by the U.S. Department of Education (2012b) indicate that only six out of ten students with learning disabilities graduate from high school with a regular diploma while almost 25 percent drop out of school—the second highest dropout rate of all pupils with disabilities. One can only conclude that our schools are failing to appropriately serve the vast number of these students.

One means of remedying this situation is through the development of a customized transition plan. PL 108–446 mandates that a transition plan be part of each adolescent's IEP. The purpose of this document is to develop goals and activities that

VIDEO

Inclusion

FIRST PERSON: CHRISTOPHER

In His Own Words

What can you tell us about yourself and your family?

My name is Christopher. I am a freshman at Oak Mountain High School. I am dyslexic and have a hard time reading and spelling. I have to get audiobooks or friends and family to help me with reading. I enjoy hands-on activities like building and drawing. I play football, lacrosse, and I also wrestle.

I have a brother and a sister who are also into sports and, like me, enjoy playing video games. My brother is visually impaired (around 20/600) from cone and rod dystrophy. I have to help him a lot with simple tasks at home and wherever we go. He helps me with spelling and math because he is really smart. He would help me more with reading if he could see better. My sister loves animals and rides English style in horse shows.

We go up to Pennsylvania once a year during Thanksgiving or Christmas to visit my relatives on my mom's side. All of my relatives on my dad's side live in Alabama, so I get to see them a lot.

What do you like to do in your free time?

I spend most of my free time playing sports and video games. For football, I play on the defensive line (noseguard) and started last fall for the Oak Mountain freshman team.

I also wrestle for Oak Mountain High School. Although my weight (194 pounds) is in the bottom of the 215-pound weight division, I sometimes have to wrestle in the heavyweight division (up to 285 pounds) for junior varsity because there is no one else that size on our team. This means that I sometimes wrestle people who are up to 90 pounds heavier than I am!

This is my first year to play lacrosse. I play for the Altamont Knights because my high school does not yet have a lacrosse team. I play "attack," which is the offensive side that is trying to score goals on the other team's defense.

When not playing sports, I like to play on my Xbox 360. I especially enjoy playing online with all my friends. My favorite game is *Call of Duty: Modern Warfare 2*.

I also enjoy traveling during breaks from school. I have gone to Australia and Europe with an organization called People to People Student Ambassadors. I also go on a lot of fun trips with my family like to Las Vegas, New York, or the beach.

I also volunteer with Special Equestrians where I help kids with physical and mental challenges ride horses. I really enjoy it and have made many new friends.

What can you tell us about your experience at school?

I go to school like every other normal 15-year-old. I take the same classes that everyone else takes except I have a help period where I get extra time for tests and have teachers read the tests to me. My favorite thing

about school is seeing all of my friends and talking with them. My least favorite thing about school is homework because it takes me two times longer to do it than regular kids. I also count studying as homework. Unlike all of my friends (my friends don't consider studying homework and don't study!), I will study for several hours, sometimes staying up late at night and waking up very early in the morning before school.

One of my favorite memories of school is yelling my lungs out with my football friends at the pep rallies. My favorite subjects in school are science and history. I have all As in school.

What can you tell us about your work background?

The only work experience I really have is refereeing soccer games. I started refereeing when I was 12 years old. Unlike other jobs, I get to pick my own schedule, and the pay is good. I enjoy working with other referees I have gotten to know. I usually referee four or five games a week when I don't have a conflict.

What do you see yourself doing in the future?

I am not exactly sure what kind of job I want, but I know I want to do something hands-on. I plan on going to college, but I am not sure what my major would be at this time. As a part of my IEP, I will be researching possible career opportunities next year.

What is one thing you want people to remember about you?

I want people to remember that I am a hard worker and will do whatever it takes to get the job done.

❖

It was quite shocking to discover that our son Christopher had dyslexia. It was difficult to know what we could do for him. We kept him at a Montessori school through sixth grade because we believed that the small class and school size would benefit him. However, the Montessori school full-sized classes ended at sixth grade. Also, after sixth grade, we knew his sports opportunities would be severely limited if he did not attend a public school. So, the decision was made to transfer Christopher to Oak Mountain Middle School.

I was pleasantly surprised at how well Christopher was able to fit into the school and how accommodating the faculty was. He worked hard, and his grades have been exceptional. In addition to his great academic work, Christopher won a character award from the school's faculty, presented to him and a few other students at a schoolwide assembly. We are as proud of that award as we are of his grades.

I am not sure what the future holds for Christopher, but I feel good about it knowing the character and work ethic that Christopher has! ∎

Adolescence can be an especially difficult time for students with learning disabilities.

are individually tailored to fulfill the student's postschool aspirations. Developing a meaningful individualized transition plan is a team effort requiring the active involvement of professionals, parents, and, perhaps most important, the student—after all, it is his or her life goals that the document addresses. Transition planning typically focuses on several different streams or options, including vocational training, preparation for postsecondary educational opportunities, or various employment possibilities.

Careful transition planning is crucial for successful adjustment later in life. The secondary school curriculum must not only prepare adolescents with learning disabilities academically, but it should also focus on preparation for future challenges such as independent living, employment options, and postsecondary schooling. Additionally, we believe that transition plans, after considering the individual needs of the student, should focus on self-determination, social skills, and assistance with understanding and adjusting to one's lifelong disability.

IDEA 2004 added a new step in transition planning for students exiting high school either by fulfilling graduation requirements or because they exceed the age of eligibility. These adolescents are to receive a summary of performance or SOP. This document reviews the individual's academic accomplishments as well as functional performance while also offering specific recommendations on the steps necessary to meet his or her postsecondary goals. The SOP, which identifies needed supports and services in the community, is a vital planning document designed to ensure future success as the young person moves forward toward adulthood (Austin & Wittig, 2013).

Adults With Learning Disabilities

The needs of adults with learning disabilities have traditionally received little attention; only recently have professionals begun to focus on this group. In many instances, however, a learning disability is a lifelong problem; many of the characteristics of learning disabilities persist into adulthood (Lewis et al., 2013). Adults with learning disabilities sometimes have great difficulty "finding their niche in the world" (Lerner & Johns, 2012, p. 294). A learning disability typically interferes with living independently, obtaining and maintaining employment, maintaining social relationships, and experiencing satisfaction with life in general (Tymchuk, Lakin, & Luckasson, 2001; Witte, Philips, & Kakela, 1998).

One should not necessarily paint a bleak picture for adults with learning disabilities. Many of these individuals achieve success and enjoy a life of quality. Successful adults establish goals, work hard, and exhibit a high degree of perseverance while also acknowledging their limitations (Scanlon, Patton, & Raskind, 2011; Wiener & Timmermanis, 2012). Table 7.5 identifies some of the characteristics exhibited by successful and unsuccessful adults with learning disabilities.

Postsecondary educational opportunities are becoming increasingly common for adults with learning disabilities. Researchers estimate that about 16 percent of students with learning disabilities are enrolled in four-year colleges or universities; an

summary of performance (SOP): Required by federal regulation for each student who exits secondary school, a summary of the individual's academic achievement and functional performance with recommendations for supports and services aimed at assisting the adolescent in achieving his or her transition goals.

AUDIO

Adults with Learning Disabilities

Successful Adults	Unsuccessful Adults
Maintain perseverance in dealing with life events	Do not understand or accept their learning disability
Develop coping strategies and know how to reduce stress	Fail to take control of their lives
Maintain emotional stability	Maintain a sense of learned helplessness and fail to assume responsibility
Have and use support systems	Seek and promote dependent relationships
Demonstrate motivation and persistence	Exhibit a lack of drive and motivation
Pursue careers that maximize their strengths and minimize their weaknesses	Fail to establish social support systems
Develop creative ways to compensate and problem-solve	Drop out of secondary school
Maintain a positive attitude toward learning	

SOURCE: Adapted from C. Mercer, *Students with Learning Disabilities,* 5th ed. (Upper Saddle River, NJ: Prentice Hall, 1997), p. 400. Reprinted by permission of Pearson Education, Inc., Upper Saddle River, NJ.

additional 35 percent attend two-year institutions such as community colleges while 22 percent are enrolled in vocational/technical schools (Newman, Wagner, Cameto, & Knokey, 2009). These figures may appear small, but they represent a dramatic increase in the number of college-bound students with learning disabilities. Unfortunately, many young adults with learning disabilities do not fully consider their postsecondary options. The Americans with Disabilities Act (PL 101–336) along with Section 504 of PL 93–112, which prohibits discrimination against individuals with disabilities, requires colleges and universities to offer reasonable accommodations to students with learning disabilities (and other impairments). Accessing support and services, however, requires that individuals self-disclose their learning disability—which some students may be reluctant to do. Typical accommodations for college students with a learning disability include extra time on exams, taking exams in a different format (for example, substituting an oral exam for a written one), waiving or substituting certain course requirements (for example, a foreign language), and using volunteer note takers for lectures (Hallahan et al., 2005).

Success in college obviously requires more than just course accommodations. Students must exhibit appropriate social skills, learn time management and organization skills, and develop self-discipline, effective study habits, and, perhaps most important, self-advocacy. Most institutions of higher education have an office of disability support services that provides students with disabilities with an array of special services designed to meet their unique requirements and enhance their chances of earning a degree.

Employment and vocational accomplishment is another concern for adults with learning disabilities. Gainful employment is a goal that many individuals with learning disabilities seek (Cortiella, 2011). In most instances, this goal is achieved. Research indicates that between 62 and 77 percent of individuals with a learning disability are competitively employed with males having a higher success rate of employment (Gonzalez, Rosenthal, & Kim, 2011; Lewis et al., 2013). Employment success is often dependent on the individual's literacy skills, his or her ability to self-advocate, and the development of work-related social competencies so that he or she becomes workplace savvy or literate.

Family Issues

A learning disability is a family affair; it affects not only the individual but, in many instances, parents, siblings, grandparents, and extended family members. Parents pay a heavy emotional toll as they deal, on a daily basis, with their son's or daughter's learning and behavioral difficulties. Yet most families of children with learning disabilities are not dysfunctional but well adjusted (Dyson, 1996).

Brothers and sisters of an individual with learning disabilities may also be affected by their sibling's disability. Feelings of embarrassment, anger, and resentment are not unusual. Although in some families siblings are adversely affected, in others brothers and sisters adjust well and seem to positively benefit from their relationships (Dyson, 1996). Positive sibling adjustment appears to be associated with parental acceptance of the child with a disability.

In keeping with the idea that parents are crucial to the well-being and adjustment of the family, Lerner and Johns (2012) offer the following recommendations for parents:

- Become an informed consumer—educate yourself about learning disabilities.
- Be an assertive advocate—protect your child's legal rights while also seeking appropriate programs in the community as well as schools.
- Be firm yet empathetic in managing the child's behavior.
- Devote time and attention to other family members.
- Make a life for yourself.

Issues of Diversity

Currently, more than four out of every ten U.S. students is black, Hispanic, or Asian American (National Center for Education Statistics, 2012b). Researchers believe that by the year 2020 students of color will represent about half of the entire school-age population in the United States (Gollnick & Chinn, 2013).

Teachers, therefore, will very likely confront significant challenges in their attempts to meet the educational needs of students from culturally and linguistically diverse backgrounds, but especially pupils with limited English language skills. One major issue for educators working with these students is distinguishing between learning problems that may arise from cultural or language differences and those that are truly due to a learning disability. It is crucial that teachers make every effort to differentiate between differences and disabilities; cultural and linguistic differences must not be interpreted as a disability.

Recent federal data reveal that 54 percent of Hispanic students with a disability are considered to have a learning disability closely followed by American Indian/ Alaskan Native pupils with a disability where 49 percent of these individuals are identified as learning disabled. Likewise, 44 percent of black students receiving a special education are recognized as having a learning disability. By way of comparison, four out of ten white students with a disability are learning disabled while 34 percent of Asian/Pacific Islanders with a disability are acknowledged to have a learning disability (U.S. Department of Education, 2012b). These statistics seem to suggest that, in some instances, we need to vastly improve our assessment procedures when evaluating culturally and linguistically diverse students for a possible learning disability.

REFERENCE

Family and Learning Disabilities

REFERENCE

Diversity

Technology and Individuals With Learning Disabilities

Students with learning disabilities can benefit from the use of assistive technology. Often for students with learning disabilities, assistive technology can serve as a cognitive prosthesis—helping students to compensate for challenges as well as become more effective and efficient learners (Bryant & Bryant, 2003; Cavalier, Ferretti, & Okolo, 1994; Edyburn, 2006). Much of the assistive technology considerations for students with learning disabilities address content-area learning (see Chapter 5 for a more in-depth discussion). For example, audiobooks or text-to-speech can help students compensate for reading challenges. Similarly, computers (word processing programs) and their related software (for example, speech-to-text, word prediction, spell-checkers) can benefit students with writing challenges. Finally, calculators can aid students with learning disabilities who struggle in calculation or the processing of basic mathematics facts. Aside from content-area support, assistive technology can also help students with learning disabilities with regard to organization and self-management (Courtad & Bouck, 2013). Students with learning disabilities can use technology such as Livescribe™ smartpens to take notes; the pen has the capability of recording the audio of a lecture or discussion while the students simultaneously take notes on its accompanying special paper. Smartphones and other portable, mobile technologies can also help students with memory problems (for example, alarms, reminders, calendars).

Trends, Issues, and Controversies

The field of learning disabilities abounds with issues and controversies. We have chosen to briefly examine one contemporary issue that confronts the field today: full inclusion.

Challenges in Service Delivery: The Full Inclusion Movement

The subject of serving students with learning disabilities in full inclusion classrooms is one of the most controversial issues confronting the field of learning disabilities. Parents, policy makers, educators, and administrators alike continue to wrestle with this emotionally charged topic, and we find powerful arguments on both sides of this issue (Spence-Cochran, Pearl, & Walker, 2013; Vaughn et al., 2014).

The issue of full inclusion is sometimes portrayed as one of equity—a belief that individuals with disabilities have a right to participate in normalized educational experiences and should not be excluded from this opportunity simply on the basis of their impairment(s). Some proponents (Peterson & Hittie, 2010; Sailor & Rogers, 2005) argue that students with learning disabilities deserve to be educated in the general education setting while others view full inclusion as a moral imperative (Specht, 2013).

As we saw earlier in this chapter, the regular classroom is currently the most popular placement for serving students with learning disabilities. Promoters of full inclusion believe that full-time placement in the general education classroom will result in enhanced academic performance, greater acceptance by typical peers, and better coordination between regular and special educators. However, those who advocate maintaining a continuum of service delivery options point out that pupils with learning disabilities are often poorly served in general education settings (McLeskey, Hoppery, Williamson, & Rentz, 2004; McLeskey & Waldron, 2011; Zigmond, 2003). The research evidence also fails to support the efficacy of full inclusion for all students with

INSIGHTS

Learning Disabilities Association of America

Position Paper on Full Inclusion of All Students with Learning Disabilities in the Regular Education Classroom January 1993, Updated June 2012

The Learning Disabilities Association of America does not support full inclusion or any policies that mandate the same placement, instruction, or treatment for ALL students with learning disabilities. Many students with learning disabilities benefit from being served in the regular education classroom. However, the regular education classroom is not the appropriate placement for a number of students with learning disabilities who may need alternative instructional environments, teaching strategies, and/or materials that cannot or will not be provided within the context of a regular class placement.

LDA believes that decisions regarding educational placement of students with disabilities must be based on the needs of each individual student rather than administrative convenience or budgetary considerations and must be the result of a cooperative effort involving educators, parents, and the student when appropriate.

LDA believes that the placement of ALL children with disabilities in the regular education classroom is as great a violation of IDEA as the placement of ALL children in separate classrooms on the basis of their type of disability.

SOURCE: Adapted from the Learning Disabilities Association of America. (1993/2012). Retrieved May 21, 2013, from http://www.ldanatl.org/about/position/papers/120614_Full-Inclusion-LDA_June- 2012-Update.pdf

learning disabilities (Fuchs & Fuchs, 2009; Zigmond & Kloo, 2011). Concerns about a lack of individualization of instruction (Zigmond & Baker, 1996) and apprehension about the appropriateness of exclusive exposure to the general education curriculum (Fuchs & Fuchs, 2009; Martin, 2002) are among the reasons that some special educators do not fully embrace full inclusion. Many national and international professional organizations and groups concerned with learning disabilities (for example, the National Joint Committee on Learning Disabilities, the Learning Disabilities Association of Canada) have adopted policy statements in opposition to full inclusion. The accompanying Insights feature presents one such position paper.

We believe that a balanced approach to this controversy is necessary. With skillful planning, equitable allocation of resources, a clear delineation of responsibilities, and careful attention to what will be taught and how it will be evaluated, full inclusion is not only feasible but also beneficial for some students with learning disabilities (Hallahan et al., 2005). Inclusive educational experiences are considered "best for children" when they provide access to the general education curriculum and opportunities to interact with typical peers in meaningful ways, as well as offering instruction that is purposefully planned, intensive, research based, and goal directed (Spence-Cochran et al., 2013).

We strongly encourage educators and other stakeholders to keep in mind the principle of individualization, which is the benchmark of special education. One size (program) does not fit all; it is a matter of a "goodness of fit." This means that for some children with learning disabilities, full inclusion is appropriate, but other students may be better served in a resource room or other setting. Perhaps our energy and attention should focus on improving the quality of our instructional practices for *all* learners with an emphasis on the individual needs of our students and the outcomes of our instruction rather than the place or location where services are provided.

AUDIO

Chapter 7 Summary

Defining Learning Disabilities

- Persons with learning disabilities are a diverse group of individuals who, despite normal intelligence, fail to learn as easily and efficiently as their classmates and peers.
- The current IDEA definition contains two key concepts: (1) a discrepancy between the student's academic performance and his or her estimated or assumed ability or potential and (2) the proviso that a learning disability cannot be due primarily to factors such as sensory impairments, intellectual disability, emotional problems, or environmental, cultural, or economic disadvantage (the exclusionary clause).

Prevalence of Learning Disabilities

- Learning disabilities is the largest category within special education, accounting for about 40 percent of all individuals receiving services.
- Government figures indicate that about 2.35 million pupils are identified as learning disabled.

Etiology of Learning Disabilities

- In the vast majority of instances, the cause of a person's learning disability is unknown.
- Researchers offer four possible factors for explaining the etiology of learning disabilities: injury or damage to the central nervous system, heredity, biochemical abnormalities, and environmental factors.

Characteristics of Individuals With Learning Disabilities

- Persons with learning disabilities are a very heterogeneous population.
- The primary characteristics of students with learning disabilities are deficits in academic performance.
- Reading is the most common problem encountered by children identified as learning disabled.
- Some individuals who are learning disabled have difficulty attending to tasks, and some exhibit excess movement and activity or hyperactive behavior. This condition is often identified as attention deficit hyperactivity disorder.

Assessment of Learning Disabilities

- State and local school districts now have the option of making eligibility decisions on the basis of how a pupil responds to research-based educational interventions, a process known as response to intervention or RTI.
- Norm-referenced assessments compare an individual's performance to that of a normative group of peers.
- Criterion-referenced assessments provide educators with a description of the student's abilities, measured against a predetermined mastery level.
- Curriculum-based measurement is a type of criterion-referenced assessment.

Educational Considerations

- About nine out of every ten students with learning disabilities spend at least part of their day in the general education classroom.
- There is no one best or correct way to teach individuals with learning disabilities.
- Cognitive training is an approach concerned with the manipulation or modification of a student's underlying thought patterns; self-instruction and mnemonic strategies are examples of cognitive training.
- Direct Instruction focuses on analyzing the characteristics or components of the task to be learned and actively involving the student in the learning process.
- Learning strategies focus on teaching students how to learn by meaningfully involving them in the instructional process.

Adolescents and Adults With Learning Disabilities

- Many adolescents with a learning disability exit school prior to graduation. Effective transition planning is one possible remedy for this problem.
- Adults with learning disabilities are increasingly taking advantage of postsecondary educational opportunities.
- Competitive employment is a realistic goal for many adults with a learning disability.

Technology and Individuals With Learning Disabilities

- Assistive technology offers many options to the challenges faced by students with learning disabilities.

STUDY QUESTIONS

1. Developing a definition of learning disabilities has proven to be problematic. Describe three reasons why this process has been so challenging.

2. What are the main components of most definitions of learning disabilities?

3. Identify the four historical phases and their respective contributions to the development of the field of learning disabilities.

4. List four possible causes of learning disabilities. Give an example of each.

5. Identify and describe five learning and behavioral characteristics common to individuals with learning disabilities. In your opinion, which one of these deficits is most debilitating? Why?

6. What is RTI? Describe the intervention process typical of most RTI models.

7. Distinguish between norm-referenced and criterion-referenced assessments. What type of information does each test provide?

8. What is the current trend in educational placement of students with learning disabilities? Do you agree with this trend? Why or why not?

9. Identify the major components of the following instructional approaches used with students who are learning disabled: cognitive training, direct instruction, and learning strategies. What are the advantages and disadvantages of each approach?

10. Why is it difficult to determine if a preschooler is learning disabled?

11. What unique problems confront secondary students with learning disabilities? How can public schools help adolescents meet these challenges?

12. Describe the variables that contribute to the successful adjustment of adults with learning disabilities.

13. In what ways might an individual with learning disabilities affect his or her family?

14. Why is it difficult to distinguish between cultural/linguistic differences and a learning disability?

15. How can technology be used to benefit individuals with learning disabilities?

16. Summarize the controversy surrounding the issue of full inclusion for students with learning disabilities.

KEY TERMS

learning disabilities   207

discrepancy   209

response to intervention (RTI)   209

exclusionary clause   209

familiality studies   215

heritability studies   215

dyslexia   217

phonological awareness   217

phonemic awareness   217

phonemes   217

pragmatics   220

short-term memory   220

working memory   220

metacognition   220

outer-directedness   221

learned helplessness   221

attention deficit hyperactivity disorder (ADHD)   222

progress monitoring   224

norm-referenced assessments   226

criterion-referenced assessments   226

curriculum-based measurement (CBM)   227

authentic assessment   227

portfolio assessment   227

self-instruction   230

mnemonic strategies   230

Direct Instruction (DI)   231

learning strategies   232

summary of performance (SOP)   238

1. Obtain a copy of the definition of learning disabilities from your state department of education, and compare it with the IDEA definition. In what ways are these definitions similar and dissimilar? Pay particular attention to eligibility criteria. How would you improve your state's definition?

2. Interview a school psychologist or educational diagnostician and inquire about the assessment and identification procedures used to determine if a student is learning disabled. Ask about the strengths and weaknesses of the various assessment instruments. Do the evaluation procedures differ depending on the grade level of the pupil? How is a discrepancy between intelligence and achievement determined? What strategies does this professional use to gather information from parents and teachers? How are children from culturally and linguistically diverse backgrounds assessed? Are RTI procedures being used to identify students with a possible learning disability?

3. Visit an elementary school, a middle school, and a high school in your community that serve individuals with learning disabilities. Observe the students in the classrooms, and interview the general educators and special educators who work with these students. What instructional approaches are used? How are the students evaluated? Does the delivery system vary according to grade level? How do the general and special educators work together? In your opinion, are the children with learning disabilities accepted by their classmates? Identify strengths and weaknesses of the learning disabilities program at each site. Would you want to be a teacher in these schools? Why or why not?

4. Interview a college student with learning disabilities. What types of supports and services does the college/university provide to students with learning disabilities? What academic and/or social areas pose the greatest challenge for this individual? What learning strategies work best for him or her? Ask the person to identify areas of strength both in and out of school. Does the individual require accommodations in the workplace? If so, what types of modifications are necessary? Inquire about the person's postschool plans and the availability of support services in the community.

5. Attend a local chapter meeting of a sibling and/or parent group for individuals with learning disabilities. What issues and concerns were addressed at this meeting? Determine what types of services and supports are available in your community for individuals with learning disabilities across the life span. Ask siblings and/or parents about the challenges and rewards of living with a person with a learning disability.

ORGANIZATIONS CONCERNED WITH LEARNING DISABILITIES

Council for Learning Disabilities

www.CLDinternational.org

Division for Learning Disabilities, Council for Exceptional Children

www.teachingLD.org

International Dyslexia Association

www.interdys.org

Learning Disabilities Association of America

www.ldanatl.org

National Center for Learning Disabilities

www.ncld.org

REFLECTING ON STANDARDS

The following exercises are designed to help you learn to apply the Council for Exceptional Children (CEC) standards to your teaching practice. Each of the reflection exercises below correlates with knowledge or a skill within the CEC standards. For the full text of each of the related CEC standards, please refer to the standards integration grid located in Appendix B.

Focus on Learner Development and Individual Learning Differences (*CEC Initial Preparation Standard 1.2*)

Reflect on a time when you weren't able to learn a skill or concept as quickly as you wanted to (for example, playing a sport or musical instrument or a particular subject in school). How did you feel about yourself? How did people treat you? What did you learn from that experience that will help you as you work with individuals who have learning disabilities?

Focus on Instructional Planning and Strategies (*CEC Initial Preparation Standard 5.2*)

Reflect on what you have learned in this chapter about students with learning disabilities. If you were to have a student with a learning disability in your general education class, how might you utilize technology to meet the various demands of your learning environment?

STUDENT STUDY SITE

⑤SAGE edge™

Sharpen your skills with SAGE edge at **edge.sagepub.com/gargiulo5e. SAGE edge for students** provides a personalized approach to help you accomplish your coursework goals in an easy-to-use learning environment.

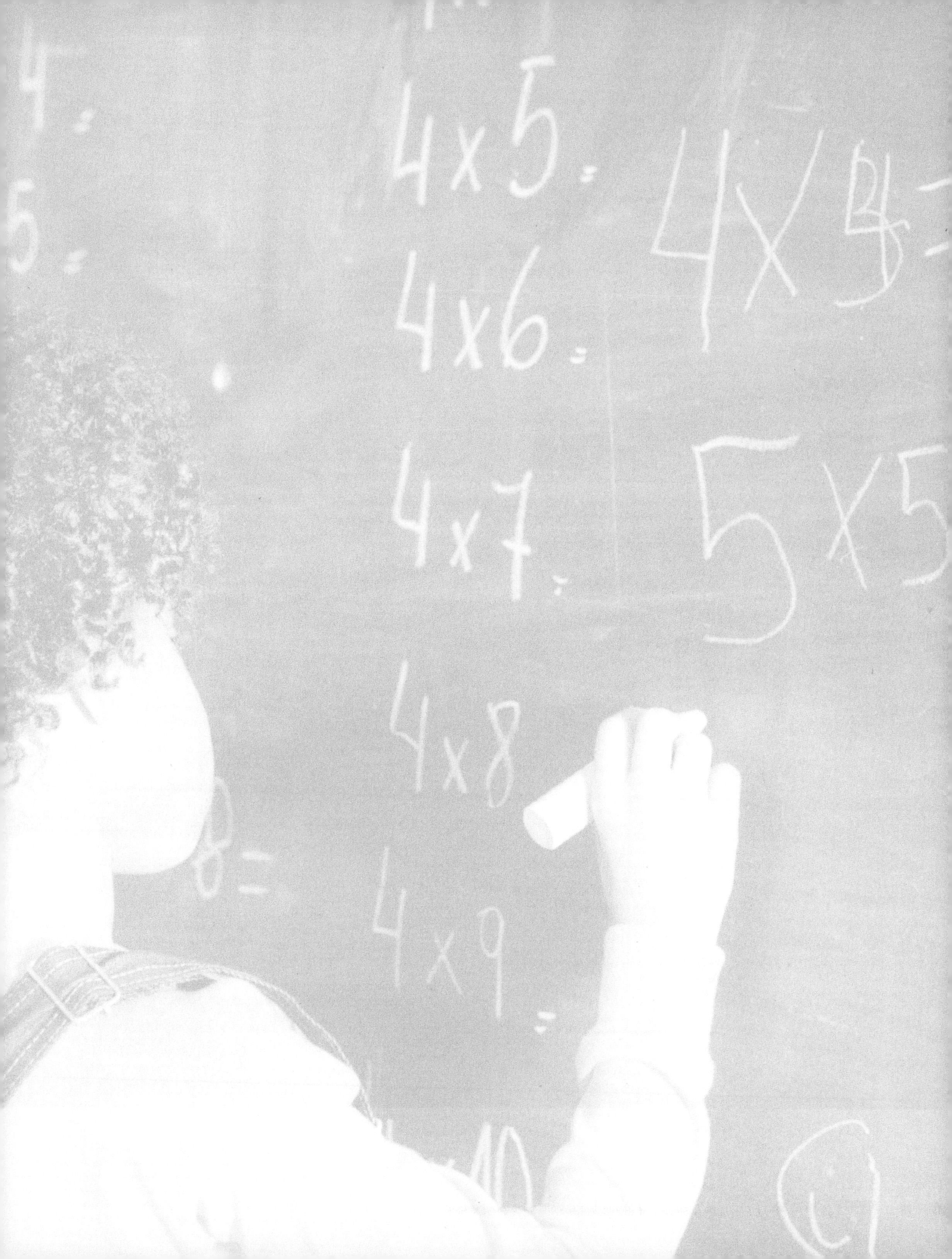
4x5 =
4x6 =
4x7 =
4x8
4x9 =
5x5

Individuals With Attention Deficit Hyperactivity Disorder

LEARNING OBJECTIVES

After reading Chapter 8, you should be able to:

- **Define** attention deficit hyperactivity disorder (ADHD).
- **Describe** the historical evolution of the concept of ADHD.
- **List** possible etiological factors associated with ADHD.
- **Identify** learning characteristics and social-emotional issues typical of persons with ADHD.
- **Explain** how ADHD is diagnosed.
- **Define** multimodal intervention.
- **Outline** instructional and environmental modifications typically used with pupils who have ADHD.
- **Describe** the role of stimulant medication in treating individuals with ADHD.
- **Summarize** the impact of ADHD on adolescents and adults.

A "Buffer Boy" With a PhD

I am Rick Parsons. By title I am a professor of counseling and educational psychology at West Chester University outside Philadelphia, Pennsylvania; a licensed psychologist with a practice in suburban Philly; and an author of more than twenty books and fifty professional articles. From a brief review of my professional accomplishments one might conclude that I have had a relatively successful career. I should also tell you that in my childhood I was a student with undiagnosed attention deficit hyperactivity disorder (ADHD).

I went to a Catholic grade school at a time when those with unique learning needs were neither recognized nor diagnosed, nor did they receive services. The idea of ADHD was not a mainstay in the early to late 1950s. Children who were easily distracted, impulsive, often engaging and annoying of class-mates, and most often itchy or squirmy were viewed as bad, out of control, or having strange diseases. The "treatment" of the day was most often of a punitive nature—detention, suspension, and even expulsion. Yet, I was one of the "lucky" ones. I was not suspended or expelled.

I can remember to this day the report cards. The grades were always medi-ocre, mostly 80s and a few 90s. The comments always pointed to how I could do better if I did my homework. There was always the direction that I needed to work on my *self-control and think before I acted!* You see I was, and still can be, a bit impulsive.

In the first few years of school I struggled with reading, being unable to really focus and attend. As a result, I was put in the slow reading group, believ-ing I wasn't very bright. In later years, as we would stand for recitation or spell-ing bees, I would often become the object of the teacher's negative attention because of my talking in line, goofing around, and most often simply moving. At times I could be in constant motion—moving my hands, swaying back and forth, tapping and drumming with my fingers, and moving to the distraction and sometimes entertainment of those near me, almost always to the frustration of the teacher attempting to run the class.

Back then the teachers employed various "interventions." I was publicly reprimanded and sent to the principal. I had notes sent home to my parents,

VIDEO

ADHD

and I even was put in time-out. Time-out for me often took the form of simply being asked to sit in the back of the class, the very back; or if need be, I could take up temporary residence in the coat closet, and even once under the teacher's desk.

Yes, the experience was one in which the message was clear. There was something wrong with this boy. After all, he came from a nice family that was actively involved in the parish, he had an older sister and brother who were excellent students, and even he had his moments in which he would shine. But this child completely lacked self-control; he was a red C student.

The poor attention and impulsive behavior were not restricted to school or bounded by the classroom. My parents had to deal with a 5-year-old who took a bus trip to the local town—just because. They parented me through years of behaviors such as climbing onto the rooftops of local stores, helping myself to penny candy, and never watching where I was going or what I was doing and therefore constantly having accidents, breaking things, or simply appearing to be a klutz. The words *pay attention, stand still, slow down,* and *watch what you're doing* became my mantra and the directive from most who knew me. And these messages took their toll.

Experience after experience had me doubt my educational abilities, my social acceptability, my emotional maturity, and even my fundamental goodness. That all changed when I met a wonderful nun, my seventh-grade teacher, Sister Mary. Without formal training in special education—simply having a respect for all of life and its uniqueness—Sister Mary helped me to understand that I wasn't bad, or immature, or ill; rather I just had a different way of learning and lots of energy to channel. It was during this seventh grade that "buffing" became more than a possible future career. Sister Mary structured my seatwork so that as soon as I finished my work, and if I could wait patiently while she checked my work and assuming it was correct, I could exit the class and operate the buffing machine. Running the buffer became a way to release energy. Operating that machine became a statement of personal competence. The fact that running the buffer was contingent on successfully completing my work helped me to attend to my work, increase my success, and eventually believe in my academic abilities.

And even though today I can still easily be distracted by external stimuli, the unconditional guidance from teachers like Sister Mary has helped me accept that it's OK to be me—it's just a challenge.

—*Rick Parsons*

Attention deficit hyperactivity disorder (ADHD) is one of the most common disorders of childhood but often continues into adolescence and adulthood (Goldstein, 2011; National Institute of Mental Health, 2008). It is believed to affect approximately 5 percent of the school-age population (American Psychiatric Association, 2013; Dopheide & Pliszka, 2009). Despite the relatively high estimate of prevalence, ADHD is not recognized as a separate disability category under the current IDEA legislation (PL 108–446). However, youngsters who have ADHD may still be eligible for a special education. In response to the lobbying efforts of parents, professionals, and advocates, in 1991 the U.S. Department of Education issued a memorandum directed to state departments of education, stating that pupils with ADHD could receive

VIDEO

Parent Interview

a special education and related services under the disability category *other health impairments* (OHI). In fact, the regulations that accompany PL 108–446 specifically mention ADHD as a condition that renders an individual eligible for services under the rubric *other health impairments*. Children with ADHD are also eligible for accommodations in general education classrooms under the protections of Section 504 of the Rehabilitation Act of 1973 (PL 93–112).

Because of the high degree of overlap or comorbidity among ADHD, learning disabilities, emotional disorders, and other conditions (Glanzman & Sell, 2013; National Institute of Mental Health, 2008) and the academic and social difficulties frequently

Students with ADHD frequently exhibit other academic and behavioral difficulties.

experienced by individuals with ADHD, we have chosen to explore this topic in greater detail in a separate chapter while acknowledging that ADHD is *not* identified by the federal government as a discrete disability category. We believe, however, it is important for educators and other professionals to be able to recognize these students and offer services, supports, and accommodations regardless of how they might (or might not) be labeled.

ADHD is frequently misunderstood; it is a disability plagued by misconceptions and myths. The behavior of individuals with ADHD is also often misinterpreted, with their actions being seen as indicators of laziness, disorganization, and even disrespect (Smith, Polloway, Patton, & Dowdy, 2012). Some people even question the legitimacy of this disability, believing that it has only been created to absolve parents (and teachers) of any responsibility for the child's conduct (Cohen, 2006).

The goal of this chapter is to examine several concepts and issues associated with ADHD. We will answer a variety of questions, such as "What is ADHD, and what causes it?" "How can I help students with ADHD?" and "What role does medication play in the treatment of ADHD?" We begin our examination by defining the term *attention deficit hyperactivity disorder*.

Defining Attention Deficit Hyperactivity Disorder

Because IDEA does not define ADHD, we use the definition put forth by the American Psychiatric Association (2013), which classifies this condition as a neurodevelopmental disorder portrayed as "a persistent pattern of inattention and/or hyperactivity-impulsivity that interferes with functioning or development" (p. 61). This description, derived from the *Diagnostic and Statistical Manual of Mental Disorders* (5th ed.) commonly referred to as DSM-5, also contains criteria to assist professionals, mainly physicians, in determining whether a child has ADHD. Examples of these characteristics are listed in Table 8.1. In examining the table, you may recognize yourself (we are all forgetful at times and occasionally easily distracted); but in individuals with ADHD, it is the chronic nature of the characteristics and their duration that often lead to impaired functioning in activities of daily living.

comorbidity: The simultaneous existence of two or more conditions within the same person.

Representative Characteristics of Attention Deficit Hyperactivity Disorder

Inattention
• Fails to pay close attention to details, often makes careless mistakes
• Difficulty sustaining attention to tasks or while playing
• Does not seem to listen when directly spoken to
• Fails to complete tasks
• Difficulty organizing tasks or activities, schoolwork is often messy and disorganized
• Avoids or resists situations requiring sustained attention
• Loses items necessary for task completion (pencils, books, tools)
• Easily distracted by extraneous stimuli
• Often forgetful in daily activities

Hyperactivity
• Fidgeting or squirming, cannot sit still
• Inability to remain seated for periods of time
• Excess running or climbing
• Difficulty engaging in quiet leisure activities
• Talks excessively
• Always on the go as if "driven by a motor"

Impulsivity
• Blurts out answers
• Difficulty waiting in line or his or her turn
• Interrupts or intrudes on others—butts into conversations or activities
• Acts without thinking, impatient

SOURCE: Adapted from the American Psychiatric Association, *Diagnostic and Statistical Manual of Mental Disorders*, 5th ed. (Arlington, VA: Author, 2013).

The preceding characteristics or symptoms must be present before the age of 12 and occur in two or more settings (for example, home and school) for at least six months. Children must present at least six symptoms from either the inattention group or the hyperactivity and impulsivity criteria. Adolescents and adults (those over age 17) must evidence five criteria. The characteristics must significantly impact or impede academic, social, or occupational functioning and not result from another mental disorder.

The American Psychiatric Association (2013) definition recognizes three subtypes of ADHD based on the individual's unique profile of symptoms: (1) predominantly inattentive type; (2) predominantly hyperactive-impulsive type; and (3) combined type. The majority of individuals with ADHD exhibit the combined type (Glanzman & Sell, 2013).

A Brief History of the Field

Individuals with attention deficit hyperactivity disorder have been recognized for more than a hundred years. In 1902, George Still, a London physician, described a group of youngsters who had average or above-average intelligence yet were disobedient toward

VIDEO
ADHD Facts

adults, acted impulsively, and exhibited inattention along with hyperactivity. He identified these children as manifesting "defective moral conduct." Still speculated that there was a hereditary foundation to their condition and that these children had neurological impairments. In the late 1930s it was discovered that administering stimulant medication to individuals with characteristics similar to those described by Dr. Still decades earlier had a calming effect on their behavior (Bradley, 1937).

Our early understanding of persons with ADHD was also aided by the work of Heinz Werner and Alfred Strauss, who had worked with children with intellectual disability in Germany. These scientists, having left Germany and immigrated to the United States, observed that some institutionalized children with intellectual disability exhibited behavior patterns of distractibility and hyperactivity not unlike those attributed to persons with brain injury. In a series of experiments comparing the performance of supposedly brain-injured children with intellectual disability to that of youngsters who were intellectually disabled but without brain injury, Werner and Strauss found that children with brain injury were more likely to focus on background objects than on the target stimulus (Strauss & Werner, 1942; Werner & Strauss, 1941). Their "figure-ground" investigations, although methodically flawed, offered evidence of the detrimental effects that distractibility and hyperactivity can have on a child's cognitive performance. Youngsters who displayed high levels of distractibility and hyperactivity were commonly referred to as exhibiting the Strauss syndrome.

The work of Werner and Strauss was replicated several years later by Cruickshank and his colleagues. These investigators (Cruickshank, Bice, & Wallen, 1957) extended the earlier figure-ground research of Werner and Strauss to children with cerebral palsy. Conceptually, this was an important extension. The youngsters in the Werner and Strauss study were assumed to have brain damage, whereas the children in the Cruickshank experiment all had cerebral palsy—a disability characterized by motor impairments resulting from brain damage (see Chapter 14). Additionally, the individuals evaluated by Werner and Strauss were intellectually disabled, but the Cruickshank et al. subjects primarily exhibited normal or near-normal intellectual ability. The finding of hyperactivity and inattention in children without intellectual disability was important because it established a link between attentional difficulties and learning problems (Hallahan, Lloyd, Kauffman, Weiss, & Martinez, 2005).

Cruickshank extrapolated his findings into educational recommendations for students who today would likely be recognized as exhibiting ADHD. He called for reducing nonessential classroom stimuli, following a highly structured teacher-directed program, and enhancing the stimulus value of instructional materials (Cruickshank, Bentzen, Ratzeburg, & Tannhauser, 1961). Although these suggestions form the nucleus of many of today's interventions for pupils with ADHD, there is a lack of scientific support for their efficacy (Barkley, 2006).

In the 1950s and 1960s, minimal brain injury was the label typically used to describe individuals with distractible, impulsive, and/or hyperactive behavior but no discernible neurological abnormalities. Use of this term soon faded because professionals believed that the designation *minimal* depreciated the difficulties experienced by these individuals. Additionally, in many instances, there was insufficient neurological evidence that the brain tissue was actually damaged (Hallahan et al., 2005).

The 1960s were known as the "Golden Age of Hyperactivity" (Barkley, 1998). During this era the label hyperactive child syndrome came into vogue, replacing *minimal brain injury* as the term of choice. Professionals favored this description because it focused attention on observable behaviors rather than relying on speculative indicators of brain injury. Eventually, during the 1980s, the *hyperactive child syndrome* label lost its position of prominence as investigators focused their interest on

Strauss syndrome: A historical term applied to individuals with intellectual disabilities who exhibit high levels of distractibility and hyperactivity.

minimal brain injury: A once popular term referring to individuals who exhibit behavioral signs of brain injury (such as distractibility or impulsivity) but with no neurological evidence.

hyperactive child syndrome: A historical term commonly used to describe youngsters who exhibit impulsivity, inattention, and/or hyperactivity.

the inattention component of ADHD as the major deficit exhibited by children with ADHD (Hallahan et al., 2005).

Prevalence of Attention Deficit Hyperactivity Disorder

As we noted earlier, ADHD is believed to affect approximately 3 to 9 percent of the school-age population or an estimated parent-reported 5.4 million children (Centers for Disease Control and Prevention, 2013a). Nationally, almost 9.5 percent of children 4 to 17 years of age exhibit ADHD, with significant variation found among the states. In Nevada, for instance, only 5.6 percent of youth were diagnosed with ADHD while Alabama reported a prevalence of over 14 percent (Centers for Disease Control and Prevention, 2013d). Despite significant variation in prevalence, the number of individuals with ADHD continues to grow, most likely because of greater awareness on the part of parents and professionals along with improved diagnostic procedures.

Recall that ADHD is not one of the thirteen disability categories recognized by the federal government; these pupils may be served, however, under the label *other health impairments*. During the 2011–2012 school year, over 734,000 students were identified as having OHI. In the past decade, this category has seen an increase of almost 396,000 children, or an astonishing 117 percent increase (U.S. Department of Education, 2005, 2013b). Of course, not all of this gain can be attributed to pupils with ADHD. We suspect, however, that individuals with ADHD are largely responsible for the dramatic growth of this category. In fact, because of this growth,

ADHD affects males more than females.

some authorities in special education now consider OHI to be a high-incidence disability.

The research literature generally suggests that ADHD is more readily identified in males than in females. This condition is diagnosed three to four times more often in boys than in girls (Centers for Disease Control and Prevention, 2013a; Lerner & Johns, 2012). These statistics suggest the possibility of a gender bias in identification and diagnosis, that boys may be overidentified and girls underidentified. We believe that this situation exists because ADHD manifests itself differently in males and females. Boys are more likely to exhibit disruptive, hyperactive behavior, thus being more noticeable to teachers. Girls, on the other hand, are more likely to be withdrawn and exhibit inattention; consequently, they are less likely to be identified (Vaughn, Bos, & Schumm, 2014; Wicks-Nelson & Israel, 2013). Though gender bias may explain part of the discrepancy between males and females, scientific evidence points to actual biological differences as the primary contributing factor (Barkley, 2006).

Etiology of Attention Deficit Hyperactivity Disorder

The precise cause of attention deficit hyperactivity disorder is unknown. To date, no single etiological factor has been discovered, although researchers are exploring several possibilities, including neurological foundations, hereditary contributions, and

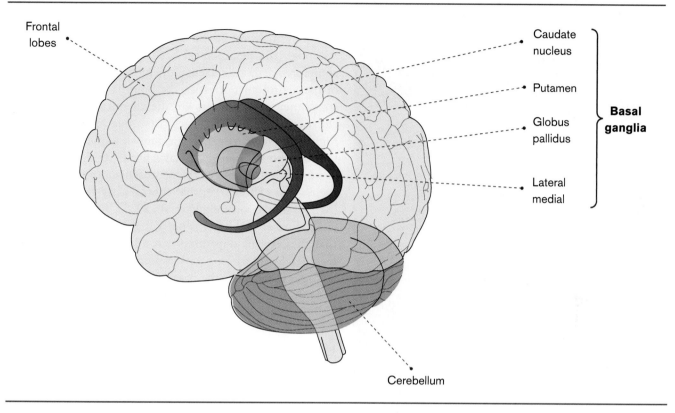

Frontal lobes

Caudate nucleus

Putamen

Globus pallidus

Lateral medial

Basal ganglia

Cerebellum

environmental conditions. As scientists learn more about ADHD, it is likely that multiple causes will be identified.

Neurological Dysfunction

Research suggests that neurological dysfunction plays a key role in individuals with ADHD. Anatomical differences and imbalances in brain chemistry are being closely examined as etiological possibilities (Floet, Scheiner, & Grossman, 2010; Makris, Biederman, Monuteaux, & Seidman, 2009; Vaidya & Stollstorff, 2008). In recent years, neuroscientists have been able to advance our understanding of the functioning of the human brain—particularly as it relates to individuals with ADHD. Aided by advances in neuroimaging technology, researchers are using scans of the brain such as positron emission tomography (PET) and magnetic resonance imaging (MRI) procedures, as well as other techniques, to learn about brain structure and activity. Several regions of the brain, specifically the frontal lobes, parts of the basal ganglia, and the cerebellum, appear to consistently exhibit abnormalities in persons with ADHD (Glanzman & Blum, 2008; Glanzman & Sell, 2013; Shaw & Rubin, 2009). See Figure 8.1 for regions of the brain thought to be affected.

The prefrontal and frontal lobes, located in the far forward region of the brain, are responsible for control of executive functions—behaviors such as self-regulation, working memory, inner speech, and arousal levels, among other dimensions. The basal ganglia, consisting of several parts (caudate and globus pallidus), is responsible for control and coordination of motor behavior. The cerebellum is also involved in controlling motor behavior (Glanzman & Sell, 2013). Disorganization and inattention, frequently implicated with ADHD, are believed to be associated with impairments

executive functions: Internal regulation of one's behavior through control of emotions, inner speech, working memory, arousal levels, and motivation. Considered impaired in individuals with attention deficit hyperactivity disorder.

AUDIO

ADHD and Neurofeedback

The neurological basis of ADHD is not fully understood.

in the prefrontal and frontal cortex, whereas hyperactive behavior is thought to be due to abnormalities in the cerebellum and/or basal ganglia (Glanzman & Blum, 2008).

Scientists are also exploring the possibility of chemical abnormalities in the brain as a reason for ADHD. Although the neurological basis for ADHD is not fully comprehended, a deficiency or imbalance in one or more of the neurotransmitters in the brain is suspected. Simply stated, neurotransmitters are the chemicals that transport electrical impulses (messages) from one brain cell or neuron to another across tiny gaps known as the synaptic cleft. Current thinking suggests that ADHD results from a deficiency or dysfunction of the neurotransmitter dopamine in the regions of the brain that control activity and attention (Mill et al., 2006; Volkow et al., 2007). Although the precise nature of the defect is not known, investigators believe that the level of dopamine is too low in the frontal cortex, thereby interfering with aspects of executive functioning, and elevated in the basal ganglia region, contributing to impulsive and hyperactive behavior (Castellanos, 1997; Volkow et al., 2009).

Hereditary Factors

There is strong evidence of the role of heredity in contributing to ADHD. Hereditary factors are believed to account for a large percentage of hyperactive-impulsive behavior (Ficks & Waldman, 2009; Glanzman & Blum, 2007, 2008; Glanzman & Sell, 2013). Approximately one out of three persons with ADHD also has relatives with this condition (Barkley, 2006). Family studies further reveal that a child who has ADHD is much more likely to have parents who exhibit ADHD (Floet et al., 2010; Hammerness, 2009). Additionally, researchers investigating monozygotic (identical) and dizygotic (fraternal) twins have consistently found a higher concordance of ADHD in identical twins than in fraternal twins, strongly suggesting a genetic link (Martin, Levy, Pieka, & Hay, 2006; Nikolas & Burt, 2010).

Environmental Factors

Various pre-, peri-, and postnatal traumas are also implicated as contributing to ADHD (Barkley, 2006; Glanzman & Sell, 2013; U.S. Department of Education, 2008a). Examples of environmental factors include maternal smoking, alcohol abuse, illicit drug use, lead poisoning, complications of birth, low birth weight, and prematurity. Many of these factors are suspected of contributing to intellectual disability as well as learning disabilities.

Research (Hallahan et al., 2005; U.S. Department of Education, 2008a) has discounted many other environmental explanations. Among the popular myths regarding suspected causes of ADHD, but lacking in scientific support, are too much/too little sugar, food additives/coloring, yeast, fluorescent lighting, bad parenting, and too much television.

Characteristics of Individuals With Attention Deficit Hyperactivity Disorder

Characteristics of persons with attention deficit hyperactivity disorder vary considerably. This disorder generally manifests itself early in a child's life. In fact, some precursors have been noted in infancy (Barkley, 2000). It would not be uncommon for behaviors associated with ADHD to be exhibited as early as kindergarten or first grade (Vaughn et al., 2014). Though many young children are sometimes inattentive, fidgety, or somewhat impulsive, the developmental features that distinguish ADHD from typical patterns of behavior in young children include the following:

- Chronic over time
- Generally pervasive behaviors across situations
- Deviant from age-based standards
- Increased likelihood of having another difficulty such as a learning or psychiatric disorder (Vaughn et al., 2014, p. 169)

ADHD presents itself in many different ways. In some students, inattention is the primary deficit. These pupils have difficulty concentrating on a specific task; they are forgetful and easily distracted. Students who exhibit hyperactive-impulsive disorder are constantly in motion; racing from one activity to another, they have difficulty sitting still or playing quietly. Individuals with a combined type of ADHD manifest aspects of both types. Review Table 8.1 (page 252) for examples of other characteristics typical of students with ADHD. (See the accompanying First Person feature.)

Behavioral Inhibition and Executive Functioning

Contemporary thinking suggests that problems with behavioral inhibition are the primary characteristic of persons with ADHD (Barkley, 2006). Behavioral inhibition consists of three elements that affect the ability to (1) withhold a planned response, (2) interrupt a response that has already been initiated, and (3) protect an ongoing activity from competing or distracting stimuli (Barkley, 2006; Vaughn et al., 2014). Problems with behavioral inhibition can lead to a variety of difficulties in the classroom. According to Hallahan et al. (2005), students may have trouble, for example, waiting their turn, resisting distractions, delaying immediate gratification, or interrupting a faulty line of thinking.

Researchers (Barkley, 2006; Glanzman & Sell, 2013; Weyandt, 2009) note that individuals with ADHD also often have difficulty with executive functions. Recall from our earlier discussion of the etiology of ADHD that executive functions involve a number of self-directed behaviors, such as self-regulation, working memory, inner speech, and arousal levels, among other dimensions. Impaired executive functioning in children with ADHD affects a wide range of performance. Difficulty following rules or directions, forgetfulness, and a lack of emotional control are just a few of the ways that students are affected.

Social and Emotional Issues

Social problems and emotional difficulties are not uncommon among individuals with ADHD. Children with ADHD often experience difficulty making friends and maintaining appropriate relationships with peers (Glanzman & Blum, 2007; Wicks-Nelson & Israel, 2013). Diminished self-confidence, low self-esteem, and feelings of social

behavioral inhibition: A characteristic common in persons with ADHD; impacts executive functions. Typically affects the ability to (1) withhold a planned response; (2) interrupt an ongoing response; and (3) protect an ongoing response from distractions.

AUDIO
ADHD Characteristics

FIRST PERSON: HELEN

Good Things Come in Small Packages

Like any expectant first-time mom, I was thrilled at the thought of becoming a parent. My joy, however, quickly turned to fear when I went into premature labor. My concerns were multiplied when I developed pulmonary edema and could barely breathe. The only thing that kept me sane was the constant, rhythmic heartbeat of my baby girl coming through loud and clear on the fetal monitor. My family knew how serious my condition was, but I was in a total fog—completely unaware that the doctor had addressed the possibility of my husband having to choose between my life and that of our unborn child. Six days after entering the hospital, and four days after our life-threatening ordeal, our daughter Helen was born.

Five weeks premature and weighing only 4 pounds, 12 ounces, she made a feisty entrance into the world. My husband and I were able to take her home just two days later. With the exception of developing jaundice, she had no health problems whatsoever. Developmental milestones such as rolling over, sitting alone, and pulling up were reached well within normal limits. She even took her first step on her first birthday. Although she was tiny, we had no concerns for her physical development.

Helen's intellectual and emotional growth initially appeared right on track as well; sometimes she was even ahead of the norm. She talked at a very young age. She used simple but complete sentences by the time she was 18 months old and could carry on a decent conversation by age 2.

When the time came for her to start kindergarten, we had some reservations about her beginning school; but at the time, her starting public school was the best option for our family. Helen was one of the youngest children in her class and was definitely the smallest. Our first hint of trouble came during this year. She struggled with reading and math, but her teacher had no worries about her moving on to first grade. She saw no problem that a little maturity couldn't fix.

Helen made great strides in first grade but still struggled. Approximately one month before the year was over, the light seemed to turn on—she got it! Her teacher lamented the fact that she could not keep her another six weeks. Much as in kindergarten, my husband and I discussed the possibility of either having her tested for a learning disability or repeating the grade, but her teacher believed she would be fine.

Second grade was a repeat of first. No problems at the beginning of the school year, then increasing struggles as the year progressed, and of course the

"eureka" moment near the end of the year. As in both kindergarten and first grade, Helen's teacher strongly recommended against holding her back, citing the social stigma of repeating while crediting many of her problems to her immaturity. Yet again, a referral for special education was discouraged.

It was not until third grade that we had a major turning point. The work was becoming more difficult, and her frustration was growing. The final straw came one evening when, after a long and confusing homework session, Helen put her head down on the table and began to cry. When I asked her what was wrong, she began to sob uncontrollably, then threw herself into my arms and pleaded with me, "Mommy, why can't I learn like everybody else?" I honestly don't remember what I told her. All I could really think of was getting to school the next day to talk with her teacher. Thus began the long saga of figuring out exactly where the problems were and how we would address them.

After multiple tests to determine her eligibility for special education, all the assessments indicated "normal" results. But thank goodness the principal, the counselor, and her teacher saw past the scores and into the eyes and heart of a little girl who was quickly losing any belief in herself. We hired a tutor, we made modifications in the classroom, and Helen took more diagnostic tests—still nothing that would qualify her for services under special education. About two thirds of the way through the school year, Helen's pediatrician diagnosed her with ADHD; thus, she was eligible to receive a special education under the label *other health impairments*. She began taking Ritalin, and we saw a gradual improvement in her schoolwork.

The improvement we saw did not come without a price. Helen was very angry with her father and me when she realized why she was taking medication every day. She was truly terrified of not having any friends if they found out she had ADHD.

About halfway through fourth grade, we decided to try the extended release form of her medication. We did this in hopes that she would not feel as though she was being "watched" by her classmates when she had to go take medicine in the middle of the day, and also to help with her homework in the late afternoon and early evening. Unfortunately, coming off the medication in the evening turned into a "crash and burn" event most nights. Helen even began to have suicidal ideation and one night did not eat dinner because, as she put it, she "could control herself" (in reference to living or dying).

We of course changed medications, and the emotional outbursts tapered off. The remainder of fourth and fifth grade was an up-and-down roller coaster, ending with yet another twist in the ride. Helen's younger sister was identified as gifted, thus creating a new set of struggles with self-confidence and self-esteem.

Currently, as a seventh grader (but the size of a third grader), she is developing new friends and her own sense of style and self. Academics continue to be a daily struggle. She tends to get lost in lengthy operations and has a great deal of trouble focusing attention and identifying pertinent information. Helen has a tremendous problem with spelling and grammar. She also has trouble transferring and assimilating knowledge from one situation to another. Helen is very rules oriented and desperately needs structure, but she cannot provide that structure for herself. She tends to vacillate from overly focused to airhead. At times, Helen appears almost belligerent—she is unable to

"shift gears" as circumstances change. We frequently see this with her schoolwork. She continues to make the same mistakes over and over again because of her unwillingness (inability) to adopt a different strategy—because, in her eyes, her way is the correct way.

Her father and I continue to try to instill the idea of effort being more important than grades, but she holds herself to a higher standard. I am not sure what the next eight to ten years hold. Helen is a very hard worker, but at this point in time a four-year college degree may or may not be in her future. Our biggest concern is that she find something she enjoys and that she can excel in. Our goal is not for her to make the honor roll or be rich, but for Helen to be a self-confident and fulfilled young woman. ■

–Anonymous

isolation/rejection are fairly typical in some individuals with ADHD (Friend & Bursuck, 2012). In some instances, in their attempts to be popular and gain friends, students with ADHD, because of their impaired impulse control, actually wind up aggravating peers and further ostracizing themselves from the very individuals with whom they are attempting to establish relationships.

Persons with ADHD may manifest a wide variety of emotional difficulties. Some individuals may exhibit aggression and antisocial behaviors; in others, withdrawn behavior, depression, and anxiety disorders are typical (Brown, 2006; Glanzman & Sell, 2013; National Institute of Mental Health, 2008). A majority of parents of children with recognized emotional disorders report that their child also exhibits ADHD (U.S. Department of Education, 2008b).

Comorbidity

Students with ADHD frequently have other academic and behavioral difficulties. Learning disabilities, for example, are very common among individuals with ADHD (Bender, 2008; Glanzman & Sell, 2013). In an interesting distinction, Silver (1990) observes that a learning disability affects the brain's ability to learn, whereas ADHD interferes with a person's availability to learn. On the other hand, pupils who are gifted and talented (see Chapter 15) are also frequently recognized as having ADHD. Some of these students, in fact, exhibit intense curiosity, creativity, and concentration (Dodson, 2002; Honos-Webb, 2005). Additionally, researchers have found that children with ADHD have coexisting psychiatric disorders at a much higher rate than their peers without ADHD (Atkins & Mariñez-Lora, 2008; Kauffman & Landrum, 2013; Stein & Shin, 2008). Unfortunately, at the present time, investigators are unable to fully explain the reasons for the high degree of overlap between ADHD and other impairments.

VIDEO

ADHD Challenges

Assessment of Attention Deficit Hyperactivity Disorder

Identifying pupils with attention deficit hyperactivity disorder is not always easy, although many teachers will say "you know it when you see it." Valid and reliable assessment of ADHD is difficult; there is no single, definitive medical or psychological test that clearly distinguishes these children from others. Identifying a child as having ADHD is a multidimensional process. Typical strategies for assessing this condition involve direct observation of the youngster and the use of behavior rating scales and other types of observation instruments completed by parents, teachers, and other professionals. Teachers, in particular, represent a valuable source of information about the child as they are involved with this student in a variety of academic and social situations.

Assessment and diagnosis of ADHD is a multifaceted endeavor involving the gathering of specific medical, behavioral, and educational data (U.S. Department of Education, 2008a). The intent of these efforts is to glean as much useful information as possible in order to accurately assess the child's condition.

Medical Evaluation

Generally speaking, a medical evaluation is designed to rule out medical conditions that might be contributing to the pupil's hyperactivity and/or inattention. Examples of these conditions include epilepsy, thyroid problems, and brain tumors (Hallahan et al., 2005; National Institute of Mental Health, 2008). Knowledge of a child's health status can also assist the health care professional in deciding which type of medication to prescribe, should that be a treatment option.

Medical professionals confronted with making a diagnosis of ADHD often utilize guidelines disseminated by the American Academy of Pediatrics (2011). These guidelines, which vary by the age of the child, offer specific direction and guidance to the doctor for the diagnosis as well as treatment of ADHD.

An interesting phenomenon is sometimes observed during the clinical interview. In novel and structured situations, such as a physician's office, it is not unusual for the child to be symptom-free of characteristics typically associated with ADHD—much to the bewilderment and dismay of his or her parents or caregivers. This phenomenon, recognized many years ago, is commonly referred to as the doctor's office effect (Cantwell, 1979).

Behavioral/Educational Evaluation

Rating scales provide another important source of information about the student suspected of having ADHD. These scales assess the presence of ADHD symptoms and offer an objective way of quantifying the severity of the behaviors (Smith et al., 2012). Evaluation of the child's performance in the classroom and his or her behavior at home will assist professionals in establishing a complete picture of the pupil's condition and ensure that the data are as accurate as possible. Although behavioral rating scales can accurately distinguish between children with and without ADHD (U.S. Department of Education, 2008a), their usefulness and accuracy are largely dependent upon raters' knowledge of the individual and their perception of his or her behavior. Despite the standardized nature of these instruments, bias is a real concern.

One example of a reliable and valid assessment measure is the ADHD Rating Scale–IV (DuPaul, Power, Anastopoulos, & Reid, 1998). As with other rating indices, informants rate an individual's performance using a Likert scale (*never or rarely*, *sometimes*, *often*, or *very often*). The Conners 3 (Conners, 2009) is another representative example of a commonly used standardized rating scale. This instrument allows the

doctor's office effect: The absence of symptoms of ADHD when the individual is evaluated in a structured environment such as a physician's office.

Table 8.2 **Sample Test Items From the "Strengths and Limitations Inventory: School Version"**

		Never Observed	Sometimes Observed	Often Observed	Very Often Observed
Attention/ Impulsivity/ Hyperactivity	Exhibits excessive nonpurposeful movement (can't sit still, stay in seat).				
	Does not stay on task for appropriate periods of time.				
	Verbally or physically interrupts conversations or activities.				
	Does not pay attention to most important stimuli.				
Reasoning/ Processing	Makes poor decisions.				
	Makes frequent errors.				
	Has difficulty getting started.				
Memory	Has difficulty repeating information recently heard.				
	Has difficulty following multiple directions.				
	Memory deficits impact daily activities.				
Executive Function	Has difficulty planning/organizing activities.				
	Has difficulty attending to several stimuli at once.				
	Has difficulty monitoring own performance throughout activity (self-monitoring).				
	Has difficulty independently adjusting behavior (self-regulation).				
Interpersonal Skills	Has difficulty accepting constructive criticism.				
	Exhibits signs of poor self-confidence.				
Emotional Maturity	Inappropriate emotion for situation.				
	Displays temper outbursts.				
	Does not follow classroom or workplace "rules."				

SOURCE: C. Dowdy, J. Patton, T. Smith, and E. Polloway, *Attention Deficit/Hyperactivity Disorder in the Classroom* (Austin, TX: Pro-Ed, 1998), pp. 112–113.

evaluator to rate a variety of ADHD characteristics on the basis of how closely the statement portrays the student. While some assessment instruments primarily assess symptoms of ADHD, other scales are multidimensional. Table 8.2 shows sample test items from one such measure. This instrument, which is typically completed by teachers, evaluates the impact of ADHD on cognitive processes, social-emotional behaviors, and impulsivity-hyperactivity.

Educational Considerations

How does a teacher assist the student who exhibits attention deficit hyperactivity disorder? With an estimated 5 million school-age children exhibiting this disorder (National Center for Health Statistics, 2010), this is an important issue for many classroom teachers and parents. Many pupils with ADHD experience significant difficulty in school, where attention and impulse control are prerequisites for success. In fact, academic underachievement is one of the most salient features of this disability. Many students with ADHD are at risk for chronic school failure (McKinley & Stormont, 2008; Scheffler et al., 2009; Wicks-Nelson & Israel, 2013).

Most children with ADHD respond to a structured and predictable learning environment where rules and expectations are clearly stated and understood, consequences are predetermined, and reinforcement is delivered immediately (National Dissemination Center for Children with Disabilities, 2012). Of course, environmental modifications alone are not the key to success. Educational researchers believe that multimodal interventions, or concurrent treatments, are generally more effective for individuals with ADHD than any one particular strategy (Lerner & Johns, 2012; Mercer & Pullen, 2009). Instructional adaptations, behavioral interventions, home-school communication, medication, and counseling represent some of the available intervention options for individuals with ADHD. We have chosen to highlight four of these treatment approaches, including a concluding examination of the role of medication in the treatment of ADHD. But first we look at the issue of the educational setting that is most appropriate for pupils with ADHD.

Where Are Students With Attention Deficit Hyperactivity Disorder Educated?

Because the federal government does not recognize attention deficit hyperactivity disorder as a discrete disability, information usually provided by the U.S. Department of Education on the educational settings in which these pupils are served is unavailable. Individuals with ADHD who qualify for a special education are eligible for services under the category *other health impairments*. It is not possible, however, to distinguish which students in this group have ADHD.

Given our current educational climate of emphasizing inclusionary placement for individuals with disabilities, it is safe to assume that large numbers of students with ADHD receive services in the general education classroom. Mercer and Pullen (2009) as well as Lerner and Johns (2012) offer support for this assumption, citing evidence that the majority of students with ADHD are appropriately served in the general education classroom. Sometimes this placement involves general education teachers and special educators working together as a collaborative team. Of course, the most appropriate setting for a student with ADHD must be decided on a case-by-case basis.

Recall that not all students with ADHD qualify for special education services under IDEA (PL 108–446). These individuals will most likely receive accommodations in the general education classroom through the protections afforded them under Section 504 of PL 93–112. See the accompanying Suggestions for the Classroom feature for a list of accommodations appropriate for designing 504 plans and individualized education programs (IEPs).

multimodal interventions: The use of concurrent treatment approaches with students who exhibit attention deficit hyperactivity disorder.

REFERENCE
Parents' Perspectives

VIDEO
Accommodations

Teachers who are successful in working with children with ADHD, regardless of the educational setting in which they are served, typically incorporate a three-pronged strategy. They begin by identifying the unique needs of the child. For example, the teacher determines how, when, and why the pupil is inattentive, impulsive, and hyperactive. The teacher then selects different educational practices associated with academic instruction, behavioral interventions, and classroom accommodations that are appropriate to meet the child's needs. Finally, the teacher combines these practices into an IEP or other individualized plan and integrates this program with educational activities provided to other students. The three steps, which summarize this strategy, are as follows:

- Evaluate the child's individual needs and strengths.
- Select appropriate instructional practices.
- Integrate practices within the IEP if the student is receiving a special education.

"Because no two children with ADHD are alike, it is important to keep in mind that no single educational program, practice, or setting will be best for all children" (U.S. Department of Education, 2008b, p. 4).

We will now examine several different treatment approaches typically used to meet the unique needs of students with ADHD.

Self-regulation is a common intervention strategy used with students with ADHD.

Functional Behavioral Assessment

Behavioral strategies are an effective intervention technique for students with ADHD. One example of this approach is the use of functional behavioral assessment. A functional behavioral assessment focuses on determining the purpose or function that a particular behavior serves. This process entails, according to Alberto and Troutman (2006), "detailed observation, analysis, and manipulation of objects and events in a student's environment to determine what is occasioning and maintaining the [inappropriate] behaviors" (p. 62). Once this analysis is completed, the goal is to construct interventions that modify the antecedent or triggering behaviors and/or the consequences that are reinforcing and maintaining the undesirable performances.

Self-Regulation/Monitoring

Self-regulation is a behavioral self-control strategy drawn from the early work of Glynn, Thomas, and Shee (1973) on self-monitoring. It is a highly effective intervention strategy for students with ADHD (DuPaul & Weyandt, 2006; Graham-Day, Gardner, & Hsin, 2010; Harris, Friedlander, Saddler, Frizzelle, & Graham, 2005; Weiss & Illes, 2006). "Self-regulation requires students to stop, think about what they are doing, compare their behavior to a criterion, record the results of their comparison, and receive reinforcement for their behavior if it meets the criterion" (Johnson & Johnson, 1999, p. 6). Self-monitoring includes all of the preceding steps with the exception of dispensing reinforcement. Self-regulation techniques can be used

functional behavioral assessment: A behavioral strategy that seeks to determine the purpose or function that a particular behavior serves—what is occasioning and maintaining the behavior.

self-regulation: The ability of an individual to manage or govern his or her own behavior.

REFERENCE

Functional Behavior Assessment

REFERENCE

Self-Regulation

SUGGESTIONS FOR THE CLASSROOM

Accommodations to Help Students With Attention Deficit Hyperactivity Disorder

Children and youth with attention deficit hyperactivity disorder (ADHD) often have serious problems in school. Inattention, impulsiveness, hyperactivity, disorganization, and other difficulties can lead to unfinished assignments, careless errors, and behavior that is disruptive to oneself and others. Through the implementation of relatively simple and straightforward accommodations to the classroom environment or teaching style, teachers can adapt to the strengths and weaknesses of students with ADHD. Small changes in how a teacher approaches the student with ADHD or in what the teacher expects can turn a losing year into a winning one for the child. Examples of accommodations that teachers can make to adapt to the needs of students with ADHD are grouped below according to areas of difficulty.

Inattention

→ Seat student in quiet area.

→ Require fewer correct responses for grade.

→ Seat student near good role model.

→ Reduce amount of homework.

→ Seat student near "study buddy."

→ Instruct student in self-monitoring using cueing.

→ Increase distance between desks.

→ Pair written instructions with oral instructions.

→ Allow extra time to complete assigned work.

→ Provide peer assistance in note taking.

→ Shorten assignments or work periods to coincide with span of attention; use timer.

→ Give clear, concise instructions.

→ Break long assignments into smaller parts so student can see end of work.

→ Seek to involve student in lesson presentation.

→ Assist student in setting short-term goals.

→ Cue student to stay on task (i.e., private signal).

→ Give assignments one at a time to avoid work overload.

Impulsiveness

→ Ignore minor inappropriate behavior.

→ Acknowledge positive behavior of nearby students.

→ Increase immediacy of rewards and consequences.

→ Seat student near role model or near teacher.

→ Use time-out procedure for misbehavior.

→ Set up behavior contract.

→ Supervise closely during transition times.

→ Instruct student in self-monitoring of behavior (i.e., hand raising, calling out).

→ Use "prudent" reprimands for misbehavior (i.e., avoid lecturing or criticism).

→ Call on only when hand is raised in appropriate manner.

→ Attend to positive behavior with compliments, etc.

→ Praise when hand raised to answer question.

Motor Activity

→ Allow student to stand at times while working.

→ Supervise closely during transition times.

→ Provide opportunity for "seat breaks" (run errands, etc.).

→ Remind student to check over work product if performance is rushed and careless.

→ Provide short breaks between assignments.

→ Give extra time to complete tasks (especially for students with slow motor tempo).

Academic Skills

→ If reading is weak: Provide additional reading time; use "previewing" strategies; select text with less on a page; shorten amount of required reading; avoid oral reading.

→ If written language is weak: Accept nonwritten forms for reports (i.e., displays, oral reports); accept use of typewriter, word processor, tape recorder; do not assign large quantity of written work; test with multiple-choice or fill-in questions.

→ If oral expression is weak: Accept all oral responses; substitute a display for an oral report; encourage student to tell about new ideas or experiences; pick topics easy for student to talk about.

→ If math is weak: Allow use of calculator; use graph paper to space numbers; provide additional math time; provide immediate corrective feedback and instruction via modeling of the correct computational procedure.

SUGGESTIONS FOR THE CLASSROOM (CONTINUED)

Organization Planning

→ Ask for parental help in encouraging organization.

→ Allow student to have extra set of books at home.

→ Provide organization rules.

→ Give assignments one at a time.

→ Encourage student to have notebook with dividers and folders for work.

→ Assist student in setting short-term goals.

→ Provide student with homework assignment book.

→ Do not penalize for poor handwriting if visual-motor defects are present.

→ Supervise writing down of homework assignments.

→ Encourage learning of keyboarding skills.

→ Send daily/weekly progress reports home.

→ Allow student to tape-record assignments or homework.

→ Regularly check desk and notebook for neatness; encourage neatness rather than penalize sloppiness.

Compliance

→ Praise compliant behavior.

→ Supervise student closely during transition times.

→ Provide immediate feedback.

→ Seat student near teacher.

→ Ignore minor misbehavior.

→ Set up behavior contract.

→ Use teacher attention to reinforce positive behavior.

→ Implement classroom behavior management system.

→ Use "prudent" reprimands for misbehavior (i.e., avoid lecturing or criticism).

→ Instruct student in self-monitoring of behavior.

→ Acknowledge positive behavior of nearby students.

Mood

→ Provide reassurance and encouragement.

→ Make time to talk alone with student.

→ Frequently compliment positive behavior and work product.

→ Encourage social interactions with classmates if student is withdrawn or excessively shy.

→ Speak softly in nonthreatening manner if student shows nervousness.

→ Reinforce frequently when signs of frustration are noticed.

→ Review instructions when giving new assignments to make sure student comprehends directions.

→ Look for signs of stress buildup and provide encouragement or reduced workload to alleviate pressure and avoid temper outburst.

→ Look for opportunities for student to display leadership role in class.

→ Spend more time talking to students who seem pent up or display anger easily.

→ Conference frequently with parents to learn about student's interests and achievements outside of school.

→ Provide brief training in anger control: encourage student to walk away; use calming strategies; tell nearby adult if getting angry.

→ Send positive notes home.

Socialization

→ Praise appropriate behavior.

→ Encourage cooperative learning tasks with other students.

→ Monitor social interactions.

→ Provide small-group social skills training.

→ Set up social behavior goals with student and implement a reward program.

→ Praise student frequently.

→ Prompt appropriate social behavior either verbally or with private signal.

→ Assign special responsibilities to student in presence of peer group so others observe student in a positive light.

–Harvey C. Parker

SOURCE: A.D.D. Warehouse, 304 Northwest 70th Avenue, Plantation, FL 33317; (800) 233-9273. Available online at http://www.addwarehouse.com/shopsite_sc/store/html/article4.htm

across all grade levels and are appropriate for children in both special education and general education classrooms.

Self-regulatory strategies are frequently used to modify common classroom behaviors such as working independently, staying on task, completing assignments, or remaining at one's desk. These strategies, which should focus on a positive target behavior, teach pupils to monitor their own behavior, engage in self-reinforcement, and direct their own strategic learning (Alberto & Troutman, 2013; Johnson & Johnson, 1999; Smith et al., 2012). After the teacher determines the student's current level of performance, the pupil executes the following steps:

1. **Self-observation**—looking at one's own behavior, given a predetermined criterion

2. **Self-assessment**—deciding if the behavior has occurred, through some form of self-questioning activity

3. **Self-recording**—recording the decision made during self-assessment on a private recording form

4. **Self-determination of reinforcement**—setting a criterion for success, and selecting a reinforcer from a menu of reinforcers

5. **Self-administration of reinforcement**—administering a reinforcer to oneself

Before allowing students to follow these steps independently, it is recommended that teachers teach self-reinforcement strategies by first demonstrating the necessary steps through modeling or guided practice. Self-monitoring of behavior has been shown to increase academic productivity and on-task behavior of students in both elementary and secondary classrooms (DuPaul & Weyandt, 2006; Hallahan et al., 2005; Weyandt, 2007).

Home-School Collaboration

Home-school collaboration is essential for all pupils, but especially for those with ADHD; it is an important ingredient for promoting their success at school (Jones & Teach, 2006). As illustrated in Figure 8.2, this partnership must be "ongoing, reciprocal, mutually respectful, and student centered" (Bos, Nahmias, & Urban, 1999, p. 4).

Parents have played a key role in their children's education ever since the enactment of PL 94–142 in 1975. Their involvement has recently been expanded, however, as part of IDEA 2004 (PL 108–446), and input from parents is now solicited during prereferral and eligibility meetings as well as when planning positive behavioral interventions. Bos et al. (1999) note that home-school collaboration can be used in many areas of school life, but it is especially appropriate for students with ADHD when parents and teachers communicate about monitoring medication effects, completing homework assignments, establishing goals and rewards, assessing intervention effectiveness, and developing behavior management plans. The communication techniques themselves can range from simple (daily checklists or rating scales) to more sophisticated strategies, such as weekly journals or traveling notebooks (communication folders). What is important is not the method used but that consistent and meaningful communication occurs. Parents and teachers should use whatever strategies work best for them.

VIDEO

Collaboration

Instructional Modification

As noted earlier, environmental modifications are often crucial if the student with ADHD is to succeed in the classroom. Instructional adaptations coupled with modifications of the learning environment are powerful tools that can help the pupil sustain attention while cultivating a climate that fosters learning and encourages the child to control his or her behavior. The following list of adaptations may benefit the individual with ADHD, regardless of educational placement.

As noted earlier in this chapter, even if a student is ineligible for a special education, general educators are required, under Section 504 of PL 93–112, to accommodate individual differences and learning styles of children who exhibit an impairment (such as ADHD) that substantially limits a major life activity such as learning. Lerner and Lowenthal (1993) offer the following suggestions for teachers, which are still appropriate in twenty-first-century classrooms:

1. Place the youngster in the least distracting location in the class. This may be in front of the class, away from doors, windows, air conditioners, heaters, and high-traffic areas. It may be necessary for the child to face a blank wall or be in a study carrel to enable the child to focus attention.

2. Surround the student with good role models, preferably peers that the child views as significant others. Encourage peer tutoring and cooperative learning.

3. Maintain a low pupil-teacher ratio whenever possible through the use of aides and volunteers.

4. Avoid unnecessary changes in schedules and monitor transitions because the child with ADHD often has difficulty coping with changes. When unavoidable disruptions do occur, prepare the student as much as possible by explaining the situation and what behaviors are appropriate.

5. Maintain eye contact with the student when giving verbal instructions. Make directions clear, concise, and simple. Repeat instructions as needed in a calm voice.

6. Combine visual and tactile cues with verbal instructions since, generally, multiple modalities of instruction will be more effective in maintaining attention and increasing learning.

7. Make lists that help the student organize tasks. Have the student check them off when they are finished. Students should complete study guides when listening to presentations.

■ ■ ■ ■ ■ Figure 8.2 **Components of Effective Home-School Collaboration**

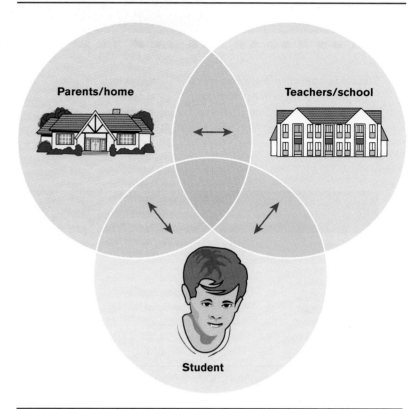

SOURCE: From "Targeting Home-School Collaboration for Students with ADHD" by C. Bos, M. Nahmias, and M. Urban, *Teaching Exceptional Children, 31*(6), p. 4. Copyright © 1999 by the Council for Exceptional Children. Reprinted with permission.

Classwide interventions are time-efficient strategies for managing students with ADHD without singling out or stigmatizing the child. They also have the advantage of benefiting *all* pupils, not just the pupil with ADHD. Classwide interventions can have a positive effect on the academic and behavioral difficulties frequently associated with ADHD. Some of these instructional options are listed below.

	Intervention	Key Features	Pros	Cons	Behavior Outcomes	Academic Outcomes
Behavioral	Contingency Management	Positively state rules Clear expectations and guidelines Identify reinforcers and punishers	Effective Flexible Adaptive Engaging, fun	Requires consistency to be effective Setup time	↓ Hyperactivity, inattentive, disruptive behavior ↑ Compliance, time on task	↑ Work accuracy and completion
	Therapy Balls	Replacing child's seat with a gym ball	Effective Socially valid Simple to implement	Costly ($$) May not be practical for whole class	↑ In-seat behavior	↑ Written work
	Self-Monitoring	Identify target behavior Explicitly teach rating scale Decisions on when and how to monitor the behavior	Teaches autonomy and responsibility One-to-one teacher attention Inexpensive	Setup time Gradual shift toward positive behavior	↑ Time on task ↓ Inattentive and inappropriate behaviors	
	Peer Monitoring	Outline appropriate and inappropriate behaviors Practice system before use Clear guidelines and rules	Focus on prosocial behaviors Use of peers to improve behavior	Requires vigilance and practice to prevent peer rejection	↓ Talking out	
	Instructional Choice	Teacher-developed menu of assignments or tasks Student choice of task	Simple to implement Inexpensive	Preparation Possible student expectancy	↓ Behavior problems	↑ Academic engagement

**Instructional Modifications
for Students With ADHD**

Effective Instructional Practices (continued)

	Intervention	Key Features	Pros	Cons	Behavior Outcomes	Academic Outcomes
Academic	Classwide Peer Tutoring	Pair students together Alternate tutor and learner roles	Teacher can monitor whole class	Setup time Initial training period	↑ Time on task ↓ Disruptive behavior	↑ Performance in math, reading, and spelling
		Provides immediate corrective feedback	Peer attention Immediate feedback Self-selected pace Inexpensive			
	Instructional Modification	Altering the assignment	Personalized to target students' needs	Time-consuming Challenging to find adequate modifications	↓ Disruptive behavior ↑ Task engagement	↑ Performance in reading and writing
	Computer-Assisted Instruction	Use of computer programs to supplement instruction Align with curriculum	Provides additional instruction Fun, engaging Builds fluency	Expensive Need computer access Some programs may not be appropriate	↑ Time on task	↑ Math performance

NOTE: ↑ indicates increase, ↓ indicates decrease.

SOURCE: Adapted from J. Harlacher, N. Roberts, and K. Merrell, "Classwide Interventions for Students with ADHD," *Teaching Exceptional Children, 39*(2), 2006, pp. 6–12.

8. Adapt worksheets so that there is less material on each page.

9. Break assignments into small chunks. Provide immediate feedback on each assignment. Allow extra time if needed for the student to finish the assignment.

10. Ensure that the student has recorded homework assignments each day before leaving school. If necessary, set up a home-school program in which the parents help the child organize and complete the homework.

11. If the child has difficulty staying in one place at school, alternate sitting with standing and activities that require moving around during the day.

12. Provide activities that require active participation, such as talking through problems or acting out the steps.

13. Use learning aids such as computers, calculators, tape recorders, and programmed learning materials. They help to structure learning and maintain interest and motivation.

14. Provide the student opportunities to demonstrate strengths at school. Set up times in which the student can assist peers. (pp. 4–5)

Medication

Many professionals believe that medication, particularly psychostimulants, can play an important role in the treatment of ADHD. It is our opinion that the use of medication should always be in conjunction with educational and behavioral interventions; medication represents only one part of a total treatment package and should not be seen as a panacea for dealing with ADHD. In fact, instructional and environmental accommodations should always be the first intervention tactic used to assist pupils with ADHD (U.S. Department of Education, 2008a, 2008b). Although medication may play a vital role in treating ADHD, teachers should *never* recommend to parents that their son or daughter needs to be on medication. Only the child's health care professional can make such a determination. Interestingly, despite the importance of medication in helping children with ADHD, few educators are knowledgeable about ADHD and the use of stimulant medication (Snider, Busch, & Arrowood, 2003). (See the accompanying Insights feature on the myths and misunderstandings surrounding stimulant medication on page 273.)

The Centers for Disease Control and Prevention (2013a) estimates that approximately 2.7 million children take medication due to ADHD. Children between 11 and 17 years of age are the most frequent users, with males more likely to take medication than females.

One of the more popular stimulant medications is Ritalin, with Dexedrine and Adderall also commonly prescribed. See Table 8.3 for an overview of these and other medications. It is estimated that 70 to 80 percent of children with ADHD respond favorably to medication (Glanzman & Sell, 2013; Lerner & Johns, 2012; MTA Cooperative Group, 2004), especially when combined with other interventions. Researchers attribute the effectiveness of stimulant medication to the drug's ability to activate or enhance particular aspects of neurological functioning. By increasing the arousal level of the central nervous system (CNS), these drugs enable individuals with ADHD to concentrate better, to control their impulsivity and distractibility, and to increase their attention span (Barkley, 2006). An analysis of the chemical and neurological effects on the CNS of stimulant medication is beyond the scope of this discussion; simply stated, scientists believe that psychostimulants operate by increasing the production of dopamine and norepinephrine, chemical neurotransmitters, which in turn activate the executive functioning capabilities of the brain—areas involved in organizing, planning, and attention (Arnsten, Berridge, & McCracken, 2009; Floet et al., 2010; Lerner & Johns, 2012; U.S. Department of Education, 2008a).

After reviewing scientific evidence, the National Institute of Mental Health (2008) concluded that stimulant drugs are quite safe when taken as directed and at normal prescription dosages. In the vast majority of youngsters who take psychostimulants for ADHD, significant improvement in behavior is observed (Barkley, 2006). Greater benefits are generally found, however, for behavioral outcomes in comparison to academic performance (DuPaul & Kern, 2011; Glanzman & Sell, 2013). The student is less distractible and exhibits greater attention to task, but psychostimulants do not make the child smarter or necessarily result in improved academic achievement.

psychostimulants: Medications typically prescribed for persons with ADHD. These drugs activate or enhance specific aspects of neurological functioning that in turn affect executive functions.

REFERENCE
ADHD Treatment Approaches

■ ■ ■ ■ ■ Table 8.3 **Representative Medications Used in Treating Attention Deficit Hyperactivity Disorder**

Brand Name	Generic Name	Approved Age of Use	Onset of Effectiveness	Duration of Effectiveness	Comments
Ritalin	Methylphenidate	6 and older	Less than 30 minutes	Approximately 4 hours	Most frequently prescribed. Excellent safety record.
Dexedrine	Dextroamphetamine	3	Less than 30 minutes	Approximately 4–5 hours	Must be administered frequently. Excellent safety record.
Focalin	Dexmethylphenidate	6 and older	Approximately 30 minutes	Approximately 5 hours	Potential adverse side effects.
Adderall	Dextroamphetamine sulfate	3	Approximately 30 minutes	Approximately 4–6 hours	Requires only one daily dose.
Concerta	Methylphenidate HCL	6	Approximately 30 minutes	Approximately 12 hours	One daily dose. Minimal side effects.
Vyvanse	Lisdexamfetamine	6 and older	Usually 2–12 hours for children ages 6–12; 2–14 hours for adults ages 18–55	Approximately 10–12 hours	One daily dose. Low potential for misuse.
Strattera	Atomoxetine HCL	6 and older	Usually within 24 hours; therapeutic level reached in 3–4 weeks	Approximately 20 hours	Nonstimulant medication. Typically one daily dose. Clinically proven effective for adults.

NOTE: Long-acting and extended-release varieties are available.

SOURCE: Adapted from J. Lerner and B. Johns, *Learning Disabilities and Related Mild Disabilities,* 12th ed. (Belmont, CA: Wadsworth/Cengage Learning, 2012), p. 212.

Medical management of ADHD is not without its drawbacks and critics. It has also been shown to be ineffective for about 25 to 30 percent of individuals who take psychostimulants (Barbaresi et al., 2006; Barkley, 2006). Typical side effects of using psychostimulants include, in some instances, loss of appetite, insomnia, drowsiness, tics, irritability, abdominal pain, headaches, and growth retardation (Barkley, 2010; Glanzman & Sell, 2013). Fortunately, most of the side effects are of short duration. It is important that parents working in conjunction with teachers and health care providers determine which medication is most effective with the least adverse consequences.

A rebound effect is sometimes observed in children using psychostimulants. As the effects of the medication gradually wear off, typically in the late afternoon or early evening, the children's behavior significantly deteriorates—they temporarily display greater impulsivity, distractibility, and hyperactivity than what was previously observed (Glanzman & Sell, 2013; Lerner & Johns, 2012).

Home-school communication is vitally important for monitoring medication effectiveness. Once a child is placed on medication, school personnel are often asked to provide feedback regarding the student's behavior, academic performance, and social

rebound effect: The behavioral deterioration sometimes observed in persons with ADHD as the effect of psychostimulant medication gradually wears off.

Stimulant medication plays an important role in the treatment of ADHD.

adjustment, as well as any side effects from the medication. Information gleaned from both parents and teachers is useful to the physician in determining the overall effectiveness of the medication regime. Because teachers cannot contact a youngster's physician without parental permission, communication between teachers and caregivers is essential. Parent-teacher communication can take many forms—telephone calls, notes, or having teachers complete checklists and rating scales.

We encourage schools to establish written policies regarding the administration and storage of any medication given to pupils by school personnel. We also recommend that any adult who administers medication to a child complete a daily medication log; at a minimum, this log should include the medication name, dosage, time, and signature of the person administering the drug. Finally, parents and teachers need to be careful that they do not send a message to the student that medication is a substitute for self-responsibility and self-initiative; nor does the use of psychostimulants absolve the parents and teachers of their responsibilities for dealing with individuals with ADHD (Hallahan et al., 2005).

Finally, we should point out that not all professionals and parents are in favor of using psychostimulants. Some individuals are fearful that prescribing these medications will lead to the illicit use of drugs in later years. Fortunately, this is a misconception. It is true that teenagers with ADHD exhibit a higher incidence of drug abuse when compared to adolescents without ADHD, but there is no scientific evidence that this is the result of using psychostimulants (Glanzman & Sell, 2013). Research, in fact, suggests that just the opposite is true. Individuals taking psychostimulant medication as children are not at increased risk for substance abuse as teenagers (Katusic et al., 2005; Wilens, Faraone, Biederman, & Gunawardene, 2003).

Adolescents and Adults With Attention Deficit Hyperactivity Disorder

Attention deficit hyperactivity disorder is, in most instances, a lifelong struggle, despite the popular misconception that youngsters "outgrow it" as they mature. This certainly is not true for vast numbers of individuals who continue to exhibit symptoms well into adolescence and adulthood (Barkley, 2010; Barkley, Fischer, Smallish, & Fletcher, 2006; Smith et al., 2012). Approximately seven out of ten children with ADHD will continue to display symptoms in adolescence (Glanzman & Sell, 2013; Hammerness, 2009). Although the signs may become subtler (see Table 8.4 on page 276), academic difficulties persist, and impaired social skills remain common (Friend & Bursuck, 2009). More than one third of adolescents with ADHD eventually drop out of school (Barkley, 2000).

When one considers the preceding facts, the prognosis for adults with ADHD is not overly promising in most cases. Well over half of individuals who experience ADHD in childhood will continue to be challenged by symptoms of impulsivity,

idea INSIGHTS

Myths and Misunderstandings About Stimulant Medication: A Quiz for Teachers

After the following statements, circle T (true) if you agree or F (false) if you do not agree.

	True	False
1. ADHD is the most commonly diagnosed psychiatric disorder of childhood.	T	F
2. There are no data to indicate that ADHD is caused by a brain malfunction.	T	F
3. ADHD symptoms (e.g., fidgets, does not follow through on instruction, easily distracted) may be caused by academic deficits.	T	F
4. Stress and conflict in the student's home life can cause ADHD symptoms.	T	F
5. Diagnosis of ADHD can be confirmed if stimulant medication improves the child's attention.	T	F
6. Stimulant medication use may decrease the physical growth rate.	T	F
7. Stimulant medication use may produce tics in students.	T	F
8. Adderall, Ritalin, and Dexedrine have abuse potential similar to Demerol, cocaine, and morphine.	T	F
9. The long-term side effects of stimulant medications are well understood.	T	F
10. Over time, stimulant medication loses its effectiveness.	T	F
11. While on stimulant medication, students exhibit similar amounts of problem behaviors as their normally developing peers.	T	F
12. Short-term studies show that stimulant medication improves the behaviors associated with ADHD.	T	F
13. Studies show that stimulant medication has a positive effect on academic achievement in the long run.	T	F

(Answers on page 279)

SOURCE: Adapted from V. Snider, T. Busch, and L. Arrowood, "Teachers Knowledge of Stimulant Medication and ADHD," *Remedial and Special Education, 24*(1), 2003, p. 50.

inattention, and hyperactivity as adults (Barkley, 2010; National Institute of Mental Health, 2008).

Because professionals wrongly assumed that ADHD was primarily a childhood disorder, little attention was paid to this condition in adults. Only in recent years has ADHD in adolescents and adults become an area of interest for physicians, researchers, and others.

As noted previously, there is no definitive medical or psychological test to determine ADHD; this statement is equally valid for adults with ADHD. What is often quite revealing and most helpful to clinicians is the individual's personal history (see the chapter opener). Although subjective in interpretation, it does provide professionals with a starting point for recognizing this condition.

VIDEO

Misuse of ADHD Medication

I recall seeing a cartoon once where a student with attention deficit hyperactivity disorder (ADHD) was portrayed as a tornado sitting in a desk (something a student with ADHD can possibly relate to). A tornado is something that gets a lot of attention, but all of it is negative. As I enter my tenth year of teaching, I reflect back on those students I worked with and the varying degrees of ADHD I encountered. I clearly remember one particular student and parent. This child was new to our school, but not new to special education. His mother finally admitted in December that she had no insurance but wanted desperately to fill her son's prescription because by this time he was constantly in trouble. After we helped her locate free medical insurance, she quickly took him to his pediatrician.

Medication helped him control his impulsiveness, and he made more than a year's progress in the few short months left in school that year. The child didn't return the following year, and I've always wondered how he was doing. Then there are the parents that I've known who have ADHD themselves. Despite facing the same issues, many of these parents still did not know how to help their child. I also recall interacting with my colleagues, wondering how some teachers can be so understanding while others are absolutely oblivious to the effects that this disability has on the educational performance of their pupils. I realized then that it was going to be my job, as a special educator, to educate my fellow teachers as well as the students.

Inclusive Education Experience

Including students with ADHD in the general education classroom is just the right thing to do. A pullout or resource room setting typically does not benefit these students. Best practices, accommodations, and a great deal of patience are all that is usually required. Depending on the severity of the disorder, behavioral interventions may be necessary, but these too are best done in the least restrictive environment. At the same time, the least restrictive environment can become overly restrictive if traditional self-control, self-direction, and adherence to inflexible classroom rules are required of the learner with ADHD. The extent to which the student's needs are matched to the teacher's expectations is important to success; and the extent to which home and school expectations mirror each other builds on that positive inclusive experience. Typically, you are not going to change the child to fit the learning environment; rather, the classroom needs to accommodate the learner's unique needs and learning style.

Strategies for the Inclusive Classroom

Most classroom strategies that can be used for pupils with ADHD are good for all students. Having an example of an organized notebook with all the required assignments in it, for instance, is a great way to give students a means of organizing themselves. Assigning a dependable peer to help with this activity will ensure that the student with ADHD stays organized while also giving him or her ownership of the task. That same notebook can help children who were absent be sure they get everything they missed.

Another classroom practice that may benefit all students is repeating instructions or assignments several times, simplifying instructions, or giving directions in multiple ways.

Most kids today love technology; therefore, teachers should incorporate what the children love. Today's technologies such as iPods, audiobooks, and computers that give constant/instant stimulation or feedback are great ways for teachers to supplement their instruction.

Successful Collaboration

To make collaboration a success it is important to appreciate the challenges frequently encountered by the general educator who works with pupils with ADHD. Co-teaching is but one example of a collaborative activity that may provide the general education teacher with the opportunity to focus on the particular needs of the student with ADHD while the special educator instructs

As adults, persons with ADHD exhibit a variety of characteristics:

- Feelings of restlessness
- Difficulty engaging in quiet, sedentary activities
- Frequent shifts from one uncompleted activity to another
- Frequent interrupting or intruding on others
- Avoidance of tasks that allow for little spontaneous movement
- Relationship difficulties

AUDIO
Adults with ADHD

VIDEO
Future Goals

the entire class. On the other hand, the special educator may work with a small group of children while the general education teacher delivers whole-group instruction. Cooperative learning groups of specifically chosen peers is another way of engaging students with ADHD. The keys to a successful collaborative relationship are listening, acknowledging the teacher's concerns, meeting the teacher's needs as well as those of the students, and doing all of this in a timely manner.

Working With Parents and Families

A close relationship with the parents and families of students with ADHD is vital to the child's success at school. Recently I e-mailed a parent about extreme changes in her son's behavior. The classroom teacher first brought it to my attention, and the paraprofessional who works with him noticed the changes as well. I also observed the changes, but working with this student for only fifteen minutes each day I failed to put it all together. I simply informed his mother that we had seen some changes and wanted to address them with her before it began to affect his progress and ultimately his grade. Later that same day she stopped by my classroom and said she had brought him his medicine. It seems that she had simply stopped giving her son his medication and wanted to see if we would notice any changes. While medication should not be the first line of defense in dealing with ADHD, for many students medication is a necessity. Some parents, however, do not believe in the benefits of medication for their child. It is important for teachers to realize that this is a very personal decision, and they must respect the wishes of the parent. Parents who feel that their voice is not being heard are more likely to become defensive and uncooperative when problems do arise.

Follow-through and consistency of routines across environments are crucial for the child with ADHD. At home there should be a schedule similar to the one used at school. There should be consequences and rewards that mirror what is done in the classroom. A clear understanding of expectations that are consistent across environments will often enhance success.

Homework is often a huge source of frustration for both parents and the child. Teachers can usually suggest ways to minimize frustration. For example, it may not always be necessary to complete each and every homework problem if the student is able to demonstrate an understanding of the concept. Breaking homework into manageable chunks or giving due dates for assignments early will allow parents additional time to help their child and possibly keep the student from feeling overwhelmed. Sometimes students are good at certain parts of an assignment, and these can possibly be omitted. A student, for instance, who is great at computation facts but weak at deciphering word problems may be required only to determine the equation but not expected to work it out. The bottom line is two-way communication. It is important that parents and teachers view each other as a team.

Advice for Making Inclusion Work

Special educators often assist the general education teacher as much as they do the student. Being available when assistance is required and serving as a source of effective instructional and behavioral interventions are very important for making inclusion work. I often send my colleagues useful articles and short weekly e-mails with instructional suggestions. I also remind them that ADHD is real and that the child is not trying to drive them crazy.

Students with ADHD lack the ability to focus and are distracted by anything overly stimulating, so finding ways to make learning fun is a key component of success. In an inclusive setting the special educator has to help the general education teacher find ways to make the learning environment less stimulating and his or her teaching more stimulating. Again, this works for *all* students, not just the child with ADHD. Be sure that you facilitate open lines of communication between home and school. View inclusion as a partnership among the general education teacher, the special educator, and the family for the benefit of all, but especially the student with ADHD.

–Lisa Cranford
Instructional Support Teacher
National Board Certified Teacher
2009 Alabama CEC Special Education Teacher of the Year
Hoover (Alabama) City Schools

- Anger management difficulties
- Frequent changes in employment (Weyandt, 2007, p. 24)

These symptoms have the potential for significantly affecting a wide range of life activities, particularly employment opportunities. Yet medication, especially extended-release forms, coupled with psychotherapy, has proven to be beneficial for adults with ADHD (National Institute of Mental Health, 2008).

VIDEO
Inclusion

VIDEO
Inclusion Strategies

Table 8.4 **Representative Characteristics of Attention Deficit Hyperactivity Disorder in Adolescents**

• Excessive talking	• Impulsiveness	• Difficulty following through on tasks
• Restlessness	• Depression	• Alcohol and drug abuse
• Antisocial behavior	• Academic failure	• Difficulty following instructions
• Low self-concept/self-esteem	• Impaired social relationships	• At risk for school suspension, dropping out
• Inattentiveness	• Difficulty maintaining employment	

SOURCE: R. Barkley, *Attention-Deficit Hyperactivity Disorder: A Handbook for Diagnosis and Treatment*, 3rd ed. (New York, NY: Guilford Press, 2006).

Educational/Vocational Outcomes

It is not unusual for individuals with ADHD to experience employment difficulties. Barkley (2010) notes that adults with ADHD are more likely than those without ADHD to be fired, and they also change jobs three times more often than peers without ADHD. At age 35, more than one third of adults with ADHD are self-employed (Smith, Polloway, Patton, & Dowdy, 2008). When one considers the characteristics of adults with ADHD, this is not too surprising. Successful employment for adults with ADHD often depends on a "goodness of fit"—that is, matching the job requirements with the individual's unique profile of symptoms. It would probably be unwise to encourage an adult who is hyperactive and has difficulty sustaining attention to task to seek a sedentary career path such as an accountant or a proofreader.

Educationally, young adults with ADHD are less likely than those without ADHD to graduate from college (Murphy, Barkley, & Bush, 2002). This finding points out the need for supportive services and accommodations for these individuals. Postsecondary institutions are legally required (Section 504 of PL 93–112 and the Americans with Disabilities Act, PL 101–336) to provide special services for their students with ADHD (and other disabilities), but students need to self-advocate and inform school officials of their requirements.

Issues of Diversity

Attention deficit hyperactivity disorder affects people of all ages, social classes, races, and cultures (Hammerness, 2009; Weyandt, 2007). When ADHD coexists with cultural and linguistic diversity, it can, according to Smith et al. (2008), present a special set of challenges to teachers. Recall from Chapter 3 that teachers must be sensitive to the values, customs, and heritage of students from culturally and linguistically diverse backgrounds. This statement is especially valid when talking about pupils who exhibit ADHD.

One area of particular concern for professionals is the identification of ADHD in individuals from culturally and linguistically diverse backgrounds. Some are fearful that ethnic and cultural factors may lead to the overdiagnosis of ADHD in some groups, especially African American boys. Because this disorder is frequently identified by means of behavior rating scales, which rely on the subjective opinions of the evaluators, the issue of bias may arise. This concern is especially troublesome when the rater's background differs from that of the student. Differences have been found in how teachers evaluate for ADHD in European American versus African American

AUDIO

Chapter 8
Summary

youngsters. African American boys, for example, were thought to exhibit the most severe symptoms of ADHD, and European American girls were seen as manifesting the least severe symptoms (Weyandt, 2007). Interestingly, Hispanic children are less likely than white and African American children to be diagnosed with ADHD (Centers for Disease Control and Prevention, 2013a).

The intriguing question then is "Are these authentic group differences (which likely reflect normative behaviors) or an indicator of possible rater bias?" Unfortunately, this issue currently remains unresolved.

Technology and Individuals With ADHD

Although many of the assistive technologies discussed in Chapter 5 regarding content-area instruction can benefit students with ADHD, other types of assistive technology can also specifically support students with ADHD. For example, students with ADHD may benefit from using a seat cushion or a fidget toy (for example, silly putty, squeeze ball). Seat cushions can provide extra stimulation while seated, and fidget toys allow hand movements that can assist students in concentrating (Aune, Burt, & Gennaro, 2010; Denton & Silver, 2012). Students with ADHD may also benefit from self-monitoring. While traditionally self-monitoring involves paper and pencil, students can use technology to self-monitor, such as student response systems (Szwed & Bouck, 2013) as well as smartphones and other mobile technologies (for example, iPod).

CHAPTER IN REVIEW

Defining Attention Deficit Hyperactivity Disorder

- Attention deficit hyperactivity disorder (ADHD) is not recognized as a discrete disability under current IDEA legislation.
- Students with ADHD may receive a special education, if eligible, under the category *other health impairments*.
- The American Psychiatric Association definition considers inattention, impulsivity, and hyperactivity to be key components of this condition.

Etiology of Attention Deficit Hyperactivity Disorder

- Neurological dysfunction, heredity, and environmental factors are suspected of causing ADHD.

Characteristics of Individuals With Attention Deficit Hyperactivity Disorder

- ADHD presents itself in many different ways. Problems with behavioral inhibition are seen as one of the primary characteristics of persons with ADHD.
- Executive functions are often impaired in individuals with ADHD.
- Students with ADHD frequently experience other academic, social, and behavioral problems. This overlap is called comorbidity.

Assessment of Attention Deficit Hyperactivity Disorder

- The assessment and diagnosis of ADHD is a multifaceted endeavor typically involving a medical evaluation and input from parents and teachers via behavioral rating scales.

Educational Considerations

- It is generally believed that most students with ADHD receive services in the general education classroom.
- Multimodal interventions, or concurrent treatments, are generally more effective for individuals with ADHD than any one particular strategy.
- Behavioral interventions, instructional adaptations, home-school collaboration, and the use of medication are some of the intervention options available to students with ADHD.
- Psychostimulants should be used only in conjunction with behavioral and educational interventions.

Adolescents and Adults With Attention Deficit Hyperactivity Disorder

- In most instances, ADHD is a lifelong condition.

STUDY QUESTIONS

1. Do you think attention deficit hyperactivity disorder (ADHD) should be recognized as a separate disability category according to IDEA? Support your position.

2. What are the three subtypes of ADHD? List three symptoms typical of each subtype.

3. Identify three possible causes of ADHD. Give an example of each.

4. Give five examples of characteristics typical of children and adolescents with ADHD.

5. Why do you think pupils with ADHD frequently exhibit other academic and behavioral difficulties?

6. How is ADHD diagnosed? What role do parents and teachers play in the diagnostic process?

7. What role does medication play in the treatment of ADHD? Why is this approach controversial? Describe three other intervention options for students with ADHD.

8. ADHD is usually a lifelong condition. In what ways might this disorder affect the lives of adults with ADHD?

9. Why are some professionals concerned about the identification of ADHD in students from culturally and linguistically diverse backgrounds?

KEY TERMS

comorbidity   251
Strauss syndrome   253
minimal brain injury   253
hyperactive child syndrome   253

executive functions   255
behavioral inhibition   257
doctor's office effect   260
multimodal interventions   262

functional behavioral assessment   263
self-regulation   263
psychostimulants   270
rebound effect   271

LEARNING ACTIVITIES

1. Observe students with ADHD in both elementary and secondary classrooms. Ask their teachers what accommodations they typically provide to these pupils. Discover if there are particular instructional strategies that these educators prefer.

2. Interview two adults with ADHD. Learn how this condition has affected their lives. What kinds of strategies have these individuals developed for dealing with their disorder?

3. Attend a local chapter meeting of CHADD (Children and Adults with Attention-Deficit/Hyperactivity Disorder). What issues and concerns were addressed at this meeting? What resources are available in your community for persons with ADHD across the life span?

ORGANIZATIONS CONCERNED WITH ATTENTION DEFICIT HYPERACTIVITY DISORDER

A.D.D. WareHouse

www.addwarehouse.com

Attention Deficit Disorder Association (ADDA)

www.add.org

Attention Deficit Disorder Information Network

www.addinfonetwork.com

CHADD (Children and Adults with Attention-Deficit/Hyperactivity Disorder)

www.chadd.org

The following exercises are designed to help you learn to apply the Council for Exceptional Children (CEC) standards to your teaching practice. Each of the reflection exercises below correlates with knowledge or a skill within the CEC standards. For the full text of each of the related CEC standards, please refer to the standards integration grid located in Appendix B.

Focus on Learning Environments (*CEC Initial Preparation Standard 2.2*)

Reflect on what you have learned about self-regulation and monitoring in this chapter. If you were to have a student in your class who needed to learn new techniques for self-regulation, what might be some self-reinforcement strategies you could teach him or her? What types of reinforcement do you think would be effective?

Focus on Curricular Content Knowledge (*CEC Initial Preparation Standard 3.3*)

Reflect on what you have learned in this chapter about students with ADHD. If you were to have a student in your class who got distracted easily by his or her peers, how might you modify your student's learning environment?

Sharpen your skills with SAGE edge at **edge.sagepub.com/gargiulo5e. SAGE edge for students** provides a personalized approach to help you accomplish your coursework goals in an easy-to-use learning environment.

Answer Key to Myths and Misunderstandings About Stimulant Medication: A Quiz for Teachers on p. 273

1. True
2. False
3. True
4. Ture

5. False
6. True
7. True

8. True
9. False
10. True

11. False
12. True
13. False

Individuals With Emotional or Behavioral Disorders

■ ■ ░ ■ ■ ░ ■ ■ ░ ■ ░ ▪ ■ ░ ▪ ░ ░ ▪ ░ ░ ▪ ■

Mike

Mike was a happy baby who was constantly moving—not running all over the place, but he would rock when he played or sat or rode in a car. He even rocked himself to sleep on his hands and knees as a baby in his crib. Mike appeared to be very bright and very verbal. He could converse better than most children his age. The problem we had was that he couldn't sit still.

By the time he was in kindergarten, he was diagnosed with attention deficit hyperactivity disorder (ADHD). He was prescribed Ritalin, and then clonidine was added because he had such emotional mood swings. His kindergarten teacher was wonderful about communicating with us and working with him. I don't know how we'd have managed without her. I felt she had his best interest at heart in all that she did, and she treated him with love and kindness, but Mike was held back in kindergarten due to his immaturity. The school convinced us it would be the best thing for him. Yet, I had no idea how devastating this would be for Mike's self-esteem.

During his second year of kindergarten, he began having thoughts he couldn't control. His teacher called us because he told her he was having thoughts of killing his brother with a knife and said he would never do that but couldn't stop thinking about it. This was the beginning of his obsessive thoughts. During the next two to three years of school, Mike developed frequent outbursts of anger that were incredible to see in a child so small. He would fly into a rage over the least thing, rant and rave loudly, occasionally throw things, and then suddenly be as calm as a kitten. He frequently blamed all of his problems on the fact that he "failed" kindergarten and was stupid. His schoolwork began to suffer drastically. Mike's obsessive thoughts included burning down the house, killing his beloved cat, and a fear that someone was going to break into the house and kill him.

By the third grade, Mike was exhibiting eye twitches, grunts, sniffing, and throat clearing. He would pull his hair when he became frustrated, and when he couldn't do his schoolwork, he hit himself or bit his arms. He occasionally

LEARNING OBJECTIVES

After reading Chapter 9, you should be able to:

- **Outline** the issues surrounding our understanding of emotional or behavioral disorders.
- **Define** socially maladjusted and conduct disorders.
- **Distinguish** between clinically derived and statistically derived systems for classifying emotional or behavioral disorders.
- **Explain** how society has historically dealt with persons with emotional or behavioral disorders.
- **Identify** biological and psychosocial risk factors of emotional or behavioral disorders.
- **List** the learning and social characteristics typical of students who exhibit emotional or behavioral disorders.
- **Describe** contemporary approaches for assessing pupils with emotional or behavioral disorders.
- **Provide** examples of academic and behavioral interventions often used with individuals with emotional or behavioral disorders.
- **Define** time management, transition management, proximity and movement management, and classroom arrangement.
- **Summarize** educational services for persons with emotional or behavioral disorders across the life span.

came home with teeth prints on his forearm or other forms of self-injurious behavior. He began to show signs of depression, and we decided it was time to switch from his pediatrician to a specialist. While these behaviors seem bizarre, they weren't frequent at first and only gradually got to the point that they were interfering with his life. Then they seemed to go from occasional to constant in the space of a couple of weeks. He had frequent headaches, stomachaches, and vomiting episodes, and he began picking at his fingers and lips until they bled. We saw a pediatric neurologist who diagnosed him with Tourette syndrome, obsessive-compulsive disorder (OCD), ADHD, and depression. He was placed on new medicines, and in spite of (or because of) them, we saw a whirlwind of worsening behaviors. He began crouching on the floor in church, in the car, and under his desk at school. He was very upset that he wasn't normal like everyone else. It was heartbreaking to see our child go through these things and not be able to "make it go away." Although my faith had been my mainstay in all that we went through, it was put to the test the day we drove home with Mike crouching on the floorboard and crying. He looked up and said, "If God really loves me, why did He make me this way? Why do I have to have all these problems?"

Mike's grades worsened, and so did his relationships with classmates. He began to come home telling me that kids made fun of him for clearing his throat and other behaviors. He got into frequent arguments with classmates and sometimes told me about things that they had said or done to him, which proved to be untrue. He seemed to believe the stories that he told. He usually held in his outbursts at school but began to come apart as soon as I picked him up. His teacher was wonderfully patient with him and tried everything imaginable. She gave him tests orally, which helped, and allowed him to run an errand to calm him down or wake him up as the situation warranted (he began to sleep to escape when he felt stressed out).

His home life worsened. He began to cry easily when he had anger outbursts, and sometimes he said he wanted to kill himself. He also said he wanted to kill me a time or two and stormed off listing horrifyingly descriptive ways he would do this under his breath. I remember thinking that if he were a little older, I would be afraid for my safety.

Within a few weeks of starting yet another round of medications for depression/OCD, hallucinations, and ADHD, we began to see improvement. It took a year to get somewhat back on track; his grades were still awful, but he felt better, and that was all I cared about at that point. We finished the fourth grade somehow and changed schools for the fifth grade.

When Mike went to junior high, we had to fight for everything we got in his IEP (individualized education program) meetings. We got him in special education under the umbrella *other health impairments*. We also fought for and got resource room services for the subjects we felt he needed. Gradually we were able to pull him from the resource classes and put him back into general education classes. By the end of the eighth grade he was in all regular classes, but we held our breath each time report cards came out.

Mike is now nearing the end of the tenth grade, and I look back with amazement at how far he/we have come. He is enrolled in all regular classes now and on the general diploma track. After years of hounding and consequences for lost/undone homework, he is managing his grades with almost no intervention from us and has earned mostly As and Bs (with an occasional C in algebra or English). He is happy now, and although he is almost 17, he rarely asks to go out or do things with friends. We are working on getting him to drive, but he has been hesitant and a little fearful.

When I look back, I think that what has helped Mike the most is the right combination of medications and caring, dedicated teachers who went the extra mile. We don't know what the future holds for Mike, but we will face it with him as it comes, and we'll all be the stronger for it in the long run.

—Anonymous

The education of children and youth with emotional and behavioral disorders has long been a subject of controversy. As the chapter opener demonstrates, many individuals struggle to effectively address the needs of these children in home, school, and community settings. The child in this feature, Mike, has a history of behavioral problems, including aggressive behavior, that have been of concern to his mother and school officials for many years. These concerns are legitimate, as we all want our children to reach their full potential. Mike, however, was fortunate in that he had access to appropriate educational, medical, and psychological services. Too many children and youth with emotional and behavioral disorders do not have access to early and appropriate interventions. Without effective interventions, these individuals may not experience positive outcomes. Left untreated, students with emotional or behavioral disorders are at high risk for experiencing negative long-term outcomes, including academic failure, school dropout, incarceration, and under- or unemployment (Kauffman & Landrum, 2013).

This chapter focuses on students with problematic behaviors. It would be a mistake, however, to assume that all children and youth with emotional or behavioral disorders exhibit acting-out, aggressive behaviors. In fact, students with these disabilities represent an extremely heterogeneous group exhibiting a wide range of behaviors, including those related to such debilitating disorders as schizophrenia, depression, anxiety, and conduct disorders. Despite this heterogeneity, however, they share at least three experiences in common. First, their behaviors are almost always upsetting and troubling to those who teach, live with, and work with them. Second, they are often blamed for their disability by those around them, who do not recognize that they are disabled and believe they are capable of changing their behavior if they so desire. Finally, these students encounter ostracism and isolation because of the stigma associated with individuals considered to be mentally ill—a generic term used by many professionals outside the field of special education for individuals with emotional or behavioral disorders. In fact, the reactions of those who encounter students with emotional or behavioral disorders are often more debilitating than the disability itself.

Defining Emotional or Behavioral Disorders

There is no universally accepted definition of emotional or behavioral disorders (Kauffman & Landrum, 2013; Landrum, 2011). Disagreements among professionals stem from many factors, including a diversity of theoretical models (for example, psychodynamic, humanistic, behavioral), the fact that all children and youth behave inappropriately at different times and in different situations, the difficulty of

mentally ill: A generic term often used by professionals outside of the field of special education to refer to individuals with emotional or behavioral disorders.

emotional or behavioral disorder: A chronic condition characterized by behaviors that significantly differ from age norms and community standards to such a degree that educational performance is adversely affected.

measuring emotions and behavior, and the variance across cultures in terms of what is acceptable and unacceptable behavior. Similarly, the terms we use to describe this population are many and diverse: *emotionally disturbed, behaviorally disordered, emotionally conflicted, socially handicapped, personally impaired, socially impaired,* and many others. This diversity of definitions and terms is compounded by the marked variability in people's definitions of "normal" behavior. We each view behavior through personal lenses that reflect our own standards, values, and beliefs. What appears to you as abnormal behavior may appear to another person as within the range of normal human behavior (Webber & Plotts, 2008).

Four Dimensions of Behavior

At least four dimensions of behavior are common to most definitions of emotional or behavioral disorders: (1) the frequency (or rate) at which the behavior occurs, (2) the intensity of the behavior, (3) the duration of the behavior, and (4) the age-appropriateness of the behavior (Scheuermann & Hall, 2012; Webber & Plotts, 2008). Frequency of behavior indicates how often a behavior occurs. For example, many students talk out in class from time to time; however, the student who talks out thirty times during a class period may be engaging in atypical behavior. Intensity refers to the severity of behavior. Temper tantrums, for example, can range from whining that is irritating to others to more serious acts of physical aggression. Duration refers to the length of time a behavior occurs. For example, out-of-seat behavior can range from relatively brief (and mildly problematic) episodes to substantially longer episodes that create major disruptions in classroom learning. Finally, age-appropriateness must be considered. For example, sexual acting-out behavior among adolescents may be disturbing to many adults, but it is a fairly common, if problematic, behavior at this age. At the preschool and early elementary levels, however, sexual acting-out behavior is of much greater concern. It is important for teachers to remember that behavior viewed as problematic at one developmental level may be fairly typical or common at another age.

Disturbed and Disturbing Behavior

In 1981, James Kauffman, a noted authority in the field of emotional or behavioral disorders, made a critical distinction between *disturbed* behavior and *disturbing* behavior. He noted that some behaviors are inappropriate in some instances and not in others, simply because of differences in setting expectations. For example, the use of profanity may be within the range of acceptable behavior to a group of adolescents out "cruising" on a Saturday night, but most teachers would find such language unacceptable in the classroom. Likewise, drinking alcohol during adolescence is relatively common and is highly influenced by one's peers. This behavior, while disturbing to many adults, may not constitute disordered behavior. According to Kauffman, these behaviors are *disturbing* because they occur in a certain place and time and in the presence of certain individuals. In contrast, *disturbed* behavior occurs in many settings, is habitual, and is part of the individual's behavior pattern. For example, stealing, if it occurs in many settings over a long period of time, may be indicative of disordered behavior.

Transient Nature of Problematic Behavior

The transient nature of problematic behavior has been the focus of research for many years. For example, a landmark study by Rubin and Balow (1971) found that more than 50 percent of all school-age children were perceived by their teachers to have behavior problems at some point during their elementary years. In this same study, 7.5 percent of school-age children were consistently perceived by their teachers to exhibit problematic behavior. These findings suggest that it is common for children and youth (as well as adults) to have periods in their lives that are characterized by conflict, crisis, depression, stress, and ineffective decision making. These difficult periods may occur at vulnerable points in an individual's life—for example, when a family member or friend has died. The resulting acting-out behavior, though disturbing, may be transient and may disappear altogether after sufficient time to grieve has elapsed (Newcomer, 2011).

Typical and Atypical Behavior

Some children with emotional or behavioral disorders exhibit unusual, or qualitatively different, behaviors—behaviors that are not typical at *any* age. For example, children and youth with Tourette syndrome exhibit peculiar behaviors such as uncontrollable motor movements (tics) and inappropriate vocalizations such as barking, profanity, or other socially inappropriate comments that are not developmentally typical at any age. These atypical behaviors are considered by some professionals to be disordered or disturbed. See the accompanying First Person feature.

Variability in Cultural and Social Standards of Behavior

Kauffman and Landrum (2013) observe that only a few behaviors are universally recognized as abnormal in every cultural group and across all social strata. Examples of behaviors that appear to deviate from nearly all cultural norms are muteness, serious self-injury, eating one's feces, and murder. In contrast, the majority of behaviors considered to be disordered are labeled as such because they violate standards that are specific to an individual's culture and social milieu. Hitting others, swearing, sexual behavior, and physical aggression are but a few of the behaviors in which normative standards vary markedly across cultures.

Federal Definition

The Individuals with Disabilities Education Improvement Act (IDEA), or PL 108–446, uses the term emotional disturbance to describe the population referred to in this chapter as individuals with emotional or behavioral disorders. The federal definition of emotional disturbance, modeled after one proposed by Eli Bower (1960), is as follows:

(i) The term means a condition exhibiting one or more of the following characteristics over a long period of time and to a marked degree that adversely affects a child's educational performance:

(A) An inability to learn that cannot be explained by intellectual, sensory, or health factors.

(B) An inability to build or maintain satisfactory interpersonal relationships with peers and teachers.

(C) Inappropriate types of behavior or feelings under normal circumstances.

(D) A general pervasive mood of unhappiness or depression.

(E) A tendency to develop physical symptoms or fears associated with personal or school problems.

Tourette syndrome: A neurological disorder characterized by motor tics and uncontrollable verbal outbursts.

(ii) The term includes schizophrenia. The term does not apply to children who are socially maladjusted, unless it is determined that they have an emotional disturbance. [34 C.F.R. § 300.8(c)(4)]

emotional disturbance: A term often used when referring to individuals with emotional or behavioral disorders.

REFERENCE
Tourette's Syndrome

FIRST PERSON: MY EAGLE SCOUT

We are at my son's Eagle recognition ceremony, an accomplishment that so few young men ever achieve. He has been in scouting since first grade, before we knew there were issues in his life that might make getting to this point a problem for him. He is sitting on the opposite side of this very large church, waiting to be called forward to receive his award. I am standing near the wall, poised to take his picture and thinking that he has no idea where I am. But in true fashion, he spies me and acknowledges my presence, just like he does at all his functions. We are connected, he and I. He is not embarrassed to be seen with his mom. What a joy he is—gentle, kind, loving, and totally uninhibited in his expression of joy or excitement. I tell my other children that while I love them all, I like him the best. For what is there about him that you wouldn't like? At 15 he is tall and handsome, a musician, an Eagle Scout, an avid Bama fan, a good student, a young man of faith, and a friend to anyone who will simply give him a chance. At times like this I often pause to reflect on how blessed we are to have him in our lives. Life has not been easy for him academically or, perhaps more important, socially. He has severe learning disabilities in some major areas such as math and reading, which impact every aspect of learning. He also has Tourette syndrome, which impacts him socially, and this is perhaps what hurts him the most.

Having a child diagnosed with anything that means his or her life is going to be more difficult is a blow to a family. Hearing a doctor or a group of educators tell you that your child will likely not have the academic skills to go on to college is hard to hear. Watching peers shun and make fun of your child because of his speech and social skills is even more painful, and you are left trying to figure out how to proceed. How to help your child achieve his or her goals? It is like trying to negotiate a complex maze. You don't know where to go or what to do, and you often have no one in particular to ask about what to do or where to go. Parents often have to learn as they travel this course, and having educators who are willing to work with them can make all the difference in the outcome.

Reflecting back fifteen years, there was nothing unusual about my son's birth or development—well, for the most part. As a young child he was always a bit intense. He would pick up and put away everything he got out—not a bad habit, but unusual for a 2-year-old. He would try and clean the glass doors if he saw they needed it. He was extremely sensitive to loud noises and to light. Once he was even called an ugly name by an

adult because he began to cry while in the gym at our church when the noise level had become unbearable to him.

So up until he was around 2 years old we thought, "Great, a child that will just move on easily." He was sweet and gentle and developing in a normal fashion. Then we began to notice that his speech was not coming along as it should. I was not blind. I was the mom of three kids, one of whom already had problems, and I was not about to wait to see if everything would turn out OK. So we began our struggle to find out what was going on.

Speech therapy was first. This was when the educational system first began to help. Therapy was provided by the school system, and he improved. But kindergarten started, and concerns began to surface. His reading was slow. He had difficulty making eye contact with his peers. He overreacted to being touched and didn't seem to know how to respond when socializing with his classmates. If his hands were dirty or sticky, he simply had to wash them and could not focus on anything else until that task was complete. In fact, if he got something in his mind that had to be done, then it had to be done before he could move on to the next thing.

In first grade he was tested by his school, and indeed, what we suspected was true. There were some issues with academics. But it seemed to be more than this. At this point I should say that the school was wonderful. It was at this time I realized just what an ally a good school system could be. Over time, more tests, outside consultations, and meetings were held until, finally, a diagnosis of Asperger syndrome was given. This diagnosis, however, never seemed to fit. As a parent, I continued to try and figure out if the experts were right. As it turns out, they were not. Around 7 years of age, my son was diagnosed with Tourette syndrome. Subsequently, he was diagnosed with a severe reading and math disability. This made sense and finally fit what we had been seeing. In every other aspect of his life, though, he did fine.

As a parent, it was like being hit in the stomach. I was sad for my child, and irritated at others around me who had children that seemed to be developing fine and who seemed unwilling to give my child a chance. I was angry with adults who wouldn't invite him over or include him in activities. Even relatives who thought he acted strange were the subjects of my irritation. You just want others to see in your child what you see. You find yourself defensive and trying to prevent your child, at least initially, from seeing himself as different. And then the work began with the school—the place he was to spend the majority of his life until age 18.

I have to say that my involvement with our school system has been, for the most part, excellent but, at times, very frustrating. As a parent, I was a bit intimidated by my son's teachers and by the administrative staff. While I trusted the school system, I wasn't about to sit back and let it totally direct his education. We had him evaluated outside the school system by a private therapist and had him seen by a pediatric neuropsychologist, who subsequently came to the school to meet with the faculty. I attended all meetings and read everything I could get my hands on. I volunteered for everything so I could be nearby, and I even acted as his aide in math class. His teachers were more than happy to have me, and I always felt welcomed by them in the classroom.

By educating myself I was able to be a key member of his educational team and not just a bystander, letting others call the shots. Because the educational team members knew I was involved, they made every effort to include me and to keep me completely informed. We did not always agree, however, on the direction his education should take, but it was not just academics that were at issue here.

I learned early on that sometimes academics had to come second to activities that allowed him a social outlet. Our son had difficulty understanding social cues. He had trouble with peer relationships. He wanted so much to have friends, but for the most part his peers had little to do with him. He was made fun of, laughed at, and rarely included in social events such as spend-the-night gatherings, parties, or even groups on the playground. You see, he had a hard time understanding and learning the rules of games, such as football. The light hurt his eyes, and the noises hurt his ears. He has trouble even now remembering information. He does not feel the passage of time and cannot tell you how many days there are in a year or a month, nor can he easily figure out how to divide something in half. Yet, he presents to the world as being very "normal." Everyone expects him to be able to do those things, and when he can't, they laugh and call him names. He has been bullied in the halls, at lunch, out in public, and on the Internet to the point where we had to threaten to bring charges against some of his peers.

The school has been an ally for us. Teachers and administrators have been available to answer my questions and to advocate for him. They have made sure that tests and study guides are appropriate and, when they are not, have allowed him extra time to study or to retake tests. They have provided guidance to me so that I can help from home, and I think, most important, they recognize that he is trying and that he does the best he can. They have, on many occasions, tried to educate other students about how to treat others and have allowed me time to talk to his peers about Tourette syndrome in an attempt to educate them.

It hasn't always been easy. There have been times that I have had to go to war over him. Middle school was particularly hard. Part of the difficulty may have been because we had such a good experience in elementary school. Going from the protected environment of elementary school to middle school where he knew so few of the children in his class, where he was made fun of in the halls, and where he had so many different teachers was extremely difficult to deal with. But he survived, and things are better now that we are in high school.

For now at least, my son is doing well. He has made the transition to high school and has found his niche. He is in the marching band and loves it. He no longer has to participate in classes that are so over his head as to be embarrassing for him. He has a case coordinator who works well with him and who helps us with his class schedule. Because he will graduate with a diploma that is vocational in nature, he takes classes that are geared to his individual needs and not college prep courses. Vocational rehabilitation will start working with him, and he will soon begin to decide what kind of job he wants and begin training toward that goal. His teachers are very helpful and have shown tremendous flexibility with him.

As his parents, we are still protective and still very much involved in his life. But even I am having to back off a bit. He is a teenager now and will soon be driving (he just got his permit), which is a bit scary, but I realize he is growing up and must learn to stand on his own. He will do well. After all, school is the only time in your life where you are expected to be good at everything. He will soon start choosing his path in life. I find that my anger has finally begun to subside and that I am growing more comfortable all the time with the outlook for his future. He has friends, particularly those at church, who love him. He has siblings who watch out for him. He is growing up quite nicely and is truly a young man with a mind and faith of his own. I could not be more proud. ∎

–Anonymous

Excluding students thought to be socially maladjusted from the IDEA definition of emotional disturbance is controversial.

Since the passage of PL 94–142 in the mid-1970s, only two changes have been made to this definition: (1) Autism, originally included in this category, became a separate disability category in 1990. (2) The term *seriously emotionally disturbed* was changed to *emotional disturbance* via PL 105–17 in 1997.

In contrast to the current federal definition, Bower's (1960, 1981) definition did *not* exclude students considered to be socially maladjusted. Rather, Bower intended for the five components of the definition to be indicators of social maladjustment (Bower, 1982). Social maladjustment is often equated with conduct disorders, one of the most common psychiatric disorders among children and youth (Wicks-Nelson & Israel, 2013). In your classroom, you may have a difficult time understanding why these students may not qualify for special education and related services, as you will probably perceive them as being very disabled by their behavior. You will not be alone in this perception. The Council for Children with Behavioral Disorders (CCBD) and others have been most vocal and active in advocating for the inclusion of students with conduct disorders in the federal definition (Council for Children with Behavioral Disorders, 1990; Forness & Kavale, 2000).

Subsequent research has supported neither the five criteria nor the "socially maladjusted" exclusionary clause in the current federal definition (Cullinan, 2007). Many have argued that the federal definition is vague, equivocal, and insufficient for identifying the full range of emotional or behavioral disorders found among children and youth (Crundwell & Killu, 2007; Newcomer, 2011; Vaughn, Bos, & Schumm, 2014). Other criticisms have targeted the ambiguity of such terms as *a long period of time, to a marked degree, inability to learn*, and *pervasive* (Kauffman & Landrum, 2013; Kerr & Nelson, 2010). The phrase *adversely affects a child's educational performance* has been criticized because at times it has been narrowly interpreted to mean only academic performance and not performance related to critical behavioral, social, and vocational skills. Rosenberg, Wilson, Maheady, and Sindelar (2004) criticize the phrase *inability to learn* because it may give the impression that children and youth with emotional or behavioral disorders do not have the capacity to learn—a conclusion that is simply untrue.

An Alternative Definition

Because of perceived difficulties inherent within the federal definition, the Council for Children with Behavioral Disorders (2000) proposed a more functional and workable definition that paralleled the earlier thinking of the National Mental Health and Special Education Coalition (Forness & Kavale, 2000), a group of professionals representing thirty different mental health, education, and child advocacy organizations. One of the recommendations contained in this document was to change the term *emotionally disturbed* to *emotional or behavioral disorders*. The latter term is generally more accepted in the field today because it (1) has greater utility; (2) is more representative of the students who experience problems with their emotions, their behavior, or both; and (3) is less stigmatizing than *emotional disturbance*.

socially maladjusted: Individuals whose social behaviors are atypical; often regarded as chronic social offenders.

conduct disorder: A common psychiatric disorder among children and youth characterized by disruptive and aggressive behavior as well as other actions that violate societal rules.

According to the CCBD, the term *emotional or behavioral disorders* means a disability that is

- characterized by behavioral or emotional responses in school programs so different from appropriate age, cultural, or ethnic norms that the responses adversely affect educational performance, including academic, social, vocational, and personal skills;
- more than a temporary, expected response to stressful events in the environment;
- consistently exhibited in two different settings, at least one of which is school related; and
- unresponsive to direct intervention applied in general education, or the condition of the child is such that general education interventions would be insufficient.

The term includes such a disability that coexists with other disabilities.

The term includes a schizophrenic disorder, affective disorder, anxiety disorder, or other sustained disorder of conduct or adjustment, affecting a child if the disorder affects educational performance as described [above]. (McIntyre & Forness, 1996, p. 5)

Despite the many advantages of this proposed alternative definition, little progress has been made toward incorporating it into federal law.

Classification of Individuals With Emotional or Behavioral Disorders

The term *emotional or behavioral disorders* encompasses a wide range of disorders. When a student is given this broad label, educators know very little about the specific nature or characteristics of the student's disability. To provide greater clarity and specificity, educators and mental health professionals have attempted to classify the many different types of emotional or behavioral disorders. Thus, for example, if a student is identified as having a conduct disorder, educators can anticipate that the student's behavior will be characterized by acting-out, aggressive, and rule-violating behavior. This pattern can be distinguished from schizophrenia, which is characterized by disturbances in thought processes, hallucinations, and bizarre behavior.

Two widely used classification systems are pertinent to the field of education. Clinically derived classification systems have been developed by psychiatrists and mental health professionals to describe childhood, adolescent, and adult mental disorders. The most widely used psychiatric, or clinically derived, classification system in the United States is the *Diagnostic and Statistical Manual of Mental Disorders* (5th ed., or DSM-5), which was revised by the American Psychiatric Association (APA) in 2013. Statistically derived classification systems are developed using sophisticated statistical techniques to analyze the patterns or "dimensions" of behaviors that characterize children and youth with emotional or behavioral disorders.

clinically derived classification system: A system frequently used by mental health professionals to describe childhood, adolescent, and adult mental disorders.

statistically derived classification system: A system developed to analyze patterns of behaviors based on statistical procedures that characterize children and youth with emotional or behavioral disorders.

Clinically Derived Classification Systems

In general, there are no "tests" available to medical professionals to diagnose emotional or behavioral disorders among children and youth. For many years, psychiatrists and other mental health professionals have relied on clinically derived classification systems, such as the DSM-5, to assist them in making psychiatric diagnoses. These systems group behaviors into diagnostic categories and provide criteria useful for making diagnoses. Clinically derived systems also include descriptions of symptoms, indicators of severity, prevalence estimates, and information about variations of disorders. To make a diagnosis, psychiatrists and other mental health professionals may observe an individual's behavior over time and across different settings and then compare these behaviors to diagnostic criteria provided in a classification system.

Although such systems in the past have focused primarily on adult disorders, in recent years they have increasingly included disorders found among children (Wicks-Nelson & Israel, 2013); for example, attention deficit hyperactivity disorder, conduct disorder, anxiety disorders, and depressive disorders. A psychiatric diagnosis does not mean, however, that a child will automatically qualify for a special education (Kauffman & Landrum, 2013). Although many students with psychiatric diagnoses are eligible for special education, such eligibility is independent of, and uses criteria different from, those criteria found in the DSM-5.

Statistically Derived Classification Systems

Some researchers use sophisticated statistical techniques to establish categories, "dimensions," or patterns of disordered behavior that appear to be common among children and youth with emotional or behavioral disorders. Using these methods, researchers have been able to develop normative standards across a variety of dimensions to assist in making important decisions, such as eligibility for special education and related services.

Two global dimensions that have been consistently identified are externalizing disorders and internalizing disorders. Externalizing disorders, sometimes referred to as "undercontrolled" disorders, are characterized by aggressiveness, tempter tantrums, acting out, and noncompliant behaviors. Externalizing disorders are disturbing to others and generally result in considerable disruption in the classroom. In contrast, internalizing disorders, sometimes referred to as "overcontrolled" disorders, are characterized by social withdrawal, depression, compulsions, and anxiety. Children and youth with internalizing disorders are far less likely to be identified by their teachers and families as having an emotional or behavioral disorder because they do not create the "chaos" that often characterizes children and youth with externalizing disorders. These internalizing disorders, however, are equally serious; if left untreated, they can lead to a variety of negative long-term outcomes, including suicide (U.S. Department of Education, 2000a). In general, males tend to be at more risk for developing externalizing disorders, whereas females appear to be at greater risk for developing internalizing disorders (Webber & Plotts, 2008; Young, Sabbah, Young, Reiser, & Richardson, 2010). However, when females with externalizing disorders are identified, their problems may be more severe than those of their male counterparts (Nelson, Benner, & Rogers-Adkinson, 2003).

Other dimensions have also emerged from statistically derived procedures. Perhaps the best-known dimensions are those reported by Quay and Peterson (1996), reflected in the six scales of their Revised Behavior Problem Checklist (see Table 9.1). This behavioral rating scale is used by many educators to identify children and youth with emotional or behavioral disorders.

Some interesting findings in current research suggest that children and youth with emotional or behavioral disorders rarely exhibit problems along a single dimension. Rather, they often have elevated levels along two or more dimensions (Kauffman & Landrum, 2013; Wicks-Nelson & Israel, 2013). In fact, the co-occurrence of disorders may be the norm rather than the exception. For example, a student may have both a conduct disorder and attention problems. The fact that disorders often co-occur means

externalizing disorders: A behavior disorder characterized by aggressive, disruptive, acting-out behavior.

internalizing disorders: Behavior disorders characterized by anxiety, withdrawal, fearfulness, and other conditions reflecting an individual's internal state.

AUDIO

Mental Illness and Children

Dimension	Behavior
Conduct Disorder	This dimension is characterized by physical aggression, difficulty controlling anger, open disobedience, and oppositionality.
Socialized Aggression	This dimension includes behaviors similar to conduct disorders except that children and youth display these behaviors in the company of others. Behaviors include stealing and substance abuse in the company of others, truancy from school, gang membership, stealing, and lying.
Attention Problems/ Immaturity	This dimension is often associated with attention deficit disorder. It includes behaviors such as short attention span, diminished concentration, distractibility, and impulsivity, as well as behaviors such as passivity, undependability, and childishness.
Anxiety/Withdrawal	This dimension is related to internalizing disorders. It includes behaviors related to poor self-confidence and self-esteem, hypersensitivity to criticism and rejection, generalized fearfulness and anxiety, and reluctance to try new behaviors because of fear of failure.
Psychotic Behavior	This dimension includes psychotic symptoms such as speech disturbance, bizarre ideation, delusions, and impaired reality testing.
Motor Tension Excess	This dimension is characterized by overactivity, including restlessness, tension, and "jumpiness."

SOURCE: Adapted from H. Quay and D. Peterson, *Manual for the Revised Behavior Problem Checklist* (Odessa, FL: Psychological Assessment Resources, 1996), p. 1. Reproduced by special permission of the publisher, Psychological Assessment Resources, Inc., 16204 North Florida Avenue, Lutz, Florida 33549, from the *Revised Behavior Problem Checklist* by Herbert Quay, PhD. Copyright 1983, 1996 by PAR, Inc. Further reproduction is prohibited without permission of PAR, Inc.

that the students in your classroom will often present very complex behaviors, frequently requiring multifaceted interventions designed to address a wide range of behaviors.

A Brief History of the Field

The inclusion of students with emotional or behavioral disorders in public schools is a relatively recent phenomenon. Throughout history, the nature of this disability has frequently resulted in stigma and ostracism by society in general, and exclusion from education in particular. Even today, there is debate and controversy regarding whether or not these students should be educated in our public schools.

The historical roots of the field of emotional or behavioral disorders are intertwined with the history of other fields of study—most notably, intellectual disability, psychiatry, and psychology (Kauffman & Landrum, 2013). Not until 1886 was a legal distinction made between "insanity" and "feeblemindedness" (Hayman, 1939). This distinction was an important one, as it marked the separation of emotional or behavioral disorders from intellectual disability. Differentiating the history of emotional or behavioral disorders from that of intellectual disability before that time is difficult. Because this common history is detailed in the chapter on intellectual disability (Chapter 6), this historical review (see Table 9.2) begins with the nineteenth century. Unless otherwise noted, the historical account that follows is based on a synthesis of several substantive resources: Despert (1965), Kauffman and Landrum (2013), Lewis (1974), Rie (1971), and Safford and Safford (1996).

Prevalence of Emotional or Behavioral Disorders

How prevalent are emotional or behavioral disorders among school-age children and youth? The answer to this question is not a simple one; prevalence estimates for this

Table 9.2 A Timeline of Representative Historical Events in the Field of Emotional or Behavioral Disorders

Date	Individual or Event
1817	First private psychiatric hospital opens in Pennsylvania operated by the Quakers, known today as Friends Hospital.
1892	American Psychological Association founded.
1908	Clifford W. Beers authors *A Mind That Found Itself*, an autobiographical account of being institutionalized in a mental hospital.
1909	National Committee for Mental Hygiene established.
1909	Juvenile Psychopathic Institute opens in Chicago to investigate causes of juvenile delinquency; treatment based on Freudian or psychodynamic principles.
1914	First special education teacher training program established in Michigan.
1922	Forerunner of the Council for Exceptional Children organized at Teachers College, Columbia University.
1923	American Orthopsychiatric Association founded.
1928	First training program in school psychology offered at New York University.
1931	First psychiatric hospital specializing in the treatment of children and adolescents with emotional or behavioral disorders opens in Rhode Island. Operates today as the Bradley Hospital.
1934	Lauretta Bender begins her pioneering work with children with schizophrenia at the Bellevue psychiatric clinic in New York City.
1936	Leo Kanner publishes *Child Psychiatry*, the first textbook on child psychology published in the United States.
1944	Pioneer House for delinquent and emotionally disturbed boys opens in Detroit. Established by Fritz Redl and David Wineman who pioneered the Life Space Interview.
1944	Bruno Bettelheim, a psychoanalyst, serves as the director of the Orthogenic School, a residential school in Chicago for children identified as emotionally disturbed.
1960	Eli Bower offers an early definition of emotional disturbance.
1960s	Emergence of conceptual models guiding educational programs, practices, and curricula for children and youth with emotional or behavioral disorders. (See companion Table 9.3.)
1964	Council for Children with Behavioral Disorders becomes a division within the Council for Exceptional Children.
1975	Herbert Quay and Donald Peterson develop an assessment tool (*Behavior Problem Checklist*) for identifying children with emotional or behavioral disorders.
1975	Public Law 94–142 enacted.

population vary widely. Among the reasons for this variance are conflicting definitions and a lack of consensus on what constitutes acceptable behavior.

From a historical perspective, the percentage of public school students receiving special education under this category grew from 0.5 percent in the mid-1970s to 1.0 percent in the mid-1980s. Since that time, however, growth in this category has been negligible (Kauffman & Landrum, 2013). The number of students being served under this category is far lower than the original federal estimate of 2 percent (U.S. Department of Education, 1980). Moreover, this estimate is considered extremely conservative by many professionals in the field (Cullinan, 2007). Students with emotional or behavioral disorders are considered to be the most underidentified of all IDEA disability categories (Landrum, Katsiyannis, & Archwamety, 2004).

Table 9.3 **Conceptual Models of Emotional or Behavioral Disorders**

Model	Approach
Behavioral	Based on the work of B. F. Skinner and other behavioral psychologists, this model assumes that behavior is a function of environmental events. Maladaptive behaviors are thought to be learned and maintained by the environment. Seeks to establish a replicable cause-and-effect relationship. Uses systematic observations and data collection procedures. Behavior can be modified by changing antecedent or consequent events. Frank Hewett's "engineered" classroom, described in his book *The Emotionally Disturbed Child in the Classroom* (1968), was constructed around a behavioral approach.
Psychodynamic	Based on the thinking of Sigmund Freud and his followers, this model proposes that disturbed behaviors are symptomatic of underlying conflict between hypothetical mental functions (id, ego, superego) that are in dynamic interaction. Unconscious motivation for behavior must be understood in order for intervention to be successful. Individual psychotherapy for the student (and sometimes the parents) is frequently used to uncover deep-rooted problems typically originating in the child's past. A permissive classroom environment and an accepting teacher are also called for.
Psychoeducational	Like the psychodynamic model this approach emphasizes unconscious motivations and underlying conflicts, but it is balanced by the realistic demands of functioning at home, at school, and in the community. Teachers attempt to gain an understanding of the child's unconscious motivation for problem behaviors through therapeutic conversations (Life Space Interviews) and try to help the student gain insight and acquire self-control through planning and reflection. *Conflict in the Classroom* (1965) by Nicholas Long, William Morse, and Ruth Newman offers a perspective on the psychoeducational model.
Ecological	This model attributes behavioral problems to the student's interactions in the family, at school, and in the community. Problematic behavior results from a lack of a "goodness of fit" between the student and the particular social milieu. Intervention attempts to alter the social settings and the transactions occurring therein. Project Re-ED, a residential treatment program established by Nicholas Hobbs in 1961, is an example of this approach.
Humanistic	This model, arising from the social-political movement of the 1960s and 1970s, stresses self-direction, self-fulfillment, and self-evaluation. Pupils are encouraged to be free and open. It is assumed that children are capable of generating their own solutions to their problems when provided with a caring and supportive environment where teachers are nonauthoritarian.
Biological	Underlying this model is a belief that emotional or behavioral disorders, such as depression or hyperaggression, are the result of physiological flaws. Treatments, therefore, may consist of drug therapy, biofeedback, dietary management, or even surgery. The Feingold diet, popular in the 1970s as a treatment for hyperactivity, is an example of this model.

SOURCE: J. M. Kauffman, *Characteristics of Emotional and Behavioral Disorders of Children and Youth*, 8th ed., © 2005. Adapted with permission of Pearson Education, Inc., Upper Saddle River, NJ.

The U.S. Department of Education (2013a) reports that during the 2011–2012 school year, 371,600 students ages 6–21 were receiving a special education and related services because of an emotional disturbance. This number represents 6.4 percent of the total number of students served in special education, making this the sixth largest disability category for students in this age range.

At the preschool level, the U.S. Department of Education (2013a) reports that only 3,128 children ages 3–5 were identified as emotionally disturbed during the 2011–2012 school year. This low level of identification may be due to at least two factors. First, because there is an emphasis on noncategorical labeling at the preschool level and in the early elementary grades, many students who ultimately are identified as emotionally disturbed may be labeled as developmentally delayed during the early childhood years. Second, school personnel may be hesitant to identify a youngster as exhibiting emotional or behavioral disorders during the early childhood years.

Although only about 0.5 percent of the school-age population currently receives special education services for emotional or behavioral disorders (U.S. Department of Education, 2013a), credible studies in the United States indicate that at least 3 to 6 percent of children and youth exhibit serious and persistent problems (Kauffman & Landrum, 2013). Numerous reasons have been offered for the underidentification of students with emotional or behavioral disorders. One possible reason is the marked variability across states in identifying pupils with emotional or behavioral disorders. The range of students receiving a special education during the 2011–2012 school year varies from a low of 0.11 percent in Arkansas to a high of 1.44 percent in Vermont (U.S. Department of Education, 2013a). Recall that IDEA allows states to adopt their own definitions, provided that state definitions identify an equivalent group of students. In fact, state definitions vary so widely that identification may be a function more of where an individual lives than of any other factor. Kauffman and Landrum (2013) believe that social policy and economic factors also play critical roles in underidentification.

Etiology of Emotional or Behavioral Disorders

Our understanding of the causes of emotional or behavioral disorders has increased substantially in recent years. A major milestone was the publication in the late nineties of a national report, *Mental Health: A Report of the Surgeon General* (Satcher, 1999). For the first time in history, the country's most prominent health care leader, the surgeon general, recognized that addressing the needs of both children and adults with mental illness is a pressing national concern.

This report describes the research regarding many of the risk factors associated with mental disorders of childhood. These risk factors often interact in a synergetic fashion; as the number of risk factors increases, so do the chances of negative outcomes such as emotional or behavioral disorders.

Biological Risk Factors

Although many professionals agree that the development of emotional or behavioral disorders is due to both biological and environmental factors (Kauffman & Landrum, 2013; Landrum, 2011; Rutter, 2006), there is a growing consensus that biological factors are particularly influential in the etiology of several disorders. These emotional or behavioral disorders can be the result of either genetic influences or biological insults. Disorders that likely have a genetic influence include, for example, bipolar disorder, schizophrenia, obsessive-compulsive disorder, and Tourette syndrome (Wicks-Nelson & Israel, 2013). Biological insults such as injury, infection, lead poisoning, poor nutrition, or exposure to toxins (including intrauterine exposure to alcohol, illicit drugs, or cigarette smoke) may also influence the development of emotional or behavioral disorders.

Numerous studies also suggest that infant temperament (that is, an infant born with a "difficult" temperament) may precede the development of emotional or behavioral disorders (Rosenblum, Dayton, & Muzik, 2009; Shaw, Gilliom, & Giovannelli, 2005; Webber & Plotts, 2008). Despite the early research in this area, more recent studies indicate that "difficult" infant temperament may be mediated to some extent by the environment (Kauffman & Landrum, 2013).

Research indicates that nearly half of individuals with emotional or behavioral disorders have additional disabilities (National Institute of Mental Health, 2013). For example, some students with conduct disorders are also depressed; in fact, these children often have a family history of depression (National Institute of Mental Health,

Behavior	Manifestations
Quiet, withdrawn, few friends	Often not recognized because the individual is not noticed and makes no obvious trouble.
Changes in behavior	Personality changes—e.g., from friendliness to withdrawal, lack of communication, and sad and expressionless appearance, or from a quiet demeanor to acting out and troublemaking.
Increased failure or role strain	Often pervasive in school, work, home, friends, and love relationships, but often manifested clearly in school pressures for young people.
Recent family changes	Illness, job loss, increased consumption of alcohol, poor health, etc.
Recent loss of a family member	Death, divorce, separation, or someone leaving home.
Feelings of despair and hopelessness*	Shows itself in many forms, from changes in posture and behavior to verbal expression of such feelings.
Symptomatic acts	Taking unnecessary risks, becoming involved in drinking and drug abuse, becoming inappropriately aggressive or submissive, giving away possessions.
Communication*	Such statements as "Life is not worth living," "I'm finished," "Might as well be dead," or "I wish I were dead."
Presence of a plan*	Storing up medication, buying a gun.

*To be viewed with heightened concern.

SOURCE: Adapted from the Crisis Center, *Ten Behavioral Suicide Warning Signs* (Birmingham, AL: n.d.).

2010). Parental depression also increases the risk of children and youth developing anxiety disorders, conduct disorder, and alcohol dependency.

Suicide among depressed children and youth is a major concern in our society. Research suggests that a high percentage of children and adolescents who have committed suicide had an apparent, though not identified, emotional or behavioral disorder before their deaths (Kauffman & Landrum, 2013; Wicks-Nelson & Israel, 2013). Table 9.4 lists some of the warning signs of an impending suicide. As an educator, you need to be especially alert to these warning signs and be sure to report them to parents, counselors, administrators, and other appropriate professionals.

Psychosocial Risk Factors

Conduct disorders typically have both biological and environmental components, with substantial psychosocial risk factors involved in their development. Environmental factors such as parental discord, a parent's mental illness or criminal behavior, overcrowding in the home, and large family size may result in conditions conducive to the development of conduct disorders—especially if the child or youth does not have a loving, nurturing relationship with at least one parent. Other risk factors include early maternal rejection and neglect and abuse.

Poverty has been shown to be a significant risk factor for the development of emotional or behavioral disorders, as it often translates into increased family stress, poor health care, underachievement, and other negative outcomes. The United States has one of the highest poverty rates of all developed countries (Children's Defense Fund, 2012). Although emotional and behavioral disorders occur among all socioeconomic classes, children who live in poverty may be at especially high risk (Kauffman & Landrum, 2013).

Table 9.5 Four Main Types of Child Maltreatment

Term	Definition
Physical abuse	Characterized by the infliction of physical injury as a result of punching, beating, kicking, biting, burning, shaking, or otherwise harming a child. The parent or caretaker may not have intended to hurt the child; rather, the injury may have resulted from overdiscipline or physical punishment.
Child neglect	Characterized by failure to provide for the child's basic needs. Neglect can be physical, educational, or emotional.
Physical neglect	Includes refusal or delay in seeking health care, abandonment, expulsion from the home or refusal to allow a runaway to return home, and inadequate supervision.
Educational neglect	Includes the allowance of chronic truancy, failure to enroll a child of mandatory school age in school, and failure to attend to a special educational need.
Emotional neglect	Includes such actions as marked inattention to the child's need for affection, refusal or failure to provide needed psychological care, spousal abuse in the child's presence, and permission of drug or alcohol use by the child. This assessment of child neglect requires consideration of cultural values and standards of care as well as recognition that the failure to provide the necessities of life may be related to poverty.
Sexual abuse	Includes fondling a child's genitals, intercourse, incest, rape, sodomy, exhibitionism, and commercial exploitation through prostitution or the production of pornographic materials. Many experts believe that sexual abuse is the most underreported of child maltreatment because of the "conspiracy of silence" that so often characterizes these cases.
Emotional abuse (psychological abuse/ verbal abuse/mental injury)	Includes acts of omission by the parents or other caregivers that have caused, or could have caused, serious behavioral, cognitive, emotional, or mental disorders. In some cases of emotional abuse, the acts of parents or other caregivers alone, without any harm evident in the child's behavior or condition, are sufficient to warrant Child Protective Services intervention.

SOURCE: Based on 42 U.S.C. § 5101 *et seq.* Child Abuse Prevention and Treatment Act. Public Law 101–36, 2003.

Child maltreatment is often associated with a number of emotional or behavioral disorders (Wicks-Nelson & Israel, 2013). Child maltreatment has been linked to internalizing disorders such as depression and externalizing disorders such as conduct disorders (Kauffman & Landrum, 2013). Child maltreatment includes neglect, physical abuse, sexual abuse, and emotional abuse. Table 9.5 describes these four main types of child maltreatment. As a teacher, your role is critical in identifying and reporting your suspicions of child maltreatment to law enforcement and social service agencies.

It is important to remember that no one cause or single event in an individual's life directly contributes to the development of emotional or behavioral disorders; rather, it is the result of a complex, multidimensional interaction of various risk factors that may lead to the development of maladaptive and other challenging behaviors. The greater the number of risk factors and the longer the child is exposed, the greater the likelihood of long-term destructive consequences (Sprague & Walker, 2000). Still, we caution that "causality in the world of emotional and behavioral disorders is rarely linear; it rarely proceeds unambiguously from event A to outcome B" (Oswald, 2003, p. 202). Figure 9.1 portrays one possible pathway to long-term and destructive outcomes.

Prevention of Emotional or Behavioral Disorders

How do we prevent the onset of emotional or behavioral disorders? How do we minimize the risk of negative long-term outcomes for those students who do develop these disorders? This section will describe two bodies of research focusing on the prevention of emotional and behavioral disorders among children and youth.

child maltreatment: The neglect and/or physical, emotional, or sexual abuse of a child.

Exposure to family, neighborhood, school and societal risk factors

- Poverty
- Abuse and neglect
- Harsh and inconsistent parenting
- Drug and alcohol use by caregivers
- Emotional and physical or sexual abuse
- Modeling of aggression
- Media violence
- Negative attitude toward schooling
- Family transitions (death or divorce)
- Parent criminality

Leads to development of maladaptive behavioral manifestations

- Defiance of adults
- Lack of school readiness
- Coercive interactive styles
- Aggression toward peers
- Lack of problem-solving skills

Risk Pathway

Produces negative short-term outcomes

- Truancy
- Peer and teacher rejection
- Low academic achievement
- High number of school discipline referrals
- Large number of different schools attended
- Early involvement with drugs and alcohol
- Early age of first arrest (under 12 years)

To negative, destructive long-term outcomes

- School failure and dropout
- Delinquency
- Drug and alcohol use
- Gang membership
- Violent acts
- Adult criminality
- Lifelong dependence on welfare system
- Higher death and injury rate

SOURCE: Redrawn from H. Walker and J. Sprague, "The Path to School Failure, Delinquency, and Violence: Causal Factors and Some Potential Solutions," *Intervention in School and Clinic, 35*(2), 1999, p. 68.

Research on Resiliency

How do we explain the fact that some children and youth, despite the most adverse circumstances, do not develop emotional or behavioral disorders? How is it that these resilient individuals become healthy, well-adjusted adults? Janas (2002) and Milstein and Henry (2000) identified four attributes of resilient children. First, resilient children appear to be socially competent; they are adept at establishing and maintaining positive relationships with both peers and adults. Second, resilient children have excellent problem-solving skills; they seek resources and help from others. Third, resilient children are autonomous; they have a strong identity and are able to act independently. Finally, resilient children develop clear goals and high aspirations; they see their futures as hopeful and bright.

Children who live in poverty may be at especially high risk for developing emotional or behavioral disorders.

What are the implications of this research for you as an educator? Resilient adults often report that, as children, they established a close, loving relationship with a supportive adult; many times, these adults were their teachers. Just one loving, caring relationship with an adult can foster resiliency in a student who is at risk for developing emotional or behavioral disorders, and thus possibly help prevent negative long-term outcomes. Research (Abelev, 2009) suggests that children who evidence resiliency do not experience long-term negative consequences from exposure to environmental risk factors. Intervention programs are now focusing on developing resilient behaviors in children who are at risk and their families (Singer, Maul, Wang, & Ethridge, 2011).

Research on Positive Behavioral Support

Educators have many approaches at their disposal for responding to students who exhibit problematic behavior in the classroom. The traditional school response has been punishment, which often includes reactive responses such as reprimands, corporal punishment, suspension, and even expulsion from school. The behaviors of children with emotional or behavioral disorders are often so chronic and intense that these children are at high risk for receiving significant amounts of punishment. Although punishment will often reduce undesirable behavior, it is generally regarded as an ineffective and unproductive behavior reduction strategy (Kauffman & Landrum, 2013; Scheuermann & Hall, 2012).

Despite its ineffectiveness, punishment is still very common in our schools. A contemporary alternative strategy for responding to problematic behavior is positive behavioral support. This is a schoolwide approach designed to prevent problem behaviors before they occur and, when they do occur, to intervene early to prevent them from escalating further. The idea is to respond *proactively* rather than *reactively*, which is typical of punishment (Chitiyo & Wheeler, 2009; Scheuermann & Hall, 2012). Positive behavioral support can be described as a systematic, evidence-based, problem-solving intervention strategy for dealing with problematic behaviors. Eber and her colleagues (Eber, Sugai, Smith, & Scott, 2002) define positive behavioral support as "a systems approach for establishing a continuum of proactive discipline procedures for all students and staff members in all types of school settings" (p. 171). A more contemporary interpretation views positive behavioral support as

> a data-driven, team-based framework or approach for establishing a continuum of effective behavioral practices and systems that (a) prevents the development or worsening of problem behavior and (b) encourages the teaching and reinforcement of prosocial expectations and behavior across all environments for all students by all staff. (Sugai, Simonsen, & Horner, 2008, p. 5)

positive behavioral support: An alternative approach to punishment; a schoolwide, proactive way of addressing problematic behaviors.

VIDEO
Student View of Positive Behavioral Support

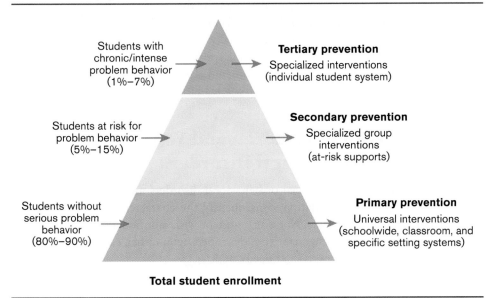

Tertiary prevention
Specialized interventions
(individual student system)

Students with
chronic/intense
problem behavior
(1%–7%)

Secondary prevention
Specialized group
interventions
(at-risk supports)

Students at risk for
problem behavior
(5%–15%)

Primary prevention
Universal interventions
(schoolwide, classroom, and
specific setting systems)

Students without
serious problem
behavior
(80%–90%)

Total student enrollment

SOURCE: Adapted from G. Sugai, R. Horner, G. Dunlap, M. Hieneman, T. Lewis, C. Nelson, et al., *Applying Positive Behavior Support and Functional Assessment in Schools* (Washington, DC: Office of Special Education Programs, Center on Positive Behavioral Interventions and Supports, 1999), p. 11.

A positive behavioral support model is designed to address the complexity of problematic behaviors through such efforts as promoting academic achievement; involving the family; emphasizing positive, nurturing relationships between students and staff; and identifying problematic behaviors *before* they become chronic and/or severe. This approach recognizes that problematic behaviors are often the result of both student and environmental variables (Scheuermann & Hall, 2012). PL 108–446 requires individualized education program (IEP) team members to consider using positive behavioral supports when addressing behaviors that impede the learning of a student with a disability and/or the learning of others. Positive behavioral support has been shown to be effective in decreasing as well as preventing problematic behaviors (Bradshaw, Mitchell, & Leaf, 2010; Lane, Kalberg, & Edwards, 2008; Lane, Robertson, & Graham-Bailey, 2006; Simonsen, Britton, & Young, 2010; Simonsen et al., 2012).

The focus of the positive behavioral support model is prevention. The prevention model depicted in Figure 9.2 identifies three critical levels of prevention. The goal of the schoolwide intervention team at the primary prevention or universal level is to reduce the number of new cases of problem behavior. Examples of such prevention efforts include schoolwide social skills training programs, clearly identified and implemented incentives for positive behavior (such as giving points, tied to identified reinforcers, for following school and classroom rules), and manipulation of environmental factors that may be contributing to problematic behavior (such as a lack of sufficient adult supervision on the playground). This requires a team effort involving staff and teachers reinforcing expectations of appropriate behavior across multiple settings like hallways, classrooms, and restrooms (Kauffman & Landrum, 2013). The secondary prevention or targeted level is designed to minimize the possibility that students at high risk will engage in misbehavior. Examples of approaches at this level include targeting small groups of students with common concerns, such as those who have experienced significant losses (death of a parent or sibling, parental divorce) and those who need more intensive instruction in specific areas (social skills, academic tutoring,

primary prevention: Activities aimed at eliminating a problem or condition prior to its onset; may also refer to reducing the number of new instances of problematic behavior.

secondary prevention: Efforts focusing on minimizing or eliminating potential risk factors in regard to persons with emotional or behavioral disorders; refers to minimizing the possibility that maladaptive or inappropriate behaviors will occur.

REFERENCE

Positive Behavioral Support

conflict resolution). The third and most intensive level of prevention is tertiary prevention, which includes interventions designed for the individual student. Examples of this level of prevention include the development and implementation of a token economy, individual counseling, and individually tailored self-monitoring programs. The purpose of tertiary prevention is to provide appropriate supports and interventions for students with chronic and intensive problem behaviors, thereby assisting them to engage in more appropriate and productive behaviors.

Characteristics of Children and Youth With Emotional or Behavioral Disorders

Children and youth with emotional or behavioral disorders are, as we have seen, an extremely heterogeneous population; consequently, the characteristics they display in the classroom are highly diverse. Not every student with emotional or behavioral disorders will exhibit all of the characteristics described here; rather, each student will be unique in terms of both strengths and needs.

Learning Characteristics

Although, intellectually, students with emotional or behavioral disorders may include individuals who are identified as gifted and those with an intellectual disability, a consistent finding of research has been that pupils with emotional or behavioral disorders typically score in the low-average range on measures of intelligence (Kauffman & Landrum, 2013; Wagner, Kutash, Duchnowski, Epstein, & Sumi, 2005).

A major concern among educators is the chronic school failure, despite about average intellectual ability, encountered by many of these students. Pupils with emotional or behavioral disorders typically experience significant academic deficits. Many of these students perform one or more years below grade-level expectations (Cullinan, 2007; Griffith, Trout, Hagaman, & Harper, 2008; Lane, Carter, Pierson, & Glaeser, 2006; Lane & Menzies, 2010). Researchers report that individuals with emotional or behavioral disorders fare much worse than average in terms of grades, grade retention, high school graduation rates, dropout rates, and absenteeism (Mihalas, Morse, Allsopp, & McHatton, 2009; Wagner & Davis, 2006). It is uncertain whether students with emotional or behavioral disorders experience academic difficulty because of a lack of motivation or maladaptive behaviors, especially those associated with externalizing disorders; regardless, these pupils are at very high risk for poor academic performance and subsequent school failure (Kauffman & Landrum, 2013; Smith, Polloway, Patton, & Dowdy, 2012).

Social Characteristics

Perhaps the most salient characteristic of students with emotional or behavioral disorders is their difficulty building and maintaining satisfactory interpersonal relationships. Many of these children, especially those exhibiting aggressive behavior, often experience rejection by both peers and adults (Dunlap et al., 2006). Moreover, it appears that the presence of aggressive behavior is a major predictor of future delinquency and incarceration, particularly if it appears in early childhood. Research on adolescents with emotional or behavioral disorders suggests high rates of incarceration for this population (Mihalas et al., 2009; Quinn, Rutherford, Leone, Osher, & Poirer, 2005).

tertiary prevention: Efforts that attempt to limit the adverse consequences of an existing problem while maximizing a person's potential; in regard to persons with emotional or behavioral disorders, refers to an intense level of intervention using strategies and supports designed for individuals with chronic and intense behavior problems.

VIDEO
Behavior Management Strategies

Language/Communication Characteristics

Over the years researchers have noted that expressive, receptive, and pragmatic language deficits (the social use of language) appear to be relatively common in individuals with emotional or behavioral disorders (Nelson, Benner, & Cheney, 2005; Nelson, Benner, Neill, & Stage, 2006; Wagner et al., 2005). Studies suggest that students with emotional or behavioral disorders use fewer words per sentence, have difficulty staying on a topic, and use language that is inappropriate to social conversation (Nelson et al., 2003; Rogers-Adkinson, 2003). It is believed that these language impairments contribute significantly to the challenging and disruptive behaviors common in some students with emotional or behavioral disorders.

Children and youth with emotional or behavioral disorders are an especially heterogeneous population.

Assessing Students With Emotional or Behavioral Disorders

As an educator, you will encounter many challenging student behaviors. These behaviors may puzzle you, and you may experience difficulty differentiating between behaviors that are "disturbing" and those that are "disturbed." Your ability to make this distinction is crucial if students with emotional or behavioral disorders are to be identified and appropriately served in a timely manner. Some children, particularly those with externalizing disorders, are hard to overlook because their behaviors result in considerable havoc and disruption in the classroom. Other students may exhibit behaviors that are more difficult to judge. For example, because the behaviors of young children change so quickly, you may find it difficult to determine whether their problematic behaviors are indicative of an emotional or behavioral disorder or are simply developmentally appropriate actions. Finally, you may overlook the behaviors of pupils with internalizing disorders because these behaviors typically do not disrupt the learning process. Your ability to identify potentially problematic behaviors represents an important first step in the assessment process.

Assessment Strategies

The assessment of children and youth with emotional or behavioral disorders is a complex process that necessitates a multimethod, multisource approach. Assessment strategies typically include a variety of methods and instruments (for example, rating scales, interviews, classroom observations) gathered from multiple sources or informants (the student, teachers, parents, peers). Each strategy has its own unique advantages and disadvantages. A multimethod approach is essential because of the transient nature

VIDEO
Student Needs

AUDIO
Mental Health Assessment

of behavior, developmental variations, and the variability of cultural and social standards of normalcy. Data from these multiple sources are typically aggregated in order to obtain a complete and authentic picture of the student's strengths as well as areas of need.

Recent Trends in Assessment of Students With Emotional or Behavioral Disorders

Over the years, three initiatives have strengthened the assessment process as it relates to students with emotional or behavioral disorders: person-centered planning, strength-based assessment, and functional behavioral assessment.

In **person-centered planning** (Austin & Wittig, 2013) the IEP team, including the parents, the student, and other stakeholders, begins the IEP process by creating a "vision" for the student's future. The student's input is vital to the success of this process. Typically, this vision includes an analysis of the individual's strengths, preferences, needs, and needed supports. By collaboratively articulating this vision *before* developing the IEP, the team seeks to address the pupil's long-term goals and aspirations. Person-centered planning forces IEP team members to look beyond the "next year" and to consider long-term solutions and interventions that will successfully address the student's "vision" and ensure a self-directed life upon leaving school.

Strength-based assessment is a reaction against the deficit-oriented model common in traditional assessment approaches (Donovan & Nickerson, 2007; Smith et al., 2012). It is based on the assumption that all children and youth have strengths and that deficits are not static but, rather, viewed as opportunities to learn (Harniss & Epstein, 2005). For example, behavior rating scales, which are commonly used throughout the assessment process, often include only items that identify behavioral deficits; they do not address the student's behavioral strengths. Epstein (2002) defines strength-based assessment as

> the measurement of the emotional and behavioral skills, competencies, and characteristics that create a sense of personal accomplishment; contribute to satisfying relationships with family members, peers, and adults; enhance one's ability to deal with adversity and stress; and promote one's personal, social, and academic development. (p. 3)

Functional behavioral assessment acknowledges that pupils engage in inappropriate behavior for multiple reasons. Likewise, several factors often influence or trigger a student's misbehavior. These precursors or antecedents to problematic behaviors may include (1) physiological factors such as illness, medication side effects, or fatigue; (2) classroom environmental factors such as seating arrangements, noise levels, or disruptions; and (3) curriculum and instructional factors such as assignments that are too difficult or unclear directions. By identifying the antecedents to problematic behavior, the teacher can then take a preventive or proactive approach to intervention. For example, by knowing that assignments are too difficult for the learner, the teacher can provide appropriate adaptations to facilitate the pupil's success and prevent acting-out behavior from ever occurring.

The consequences that follow an individual's behavior are also important factors to consider when choosing appropriate interventions for children and youth with emotional or behavioral disorders. A student who finds work too difficult, for example, may act out in an effort to avoid or escape the task. If the pupil is successful in avoiding the task, he or she is then reinforced for this acting-out behavior. As a teacher, you need

person-centered planning: Useful when developing a student's individualized education program; creates a vision for pupil's future based on an analysis of his or her strengths, needs, and preferences.

strength-based assessment: An assessment model that looks at an individual's strengths, abilities, and accomplishments rather than focusing on his or her deficits.

functional behavioral assessment: A behavioral strategy that seeks to determine the purpose or function that a particular behavior serves—what is occasioning and maintaining the behavior.

REFERENCE

Assessment of Emotional Disturbance

to be aware of your own possible role in the maintenance or escalation of a student's misbehavior. The consequences that follow a student's actions may inadvertently reinforce the very behaviors you want to decrease.

Functional behavioral assessment has historically been used with individuals with severe developmental disorders. Now, however, due to PL 108–446, it is a required component of the assessment process for students with disabilities who present behavioral challenges.

A functional behavior assessment examines the circumstances surrounding the occurrence and/or nonoccurrence of the challenging behavior, seeking to identify variables and events that are consistently present in those situations. The student's behavior during these times is examined to determine the function of the challenging behavior and to identify which variables might be maintaining it (Alberto & Troutman, 2013; Erickson, Stage, & Nelson, 2006; Lane, Weisenbach, Phillips, & Wehby, 2007). By understanding and manipulating the variables that precede and follow misbehavior, educators and parents can design interventions that will assist them in developing and implementing positive behavior supports for students. In fact, a functional behavioral assessment is considered to be a cornerstone or foundation of positive behavior supports (Alberto & Troutman, 2013; Chandler & Dahlquist, 2010; Lerner & Johns, 2012; Scheuermann & Hall, 2012).

Identification of antecedents and consequences is directly tied to the development of a behavioral intervention plan, required by PL 108–446 for students with disabilities who exhibit problematic behaviors in school. In developing this plan, the IEP team must consider the use of positive behavioral interventions, strategies, and supports to address the problematic behaviors. In effect, the IEP team must develop a proactive plan of intervention. This approach contrasts with more traditional approaches to student discipline, which are primarily reactive and punitive in nature.

Educational Considerations

Children and youth with emotional or behavioral disorders present unique challenges in terms of educational placement and programming. Interventions for students with emotional or behavioral disorders can be divided into three broad categories: physical environment interventions, academic and instructional interventions, and behavioral and cognitive-behavioral interventions. These categories represent an array of interventions reflecting various conceptual and theoretical models and include a range of primary, secondary, and tertiary intervention approaches.

Where Are Students With Emotional or Behavioral Disorders Educated?

In passing the 2004 amendments to IDEA, Congress voiced its preference that students with disabilities be educated in normalized educational environments. Clearly, this preference has not been fully implemented for students with emotional or behavioral disorders, who represent one of the more segregated groups of all students with disabilities. Currently, almost 40 percent of students with emotional or behavioral disorders receive a special education and related services in environments that segregate them from their typical peers for all or part of the school day (U.S. Department of Education, 2013a). During the 2011–2012 school year, slightly more than four out of ten students (43.1%) with emotional or behavioral disorders were receiving a special education in the general education classroom (see Figure 9.3). Relative to other

behavioral intervention plan: A plan required by Public Law 105–17 for students with disabilities who exhibit problematic behavior; a proactive intervention approach that includes a functional behavioral assessment and the use of positive behavioral supports.

Figure 9.3 Educational Placements for Students With Emotional or Behavioral Disorders

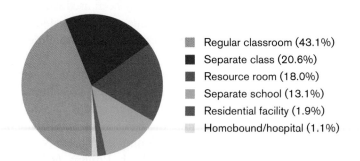

- Regular classroom (43.1%)
- Separate class (20.6%)
- Resource room (18.0%)
- Separate school (13.1%)
- Residential facility (1.9%)
- Homebound/hospital (1.1%)

NOTE: Figure represents percentage of enrollment of students with emotional or behavioral disorders during the 2011–2012 school year. Excludes pupils enrolled in parentally placed private schools and individuals in correctional facilities.

SOURCE: U.S. Department of Education. (2013). *Historical state-level IDEA data files*. Retrieved November 14, 2013, from http://tadnet.public.tadnet.org/pages/712

students with disabilities, children and youth with emotional or behavioral disorders are more likely to be educated in separate schools, residential settings, and home/hospital settings.

Physical Environment Interventions

A number of proactive interventions related to management of the physical environment are appropriate for use with students with emotional or behavioral disorders. Most of these interventions are at the primary level of prevention; that is, they are appropriate for *all* students, not just those with emotional or behavioral disorders.

Time management involves proactive interventions such as maximizing student engagement time, scheduling appropriately, and teaching time management skills. Because students with emotional or behavioral disorders experience considerable academic failure, teachers should endeavor to maximize the time spent in instruction and make every effort to keep their students on task as much as possible. "One of the most powerful tools for improving learning is the careful use of instructional time . . . effective time management becomes an essential part of designing and providing effective instruction" (Vaughn & Bos, 2012, p. 26). This means that you should make every effort to prepare for instruction in advance, minimize classroom interruptions, and interact substantively with students to keep them focused on the task. By creating and developing effective schedules, teachers can minimize the likelihood of disruptive behavior. For suggestions on effective scheduling, see the accompanying Suggestions for the Classroom.

Educators should also teach time management skills directly to students. Strategies include requiring students to maintain calendars on which they list their assignments and activities, helping students establish and prioritize goals for assignment completion, and allocating time during the school day to help students develop timelines and plan for completing assignments (Friend & Bursuck, 2012; Salend, 2011).

Closely related to time management is transition management. Transition times are those periods during the day when students are moving from one activity to another, such as changing classes, moving from one assignment to another, or beginning or ending the school day. Considerable academic learning time is wasted by poorly managed

time management: A proactive intervention strategy that attempts to maximize student engagement time and appropriately schedule class activities in addition to instruction in time management skills.

transition management: The regulating of students as they move from one assignment to another or from one activity to another; a proactive behavioral intervention strategy.

VIDEO

Physical Environment Interventions

SUGGESTIONS FOR THE CLASSROOM

Suggestions for Effective Scheduling

→ Place class schedule in a prominent location.

→ Intersperse more challenging tasks with less difficult ones.

→ Alternate lecture, discussion, and movement types of activities.

→ Adjust the length of activities and/or the schedule to meet the attention, developmental, and ability level of students.

→ Review and discuss the schedule frequently with students.

→ Inform students in advance of any schedule changes.

→ Schedule routine opening and closing activities each day.

SOURCE: Based on E. Polloway, J. Patton, L. Serna, and J. Bailey, *Strategies for Teaching Learners with Special Needs,* 10th ed. (Upper Saddle River, NJ: Pearson Education, 2013); S. Salend, *Creating Inclusive Classrooms,* 7th ed. (Upper Saddle River, NJ: Pearson Education, 2011).

transitions (Friend & Bursuck, 2012). Transitions also create situations in which disruptive student behavior is increased. According to Polloway, Patton, Serna, and Bailey (2013), teachers can minimize disruptive behavior during transition times by (1) giving students specific directions about how to move from one activity to another; (2) establishing, teaching, and having students rehearse transition routines; and (3) rewarding students for making orderly and smooth transitions.

Teachers can also use cues or signals to help students make transitions successfully, thereby minimizing disruptions. Examples include verbal cues, physical cues (light blinking, buzzer sounding, hand gestures), and creative dismissal cues ("All students with green eyes may line up for lunch"). Examples of two cueing systems (one picture cue and one physical cue) are shown in Figure 9.4. These systems, if taught and routinely used with students, may assist teachers in helping students to settle down quickly and get started on the next activity or assignment.

Proximity and movement management includes making sure that high-traffic areas are free from congestion, developing clear procedures for the use of classroom space and equipment, and ensuring sufficient separation of students to minimize inappropriate behavior (Salend, 2011). Gunter, Shores, Jack, Rasmussen, and Flowers (1995) suggest that teachers can use both proximity and movement to facilitate desired student behavior by

- placing the desks of disruptive students near the teacher's desk or main work area;
- interacting briefly and frequently with students; and
- providing praise, reprimands, and consequences when in close physical proximity to students.

Classroom arrangement includes the physical layout of the classroom as well as classroom décor. Physical layout includes student seating and grouping arrangements; location of materials, equipment, and personal items; removal of tempting or

proximity and movement management: A classroom management strategy focusing on the effective use of classroom space and the arrangement of the physical environment as a means of minimizing disruptive behavior.

classroom arrangement: The physical layout of the classroom and its décor; a proactive intervention technique designed to minimize disruptions while increasing pupil engagement.

Figure 9.4 **Examples of Cueing Systems**

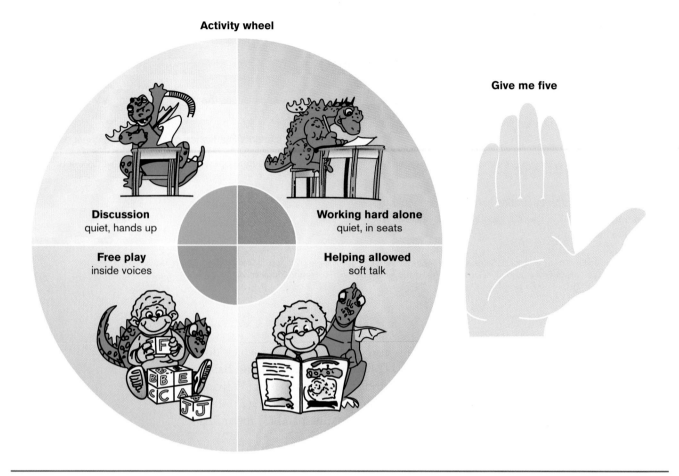

Activity wheel

Give me five

Discussion
quiet, hands up

Working hard alone
quiet, in seats

Free play
inside voices

Helping allowed
soft talk

SOURCE: C. Webster-Stratton, *How to Promote Children's Social and Emotional Competence* (Thousand Oaks, CA: Sage, 1999), pp. 56, 149. Copyright © 1999 by Sage Publications, Inc. Reprinted by permission of Sage Publications, Inc.

dangerous items; and location of the teacher's desk. The following suggestions have been made regarding seating and grouping arrangements:

- Students should be seated in locations that provide teachers with easy visual and physical access at all times (Salend, 2011).
- Savage (1999) recommends using rows for direct instruction, circular patterns for discussions, and clustered arrangements for group work.
- Place disruptive students in the "action zone" in the classroom. The action zone consists of seats across the front of the classroom and down the center. Research reviewed by Savage (1999) suggests that students seated in the action zone attend more to tasks, participate more, have higher levels of achievement, and demonstrate more positive attitudes.
- Disruptive students should be seated near the teacher to allow for proximity control and frequent monitoring.

Teachers can also minimize the likelihood of disruptive behavior by removing items that are physically tempting, distracting, or dangerous. The location of the teacher's desk may influence student behavior. The teacher's desk should have a barrier-free view of all students and be positioned to allow the teacher to move quickly if a situation necessitates (Salend, 2011).

For students who need a quiet, distraction-free place to study, the use of study carrels may be helpful. If study carrels are used, teachers should make sure their use is continuously monitored and be cautious not to overuse them as they may isolate or stigmatize students if used excessively (Salend, 2011).

Academic and Instructional Interventions

Positive behavioral supports include providing effective academic content and instruction to students with emotional and behavioral disorders (Scheuermann & Hall, 2012). Although there has been much research on effective social-emotional behavioral interventions for

Classroom arrangements can influence students' behavior in positive ways.

students with emotional or behavioral disorders, the research on effective academic curriculum and instructional practices for these students is limited.

The paucity of research on academic and instructional interventions is unfortunate given the high rates of academic failure experienced by these students (Smith et al., 2012). One significant way in which educators can help to minimize these negative long-term outcomes is through the provision of a sound academic program. There is a strong correlation between poor academic achievement and juvenile delinquency (Allen-DeBoer, Malmgren, & Glass, 2006; Cagnon & Barber, 2010). The hope is that if educators can design academic programs that strengthen the achievement levels of this population, delinquency rates will decrease. Academic achievement may serve as a critical protective or preventive factor for students with emotional or behavioral disorders.

Several researchers (Barton-Arwood, Wehby, & Falk, 2005; Lane, Little, Redding-Rhodes, Phillips, & Welsh, 2007) recommend a primary focus on academic interventions rather than social-emotional-behavioral interventions. Effective academic interventions may result not only in higher academic achievement but also in improved behavior (Nelson, Benner, Lane, & Smith, 2004; Wehby, Falk, Barton-Arwood, Lane, & Cooley, 2003). Research suggests, however, that interventions that focus solely on improving behavior are not always accompanied by simultaneous improvement in academics. It is difficult for a student to be academically successful while simultaneously engaging in inappropriate behavior. To be effective, academic intervention must address two areas of concern: academic curriculum and instructional delivery. Academic curriculum includes the instructional programs or materials used by classroom teachers to teach specific content while instructional delivery refers to teaching strategies and tactics.

Academic Curriculum

In many respects, the academic curriculum for students with emotional or behavioral disorders mirrors that of their typical classmates. Because this population varies

One of the benefits of spending many years in special education has been the opportunity to vicariously ride the swinging pendulum regarding the inclusion of students with special needs. As a teacher, counselor, and coordinator, all in the field of special education, I have seen and experienced the continuum of inclusion from the worst of times to what I consider the beginning of the best of times. What a great opportunity we have to grant each and every student the right to success they so desperately desire and deserve.

My very first job was teaching students with emotional or behavioral disorders attending a separate special education school. Fourteen students, eleven boys and three girls, were brought by bus to our county school and somewhat thrown together in a self-contained classroom. The students' ages ranged from 14 through 21, and although they were diagnosed as having emotional or behavioral disorders, their disabilities and needs varied greatly. As a first-year teacher, survival was my objective, not teaching anyone to read or divide. Unfortunately,

it was a terrifying, difficult year. As a teacher, I did not have the training or support needed to properly meet the needs of the students in my classroom. Students already typically deficient in social skills and academics were given scant opportunity for practice or success. In addition, there were virtually no positive peer role models within the classroom. I was discouraged because I knew we were letting these students down by separating them from the rest of the children. Needless to say, progress was minimal.

Fast-forward several years. I thankfully work in a society with an educational and legal system that now recognizes the benefits and need for inclusion of all students. It is a pleasure and honor to work with students and teachers preparing the way for meaningful inclusion of students. Not only do I get to work as a counselor and behavior interventionist with many students who have special needs, but I also teach at the university level, training preservice general education and special education teachers. Whether I am in a public school or university classroom, I seize the occasion to champion the benefits of inclusion for students and teachers alike.

A predominant concern teachers have shared with me over the years is that they are willing to welcome most children with special needs into their classrooms if they are told how to include the students and what to do! The exception, however,

widely in achievement and ability levels, educators must adapt or modify the curriculum accordingly. PL 108–446 mandates that, to the maximum extent appropriate, students with disabilities have access to the general education curriculum. For students with emotional or behavioral disorders, this may necessitate appropriate supports and curriculum modifications. By incorporating students' interests into the curriculum, educators can enhance both the behavior and the academic engagement of these students. Thus, teachers should endeavor to design a curriculum that is both relevant and motivating for students with emotional and behavioral disorders.

Instructional Delivery

Instruction is a critical component in preventing behavior problems. How teachers instruct children and youth with emotional or behavioral disorders influences not only their academic performance but their behavior as well (Scheuermann & Hall, 2012). Three instructional strategies that typically benefit these students (and other learners) are mnemonics, self-monitoring strategies, and content enhancements.

Mnemonic strategies are tools for helping students recall facts and relationships. Mnemonic strategies have been found to be extremely effective in promoting academic achievement among students with disabilities, including those with emotional or behavioral disorders (Scruggs & Mastropieri, 2000; Vaughn & Bos, 2012). There are many different types of mnemonic strategies; a few of these are illustrated in Figure 9.5.

Self-monitoring strategies, such as assignment checklists and self-monitoring checklists, can be used to assist students with emotional or behavioral disorders. These strategies help students by providing the cues necessary to complete a task successfully. You may want to incorporate these strategies for all your students, not

mnemonic strategies: A cognitive approach used to assist pupils in remembering material; the use of rhymes, pictures, acronyms, and similar aids to help in recall.

self-monitoring strategies: A behavioral self-control strategy; pupils compare their performance to a criterion, record their efforts, and obtain reinforcement if appropriate.

VIDEO
Inclusion

VIDEO
Additional Strategies

is usually students with emotional or behavioral disorders. The majority of these students want to be in a safe environment, and they crave structure, consistency, and predictability. An attitude geared toward welcoming any student into a safe learning environment is half of the formula for successful inclusion. Students will know if they are welcome in your classroom. They will likely feel welcomed and safe if you are clear about your expectations, are consistent, and are well prepared. Avoid assuming the worst and that students "can't." Assume they "can" with careful planning and preparation. Say what you mean and always mean what you say—follow through.

Preparation is so very important and may include modification of the curriculum, teaching styles, and classroom management procedures and practices. Does this mean you must change everything you do for one student? Absolutely not. It does mean that having students with special needs in your classroom should give you cause to reflect on your personal teaching style, strategies, tolerance levels, expectations, procedures, and behavior management style. Reflection on your practices as a teacher will shed light on your readiness to include all students, and you will be well on your way to making preparations for students with special needs.

Although this may all sound a bit overwhelming, the best news is that you are not alone. Collaboration may very well be the biggest key to successful inclusion. You will have access to a host of wisdom, knowledge, and experience from the professionals with whom you work. Take advantage. Be proactive with teachers and parents and learn as much about each student as possible. Access the special educators in your building and seek their knowledge regarding the special needs of your students. You may need to take the first step and ask for help. The special educator in your building may be hesitant as well, for fear of stepping on your turf. It is also important to establish your own relationship with the parents and well worth the effort to do so before the need arises to discuss a problem. Time spent getting to know each student personally is possibly the best investment. Once you know what interests a student, meaningful engagement in academics is more likely, and building of relationships will be easier. Collaborating and preplanning for the arrival of a student with special needs may mean the difference between success and failure for everyone.

–Teresa (Tracy) Teaff
Former behavior interventionist,
Arlington (Texas) Independent School District
Currently Chief Liaison Officer
Texas A&M University–Central Texas

just those with emotional or behavioral disorders. See Figure 9.6 for an example of an academic self-monitoring checklist.

Content enhancements include graphic organizers, content diagrams, semantic maps, advance organizers, guided notes, and study guides. Content enhancements help students understand major concepts, ideas, and vocabulary in a manner that is conducive to knowledge acquisition, organization, and retrieval. These enhancements make explicit the content to be learned, link concepts together, and help students link new content to previously learned content.

Behavioral and Cognitive-Behavioral Interventions

Researchers (Cooper, Heron, & Heward, 2007) have identified two broad-based intervention approaches that have substantial support: behavior modification and cognitive-behavior modification. These two intervention approaches share many common features, including positive reinforcement, ongoing monitoring, and contingency management. There is one primary difference, however. Whereas strict behavioral approaches rely on *external* sources of behavioral control (in school settings, this external source of control is often teacher mediated), cognitive-behavioral approaches seek to promote students' *internal* control or self-regulatory behavior (that is, these strategies are self-mediated or self-managed) (Gumpel & David, 2000; Janney & Snell, 2008).

Both behavioral and cognitive-behavioral interventions range from primary to tertiary levels of prevention. These interventions can also be placed on a continuum in terms of their intrusiveness and restrictiveness. The intervention ladder pictured in Figure 9.7 suggests that most students will respond to mildly intrusive and restrictive

content enhancements: Instructional aids designed to assist pupils in understanding major concepts, ideas, and vocabulary in a way that aids the acquisition, organization, and recall of material.

The Keyword Method

To help a student remember that the word "barrister" is another word for lawyer . . .

Your Honor, my client is INNOCENT!

The Keyword Method

To help students remember that insects have six legs . . .

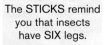

The STICKS remind you that insects have SIX legs.

Look at the insects on these sticks!

Reconstructive Elaborations

To help students remember that early bridges often rotted and washed away . . .

Dang! These old bridges are no good!

Letter Strategies

Letter strategies include both **acronyms** and **acrostics**. Acronyms create new words by combining the first letters of a list or series of words. For example, the acronym HOMES is tied to the Great Lakes:

H = Huron
O = Ontario
M = Michigan
E = Erie
S = Superior

Acrostics are similar to acronyms, but they consist of sentences. The first letter of each sentence represents a different word, a strategy that can be useful when information must be remembered in sequence. For example, "My very educated mother just served us nine pizzas," to remember the names of the planets (Mercury, Venus, Earth, Mars, etc.).

SOURCE: Adapted from M. A. Mastropieri and T. E. Scruggs, *Teaching Students Ways to Remember: Strategies for Learning Mnemonically* (Cambridge, MA: Brookline Books, 1990).

interventions and only a few will require more intensive and restrictive interventions. Teachers should attempt less intensive and restrictive interventions first and proceed to the next level only if these interventions are unsuccessful.

One example of a mildly intrusive intervention strategy is classroom rules and routines. Students may misbehave because they do not understand the behavior expected of them. For example, a student may not understand that talking out is inappropriate during teacher-led presentations but may be permitted during cooperative learning activities. Teachers can do much to prevent misbehavior in their classrooms by making their expectations clear. This means that teachers should pay particular attention to the establishment and consistent enforcement of classroom rules and routines. Classroom rules provide structure for acceptable and unacceptable student behaviors (Vaughn et al., 2014); for guidelines on establishing classroom rules, see the accompanying Suggestions for the Classroom. Classroom routines are those procedures that occur periodically throughout the school day—for example, sharpening pencils, class dismissal,

Name _____   Date _____

Assignment checklist

1. Is my name on the paper?   Yes ____   No ____
2. Do all sentences begin with a capital letter?   Yes ____   No ____
3. Do all my sentences end with the correct punctuation? Yes ____   No ____
4. Did I answer all of the questions?   Yes ____   No ____
5. Do I need extra help?   Yes ____   No ____
6. Do I need more time?   Yes ____   No ____
7. Do I understand the assignment?   Yes ____   No ____
8. Did I finish all of my work?   Yes ____   No ____
9. Did I follow teacher directions?   Yes ____   No ____
10. Did I turn in my assignment?   Yes ____   No ____

SOURCE: From "Self-Monitoring, Cueing, Recording, and Managing: Teaching Students to Manage Their Own Behavior" by M. McConnell, *Teaching Exceptional Children, 32*(2), p. 18. Copyright © 1999 by the Council for Exceptional Children. Reprinted with permission.

turning in assignments, or making up work during absences—that allow the classroom to run smoothly and efficiently. In addition, the Effective Instructional Practices feature provides some tips for managing behavioral issues in the classroom.

Other Interventions

The behavior characteristics of students with emotional or behavioral disorders often necessitate that careful thought be given to the development and implementation of specialized intervention strategies. Three examples of these interventions include social skills training, interpersonal problem solving and conflict resolution, and management of behavioral crises at school.

Social Skills Training

Many students with emotional or behavioral disorders have difficulty interacting successfully with their peers, teachers, and other adults they daily encounter. Deficits in social skills can lead to alienation from peers, impaired interpersonal relationships, and academic failure in addition to difficulties with independent living in adulthood (Kauffman & Landrum, 2013; Maag, 2006).

Social skills training can occur at any level of prevention—primary, secondary, or tertiary—and some professionals have called for the implementation of primary (schoolwide) social skills training programs and the infusion of social skills instruction into the curriculum (Forgan & Gonzalez-DeHass, 2004; Scheuermann & Hall, 2012). "The goal of social skills training is to teach

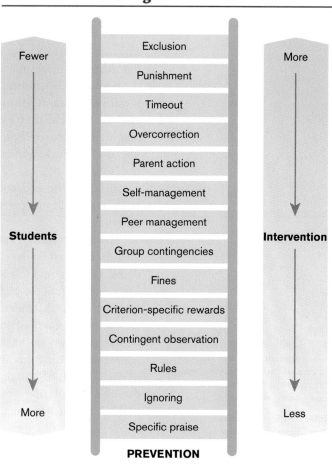

■ ■ ■ ■ ■ Figure 9.7 **A Ladder of Intervention Strategies**

Fewer / More

Students / Intervention

More / Less

Exclusion
Punishment
Timeout
Overcorrection
Parent action
Self-management
Peer management
Group contingencies
Fines
Criterion-specific rewards
Contingent observation
Rules
Ignoring
Specific praise

PREVENTION

SOURCE: Adapted from D. Smith and D. Rivera, *Effective Discipline*, 2nd ed. (Austin, TX: Psycho-Educational Services, 2001), p. 17. Reprinted with permission.

SUGGESTIONS FOR THE CLASSROOM

Guidelines for Establishing Classroom Rules

→ Keep the wording of rules simple and clear.

→ Select the fewest possible number of rules (three to six).

→ Use different rules for different situations.

→ Rules should be stated behaviorally, and they should be enforceable.

→ Rules should be stated positively.

→ Rules should be reasonable.

→ Specify consequences for both rule adherence and rule infraction, and provide consequences consistently.

→ Give examples and nonexamples of each rule.

→ Discuss the need for rules in the classroom.

→ Check for student understanding of rules.

→ Review rules regularly.

→ Post the rules in a prominent location in the room.

→ Obtain written commitments from students that they will follow the rules.

SOURCE: Adapted from B. Burden, *Powerful Classroom Management Strategies* (Thousand Oaks, CA: Corwin Press, 2000); M. Kerr and C. Nelson, *Strategies for Managing Behavior Problems in the Classroom*, 6th ed. (Upper Saddle River, NJ: Pearson Education, 2010).

students a complex response set that allows them to adapt to the numerous problems that occur in social situations" (Vaughn & Bos, 2012, p. 112).

Social skills training often uses direct instruction to teach students appropriate social behaviors. It assumes that behavioral problems in the classroom reflect social skill deficits and that social skills are learned behaviors; consequently, they can be taught. Examples of these skills include correctly interpreting body language, receiving negative feedback, understanding the feelings of others, and maintaining a conversation (Vaughn & Bos, 2012). Social skills training attempts to develop pupils' social competence. The end goal is to increase their social acceptance, friendship-making skills, and ability to participate successfully in school and community activities and functions.

The importance of teaching social skills to students with emotional or behavioral disorders cannot be overstated, as adequate social skills are critical precursors to academic instruction. Unless children have the basic social skills—asking for assistance, following directions, and adhering to classroom rules, routines, and procedures— attempts to teach academics to these students will be largely unsuccessful. Research on the effectiveness of social skills training has yielded mixed results (Lane, Wehby, & Barton-Atwood, 2005; Maag, 2006; Miller, Lane, & Wehby, 2005). Most of the concerns regarding this approach have centered on the generalization and maintenance of social skills. Although a student may be able to demonstrate a specific social skill during a role-playing situation, that same skill may not be demonstrated in more natural settings such as the classroom or playground.

Interpersonal Problem Solving and Conflict Resolution

Closely related to social skills training is the teaching of interpersonal problem solving and conflict resolution. **Interpersonal problem solving** focuses on teaching students the

social skills training: Using direct instruction to teach students appropriate social behaviors; goal is to increase individual's social competency and acceptance.

interpersonal problem solving: Teaching pupils the cognitive skills needed to avoid and resolve interpersonal conflicts, peer pressure, and ways of coping with stress and their own feelings.

VIDEO

Additional Suggestions

Effective Instructional Practices
Behavioral Principles

Principles for Strengthening (or Increasing) Existing Behavior

Response increment principles include the following:

PRINCIPLE 1: Positive Reinforcement Principle

Provide positive reinforcement immediately after desired behavior occurs.

EXAMPLE: Praise the child following task completion.

PRINCIPLE 2: Premack Principle (First you work, then you play.)

Allow the child to engage in a favored activity immediately following the occurrence of the desired behavior.

EXAMPLE: After completion of a disliked math assignment, permit the child to complete a favored activity such as putting a puzzle together.

PRINCIPLE 3: Contingency Contracting Principle

Specify in writing the desired behavior and the positive consequences that will follow if the child engages in the desired behavior.

EXAMPLE: Allow the child to listen to preferred music following the observance of the desired behavior.

Principles for Developing New Behavior

Response acquisition principles include the following:

PRINCIPLE 1: Successive Approximations Principle

Reward successive steps to the desired behavior.

EXAMPLE: For problematic off-task behavior, first reward the child for staying on task for five minutes, then ten minutes, then fifteen minutes, and so on.

PRINCIPLE 2: Modeling Principle

Allow the child to observe a prestigious person engaging in the desired behavior.

EXAMPLE: For problematic handwriting behavior, have a peer demonstrate the correct letter formation and have the student model the formation.

PRINCIPLE 3: Cueing Principle

To teach a child to engage in a particular behavior at a certain time, provide a cue or prompt just before the desired behavior is expected.

EXAMPLE: Teacher and child mutually develop a signal to cue the child to begin a task.

PRINCIPLE 4: Discrimination Principle

To teach a child to engage in a specific behavior under one set of circumstances but not another, help the child only when his or her behavior is appropriate to the cue.

EXAMPLE: Reinforce the use of an "inside" voice when the child is in the classroom but not on the playground.

Principles for Decreasing or Extinguishing Undesired Behavior

Response decrement principles include the following:

PRINCIPLE 1: Extinction

Arrange conditions so that the child receives no reinforcement following the undesired behavior.

EXAMPLE: Ignore talking-out behavior.

PRINCIPLE 2: Reinforcement of Incompatible Behavior

Reinforce an alternative or desired behavior that is inconsistent with the undesired behavior.

EXAMPLE: Reinforce on-task behavior to decrease the child's out-of-seat behavior.

PRINCIPLE 3: Response Cost

Arrange conditions so that something the child considers reinforcing is taken away when the undesired behavior occurs.

EXAMPLE: Take away television privileges when a child hits another child.

Students with emotional or behavioral disorders often have difficulty interacting appropriately with peers.

"thinking" skills necessary to avoid and resolve interpersonal conflicts, resist peer pressure, and cope with their emotions and stress. Students are taught to identify their problems, consider and select from a range of alternative solutions, and evaluate the results of their selection. One example of interpersonal problem solving is the FAST strategy, developed by Vaughn and Lancelotta (1990):

F = Freeze and think! What is the problem?

A = Alternatives? What are my possible solutions?

S = Solution evaluation. Choose the best solution. Is it safe? Is it fair?

T = Try it! Slowly and carefully. Does it work?

Strategies such as this one can be taught to both large and small groups, as well as to individual students. Students are taught to go through the steps of problem solving, such as those detailed in the FAST strategy, whenever they encounter a problem or conflict.

Conflict resolution programs are similar to problem-solving approaches. However, conflict resolution programs are designed to teach not only problem-solving skills but skills related to negotiation, mediation, and communication (Larrivee, 2009).

Management of Behavioral Crises at School

Some students identified as having emotional or behavioral disorders will, on occasion, become physically aggressive toward others while in other instances they may evidence self-injurious behavior. In recent years, crisis prevention and management programs have been implemented to teach educators how to effectively and proactively address pupils' violent, aggressive, and/or self-injurious behaviors. Crisis management programs typically are preventive and proactive in orientation; educators are taught verbal mediation strategies to defuse acting-out behavior before it reaches the point of a physical crisis. If these verbal mediation strategies are unsuccessful, educators are instructed to use physical restraint and employ safety techniques to protect the welfare of both the acting-out individual and those around him or her.

conflict resolution: Program designed to teach problem-solving skills along with strategies for negotiation and mediation.

crisis prevention and management programs: Techniques taught to teachers on how to effectively and proactively deal with students' violent, aggressive, and/or self-injurious behaviors; a proactive preventative approach.

Services for Young Children With Emotional or Behavioral Disorders

A growing body of research suggests a clear developmental pattern of emotional or behavioral disorders that typically begins at a very early age and appears to persist throughout adolescence and adulthood (Stichter, Conroy, & Kauffman, 2008; Wakschlag & Danis, 2009). Infants and toddlers who are born with a "difficult temperament"—those who are frequently irritable, display irregular patterns

VIDEO

Safety

of sleeping and eating, and are highly emotional—may be at especially high risk for progressing to more acting-out aggressive behaviors, even before they reach their elementary years. Although many believe that very young children who exhibit these antisocial behaviors will outgrow them, research suggests that this is often not the case. In fact, early antisocial behavior appears to be a particularly potent precursor or antecedent to such negative long-term outcomes as dropping out of school, delinquency, drug abuse, and adult incarceration (Dunlap et al., 2006; Kendziora, 2004; Whitted, 2011).

Early intervention is crucial for young children with emotional or behavioral disorders (Kauffman & Landrum, 2013; Wehman, Sutherland, & Achola, 2013). Although early intervention services are clearly beneficial, both in preventing emotional or behavioral disorders from developing and in minimizing their impact once they do develop, these vital services are often lacking (Kauffman & Brigham, 2009; Kauffman & Landrum, 2013). In some instances, it is because of a lack of resources, except for those young children with the most severe disorders. On the other hand, some teachers are hesitant to identify very young children with problematic behaviors (Kauffman, 2010), despite the fact that educators are very capable at identifying youngsters who are at risk for antisocial behavior (Kauffman & Landrum, 2013; Lane, 2003).

A few early intervention programs are available to help young children at risk for emotional or behavioral disorders. One example of a successful program is First Step to Success (Beard & Sugai, 2004; Walker et al., 1997). First Step to Success is a comprehensive and collaborative school-home early intervention program designed for kindergartners who exhibit emerging antisocial behaviors. This program, involving the combined efforts of teachers, parents, and peers, has been shown to be effective in helping youngsters who exhibit early-onset antisocial behavior achieve success in school (Walker et al., 2012).

Emotional or behavioral disorders that develop at an early age are likely to persist throughout adolescence and adulthood.

Transition Into Adulthood

Research suggests that the presence of emotional or behavioral disorders in children is an accurate predictor of school failure, delinquency, adult psychiatric problems, substance abuse, and other problems (Lane et al., 2007). Youth who exhibit externalizing as well as internalizing disorders are at heightened risk for impaired functioning and negative, long-term consequences (Kauffman & Landrum, 2013; Stichter et al., 2008).

A particularly alarming statistic is that approximately 45 percent of students with emotional or behavioral disorders leave school before graduation—the highest dropout rate among all categories of students with disabilities (U.S. Department of Education, 2012b). An equally disturbing finding is that the majority of students with emotional or behavioral disorders are not identified and served until their adolescent years. In stark contrast to students in other disability categories, who are identified and served at much earlier ages, the U.S. Department of Education (2013a) reports that over 50 percent of all students receiving special education and related services because of emotional or behavioral disorders are adolescents. During the 2011–2012 school year, the peak age for placement of these students was 16 years of age. Clearly, educators need to work more aggressively to identify and serve this population at earlier ages and to implement effective dropout prevention and transition programs.

Transitioning from school to adulthood is particularly difficult for individuals with emotional or behavioral disorders (Wehman et al., 2013). Educators need to understand that these students have a developmental disability that will require intervention throughout their life span. This means that transition planning needs to be comprehensive and broad based. Transition services need to go well beyond just preparing these students for employment. Rather, there is a need to view transition in terms of postsecondary educational opportunities, independent living choices, and community participation in addition to vocational possibilities. Middle school and secondary school educators need to provide instruction in such diverse areas as personal management, personal health, leisure skills, citizenship, and social skills (Sabornie & deBettencourt, 2009). Effective transition planning includes vocational training, parental and student involvement, interagency collaboration, paid work experience, follow-up employment services, community-based instruction, and community-referenced curriculum.

One promising approach is a wraparound plan, which should begin in the elementary years and continue throughout the secondary years and adulthood. *Wraparound* refers to an approach that "wraps" services and supports around the student and his or her family. This network of comprehensive and coordinated interagency services is provided in school, home, and community environments (Eber, Breen, Rose, Unizycki, & London, 2008; Vaughn et al., 2014). Such a plan allows for the integrated involvement of multiple agencies to facilitate the successful transition from school to adulthood for adolescents with emotional or behavioral disorders. Such wraparound plans may be essential for adolescents because many do not have access to the many critical services offered in their communities.

Adults With Emotional or Behavioral Disorders

Once a student with emotional or behavioral disorders leaves secondary education and enters postsecondary education or employment, the protections offered by IDEA no longer apply. Two other legislative acts protect these young adults in the areas of education and employment: Section 504 of the Rehabilitation Act of 1973 (PL 93–112) and the Americans with Disabilities Act (ADA) (PL 101–336). Both Section 504 and ADA guarantee individuals with disabilities "equal access" to postsecondary programs if they are "otherwise qualified." This does not mean that individuals with disabilities are automatically guaranteed access to postsecondary institutions; they must meet the admission criteria for the institution to which they apply. It does mean that postsecondary institutions cannot deny admission simply because the individual has a disability. If an individual with a disability is admitted to a federally funded postsecondary institution, he or she is entitled to "reasonable accommodations." These accommodations might include, for example, extended time on assignments, texts on audiotapes, and peer tutoring.

Postsecondary program options for students with emotional or behavioral disorders include vocational and technical programs, trade schools, adult education programs, two-year community colleges, and four-year colleges and universities. Given the alarming dropout rates among students with emotional or behavioral disorders, however, many of these students never enter, much less complete, postsecondary programs that

wraparound plan: A coordinated interagency effort at providing supports and services to a student and his or her family in the natural environment—school, home, or community.

will prepare them for meaningful careers (Wehman et al., 2013; Zigmond, 2006).

For those students who do pursue postsecondary education opportunities, preparation must begin early in their secondary years. Areas of instruction that will need to be addressed include time management skills, organizational skills, study skills, and self-advocacy. Another important area is helping students learn about the types of support services they may need during their years in higher education, such as writing centers, counseling services, tutoring, and instructional supports. Learning how to advocate for these services and apply for disability services in higher-education settings is a critical skill that should be incorporated into an individualized transition plan early during a student's secondary years.

Postsecondary institutions cannot deny admission simply because a student has a disability.

Employment training is available to many young adults with emotional or behavioral disorders through vocational rehabilitation services. Not all individuals, however, will receive these services. Vocational rehabilitation is an eligibility program, not an entitlement program, and eligibility criteria differ from those in IDEA. For young adults who do qualify for vocational rehabilitation services, an individualized rehabilitation plan is developed and implemented. This plan addresses areas such as basic skill development, communication skills, and specific on-the-job skills.

Family-Centered Interventions

Some professionals, including educators, blame parents for the behavioral problems exhibited by their children. This blaming, however, often creates a significant barrier to working effectively and collaboratively with families (Jensen, 2005). Rather than blaming parents, effective programs for children and youth with emotional or behavioral disorders seek to meaningfully involve parents and other caregivers in providing interventions and services that meet the needs of the student and his or her family. Many of these programs incorporate family-centered early intervention. This approach recognizes the central role that the family plays in the lives of individuals and focuses on the strengths and assets of the family unit (Gargiulo & Kilgo, 2014; Turnbull, Turnbull, Erin, Soodak, & Shrogren, 2011).

Raising a child with emotional or behavioral disorders can be extraordinarily difficult and highly stressful. A child with a disability may affect family finances, put a strain on marital and sibling relationships, create a need for respite care, and disrupt family routines and schedules (Turnbull et al., 2011). Another common stressor is the isolation that caretakers often experience because of the negative reactions of others to the child's behaviors (Taylor-Richardson, Heflinger, & Brown, 2006). These negative reactions from extended family members, neighbors, friends, and others can be emotionally and physically draining. As an educator, you need to interact positively with parents as much as possible and be careful that your communications with parents are positive.

family-centered early intervention: A philosophy of working with families that stresses family strengths and capabilities, the enhancement of skills, and the development of mutual partnerships between service providers and families.

Figure 9.8 **School–Home Daily Report**

Date _____   **Missy's School–Home Daily Report**

_____   _____
Teacher's signature   **Parent's signature**

___Yes ___No Completed assignments   ___Yes ___No Completed chores
___Yes ___No Followed teacher's directions ___Yes ___No Followed parent's directions
___Yes ___No Handed in completed homework   ___Yes ___No Completed homework
___Yes ___No Followed classroom rules   ___Yes ___No Followed home rules
___Yes ___No Interacted well with peers   ___Yes ___No Interacted well with siblings

Teacher's comments: **Parent's comments:**

Missy's self-evaluation
How did I do?

___My day was great! (more than 8 "Yes")
___My day was okay. (6–8 "Yes")

Totals ___Yes ___ No

___Today was not so great. (below 6 "Yes")

Missy's comments:

One strategy for increasing positive (and two-way) communication with parents is the development of a school-home communication system. Such a system, illustrated in Figure 9.8, fosters positive and constructive communication regarding a child's progress both at home and at school. These systems enable educators and parents to address behaviors of mutual concern and to implement interventions consistently in both environments.

Issues of Diversity

A continuing, yet unresolved, issue confronting educators is the overrepresentation of African American students, particularly males, in special education programs for pupils with emotional or behavioral disorders (DeValenzuela, Copeland, Qi, & Park, 2006; Smith et al., 2012; U.S. Department of Education, 2012b). Explanations for this situation are multifaceted ranging from culturally insensitive assessment practices, to an incongruity between educators' values (primarily white women) and those of their students, and the consequences of residing in poverty (Gollnick & Chinn, 2013).

In contrast to the overrepresentation of African Americans, relatively little has been written about the underrepresentation of females. Research indicates that girls are seldom referred, identified, or placed in special education programs for students with emotional or behavioral disorders (Nelson et al., 2003). One suggested explanation is that girls are much more likely to exhibit internalizing disorders such as depression or anxiety, whereas boys are more likely to display externalizing behaviors such as aggression (Cullinan, Evans, Epstein, & Ryser, 2003). Because internalizing disorders are not typically disruptive to the learning process, educators may not consider these behaviors to be as serious; hence, they are less likely to initiate a referral for special education (Wicks-Nelson & Israel, 2013). This suggests that when girls are identified as having emotional or behavioral disorders, they may evidence more severe problems and require more intensive intervention.

Technology and Individuals With Emotional or Behavioral Disorders

Although little attention is specifically given to technology and pupils with emotional or behavioral disorders, these students can often benefit from the assistive technologies discussed in Chapter 5 that support accessing and learning in the content areas (for example, speech-to-text, concrete manipulatives) (Courtad & Bouck, 2012; Fitzpatrick & Knowlton, 2009). Another increasing area of technology use for individuals with emotional or behavioral disorders is self-management or self-monitoring. Self-monitoring, or regulating one's own behaviors, has a strong evidence base with regard to educating students with emotional or behavioral disorders (Fitzpatrick & Knowlton, 2009; Lee, Palmer, & Wehmeyer, 2009). Although historically self-monitoring involves the use of paper and pencil, more high technology is currently being used to help students monitor their behavior. Pupils with emotional or behavioral disorders have successfully used a pager, a MotivAider (a handheld device that vibrates to provide reminders), an MP3 player, an iPod Touch, and student response systems to self-monitor their behavior (Amato-Zech, Hoff, & Dorepke, 2006; Blood, Johnson, Ridenour, Simmons, & Crouch, 2011; Epstein, Willis, Conners, & Johnson, 2001; Gulchak, 2008; Szwed & Bouck, 2013). In addition to self-monitoring, technology is often used as a reinforcer in behavior intervention plans for individuals with emotional or behavioral disorders. Students often find computers reinforcing, motivating, and/or engaging (White, Palmer, & Huffman, 2003).

Trends, Issues, and Controversies

Throughout this chapter, considerable attention has been paid to the very poor outcomes experienced by children and youth with emotional or behavioral disorders. Although the outcomes for this population are generally dismal, the twenty-first century has brought proven strategies and practices that can greatly improve these outcomes. Professionals now have available an arsenal of intervention strategies at their disposal. One contemporary example is the use of response to intervention (RTI), which we introduced in Chapter 7. You may recall that RTI is a data-driven approach whereby a pupil receives increasingly intensive levels of evidence-based intervention matched to his or her individual needs. Typically associated with students with learning disabilities, RTI has intuitive appeal for individuals who exhibit emotional or behavioral disorders (Fairbanks, Sugai, Guardino, & Lathrop, 2007). RTI is increasingly being used with students who present challenging behaviors in the classroom (Kauffman, Nelson, Simpson, & Mock, 2011; Smith et al., 2012; Vaughn & Bos, 2012). "Key to RTI are the goals of early identification of emotional or behavioral disorders, appropriate intervention, and the monitoring of student progress" (Vaughn et al., 2014, p. 221).

response to intervention (RTI): A strategy used for determining whether a pupil has a learning disability. Student is exposed to increasing levels of validated instructional intervention; responsiveness to the instruction is assessed; a lack of adequate progress typically leads to a referral for possible special education services.

1. Every effort should be made to prevent the need for the use of restraint and for the use of seclusion.

2. Schools should never use mechanical restraints to restrict a child's freedom of movement, and schools should never use a drug or medication to control behavior or restrict freedom of movement (except as authorized by a licensed physician or other qualified health professional).

3. Physical restraint or seclusion should not be used except in situations where the child's behavior poses imminent danger of serious physical harm to self or others and other interventions are ineffective and should be discontinued as soon as imminent danger of serious physical harm to self or others has dissipated.

4. Policies restricting the use of restraint and seclusion should apply to all children, not just children with disabilities.

5. Any behavioral intervention should be consistent with the child's rights to be treated with dignity and to be free from abuse.

6. Restriction or seclusion should never be used as punishment or discipline (e.g., placing in seclusion for out-of-seat behavior), as a means of coercion or retaliation, or as a convenience.

7. Restraint or seclusion should never be used in a manner that restricts a child's breathing or harms a child.

8. The use of restraint or seclusion, particularly when there is repeated use for an individual child, multiple uses within the same classroom, or multiple uses by the same individual, should trigger a review and, if appropriate, revision of strategies currently in place to address dangerous behavior; if positive behavioral strategies are not in place, staff should consider developing them.

9. Behavioral strategies to address dangerous behavior that results in the use of restraint or seclusion should address the underlying cause or purpose of the dangerous behavior.

10. Teachers and other personnel should be trained regularly on the appropriate use of effective alternatives to physical restraint and seclusion, such as positive behavioral interventions and supports, and, only for cases involving imminent danger of serious physical harm, on the safe use of physical restraint and seclusion.

11. Every instance in which restraint or seclusion is used should be carefully and continuously and visually monitored to ensure the appropriateness of its use and safety of the child, other children, teachers, and other personnel.

12. Parents should be informed of the policies on restraint and seclusion at their child's school or other educational setting, as well as applicable federal, state, or local laws.

13. Parents should be notified as soon as possible following each instance in which restraint or seclusion is used with their child.

14. Policies regarding the use of restraint and seclusion should be reviewed regularly and updated as appropriate.

15. Policies regarding the use of restraint and seclusion should provide that each incident involving the use of restraint or seclusion be documented in writing and provide for the collection of specific data that would enable teachers, staff, and other personnel to understand and implement the preceding principles.

SOURCE: U.S. Department of Education, *Restraint and Seclusion: Resource Document* (Washington, DC: Author, 2012), pp. 12–13.

(One example of an evidence-based practice or intervention for pupils with emotional or behavioral disorders is positive behavioral support. See page 298 for a description of this strategy.) Some investigators (Kauffman, Bruce, & Lloyd, 2012) believe, however, that while elements of RTI are supported by a solid research base, the benefit of RTI for students with emotional or behavioral disorders is waiting further validation.

Another issue attracting considerable attention is the use of physical restraint and seclusion with students with emotional and behavioral disorders. Reports of abuse and misuse of these two intervention tactics have led to calls for legislation and policy statements in an effort to regulate, and in some instances outright forbid, their use. Although there is a lack of consensus among professionals as to whether or not these control techniques are necessary or appropriate, there is general agreement that oversight and supervision is needed (Alberto & Troutman, 2013).

AUDIO

Chapter 9 Summary

Physical restraint (also known as manual restraint) typically refers to restricting an individual's freedom of movement, physical activity, or access to his or her body (Council for Children with Behavioral Disorders, 2009a). Unfortunately, there is a paucity of research on the effectiveness, frequency, and application of physical restraint. Furthermore, almost no research is available on the use of this strategy in schools (Council for Children with Behavioral Disorders, 2009a).

Seclusion is considered to be "the involuntary confinement of a student alone in a room or area from which the student is physically prevented from leaving" (Council for Children with Behavioral Disorders, 2009b, p. 1). This includes situations where a door is locked, held shut by an adult, or barricaded by objects. Most schools view seclusion as a behavior change strategy and use it as a consequence when a pupil is out of control. Very little research exists on the use of seclusion in educational settings. Many professionals suspect that its use is on the increase as more students with significant behavioral and emotional needs are being served in inclusive learning environments (Council for Children with Behavioral Disorders, 2009b).

Due to the ongoing controversy surrounding the use of physical restraint and seclusion in our schools, the U.S. Department of Education developed a set of guidelines for educators, parents, and other stakeholders. The principles contained within this resource document are portrayed in Table 9.6.

Like many professionals, we question whether or not restraint and seclusion are appropriate intervention strategies and represent best practice for children and youth with emotional and behavioral disorders. Certainly these are controversial procedures. We recommend, therefore, that teachers carefully read their school district's policy and procedures manual on this topic. Physical restraint and seclusion should only be considered when a child's behavior poses imminent danger of serious physical harm to him- or herself or when the safety and well-being of other students or staff is in jeopardy. These procedures should never be a teacher's initial attempt at controlling a pupil's inappropriate behavior.

physical restraint: The restriction of a student's freedom of movement, physical activity, or access to his or her body.

seclusion: The involuntary confinement of a student to a room or area from which he or she is physically prevented from leaving.

CHAPTER IN REVIEW

Defining Emotional or Behavioral Disorders

- There is no universally accepted definition of emotional or behavioral disorders.
- Terms used to describe individuals with emotional or behavioral disorders are very diversified and compounded by the variability in our understanding of what constitutes "normal" behavior.
- The current IDEA definition of emotional disturbance is controversial.

Classification of Individuals With Emotional or Behavioral Disorders

- Clinically and statistically derived classification systems are frequently used to classify the many different types of emotional or behavioral disorders.

- Externalizing disorders are sometimes referred to as "undercontrolled" behaviors, and internalizing disorders are sometimes referred to as "overcontrolled" behaviors.

Prevalence of Emotional or Behavioral Disorders

- Students with emotional or behavioral disorders represent an underidentified population. Currently, fewer than 1 percent of all pupils in public schools are recognized as having emotional or behavioral disorders.

Etiology of Emotional or Behavioral Disorders

- Most professionals believe that the development of emotional or behavioral disorders is related to both biological and psychosocial risk factors.

Prevention of Emotional or Behavioral Disorders

- Positive behavioral support is a schoolwide approach designed to prevent problem behaviors from occurring and, if they do occur, to intervene early to prevent escalation. It represents a proactive rather than reactive approach to dealing with problematic behaviors.

Characteristics of Children and Youth With Emotional or Behavioral Disorders

- Research indicates that pupils with emotional or behavioral disorders typically score in the low-average range on measures of intelligence.
- Perhaps the most salient characteristic of students with emotional or behavioral disorders is their difficulty in building and maintaining satisfactory relationships with peers and adults.

Assessing Students With Emotional or Behavioral Disorders

- Person-centered planning, strength-based assessment, and functional behavioral assessment are representative of the contemporary trends in assessment of pupils with emotional or behavioral disorders.
- A behavioral intervention plan is mandated by PL 108–446 for those individuals who exhibit problematic behaviors in school.

Educational Considerations

- Students with emotional or behavioral disorders represent one of the more educationally segregated groups of students with disabilities.
- Effective management of the physical environment includes proactively addressing such areas as time management, transition management, and proximity and movement management, along with classroom management.
- Mnemonics, self-monitoring strategies, and content enhancements are examples of effective instructional strategies designed to assist students with emotional or behavioral disorders in accessing the general education curriculum.
- At the classroom level, educators can tap an array of interventions including social skills training, interpersonal problem solving, and conflict resolution, in addition to crisis prevention and management programs.

Transition Into Adulthood

- Students with emotional or behavioral disorders have the highest dropout rate among all categories of pupils with disabilities.
- To improve the outcomes for both adolescents and adults with emotional or behavioral disorders, research suggests that wraparound planning is necessary. This model incorporates a family-centered approach designed to actively involve the student and his or her family in planning integrated services.

Family-Centered Interventions

- A family-centered approach for working with students with emotional or behavioral disorders recognizes the importance of the individual's family and focuses on the strengths of the family unit.

Issues of Diversity

- Students who are African American are overrepresented in programs for pupils with emotional or behavioral disorders while females are underrepresented.

STUDY QUESTIONS

1. Explain why each of the following factors should be taken into consideration when defining emotional or behavioral disorders:
   a. Dimensions of behavior (frequency, intensity, duration, age-appropriateness)
   b. "Disturbed" versus "disturbing" behavior
   c. Transient nature of problematic behavior
   d. "Typical" versus "atypical" behavior
   e. Variability in cultural and social standards of behavior

2. Why is the federal definition of emotional disturbance controversial? How does this definition differ from the one proposed by the Council for Children with Behavioral Disorders? Discuss the pros and cons of each definition.

3. Compare and contrast clinically and statistically derived classification systems. Give examples of each.

4. Define externalizing and internalizing disorders. Give an example of behaviors reflecting each of these two dimensions.

5. Describe the various conceptual models in the field of emotional or behavioral disorders.

6. List four causes of, and risk factors associated with, emotional or behavioral disorders.

7. How does a positive behavioral support model differ from traditional disciplinary methods?

8. What are some of the significant learning, social, and language/communication characteristics of children and youth with emotional or behavioral disorders?

9. Give examples of three strategies typically used to assess students with emotional or behavioral disorders.

10. How can a teacher manipulate the physical environment to assist students with and without emotional or behavioral disorders?

11. Give examples of instructional interventions that are effective with pupils with emotional or behavioral disorders.

12. Describe how you would use the following intervention strategies with students with emotional or behavioral disorders: social skills training, interpersonal problem solving and conflict resolution, and crisis prevention and management programs.

13. Provide an argument for providing early intervention services for students who have, or who are at risk for developing, emotional or behavioral disorders.

14. What does research say about the long-term outcomes for students with emotional or behavioral disorders?

15. What issues need to be considered when planning for the transition of adolescents with emotional or behavioral disorders?

16. Why is disproportionate representation an issue for students with emotional or behavioral disorders?

17. Define the term *wraparound planning*.

KEY TERMS

mentally ill   283
emotional or behavioral disorders   283
Tourette syndrome   285
emotional disturbance   285
socially maladjusted   288
conduct disorders   288
clinically derived classification systems   289
statistically derived classification systems   289
externalizing disorders   290
internalizing disorders   290
child maltreatment   296

positive behavioral support   298
primary prevention   299
secondary prevention   299
tertiary prevention   300
person-centered planning   302
strength-based assessment   302
functional behavioral assessment   302
behavioral intervention plan   303
time management   304
transition management   304
proximity and movement management   305
classroom arrangement   305

mnemonic strategies   308
self-monitoring strategies   308
content enhancements   309
social skills training   312
interpersonal problem solving   312
conflict resolution   314
crisis prevention and management programs   314
wraparound plan   316
family-centered early intervention   317
response to intervention (RTI)   319
physical restraint   321
seclusion   321

LEARNING ACTIVITIES

1. Break into small groups to debate whether or not Mike is "socially maladjusted" as defined by the current federal definition of emotional disturbance.

2. Visit a local mental health center and interview a counselor, psychologist, or social worker. Determine the extent to which this mental health center has created linkages with the public schools.

3. Work with a group to develop a presentation on promoting resiliency among children and youth.

4. Visit a local school. Investigate the extent to which a positive behavioral support model is being implemented. Identify ways in which such a model might be integrated into the

school at the primary, secondary, and tertiary levels of prevention.

5. Interview a special educator who teaches students with emotional or behavioral disorders. Ask him or her to describe the types of assessment strategies typically used with this population in the school setting.

6. Prepare a class presentation on one of the following:

   a. Conduct disorders

   b. Schizophrenia

   c. Obsessive-compulsive disorder

   d. Depression and/or suicide

ORGANIZATIONS CONCERNED WITH EMOTIONAL OR BEHAVIORAL DISORDERS

American Psychiatric Association

www.psych.org

American Psychological Association

www.apa.org

Council for Children with Behavioral Disorders (CCBD), Council for Exceptional Children

www.ccbd.net

Mental Health America

www.nmha.org

National Federation of Families for Children's Mental Health

www.ffcmh.org

REFLECTING ON STANDARDS

The following exercises are designed to help you learn to apply the Council for Exceptional Children (CEC) standards to your teaching practice. Each of the reflection exercises below correlates with knowledge or a skill within the CEC standards. For the full text of each of the related CEC standards, please refer to the standards integration grid located in Appendix B.

Focus on Curricular Content Knowledge (*CEC Initial Preparation Standard 3.1*)

Reflect on what you have learned about behavior management in this book thus far. Based on what you have learned, how would you establish your classroom rules? What kinds of rules

do you think are important to have in your class? How do you plan to assess which classroom rules are best suited for your particular students?

Focus on Learning Environments (*CEC Initial Preparation Standard 2.2*)

Reflect on a teacher you have had who used his or her instructional time in class effectively. Why was he or she effective? How did he or she schedule the instructional time in class to make things flow well? What steps do you plan to take in your instructional planning to make sure to use instructional time wisely?

STUDENT STUDY SITE

Sharpen your skills with SAGE edge at **edge.sagepub.com/gargiulo5e. SAGE edge for students** provides a personalized approach to help you accomplish your coursework goals in an easy-to-use learning environment.

Individuals With Autism Spectrum Disorders

■■■■■■■■■■■■ ■■■■■■■■

Autism From a Personal Perspective: A True Story of Beating the Odds and Winning

I would like to begin by dedicating my story to my parents, who never gave up, and to the loving memory of my grandmother, who would become a very instrumental person in my life. May her legacy live on through my words and testimony.

When I was 18 months old, a military psychiatrist diagnosed me with early childhood autism. My parents and I were living in Germany while my dad was serving in the army. My parents were told that the military could not provide any treatment or intervention, but if it found a program that I could benefit from that was located near a military base, the army would take care of relocating us. We came back to Anniston (Alabama), which is my hometown, and we lived with my grandmother for a few months until we knew what to do and where we were going. My first symptoms started with being nonverbal, rocking, sound sensitivity, and resistance to change.

However, I had some special abilities such as drawing, and I loved music. I'm also visually impaired, which has bothered me since birth but never had anything to do with autism. This was a disability I already had. I got my first pair of glasses after I turned a year old. I no longer drive because of my extremely low vision. I currently use public transportation services to get around town. After coming home from Germany, my mother started taking me to see some doctors, which did little good. Some would say, "Well, he's just a baby going through some phases, and he'll come out of it soon." Well, that wasn't enough for my mother. She knew there was something more wrong with me, and nobody was listening yet. I still wasn't talking, and I kept to myself a lot. My grandmother took this pretty hard because the last time she saw me, I was only a few months old. Now I was already walking and playing.

I have a favorite story that I would like to share. The story is about how my grandmother got me to speak my first words. This would be a pioneering example of how important early intervention is to children with disabilities. Every night when she put me to bed, she would look at me and say, "Say

- **Describe** the evolution of the definition of autism spectrum disorders.
- **Identify** the key features of the DSM-5 definition of autism spectrum disorder.
- **Provide** examples of etiological possibilities of autism spectrum disorders.
- **Outline** the behavioral, social, and communication characteristics typically associated with individuals with autism spectrum disorders.
- **Explain** how autism spectrum disorders are diagnosed.
- **Describe** instructional strategies often used with students with autism spectrum disorders.
- **Summarize** services for young children with autism spectrum disorders.
- **Characterize** adult services for individuals with autism spectrum disorders.
- **Explain** how low-tech and high-tech devices are used to facilitate communication in pupils with autism spectrum disorders.

'Mama,' say 'Mama'" at me. She would do this every night until one night I looked up at her, and I said, "Mama" back to Grandma. That was how I finally began talking. This was the greatest joy that my grandmother ever had, and that's how my silence was broken. I was 3 years old at the time, and this was just the beginning. After having no luck with the doctors on trying to learn more about my situation, my mother took me to the mental health center in Anniston and met with a social worker. After meeting with this person, my mother learned about the Autism Society of Alabama, and then she learned about the TEACCH program at the University of North Carolina located in Chapel Hill. We tried a few programs while living in Anniston and had no success. These programs were only experimental at the time. I recall one scenario where they had me do a task, and when I didn't cooperate or understand, I got squirted with a water gun for punishment. There was another scenario where I was held down in a chair, and I would be kickin' and screamin' because I didn't like the feeling of being restrained. None of these scenarios was working or providing any results, and it all seemed to be set toward punishment rather than praise.

My parents decided to move to North Carolina and have me enrolled in the TEACCH program. We moved to Fayetteville, and my father got reassigned to Fort Bragg Military Reservation. They also put me into a preschool devoted to working with children with disabilities that had ties to the TEACCH program. This program was unique and in a class by itself. I really believe it was one of the only renowned programs in the whole country to provide a different approach to autism. I would go through three and a half years of various sessions with TEACCH to help improve my language, communication, and social skills. The major emphasis was to train my parents on how to work with me and have a better understanding of autism. The program would give my parents a variety of tasks to perform with me at home because my therapists felt the home was a better environment to learn in rather than sending me away to an institution. We would travel to the TEACCH center once a month for progress reports and meetings, and get new home assignments. The TEACCH center was a two-hour drive from Fayetteville and is located outside of the Raleigh area. There were also times where my therapists came and worked with me in our house. They would conduct behavioral observations and give ideas and suggestions.

This was a very coordinated program among my parents, my teachers, my therapists, and anyone involved with me. I would like to stress that TEACCH was not a cure for autism. But it did reduce the severity, and I made a lot of progress along the way. I believe what has helped me the most is the early diagnosis and early intervention. You really have to play your part and be supportive, which proved to be crucial in my overcoming autism. Everybody was in it together, and it's like a team—that's what I remember most about the program.

After leaving TEACCH, it was recommended that I be put in special education classes when I got ready to enroll in school, and I would remain there until I graduated. But I made a lot more progress than anticipated. Although I was in special education classes most of my life, I did participate in regular classes and after-school programs. My high school was very helpful and supportive in making it possible for me to be a part of any program offered by my school that I desired to be involved in. I played basketball and became team manager. I also took art and speech classes, which I enjoyed very much.

After graduating high school I got involved with vocational rehabilitation. I spent some time in Talladega, Alabama, at E. H. Gentry Technical Facility, which is affiliated

VIDEO

Teacher Interview

with the Alabama Institute for Deaf and Blind, to study electronics, and then I got a computer and taught myself how to use some of the Microsoft Office programs. My efforts led me to getting a job and moving to Birmingham to live on my own and have an independent life. I have lived successfully on my own for eight years.

I'm now currently employed with the Alabama Department of Rehabilitation Services (ADRS) as a telephone operator. I've been with the agency for seven years, and it's been a very exciting time for me, with many great opportunities to get involved in. For a long time, I didn't like to talk to others about my experiences with autism because I was afraid of the prejudices and negative reactions that people might have. When I began working with ADRS, I slowly began to share my experiences with my colleagues, and those fears began to diminish. I realized there was a need for firsthand perspectives about autism. With the support and courage from my friends at ADRS and the Autism Society of Alabama, I have found my courage to speak to others and be a voice of hope to our community. I have already had some great opportunities come my way, and the best is yet to come.

I also own a disc jockey business. I play at weddings, private parties, school dances, and a variety of other entertainment functions. I've had a wonderful life, and I wouldn't change a thing. If I could do it over again, I would. Learning from these experiences has prepared me for many challenges that came later in my life, and it's kept me strong during these times. I would like to thank those who have helped and supported me through it all.

–Jerimie Goike

Although most people have heard the term **autism spectrum disorders**, their perceptions may be colored by television shows and movies. For example, did you see the classic movie *Rain Man* or perhaps *Mercury Rising?* In these two movies, individuals with autism spectrum disorders (commonly referred to as ASD) are portrayed as possessing very special recall and mathematical skills. You may believe that all individuals with ASD possess these unique abilities. This is a common misperception; only rarely do individuals with autism spectrum disorders actually demonstrate these special skills.

In contrast to the movies, some television shows portray individuals with ASD as being locked into their own world, unable to communicate or to give or receive affection. Often, it is implied that if someone could just break through their isolation, there would be a genius inside. In addition, individuals with ASD are often shown as being aggressive and/or self-injurious. These are all common myths about ASD. Most individuals with autism spectrum disorders learn to speak or communicate with sign language, picture symbols, and, often, assistive technology. Although their deficits may impair the way they give and receive affection, even the most severely impaired individuals with autism spectrum disorders demonstrate and accept affection from the significant people in their lives. The belief that a genius exists inside each individual with ASD is fueled by the presence of unevenly developed skills. For example, a child may be able to read fluently but may not understand a word he or she has read.

What does ASD really look like? Although all individuals with autism spectrum disorders show characteristic deficits in communication and social skills, as well as

autism spectrum disorder:
A developmental disorder characterized by abnormal or impaired development in social interaction and communication and a markedly restricted repertoire of activity and interests.

restrictive behaviors and interests, each person is unique. A range of behavioral characteristics is often associated with autism spectrum disorders including hyperactivity, short attention span, impulsivity, aggressiveness, and sometimes self-injurious behaviors. The degree to which these features are demonstrated, in combination with intellectual ability, helps to define the person's strengths and challenges. It is the variability of these behaviors that has resulted in professionals referring to autism as a spectrum disorder with features ranging from mild to severe.

Despite their deficits, individuals with autism spectrum disorders can lead meaningful and productive lives and be an integral part of their family, school, and community. Students with ASD benefit from educational interventions; they also learn from social opportunities and community inclusion. This chapter will explore these topics and others in greater detail, beginning with the evolution of the disorder.

Defining Autism Spectrum Disorders: An Evolving Process

Autism spectrum disorders are among the least understood and most mysterious disabilities in special education. Although an estimated 1 to 1.5 million individuals in the United States today have autism spectrum disorders (Autism Society of America, 2013a), most people have never met a person with ASD. Therefore, it may surprise you that ASD is the fastest-growing developmental disability (Xin & Sutman, 2011).

The Early Years

First described in the early 1800s (Volkmar & Wiesner, 2009), it was not until 1943 that Leo Kanner, a psychiatrist at Johns Hopkins Hospital in Baltimore, identified the symptoms that characterize autism. Kanner (1943/1985) described eleven children with an "inability to relate themselves in the ordinary way to people and situations" (p. 41). Kanner used the term *autistic*, which means "to escape from reality," to describe this condition. Prior to Kanner's work, individuals with autism spectrum disorders were given many labels, including *childhood schizophrenia, feebleminded, idiot, mentally retarded,* and *imbecile*. Kanner believed that these children came "into the world with innate inability to form the usual, biologically affective contact with people, just as other children come into the world with innate physical or intellectual handicaps" (p. 50). In addition, Kanner described these children as having an excellent rote memory, delays in the acquisition of speech and language (including pronoun reversals, echolalia, and extreme literalness), and an anxiously obsessive desire for the maintenance of sameness.

The word *autistic* was borrowed from a term used to describe schizophrenia that means a withdrawal from relationships. Kanner (1943/1985) used the term to describe an "inability to relate to themselves," and noted that the disorder starts as an "extreme autistic aloneness that, whenever possible, disregards, ignores, [or] shuts out anything that comes to the child from outside" (p. 41). Kanner differentiated autism from schizophrenia in three areas: an extreme aloneness from the very beginning of life, an attachment to objects, and a powerful desire for aloneness and sameness.

Despite Kanner's distinction between autism and schizophrenia, for many years children with autism were described in the literature as having childhood schizophrenia, early infantile autism, or childhood onset pervasive developmental disorder. It was hypothesized that many of these children would develop schizophrenia as adults, which clinicians now know is not true. The use of these terms added to the diagnostic confusion and lack of understanding regarding ASD.

REFERENCE

Autism Spectrum

Individuals With Disabilities Education Act

Fortunately, a lot has changed in the field since 1943. Autism is now one of the specific disability categories defined in the Individuals with Disabilities Education Act (IDEA). With the reauthorization of IDEA in 1990 (PL 101–476) autism was added as a discrete category. The 2004 amendments to IDEA define autism as follows:

Children with autism spectrum disorders are guaranteed a free appropriate public education.

(i) Autism means a developmental disability significantly affecting verbal and nonverbal communication and social interaction, usually evident before age three, that adversely affects a child's educational performance. Other characteristics often associated with autism are engagement in repetitive activities and stereotyped movements, resistance to environmental change or change in daily routines, and unusual responses to sensory experiences.

(ii) Autism does not apply if a child's educational performance is adversely affected primarily because the child has an emotional disturbance . . .

(iii) A child who manifests the characteristics of autism after age three could be diagnosed as having autism if the criteria in paragraph (c) (1) (i) of this section are satisfied. (34 C.F.R. §300.8 [c] [1])

American Psychiatric Association Definition

The American Psychiatric Association (APA) periodically updates the diagnostic and statistical manual (DSM) that defines mental disorders and general medical conditions. Autism first appeared in the third edition of the DSM, published in 1977; before that time, the APA did not recognize autism as a separate disorder. The Autism Society of America was instrumental in the inclusion of autism in the DSM-III and influenced the definition that was ultimately used (Freeman, 1999). Since 1980, autism has been characterized in the DSM as a pervasive developmental disorder to highlight the fact that autism is a developmental disorder of childhood, not a psychotic disorder like schizophrenia. The APA radically revised its thinking about autism spectrum disorders with the publication of the fifth edition of the DSM in May 2013. The new terminology of choice is *autism spectrum disorder*, which is now characterized as a neurodevelopmental disorder (along with, for example, intellectual disability, attention deficit hyperactivity disorder, learning disabilities, and other disorders) rather than a pervasive developmental disorder. The new edition consolidates autistic disorder (autism), Asperger disorder (syndrome), and pervasive developmental disorder under the heading of autism spectrum disorder. The rationale for this change is that "these disorders represent a single continuum of mild to severe impairments in the two domains of social communication and restrictive/repetitive interests rather than being distinct disorders" (American Psychiatric Association, 2013, p. xliii).

> **VIDEO**
> New Autism Definition

■ ■ ■ ■ ■   Table 10.1 **Diagnostic Criteria for Autism Spectrum Disorder**

A. Persistent deficits in social communication and social interaction across multiple contexts, as manifested by the following, currently or by history:
   1. Deficits in social-emotional reciprocity, ranging, for example, from abnormal social approach and failure of normal back-and-forth conversation; to reduced sharing of interests, emotions, or affect; to failure to initiate or respond to social interactions.
   2. Deficits in nonverbal communicative behaviors used for social interaction, ranging, for example, from poorly integrated verbal and nonverbal communication; to abnormalities in eye contact and body language or deficits in understanding and use of gestures; to a total lack of facial expressions and nonverbal communication.
   3. Deficits in developing, maintaining, and understanding relationships, ranging, for example, from difficulties adjusting behavior to suit various social contexts; to difficulties in sharing imaginative play or in making friends; to absence of interest in peers.

B. Restricted, repetitive patterns of behavior, interests, or activities, as manifested by at least two of the following, currently or by history:
   1. Stereotyped or repetitive motor movements, use of objects, or speech (e.g., simple motor stereotypies, lining up toys or flipping objects, echolalia, idiosyncratic phrases).
   2. Insistence on sameness, inflexible adherence to routines, or ritualized patterns of verbal or nonverbal behavior (e.g., extreme distress at small changes, difficulties with transitions, rigid thinking patterns, greeting rituals, need to take same route or eat same food every day).
   3. Highly restricted, fixated interests that are abnormal in intensity or focus (e.g., strong attachment to or preoccupation with unusual objects, excessively circumscribed or perseverative interests).
   4. Hyper- or hyporeactivity to sensory input or unusual interest in sensory aspects of the environment (e.g., apparent indifference to pain/temperature, adverse response to specific sounds or textures, excessive smelling or touching of objects, visual fascination with light or movements).

C. Symptoms must be present in the early developmental period (but may not become fully manifest until social demands exceed limited capacities, or may be masked by learned strategies later in life).

D. Symptoms cause clinically significant impairment in social, occupational, or other important areas of current functioning.

E. These disturbances are not better explained by intellectual disability (intellectual developmental disorder) or global developmental delay. Intellectual disability and autism spectrum disorder frequently co-occur; to make comorbid diagnoses of autism spectrum disorder and intellectual disability, social communication should be below that expected for general developmental level.

SOURCE: *Diagnostic and Statistical Manual of Mental Disorders*, 5th ed. (Arlington, VA: American Psychiatric Association, 2013), pp. 51–53.

The APA characterizes autism spectrum disorder as

persistent deficits in social communication and social interaction across multiple contexts, including deficits in social reciprocity, nonverbal communicative behaviors used for social interaction, and skills for developing, maintaining, and understanding relationships. In addition to the social communication deficits, the diagnosis of autism spectrum disorder requires the presence of restricted, repetitive patterns of behavior, interests, or activities. (American Psychiatric Association, 2013, p. 31)

See Table 10.1 for an expansion of this definition.

A child diagnosed with autism spectrum disorder can be assigned one of three levels of severity, recognizing that severity may fluctuate over time and vary by context. Classification is based on the amount of support required by the individual to counteract impairments in everyday functioning. The DSM-5 offers the following three levels: Level 1: requiring support; Level 2: requiring substantial support; and Level 3: requiring very substantial support.

Asperger Syndrome

Although the DSM-5 no longer classifies Asperger disorder (more commonly known as Asperger syndrome) as a discrete disability due to considerable overlap with autism spectrum disorder, we believe that individuals with this impairment merit attention. First described in 1944 by Hans Asperger, an Austrian pediatrician and contemporary of Leo Kanner, his work, written in German, was later popularized by English psychiatrist Lorna Wing (1981), who referenced his earlier investigation of children he identified as "little professors."

Individuals with Asperger syndrome, which is foremost a social disorder (Myles & Simpson, 2002), have no significant delay in language development, and the majority of students with Asperger syndrome have average to above-average intellectual abilities (Hall, 2013; Ryan, Hughes, Katsiyannis, McDaniel, & Sprinkle, 2011). Children with Asperger syndrome are typically not diagnosed until they attend school and the social demands of the classroom cause their limitations to become apparent (Hyman & Levy, 2013). Unique characteristics and qualities typical of individuals with Asperger syndrome include the following:

- Auditory and tactile hypersensitivity
- Concrete and literal thinking
- Coordination and balance problems
- Decreased sensitivity to pain
- Difficulty comprehending abstract materials
- Difficulty understanding and appreciating the feelings and thoughts of others
- Difficulty understanding nonverbal social cues
- Extensive vocabulary within a narrow area of interest ("little professor")
- Formal pattern of speaking
- Inflexibility
- Poor motor skills
- Poor self-concept and low self-esteem
- Restricted range of interests
- Rigid adherence to rules and routines
- Significant academic problems
- Social awkwardness
- Superior rote memory skills (Boutot & Myles, 2011; Heflin & Alaimo, 2007; Myles & Simpson, 2002)

It is important to remember, however, that individuals with Asperger syndrome represent a very heterogeneous population, and very few generalizations can be made that adequately describe any one individual (Heflin & Alaimo, 2007).

Given the benefits of early intervention, it is essential that educators are aware of the possible indicators of Asperger syndrome. The presence of a cluster of these characteristics, over a period of time, should result in a formal referral for special education services (Dahle & Gargiulo, 2003). If found eligible for services, students with Asperger syndrome may qualify for eligibility through a multitude of classifications because Asperger syndrome is not a distinct educational category identified by IDEA 2004.

A Brief History of the Field[1]

The field of autism has continued to grow since Kanner (1943/1985) identified the first eleven children with autism. We now turn our attention to some of the early researchers

Asperger syndrome: A pervasive developmental disorder with severe and sustained impairments in social interaction and the development of restricted, repetitive patterns of behavior, interests, and activities. Disorder causes clinically significant impairments in other important areas of functioning.

---

[1]We have chosen to use the term *autism* in this section of the chapter because it was the terminology of choice in earlier decades.

VIDEO

Asperger Syndrome

in the field and early theories about the etiology of autism and conclude with a brief examination of more contemporary thinking about causes of autism.

Psychogenic Theories

Following Kanner's initial research on autism, many researchers focused on inappropriate or bad parenting as a cause of autism. Rank (1949), for example, blamed "bad mothering" and emphasized deviant maternal characteristics. These theories, known as psychogenic theories, were embraced by Freudian therapists. They hypothesized that if certain basic psychological bonds were not established between parent and child, the child would not be able to establish relationships with others and would fail to progress. Individual psychotherapy was recommended for the child and the parents. In *The Empty Fortress: Infantile Autism and the Birth of Self*, Bruno Bettelheim (1967) speculated that during infancy some parents, particularly mothers, withheld affection or exhibited extremely negative feelings toward their son or daughter; consequently, the youngster retreated into an autistic "empty fortress." Bettelheim's book further contributed to the idea of blaming parents as the cause of the child's autistic condition.

In 1985, Bernard Rimland disputed these psychogenic theories of autism. An advocate for families with children with autism and the father of an individual with autism, Rimland reacted to the idea that parents, particularly mothers, were judged to be guilty of causing their child's autism based on a hypothesis that had not been proved. Rimland set forth nine points as evidence for the biological origins of autism that are still considered valid today. Nevertheless, the controversy over the causes of autism did not stop with Rimland's work. It was the continued research on the biological causes of autism and the advocacy of the Autism Society of America (formerly the National Society for Autistic Children founded by Bernard Rimland) that eventually quieted the psychogenic theories of causation.

Organic Theories

In the 1940s and 1950s, Lauretta Bender and other researchers suggested that autism may be organically based and that the mother's behavior was a reaction to the child's condition (Rutter, 1978). The high incidence of seizures in individuals with autism, documented in the 1960s, continues to support an organic framework for autism (Hyman & Levy, 2013; Volkmar & Nelson, 1990). Finally, the biological basis of autism is no longer in question because of its association with intellectual disability (Volkmar & Pauls, 2003).

psychogenic theories: Freudian perspective that if basic psychological bonds are not established between the parent and the child, the child will not be able to establish relationships with others and will fail to progress. Individual psychotherapy recommended as the treatment of choice.

applied behavior analysis (ABA): Application of learning principles derived from operant conditioning; used to increase or decrease specific behaviors.

Behavioral Theories

Charles Fester was one of the first behavioral psychologists to propose that autism was environmentally determined (LaVigna, 1985). Behavioral psychologists such as Fester believed that the child with autism was not conditioned properly by his or her parents. Fester, and those who followed, provided the foundation for what is known today as applied behavior analysis (ABA). The work of Ivar Lovaas (1987, 1993) with individuals with autism grew out of Fester's investigations in behavior modification. A major focus of Lovaas's work initially was in the area of self-injurious behavior. At first, Lovaas used forms of punishment, such as shock, to reduce self-injurious behaviors.

Later, Lovaas learned that individuals with autism adapted to these forms of punishment, which did not reduce the self-injurious behaviors. Today, physical punishment is no longer used to decrease self-injurious behaviors, although the command *no* and time-out are still used.

The use of positive reinforcement is currently the intervention of choice for many professionals.

Prevalence of Autism Spectrum Disorders

As noted earlier, autism spectrum disorders is the fastest-growing developmental disability. Yet, there is debate about the prevalence of ASD and the reasons for the recent marked increase (Hyman & Levy, 2013). As recently as 2009, the reported prevalence was nearly 1 in 110 children ages 3–17 (Kogan et al., 2009). A more recent estimate from the Centers for Disease Control and Prevention (CDC, 2012) suggests that 1 in every 88 children at age 8 is identified with autism spectrum disorders. According to the CDC, the risk for ASD is almost five times more likely in males than in females. The CDC cautions that the data do not represent a nationally representative sample and, therefore, cannot be generalized to the country as a whole. Still, these numbers give rise to the cry of an "autism epidemic."

Recent statistics compiled by the U.S. government indicate that approximately 407,000 pupils ages 6–21 were identified as having autism in the 2011–2012 school year (U.S. Department of Education, 2013a). Data about individuals with autism were first reported in the 1991–1992 school year with just over 5,400 students recognized (U.S. Department of Education, 2000b). Since that time, the number of pupils with autism receiving a special education has increased more than 7,700 percent.

There are currently almost 51,000 preschoolers identified with autism as their primary disability. This number represents 6.8 percent of all youngsters with a disability (U.S. Department of Education, 2013a).

The Centers for Disease Control and Prevention (2013b) considers autism spectrum disorders to be a national health concern because of the number of individuals who are being identified as having ASD and the associated financial costs of dealing with this disability. The number of individuals identified with autism spectrum disorders is, without a doubt, on the rise, although the reasons for this phenomenon are complex and not completely clear (Hyman & Levy, 2013; Saracino, Noseworthy, Steiman, Reisinger, & Frombonne, 2010). We offer several possibilities. First, clinicians are evaluating and diagnosing individuals more accurately, including individuals with milder forms of the disability that would have gone undiagnosed previously. Second, special education legislation has mandated early intervention and specialized services, bringing more individuals with ASD to the attention of the public schools. In addition, IDEA added a separate category for autism; individuals who were previously labeled as intellectually disabled, learning disabled, or emotionally disturbed are now being appropriately identified as having autism. Third, there is greater public awareness of ASD resulting from increased attention in the popular press and other types of media. Parents are becoming proactive and noticing delays and/or differences in their child's development, and they are bringing their concerns to the attention of professionals. Finally, changing diagnostic criteria used to identify autism spectrum disorders may also account for the increasing prevalence data. Regardless of the explanations put forth, it seems safe to conclude that an authentic increase in the number of children with ASD is occurring.

VIDEO
Applied Behavior Analysis

VIDEO
History of Autism

Etiology of Autism Spectrum Disorders

The etiology of autism spectrum disorders is complex, and in most cases, the underlying pathologic mechanisms are unknown. While the precise cause of ASD may be unknown, current thinking suggests that multiple etiologies are involved. The primary suspected contributing factors include genetic predispositions and abnormal brain chemistry and development in addition to environmental variables (National Institute of Mental Health, 2013b; Ryan et al., 2011; Williams & Williams, 2011).

The evidence for a genetic contribution to autism spectrum disorders is incontrovertible. Although the exact mode of transmission is unclear, multiple genes are believed to be involved (Gong, Yan, Xie, Liu, & Sun, 2012; Hall, 2013; Heflin & Alaimo, 2007; Rapin, 2008; Volkmar & Pauls, 2003). Family studies as well as studies of twins clearly support an underlying genetic vulnerability to ASD (Hyman & Levy, 2013; Wicks-Nelson & Israel, 2013). In a small percentage of instances, autism spectrum disorders are caused by medical conditions such as fragile X syndrome and tuberous sclerosis (Hyman & Levy, 2013).

Neuroimaging studies implicate structural abnormalities of the brain in individuals with ASD (Hall, 2013; Hyman & Levy, 2013; Muller, 2007; Volkmar & Pauls, 2003). The cerebellum, cerebral cortex, and brain stem are just some of the regions of the brain in which anomalies are being investigated. Autism spectrum disorders are not the result of abnormalities in just one specific location of the brain; rather, multiple regions are likely involved (Minshew, Scherf, Behrmann, & Humphreys, 2011). Figure 10.1 illustrates major brain structures implicated in ASD.

Neurochemical research is also focusing on neurotransmitters such as serotonin, dopamine, and epinephrine and their role in contributing to autism spectrum disorders (Dougherty et al., 2013; Heflin & Alaimo, 2007; Toma et al., 2013; Volkmar & Wiesner, 2009).

Finally, a great deal of attention has focused on a controversial connection between vaccinating children for measles, mumps, and rubella (MMR) and autism spectrum disorders. It was believed that there was a link between thimerosal, a mercury-containing preservative used in pediatric vaccines like the MMR vaccine, and the onset of ASD. (Vaccines developed after 2001 no longer contain thimerosal.) A significant body of empirical research has refuted a causal relationship between the vaccine and the development of autism spectrum disorders; in fact, the original research study was retracted by medical journal *The Lancet* due to investigative improprieties (Hall, 2013; Hyman & Levy, 2013; Institute of Medicine, 2004, 2011; Ryan et al., 2011; Schechter & Grether, 2008).

At the present time, the specific cause of autism spectrum disorders is unknown; most likely multiple biological etiologies are involved. Scientists, however, continue to unravel the complexities of this disorder, and hopefully answers will soon be discovered.

Characteristics of Individuals With Autism Spectrum Disorders

Intellectual Functioning

Autism spectrum disorders are generally described as mild, moderate, or severe depending on the cognitive functioning level of the individual. Emerging research suggests that individuals within the spectrum may exhibit a full range of cognitive development (Edelson, 2006; Ryan et al., 2011; Wicks-Nelson & Israel, 2013). Many individuals

AUDIO
Increased Identification

AUDIO
Etiology

Figure 10.1 **Regions of the Brain Implicated in Autism**

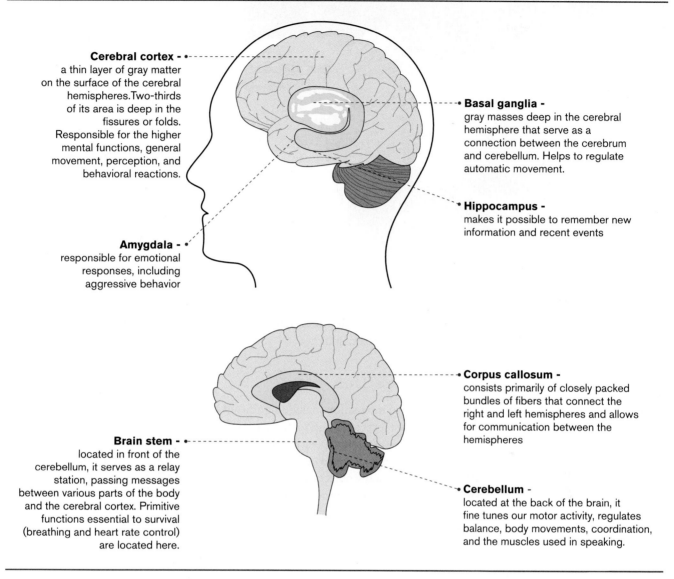

Cerebral cortex -
a thin layer of gray matter on the surface of the cerebral hemispheres. Two-thirds of its area is deep in the fissures or folds. Responsible for the higher mental functions, general movement, perception, and behavioral reactions.

Amygdala -
responsible for emotional responses, including aggressive behavior

Basal ganglia -
gray masses deep in the cerebral hemisphere that serve as a connection between the cerebrum and cerebellum. Helps to regulate automatic movement.

Hippocampus -
makes it possible to remember new information and recent events

Brain stem -
located in front of the cerebellum, it serves as a relay station, passing messages between various parts of the body and the cerebral cortex. Primitive functions essential to survival (breathing and heart rate control) are located here.

Corpus callosum -
consists primarily of closely packed bundles of fibers that connect the right and left hemispheres and allows for communication between the hemispheres

Cerebellum -
located at the back of the brain, it fine tunes our motor activity, regulates balance, body movements, coordination, and the muscles used in speaking.

SOURCE: Available at http://neurosciencenews.com/neuroscience-topics/autism/page/2/

with ASD, however, exhibit some degree of intellectual impairment (Klinger, O'Kelley, & Mussey, 2009).

About 10 percent of individuals with ASD demonstrate extraordinary skills and talents in areas such as mathematical calculations, memory feats, artistic or musical abilities, and reading. These individuals were originally described as "idiot savants." At one time, *idiot* was the accepted label for someone with an intelligence quotient below 25, and *savant* was derived from the French word *savoir* meaning "to know" (Treffert, 2013). Due to its pejorative connotation, the term autistic savant was introduced to describe someone with these highly specialized skills (Edelson, 2000). Other professionals describe these individuals as exhibiting savant syndrome. These "islands of genius" stand in stark contrast to the person's overall limitations (Treffert, 2013). One example of a savant skill was portrayed in the popular movie *Mercury Rising*, where

autistic savant: An individual with autism who possesses special skills in areas such as mathematical calculations, memory feats, artistic and musical abilities, or reading.

Some young children with autism spectrum disorders are able to read at an early age.

an individual with autism spectrum disorder demonstrated unusual skills in the area of memory and code breaking. In comparison to these autistic savants, only 1 percent of the general population and individuals with intellectual disability possess these skills (Edelson, 2000).

Theory of Mind

The theory of mind is a cognitive hypothesis that seeks to explain the inability of the individual with autism spectrum disorders to realize that other people have their own unique points of view about the world. Specifically, many individuals with ASD do not understand that others may have different thoughts, plans, emotions, and perspectives from their own (Boucher, 2012; Williams, 2010). Typically developing children appear to acquire this skill by age 4 (Astington & Barricult, 2001).

Social Interaction

Deficits in social interaction include significant impairment in the use of multiple nonverbal behaviors (eye-to-eye gaze, facial expression, body postures and gestures), failure to develop age-appropriate peer relationships, a lack of spontaneous sharing with others, and the absence of social or emotional reciprocity. Often the individual with ASD does not point or show objects of interest to others, shows little or no expressed pleasure in interaction, and lacks coordinated gaze. This person rarely or never directs appropriate facial expressions to others and does not show interest in an object or activity even when reference to the object is accompanied by pointing or facial cues. Joint attention is the term typically applied to this deficit in social communication. Impairments with this skill possibly account for the difficulty individuals with autism spectrum disorder encounter with observational learning—they do not readily learn by observing others.

Difficulties with social interaction are often devastating to individuals with autism spectrum disorders. Professionals (Heflin & Alaimo, 2007; Hyman & Levy, 2013; Wicks-Nelson & Israel, 2013) note that even the highest-functioning individuals often experience significant difficulties in developing friendships and relating to others. Persons with ASD also have problems with social exchanges. They may fail to take social norms or the listener's feelings into account. They may rely exclusively on limited conversational strategies or stereotyped expressions, elaborating on some idiosyncratic interest or echoing a previous statement. For example, an individual with ASD may tell a coworker she smells whenever she wears a particular perfume to work. Another person may only interact with you if you talk about his favorite topic—pizza! The individual shows relatively little interest in others unless he or she needs help or responds to questions; there is little or no reciprocal social communication. An individual with these deficits will not ask you how you are feeling or seem to notice if there has been a change in mood. Social impairments in persons with autism spectrum disorders significantly affect their involvement with others in educational, vocational, and social settings (National Education Association, 2006).

theory of mind: A hypothesis that attempts to explain the inability of the individual with autism to realize that other people have their own unique point of view about the world—different thoughts, plans, and perspectives from their own.

joint attention: A social communication deficit common in individuals with autism spectrum disorders, the failure to respond to a gaze or pointing by another person.

Communication

A lack of speech has long been considered a hallmark of autism spectrum disorders. It is estimated that 25 to 30 percent of children with ASD never develop language (Tiegerman-Farber, 2009; Wicks-Nelson & Israel, 2013). In individuals with ASD who do speak, "their speech may not be functional or fluent and may lack communicative intent" (Johnson & Myers, 2007, p. 1192). Typical communication deficits include a delay in receptive and expressive language, improper use of pronouns, marked impairment in conversational skills, and stereotyped and repetitive use of language, in addition to echolalia or "parroting" the speech of others (Hyman & Levy, 2013; Owens, 2014; Wicks-Nelson & Israel, 2013).

The speech of individuals with ASD is clearly abnormal in rhythm, has an odd intonation or inappropriate pitch, and may sound toneless or mechanical. Deficits in the pragmatic or social use of language are also common (Owens, 2014; Volkmar & Pauls, 2003). Approximately 25 to 30 percent of youngsters with autism spectrum disorders begin to use words and then suddenly cease to speak, often between 15 and 24 months of age (Johnson & Myers, 2007).

A lack of appropriate social skills is a common problem among individuals with autism spectrum disorders.

Some of the early prespeech deficits that may facilitate an early diagnosis and thus early intervention include

- lack of recognition of mother's (or father's or consistent caregiver's) voice;
- disregard for vocalizations (e.g., lack of response to name), yet keen awareness of environmental sounds;
- delayed onset of babbling past 9 months of age;
- decreased or absent use of prespeech gestures (waving, pointing, showing);
- lack of expressions such as "oh oh" or "huh"; [and]
- lack of interest [in] or response of any kind to neutral statements (e.g., "Oh no, it's raining again!"). (Johnson & Myers, 2007, p. 1192)

Repetitive and Restrictive Behaviors

Repetitive and restrictive behaviors (see Table 10.1, p. 332) include preoccupation with at least one stereotyped and restricted pattern of interest to an abnormal degree, strict adherence to nonfunctional rituals or routines, stereotyped and repetitive motor mannerisms, and preoccupation with parts of objects. Individuals with ASD may

- play with toys in an unintended fashion;
- be rigid about routines or object placements;

VIDEO

Parent Interview

Many individuals with autism spectrum disorders engage in stereotypical and repetitive behaviors.

- eat few foods or only foods with a certain texture;
- smell food;
- be insensitive to pain;
- be unaware of danger;
- show unusual attachment to inanimate objects; and
- exhibit repeated body movements (hand flapping, rocking, finger licking, spinning, etc.).

Other Characteristics

In addition to the two primary characteristics of autism spectrum disorders, other features that often coexist (comorbid conditions) include problems with concentration, attention, and activity level; anxiety disorders; affective or mood disorders; and learning difficulties. These behaviors are briefly summarized in Table 10.2.

Assessment of Autism Spectrum Disorders

The assessment of an individual with autism spectrum disorders is confounded by the fact that the very behaviors necessary for valid testing—the ability to sit still, pay attention, follow directions, and respond verbally—are often difficult for the individual with ASD. Some professionals believe that these deficits render children with ASD untestable, and they generally disregard the results of formal cognitive and achievement tests. However, most researchers believe that intellectual assessments and achievement tests can be administered effectively and used in planning programs for students with ASD. Behavioral assessments and rating scales can also generate useful information about the individual with autism spectrum disorders without the problems associated with a formal testing situation.

Although medical tests cannot diagnose autism spectrum disorders, a medical examination is often helpful in ruling out specific disabilities such as hearing or vision loss and in diagnosing any associated neurological disorders such as epilepsy, fragile X syndrome, or tuberous sclerosis. Because the characteristics and associated conditions of autism spectrum disorders vary so much, a child suspected of having ASD should ideally be evaluated by a multidisciplinary team including a neurologist, a psychologist, a developmental pediatrician, and a speech-language pathologist in addition to a special educator (Dahle, 2003a). An accurate diagnosis is important in order for the student to receive appropriate interventions and gain access to customized special educational services (Handleman & Harris, 2008; Myers & Johnson, 2007).

Intellectual Assessment

As we noted earlier, one common myth about autism spectrum disorders is that inside each child is a genius. This myth may have arisen because of the presence of extraordinary abilities in a small number of children. Despite the existence of unusual talents,

VIDEO

Characteristics

Table 10.2 **Associated Characteristics of Individuals With Autism Spectrum Disorders**

Areas of Concern	Behaviors
Concentration and Attention	• Hyperactivity • Short attention span • Impulsivity • Stimulus overselectivity (selective attention)
Anxiety Disorders	• Self-injurious behaviors • Excessive scratching or rubbing • Limiting diet to a few foods • Eating inedible items (pica) • Obsessive-compulsive disorder
Affective Disorders	• Abnormalities of mood or affect (giggling or crying for no apparent reason) • Sleeping problems (difficulties falling asleep, frequent awakening, early morning awakening) • Bed-wetting • Depression, suicidal ideation
Learning Difficulties	• Uneven achievement • Impaired executive functioning • Poor reading comprehension • Inadequate receptive/expressive language skills • Difficulty generalizing skills or information

many individuals with ASD exhibit significant cognitive deficits, although a growing number of children with ASD portray typical cognitive abilities (Hyman & Levy, 2013).

For all individuals with ASD, we know that the severity of the symptoms affects the individual's overall level of functioning, particularly in the areas of language and social skills. What is most important is not the person's intellectual capacity but his or her ability to function independently in society. Nevertheless, intellectual assessments are important components in determining a child's eligibility for a special education and other needed services. Therefore, tests measuring intellectual ability as well as checklists assessing adaptive levels of functioning are typically administered as part of an overall assessment battery.

Screening and Diagnosis

There is no specific test to diagnose autism spectrum disorders. Physicians look for behavioral symptoms to make a diagnosis. These symptoms may be noticeable within the first few months of life, or they may appear anytime prior to age 3. In some instances, it is not unusual to find characteristics being recognized later primarily because they were likely confused with the symptoms of other disorders.

In the past decade, researchers have identified several characteristics that are helpful in making an early diagnosis of ASD. It has been shown that a diagnosis of autism spectrum disorders at age 2 is reliable, valid, and stable (Johnson & Myers

REFERENCE

Identifying Autism

2007; Levy, Hyman, & Pinto-Martin, 2008; National Institute of Mental Health, 2013b).

The diagnosis of ASD should include two steps. The first step is a developmental screening (a brief assessment designed to identify youngsters who should receive a more thorough evaluation) and surveillance (a process whereby health care professionals monitor children who may have a developmental disability). It is recommended that screening tests be given to *all* children during their well-child visits at 9, 18, 24, and 30 months of age. Additional screening is warranted if the youngster is at high risk (for example, has a sibling or parent with ASD) or presents characteristics suggestive of autism spectrum disorders.

The second step in the diagnostic process is a comprehensive evaluation by a multidisciplinary team of professionals. Typical evaluations include clinical and educational observations, caregiver interviews, developmental histories, psychological testing, speech-language assessments, and possibly one or more diagnostic scales. Because ASD is a complex disorder, neurological and genetic testing may be appropriate.

Many instruments have been developed for assessment of autism spectrum disorders, yet no single tool should be used for diagnosing ASD. Diagnostic instruments typically rely on caregivers' descriptions of the child's development as well as direct observation of the individual in both structured and unstructured situations. The "gold standards" of diagnostic assessments include the Autism Diagnostic Observation Schedule (ADOS-2) (Lord et al., 2012) and the Autism Diagnostic Interview–Revised (ADI-R) (Rutter, Le Couteur, & Lord, 2003). The ADOS-2 is a focused interaction with the individual with ASD, which is balanced by parental concerns as reflected in the ADI-R interview. The findings offer a description of the characteristics of the individual and the consistency of the symptoms with the features identified by the American Psychiatric Association.

Screening for Asperger Syndrome

Until recently, screening instruments often did not identify children with mild ASD, such as those youngsters with more functional adaptive skills, intellectual flexibility, or Asperger syndrome. Today, however, the Autism Spectrum Screening Questionnaire (Ehlers, Gillberg, & Wing, 1999) and the Childhood Asperger Syndrome Test (Williams et al., 2005) provide a reliable means for identifying school-age children with Asperger syndrome or milder forms of ASD. These two tools focus on social and behavioral impairments in children without significant language delays.

Educational Considerations

Where Are Individuals With Autism Spectrum Disorders Educated?

During the 2011–2012 school year, one third (33.7%) of school-age students with ASD received services in a self-contained classroom while four out of ten students (39.9%) were assigned to the general education classroom (U.S. Department of Education, 2013a). Figure 10.2 profiles where pupils with autism spectrum disorders receive a special education. It is interesting to note that almost twice as many individuals with ASD are educated in a resource room as compared to students receiving services in a separate school.

VIDEO

Differentiated Instruction

Figure 10.2 Educational Placement of Students With Autism Spectrum Disorders

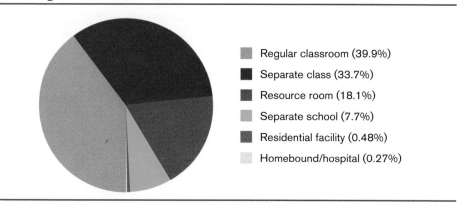

- Regular classroom (39.9%)
- Separate class (33.7%)
- Resource room (18.1%)
- Separate school (7.7%)
- Residential facility (0.48%)
- Homebound/hospital (0.27%)

NOTE: Figure represents percentages of enrollment of students with autism during the 2011–2012 school year. Excludes pupils enrolled in parentally placed private schools and individuals in correctional facilities.

SOURCE: U.S. Department of Education. (2013). *Historical state-level IDEA data files.* Retrieved November 14, 2013, from http://tadnet.public.tadnet.org/pages/712

Instructional Approaches

Individuals with autism spectrum disorders represent a very heterogeneous population. These students typically require a diversity of educational interventions and teaching strategies. It is well documented that effective instructional approaches are structured, predictable, and geared to the person's level of functioning (Autism Society of America, 2013b; Heflin & Alaimo, 2007). Most individuals with ASD demonstrate appropriate behaviors in structured rather than in unstructured situations, and special education programs with more structure are generally associated with better outcomes.

Generally speaking, the most successful programs for pupils with autism spectrum disorders are those that begin early and are intensive, continuous, and multidisciplinary (Hyman & Levy, 2013; Levy, Hyman et al., 2008). Many of these effective programs incorporate evidence-based practices, use principles of applied behavior analysis, or rely on structured teaching methodologies. It is not too surprising that the field of ASD is filled with treatment fads and programs that claim to be effective; however, many of these interventions lack empirical support. Fortunately, there is a growing body of research, albeit limited, identifying best practice interventions (Hall, 2013; National Autism Center, 2009; Ryan et al., 2011). See Table 10.3 for a description of some of these programs. Regardless of the approach used, effective instructional programs for pupils with autism spectrum disorders build on the child's strengths while also focusing on the child's areas of interest.

Although no one instructional strategy is effective with all students with autism spectrum disorders (Autism Society of America, 2013b; Smith, Polloway, Patton, & Dowdy, 2012), an emphasis on developing functional communication abilities and appropriate social skills is characteristic of most approaches. For other pupils with ASD, their individualized education programs (IEPs) might focus on self-help skills along with functional academics. In most instances, the various instructional interventions aim to maximize the individual's independence and future integration in the community. Refer to the Suggestions for the Classroom feature for hints on teaching high-functioning students with autism spectrum disorders.

REFERENCE

Supporting Students

■ ■ ■ ■ ■ Table 10.3 **Evidence-Based Interventions for Students With Autism Spectrum Disorders**

Intervention	Program Description	Demonstrated Efficacy	Website
Developmental, Individual-Difference, Relationship-Based Model (DIR®/Floortime)	Through challenging yet child-friendly play experiences, clinicians, parents, and educators learn about the strengths and limitations of the child, therefore gaining the ability to tailor interventions as necessary while strengthening the bond between the parent and the child and fostering social and emotional development of the child. Time requirement: 14–35 hours per week.	Increased levels of: • Social functioning • Emotional functioning • Information gathering For ages: Approximately 2–5 years.	www.icdl.com
Discrete Trial Training (DTT)	Intervention that focuses on managing a child's learning opportunities by teaching specific, manageable tasks until mastery in a continued effort to build upon the mastered skills. Time requirement: 20–30 hours per week across settings.	Increased levels of: • Cognitive skills • Language skills • Adaptive skills • Compliance skills For ages: Approximately 2–6 years.	www.aba.insightcommerce.net
Lovaas Method	Intervention that focuses on managing a child's learning opportunities by teaching specific, manageable tasks to build upon the mastered skills. Time requirement: 20–40 hours per week.	Increased levels of: • Adaptive skills • Cognitive skills • Compliance skills • Language skills • IQ • Social functions For ages: Approximately 2–12 years.	www.lovaas.com
Picture Exchange Communication System® (PECS®)	Communication system developed to assist students in building fundamental language skills, eventually leading to spontaneous communication. The tiered intervention supports the learner in learning to identify, discriminate between, and then exchange different symbols with a partner as a means to communicate a want.	Increased levels of: • Speech and language development • Social-communicative behaviors	www.PECS.com
Social Stories™	Personalized stories that systematically describe a situation, skill, or concept in terms of relevant social cues, perspectives, and common responses, modeling and providing a socially accepted behavior option. Time requirement: Time requirements vary per story; approximately 5–10 minutes prior to difficult situation.	Increased levels of: • Prosocial behaviors For ages: Approximately 2–12 years.	www.thegraycenter.org

Intervention	Program Description	Demonstrated Efficacy	Website
TEACCH Model	Intervention that supports task completion by providing explicit instruction and visual supports in a purposefully structured environment, planned to meet the unique task needs of the student. Time requirement: Up to 25 hours per week (during the school day).	Increased levels of: • Imitation • Perception • Gross motor skills • Hand-eye coordination • Cognitive performance For ages: Approximately 6 years–adult.	www.teacch.com

SOURCE: Adapted from J. Ryan, E. Hughes, A. Katsiyannis, M. McDaniel, and C. Sprinkle, "Research-based Educational Practices for Students with Autism Spectrum Disorders," *Teaching Exceptional Children, 43*(3), 2011, p. 59.

Services for Young Children With Autism Spectrum Disorders

There is no known cure for autism spectrum disorders, but developmentally appropriate educational programming in the early years can play a significant role in enhancing functioning in later life (Lipkin & Schertz, 2008). Identifying and diagnosing ASD early can provide access to appropriate services and interventions that result in a better prognosis (Autism Society of America, 2013a; Centers for Disease Control and Prevention, 2013). In addition to receiving appropriate services, another benefit of early identification is the decreased need for restrictive educational placements in the future (Gargiulo & Kilgo, 2014).

Early Intervention Services

Federal law mandates services for young children with disabilities, including identification, assessment, and customized interventions. Early intervention services, tailored to the youngster's unique needs, typically include a structured educational and behavioral approach with related and specialized services provided as necessary. Examples of these related and specialized services may include, but are not limited to, the following:

- Nutrition services
- Occupational therapy
- Parent counseling
- Recreational therapy
- School nursing services
- Speech and language therapy

Early intervention for the young child with autism spectrum disorder begins with the development of an individualized family service plan (IFSP), which typically addresses needs in the areas of social skills, functional skills (dressing, toilet training, self-feeding), communication, and behavior. No one program is applicable to all children with ASD; the strengths and needs of each child, and the wishes of his or her family, must be considered in the development of an IFSP.

SUGGESTIONS FOR THE CLASSROOM

Tips for Teaching High-Functioning Individuals With Autism Spectrum Disorders

→ **Avoid abstract ideas whenever possible.** Individuals with autism spectrum disorders frequently have problems with abstract and conceptual thinking. While some students may eventually acquire a few abstract skills, others never will. When abstract concepts must be used, use visual cues, such as gestures or written words, to augment the abstract ideas.

→ **Avoid speech students might misinterpret.** Most high-functioning people with autism spectrum disorders use and interpret speech literally. Until you know the capabilities of the individual, it is recommended that you avoid
- idioms (save your breath, jump the gun, second thoughts, etc.);
- double meanings (most jokes have double meanings);
- sarcasm, such as saying, "Great!" after someone has just spilled a soft drink all over the table; and
- nicknames.

→ **Break down tasks.** If a pupil doesn't appear capable of learning a task, break it down into smaller steps, or present the task in several different ways (e.g., visually, verbally, and physically).

→ **Assist students with organizational skills.** Individuals with autism spectrum disorders often have difficulty with organizational skills, regardless of their intelligence and/or age. Even a "straight A" student with autism spectrum disorders who has a photographic memory can sometimes be incapable of remembering to bring a pencil to class or remembering a deadline for an assignment. In such cases, assistance should be provided in the least intrusive way possible.

Strategies could include putting a picture of a pencil on the cover of the student's notebook or reminders at the end of the day of assignments that are to be completed at home. Always praise the pupil when he or she remembers something he or she has previously forgotten.

→ **Prepare students for change.** It is important to prepare the student for all unexpected changes, such as an assembly, a substitute teacher, rescheduling of classes, and so forth. Use a written or visual schedule to prepare for change.

→ **Make adjustments for auditory and visual distractions.** Be aware that normal levels of auditory and visual input can be perceived by individuals with autism spectrum disorders as too much or too little. For example, the hum of fluorescent lighting is extremely distracting for some people with autism spectrum disorders. Consider environmental changes, such as removing some of the visual clutter from the room, or seating changes if the student seems distracted or upset by his or her classroom environment.

→ **Facilitate group work.** If a class activity involves pairing off or choosing partners, draw numbers or use some other arbitrary means of pairing. You could also ask a class leader whether he or she would agree to choose the individual with autism spectrum disorder as a partner. This should be arranged prior to pairing. The pupil with autism spectrum disorders is most often the individual left with no partner. This is unfortunate because this student could benefit most from having a partner.

→ Most importantly, be positive, be creative, and, most of all, be flexible!

SOURCE: Adapted from S. Moreno, "Tips for Teaching High-Functioning People with Autism." Available at http://www.aspergersyndrome.org/Articles/Tips-for-Teaching-High-Functioning-People-with-Aut.aspx. Used by permission.

Preschool Children With Autism Spectrum Disorders

Many preschool children with autism spectrum disorders lack even the most basic communication skills. For instance, they may not come when they are called, may not recognize their name, may have no idea of the notion of carrying out an activity upon either verbal or nonverbal request, and may have no concept of "First you do this, and then this happens." Safety also becomes an issue, as preschool children with ASD are able to run, open doors, and climb, but do not come when called, understand "no," or comprehend the possible dangers of busy streets or getting lost.

In planning for preschool children versus older children with ASD, the curriculum is usually less well defined. Even structured teaching needs special adaptation at the preschool level because of the behaviors that are targeted. Behavioral models provide useful starting points for establishing control of young children's attention and reducing interfering behaviors. It is important, however, to teach both communication and social skills as part of the overall program. Classroom adaptations for preschoolers with autism spectrum disorders are an important component for ensuring academic success (Dahle, 2003b).

Multiple instructional programs are available for preschool children with autism spectrum disorders. The most effective interventions incorporate a combination of developmental and behavioral approaches (Hyman & Levy, 2013). Highly structured programs, like those associated with behavioral strategies, produce long-lasting and significant gains for many young children with autism spectrum disorders (Hall, 2013; Myers & Johnson, 2007).

Many professionals recommend a minimum of twenty-five hours per week of intervention (Levy, Kruger, & Hyman, 2008). Effective programs for preschoolers with ASD typically share the following representative features:

- An emphasis on developing communication as well as social skills
- High degree of parent involvement
- Intensive behavioral interventions
- Involvement with typically developing children
- Interdisciplinary interventions
- Low teacher (staff)–student ratios
- Structured/organized learning environment
- Well-planned transition experiences (Levy, Kim, & Olive, 2006; Volkmar & Wiesner, 2009)

Transition Into Adulthood

As adolescents with autism spectrum disorders mature, they face the same developmental, psychological, social, and personal issues as their typical peers. However, their ability to deal with these issues is confounded by their unresolved communication, behavior, and social deficits. While adolescents with ASD may show a greater interest in other people, many still lack the most fundamental skills to form friendships (Hendricks & Wehman, 2009; Schall, Targett, & Wehman, 2013). Unfortunately, as their interest in others increases, their opportunities for structured social interactions usually decreases as they begin to transition from high school. Opportunities to participate in community programs are also frequently limited by the individual's lack of leisure and recreational skills and the limited availability of programs.

IDEA 2004 requires that school personnel assist the family with planning for transition from school beginning no later than age 16. It is important that both families and school personnel begin the transition planning as early as possible to address the myriad of potential problems that often confront adolescents with autism spectrum disorders.

The movement from the secure world of school to the uncertainty of adulthood is often challenging and stressful. For the adolescent with autism spectrum disorder

VIDEO

Classroom Suggestions

Working with children with autism spectrum disorders is often like riding a roller coaster without a seat belt—you never know what will be around the next corner or if the next bump will dump you out of the car. I have found that no two children and no two days are the same where ASD is involved. The needs of our children change on a daily, sometimes hourly, basis. Striving to meet these needs (sensory, anxiety, and food based) and provide an education is a full-time job. In my classroom there are five adults and ten children ages 5–11. Most of the children are included in the general education setting for some part of their day. Next year four of our kindergartners and I will take on the challenge of full inclusion for the first time in our county.

Inclusive Education Experience

I find the most difficult challenge facing my students is a fear of autism spectrum disorders. Most general education teachers have no experience with ASD; their only reference is the movie *Rain Man*. Many teachers will refuse to work with my students simply because of their label. To dispel this fear I arrange for my students to meet with their general education teachers in the week before school starts. This gives the teacher and the child a chance to check each other out. The teachers can see that this student is just a kid, a little odd sometimes, but nothing scary. This also gives the students a chance to see their new room and new teacher before the chaos of the first day. It gives them a reference point to start the year.

When I begin a year with a new teacher, I provide him or her with information about ASD, samples of the child's work, appropriate modifications, and the student's present level of performance. Then we meet over lunch or a snack during the week before school starts and discuss the student. Once

teachers put a face to the child's name they tend to be less afraid of the "autism" part of the experience.

Currently all of my students receive constant support in the general education setting (an aide or myself), and this seems to help the general education teachers feel more comfortable. Sometimes students will need to leave the room because of behavioral outbursts or breakdowns. Many teachers outside of special education do not feel qualified to handle these situations. I try to model the appropriate responses and encourage the other teachers to ask me questions. Prior to the school year I make emergency plans with the IEP team for each child. During our planning sessions I tell everyone that no one should attempt to restrain a child if he or she has not been trained. I take responsibility in most emergency situations.

When providing students with sensory strategies in the general education setting, I take into account how distracting the item will be. Sensory strategies should be discussed prior to implementation. General education teachers might not understand the importance of an item and take it away because it is a toy or the child is fidgeting. Strategies used within the general education setting should be discrete and small. Sometimes it is necessary to go in and explain the importance of a sensory item to the other students in the classroom. I have found that doing this eliminates the "I want what he has" battles.

I also provide an in-service for teachers in our county on autism spectrum disorders. This is a great way to reach a wider audience and help teachers who are not in my school. Offering experiences like this helps teachers become more comfortable with the disability. I encourage all of the teachers I work with to attend and am happy to have had several general education teachers from other schools participate. Providing learning experiences like this is a good way to bridge the gap between general and special education.

My students will be in the school system for at least 12 years. Their needs and cognitive skills will change over time; some of our boys will be in general education classes with no support by the time they reach the fifth grade. Part of my job as a special educator is to educate my colleagues about the

it may seem to be an especially demanding and complex task. Transition planning is designed to help facilitate the movement from school to adulthood. It is a coordinated process that includes the student, his or her family, education professionals, and representatives from a variety of community and social service agencies. Transition planning must be based on the individual's current and future needs, taking into account the student's abilities, preferences, and interests (see the accompanying Insights feature). To ensure that long-term goals are fulfilled it is vitally important that the individual with ASD meaningfully participate in the development of his or her own transition plan. The student's involvement is often critical to the success of the planning process.

VIDEO
Inclusion

disorder. If we are to advocate for the rights of our students, we have to educate the general population. Autism spectrum disorders are nothing to be afraid of.

Strategies for Inclusive Classrooms

- Bring models of modifications and accommodations to planning sessions—for example, a visual schedule, a test with a word bank. It is more effective to be able to show someone what you are suggesting.
- Provide brief articles about ASD to those teachers who are interested in learning more about the disability.
- Make sure fidgets and other small sensory items meet the students' needs without disrupting the rest of the class.
- Let other students try out the sensory items you bring in.
- Meet with the general education teachers as much as possible and let them know they can ask you to help prepare general lessons as well as modified lessons.
- Constantly assess the success of your students in the general education setting.
- Data are extremely important. Carry a clipboard or sticky notes. You should be able to back up any statement you make about your students.
- Provide social skills training for the students outside the general education setting. It may embarrass students to have social skills lessons with their peers. Sometimes it is better to practice the lesson outside the room and then bring it into the classroom.
- It is imperative to share the responsibilities of the classroom for inclusion to work. The students need to be a shared responsibility; there should be no "my" students and "your" students. Let the teacher know that you are there for all students.

Working With Parents and Families

In the field of autism spectrum disorders, working with the parents is essential to success. I often go on home visits with the younger students. This way I can model the responses to certain outbursts or inappropriate behavior. I have also gone to restaurants and grocery stores with the families to model behaviors. I have found that it is more successful to model than to just tell a parent what to do.

It is also important for the parents to become familiar with the general education teacher and classroom. In an inclusive program the parents should feel comfortable talking to the general education teacher as well as the special education teacher. When the special education teacher serves as a go-between (with parents and other teachers), communication breaks down. Parent-teacher conferences should be held with all the members of the team and not just one teacher. It is important to have the parents support each other. We started a parent support group this year. This provided the parents with someone other than me to turn to with questions and problems. I began it at the beginning of school, and then a parent took over. Parents need to talk to each other and compare experiences; having a child with such an intense disability can sometimes make parents feel isolated and helpless.

Special education teachers should familiarize themselves with the local resources for parents and families. Social services, food banks, and local agencies can be excellent resources. However, many families are too overwhelmed and do not know where to look for outside help.

Advice for Making Inclusion and Collaboration Work

My advice would be to always remember that kids are kids. A disability is only part of a child, and while it may shape most of his or her world, a kid is still a kid. Children still need love and support. You as the teacher need to know how to provide these things to your students and still encourage academic growth. Learn about the disability as much as possible, but learn everything about the kids.

—Sarah Reynolds
Leslie Fox Keyser Elementary School, Warren County, VA
Kindergarten–fifth grade

Regrettably, the overwhelming majority of transition planning meetings fail to include the individual with autism spectrum disorder (Hendricks & Wehman, 2009). Transition plans for the adolescent with ASD may include daily living skills, communication and social skills, living arrangements, community participation, and the development of vocational competencies, including interpersonal skills appropriate to the workplace (Hendricks & Wehman, 2009; Schall et al., 2013). Collaboration and coordination between the high school and community agencies, along with the involvement of the individual and his or her family, are crucial to ensure the future success of the student with ASD.

VIDEO
Making Inclusion Work

VIDEO
Inclusion Strategies

Effective Instructional Practices

Social Stories ™

Students with autism spectrum disorders typically experience difficulty interpreting social situations. These individuals are frequently unable to accurately assess and respond to various social, behavioral, and environmental cues. Social Stories represent an increasingly popular strategy for ameliorating these deficits and, in turn, enhancing the social skills of students with autism spectrum disorders. This intervention technique is also particularly helpful in facilitating the integration of pupils with ASD in inclusive learning environments.

A Social Story is an individually designed story aimed at increasing the individual's awareness and understanding of social situations and the perspectives of others while teaching appropriate responses and self-management techniques.

Researchers have identified the basic steps necessary for developing a Social Story:

1. Target a specific problematic social situation.

2. Identify salient features of context and setting.

3. Share this information with the individual and others.

The following is an example of a Social Story that is designed to explain to a student when it is appropriate to run at school:

Running

I like to run. It is fun to go fast.

It is OK to run when I am playing outside.

I can run when I am on the playground.

I can run during P.E.

It is not OK to run when I am inside, especially at school.

Running in the hallways is not safe.

Teachers worry that someone may get hurt if I run into them.

When people are inside, they walk.

I will try to walk in the hallways and only run when I am outside on the playground.

Writing a Social Story

Begin by observing the student in the situation you hope to address. Let the pupil's perspective tell you which aspects of the situation should be the focus of the story. Include those things that usually occur in the social situation, but also consider possible variations.

There are generally four types of sentences used in writing Social Stories:

- *Descriptive* sentences objectively define where a situation occurs, who is involved, what that person is doing, and why.
- *Perspective* sentences describe the reactions and feelings of others in a given situation.
- *Directive* sentences are positively stated, individualized statements of desired responses. They may begin with "I can try . . ." or "I will work on . . ." Try to avoid sentences starting with "Do not . . ." In the above example, the final sentence is the directive sentence.
- *Affirmative* sentences express a commonly shared cultural belief, opinion, or value.

A Social Story needs to have three to five descriptive and perspective sentences for each directive sentence. Avoid using too many directive sentences. They may be lost without adequate context.

Presenting a Social Story

Customize the language and the presentation to students' abilities. Young children and nonreaders will need pictures to accompany the story. The pictures need to be very simple and very specific. Delete extraneous details and backgrounds. These children will also require larger fonts and less information on each page. A storybook is a good idea. For older pupils and readers, the story can be presented on one page. Alternatively, each sentence can be mounted on black construction paper and bound in book format.

Present the story in a calm, stress-free environment. Be consistent. Present the story once each day, preferably right before the particular event. Once the story is mastered and the individual has incorporated it into his or her social repertoire, slowly decrease its use.

The empirical evidence on the effectiveness of Social Stories is growing. It is currently considered a validated or evidence-based practice.

SOURCE: Adapted from "Social Stories," Center for Autism and Related Disabilities, University of Florida. Retrieved February 8, 2010, from http://www.card.ufl.edu/socialstories.htm

For additional information on using Social Stories with children with autism spectrum disorders, see J. Xin and F. Sutman, "Using the Smart Board in Teaching Social Stories to Students with Autism," *Teaching Exceptional Children, 43*(4), 2011, pp. 18–24. Also visit The Gray Center for Social Learning and Understanding at http://www.thegraycenter.org.

When thinking about transition from high school, sometimes it is helpful to start the process with a list of questions to act as a springboard for discussion. The following questions can guide the IEP team in transition planning for young adults with ASD anticipating life beyond high school.

1. To what degree is the individual self-determined, that is, able to make personal decisions and accept responsibility for those decisions?

2. What is the student's and family's vision for this person's future?

3. Where does he or she wish to live and work as an adult?

4. What critical skills and abilities are needed to create an enviable life for this person?

5. What skills and abilities does the student currently possess that match his or her vision?

6. What additional training or skills does the individual require in order to fulfill his or her vision?

7. Is this person able to live independently and care for him- or herself?

8. What is the depth of the student's experiences in the community and world of work?

9. What resources are available that will increase the likelihood that this individual will achieve his or her vision?

10. What experiences, linkages, and resources are needed to ensure a smooth transition to adult life?

SOURCE: Adapted from C. Schall, P. Targett, and P. Wehman, "Application for Youth with Autism Spectrum Disorders," in P. Wehman (Ed.), *Life Beyond the Classroom*, 5th ed., (Baltimore, MD: Paul H. Brookes, 2013), p. 457.

Adults With Autism Spectrum Disorders

Because ASD is a lifelong developmental disorder, many individuals with autism spectrum disorders are unable to either live or work independently as adults. Although symptoms may decrease with age, a majority of adults with ASD continue to manifest significant impairments (Gabriels, 2011; Seltzer et al., 2011). Only a small number of individuals with autism spectrum disorders are able to achieve a degree of independence in adulthood (American Psychiatric Association, 2013; Howlin, Goode, Hutton, & Rutter, 2004).

Adults with ASD, and their families, are typically confronted with two main issues of adulthood—living arrangements and employment possibilities. In both instances, the unique characteristics and ability level of the individual will influence decisions and options.

Regarding living arrangements, if the person is unable to live independently, families and the individual, if capable, have many decisions to make. Choices range from residential (institutional) care, to foster care, to group home settings, to supervised apartment living. In some situations there is the possibility of living with an adult sibling as parents age. Generally speaking, there is no one "best" or "correct" placement. The needs of the adult with ASD and the availability of community resources will likely influence decisions keeping in mind that maximum independenceand integration in the community is a goal for many adults with autism spectrum disorders.

Employment Options

Large numbers of adults with autism spectrum disorders experience high unemployment or underemployment despite the fact that many of these individuals are capable

VIDEO

Transitions

Some adults with autism spectrum disorders live in group homes located in residential neighborhoods.

of work (Gerhardt & Lainer, 2011; Hendricks & Wehman, 2009). Persons with ASD often possess the job skills needed to be successful in the workplace especially if the requirements of the job are aligned with the individual's strengths and interests. Yet some adults experience difficulty in managing the social requirements of the work site; for instance, they may greet a coworker with a hug rather than a handshake. "Soft job skills," like how to appropriately interact with a supervisor, tolerating change, and appropriate conversational topics during a break, may be as crucial or slightly more important for successful employment than the actual job or "hard" skills (Schall et al., 2013).

Two common employment options for the adult with ASD who cannot work independently are sheltered workshops and supported employment. Sheltered workshops are supervised, structured settings that provide training in specific job skills. Typically, businesses contract with a sheltered workshop to complete a particular task in a contracted length of time. Sheltered workshops have many disadvantages, including low wages, minimal vocational training, and a lack of interaction with typical peers (Gerhardt & Holmes, 2005). Unfortunately, for many adults with autism spectrum disorders, sheltered workshops tend to be a final job placement rather than a step toward employment in the community.

In a supported employment model, the adult with autism spectrum disorder works at a job in the community alongside typical coworkers. Intensive training, assistance, and support are provided by a job coach or supported employment specialist. As the individual with ASD gains competency on the job, support is gradually faded. A job coach may supervise one or more adults for all or part of the day. In addition to offering on-site training, the employment specialist may assist with transportation needs, provide information to typical coworkers about individuals with ASD, and act as a liaison between family members and the employer. Over the years, an increasing number of individuals with autism spectrum disorders have secured employment in the community as a result of supported employment initiatives (Gerhardt & Holmes, 2005; Hendricks & Wehman, 2009). Employment opportunities typically range from food services worker, to retail possibilities, to custodial and housekeeping positions as well as entry-level white-collar jobs.

Family Issues

Autism spectrum disorders can affect the entire family constellation. Parents, as well as siblings, are often confronted with significant and potentially lifelong challenges. Usually by the infant's first birthday parents and other family members are aware that something is different with the child. In some instances, by the time the parents receive a diagnosis of ASD, they have spent years dealing with various professionals searching for answers and the cause of their child's disability. As a consequence, confusion, frustration, and even anger are part of their daily existence. A diagnosis of ASD is an important step in parents' quest to understand their son or daughter's disability. It can also give parents a sense of direction and permits them to seek needed services and support, not only for their child but also for themselves.

Mothers are typically the primary caregivers for the child with autism spectrum disorders, although fathers are often helpful with specific tasks. Not surprisingly, the presence of a child with ASD sometimes exerts a pervasive and stressful effect on mothers and other family members while directly or indirectly impacting many aspects of family life (Brobst, Clopton, & Hendrick, 2009; Ekas & Whitman, 2011; Seligman & Darling, 2007). Some parents find benefit from joining a support group. Other parents of children with ASD are often a tremendous source of information, resources, and emotional support.

Many parents struggle with the demands placed on their typical children by their brother or sister with ASD. It is important that siblings understand the diagnosis of ASD on a developmentally appropriate level. As typical children grow, information needs to be continually presented and discussed with them rather than relying on a "one-shot" explanation (Autism Society of America, 2013b). Also, as parents age, siblings need to understand what plans have been made for the individual with ASD and what, if any, is their responsibility (Gallagher, Powell, & Rhodes, 2006).

Research on siblings of children with autism spectrum disorders is somewhat limited, and it has produced mixed results (Marcus, Kunce, & Schopler, 2005; Meadan, Stoner, & Angell, 2010). Studies suggest that some siblings show no negative effects while other research has shown that siblings of children with ASD develop adjustment problems. Sibling support groups are a popular vehicle for supporting siblings and giving them needed information about ASD. These support groups encourage the siblings of individuals with autism spectrum disorders to express their feelings and to ask questions about ASD.

Issues of Diversity

Autism spectrum disorders know no racial, ethnic, or social boundaries. ASD occurs in all races, societies, socioeconomic groups, and types of families (Centers for Disease Control and Prevention, 2013). As we saw earlier, no social or psychological characteristics of parents or families have proven to be associated with autism spectrum disorders.

Technology and Individuals With Autism Spectrum Disorders

Technology for students with autism spectrum disorders falls along multiple lines, including augmentative and alternative communication (AAC) devices, prompting devices (for example, video modeling, audio prompting), and computer-assisted instruction (CAI) (Bouck, Satsangi, Doughty, & Courtney, 2013). Additionally, considerable attention is focusing on using mobile technology devices for pupils with autism spectrum disorders, including cell phones, iPods, and iPads (Ayres, Mechling, & Sansosti, 2013).

AAC is commonly used for individuals with autism spectrum disorders and, like all technology for students with disabilities, runs the gamut from low-tech to high-tech. One popular low-tech AAC device is the Picture Exchange Communication System® (PECS®) (Bondy, 2012). PECS® involves the presentation or selection of a picture as a means of communication. Not only can picture symbols be used for communication for students with autism spectrum disorders, but also picture symbols are commonly used to create picture schedules (Bondy, 2012) (see Figure 10.3).

augmentative and alternative communication (AAC): Symbols, aids, strategies, and techniques used as a supplement or alternative to oral language.

computer-assisted instruction (CAI): The application of computer technology to deliver instruction.

VIDEO
Advice for Parents

Figure 10.3 **Picture Communication Aids**

SOURCE: Courtesy of Pyramid Educational Products, Inc.

High-tech AAC devices such as speech-generating devices (SGDs) or voice output communication aids (VOCAs) are also frequently used by individuals with autism spectrum disorders who do not possess verbal communication skills (see Figure 10.4). High-tech AAC devices are tools that present speech when an icon or button is selected or words are typed. These devices vary in cost and functionality; for some technologies an individual needs to record the words or phrases into the tool while in other instances synthesized speech is produced (Ball, Bilyeu, Prentice, & Beukelman, 2005). AAC devices are increasingly being accessed through mobile technologies (for example, iPod, iPad), through an app called Proloquo2Go® (Sennott & Bowker, 2009). Proloquo2Go involves students selecting symbols to generate speech, similar to stand-alone, high-tech AAC devices.

Self-operated prompting devices are another example of popular technology for students with autism spectrum disorders. Prompting devices are tools that provide prompts to individuals as they work to complete a task. Over the years, prompting devices have undergone transformations—beginning as static picture-based tools (for example, picture symbols), and then moving to audio tools (for example, audio recorders), and now, video tools (for example, DVD players) (Mechling, Gast, & Seid, 2010). Today, as with other AAC devices, prompting devices utilize mobile technologies (for example, iPad) (Ayres et al., 2013).

speech-generating device (SGD): A high-tech augmentative or alternative communication device capable of generating speech.

voice output communication aid (VOCA): Device that can be programmed to produce speech.

Figure 10.4 **Example of a High-Tech AAC Speech-Generating Device**

SOURCE: Proloquo2Go® is an AssistiveWare® product. Used with permission.

AssistiveWare is a registered trade name of AssistiveWare B.V. Proloquo2Go and AssistiveWare are registered trademarks of AssistiveWare B.V. in the U.S. and other countries.

Finally, CAI is an area where technology is often incorporated for learners with autism spectrum disorders. Researchers support the use of CAI in the academic domains of literacy, science, and mathematics (Bouck et al., 2013; Pennington, 2010; Smith, Spooner, & Wood, 2013). Bouck and her colleagues (2013), for example, successfully taught elementary students with autism spectrum disorders addition and subtraction through use of virtual manipulatives with the National Library of Virtual Manipulatives (http://nlvm.usu.edu/en/).

Trends, Issues, and Controversies

Parents of individuals with autism spectrum disorders are exposed to a variety of treatments that promise dramatic improvement or "cures" for their child. With so many possible causes of ASD, there are likely as many possible treatments that may help the family in caring for its child. Unfortunately, research has not advanced to the point that the cause can always be matched to an appropriate treatment. Families often rely on anecdotal reports of treatments rather than waiting for the research to support the claims of improvement. Who can blame them? As long as the treatment does not harm the child, some families do not believe they can wait for science to catch up and miss an opportunity that could make a difference in the life of their child. Many parents stay up-to-date on treatment methodologies and current debates using the Internet. Unfortunately, these parents frequently "become susceptible to the promotions of specific therapies that usually have little to offer other than hope" (Marcus et al., 2005, p. 1058).

AUDIO

Chapter 10 Summary

AUDIO

Controversies

In the language of the ASD community, unproven techniques and therapies fall under the heading of complementary and alternative medicine (CAM) (Myers & Johnson, 2007; Volkmar & Wiesner, 2009; Warren & Stone, 2011; Zimmer, 2013). A multitude of treatment options, both biological and nonbiological, are considered CAM therapies, including, for example, dietary and vitamin treatments, hormone injections, facilitated communication, music therapy, and auditory integration training, along with optometric training. While case reports and anecdotal evidence lend credence to the popularity of these interventions, the scientific literature, which requires the use of a randomized, double-blind, placebo-controlled study, does not support these treatments (Challman, Voigt, & Myers, 2008; Hyman & Levy, 2011, 2013; Levy, Kruger et al., 2008). What is regrettably lacking in the field of autism spectrum disorders are "large-scale, rigorously designed, replicated intervention studies that compare the major autism intervention approaches" (Marcus et al., 2005, p. 1059). Until this evidence is available, parents and professionals alike need to carefully evaluate treatment options for individuals with autism spectrum disorders. Families should be especially cautious of a treatment strategy or intervention if they encounter

- treatments that are based on overly simple scientific theories;
- therapies that claim to be effective for multiple, unrelated conditions or symptoms;
- claims that children will respond dramatically and some will be cured;
- use of case reports or anecdotal data rather than carefully designed studies to support claims for treatment;
- lack of peer-reviewed references or denial of the need for controlled studies; or
- treatments that are said to have no potential or reported adverse effects. (Myers & Johnson, 2007, p. 1173)

Parents and professionals alike can locate current information about autism spectrum disorders by visiting the Healing Thresholds website (http://autism.healing-thresholds.com). Here you will find the latest scientific research on ASD explained in terms understandable by a layperson. Additionally, the federal government via the National Institutes of Health offers parent-friendly information regarding the scientific validity of CAM treatments at http://nccam.nih.gov.

complementary and alternative medicine (CAM): Treatment strategies and interventions for individuals with autism spectrum disorders that lack empirical support.

CHAPTER IN REVIEW

Defining Autism Spectrum Disorders: An Evolving Process

- The field of autism spectrum disorders is still relatively new, with the first clinical description of ASD appearing in the literature in 1943.
- Autism spectrum disorders were not described as a distinct clinical category until 1977.
- The DSM-5 characterizes ASD as a neurodevelopmental disorder.

- IDEA included autism as a separate diagnostic category in 1990. The definition of autism in IDEA 2004 parallels the description of autism spectrum disorder in the DSM-5.

Prevalence of Autism Spectrum Disorders

- According to the federal government, approximately 458,000 pupils ages 3–21 were identified as having autism during the 2011–2012 school year.
- The number of individuals exhibiting ASD has risen dramatically.

Etiology of Autism Spectrum Disorders

- At the present time we do not know the cause of ASD.
- Current research suggests genetic contributions, structural abnormalities of the brain, and environmental variables as possible causes of autism spectrum disorders.

Characteristics of Individuals With Autism Spectrum Disorders

- Three cardinal characteristics portray autism spectrum disorders: impaired social interaction, repetitive and restricted behaviors, and communication deficits.
- Many individuals with autism spectrum disorders exhibit some degree of intellectual impairment.

Assessment of Autism Spectrum Disorders

- There is no specific test to diagnose ASD. A multidisciplinary team of professionals is often involved in assessing individuals suspected of having autism spectrum disorders.
- Behavioral assessments and ratings scales are frequently used when evaluating individuals with autism spectrum disorders.

Educational Considerations

- Slightly more than one third of all school-age students with autism spectrum disorders receive services in a self-contained classroom with an approximately equal number of pupils educated in the general education classroom.
- Individuals with ASD require structured educational programs. Behavior intervention strategies are often used with students with autism spectrum disorders.
- There are a growing number of evidence-based practices.

Services for Young Children With Autism Spectrum Disorders

- Early intervention makes a positive difference in the life of youngsters with autism spectrum disorders.
- Early intervention programs typically address social skills, communication deficits, and behavioral issues.

Adolescents and Adults With Autism Spectrum Disorders

- Transition planning for adolescents with ASD must be based on the individual's current and future needs and goals.
- Transition plans often focus on daily living skills, communication and social skills, living arrangements, community participation, and the development of vocational competencies.
- Living arrangements and employment options are two areas of concern for many adults with ASD.

Technology and Individuals With Autism Spectrum Disorders

- Various low- and high-tech devices are assisting individuals with autism spectrum disorders overcome communication deficits and experience success in the classroom.

Trends, Issues, and Controversies

- The field of autism spectrum disorders is replete with unproven therapies and strategies that are identified as complementary and alternative medicine.

STUDY QUESTIONS

1. Describe the DSM-5 definition and compare it to the IDEA definition of ASD.

2. Prior to the acknowledgment of genetic and neurological causes of autism spectrum disorders, what were the prevailing theories and treatments?

3. Why is the prevalence of ASD increasing?

4. List three possible causes of autism spectrum disorders.

5. What does the term *autistic savant* mean?

6. Identify the three cardinal characteristics of ASD.

7. Detail the characteristics of the most common interventions used to educate individuals with autism spectrum disorders.

8. What are the key issues related to transitioning into adulthood for individuals with ASD?

9. Describe the issues that families typically deal with when they have a child with autism spectrum disorders.

10. How is technology being used with individuals with ASD?

11. What is complementary and alternative medicine? Describe the type of research that is needed to rigorously evaluate treatment options for individuals with autism spectrum disorders.

autism spectrum disorders,   329

Asperger syndrome,   333

autistic savant,   337

psychogenic theories,   334

applied behavior analysis (ABA),   334

theory of mind,   338

joint attention,   338

augmentative and alternative communication (AAC),   353

computer-assisted instruction (CAI),   353

speech-generating device (SGD),   354

voice output communication aid (VOCA),   354

complementary and alternative medicine (CAM),   356

LEARNING ACTIVITIES ▪▪▪▪▪▪▪▪▪▪▪▪▪▪▪▪▪▪▪▪▪▪▪▪▪▪▪▪▪▪▪▪▪▪

1. Observe students with autism spectrum disorders in a special education setting and in an inclusive learning environment. What are the advantages and disadvantages of both educational settings? What kinds of educational interventions did you observe in each location? Which type of educational environment would you want for your child?

2. Participate in a local support group for individuals with autism spectrum disorders. Listen to the families' concerns and needs. Is there something you or your friends could do to help, such as providing respite care? Have you ever considered extending your friendship to an adult with ASD? Consider joining a support group.

ORGANIZATIONS CONCERNED WITH AUTISM SPECTRUM DISORDERS

Autism Society of America

www.autism-society.org

Autism Speaks

www.autismspeaks.org

Indiana Resource Center for Autism

www.iidc.indiana.edu/index.php?pageId=32

Kennedy Krieger Institute

www.kennedykrieger.org

Ohio Center for Autism and Low Incidence

www.ocali.org

REFLECTING ON STANDARDS ▪▪▪▪▪▪▪▪▪▪▪▪▪▪▪▪▪▪▪▪▪▪▪▪▪▪▪▪▪▪

The following exercises are designed to help you learn to apply the Council for Exceptional Children (CEC) standards to your teaching practice. Each of the reflection exercises below correlates with knowledge or a skill within the CEC standards. For the full text of each of the related CEC standards, please refer to the standards integration grid located in Appendix B.

Focus on Learning Environments (*CEC Initial Preparation Standard 2.2*)

Reflect on what you have learned about the social interaction difficulties individuals with autism spectrum disorders sometimes

have. If you were to have a student with autism spectrum disorders in your class, how might you encourage him or her to participate in group and one-on-one interactions with other students? How might you modify assignments to allow for positive social interaction?

Focus on Collaboration (*CEC Initial Preparation Standard 7.3*)

Reflect on what you have learned about inclusion of students with autism spectrum disorders in a general education classroom. If you were to teach at a school where students with autism spectrum disorders received services in a self-contained special education classroom, how might you coordinate with the special education teacher to involve his or her students in your classroom? How might you be able to involve students with autism spectrum disorders to help them learn affective, social, and life skills while working with general education students?

Individuals With Speech and Language Impairments

▪▪▪▪▪▪▪▪▪▪▪▪▪▪▪▪▪▪▪▪

A Parent's Story

Adam's life started with my pregnancy. It was a normal pregnancy with no complications. I had a caesarean section when Adam was a week overdue. He weighed 9.5 pounds, a very healthy baby. Adam reached all of his developmental milestones at normal times. He crawled at 6 months, walked at 10 months, and said his first word at 12 months. His speech and language continued to develop at a normal pace.

When it was time to eat solid foods, we had a problem. Adam had a strong gag reflex and did not seem to want to eat any foods that were not pureed. I came to the conclusion that he was not just picky. In addition, Adam drooled a great deal until he turned 3. I knew this was a lot longer than normal. I talked to the pediatrician about the eating and drooling. He said it was probably from teething and told me to keep introducing foods—eventually Adam would eat them.

When Adam was about 2 years old, I noticed that he could not pronounce *n, t, d, l,* and *s* correctly. I knew that *l* and *s* were not supposed to be mastered until the age of 4. I just thought he would master these by the time he was 4.

My husband, Rick, and I started to notice a great deal of frustration in Adam, who was now 3. What was the cause of it? We did not know and assumed it was age related. He did not seem to understand punishment. We would ask him why he was on his "thinking bench," and he could never answer. He would get more upset and answer something inappropriate. We would go to the pool during the summer. Adam would ask at least ten times, "Where are we going?" I would answer and could tell he just did not understand. I would try to rephrase, and sometimes this would help. Adam did not seem to understand simple directions, question words (*why, how*), sequencing, verb tense, and common language concepts. All of these things were very subtle, and other people did not notice. He was not acquiring language concepts that children learn without formal teaching, and his pronunciation was not getting better.

In the fall, Adam started preschool. At this time I was starting to put some of the pieces together and had some concerns. In October I had a teacher conference and told the teacher of my concerns and asked her if she noticed anything. She did. I told her I felt like he would hear me but not understand

LEARNING OBJECTIVES

After reading Chapter 11, you should be able to:

- **Define** speech, language, and communication.
- **Identify** the five components of language.
- **List** three different types of speech impairments and five forms of language disorders.
- **Define** central auditory processing disorder.
- **Distinguish** between functional and organic causes of speech and language impairments.
- **Explain** the differences between receptive and expressive language impairments.
- **Describe** procedures used for assessing speech and language impairments.
- **Explain** the function of augmentative and alternative communication devices.

VIDEO

Speech Impairments

what I said. She noticed that he did not understand *yes* and *no* questions and, when asked simple things that she knew he knew, he would say, "I don't know." He was still a very picky eater but would try a few new things and only eat a very small bite. The teacher recommended that we have him screened by the speech pathologist who was coming to the school in a few weeks.

Adam went to the speech and language screening, and we waited for the results. The speech pathologist sent home a brief report that gave his results and called us that night to discuss them. I remember it vividly, even that it was raining that night. She told me he had scored very low, in the 1 percent range for some of the tests, matter-of-factly telling me he needed to be evaluated fully and would possibly need to go to a special school. I was floored! I wish my husband had been on the phone with me to hear it for himself; I knew there were going to be many questions that I did not ask or have an answer for. I wondered how this could be so severe and how I could be that blind to the severity. I knew something was wrong, but I did not realize that it was this bad.

Adam was scheduled at a facility known in town for being on the cutting edge and recommended on the school list of places for referral. Rick and I both went to the evaluation and met with the speech pathologist afterward. She was very kind and supportive, giving us books to read and scheduling Adam's therapy. Adam was diagnosed with a mild to moderate language disorder, mild articulation difficulty, and low facial muscle tone. I felt very overwhelmed. What do we do now? How can I help? Does this mean he will have to struggle his whole life? How can I manage this? Rick was upset as well, but in a different way. He was defensive. He asked if Adam was stupid, and would he go to college? We were both dealing with fear and sadness that something was wrong with our child. After we talked more to each other and learned more about what was wrong, things settled down. The overall experience with the first speech pathologist was terrible, and the second time we felt very supported.

Adam is now 4 and has made great progress. He has matured socially, has improved his speech and language skills, and goes to occupational therapy as well. Both Rick and I incorporate therapy into everyday happenings. I feel like this is just a part of my everyday normal life and not a big problem. I primarily take Adam to therapy. Rick takes him sometimes as well. It has been important for both of us, as parents, to stay involved with his therapy.

I still wonder about the future and how this will affect Adam. I have to put that aside and do the best that I can now, hoping for the best later. Adam likes to go to therapy and is much less frustrated. Because he was diagnosed and started therapy at such a young age, his future will be bright.

—Lori Smith

■□■■■■■□■■□■■■■■□■□■■□■■■■□■■□■■■□■■■□■□■■■■□■■□

Although Adam's mother does not mention an individualized education program (IEP), Adam may have been one of the more than 342,000 preschoolers who received services under the speech or language impairment category of the Individuals with Disabilities Education Improvement Act (IDEA, 2004) during the 2011–2012 school year (U.S. Department of Education, 2013a). Services for young children like Adam will be described later in this chapter.

VIDEO

Speech Therapist
Interview

The main focus of this chapter is on students who demonstrate communication difficulties that are not the result of or directly associated with another disability. The disability category under which these children are served is *speech or language impairment*. The communication difficulties of children who have a primary disability other than speech or language impairment are noted but not discussed as they are addressed in other chapters. First, we will introduce the discussion of speech and language delays and disorders with a review of the nature of speech, language, and communication.

The Nature of Speech, Language, and Communication

Of all the singular gifts bestowed on humans, the acquisition and use of language is undoubtedly the most miraculous. Most people give little thought to this remarkable achievement that begins in the womb. Even before they are out of diapers, most children have a vocabulary of fifty words or more, and by age 2, they are producing short but intelligible sentences. Three-year-olds are chatty and engaging as they begin to acquire the rules for tense and number, often overextending them to produce amusing statements like "I seed two mouses in the picture." At this age they are also discovering that words have different meanings depending on how you string them together. By kindergarten, most children have an impressive vocabulary, typically in excess of two thousand words. Table 11.1 shows the amazing accomplishments of language learning. When attainment of any of the milestones shown in Table 11.1 is delayed or there is a disturbance in one or more of the components necessary for communication, the child is at risk for a language disorder.

It is important to begin by differentiating the concepts *speech, language,* and *communication* so that you can be as precise as possible when you talk about speech and language impairments with other professionals. You are familiar with the three terms, but you may have used them interchangeably, and they have very distinct meanings. Speech is the expression of language with sounds—essentially the oral modality for language. Compared to other ways of conveying ideas and intentions (for example, manual signing, writing, gesturing), speech is probably the most difficult. Humans are not the only species to produce sounds, but we are the only species with a vocal tract that permits production of the variety and complexity of sounds required for speech. Speech production depends on precise physiological and neuromuscular coordination of (1) respiration (the act of breathing), (2) phonation (production of sound by the larynx and vocal fold), and (3) articulation (use of the lips, tongue, teeth, and hard and soft palates to form speech sounds). Speech is considerably more than a motor behavior. It is willed, planned, and programmed by the central nervous system—the brain, spinal cord, and peripheral nervous system.

Language is a "rule-based method of communication involving the comprehension and use of signs and symbols by which ideas are represented" (Bryant, Smith, & Bryant, 2008, p. 56). The main purpose of language, according to experts (Hoff, 2014; Owens, 2012; Vaughn & Bos, 2012), is communication or self-expression. Essentially, language is a social tool (Owens, 2012, 2014). In many ways language can be thought of as a code. It is a code in the sense that it is not a direct representation of the world but, rather, something with which to represent ideas and concepts about the world. It is a very complex and multidimensional system of symbols and the rules for appropriately using these symbols.

What does it mean to *know* a language? It means that you are able to apply the basic units and the complex rules governing relationships among sounds, words, sentences, meaning, and use of the language. Language contains five major interrelated

speech: The expression of language via sounds; the oral modality for language.

language: A code used to communicate ideas via a conventional system of arbitrary signals.

Table III.I **Milestones for Acquiring Language**

Age Range	Milestones in Language Development
By Age 1	• Recognizes name • Says first words • Imitates familiar words (echolalia) • Understands simple instructions • Recognizes words as symbols for objects: hears "ball"—points to ball
Between 1 and 2 Years of Age	• Understands "no" • Uses 10 to 20 words, including names • Combines two words such as "Daddy bye-bye" • Waves good-bye and plays pat-a-cake • Makes the "sounds" of familiar animals • Gives a toy when asked • Uses words such as "more" to make wants known • Points to his or her toes, eyes, and nose • Brings object from another room when asked
Between 2 and 3 Years of Age	• Identifies body parts • Carries on "conversation" with self and dolls • Asks "What's that?" and "Where's my?" • Uses two-word negative phrases such as "No want" • Forms some plurals by adding "s": "book," "books" • Has a 450-word vocabulary • Gives first name, holds up fingers to tell age • Combines nouns and verbs: "Mommy go" • Understands simple time concepts: "last night," "tomorrow" • Refers to self as "me" rather than by name • Tries to get adult attention: "Watch me" • Likes to hear same story repeated • May say "no" when means "yes" • Talks to other children as well as adults • Solves problems by talking instead of hitting or crying • Answers "where" questions • Names common pictures and things • Uses short sentences like "Me want more" or "Me want cookie," matches 3–4 colors, knows big and little
Between 3 and 4 Years of Age	• Can tell a story • Has sentence length of 4–5 words • Has a vocabulary of nearly 1,000 words • Names at least one color • Understands "yesterday," "summer," "lunchtime," "tonight," "little/big" • Begins to obey requests like "Put the block under the chair" • Knows his or her last name, name of street on which he or she lives, and several nursery rhymes
Between 4 and 5 Years of Age	• Has sentence length of 4–5 words • Uses past tense correctly • Has a vocabulary of nearly 1,500 words • Points to colors red, blue, yellow, and green • Identifies triangles, circles, and squares • Understands "in the morning," "next," "noontime" • Can speak of imaginary conditions such as "I hope" • Asks many questions, including "Who?" and "Why?"
Between 5 and 6 Years of Age	• Has a sentence length of 5–6 words • Has a vocabulary of around 2,000 words • Defines objects by their use (you eat with a fork) and can tell what objects are made of • Knows spatial relations like "on top," "behind," "far," and "near" • Knows his or her address • Identifies a penny, nickel, and dime • Knows common opposites like "big/little" • Understands "same" and "different" • Counts 10 objects • Asks questions for information • Distinguishes left and right hand • Uses all types of sentences—for example, "Let's go to the store after we eat"

NOTE: Some variation in reaching developmental milestones is common.

SOURCE: Adapted from Learning Disabilities Association of America, *Speech and Language Milestone Chart*, 1999. Available from http://www.ldonline.org/article/6313/

yet distinct elements (see Figure 11.1)—phonology, morphology, syntax, semantics, and pragmatics—that are present at both the receptive and expressive levels. These components, according to Owens (2012), represent the basic rule systems found in language. *Form* incorporates phonology, morphology, and syntax, or the elements that connect sounds or symbols with meaning. *Content* encompasses the meaning of words and sentences (semantics), while *use* addresses the social aspects of language, or pragmatics.

Form. The phonology of language includes the sounds that are characteristic of that language, the rules governing their distribution and sequencing, and the stress and intonation patterns that accompany sounds. There are approximately forty-five different speech sounds in the English language, which we call phonemes.

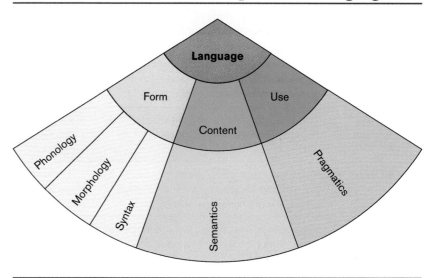

Figure 11.1 **Basic Components of Language**

SOURCE: Adapted from R. Owens, *Language Development: An Introduction,* 8th ed. (Boston, MA: Allyn & Bacon, 2012), p. 19.

The morphology of a language includes the rules governing how words are formed from meaningful units called morphemes.

The syntax of language contains rules for how to string words together to form phrases and sentences, what sentences are acceptable, and how to transform sentences into other sentences. Knowledge of the syntax of a language allows a speaker to generate an infinite number of new sentences and recognize sentences that are not grammatically acceptable.

Content. At the most basic level, semantics is the linguistic realization of what the speaker knows about the world—what people talk about. Semantics is concerned with relationships (1) between words and meanings, (2) between words, (3) between word meanings and sentence meanings, and (4) between linguistic meaning and nonlinguistic reality.

Use. The major concern in pragmatics is the effectiveness of language in achieving desired functions in social situations. Attitudes, personal history, the setting, the topic of conversation, and the details of the preceding discourse are among the social and contextual factors that determine how speakers cast their sentences (and how listeners interpret them). Table 11.2 summarizes these five components of language. You may wish to refer back to this table when you are reading about specific disorders later in this chapter.

Communication is the exchange of ideas, information, thoughts, and feelings. It does not necessarily involve speech. Examples of nonlinguistic communication behaviors are gestures, posture, eye contact, facial expression, and head and body movement. Nonlinguistic communication modes may be used as the only method of communication, or they may be used in conjunction with oral language. The communication process begins when a person has an idea or intention and wants to share it. The idea or intention is formulated into a message and then expressed to another person or persons. The other person receives the message and reacts to or acknowledges it. In any communication there is always a potential for message distortion because of the many possible message modalities and the many possible connotations and perceptions of the communication partners.

The accompanying Insights feature illustrates one contemporary viewpoint on how young children acquire language (page 367).

phonology: The sound system of a language, including the use of sounds to create meaningful syllables and words.

morphology: Dictates how the smallest meaningful units of our language (morphemes) are combined to form words.

syntax: A series of linguistic rules that determine word order and combinations to form sentences and how such word order is used in the communication process.

semantics: A psycholinguistic system that involves word meanings and word relationships and their use in communication.

pragmatics: A sociolinguistic system involving the use of communication skills in social contexts.

communication: The sharing or exchange of ideas, information, thoughts, and feelings. Does not necessarily require speech or language.

Table 11.2 **Components of Language**

Component	Definition	Receptive level	Expressive level
Phonology	The sounds characteristic of a language, the rules governing their distribution and sequencing, and the stress and intonation patterns that accompany sounds	Discrimination of speech sounds	Articulation of speech sounds
Morphology	The rules governing how words are formed from the basic element of meaning	Understanding of the grammatical structure of words	Use of grammar in words
Syntax	Rules for how to string words together to form phrases and sentences—the relationships among the elements of a sentence	Understanding of phrases and sentences	Use of grammar in phrases and sentences
Semantics	The linguistic realization of what the speaker knows about the world—the meanings of words and sentences	Understanding of word meanings and word relationships	Use of word meanings and word relationships
Pragmatics	The social effectiveness of language in achieving desired functions—rules related to the use of language in social contexts	Understanding of social and contextual cues	Use of language to affect others

SOURCE: Adapted from L. McCormick, "introduction to language acquisition," in L. McCormick, D. Loeb, and R. Schiefelbusch (eds.), *Supporting Children with Communication Difficulties in Inclusive Settings,* 2nd ed. (Boston, MA: Allyn & Bacon, 2003).

Defining Speech and Language Impairments

Speech and/or language impairments are problems in communication and related areas such as oral motor function. Delays and disorders may range from those so subtle that they have little or no impact on daily living and socialization to the inability to produce speech or to understand and use language. Fortunately, only a very small percentage of children are at the most extreme level of severity. However, because of the importance of language and communication skills in a child's life (or, for that matter, in anyone's life), even mild to moderate disorders or disturbances can have a profound effect on all aspects of life, sometimes isolating children from their peers and their educational environments.

Severe communication and language disabilities are most likely to occur secondary to pervasive cognitive, neurological, or physical disabilities. Table 11.3 provides an overview of language difficulties that are secondary to learning disabilities, autism spectrum disorders, intellectual disability, and traumatic brain injury. These communication difficulties are described in more depth in their respective chapters.

The IDEA 2004 (PL 108–446) label for students with communication difficulties is *speech or language impairment*. Children are eligible for services in this category if they have "a communication disorder, such as stuttering, impaired articulation, a language impairment, or a voice impairment, that adversely affects a child's educational performance" (34 C.F.R. § 300.8 [c] [11]). IDEA includes speech and language disorders under both special education and related services.

The American Speech-Language-Hearing Association (1993) defines a communication disorder as "an impairment in the ability to receive, send, process, and comprehend concepts or verbal, nonverbal, and graphic symbols systems. A communication disorder may be evident in the processes of hearing, language, and/or speech" (p. 40).

INSIGHTS

The Genetics of Speech

How Do We Learn Language?

It is safe to say that most 4-year-olds know nothing about subjects and verbs, direct and indirect objects, gerunds, participles, and infinitives. Yet they can talk your ear off in complete, complex sentences. So how do children learn to speak language so easily and with almost no adult instruction? Do they absorb it, or is it inborn knowledge?

According to University of Alabama at Birmingham linguist David Basilico, PhD, it's simply human nature. "Having and acquiring language is a biological property of being human, like having opposable thumbs," he says. Fifty years ago, however, behaviorists theorized that children learn everything they need to know from their environments. The problem with that conclusion is the "poverty of stimulus," Basilico explains. "There's just not enough information in what children hear in ordinary conversation to generate a full knowledge of English." Basilico says that most linguists now agree that humans have some genetic knowledge that makes learning language easy and natural, much like learning to walk. Babies aren't born with the complete English lexicon, of course, but they have an intuitive understanding of the rules and principles that underlie language, a concept known as "universal grammar." Basilico describes universal grammar as a menu of language possibilities. It provides a variety of options for the logical construction of a language—but not an infinite variety.

"Language picks and chooses from that menu," Basilico says. The constrained variation means that children don't have to listen to many sentences before they figure out the grammar for the entire language.

Clock Ticking on Talking

This remarkable ability has a time limit, however. "To acquire a language as a native, you have to be exposed to it very early," Basilico explains. Linguists once considered puberty the time when the language-learning system would "sort of freeze up," but now many believe it happens at a younger age, Basilico says. "Beyond this window, known as the critical period, you cannot learn a language as a native." That is why adults often face difficulties in becoming fluent in a foreign language.

Universal grammar also implies that all of the world's languages share an underlying system of rules and principles. "All human societies have language, and all languages are of equal complexity," Basilico says. "The more you study languages, the more you realize they have much in common." He adds that languages seem different due to their unique vocabulary choices and other superficial differences, "but on a deeper level, there are many similarities."

Universal grammar also does not apply to written language, which doesn't exist in all societies, Basilico notes.

Plug and Say

The theory that spoken language springs from a genetic source could have broad ramifications. Basilico and many other linguists believe that our innate language knowledge is "modularized"—that is, that the brain has a built-in "language module" in the same way that it has specialized modules for visual perception and other functions. But others argue that our language abilities are "a property of an all-purpose, general cognitive mechanism," he says.

That raises new questions about the relationship between language and thought; for example, does the language we speak shape the way we think, and vice versa? Basilico is skeptical, but he says both the modular and general hypotheses present intriguing examples of how genes can shape behavior. "If we can answer questions about language," he muses, "who knows what that could lead to?"

SOURCE: Adapted from C. Burgess, "The Genetics of Speech," *UAB Magazine, 29*(1), Spring 2010, p. 10. Used by permission of the Board of Trustees of the University of Alabama System for the University of Alabama at Birmingham.

Classifying Speech and Language Impairments

Speech Disorders

Speech is the most common and the most complex mode for expression of language. It requires coordination of the neuromusculature of the breathing and voice-producing mechanisms, as well as integrity of the mouth or oral cavity. Figure 11.2 shows the organs used in speech production.

Simply stated, a speech impairment is present when the individual's speech deviates to such a degree that it interferes with communication, attracts unfavorable attention, and adversely affects the listeners, the speaker, or both (Bernthal, Bankson, & Flipsen,

	Phonology	Morphology/Syntax
Learning Disabilities	• Delayed acquisition of sounds • Inferior perception and/or production of complex sounds • Inefficient use of phonological codes in short-term memory • Impaired sensitivity to sounds	• Shorter and less elaborate sentences • Failure to encode all relevant information in sentences • Difficulties with negative and passive constructions, relative clauses, contractions, and adjectival forms • Confusion of articles (*a, an, the*) • Difficulty with verb tense, plurality, possession, and pronouns • Delayed acquisition of morphological rules • Difficulty with rules for auxiliaries, modals, prepositions, conjunctions, and other grammatical markers
Autism Spectrum Disorders	• Difficulties with expressive prosody (e.g., fluctuations in vocal intensity, monotonous pitch, tonal contrasts inconsistent with meanings)	• Confusions of pronominal forms (e.g., gender confusion [*he for she or it*], case substitution [him for he], first- and second-person singular forms [you for I or me]) • Less complex sentences than peers
Intellectual Disability	• Delayed development of phonological rules • Problems with speech production	• Production of shorter, less complex sentences with fewer subject elaborations or relative clauses • Delayed morpheme development • Delayed development of syntax
Traumatic Brain Injury	• Sound substitutions and omissions • Slurred speech • Difficulties with speech prosody (pitch, loudness, rate, and rhythm)	• Deficits in syntactic comprehension • Fragmented, irrelevant, and lengthy utterances • Mutism immediately after the injury, followed by telegraphic production
	Semantics	**Pragmatics**
Learning Disabilities	• Word-finding and definitional problems • Restricted word meanings (too literal and concrete) • Difficulty with multiple word meanings • Excessive use of nonspecific terms and indefinite reference • Difficulty comprehending certain conjunctions (but, or, if, then, either)	• Difficulty with questions and requests for clarification • Difficulty initiating and maintaining conversation • Difficulty with relational terms (*comparative, spatial, temporal*)
Autism Spectrum Disorders	• Word-finding problems • Inappropriate answers to questions	• Limited range of communicative functions • Difficulty initiating and maintaining conversation • Few gestures • Failure to make eye contact prior to or during communicative interactions • Preference to follow rather than lead in a conversation • Failure to engage communication partners at a level that requires sharing
Intellectual Disability	• Use of more concrete word meanings • Slower rate of vocabulary acquisition	• Difficulty with speech-act development • Difficulty with referential communication • Difficulty initiating and maintaining a conversation • Difficulty repairing communication breakdowns
Traumatic Brain Injury	• Small, restricted vocabulary • Word-finding problems	• Difficulty with organization and expression of complex ideas • Socially inappropriate and off-topic comments • Less use of the naming function

SOURCE: Adapted from L. McCormick and D. Loeb, "Characteristics of Students with Language and Communication Difficulties," in L. McCormick, D. Loeb, and R. Schiefelbusch (Eds.), *Supporting Children with Communication Difficulties in Inclusive Settings,* 2nd ed. (Boston, MA: Allyn & Bacon, 2003).

REFERENCE

Communication Disorders

REFERENCE

Speech Impairments

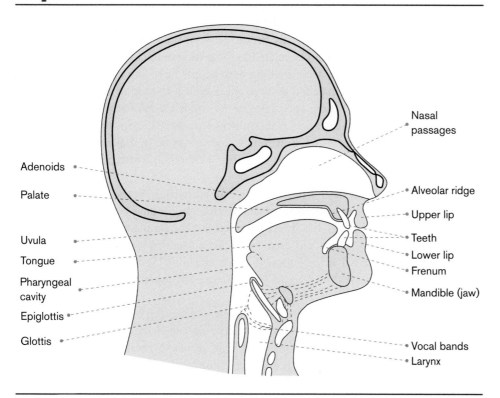

2013). There are three basic types of speech impairments: articulation disorders, fluency disorders, and voice disorders.

One of the most prevalent of all speech problems is **articulation disorders** (Owens, Metz, & Farinella, 2011). Articulation disorders are errors in the production of speech sounds. They include **omissions** (*han* for *hand*), **substitutions** (*wabbit* for *rabbit*), **additions** (*footsball* for *football*), and **distortions** (*shlip* for *sip*). A lisp is a good example of a distortion. Common difficulties are often associated with the mispronunciation of /*ch*/, /*s*/, /*sh*/, and /*z*/ phonemes (Plante & Beeson, 2013).

Articulation errors may be related to anatomical or physiological limitations in the skeletal, muscular, or neuromuscular support for speech production, or to other factors (for example, cerebral palsy, hearing loss). The etiology of most articulation problems, however, is unknown.

A child has a severe articulation disorder if pronunciation is so poor that his or her speech is unintelligible most of the time to family members, teachers, and peers. The focus of therapy for articulation disorders is acquisition of the correct speech sound(s), generalization of the sound(s) to different settings, and maintenance over time. For additional information on articulation disorders, see the accompanying Insights feature (page 371).

Fluency disorders are difficulties with the rhythm and timing of speech. A fluency disorder is basically "an interruption in the flow of speaking characterized by atypical rate, rhythm, and repetitions in sounds, syllables, words, and phrases. This may be accompanied by excessive tension, struggle behavior, and secondary mannerisms" (American Speech-Language-Hearing Association, 1993, p. 40). **Stuttering** is the most familiar fluency disorder. It is marked by rapid-fire repetitions of consonant or

articulation disorders: Errors in the formation of individual sounds of speech.

omissions: Articulation disorder that occurs when a sound is not pronounced in a word (e.g., *han* for *hand*).

substitutions: Articulation disorder that occurs when one sound is substituted for another in the pronunciation of a word (e.g., *wabbit* for *rabbit*).

additions: An articulation disorder wherein the speaker inserts extra sounds in spoken words.

distortions: Articulation disorder in which a sound is said inaccurately, but resembles the intended sound (e.g., *shlip* for *sip*).

fluency disorders: Disorders that involve the flow of speech, influencing the rate and smoothness of an individual's speech.

stuttering: Type of fluency disorder in which word sounds are repeated.

vowel sounds especially at the beginning of words, prolongations, hesitations, interjections, and complete verbal blocks. Examples of famous personalities affected by fluency disorders include Winston Churchill, King George VI of England, Tiger Woods, and Marilyn Monroe (Ramig & Pollard, 2011).

Developmental stuttering typically begins between the ages of 2 and 6. Stuttering is situational in that it appears to be related to the setting or circumstances of speech. A child is more likely to stutter when talking with people he or she considers important (parents, teachers) and when called upon to speak before a group of people (for example, in front of the class). There appears to be no single cause of stuttering; for many children, the etiology of stuttering is unknown (Ratner, 2013; Smith, Polloway, Patton, & Dowdy, 2012). Stuttering, however, is more common in males than in females. Investigators also note that a child has a greater likelihood of stuttering if he or she is a twin (Ramig & Pollard, 2011).

No single therapy method is most effective for stuttering. As they mature, children can learn to manage their stuttering by deliberately prolonging certain sounds or by speaking slowly to get through a "block." Sometimes the problem disappears without treatment. In many instances, children who stutter seem to recover or outgrow the condition without formal intervention (Owens et al., 2011; Ratner, 2013). See the accompanying Insights feature (page 373) for frequently asked questions and answers about stuttering.

Individuals who stutter may also be clutterers. Cluttering is a related fluency disorder characterized by excessively fast and jerky speech. Like stuttering, cluttering interferes with the flow of a person's speech. It seems to result from disorganized speech planning, talking too fast or in spurts, or simply being unsure of what one wants to say. Speech may initially be clear; then it gradually increases in speed, shifts to an irregular rhythm, and becomes mumbled. Symptoms of cluttering may include reading and writing disorders, word repetitions, short attention span, and grammatical errors. A difference between stutterers and clutterers is that the stutterer is usually very aware of his or her fluency problem, whereas the clutterer may seem oblivious to the problem. Speech-language pathologists typically collaborate with special education teachers who have expertise in learning disabilities and behavior disorders when working with children who demonstrate cluttering.

Voice disorders are problems with the quality or use of one's voice that result from disorders of the larynx. They are characterized by "the abnormal production and/or absences of vocal quality, pitch, loudness, resonance, and/or duration, which is inappropriate for an individual's age and/or sex" (American Speech-Language-Hearing Association, 1993, p. 40). Speech may be excessively hoarse, or lack appropriate inflection. Voice disorders may be caused by temporary conditions such as colds or allergies, chemically induced irritation, or vocally demanding activities, or more permanent abnormalities such as vocal nodules. Although voice disorders are more common in adults than in children, there are cases in which a child's voice is difficult to understand or unpleasant. The two types of voice disorders are phonation disorders and resonance disorders. The characteristics of a phonation disorder are breathiness, hoarseness, huskiness, and straining. In severe cases, the individual may not have any voice at all.

A resonance disorder may be characterized by hypernasality (too many sounds coming through the air passages of the nose) or hyponasality (too little resonance of the nasal passages). Hypernasality is often a result of cleft palate. Too much air passes through the nasal cavities during production of sounds, giving the speaker a distinctive "twang." Because the flow of air through the nostrils is impeded, the speaker with hyponasality sounds as if his nose is clamped or she has a cold.

cluttering: Type of fluency disorder involving cognitive, linguistic, pragmatic, speech, and motor abilities.

voice disorders: May result from disorders of the larynx or disorders in phonation.

phonation: Includes speech factors of pitch, loudness, and quality.

resonance: Sound quality of speech.

hypernasality: Disorder of voice resonance, frequently observed as a result of cleft palate, in which too much air passes through the nasal cavities during the production of sounds, giving the speaker a distinctive nasal quality or "twang."

hyponasality: Disorder of voice resonance in which there is a restricted flow of air through the nostrils, often resulting in the speaker's sounding as if his or her nose is being held.

INSIGHTS

Questions and Answers About Articulation Problems

Q. Will a child outgrow a functional articulation problem?

A. A child's overall speech pattern will usually become more understandable as he or she matures, but some children will need direct training to eliminate all articulation errors. The exact speech pattern of the individual child will determine the answer to this question.

Q. Do children learn all sounds at once?

A. Sounds are learned in an orderly sequence. Some sounds, such as *p, m,* and *b,* are learned as early as 3 years of age. Other sounds, such as *s, r,* and *l,* often are not completely mastered until the early school years.

Q. At what age should a child be producing all sounds correctly?

A. Children should make all the sounds of English by 8 years of age. Many children learn these sounds much earlier.

Q. How can I help a child pronounce words correctly?

A. By setting a good example. Don't interrupt or constantly correct the child. Don't let anyone tease or mock (including friends or relatives). Instead, present a good model. Use the misarticulated word correctly with emphasis. If the child says, "that's a big wabbit," you say, "yes, that is a big rabbit. A big white rabbit. Would you like to have a rabbit?"

Q. Can an adult with an articulation problem be helped?

A. Most articulation problems can be helped regardless of a person's age, but the longer the problem persists, the harder it is to change. Some problems, such as those relating to nerve impulses to the muscles of articulation (dysarthria), are particularly difficult and generally require a longer period of help than a functional disorder. Other conditions that may influence progress in a child or an adult include hearing ability, condition of the oral structures such as the teeth, frequency of help obtained, motivation, intelligence, and cooperation.

Q. Who can help?

A. Contact a speech-language pathologist if you are concerned about speech. A speech-language pathologist is a professional trained at the master's or doctoral level to evaluate and help the child or adult with an articulation problem as well as other speech and/or language disorders. The speech-language pathologist can advise whether professional help is indicated and how to arrange for assistance. The speech-language pathologist can also give you guidance or provide services to help prevent or eliminate a problem. Early help is especially important for more severe problems.

Q. Is it important to correct an articulation problem?

A. When you consider the possible impact an articulation problem may have on one's social, emotional, educational, and/or vocational status, the answer becomes obvious. Our speech is an important part of us. The quality of our lives is affected by the adequacy of our speech.

SOURCE: Adapted from American Speech-Language-Hearing Association, *Answers and Questions about Articulation Problems* (Rockville, MD: n.d.).

Language Disorders

How well children understand and use language affects not only their ability to learn to read and write but also the perceptions of peers, family members, teachers, and society at large. When a child starts school, the perception of his or her language skills becomes particularly influential. When children's communication skills do not match others' expectations, children are likely to be perceived negatively and may consequently experience less academic and social success (Owens, 2014; Turner, 2008). Speech-language pathologists and teachers have two responsibilities: (1) to address children's specific language difficulties and (2) to minimize the social impact of particular speech-language characteristics by promoting understanding of and acceptance of language difficulties in the classroom.

Recall the components of language as reviewed in Table 11.2 (page 366). Each of these five components of language (phonology, morphology, syntax, semantics, pragmatics) has rules that must be mastered if the child is to have language competence. Language disorders occur when there is delay or difficulties with mastery in one or more of these areas.

REFERENCE

Speech Disorders

Children learn the rules of language by listening and imitating what they hear.

A **phonological disorder** is defined as abnormal organization of the phonologic system or a significant deficit in speech production or perception. A developmental phonological disorder is the difficulty of organizing speech sounds into patterns. A child with a phonological disorder may be described as hard to understand or as not saying the sounds right—the child is likely to have difficulty decoding spoken language and may make substitutions for sounds. A child has a phonological disorder (as opposed to an articulation disorder) if he or she has the ability to produce a given sound and does so correctly in some instances but fails to produce the sound correctly at other times. Unlike articulation disorders, a phonological disorder reveals a pattern of responses and is therefore a rule-based phenomenon. Assessment for these children focuses on determining which sounds the child can produce, the contexts of correct and incorrect sound production, and the child's use or overuse of phonological processes. The focus of therapy for phonological disorders is to help the child identify the error pattern(s) and gradually produce more linguistically appropriate sound patterns.

Apraxia of speech is a neurological phonologic disorder that results from impairment of the capacity to select, program, or execute the positioning of the speech muscles to produce speech sounds. The speech mechanisms are operating, but the child cannot get them to operate properly—when the child wants to speak, he or she has difficulty planning what to say and which motor movements to use. The weakened or slowed processes affect speech prosody, stress intonation, and rhythm. The speech of these children is characterized by groping attempts to articulate sounds correctly. There are frequent speech-sound substitutions and omissions with sound-sequencing difficulties and distortions and obvious struggle to retrieve desired sounds and patterns.

Disorders involving morphology involve difficulties with morphological inflections. Morphological inflections (also called grammatical morphemes) are inflections on nouns, verbs, and adjectives that signal different kinds of meanings. For example, when you add the morphological inflection -*s* to dog, this signals plurality. Children with a **morphological disorder** have problems learning and using morphological rules. They use fewer grammatical morphemes and produce more grammatical errors than same-age peers.

Children with **syntactical deficits** have difficulty acquiring the rules that govern word order and other aspects of grammar such as subject-verb agreement. They have problems processing sentences, even relatively simple ones, and they typically produce shorter and less elaborated sentences with fewer cohesive conjunctions than their peers. Most evident is their inability to organize and express complex ideas.

Semantic disorders are characterized by poor vocabulary development, inappropriate use of word meanings, and/or inability to comprehend word meanings. Most evident are problems with word finding, the ability to generate a specific word that

phonological disorder: Abnormal organization of phonological system resulting in a significant deficit in speech production or perception.

apraxia of speech: Speech and language disorder comprised of both a speech disorder, caused by oral-motor difficulty, and a language disorder, characterized by the resultant limitations of expression.

morphological disorder: Difficulty learning and using morphological rules of language.

syntactical deficits: Difficulty in acquiring the rules that control word order and other aspects of grammar.

semantic disorder: Language difficulty associated with poor vocabulary development, inappropriate use of word meanings, and/or inability to comprehend word meanings.

VIDEO

Components of Language

Questions and Answers About Stuttering

Q. What is stuttering?

A. Stuttering is the condition in which the flow of speech is broken by abnormal stoppages (no sound), repetitions (st-st-stuttering), or prolongations (ssssstuttering) of sounds and syllables. There may also be unusual facial and body movements associated with the effort to speak.

Q. Aren't all people nonfluent to some extent?

A. Yes. Almost all children go through a stage of frequent nonfluency in early speech development. Adults may interject syllables ("uh") and occasionally repeat words, phrases, and sounds, but these nonfluencies are accepted as normal and usually are not a cause for concern.

Q. Does stammering mean the same thing as stuttering?

A. Most people use the terms interchangeably.

Q. What causes stuttering?

A. We still do not know what causes stuttering. It may have different causes in different people, or it may occur only when a combination of factors comes together. It is also possible that what causes stuttering is different from what makes it continue or get worse. Possible influences include incoordination of the speech muscles, rate of language development, the way parents and others talk to the child, and other forms of communication and life stress.

Q. Is stuttering caused by emotional or psychological problems?

A. Children who stutter are no more likely to have psychological problems than children who do not stutter. There is no evidence that emotional trauma causes stuttering.

Q. At what age is stuttering likely to appear?

A. Stuttering typically begins between 2 and 5 years of age, but occasionally begins in a school-age child and, more rarely, in an adult.

Q. If I think my child is beginning to stutter, should I wait or seek help?

A. You should seek a professional evaluation. Most children outgrow their nonfluency, but others will not. The problem of stuttering may be prevented from developing if treated early enough.

Q. Once stuttering has developed, can it be treated?

A. Yes. There are a variety of successful approaches for treating both children and adults.

Q. Can stuttering be "cured"?

A. Stuttering is not a disease. Rather than thinking in terms of an absolute "cure" for stuttering, the goal should be to progress toward improved fluency and success in communicating.

Q. What should I do when I hear a child speaking nonfluently?

A. Children may be unaware that they are speaking nonfluently. Do not call attention to the nonfluent speech pattern or allow others to do so.

Do not say, "stop and start over," "think before you talk," "talk slower," or "cat got your tongue?" Listen patiently and carefully to what the child is saying, and do not focus on how it is being said.

Q. What should I do when I hear an adult stuttering?

A. Adults who stutter need the same patience and attention to their ideas as speakers who don't stutter. Don't look away, and don't hurry them or fill in words. This attempt to help can create anxiety and self-consciousness and make the problem worse.

SOURCE: Adapted from American Speech-Language-Hearing Association, *Answers and Questions about Stuttering* (Rockville, MD: n.d.).

is evoked by a situation, stimulus, sentence, context, or conversation. Children with semantic difficulties also demonstrate restrictions in word meanings, difficulties with multiple word meanings, excessive use of nonspecific terms (for example, *thing, stuff*) and indefinite references (for example, *that* and *there*), and difficulties with comprehension of conjunctions and relational terms.

Children with **pragmatic difficulties** have problems understanding and using language in different social contexts. They do not understand how to infer their listeners' needs, so they do not know what and how much information they need to provide in an interaction. Other weaknesses include lack of understanding of the rules for (1) when and how to make eye contact, (2) how close it is permissible to stand when talking to someone, (3) when to request clarification of information, (4) how to interpret direct and indirect requests, and (5) how to introduce topics.

pragmatic difficulties: Problems in understanding and using language in different social contexts.

REFERENCE
Language Disorders

Table 11.4 presents indicators of a possible language impairment. These behaviors might suggest the need for an evaluation by a speech-language pathologist.

Central Auditory Processing Disorder

Defining central auditory processing disorder (CAPD) presents some difficulty because it has been the center of considerable controversy in the field of language disorders. Most authorities agree, however, that it is a problem in the processing of sound, not attributed to hearing loss or intellectual capacity. Simply stated, central auditory processing involves how we use and interpret auditory information. CAPD occurs when the ear and the brain do not work together as smoothly as they should. CAPD varies in degree from mild to severe. It may be the primary or secondary disorder, and involves aspects of listening skills necessary for language development. In children with CAPD, these deficits are not the result of a hearing loss; hearing is usually normal. These children demonstrate problems with auditory figure-ground (difficulty attending to a speaker when there is noise in the background), auditory memory, auditory discrimination (hearing the difference between similar sounds or words), auditory attention (maintaining listening focus), and auditory cohesion (for example, drawing inferences from conversations, understanding riddles, comprehending verbal math problems).

Children with CAPD process auditory input in a way that is slow and inaccurate, and they work harder to interpret what they hear than their classmates do. These children are at risk for noticeable listening difficulties in many classroom situations. For example, spelling tests and note taking are activities often adversely affected by CAPD. Behavioral characteristics of children exhibiting signs of CAPD may also mimic those of children with learning disabilities, attention deficit hyperactivity disorder, or dyslexia.

The causes of CAPD are many and varied and may include head trauma, lead poisoning, and chronic ear infections, as well as unknown etiologies. A neurophysiological basis for this disorder is likely.

Historical Perspectives

For many years, individuals with speech and language impairments and other disabilities were referred to as "handicapped," the origin of the word referring to the image and practice of individuals with disabilities begging on streets with a cap in hand to catch donations. The work of Itard, referenced in Chapter 6, is considered classic early speech and language research. There was great fascination and curiosity regarding the "wild boy of Aveyron's" development of fundamental speech sounds and gradual use of these sounds in language for communication of his wants and needs. Early language deprivation, like that experienced by Victor, is one of the many etiologies identified for speech and language disorders.

Van Riper and Emerick (1996) have classified historic reactions toward individuals with disabilities into three categories:

- Rejection—being thrown from mountain peaks in ancient Sparta
- Objects of pity—frequently used within the context of religious practices throughout the ages
- A rewarding source of humor—"balbus blaesius," an individual who stuttered and was caged and displayed on the Appian Way along with other individuals with disabilities

central auditory processing disorder (CAPD): A problem in the processing of sound not attributed to hearing loss or intellectual capacity, involving cognitive and linguistic functions that directly affect receptive communication skills.

■ ■ ■ ■ ■ Table 11.4 **Behaviors Indicative of a Possible Language Impairment in Children**

Child mispronounces sounds and words.
Child omits word endings, such as plural -s and past-tense -ed.
Child omits small unemphasized words, such as auxiliary verbs or prepositions.
Child uses an immature vocabulary; overuses empty words, such as one and thing; or seems to have difficulty recalling or finding the right word.
Child has difficulty comprehending new words and concepts.
Child's sentence structure seems immature or overreliant on forms, such as subject–verb–object. It's unoriginal, dull.
Child's question and/or negative sentence style is immature.

Child has difficulty with one of the following:

- Verb tensing
- Pronouns
- Word order
- Articles
- Irregular verbs
- Irregular plurals
- Auxiliary verbs
- Prepositions
- Conjunctions

Child has difficulty relating sequential events.
Child has difficulty following directions.
Child's questions are often inaccurate or vague.
Child's questions are often poorly formed.
Child has difficulty answering questions.
Child's comments are often off-topic or inappropriate for the conversation.
There are long pauses between a remark and the child's reply or between successive remarks by the child. It's as if the child is searching for a response or is confused.
Child appears to be attending to communication but remembers little of what is said.

Child has difficulty using language socially for the following purposes:

- Request needs
- Greet
- Respond/reply
- Relate events
- Pretend/imagine
- Request information
- Share ideas, feelings
- Entertain
- Protest
- Gain attention
- Clarify
- Reason

Child has difficulty interpreting the following:

- Figurative language
- Emotions
- Humor
- Body language
- Gestures

Child does not alter production for different audiences and locations.
Child does not seem to consider the effect of language on the listener.
Child often has verbal misunderstandings with others.
Child has difficulty with reading and writing.
Child's language skills seem to be much lower than other areas, such as mechanical, artistic, or social skills.

SOURCE: Adapted from R. Owens, *Language Disorders: A Functional Approach to Assessment and Intervention,* 6th ed. (Boston, MA: Pearson Education, 2014), P. 337.

Although contemporary society has moved forward in the treatment of individuals with disabilities, these early reactions persist. Consider your own reactions to persons with speech and language impairments.

- Rejection. How many friends with significant speech and language disorders did you have in school? How many individuals with speech and language impairments were class leaders or had parts in school plays? How many of these individuals dated?
- Objects of pity. What happened when it was time to read aloud in class? How did you feel when these students were asked to present projects in class and had difficulty with the speech and language aspects of their presentation? Were you uncomfortable? Did you feel sorry for them? Did they give oral presentations?
- A rewarding source of humor. Have you ever laughed at jokes or imitations of these individuals behind their backs? Have you laughed at the "humor" created by the speech and language disorders of cartoon characters such as Tweety Bird, Sylvester, Elmer Fudd, Porky Pig, and Donald Duck? Would it be funny to you if you had the same speech and language impairment as one of these cartoon characters? How would you feel as you watched everyone around you laugh at the cartoon?

Educational programming and intervention for students with speech and language impairments have been available since the early twentieth century. In 1910, the Chicago public schools hired the first "speech correction teachers." Until the 1950s, school-based speech-language pathologists had many titles, including *speech correctionists, speech specialists,* and *speech teachers.* Van Hattum (1969) credits a growing understanding of language development and skills in the identification and remediation of language disorders for the change to the term *speech therapist.* Students typically worked with speech therapists in large groups, primarily at the elementary school level.

As the profession continued to expand, and professionals in the field of speech and language disorders practiced in a wider variety of settings, specialists generally adopted a medical/clinical model, leading to the presently used term, *speech-language pathologist.* Today speech-language pathologists work in a wide variety of settings, including rehabilitation centers, nursing care facilities, health departments, and, of course, public and private schools. General and special education teachers work most frequently with school-based speech-language pathologists.

Prevalence of Speech and Language Impairments

Speech and language impairments are considered a high-incidence disability. According to the U.S. Department of Education (2013a), slightly less than 20 percent of students receiving special education services are receiving services for speech and language impairments. This estimate does not include children who receive services for speech and language impairments that are secondary to other conditions such as deafness. During the 2011–2012 school year, a total of 1,071,555 individuals ages 6–21 were identified as having speech and language impairments (U.S. Department of Education, 2013a).

AUDIO

Stuttering

Youngsters with speech and language disorders represent almost half of all preschoolers receiving a special education. Approximately 46 percent of all 3-, 4-, and 5-year-olds with a disability exhibit speech and language impairments. The U.S. Department of Education (2013a) reports over 342,000 preschoolers in this category.

Etiology of Speech and Language Impairments

The etiologies, or causes, of speech and language impairments can be broadly subdivided in several different ways. One way is to classify them into functional versus organic etiologies. Functional etiologies have no obvious physiological foundation, and the cause of the impairment is often unknown. An articulation disorder, for example, without a physical basis would be classified as a functional etiology. Organic etiologies, such as cleft palate can be linked to a physiological deficit.

Additionally, impairments may be classified as congenital, developmental, or acquired. Congenital disorders are those existing at birth; developmental disorders emerge during the preschool years. Acquired disorders are usually the result of injury, disease, or environmental insult; they most frequently result in childhood aphasia, which is a loss or impairment of language functions. Causative factors for developmental disorders are largely unknown, but may involve brain dysfunction, or can be secondary to hearing loss or autism spectrum disorders. Such factors have important implications for prognosis and service delivery. Speech and language impairments can also be classified by age of onset, severity, and behavioral characteristics of the disorder (symptoms).

The etiologies of communicative disorders are frequently complex. Although the vast majority of children evaluated by speech-language pathologists in schools exhibit functional disorders (Smith et al., 2012), familiarity with organic factors is also important for educators. Etiologies may include congenital malformations, prenatal injury, tumors, and problems with the nervous or muscular systems, the brain, or the speech mechanism itself. Exposure to teratogens, including X-rays, viruses, drugs, and environmental toxins, can also cause congenital disorders. During the first six to twelve weeks of embryonic life, many organs are being formed. Any agent capable of damaging one organ may affect various systems developing simultaneously. A prime example of such an agent is maternal rubella (German measles). When contracted during the first trimester of pregnancy, this teratogen is capable of causing multiple and concurrent congenital problems such as cardiac defects, cataracts, intellectual disability, microcephaly, short stature, hearing loss, and a variety of concurrent speech and language pathologies (Bell, 2007).

Communication problems that result from disease or traumatic insult after birth are acquired disorders. Traumatic brain injury following a motor vehicle accident is an example of an acquired disorder that frequently has negative implications for speech and language abilities. Meningitis, a disease resulting in inflammation of brain tissue, is a relatively common pediatric disorder. Complications of meningitis can result in hearing loss and associated communication deficit. Speech and language problems resulting from such an illness would represent an acquired communication disorder.

Articulation, voice quality, and fluency can be influenced by abnormalities in respiration (airflow in and out of the lungs), phonation (sound produced by the larynx), and vocal resonance (vibration within the vocal tract). Such disorders vary in degree and can occur in isolation, in combination with each other, or in conjunction with other language pathologies. Normal neurophysiology, as well as skeletal and muscular

functional: Etiologies of speech and language disorders that have no obvious physical basis (such as environmental stress).

organic: Etiologies of speech and language disorders that can be linked to a physiological deficit (such as cleft palate).

aphasia: Loss or impairment of language functions.

support for respiration and phonation, is necessary for speech skills to develop properly. The clinical entities presenting structural hazards to articulation include lips, teeth, and limited tongue mobility as well as a cleft lip and/or cleft palate. A cleft lip or cleft palate is a congenital abnormality that occurs in about 1 in every 750 births (Owens et al., 2011), making it one of the most common birth defects in the United States (American Speech-Language-Hearing Association, 2013a). Simply stated, a cleft lip/palate, which is recognized as an organic etiology, results from the failure of bone and palate tissue to correctly fuse during the early weeks of fetal development. Some infants are born with an opening in the roof of their mouth while others have a gap (cleft) in their upper lip. In some instances, babies have both. The severity of these conditions can greatly vary. Unfortunately, the etiology of these birth defects is not well understood (March of Dimes, 2013a). Hypernasal speech is fairly common in youngsters with a cleft palate. Surgery and/or the use of a prosthetic, however, can often correct or minimize the impact of these structural defects.

Hearing loss, intellectual disability, learning disabilities, and emotional disturbance are also commonly associated with communicative disorders and have implications for language as well as speech development.

Prevention of Speech and Language Impairments

It is difficult to assign differential responsibility to hereditary versus environmental factors (nature versus nurture) when language is disordered. Because linguistic skills are so closely linked to academic performance, determinants of language abilities are of interest to all educators.

Any risk factor or disability that affects a child's cognitive, motor, and/or social development is also very likely to affect that child's language development; yet attempts to determine specific etiology are often not very productive. From the standpoint of prevention, however, it is useful to keep in mind the factors necessary for normal language acquisition. Four sets of variables seem to have a profound influence on language learning: (1) biological preparation, (2) successful nurturance, (3) sensorimotor experiences, and (4) linguistic experiences (McCormick, 2003a). The strongest evidence for the contention that language is a biologically determined capability comes from the fact that all cultures have language and all humans learn to talk (unless limited by sensory, neuromuscular, or cognitive impairment). As discussed earlier in this chapter, infants arrive in this world prepared to understand and use language. Their biological preparation includes neuromotor capabilities, an impressive supply of attentional and perceptual abilities, and a strong desire to interact with others. Successful nurturance requires a nurturing environment in which responsive adults carefully mediate the introduction of new stimuli. The dynamic regulation of stimuli is evident in caregiving rituals such as feeding and diapering, joint action routines (for example, peek-a-boo), and a variety of other daily interactions. Adults use these exchanges to help infants learn the rules of turn taking, the meaning of particular gestures, imitation of sounds and gestures, and mutuality. Sensorimotor experiences are the means through which infants construct their understanding of the world by acting on it, both physically and mentally (Piaget, 1952). These experiences make it possible for infants to progress, in less than two short years, from being totally reflexive and largely immobile to becoming planful thinkers who can move about independently and communicate their intentions. Finally, linguistic experiences (called child-directed speech) undoubtedly play an important role in language learning. Caregivers facilitate language learning by continuously adjusting the phonologic,

cleft lip/cleft palate: A congenital defect in which the upper lip is split or there is an opening in the roof of the mouth. Can often be surgically corrected. Hypernasality is common.

Language develops within the context of social relationships.

semantic, syntactic, and pragmatic characteristics of their speech when they address infants. If any one or some combination of these factors is lacking or deficient, the child is at risk for language delay and/or disorders.

Language is possibly the most complex human behavior. Yet despite significant differences in child-rearing practices across cultures, almost all normal children develop native language at about the same chronological age. Most children appear to learn their language system in a matter of a few years without formal instruction. However, development of mature language skills requires an environment that provides substantial communicative interaction. In virtually every known culture, language develops within the context of social relationships—primarily the parent or caretaker relationship. Research suggests that variability in such relationships may account for at least some differences in linguistic skills.

Months of rich social and communicative exchange precede actual production or expression of language by the child. During infancy and early childhood, caregivers respond to nonlinguistic communications, decode linguistic attempts, and provide adequate models for and shaping of the expressions of language. When these interactions fail to occur, the child is at risk for developmental language delay. Delayed language means that a child is slow to develop adequate vocabulary and grammar, or language age does not correspond to the child's chronological age. Refer back to Table 11.1 (page 364), which lists some normal developmental milestones in language. Awareness of basic developmental guidelines is of the utmost importance for professionals involved in the education of the very young child, as communication

developmental language delay: Slowness in the development of adequate vocabulary and grammar, or when a child's language age does not correspond to the child's chronological age.

disorders linked to developmental delays are less amenable to modification with increasing age.

Characteristics of Individuals With Speech and Language Impairments

Language, as well as its associated pathologies, can be broadly categorized into two basic types: receptive language, or the ability to understand what is meant by spoken communication, and expressive language, which involves production of language that is understood by and meaningful to others (Friend & Bursuck, 2012). Children with language disorders have difficulty expressing thoughts or understanding what is said. Expressive language skills and possible areas of deficit include grammar, syntax, fluency, vocabulary, and repetition. Receptive language deficits address response, abstraction, retention, and recall issues. A student who is unable to follow directions efficiently in the classroom may have a receptive language disorder; the child who cannot communicate clearly because of poor grammar, insufficient vocabulary, or production problems such as an articulation disorder suffers from an expressive language disorder.

Children with language impairments frequently struggle in the classroom as well as at home and in other community settings. (See the accompanying First Person feature.) Some of the difficulties (Vaughn & Bos, 2012) you may observe in children with expressive language disorders include

- Limited vocabulary;
- Incorrect grammar or syntax;
- Excessive repetition of information; and
- Difficulty in formulating questions.

Youngsters with receptive language problems typically have difficulty

- Following oral directions;
- Understanding humor or figurative language;
- Comprehending compound and complex sentences; and
- Responding to questions appropriately.

How do young children learn language? The answer to this question still eludes researchers, and conflicting theories abound. Beginning before age 2 and largely before age 4, most children acquire intelligible speech and possess a basis for development of adult grammar (McCormick, 2003a). However, there is substantial variability in the normal development of speech and language in children. For example, the age of mastery of various speech sounds may vary by as much as three years. By age 8, however, virtually all speech sounds in the child's native language should be correctly produced (see Figure 11.3).

Assessing Speech and Language Impairments

Assessment is an important step in the habilitation and management of communication disorders. The purpose of assessing the child in whom language or speech problems is

receptive language: The ability to understand what is meant by spoken communication.

expressive language: The formation and production of language, verbal and nonverbal, that is understood by and meaningful to others.

Figure 11.3 Age of Acquisition of Speech Sounds

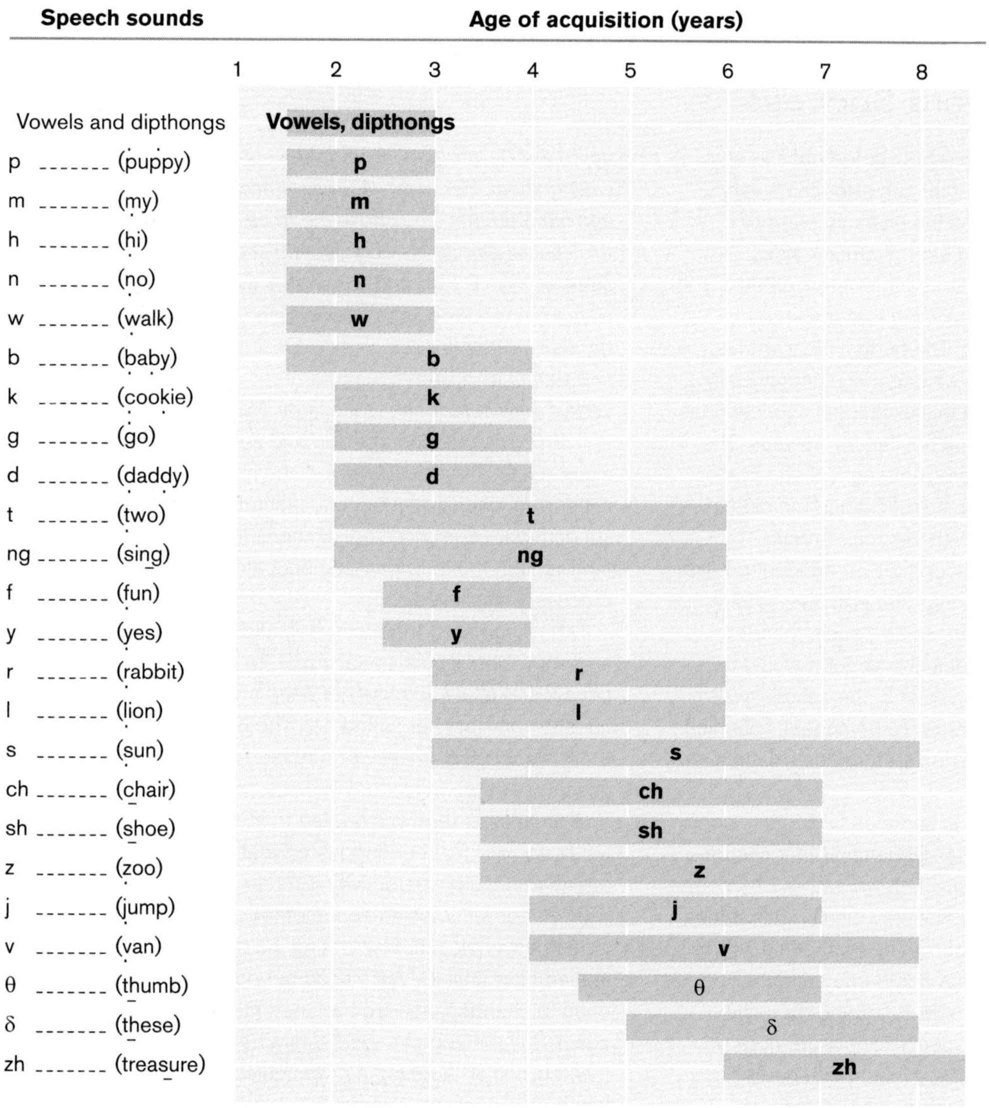

Speech sounds	Age of acquisition (years)
Vowels and dipthongs	Vowels, dipthongs (≈1–2)
p (puppy)	p
m (my)	m
h (hi)	h
n (no)	n
w (walk)	w
b (baby)	b
k (cookie)	k
g (go)	g
d (daddy)	d
t (two)	t
ng (sing)	ng
f (fun)	f
y (yes)	y
r (rabbit)	r
l (lion)	l
s (sun)	s
ch (chair)	ch
sh (shoe)	sh
z (zoo)	z
j (jump)	j
v (van)	v
θ (thumb)	θ
δ (these)	δ
zh (treasure)	zh

NOTE: Beginning of bar represents age at which children begin to acquire each sound. End of bar represents age at which most children have mastered each sound.

SOURCE: D. Sindrey, *Listening Games for Littles II* (London, Ontario: Wordplay Publications, 2002).

suspected should be to gain insight into his or her functional abilities, limitations, and perceived needs. A wide range of assessment tools, both formal and informal, is available to assess language and speech. Some of these tools are also available in Spanish. Most of these evaluation procedures are conducted by a speech-language pathologist within the educational system or in private practice.

One of the most important tools in the assessment process for speech and language impairments is the case history. Amassing identifying information such as gender, age, natural or adoptive parents, and pertinent family status information is helpful. The initial family interview is of paramount importance to the assessment and rehabilitative effort, and sets the tone for future interactions between professionals and families.

VIDEO
Age of Acquisition

A Journey Toward Success

The day my child became special started out like any ordinary day. She was a toddler and attended a very prestigious preschool. It was the biannual parent-teacher meeting, which had been the norm since she was an infant. My husband and I were excited to see her drawings and scribbling that marked the beginning stages of writing. The normal pleasantries were exchanged, and then we began looking at Emily's work. At some point during this exchange, I noticed that the teachers were somewhat hesitant or nervous. The topic was color identification. The teachers stated that Emily wasn't retaining color identification. She did not associate the word green with the color green.

The suggestion was made that we needed to have her tested. The teachers stated that probably nothing was wrong; but, if there were some issues, then the earlier that intervention began, the better it would be for Emily. Since Emily was almost 3, the school system provided testing free of charge. To be honest, I handled this situation like any grown-up mature adult—I cried and cried.

I began flashing back to some early warning signs. Emily walked and talked later than most other children, and she would get confused when I would say, "Go get your toy in the living room." She also didn't understand the concepts of up/down, above/below, behind/in front of, and so forth, and with that our journey began.

The test results confirmed a learning disability. Emily was also eligible for speech-language therapy. Although the school system provided free speech-language therapy, the location to my employment wasn't convenient. Therefore, the decision was made to hire a private speech-language therapist to come to her preschool two days per week. Therapy was fairly smooth at first as I waited for this therapist to "cure" my child. She would share funny stories with me but always seemed to focus on Emily's disability rather than her abilities. She also failed to fully communicate with Emily's preschool teachers.

This therapist soon relocated to another state, and we started working with a new speech-language pathologist. Emily and I immediately clicked with her. She laid out a plan of action and regularly met with Emily's teachers and me. She e-mailed me after each session and would tell me the great things Emily achieved during the session. She loved Emily, and, most important, she saw her abilities.

As I am writing this it has occurred to me that I am writing all about what I went through. I haven't appropriately introduced you to the special girl that I am writing about. Her name is Emily Grace, and I am proud and honored that God chose me to be the mother of this special girl. She is 10 years old and doesn't meet a stranger. She is kind and has always been the caretaker of all her friends. When she sees a friend, she almost knocks her down with big hugs. Seeing Emily, you would never know she has a language impairment. She doesn't look a certain way; in fact, she is a beauty! Now back to the story.

Emily began kindergarten and a totally new experience. This time, however, she had an instructional support teacher, a general education teacher, and a speech-language pathologist. I became increasingly familiar with the individualized education program (IEP) process. Emily loved school.

Emily entered the first grade and continued to be happy. She is very social but at the same time well behaved. She would raise her hand and answer any question her teacher asked her. The problem was that Emily would give an answer that didn't pertain to the question or the subject being discussed. She would give an answer that was related to the last thought in her head. Her teacher suggested that maybe Emily had attention deficit hyperactivity disorder (ADHD). So off we went to her pediatrician and another battery of tests with a neuropsychologist. The testing indicated that Emily did indeed have ADHD. We placed her on medication but nothing changed, and we switched medication again and again. Still nothing changed. Emily, however, changed—this fun, social, laughing girl was quiet. My husband and I made the decision, against the wishes of her teacher and neuropsychologist, to remove Emily from medication.

Teachers who are not familiar with Emily's disability think she is not listening. Directions are hard for her. Something as simple as "Get your books out and write down your homework assignments" is a hard concept for Emily to follow. The teacher doesn't know that for Emily she needs to say, "Emily, open the book," and, once the book is opened, she has to point to the homework assignment and say, "Write this down in your book."

Reading comprehension is extremely difficult for Emily. She reads at a level higher than her comprehension. She can read a paragraph, but when asked what she just read she would repeat some words from the last sentence of that paragraph.

Second grade began, and her teacher wasn't one who was "warm and fuzzy." My sense was that she felt inconvenienced by having Emily included in her class. During one of our many conferences, she remarked that

Emily was unorganized; she wasn't able to come in, put her backpack down, and get her books out. She held the entire class up. The teacher told me that Emily's peers were pulling away from her, and she described a child with whom I was not familiar. She also told me that Emily would embarrass herself by responding to questions with answers that didn't pertain to the subject being discussed. I wanted to scream, "Don't you think I know this?" Fortunately, for me, the saving grace that year was Emily's instructional support teacher and her speech-language pathologist. Her instructional support teacher made laminated picture cues for Emily that visually showed her the correct sequence to follow upon arriving in class. I am proud to say that Emily got the hang of it. She learned! You see, Emily can learn. She just learns a bit slower and differently than most children, but, nonetheless, she learns.

Blessings occurred many times in our lives, and another arrived the day Emily entered third grade. She had a new teacher. This teacher was new to the school system, and she was young. "Oh boy, I bet you she doesn't have a clue about language delay" was my initial reaction. In addition, Emily was assigned a new instructional support teacher. I thought, "Here we go again." I didn't want to have the typical three-month recoupment period that both Emily and I faced each year, so I decided to tell them how Emily learns. This third-grade teacher got it. She read my notes and focused from the beginning on Emily's abilities. She introduced me to a new concept called frontloading. She would take Emily aside and preteach her a subject while classmates were reading. When the teacher went over the lesson with the remainder of the class, Emily would be hearing it the second time. It helped to reinforce the subject. By far, this teacher has been the best teacher to date for Emily.

Her new instructional support teacher was also wonderful. Because she was familiar with receptive/expressive language delays, she taught concepts to Emily visually. She actually knew Emily and understood her struggles. She worked closely with the classroom teacher and gave her ideas to help Emily respond properly to questions. It was also done in a way that didn't embarrass Emily in front of her peers.

This instructional support teacher also challenged the school administrators about the Honors Day program. She asked, "Why can't children in instructional support be included on the AB honor roll? After all, they learn and do well at their level. Are only A students successful in life?"

Emily entered fourth grade; fortunately, her support team remained intact. Still the old, familiar three-month lag raised its ugly head. Her grades typically slipped during this time frame as her teachers tried to understand and respond appropriately to her disability.

E-mails and constant communication with her teacher and the familiarity of her instructional support teacher helped tremendously. Emily worked extremely hard, and her efforts paid off. She received the Principal's Leadership Award during the Honor Ceremony that year.

Emily is now in fifth grade. To be honest, this has been an extremely difficult year. Two conferences with her teacher were required, and things were still difficult. The issue is communication. The teacher assured the parents during orientation that all homework would be included on his website, and it was—partially. For instance, he would tell the class, "Do page 2 in your math book." Emily wouldn't bring the book home, or each unit in the book had a page 2. So which unit? While most kids could tell you which unit, Emily can't. Another example: She would often bring home books but didn't bother to write the assignments in her planner. The website would have homework assignments for the class that didn't pertain to Emily. During one of our conferences, the teacher remarked, "I told her several times to make sure that she had all her books to take home." (He didn't realize that all Emily heard was books.) Her instructional support teacher would tactfully remind him that this is a product of her disability.

A thirty-minute reading assignment is brutal for Emily. It takes Emily well over an hour to complete the assignment. She slowly sounds out the words, and then can't tell you one thing she just read. Once again, her instructional support teacher stepped in. Emily was given a notebook (to keep at home) that had short stories with questions to answer. Her teacher taught her to number the paragraphs and then break them down. Last night, we completed four stories in thirty minutes! Success!

It is helpful that the instructional support teacher e-mails me each Monday with the teacher's weekly plan. She answers my e-mails daily. She understands my frustrations. I lean heavily on her during these tough times. I have left her phone messages as I cried with frustration on trying to understand what the classroom teacher was expecting of my child.

My worries are now with the transition to the middle school. In life, the smart kids, the popular kids, and the enrichment kids are favored. Some teachers are inconvenienced that they have to teach another way to my child, and I get that. It has to be hard and time-consuming. But isn't that what the calling of a teacher is? To teach? Learning to teach students doesn't mean teaching only smart students. Emily will have to fight to make her way, to stand out in life. It is regrettable that it takes some teachers four months to get it. Will you be the type of teacher who extends his or her hand and pulls Emily to the top? Will you get it? I hope so. Emily and others like her need you. ∎

–Anonymous

Assessment is an important first step in the habilitation and management of communication disorders.

Asking parents of young children questions such as "What issues have prompted you to have your child evaluated?" or "What would be most helpful for me to know about your child?" can aid in determining parental concerns. Family-directed assessment focuses on information that families choose to provide regarding needs, concerns, resources, and priorities. This type of assessment is useful for infants, toddlers, and preschool-age youngsters. In this procedure, families participate in the assessment process by identifying strengths and needs and are empowered in the process of determining which support services are most necessary (Gargiulo & Kilgo, 2014).

Effective assessment should be holistic, including both formal and informal measures (Turner, 2008). Information relative to the child's hearing, motor skills, oral and respiratory mechanisms, general physical condition, educational records, and social and developmental histories must be amassed and reviewed. In addition to physical, educational, and communicative ability, consideration of the child's psychological and social status, as well as family dynamics, will affect decisions regarding effective intervention strategies. IDEA 2004 mandates that information provided by parents be included in the assessment process. While testing is important, asking questions, gathering information, observing, and directly interacting with the child also yield critical insights. This type of informal assessment requires input from the child's family members, caregivers, and significant others. Open-ended questions such as "What concerns prompted you to seek evaluation of your child?" allow professionals to explore various social, cultural, and family issues that need to be considered in designing meaningful and individualized approaches to remediation. Awareness of these issues and their relationship to the communication difficulties provides a framework for effective treatment.

Observing the child's general appearance may also identify significant but subtle physical anomalies consistent with some congenital abnormalities that impair the communication process. Such markers might include low-set ears and peculiarities of the head, jaw, teeth, and tongue and should also be noted during the initial interview.

A speech assessment evaluates articulation, voice, and fluency abilities of the child. The articulation test is a formal evaluation procedure designed to identify sounds or phonemes that are not produced correctly in light of the student's age. The Goldman-Fristoe Test of Articulation 2 (Goldman & Fristoe, 2000) is a commonly used measure of articulation. When determining accuracy of production, test items evaluate various consonants in initial, middle, and final positions (for the sound /t/, for example, position varies in the words *two, platter,* and *cat*).

The professional who seeks to assess language pathology faces a formidable task, however, in determining what constitutes "normalcy" for language. Evaluating children in our culturally diverse society is particularly difficult. Care must be taken that normative data account for individual and cultural differences that affect language acquisition. How can we effectively distinguish speech and language pathology in the midst of

family-directed assessment:
A form of assessment, useful for infants, toddlers, and preschool-age youngsters, that focuses on information that families choose to provide regarding needs, concerns, resources, and priorities.

Effective Instructional Practices
Teaching Language Skills

The teacher's use of effective teaching strategies will help students with language difficulties gain the concepts and content that they need for success in content-area classes. Key strategies that can be used in teaching language concepts or patterns include the following:

- Gear the activities to the student's interests and cognitive level.
- Get the student's attention before engaging in communication activities.
- Bombard the student with the concept or skill frequently throughout the day in a functional manner.
- When speaking, place stress on the target concept or language pattern.
- Pause between phrases or sentences so that the student has time to process the new concept or language pattern.

- Decrease the rate of presentation when first introducing the concept or language pattern.
- When introducing a new concept or language pattern, use familiar vocabulary that can be readily visualized.
- If possible, present the new concept or language pattern by using more than one input mode (e.g., auditory, visual, kinesthetic). Gestures and facial expressions that are paired with a specific language pattern often assist students in understanding the form. For example, giving a look of puzzlement or wonder when asking a question can serve as a cue to the students.
- Pair written symbols with oral language. For instance, demonstrating morphological endings such as -s (plurals) and -ed (past tense) can be done in writing. The students can then be cued to listen for what they see.

SOURCE: S. Vaughn, C. Bos, and J. Schumm, *Teaching Students Who Are Exceptional, Diverse, and at Risk,* 8th ed. (Upper Saddle River, NJ: Pearson Education, 2014), p. 200.

---

cultural diversity? Educational professionals must observe the child's speech production and compare its quality and content to that of the child's own peers. Informal measures, such as conversational sampling of speech, often provide more useful information than do formal assessment tools. Educators are encouraged to use such informal evaluation methods to enhance the evaluation process (Turner, 2008). Obtaining a **language sample** from a very young child is sometimes impossible because the child does not have speech that is sufficiently developed to provide such a sample. In this case, **prelinguistic** communicative behaviors can be used; these are frequently obtained by parent interview as well as by direct observation. A variety of scales and checklists have been designed for this purpose. The BRIGANCE® Inventory of Early Development III (Brigance, 2013) is an excellent example of a criterion-referenced assessment that can be used in this way.

Any comprehensive assessment of linguistic ability will require a variety of assessment measures that consider developmental level, maturity, gender, ethnicity, and cultural background (Cohen & Spenciner, 2011). On the basis of such findings, objectives can be designed for the child and his or her family. Results of assessment may provide a baseline for pre- and postintervention comparisons, as well as indicating a need for referral to various other professional disciplines. Well-designed and -implemented evaluation techniques help determine whether linguistic competence is outside the range of normalcy, as well as clarify what communication problems are amenable to change, how much improvement can be expected, the need for a range of professional services, and variables that will influence treatment outcomes.

language sample: An observational evaluation that includes observing the speech and language characteristics of a child actively communicating.

prelinguistic: Communicative behaviors used by children before the formation of formal speech and language characteristics.

REFERENCE
Student Performance

SUGGESTIONS FOR THE CLASSROOM

Educational and Treatment Approaches for Central Auditory Processing Problems

One approach focuses on training certain auditory and listening skills, such as auditory discrimination (for example, telling the difference between *peas* and *bees*), localization of sound, sequencing sounds, or identifying a target sound in a noisy background. Training these skills in isolation, however, may not help a child understand complex language, such as a teacher's instructions. Therefore, another approach concentrates on teaching more functional language skills (vocabulary, grammar, conversational skills) and uses strategies (visual aids, repeating directions) to facilitate the processing of language.

Changes at home and in the classroom can also help a child with central auditory processing problems.

- **Seating:** to help the child focus and maintain attention, select seating that is away from auditory and visual distractions. A seat close to the teacher and the blackboard and away from the window and the door may be helpful.

- **Setting:** reduce external visual and auditory distractions. A large display of posters or cluttered bulletin boards can be distracting. A study carrel in the room may help. Earplugs may be useful to block distracting noise from a heater or air conditioner, the pencil sharpener, or talking in the hallway. Check with an audiologist to find out if earplugs are appropriate and which kind to use. Placing mats and cloth poster boards on classroom walls has been shown to decrease the reverberation of noise. A structured classroom setting may be more beneficial than an open classroom situation.

To improve the listening environment, an audiologist may recommend the use of a device that transmits the teacher's voice directly to the student's ear while blocking out background noise. The audiologist can provide recommendations on the potential benefit of available options based on the child's individual needs.

Speaking:

- Gain the child's attention before giving directions.

- Speak slowly and clearly, but do not overexaggerate speech.

- Use simple, brief directions.

- Give directions in a logical, time-ordered sequence. Use words that make the sequence clear, such as *first, next,* and *finally.*

- Use visual aids and write instructions to supplement spoken information.

- Emphasize key words when speaking or writing, especially when presenting new information. Pre-instructions with emphasis on the main ideas to be presented may also be effective.

- Use gestures that clarify information.

- Vary loudness to increase attention.

- Check comprehension by asking the child questions or asking for a brief summary after key ideas have been presented.

- Paraphrase instructions and information in shorter and simpler sentences rather than just repeating them.

- Encourage the child to ask questions for further clarification.

- Make instructional transitions clear.

- Review previously learned material.

- Recognize periods of fatigue and give breaks as necessary.

- Avoid showing frustration when the child misunderstands a message.

- Avoid asking the child to listen and write at the same time. For children with severe central auditory processing problems, ask a buddy to take notes, or ask the teacher to provide notes. Audio- or video-recording classes is another effective strategy.

Central auditory processing problems can affect learning, particularly in areas such as spelling and reading. It is important to identify problems early and help the child acquire adaptive strategies to compensate. If your student is a "poor" listener, frequently misunderstands speech, and has difficulty following directions, direct his or her parents to consult an audiologist or speech-language pathologist to determine if a problem exists.

SOURCE: Adapted from D. Kelly, *Processing Problems in Children* (San Antonio, TX: Communication Skills Builders, 1995), p. 25.

Figure 11.4 **Educational Placement of Students With Speech and Language Impairments**

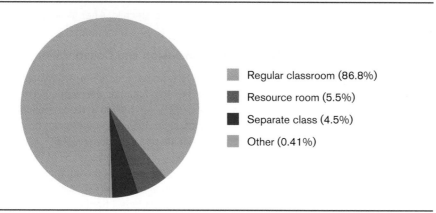

- Regular classroom (86.8%)
- Resource room (5.5%)
- Separate class (4.5%)
- Other (0.41%)

NOTE: This figure represents the percentages of enrollment of students with speech and language impairments during the 2011–2012 school year. Excludes pupils enrolled in parentally placed private schools and individuals in correctional facilities.

Other placements include separate schools, residential facilities, and homebound/hospital settings.

SOURCE: U.S. Department of Education. (2013). *Historical state-level IDEA data files.* Retrieved November 14, 2013, from http://tadnet.public.tadnet.org/pages/712

Educational Considerations

Educational planning for children with speech and language impairments involves many factors. Planning concepts that need to be considered in the classroom setting include seating arrangements, reducing distractions in the physical environment, and interactive techniques to enhance the teaching/learning process. The accompanying Suggestions for the Classroom feature outlines some suggestions and techniques that can be used by parents, general and special educators, and speech-language pathologists to help children with central auditory processing disorders. These approaches are also appropriate for many other speech and language impairments discussed in this chapter.

Where Are Students With Speech and Language Impairments Served?

The overwhelming majority of children with speech and language impairments are served in the regular or general education classroom. Figure 11.4 graphically represents the educational placements typically used with pupils who have a speech or language impairment.

Services for Young Children With Speech and Language Impairments

The very young child with a linguistic disorder represents a unique population. As knowledge regarding pediatric speech and language pathologies continues to expand, it has been noted repeatedly that there are time-locked "critical periods" for acquisition of communication skills. These windows of opportunity for language learning have historically been the subject of much study and debate. Is there an optimal time frame for providing intervention for communication disorders? Is there a point at which such intervention is really too late to be effective? Research suggests that for virtually

VIDEO
Classroom Suggestions

I realized I wanted to pursue a career as a speech-language pathologist when I was a high school senior working with a young neighbor. I earned an undergraduate degree in speech-language pathology as well as a master's degree in elementary education from the University of Montevallo. I am currently pursuing a second master's degree in special education. I have worked in public schools for many years teaching speech to preschool children and elementary-grade students. The children I have worked with had articulation disorders, delayed language development, and social skill deficits in addition to speech dysfluencies that hindered proper communication. I have led social groups to help pupils learn how to appropriately communicate and interact with their peers. I have been greatly blessed to be a part of the lives of these children and their families, and I will always be grateful that I have been able to walk with them on this journey.

I find that the most important thing I can do to help my students is to develop a good rapport with their parents. I invite parents to become a part of my class and to observe therapy with their children. I send frequent progress reports home and respond quickly to any notes, phone calls, or e-mails. As much as I am dedicated to being an effective speech-language pathologist, I deeply care about the daily stresses and struggles these parents encounter in raising their child. It is not an easy task, but every educator needs to remember that parents are the experts, and they need to be respected as such. In most instances, they have invested their entire lives in helping their son or daughter, and they often know what does and does not work with their child. After all, they were their child's first teacher.

Strategies for Inclusion and Collaboration

Collaboration begins with the referral process. While the special educator is often the team member who writes the individualized education program (IEP), information and observations from other teachers, therapists, and paraprofessionals are gathered to construct an appropriate and individualized IEP. Working and planning collaboratively with all of the teachers and professionals who are a part of the student's day help the child to work on speech and language goals throughout the day in his or her natural settings. I frequently meet with my students' teachers to share IEP goals and the progress each child has made. When teachers are aware of the success a student has had in learning a particular speech sound or language skill, they are able to follow up and help the student in their classroom as well.

The general education teacher is not the only person who works with the student who has a speech and language impairment. I inform all of the individuals who work with my students of ways that they can help support the child. Physical education teachers, lunchroom workers, the teacher in the computer lab, the media specialist, the guidance counselor, the music teacher, and any other therapists who work with my pupils are all aware of the strategies and techniques that they can use to support and encourage my students. In this way, the children are able to practice the skills that are needed in more than one environment. Furthermore, I believe it helps others who work with these children to be more compassionate and understanding.

Speech-language pathologists often remove pupils from their classroom due to the students' need for individualized and specialized therapy; however, a great deal can be accomplished in the general education classroom. I often teach language skills as a whole-class activity, and all the children

all communication deficiencies, the younger the child at the time of intervention, the more positive the outcome (Guralnick, 2011; Paul & Roth, 2011).

Early intervention to address communication problems in the young child is grounded by four guiding principles put forth by the American Speech-Language-Hearing Association (2008): Services are (1) family centered and culturally and linguistically responsive; (2) developmentally supportive, promoting children's participation in their natural environment; (3) comprehensive, coordinated, and team based; and (4) based on the highest-quality evidence available.

To provide effective intervention for the young child, we must first be able to identify those with speech and language impairments. Those at risk for having a delay in speech or language need to be screened early and at regular intervals.

benefit from the experience. In one instance, I had a child working on understanding figurative language. I went to his classroom and taught the entire class this skill while planning a lesson around the book *Amelia Bedelia*. It was a lot of fun for everyone.

I often start with students learning and practicing social skills. I then share with other teachers the skills under development, and together we find ways for the children to practice the skills throughout their school day. One of my students, who had been diagnosed with Asperger syndrome, was having a difficult time at lunch interacting with his peers and choosing appropriate topics to discuss, and was frequently bothering his teacher with unnecessary comments and requests. His classroom teacher, his special education teacher, his paraprofessional, and I met to help him with this problem. I taught him appropriate topics to ask about and discuss with his friends at lunch, and encouraged him to only talk to his teacher when absolutely necessary. We all took turns having lunch with him and his classmates so that we could prompt him to ask questions and participate in the natural conversation at the table. We were also able to help him with deciding what things did or did not need his teacher's attention, giving her a much-needed break. More important, this student was able to maintain and strengthen friendships with his classmates that were previously deteriorating. His mother also gave permission for the teacher to discuss her son's condition with his classmates. This made a tremendous difference. The children responded positively and openly to his uniqueness. I know that working collaboratively made a tremendous difference in this child's daily experiences at school.

I have also seen successful collaboration in our sensory motor group. This is a small group of students that meets with the occupational therapist, the special education teacher, and myself. This is an hour-long group where the children practice proprioceptive, vestibular, and balance activities. The pupils also listen to short stories that encourage proper questioning and responses in addition to learning vocabulary, recalling of events, and sequencing skills. We finish with a craft activity that addresses their individual sensory and tactile issues.

Participating in grade-level planning meetings is important as well. This has been very helpful in planning my own lessons for the children. I am able to plan lessons dealing with the same science and social studies topics that they are learning in the classroom, making the time they spend in therapy a more meaningful experience. Meeting with teachers regularly keeps me informed of how my students are performing in their classroom.

A Concluding Thought

While I sometimes find a need for a few of my students to practice articulation, language, and social skills in my classroom, I also find a very real benefit in providing therapy in inclusive settings.

Doing so provides appropriate peer models for the pupil with a speech and language impairment, and it allows me the opportunity to work with all the students while being a consultant to the other teachers and paraprofessionals on my team. Children are able to learn in their least restrictive environment and have more opportunities to practice skills while being full-fledged members of their classrooms. Their peers also learn to be understanding of individual differences, and all of the children benefit from the extra adult support in the classroom. I believe that I have learned as much as my students have from my inclusive education experience. I have developed so much professionally by watching my colleagues in action. Inclusion has helped me to become a better speech-language pathologist.

–Brooke T. Bunn
Former Speech-Language Pathologist
Jefferson County (Alabama) Schools

Children identified as high risk include, for example, youngsters from neonatal intensive care units, children with chronic ear infections, those with known genetic defects, and children with fetal alcohol syndrome, neurological defects, or delayed language.

Public Law 99–457 mandates that speech-language pathologists evaluate and treat children between the ages of 3 and 5; fortunately, all states currently serve youngsters from birth to 5 years of age. When providing services to infants, toddlers, and pre-schoolers, assessment of the family—its strengths, needs, and interaction patterns—is as important as the evaluation of the child. Because the structure of the American family is changing, caregivers other than parents may be involved in treatment strategies. Many of the newly developed rating scales, which specifically analyze

VIDEO
Inclusion

communication-promoting behaviors between a child and his or her caregiver, reflect the importance of this relationship. This type of observation is a valuable tool in quantifying strengths and weaknesses in daily communicative interactions—for example, the level of vocabulary used with the child, the number of attempts to engage the child in communication, the quality of voice animation and body language, responses to the child's attempts to communicate, and imitation of the child's efforts—and planning appropriate remediation strategies.

Evaluation of language skills in the preschool child should always include such measures as adaptive behavior scales, parent interviews, and informal language sampling. More formal assessment tools for examining language in very young children are increasing in number. Many of these tests are developmental scales that look at language as part of the assessment process.

Preschoolers with speech and language impairments (whether as a primary or secondary disability) generally thrive in general education classrooms. These settings provide daily interactions with peer models and exposure to a rich variety of experiences. Children have the opportunity to observe, learn, and practice age-appropriate social, communication, and cognitive skills. The single most essential element of language intervention in these settings is arranging the environment (McCormick, 2003b). Environmental arrangement entails selection and use of materials, arrangement of the physical space, and the provision of structure to activities.

Adolescents and Adults With Speech and Language Impairments

Transitioning from high school to the adult world presents a special challenge for professionals involved with adolescents with speech and language impairments. Many of these individuals encounter situations and issues that are similar to those faced by other young adults with and without disabilities such as employment decisions, living arrangements, and postsecondary educational choices to mention only a few. This is a period of rapid change that is compounded by a host of social, emotional, and psychological factors. Searching for one's own identity, coping with emerging sexuality, and striving for independence are just some of the complex issues that are exacerbated by communication difficulties. Working effectively with adolescents who exhibit speech and language impairments requires tremendous understanding and empathy from the speech-language pathologist. The intense desire of the adolescent to be like others can often hinder well-intentioned diagnostic and rehabilitative efforts.

Family Issues

Families with children who have speech and language impairments, like all families, exhibit complicated dynamics. When a problem affects one member of the family, other members are likely affected. It is important for professionals to understand and appreciate the emotional issues and stress that the some families of children with communication disorders confront. Luterman (2008), for instance, describes the medical model of assessment as "diagnosis by committee." In this model, parents are confronted by an array of professional "experts" delivering reports filled with technical jargon, much of which is neither understood nor retained. Indeed, many parents of children with speech and language impairments describe the initial assessment of their son or daughter as very unpleasant or upsetting. Unfortunately, contemporary medical and educational models for assessment and treatment of speech and language impairments are largely child centered in their approach. By ignoring the needs of the family, they often fail to address the concerns of those who are most significantly affected by the impairment.

Appropriately designed family-centered intervention is based only in part on formal assessment. The value of any assessment procedure is only as good as the intervention that accompanies it. Allowing parents to "tell their story," share concerns, and "be the expert" regarding their child is essential to empower them as partners in the habilitation process. Including parents and family members as active participants in both assessment and habilitation encourages involvement from those most intimately involved with the child, increasing effectiveness in treating communication disorders. Ideally, parents then emerge as actual partners in the rehabilitative process.

The hour or two a week that a child with a speech or language impairment might spend with a speech-language pathologist is infinitesimal compared to the time spent with other adults (parent, teachers) and peers. The speech-language pathologist attempts to learn as much as possible about the child's activities in various environments so that all of the child's communication partners can be involved in the intervention process. For instance, the speech-language pathologist works with family members to develop a better understanding of the child's needs and how best to facilitate interaction and communication. Specifically, the speech-language pathologist collaborates with family members to help them learn how to keep conversations with the child focused on the present, reduce distractions during conversations, slow the rate and decrease the complexity of language directed to the child, and maximize nonlinguistic cues.

The sooner early intervention begins for a youngster with communication disorders, the more promising the outcomes.

Issues of Diversity

The United States is currently experiencing record immigration. The number of foreign-born residents living in the United States is at its highest level in history, reaching 40 million citizens (Wasem, 2013). One result of this influx of new citizens is that one in five U.S. children has a parent who is an immigrant (Urban Institute, 2013). This most likely means that vast numbers of children who do not speak standard American English as their first language will likely need help with one aspect of language or another. Recent estimates suggest that approximately 4.7 million public school students are considered English learners (National Center for Education Statistics, 2013).

Over the past few years, the descriptor for individuals who are second-language learners has been changing. The term *limited English proficient* (LEP) is common in some educational circles; in fact, both IDEA 2004 and the No Child Left Behind Act incorporate this term when addressing the needs of students whose primary language is not English. Due to the perceived pejorative connotation associated with this term, the more contemporary label, *English learner* (EL), is now gaining in popularity among professionals.

How families interact with their children and the prelinguistic skills that develop from these interactions vary considerably across cultures (Johnson & Wong, 2002). Observations of non-Western cultural groups make it clear that the large literature on child-directed talk primarily describes Western parent-child interaction patterns. When working with children from culturally and linguistically diverse populations, the speech-language pathologist may draw teaching materials directly from the children's homes and communities, capitalizing on whatever communication skills they have, regardless of whether they are verbal or nonverbal, in English or another language.

The lack of reliable and valid assessments often makes it extremely difficult to accurately and fairly identify speech and language impairments in children from culturally and linguistically diverse populations (Guiberson & Atkins, 2012; Turner, 2008). There is always the issue of whether speech and language variations are due to a disability or to the child's competency in the second language (Bunce, 2003). Too often EL children are mistakenly placed in special education classes based on test scores that are normed on English-speaking students. Many of these students are misdiagnosed and incorrectly labeled as having an intellectual disability or a learning disability.

Intervention for EL children who have language impairments depends on their age, the severity of the disability, the goals of the family, and available social interactions along with vocational expectations (Bunce, 2003). Most intervention programs incorporate a variety of techniques similar to those used with monolingual children with language impairments, combined with techniques for second-language learners. These programs focus on the different components of language—phonology, morphology, syntax, semantics, and pragmatics. Additional techniques for second-language learners include (1) teaching vocabulary and syntax in the context of ongoing activities, (2) allowing time for comprehension to develop before insisting on production, (3) using predictable books, (4) using peer buddies, and (5) incorporating parents and other family members as teaching partners.

Technology and Individuals With Speech and Language Impairments

Children with speech and language impairments represent a very heterogeneous group of individuals. When one considers technology for pupils with speech and language impairments it is typically for students who cannot use their speech all or part of the time (American Speech-Language-Hearing Association, n.d.). Technology use for these students is referred to as augmentative and alternative communication (AAC). In other words, AAC is typically used by pupils with severe speech and language impairments. "Augmentative communication systems attempt to compensate for, temporarily or permanently, the impairment and disability patterns of individuals with severe expressive and receptive language disorders" (Vaughn, Bos, & Schumm, 2014, p. 197). Research suggests that AAC has significant benefits for individuals with speech and language impairments (Clarke et al., 2012; Owens, 2014).

AAC is actually a diverse range of technology. AAC not only includes low-tech, mid-tech, and high-tech options, as discussed in Chapter 5, but also is typically categorized into aided and unaided technology. Aided technology refers to tools external to a person (for example, picture symbols, Proloquo2Go® on an iPad), whereas unaided technology consists of nonverbal means of communication such as facial expressions or

augmentative and alternative communication (AAC): Symbols, aids, strategies, and techniques used as a supplement or alternative to oral language.

AUDIO
Computerized Voices

gestures as well as American Sign Language (ASL) (American Speech-Language-Hearing Association, n.d.; Owens, 2014).

Low-tech AAC includes the use of picture symbols, such as Picture Communication Symbols (PCS) by Mayer-Johnson or Blissymbols (American Speech-Language-Hearing Association, n.d.; Bondy, 2012). With picture symbols, students often use a communication board or book to select symbols to communicate. Mid-tech and high-tech AAC involves the selection of symbols or words to generate speech, using devices referred to as **speech-generating devices (SGDs)**. With mid-tech AAC, typically another individual records a finite set of words or phrases that a student can then select

Augmentative and alternative communication technology has opened a world of opportunity for individuals with speech and language impairments.

to communicate (for example, GoTalk by Attainment Company or Cheap Talk 8). With high-tech AAC, a pupil selects symbols or words to produce synthesized (digital) speech (for example, Accent by PRC or Tango by DynaVox). Increasingly, AAC is using mobile technologies, such as iPods, iPads, and even smartphones. Proloquo2Go®, for example, is a mobile technology app that involves individuals selecting symbols to generate speech output, similar to high-tech aided AAC devices (Sennott & Bowker, 2009).

Trends, Issues, and Controversies

Speech and language impairments represent a *high-incidence disability*—an impairment that has far-reaching and pervasive effects. Advances in the areas of early intervention, genetic research, and enhanced assistive technology continue to improve the prognosis for those with speech and language disorders. As research data confirm the merits of early intervention for children with communication disorders, particularly language disorders (Lipkin & Schertz, 2008), medical and educational professionals have become increasingly aware of the urgent need for early and accurate diagnosis and timely, well-designed interventions.

Cultural diversity and nonstandard English have come to the forefront of the educational arena because of their implications for linguistic performance. Common tools for assessing speech and language skills will continue to be reviewed for their adequacy in measuring linguistic abilities of children who are increasingly multicultural.

Controversy persists regarding the etiologies of various speech and language disorders such as CAPD and stuttering. With increased understanding of the underlying neurophysiological basis of such problems, educational management strategies for these and other disorders will continue to improve.

Digital technology has certainly enlarged the array of electronic devices that increase message redundancy or offer viable alternatives to conventional methods of communication. Assistive technology now provides avenues for communication that did not exist only a few years ago.

speech-generating device (SGD): A high-tech augmentative or alternative communication device capable of generating speech.

The Nature of Speech, Language, and Communication

- Speech is the expression of language with sounds—essentially, the oral modality for language.
- Language is a code whereby ideas about the world are represented through a conventional system of arbitrary signals for communication.
- Language has five components—phonology, morphology, syntax, semantics, and pragmatics—that are present at both the receptive and expressive levels.
- Communication is the exchange of ideas, information, thoughts, and feelings. It does not necessarily require speech or language.

Defining Speech and Language Impairments

- The most common speech problem is an articulation disorder, which includes substitutions, omissions, distortions, and additions.
- Stuttering and cluttering are examples of fluency disorders.
- Voice disorders are associated with the larynx. Phonation and resonance are illustrations of this disorder.
- Apraxia of speech involves both speech and language disorders. It results from the inability to position speech muscles necessary to produce speech sounds.
- Central auditory processing disorder (CAPD) is a problem in the processing of sound not attributed to hearing loss or intellectual ability.

Prevalence of Speech and Language Impairments

- About 20 percent of children receiving special education services are receiving services for speech and language impairments.

Etiology of Speech and Language Impairments

- Speech and language problems can result from functional (without an obvious physical basis) or organic (associated physiological deficit) etiologies.
- Disorders may be congenital or the result of an acquired insult.
- Aphasia is the loss or impairment of language functions.

Characteristics of Speech and Language Impairments

- The ability to understand what is meant by spoken communication is known as receptive language; the production of language that is understood by and meaningful to others is identified as expressive language.

Assessing Speech and Language Impairments

- Identifying speech and language impairments frequently involves collaborative teams using formal and informal performance measures.

Educational Considerations

- The vast majority (almost 87%) of pupils with speech or language impairments receive services in the general education classroom.

Technology and Individuals With Speech and Language Impairments

- Augmentative and alternative communication (AAC) devices include symbols, aids, strategies, and techniques used as a supplement or alternative to oral language. Sign language and communication boards, both manual and electronic, are two examples of these devices.

1. What are the two main categories of communication disorder?

2. How does IDEA define speech and language impairments?

3. List the three broad categories of speech disorders, and give an example of each.

4. Define language, and explain how it is different from speech.

5. List several factors that cause or contribute to voice disorders.

6. At what age should a child be pronouncing all sounds correctly? What course of action should be taken if he or she is not?

7. List the five rules that must be learned for successful language acquisition to occur.

8. Define central auditory processing disorder. What types of intervention strategies are most effective with this population?

9. Describe the evolution of the role of the speech-language pathologist during the twentieth century.

10. How does a developmental disorder differ from one that is acquired?

11. How has family-centered early intervention influenced remediation strategies for young children with speech and language impairments?

12. Define expressive and receptive language.

13. Describe an effective informal measure of communication skills for the young child.

14. What difficulties are inherent to assessment of speech and language skills in a culturally diverse population?

15. Define AAC and describe its use by children with speech and language impairments.

KEY TERMS

speech, 363

language, 363

phonology, 365

morphology, 365

syntax, 365

semantics, 365

pragmatics, 365

communication, 365

articulation disorders, 369

omissions, 369

substitutions, 369

distortions, 369

additions, 369

fluency disorders, 369

stuttering, 369

cluttering, 370

voice disorders, 370

phonation, 370

resonance, 370

hypernasality, 370

hyponasality, 370

phonological disorder, 372

apraxia of speech, 372

morphological disorder, 372

syntactical deficits, 372

semantic disorders, 372

pragmatic difficulties, 373

central auditory processing disorder (CAPD), 374

functional, 377

organic, 377

aphasia, 377

cleft lip, 378

cleft palate, 378

developmental language delay, 379

receptive language, 380

expressive language, 380

family-directed assessment, 384

language sample, 385

prelinguistic, 385

augmentative and alternative communication (AAC), 392

speech-generating devices (SGD), 393

LEARNING ACTIVITIES

1. Visit an educational setting serving students with speech and language impairments. How was the students' classroom performance affected by their communication difficulty? How were their social interactions with other students and teachers affected? Were any special teaching techniques used or classroom modifications made to enhance their performance? Was therapy given outside of the general education classroom? Was this arrangement positive or negative? How did intervention differ for older children? What was your overall impression of the services provided?

2. Visit a clinic or hospital in your community providing services to persons with speech and/or language impairments. Interview the speech-language pathologist. What types of disorders are served? Are there special challenges in assessment techniques? What types of intervention strategies are used? What interaction does this professional have with the community at large and with area schools? Is there a team approach in use? Is there a family-centered remediation model for implementing therapy?

3. Prepare a resource book for your class that describes common types of speech and language impairments and their characteristics. Include appropriate assessment, referral, and remediation strategies. Provide information on causes and prevention, assistive technology, need for early intervention, and classroom strategies. Provide websites appropriate to each disorder.

4. Compile a list of local agencies (public and private), medical facilities, and civic groups that provide services to

persons with speech and language impairments. Be sure to include contact information as well as a brief description of services provided.

5. Visit a local preschool program for children at risk for language delay. Interview a staff member. Find out how young children are screened for speech and language problems, and describe the process. Volunteer to help with screenings if possible. What types of language stimulation activities are used? How are families included in this process? What is your opinion regarding the effectiveness of the program?

ORGANIZATIONS CONCERNED WITH SPEECH AND LANGUAGE IMPAIRMENTS

Alliance for Technology Access

www.ataccess.org

American Speech-Language-Hearing Association (ASHA)

www.asha.org

Cleft Palate Foundation

www.cleftline.org

Division for Communicative Disabilities and Deafness (DCDD), Council for Exceptional Children

www.dcdd.us

National Craniofacial Association

www.faces-cranio.org

National Easter Seals Society

www.easterseals.com

REFLECTING ON STANDARDS

The following exercises are designed to help you learn to apply the Council for Exceptional Children (CEC) standards to your teaching practice. Each of the reflection exercises below correlates with knowledge or a skill within the CEC standards. For the full text of each of the related CEC standards, please refer to the standards integration grid located in Appendix B.

Focus on Professional Learning and Ethical Practice (*CEC Initial Preparation Standard 6.3*)

Reflect on what you have learned about how students with speech and language impairments are diagnosed. If you had a student in your class with a culturally or linguistically diverse background who exhibited signs of speech or language impairments, what kinds of issues might you have in defining and identifying if he or she had exceptional learning needs?

How might you need to work with families and school personnel to make sure to address the student's learning needs?

Focus on Instructional Planning and Strategies (*CEC Initial Preparation Standard 5.4*)

Reflect on what you have learned about students with speech and language impairments. If you were to have a student in your class who needed to daily meet with a speech-language pathologist, how might you support the student's attendance at therapy? How do you think the student might feel about standing out from his or her peers? How might his or her exceptional learning needs affect his or her relationships with peers? What can you, as a teacher, do to help alleviate any discomfort for the student?

⑤SAGE edge™

Sharpen your skills with SAGE edge at **edge.sagepub.com/gargiulo5e. SAGE edge for students** provides a personalized approach to help you accomplish your coursework goals in an easy-to-use learning environment.

Individuals With Hearing Impairments

A Parent's Story

We didn't think we would ever have a child. We were married for eleven years before the magic day. Christine is our little miracle child. Preparing for parenthood was lots of fun. We decorated a nursery, went shopping for furniture and clothes, and set up a college fund. Baby showers and teas were an exciting end to an uneventful pregnancy. My pregnancy was normal with no complications. The delivery was induced since my blood pressure was rising at the end. I had natural childbirth. She was beautiful—two eyes, one nose, one mouth, ten fingers, ten toes, and all in the right places. All the early checkups were routine, with no problems.

I didn't start to worry until Christine was about 6 months of age. My pediatrician listened to my concerns. At an office visit, Christine was playing with the paper on the exam table when the doctor came in. He clapped his hands loudly. I almost jumped out of my skin, but our little girl never knew he was in the room. He examined her ears and found nothing wrong. He sent us to an ENT (ear, nose, and throat specialist).

The first ENT said that there must be fluid behind her eardrums, so we got tubes. That didn't seem to make any difference. That ENT sent us to another ENT. The second ENT told me I was a hypochondriac and there was nothing wrong with my child. Finally, we were sent to another ENT, who diagnosed Christine as being hearing impaired, but because of her age, he was not sure of the severity. Let the grieving begin—no one plans on having a child with a disability. All our hopes and dreams popped like a balloon. What were we going to do? Where would we find help?

We started reading and calling, talking to everyone. Christine got her first set of hearing aids before her first birthday, but they were not strong enough. Each time we got bigger and more powerful hearing aids. At age 1, she was finally diagnosed as profoundly hearing impaired. We wanted her to talk. We wanted her to be independent. I didn't want to send her to a special school, isolated from society.

We started auditory-verbal therapy. We made it a part of our daily life. It was once told to us that auditory-verbal therapy was living your life but

VIDEO — Hearing Impairment

VIDEO — Parent Interview

VIDEO — Individual Interview

LEARNING OBJECTIVES

After reading Chapter 12, you should be able to:

- **Define** hearing impairment, deaf, and hard of hearing.
- **Distinguish** between conductive and sensorineural hearing loss.
- **Explain** the various assessment procedures used to measure hearing loss.
- **Describe** the difference between prelingual and postlingual hearing impairments.
- **Outline** the historical evolution of educational services for children and youth with hearing impairments.
- **List** possible causes of hearing loss.
- **Identify** representative academic, social, and language characteristics of individuals with hearing impairments.
- **Distinguish** among oral, manual, and total communication approaches for instructing students with hearing impairments.
- **Describe** the concept of the Deaf culture.
- **Summarize** educational services for persons with hearing impairments across the life span.
- **Explain** how technology benefits individuals with hearing impairments.

narrating everything you see and do. After about six months with the most powerful hearing aids made, we didn't see any or very much progress.

Being in the medical profession, we started reading and talking to people about cochlear implants. That would be the next step. We talked to several surgeons in Georgia, Texas, and Tennessee, and here at home in Alabama. Christine was implanted at 2 years, 4 months of age, and the implant was turned on the first of November. It was a frightening time for all of us. She was our little miracle child, and we had waited so very long for her. Christine's and our lives began again after her implant was stimulated. It worked! The first month was very hard on all of us, with lots of tears from us all. It was a new world with sound. Christine was turning to her name within two weeks. We worked with her every day, all waking hours. We sang, talked, and babbled.

Christine was enrolled in a church preschool with normally hearing kids. We pushed her out there, but we were always right behind her all the way. Currently, Christine is in a mainstreamed elementary school with a sound field system in the classroom. She gets some help from a teacher of the hearing impaired when she needs it. We are there to help with anything she might not understand and to reinforce what is taught in the classroom. She is making straight As so far. Christine enjoys dancing competitively. We don't know how she does it.

If you were to sit and talk to her today, you would never know she had a disability. She has beautiful speech with great inflections in her voice. We were at a company party, and there were a lot of people we didn't know and who didn't know us. The kids were all swimming in the lake. I overheard one little boy ask his mother why Christine didn't talk to him, as she did earlier that day. I interrupted and asked the little boy if she had her back to him while he was talking. We told him she was deaf and could not hear him without her processor on. All the other parents were astonished. "But she talks so well—she doesn't sound deaf or sign," people said. We had to tell them all about cochlear implants and what a huge change it made in our life. Christine sounds like any other normally hearing child. That made us feel great. Strangers couldn't tell she was hearing impaired.

If we can tell anyone about cochlear implants, it would be to say that it was the best thing that happened to us. It is worth looking into and doing. It is a lot of hard work. As a family, we have dedicated many hours and much money to the rehabilitation of Christine.

We are very grateful for having a child like her. She is a joy to be with, and watching her now—all the hard work we did early on has paid off. Granted, she will never have normal hearing and has to work harder than anyone in her classes, but we wouldn't change a thing. She is a great example of what a cochlear implant at an early age can do for someone.

—Kitty McBride

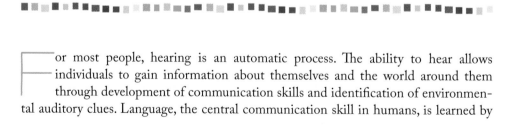

For most people, hearing is an automatic process. The ability to hear allows individuals to gain information about themselves and the world around them through development of communication skills and identification of environmental auditory clues. Language, the central communication skill in humans, is learned by

Chapter contribution written by Betty Nelson, University of Alabama at Birmingham

VIDEO

Individual Interview

interacting with the environment and associating stimuli in numerous ways (Allen & Cowdery, 2012). Typically, an individual's language is refined and speech is developed through a series of activities: observing, listening, understanding, imitating others, hearing oneself, and comparing and perfecting speech and language components of the communication process. Parts of these activities and the development of language and speech may be difficult for individuals with hearing impairments.

Definitions and Concepts in the Field of Hearing Impairment

Hearing impairment is a general term used to describe disordered hearing. We should point out that the use of this term is offensive to some individuals who are deaf and hard of hearing because the word *impairment* implies a deficiency. Although we acknowledge this viewpoint, the label *hearing impairment* is preferred by the federal government when describing this disability category. We have chosen to be consistent with the terminology used by the U.S. Department of Education.

Hearing sensitivity loss refers to a specific aspect of hearing impairment, and is ordinarily described as ranging in severity from mild to profound. The term deaf is often overused and misunderstood, and may be applied inappropriately to describe the various types of hearing loss. It can be defined as referring to those for whom the sense of hearing is nonfunctional for the ordinary purposes of life. IDEA 2004 (the Individuals with Disabilities Education Improvement Act, or PL 108–446) describes deafness as a hearing loss that adversely affects educational performance and is so severe that the child is impaired in processing linguistic information (communication) through hearing, with or without amplification (hearing aids). The term *Deaf,* used with a capital *D*, refers to those individuals who want to be identified with Deaf culture. It is inappropriate and misleading to use the term *deaf* in reference to any hearing loss that is mild or moderate in degree.

Persons who are hearing impaired but possess enough residual hearing (remaining usable hearing) to hear and understand speech may be described as hard of hearing. Individuals who are hard of hearing are those in whom the sense of hearing, although defective, is functional either with or without a hearing aid. For these persons, the use of a hearing aid is frequently necessary or desirable to enhance residual hearing (Kuder, 2013).

The extent to which persons with hearing impairment have difficulty in developing speech and language is heavily influenced by the degree of hearing loss.

The Anatomy of the Auditory System

The ear is divided into four connected sections: the outer ear (also known as the auricle), the middle ear, the inner ear, and the central auditory nervous system (see Figure 12.1). The outer ear functions to protect the middle ear, direct sound into the ear canal, and enhance sound localization. In addition, the outer ear serves to enhance the intensity of sounds in the midfrequency range where the sound spectrum of speech is located.

Sound waves enter the outer ear and travel through the ear canal to the tympanic membrane (eardrum), causing a vibrating action. The tympanic membrane is attached to one of the three smallest bones in the body, the malleus (hammer), through which the sound vibrations are transmitted to the second and third of the smallest bones, the incus (anvil) and the stapes (stirrup). These three bone structures form the ossicular chain, a bridge of bones across which sound vibrations travel to the inner ear.

---

hearing impairment: Less than normal hearing (either sensitivity or speech understanding) resulting from auditory disorder(s).

hearing sensitivity loss: Poorer than normal auditory sensitivity for sounds; usually measured in decibels (dB) using pure tones.

deaf: Limited or absent hearing for ordinary purposes of daily living.

hard of hearing: Refers to a person who has a hearing loss but uses the auditory channel as the primary avenue for oral communication, with or without a hearing aid.

outer ear: The most visible (external) part of the ear, useful in funneling sound to the ear canal and in localizing the source of sound.

middle ear: The air-filled space behind the eardrum that contains three tiny bones (ossicles) that carry sound to the inner ear.

inner ear: The snail-shaped part of the ear (cochlea) containing the organs of hearing and balance.

central auditory nervous system: Part of the hearing mechanism connecting the ear to the brain.

tympanic membrane: A thin, membranous tissue between the ear canal and the middle ear that vibrates when struck by sound waves; also called the eardrum.

malleus: The first and largest of the three middle ear bones for conducting sound to the inner ear. Also called the hammer, it is attached to the tympanic membrane.

incus: The second of the three middle ear bones for conducting sound to the inner ear, located between the malleus and the stapes; also called the anvil.

stapes: The third of the middle ear bones for conducting sound to the inner ear. It resembles a stirrup in shape and is sometimes called the stirrup. It is the smallest bone in the body.

ossicular chain: Three bones in the middle ear (malleus, incus, and stapes) that connect the eardrum to the inner ear and help to amplify sounds.

Figure 12.1 **A Cross Section of the Human Ear**

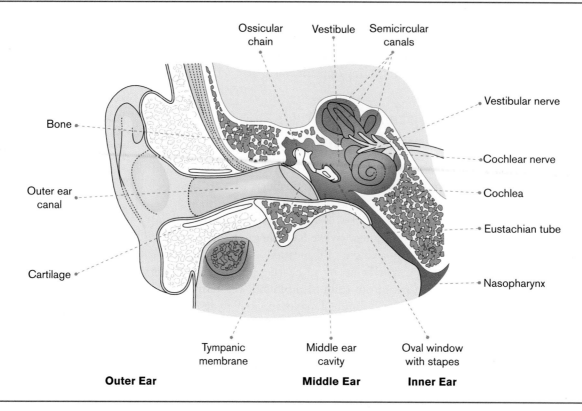

Ossicular chain · Vestibule · Semicircular canals

Bone

Outer ear canal

Cartilage

Vestibular nerve

Cochlear nerve

Cochlea

Eustachian tube

Nasopharynx

Tympanic membrane · Middle ear cavity · Oval window with stapes

Outer Ear · **Middle Ear** · **Inner Ear**

SOURCE: Redrawn from J. Northern, *Hearing Disorders,* 3rd ed. (Boston, MA: Allyn & Bacon, 1996), p. 16.

Together with the tympanic membrane, the ossicles convert airborne sound waves into mechanical (vibratory) energy and transfer this to the inner ear.

The footplate of the stapes, the smallest of the three middle ear bones, fits into the oval window, an opening into the inner ear. The vibratory motion of the stapes footplate in the oval window transmits mechanical energy to fluid-filled channels within the snail-like structure of the cochlea (inner ear). The cochlea houses the end organ of hearing, called the organ of Corti. Waves set up in the cochlear fluid, the result of vibratory energy from the tympanic membrane and ossicular chain, stimulate nearly 20,000 tiny hair cells in the organ of Corti arrayed along the length of the cochlea. This mechanical energy is transformed into electrical nerve impulses. The hair cells near the oval window respond to high-frequency energy, and those in the middle and at the apex of the cochlea respond to low-frequency energy. The resultant nerve impulses course through the auditory nervous system pathways to the auditory cortex, located in the temporal lobe of the brain, for message decoding (Buethe, Vohr, & Herer, 2013).

Classifications of Hearing Loss

The classification or type of hearing loss refers primarily to the site of disorder in the auditory system causing the hearing impairment. A conductive hearing loss is caused by a blockage or barrier to the transmission of sound through the outer or middle ear. It is referred to as a conductive loss because sound is not conducted normally through the mechanical sound-conducting mechanisms in the disordered outer or middle ear

oval window: The link between the inner ear and the middle ear.

cochlea: Shell- or spiral-shaped structure in the inner ear that is responsible for hearing.

organ of Corti: Organ of hearing found within the cochlea.

conductive hearing loss: The loss of sound sensitivity produced by abnormalities of the outer ear and/or middle ear.

REFERENCE

Audiology

(Stach, 2010). As a result, sounds are soft or attenuated in some way for the listener, but clearly heard when loud enough. Common causes of a conductive loss include inflammation, infection of the middle ear (otitis media), objects in the ear, or malformations of the outer or middle ear. Typically, a conductive loss can be reversed by medical or surgical intervention.

A **sensorineural hearing loss** is caused by disorders of the inner ear (cochlea), the auditory nerve that transmits impulses to the brain, or both. In this type of hearing loss, there is not only a loss of hearing sensitivity, but sounds are usually distorted to the listener and speech often is not heard clearly. This type of hearing loss may be congenital or may occur as a result of accident, illness, or disease. Although a small percentage of sensorineural hearing losses can be medically or surgically treated, most cannot be and are permanent in nature (Bess & Humes, 2008).

A **mixed hearing loss** is a combination of both a conductive and a sensorineural loss. In many cases, the conductive portion of the hearing loss may respond to medical or surgical treatment. Typically, however, the listener continues to experience the effects of the residual sensorineural impairment and may be a candidate for a hearing aid (Bess & Humes, 2008).

A **central hearing disorder** is one resulting from disorder or dysfunction in the central auditory nervous system between the brain stem and the auditory cortex in the brain. A hearing loss may or may not accompany this type of hearing impairment. The listener with this impairment may be able to hear, but cannot make sense of or understand speech. Additional problems, such as short- and long-term auditory memory and reading comprehension disability (Salvia, Ysseldyke, & Bolt, 2013), may also be present. This impairment may be referred to as a central auditory processing disorder, as described in Chapter 11 (Stach, 2010).

Measurement of Hearing Impairment

An **audiologist** is a professional who holds certification and/or licensure and provides evaluation, rehabilitation, and prevention services to persons with hearing impairments. Audiologists are the primary specialists in evaluating hearing loss and determining the extent to which that loss constitutes an impairment and disability. Typically, the assessment of hearing begins with the goal of accurately measuring hearing threshold levels. If a hearing loss exists, the audiologist uses test and measurement procedures to determine the extent of the deficit, the impact on communication function, whether the hearing loss can be treated medically or surgically, and whether the use of hearing aids or other amplification systems is indicated.

Auditory threshold measures obtained by the audiologist during a hearing evaluation are plotted on a graph called an **audiogram** (see Figure 12.2). The horizontal axis of an audiogram is divided into octave intervals corresponding to the principal test

Accurate assessment of a hearing loss is important for determining its impact on communication.

sensorineural hearing loss: The loss of sound sensitivity produced by abnormalities of the inner ear or nerve pathways beyond the inner ear to the brain.

mixed hearing loss: Hearing losses resulting from both conductive and sensorineural hearing impairments.

central hearing disorder: Difficulty in the reception and interpretation of auditory information in the absence of a hearing loss.

audiologist: A professional who studies the science of hearing, including anatomy, function, and disorders, and provides education and treatment for those with hearing loss.

audiogram: A graphic representation of audiometric findings showing hearing thresholds as a function of frequency.

Figure 12.2 **Audiograms Demonstrating Types of Hearing Loss**

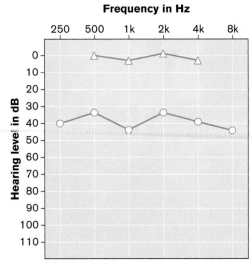

Panel A

An audiogram demonstrating that when the outer or middle ear is not functioning normally, resulting in a conductive hearing loss, the intensity of the air-conducted signals must be raised before threshold is reached while the bone-conduction thresholds remain normal.

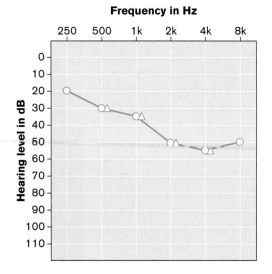

Panel B

An audiogram demonstrating that when a hearing loss is of cochlear origin, resulting in a sensorineural hearing loss, both air- and bone-conduction thresholds are affected similarly.

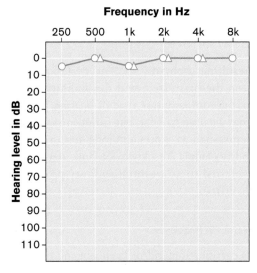

Panel C

An audiogram showing that when the outer and middle ear are functioning normally, air-conduction and bone-conduction thresholds are the same.

○ Air conduction   △ Bone conduction

SOURCE: Adapted from B. Stach, *Clinical Audiology: An Introduction,* 2nd ed. (Clifton Park, NY: Delmar/Cengage Learning, 2010), pp. 89–91.

Noise levels are measured in decibels (dB). The higher the decibel level, the louder the noise. Sounds louder than 80 dB are considered potentially hazardous. The noise chart below gives an idea of average decibel levels for everyday sounds around you.

Human Perception	Decibel Level
Painful	• 150 dB = rock music peak • 140 dB = firearms, air raid siren, jet engine • 130 dB = jackhammer • 120 dB = jet plane takeoff, amplified rock music at 4–6 feet, car stereo, band practice
Extremely Loud	• 110 dB = rock music, model airplane • 106 dB = timpani and bass drum rolls • 100 dB = snowmobile, chain saw, pneumatic drill • 90 dB = lawnmower, shop tools, truck traffic, subway
Very Loud	• 80 dB = alarm clock, busy street • 70 dB = busy traffic, vacuum cleaner • 60 dB = conversation, dishwasher
Moderate	• 50 dB = moderate rainfall • 40 dB = quiet room
Faint	• 30 dB = whisper, quiet library

SOURCE: Adapted from the American Speech-Language-Hearing Association. Available at http://www.asha.org/public/hearing/disorders/noise.htm

frequencies of interest during the evaluation. The frequency of a particular sound is a measure of the rate at which the sound source vibrates and is measured in hertz (Hz), so named in honor of a German scientist. The frequency of sounds can be precisely measured electronically. Pitch is the psychological correlate of frequency and cannot be measured as precisely because it is perceived differently from one person to the next. But in general, as the frequency of a sound increases, a listener perceives the sound as having increased in pitch. The audiogram typically displays a range of frequencies from about 250 Hz to 8,000 Hz. Most sounds important to human beings fall between 125 and 8,000 Hz, with most of the energy in human speech concentrated in the range of 500 to 3,000 Hz (Berk, 2013).

The vertical axis of the audiogram displays hearing threshold levels (HTLs) in increments of 10 decibels (dB), with 0 dB at the top (representing no hearing loss). As the hearing loss increases, the hearing thresholds are plotted lower down on the audiogram. Decibels are units of sound pressure. Sound pressure is a physical measure that can be precisely determined. It is associated with the psychological sensation of loudness, which is not perceived identically by all persons. In general, as sound pressure in decibels increases, the sensation of loudness increases. Human speech normally ranges between a 40- and 60-dB sound pressure level; any sound above a 130-dB sound pressure level, such as large electrical turbines (145 dB), can be extremely painful and damaging (Bess & Humes, 2008). Table 12.1 presents the decibel levels of everyday sounds from our environment.

During the basic hearing evaluation process, pure-tone audiometry is conducted through earphones or other means to obtain an audiogram. Stimuli are delivered to the listener until a test signal of a particular frequency is barely audible 50 percent of the time. It is then presented to the person being evaluated, and a hearing threshold level for that signal can be plotted on the audiogram. This is a convenient and well-accepted measurement technique permitting an efficient determination of hearing threshold

frequency: The number of vibrations per second of a given sound wave; typically measured as cycles per second (cps) or hertz (Hz).

hertz (Hz): A unit of measurement for sound frequency, expressed as cycles per second (cps).

pure-tone audiometry: A procedure for measuring hearing sensitivity at certain frequencies using tones that are presented at various intensities.

levels across the frequency range most important for hearing and understanding speech and environmental sounds. Ordinarily, pure-tone audiometry will be conducted in two modes, air conduction and bone conduction. Air-conduction audiometry is carried out with earphones or speakers and reflects hearing thresholds measured through the outer, middle, and inner ears. In contrast, bone-conduction audiometry is carried out with a small vibrator placed on the forehead or on the bone behind the ear, stimulating the inner ear directly. This reflects hearing sensitivity as measured primarily from the inner ear, not from the conductive mechanism in the outer and middle ears. A comparison of air- and bone-conduction hearing threshold levels forms the basis of determining the type of hearing loss present.

For example, Panel A in Figure 12.2 (page 404) shows a conductive hearing loss. When the audiogram is examined closely, the bone-conduction HTLs can be seen to be clustered around the 0-dB level, suggesting no hearing loss for these stimuli. On the other hand, Os, representing air-conduction HTLs, cluster around the 40-dB hearing level. These results suggest that, when the inner ear is stimulated directly by bone conduction, hearing thresholds are normal. However, when the test stimuli are delivered through the ear canal, a 40-dB hearing loss is present. This leads the audiologist to suspect the presence of some conductive disorder affecting the outer or middle ear transmission system that may be causing the hearing loss. Panel B displays findings for an individual with similar bone- and air-conduction deficits, indicating mild to moderate sensorineural hearing loss. Panel C in Figure 12.2 illustrates normal hearing threshold levels. It can be seen that both triangles (bone conduction) and Os (air conduction) cluster around the 0- to 10-dB range at each test frequency, suggesting no hearing loss.

Other Types of Hearing Assessment

Often, a hearing screening is the initial point at which hearing loss is suspected, and more sophisticated audiological procedures may be required. The American Speech-Language-Hearing Association (ASHA, 2002) has developed guidelines for hearing screening. ASHA suggests that the process involve (1) a case history; (2) visual inspection of the outer ear, ear canal, and eardrum; (3) pure-tone audiologic hearing screening; and (4) tympanometry screening. It is important to note that hearing screening aims to determine only whether a hearing loss may be present, not the degree or type of hearing impairment.

Audiologists are trained to conduct hearing screening programs in hospital newborn nurseries, in schools, and for adults. Some school systems employ audiologists, and hearing screening programs may fall within their purview. However, in most school settings, it is the speech-language pathologist who is best equipped to conduct hearing screening, refer students who are suspected of having a hearing loss for further audiologic evaluation, and make recommendations for school placement. Audiologic assessment is an essential component in the determination of a hearing loss and its impact on communication. However, a thorough assessment battery, including assessment of cognitive functioning, speech and language skills, social-emotional adjustment, and academic achievement, is required for appropriate school placement (Simeonsson & Rosenthal, 2001).

Hearing is a complex hierarchy of functions, the assessment of which requires highly sophisticated instrumentation and procedures in a clinical setting. Furthermore, testing procedures appropriate for adults are not useful with young children and individuals with special needs. For example, play audiometry is often used with children who are difficult to test or unable to follow simple commands. In this procedure, the child is conditioned to respond to sounds in specific ways in order to determine the hearing threshold levels. Speech audiometry measures an individual's speech recognition threshold (SRT), as

air-conduction audiometry: A procedure for measuring hearing sensitivity at certain frequencies using pure tones presented to the listener through earphones or speakers.

bone-conduction audiometry: A procedure for measuring hearing sensitivity at certain frequencies using pure tones presented through an oscillator placed on the forehead or mastoid bone of the listener. Sound is conducted to the inner ear through the bones of the skull.

play audiometry: A method for measuring hearing sensitivity in young children by rewarding correct responses; turning the evaluation situation into a game in order to maintain interest and cooperation.

speech audiometry: A set of procedures for measuring auditory perception of speech, including syllables, words, and sentences.

speech recognition threshold (SRT): A measure of threshold sensitivity for speech. The SRT represents the softest sound level at which a listener can identify the stimuli 50 percent of the time.

VIDEO

Hearing Loss

well as that person's speech recognition ability in various listening conditions. Other types of auditory system assessment include electrophysiological measures of auditory function from the inner ear through the auditory brain stem to the cortex of the brain (**auditory evoked potentials**). **Evoked otoacoustic emissions** from the inner ear can be measured with sensitive microphones to examine functions in the inner ear far beyond the understanding of scientists in the past. To detect possible problems in the middle ear, **acoustic immittance** measures are used, placing a small probe in the ear to measure the transmission of sound through the eardrum and ossicular chain (American Speech-Language-Hearing Association, 2010). Using all of these procedures, audiologists have opened new windows into mechanisms to evaluate human hearing, leading to better assessment and remediation for those with hearing impairments.

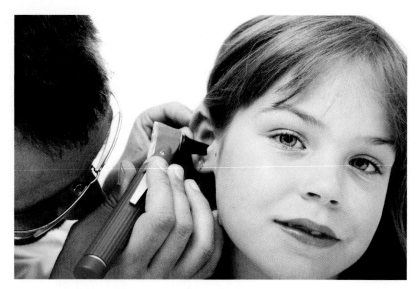

Special assessments are often used when evaluating the hearing of young children or students with special needs.

Age of Onset

The effects of hearing impairment depend significantly on the age at which the impairment occurs. **Prelingual** hearing impairment refers to disordered hearing present at birth or occurring before the development of speech and language. **Postlingual** impairment describes an auditory deficit acquired after the acquisition of speech and language (Berk, 2013). The age at which the hearing loss occurs is critical because normal language development is very much dependent on an intact auditory system.

Not surprisingly, postlingually deaf children generally develop better speech, language, reading, and writing skills than prelingually deaf youngsters. Currently, great importance is placed on the early identification of hearing impairment in neonates and infants so that early intervention can reduce the effects of the hearing impairment on these skills, as well as on other areas such as social/cognitive development and academic achievement (Gallagher, Easterbrooks, & Malone, 2006).

The American Speech-Language-Hearing Association (2013c) estimates that hearing loss affects 12,000 children born in the United States each year; approximately 3 in 1,000 babies are born with permanent hearing loss. Hearing loss is the most common congenital disorder in newborns. All states screen newborns for hearing loss, and forty-seven states have legislation that mandates hearing screening of newborns prior to discharge from the hospital (Buethe et al., 2013).

A Brief History of the Field

The history of education of the hearing impaired is complex and controversial. Hearing impairments have probably existed in North America since the early settlement of this area by diverse Native American populations. Despite occasional references to provision of educational services for individuals with hearing impairments, however, there is no evidence of any organized program development until the nineteenth century (Moores, 2001).

auditory evoked potentials: Neural impulses produced from within the auditory system in response to stimulation of the auditory pathway and recorded as bioelectric events using a special computer.

evoked otoacoustic emissions: Sounds produced by the inner ear in response to auditory stimulation and measured in the ear canal.

acoustic immittance: A technical term for measurements of middle ear function.

prelingual: Referring to the period of time prior to a child's development of language.

postlingual: Referring to the period of time after a child has developed language.

VIDEO
Parent Interview

In 1817, the first school in the United States for students with significant hearing impairments, the Connecticut Asylum for the Education and Instruction of Deaf and Dumb Persons, was established in Hartford, Connecticut. This institution was begun through the efforts of a young divinity student named Thomas Hopkins Gallaudet. The name of the school was eventually changed to the American School for the Deaf, and the student population broadened to include individuals with hearing impairment from other states (Moores, 2001).

During this time period in France, a number of schools for the hearing impaired were experimenting with l'Epée's methods of communication, which were primarily manual. Gallaudet visited these schools and was greatly influenced by the work of l'Epée. In an effort to establish effective systems of manual communication in the United States, Gallaudet brought Laurent Clerc, a deaf Frenchman and well-known educator of the hearing impaired, to the United States. However, other American deaf educators went to Europe and were impressed by the oral approaches and philosophies. Of special interest were those methods that discouraged the use of any form of manual communication or sign language (Van Hasselt, Strain, & Hersen, 1988).

Many parents of children with significant hearing impairments assumed that living and learning with other individuals with similar problems was best for their children, and early formal education efforts were centered primarily in residential schools. Residential schools at this time were selective and would not serve all students with significant hearing impairments, especially those from minority groups or those with other significant disabilities. Day schools gained popularity partly because of these restrictive policies.

In 1864, Abraham Lincoln signed legislation establishing the nation's first college for the hearing impaired, known today as Gallaudet University. However, the debate over which method (oral or manual) was more appropriate for the instruction and communication of individuals with significant hearing impairments was now in full force. The two central figures in this debate were Thomas Gallaudet's son Edward, a renowned legal scholar, and Alexander Graham Bell, known to most as the inventor of the telephone and audiometer, who was an internationally recognized educator of the deaf. Bell's position centered on the issue of segregation in policy and practice. He believed that the manual philosophy, particularly in residential schools, as well as the use of sign language, fostered segregation of individuals with significant hearing impairments from the mainstream of society. Bell proposed a number of radical pieces of legislation that would (1) eliminate residential schools, (2) ban the use of manual communication in any form, (3) legislate that no adult with a significant hearing impairment could become a teacher of the deaf, and (4) forbid two adults with significant hearing impairments to marry. Interestingly, for many years the oral approach was more widely accepted than the manual position.

Edward Gallaudet strongly opposed these positions from both a moral and a methodological point of view. He believed that those who used the manual method (1) could learn when expectations were appropriately high, (2) would not feel isolated from society, (3) could and would participate in general life activities, and (4) would benefit socially by having friends with common interests (Moores, 2001). Eventually, Gallaudet's position gained support in Congress through appropriations to establish teacher preparation programs emphasizing the manual approach.

In the 1970s, total communication (TC)—combining a number of sensory modalities with manual and oral communication—was adopted by many professionals as the best approach to working with individuals with significant hearing impairments. Those who argued for TC criticized the practice of keeping many children with hearing impairments in oral programs until 9 or 10 years of age, especially those who had limited early success, because critical periods for attaining the basic linguistic principles were potentially missed. Those who argued against TC expressed concern that it would be difficult to emphasize all methods of communication and do justice

manual communication: Communication methods that utilize fingerspelling, signs, and gestures.

oral approaches: Methods of instruction for children with hearing impairments that emphasize spoken language skills. Methodology attempts to use the child's residual hearing and employs auditory training and speechreading.

total communication: A method of communication for students with hearing impairments, designed to provide equal emphasis on oral and signing skills to facilitate communication ability.

AUDIO
Loss of Hearing

The issue of what constitutes the least restrictive environment for students with hearing impairments is controversial.

to all. They further argued that the manual method would be the primary avenue of communication because it was significantly quicker and easier to learn. The debate continues today, indicated by the fact that Gallaudet University publishes a journal with a total communication orientation (*American Annals of the Deaf*), and the AG Bell Association publishes one with an oral orientation (*Volta Review*). Both journals are world renowned for their quality of content and research articles.

The educational placement options available for children with hearing impairments today are a result of historical, political, and cultural forces. Since the 1980s, there has been a significant increase in the visibility of cultural advocacy groups for individuals who are hearing impaired. The "deaf rights" movement, embraced by many residential schools and deaf communities, increasingly polarized proponents of various methodologies. Advanced medical interventions such as gene therapy and cochlear implantation were not initially embraced by many culturally deaf adults, further complicating the cultural controversy. Educators today struggle to determine what constitutes the least restrictive environment (LRE) within the public school arena for children with significant hearing impairment. Although a number of educational placement options are available to facilitate LRE, parents as well as professionals frequently find themselves drawing legal and educational battle lines simply trying to *define* what constitutes such an environment.

The 1997 amendments to IDEA (PL 105–17) introduced a requirement to consider the communication needs of children with hearing impairments when making educational placement decisions. IDEA 2004 continues this stipulation. Communication-rich environments are an essential element in the education of children who are deaf and hard of hearing (Katz & Schery, 2006). What might be the LRE for many other children with disabilities may not be the LRE for a student with a hearing impairment because of the child's unique communication needs. Are there peers at the recommended placement site who can communicate with the child? Does the teacher have adequate skills in the communication mode typically used by the child? Does the teacher possess the skills necessary to meet the unique instructional needs of a student with hearing impairments? There are many questions regarding the implementation of the LRE requirement to consider—especially the communication needs of the pupil. Unfortunately, personnel responsible for making placement recommendations frequently do not have an adequate understanding of the educational needs of children who are deaf or hard of hearing (Easterbrooks & Baker, 2001; Katz & Schery, 2006).

Prevalence of Hearing Impairment

The number of Americans with a hearing loss has nearly doubled in the past three decades. Investigators estimate that hearing loss affects over 28 million people (American Speech-Language-Hearing Association, 2013e). Current information suggests that hearing loss increases as people age; 18 percent of "baby boomers" (individuals in their mid-40s to mid-60s) experience hearing loss while 29 percent of 65-year-olds have a hearing loss. By way of comparison, less than 2 percent of children under age 18 have a hearing loss (Kochkin, 2013).

According to the U.S. Department of Education (2013a), approximately 69,300 students between the ages of 6 and 21 were considered to have a hearing impairment during the 2011–2012 school year. These students represent 1.1 percent of all pupils with disabilities. At the same time, over 9,300 preschoolers were receiving a special education because of a hearing impairment. This figure represents 1.2 percent of all preschoolers with a disability.

Etiology of Hearing Impairment

Causes of hearing loss can be classified in several ways. For example, hearing losses may be congenital (occurring before birth) or acquired (occurring after birth). Hearing losses occurring around the time of birth are generally considered to be congenital, whether or not the loss was actually documented at that time. Further, hearing losses may be classified as genetic or nongenetic. Genetic or hereditary factors are one of the leading causes of hearing impairments in children. It has been estimated that in approximately one third of all persons with hearing loss greater than about 55 dB, the origin of the loss is hereditary (Toriello & Smith, 2013). Adventitious (acquired) hearing losses of this magnitude constitute roughly another third of all cases, and unknown factors are responsible for the remaining third. The etiology of hearing loss is an important variable in determining immediate and long-range educational strategies.

Genetic/Hereditary Factors

Genetic causes are thought to account for more than two hundred different types of deafness (Buethe et al., 2013). Researchers estimate that about one half of all congenital deafness is the result of genetic factors (Petersen & Willems, 2006). Of the several known modes of genetic inheritance, three mechanisms are most important. Autosomal dominant inheritance is characterized by expression of a trait (for example, hearing loss) even if the gene for it is carried on only one chromosome of a matched pair. Waardenburg syndrome is an example of autosomal dominant hearing loss.

In autosomal recessive inheritance, both genes of a pair must carry the characteristic in order for it to be expressed. Usher syndrome is an example of autosomal recessive inheritance.

adventitious (acquired) hearing loss: Hearing loss that is acquired after birth, not inherited.

autosomal dominant: A genetic form of inheritance involving the non–sex-linked chromosomes in which the individual has one normal and one abnormal gene in a gene pair.

autosomal recessive: A genetic form of inheritance involving the non–sex-linked chromosomes in which both genes of a gene pair must be affected for the trait to be expressed.

Table 12.2 **Disorders Associated With Hearing Loss in Children**

Disorder	Description
Cytomegalovirus (CMV)	• Most common congenital viral infection causing hearing loss today, occurring in 1 in 1,000 live births • Contracted in utero or postnatally from the mother • Can result in sensorineural hearing loss as well as central nervous system, cardiac, optic, and growth abnormalities • Symptoms may not be apparent at birth, with onset about 18 months of age • Progresses rapidly during the first year
Down Syndrome	• Congenital chromosomal abnormality (trisomy 21) • Frequently have low-set small ears, external canal stenosis, middle ear deformities, and facial nerve abnormalities • 30% of these children have sensorineural hearing loss • Most have poor Eustachian tube function, resulting in chronic middle ear disease with associated conductive hearing loss
Meningitis	• Neonatal infection, can be viral or bacterial • Most common cause of acquired sensorineural hearing loss • Hearing loss can range from mild to profound, and may be progressive • Symptoms may include headache, neck stiffness, photophobia, and suppurative otitis media
Ototoxicity	• Can be caused by a wide variety of strong antibiotics, chemotherapeutic agents, or loop diuretics • Can also result from exposure to various chemical agents in the environment • Characterized by a progressive high-frequency sensorineural hearing loss following such exposure
Usher Syndrome	• Autosomal recessive • Occurs in 6%–12% of congenitally deaf children, and 3 in 100,000 of the general population • Involves retinitis pigmentosa and progressive moderate to severe sensorineural hearing loss • Can vary greatly in age of onset, severity, and progression
Waardenburg Syndrome	• Autosomal dominant • 20% have white forelock, 99% have increased distance between the eyes, 45% have two differently colored eyes (typically one brown and one blue) • Depigmentation of the skin and eyebrows that meet over the bridge of the nose • 50% have mild to severe sensorineural hearing loss, which can be unilateral or bilateral and is progressive

The third major mechanism of genetic transmission is **X-linked** inheritance. In the X-linked recessive form of this transmission mode, the parents are apparently normal, and the altered gene is associated with the X chromosomes of the male offspring. Most X-linked recessive hearing losses are sensorineural (Toriello & Smith, 2013).

Table 12.2 summarizes some of the disorders, both genetic and acquired, associated with hearing loss in children.

Infections

Many infectious agents that cause hearing loss are well documented; they can occur prenatally (before birth), at or around the time of birth (perinatally), or later in life (postnatally). During the mid-1960s, a rubella (German measles) outbreak caused an inordinate number of infants to be born with a hearing impairment. During that time span, approximately 10 percent of all congenital deafness was attributed to this disease, with half of these cases involving a severe sensorineural hearing loss. Fortunately, with the development of rubella vaccines, the incidence of this disease has dramatically decreased.

Common perinatal infections that may result in hearing impairment include cytomegalovirus (CMV), hepatitis B virus, and syphilis. Today, CMV infection is the

X-linked: A pattern of inheritance involving the X chromosome, one of an individual's two sex chromosomes.

leading viral cause of sensorineural hearing loss in children (Picard, 2004; Stach, 2010). Most children do not show clinical signs of the infection at birth but begin to demonstrate progressive evidence of it in the early years of life.

Measles and mumps viruses are examples of viral infections that can cause sensorineural hearing loss later in life, but for which there are now preventive vaccines. Hearing losses due to these viruses were all but completely eliminated, but failure to inoculate all children against these diseases has put them on the rise again and raised the risk of increased incidence of associated hearing loss.

Many nonviral infections can cause significant hearing loss. Bacterial meningitis can cause severe bilateral sensorineural hearing loss. Although viral meningitis can also cause hearing loss, most instances of hearing loss due to meningitis result from the bacterial form.

Otitis media is one of the leading causes of mild to moderate conductive hearing loss in children (Roizen, 2008). Fluid accumulation in the middle ear resulting from this disease typically causes a 15- to 40-dB conductive hearing loss and, if not treated, can lead to sensorineural impairment. Otitis media is most often treated by administering antibiotics or, in some instances, through placement of tubes in the ears.

Developmental Abnormalities

Some congenital causes of hearing loss involve abnormal development of outer or inner ear structure. Atresia (a narrowing or closure of the external ear canal and/or malformation of the middle ear) is a developmental disorder that affects the fetus early in pregnancy and results in malformation of the outer and/or middle ears. This frequently results in a conductive hearing loss that may or may not be treated successfully with surgical intervention.

Environmental/Traumatic Factors

Low birth weight, and its associated conditions, and asphyxia (breathing difficulties) are causes of serious hearing loss that frequently occur at birth or shortly thereafter. Both factors can result in conditions that actually cause hearing loss by traumatizing the ear. Some prescription drugs (including antibiotic medications) are known to be toxic to the inner ear, and the resulting hearing loss can occur prenatally when drugs are administered to the mother or during medical treatment later in life. The resulting hearing loss is typically sensorineural in type and permanent once damage is done. Intense noise, head injuries involving fractures of the skull, and dramatic pressure changes in the middle ear are all examples of traumatic causes of damage to the ear and hearing loss.

Characteristics of Individuals With Hearing Impairments

Variations in etiology, onset, degree, and type of hearing loss, as well as family and educational situations, result in a widely diverse hearing-impaired population. However, children and adults with hearing disabilities characteristically experience significant issues with regard to social and intellectual development, speech and language, and educational achievement.

Intelligence

Over the past several years, reviews of the research on the intellectual characteristics of children with a hearing impairment have suggested that the distribution of

otitis media: Infection of the middle ear space, causing conductive hearing loss.

atresia: The absence or closure of the ear canal; can be congenital or acquired from injury or disease.

intelligence or IQ scores for these individuals is similar to that of their hearing counterparts (Simeonsson & Rosenthal, 2001; Williams & Finnegan, 2003). Findings suggest that intellectual development for people with a hearing impairment is more a function of language development than cognitive ability. Any difficulties in performance appear to be closely associated with speaking, reading, and writing the English language, but unrelated to level of intelligence (Marschark, 2006).

Speech and Language

Speech and language skills are the areas of development most severely affected for those with a hearing impairment, particularly for children who are born deaf. The majority of children who are deaf have a very difficult time learning to use speech (McLean, Wolery, & Bailey, 2004). Research on the speech skills of children with hearing impairments suggests that the effects of a hearing loss on English language development vary considerably (Berk, 2013). For individuals who experience mild to moderate hearing losses, the effect may be minimal. Even for those with a prelingual moderate loss, effective communication skills are possible because the voiced sounds of conversational speech remain audible. Although the person with this type of hearing loss cannot hear unvoiced sounds and distant speech, language delays can be reduced or prevented by early diagnosis, the use of advanced technologies such as a cochlear implant, and intervention. Thus, a vast majority of these individuals are able to use speech as the primary mode for English language acquisition.

For the individual with profound congenital deafness, who does not have a cochlear implant, most loud speech is inaudible, even with the use of the most sophisticated hearing aids. These individuals are unable to receive information through speech unless they have learned to speechread (lipread). Sounds produced by the individual who is deaf are often difficult to understand. Children who are deaf exhibit significant articulation, voice quality, and tone discrimination problems. Researchers have found that, even as early as 8 months of age, babies who are deaf appear to babble less than their hearing peers (Allen & Cowdery, 2012). This has been attributed to the fact that infants who are deaf do not experience the same auditory feedback from babbling as their hearing counterparts and therefore are not as motivated to continue the activity.

In 1990, the U.S. Food and Drug Administration approved cochlear implants for children between the ages of 2 and 17. Implants are now being used at an even earlier age. Research indicates that the optimal age to implant a youngster is 10–15 months. Studies show that children who receive an implant prior to age 2 experience gains in language development and will more likely succeed in an inclusive classroom. Approximately 40 percent of children with a profound hearing loss receive a cochlear implant—a 25 percent gain in the last five years (U.S. Department of Health and Human Services, 2013). New debates surround the potential benefit of early bilateral implantation. Early research indicates that pediatric implant users are receiving substantial benefit that will be evident in their development of speech and language (Berg, Ip, Hurst, & Herb, 2007).

Social Development

Social-emotional development in young children with hearing impairments shows the same developmental patterns as in those without a hearing loss with regard to preschool friendships and ethnic, age, and gender preferences. Social-emotional development, however, also depends heavily on the ability to use communication skills. A hearing loss modifies one's capacity to receive and process auditory stimuli; thus, the individual who is deaf or hard of hearing receives reduced auditory information and/or

cochlear implant: A surgically implanted device that allows individuals who are deaf to hear environmental sounds and understand speech.

VIDEO

Social Development

DEAF DONALD

Deaf Donald met Talkie Sue

But  was all he could do.

And Sue said, "Donald, I sure do like you."

But  was all he could do.

And Sue asked Donald, "Do you like me too?"

But  was all he could do.

"Good-bye then, Donald, I'm leaving you."

But  was all he did do.

And she left forever so she never knew

That  means I love you.

information that is distorted. As a result, there appear to be some differences in the way young children who are deaf play as compared to their hearing counterparts.

Young children who are deaf typically have less language interaction during play and appear to prefer groups of two rather than larger group sizes. These patterns may be attributed to the difficulty of dividing their attention, which is so visual in its nature, and their poorer knowledge of language appropriate to play situations. They also engage in less pretend play, possibly because language deficits impede their ability to script elaborate imaginary situations. Children who are deaf spend less time in cooperative peer play when they are with other children who are deaf; even though they are interested in and initiate the interaction, they frequently get no response from their play partner because of language deficits. When deaf and hearing children attempt to play but do not share a common communication system—both relying on oral skills or both relying on sign skills—they demonstrate little interest in playing together or sustaining a friendship (Marschark, 2006). This suggests a need to develop communication skills within the hearing peer group and among all teachers if children placed in inclusive classroom settings are to avoid social isolation. The poem "Deaf Donald" by Shel Silverstein is a poignant example of what may happen without such support (see Figure 12.3).

There is an increasing awareness and acceptance of children with disabilities by their peer group. This is recognized and promoted by toy manufacturers as more "awareness" products become available. Mattel, for instance, has assisted in awareness of hearing impairments through the introduction of the "Sign Language Barbie," which is distributed through Toys "R" Us.

As children with a hearing impairment grow and mature, their capacity for receiving and using language often hinders their overall social-emotional growth. Reviews of the literature on social and psychological development in adolescents who are deaf suggest distinct differences from their hearing peers in such areas as maturity, awareness of social mores and attitudes, and social interactions (Marschark, 2007). It is not unusual for children who are deaf to experience difficulty in developing social relationships due to their lack of language skills or absence of socially appropriate behaviors (Luckner, Slike, & Johnson, 2012). Yet, smartphones and tablets combined with social media outlets like Facebook and Twitter now offer new opportunities for interaction between and among individuals who are hearing impaired as well as with their typical peers and others.

Social and emotional development depend, in part, on a person's ability to communicate.

Educational Achievement

The educational achievement of students with hearing impairments may be significantly delayed in comparison to that of their hearing peers. Students who are deaf often encounter considerable difficulty succeeding in an educational system that depends primarily on the spoken word and written language to transmit knowledge. Low achievement is characteristic of students who are deaf (Shaver, Newman, Huang, Yu, & Knokey, 2011), typically averaging three to four years below their age-appropriate grade levels.

Reading is the academic area most negatively affected for students with a hearing impairment. Any hearing loss, whether mild or profound, appears to have detrimental effects on reading performance. Research suggests that pupils who are hearing impaired read at approximately a third- to fourth-grade level (Gallaudet Research Institute, 2003; Traxler, 2000; Trezek, Wang, & Paul, 2010). Consequently, many of these individuals will encounter difficulty reading a typical newspaper.

Although researchers report slight variations in educational achievement scores, there is no question that high-stakes assessment is of great concern for this group of children. The difficulty the majority of students with hearing impairments experience taking high school exit exams and the fact that most of them do not pass these tests are issues of profound concern among educators (Johnson, 2003).

Assessment of Individuals With Hearing Impairments

The primary objective of an assessment of individuals with a hearing impairment is to put together an accurate picture of cognitive, communicative, and personal characteristics (Simeonsson & Rosenthal, 2001). This information is central to designing individualized instructional plans and other experiential activities to promote development.

Cognitive Assessment

It is crucial that the intellectual assessment of students with hearing impairments use measures that do *not* rely primarily on verbal abilities as indicators of cognitive functioning. There are several nonverbal assessment options considered appropriate for individuals with hearing impairments. These include the nonverbal portion of the Kaufman Assessment Battery for Children (2nd ed.) (Kaufman & Kaufman, 2004) and the performance section of the Wechsler Intelligence Scale for Children (4th ed.) (Wechsler, 2003). Because of the nonverbal nature of these instruments, however, they have limited predictive validity in relation to achievement that requires verbal skills (Schum, 2004). As a result, their usefulness has yet to be determined for educational practice.

The two most widely used measures of academic achievement with this population are the Stanford Achievement Test (SAT-10) (Pearson Assessment, 2008) and state achievement tests. The psychometric qualities of the SAT include excellent data representing diverse performance levels of individuals with hearing impairments (Luckner & Bowen, 2006).

Communication Assessment

The most serious negative aspect of a hearing impairment is its effect on language and speech development. Inadequate auditory stimulation during early development almost always leads to marked problems in language acquisition and speech production (Allen & Cowdery, 2012). Language assessment with this population should examine both receptive and expressive communication skills, including (1) form of language, (2) content of language, and (3) use of language. However, most language assessments do not assess all these areas. In most cases, several different assessment tools and techniques (such as language sampling) are needed to accurately determine the individual's language abilities (Simeonsson & Rosenthal, 2001).

Speech assessment with this population should include a battery of tools designed to ascertain the individual's articulation, pitch, loudness, quality, and rate. Analysis of these speech functions will provide a basis for designing speech therapy objectives as part of the individualized education program (IEP) for the student with a hearing impairment.

Personal/Social/Behavioral Assessment

A number of measures of personal, social, and behavioral functioning are being used with individuals with hearing impairments. The assessment of personal/social characteristics with this population is very challenging given the language content of most of the measures in this area, which are designed to be completed by a rater in response to items in the domains of social adjustment, self-image, and emotional adjustment. Sattler and Hoge (2006) urge caution when inferring development in these areas. Individuals with a hearing impairment may respond atypically to a personality measure, not because they exhibit aberrant social-emotional development, but as a result of their linguistic difficulties.

Educational Considerations

One method of classifying hearing impairment is by degree. Hearing loss can range from mild to profound based on the level of intensity required (measured in decibels, or dB) at various frequencies (described in hertz, or Hz) to establish hearing threshold. This classification system is directly related to the individual's ability to hear and comprehend speech. Factors such as these, as well as whether the hearing loss is pre- or postlingual, clearly have significant educational implications (see Table 12.3).

REFERENCE

Assessment Practices

VIDEO

Parent Perspective

Degree of Hearing Loss	Possible Psychosocial Impact of Hearing Loss	Effect of Hearing Loss on Speech and Language	Possible Educational Needs
Minimal or borderline: 16- to 25-dB loss	May be unaware of subtle conversational cues, causing student to be viewed as inappropriate or awkward. May miss portions of fast-paced peer interactions, which could begin to have an impact on socialization and self-concept. May exhibit immature behavior. Pupil may be more fatigued than classmates because of greater listening effort.	May have difficulty hearing faint or distant speech. At 15 dB student can miss up to 10% of speech when teacher is at a distance greater than 3 feet or when the classroom is noisy.	May benefit from a hearing aid, personal FM system, favorable seating, or sound field amplification if classroom is noisy. May need attention to vocabulary or speech, especially with recurrent otitis media history. Teacher in-service required.
Mild: 26- to 40-dB loss	Barriers beginning to build, with negative impact on self-esteem as student is accused of "hearing only when he or she wants to," "daydreaming," or "not paying attention." Begins to lose ability for selective hearing and has increasing difficulty suppressing background noise, which makes the learning environment stressful. Is more fatigued than classmates because of required listening effort.	At 30 dB may miss 25%–40% of speech. The degree of difficulty experienced will depend upon the noise level in the classroom, the distance from the teacher, and the configuration of the hearing loss. Without amplification, the pupil with a 35- to 40-dB loss may miss at least 50% of class discussions, especially when voices are faint or speaker is not in line of vision. Will miss consonants, especially when a high-frequency hearing loss is present.	Will benefit from a hearing aid, personal FM system, or sound field system. Favorable seating and lighting required. Needs auditory skill building and attention to vocabulary and language development, as well as articulation and speechreading. Teacher in-service required.
Moderate: 41- to 55-dB loss	Communication is often significantly affected, and socialization with hearing peers becomes increasingly difficult. With full-time use of hearing aids or FM systems, student may be viewed as a less competent learner. Increasing impact on self-esteem.	Understands conversational speech at a distance of 3–5 feet (face-to-face) only if structure and vocabulary controlled. Without amplification, the amount of speech missed can be 50%–75% with a 40-dB loss and 80%–100% with a 50-dB loss. Is likely to have delayed or defective syntax, limited vocabulary, imperfect speech production, and atonal voice quality.	Amplification is essential (hearing aids and FM system). Special education support may be needed, especially for primary grade students. Attention to oral language development, reading, and written language. Auditory skill development and speech therapy is usually needed. Teacher in-service required.
Moderate to severe: 56- to 70-dB loss	Full-time use of hearing aids or FM systems may result in pupil being judged by peers and adults as a less competent learner. Poor self-concept and diminished social maturity may contribute to feelings of rejection.	Without amplification, conversation must be very loud to be understood. A 55-dB loss can cause student to miss up to 100% of oral information. Will have marked difficulty in situations requiring verbal communication in both one-to-one and group situations. Delayed language, syntax, reduced speech intelligibility, and atonal voice quality are likely.	Full-time use of amplification is essential. Will need a resource teacher or special class placement depending on the magnitude of language delay. Will likely require assistance with language skills and academic subjects. In-service of general educators required.

(Continued)

Degree of Hearing Loss	Possible Psychosocial Impact of Hearing Loss	Effect of Hearing Loss on Speech and Language	Possible Educational Needs
Severe: 71- to 90-dB loss	Student may prefer other children with hearing impairments as friends. This may further isolate the individual from his or her classmates; however, these peer relationships may foster an improved self-concept and a sense of cultural identity.	Without amplification, may hear loud voices about 1 foot away. When amplified optimally, a student with hearing ability of 90 dB or better should be able to identify environmental sounds and detect all the sounds of speech. If loss is prelingual, oral language and speech may not develop spontaneously or will be severely delayed. If hearing loss is of recent onset, speech is likely to deteriorate with quality becoming atonal.	Emphasis placed on auditory language skills, speechreading, concept development, and speech. As loss approaches 80–90 dB, student may benefit from a total communication approach. Individual hearing aid or personal FM system is essential. Regular class placement is preferred, but teacher in-service is vital.
Profound: 91-dB loss or greater	Depending on auditory/oral competence, peer use of sign language, parental attitude, and other factors, student may or may not increasingly prefer association with the Deaf culture.	Aware of vibrations more than tonal pattern. Will likely rely on vision rather than hearing as primary avenue for communication and learning. Detection of speech sounds dependent upon loss configuration and use of amplification. Speech and language will not develop spontaneously and are likely to deteriorate rapidly if hearing loss is of recent onset.	May need special program with an emphasis on language skills and academic subjects along with comprehensive support services. Early use of amplification likely to help. May be a candidate for a cochlear implant. Requires continual appraisal of communication needs and learning modality. Part-time placement in general education classes as benefits student.

SOURCE: Adapted from Supporting Success for Children with Hearing Loss, *Impact of Listening on Learning*, 2013. Available at http://successforkidswithhearingloss.com/impact-on-listening-and-learning

Individuals with a mild hearing loss may encounter difficulty hearing in a noisy classroom setting or distinguishing distant sounds; however, their speech discrimination ability is often within normal limits. Appropriate accommodations for such a student may include preferential seating, possible use of a hearing aid or personal FM system, greater redundancy of instruction, and increased collaboration with parents to facilitate learning.

The individual with a moderate hearing loss—depending on type, degree, and age of onset—may experience significant delays in speech and language. Articulation deficits, reduced vocabulary, difficulty mastering various grammatical and syntactical concepts, and poor voice quality are common problems. Hearing aid use coupled with personal FM systems is necessary for such students, in addition to the intervention strategies cited previously.

A severe or profound hearing loss, again depending on the type, degree, and age of onset, may severely impede speech and language development. Individuals with severe to profound losses frequently have poor auditory discrimination, which often limits

VIDEO
Student Story

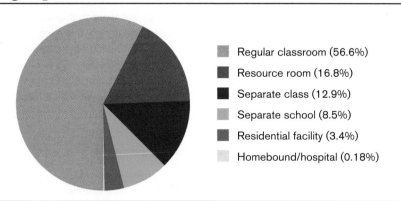

■ ■ ■ ■ ■   Figure 12.4 **Educational Placement of Children With Hearing Impairments**

- Regular classroom (56.6%)
- Resource room (16.8%)
- Separate class (12.9%)
- Separate school (8.5%)
- Residential facility (3.4%)
- Homebound/hospital (0.18%)

NOTE: Figure represents percentages of enrollment of students with hearing impairments during the 2011–2012 school year. Excludes pupils enrolled in parentally placed private schools and individuals in correctional facilities.

SOURCE: U.S. Department of Education. (2013). *Historical state-level IDEA data files.* Retrieved November 22, 2013, from http://tadnet.public.tadnet.org/pages/712

the effectiveness of conventional amplification devices. A team approach to remediation should be used, which involves substantial interaction with the child's audiologist to ensure accuracy of diagnostic information as well as appropriateness of amplification. Students with this degree of hearing loss will need significant accommodation in the educational environment to be successful, including intense visual language reinforcement for the instruction of grammar and syntax. See the accompanying Suggestions for the Classroom (page 425) on teaching students with hearing impairments.

Where Are Students With Hearing Impairments Served?

Figure 12.4 portrays the various educational environments providing a special education to children with hearing impairments. Approximately 90 percent of these students were enrolled in public schools during the 2011–2012 school year, with the majority of individuals served in the regular classroom. This represents a dramatic shift from the historical placement of pupils with hearing impairments in residential facilities. Before 1975, when PL 94–142 was enacted, about 80 percent of students with hearing impairments were served in special schools, typically state residential schools for the deaf. This shift has caused great concern among adults who are deaf because residential schools have long been the foundation of the Deaf culture (Scheetz, 2012).

Educational placement decisions may be influenced by such factors as the degree of loss, age of onset, mode of communication, presence of other disabilities, and available resources. (See the accompanying First Person feature on page 427.)

Instructional Interventions

Methods of Communication

Communication implies a transfer or exchange of knowledge, ideas, opinions, and feelings; it involves encoding and decoding messages. The basic foundation for communication is language, which is often defined as a system of rules governing sounds,

REFERENCE
Deaf Education

VIDEO
Parent–Teacher Relationship

VIDEO
Educational Settings

My name is Catherine Davis, and I have been a teacher of the deaf and hard of hearing in the Blue Valley School District in Overland Park, Kansas, for four years. The first year I worked as an itinerant deaf education teacher serving six schools. Then I was lucky enough to get to start a center-based resource room program in a brand-new elementary school. There I teach preschool through fifth-grade students whose IEP teams have decided that due to the educational impact of their hearing loss—often accompanied by additional disabilities such as attention deficit hyperactivity disorder (ADHD) and/or cognitive, motor, and/or vision impairments—they would be best served in this program rather than in their neighborhood school. My students spend the majority of their day in the general education classroom but come to me for academic support as well as auditory training, speechreading, and sign language instruction.

I grew up in a small Midwestern town where there was not a lot of diversity. One boy in my high school was deaf, and I watched the other kids tease him, thinking he couldn't understand what they were saying because he couldn't hear them. He could. I decided to become his friend, learned to sign, and eventually started tutoring him. Thus, my love of teaching, combined with an interest in deafness and signing, began. After graduating from high school in 1992, I attended an interpreter-training program at the University of Kansas. Seeking to utilize my skills and have an adventure at the same time, I set out for Homer, Alaska, where I accepted a job interpreting for two Native Alaskan students. Miles from home, I encountered beauty and adventure, but also a challenge for which I was definitely unprepared. The two students with whom I worked had multiple disabilities and needed significant support. Unfortunately, the itinerant teacher was not always there to provide this support. Even though I loved Alaska and my job, this experience solidified my desire to teach, and I knew I needed more training. So after a year I returned to Kansas. I completed a BS in elementary education and an MS in deaf education, and I am now in my final year of my PhD in special education with a focus on deaf education.

Inclusive Education Experience

The group of kids that I currently work with is truly representative of the type of caseload that a future teacher of the deaf can expect to have. My students are as different as they could be. I have one first grader who has a cochlear implant and communicates solely through sign language and another first-grade student who is hard of hearing, wears hearing aids, and uses an FM system. She is oral but learning to sign. A second-grade student has multiple disabilities including ADHD, aphasia, and vision loss. She wears hearing aids and an FM system, and uses both verbal and sign language. The fifth grader I teach has a severe hearing loss, wears hearing aids, uses an FM system, and also has multiple disabilities including motor, cognitive, and vision impairments. Her predominant mode of communication is oral.

At the beginning of every year I do an in-service for the entire staff in order to provide suggestions for working with students with a hearing loss. I also go into the general education classrooms and do lessons with all of the students explaining hearing loss, sign language, and Deaf culture. Often these lessons occur only with the classroom teacher or the special education teachers. However, I believe the whole school needs to be educated to really ensure that my students are fully included. I find that the more people know, the less apprehensive they are to interact with these kids. I let them try on hearing aids, listen to an FM system, watch a video on cochlear implants, learn some sign language, and even try to take a spelling test by reading lips to simulate what it might be like for students with a hearing loss.

words, meaning, and use. When a child is born with a hearing impairment, depending on the severity of the hearing problem, normal language acquisition is disrupted. Other means of communication are viable alternatives to spoken language. Sign language, in one of its multiple forms, and fingerspelling using the manual alphabet (see Figure 12.5) are examples of such alternatives. See Table 12.4 for a description of the three sign language systems that are most commonly used. Other methods of instruction include oral, auditory verbal, cued speech, total communication, and the Rochester Method (fingerspelling). For educators of the deaf and the Deaf culture, which method of communication to use is at the root of the current philosophical debate.

Within the educational placement options previously described, three different approaches to communication may be used: (1) a bilingual-bicultural (bi-bi) approach, (2) total communication (TC), or (3) an auditory-oral approach. See Table 12.5 for a description of these approaches. The majority of public school programs using TC employ

fingerspelling: A form of manual communication; different positions or movements of the fingers indicate letters of the alphabet.

Strategies for Inclusive Classrooms

Because of the diverse student needs, I am required to be versatile in my communication style. My philosophy on communication modality is not to have one! Instead, I go forward based on where the student is when he or she enters my program. At any given time, I use an eclectic combination of anything that works—sign, voice, gestures, drawing pictures, writing, acting—whatever it takes. In addition to working with the student at his or her level, it is critical to develop a good working relationship with the family.

One of the first things that I tell classroom teachers who are going to have a student who is deaf or hard of hearing in their classroom is that most accommodations are pretty simple. They shouldn't be scared! First of all, students with a hearing loss should be given priority seating so they will have a better opportunity to hear as well as have visual access to the teacher's mouth for lipreading or see their interpreter if they use one. I also tell teachers that anytime they can make their teaching more visual they should do so. This can be accomplished by writing new vocabulary on the board or accompanying it with a picture, or by using visual schedules. The students will have a much easier time following along with these visual cues added. If the child uses sign language, one of the best ways for the teacher and student to learn is to make it a part of the lesson for all students. I worked with a kindergarten teacher last year who really embraced this concept. She often invited me into her classroom to do lessons with her class. Eventually she and the interpreter took over the teaching. Anytime her class learned a new sight word, they paired it with the sign. She said that using this extra modality really accelerated the child's learning. A preschool teacher I worked with two years ago used sign language so much, and also encouraged her kids to sign, that a visiting parent had to ask which one of the students was deaf!

Our school music teacher is another good example of someone with whom I collaborate often. The school put on a musical last year, and the whole student body learned to sign the songs. The parent of one of my students came to my room the next day to thank me; she was nearly in tears. She said that she never thought that she would see her child up on a stage singing and signing with everyone else, just like one of the other kids. Obviously, this kind of integration and collaboration benefits not only the student who is deaf, but everyone involved as well.

Another thing I do is to encourage teachers to be good advocates for their students. This often takes sustained determination to educate others about the child's needs. Although the many meetings and abundance of paperwork that this can require can seem overwhelming at times, the results are worth it. Teachers also need to teach the children with hearing loss to be good advocates for themselves. Fostering independence in students with disabilities is a component that is sometimes overlooked. In order for them to have a quality life within their educational setting, and also outside of school, students need to know how to request an interpreter, manage their audiological equipment, and educate people about their hearing loss.

The reality is that hearing loss is a low-incidence disability. In my experiences in rural settings, both in Kansas and Alaska, I have seen how isolating it can be for the student to be the only one who is deaf or hard of hearing, or one of few, in his or her school. Therefore, it is especially important to me that I do everything I can to make sure the students I work with are included as much as possible. By being flexible and adaptable both in my teaching and in my communication style; by collaborating with staff, students, and parents; and by being a good advocate for my students and encouraging them to be good advocates for themselves, I find that my students are very successful in an inclusive setting.

–Catherine Davis
Liberty View Elementary School, Overland Park, Kansas
Teacher of the Deaf and Hard of Hearing

a form of Signed English for the sign language component. Many residential programs and postsecondary programs for the deaf, however, endorse the bi-bi approach, which uses American Sign Language (ASL). There are few data suggesting that one instructional approach is significantly better than another (Swanwick & Marschark, 2010).

Audiologists

Audiologists have served students with hearing impairments in educational settings for many years and are often included as a member of the educational team. Using a collaborative approach, audiologists frequently provide support to general educators, speech-language pathologists, teachers of the hearing impaired, and other special educators as well as interpreters. The American Speech-Language-Hearing Association (2002) recommends in its *Guidelines for Audiology Service Provision in and for Schools* that there be at least one audiologist for every 10,000 students in a school system.

Figure 12.5 **The Manual Alphabet**

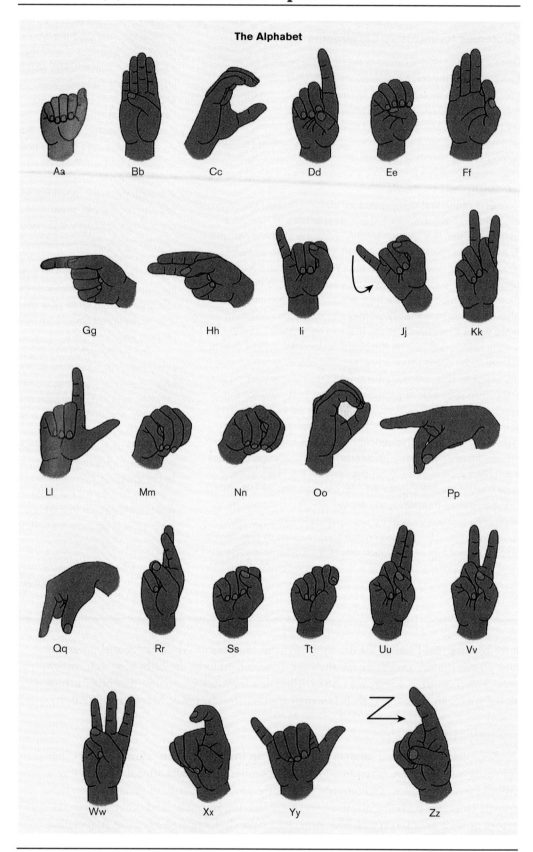

The Alphabet

SOURCE: G. Gustason and E. Zawolkow, *Signing Exact English* (Los Alamitos, CA: Modern Signs Press, 1993), pp. xxvi, 1.

Sign System	Description	Advantages/Disadvantages
American Sign Language (ASL)	• Considered the natural language of the deaf • Has a unique syntax system, not a word-by-word interpretation • System most frequently used by interpreters in public settings (churches, concerts, ceremonies, etc.)	• Unique syntax could make transition to English more challenging
Signing Exact English	• Most like spoken English • Close match to ASL • Uses English word order • System most commonly used in public schools	• Can be understood by ASL users • English word order should make the transition to English less challenging
Signed English	• Uses ASL signs in English word order patterns	• Even closer match to ASL but with the advantage of English word order

SOURCE: Adapted from S. Kuder, *Teaching Students with Language and Communication Disabilities*, 3rd ed. (Boston, MA: Allyn & Bacon, 2008), p. 235.

Interpreters

When an **interpreter** is used, three people are involved in the communication experience: the interpreter, the person who is deaf or hard of hearing, and the hearing person. The primary role of the educational interpreter is to relay to the student anything that is said in class by employing communication processes such as repetition, sign language, fingerspelling, body language, and verbal expressions. Many sign language systems (such as ASL, Signed English, or Signing Exact English) may be used, depending on the preferred communication mode or need of the individual with a hearing impairment. An **oral interpreter** may be used for cochlear implant users or individuals with a great deal of residual hearing. Oral interpreters use clear enunciation, slightly slower speech, and expressive mouth and facial movements to improve the visibility of the spoken message. In conjunction with the communication process, an interpreter may also use **transliteration**. For example, the interpreter may change the exact wording of the hearing person's communication in order to help the individual with a hearing impairment to better understand the context of the message. However, the interpreter is never a contributing member in the communication exchange.

Educational interpreters play diverse roles at all grade levels. They may assist students in the classroom, tutor individual students, assist regular and special educators in classroom activities, or interpret lectures. As increasing numbers of individuals with a hearing impairment choose to attend regular schools, the demand for interpreters is growing. A critical shortage of qualified interpreters exists in many educational settings, especially in rural areas. There is also a nationwide shortage of qualified interpreter preparation programs.

Services for Young Children With Hearing Impairments

Early intervention for the child with a hearing impairment is grounded in the same basic concepts as early intervention and early childhood special education programs for youngsters with other disabilities. Screening programs designed to detect hearing

interpreter: A professional who signs, gestures, and/or fingerspells a speaker's message as it is spoken to enable individuals with hearing impairments to understand spoken language.

oral interpreter: A professional who silently repeats a speaker's message as it is spoken so that a hearing-impaired person can lipread the message.

transliteration: Altering an interpreted message to facilitate understanding by a person who is hearing impaired.

Table 12.5 Communication Approaches Used With Students With Hearing Impairments

	Basic Position	Objective	Method of Communication
Bilingual-Bicultural	Considers American Sign Language (ASL) to be the natural language of the Deaf culture and urges recognition of ASL as the primary language choice with English considered a second language	To provide a foundation in the use of ASL with its unique vocabulary and syntax rules; English as a second language (ESL) instruction provided for English vocabulary and syntax rules	ASL
Total Communication	Supports the belief that simultaneous use of multiple communication techniques enhances an individual's ability to communicate, comprehend, and learn	To provide a multifaceted approach to communication to facilitate whichever method(s) work(s) best for each individual	Combination of sign language (accepts the use of any of the sign language systems), fingerspelling, and speechreading
Auditory-Oral	Supports the belief that children with hearing impairments can develop listening/receptive language and oral language expression (English) skills; emphasizes use of residual hearing (the level of hearing an individual possesses), amplification (hearing aids, auditory training, etc.), and speech/language training	To facilitate the development of spoken (oral) English	Spoken (oral) English

loss in school-age populations have existed for years. However, for children born with a hearing impairment, identification and early intervention is critical. There is an obvious relationship between expressive and receptive communication skills and the hearing mechanism that facilitates such skills, which begin long before a child's first words are ever spoken. Because more children are being identified as hearing impaired at an earlier age, the emphasis of many early intervention programs has changed in order to meet the needs of younger children with hearing impairments, many of whom will receive cochlear implants.

Failure to identify and provide appropriate services for children who are hearing impaired has a profoundly negative impact on the development of language and speech, as well as educational achievement (Buethe et al., 2013). Only about 50 percent of infants with hearing loss are identified using a high-risk register (Johnson & Seaton, 2012). With the use of sophisticated diagnostic technology, universal newborn screening programs designed to identify hearing loss in infants have increased in number and scope. States that have legislated universal newborn screening programs, however, have encountered substantial difficulty with family compliance for follow-up testing. Because of this limitation, providing timely services to families of infants with hearing impairments has been difficult.

Early intervention programs provide families with information on language development, communication skills, the use of residual hearing, amplification, self-help skills, and the social-emotional development of a youngster with a hearing loss. These programs place a strong emphasis on family involvement. Meeting the needs of each individual family requires customized intervention strategies.

The vast majority (over 90%) of infants with hearing impairments have parents with normal hearing (Buethe et al., 2013). Whether a child with a hearing loss is born

high-risk register: A list of factors placing infants at increased risk for hearing impairment, including, but not limited to, low birth weight, congenital perinatal infections, a family history of childhood hearing impairment, severe asphyxia, and bacterial meningitis.

Table 12.4 **Sign Language Systems**

SUGGESTIONS FOR THE CLASSROOM

Suggestions for Teaching Students With Hearing Impairments

Suggestion #1: Promote acceptance of your students. Your student will benefit from a classroom where he or she feels accepted and where modifications are made without undue attention.

→ Welcome the student to your class. Your positive attitude will help other students accept him or her.

→ Discuss your student's hearing loss with him or her; let him or her know you are willing to help.

→ As appropriate, have your student, the audiologist, or another person explain the student's hearing loss to your entire class.

→ Make modifications seem as natural as possible so the student is not singled out.

→ Accept your student as an individual; be aware of his or her assets as well as his or her limitations.

→ Encourage your student's special abilities or interests.

Suggestion #2: Be sure hearing aids and other amplification devices are used when recommended. This will enable your student to use his or her hearing maximally.

→ Realize that hearing aids make sounds louder, but not necessarily clearer. Hearing aids don't make hearing normal.

→ Be sure your student's hearing aids or other devices are checked daily to see that they are working properly.

→ Encourage the student to care for his or her hearing aid(s) by putting it on, telling you when it is not functioning properly, and so forth.

→ Be sure your student always has a spare battery at school.

→ Know whom to contact if your student's device is not working properly.

Suggestion #3: Provide preferential seating. Appropriate seating will enhance your student's ability to hear and understand what is said in the classroom.

→ Seat your student near where you typically teach. It will be helpful if your student is at one side of the classroom so he or she can easily turn and follow classroom dialogue.

→ Seat your student where he or she can easily watch your face without straining to look straight up. Typically the second or third row is best.

→ Seat your student away from noise sources, including hallways, radiators, pencil sharpeners, and so forth.

→ Seat your student where light is on your face and not in your student's eyes.

→ If there is a preferred ear, place it toward the classroom.

→ Allow your student to move to other seats when necessary for demonstrations, classroom discussions, or other activities.

Suggestion #4: Increase visual information. Your student will use speechreading and other visual information to supplement what he or she hears.

→ Remember that your student needs to see your face in order to speechread!

– Try to stay in one place while talking to the class so your student does not have to speechread a "moving target."

– Avoid talking with your face turned downward while reading.

– Keep the light on your face, not at your back. Avoid standing in front of windows where the glare will make it difficult to see your face.

→ Use visual aids, such as pictures and diagrams, when possible.

→ Demonstrate what you want the student to understand when possible. Use natural gestures, such as pointing to objects being discussed, to help clarify what you say.

→ Use the board—write assignments, new vocabulary words, key words, and so forth on it.

Suggestion #5: Minimize classroom noise. Even a small amount of noise will make it very difficult for your student to hear and understand what is said.

→ Seat your student away from noisy parts of your classroom.

→ Wait until all your students are quiet before talking to them.

(Continued)

SUGGESTIONS FOR THE CLASSROOM (CONTINUED)

Suggestions for Teaching Students With Hearing Impairments

Suggestion #6: Modify teaching procedures.
Modifications will allow your student to benefit from your instruction and will decrease the need for repetition.

→ Be sure your student is watching and listening when you are talking to him or her.

→ Be sure your student understands what is said by having him or her repeat information or answer questions.

→ Rephrase, rather than repeat, questions and instructions if your student has not understood them.

→ Write key words, new words, new topics, and so forth on the board.

→ Repeat or rephrase things said by other students during classroom discussions.

→ Introduce new vocabulary to the student in advance. The speech-language pathologist or parents may be able to help with this.

→ Use a "buddy" to alert your student to listen and to be sure your student has understood all information correctly.

Suggestion #7: Have realistic expectations. This will help your student succeed in your classroom.

→ Remember that your student cannot understand everything all of the time, no matter how hard he or she tries. Encourage him or her to ask for repetition.

→ Be patient when your student asks for repetition.

→ Give breaks from listening when necessary. Your student may fatigue easily because he or she is straining to listen and understand.

→ Expect your student to follow classroom routine. Do not spoil or pamper your student.

→ Expect your student to accept the same responsibilities for considerate behavior, homework, and dependability as you require of other students in your classroom.

→ Ask your student to repeat if you can't understand him or her. Your student's speech may be distorted because he or she does not hear sounds clearly. Work with the speech-language pathologist to help your student improve his or her speech as much as possible.

SOURCE: Adapted from C. Johnson and J. Seaton, *Educational Audiology Handbook*, 2nd ed. (Clifton Park, NY: Delmar/Cengage Learning, 2012), pp. 195–196.

to deaf or hearing parents may influence social, educational, and cultural issues. For example, many hearing parents of children who are severely hearing impaired probably do not know or use sign language. They may be unaware of cultural issues related to the Deaf community, and how such issues might relate to their own child's education options. Some research indicates that parents who are deaf are more likely to view children with hearing impairments in a positive way, which may result in greater normalization of the parent-child relationship (Katz & Schery, 2006). Allen and Cowdery (2012) suggest that early intervention programs focus on helping the child with a hearing impairment develop within the structure of his or her family, just as a child with normal hearing develops within this context.

Transition and Individuals With Hearing Impairments

The process of transition, enabling the person with a hearing impairment to make a successful change from one environment to another, requires systematic planning

VIDEO
Parents' Experiences

FIRST PERSON: MINDY

Believing in Yourself

My experience growing up as a person who is deaf has been enriching. I have a successful career thanks to supportive parents who always treated me like a typical child. During my difficult times, they supported me wholeheartedly. Some parents of children who are deaf tend to be overprotective, but not my parents. They encouraged me to make my own decisions. I do not think that I would be as successful as I am today without them.

After my parents found out that I was deaf, they enrolled me in a preschool where I learned cued speech. A new teacher arrived and told my parents that Signing Exact English (SEE) would be more useful and social than cued speech. My parents then enrolled in sign language classes so that they could communicate with me.

In elementary school I was in a self-contained room with other students who were deaf and a teacher who used SEE. I loved that environment. At the time that I was about to enter the sixth grade, I was faced with a decision. Did I want to attend the Alabama School for the Deaf or an integrated middle school? I do not remember how I decided, but I chose the local middle school. I was in culture shock. My classroom was full of thirty hearing students. I was the only student who was deaf in the entire grade. (There were a few other students who were deaf, but they were in different grades.) I had to rely on my interpreter for everything, so I became shyer and less outgoing than I was in elementary school. Many of my classmates learned to sign or fingerspell, but I still missed so much information vital to socialization. I remember walking through the hallways, and my interpreter would walk with me and tell me all kinds of gossip she heard. I was shocked; I had no idea what the students were talking about. As I entered high school, I became very unhappy. I noticed that high school students were more into cliques. I felt as though I did not belong.

At a summer camp for children who are deaf, a camp counselor told me about the Model Secondary School for the Deaf (MSSD) at Gallaudet University in Washington, DC. I was interested, so I mentioned it to my parents. Of course, they said I was too young to be so far away. Yet the thought of attending this school stayed with me. I wrote a letter to Gallaudet asking for information about the school. They sent me a colorful, fancy brochure, and I was impressed. I brought it up once again with my parents, but they shrugged it off. I filled out the application anyway and asked them to sign the papers just in case. I think my parents thought that I would change my mind if things got serious. When MSSD called my parents to come for an intake interview, they kept asking me if I really wanted to do this. I was determined as ever to go. We made the trip to MSSD, and I fell in love with the school immediately. Once again, however, I was in culture shock because I was not aware of the Deaf culture. The students made fun of my clothes, my makeup, and my use of SEE. I was bewildered by all of this. I eventually learned American Sign Language, which was the language of choice. A friend once charged me a penny every time I signed using SEE. I loved the social aspects of being at MSSD. Unlike my middle school, I was able to be involved in any activity that I wished. I was viewed as the "deaf" girl at my middle school, but at MSSD, I was looked at as "Usher syndrome" girl.

I am currently a counselor at a school for the deaf, where I have worked for the past eight years. I have had to face many obstacles as I moved to a town where I knew no one. I chose to face my challenges rather than staying home and believing that things would not work out for me. I still face challenges now as a person who is deaf-blind. I am not completely blind yet, but my vision is slowly deteriorating. I have learned how to use Grade 1 Braille, and I am currently learning Grade 2. I have also completed orientation and mobility training so that I can become somewhat independent in challenging areas such as heavy traffic. I have learned everything possible in order to be independent in case I lose my sight completely.

In the summer of 2006 I had a cochlear implant because of concerns about my safety in the future. I will need to depend upon environmental sounds if and when I lose my vision. I now enjoy hearing the birds sing and water running. When the audiologist turned on my cochlear implant, it was the strangest sensation. The first sounds I heard were my husband's voice and that of the audiologist. Then I entered the bathroom. I did not realize that bathrooms were so noisy! Funny, I always thought that bathrooms were silent. After I got home, I noticed that flushing toilets even had a sound, so I was incredulous of that. I had never heard those sounds until I received my implant. It was one of the best decisions I ever made for myself.

I know I will face additional challenges as my vision deteriorates, but I have a wonderful support system consisting of my husband, family, and friends. I am confident that I will be able to overcome whatever obstacles come my way. ■

–Anonymous

Effective Instructional Practices
Promoting Language Development in Young Children With Hearing Impairments

- **Speak using an ordinary tone/volume.** Make sure the student's attention is focused on the speaker. Talk naturally and clearly and use simple phrases or simple but complete sentences, depending on the pupil's language level. Do not shout or exaggerate words or slow down your speech unnaturally. Highlighting lips with lipstick can assist a young child in following speech. A mustache or long hair obscuring the face can cause loss of visual information.

- **Clarify idioms.** Explain idioms in context (for example, explain "It's raining cats and dogs" when you have used the expression after dashing inside during a cloudburst). This prevents misunderstandings and enriches the child's language.

- **Check with the student to ensure comprehension.** Sometimes saying "Tell me what I just said" provides information about how much a child understands. However, many children with a hearing loss have difficulty articulating their responses. Therefore, you may need to observe the child's actions for a short period to check for understanding. A perplexed look or doing nothing may indicate lack of understanding, and you will need to find additional, preferably visual, methods for getting the message across.

- **Institute a buddy system to facilitate a child's understanding of directions and curriculum content.** Many times children understand another child better than they do an adult, so have a child's buddy explain the information again after you have finished. Furthermore, attentive peer modeling of both speech and behavior is an excellent resource for the child with hearing deficits.

- **Show real-life pictures when reading or talking about a topic, and use simple signs, point, or have an example of the object you're explaining.** Pupils with a hearing loss need visual information to learn. Acting out experience-based language lessons or stories is helpful. Using environmental labels around the classroom can start such children on the road to learning language through print.

- **Provide language boards or books for children who have difficulty producing intelligible speech or manual signs.** Try providing a flannel board with pictures, words, or other graphic symbols to help communicate information such as available interest centers or answers to routine questions. The child can point to the board to indicate a response or choice. Preteach key vocabulary words from a story that will be read to the class, or send the book home with the child beforehand so that the words can be introduced by the family (and reinforced afterward).

and evaluation. IDEA mandates individualized transition plans for students with disabilities age 16 and older. It also requires periodic revisions in order to remain current and sensitive to the needs of these individuals and their families. As we noted previously, many students with severe to profound hearing impairments lag behind their peers in personal, social, and behavioral maturity, which affects the structure and outcome of transition planning.

Stress is often associated with change, and transition can be especially difficult for the family as well as the pupil. Families learning to adjust to the new challenges of having an adolescent or a young adult who is deaf or hard of hearing are often assisted by teachers, counselors, or other specialists. Family life plays a key role in the transition process for adolescents who are deaf. Many times, an audiologist, rehabilitation specialist, speech-language pathologist, or special education teacher are able to assist the student and his or her family in making transition decisions about postsecondary educational programs or employment opportunities. The Laurent Clerc National Deaf Education Center, located at Gallaudet University, provides excellent information families and teachers can use to promote transition and independence.

Legislation facilitating transition as a national priority for the hearing impaired began with the passage of PL 89–36 in 1968, which established the National Technical

Institute for the Deaf (NTID) at the Rochester Institute of Technology, and the enactment of Section 504 of the Rehabilitation Act of 1973 (PL 93–112), which mandated that institutions of higher education provide accessible facilities and support services for individuals with disabilities. In addition to funding Gallaudet University and the NTID, Congress funds regional postsecondary education programs for the deaf. Programs at California State University at Northridge and the University of Tennessee Center on Deafness are two examples of this activity.

The transition for many individuals with a hearing impairment also involves personal, social, and community adjustments. The new experiences are intensified not only by communication difficulties but also by the diverse literacy skills needed in the new environment. Transition to postsecondary education, vocational training, and/or employment can be eased by career counseling and coursework centered on vocational skills and independent living, as outlined in the student's transition plan. For students desiring a college degree, in addition to stressing academic achievement, a successful college preparatory training program often involves instruction regarding dorm life, responsible social behavior, and problem-solving strategies for coping with the multitude of problems that college students with hearing impairments are likely to encounter (King, De Caro, Karchmer, & Cole, 2001).

Adolescence can be a stressful time for individuals with a hearing impairment.

Services for Adults With Hearing Impairments

Adult support services often provide a vital link between the hearing impaired and the hearing world. These diverse services may be used to enhance public knowledge regarding deafness, facilitate communication, or aid in the transfer of information.

Two basic types of mandated services are offered statewide for adults who are deaf or hard of hearing. The first is a state commission or office on deafness, whose services include advocacy, information gathering and dissemination, referral to appropriate agencies, interpreting services, and job placement and development. The second type of service is offered through each state's vocational rehabilitation service. A coordinator of rehabilitation services for the deaf and hard of hearing provides vocational evaluation, job placement, and counseling, often in conjunction with the transition plan while the student is still in high school. State rehabilitation offices can also help students preparing to enter postsecondary academic environments. Under the Americans with Disabilities Act, colleges and universities are required to provide qualified sign language interpreters and other auxiliary aids needed to ensure effective communication opportunities for students who are deaf or hard of hearing, even if these services are not provided by the state vocational rehabilitation system.

For almost a hundred and thirty-five years, the National Association of the Deaf (NAD), the nation's premier civil rights organization for people who are deaf or hard of hearing, has been championing the rights of individuals with hearing impairments. NAD provides a wide range advocacy at the state and federal levels on issues of importance to individuals with hearing loss, including the preservation of American Sign Language (National Association of the Deaf, 2013).

VIDEO

Student Perspective

Another significant organization promoting the integration of the hearing impaired population into mainstream society is the Alexander Graham Bell Association. The philosophy of the AG Bell Association is based on the improvement of oral speech communication. This association serves as a clearinghouse of materials and information concerning oral teaching methods, technology, and related topics.

Family Issues

Family dynamics can be severely disrupted when a child is born with a significant hearing impairment. Parental, sibling, and grandparenting roles are often dramatically altered by such an event. Because the effects of hearing impairment are so pervasive, particularly with regard to communication, accepting and "normalizing" the child's disability can be quite difficult. The expected or fantasized child does not arrive, and the family experiences an initial state of emotional shock and disbelief. The level of impact on the family may vary, but for most families such an event can create a crisis atmosphere of considerable magnitude.

Family Reaction

Interpreters provide a vital service to college students with hearing impairments.

As we mentioned, approximately 90 percent of all children with hearing impairments have hearing parents. After the initial emotional states of shock and disbelief, stresses on the family can increase as individual members come to understand that communicating with the child who is hearing impaired is different and likely always will be. From these initial reactions, some parents go through different stages of grieving such as frustration, denial, depression, and anxiety. They may initially blame their spouse, fate, or the professional community, or even misdirect anger and frustration toward themselves. Parents may have difficulty accepting assistance or recommendations from professionals, extended family, and friends. Some may become overprotective of the child and turn their attention away from other family members. Others may withdraw, finding isolation easier than coping with the child care demands placed upon them (Gargiulo & Kilgo, 2014).

Perhaps the greatest factor in positive resolution of such emotionally charged issues is acceptance of the hearing impairment. Achieving genuine acceptance of any disability is, for most families, an ongoing process. Stages of this process are not necessarily completed independently and in successive order, just as achieving a measure of acceptance does not prevent certain situations from reopening old emotional wounds. Grieving and uncertainty may emerge time and again during the child's development, but will be less severe as the family's coping mechanisms improve. The stages of grieving that follow the birth of a baby with a hearing loss are healthy expressions of normal emotional reactions. The process of working through such feelings should not be hurried; it allows the family members opportunities to recognize and acknowledge change in their lives, as well as time to formulate positive strategies for accommodating the child with the hearing impairment (Gargiulo & Kilgo, 2014). In this process, the development of positive relationships is individually and collectively encouraged. Parental support groups provide a very effective arena for expressing concerns, offering support and encouragement, and formulating effective parenting strategies.

> VIDEO
> **Parent Interview**

> VIDEO
> Family

Siblings and Grandparents

Siblings and grandparents are not immune to the emotional issues that accompany the birth of a child with a hearing impairment. There is little formal research that examines the emotional impact of hearing impairment on either group. Siblings may feel unspoken pressure to compensate for perceived parental uncertainty and disappointment. Such perceptions may result in attempts to excel academically or socially. Some siblings describe very close relationships with their brother or sister who is hearing impaired, assuming a great deal of responsibility for the child, and describe the relationship as almost a parental one. Others resent the time and attention parents devote to their sibling with a hearing impairment.

Siblings can play an important role in families that have a child with a hearing impairment.

This resentment may take the form of jealousy or anger. Because of these and other factors, siblings of children with hearing impairments or are often at risk for behavior problems. Perhaps the best way to help siblings is for parents to communicate with them, ask about concerns, talk openly about family issues, have uniform behavioral expectations, and ensure that family responsibilities are equally shared.

Luterman (2008) describes grandparents of children with hearing impairments as "the forgotten people." Grandparents experience a "double hurt," stemming from both the emotional pain of having a grandchild with a hearing impairment and the pain experienced by their own child, the grieving parent. However, the role of grandparents can often provide much-needed emotional, logistical, and financial support for the family unit (Clark & Martin, 1994). Parent support groups often incorporate siblings, caregivers, and extended family members, affording them the opportunity to address the various dynamics of families dealing with hearing loss in a group setting.

Issues of Diversity

According to data from the Gallaudet Research Institute (2011), almost 50 percent of all students in programs for the deaf and hearing impaired are persons from culturally diverse groups. Similarly, statistics from the U.S. Department of Education (2013a) indicate that approximately 49 percent of students with hearing impairments, ages 6–21, represent culturally diverse populations. Serving students with hearing impairments whose primary language at home is not English creates unique, and sometimes difficult, challenges for educators.

A contemporary issue of diversity involves the Deaf culture. Many individuals who are deaf or hard of hearing tend to identify with the Deaf community. They contend that they should be viewed not as deficient or pathological, but as members of a different culture with its own language, traditions, values, and literature. The Deaf culture does not use the term *hearing impaired*. Its adherents view spoken English as an optional second language but ASL as the language of choice. This bilingual-bicultural

Deaf culture: Refers to individuals who are deaf who share similar values, attitudes, and practices; view American Sign Language as their natural language.

AUDIO
Siblings

REFERENCE
Teaching Deaf English Language Learners

approach stands in opposition to oralist philosophies and forms of sign language other than ASL. Generally speaking, proponents of the Deaf culture have delayed accepting cochlear implants, which seek to restore or enhance auditory information through surgery (see page 435).

Technology and Individuals With Hearing Impairments

Modern technology is an important component in the lives of many individuals with disabilities. Today's technological advances are especially evident in the area of hearing impairment. Sophisticated hearing aids, computers, alerting devices, cochlear implants, captioned media, and adaptive equipment are only a few of the items that have revolutionized the education of children with hearing impairments.

Hearing Aids and Auditory Training Devices

There are several different types of hearing aids including in-the-ear and behind-the-ear aids (see Figure 12.6). Hearing aids are individually prescribed based on an audiologist's determination of the degree and nature of hearing impairment, along with age, additional disabilities or physical limitations, the individual's speech and language skills, cost considerations, and the environment in which the hearing aid will be used. The audiologist determines how much amplification—the difference between the level of acoustical input at the microphone and the level of acoustical output at the speaker—the hearing instrument will provide. All hearing aids contain miniaturized electronic components consisting of a microphone, an amplifier, a receiver, and a power source. The audiologist also determines the frequency response of the aid—that is, the range of frequencies amplified (usually between 250 Hz and 6,000 Hz). In the past, hearing aids simply amplified all incoming sounds equally. Recent technological advances have allowed for differential amplification so that hearing aid output depends somewhat on the nature of the incoming sound. In other words, the hearing aid does not respond to all incoming sounds in the same way. Programmable hearing aids can be linked to a computer and adjusted by the audiologist. Sound outputs at certain frequencies, or at various levels of loudness, can be varied during programming sessions. Today's increasingly sophisticated programmable hearing aids are individually tailored to closely match the configuration of an individual's hearing loss. The Insights feature (page 434) provides a basic hearing aid checklist for the classroom teacher.

Although current hearing aid technology offers substantial improvement over previously available personal amplification, such devices will not necessarily meet all of the listening needs of an individual with a significant degree of hearing loss. Assistive listening devices may be used to enhance the performance of people with hearing impairment in a variety of situations. Children with hearing impairments often use auditory trainers, particularly FM systems, in their educational settings. These amplification systems are easy to use and are often more effective than hearing aids in managing the acoustical problems inherent in most classrooms. Speech understanding in the presence of background noise presents a significant dilemma for pupils with hearing impairments, particularly those wearing some type of hearing aid. The signal-to-noise ratio, or loudness level of the desired sound source relative to unwanted noise, can be greatly enhanced by these systems. An FM system consists of a small transmitter with a tiny directional microphone worn by the teacher. A receiver can be worn separately by the

assistive listening devices: Devices such as FM or sound field systems that improve the clarity of what is heard by an individual with hearing impairments by reducing background noise levels.

auditory trainer: Type of amplification system used by children with hearing impairments in place of their hearing aids in educational settings.

FM system: A wireless system that allows the transmission of a signal from the teacher wearing a microphone to the student wearing a receiver, increasing the volume of the teacher's voice over the volume level of classroom noise.

VIDEO

Hearing Aids

student or in conjunction with his or her personal hearing aid. When using the FM system, the teacher's voice is heard directly and clearly regardless of his or her location in the classroom.

Sound field systems can also enhance signal-to-noise ratio in the classroom. With this type of system, the teacher wears a lavalier microphone, and his or her voice is transmitted to various speakers strategically placed about the room, or on the desktop for a particular student. These systems have proven particularly successful for individuals with minimal hearing loss, recurrent otitis media, cochlear implants, and a variety of other communication problems.

Computers

Computers have many applications for educating children with hearing impairments. Computer-assisted instructional programs offer students with hearing impairments the opportunity to individualize the learning process at their own comfort level and pace, placing them in control of the interactive process with a variety of subjects. Special programs are also available on CD-ROM as well as on the Internet for speech drill, auditory training, sign language instruction, speechreading, and supplemental reading and language instruction. Computers can now synthesize speech from keyboard input and transcribe speech onto a printed display screen. This technology makes it easier for students with hearing impairments and limited speechreading skills to understand verbal communications and to communicate verbally with others.

Alerting Devices

Many everyday devices have been adapted to meet the needs of persons with hearing impairments. Wristwatches can be equipped with vibratory devices rather than auditory alarms. Doorbells, fire alarms, and alarm clocks are available with vibratory mechanisms or flashing lights in addition to auditory signals. Flashing-light clocks are useful for those individuals who sleep lightly. For heavy sleepers or individuals who are deaf-blind, flashing lamps (eighty-five flashes per minute) or special pillow vibrators are available. For parents who are hearing impaired, alerting devices are available with lights that flash in response to a baby's cry. Certain high-frequency alarms, such as a smoke detector, can be converted to a lower frequency, ensuring that the signal falls within the frequency range where there is sufficient residual hearing for detection.

Real-Time Captioning/Interpreting Technology

Technological advancements, some of which were originally intended for different applications, have made information more available to students with hearing impairments.

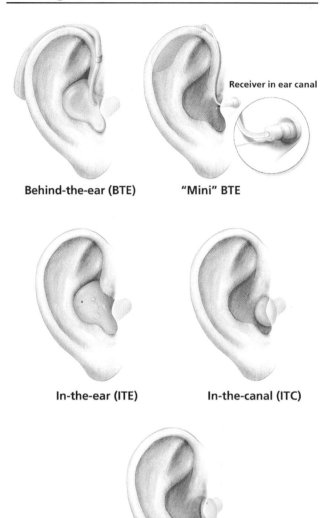

◼ ◼ ◼ ◼ ◼ Figure 12.6 **Styles of Hearing Aids**

Receiver in ear canal

Behind-the-ear (BTE)   **"Mini" BTE**

In-the-ear (ITE)   **In-the-canal (ITC)**

Completely-in-canal (CIC)

SOURCE: From the National Institute on Deafness and Other Communication Disorders (National Institute of Health).

sound field system: A system to assist students with hearing impairments in which the teacher wears a microphone that transmits a signal to a speaker strategically placed in the classroom rather than to a body-worn receiver.

How to Check a Hearing Aid

For children who use hearing aids, it is helpful to check the aids on a regular basis to ensure functioning. With minimum effort and a few minutes a day, teachers can help students check their hearing aids. Depending on the age of the child, students should take appropriate responsibility for the checking process.

Know Background Information

Basic information on the child's hearing aid should be supplied by the audiologist or parents. Things to know about the aid include the following:

- Brand and model
- Recommended volume
- Internal settings
- Battery type

Check Hearing Aid Functions

Two inexpensive pieces of equipment—a hearing aid stethoscope and a battery tester—should be kept in the classroom and used to check hearing aids. Stethoscopes can usually be purchased through local hearing aid dealers. The stethoscope is used to check the quality of sound provided by the hearing aid. Listen for the following problems:

- Sound cuts on/off when the volume control is changed.
- Sound cuts on/off when the cord of an FM system is jiggled.
- Voice quality sounds distorted.

Battery testers are also available through hearing aid dealers or local commercial outlets, such as Radio Shack. Depending on their quality and sophistication, testers are usually inexpensive. Use them according to directions to test hearing aid batteries. Only batteries working at full power will provide good hearing aid function.

Check Student Function With Hearing Aid

Described below is a quick, efficient check of how a child functions with a hearing aid. In addition to including if the hearing aid is working, this check can detect other possible problems a child may be experiencing such as a change in hearing levels related to outer or middle ear problems or a change in sensorineural hearing levels.

- Have the student sit facing you at a distance of about three feet, wearing the aid.
- Cover your mouth with an index card or piece of paper.
- Individually present each of the following five sounds: *ah, oo, ee, sh, s*. (These sounds represent the variety of the frequencies present in speech.)

- Have the student raise one hand or place a block into a container when the sound becomes audible.
- Set a baseline for each student, consisting of the sounds the student can perceive from three feet away, using a functioning hearing aid with a good battery. Not all students will hear all five sounds.
- Check each student's awareness of the five sounds on a regular basis. If hearing deviates from the student's baseline, check the aid more carefully.
- If a thorough check of the aid confirms that it is working well, poor performance on the five-sound test may indicate that a problem such as fluid in the middle ear is impairing the student's ability to hear at baseline levels. Notify the student's family if you strongly suspect that middle ear fluid is causing problems.

Troubleshoot Hearing Aid Problems

When a student seems to be having difficulty with a hearing aid, some of the following signs may help you find or eliminate the problem. If you uncover any hearing aid problems that cannot be resolved in the classroom, let the student's family know so the aid can be repaired or replaced as necessary.

Problem: No Sound

- Try a new battery.
- Make sure the battery is properly placed. Match the positive (+) on the battery to the (+) in the battery compartment.
- The battery compartment may be corroded. Clean it gently with a pencil eraser, then try a new battery.
- Make sure the hearing aid is set at ON, not at T for telephone.
- Look for wax or dirt in the earmold. Clean the mold with a pipe cleaner, then with warm soapy water. Dry it completely before reattaching it to the aid. Do not use alcohol.
- Look for twists in the tubing.

Problem: Squealing/Feedback

- Check to see if the earmold fits properly. If it looks too small, inform the student's parent or audiologist.
- Check the volume and turn it down to the appropriate setting. If it still squeals, the mold is too small or there is an internal problem in the aid.
- Check for loose tubing, or for cracks in the tubing attached to the aid or mold.

SOURCE: Laurent Clerc National Deaf Education Center, Gallaudet University, *How to Check a Hearing Aid, Series #5004*. Available at http://clerccenter.gallaudet.edu/SupportServices/series/5004.html

Software that uses voice recognition and converts the spoken word to printed files is one such example. In this application, the teacher uses a microphone connected to a computer with voice recognition software, which picks up the instruction as spoken and translates it to a print file on a computer screen viewed by the student. Students with hearing impairments can follow the real-time instruction on the computer monitor and then save the print file to the computer when finished. The print file can then be reviewed, sorted into notes and study guides, and saved for the student to use whenever needed.

For students who function better with sign language than with print, a software program is now available that works just as the voice recognition software does, with one significant difference. Instead of having

Children who are hearing impaired frequently use auditory trainers in the classroom.

a print file appear on the screen viewed by the student, the instruction from the teacher is presented by a computer-based character that signs the information in real time.

Another example of real-time interpreter/print technology is the CART (Communication Access Realtime Translation) program. CART uses the paid services of trained court reporters to record instruction in the classroom. The student is able to follow the instruction on a computer screen in real time and then save and use files of information later, just as with the voice recognition files described previously.

Captioning

Many current television programs and feature films are captioned to make entertainment more accessible to audiences with hearing impairments. Federal law now requires that all new televisions with screens thirteen inches and larger have built-in caption functions.

Telecommunication Devices

Individuals with severe hearing impairments can communicate by telephone with a **telecommunication device for the deaf (TDD)**. A TDD is a small keyboard with an electronic display screen and modem attached. The telephone receiver is placed in the modem, and messages typed onto a keyboard are carried as different sets of tones on the telephone line to the other party's telephone, which must be linked to a TDD in order to complete the call. Today, however, many individuals with hearing impairments rely on text messaging and other social media outlets as their primary means of communicating.

Cochlear Implants

Many persons have sensorineural hearing loss so severe that they may not derive significant benefit from conventional amplification devices. The cochlear implant (see Figure 12.7) is a surgically implanted device designed to make sounds audible for these individuals. Although somewhat controversial in the past, particularly with the

telecommunication device for the deaf (TDD): An instrument for sending typewritten messages over telephone lines to be received by a person who is deaf or severely hearing impaired as a printed message. Sometimes called TT, TTY, or TTD.

AUDIO

Technology

Figure 12.7 **Cochlear Implant**

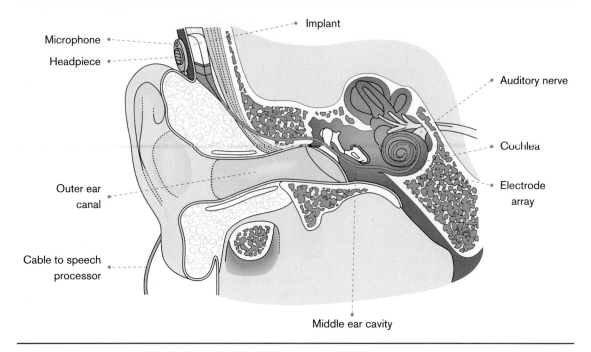

Microphone

Headpiece

Implant

Auditory nerve

Cochlea

Electrode array

Outer ear canal

Cable to speech processor

Middle ear cavity

SOURCE: Based on drawing from Advanced Bionics Corporation, Sylmar, CA.

Deaf culture community, large numbers of children and adults have been implanted, with favorable results. Approximately 38,000 children and 58,000 adults in the United States have received cochlear implants (National Institute on Deafness and Other Communication Disorders, 2013). Research indicates that cochlear implant users, particularly adventitiously deaf adults and children implanted at an early age, perform significantly better on a variety of tasks than most hearing aid users with a similar degree of hearing loss. When comparing the level of speech intelligibility between children with cochlear implants and children with normal hearing, distinct differences have been noted. By age 4, children with normal hearing develop adult or near adultlike speech intelligibility. Children with cochlear implants do not develop a similar ceiling of competence at such a rapid rate. Instead, they have a continuum of improvement that correlates to increased age and length of use of their implant. They continue to have a speech that is less intelligible than that of their same-age peer group with normal hearing. The question of how to bring them to the same level of intelligible speech as a normally hearing 4-year-old remains a challenge (Chin, Tsai, & Gao, 2003). Despite high variability in performance among users, cochlear implant technology is revolutionizing educational management of the child who is profoundly deaf.

A cochlear implant is not a hearing aid but rather a tiny array of electrodes that is implanted surgically in the inner ear (cochlea) and is attached to a receiver-stimulator implanted just behind the ear at the base of the skull. The individual wears a microphone and a small computer for speech processing, connected by electrical wiring. The transmitter is held in place over the implant site using a special magnet. Although many implant users wear larger processors similar in appearance to a body-type hearing aid, newer devices are a great deal smaller, fitting completely behind the ear, and are generally more cosmetically appealing. Continuous advancements in technology

VIDEO

Cochlear Implants

■ ■ ■ ■ ■ Table 12.6 **Guidelines for Cochlear Implants: Who Might Benefit?**

Age Range	Guidelines
Young Children: 12 months to 2 years	Does your child have: • Profound sensorineural hearing loss (nerve deafness) in both ears? • Lack of progress in development of auditory skill with hearing aid or other amplification? • High motivation and realistic expectations from family? • Other existing medical conditions that won't interfere with cochlear implant procedure?
Children: 2 to 17 years	Do you have: • Severe-to-profound sensorineural hearing loss (nerve deafness) in both ears? • Little or no benefit from hearing aids? • Lack of progress in the development of auditory skills? • High motivation and realistic expectations from family?
Adults: 18 years and older	Do you have: • Severe-to-profound sensorineural hearing loss in both ears? • Little or no useful benefit from hearing aids? • Scores of 50% or less on sentence recognition tests in the ear to be implanted and 60% or less in the nonimplanted ear or bilaterally?

SOURCE: From *Introduction to Cochlear Implants*. Retrieved November 23, 2013, from http://www.cochlearamericas.com/378.asp

present ever-changing improvements in the options and results available to those opting for implantation (Chute, 2004).

Guidelines for implantation have become increasingly liberal (see Table 12.6). A number of factors affect the probability of success with implantation, including degree of hearing loss, age of onset, age at implantation, previous experiences with amplification, family support, and educational methodology. The earlier the child is implanted, the better the prognosis for success—especially for acquisition of intelligible speech (American Speech-Language-Hearing Association, 2013b). Implantation of older children (above 6 years) has shown some success, but improvement may be more limited.

The responsibility of public schools to children with cochlear implants was addressed in the final IDEA 2004 regulations. Because a cochlear implant is surgically implanted, it is not considered to be an assistive technology device. Therefore, schools are not required to pay for this appliance. The student, however, is still entitled to receive related services as specified in his or her IEP. This can include speech-language as well as audiology services (American Speech-Language-Hearing Association, 2013d).

Because cochlear implantation provides such an increase in residual hearing for the child who is deaf, educational management strategies are more likely to mirror those provided for children with a mild to moderate degree of loss. For example, children who are profoundly deaf often simply cannot hear many high-frequency consonants, even with technologically advanced amplification. Teaching such students to produce these sounds correctly in speech is extremely difficult. Children using cochlear implants generally have much better high-frequency hearing ability; as a consequence, encouraging correct production of high-frequency consonants becomes much easier. Although these children still have limitations with regard to complex grammatical structure, sophisticated vocabulary, and certain auditory skills, if implantation is done early and appropriate rehabilitative and educational supports are in place, linguistic and educational progress is generally more rapid for children using cochlear implants.

AUDIO

Cochlear Implants

Trends, Issues, and Controversies

The debate regarding the most appropriate methodology for educating children with hearing impairments has raged for more than two hundred years and continues to be an emotionally charged issue. Overall, the research findings on efficacy of various communication styles and educational philosophies are inconclusive. It does appear that infants with hearing impairments born to parents who are deaf and who use American Sign Language exhibit significantly better language development (Hunt & Marshall, 2013). Determining the most appropriate methods for enhancing language acquisition, expressive and receptive communication skills, and educational achievement of children with hearing impairments is an issue of paramount importance. This issue has two critical elements: (1) kind of language and (2) form of communication. More specifically, there are two languages, ASL and Signed English systems, and two communication forms, oral and manual, to be considered. Any combination can produce a variety of approaches. The acquisition of one's native language is central to the development of functional literacy, which in turn provides the platform for future academic and societal success.

Research conducted by Moores (2001) suggests that parents who use a total communication approach, including manual signs, fingerspelling, and spoken language, with their child and with each other enhance their child's acquisition of language. Traditionally, the severity of hearing impairment has been viewed as a primary determinant of methodology. The merits of various methodologies are now being reexamined in light of recent advances in amplification and the use of cochlear implants.

Total communication is currently the communication approach of choice in many public school classrooms. Proponents of TC contend that by placing equal emphasis on signing, speaking, and speechreading skills, this method ensures a more normal rate of language acquisition and use of English as the primary language. Yet, total communication has met with some opposition. Although many educational programs purport to use total communication, in reality little emphasis is given to oral skills. It has been argued that learning English as a primary language denies children with hearing impairments their cultural birthright by limiting their exposure to Deaf culture and ASL, its native language. Opponents of TC point to the early research of Strong and Prinz (1997), which suggests that exposure to ASL correlates positively with enhanced literacy and academic performance and may actually facilitate learning English as a second language.

Current ideological and cultural controversies fueled by Deaf culture advocates and rigid proponents of various methodologies have polarized many educators. The bilingual–bicultural philosophy, often referred to as bi-bi, contends that deafness is a separate and viable culture within society, with ASL as its own unique and natural language. ASL has a unique grammar and syntax, and in the bi-bi approach English is learned as a second language. Advocates for Deaf culture consider hearing impairment to be nonpathological and, therefore, not a condition requiring medical intervention (for example, a cochlear implant). Individuals with significant hearing loss often work in the hearing world, but their family/social lives are usually sequestered within the deaf world. Proponents of Deaf culture claim that, when given a choice, individuals with significant hearing impairments would most often choose to spend the majority of their lives in the comfort of their own culture (Moores, 2001). Regrettably, the two societies, one deaf and the other hearing, often experience limited interaction and contact.

Full inclusion is another area of controversy. A number of educators, parents, and advocates have challenged full inclusion as a viable placement option for individuals

AUDIO

Chapter 12 Summary

with hearing impairments. The main points of debate are that in full inclusion classrooms teachers are often unfamiliar with the dynamics of deafness, they are not skilled in different communication techniques, and students are frequently stigmatized and often isolated socially (Moores, 2005).

Definitions and Concepts in the Field of Hearing Impairment

- *Hearing impairment* is a generic term indicating a hearing disability that may range in severity from mild to profound.
- The term *deaf* refers to those in whom the sense of hearing is nonfunctional for the ordinary purposes of life. Deafness precludes successful processing of linguistic information through audition, with or without a hearing aid.
- An individual may be either congenitally deaf (born deaf) or adventitiously deaf—born with normal hearing that has become nonfunctional through illness or accident.
- Persons who are hard of hearing are those in whom the sense of hearing is defective but functional, either with or without a hearing aid, for the purpose of processing linguistic information.
- The ear is divided into three connected sections: the outer, the middle, and the inner ear. Hearing impairments are commonly classified according to their location in the hearing process and the severity of the loss.
- A conductive hearing loss is the interference of sound through the outer and middle ear.
- A sensorineural hearing loss is caused by defects of the inner ear (the cochlea), the auditory nerve that transmits impulses to the brain, or both.
- A mixed hearing loss involves both conductive and sensorineural loss.
- A central hearing loss is the result of damage to the central nervous system; an individual with this type of hearing loss may hear but not understand speech.
- Hearing loss is measured through testing procedures conducted by an audiologist and is graphed on an audiogram.
- The degree of hearing is usually reported in decibels (dB), a measure of sound intensity. It is also measured in hertz (Hz), or frequency of the sound.
- A hearing impairment is usually classified according to degree, ranging from mild to profound loss, based on different levels of intensity (dB) at different frequencies (Hz).
- One of the most common types of audiological tests is puretone audiometry, which is the practice of delivering sound

tones to an individual via air conduction (headphones) and measuring recognition on an audiometer.
- Another common test is bone-conduction audiometry, which allows the signals to bypass the middle ear and be transmitted directly to the inner ear by vibrating the bones of the skull. It is used to ascertain whether there is a possible sensorineural or conductive hearing loss.
- More specialized types of hearing tests include play audiometry and speech audiometry.

Prevalence of Hearing Impairment

- Over 69,000 students between the ages of 6 and 21 were receiving some type of specialized services because of a hearing impairment in the 2011–2012 school year. This accounts for approximately 1.2 percent of the students receiving services under IDEA.

Etiology of Hearing Impairment

- The cause of approximately one third of all hearing loss remains unknown; however, the known major causes are genetic or chromosomal anomalies, disease, and trauma.
- The etiology, location, and severity of the hearing loss are variables used in determining immediate and long-range treatment and programming.

Characteristics of Individuals With Hearing Impairment

- Children with hearing impairments have IQs similar to those of their typical peers.
- Educational achievement in students with hearing impairments may be significantly delayed in comparison to that of their hearing peers, averaging three to four years below their age-appropriate grade levels.
- Play situations and the development of friendships are affected by difficulty with language development.

Educational Considerations

- The two principal educational settings for students with hearing impairment are public schools and special schools.

- There are three main instructional approaches to providing educational services to a child with a hearing impairment: (1) the auditory-oral method, (2) total communication, and (3) the bilingual-bicultural method.
- Currently a significant majority of educational and related service programs are using total communication.

Issues of Diversity

- Many persons who are deaf and hard of hearing contend that they should be viewed not as deficient or pathological, but rather as members of the Deaf culture with its own language, traditions, and values.

Technology and Individuals With Hearing Impairments

- Technology tremendously benefits the lives of individuals with hearing impairments.

STUDY QUESTIONS

1. Define the terms *deaf* and *hard of hearing*.
2. Why is it important to know the age of onset, type, and degree of hearing loss?
3. What is the primary difference between prelingual and postlingual hearing impairments?
4. List the four major types of hearing loss.
5. Describe three different types of audiological evaluations.
6. What are some major areas of development that are usually affected by a hearing impairment?
7. List three major causes of hearing impairment.
8. What issues are central to the debate over manual and oral approaches?
9. Define the concept of a Deaf culture.
10. What is total communication, and how can it be used in the classroom?
11. Describe the bilingual-bicultural approach to educating pupils with hearing impairments.
12. In what two academic areas do students with hearing impairments usually lag behind their classmates?
13. Why is early identification of a hearing impairment critical?
14. Why do professionals assess the language and speech abilities of individuals with hearing impairments?
15. List five indicators of a possible hearing loss in the classroom.
16. What are three indicators in children that may predict success with a cochlear implant?
17. Identify five strategies a classroom teacher can use to promote communicative skills and enhance independence in the transition to adulthood.
18. Describe how to check a hearing aid.
19. How can technology benefit individuals with a hearing impairment?

KEY TERMS

hearing impairment, 401

hearing sensitivity loss, 401

deaf, 401

hard of hearing, 401

outer ear, 401

middle ear, 401

inner ear, 401

central auditory nervous system, 401

tympanic membrane, 401

malleus, 401

incus, 401

stapes, 401

ossicular chain, 401

oval window, 402

cochlea, 402

organ of Corti, 402

conductive hearing loss, 402

sensorineural hearing loss, 403

mixed hearing loss, 403

central hearing disorder, 403

audiologist, 403

audiogram, 403

frequency, 405

hertz (Hz), 405

decibels (dB), 405

pure-tone audiometry, 405

air-conduction audiometry, 406

LEARNING ACTIVITIES

1. Observe an audiological examination of a student.

   a. Describe the individual being tested.

   b. What tests were administered?

   c. Were any hearing difficulties identified? If so, what kind of hearing loss was detected?

   d. What were your reactions to the assessment?

2. Observe an infant/toddler program as well as a school-age program for students with hearing impairments.

   a. Where did you observe the program?

   b. Describe the learning environment.

   c. Describe the activities you observed.

   d. What type(s) of communication modes were used?

   e. What were your reactions? What differences did you observe between the two programs?

3. Interview a general education teacher who has students who are deaf or hard of hearing in his or her class.

   a. How long has the teacher been educating students with hearing impairments?

   b. What type of professional training (preparation) does the teacher have?

   c. Ask the teacher about the primary purposes of the program and what kinds of problems he or she encounters.

   d. How would the teacher describe his or her classroom: as mainstreamed or fully inclusive?

   e. What communication modes are used?

   f. How is technology used in the classroom?

   g. Describe your personal and professional reactions to this experience.

ORGANIZATIONS CONCERNED WITH HEARING IMPAIRMENTS

Alexander Graham Bell Association for the Deaf and Hard of Hearing

http://listeningandspokenlanguage.org/

American Speech-Language-Hearing Association

www.asha.org

Division for Communicative Disabilities and Deafness (DCDD), Council for Exceptional Children

www.dcdd.us

National Association of the Deaf

www.nad.org

REFLECTING ON STANDARDS

The following exercises are designed to help you learn to apply the Council for Exceptional Children (CEC) standards to your teaching practice. Each of the reflection exercises below correlates with knowledge or a skill within the CEC standards. For the full text of each of the related CEC standards, please refer to the standards integration grid located in Appendix B.

Focus on Learning Environments
(*CEC Initial Preparation Standard 2.2*)

Reflect on what you have learned about students with hearing impairments. If you were to have a student in your class with a hearing impairment, how might you help him or her learn skills for self-advocacy? In what ways might you be able to help your student better understand his or her disability and communicate his or her learning needs?

Focus on Instructional Planning and Strategies
(*CEC Initial Preparation Standard 5.2*)

Reflect on what you have learned about the various assistive technologies available for students with hearing impairments. If you had a student in your class with a hearing impairment, how might you work with the student and his or her family to assess which assistive technologies might be best to use in your classroom? Who else might you need to involve from the school district to implement any new technologies?

STUDENT STUDY SITE

Sharpen your skills with SAGE edge at **edge.sagepub.com/gargiulo5e. SAGE edge for students** provides a personalized approach to help you accomplish your coursework goals in an easy-to-use learning environment.

Individuals With Visual Impairments

Carrie

The series of whistles sounds. She steps onto the starting block and bends into position as the official instructs. The beep of the starter propels the swimmers into the water. It is a good start. She and Jennifer surface at the same time, just short of Beth. Steadily Jennifer pulls ahead. "C'mon, Carrie, you can do it!" I think to myself. Jennifer's lead widens. I turn my head; I can't watch. She's worked so hard to not succeed now. At the turn, she flips just as Jennifer starts back for the last 50 meters. It's now or four more years. Suddenly she begins to narrow the margin. Is it too little too late? Maybe. I begin to yell (as do others around me). Please, dear God! She's doing it! Oh, no, the flags. It's so close. Yes, she does it! She out-touches Jennifer by hundredths of a second. But the clock does not register. Quickly the judges check the computers. Yes, she really did it! She doesn't know. Frantically I send word by a friend. When she hears the news, she stops in disbelief, and then her right arm shoots straight up with joy.

She came through again. I don't know why I'm surprised. She has done it time and time again. That's just Carrie. All of her life she has amazed me as well as others she has encountered. While second place does not sound like much of an accomplishment, it is to a disabled child. Perhaps *disabled* is not the right word.

Carrie, now 22, was born with oculocutaneous albinism. As with all disabilities, this has a complex definition. For Carrie, it means she has no pigment in her eyes, skin, or hair; she is extremely sensitive to light; she has nystagmus; and she is legally blind. She has also had some other physical problems along the way, but has developed into an outstanding young lady earning her place on the U.S. Paralympic Team.

The road to victory has not been easy, and sometimes Carrie did not choose the easy route. Even as a small child many people saw the special qualities in Carrie and encouraged and guided her. Others have been unable to see beyond her shortcomings. The key to her success has been her strength of character to focus on her abilities, not her disabilities. Her favorite saying is "I may not have eyesight, but I have vision."

VIDEO
Visual Impairment

LEARNING OBJECTIVES

After reading Chapter 13, you should be able to:

- **Define** legally blind, functionally blind, deaf-blind, and low vision.
- **Explain** the vision process and associated vision disorders.
- **List** the most common visual impairments affecting school-age children.
- **Outline** the historical evolution of educational services for children and youth with visual impairments.
- **Provide** examples of observable characteristics of vision difficulties.
- **Describe** how visual acuity is assessed.
- **Define** literacy medium and learning medium.
- **Summarize** educational services for persons with visual impairments across the life span.
- **Explain** how technology benefits individuals with visual impairments.

Her academic life has definitely had its ups and downs. Her level of success and happiness seems to have been determined by her attitude, which is closely related to the attitude of her teachers and her classmates. The more creative and open the atmosphere, the more Carrie has achieved. Quite often the more creative teachers found ways to minimize her visual limitations and maximize her intellectual and creative abilities.

Swimming is not her only accomplishment. She is a college senior majoring in liberal arts with a concentration in visual arts. She is an award winner not only in the disabled world, but also in the "real world." Of all her talents, gifts, awards, recognitions, and other achievements, the one I am most proud of is the Right Stuff Award that she received at Space Camp in Huntsville, Alabama. This award is presented each camp session to one female and one male who have demonstrated outstanding leadership and personal effort. This shows me that she has developed into the kind of person who will contribute to society in a positive manner.

—Jane Willoughby

NOTE: For additional coverage of Carrie, check out the First Person feature on page 467, written in her own words about her experience with her visual impairment.

■ ■

Visual impairment is a term that describes people who cannot see well even with correction. Throughout history, *blindness* has been used as a term to mean that something is not understood, such as "I was blind to that idea" or the aged person is "old and blind." How many times do we use the stereotypes of the blind beggar on the street corner and the blind person groping for mobility in the environment? The stigma associated with loss of vision affects encounters with others, who may assume that the person is dependent on others for everything.

Famous success stories about persons who are blind include those of Helen Keller and Mary Ingalls. Helen Keller and her teacher, Annie Sullivan, pursued their lifelong journey from Tuscumbia, Alabama, to Perkins Institute for the Blind (now known as Perkins School for the Blind), to Radcliffe College, and then to employment with the American Foundation for the Blind. Keller helped develop schools for the blind all over the world (Lash, 1980).

Mary Ingalls was a student at Iowa College for the Blind (now Iowa Braille and Sight Saving School) in 1881. Her scholastic endeavors were made famous through Laura Ingalls Wilder's *Little House on the Prairie*, which later became a television series. Laura's portrayal of the determination of her sister Mary and their family to continue her education after she lost her vision at age 14 showed the world the success a person who is blind can achieve.

Movies about persons with visual impairments and publicity about musicians and athletes who are visually impaired have helped to change the image of persons with visual impairments. Braille in elevators, voice output on computers, and access to restaurant hosts who read the menu reflect a recognition that the person with vision

visual impairment: An impairment in vision that, even with correction, adversely affects an individual's educational performance. The term includes both partial sight and blindness.

Chapter contribution written by Carol Allison and Mary Jean Sanspree formerly with the University of Alabama at Birmingham.

loss is competent with only a visual acuity difference. Such changes allow for independence in the everyday world with only a few accommodations.

The goal of this chapter is to provide an understanding of the visual process, vision loss, the effects of vision loss on school performance and vocation, and the roles of the family and community. Historical foundations, classifications of vision loss, educational practices, and technological interventions are presented for you to examine how the general educational curriculum may be adapted for the student with a visual impairment.

Defining Visual Impairments

Visual impairment including blindness is defined in the Individuals with Disabilities Education Improvement Act (IDEA 2004, PL 108–446) as an impairment in vision that, even with correction, adversely affects an individual's educational performance. The term includes both partial sight and blindness. Educational services for students with visual impairments are determined by variations of the definition specified in IDEA. This definition encompasses students with a wide range of visual impairments, who may vary significantly in their visual abilities. One student may have no functional vision and must learn through tactual means; another may be able to read and write print with modifications such as enlarged print; still others may use a combination of both Braille and print. An appropriate learning medium for each student must be determined by the student's ability to use each of these means or a combination of both.

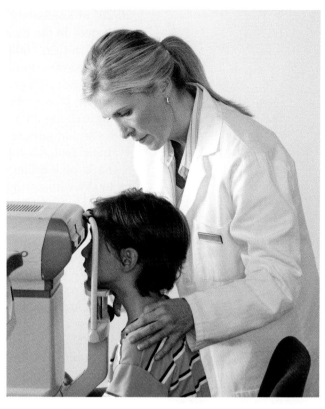

Legal blindness is visual acuity of 20/200 or less in the better eye after correction or a visual field that is no greater than 20 degrees.

Visual impairments may include a reduction of **visual acuity** (the ability to visually perceive details) of near or distant vision or a restriction in the field of vision. In other words, acuity affects how well a child sees materials presented up close or how accurately the child can see work presented on chalkboards or maps across the room. An impairment involving the **visual field** refers to the amount of vision a student has in the quadrant regions to the right, to the left, above, and below while gazing straight ahead. Students may exhibit unusual head turning or positioning in order to view materials with the portion of the visual field that is functional. Students with a **field loss**, or a restriction to the visual field, must be taught to use auditory cues for safety purposes on the playground, in the classroom, and in other environments.

Other areas of consideration in understanding a student's visual abilities include the age of the student at the time of the vision loss, the severity and stability of the eye condition, and whether the condition is the result of hereditary or congenital conditions. This information is usually obtained through a medical or clinically based assessment by an optometrist or ophthalmologist and does not necessarily include how the person functions in various settings throughout the school, home, or community.

Understanding the definitions of visual impairments is critical for the educational team in developing an appropriate educational program. Over the years, the term **legally blind** has been used as a federal definition of blindness. This definition involves using a **Snellen chart**, which is a clinical measurement of the true amount of distance vision an individual has under certain conditions. Legal blindness is a visual acuity of

visual acuity: The ability to visually perceive details of near or distant objects.

visual field: The amount of vision in the quadrant regions to the right, left, up, and down while gazing straight ahead.

field loss: A restriction to the visual field within the quadrant regions to the right, left, up, and down while gazing straight ahead.

legally blind: A visual acuity of 20/200 or less in the better eye with correction or a visual field that is no greater than 20 degrees.

Snellen chart: An eye chart of clinical measurement of the true amount of distance vision an individual has under certain conditions.

20/200 or less in the better eye with correction or a visual field that is no greater than 20 degrees. In this definition, 20 feet is the distance at which visual acuity is measured. The *200* in this definition indicates the distance (200 feet) from which a person with normal vision would be able to identify the largest symbol on the eye chart. The second part of the definition refers to field restriction, which involves the amount of vision a person has to view objects peripherally. The legal definition is considered in education, but by itself has little value in planning a functional educational program for students with visual impairments.

Individuals identified as blind use tactile and auditory abilities as the primary channels of learning. They may have some minimal light or form perception or be totally without sight. Braille or other tactile media are commonly the preferred literacy channel. Orientation and mobility training is required for all students who are blind.

Individuals are considered functionally blind when the primary channel of learning is through tactile or auditory means. They may use limited vision to obtain additional information about the environment. These individuals usually use Braille as the primary literacy medium (most frequently used method of reading) and require orientation and mobility training.

A person is described as having low vision when the visual impairment interferes with the ability to perform daily activities. The primary channel of learning is through visual means with the use of prescription and nonprescription devices. The literacy medium varies with each individual according to the use of the remaining vision and the use of low vision devices. Orientation and mobility training is required for students to learn to use residual vision (usable vision).

Persons with deaf-blindness have limited vision and hearing that interfere with visual and auditory tasks. According to IDEA 2004 (PL 108–446), deaf-blindness means concomitant hearing and visual impairments, the combination of which causes such severe communication and other developmental and educational needs that the student who is deaf-blind cannot be accommodated in special education programs solely for children with deafness or children with blindness. Individuals who are deaf-blind learn tactually. Braille and sign language are the preferred literacy and communication media. A sign language interpreter and orientation and mobility training are required for persons with deaf-blindness. The use of a variety of ways to communicate facilitates direct learning experiences for the person with deaf-blindness (Chen & Downing, 2006).

The Eye and How It Works

The human eye is the organ that gives us the sense of sight, which allows us to learn more about the surrounding world than any of the other four senses. We use our eyes in almost every activity we perform, whether reading, working, watching television, writing a letter, or driving a car. The eye allows us to see and interpret the shapes, colors, and dimensions of objects by processing the light. Light enters the eye first through the clear cornea and then through the circular opening in the iris called the pupil. Next the light is converged by the crystalline lens. The light progresses through the gelatinous vitreous humor to a clear focus on the retina, the central area of which is the macula. In the retina, light impulses are changed into electrical signals and sent along the optic nerve to the occipital (posterior) lobe of the brain, which interprets these electrical signals as visual images.

When an eyeball is longer than normal from front to back, the incoming rays of light focus in front of the retina instead of on the retina. This condition is known as

functionally blind: An educational description when the primary channel of learning is through tactile and auditory means.

primary literacy medium: An individual's most frequently used method of reading and writing.

low vision: A visual impairment that interferes with the ability to perform daily activities and in which the primary channel of learning is through the use of prescription and nonprescription devices.

residual vision: An individual's usable vision.

deaf-blindness: Concomitant hearing and visual impairments.

cornea: The transparent outer portion of the eyeball that transmits light to the retina.

iris: The colored, circular part of the eye in front of the lens that controls the size of the pupil.

pupil: The circular opening at the center of the iris that controls the amount of light allowed into the eye.

lens: The transparent disc in the middle of the eye behind the pupil that brings rays of light into focus on the retina.

vitreous humor: A colorless mass of soft, gelatinlike material that fills the eyeball behind the lens.

retina: The inner layer of the eye containing light-sensitive cells that connect with the brain through the optic nerve.

macula: The area of best central vision.

optic nerve: The nerve at the posterior of the eye that carries messages from the retina to the brain.

Table 13.1 Terminology Describing Eye Functioning

Term	Definition
Aqueous humor	A clear, watery fluid that fills the front part of the eye between the cornea, lens, and iris.
Choroid	The middle layer of the eyeball, which contains veins and arteries that furnish nourishment to the eye, especially the retina.
Conjunctiva	A mucous membrane that lines the eyelids and covers the front part of the eyeball.
Cornea	The transparent outer portion of the eyeball that transmits light to the retina.
Iris	The colored, circular part of the eye in front of the lens. It controls the size of the pupil.
Lens	The transparent disc in the middle of the eye behind the pupil that brings rays of light into focus on the retina.
Optic nerve	The important nerve that carries messages from the retina to the brain.
Pupil	The circular opening at the center of the iris that controls the amount of light allowed into the eye.
Retina	The inner layer of the eye containing light-sensitive cells that connect with the brain through the optic nerve.
Sclera	The white part of the eye; a tough coating that, along with the cornea, forms the external protective coat of the eye.
Vitreous body	A colorless mass of soft, gelatinlike material that fills the eyeball behind the lens.

myopia or nearsightedness. In this situation, a pupil can see near objects (for example, his or her textbook), but viewing objects at a distance—the chalkboard—may be problematic. If the eyeball is too short, the image will focus behind the retina. This condition is commonly referred to as hyperopia or farsightedness. A child with hyperopia typically has no problem seeing distant objects but encounters difficulty seeing near objects. Hyperopia is the most common refractive error in children (Geddie, Bina, & Miller, 2013).

In the case of astigmatism, one or more surfaces of the cornea or lens (the eye structures that focus incoming light) are not spherical (shaped like the side of a basketball) but cylindrical (shaped like the side of a football). As a result, there is no distinct point of focus inside the eye but, rather, a smeared or spread-out focus.

The eyeball, which measures approximately one inch in diameter, is set in a protective cone-shaped cavity in the skull called the orbit or socket. The orbit is surrounded by layers of soft, fatty tissue that protect the eye and enable it to turn easily. Three pairs of muscles regulate the motion of each eye.

Figure 13.1 shows the anatomy of the human eye while Table 13.1 presents key terminology associated with the functioning of the eye.

Classification of Visual Impairments

Children are eligible for special education services according to the amount of vision loss and how that vision loss affects educational performance. The most common visual impairments affecting the school-age child include cataracts, glaucoma, optic nerve atrophy, myopia, albinism, eye injury, cortical visual impairment, and retinopathy of prematurity (ROP). Examples of how children see with different eye diseases are shown in Figure 13.2.

Some visual impairments are secondary to systematic diseases such as diabetes, cancer, muscular dystrophy, and arthritis. A list of these visual impairments and their characteristics can be found in Table 13.2.

myopia: Elongation of the eye that causes extreme nearsightedness and decreased visual acuity.

hyperopia: Change in the shape of the eye, which shortens the light ray path and causes farsightedness.

astigmatism: One or more surfaces of the cornea or lens are cylindrical, not spherical, resulting in distorted vision.

orbit: A protective cone-shaped cavity in the skull, sometimes called the socket.

cataracts: Lenses that are opaque or cloudy due to trauma or age.

glaucoma: A disease caused by increased pressure inside the aqueous portion of the eye with loss in the visual field.

optic nerve atrophy: Degeneration of the optic nerve, which may be congenital or hereditary, causing loss of central vision, color vision, and reduced visual acuity.

albinism: A hereditary condition with partial or total absence of pigment in the eye.

Figure 13.1 **Schematic of the Eye**

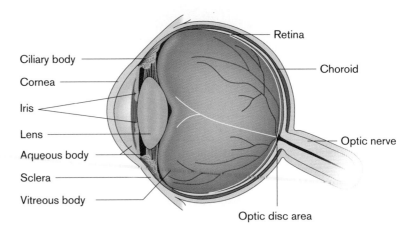

SOURCE: National Eye Institute. (2013). *Photograph and Image Catalog: Normal Eye Anatomy.* Available at http://www.nei.nih .gov/photo/eyean/images/NEA13_72.jpg

A Brief History of Visual Impairments

Education for and changes of attitudes toward persons with visual impairments were of great interest to Diderot (1749), who wrote to King Louis of France a philosophical work called *Letter on the Blind for the Use of Those Who See.* Diderot had contact with two people who were blind: Nicholas Saunderson, a mathematics professor, and Maria Theresia von Paradis, a Viennese pianist and music teacher. Diderot was one of the early champions of the visually impaired and believed that persons who were blind could lead normal lives.

In 1784, Valentin Haüy established the Institut National des Jeunes Aveugles in Paris. This institution for blind youth was the first school for the education of children with vision loss. Haüy used Roman letters to teach students who were blind. His students, however, were using night writing codes within the school. In the 1800s, one of Haüy's students, Louis Braille, developed an embossed communication system so he could write to his friends in a simpler manner than using raised letters (Scholl, Mulholland, & Lonergan, 1986). His system of embossed dots was not accepted by educators until later, but his system of Braille dots remains today as the literacy code accepted throughout the world.

The first schools for the blind in the United States were financially supported through the school in Paris. These schools included the Perkins School for the Blind in Boston, established in 1829; the New York Institution for the Blind, incorporated in 1831; and the Overbrook School for the Blind in Philadelphia, opened in 1833. These residential schools, modeled after the Institut National des Jeunes Aveugles in Paris, were the brainchild of Samuel Gridley Howe, who had visited European schools to learn how to provide education for the blind in the United States (Scholl et al., 1986).

Residential programs were designed to prepare students with visual impairments for daily living skills and menial jobs. Students were expected to function within a sheltered environment and go into life as members of a separate society that was labeled as "helpless" or dependent. The schools were a type of experiment to see if students with disabilities could learn community skills and function as participating citizens instead of dependents of society.

retinopathy of prematurity (ROP): An interruption in the vascular system of the eye, due to premature birth, in which veins and arteries begin to grow in an unorganized manner and cause bundles that pull together and detach the retina, resulting in loss of peripheral vision or total blindness.

Braille: A communication system utilizing raised representation of written materials for tactual interpretation.

Figure 13.2 **Examples of Eye Diseases**

(a)

Normal vision

(b)

Glaucoma

(c)

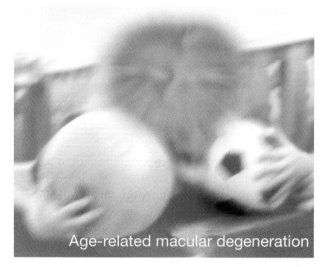

Age-related macular degeneration

(d)

Cataract

(e)

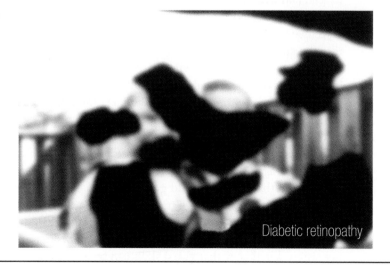

Diabetic retinopathy

SOURCE: National Eye Institute. (2013). *Photograph and Image Catalog: Eye Disease Simulation.* Available at http://www.nei.nih.gov/health/examples

Common Visual Impairments of School-Age Children

Condition	Cause	Characteristics
Congenital cataracts	Congenital anomaly, infection, severe malnutrition, systemic disease, or trauma	Blurred vision, nystagmus
Congenital glaucoma	Increased pressure of the eye	Excessive tearing, cloudy lens, pain, restricted visual fields
Eye injury	Trauma	Poor visual acuity or blindness resulting from injury
Myopia	Elongation of the eye	Extreme nearsightedness, decreased visual acuity
Ocular albinism	Total or partial absence of pigment, hereditary condition	Nystagmus, light sensitivity, decreased visual acuity
Optic atrophy	Degeneration of the optic nerve, may be congenital or hereditary	Loss of central vision, color vision, and reduced visual acuity
Retinopathy of prematurity (ROP)	Prematurity and low birth weight	Loss of peripheral vision; total blindness may occur
Coloboma	Congenital genetic anomaly	Hole in one of the structures of the eye such as the iris, retina, choroid, or optic disc
Cortical visual impairment (CVI)	Congenital anomaly	Lesion to the cortex of the brain that is related to vision, not the eye structure

SOURCE: Adapted from National Dissemination Center for Children with Disabilities (NICHCY). *Visual Impairment, Including Blindness* (Fact Sheet 13). Available at http://nichcy .org/disability/specific/visualimpairment

In the early 1900s, children with visual impairments were served by various agencies such as hospitals, children's services for rehabilitation, and residential schools; there were no laws mandating services. Children were often recruited to attend residential schools where they would learn vocational skills so they could become active members of the community (Best, 1919). In the 1950s and 1960s, vision professionals endorsed "sight-saving" classes located in public schools that "saved" children's remaining vision by not allowing them to use their residual vision. Children were blindfolded and taught to read and write tactually.

In the 1950s and 1960s, parents and educators also saw a need for an array of school placement options for students with visual impairments. Focusing on individual rights, this movement was related to the civil rights movement, the development of the Head Start program, and the growing needs of young children who were born with visual impairments during the baby boom following World War II (Lang, 1992). Residential and public school options developed to meet the educational needs of the child and his or her rights within the community.

In the 1970s, professionals accepted the theory that vision should be stimulated and children should be taught to more efficiently and effectively use remaining vision. Natalie Barraga (1973) shared the opinion that children could learn to use vision that was left and that this use would get better with practice. The training of residual vision to gather information through tracking, focusing, and eye teaming was known as visual efficiency (Optometric Center of Los Angeles, 2013). The child was taught to use spectacles, magnifiers, and any other assistive devices to improve the use of any remaining vision. The theory that visual skills can be learned is still discussed today.

visual efficiency: How well an individual uses remaining visual acuity at a distance or close up.

At this time, children with visual impairments were attending both residential and public schools; however, legislation such as PL 94–142 required school districts to identify and serve children with visual impairments in the local community. Many of these students were placed in the general education classroom with assistance provided by vision specialists serving as consultants. Vocational training was not emphasized because integration of children with visual impairment allowed for access to the general education curriculum. Today, students with visual impairments are able to receive specialized vision services from infancy through young adulthood.

Prevalence of Visual Impairments

Visual impairments are relatively rare among children and youth. It is estimated that 2.4 percent of school-age children in the United States experience a vision loss significant enough to require specialized support in their educational program (National Eye Institute, 2013). The U.S. Department of Education (2013a) reports that approximately 25,700 children ages 6–21 were receiving services in the 2011–2012 school year because of a visual impairment. When compared to the total number of school-age children who are receiving a special education, students with visual impairments constitute only 0.4 percent of pupils with a disability. Visual impairment, therefore, is one of the least prevalent disabilities.

Recent data from the U.S. Department of Education (2013a) indicate that slightly fewer than 3,400 preschoolers were receiving a special education in the 2011–2012 school year because of visual impairments. This group of youngsters represents 0.4 percent of all preschoolers with a disability.

Vision specialists believe that one half to two thirds of children with a visual impairment also have concomitant developmental or physical disabilities (Geddie et al., 2013). Vision loss may be associated with cerebral palsy, muscular dystrophy, arthritis, or other childhood diseases. As a result of improvements in neonatology and advanced medical procedures, this population of children continues to grow. Students in these circumstances are often reported to the U.S. Department of Education in disability categories other than visual impairment; visual impairment, however, is recognized as a secondary disability.

The Vision Process and Etiology of Visual Impairments

In working with students with visual impairments, it is important to understand what can happen when the parts of the visual system do not perform as they should. Here we review some of the causes of visual impairments and how they can affect the student's functional vision.

Light enters the eye through the cornea (see Figure 13.1, page 450), which is the clear, transparent covering at the front of the eye. The cornea is curved in shape and serves as a strong protective structure for the inner parts of the eye. It assists in focusing the optical image that will reach the brain. If the cornea is damaged through trauma or disease and attention is not given to the disturbance, then the inner area may become infected, which can result in permanent visual impairment and even total blindness.

As light passes through the cornea, it goes into an area called the anterior chamber, which is filled with aqueous fluid. This fluid helps bring nutrients to and remove waste from the back surface of the cornea. It also helps maintain the shape of the eye. The major disease that occurs in the aqueous humor is glaucoma, which can result in a loss of visual acuity as well as a loss in the visual field. Students with glaucoma often have headaches and require frequent periods of rest. Students may also need medication to treat this disease. Student health care plans should include this information.

The next section of the eye that light must travel through is the iris. The iris is the colored, circular muscle of the eye that controls the amount of light that comes into the eye by regulating the size of the pupil. The pupil is the opening in the iris where light enters the eye. If the iris is malformed, the function of light control will be interrupted, and the child can become photophobic (sensitive to light). Students may require sunglasses or other optical devices to reduce the amount of light reaching the retina. Close work may result in fatigue and blurring. Mobility training should be provided, if required, to work with depth perception in moving about the environment. Teachers should be aware of children with abnormalities to the iris and refer them for further medical attention.

The lens is a colorless, transparent oval structure suspended behind the iris. The function of the lens is to filter and bend the light rays before they reach the back part of the eye. Cataracts are lenses that are opaque or cloudy as a result of trauma or age. Children with congenital cataracts often have the cataracts removed. If needed, this should be done as early as possible to allow for normal vision development. In the absence of the lens, the eye will appear flat (aphakic), and light will not be filtered appropriately. The child will be photophobic and may complain of serious glare problems. Depending on the location of the cataract, a child's color vision may also be distorted. Squinting, caused by a lack of visual stimulation and resulting in reduced visual acuity, can be a characteristic of a child with cataracts. Low illumination may be preferred. Additional time may be required to move from one activity to another to accommodate lighting needs. Cataracts may also be associated with Down syndrome, Marfan syndrome, and rubella.

Behind the lens, light must travel through a clear liquid gel (vitreous body). This thick fluid serves as a filter for light and helps maintain the shape of the eye. If the lens becomes infected and cloudy, the light rays to the back of the eye will be distorted, resulting in reduced visual acuity. In diabetes, this part of the eye often contains particles or tissue from vascular bleeding, which can distort vision, affecting peripheral vision as well as central visual acuity. The child sees blurry and distorted images and has difficulty reading and observing objects at a distance.

After the light goes through the vitreous fluid, it reaches the retina. The retina, located in the innermost part of the eye, contains layers of light-sensitive nerve cells. It is very thin and has an intricate vascular system. This is the area where the light is sent to the optic nerve for transmission to the brain. Most retina disorders result in blurred vision. Unlike other eye diseases associated with pain, the retina has no pain fibers or other physical characteristics such as red and inflamed eyes. The purpose of the retina is to receive the light image and send it to the brain through the optic nerve. The optic nerve carries the light messages (electrical signals) to the brain, where they are interpreted as visual images known as sight.

Rods and cones are photoreceptive cells found in the retina. Rod cells, located mainly in the peripheral areas, are extremely light sensitive. Responsible for shape and motion, they function best in reduced illumination. Rod cells are not responsive to color. Cone cells are located mainly in the central area of the retina. Color is defined in the cone cells. Only special cones are found in the macula area, which is the area of best central vision, and the fovea area, which is the area of most acute vision. Macular degeneration is a common eye disease in adults, but it may also occur in young people. This disease involves damage to the central part of the retina cones, affecting central vision, photophobia, and color vision.

photophobic: Sensitive to light.

aphakic: Absence of the lens, causing light sensitivity and loss of visual acuity.

rod cells: Light-sensitive cells located mainly in the peripheral areas of the retina that are responsible for shape and motion, function best in reduced illumination, and are not responsive to color.

cone cells: Light-sensitive cells located mainly in the central area of the retina that define color.

macular degeneration: A common eye disease in adults, which may also occur in young people, involving damage to the central part of the retina cones, affecting central vision, light sensitivity, and color.

If a child has retinopathy of prematurity (ROP), vascular growth has been interrupted by premature birth. The veins and arteries begin to grow in an unorganized manner causing bundles, which pull together and detach the retina. The child first loses peripheral vision and then the whole field of vision unless surgical intervention is immediate. Spotty vision, retinal scarring, field loss, and glaucoma may also be present. Training in early intervention and sensory stimulation is an area of concern.

According to the Texas School for the Blind (2007), other retinal diseases include the following:

- **Retinitis pigmentosa** is a hereditary condition involving gradual degeneration of the retina, which can result in night blindness, photophobia, and eventually loss of macular vision.
- Toxoplasmosis is a severe infection transmitted through contact with domestic animals such as cats or chickens. Lesions on the retina can reduce visual acuity and field vision. Squinting is an observable characteristic of children with toxoplasmosis.
- Albinism is a congenital condition characterized by a lack of pigment (skin, hair, or eyes). If the eyes are the only area affected, it is called ocular albinism. These children may be extremely photophobic and sensitive to glare, both in the classroom and outdoors. They may have high refractive problems, but the visual fields are usually normal. Fatigue may become a factor in close work.
- **Coloboma** is a congenital condition that results in a teardrop shape of the pupil, iris, lens, retina, choroid, or optic nerve. Field of vision may be affected, problems with glare may also be present, and problems with depth perception may occur.
- Optic nerve atrophy is caused by a variety of diseases. Early treatment can prevent a loss of visual acuity. Without treatment, optic atrophy can result in conditions from low visual acuity to total blindness.
- Retinopathy of prematurity is disorganized growth of blood vessels in the retina, which may result in scarring and retinal detachment. Various levels of visual field loss may be a factor.

Prevention of Visual Impairments

Most visual impairments are genetic in source, but others can be prevented or controlled. Prenatal care can prevent eye problems secondary to sexually transmitted diseases, prematurity, or known hereditary problems. Screening of babies in the hospital nursery, youngsters in the preschool setting, and older students on a regular basis can help detect and prevent eye diseases that cause visual impairments.

Eye safety is a preventive measure against eye injuries that can hinder visual acuity and even cause blindness. Ocular trauma can affect the orbit, the eyelids, and other structures of the eye, and immediate intervention is necessary. Some trauma causes infections, changes in the appearance of the eye, and even blindness.

Early Detection

Vision problems affect one in twenty preschoolers and one in four school-age children (Prevent Blindness America, 2013a). Early screening and diagnosis can determine the prognosis for visual impairments. Eye examinations should take place shortly after birth, at 6 months of age, before entering school, and periodically throughout the school years.

retinitis pigmentosa: Pigmentation of the retina that can result in night blindness, photophobia, and eventual loss of vision in various parts of the periphery.

coloboma: A congenital condition that results in a teardrop shape of the pupil, iris, lens, retina, choroids, or optic nerve; may involve loss of field vision as well as problems with glare and depth perception.

VIDEO
Etiology of Visual Impairment

Eye Safety

Eye injuries are common. They can range from a mild abrasion with bleeding in the front of the eye to retinal detachment, penetration of the eye, or actual rupture of the globe (eyeball). Some injuries heal without loss of vision; others result in the loss of the eye. At least 90 percent of all eye injuries to children can be prevented by understanding the dangers, identifying and correcting hazards, and using greater care when supervising children (Prevent Blindness America, 2013b). Some of the most frequent causes of eye injuries are listed as follows:

Many types of eye injury can be prevented.

- Misuse of toys or altering toys
- Falls involving home furnishings and fixtures such as beds, stairs, tables, and toys
- Misuse of everyday objects, such as home repair and yard care products, personal use items, kitchen utensils, silverware, pens, and pencils
- Accidental exposure to harmful household and cleaning products, such as detergents, paints, pesticides, glues, and adhesives
- Automobile accidents (a leading cause of eye injuries to young children)
- Fireworks, which may cause injury to the user and bystanders alike

Characteristics of Individuals With Visual Impairments

Visual impairment affects the type of experiences the child has, the ability to travel within the environment, and actual involvement in the immediate and secondary communities. These factors will be affected differently depending on the amount of vision loss. The child with low vision has experiences that are different from those of the child who is legally blind or totally blind. The Optometric Extension Program Foundation has developed a checklist of observable characteristics of vision difficulties in children to assist teachers in making reliable observations of children's visual behavior (see Table 13.3).

Academic Performance

At one time it was believed that visual impairments were associated with lowered intellectual abilities, but we now know that this is not true. In fact, in many instances, the intellectual capabilities of students with visual impairments are similar to those of their sighted peers (Gargiulo & Metcalf, 2013). Despite this, significant academic delays are not uncommon in learners with visual impairments. This is most likely due to their restricted opportunity to obtain information visually (Pogrund & Fazzi, 2007). For these children, unlike their sighted classmates, incidental learning derived from interacting with the environment is severely limited (Liefert, 2003). As a result, conceptual development and other learning in pupils with visual impairments primarily depend on tactile (touch) experiences and the use of sensory modalities other than vision (Bishop, 2004; Chen & Downing, 2006; Gargiulo & Metcalf, 2013).

■ ■ ■ ■ ■ Table 13.3 **Behavioral Characteristics in Vision Function Problems**

Unusual turning of the head, body, or eye
Holding reading material extremely close to the face
Excessive rubbing of the eye
Watery eyes
Eye fatigue
Frequent eye pain
Frequent headaches
Squints or shades the eye to view objects
Constantly having difficulty in keeping up when reading and writing
Using markers such as pencils and fingers when reading
Difficulty copying from the board or transparencies
Confusion in writing letters and numbers appropriately
"Clumsy" movement from one environment to another
Poor posture in both standing and sitting
Reluctance to participate in social and physical activities
Poor grades
Difficulty with color identification or color coordination
Sensory perceptual coordination
Misaligns columns when writing math problems
Requires additional time to complete a task
Fails to make eye contact when talking to people
Behavior problems

SOURCE: Optometric Extension Program Foundation, *Educator's Guide to Classroom Vision Problems.* Available at http://oep.excerpo.com/index.php?action=show_details&product_id=3056

Social and Emotional Development

The everyday experiences of children who have visual impairments are affected because these children do not respond visually to people in the environment. Maintaining eye contact during speech, smiling at someone in a friendly manner, and reaching out to touch someone nearby are not innate skills for the child who cannot see details in the immediate surroundings. For the child with visual impairment, knowledge about body parts, eating skills, age-appropriate behavior, clothing, and other social skills are not learned by viewing others in the family or community. Socially appropriate behaviors must be intentionally taught to the person with a visual impairment so that other people will be at ease during communication.

A child who has low vision will display more visual and tactual skills in the social situation. The appropriate responses shown because of paired visual and tactile experiences will often make the child with low vision appear to have less of a vision loss than is

It is important that children with visual impairments feel accepted by their classmates.

really present. However, the child with low vision may have optical devices, enlarged materials, mobility devices, and technology for reading and writing with print. This may cause frustration for the child because of the complexity of the devices and materials needed to obtain information visually and auditorily.

Travel Skills

The child with vision loss may travel with a cane, a dog, or a sighted guide and will require training in orientation and mobility (O&M). O&M teaches skills to orient a person to the surroundings and to move independently and safely in the environment. O&M is necessary for the child who is totally blind, with no light perception or possibly with prosthetic eyes, since there is a dependence on tactual and auditory skills for all information.

The child who is legally blind will retrieve information tactually and auditorily, with minimal use of vision for tasks where large objects or light affects mobility decisions. Many parents notice that the young child does not turn his or her head toward the person talking and seems to grope for toys on the floor, hold onto the wall, or sit alone rather than explore the room. The child may have difficulty reacting to visual cues, sit in one place until guided to another setting, and become dependent on others for stimulation within the immediate environment. The child may also concentrate on items within the immediate environment, talk out when it is not appropriate, and ask questions to maintain voice contact with people in the room.

Vocational Skills

Children with visual impairments begin vocational skills training at an early age if early intervention is provided or a preschool class is available. Children learn about dressing, eating, cooking, telling time, and using calendars for scheduling events in daily life. As the child progresses through school, a specialized curriculum may be introduced to teach about earning money, having a job, and traveling within the community.

Entering the world of work is an issue for vocational development. The student must know how to bathe, dress, prepare a meal, and plan the travel details to get to a job. After arriving at the workplace, the student must learn the building layout and the location of necessary sites such as the main office, restroom, lunchroom, and other important places within the company. Job duties and responsibilities must be explained so that job tasks can be completed successfully. Ethical behavior within the workplace must be learned before the first day of work. Ways to communicate with people within the work setting are also an educational issue.

The child with visual impairments faces quality-of-life issues that may differ from those faced by persons with other disabilities. The amount of vision loss, the intervention strategies, and the quality of life should all be taken into account. Independence begins in the early years and continues throughout life, affecting the

VIDEO

Social Development

quality of life at work, at home, and in the community. Vocational skills are a part of the preschool plan, the educational program, and the transition to adulthood so that age-appropriate skills are learned and used for independence.

Assessment of Students With Visual Impairments

Public Law 108–446 ensures that all students with disabilities will have available a free appropriate public education. A comprehensive assessment is required to determine eligibility for special education services and to develop an educational program that provides for the individual needs of each pupil. In developing an educational program for children with visual impairments, the assessment process must comply with the equivalent guidelines for other areas of exceptionality while also diagnosing and determining the unique needs and abilities of students with visual impairments.

Some children may be identified at birth as having a visual impairment through routine medical examinations, but many others are not identified as visually impaired until later. Parents or caregivers may notice unusual developmental behaviors caused by a vision loss. Some children may be diagnosed with a visual impairment following an accident or childhood illness. Other children may be identified through preschool or kindergarten vision screening programs.

A screening for visual acuity is often provided at school or in the physician's office. The acuity chart most often used for testing and reporting vision loss is the Snellen chart (see Figure 13.3). An example of a distance loss on the Snellen chart is 20/70, meaning that the person has to be 20 feet away from the chart to see what the normal eye can see from 70 feet. This chart is a 20-foot distance test; other tests are given for near vision and other vision problems.

Any student identified with a suspected vision problem should be referred to a licensed ophthalmologist or optometrist for further evaluation, including a medical examination and report. The information in this report should include etiology, medical history and diagnosis, ocular health, visual abilities, recommended low vision devices, orientation and mobility needs, and a reevaluation date. This information may be provided to the educational system through a written ocular report (see Figure 13.4).

Interpretation of these data for the educational team should be by a trained and certified teacher of the visually impaired. This information is crucial to the development of an appropriate educational experience. If conditions warrant, further assessment should be obtained and considered by the multidisciplinary team.

In addition to a medical examination, a clinical low vision evaluation is necessary to determine if a student could benefit from other optical or nonoptical low vision devices. The low vision examination involves acuity tests, visual field testing for peripheral or central vision loss, and an interview with the individual to see what he or she would like to do for work, school, or leisure activities. A personal prescription for low vision devices, technology, or referrals to community agencies is part of the low vision

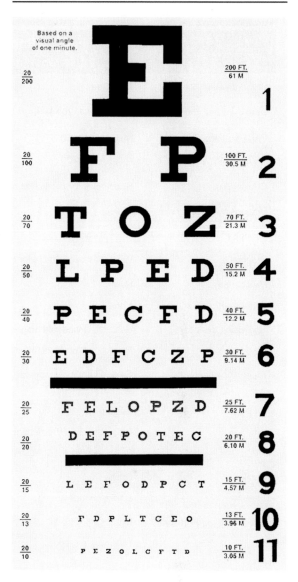

Figure 13.3 **Snellen Chart**

SOURCE: National Eye Institute. (2013). *Photograph and Image Catalog: Eye Charts* (Ref#EC01). Available at http://www.nei.nih.gov/photo

VIDEO

Visual Impairment Simulations

Figure 13.4 **Ocular Report**

Report From Eye Physician This report is to be used in educational planning.				
Student name:	John Doe		Age:	10 years
Date of examination:	November 4, 2014		Physician name:	David Seebetter, MD
Visual acuity without Rx	Near: 20/350	Far: 20/400		
Visual acuity with Rx	Near: 20/200	Far: 20/400		
Current Rx:	Spectacles for protection only. UV sunglasses recommended.			
Diagnosis/etiology:	Affects:			
Retinopathy of prematurity	Central vision _____	Peripheral vision __X__		
Prognosis:	Vision has been stable for the past year; return visit in one year for follow-up examination.			
Medication:	None			
Other treatment:	None			
Low vision devices:	Near: Handheld magnifier–8x magnification; closed circuit TV			
	Far: Monocular telescope			
Technology needed:	Closed circuit TV, speech reader on computer, radio reading service, slow-speed tape recorder, talking watch, talking calculator			
Print size:	Large print	_____		
	Closed circuit TV/size print	__X__	Self-adjust	
	Bold line paper	__X__		
Braille	Braille	__X__	Braille should be considered for speed of reading and comprehension.	
	Books on tape	__X__		
Classroom modifications	Lighting	_____		
	Seating preference	__X__	Near teacher or class activity; special table for Brailler, CCTV	

plan. If low vision devices cannot assist the student with reading, writing, or distant viewing, then auditory and tactual prescriptions are recommended as pre-Braille or listening skill practice. The student's vision teacher can attend this evaluation and bring materials relevant to the scheduled daily activities. Examples of educational materials pertinent to the student with visual impairments are reading texts, technology adaptations, daily writing journals, workbooks, maps, and charts.

Functional Vision Evaluation

Each child's ability to use vision is unique, and the ability to use what vision the child has (visual efficiency) may be improved through specific programs of instruction. An important element in planning an educational program for children with visual impairments is assessment of a student's present functional vision. In other words, an assessment is needed to see how well each student uses vision to complete a specific task.

functional vision: How well students use the vision they have to complete a specific task.

Because of the role that vision plays in the overall development of each child, a functional vision evaluation must be performed before all other educational evaluations. This is to ensure that each child will have access to the materials and equipment needed to participate and perform to the best of his or her abilities. Under the supervision of a teacher of students with visual impairments, each pupil must be observed in a variety of environments that occur throughout the student's daily routine. This observation must include the student performing various tasks that require both near and distant visual abilities. Observations should encompass both individual and group activities, including oral and silent reading groups, desk work, and board work. The functional vision evaluation should also include travel within the school environment—playground, restroom, music room, lunchroom, and physical education sites—as well as accessing modes of transportation (Zimmerman & Zebehazy, 2011). The evaluation should also include samples of the student's work and reports of activities in the home and community.

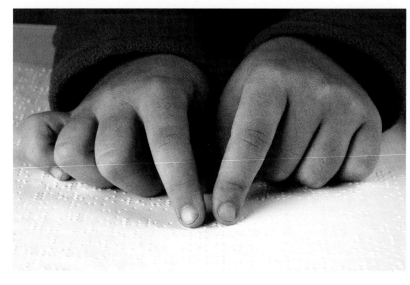

Braille is usually the reading medium of choice for pupils who are totally blind.

The functional vision evaluation is a collaborative effort of the educational team for purposes of program planning. Specific recommendations, accommodations, modifications, and intervention strategies for the student in all environments can be based on a comprehensive evaluation. The team approach to the functional evaluation can provide a continuum of appropriate strategies in the educational and community settings.

Learning Media

Another important component in the assessment process is to determine the most effective learning and literacy media. Literacy medium refers to sensory channels and is based on the student's preferred method of reading and writing—print, Braille, or both. Regardless of the level of vision a student has or whether the pupil has an additional disability, a learning medium assessment must be conducted to determine the student's preferred mode of learning and literacy (American Foundation for the Blind, 2013a).

Learning media include the materials and methods a student uses in conjunction with the sensory channels in the process of learning. Visual learning media include pictures, videos, imitation, and demonstration. Tactual learning media include models, real objects, and physical prompting. Auditory learning media include verbal communication, taped information, and environmental sounds (American Foundation for the Blind, 2013b; Paths to Literacy, 2013). A hearing evaluation is required as a part of the auditory media determination. Determination of print size is important so that the child with a visual impairment can readily use low vision devices prescribed for reading, writing, and leisure activities. A vision specialist can inform the child and family about specific low vision devices, where to use them, and what size print is required for each device. The standard print sizes recommended range from 6 point, the size used in telephone directories, to 24 point, used in large-print texts.

literacy medium: The student's preferred method of reading and writing.

learning media: The materials and methods a student uses in conjunction with the sensory channels in the process of learning.

AUDIO
Learning Media

Figure 13.5 **Braille Card**

"This is 13-point type."

"This is 18-point type."

"This is 24-point type."

Braille Alphabet and Numbers
Used by the Blind
Close your eyes and read this with your fingers.

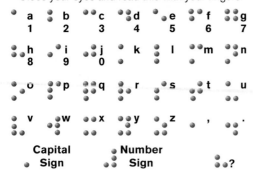

The Braille system is comprised of signs formed by the use of all the possible combinations of 6 dots numbered and arranged thus:

```
1 ● ● 4
2 ● ● 5
3 ● ● 6
```

Letters are capitalized by prefixing dot 6. The first ten letters preceded by the number sign represent numbers. Punctuation marks are formed in the lower part of the cell.

In addition to ordinary print the Braille system provides for the writing of foreign languages, musical scores, mathematical and chemical notations, and other technical matter.

This is

SOURCE: American Printing House for the Blind, Inc., Louisville, KY.

Braille as a literacy medium is used together with print and auditory input if the child has any residual vision. This enables the student to read print for survival skills, and to sign documents. An individual who is totally blind will use Braille and listening skills for input. Braille is addressed in the individualized education program (IEP) so that the child with a visual impairment will have ongoing consideration of Braille as a reading medium.

Braille consists of patterns of six possible dots arranged in two columns of three (see Figure 13.5). The combination of dots indicates a certain letter of the alphabet. Each language has a Braille code that matches the letters in the alphabet of that language. American Braille has two "grades." In Grade 1 Braille, each letter of a word is spelled out using the Braille letter corresponding to the print letter. This is the first level taught so that the complete alphabet is learned. Grade 2 Braille is made up of contractions representing parts of words or whole words, similar to print shorthand. The primers begin with words contracted so that the child learns the spelling of the word with Grade 1 and the whole word in a sentence with Grade 2. Many elevators and signs use Grade 2, because that is the standard for Braille readers. Examples of Grade 1 and Grade 2 Braille are presented in Figure 13.6.

Unfortunately, over the years, there has been a steady decline in Braille literacy rates among school-age children. Forty years ago more than 50 percent of children read Braille; today, however, only 12 percent read Braille. Yet, research suggests that Braille helps students learn language and grammar as well as math and science (National Braille Press, 2013).

Educational Assessment and Program Planning

Appropriate assessment strategies are a prerequisite to effective teaching. Assessments can provide critical information on the ways in which various visual impairments can affect learning and the need for instructional adaptations. Many students with visual impairments have the same educational goals as other pupils and can often be successfully included in the general education classroom. In planning an educational program for a student with visual impairments, other assessments must also be considered. However, educational assessments must be modified for accessibility, with larger print, Braille, oral presentation, or omission of items that test visual skills. The evaluation must measure the skills of the student using the modifications

Grade 1 Braille: A beginning level of Braille in which a word is spelled out with a Braille letter corresponding to each printed letter.

Grade 2 Braille: A more complex level of Braille in which contractions are used to represent parts of words or whole words.

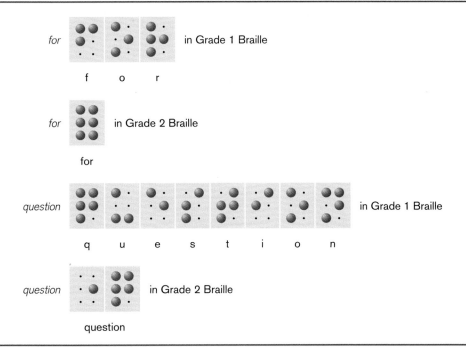

with which the student is familiar so that the results will paint a picture of academic functioning level.

Students who have a visual impairment also have unique educational needs and should be evaluated in these areas to determine the appropriate educational placement and program. According to the American Foundation for the Blind (2013b), formal assessments used to determine strategies and needs in particular areas of instruction may include the following:

- Basic academic skills
- Career/vocational skills
- Independent living skills
- Learning and literacy media
- Orientation and mobility skills
- Social interaction skills
- Use of assistive technology
- Verbal and nonverbal communication skills
- Visual efficiency skills

Eligibility Determination

Recall that to determine eligibility for special education because of a disability, the IEP team must base its decision on data from multiple sources. A functional vision evaluation and a learning media assessment should be part of the initial evaluation for individuals with visual impairments. However, a student with a visual disorder may not be eligible for or need specialized services if the disorder has no adverse effect on the student's educational progress.

Proctor for Braille transcription (recording or transfer scores)
Large-print materials and tests
Oral presentation of materials (reader assistance for texts and other materials)
Assistive technology
Fxtended time limits (1.5 or twice the time is usually recognized for individuals with low vision or blindness)
Small or individual group assessment
Preferred seating
Shorter periods of testing with rest breaks between sessions

Instructional planning requires a comprehensive assessment to establish current levels of performance. Using the information from multiple assessments, the team determines the student's current levels of performance and develops an IEP. In keeping with the requirements of IDEA, parents and students are informed and involved in all areas of the planning process.

The success of the IEP depends on selecting and using appropriate instruments that address issues or concerns relevant to the needs of the student with a visual impairment. This process may be completed by having appropriately trained personnel use both formal and informal assessment instruments. Few formal instruments are available, however, because children with visual impairments are diverse in age, background, and environmental influences, as well as in levels of visual abilities. Numerous factors, such as acuity, color blindness, age of onset, field vision restrictions, and other disabilities, affect a child's visual ability. Given the unique needs and diversity of these students, trained teachers of the visually impaired must be involved in the assessment process and the interpretation of test results.

Students with visual impairments are not usually included in standardized testing; however, they should participate with needed modifications or accommodations (see Table 13.4). Although the validity and reliability of the assessment may be compromised if too many modifications are made, instructional planning, including pupil and program evaluation, can be enhanced. In reporting test results, any modification or accommodations that were made should be recorded.

Many states require all students to participate in statewide testing programs, developed with specific guidelines and scores, to progress to the next grade or academic level. IDEA requires the IEP team to determine a student's participation in state- and districtwide assessment programs. The team must verify that the student is in need of modifications in order to participate, or if the student will not participate, the team must state why the assessment is not appropriate and what alternate assessments will be used.

Educational Considerations

Students with visual impairments require an educational plan to prepare for independent and productive lives. Educational goals delineate the needs of the child and the family. Appropriate accommodations allow for acquisition of information through incidental learning, observation and imitation, exploration, and social behavior.

REFERENCE

Assessment

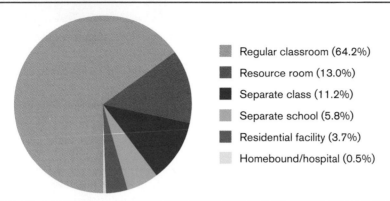

- Regular classroom (64.2%)
- Resource room (13.0%)
- Separate class (11.2%)
- Separate school (5.8%)
- Residential facility (3.7%)
- Homebound/hospital (0.5%)

NOTE: This figure represents the percentages of enrollment of students with visual impairments during the 2011–2012 school year. Excludes pupils enrolled in parentally placed private schools and individuals in correctional facilities.

SOURCE: U.S. Department of Education. (2013). *Historical state-level IDEA data files.* Retrieved October 13, 2013, from http://tadnet.public.tadnet.org/pages/712

Where Are Students With Visual Impairments Educated?

Both the passage of IDEA and policy statements from professional organizations and agencies reinforce the principle that in order to meet the unique needs of children with sensory impairments and help them become responsible and independent members of a fully integrated society, we must offer a full continuum of services. According to the U.S. Department of Education (2013a), almost two thirds of all students with visual impairments received services in the general education classroom during the 2011–2012 school year. Approximately one out of ten pupils with visual impairments was assigned to a resource room, and less than 5 percent were placed in a residential facility (see Figure 13.7). The IEP team should determine the educational setting that is most appropriate for each student, keeping in mind current levels of academic, psychosocial, physical, and vocational functioning and the materials and instructional techniques that are successful with that child. (See the accompanying First Person feature, page 467.)

Instructional Considerations

Instructional goals for most students with visual impairment include communication skills, social competency, employability, and independence, in addition to academic progress (American Foundation for the Blind, 2013b). The IEP team must decide how these goals will be accomplished.

Many students with visual impairments are able to participate in testing programs when appropriate modifications are made.

Examples of Expanded Common Core Curriculum-Specific Equipment

Setting	Assistive Technology
Academics	Magnifiers, glasses, closed-circuit television (CCTV), Braille, bookstands, video, scanners, optical character recognition system
	Word processing programs, slate and stylus, electronic spell-checkers, bold line writing paper, embossed writing paper, signature writing guides
	Abacus, scientific calculator, talking clock, Braille/print protractors and rulers, embossed and bold line grid pattern sheets, spreadsheet software
	Tactile globes, relief maps, Braille and large-print maps, tactile anatomy atlas, speech output devices such as thermometers and environmental controls
Leisure Time and Recreational Activities	Adapted games, large-print books, radio reading services, beeper balls, buzzers, wheelchair adapted for basketball and tennis play, lifts for swimming pools, adapted snow- and water-skiing equipment, descriptive video
Daily Living and Self-Help	Walkers, feeding adaptations, Braille labels, voice-activated switches, button switches, large-print telephone buttons, automatic thermostats, Braille calendars, electronic address books and calendars, magnifiers for hand sewing and sewing machines, electronic mobility devices, lifts for automobiles and chairs

Often an array of low vision devices will be required, depending on the needs of the student. The team will have to decide whether the child requires materials to be read, enlarged, or put into Braille and whether low vision devices or technology such as an abacus or a talking calculator will be used.

The vision-related needs of the pupil should be supported within the general education curriculum wherever appropriate. The need for direct, specialized services also varies throughout the child's education, depending on the goals of the educational program and the way in which these goals are met in the classroom. Table 13.5 describes some types of equipment that can be used to meet the needs of students with visual impairments in the general education classroom.

Individuals who are visually impaired should acquire compensatory skills and experiential learning by accessing the expanded core curriculum (American Foundation for the Blind, 2013b; Huebner, Merk-Adam, Stryker, & Wolffe, 2004). The expanded core curriculum is the body of knowledge and skills that are needed by pupils with visual impairments because of their unique disability-specific needs. Students who are visually impaired need the expanded core curriculum in addition to the core academic curriculum found in general education. The expanded core curriculum should be used as a framework for assessing pupils, planning individual goals, and providing instruction. According to Huebner et al. (2004), the expanded core curriculum typically includes the following:

- Assistive technology
- Career education
- Compensatory skills
- Independent living skills
- Orientation and mobility
- Recreation and leisure skills
- Self-determination
- Social skills
- Visual efficiency skills

VIDEO
Teaching Strategies

FIRST PERSON: CARRIE

The Face of "Different"

It was a bright sunny day outside. The kids were going out to play, but a few of us were staying inside. I started to draw after staring at a friend's face. It was just a line with some curves. "That's different," remarked a classmate. "Wow, that's really good," said Mr. Tom. "Thank you," I replied.

At that point, I realized that I was good at something and at the same time realized that there was something "different" about me. I was drawing someone's face as if it were a silhouette. It was different from my classmates' drawings. These words of encouragement and approval would have seemed small to most, but to a 6-year-old they were awesome. I was just drawing what I saw. How could that have been different from anyone else, or even that good?

I was born with oculocutaneous albinism, which is the lack of pigment in the eyes, the skin, and the hair. A common side effect is a visual impairment, but this varies in severity from one person to another. The idea of being visually impaired and able to draw astounded Mr. Tom. He was surprised by my ability to depict how I saw the world. I enjoyed arts and crafts time during elementary school and still amazed many teachers by this talent. It was as if I was redefining their perception of my abilities.

In second grade there was a test to see how many addition problems we could solve correctly in two minutes. The teacher remarked that I would need extra time. Full of embarrassment, I wanted to prove her wrong. And I did. The same type of situation occurred in middle school. The challenge was reading maps for geography class. The maps were small with many black lines. "How is she going to do this with a visual impairment?" many remarked. I could see shapes and color. So I colored them in and then labeled them as I studied. It made things more difficult and was a different approach, but it worked. The test came back with a 97, and I was excited.

There were many times that I needed to take a different approach in my study tactics. I was more successful in class with teachers who were open-minded or who accentuated my strengths and minimized my weaknesses. My senior year in high school I read the book *The Strange Case of Dr. Jekyll and Mr. Hyde* by Robert Louis Stevenson. Reading a novel was difficult because it took me longer to read than most students. I would feel discouraged and defeated, therefore losing motivation in the class. My teacher asked me to draw or paint how I envisioned the main characters, Dr. Jekyll and Mr. Hyde. The two characters are really one person but with a different look and contrasting personalities. She was pleased by the end result and distributed the grade on the ability to envision the description rather than the test alone.

There is not a map or a face that can guide and show a teacher how to educate a student with a visual impairment. I learned by doing and trying things by myself and with others. I was not the face of "different" as a child. Different is not a face to identify or a point to relate to; different is the line with curves between two points. Different is the process in which children as individuals learn, create, grow, and therefore succeed. It is the path and our attitude that depict our face. "We are all 'different,' and I thank you!" ■

–Carrie Willoughby

The expanded core curriculum essentially creates a parallel curriculum of disability-specific skills supplementary to the general education curriculum. The academic curriculum must be modified to meet the individual needs of each student so that progress is based on skill level and successful completion of expectations in each subject area. Specialized areas of the regular curriculum, such as art, music, and home economics, are also considered appropriate for pupils with visual impairments. Modifications and accommodations of lessons can often be achieved through the use of visual, auditory, or tactual experiences.

Adaptations of materials and the environment may be necessary to enable students who are visually impaired to participate in the educational program and derive maximum benefit from the experience (see Table 13.6). Adaptations may vary according to individual needs, which should be assessed before making special provisions available to the student.

During the spring of my senior year as an undergraduate student in elementary education, I was required to complete a twenty-four-hour practicum for a special education course. The site I chose was the North Dakota School for the Blind. After my experiences at the school, I realized that I was very interested in working with children who were blind and visually impaired. This led me to search for graduate programs in the field of blindness. I was fortunate enough to locate the vision program at the University of Alabama at Birmingham. From my first day in the program, I had the opportunity to work with children of varying degrees of visual impairment, as well as additional disabilities. After completing my master's degree, I worked as an itinerant teacher for the visually impaired in southwestern Iowa for four years and went on to become the state consultant for children with deaf-blindness. I then returned to graduate school and earned my doctorate at Iowa State University.

Inclusive Education Experience

Working with children with visual impairments and multiple disabilities is definitely challenging, yet very rewarding. This is especially true when working with general education teachers in inclusive settings. You have to have a starting point that everyone can agree upon, including acceptance of the child with special needs as a full member of the general education class and an understanding that the general education teacher is that child's full-time teacher—not the five other service providers

---

Table 13.7 presents some general guidelines for working with students who have a visual impairment. These suggestions are offered using a "Do" and "Don't" format.

Orientation and Mobility

Students with visual impairments require instruction in orientation and mobility, which is a related service according to IDEA. Orientation is being aware of where you are, where you are going, and the route to get there. Mobility is moving from place to place. A child must be able to put the orientation and mobility together to travel independently. Orientation and mobility training includes sensory training, concept development, and motor development. A certified orientation and mobility specialist can evaluate the child's functional level and prescribe specific training. See the accompanying Suggestions for the Classroom (page 472) for orientation and mobility tips for the general educator.

A child must be empowered to negotiate the environment skillfully and confidently. Opportunities for exploration must be provided for good posture, good health, and flexible muscles. With confident movement, the child can achieve good self-esteem and master independent travel within the community.

Young Children With Visual Impairments

The focus in early childhood education is not only on visual and auditory tasks, but also on the whole realm of developmental skills that must be taught, with modifications, to the child with visual impairments. These basic readiness skills should be integrated for age-appropriate cognitive development:

- Expressive language development
- Fine motor development
- Gross motor development
- Receptive language development

orientation and mobility:
Systematic techniques to plan routes and move from place to place for persons with visual impairments.

REFERENCE

Motor Skill Development

who also work with the child once a week. If the IEP team can come to such an agreement, then everything else seems to fall into place. For example, it may be that a teacher of the visually impaired works with the general education teacher to adapt lessons by creating tactile materials or story boxes, or even works with the entire class by teaching a class lesson.

One of my more memorable teaching experiences was collaborating with a first-year teacher who was working with a kindergartener, Andrew, who had multiple disabilities, including deaf-blindness. I taught a cooking lesson to the class once a month, in order to model interacting with Andrew for the other children and adults in the classroom. This worked well for the kindergarten teacher because it incorporated math, reading, and social skills. It was a wonderful opportunity, however, for the other children to see that Andrew could be an active and important member of the class, as they worked in small groups to get to know Andrew. By the end of the school year, the children were able to tell the adults what Andrew liked and disliked. The students also knew how to interact with Andrew so that he could respond to them with facial expressions and vocalizations.

Overall, as a teacher of the visually impaired, being able to work with the kindergarten class took extra time and preparation on my part. However, classrooms today are changing, as are the instructional expectations of both general education and special education teachers. It takes teamwork and collaboration to make programs work for children with special needs and to give them the best possible start to being active and contributing members of their community.

–Susan A. Brennan
Former teacher of students with visual impairments
Project Coordinator/Statewide Consultant at Iowa
Educational Services for the Blind and Visually Impaired

- Self-help development
- Sensory development
- Social development

The early intervention team can assist the family with activities that stimulate each of the developmental areas. Children are referred through state child-find activities, physicians, and other agencies to early intervention services, which are available for children from birth to age 3. Services are provided according to the youngster's IFSP (individualized family service plan), with the child receiving services prescribed by the specialists involved on the team. The specialists who work with the child and family act as consultants, and some may provide direct services. Intervention may be offered in the youngster's home or an early childhood education program in the community.

At age 3, the child should transition to an early childhood class for youngsters with vision loss. A well-designed transition plan includes planning with the school administrators, general educators, parents or other caregivers, and related services personnel in support of the move to school. The service coordinator and vision specialist should also have input into the construction of the IEP. This will ensure that the receiving teacher knows about the child's progress and goals for the future. Age-related needs that should be addressed by the team when designing a transition plan include travel, low vision devices, educational activities, and leisure activities. Other services that family and school officials should consider include the following:

- Access to an equipment resource center
- Activities of daily living
- Adaptive technology services
- Community education
- Low vision examination
- Orientation and mobility
- Reader services
- Transcription services

VIDEO
Mobility

VIDEO
Orientation and Mobility

	Lighting	Color and Contrast	Size and Distance	Time
What to observe	• Variety of lighting situations • Lighting at different times of day • Low vision devices used	• Contrast between object and background • Color contrast • Tactile tasks such as locker for books	• Placement and size of objects at near • Placement and size of objects at far	• Time for completion of visual discrimination during tasks
What to use	• Light sensitivity: shades, visors, tinted spectacles • Low light: lamp or illuminated low vision device • Room obstructions: preferential seating, furniture placement • Glare: nonglare surface on areas such as chalkboards, computer screens, desktop, paper, maps, globes	• Bold line paper • Black print on white background • Dark markers • One-sided writing on paper • Dark placemat for contrast during eating • Floor contrast for mobility ease • Tactile markings for outline discrimination • Contrast to define borders on walls • Lock and key is preferred over combination locker	• Enlarged materials • Preferred seating • Electronic devices • Magnification • Optical character recognition • Adjustment of desks, tables, and chairs • Additional storage space for Braille, large-print books, low vision devices near each workstation	• Verbal cues for actions in classroom • Increased time for task completion • Calling student by name • Announcements when entering or leaving room • Encourage participation in demonstrations • Opportunity to observe materials prior to lesson • Authentic manipulative objects • Schedule instructional time in early part of day • Convenient use and storage of materials
Desired results	• Better posture • Greater concentration • Less fatigue	• Better visual efficiency • Less fatigue • Safer travel	• Ease of viewing • Appropriate adaptations for specific vision loss	• Less fatigue • Inclusion in class activities • Time efficiency

Transition Into Adulthood

IDEA mandates that an individualized education program include a transition plan for adolescents with disabilities. A transition plan must be designed no later than age 16 and reviewed at least annually. Best practice suggests that a full range of options, services, and supports be explored by the IEP team. The student's preferences and vision for his or her future along with meaningful family involvement and input from professionals are integral components of a successful transition plan.

The goals for adolescents and young adults with a visual impairment often include vocational choices, postsecondary educational opportunities, travel skills, the use of technology, reading options, community participation, activities of daily living, independence on the job, and the acquisition of social/interpersonal skills among other critical areas. The wide spectrum of individual needs typically defines the goals for the young adult.

Planning transition of a student into higher education or vocational programs involves assessing the individual's level of functioning. The transition team, including the family, must be familiar with and prepared to respond to the adolescent's strengths

Table 13.7 Suggestions for Working With Students Who Are Visually Impaired

DO	DON'T
• Feel comfortable using vision words such as *look*, *see*, and *watch*.	• Be fearful of touching a student who is visually impaired. Be sure to tell the student, however, that you are about to touch him or her. Be respectful of the individual's personal preference about being touched.
• Use the pupil's name when addressing a student.	• Overprotect. Allow the pupil to attempt as many things as desired.
• Read aloud when writing on the board.	• Worry about personal feelings of awkwardness. A student with vision loss requires consistent directions.
• Encourage independence.	• Be afraid of having high expectations and demanding the pupil's best work.
• Include the pupil in all class activities as feasible.	• Tolerate unacceptable behavior.
• Give explicit instructions.	
• Provide extra space for storage of equipment and specialized materials.	
• Encourage the use of supplementary devices when necessary.	

SOURCE: Adapted from V. Bishop, *Teaching Visually Impaired Children*, 3rd ed. (Springfield, IL: Charles C Thomas, 2004), pp. 93–94.

and needs with respect to functional domains such as cognitive, social, and daily living skills. Professionals, in conjunction with the adolescent and his or her family, also need to identify the specific community resources needed to assist the young adult in preparing for life after school. This mapping for the future should include information about postsecondary educational opportunities as well as vocational, recreational, and independent living options (American Foundation for the Blind, 2013c).

The goal of transition to adulthood is success in the community. Success is measured by the young adult, the family, and the employer. Continuous observation of a student's performance is an integral part of educational and vocational training. These observations and reported skills or behaviors enable a college and career habilitation plan to be designed and regularly updated.

Adults With Visual Impairments

Adults with visual impairments are often isolated from peers in the community. Some of the specific needs of adults with visual impairments are transportation, low vision evaluation and prescription, technology support, social opportunities, and orientation and mobility training. Without leisure and work support, successful integration into the community becomes difficult. Adults should have access to radio reading services, auditory books, low vision devices, leisure activities, and other community support. Adults who have a vision loss late in life are often dramatically affected. In some instances, loss of self-esteem, depression, and loneliness are typical consequences. Community information and referral systems, however, can make a difference for the adult with a visual impairment.

The adult who has a vision loss will often need job training accommodations, transportation to the workplace, and possibly housing near the job site. The

AUDIO

Adults and Visual Impairment

SUGGESTIONS FOR THE CLASSROOM

Orientation and Mobility Tips

→ Eliminate unnecessary obstacles; inform student of changes in room arrangement or of any temporary obstacles.

→ Keep doors completely closed or completely open to eliminate the possibility of the student's running into a partially open door.

→ Allow the student to travel with a companion to frequently used rooms such as the library, school office, restroom, and gym. Discuss routes with turns and landmarks.

→ Allow the student to move about freely until the room and route are familiar.

→ Encourage the use of a sighted guide for fire drills, field trips, assemblies, and seating in rooms that ordinarily have no assigned seats.

→ Encourage independent travel in the familiar settings at school.

SOURCE: Adapted from R. Craig and C. Howard, "Visual Impairment," in M. Hardman, M. Egan, and D. Landau (Eds.), *What Will We Do in the Morning?* (Dubuque, IA: W. C. Brown, 1981), p. 191.

accommodations should be individualized, match the job description and responsibilities, and be appropriate for a person with a vision loss. Some job descriptions specify the visual acuity needed for the job, and some include options for vision loss adaptations.

An individual with a vision loss that occurs in adulthood usually has job skills that were learned prior to the loss. In this case, the individual can assist the employer with reasonable adaptations to the work area. If the job requires good vision, the worker may have to compete for another job within the agency or in the community. Sometimes the person with a visual impairment will need to obtain job training through the state vocational rehabilitation services.

The adult with vision loss should be independent within the workplace unless the setting is a sheltered workshop or another specialized work environment. Independence can be achieved through training with low vision devices, orientation and mobility training, job coaching to help find areas of the job where modifications must be made, and reasonable changes to the workstation to accommodate the person with a vision loss.

Family Issues

Families of persons with visual impairments face issues that are directly related to the independence of the family member with a vision loss. If a child is born with a visual impairment, the parents and other family members confront issues at every developmental age level. The family of the infant and toddler must address the nature of the visual impairment, the services available for the family, and the educational needs of the youngster during the early developmental years. As the child enters school, the family often becomes a partner in educational planning and the primary source of leisure activities. As the child begins to participate in school and interact with classmates, the family role often changes to that of an advocate supporting the needs of children with visual impairment.

Effective Instructional Practices
Accommodations for Students With Visual Impairments

Communication and accessibility are keys to providing an environment in which the student with visual impairments can realize his or her academic potential. Accommodations should provide the pupil with the ability to fully participate in the classroom as well as reduce the effects of the visual impairment.

Instructional Area	Accommodations
Reading	• Consult with the teacher of students with visual impairments on any optical devices the student may need to read printed materials. • Allow extra time for low vision readers, as they may experience eye fatigue. • Provide reading materials to the teacher of students with visual impairments in advance to be enlarged, scanned, Brailled, or recorded. • Textbooks and books commonly used in educational settings are available electronically. • Recreational books in recorded or Braille format can be ordered through the National Library Service for the Blind and Physically Handicapped (www.loc.gov/nls). This is a free service, but users must be registered before ordering. • Many local library systems have popular books available electronically.
Writing	• Some pupils with low vision need dark, bold, or raised lined paper for writing assignments. • Some individuals will need to use an electronic device for completing written assignments. • Braille readers may Braille assignments and transcribe them into print. • Some Braille readers use an electronic Braille note taker for written assignments. The assignment is entered in Braille and then translated into a print copy for the classroom teacher.
Note-taking	• Students with visual impairments may take notes on their Brailler, electronic note taker, or computer. • Any notes written on the board should be spoken aloud for the pupil who is visually impaired. • Students with visual impairments should be seated as close to an object or a display as possible. • Keep information in a visually simple and organized format for all students with visual perceptual difficulties. • Use high-contrast writing tools when using an overhead, a chalkboard, or a dry-erase board. • Use of a touch screen attached to the student's or the classroom computer can provide the individual with an accessible version of the notes. • Use of a touch screen with text conversion software allows the student to access the electronic version of the notes with a screen reading or voice output program.

SOURCE: Adapted from L. Schrenko, *Visual Impairment* (Georgia Department of Education, February 2002). Available at http://www.glc.k13.ga.us/passwd/trc/ttools/attach/accomm/visimp.doc

If a person loses vision in adolescence, issues related to the teen years begin the family advocacy process. Secondary special educators and families frequently work together on independent living, postsecondary education, employment options, and linkages with adult services. Issues such as accepting that a person will not obtain a driver's license and may encounter difficulty with employment, dating, or entry to

Vocational training is an important component of transition planning for adolescents who are visually impaired.

postsecondary education are typical concerns of most families. If the person with a vision loss is an adult, issues of employment, mobility, independence, and community living are some of the areas of concern.

The family is the core community for the person with vision loss and frequently assumes an advocacy role. Advocacy for persons with visual impairment is provided through parent organizations, service agencies, and professional organizations. As a field, special education has a long and rich history of advocacy for individuals with disabilities. Professionals as well as families work together as a voice for persons with special needs. Families and persons with visual impairments advocate for educational and vocational needs and help to implement needed legislation.

Parent and professional organizations, support groups, and advocacy groups can provide information about local and national resources for families. The benefit of parent groups is that families within a community join hands to learn from and offer support to one another. These support groups also serve as a resource for educators, rehabilitation professionals, employers, and legislators on issues affecting persons with visual impairments.

Issues of Diversity

In planning the educational program for the student with visual impairments, the team must have an appreciation and understanding of cultural diversity. Certain cultures may have a greater susceptibility to eye diseases such as glaucoma or diabetes; others may have diets that cause eye disease specific to vitamin deficiency. Children from low socioeconomic communities tend to have less access to medical intervention. Eye care may be difficult to obtain, and issues of cost or availability may prevent follow-up on medications.

A diversity of backgrounds often means a diversity of skills. Diversity issues for children with visual impairments are multifaceted because of the many eye diseases, different ages of onset, and accommodations that are needed for the student to succeed. Educational plans should address cultural and linguistic differences and how the family and school personnel can work together to achieve the goals for the child. Diversity issues must be recognized prior to assessments and evaluations so that eligibility and placement will be appropriate for the child.

Language difference may present problems in assessment and placement, as well as in program progress. Ongoing family and school communication may become a problem if the language barrier is not considered in each aspect of the educational plan. Cultures and customs may create barriers for educational planning in social skills and in orientation and mobility. In some cultures, conversation is face-to-face, and it is considered impolite to walk while conversing. This could be a problem for the child and the family when learning orientation and mobility.

VIDEO
Diversity

VIDEO
Family Resources

Integration of skills such as Braille into the home may be difficult if the family does not understand the reasons for or mechanism of certain activities. On the other hand, if the parents also have a visual impairment, they may require Braille or large print for written documents and may also need translation into the family's native language. Either situation must be addressed as a diversity issue demanding sensitivity and cooperation of all parties who have an interest in the child.

Technology and Individuals With Visual Impairments

Advances in technology have provided opportunities for students with visual impairments to participate in educational programs on a level with sighted peers. After determining the individual needs of the pupil with a visual impairment, the educational team must consider the array of specialized materials and equipment that allows the student full participation in the least restrictive environment. Identification and use of these resources can make a notable difference in the educational program and future of the student with a visual impairment.

The American Printing House for the Blind in Louisville, Kentucky, is a valuable resource for special media, tools, and materials needed for an educational program. The American Foundation for the Blind has many publications on technology for consumers with visual impairments. Learning Ally (previously known as Recording for the Blind & Dyslexic) is a national educational library for people with print disabilities, including blindness and visual impairments. It provides audio textbooks along with reference and professional materials for people who cannot read standard print because of a disability.

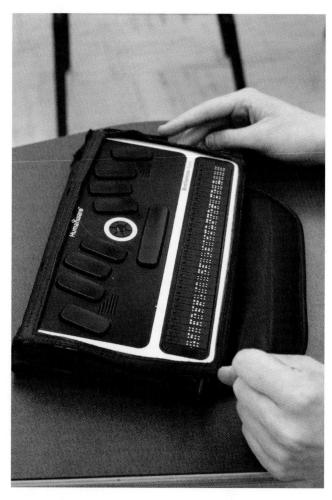

Technology plays a vital role in the lives of students who are visually impaired.

IDEA Requirements

IDEA 2004 requires the IEP team to consider the provision of assistive technology devices and services in the development of the student's IEP. Many twenty-first-century classrooms are increasingly relying on technology to enhance student learning. Pupils with visual impairment especially benefit from the use of technology, which runs the gamut from low-tech to high-tech. See Table 13.8 for examples of these technologies.

Despite the increase in use of technology, one form of low-tech technology retains its importance for some students with visual impairments—Braille. Braille has, and will continue to be, an important component of the educational program for individuals with vision loss. Under IDEA, Braille instruction is required unless the IEP team determines that it is not appropriate after evaluation of the student's reading and writing skills, needs, and appropriate reading and writing media (Mittler, 2007).

REFERENCE

Theater Accommodations

Technology Tool	Example
Adaptive Hardware	• Refreshable Braille displays • Screen enlargement peripherals • Speech synthesizers • Printers • Braille embosser • Electronic note takers • Braille input/output devices
Adaptive Software	• Braille translation software • Screen readers (e.g., JAWS) • Screen magnification software (e.g., MAGic) • Speech recognition software (e.g., Dragon NaturallySpeaking)
Adapted Output Systems	• Enhanced image systems (e.g., CCTV) • Screen readers (e.g., JAWS, NaturalReader) • Refreshable Braille displays • Use of Braille printers • Use of optical character recognition (OCR) systems (e.g., ReadingPen, Kurzweil 1000)
Adapted Input Systems	• Braille input devices • Use of speech recognition systems (e.g., Dragon NaturallySpeaking)
Global Positioning Systems (GPS)	• Portable travel tools (e.g., BrailleNote GPS, Trekker GPS) that permit individuals the freedom to independently navigate their environment

SOURCE: Adapted from J. Gense and M. Gense, "Using Assistive Technology for Learners Who Are Blind or Visually Impaired," in Pennsylvania College of Optometry (Eds.), *Increasing Literacy Levels: Final Report* (Starkville: Mississippi State University Rehabilitation Research & Training Center on Blindness and Low Vision, 1997).

Technology and Literacy

Technology plays an integral role in learning and all aspects of daily living, from literacy and mathematics to mobility to independent living. Students with visual impairments must have technology prescribed so that specialized equipment and devices are accessible in daily activities. Today, many children and young adults are learning to use various forms of technology despite their loss of vision. Table 13.9 illustrates some of the options available for persons who are visually impaired.

Literacy is an essential component of any student's educational program, including pupils with visual impairments. According to scholars (Erin, 2000), literacy can be demonstrated in four ways:

- When an individual is successful in communicating through writing
- When an individual is successful in communicating with a desired audience
- When an individual can successfully apply reading and writing skills
- When an individual is successful in reading and writing at different levels throughout the life span

Each student needs to have the opportunity to access information according to his or her unique requirements. Accessing and correctly using appropriate technology is a

AUDIO

Technology and Visual Impairments

Table 13.9 Representative Literacy Technologies for Individuals With Visual Impairment

Method of Access	Device	Description
Braille Embosser	Mountbatten Brailler	Electronic Braille embosser that translates text from a Braille keyboard to a printer
Braille Translator	Duxbury Braille Translator	A software program that takes a computerized text file and converts and formats the document properly for printing
Braille Writer	Perkins Brailler	A machine with keys corresponding to each of six dots of the Braille code to create all characters of the code
Optical Character Recognition (OCR)	Kurzweil 1000, OpenBook	A system that provides the capacity to scan printed text, have it spoken in synthetic speech, save it to a computer file, or render it in Braille
Synthetic Speech	JAWS, Window-Eyes	Screen reading software that allows text to be converted to speech
Video Magnifier	Closed-circuit television (CCTV)	Hardware used to project magnified images onto a video monitor

developmental process that should result in providing these students with the ability to become as independent as their sighted peers. With appropriate assessment and training in technology, students who are blind or visually impaired can compete successfully in educational programs. To do so, however, these pupils must have access to various technology tools. For example, if a teacher assigns the class a book to read from an approved list and then to write a report, a student with a visual impairment may read this book through a digital text or e-text, with his or her computer or other digital text reader (for example, iPad, Nook, or Kindle). The student could also elect to access the book via an audio recording from Learning Ally. The student may type his or her report by using a standard keyboard or a Braille input device, or may dictate his or her paper through a speech or voice recognition program.

Technology and Mathematics

While multiple options are available for helping students with visual impairment access written material, mathematics, especially advanced mathematics such as algebra, can present challenges. Sometimes typical options for accessing standard text such as scanned textbooks, audiobooks, and even Braille have difficulty with mathematical language. Some of these obstacles include ambiguity, poor translations, and pacing (Bouck & Meyer, 2012; Isaacson, Schleppenbach, & Lloyd, 2010/2011). Digital talking book players with specialized language provide one solution to these problems. Figure 13.8 illustrates an example of the ambiguity that can occur with mathematics and how one technology, ReadHear (gh, LLC, 2006), with its mathematics language, MathSpeak, can resolve this challenge.

Mobile Computing Devices

Mobile computing devices are growing in popularity with students with visual impairments, and increasingly standardly equipped with accessibility features. For example,

Figure 13.8 **Algebraic Ambiguity and Technological Resolution for Students With Visual Impairments**

Consider the orally read algebraic equation:

y equals 2 over *x* + 2

What does that equation look like?

Correct interpretations are:

$$y = \frac{2}{x+2} \text{ or } y = \frac{2+2}{x}$$

The MathSpeak language with the ReadHear technology results in the following output:

"*y* equals BEGIN FRACTION 2 over *x* + 2 END FRACTION"

The correct interpretation is then clear:

$$y = \frac{2}{x+2}$$

---

the operating system (iOS) for iPhones, iPads, and iPods has a built-in screen reader, speech-to-text (dictation), text-to-speech, and zooming capabilities. In addition, colors can be inverted and text can be enlarged. Finally, Braille displays can be used with iOS devices (Apple, 2013a). In addition to the device's own features, apps can be installed on mobile computing devices to assist students with visual impairments with various facets of life, including mobility and orientation—critical curriculum for students with visual impairments.

Technology Competency

In many public and residential schools, competence with computers and other types of technology is a prerequisite skill for accessing the academic curriculum and attainment of grade-level academic standards. Because computer technology must often be adapted for students with visual impairments, a computer proficiency requirement is frequently a part of an individualized education program. A vision specialist assists with classroom modifications and training while the general education curriculum is implemented. The vision specialist also needs to be knowledgeable about changing technology necessary to ensure meaningful participation in the general education classroom (Johnson, 2003).

Based on diagnostic information about the student's desires and needs in the classroom and community, an individualized technology plan can be designed for each pupil. To ensure that the individualized plan is thorough and up-to-date, an assistive technology team should develop a blueprint for the student's program (American Foundation for the Blind, 2010; Griffin, Williams, Davis, & Engleman, 2002). Team members typically include the following persons:

- Eye care professional
- General education teacher
- Occupational therapist
- Orientation and mobility specialist
- Parent or primary caregiver
- Physical therapist
- Product vendors
- Rehabilitation specialist
- Student
- Technology specialist
- Vision teacher

Trends, Issues, and Controversies

Trends, issues, and controversies directly affecting children with visual impairments include teacher shortages, access to certified orientation and mobility specialists, number of students assigned to teachers of the visually impaired, reading and literacy media assessment, and vocational training. Issues and trends, as well as controversies, are addressed by professional groups such as the Council for Exceptional Children Division on Visual Impairments, the Association for Education and Rehabilitation of the Blind and Visually Impaired, the National Association of State Directors of Special Education, and the American Foundation for the Blind. Consumer groups such as the National Federation of the Blind and the American Council of the Blind address issues from the perspective of the person with a visual impairment. These groups work to address these issues with the U.S. Department of Education, special educators, university faculty, and local and state directors of special education.

The profound teacher shortage in the field of visual impairment is an issue affecting all school districts in the United States. Few colleges and universities have the necessary resources to prepare teachers in a profession with a relatively small number of public and residential school students. Only about 250 new teachers of the visually impaired graduate college each year, thus contributing to the shortage of these professionals (Ferrell, 2007). Many of these individuals work in large urban school districts. Rural parts of the United States, with smaller school districts and fewer students with visual impairments, often lack certified teachers.

Just as there is a shortage of teachers of the visually impaired, there is also a shortage of orientation and mobility specialists. IDEA requires mobility evaluation and education for children with special needs. With only a small number of universities training orientation and mobility professionals, the need for these specialists by public and residential schools continues to grow. As a result, these services are often lacking, especially in rural areas. Since orientation and mobility instructors are not usually educators, they are hired in the same category as related service personnel and are costly for school districts. They often serve all students with visual impairments in the district, whereas the teacher of the visually impaired has a lighter caseload to teach. The suggested caseload for a teacher is six students to one teacher (Pugh & Erin, 1999).

The caseload of teachers of the visually impaired as well as orientation and mobility specialists continues to grow because of the shortage of qualified professionals. Larger caseloads affect the number of hours available to fulfill the IEP for each child. When a teacher has more than twenty students, distributed in general education classrooms at several different schools, time for travel and planning detracts from actual class time with the students. A reduction in class caseloads would enable teachers to fulfill IEP goals with more stable outcomes.

Prescriptions for reading and literacy media require a team approach based on the physician's and the teacher's educational recommendations. Reading media assessment is necessary to determine the appropriate low vision devices, enlargements, technology, or Braille use for each student. Some students need large print; others may require magnification or Braille; still others use books on tape. IDEA requires that the use of Braille be assessed in each student's IEP. Appropriate assessments of reading and writing media needs are limited. Teachers often use observations, work samples, and physician suggestions to validate media needs because functional levels are important for daily needs. With few certified teachers, it is difficult to provide this assessment for all students who are visually impaired.

Issues of transition center on evaluation and prognosis, vocational preparation, and how outcomes will be measured. Independence of students as they move into higher education or vocational training is a responsibility of the school and family and is often

AUDIO

Chapter 13 Summary

a problem with transition into the community. Because so many jobs require vision to complete the task, job training and higher education choices are sometimes difficult to select and implement. School representatives and families must construct a life plan with the student so that the benchmarks for success are attainable and reasonable and provide a meaningful and independent life of quality. Issues of community support also affect the successful outcomes of transition plans.

CHAPTER IN REVIEW ●

Defining Visual Impairments

- The educational definition of *visual impairment* is vision impairment that, even with correction, adversely affects an individual's educational performance.
- Visual impairment includes both partial sight and blindness.

The Eye and How It Works

- Light enters the eye first through the clear, transparent area in front of the eye known as the cornea and passes through the other structures to the retina.
- In the retina, light impulses are changed into electrical signals and travel along the optic nerve and back to the occipital lobe of the brain, which interprets the electrical signals as visual images.

Classification of Visual Impairments

- The most common visual impairments affecting school-age children are cataracts, glaucoma, optic nerve atrophy, myopia, albinism, eye injury, and retinopathy of prematurity (ROP).

Prevalence of Visual Impairments

- Visual impairment is one of the least prevalent disabilities, accounting for only 0.4 percent of pupils with a disability who are receiving a special education.

The Vision Process and Etiology of Visual Impairments

- If the cornea is damaged through trauma or disease, then the inner area may become infected, which could result in permanent visual impairment.
- Glaucoma is the major disease that occurs in the aqueous humor. This may result in a loss of visual acuity as well as a loss in the visual field.
- If the iris is malformed, the function of light control will be interrupted, and the child can become photophobic (sensitive to light).
- Cataracts are lenses that are opaque or cloudy due to trauma or age. Children with congenital cataracts often have the cataracts removed.
- Macular degeneration is a common eye disease in adults, but it may also occur in young people.

- Rods and cones are photoreceptive cells found in the retina.
- If a youngster has retinopathy of prematurity (ROP), vascular growth has been interrupted by premature birth.
- Retinitis pigmentosa is a hereditary condition involving gradual degeneration of the retina.

Prevention of Visual Impairments

- Most visual impairments are genetic in origin, but others such as injury can be prevented.

Assessment of Students With Visual Impairments

- The acuity chart that is most often used for testing and reporting vision loss is the Snellen chart.
- An important first step in planning an educational program for a child with visual impairments is to assess the pupil's present functional vision.
- Another important component in the assessment process is to determine the most effective learning and literacy media.
- Braille is used as a literacy medium along with print and auditory input if the child has any residual vision.

Educational Considerations

- Over six out of ten pupils with visual impairments are served in the general education classroom.
- Many students with visual impairments have the same education goals as other pupils.
- Instructional goals for most students with visual impairment include communication skills, social competency, employability, and independence, in addition to academic progress.
- Students with visual impairments may also require instruction in orientation and mobility.

Technology and Individuals With Visual Impairments

- With appropriate assessment and training in technology, students who are blind or visually impaired can compete successfully in educational programs.
- Technology plays an integral role in learning and all aspects of daily living, from literacy to mobility to independent living.

1. What is the legal definition of blindness? How does it differ from the IDEA definition?

2. What does the Snellen chart assess? What does 20/200 mean?

3. Describe how the eye functions.

4. Define the terms *myopia*, *hyperopia*, and *astigmatism*.

5. List five eye problems common to school-age children.

6. Why is early detection of vision problems important?

7. Describe the social and emotional characteristics of persons with visual impairments.

8. What is functional vision, and how is it evaluated?

9. Define the term *learning media*. Give three examples of different forms of learning media.

10. In what two educational settings do the majority of students with a visual impairment receive a special education?

11. What are some common educational accommodations that a student with visual impairments may require?

12. List five signs of possible vision problems in children.

13. Identify three critical issues that must be addressed if an adolescent is to successfully transition to postsecondary education or enter the workforce.

14. Besides cultural differences, what diversity issue must be addressed for parents who are also visually impaired?

15. Identify five technology accommodations that can be provided in high school for a student who is legally blind.

16. Discuss the shortage of orientation and mobility specialists and how a child's educational plan is affected by a shortage of personnel.

KEY TERMS

visual impairment, 446

visual acuity, 447

visual field, 447

field loss, 447

legally blind, 447

Snellen chart, 447

functionally blind, 448

primary literacy medium, 448

low vision, 448

residual vision, 448

deaf-blindness, 448

cornea, 448

iris, 448

pupil, 448

lens, 448

vitreous humor, 448

retina, 448

macula, 448

optic nerve, 448

myopia, 449

hyperopia, 449

astigmatism, 449

orbit, 449

cataracts, 449

glaucoma, 449

optic nerve atrophy, 449

albinism, 449

retinopathy of prematurity (ROP), 450

Braille, 450

visual efficiency, 452

photophobic, 454

aphakic, 454

rod cells, 454

cone cells, 454

macular degeneration, 454

retinitis pigmentosa, 455

coloboma, 455

functional vision, 460

literacy medium, 461

learning media, 461

Grade 1 Braille, 462

Grade 2 Braille, 462

orientation and mobility, 468

LEARNING ACTIVITIES

1. Spend a day traveling with an itinerant teacher of the visually impaired. Describe the types of instruction this professional provided for one or two of the pupils. What IEP goals were addressed? How was technology used to adapt the general education curriculum? How did classmates relate to the child with a visual impairment? What type of assistance did the vision specialist offer to the general educator? What problems or difficulties, if any, did you observe? Write a summary of your experience and share it with your classmates.

2. Search the Internet for information about the following three educational tools: an electronic Brailler, screen readers, and optical character recognition systems. Develop IEP goals and accompanying benchmarks for a secondary student who is legally blind and preparing to transition to a community college. How will this equipment be used to assist the adolescent in adapting to the general education curriculum? What individuals should be involved in planning the transition experience?

3. Interview an adult with a visual impairment. Find out about the type and age of onset of the vision loss. Ask about personal and family reactions to the loss of vision. What type of low vision devices or technology does this individual use on a daily basis? If possible, identify any adjustment concerns about independence, mobility, vocational and career issues, community involvement, and personal relationships. Share your impressions of this interview with your fellow students.

4. Travel with an orientation and mobility specialist and observe the training of a person with a visual impairment. What type of equipment was used? What travel techniques were addressed during the lesson? How did the orientation and mobility specialist evaluate the individual? Ask if you can use the various devices. How did it feel to navigate about the environment while simulating a visual impairment?

ORGANIZATIONS CONCERNED WITH VISUAL IMPAIRMENTS

American Council of the Blind

www.acb.org

American Foundation for the Blind

www.afb.org

American Printing House for the Blind

www.aph.org

Learning Ally

www.learningally.org

The National Braille Press

www.nbp.org

National Federation of the Blind

www.nfb.org

The National Library Service for the Blind and Physically Handicapped

www.loc.gov/nls

The Seeing Eye, Inc.

www.seeingeye.org

The following exercises are designed to help you learn to apply the Council for Exceptional Children (CEC) standards to your teaching practice. Each of the reflection exercises below correlates with knowledge or a skill within the CEC standards. For the full text of each of the related CEC standards, please refer to the standards integration grid located in Appendix B.

Focus on Learning Environments (*CEC Initial Preparation Standard 2.1*)

Reflect on what you have learned about accommodations needed for students with visual impairments. If you were developing a reading program for your class and you had a student in your class with a visual impairment, in what ways might you modify your instruction to take into account all of your students' learning needs? How might you need to integrate assistive technology into your instruction?

Focus on Instructional Planning and Strategies (*CEC Initial Preparation Standard 5.4*)

Reflect on what you have learned about students with visual impairments. If you were to have a student in your class with a visual impairment, how might you help him or her develop increased independence? How might you modify your classroom or your teaching strategies to create an environment where a student with visual impairments would feel comfortable? How might your other students assist you in creating this type of environment?

Sharpen your skills with SAGE edge at **edge.sagepub.com/gargiulo5e. SAGE edge for students** provides a personalized approach to help you accomplish your coursework goals in an easy-to-use learning environment.

Individuals With Physical Disabilities, Health Disabilities, and Related Low-Incidence Disabilities

Natalie's Story

Natalie is an amazing young lady who has exceeded most of the expectations of those who made assumptions based on her "labels" and therefore had lowered expectations for her. Fortunately, she did not live down to their expectations! Natalie has cerebral palsy (severe spastic quadriplegic and athetoid) with poor head and trunk control and only some limited use of her left hand and arm. She has undetermined visual acuity, has a questionable degree of intellectual disability, used to have seizures of varying types, and has a G-tube for most of her nutrition and caloric intake. She has had braces, splints, eye patching, and numerous surgeries (including spinal fusion).

Although Natalie is nonverbal, she can make approximately thirty words or sounds (that can mean up to two hundred different things, depending on the context or situation), and she uses an electronic augmentative communication device. Using a combination of two to four symbols, she can say approximately fifteen hundred sentences, three hundred words, and one hundred names!

Natalie is our third of three girls. She was born in 1975, five to six weeks premature. She was bluish-gray at birth, indicating a lack of oxygen, and had facial bruising, indicating a traumatic birth (face presentation). So she had the three leading causes of cerebral palsy going against her! She was diagnosed at 6 and a half months. She started therapy at 8 and a half months. At 6 and a half years, Natalie was given her first psychological test, which indicated an IQ of 65. Natalie was to be educated as if she had potential for normal intelligence, and she started school in an academically based class for students with orthopedic impairments.

Our family had to move, and it was then "determined" that Natalie would be placed in a self-contained, center-based class for students with severe mental retardation because all of the therapies were conveniently located there. I, of course, objected. We were told that she wouldn't really "fit" into the orthopedically impaired program, as those kids were more "advanced." (Please note that the terms *convenient* and *fit into* seem in direct contradiction to what is stated for an IEP, or *individualized* education program.)

LEARNING OBJECTIVES

After reading Chapter 14, you should be able to:

- **List** the disabilities associated with physical impairments.
- **Identify** disabilities associated with other health impairments.
- **Define** deaf-blindness.
- **Summarize** society's reaction to and treatment of persons with physical or health impairments.
- **Provide** examples of common causes of physical disabilities and health impairments.
- **Outline** representative conditions associated with orthopedic impairments, multiple disabilities, traumatic brain injury, other health impairments, and deaf-blindness.
- **Describe** the impact of a physical or health impairment on school performance.
- **Explain** the procedures that teachers and other professionals use to meet the educational needs of pupils with physical/health disabilities and deaf-blindness.
- **Summarize** educational services for individuals with physical or health impairments across the life span.
- **Give** examples of how technology benefits individuals with a physical or health disability.

Physical, Health, and Low Incidence Disabilities

Parent Interview

From 1985 to 1987, we were fortunate to have a teacher who, despite the label of severe intellectual disability, knew Natalie had capabilities and academic potential. This teacher's philosophy was that if Natalie was having a problem with something, it was not that Natalie couldn't learn it, but more likely that she just needed to change her approach. She worked with sight words and numbers and picture boards that increased in complexity as Natalie became proficient using them. As Natalie's skills developed, we started our search for the "right" augmentative communication device. After a year-long assessment we found the ideal augmentative communication device for Natalie, a Touch Talker. Within six months, I had programmed two thirds of what is currently in her device. People began to see Natalie in a totally different way and to recognize her intelligence and humor and emotions, and lots of frustrations. They began to relate to her in a totally different way—all because she could finally communicate!

Natalie's label changed, and she was moved from the severe mental retardation class into a moderate mental retardation class in a public middle school. We tried again for placement in an orthopedic impairments class, and were again denied.

Finally, she was placed into an orthopedically impaired class her last year of middle school. It was probably her best year for academic learning, as she worked one-on-one on her individual goals, but also was part of group learning. She thrived in the group setting, and quite often had to be reprimanded for answering other students' questions!

Unfortunately, inclusion in high school, with the opportunity to go into general education classes, did not work for Natalie—it came too late. We tried, but it's a little hard to start with high school curriculum when you haven't had the basics! She was, for the most part, in a self-contained orthopedically impaired class for her last seven years. Her teacher involved peer tutors in much of Natalie's program, which was very motivating for Natalie and gave her the opportunity to make friends. It was kind of like bringing inclusion to Natalie. They definitely were a benefit to her, both socially and academically.

Transition planning for Natalie was a challenge because of the severity of Natalie's disabilities and the lack of experience with this type of student. We stressed the need to develop assertiveness, as Natalie—like so many folks with disabilities—was too often passive in situations that were not to her liking, but there was no such program. We encouraged goals based on our vision for Natalie's future, which was living and working in the community with supports.

Through school, she did participate in community-based vocational training and worked in several locations. Although these were not jobs that she could actually do independently, they did offer an opportunity to work on her communication and mobility goals. And she brought an awareness to those stores—and the community that frequented them—of the possibility that a person with severe disabilities could work, wanted to work, and was excited about it!

One of our proudest moments was when Natalie received a standing ovation as she graduated from high school, and there have been many proud moments since. Natalie has had two paying jobs. She lives in her own home with a roommate and a live-in care provider. She is working on understanding and accepting more independence each day. She has given many presentations to community groups and is an active advocate for people who can't speak for themselves.

Through the years, Natalie has been blessed by many wonderful teachers, aides, therapists, and specialists who gave so much of themselves for her benefit. I hope that

VIDEO

**Individual Interview: Woman
With Traumatic Brain Injury**

they will someday realize the impact that each one of them has had, individually and collectively, on Natalie and—through her—on the community as a whole. Natalie is an inspiration, and a wonderful example of what can be!

—Beth Tumlin

■▨■▨▨■▨■▨▨▨ ▨▨■▨▨■▨■■▨ ■▨■▨■▨▨▨▨ ▨ ▨▨▨■▨▨■▨▨■▨■▨▨▨▨▨▨▨ ▨

Students who have physical or health disabilities comprise one of the most diverse categories of learners in special education because of the wide range of diseases and disorders included in this category. Pupils with physical disabilities may range from those with severe physical conditions resulting in an inability to talk, walk, point, or make any purposeful movement to those students with only some difficulty walking or an unseen skeletal abnormality. Individuals with health disabilities may range from those with severe health problems forcing them to stay home to those with a hidden disability, such as a tumor. In addition, there are several low-incidence disabilities that can include physical or health disabilities, such as traumatic brain injury, deaf-blindness, and multiple disabilities. The term *low-incidence* generally refers to a disability that occurs infrequently. In fact, children who exhibit the three impairments listed above account for only about 2.6 percent of all pupils receiving a special education (U.S. Department of Education, 2013a). What places all of these students together in this chapter is that they frequently share some dimension or aspect of physical or health impairments.

At the beginning of this chapter, we read about Natalie, whose story is typical of many individuals who have a severe physical disability. Natalie has one of the most common physical disabilities (cerebral palsy) that occur in schoolchildren. In her case, she also has a health disability (epilepsy). She has faced several challenges in her education, such as appropriate assessment, correct educational placement, selection of appropriate curriculum, and use of specialized strategies for teaching and adapting academics for a student who is essentially unable to speak. She uses several assistive technology devices, such as an augmentative and alternative communication (AAC) device and a power wheelchair. Although she encountered problems regarding her placement and lack of inclusion, she has achieved successes in terms of acquired skills and transition to paid employment.

This chapter will examine what it means for a student to have a physical, health, or related low-incidence disability. Definitions will be given, along with a history of the field, data on the prevalence of these disabilities, and some of their causes. A sampling of some of the most common types of physical, health, and related low-incidence disabilities will be explored. A model will be presented explaining how school performance is affected by a physical, health, or related low-incidence disability, along with strategies to address these students' needs. Many other areas will also be reviewed, including services for young children, transition, adult issues, family issues, diversity, technology, and current issues in the field of physical and health disabilities. We begin by defining physical, health, and related low-incidence disabilities as they are addressed in education.

assistive technology device: Any item, piece of equipment, or product system that increases, maintains, or improves functional capabilities of individuals with disabilities.

augmentative and alternative communication (AAC): Symbols, aids, strategies, and techniques used as a supplement or alternative to oral language.

Chapter contribution written by Kathryn Wolff Heller, Georgia State University, and Richard M. Gargiulo

Defining Physical Disabilities, Health Disabilities, and Related Low-Incidence Disabilities

Many individuals with physical or health disabilities are capable of living independent and productive lives.

orthopedic impairment: A physical disability that occurs from congenital anomalies, diseases, or other causes that adversely affect a child's educational performance.

multiple disabilities: Concomitant impairments that result in such severe educational needs that a student cannot be accommodated in a special education program solely on the basis of one of the impairments.

traumatic brain injury: An acquired injury to the brain caused by an external force that results in a disability or psychosocial impairment that adversely affects educational performance.

other health impairment: A chronic or acute health problem that results in limited strength, vitality, or alertness and adversely affects educational performance.

deaf-blindness: Concomitant hearing and visual impairments.

Many students have various physical or health conditions, but only those with physical or health disabilities that interfere with their educational performance require special education services. According to the Individuals with Disabilities Education Improvement Act of 2004 (PL 108–446), students with physical impairments may qualify for special education services under three possible categories: orthopedic impairment, multiple disabilities, and traumatic brain injury. Students with health disabilities may qualify under the IDEA category of other health impairment. Children with the loss of both vision and hearing receive services under the label deaf-blindness.

The federal definition of orthopedic impairment provides examples of impairments resulting from congenital anomalies (irregularities or defects present at birth), diseases, or other causes (see Table 14.1). In our chapter opener, Natalie was classified under this definition of orthopedic impairment and received special education services because of the impact of her cerebral palsy on her school functioning. Although Natalie had other impairments (seizures), she could be accommodated under the educational program in orthopedic impairment.

When students have two or more primary disabilities that cannot be accommodated by one special education program, they may be classified as having multiple disabilities. For example, a child who has a severe physical impairment and is deaf may be classified as having a multiple disability; this pupil may require services from a teacher certified to teach students with orthopedic impairments and another teacher certified to teach students who are deaf or hard of hearing. Many possible combinations of disabilities can fall under the category of multiple disabilities, but because a physical or health disability is often involved, this category is addressed in this chapter.

Children who have an acquired brain injury as a result of external force, such as from a car accident, may be served under the category of traumatic brain injury. Traumatic brain injury may result in impairments in several different areas, including physical disabilities, sensory impairments, cognitive abnormalities, language abnormalities, and behavioral disorders. This category does not include individuals who have brain injury that occurred before or during birth or that was acquired as a result of a degenerative disease.

Students with other health impairments have limited alertness to the educational environment because of health problems that limit strength, vitality, or alertness. This health impairment may be chronic (persisting over a long period of time) or acute (having a short and usually severe course). The federal definition in Table 14.1 gives several examples of health impairments, including asthma, heart conditions, diabetes, and attention deficit hyperactivity disorder. This is only a partial listing of all of the possible conditions that may be included in this disability area.

Pupils who have visual or hearing impairments of such magnitude that they cannot be appropriately accommodated in a special education program for children with deafness or blindness are identified as deaf-blind. Most of us could not imagine what

AUDIO

Prenatal Surgery

Terms	Federal Definition
Deaf-blindness	Concomitant hearing and visual impairments, the combination of which causes such severe communication and other developmental and educational needs that students cannot be accommodated in special education programs solely for children with deafness or children with blindness.
Multiple disabilities	Concomitant impairments (such as intellectual disability–blindness, intellectual disability–orthopedic impairment, etc.), the combination of which causes such severe educational needs that students cannot be accommodated in special education programs solely for one of the impairments. The term does not include deaf-blindness.
Orthopedic impairment	A severe orthopedic impairment that adversely affects a child's educational performance. The term includes impairments caused by congenital anomaly (e.g., clubfoot, absence of some member), impairments caused by disease (e.g., poliomyelitis, bone tuberculosis), and impairments from other causes (e.g., cerebral palsy, amputations, and fractures or burns that cause contractures).
Other health impairment	Having limited strength, vitality, or alertness, including a heightened alertness to environmental stimuli, that results in limited alertness with respect to the education environment that i. Is due to chronic or acute health problems such as asthma, attention deficit disorder or attention deficit hyperactivity disorder, diabetes, epilepsy, a heart condition, hemophilia, lead poisoning, leukemia, nephritis, rheumatic fever, sickle cell anemia, and Tourette syndrome; and ii. Adversely affects a child's educational performance.
Traumatic brain injury	An acquired injury to the brain caused by an external physical force, resulting in total or partial functional disability or psychosocial impairment, or both, that adversely affects educational performance. The term applies to open or closed head injuries resulting in impairments in one or more areas, such as cognition; language; memory; attention; reasoning; abstract thinking; judgment; problem-solving; sensory, perceptual, and motor abilities; psychosocial behavior; physical functions; information processing; and speech. The term does not apply to brain injuries that are congenital or degenerative, or to brain injuries induced by birth trauma.

SOURCE: 34 C.F.R. § 300.8 (c).

it would be like to be without the use of both our hearing and our eyesight. We gather so much information about our surroundings through these two senses. The loss of both hearing and vision represents one of the most challenging of all disability categories. It would be wrong to assume, however, that students classified as deaf-blind are completely unable to see or hear—the term is not absolute. In reality, many children classified as deaf-blind experience a broad range of perceptions. Some pupils may be completely blind but only partially deaf, while in other instances a youngster might be partially sighted but have a severe hearing loss. Fortunately, a majority of these individuals possess some degree of functional hearing and vision (Miles, 2013). Only a very few pupils classified as deaf-blind are profoundly deaf *and* totally blind (Alabama Institute for Deaf and Blind, 2013).

The challenges facing this group of children are sometimes formidable and often include severe communication deficits, impaired mobility, and diminished social skills. Intellectual disabilities and physical impairments are often present in individuals who are deaf-blind (National Consortium on Deaf-Blindness, 2009). For pupils who are profoundly deaf and totally blind, their experience with and knowledge of the world is very narrow, often extending only as far as their fingertips can reach (Miles, 2013). Helen Keller said, "Blindness separates a person from things, but deafness separates him from people." Helping a child who is deaf-blind relate to the world is a tremendous undertaking, a responsibility that frequently falls to teachers, family members, and other professionals.

A Brief History of the Field

Physical and health disabilities have existed throughout history, and reactions to individuals who have this type of disability have varied across civilizations, cultures, and individual beliefs. Reactions have ranged from abandonment and extermination to providing educational, social, and medical treatment. A brief historical review of the treatment of individuals with physical or health disabilities will help to provide an understanding of present-day practices.

Early History

In ancient civilizations, individuals with physical or health impairments did not often live long. A lack of sophisticated medical treatment made it impossible to treat many of these impairments. Many cultures did not value individuals who were viewed as being incapable of contributing to group survival. Infants were often abandoned to die. Individuals who later developed injury or illness were often ostracized and forced to leave the group. However, some artifacts do indicate that some attempts were made to heal the effects of illness and disability in ancient times. For example, primitive skulls have been found with holes cut into them; evidence suggests that people were trying to cure epilepsy by cutting a hole through the skull to let "evil spirits out" (Temkin, 1971).

During the Middle Ages, religious influence typically resulted in more humanitarian care. Individuals with disabilities were often viewed as "children of God" and received protection from the Church. However, in some instances, individuals with disabilities (such as seizure disorders) were perceived as witches or possessed by evil spirits and were burned at the stake (Gargiulo, 1985).

In the 1800s, physicians and researchers showed an increased interest in physical disabilities and studied individuals with disabilities to find effective treatments. For example, in the 1860s, Dr. William Little described several cases and treatments of what is now referred to as cerebral palsy (because of his pioneering efforts, the disorder was initially named Little disease). At about this time, the first schools were opened for individuals with physical disabilities, in the form of residential institutions.

The first institution in the United States for children with physical disabilities was the Industrial School for Crippled and Deformed Children in Boston, established in 1890 (Eberle, 1922). This and other institutions were well intended, and provided a centralized place that could house needed equipment and provide specialized treatment and training. However, over the years, many institutions degenerated into providing only custodial services. Residential institutions often became places to "protect" society from "undesirables" (Macmillan & Hendrick, 1993). This practice of separating individuals with disabilities from society has been questioned in modern society, with the recognition that persons with physical and health impairments can contribute positively to society and should be allowed to do so.

Emergence of Public Education

It was not until the 1900s that public schools for "crippled children" were established (La Vor, 1976), first in Chicago and then in New York, Cleveland, and Philadelphia. These schools permitted expensive equipment to be centrally located and enabled highly trained professionals to work with these children. However, this segregated setting did not allow students with physical disabilities to interact with students without disabilities in the educational environment. Unfortunately, students with physical disabilities were not always welcome in public school. In *Beattie v. Board of Education* (1919), the courts ruled that students with physical disabilities could be excluded from school because they were said to have a "depressing and nauseating effect" on other students (Ysseldyke & Algozzine, 1982). Over time, the educational setting changed to allow for the integration of students with physical and health disabilities into neighborhood schools and general education classes. The move to more integrated school placements took a combination of legislation, shift in ideology, and advances in medical and technological practices.

Prevalence of Physical Disabilities, Health Disabilities, and Related Low-Incidence Disabilities

Reported prevalence figures for physical and health disabilities vary widely, depending on the specific condition. For example, United Cerebral Palsy (2013) estimates that 764,000 children and adults in the United States have cerebral palsy and approximately 10,000 infants and 1,200–1,500 preschool-age children are diagnosed each year. Spina bifida is a very common birth defect. Each day, approximately eight babies born in the United States have spina bifida or a related birth defect involving the brain and spine (Spina Bifida Association of America, 2013). The Epilepsy Foundation of America (2013) reports that approximately 45,000 children under the age of 15 develop epilepsy each year, and more than 3 million Americans are currently diagnosed with epilepsy. The American Lung Association (2012b) estimates that more than 7 million children under the age of 18 have asthma. The estimated number of individuals diagnosed with AIDS in the United States is over 1 million with almost 9,600 of these being children under the age of 14 (Centers for Disease Control and Prevention, 2009).

Not every school-age child with a physical or health impairment requires special education services, because the condition may not have a negative impact on the student's academic performance. The U.S. Department of Education (2013a) annually compiles information from each state on the number of school-age children receiving special education by disability category. During the 2011–2012 school year, in the area of physical and health disabilities, a total of 938,794 school-age children received services across the categories of orthopedic impairment (54,410 children), multiple disabilities (125,150 children), traumatic brain injury (24,886 children), and other health impairment (734,348 children). These four areas comprised approximately 16 percent of the students receiving a special education, with a range of 0.42 percent (traumatic brain injury) to 12.68 percent (other health impairment). Pupils with deaf-blindness (1,378 children) were reported as making up only 0.02 percent of all individuals receiving a special education. This figure, however, is thought to be underestimated because many children who are deaf-blind are placed in other categories (for example, multiple disabilities) when they have additional physical or intellectual impairments.

Etiology of Physical Disabilities, Health Disabilities, and Related Low-Incidence Disabilities

The etiology (or cause) of physical and health disabilities varies greatly according to the specific disease or disorder. Some of the most common etiologies resulting in physical and health disabilities are genetic and chromosomal defects, teratogenic causes, prematurity and complications of pregnancy, and acquired causes. In some cases, certain physical or health disabilities have multiple etiologies. For instance, infants are at risk for cerebral palsy due to preconceptional factors (for example, prior maternal diagnosis of seizures or thyroid disease), prenatal factors (for example, small for gestational age, birth defects), perinatal factors (for example, birth asphyxia where there is a lack of oxygen to the fetus), and postnatal factors (for example, presence of seizures, respiratory distress syndrome, infections) (McIntyre et al., 2013).

Chromosomal and Genetic Causes

Among the most common causes of physical and health disabilities are hereditary conditions resulting from defects in one or both parents' chromosomes or genes. Several genetic defects are believed to contribute to a range of physical and health disabilities, such as muscular dystrophy, sickle cell anemia, hemophilia, and cystic fibrosis (Heller, 2009b; Heller, Mezei, & Schwartzman, 2009). In some cases, infants may be born with several disabilities resulting from an inherited congenital syndrome (for example, Cockayne syndrome, which can result in intellectual disability, dwarfism, deaf-blindness, unsteady gait, and tremors). In these examples, the inherited gene clearly causes the disease or disorder.

Although there are about sixty genetic causes of deaf-blindness (National Consortium on Deaf-Blindness, 2013), we have chosen only two illustrative syndromes. Our first example is CHARGE association (syndrome), which represents a collection of physical irregularities present at birth. This syndrome is an extremely complex disorder typically involving extensive medical as well as physical challenges. CHARGE association is a relatively rare disorder occurring in 1 out of every 9,000 to 10,000 births. In the vast majority of cases, there is no history of CHARGE syndrome or any other similar condition in the family (CHARGE Syndrome Foundation, 2013). CHARGE is an acronym that stands for

C = coloboma, a congenital condition resulting from an unusually shaped (tear-drop) pupil and/or other abnormalities of the eye contributing to difficulties with depth perception, visual acuity, and sensitivity to light

H = heart defects, which may range from minor to life-threatening conditions

A = atresia, complications of the respiratory system

R = retarded physical growth; in some instances intellectual disability is also present

G = genital abnormalities—incomplete or underdeveloped genitals, more common in males

E = ear defects, structural deformities in the outer, middle, or inner ear; hearing loss may range from mild to profound. (Alabama Institute for Deaf and Blind, 2013; CHARGE Syndrome Foundation, 2013)

In order to make a diagnosis of CHARGE, four of the preceding six characteristics must be present. In addition, children who exhibit this syndrome frequently experience high levels of anxiety while displaying compulsive behaviors (Silberman, Bruce, & Nelson, 2004).

Our second illustration is Usher syndrome. This inherited disorder is one of the leading causes of deaf-blindness after childhood. Approximately 1 in 20,000 individuals is born with this condition (Alabama Institute for Deaf and Blind, 2013). Usher syndrome results in congenital deafness, progressive vision loss (retinitis pigmentosa), and, in some children, intellectual disability. Vision difficulties are typically noted in adolescence or early adulthood, eventually leading to night blindness and tunnel vision.

CHARGE association: A rare genetic disorder resulting in deaf-blindness, a syndrome representing a cluster of physical anomalies present at birth.

Usher syndrome: An inherited disorder resulting in deaf-blindness, deafness present at birth accompanied by progressive vision loss, sometimes associated with intellectual disabilities.

FIRST PERSON: VIRGINIA

One Day at a Time

As early as the fourth grade I became aware that I probably didn't see as well as others in the dark. But not being able to see at night just seemed like it should be normal.

However, in seventh grade, in anticipation of our Washington, DC, school trip, I was a little worried about the whole "not being able to see at night" thing, so my mom and I went to talk to the school nurse who was also going on the trip. She checked my eyes and said that I just needed glasses (not that that had anything to do with not being able to see in the dark). My mom made an appointment with the eye doctor, and he also said that I needed glasses. My dad told the doctor that the main reason for the appointment was to find out why I couldn't see in the dark. He examined my eyes again and said that I would have to take some additional tests at Emory University.

The summer before eighth grade I discovered the real reason I couldn't see in the dark: I had Usher syndrome. I couldn't believe it, and I didn't want to believe it. I didn't want to lose a sense that was so very precious to me. I used my sight not only to get around but also, because of my hearing loss, for lipreading. At such a young age, I was worried about being "normal." For the next two years I was in a state of denial. I refused to talk about my condition, and if I was forced to talk about it, it only brought pain. How could I, a person who relied so heavily on sight to communicate, lose my vision? It just didn't seem fair, and I felt so alone. No one knew or understood what I was going through. Of course, I had my family and friends supporting me, but I still felt alone.

It wasn't until I was 15 that I began to accept my deaf-blindness. Now I'm OK with my disability. While I have learned to accept my vision as something that has shaped who I am today, I am in no way completely cured of all my emotional pain. No way! I still struggle with adjusting to the changes in my vision. I worry about completing college and what the future holds. There are some days when I get so frustrated that all I want to do is run away and scream. It's hard, but all I can do is take one day at a time and trust that God has an awesome plan for my life. ■

Hearing loss is evidenced in both ears and is usually in the moderate (45- to 55-dB) to severe (71- to 90-dB) range. Significant balance difficulties are also associated with this syndrome. (See the accompanying First Person feature.)

Finally, some 17 percent of children who are deaf-blind evidence this disability at birth or within the first five years of life. The overwhelming majority of students with deaf-blindness, however, are adventitiously deaf-blind; that is, they are born with both vision and hearing but lose some or all of these senses as a result of illness or injury (Miles, 2013; National Consortium on Deaf-Blindness, 2007). How deaf-blindness impacts a child's development depends on several key variables, including age of onset, the degree and type of hearing and vision loss, the stability of each sensory loss, and, perhaps most important, the educational interventions provided (Alabama Institute for Deaf and Blind, 2013).

Teratogenic Causes

Many physical and health disabilities are caused by teratogenic agents that affect the developing fetus. Teratogens are outside causes, such as infections, drugs, chemicals, or environmental agents, that can produce fetal abnormalities.

Certain congenital infections can result in severe multiple disabilities in the unborn child. Infections are acquired by the mother and then passed on to the developing fetus. Several prenatal infections that may result in severe birth defects are referred to by the acronym TORCH—toxoplasmosis, other, rubella, cytomegalovirus, and herpes.

teratogen: Infections, drugs, chemicals, or environmental agents that can produce fetal abnormalities.

The effects of these infections on the fetus can vary from no adverse effect to severe disabilities or death. A baby who contracts one of these infections during gestation may be born with cerebral palsy, blindness, deafness, intellectual disability, and several other abnormalities, including heart defects, kidney defects, brain abnormalities, and deaf-blindness (Best & Heller, 2009b).

The fetus is also at risk of developing physical and health disabilities when exposed to certain drugs, chemicals, or environmental agents. Maternal abuse of alcohol, for example, has been linked to a range of physical, cognitive, and behavioral abnormalities that can result in lifelong damage (Merrick, Merrick, Morad, & Kandel, 2006; Tsai, Floyd, Green, & Boyle, 2007). Serious fetal abnormalities can also occur as a result of prescription medications taken for maternal illness or disease (for example, certain antibiotics and seizure medications). Environmental toxins such as radiation have been linked to birth defects, cancer, and mutations (Williams & Fletcher, 2010). Certain maternal diseases, such as diabetes, have also been associated with a higher risk of congenital malformations (Barnes-Powell, 2007).

Prematurity and Complications of Pregnancy

Infants are usually born at approximately 40 weeks of gestation, weighing approximately 7.5 pounds (Kliegman, Stanton, St. Geme, Schor, & Behrman, 2011). An infant born before 37 weeks is considered premature.

Infants who are premature and born with very low birth weight (less than 1,500 grams) are at risk of having disabilities. These infants can develop neurological problems resulting in cerebral palsy, epilepsy, vision loss, hearing loss, deaf-blindness, and/or psychosis (Valcamonico et al., 2007). Cognitive functioning can be affected, resulting in intellectual or learning disabilities, which can lead to future educational difficulties (Hille et al., 2007).

In some instances, babies who are born on time and with average weight encounter complications during the perinatal period. The most common cause of brain injury during the perinatal period is asphyxia—a decrease of oxygen in the blood. Among infants who survive an episode of asphyxia, several disabilities may occur such as cerebral palsy, epilepsy, and cognitive deficits (Rennie, Hagmann, & Robertson, 2007).

Acquired Causes

Many physical and health disabilities in addition to related low-incidence disabilities are acquired after birth by infants, children, and adults. These acquired causes include trauma, child abuse, infections, environmental toxins, and disease. For example, deaf-blindness may be caused by meningitis. Traumatic brain injury is usually due to an acquired cause resulting from some type of trauma (for example, falls, accidents, child abuse). The extent of disability depends on the cause and its severity.

Characteristics of Individuals With Physical Disabilities, Health Disabilities, and Related Low-Incidence Disabilities

The specific characteristics of an individual who has a physical or health disability will depend on the specific disease, its severity, and individual factors. Two individuals with identical diagnoses may be quite different in terms of their capabilities. Also, it is important to remember that students who have severe physical disabilities (even individuals who are unable to talk, walk, or feed themselves) may have normal

Physical Disabilities	Health Disabilities
Orthopedic Impairments	Other Health Impairments
Neuromotor impairments • Cerebral palsy • Spina bifida	Major health impairments • Seizure disorders • Asthma
Degenerative diseases • Muscular dystrophy	Infectious diseases • AIDS
Musculoskeletal disorders • Juvenile idiopathic arthritis • Limb deficiency	
Multiple Disabilities*	
Physical disability plus another disability	
Traumatic Brain Injury*	
Physical disability resulting from traumatic brain injury	

NOTE: *Multiple disabilities and traumatic brain injury can occur without a physical disability being present. They fall under the category of physical disabilities only when a physical disability is present.

or gifted intelligence. No one should judge a person's intellectual ability based on physical appearance.

A multitude of physical and health disabilities may be encountered at school. Each of them has differing characteristics, treatments, and prognoses. To illustrate the range of conditions included under physical and health disabilities, this section describes a number of sample conditions across the four IDEA categories of orthopedic impairment, multiple disabilities, traumatic brain injury, and other health impairment. Table 14.2 gives an outline of the categories, subcategories, and sample conditions that will be discussed. Characteristics of individuals with deaf-blindness will also be reviewed.

Characteristics of Students With Orthopedic Impairments

The IDEA category of orthopedic impairment contains a wide variety of disorders. These can be divided into three main areas: neuromotor impairments, degenerative diseases, and musculoskeletal disorders. Each of these areas has unique characteristics and contains many different disabilities. Following is a sampling of some of the most commonly found orthopedic impairments in the school-age population.

Neuromotor Impairments

A neuromotor impairment is an abnormality of, or damage to, the brain, spinal cord, or nerves that send impulses to the muscles of the body. Neuromotor impairments often result in complex motor problems that can affect several body systems (for example, limited limb movement, loss of urinary control, loss of proper alignment of the spine). Individuals with neuromotor impairments have a higher incidence of additional impairments, especially when there has been brain involvement

neuromotor impairments: Several types of impairments involving abnormality of, or damage to, the brain, spinal cord, or nerves that send impulses to the muscles of the body.

VIDEO
Parent Interview

REFERENCE
Cerebral Palsy

(for example, intellectual disability, seizures, visual impairments). Two types of neuromotor impairments that fall under the IDEA category of orthopedic impairment are cerebral palsy and spina bifida.

1. **Cerebral Palsy.** **Cerebral palsy** refers to several nonprogressive disorders of voluntary movement or posture that are caused by malfunction of or damage to the developing brain that occurs before or during birth or within the first few years of life (Porter, 2011). This disorder is associated with many different etiologies, including teratogens (such as the TORCH infections), prematurity, complications of pregnancy (such as lack of oxygen), acquired causes, and certain genetic syndromes.

Individuals with cerebral palsy have abnormal, involuntary, and/or uncoordinated motor movements. The severity can range from mild to severe. Some mild forms of cerebral palsy may only be noticeable when the person runs and appears to move in an uncoordinated fashion. At the other extreme, individuals with severe forms of cerebral palsy are unable to make the motor movements necessary to walk, sit without support, feed themselves, chew food, pick up an object, or speak.

The four most common types of cerebral palsy are spastic, athetoid, ataxia, and mixed. **Spastic cerebral palsy** is characterized by very tight muscles occurring in one or more muscle groups. This tightness results in stiff, uncoordinated movements. In **athetoid cerebral palsy**, movements are contorted, abnormal, and purposeless. Individuals with **ataxic cerebral palsy**, or **ataxia**, have poor balance and equilibrium in addition to uncoordinated voluntary movement. **Mixed cerebral palsy** refers to a combination of types, such as spastic and athetoid, as in the case of Natalie described at the beginning of this chapter.

Cerebral palsy is further classified by which limbs (arms and legs) are affected. This classification system is also used for other types of motor disorders and paralysis. Some of the major classifications are **hemiplegia**, in which the left or right side of the body is involved; **diplegia**, in which the legs are more affected than the arms; **paraplegia**, in which only the legs are involved; and **quadriplegia**, in which all four limbs are involved (see Figure 14.1). Natalie's spastic cerebral palsy is the type in which all four limbs are severely involved. Hence, she is described as having severe spastic quadriplegic cerebral palsy, in addition to the athetoid form.

Although cerebral palsy is considered nonprogressive because the brain damage does not progress, further complications and additional disabilities may result. Many individuals develop contractures (shortening of the muscle) that further decrease motor movement and can result in deformity. Abnormal muscle tone can result in conditions such as curvature of the spine (scoliosis) and hip displacement. Abnormal oral reflexes may result in a need for a feeding tube (a tube going into the stomach through which nutritional liquids are given when the person is unable to eat sufficient amounts of food). Individuals with cerebral palsy have an increased incidence of other disorders, including epilepsy, visual impairments, and intellectual disability (Heller & Tumlin-Garrett, 2009). However, cognitive ability can range from giftedness to intellectual disability, and accurate scores can be difficult to obtain.

At present, there is no cure for cerebral palsy. Cerebral palsy is often managed through medication (such as diazepam or baclofen) and/or surgery, which decrease the effects of tight muscles and deformity, although movement abnormalities still remain. Part of a student's treatment regime will also include the use of various braces or splints, known as **orthotics**, to help maintain alignment and decrease the development of **contractures** (shortened muscles that result in the inability to fully extend a joint, such as being unable to fully extend the arm at the elbow or completely straighten at the knees). New, experimental treatments are under investigation in the hope of improving motor function.

cerebral palsy: Several nonprogressive disorders of voluntary movement or posture that are caused by damage to the developing brain.

spastic cerebral palsy: A type of cerebral palsy in which the person has very tight muscles occurring in one or more muscle groups, resulting in stiff, uncoordinated movements.

athetoid cerebral palsy: A type of cerebral palsy in which movements are contorted, abnormal, and purposeless.

ataxic cerebral palsy (ataxia): A type of cerebral palsy that is characterized by poor balance and equilibrium in addition to uncoordinated voluntary movement.

mixed cerebral palsy: Cerebral palsy that consists of combinations of different types. A person who has both spastic and athetoid cerebral palsy would be considered to have mixed cerebral palsy.

hemiplegia: Paralysis (or spasticity) on the left or right side of the body.

diplegia: Paralysis (or spasticity) of the legs and partly the arms.

paraplegia: Paralysis (or spasticity) of the legs.

quadriplegia: Paralysis (or spasticity) of both legs and both arms.

orthotics: Various braces or splints that are used to help maintain alignment and decrease the development of contractures.

VIDEO

Parent Interview

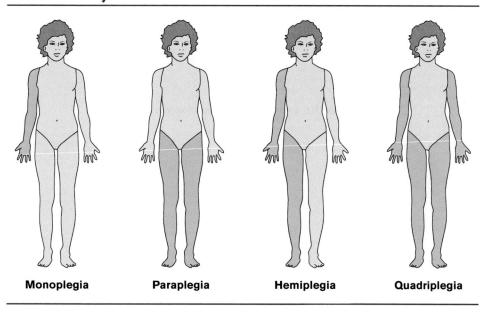

| **Monoplegia** | **Paraplegia** | **Hemiplegia** | **Quadriplegia** |

2. **Spina Bifida.** During the first twenty-eight days of pregnancy, special embryo cells form a closed tube that will become the brain and spinal cord. When this process is interrupted and the tube does not completely close, a congenital abnormality known as a neural tube defect occurs. When it occurs in the area of the spinal cord, a condition known as **spina bifida** results. In the most severe form, myelomeningocele spina bifida, the baby is born with a sac on its back and the spinal cord pouches out into the sac (see Figure 14.2). The spinal cord does not properly function at the point of the sac and below. Surgery will be performed to remove the sac when the infant is born, but the damage to the spinal cord cannot be reversed (Herring, 2007). However, research is being done to determine if the effects of spina bifida can be decreased by closing the defect with prenatal surgery during the second trimester (Management of Myelomeningocele Study, 2010).

The characteristics of myelomeningocele spina bifida depend on the location of the defect. As with a spinal cord injury, there will be a lack of movement and sensation below the area of injury. Although the defect can occur anywhere along the spinal column, it typically occurs in the lower part of the spinal cord. Usually the student will have difficulty walking, but can do so with braces, crutches, or a walker. Some children will need a wheelchair for long distances, and others may only be able to get about using a wheelchair. In addition, many students will need to catheterize themselves to empty their bladder. Also, a high incidence of latex allergies may require latex-free gloves and avoidance of latex products.

Students with spina bifida are at risk for hydrocephalus (a buildup of cerebral spinal fluid in the brain). To treat hydrocephalus, a shunt (small tube) is placed under the skin from the brain and usually into the abdominal area to drain the excess fluid. It is important for teachers to know the signs and symptoms to look for should the shunt become blocked, such as headache, irritability, vomiting, crossed eyes, inability to look up, difficulty swallowing, lethargy, worsening arm or leg function, seizure, and worsening brain function (for example, deterioration in school performance, emotional disturbances, personality change) (Dias, 2013). Sometimes the symptoms are subtle

contractures: Shortened muscles that result in the inability to fully extend a joint.

spina bifida: Failure of the neural tube to completely close during fetal development. In its most severe form, the baby is born with a sac on his or her back containing part of the spinal cord.

Figure 14.2 **Normal Development of the Neural Tube, Normal Spine at Birth, and Spina Bifida**

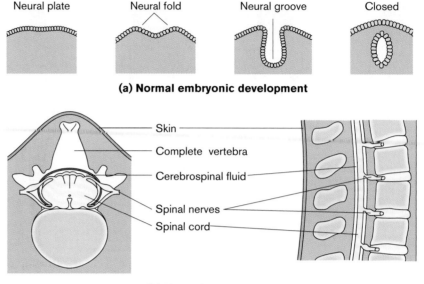

Neural plate   **Neural fold**   **Neural groove**   **Closed**

(a) Normal embryonic development

Skin
Complete vertebra
Cerebrospinal fluid
Spinal nerves
Spinal cord

(b) Normal spine at birth

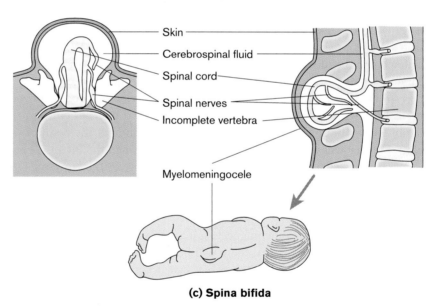

Skin
Cerebrospinal fluid
Spinal cord
Spinal nerves
Incomplete vertebra

Myelomeningocele

(c) Spina bifida

and not easily detected. However, if a shunt blockage is suspected, the teacher will need to notify the appropriate personnel immediately, and the child will need shunt repair surgery.

Many individuals with spina bifida and hydrocephalus are at risk for deficits in executive function, which impacts their learning. This may include deficits in such areas as attention, memory, recall, motor reaction times, visual-perceptual skills, and organizational skills (Heller, 2009c; Iddon, Morgan, Loveday, Sahakian, & Pickard, 2004). Some children with spina bifida have also been found to have difficulty with language comprehension, initiating conversation, maintaining conversations, and exhibiting verbosity (Holck, Nettelbladt, & Sandberg, 2009). Appropriate modifications and instructional strategies are needed to provide an appropriate education for these students.

Degenerative Diseases

The second group of disabilities within the category of orthopedic impairment is degenerative diseases that affect motor movement. Degenerative diseases are typically grouped separately because of their unique and poignant impact on individuals. The student with a degenerative disease will often need increasingly more complex adaptations and assistive technology to permit continued participation in school activities. Teachers are also confronted with emotional issues regarding the loss of capabilities, as well as issues of death and dying. One of the most common degenerative diseases found in the school population is Duchenne muscular dystrophy.

Muscular dystrophy includes a group of inherited diseases that are characterized by progressive muscle weakness from degeneration of the muscle fiber. When an infant is born with Duchenne muscular dystrophy, no disability is initially apparent. Usually by age 3, leg weakness begins to manifest in some problems walking and running; by age 5, walking may appear abnormal. Between ages 5 and 10, there is further weakness of the legs accompanied by arm weakness. Often around 10 or 12 years of age, the child can no longer walk and needs a wheelchair. Through the teenage years, muscle weakness continues; the child will no longer be able to push the wheelchair and will need an electric wheelchair. Over time, it will become increasingly difficult to move the arms or keep the head upright. As the muscles used for breathing weaken, most individuals will develop respiratory infections and die in their late teens or early 20s. It is important to note that only the muscles are degenerating, not the mind.

There is currently no effective treatment for Duchenne muscular dystrophy. The aim of treatment is to try to maintain functioning and help the person walk as long as possible. Physical and occupational therapy are used in an effort to prevent deformity of the legs and arms and may include the use of braces and splints. Medications will be prescribed for a variety of problems, such as respiratory infections, and surgery may be performed to release contractures and prevent early deformity.

Issues of death and dying often come to the surface, and students may want to discuss their fears with a teacher. Teachers need to be good listeners and give these students a chance to discuss their feelings. Programs are also available for students with terminal illness to give them support during this difficult time.

Teachers need to be observant of the disease's progression and let the special educator know if problems are occurring. Often these problems indicate that the student's assistive technology needs to be changed. For example, a student who was using a pencil to write may need to change to a keyboard and then to a smaller adapted keyboard as motor movement is lost and fatigue increases. Teachers need to have a supportive attitude and provide appropriate modifications.

Musculoskeletal Disorders

Students with musculoskeletal disorders greatly vary in the severity of their physical disability. Although some of these conditions can result in severe physical limitations, the person usually does not have cognitive, learning, perceptual, language, or sensory issues to the extent that is found in many neuromotor impairments. Two examples in this category are juvenile idiopathic arthritis and limb deficiencies.

1. **Juvenile Idiopathic Arthritis.** Juvenile idiopathic arthritis (JIA) is a chronic arthritic condition affecting the joints that occurs before 16 years of age and lasts more than 6 weeks. Although there are different types of JIA, the main features are joint effusion (swelling of the joint) that may be accompanied by reduced range of motion, pain on movement, and warmth over the affected joints. Morning stiffness and more prominent pain in the morning or after inactivity are typical. Over time, this disease

Duchenne muscular dystrophy: An inherited disease that is characterized by progressive muscle weakness from the degeneration of the muscle fiber.

juvenile ideopathic arthritis (JIA): A chronic arthritic condition affecting the joints that occurs before 16 years of age.

may go into remission, stabilize, or progress and cause permanent deformity of the joints. The disease may result in additional disabilities, such as contractures, and visual impairments. Treatment of JIA consists of aggressive treatment using a range of medications with an aim of early disease remission (Ostring & Singh-Grewal, 2013).

As with any condition that involves pain, students' learning will be affected when pain is present. Fatigue and lack of stamina may also interfere with learning. Modifications are often made to address these issues. For example, sitting too long can actually be harmful and result in pain when getting up. The student may need to stand or move about periodically in class (such as to sharpen a pencil or go to the board). Pupils with JIA may need to leave class early to get to their next class and avoid jostling in the hallways. If significant joint deformity has occurred, assistive technology (such as an adapted keyboard) may also be needed.

2. **Limb Deficiency.** A **limb deficiency** refers to any number of skeletal abnormalities in which an arm(s) and/or a leg(s) is partially or totally missing. A student may be born missing an arm or a leg or may lose a limb in an accident. Typically, individuals with limb deficiencies will be fitted with a prosthetic device (artificial limb). There are many different types of prosthetic devices with different levels of complexity. A student may have a leg prosthetic that allows for walking and running or an artificial hand that permits grasping and writing. If the limb has been missing from birth, the child may have learned to do things using other limbs. For example, some individuals who are missing both arms can write and feed themselves with their feet. Some students may type with their feet. Whether a prosthetic device is used or not, many students will still require some modifications and may need specialized instruction in such areas as one-handed keyboarding.

Characteristics of Students With Multiple Disabilities

Multiple disabilities is an umbrella term under which various educational, rehabilitation, government, and advocacy groups include different combinations of disabilities. In IDEA, this category refers to persons with concomitant impairments whose needs cannot be met in a special education program designed solely for one of the impairments. Although there is no single definition, the term does imply two or more disabilities whose combination usually creates an interactional, multiplicative effect rather than just an additive one. Some examples include learners with the following conditions:

- Behavior disorders and muscular dystrophy
- Cerebral palsy and seizures
- Deafness and AIDS
- Intellectual disability and spina bifida
- Learning disabilities and asthma

Depending on the type of multiple disabilities, cognitive functioning may vary from giftedness to profound intellectual disability. Usually there will be a need for modifications, assistive technology, and specialized teaching strategies.

Characteristics of Students With Traumatic Brain Injury

Traumatic brain injury refers to temporary or permanent injury to the brain from acquired causes such as car accidents, accidental falls, and gunshot wounds to the head;

limb deficiency: Any number of skeletal abnormalities in which an arm(s) and/or leg(s) is partially or totally missing.

it does not include congenital or degenerative conditions or birth trauma. Approximately 1.7 million people in the United States experience a traumatic brain injury each year (Centers for Disease Control and Prevention, 2013c). Although a person can acquire a traumatic brain injury at any age, one of the highest rates is among teenagers.

The effects of an injury will differ depending on the cause. A penetration injury, such as a bullet going through the brain, will result in certain specific effects. The effects of the injury are usually specific to the site of injury, with secondary effects occurring in other areas as a result of complications.

Traumatic brain injury can also be caused by car accidents and falls. This type of injury, known as an acceleration injury, results in diffuse damage throughout the

Some students may use their feet for such tasks as accessing a communication device.

brain. When the head hits the steering wheel of a car, for example, the brain (which is floating in cerebral spinal fluid) is thrown violently forward against the skull. This initial site of impact is referred to as "coup" (see Figure 14.3). The brain is then thrown backward and hits the back of the skull. This second site of impact is known as "contracoup." The brain continues to move back and forth, hitting against the skull, and suffering further damage against any sharp bony protrusions. Often the brain will be twisting as well, breaking and damaging nerve cells throughout. The result is diffuse damage across the brain. Complications such as hemorrhage (bleeding) and edema (swelling) often cause further damage to the brain.

The effects of a traumatic brain injury range from no ill effects to severe disability. Most head injuries are mild, with no abnormalities found on neurological exams, and the person often does not require medical treatment. Even following a mild injury, however, problems such as headache, fatigue, distractibility, memory problems, and perceptual motor slowing can occur and persist for months, for years, or permanently. These problems often go undetected until difficulties arise during classroom activities. In one case, a girl fell out of a window and was taken to the emergency room. Although she had no apparent damage, she failed the school year. In retrospect, the teacher and parent were able to trace the student's academic difficulties as beginning after the accident and realized that some cognitive deficits must have occurred.

Students with moderate and severe cases of traumatic head injury typically require hospital stays and rehabilitation services before reentering school. The person with a severe traumatic brain injury often enters the hospital in a coma and slowly regains some or most abilities. Typically, motor skills return first, and higher-level cognitive skills return last. Improvement can be a long process, with the most dramatic gains occurring over the first year but skills continuing to improve over about a five-year period.

Some individuals may fully recover from a traumatic brain injury, while others may have permanent disabilities. A traumatic brain injury has the potential for causing lifelong disabilities across physical, cognitive, social, behavioral, health, and sensory domains. In the area of physical disabilities, some individuals are left without the ability to walk or use their hands. However, the permanent physical disability

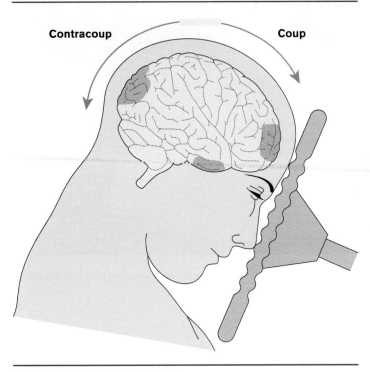

Figure 14.3 **Traumatic Brain Injury**

Contracoup

Coup

SOURCE: Adapted from S. Grandinette and S. Best, "Traumatic Brain Injury," in K. Heller, P. Forney, P. Alberto, S. Best, and M. Schwartzman (Eds.), *Understanding Physical, Health, and Multiple Disabilities,* 2nd ed. (Upper Saddle River, NJ: Pearson Education, 2009), p. 122.

is often more subtle, with decreased motor speed, balance, strength, and coordination (Davis & Dean, 2010; Katz-Leurer, Rotem, Keren, & Meyer, 2009). Although these may seem mild, they can interfere with participation in sports and activities requiring good hand control.

Cognitive deficits can remain after a traumatic brain injury. These can range from severe intellectual disability to mild cognitive impairments. Individuals may have deficits in such areas as sustaining attention, shifting attention, organization, planning, comprehension, and memory (Braine & Smith, 2013; Crowe, Catroppa, Babi, & Anderson, 2013). Impairments in these areas often result in learning problems and difficulty with setting goals, monitoring and evaluating performance, shifting strategies to address a problem, remaining focused over time, and remembering information. Teachers will need to use systematic instruction and specialized strategies to address these problems.

Impairments in social and behavioral functioning are common in individuals with traumatic brain injury. Poor social interactions can occur following a traumatic brain injury with low peer acceptance. Some individuals will have impulsive behavior and episodic aggression (Wood & Thomas, 2013). These types of behaviors are often considered the most challenging to address in the classroom setting. A behavior management plan is usually constructed to provide guidelines for how to address the behavior problems.

During the reauthorization of IDEA in 1990, traumatic brain injury was added as a separate disability category, in part because of its unique and multiple characteristics that can interfere with learning and functioning. These students need to be constantly assessed, because skill levels do improve over time. For example, one student with a three-year-old severe traumatic brain injury was being taught to use pictures to communicate when suddenly she began to laugh at a misspelled word on a bulletin board. She had regained the ability to read most words without anyone realizing it. Unlike those with developmental disabilities, students with traumatic brain injury may be left with "splinter skills," meaning that they have some advanced skills but lack other simple ones. For example, one student with severe traumatic brain injury could identify any number, no matter how large, but had difficulty with the concept that 1 plus 1 equals 2. Teachers need to use various modifications and techniques to address the many problems that can occur in a student with a traumatic brain injury; some sample strategies are provided in the accompanying Suggestions for the Classroom. The special education teacher needs to work closely with the general education teacher in helping to use the most appropriate techniques.

Characteristics of Students With Other Health Impairments

Disabilities that fall under the IDEA category of other health impairment are often divided into two areas: major health impairments and infectious diseases. Students will

VIDEO

A Family's Experience with Traumatic Brain Injury

SUGGESTIONS FOR THE CLASSROOM

Strategies That May Be Used for Students With Traumatic Brain Injury

Impairments	Strategies	Examples
Poor attention	Decrease distractions.	Move away extra pencils.
	Provide cues to attend.	Touch card that says "Listen."
	Limit amount of information.	Divide up information.
	Provide advance organizers.	Give list of important events.
Memory problems	Teach verbal rehearsal strategies.	Student repeats list of people.
	Teach use of visual imagery.	Student visualizes battle for history.
	Provide information in writing.	Give teacher's notes.
	Give a school schedule.	Put pictures by each subject.
	Repeat directions.	Repeat one direction at a time.
Decreased writing speed and accuracy	Give more time on tests.	Student takes test over two periods.
	Decrease assignment load.	Student writes two fewer papers.
	Have student type instead of writing by hand.	Student writes faster using keyboard.
Decreased stamina and endurance	Allow rest breaks.	Student rests for five minutes.
	Adjust school day.	Student comes for half day.
	Have peer carry books.	Friend helps with books.
Impulsive behavior	Encourage "thinking time."	Have student wait, then answer.
	Discuss rules each day.	Review rules.
	Redirect inappropriate behavior.	Tell student to sit, open book.
	Remove unnecessary material.	Book bags are placed at side of room.
	Role-play.	Practice different scenarios.

not typically require special education services unless these conditions are severe. These impairments often result in more absences, fatigue, and decreased stamina.

Major Health Impairments

Many major health impairments fall under the category of other health impairment. Some of these can be treated effectively; others have no cure. Many of them can give rise to emergency situations that need to be handled immediately, and some can result in death. Two of the most commonly occurring health impairments are seizure disorders and asthma.

1. Seizure Disorders. A seizure is a sudden, temporary change in the normal functioning of the brain's electrical system as a result of excessive, uncontrolled electrical activity in the brain. A seizure may be due to a high fever, ingestion of certain drugs or poisons, certain metabolic disorders, or chemical imbalances. Seizures may also be the result of a prenatal or perinatal brain injury, head trauma, infections such as meningitis, congenital malformations, or unknown causes (Porter, 2011). A person has a seizure disorder, also known as epilepsy, when the seizures are recurrent. Often the reason for the seizure disorder is unknown.

Seizures are of many different types, depending on where in the brain the abnormal electrical activity occurs. Seizures may be characterized by altered consciousness, motor activity, sensory phenomena, inappropriate behaviors, or some combination of these. Three of the most commonly encountered seizure disorders are absence seizures, complex partial seizures, and tonic-clonic seizures.

An individual who has absence seizures (formerly known as *petit mal* seizures) will suddenly lose consciousness, stop moving, and stare straight ahead (or the eyes may roll upward). The person will not fall, but simply stop and appear trancelike. Typically, these seizures are brief, lasting only seconds, and interrupt any ongoing activities. They most frequently occur between 4 and 9 years of age (Caraballo et al., 2011). Often the person is not aware of what has happened. When the seizure occurs during a teacher's lecture, the child often doesn't understand why the teacher is suddenly talking about something different. These seizures have been mistaken for daydreaming, but the student cannot be brought out of the seizure by touch or loud voices. Often it is the observant teacher who first detects that something is wrong with the student.

In a complex partial seizure, consciousness is impaired, and the person usually exhibits a series of motor movements that may appear voluntary but are beyond the person's control. For example, some individuals having a complex partial seizure will appear dazed and engage in purposeless activity such as walking aimlessly, picking up objects, or picking at their clothes. Some individuals may start laughing, gesturing, or repeating a phrase. Whatever the person's particular pattern, the same pattern will usually be repeated with each seizure. In other words, if a child walks in a circle when having a complex partial seizure, then that is what his or her seizures are expected to look like each time one occurs.

Tonic-clonic seizures (formerly known as *grand mal* seizures) are typically what people think of when they hear that a person has a seizure disorder. This is a convulsive seizure in which the individual loses consciousness and becomes very stiff. A person who is standing when the seizure occurs will drop to the floor and may sustain injuries from the fall. This stiffness is followed by a jerking phase in which the body makes rhythmic jerking motions that gradually decrease. During this phase, saliva may pool in the mouth and bubble at the lips. Breathing may become shallow or irregular. Usually there is a loss of bladder control. These seizures usually last between two and five minutes. After the seizure, the student may be slightly disoriented at first and not realize what has happened. The person is usually exhausted and will often sleep. There are many misconceptions of what to do when this type of seizure occurs. See the accompanying Suggestions for the Classroom for information on the steps to take when a tonic-clonic seizure occurs.

The most common treatment for seizures is medication. Other treatments may be used when the seizures are severe and cannot be controlled by medication, such as surgery on part of the brain, special diets, and electrical stimulation of the vagus nerve (Majkowska-Zwolińska, Zwoliński, Roszkowski, & Drabik, 2012; Saxena & Nadkarni, 2011). However, these treatments are not always effective, and seizures may still occur.

---

seizure: A sudden, temporary change in the normal functioning of the brain's electrical system due to excessive, uncontrolled electrical activity in the brain.

epilepsy: A chronic condition in which the person has reoccurring seizures.

absence seizure: A type of epileptic seizure lasting for a brief period of time whereby the individual loses consciousness and stops moving, formerly known as a petit mal seizure.

complex partial seizure: A type of epileptic seizure whereby the person exhibits purposeless motor activity for a brief period of time; consciousness is impaired.

tonic-clonic seizure: A convulsive seizure whereby the individual loses consciousness, falls, and begins making rhythmic jerking motions, formerly known as a grand mal seizure.

SUGGESTIONS FOR THE CLASSROOM

Steps for Teachers to Take When a Tonic-Clonic Seizure Occurs

What to Do

- Stay calm; note time of onset.

- Move furniture out of the way to prevent injury.

- Loosen shirt collar and put something soft under head.

- Turn student on his or her side to allow saliva to drain out of mouth.

- If seizure continues more than five minutes, or if multiple seizures occur one right after another, or if this is the first seizure, call for an ambulance.

- If seizure stops but the student is not breathing, give mouth-to-mouth resuscitation (this rarely occurs).

- After the seizure is over, reassure student.

- Allow student to rest.

What *Not* to Do

- Do not put anything in the mouth.

- Do not restrain movements.

- Do not give liquids immediately after seizure.

It is important for teachers to know the steps to take when seizures happen. Often they will have a seizure information sheet to provide them with pertinent information. When a seizure occurs, teachers will often be asked to fill out a seizure report that describes what the seizure looked like, how long it lasted, and what treatment was given. The teacher will also need to be supportive of the child and try to minimize embarrassment (especially when there is a loss of bladder control). Often classmates will think seizures are contagious or their classmate is dead. It is important to help children understand that seizures are not contagious and to explain in simple terms what has happened.

2. **Asthma.** Asthma is the most common pulmonary disease of childhood (American Lung Association, 2012a). Children who have asthma breathe normally until they come in contact with a substance or situation that triggers an asthma attack, such as pollen, air pollution, a respiratory infection, or exercise. When an asthma attack is triggered, the person has difficulty breathing. Symptoms include shortness of breath, wheezing, coughing, and labored breathing.

Asthma is treated by avoiding triggers and taking medication. In some instances, triggers can be removed or reduced. For example, if being close to the classroom hamster triggers an attack, then the hamster should be removed or placed in a different location. If exercise is a trigger, the student may need some modifications in physical education class. Medication may be taken on a regular basis to decrease the possibility of an asthma attack. When an asthma attack occurs, the student often uses a prescribed inhaler (medication delivered in a spray form). It is important that the inhaler be used immediately if an attack occurs, so the inhaler needs to be readily accessible. If the student goes on a field trip, for example, the inhaler needs to go with him or her.

For most students, the asthma attack will stop once the inhaler is used. However, for some pupils, the inhaler will help but not stop the attack. It is very important that all school personnel know what steps to take should an asthma attack occur. Although

asthma: A lung disease with acute attacks of shortness of breath and wheezing.

AUDIO
Asthma

My inspiration and passion for teaching special education stems from a lifetime of experience: growing up with a sister with severe cerebral palsy who spent time in many different programs in the school system. I began my professional career teaching in a K–1 class for students with moderate, severe, and profound intellectual disabilities after graduating with a degree in intellectual disability. After four years in that setting, I completed my master's degree in orthopedic impairments (OI). I then taught students with orthopedic impairments at the high school level for eight years. Most of my students were fully included in the general education curriculum and were college or career bound. Other students were partially included in the general elective curriculum. Since that time, I completed my PhD in physical disabilities and have worked with many educators who teach pupils with orthopedic impairments.

Inclusive Education Experience

In most cases, I favor inclusive education for students whose primary disability is physical. It is much easier to justify making physical modifications and accommodations for access to the general curriculum than it is to justify removing students due to modification and accessibility difficulties. Many different models exist for including students, ranging from intermittent checkups with the teacher to random student observations to having full-time assistance from either the OI teacher or a paraprofessional. Using an inclusion model allows teachers to collaborate, problem-solve, and inspire each other creatively. It also exposes teachers and students to a variety of teaching and learning styles. Because of multiple needs in the classroom, information is often explained in a variety of ways, and information is often presented through different modalities. Many students shine when they are given access to experiences they have not had before because of their physical limitations. Classmates are given the opportunity to look past the students' physical limitations and see their capabilities. The benefits for all students in the inclusive environment are reciprocal.

I have often run into lowered expectations and skepticism about the OI students' abilities. This is when it is necessary to get into the classroom and prove students' capabilities. The negativity usually doesn't last long. Another problem arises when OI students in inclusive environments use assistive technology (AT). Although AT often equalizes access, it can be tremendously frustrating as well. Some of the most common initial problems with inclusive OI are the general education teachers' fears of not being supported, fears of not knowing how to interact or communicate with the student, and concerns over assistive technology use. Associated medical problems can be intimidating as well. One way to overcome these problems is through education, training, and modeling by the OI teacher.

it is rare for an asthma attack to be fatal, it is a possibility. If the student is experiencing severe respiratory problems, an ambulance should be called. When the asthma attack lasts for a long period of time (for example, several days), teachers will need to assist the student in completing missed work.

Infectious Diseases

Several infectious diseases fall under the heading of other health impairment. Some infectious diseases are readily transmittable (such as tuberculosis); others may pose no threat in the school environment (such as AIDS).

Acquired immune deficiency syndrome (AIDS) is one of the newest chronic illnesses of childhood. It is caused by the human immunodeficiency virus (HIV), which destroys the immune system, leaving the person open to serious, life-threatening diseases (such as pneumocystis carinii pneumonia). Transmission generally occurs in one of three ways: (1) having sex with an infected partner, (2) sharing contaminated needles during drug use, and (3) passing on the infection from mother to infant. It cannot be acquired through casual contact because it is only transmitted in blood, semen, vaginal secretions, and breast milk (Best & Heller, 2009a). Because it is not transmitted in saliva, even sharing toothbrushes or kissing will not transmit the infection.

acquired immune deficiency syndrome (AIDS): An infectious disease caused by HIV (human immunodeficiency virus) that destroys the immune system, leaving the person open to serious, life-threatening diseases.

Strategies for Inclusive Classrooms

A good schedule can make it or break it, so scheduling is first and foremost. Schedule your students to allow for the most support from you. This might mean manipulating everyone's schedule multiple times. It is imperative that the lines of communication between collaborating teachers be two-way. It is the responsibility of the special education teacher to communicate the specific needs of the students in the class to the general education teacher. It is not solely the general education teacher's responsibility to provide instruction. Here are some helpful hints:

Provide the general education teacher with IEP-driven modifications and strategies for success as well as emergency plans. Encourage the general education teacher to keep these strategies and plans in his or her grade book or another high-use area for quick reference.

Discuss expectations of the student and each teacher or paraprofessional supporting the student before beginning collaborative teaching.

Successful Collaboration

Successful collaboration means that the teachers have developed a good, professional working relationship and that all students have been enriched by the collaborative activities. This begins with open communication and effective planning. The structure of the class typically comes from the classroom teacher, with adaptations and individualization provided by the OI teacher. It is important, however, for both teachers to be able to switch roles and interact with all students in the class.

Working With Parents and Families

I have had the unique advantage of being on both sides: family and school system. As difficult as it might be, encourage the family to plan for the future early. Along with the parents, define realistic expectations for the students and strive to meet them. Parents know their children better than anyone. Listen to them and be sensitive to their needs. Establish how you will communicate with the parents regarding timelines, grades, progress, and parent-teacher conferences.

Advice for Making Inclusion and Collaboration Work

Transitioning into teaching in the OI classroom can be overwhelming. Teachers are always multitasking, supporting multiple students with multiple disabilities across multiple subjects in the same classroom at the same time. Trying to keep up with the pace of regular education while trying to work in extended time, technology, individualization, and physical access can be a vast undertaking. The best advice is to stay organized and stay focused on the needs of the students and on providing the best education in the most productive and appropriate learning environment possible.

–Jennifer Tumlin Garrett, PhD
Former teacher of students with orthopedic impairments
Currently assistant professor, Georgia State University

Some students are born with the infection from an infected mother; adolescents may acquire the infection from sex with an infected partner or by sharing needles during drug use. Children born with HIV may have developmental delays, motor problems, nervous system damage, and additional infections. Adolescents acquiring the disease may also develop life-threatening infections, nervous system abnormalities, and other impairments (such as visual impairments). Treatment consists of a combination of medications that may slow the disease's effect on the immune system. However, the disease is considered terminal in most cases.

Often children with AIDS will not initially need any modifications in the school setting. However, as the disease progresses, they will require some modifications because of fatigue and frequent absences. A supportive attitude should be in place, especially given the social stigma surrounding the disease. Misconceptions that students or teachers have should be dispelled with accurate information.

Characteristics of Students With Deaf-Blindness

Describing the characteristics of pupils with deaf-blindness is a difficult task. This is an extremely heterogeneous population varying tremendously in individuals' needs, abilities, and educational requirements. Students with deaf-blindness vary in their combinations of hearing and vision loss, and range from normal or gifted intelligence to severe intellectual disability. They may also have additional disabilities (for example, cerebral palsy, seizures) (Downing & Eichinger, 2011).

As we stated at the beginning of this discussion, in addition to impaired hearing and vision, large numbers of students who are deaf and blind exhibit cognitive deficits (66%), physical impairments (57%), or complex health needs (38%) (Killoran, 2007). Speech and language impairments are also typical of individuals who are deaf-blind. Behavioral and social difficulties often accompany deaf-blindness. These deficits are frequently a result of the person's inability to understand language and effectively communicate with others (Miles, 2013). In addition to problems with communication, difficulties navigating the environment are common. The restrictions and challenges represented by these two areas usually lead to feelings of isolation among children and adults who are deaf-blind.

Assessment of Physical Disabilities, Health Disabilities, and Related Low-Incidence Disabilities

In order to qualify for special education services, students with a physical or health disability need to have a thorough assessment. The assessment will determine whether they qualify for special education services, and which ones are needed. The assessment for initial eligibility typically involves a medical evaluation and a series of educational evaluations. Depending on the student's medical condition and school functioning, other assessments involving related services and assistive technology will need to be performed.

First and foremost, a student will need a medical evaluation by a licensed physician that provides a diagnosis of the student's physical or health condition. The medical evaluation will typically include important information such as medications, surgeries, special health care procedures, and special diet or activity restrictions. Any sensory deficits should also be noted.

Once a medical diagnosis confirms a physical or health disability, a determination needs to be made as to whether the disability negatively affects the student's educational performance. A comprehensive educational assessment (or, for preschool children, a developmental assessment) will be performed to determine the effects of the physical or health disability. The precise educational assessment instruments will vary according to the student's age and abilities. Assessments will document deficits in areas such as preacademic functioning, academic functioning, adaptive behavior, motor development, language and communication skills, and social-emotional development.

A psychological evaluation may be given if there is a significant deficit in academic or cognitive functioning. However, it is often very difficult to evaluate cognitive functioning (possible intellectual disability) when the student has severe physical disabilities and is unable to speak. This is especially the case when the student has not yet learned to use a communication device, or cannot do so reliably because of severe motor constraints. Psychological and educational misdiagnosis and misplacement do occur, as they did in the case of Natalie.

If the educational evaluations demonstrate that the student's physical or health disability is affecting his or her educational performance, a decision will be made as to which educational category the student qualifies for: orthopedic impairment, multiple disabilities, traumatic brain injury, or other health impairment. Additional assessments will be performed based on the medical and educational evaluations. If the physician

VIDEO

Educational Placement

orders physical or occupational therapy, for example, the student will need to have assessments in these areas. If the student qualifies for speech-language pathology services, assessments will occur in that area as well. If the student has a physical disability, an assistive technology assessment may be performed by the special education teacher in conjunction with the educational team, or the school system may have a specialist or team of specialists in that area. If the student requires specialized health care procedures, such as tube feeding, an individual health (or health care) plan will be developed, and the student will be assessed to determine if he or she can be taught to self-perform the procedure. Depending on the student's needs, other assessments may be performed to provide appropriate educational services to the student.

Assessment of Students With Deaf-Blindness

The low-incidence nature of deaf-blindness coupled with the scarcity of appropriate assessment instruments presents a unique set of challenges to teachers and other professionals (Silberman et al., 2004). A team of individuals is typically needed to accurately assess the student with deaf-blindness. Valid assessment of individuals with deaf-blindness dictates collaboration among family members and professionals. The key is to conduct multiple assessments over both time and contexts.

Unfortunately, norm-referenced assessments are of little value when assessing pupils with deaf-blindness. Criterion-referenced tests, developmental scales (frequently normed on children without disabilities), and informal observations often yield useful information but may still have limitations. Experts recommend that assessments focus on what the child *has* learned as well as what he or she *needs* to learn (Silberman et al., 2004). Teachers may use authentic assessment to gain useful information. This involves obtaining information about the child during normal activities and across environments to determine what the student knows and the types of situations and settings that assist the child with deaf-blindness to learn (Malloy, 2010; Rowland, 2009). Also, tools are available to assess pupils that focus on desired outcomes. For example, the Assessment Intervention Matrix (Wolf-Schein & Schein, 2009) focuses on basic daily living skills as well as housekeeping and food preparation.

Educational Considerations

Educational considerations for individuals with physical or health disabilities include the setting in which each pupil can receive an appropriate education, the impact of the physical or health disability on the student's school performance, and the best ways of meeting his or her needs in the educational setting.

Where Are Students With Physical or
Health Disabilities Educated?

Students with physical and health disabilities are educated in a variety of settings. Settings can range from a regular classroom to a homebound or hospital setting, with several other settings in between (such as resource room, separate class, separate school, and residential facility). The appropriate setting is determined by the educational team, based on student assessments, educational goals, and planned interventions. For example, one student with cerebral palsy who is nonverbal may need special education services addressing reading and writing; this student may go to a resource room for the majority of the day to learn how to use an assistive technology device and receive specialized instruction. A second pupil with cerebral palsy may just need monitoring in regular education classes. A third student with cerebral palsy may be several grade levels behind across all areas; this individual may need to be in a separate class to meet his or her educational goals. Some children may have such severe health problems that homebound instruction is necessary; in this case, a teacher goes to the student's house to provide instruction.

Educational placement of students with physical and health disabilities varies greatly across the IDEA categories of orthopedic impairment, multiple disabilities, traumatic brain injury, other health impairment, and deaf-blindness (see Figure 14.4). The largest number of students with orthopedic impairments are educated in the regular classroom (54.0%), followed by a separate class (22.2%) and resource room (16.3%). This is not surprising, as most of this population does not have additional cognitive impairments. However, when the student's physical disability is severe, additional support is needed and may be provided in a resource room or separate class.

In contrast, the most common placement for students with multiple disabilities is a separate class (46.2%), followed by a separate school (19.2%), and then resource room (16.3%). Students with multiple disabilities often have severe physical disabilities with concomitant severe intellectual disability. Although many states are trying to phase out separate schools, they remain part of the range of options available to students.

Students with traumatic brain injury vary greatly in the severity of injury and its effects on the individual. Slightly more than five out of ten pupils with traumatic brain injury are served in the regular or general education classroom, with placement in a resource room (16.3%) or separate class (22.2%) about equally split. Functioning often improves during the first few years after injury, and the educational placement will typically change over a fairly short period of time.

Like pupils with orthopedic impairments, students with other health impairments are most likely to be educated in the regular classroom (63.4%). However, frequent absences, fatigue, inattention, pain, and other health-related factors often result in a need for placement in a resource room (22.6%) or separate class (9.9%).

At this time, individuals who are deaf-blind are often educated in more restrictive settings. Only about one out of four students (27.0%) is educated in the regular classroom, while over half of these pupils receive a special education in either a separate class (32.5%) or a separate school (18.0%).

Impact on School Performance

Several variables affect school performance for a student with a physical or health disability according to the Physical and Health Disabilities Performance Model (Heller, 2009a). These variables can be divided into three major areas: type of disability, functional effects, and psychosocial and environmental factors (see Figure 14.5). Students with physical or health disabilities will typically have one or more problems in each of these major areas, and their interaction can negatively affect the students' school performance. A better understanding of these areas and how they affect each child's school performance will help the teacher and the educational team make appropriate decisions regarding educational objectives and necessary modifications.

The first major area to affect student performance is the type of disability. Pupils with orthopedic impairments, for example, will often have problems accessing materials while students with other health impairments are more likely to have problems of endurance and stamina. The severity of the specific disability will also be a factor. The teacher will need to be familiar with the student's specific disability, its severity, and its implications for academic performance.

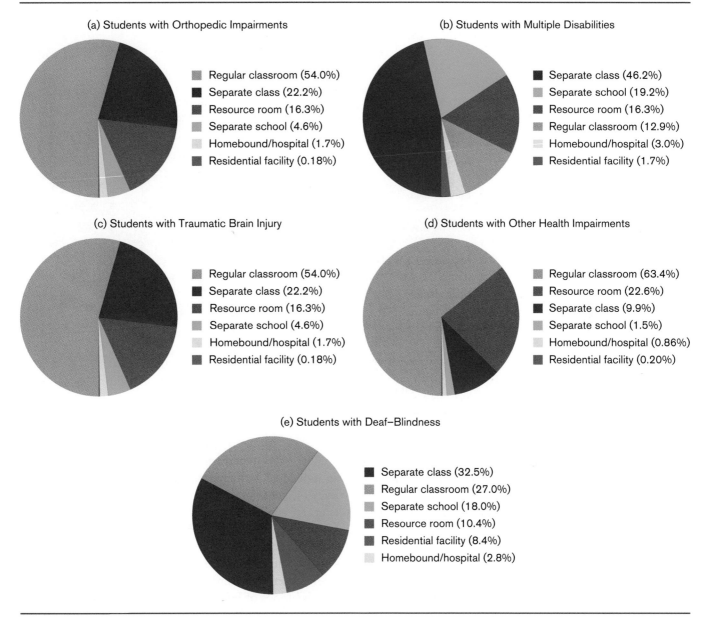

(a) Students with Orthopedic Impairments

- Regular classroom (54.0%)
- Separate class (22.2%)
- Resource room (16.3%)
- Separate school (4.6%)
- Homebound/hospital (1.7%)
- Residential facility (0.18%)

(b) Students with Multiple Disabilities

- Separate class (46.2%)
- Separate school (19.2%)
- Resource room (16.3%)
- Regular classroom (12.9%)
- Homebound/hospital (3.0%)
- Residential facility (1.7%)

(c) Students with Traumatic Brain Injury

- Regular classroom (54.0%)
- Separate class (22.2%)
- Resource room (16.3%)
- Separate school (4.6%)
- Homebound/hospital (1.7%)
- Residential facility (0.18%)

(d) Students with Other Health Impairments

- Regular classroom (63.4%)
- Resource room (22.6%)
- Separate class (9.9%)
- Separate school (1.5%)
- Homebound/hospital (0.86%)
- Residential facility (0.20%)

(e) Students with Deaf–Blindness

- Separate class (32.5%)
- Regular classroom (27.0%)
- Separate school (18.0%)
- Resource room (10.4%)
- Residential facility (8.4%)
- Homebound/hospital (2.8%)

NOTE: Figure represents percentages of enrollment of students with physical disabilities, health disabilities, and deaf-blindness during the 2011–2012 school year. Excludes pupils enrolled in parentally placed private schools and individuals in correctional facilities.

SOURCE: U.S. Department of Education. (2013). *Historical state-level IDEA data files.* Retrieved October 19, 2013, from http://tadnet.public.tadnet.org/pages/712

The second area that affects student performance is the functional effects of the disability on each particular student. This area is divided into seven categories: (1) atypical movements and motor abilities, (2) sensory loss, (3) communication impairments, (4) fatigue and lack of endurance, (5) health factors, (6) experiential deficits, and (7) cognitive impairments and processing issues (Heller, 2009a). The student's disability, its severity, and how it affects the particular student will determine which of these seven categories is a factor in affecting school performance. Several examples of how these areas can affect school performance are given in Table 14.3.

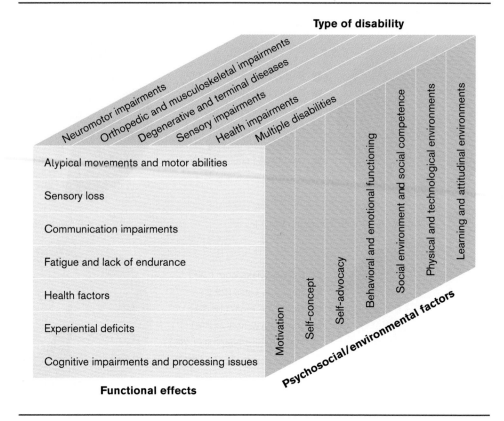

The third area that can affect school performance—the third dimension in Figure 14.5—consists of seven individual and environmental factors: (1) motivation, (2) self-concept, (3) self-advocacy, (4) behavioral and emotional functioning, (5) social environment and social competence, (6) physical and technological environments, and (7) learning and attitudinal environments (Heller, 2009a). Each of these is shaped by the pupil's personality, the student's reaction to his or her disability, and the reactions of those in the student's environment. Also, the availability of technological and educational support and an accessible environment are important factors. Table 14.4 provides several examples and explanations of how these factors can affect school performance.

Meeting Educational Needs

Meeting the educational needs of students with physical or health disabilities requires several types of modifications. These will be discussed under four main headings: (1) physical/health monitoring, (2) modifications and adaptations, (3) specialized instructional strategies, and (4) specialized expanded curriculum areas.

Physical/Health Monitoring

It is the responsibility of teachers and school officials to maintain a safe, healthy environment for their students (DPHD Critical Issues and Leadership Committee, 2013). Maintaining a safe, healthy environment includes having efficient evacuation plans,

VIDEO

Social Factors

■ ■ ■ ■ ■ Table 14.3 **Impact on School Performance: Functional Effects**

Functional Effects of the Disability	Examples of How School Performance Can Be Affected
1. Atypical Movements and Motor Abilities	Inaccurate, difficult, slow, or restricted arm movements can negatively affect access to school materials (for example, inability to use a keyboard). Even with proper adaptations, school performance may be affected (for example, can only type 12 words a minute with an adapted keyboard).
2. Sensory Loss	Many physical disabilities have an increased incidence of sensory impairments (for example, vision loss), which can impact student performance.
3. Communication Impairments	Even with an augmentative communication device, asking questions and answering questions may be limited due to what is programmed into the device or due to the student still learning to use the device accurately.
4. Fatigue and Lack of Endurance	For some students, fatigue can be so severe that they need rest breaks throughout the day or a shortened school day, which can impact the amount of school material learned.
5. Health Factors	Students experiencing pain or discomfort from their conditions (for example, juvenile idiopathic arthritis) or from their devices (for example, poorly fitted wheelchair) will not be able to attend well to the lessons being taught. Frequent illness or surgeries may also result in extended absences.
6. Experiential Deficits	Some students with physical disabilities will lack common experiences due to physical or motor issues that their peers usually have acquired. These missed experiences or concepts can be important for school success.
7. Cognitive Impairments and Processing Issues	Although students with physical disabilities can be gifted or have IQs in the normal range of intelligence, there is an increase of cognitive impairments and processing issues (for example, memory, organization, perception, motor planning) with certain physical disabilities that will affect school performance.

school emergency procedures, proper infection control procedures, and teachers trained in CPR and first aid.

Teachers must know what type of medical condition each student has, how to monitor the student's physical or health impairment for problems, and what to do if a problem occurs. For example, if a pupil has a generalized tonic-clonic seizure, the teacher should have a plan in place and be able to immediately assist the student. In this example, immediate action is needed. Some monitoring may be more subtle, such as picking up signs that the student with muscular dystrophy is deteriorating and may need further modifications. Some children may have health care procedures such as tube feeding (being fed through a tube that goes into the stomach) or suctioning (inserting a tube to get out respiratory secretions), and the teacher should know what to do if any problems occur due to the health care procedure (Heller & Avant, 2011). Good communication and collaboration with the nurse, special education teacher, parents, and team will be important in planning for any anticipated problems that might arise.

Modifications and Adaptations

Several modifications and adaptations may be needed to ensure that students with physical or health impairments are getting what they need to succeed in school. Major areas of concern include environmental arrangement, communication, instructional and curricular modifications, modifications and assistive technology for specific content areas, class participation, assignments and classroom tests, and sensory and perceptual modifications.

Psychosocial and Environmental Factors	Examples of How School Performance Can Be Affected
1. Motivation	Lack of motivation may be present due to other priorities over health issues or degenerative changes. Students may also lack motivation due to learned helplessness. These would all affect school performance.
2. Self-Concept	A poor self-concept may occur due to difficulty mastering tasks from the effects of a physical disability or due to the way others treat the student. This may interfere with school performance.
3. Self-Advocacy	Students who do not do not operate/act as advocates for themselves in the classroom may not have adequate access to material to succeed in school (for example, student with a severe physical impairment can't see the board due to poor wheelchair positioning and does not ask to be repositioned). Lack of self-advocacy skills can also be life threatening (for example, student with diabetes does not tell substitute teacher she has to have a snack).
4. Behavior and Emotional Functioning	A negative impact on school performance often occurs with students who have difficulty coping with their disability and who exhibit such emotional problems as depression, anger, or hopelessness.
5. Social Environment and Social Competence	Students may have difficulty socializing due to misunderstandings about their disability or due to delayed or maladaptive social functioning. A poor social environment may impact the student's performance in school.
6. Physical and Technological Environments	If proper accommodations and assistive technology are not in place for students with physical disabilities, their ability to succeed in the school environment will be negatively impacted.
7. Learning and Attitudinal Environments	Performance may be affected if there are negative attitudes toward the student or if proper educational supports and adaptations are not in place.

Often the special education teacher completes a checklist of needed modifications for each student with a physical or health disability and then discusses it with the general education teacher and other school personnel. Using a checklist helps ensure that a variety of modifications have been considered and that everyone is using the same modifications across environments.

1. Environmental Arrangements. Several types of environmental modifications may be needed to accommodate a student with a physical or health impairment. Fatigue or endurance issues may necessitate a modified day, rest breaks, or classrooms in close proximity. A pupil with very severe health issues may need a homeroom near an exit for easy access to an ambulance. In the classroom, a student may need widened aisles for wheelchair access or preferential seating in order to see the teacher or the board. In some cases, the student will need a special chair or desk to accommodate physical limitations. An individual with restricted or impaired arm movement may need classroom materials to be positioned in a certain location or stabilized so they do not roll around.

communication: The sharing or exchange of ideas, information, thoughts, and feelings. Does not necessarily require speech or language.

2. Communication. Most pupils with physical and health disabilities will not need any adaptations in the area of communication. However, students with conditions such as severe cerebral palsy will often have speech that is not understandable. In our chapter opener, Natalie was able to communicate approximately thirty

VIDEO
Modifications

words or sounds that could mean up to two hundred different things depending on the context. Her use of an augmentative communication device opened up her world by allowing others to understand her.

It is very important that the teacher understand how the student communicates and how the teacher should present questions. Augmentative communication devices, for example, may range from a notebook with pictures to electronic devices with voice output, and may be used along with various sounds or words that the student can say. However, some pupils may not be able to use their communication device very reliably when they are still learning how to use it. The teacher may be instructed to ask questions giving answers in a multiple-choice format when calling on these students.

Classrooms, and other environments, must be arranged so as to allow ease of access for students with physical and health disabilities.

For example, the teacher may ask the class, "On which mountain did the expedition take place?" Susan, a student with severe cerebral palsy, indicates she knows the answer. The teacher calls on her and asks, "Susan, is it (a) Mount Rainier, (b) Annapurna, (c) Mount Saint Helens, or (d) Mount Everest?" Upon hearing the correct one, Susan points to the *d* on her board to indicate her answer. The best way for communication to take place in the classroom setting will be discussed between the special and general education teachers and, once agreed upon, recorded on the modification checklist.

3. **Instructional and Curricular Modifications.** Often individuals with physical and health disabilities will require instructional and curricular modifications. Modifications in this area may include providing a study outline, extra repetition, or more frequent feedback. Students with physical disabilities who have speech impairments are often behind in their reading and may require material at a lower grade level. This may involve providing outlines at a reading level that the pupil can understand or using alternative textbooks that are easier to follow. Sometimes individual instruction from a special education teacher will be needed. Materials may need to be altered for accessibility (such as a larger calculator with bigger keys), and the curriculum may need to be altered to address the student's educational needs. Some students may need help with organizational skills, and others may need two sets of books because they are not physically capable of carrying their books back and forth between home and school.

4. **Modifications and Assistive Technology for Specific Content Areas.** Often students will require modifications or assistive technology to access different school subjects. For example, to make a computer accessible for writing, some students with cerebral palsy may need to use a larger keyboard with bigger keys to correctly select the one they want. A student with a spinal cord injury may access the keyboard by using a voice recognition program in which the words appear on the screen as the student speaks into a microphone. In Natalie's case, she needed to use her

augmentative communication device as a keyboard that connected to the computer in order to write.

5. **Class Participation.** Some modifications may be needed to allow a student with a physical or health disability to participate in class. It is important to determine how the pupil will gain the teacher's attention, especially if he is unable to raise his hand. Some students may need extra time to respond to a question in class because of motor difficulties using an augmentative communication system. Some teachers will patiently wait for the response. Others may elect to give the student some questions that will be asked the next day in class so the student can program his or her augmentative communication device with the answers. For some students, it is more appropriate to ask questions using a multiple-choice format, as described previously.

6. **Assignments and Tests.** Some learners will need assignments and tests modified because of fatigue and endurance issues—either because of a health problem or because of the physical effort involved in slowly completing an assignment or a test. Assignments may need to be abbreviated or broken up into shorter segments, or students may need extra time to complete assignments and tests. A pupil may be offered alternative ways to complete an assignment or a test, such as using a computer or telling the answers instead of writing them. Students may be unable to complete several essay questions because of the time and effort it takes to complete one question; a student with severe spastic quadriplegic cerebral palsy, for example, may take twenty minutes to type two sentences when using an alternative access mode for a computer. In these cases, the individual may be given an alternative format such as multiple choice or short answer.

7. **Other Modifications.** Some students may need modifications or assistance in the areas of mobility, using the bathroom, and eating. If a party is given in class, the teacher needs to know if a student needs a special spoon or a special feeding technique. If a pupil needs to use the restroom, the teacher needs to know if the student cannot get onto the toilet without help. Advanced planning is necessary to determine what type of help a student needs and who will provide that help.

Specialized Instructional Strategies

Teachers need to know how to implement specialized instructional strategies for students with physical and health disabilities. Such strategies include using special techniques for teaching nonverbal students phonics, adapting assessment procedures, utilizing the student's reliable means of response, using alternative approaches for learning the writing process when alternative-access keyboarding is slow, and supporting chronically ill and terminally ill children. For example, when teaching students with severe speech and physical impairments to sound out a word, the special education teacher may use the Nonverbal Reading Approach (Heller & Alberto, 2010), which teaches the individual who cannot talk to sound out the word using internal speech. Certain math algorithms that do not involve carrying a number may be advantageous for students using computers to write out their work (Heller, 2010). The special education teacher often uses these specialized approaches when teaching students with physical or health disabilities and will instruct other teachers regarding their use.

Teachers also need to know how to implement specialized strategies to prevent communication breakdowns. Often teachers and students who are using augmentative communication devices will have a communication breakdown—a misunderstanding or misinterpretation of what is being communicated. Heller and Bigge (2010) provide an example of a student (S) who was telling about a party at school, including

specialized instructional strategies: Teaching techniques specifically designed for a particular special education population to assist with learning specific material.

communication breakdown: Misunderstanding as to what is being communicated, especially as it relates to individuals who are using some form of augmentative communication.

the refreshments, activities, and people invited. The Boy Scout master (BSM) listened to the details and said, "You must have enjoyed that."

S: No.

BSM: You didn't?

S: No.

BSM: But you told me all about it. Did something bad happen?

S: No.

BSM: But you didn't enjoy it?

S: No.

BSM: Well, you did go, didn't you?

S: No.

BSM: You didn't! Why not? Were you somewhere else?

S: No.

BSM: Were you ill?

S: No.

BSM: I don't get it, then. (p. 272)

In this example, the student was trying to tell the Boy Scout master about a party that his class had planned, but that had not yet taken place. The Boy Scout master assumed that the party had already occurred.

Several strategies can be used to avoid a communication breakdown. The first is to be aware that you may be making an erroneous assumption that is leading to the breakdown. It is important to clarify or check each part of the information as it is being presented ("We are talking about a party?" "Yes." "At school?" "Yes." "That your class had?" "No."). Another strategy is to ask, "Am I missing something?" and then ask by categories, "Is it a person?" "A place?" "A feeling?" "A time?" and so on. It is also important to verify by asking, "Is that exactly right?" This will help ensure that you are understanding the message correctly. It is equally important that the student have a way of saying, "You are not understanding my message" (Heller & Bigge, 2010).

Specialized Expanded Curriculum Areas

The individualized education program (IEP) team will determine the appropriate goals for a student with a physical or health disability. In some cases, a student will be on a regular academic curriculum; in others, a student with intellectual disability may be in a functional curriculum. In either case, students may be taught additional curricular areas, referred to as *specialized expanded curriculum areas*. These areas often pertain to the technology they use, the adaptations they will need for independent living, and the health care they need because of their particular physical or health disability. For example, students may be taught to use their assistive technology and augmentative communication devices. Pupils who require health care procedures (such as tube feeding for nutrition) may be taught how to do the procedure themselves, along with other management issues related to the procedure (Heller & Avant, 2011). Independent living skills (such as cooking, cleaning, shopping, and dressing) often require adaptations, and

Recommended Classroom Adaptations

- Students with physical and health disabilities often require adaptations to accommodate their specific disabilities. This can include adaptations to the environment, instructional materials, and teaching strategies. Some effective practices are as follows:

- Make classroom adaptations to accommodate students' mobility and seating needs (e.g., widened aisles for wheelchairs, sit near side of room to see board and access computer, special desk).

- Use and properly arrange adaptations and assistive technology as determined by the special education teacher and educational team to provide access to the learning environment (e.g., slant board and stabilization of material on desk, alternative keyboard, augmentative communication device, books and worksheets scanned into the computer).

- Assist students with physical disabilities to participate as much as possible in classroom activities requiring a motor response (e.g., bring needed items to student, help student manipulate materials, partner student with peer to assist each other with task).

- Use a variety of systematic instructional strategies that effectively address the student's individual learning needs (e.g., learning strategies, content enhancement strategies, antecedent prompts, response prompts).

- Use specialized instructional strategies specifically developed for students with physical disabilities as appropriate (e.g., teach students who are nonverbal to use internal speech to decode words as in the Nonverbal Reading Approach).

- Assist students who use augmentative forms of communication to learn to use their communication devices successfully across learning and social environments during the school day. Also, allow students to answer questions using their most reliable form of communication.

- Allow more time for the student to respond, take tests, or hand in assignments when oral or written communication is affected by his or her disability.

- Modify assignments or tests to accommodate student's disability (e.g., reduce paper tasks, break up assignments into shorter segments, alternate test or assignment format).

- Maintain a safe, healthy environment by observing for health-related problems and knowing the steps to take should a problem occur (e.g., seizure, fatigue, medication side effects).

SOURCE: Adapted from K. Heller and M. Coleman-Martin, "Classroom Adaptations for Students with Physical, Health, and Multiple Disabilities," in K. Heller, P. Forney, P. Alberto, S. Best, and M. Schwartzman (Eds.), *Understanding Physical, Health, and Multiple Disabilities,* 2nd ed. (Upper Saddle River, NJ: Pearson Education, 2009).

---

students may be taught how to perform these tasks with the necessary modifications. Other possible specialized expanded curriculum areas include social skills, vocational skills, community skills, mobility skills, and leisure skills.

Meeting the Educational Needs of Students Who Are Deaf-Blind

Pupils who are deaf-blind frequently present a variety of instructional challenges for educators. The impact of the loss (or diminished capacity) of both vision and hearing results in significant educational needs. As a result, there are several important areas of instruction for these students, such as teaching concepts and curricular content utilizing effective instructional strategies and adaptations, promoting effective communication, and teaching about the environment and navigation of the environment.

VIDEO

Deaf-Blindness

Individuals with deaf-blindness require adjustments to materials and intervention strategies to accommodate their specific needs. This may include enhancing visual, auditory, and/or tactile stimuli; using tactile techniques; targeting visual and auditory skills within meaningful contexts; and teaching in small groups, in addition to one-to-one instruction (Downing & Eichinger, 2011). Children and youth with deaf-blindness often will have difficulty learning despite these adaptations due to an inability to access enough information to fully understand what is going on around them. To address this problem, some students will have an **intervener**. An intervener is a trained individual who usually works individually with the student and facilitates access of environmental information and facilitates communication (Alsop et al., 2012; Alsop, Blaha, & Kloos, 2000).

As with instruction of other students, the education of pupils with deaf-blindness addresses all domains of learning from concept development to academic subjects. Communication/language, however, is typically a priority area of these students since it is often affected by hearing and vision loss. Effective communication instruction becomes essential to meet their needs.

Communication

Learning to communicate without the ability to hear is probably the most significant challenge that students with deaf-blindness will encounter. Yet it is also their greatest opportunity—for language opens the world to them (Alabama Institute for Deaf and Blind, 2013). Pupils who are deaf-blind vary tremendously in their communication abilities and consequently their educational needs. Recall that many of these children have some residual hearing and vision, and a few are capable of speech. In many instances, however, touch, gestures, and body movements are the primary form of communication, although some individuals will learn more complex forms of communication, such as sign language.

Because communication is critical to all activities at school, at home, and in the community, it is imperative that the pupil develop an effective and efficient system of communication. This may entail acquiring tactile means of receptive and expressive communication or developing the student's residual vision and hearing for purposes of communication. Multiple forms of communication are available to both teachers and parents. For instance, if vision is sufficient, some students who are deaf-blind will use the standard manual alphabet (see Figure 12.5, page 422). However, if the pupil's vision is inadequate, the alphabet can be traced in the palm of the individual's hand.

Some of the principal communication systems used with individuals who are deaf-blind include the following:

- Braille
- Fingerspelling
- Large print
- Multiple versions of sign language
- Object symbols (using an object to represent item or activity, for example, spoon represents lunch)
- Picture symbols
- Speechreading
- Touch cues (using touch to represent an item or activity, for example, touch back of hand for "give me") (Miles, 2013)

As the student gains competency with nonverbal interactions, symbolic communication becomes a frequent adjunct to the student's system of communication. It is

intervener: A person with specialized training and skills in deaf-blindness who provides individualized assistance to students.

REFERENCE

Deaf-Blindness

often beneficial to incorporate simple gestures or objects that serve as representations or symbols for various activities. For example, a spoon may indicate mealtime, a small rubber ball could represent recess, and a sweater might mean dismissal time. These representations help the pupil understand that one thing may represent another while also enabling the child to anticipate specific events. Reliable routines are particularly important to individuals who are deaf-blind since they enhance understanding and can reduce anxiety.

Orientation and Mobility

Being able to safely and independently navigate the environment (at school, at home, and in the community) is another major area of emphasis for individuals who are deaf-blind. Mobility training becomes a significant instructional challenge for the orientation and mobility (O&M) specialist when the student exhibits a dual sensory impairment. In some instances, a lack of motivation to explore the world coupled with difficulty in establishing an effective means of communication is but one obstacle confronting this professional. Generally speaking, the earlier the instruction begins, the greater the likelihood that the pupil will be able to successfully move about with confidence and independence.

Collaborative Efforts

It should be obvious from our discussion of these two key areas that multiple professionals are involved in the education of persons with deaf-blindness. It is not unusual to find vision teachers, O&M specialists, interpreters, physical and occupational therapists, special education teachers, and other professionals all working together to ensure that the individual needs of the pupil are fully met in an integrated and coordinated fashion. Collaboration is imperative for meeting these students' needs.

Services for Young Children With Physical Disabilities, Health Disabilities, and Related Low-Incidence Disabilities

Like all school-age children, young children with physical disabilities, health disabilities, and related low-incidence disabilities typically need a collaborative approach utilizing expertise from a variety of disciplines. Professional staff, such as physical therapists, occupational therapists, speech-language pathologists, special education teachers, preschool teachers, adapted physical education teachers, nurses, and physicians, as well as families, may be involved in the education of the young child with physical or health disabilities. This team of individuals will determine the major goals and objectives for the young child, including a safe and healthy environment, motor development and positioning, communication development, concept development, and early academic and functional skills.

Maintaining a safe, healthy environment involves special considerations for the young child. Young children may not understand why they have certain restrictions (such as restricted sweets if they have diabetes) or the exact nature of their disability (what is happening when they have a seizure, and why). The teacher needs to understand what restrictions are necessary and help the young child comply with them. Also, some young children may have the misconception that they have a particular condition because they did something bad. The teacher should be alert for such misconceptions and notify the parents.

Children with physical disabilities, multiple disabilities, and deaf-blindness often show delays or little progress in motor development—rolling over, sitting, crawling, walking, reaching for items, grasping items—and may receive the services of a physical therapist and an occupational therapist. These professionals can provide positioning suggestions and equipment, mobility devices, adaptive toys, devices for daily living (such as adapted feeding utensils and toothbrushes), and orthotics (such as leg braces). They may suggest changes in the environment to eliminate architectural barriers as they seek to integrate therapy intervention strategies into the child's daily routines (Effgen, 2012). Teachers will often integrate some of the therapy goals and objectives into the preschool classroom.

When young children with physical disabilities have communication problems, one of the major emphases of early intervention is to promote communication. It is often difficult to determine if a child will be understandable using speech or if the child will require an augmentative communication system. To encourage communication and decrease frustration, augmentative communication may be combined with speech therapy, giving the child a means of communicating while also working on speech production.

Some parents may not want their child to use augmentative communication for fear that it will hinder speech production and reduce their child's motivation to speak. Augmentative communication is never meant to replace speech, but meant to supplement it. There are no data to support the idea that augmentative and alternative communication interferes with speech production; in fact, research studies suggest just the opposite (Kaiser & Grim, 2006; Sevcik & Romski, 2010).

Because many young children with physical disabilities, health disabilities, and related low-incidence disabilities lack common experiences or the ability to manipulate common items, teachers will often need to work on concept development. Although concept development (for example, *round versus square, colors*) is typically addressed with the preschool child, even more basic concepts may need to be addressed with the child with a severe physical disability. Concepts such as "an orange is soft, not hard like a rock," or "a sponge can be squeezed" may need to be introduced. Failure to address these basic concepts can interfere with comprehension of material that will be addressed later in the school curriculum.

Children with physical disabilities, health disabilities, and related low-incidence disabilities will be participating in all or part of the preschool curriculum, and it is important that appropriate adaptations and modifications be in place. For coloring and drawing, for example, the child may need an adapted crayon or may begin using a simple drawing program on a computer. The special education teacher, with input from other members of the educational team, will assist in determining the appropriate modifications and assistive technology.

Transition Into Adulthood

As students with physical disabilities, health disabilities, and related low-incidence disabilities transition into adulthood, they often face major decisions regarding college, employment, and independent living. Hopefully, these issues have been discussed for many years with preparations made well in advance to make a smooth transition from high school to the next environment. Through the help of transition planning, legislation, technological advances, and options for support, more opportunities now exist for individuals with physical and health disabilities than ever before.

With the passage of PL 101–476, each adolescent's IEP is required to include a transition plan. A transition plan identifies goals specific to that student aimed at meeting the student's needs after high school. Identification of transition needs and services is part of the planning process. Successful transition plans often base their programs

transition plan: *See* individualized transition plan.

VIDEO
Individual Interview

REFERENCE
Children With Multiple Disabilities

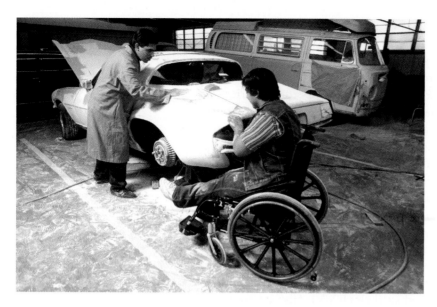

Vocational education is important for some adolescents with physical or health disabilities.

on major life areas that will be important for adulthood. These may include daily living skills, personal-social skills, and occupational guidance and preparation (Clark, Bigge, & Best, 2010).

Career preparation should occur throughout students' school years. Some pupils will be preparing to go on to vocational school, community college, or a university before seeking employment. Others will seek employment after finishing high school. Individuals with disabilities may use one of several vocational education service delivery programs, including secondary vocational education, secondary special needs vocational education, postsecondary vocational and technical education, apprenticeship programs, and vocational rehabilitation programs (Sitlington, Neubert, & Clark, 2009).

Students who are able to go to college and who decide to do so may find it very stressful to leave familiar surroundings and supports. However, colleges and universities typically offer services for individuals with physical and health disabilities to assist them with accommodations and accessibility issues. Other modifications, such as modified test taking or assignment adjustments, will also be addressed through these college and university services for individuals with disabilities. It is important in the high school years that students learn to be self-advocates and learn how to find and use available resources to make the appropriate accommodations.

Technology has made more jobs than ever before accessible for individuals with physical and health disabilities. Many jobs today are computer based, and individuals with severe physical and health disabilities can often work in these fields by adapting the computer to meet their specific needs. Modifications may be quite simple, such as having the keyboard placed in a different position for easy access or using a software program that provides a keyboard on the screen to be accessed with a joystick. Many other job opportunities are possible with often minor modifications. Being willing to figure out what is necessary to make a job possible and following through with appropriate modifications are critical for success.

Some individuals with physical disabilities, health disabilities, and related low-incidence disabilities who are unable to work in competitive employment may benefit from supported competitive employment or other employment models. In supported employment, the person with a disability works in the regular work setting and becomes a regular employee; however, training and continued support are necessary. A job coach (or job specialist) provides on-the-job assistance to the person with a disability. Often individuals who will benefit from this model have also received community-based vocational instruction during high school with a job coach. This previous training can help a student learn important job skills and also acquaints the student with a supported employment model.

It is difficult to predict the employment outlook for individuals with physical disabilities, health disabilities, or related low-incidence disabilities. When the physical or health disability is mild, it may not interfere with employment opportunities. However, students with mild physical or health disabilities may have inappropriate social behaviors or poor work habits that make finding and keeping a job difficult without

supported competitive employment: At a work site for typical workers, individuals with disabilities are employed and work alongside their typical peers but receive ongoing assistance from a job coach.

job coach: An individual who supervises a person with a disability for all or part of the day to provide training, assistance, or support to maintain a job.

VIDEO
Parent Interview

further training. Pupils who have severe physical disabilities will be unable to do many physically demanding jobs, but if they have normal cognitive functioning, they may be able to perform intellectually based jobs with the use of assistive technology. However, students with severe physical disabilities still face major barriers to employment when assistance is needed in personal skills (for example, bathroom assistance) or there are mobility or communication difficulties. These problems, among others, contribute to a significant underemployment rate for individuals with cerebral palsy and other severe physical disabilities (Clark et al., 2010; Wehman, 2012) as well as those with deaf-blindness and multiple disabilities.

Adults With Physical Disabilities, Health Disabilities, and Related Low-Incidence Disabilities

Many adults with physical disabilities, health disabilities, and related low-incidence disabilities will make a positive transition into adulthood and be integrated into work and community environments. Their success will depend partly on community acceptance and partly on the provision of necessary accommodations and support. With these kinds of disabilities, having appropriate medical and technological support will also be critical in ensuring a high quality of life.

The impact of a physical or health disability in the adult years will vary greatly, depending on the specific impairment, its prognosis, and possible complications. Many individuals who have mild physical or health disabilities may experience only minor problems resulting from their disability. At the other extreme, individuals who have a terminal illness (Duchenne muscular dystrophy, AIDS, cystic fibrosis) may die in their early adult years, or not even survive to adulthood. Many other adults, such as those with cerebral palsy, may experience complications and multiple health issues, such as scoliosis (curvatures of the spine) and contractures, further limiting movement and mobility and resulting in pain. Multiple surgeries may be needed to address these types of musculoskeletal problems.

Some problems that occur in adults with physical disabilities can be prevented. A shocking lack of preventive medical care (general medical checkups, dental care) has been found among adults with cerebral palsy. As a result, adults with cerebral palsy are more susceptible to medical problems that could have been prevented or treated in their early stages. Providing preventive and appropriate medical care is key to adult health.

Family Issues

Families with children who have physical disabilities, health disabilities, or related low-incidence disabilities can be put under tremendous stress. Sources of stress include juggling the demands of the disability and ongoing medical treatment, dealing with uncertainties about the child's future health and independence, financial strains, lack of respite care, routine changes and disruptions, and overall exhaustion (Murphy, Christian, Caplin, & Young, 2007). For example, the young woman in our chapter opener has been to more than seventy-three doctors, therapists, and rehabilitation engineers, involving countless appointments, medications, and treatments, as well as thirteen surgeries. This is not unusual for a family that has a child with a severe physical disability.

Stress can also result from the additional care and daily activities that may need to be performed for the child. Absences from school because of illness, surgeries, and medical treatments may add stress when one of the parents needs to stay home (or in

AUDIO
Long-term Care

the hospital) with the child. Day to day, the child may need help with such basic tasks as eating, toileting, and obtaining desired items. Some children will require regular medical treatments at home (such as respiratory physical therapy to decrease respiratory secretions) or at a clinic (such as dialysis). Some students may have terminal and degenerative conditions, which can increase stress.

Despite the added stress, most families are able to manage the demands of having a child with a physical or health disability with the child being a valued, loved, and contributing member of the family. Many factors contribute to the family's coping ability, including support from concerned others, positive family appraisal, spiritual support, advocacy, positive social interactions, education and information, parental involvement that enhances a sense of control, and consistency in the medical care of the child (Lin, 2000; Turnbull, Turnbull, Erwin, Soodak, & Shogren, 2011). Teachers can help families by being supportive, helping parents be an active part of the IEP team, and not being judgmental toward the parents.

Issues of Diversity

Physical disabilities, health disabilities, and related low-incidence disabilities occur in students from all backgrounds, cultures, and economic levels. Unlike other disabilities, such as intellectual and learning disabilities, physical disabilities raise no questions regarding misclassification and culture bias. However, misunderstanding can result from cultural differences in how the disability is viewed and miscommunication between parents and school.

Different families cope with illness and disability in diverse ways, and some are influenced by their particular culture. For example, some Hmong view epilepsy as a sign of distinction that could qualify them for the divine office of shaman (Fadiman, 1997). More often the cultural influences are subtler.

Misunderstandings can occur between the school and family as a result of cultural differences. In one study (Geenen, Powers, & Lopez-Vasquez, 2001), for example, culturally and linguistically diverse parents described themselves as being very involved in the transition process while school officials reported far less involvement. This discrepancy can be explained by these parents' heavy involvement in talking with their children about life after high school and caring for their disability, but lack of participation in the school-based transition process. Many of these families viewed transitioning a student into adulthood as a family and community responsibility rather than an educational one. Understanding and respecting cultural differences is important to providing positive educational experiences for the student.

Technology and Individuals With Physical Disabilities, Health Disabilities, and Related Low-Incidence Disabilities

technology productivity tools: Computer software, hardware, and related systems designed to help people work effectively.

information technology: Databases and computer-based information sources.

instructional technology: Any apparatus or device that supports the teaching-learning process, such as computers or televisions; a tool for the delivery of instruction.

Technology encountered in school settings is often grouped into several categories such as (1) technology productivity tools, (2) information technology, (3) instructional technology, (4) medical technology, (5) and assistive technology (Blackhurst 2005b; Lindsey, 2008). Most students, whether they have disabilities or not, will use technology productivity tools (such as computers), information technology (such as the World Wide Web), and instructional technology (such as software programs teaching multiplication or map skills). In addition to these forms of technology, students with physical or health impairments will often require medical and assistive technology.

VIDEO
Support Groups

Activity	Low Technology	High Technology
Reading	• Book stand, nonslip mat • Turn pages with mouthstick or eraser tip of pencil • Ruler to help keep place on page	• Electric page turner • Software to scan book into computer to easily move through book, highlight material, or read text aloud
Writing	• Pencil with built-up grip • Wider-spaced paper • Mouthstick with pencil attached	• Computer with alternative input (switch or voice recognition)
Math	• Counter • Abacus • Money cards	• Graphing calculators • Electronic worksheet program that can correctly position the cursor for regrouping
Eating	• Spoon with built-up handle • Hand splint to hold spoon • Adaptive cup • Scoop dish	• Electric feeder • Robotic arm
Leisure	• Card holder • Bigger baseball	• Sport wheelchair • Adapted bicycle • Computer games

Many students with physical or health impairments require medical technology to sustain life and functionality. Medical technology devices can range from battery-powered artificial limbs that restore movement to individuals who have lost an arm or a leg to pumps that deliver medication. Other examples of medical technology are inhalers and nebulizers for individuals with asthma, glucose monitoring devices and injection systems for individuals requiring insulin, ventilators for individuals who need additional support to breathe, and gastrostomy tubes and supporting equipment for delivery of nutrition. Teachers should be knowledgeable about their students' medical technology and know what to do should a problem arise.

Assistive technology has opened doors for students with physical or health disabilities. The Technology-Related Assistance for Individuals with Disabilities Act of 1988 defines *assistive technology* as "any item, piece of equipment, or product system, whether acquired commercially off the shelf, modified or customized, that is used to increase, maintain, or improve functional capabilities of individuals with disabilities." Thus, assistive technology can range from something as simple as a bent spoon used when eating to a sophisticated computer-based augmentative communication system. Assistive technology can be divided into low-tech and high-tech categories, according to the complexity of the device. Table 14.5 gives some examples of both categories across several different activities.

Types of assistive technology commonly used by students with physical disabilities include computer access, augmentative and alternative communication, positioning and seating devices, mobility devices, assistive technology for daily living and environmental control, and assistive technology for recreation and leisure. These various types of assistive technology can greatly improve the students' functioning and be critical in providing access to school, home, community, and work environments.

Computer Access

Individuals with physical or health disabilities use computers for communication, academic tasks, leisure, and socialization. Depending on the extent of the physical or health disability, a wide range of adaptations can be made to the computer. These adaptations can be categorized into three major categories: input modifications, increasing text entry efficiency, and output modifications.

Input Modifications

Input devices provide information to the computer; standard input devices are the keyboard and mouse. For students with physical or health disabilities who have difficulty using these, a number of alternatives are available. Some students may need to activate the accessibility options available on most computers, such as the option to make keys not repeat when held down. Simple appliances may be placed over the standard keyboard to make it accessible. For example, some students drag their hand across the keyboard and need a keyguard (a plastic cover with holes for each key) to prevent accidentally pushing an unwanted key.

Students may use alternative keyboards that are larger, smaller, or differently configured than the standard keyboard in order to accommodate their physical impairment. Some individuals may use an on-screen keyboard; that is, the keyboard is displayed on the computer screen. A pupil may control the on-screen keyboard using any number of alternative input devices, such as a trackball, joystick, touchpad, touch monitor (directly touching the keyboard on the screen), or switch.

Some students may use an alternative keyboard to access a computer.

Some input devices do not use a keyboard at all. For example, voice recognition software enables a student to talk to the computer, which writes what is said.

Increasing Text Entry Efficiency

Once a student has a way of inputting information into the computer, there may be a problem with the speed at which the student can type. Whether the individual is using a standard keyboard, using an alternative keyboard, using voice recognition software, or typing by raising an eyebrow, input may be slow. There are several techniques that can be used to increase text entry efficiency. One of these techniques is using a word prediction program (Simpson, 2013). As a student types the first letter, the computer displays a list of words commonly used by this user that start with the letter typed. If the word is displayed, the student can type the corresponding number instead of the entire word. If the word is not displayed, the on-screen list continues to change as more letters are typed.

word prediction program: A software program that provides a list of potential words that correspond to the letters the user is typing so that the user does not have to type out the entire word.

Output Modifications

Computers commonly have two types of output: the screen monitor and the printer. However, students with physical or health disabilities may require additional modifications. Some students may need to use speech synthesizers (text to speech) that allow the computer to "read aloud" what is on the screen. Others may need a larger monitor or a software program that can magnify what is on the screen. Printers can also be modified to allow for large fonts.

Augmentative and Alternative Communication

Some individuals with disabilities will be unable to effectively communicate using their voice and require augmentative and alternative communication. AAC refers to the various forms of communication that are used as a supplement or an alternative to oral or written language, such as communication behaviors, gestures, sign language, picture symbols, the alphabet, communication devices, and computers with synthetic speech. Often students will use a combination of ways to communicate. The goal of AAC is not to find a technological solution, but to enable individuals to effectively communicate and engage in a variety of interactions (Beukelman & Mirenda, 2013). The educational team will be involved in determining the most appropriate forms of augmentative communication for each individual student.

Positioning and Seating Devices

To provide access to activities, curriculum, and assistive devices, it is imperative that the student with a physical or health disability have proper positioning and seating. Position will always affect the quality and precision of a person's movement and ability to accomplish a task (Best, Reed, & Bigge, 2010). Proper positioning and seating are achieved through a wide range of special chairs and inserts that can go into a chair or wheelchair to achieve optimal positioning. Proper positioning not only helps the student move as efficiently as possible but can also reduce deformity and promote feelings of physical security. If students are unable to move themselves, their position may need to be changed frequently throughout the day to avoid any stiffness or pressure sores (skin breakdown from staying in one position for too long).

A pupil may use several different positioning devices throughout the day. Some devices may allow the student to sit a certain way, while other devices help the student lie on his or her side, stomach, or back. A prone stander may be used to support the individual in a standing position. Such positioning devices may enable students to participate in activities they would not be able to do from a wheelchair, such as wash dishes at a sink while positioned in a prone stander. They can also increase muscle strength and movement, stimulate bone growth, improve circulation, and increase the movement of food through the gastrointestinal system. The physical therapist will determine the most therapeutic positions for the individual and the types of devices to use to help the student achieve these positions.

Mobility Devices

Students with physical or health disabilities may use a wide range of mobility devices to move from one location to another. One of the most common devices is the wheelchair, either manual or power. Manual wheelchairs are pushed by the student (or someone else). Power wheelchairs have a motor that allows the wheelchair user to operate the chair by means of a joystick or other device. Self-operated wheelchairs can give their users tremendous independence.

Depending on the disability, a student may use the wheelchair all the time when moving about, or only when fatigued. Many people are surprised to see a student using a wheelchair one moment, then walking around the next. The type of chair and its frequency of use will depend on the student's disability.

Some students with cerebral palsy require the use of positioning equipment during the school day.

Individuals with physical disabilities use many other types of mobility devices. Some may use a power-operated scooter instead of a traditional wheelchair. A student who can stand and walk with support may use a walker. Others who need even less support may use canes or crutches. Older individuals may drive cars that have been modified for their use. Whichever mobility device is used, the teacher should be familiar with it and know what type of support the student needs in order to use it.

Environmental Control and Assistive Technology for Daily Living

An environmental control unit (ECU) is a device that allows the user to control electric appliances, telephones, and other items that use electric outlets. The device may be a stand-alone unit (that can be mounted onto a wheelchair) or be purchased as a software package that can be used with a computer or some electronic augmentative communication devices. The electrical appliances are equipped with receivers. The user then chooses an appliance (such as the TV or a room light) and what the user wants it to do (such as turn on or off) from a list on the ECU, which sends a signal to the appliance. ECUs can help students with physical or health disabilities to manipulate their surroundings independently.

Many other types of assistive technologies are available to help with daily living. Personal care items, such as modified toothbrushes and hairbrushes, can help the individual with a physical disability who has restricted arm and hand motion or who cannot grasp well. These items may have elongated handles, built-up handles, or Velcro straps. Modified washcloths that fit over the hand like a mitt and Velcro around the wrist may also be used.

Modifications for eating and preparing food include special cutting boards with edges and safety knives, modified dishes with one side higher than the other to help with scooping, and modified cups to help with drinking. Students who are unable to move their arms may use a mechanical feeder that scoops food onto a spoon and brings the spoon up to the mouth with the touch of a switch.

Dressing aids include special sticks with hooks on the end that can be used to pull pants and zippers up or down and devices to help put on socks when the individual cannot reach to the floor. Modified clothing, such as garments with Velcro along the seams to go over braces, can also make dressing easier.

walker: A mobility aid for individuals requiring support when walking.

environmental control unit (ECU): A device that allows the user to control electric appliances, telephones, and other items that use electric outlets from a distance.

Assistive Technology for Play and Recreation

Numerous assistive technology devices are available for play and recreation. Children who cannot manipulate toys may have battery-operated toys they can activate by a switch. Switches may also be used to turn on and off radios or televisions. Computer games can often be accessed using joysticks or other input devices. Other types of recreational games, such as card games and board games, may require the use of a simple device to hold the cards, or a dice holder that can be knocked over to roll the dice.

Individuals with physical or health disabilities can also enjoy playing sports and engaging in physical activities. Some school systems have adapted sports teams, such as wheelchair basketball or wheelchair soccer, for students with physical disabilities. Many pupils with disabilities can participate in a wide variety of sports with minor modifications and assistive technology devices—for example, hitting a ball off a tee, allowing an extra swing at bat, or using a small adapted ramp that holds a bowling ball and allows the wheelchair user to push the ball down the ramp into the bowling lane. Individuals who like to exercise may be able to use adapted tricycles, bicycles, and mobility devices.

Students with physical or health disabilities enjoy playing a variety of sports.

Trends, Issues, and Controversies

Three major issues in the field of physical disabilities, health disabilities, and related low-incidence disabilities are (1) assessing capabilities and needs of students with very severe physical disabilities; (2) provision of specialized technology, adaptations, and instructional strategies; and (3) selection of appropriate curriculum.

The first issue is appropriate assessment of students with severe physical disabilities in terms of cognitive functioning and evaluation of what the student has learned. When a young child cannot reliably move or speak, and is not yet using augmentative communication effectively, psychological testing can be of limited value or accuracy. We have come across twelve instances over the past decade in which young children with severe speech and physical impairments had been labeled as having severe intellectual disability, but whose intelligence was later determined to range from mild intellectual disability to giftedness. In our chapter opener, Natalie's category changed multiple times, although her intellectual capabilities remained the same. Assessment difficulties are also present for students with multiple disabilities and deaf-blindness.

Because of this difficulty, two major areas need to be addressed: finding a reliable response and providing an appropriate curriculum. While these students are learning augmentative communication, it is essential to find some **reliable means of response**—that is, a consistent, reliable way for the student to answer questions. This could be looking at the answer (eye gazing), touching the answer, hitting a switch to indicate the answer, or having the teacher move a finger across answers until the student makes a noise indicating a selection. Typically, this means that questions must be presented in a multiple-choice format, at least until students have literacy skills and can type out their own responses. Having a reliable means of response makes it possible to assess what the pupil knows. Given the lack of experiences and inability to communicate thoughts and questions, intelligence testing may still not be accurate, even when the student has a reliable way to respond to the questions. However, it does give the teacher an accurate way of determining if the student has learned the material.

reliable means of response: A consistent, reliable way of answering questions.

A second issue involves the provision of specialized technology, adaptations, and instructional strategies. Barriers to obtaining and using the necessary technology include funding issues, appropriate assessment, selection of devices, training to use the devices, and ongoing technical support.

The third area to consider is curriculum. Some learners with physical or health disabilities will be on an academic curriculum; others will be on a more adapted curriculum. However, when the individual has severe speech and physical impairments, it may not be obvious where the student is functioning. Pupils with severe physical and multiple disabilities should be periodically taught and assessed on more advanced skills to determine whether the student can learn them. For example, if the student is only introduced to pictures for communication, how do we know that the student is not capable of learning words? This concern is best summed up by Natalie's mom (B. Tumlin, personal communication, July 2001):

> A nonverbal child cannot provide her own opportunities to prove more than what is expected. When placement is based strictly on test scores and/or assumptions, quite often our kids end up living *down* to expectations, are isolated from normal interactions and experiences, and learn inappropriate behaviors to be what is "normal."

Placing students in inappropriate curriculums or teaching them less than they are capable of learning may be due to spread (Kirshbaum, 2000)—the overgeneralization of a disability into unrelated areas, often resulting in stereotyping. For example, people may assume that someone who uses a wheelchair has a cognitive impairment, or may react to a person who is blind by talking more loudly. It is important to interact with individuals with disabilities based on what they demonstrate, rather than on unfounded assumptions.

spread: The practice of spreading inferences to other unrelated aspects of a disability, often resulting in stereotyping.

CHAPTER IN REVIEW

Defining Physical Disabilities, Health Disabilities, and Related Low-Incidence Disabilities

- Students who have physical and health disabilities comprise one of the most diverse categories of students receiving special education services.
- Depending on their disability, they may come under one of four IDEA categories: orthopedic impairment, multiple disabilities, traumatic brain injury, and other health impairment.
- Individuals with the concomitant loss of both vision and hearing are referred to as having deaf-blindness.

Prevalence of Physical Disabilities, Health Disabilities, and Related Low-Incidence Disabilities

- Physical and health disabilities vary widely in reported prevalence figures.
- Pupils with deaf-blindness are representative of a low-incidence disability accounting for only 0.02 percent of all individuals receiving a special education.

- Children with physical or health disabilities and low-incidence disabilities comprise about 16 percent of the special education population.

Etiology of Physical Disabilities, Health Disabilities, and Related Low-Incidence Disabilities

- Physical disabilities, health disabilities, and related low-incidence disabilities have many causes.
- Some of the more common etiologies can be grouped under chromosomal and genetic causes, teratogens, prematurity and complications of pregnancy, and acquired causes.

Characteristics of Individuals With Physical Disabilities, Health Disabilities, and Related Low-Incidence Disabilities

- The characteristics of individuals with physical disabilities, health disabilities, and related low-incidence disabilities depend on the specific condition and its severity.

- Individuals with such neuromotor impairments as cerebral palsy and spina bifida have impaired motor movements and often have additional disabilities associated with their condition.
- Children with degenerative diseases, such as Duchenne muscular dystrophy, have progressive loss of control in moving their bodies and often die early in life.
- Students with orthopedic and musculoskeletal disorders, such as juvenile idiopathic arthritis and limb deficiencies, can have severe physical limitations.
- Individuals with multiple disabilities have a combination of disabilities, often including a physical or health impairment.
- Pupils with traumatic brain injury may have deficits across cognitive, motor, physical, health, sensory, language, social, and behavioral domains.
- Major health impairments (such as seizure disorders) and infectious diseases (such as AIDS) can affect an individual's endurance and attention.
- Students with deaf-blindness are an especially heterogeneous group of learners varying tremendously in their needs, abilities, and educational requirements.

Educational Considerations

- Educational placement of students with physical disabilities, health disabilities, and related low-incidence disabilities varies greatly.

- Physical and health disabilities vary in their impact on school performance according to the type of disability involved, the functional effects of the disability, and the psychosocial and environmental factors surrounding the disability.
- Meeting the educational needs of students with physical disabilities, health disabilities, and related low-incidence disabilities involves monitoring, modifications and adaptations, and specialized instructional strategies.

Technology and Individuals With Physical Disabilities, Health Disabilities, and Related Low-Incidence Disabilities

- Prominent is the role of medical and assistive technology. Advances in medical technology have helped individuals lead healthier lives.
- Types of assistive technology commonly used by individuals with physical disabilities, health disabilities, and related low-incidence disabilities include computer access, augmentative and alternative communication, positioning and seating devices, mobility devices, environmental control and daily living devices, and play and recreation devices.

STUDY QUESTIONS

1. Which IDEA categories include students with a physical or health disability, and how are they defined?

2. What are the major causes of physical disabilities, health disabilities, and deaf-blindness?

3. Explain the following conditions: cerebral palsy, spina bifida, traumatic brain injury, Duchenne muscular dystrophy, limb deficiency, seizure disorders, AIDS, and deaf-blindness.

4. Explain the steps you would take if a tonic-clonic seizure occurred in your classroom.

5. How does a physical disability, health impairment, or low-incidence disability affect school performance?

6. What does it mean to maintain a safe, healthy environment?

7. What types of modifications and adaptations may need to be used in the classroom? Include seven major areas in your discussion.

8. Identify five of the principal communication systems used with pupils who are deaf-blind.

9. Describe how communication breakdowns can occur when talking with an individual using an augmentative communication device. Describe some techniques for preventing such breakdowns from occurring.

10. What are specialized instructional strategies and specialized expanded curriculum areas? Provide examples.

11. What are some stresses that occur in families that have a child with a physical or health impairment? How are these stresses different from those experienced by families with other types of disabilities?

12. What are the major types of assistive technology available to students with physical disabilities, health disabilities, or low-incidence disabilities?

13. What is augmentative and alternative communication? Does its use interfere with speech production?

14. What is "spread," and how may it affect a person with a physical or health disability?

KEY TERMS ■■■■■■■■■■■■■■■■■■■■■■■■■■■■■■■■■■■■■■■

low-incidence disabilities,   487

assistive technology device,   487

augmentative and alternative
communication (AAC),   487

orthopedic impairment,   488

multiple disabilities,   488

traumatic brain injury,   488

other health impairment,   488

deaf-blindness,   488

CHARGE association,   492

Usher syndrome,   492

teratogen,   493

neuromotor impairment,   495

cerebral palsy,   488

spastic cerebral palsy,   496

athetoid cerebral palsy,   496

ataxic cerebral palsy
(ataxia),   496

mixed cerebral palsy,   496

hemiplegia,   496

diplegia,   496

paraplegia,   496

quadriplegia,   496

orthotics,   496

contractures,   497

spina bifida,   497

Duchenne muscular dystrophy,   499

juvenile idiopathic arthritis (JIA),   499

limb deficiency,   500

seizure,   504

epilepsy,   504

absence seizure,   504

complex partial seizure,   504

tonic-clonic seizure,   504

asthma,   505

acquired immune deficiency syndrome
(AIDS),   506

specialized instructional
strategies,   516

communication breakdowns,   516

intervener,   519

transition plan,   521

supported competitive
employment,   522

job coach,   522

technology productivity tools,   524

information technology,   524

instructional technology,   524

word prediction program,   526

walker,   528

environmental control unit (ECU),   528

reliable means of response,   529

spread,   530

LEARNING ACTIVITIES ■■■■■■■■■■■■■■■■■■■■■■■■■■■■■■■■■■■■■■■

1. Visit a website specializing in assistive technology (e.g., www.abledata.com or www.closingthegap.com). What types of assistive technology are provided on the site? Select five different assistive technology devices and describe their use, whom they are for, their price, and your overall impression of the devices.

2. Learn about your own state's disability definitions and special education certification categories. Does your state use the orthopedic impairment, traumatic brain injury, multiple disabilities, other health impairment, and deaf-blindness categories? How are they defined? What types of special education certification does your state provide, and is there specialized training in physical and health disabilities?

3. Visit a school and observe students with low-incidence disabilities. What types of modifications, adaptations, and assistive technologies are being used? What are the roles of the occupational therapist, physical therapist,

speech-language pathologist, nurse, special education teacher, general education teacher, student, and parents in determining modifications, adaptations, and selection of assistive technology?

4. Interview a high school student (or parent of a child) with a physical or health disability. Ask the student about his or her disability and its treatment. Ask the student what it is like to have the particular disability. Does he or she feel that it has interfered with school, activities, or making friends? What does the student think that teachers need to know about the disability?

5. Contact local chapters of organizations involved with physical and health disabilities, such as the Epilepsy Foundation of America or United Cerebral Palsy. Find out what services they provide. Obtain samples of literature they have for the public. Attend a support meeting to gain insight into some of the issues in their area of focus.

ORGANIZATIONS CONCERNED WITH PHYSICAL DISABILITIES, HEALTH DISABILITIES, OR RELATED LOW-INCIDENCE DISABILITIES

Brain Injury Association of America

www.biausa.org

Centers for Disease Control and Prevention

www.cdc.gov

Division for Physical and Health Disabilities, Council for Exceptional Children

www.cec.sped.org

Muscular Dystrophy Association

www.mda.org

National Organization for Rare Disorders (NORD)

www.rarediseases.org

United Cerebral Palsy

www.ucp.org

REFLECTING ON STANDARDS

The following exercises are designed to help you learn to apply the Council for Exceptional Children (CEC) standards to your teaching practice. Each of the reflection exercises below correlates with knowledge or a skill within the CEC standards. For the full text of each of the related CEC standards, please refer to the standards integration grid located in Appendix B.

Focus on Learning Environments (*CEC Initial Preparation Standard 2.1*)

Reflect on someone you know who has a physical disability or a related low-incidence disability. How is this person often misunderstood or treated by the general population? If you were to have a student in your class with a physical or related low-incidence disability, how might you need to educate your general education students so that your classroom is a safe, equitable, positive, and supportive learning environment?

Focus on Instructional Planning and Strategies (*CEC Initial Preparation Standard 5.4*)

Reflect on what you have learned in this chapter about the educational needs of students with physical disabilities and related low-incidence disabilities. If you were to have a student with cerebral palsy in your class, what strategies might you need to implement to make sure communication with your student is clear? What assistive technologies might you need to implement?

⑤SAGE edge™

Sharpen your skills with SAGE edge at **edge.sagepub.com/gargiulo5e. SAGE edge for students** provides a personalized approach to help you accomplish your coursework goals in an easy-to-use learning environment.

Individuals Who Are Gifted and Talented

It's All Up to the Parent

My mom still laughs about it—knowingly laughs at my naïveté, joyfully laughs with his possibilities. At 18 months, Jake (my firstborn and only born at the time) was splashing in the tub playing "name that alphabet letter." Randomly I held up sponge letters as he giggled and shouted their names at me. But he misidentified the *I* as an *L*. When I told Mom about it, she was thrilled! I, on the other hand, explained, "But he missed one." There was silence, then laughter on the phone.

I've learned so much in the six years since then. For example, I've learned that most 18-month-olds can't speak in full sentences, much less know all the letters by name. And I've learned that most 4-year-olds can't read. In spite of all the child development books on the market and in my personal library, I've learned that gifted children are virtually ignored. Their educational, social, and emotional needs are very different from other children's, so unless the book solely deals with the gifted, it's not very beneficial. And I guess the most important thing I've learned is that, right or wrong, it's usually all up to the parent.

Academically, I have found that very few teachers understand or even recognize the gifted child. This became painfully clear to me as day after day I had to drag my first grader, my Jake, out from behind the couch forcing him to go to school. I have found that I am the one responsible for making sure he is challenged in the classroom and at home. I vividly remember the meeting I had with his teachers, then his principal. I had researched, read numerous books, prepared sample lessons, and organized the cognitive test results from an independent psychologist. I walked a fine line between concerned parent who wants the best for her child and so offers resources and suggestions—and the pushy, domineering mother who knows best. Luckily for Jake, it worked beautifully. I met with open-minded, openhearted professionals. He now has two very caring, understanding teachers from different grades individualizing instruction and challenging him. The couch is no longer an issue—this year.

LEARNING OBJECTIVES

After reading Chapter 15, you should be able to:

- **Describe** various interpretations of giftedness.
- **Explain** the techniques typically used to assess an individual's gifts and talents.
- **Outline** the history of educational services for students who are gifted and talented.
- **List** the characteristics of persons who are gifted and talented according to the five dimensions of giftedness.
- **Summarize** the various instructional strategies used by educators to teach pupils who are gifted and talented.
- **Identify** the service delivery options available to students with gifts and talents.
- **Describe** educational opportunities for young children and adolescents who are gifted and talented.
- **Define** *twice-exceptional*.
- **Discuss** the challenges confronting girls who are gifted and talented as well as children with gifts and talents from culturally diverse backgrounds.

VIDEO

Giftedness

The academic struggles Jake has battled in no way compare to the emotional issues we deal with almost daily. I see his confusion as people constantly expect more from him than other 7-year-olds because he is so bright. I see his frustration as he tries to explain some complicated make-believe game to his age peers. I see his boredom as he brings home worksheets that force him to "practice" a math skill twenty times that he knew after three. I see his hurt as he worries about the sick and misfortunate. And I see his anger over things that aren't fair.

Oh, how I wish people understood! If administrators only knew that the best way to remove the learning ceiling is to cluster group by ability. If teachers only realized that gifted kids have very different academic and social needs. If they only knew how a little differentiation literally changes the life of a gifted child. (I well remember Jake's response to just the possibility of doing an independent project. He paced the floor rushing out his words about king cobras and books and where's the poster board! And I well remember the void of all expression when the teacher "didn't get around to it.") And if gifted kids only knew that there would be challenge, there would be intellectual peers who could share ideas, and there would be teachers and principals who just plain understood.

But until that happens, it seems to be up to the parent. I am the one who discovers the opportunities—The Center for Gifted Studies, the Super Saturdays enrichment classes, the summer reading programs, the independent learning. I am the advocate passing on information to the school, gifting the teacher with the latest curriculum book, serving on the School Council. And I see changes. I see how much information opens eyes. And I've seen how opened eyes facilitate change. And I am beginning to get the feeling I'm not alone.

—*Tracy Inman*

Stereotypes of children who are gifted and talented are numerous, and many people believe that the stereotypes represent the truth about gifted children. Some people think that a person is not gifted unless he or she is radically accelerated or that being gifted means having few or diminished social skills. Others gather their impressions about giftedness from one or a few individuals they have known or heard about, and then they generalize about people who are gifted based on this limited information. Many of the resulting stereotypes are just that—stereotypes; they are often inaccurate or misleading when applied to students who are gifted or talented and gifted individuals in general.

Some people say that every child is gifted; if they mean all children are special, then, of course, they are right. However, they are using a different meaning of *gifted* from the one used in this chapter to describe a category of exceptional children. Other people use the term *gifted* only in connection with the arts or athletics; we often read about the gifted tennis player or the gifted violinist. As the term is used in education, however, children who are gifted and talented have abilities and talents that can be demonstrated or have the potential for being developed at exceptional levels. They

gifted and talented: Persons who possess abilities and talents that can be demonstrated, or have the potential for being developed, at exceptionally high levels.

Chapter contribution written by Julia Link Roberts, Western Kentucky University

VIDEO
Interview: Parent of a Child With Giftedness

are significantly different from age-mates in their area(s) of giftedness or talent. These children have needs that differ in some degree from those of other children.

In this chapter, we examine the concept of giftedness, the characteristics of children and young people who are gifted and talented, and the special needs created by these characteristics. We will trace the historical development of the concept of giftedness; describe trends in support, and lack of support, for addressing the needs of gifted individuals; and elaborate on strategies that can be used in schools and in other settings to develop students' maximum potential. Finally, we will explore some current issues and challenges in identifying and providing services for children who are gifted and talented.

See the accompanying Insights feature (page 542) for a preview of frequently asked questions about students who are gifted and their education.

Defining Giftedness: Refining the Meaning

During the early twentieth century, the public equated giftedness with high intelligence. Terman (1925), for instance, considered individuals gifted if they had an IQ greater than 140—the top 1 percent of the population. The connection between high intelligence and giftedness remains with us today. However, this restrictive view of giftedness has been expanded to include other dimensions and categories.

Giftedness manifests itself in many different ways.

The first national report on gifted education, known as the Marland Report, offered the following definition, specifying six categories of giftedness (Marland, 1972, p. 10):

> Gifted and talented children are those identified by professionally qualified persons who by virtue of outstanding abilities are capable of high performance. These are children who require differentiated educational programs and/or services beyond those normally provided by the regular school program in order to realize their contribution to self and society.
>
> Children capable of high performance include those with demonstrated achievement and/or potential ability in any of the following areas: (1) general intellectual ability, (2) specific academic aptitude, (3) creative or productive thinking, (4) leadership ability, (5) visual and performing arts, and (6) psychomotor ability.

Many states have essentially adopted this definition, with the exception of psychomotor ability. Although individuals do demonstrate giftedness in psychomotor ability, the category has been removed because the development of athletic ability is generously funded in other ways.

The second national report on gifted education, *National Excellence: A Case for Developing America's Talent* (Ross, 1993), uses the term *talent* rather than *gifted:* "Children and youth with outstanding talent perform or show the potential for performing at remarkably high levels of accomplishment when compared with others of their age, experience, or environment" (p. 3). Like the Marland Report, it notes that "outstanding

VIDEO

Individual Interview

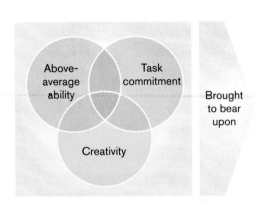

General performance areas

Mathematics	Social sciences	Music
Visual arts	Law	Life sciences
Physical sciences	Religion	Movement arts
Philosophy	Language arts	

Specific performance areas

Cartooning	Microphotography	Child care
Astronomy	City planning	Consumer protection
Public opinion polling	Pollution control	Cooking
Jewelry design	Poetry	Ornithology
Map making	Fashion design	Furniture design
Choreography	Weaving	Navigation
Biography	Play writing	Genealogy
Filmmaking	Advertising	Sculpture
Statistics	Costume design	Wildlife management
Local history	Meteorology	Set design
Electronics	Puppetry	Agricultural research
Musical composition	Marketing	Animal learning
Landscape architecture	Game design	Film criticism
Chemistry	Journalism	
Demography	Electronic music	

SOURCE: Adapted from J. Renzulli, "What Makes Giftedness? Reexamining a Definition," *Phi Delta Kappan, 60,* 1978, p. 184.

talent" can be evidenced in general intellectual ability, specific academic ability, creative thinking, leadership ability, and/or the visual and performing arts. At the same time, it stresses that "outstanding talents are present in children and youth from all cultural groups, across all economic strata, and in all areas of human endeavor" (p. 3). The recommendations contained in *National Excellence* provide a blueprint for states to use in expanding their definitions of children who are gifted and talented.

Renzulli (1978, 1998) has proposed a "Three-Ring" model of giftedness, represented visually as three intersecting circles (see Figure 15.1). Giftedness comprises three traits: creativity, above-average intellectual abilities, and task commitment. The focus of this model is on endeavors and activities that demonstrate giftedness; some examples of these behavioral manifestations are listed in Table 15.1.

Piirto (2007) provides a definition of giftedness that applies to school settings. In this context, the gifted population includes

those individuals who, by way of learning characteristics such as superior memory, observational powers, curiosity, creativity, and the ability to learn school-related subject matters rapidly and accurately with a minimum of drill and repetition, have a right to an education that is differentiated according to these characteristics because all children have a right to be educated according to their needs. (p. 37)

Gifted Behavior	Examples
Above-Average Ability (general)	• High levels of abstract thought • Adaptation to novel situations • Rapid and accurate retrieval of information
Above-Average Ability (specific)	• Applications of general abilities to specific area of knowledge • Capacity to sort out relevant from irrelevant information • Capacity to acquire and use advanced knowledge and strategies while pursuing a problem
Task Commitment	• Capacity for high levels of interest, enthusiasm • Hard work and determination in a particular area • Self-confidence and drive to achieve • Ability to identify significant problems within an area of study • Setting high standards for one's work
Creativity	• Fluency, flexibility, and originality of thought • Open to new experiences and ideas • Curious • Willing to take risks • Sensitive to aesthetic characteristics

SOURCE: J. Renzulli and S. Reis, *The Schoolwide Enrichment Model*, 2nd ed. (Mansfield Center, CT: Creative Learning Press, 1997), p. 9.

These children can be observed early, and their education should be planned to address their needs from preschool through college. Piirto also presents a model of talent development (see Figure 15.2, page 544) "in circular (not linear) form to indicate that the giftedness construct is not lines and angles, but a sphere, a circle, which enfolds all kinds of talent" (p. 37).

As you can see, definitions of *gifted* have evolved from an exclusive focus on high intelligence to a range of categories and indicators of talent. Identifying giftedness and talent in specific categories highlights the need for services to be customized to the individual's area(s) of identified strength(s). Identifying areas of giftedness is essential in order to match services and learning opportunities to need. Fairness is not offering the same educational opportunities to all children of the same age; rather, it is providing learning opportunities matched with needs, interests, and abilities.

Some examples may help. Jimmy was outstanding in many areas. He was so good at science that teachers encouraged him to become a physician or a research scientist; he was such an outstanding writer that his English teachers thought he was bound to be a journalist; he was also a talented musician and could have pursued a career in music. Jimmy was intellectually gifted, gifted in specific academic areas, and talented in the performing arts. Chin Lan was very talented in math and science and should have been identified as gifted in those specific academic areas; in other academic areas, she was ready for the academic challenges provided for others her age. Luis, who performed at grade level in academic subjects, was charismatic and had the ability to get others to do what he wanted; he was gifted in leadership and needed opportunities to develop his abilities and skills as a leader. Albert was very creative; his teachers saw his ideas as pushing the limits. Gifted in creative thinking, he was also academically talented in English and social studies. Sara was an outstanding musician and took advantage of opportunities to develop her musical talents. All of these students were recognized as

FAQs (Frequently Asked Questions) About Children and Youth Who Are Gifted and Talented

Q. Can all children become gifted?

A. From the data neurobiology is providing, it is evident that nearly all children are born with very complex and unique brain structures. Although each child is different, they all seem to have extraordinary potential. I believe that, if given the opportunity to develop optimally, most children could perform at the level we now call *gifted*, and it probably would be more natural for them to do so.

Q. Which is more important for the development of intelligence–heredity or environment?

A. Both are important, and current research recognizes that the interaction between them is complex and interdependent. At this time, few knowledgeable scientists even try to speak of one as being more important than the other.

Q. What is the biggest problem with labeling a child gifted? Would it be better to call children who are gifted by another word?

A. The word *gifted* does give an unfortunate connotation to the group of children who bear this label. People often think these children were given a gift; that is, they did nothing to earn their ability or talent. Americans tend to be suspicious of anyone who gets something for nothing. We think that people who didn't earn what they have probably do not deserve to have it, and certainly they should not have more. This line of thinking has been responsible for a lot of misunderstanding about gifted children. However, giving them a different label would still not solve the problems labeling causes. We have this label now, so perhaps the best we can do is to be sure everyone, including the child who is gifted, understands what we mean by it.

Q. Will grouping students who are gifted together result in "elitism"?

A. When this question is asked, "elitism" usually implies that the students who are gifted will become arrogant and snobbish and think they are better than other children. Research indicates that grouping gifted students together appropriately and flexibly in the areas in which they need advanced or accelerated work will not only result in their growth academically, but will give them a more realistic view of their abilities. Students who are always ahead of their classmates and do not have to study or are never challenged are in danger not only of becoming bored and dull but of falsely assuming that they are superior to other students. Because they are never challenged, they do not learn good study skills and will have problems later as they try to pursue higher education. Arrogance can come either from unrealistic appraisal of their talent or from trying to cover up for the feeling of being different and not understanding why others continually reject them. In either case, flexible and appropriate grouping with intellectual peers will decrease that type of elitism, not increase it.

Q. Considering the focus on inclusion in the regular classroom, when is it appropriate to have special programs for students who are gifted?

A. When the material and the pacing used in the classroom are not allowing students to grow and learn, special provisions must be made. When there is no provision for students who are gifted to interact with intellectual peers, ways in which such groupings can occur must be planned. Research indicates that these are the minimum provisions that pupils who are gifted must have if they are to continue to develop and not regress, losing ability and motivation. For many students who are gifted, an appropriately individualized classroom can provide the differentiated materials and instruction needed. However, for children with gifts and talents whose pace and level of learning are significantly beyond those of their classmates, the least restrictive environment will *not* be the regular classroom. These students will need special classes and mentoring to grow and learn.

---

gifted and/or talented, but each one was unique. Each pupil needed services to allow him or her to make continuous progress in his or her area of strength.

Following are some important features of giftedness and talent, as used in this chapter and applied in school settings:

- Each state establishes its own definition of children and young people who are gifted and talented. Although there are similarities, it is important to know the definition in the state where you live and/or work.
- In states in which children who are gifted constitute a category of exceptionality, laws governing special education also apply to children and young people who are gifted and talented.

Q. Which is better for a gifted learner, acceleration or enrichment?

A. Pupils who are gifted need both acceleration and enrichment, and any gifted program should be designed to provide both. When to use each will depend on the student's needs.

Q. What is the difference between differentiation and individualization?

A. *Differentiation* for learners who are gifted is the preparation that is made for the curriculum to respond to their characteristic needs, such as allowing for a faster pace of learning and choosing themes and content that allow for more complex investigation. Individualization for children who are gifted is the process of adapting that curriculum to the needs and interests of a particular student. A program for gifted learners requires both to be really successful.

Q. Are most gifted children hyperactive?

A. Many children with gifts and talents have high levels of energy; they require less sleep, and they are very, very curious. These traits can look like hyperactivity, but there is a difference. The energy of a child who is gifted is focused, directed, and intense. The energy of a hyperactive child is diffuse, random, and sporadic. Gifted children can attend to an activity of their interest for long periods of time; hyperactive children cannot. The brighter the child, the more the energy may look excessive.

Q. Why do some teachers, principals, and other school personnel seem to have negative attitudes toward gifted students?

A. Unfortunately, studies show that this is too often true. Children who are gifted do not fit easily into the structure of most schools and classrooms. Because they can be two to four years ahead of the curriculum offered at any grade level, they make it very hard for a teacher of twenty to thirty other children to find appropriate curricular experiences for them. They often question and seek more information about ideas than the teacher is prepared to give. Teachers may see children who are gifted as a challenge to their authority. They may refuse to do work that they consider boring or to repeat or practice lessons if they already understand the material. In a classroom where everyone is expected to do much the same work and cover the same material, this can be seen as a real problem. Pupils who are gifted can be demanding, challenging, intense, critical, oversensitive, highly verbal, and physically active, and they can devour material rapidly. None of these traits are problems in themselves, but they can present real problems for teachers who are not prepared to meet these needs. Some teachers do not know what to do with these youngsters and feel incompetent and threatened by them. For administrators, children who are gifted present needs for special services. This may be perceived as pressure on an already tight budget or cause special arrangements to be made that seem unnecessary. Fortunately, these attitudes often can be changed with professional development in gifted education.

Q. Do culturally diverse students require a separate curriculum?

A. If the instruction is individualized and the curriculum is differentiated, a separate curriculum is not necessary. What is important, however, is that the teacher and others involved in gifted programs in which cultural diversity exists hold positive attitudes toward cultural differences, that they be aware of cultural and ethnic history and traditions, that lots of resources related to diverse populations be made available, and that the program be flexible and responsive to each child's needs.

SOURCE: Adapted from B. Clark, Growing Up Gifted, 7th ed., © 2008. Adapted by permission of Pearson Education, Inc., Upper Saddle River, NJ.

- Being specific about the area of giftedness will make it possible to offer appropriate services and educational opportunities to allow continuous progress to be made in each category of talent or giftedness. Being specific also facilitates communication as you describe a young person as being gifted in mathematics, gifted in leadership, or intellectually gifted.
- Using giftedness and talent interchangeably will allow for concentration on the performance or potential for performance at levels that are exceptional in comparison with those of others of the same age, environment, or experience.
- Giftedness and talent will be found in children from all ethnic and racial groups and from all socioeconomic levels. Giftedness is also found among children with disabilities and English learners.

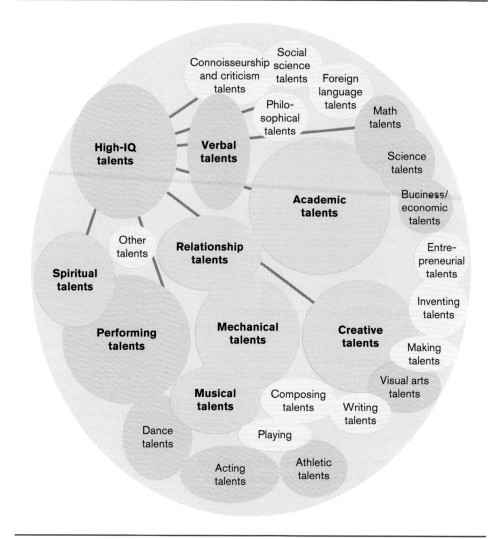

SOURCE: J. Piirto, *Talented Children and Adults: Their Development and Education,* 3rd ed. (Waco, TX: Prufrock Press, 2007), p. 46. Reprinted with permission.

Assessing Giftedness and Talent

The goal of assessment is to enable educators and parents to address the strengths and needs of children who are gifted and talented in one or in several categories. A thorough assessment paints a picture of the child, including his or her characteristics, interests, and strengths. Each category of giftedness must be assessed in different ways, using both informal and formal measures. Multifactor assessment of a student's strengths may include such diverse informal measures as a portfolio of work samples, anecdotal records, checklists or rating scales of gifted characteristics, and evaluations by experts of a pupil's creative products or performances.

A specific example of an informal measure of giftedness is the "jot-down." Jot-down forms can be used to help teachers focus on behaviors that in combination indicate giftedness. Teachers observe characteristics and behaviors and "jot down" the names of pupils they see demonstrating the behavior described in the box on a jot-down sheet. (See Figure 15.3 for an example of a jot-down.) Using jot-down sheets enables

Figure 15.3 **An Example of a Jot-Down Sheet**

Specific Academic Area Jot-Down

Brief description of   Check one: _____ Language arts   Date _____ / _____ / _____
observed activity _____   _____ Social studies   Month   Day   Year
_____   _____ Math   Teacher _____
_____   _____ Science   Grade _____ School _____

1. As students show evidence of the following characteristics in comparison with age peers, jot their names down in the appropriate box(es).
2. When recommending students for gifted services, use this identification jot-down as a reminder of student performances in this specific academic area.

Sees connections.	Asks many probing questions.	Shares what he/she knows, which may be seen as answering "too often."	Provides many written/oral details.
Is widely read or likes to read about subject area.	Absorbs information quickly from limited exposure.	Has a large vocabulary in subject area.	Benefits from rapid rate of presentation.
Displays intensity for learning within subject area.	Requires little or no drill to grasp concepts.	Generates large number of ideas or solutions to problems.	Has knowledge about things age peers may not be aware of.
Prefers to work independently with little direction.	Displays leadership qualities within subject area.	Applies knowledge to unfamiliar situations.	Offers unusual or unique responses.

SOURCE: Developed by L. Whaley and M. Evans, The Center for Gifted Studies, Western Kentucky University.

educators to observe students in class and to gather information about students as they encounter new and challenging learning activities. Behaviors in the boxes on the jot-down sheets may be seen in all children; when observed in clusters, however, they may indicate a child who is gifted and talented intellectually, academically, creatively, in leadership, or in the visual or performing arts.

Checklists provide another way of assessing a pupil's gifts and talents. The Pfeiffer-Jarosewich Gifted Rating Scales (Pfeiffer & Jarosewich, 2003) for school-age children are one example of an assessment instrument that looks at the various dimensions of giftedness. Teachers evaluate students in the areas of intellectual ability, academic ability, creativity, the arts, and motivation, as well as leadership abilities. Data gleaned from this rating scale can then be used with other sources of information to assist professionals in developing a picture of the student's strengths.

Teachers who are knowledgeable about the characteristics of children who are gifted become talent scouts as they document behaviors that are indicative of giftedness in various categories. It is important for educators to understand that giftedness comes in many different forms, each with recognized needs. The needs of students who are gifted and talented in each category arise from strengths rather than from deficits—strengths that make them children with exceptionalities when compared with age peers.

Obviously, the first step in addressing the needs of individuals who are gifted and talented is to have educators who are knowledgeable about their characteristics. Applying this knowledge allows teachers to recommend the pupil for additional informal and formal assessment and to make accommodations for the student in their curriculum. Parent and peer nominations are also useful in identifying students, and self-nomination is often a good predictor of leadership potential.

Tests of intellectual ability provide a formal measure of intellectual giftedness. No child can be fully represented by a number, but tests of intellectual ability can provide important information in identifying intellectual giftedness and planning appropriate modifications and services. Individual measures of intelligence such as the Wechsler Intelligence Scale for Children (4th ed.) (Wechsler, 2003) or the Stanford-Binet Intelligence Test (5th ed.) (Roid, 2003) are preferred to group measures for their ability to present a more comprehensive assessment. Another critical consideration is to look for instruments that are not biased. Up-to-date information on assessment measures is vital to planning and implementing an identification process that is defensible. Once formal measures indicate intellectual giftedness, further assessment should be made to identify areas of the curriculum that need to be differentiated to allow the student to be challenged academically and intellectually.

Formal assessment of specific academic ability can best be made with instruments that remove the learning ceiling. Off-level testing (the use of measures intended for older children) is important in assessing giftedness in a specific academic area. Grade-level achievement tests have a low ceiling and do not allow a child to demonstrate what he or she knows in the particular content area being tested. Examples of off-level testing are using the Woodcock-Johnson III Tests of Achievement (Woodcock, McGrew, & Mather, 2001) to measure a specific area of reading or mathematics or using the Scholastic Assessment Test (SAT) with middle school students to ascertain the level of reasoning and achievement in mathematics or verbal ability. Giftedness in a content area can be assessed through academic work, but students who are not challenged will not produce high-level products. Students who are gifted in a specific academic area will usually demonstrate their high level of work when given opportunities to take part in designing the learning experience, allowing them to pursue an aspect of the content area of great interest. Preassessing each unit will allow the assessment of knowledge and interests in a specific content area to be ongoing and to reflect the academic progress being made.

Creativity is defined in many ways—creative personality, creative products, creative thinking. Measures to assess creativity, therefore, must be chosen to match the kind of creativity that is being identified. Educators frequently assess creativity through creative products or tests of creative thinking. To assess products for creativity, it is wise to have scoring guides or rubrics available to students as they embark on creating the products. Tests by E. Paul Torrance (1966, 1998) and Frank Williams (1993) are frequently used to assess creative thinking skills. A more recent assessment instrument is

off-level testing: The use of assessment instruments designed for older students when evaluating the academic ability of a child thought to be gifted.

creativity: A term with multiple meanings, generally referring to the production of novel or original ideas or products.

AUDIO

IQ Tests

the Developing and Assessing Products (DAP) Tool (Roberts & Inman, 2009a), which uses creativity as one of four components when evaluating student work products.

Educators often equate leadership with elected positions. Being elected to office, however, is only one possible indicator of talent in leadership. It is best to identify leadership talent by observing behaviors that suggest leadership potential. Students should have the opportunity to present a leadership portfolio, including evidence of leadership opportunities outside of school. Leadership may be shown in a specific academic area or in an area of the visual or performing arts. Self-nomination through a portfolio can be coupled with peer nomination. Identifying leadership potential is important in order to match leadership opportunities with young people ready to develop their leadership skills.

Artists in a specific talent area are often appropriate individuals to assess talent in the visual and performing arts. As experts in the visual and performing arts, they are prepared to recognize talent that is exceptional for a young person when compared with others the same age. Products, sometimes assembled in a portfolio, and performances provide the means for assessing talent in the arts. Of course, recognizing and identifying talent is important in order for schools to provide learning opportunities to develop the talent to the highest levels possible.

School districts should establish policies that reflect best practices in screening and assessment (Evans, 2001; Gubbins, 2006; Johnsen, 2011; Landrum, Callahan, & Shaklee, 2001; Landrum & Shaklee, 1998):

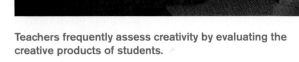

Teachers frequently assess creativity by evaluating the creative products of students.

- Each district should have a written plan for nominating and identifying students for gifted services.
- The nominating process for gifted education services should be ongoing.
- Screening for services can occur at any point in the school year.
- Assessment should be made in the language in which the student is fluent.
- Nonbiased measures should be used, taking into consideration ethnicity, culture, developmental differences, gender, economic conditions, disabilities, and environmental influences.
- Multiple measures include self-nomination, parent and teacher nomination, product and performance assessment, portfolios, and test scores.
- The school district should have written procedures on informed consent, student retention, student reassessment, student exiting, and appeals procedures.

Differences Among Children Who Are Gifted and Talented

Although individuals who are gifted and talented share many characteristics, they also differ in a variety of ways. The differences among individuals in each category of giftedness are important to recognize, for they indicate the type of instructional modifications needed for the students to make continuous progress. Knowing differences allows

Figure 15.4 **Theoretical Distribution of Intelligence**

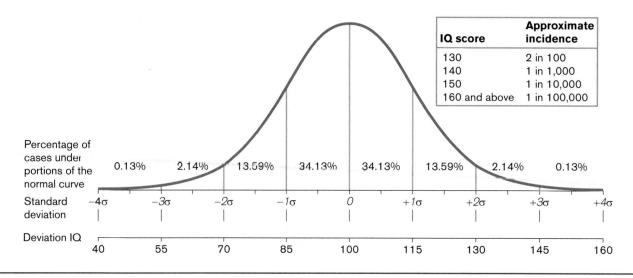

IQ score	Approximate incidence
130	2 in 100
140	1 in 1,000
150	1 in 10,000
160 and above	1 in 100,000

Percentage of cases under portions of the normal curve

0.13% 2.14% 13.59% 34.13% 34.13% 13.59% 2.14% 0.13%

Standard deviation: -4σ -3σ -2σ -1σ 0 $+1\sigma$ $+2\sigma$ $+3\sigma$ $+4\sigma$

Deviation IQ: 40 55 70 85 100 115 130 145 160

SOURCE: Boxed matter from G. Cartwright, C. Cartwright, and M. Ward, *Educating Special Learners,* 2nd ed. (Belmont, CA: Wadsworth, 1981), p. 191.

for the identification of children who do not demonstrate all of the characteristics of the stereotype of the student who is gifted and talented. Assessment provides the data and information needed to understand the degree of giftedness. Off-level testing (using measures that allow for assessing beyond-grade-level performance) is necessary to remove the ceiling effect of grade-level assessment. Individuals who perform at or show the potential to perform at the very high end for any category of giftedness and talent are often referred to as highly or profoundly gifted or talented.

As one examines individuals in each category of giftedness, the degree of giftedness is most apparent among individuals who are gifted in intellectual ability. Certainly IQ is not the only indicator of a person who is intellectually gifted, but it is one criterion that should be considered. Looking at a normal curve, an IQ score that is two standard deviations above the mean may qualify a student for gifted services, but other young people will score three and four standard deviations above the mean (see Figure 15.4). Obviously all these pupils are significantly different from the average child, but they also differ significantly from each other. The specific characteristics of each student who is gifted become important when educators are matching instruction to the needs of the individual. A "one-size-fits-all" approach to service options for students with gifts and talents is inappropriate because it does not match services to needs or allow for the continuous progress of children or young adults.

Exceptional levels of potential and performance can be found in all academic and talent categories. For example, many young people who are gifted mathematically need to work above grade level, and a few are able to work several grades above their age-mates. One young third grader successfully completed a year of algebra with eighth graders, scoring at the top of the class. A 13-year-old studied calculus on his own, and then took the College Board Advanced Placement (AP) exam in calculus. He scored a 5 on the exam, the highest score possible on an AP exam, usually earning the student six hours of college credit in calculus. Few children of these ages, even those who are gifted in mathematics, could or should be working at these levels; however, such accelerated options are as important as opportunities. Providing such advanced study is essential in order to allow these students to continue learning in their area of specific academic giftedness.

A Brief History of the Field of Gifted and Talented Education

The field of gifted and talented education in the United States has its roots in the late nineteenth century but grew and matured in the twentieth century. The twenty-first century brings both challenges and promise to the education of children who are gifted. The history of the field will be described through key events, individuals, and movements that have shaped the study of giftedness and the implementation of programming and services to address the needs of children and youth who are gifted and talented.

The First Half of the Twentieth Century: Pioneering the Field

The development of intelligence testing in the late nineteenth century and the early part of the twentieth century provided the means for the study of gifted individuals. The initial work on measuring intelligence was done by Alfred Binet in France; its purpose was not to measure high-end intelligence but rather to identify children and adults who might not benefit from schooling. William Stern, a German psychologist, developed the formula for the intelligence quotient, or IQ. With the ability to measure intelligence, cognitive science emerged as a field of study.

Lewis Terman (1925), known as the founder of gifted education, conducted a major longitudinal study of gifted children. The measure used to define giftedness was an IQ of 140 or higher. This study of 1,500 children, begun by Terman in the 1920s, continued for seventy years (beyond his lifetime by colleagues), following the children through their adult lives. The study provided information about the characteristics of gifted children and disproved widely held beliefs that gifted children were characterized by social and emotional peculiarities and that "early ripe" would lead to "early rot." Debunking the mythology about gifted individuals was a major contribution of this long-term study.

Another early pioneer in the field of gifted education was Leta S. Hollingworth, who began a longitudinal study of highly gifted children in 1916. Her study yielded information about the characteristics of this exceptional population. She also wrote *Gifted Children: Their Nature and Nurture* (1926), the first comprehensive textbook on gifted education. Hollingworth directed attention to the emotional needs of children who are gifted and believed that giftedness is influenced by both heredity and environment, a view still popular today. Hollingworth was one of the first to start classes for gifted children, believing that appropriate learning opportunities must be matched to students' needs and their readiness to learn.

The 1950s, 1960s, and 1970s: Establishing Foundations for the Field

Understanding intelligence as the *g* factor (general intelligence) is based on the belief that intelligence is a unitary trait. Founded on work begun in the 1950s, however, J. P. Guilford in 1967 published *The Nature of Human Intelligence*, in which he described multiple intelligences. Guilford's theory, the structure-of-the-intellect model, provides a theoretical foundation for the concept of intelligence. Guilford proposed a total of 120 different kinds of intelligences. His theory of multiple intelligences continues to have a tremendous impact on the understanding of children and youth who are gifted and talented.

REFERENCE

Gifted Education

The emergence of national organizations has fostered the development of the emerging field of gifted education. The National Association for Gifted Children (NAGC), started in 1954, now has affiliates in most states. The Association for the Gifted, a division of the Council for Exceptional Children, was established in 1958 and advocates appropriate educational opportunities for gifted and talented children as a category of individuals who are exceptional. Parents and educators combine their efforts in these national organizations and their state affiliates to ensure that the needs of children who are gifted and talented are considered in the development of policies and legislation.

The next important impetus to gifted and talented education came in 1957 with the Russia launched *Sputnik 1*. This demonstration of Soviet progress in science and technology shook public confidence in the United States and began the space race. Suddenly, legislators sought to provide challenging learning opportunities for young people in mathematics and science, with the goal of producing superior mathematicians and scientists. During international crises, gifted individuals often are considered valuable resources to be cultivated. During less tumultuous times, however, their value among the public diminishes, producing a roller-coaster effect.

In 1961, Virgil Ward coined the term *differential education* to describe a curriculum that would enable gifted students to learn at appropriate levels. In *Educating the Gifted: An Axiomatic Approach*, Ward set forth guidelines for writing such a curriculum. Although the curriculum does not need to be entirely different for academically talented students, it must be tied to their characteristics in order to enhance learning. It should be different in ways that encourage learning by young people who are ready to learn at more complex levels that would not be appealing to all students. By highlighting the need to design curriculum to address the needs of academically talented youth—a concept introduced decades earlier by Hollingworth—Ward's work provides a foundation for differentiating the curriculum in defensible ways.

The 1972 Marland Report, mentioned earlier, documented the lack of recognition of the needs of children who are gifted and talented. More than half the personnel in the schools surveyed responded that they had no gifted children in their districts, and twenty-one states reported no services for gifted students. This report, and materials appended to it, noted that the societal and personal costs of not providing services to this population of exceptional children are high. The Marland definition of giftedness (page 539) broadened the view of giftedness from one based strictly on IQ to one encompassing six areas of outstanding or potentially outstanding performance.

The passage of Public Law 94–142, the Education for All Handicapped Children Act, in 1975 led to an increased interest in and awareness of individual differences and exceptionalities. PL 94–142, however, was a missed opportunity for gifted children, as there is no national mandate to serve them. Mandates to provide services for children and youth who are gifted or talented are the result of state rather than federal legislation.

The 1980s and 1990s: The Field Matures and Provides Focus for School Reform

Building on Guilford's multifaceted view of intelligence, Howard Gardner and Robert Sternberg advanced their own theories of multiple intelligences in the 1980s. Gardner (1983) originally identified seven intelligences—linguistic, logical-mathematical, spatial, bodily-kinesthetic, musical, interpersonal, and intrapersonal (see Table 15.2). Describing these intelligences as relatively independent of one another, he later added

■ ■ ■ ■ ■ Table 15.2 **Gardner's Multiple Intelligences**

Intelligence	Characteristics	Possible Career Choices	Examples
Linguistic	Ability to use language effectively in written and oral expression; highly developed verbal skills; often think in words	Novelist, lecturer, lawyer, playwright	Ernest Hemingway, Martin Luther King, Jr.
Logical-mathematical	Ability to use calculation to assist with deductive and inductive reasoning; good at seeing patterns and relationships; think abstractly and conceptually; tend to be logical and systematic	Mathematician, physicist	Albert Einstein, Stephen Hawking
Spatial	Ability to manipulate spatial configurations; good at pattern recognition, sensitive to shape, form, and space; think in pictures or images	Architect, sculptor, interior decorator, engineer	I. M. Pei, Michelangelo
Bodily-kinesthetic	Ability to control and skillfully use one's body to perform a task or express feelings and ideas; able to communicate through body language; keen athletic ability	Dancer, athlete, surgeon	Mikhail Baryshnikov, Michael Jordan
Musical	Ability to discriminate pitch; sensitivity to rhythm, texture, and timbre; ability to hear themes; production of music through performance or composition	Musician, composer	Leonard Bernstein, Ludwig van Beethoven
Interpersonal	Ability to understand other individuals—their actions, moods, and motivations—and to act accordingly; sensitive to ideas and feelings of others, empathetic	Counselor, teacher, politician, salesperson	Carl Rogers, Nelson Mandela
Intrapersonal	Ability to understand one's own feelings, values, and motivations; self-reflective, inwardly motivated; insightful and self-disciplined	Therapist, religious leader	Sigmund Freud, Mother Teresa
Naturalist	Ability to understand interrelationships; capacity to discriminate and classify, recognizes patterns and characteristics; evidences a concern for the environment, sensitive to natural phenomena	Conservationist, forester	John Audubon, Charles Darwin

SOURCE: Adapted from N. Colangelo and G. Davis (Eds.), *Handbook of Gifted Education*, 3rd ed. (Boston, MA: Allyn & Bacon, 2003), p. 102. Adapted by permission.

naturalistic as an eighth intelligence (Gardner, 1993). Sternberg (1985) presented a triarchic view of "successful intelligence," encompassing practical, creative, and executive intelligences. Using these models, the field of gifted education has expanded its understanding of intelligence while not abandoning IQ as a criterion for identifying intellectually gifted children.

A Nation at Risk (National Commission on Excellence in Education, 1983) described the state of education in U.S. schools as abysmal. The report made a connection between the education of children who are gifted and our country's future. This commission found that 50 percent of the school-age gifted population was not performing to full potential and that mathematics and science were in deplorable condition in the schools. The message in this report percolated across the country and was responsible for a renewed interest in gifted education as well as in massive education reform that occurred nationally and state by state.

The field of gifted education has expanded its understanding of intelligence.

The Jacob K. Javits Gifted and Talented Students Education Act (PL 100–297) was passed in 1988. The Javits Act states that "gifted and talented students are a national resource vital to the future of the Nation and its security and well-being" [Sec. 8032 (a) (2)]. This legislation provided for the Office of Gifted and Talented Education, a national research center focusing on gifted children, and demonstration projects in gifted education. In the early '90s, the Office of Educational Research and Improvement in the U.S. Department of Education issued *National Excellence: A Case for Developing America's Talent* (Ross, 1993), the second national report on gifted children. The National Research Center on the Gifted and Talented generated research that was used by decision makers to design and implement policy and enact legislation. The demonstration projects focused on developing talents in areas with a large percentage of children who have been underrepresented in gifted services. The Javits legislation, reauthorized in 2001 as part of the No Child Left Behind Act (PL 107–110), was funded at $11.14 million in fiscal year 2004. Congress approved an appropriation of approximately $7.6 million for the Javits program in fiscal year 2008. In 2010 this funding was eliminated.

Academic standards have become increasingly important in the past decade. The National Association for Gifted Children (2010) issued the *Pre-K–Grade 12 Gifted Programming Standards*. These standards focus on student outcomes and encourage collaboration among general education teachers, special educators, and teachers of the gifted in an effort to assist students in achieving projected outcomes. In 2010, the Common Core State Standards Initiative from the National Governors Association Center for Best Practices and the Council of Chief State School Officers provided standards in mathematics and English/language arts for Grades K–12. In 2013, the Next Generation Science Standards were adopted by several states. These curriculum standards have spurred interest in ensuring a significant content focus in school linked with higher-level thinking—a "must" for all children, including those who are gifted and talented.

The Twenty-First Century: Challenges and Promise Present

Grade-level proficiency was the focus of the No Child Left Behind Act (PL 107–110). For children who are gifted, the goal of reaching proficiency was very limiting as their level of achievement was often beyond what was being taught. When this was the case, reaching proficiency required moving backward or standing still.

In the twenty-first century the standards movement continues to provide momentum in education. Professional organizations are continuing to focus on standards. Leaders in the National Association for Gifted Children and the Council for Exceptional Children have partnered to craft a set of initial teacher preparation standards for both undergraduate and graduate students in gifted education. As you just read, the first decade of the twenty-first century ended with the development of standards in mathematics, language arts, and science.

Prevalence of Giftedness and Talent

Educators believe that approximately 3 to 5 percent of the school-age population is gifted (Clark, 2008). Of course, the number of students identified as gifted or talented depends on the definition of giftedness used by each state. Many pupils exhibit gifts and talents across several areas, and this overlapping results in much higher estimates of who is gifted or talented. Some professionals (Renzulli & Reis, 2003) believe that 10 to 15 percent of the school-age population can be thought of as gifted. The National Association for Gifted Children (2013) estimates that approximately 3 million children are gifted and talented. This group represents about 6 percent of the school-age population in the United States. Likewise, statistics gathered by the federal government also mirror this estimate (National Center for Education Statistics, 2012b).

Etiology of Giftedness and Talent

What makes a child gifted and talented? No doubt giftedness results from a combination of genetic makeup and environmental stimulation. No one knows the precise role of genetics or of the environment, but it is clear that both genetic patterns and environmental stimulation play key roles in developing a child's potential to perform at exceptionally high levels. Understanding giftedness necessitates recognizing that the relationship between genes and a stimulating environment is complex. No longer is it acceptable to view intelligence as fixed at birth; rather, potential intelligence is created by a far more complex interplay between nature and nurture (Clark, 2013).

Neuroscience provides evidence of the vital role played by stimulation in increasing a child's capacity to learn. According to Clark (2013), "the development of intelligence is enhanced or inhibited by the interaction between the genetic pattern of an individual and the opportunities provided by the environment throughout the individual's lifespan" (p. 24). The brain changes physically and chemically when stimulated or challenged. Parents and educators, therefore, play significant roles in developing a child's capacity to learn at high levels.

Characteristics of Individuals Who Are Gifted and Talented

Understanding the characteristics of children and young people who are gifted and talented can help educators and parents recognize behaviors that are indicative of giftedness (see Table 15.3). Many characteristics resemble the characteristics of all children; however, the degree and intensity of the characteristic provide clues that the child may be exceptional. For example, all children are curious, but children who are intellectually gifted and talented may ask so many probing questions that adults think they may be driven to distraction.

Interestingly, the very characteristics identified in Table 15.3 sometimes result in a phenomenon known as the "paradoxical negative effect" (Blackbourn, Patton, & Trainor, 2004). In this situation, behaviors displayed by students with gifts and talents may work to their detriment. For example, high verbal abilities may lead the student to dominate class discussion, self-confidence may be misinterpreted as arrogance, and a dislike for rules and routine may be perceived as a disruptive influence.

Children who are intellectually gifted and talented often perform childhood tasks on an advanced schedule. They may talk in sentences early, read before entering school, or think abstractly before age-mates. These children display exceptional memories and learn at a rapid pace. They are knowledgeable about things about which their age peers

AUDIO

Gifted Students

Category	Attributes
Academic/Learning Characteristics	• Ability to reason and think abstractly • Acquires information easily • Enjoys learning • Highly inquisitive • Demonstrates interest in a variety of areas/activities • Generalizes knowledge to novel settings • Intellectually curious • Highly motivated, persistent learner • Sees relationships among seemingly unrelated items, facts, and ideas • Early reader • Exhibits sustained attention and concentration • Excellent memory • Highly verbal • Generates elaborate and possibly nontraditional responses to questions • Good problem-solving skills • Conceptualizes and synthesizes information quickly
Social and Emotional Characteristics	• Works well independently • High energy level • Self-confident • Exhibits qualities of leadership • Relates well to older classmates, teachers, and adults • Sensitive and empathetic • Intrinsically motivated • Risk taker • Critical of self, strives for perfection • Concern for justice and idealism • Intense • Dislike of routine, rules, and regulations • Likely to have internal locus of control

*Attributes are examples only; not all individuals identified as intellectually gifted will exhibit these features.

SOURCE: Adapted from B. Clark, *Growing Up Gifted,* 7th ed., © 2008. Adapted by permission of Pearson Education, Inc., Upper Saddle River, NJ.

are not aware. They show a propensity for learning and, if allowed to learn about areas of interest at a challenging pace, may not distinguish work from play.

A second characteristic is exceptional talent in one or more specific academic areas. One child may be exceptional in mathematics but perform on grade level in language arts; another may be a gifted writer but not evidence the same level of talent in science. Children who are gifted in a specific academic area read widely and intently about that subject area, require little or no drill to grasp concepts, and have large vocabularies in that specific subject area. This intense interest may be viewed as being "single-minded" or may be seen as an opportunity to develop the interest and talent to an exceptional level. Such focus is an advantage when choosing a college major or, later, a career.

A third category of giftedness is creativity. All children are creative; however, some are exceptionally creative. These children have many unusual ideas and vivid imaginations. They have a high level of energy that may get them in trouble. They may daydream and become easily bored with routine tasks. They have a high level of tolerance for ambiguity and are risk takers. Creative children view the world from their own vantage points. With appropriate experiences, they may be future entrepreneurs.

Leadership is another category or characteristic of giftedness. Others look to leaders when a decision needs to be made, and children who are gifted in leadership are sought after to lead activities, projects, and play. Leaders initiate activities and make plans to reach goals. They get others to work toward goals, which may be desirable or undesirable. Children who are leaders may be seen as bossy. Children who display early leadership abilities have personal qualities that make them charismatic.

A final category of giftedness and talent focuses on the visual and performing arts. Some children may display exceptional talent in art, music, dance, and/or drama. They exhibit an intense interest in one or more of the visual and performing arts. They quickly grasp concepts in the talent area, demonstrate original work in that area, and perform at exceptional levels when compared with their age-mates.

Figure 15.5 summarizes characteristics of individuals who are gifted and talented on these five dimensions of giftedness. See the accompanying Insights feature (page 556).

Educational Considerations

Research suggests that most classroom teachers make no or only minor modifications to meet the unique needs of learners who are gifted (Archambault et al., 1993). Westberg and colleagues (Westberg, Archambault, Dobyns, & Salvin, 1993) observe that little attention is given to differentiating instruction, curricular practices, or grouping arrangements when teachers are confronted with pupils who are gifted. Ten years later Westberg and Daoust (2003) replicated the earlier study. The results showed that differentiation practices were no more likely to be found in the classrooms then than they were a decade earlier. This situation is regrettable. Children who are gifted and talented need opportunities to work hard on challenging learning tasks. Instructional practices need to be modified in order to address the cognitive and social-emotional needs of students with unique talents and gifts.

■ ■ ■ ■ ■ Figure 15.5 **Characteristics of Various Areas of Giftedness**

Visual/performing arts
Outstanding in sense of spatial relationships
Unusual ability for expressing self, feelings, moods, etc., through art, dance, drama, music
Good motor coordination
Exhibits creative expression
Desire for producing "own product" (not content with mere copying)
Observant

Leadership
Assumes responsibility
High expectations for self and others
Fluent, concise self-expression
Foresees consequences and implications of decisions
Good judgment in decision making
Likes structure
Well-liked by peers
Self-confident
Organized

Creative thinking
Independent thinker
Exhibits original thinking in oral and written expression
Comes up with several solutions to a given problem
Possesses a sense of humor
Creates and invents
Challenged by creative tasks
Improvises often
Does not mind being different from the crowd

General intellectual ability
Formulates abstractions
Processes information in complex ways
Observant
Excited about new ideas
Enjoys hypothesizing
Learns rapidly
Uses a large vocabulary
Inquisitive
Self-starter

Specific academic ability
Good memorization ability
Advanced comprehension
Acquires basic-skills knowledge quickly
Widely read in special-interest area
High academic success in special-interest area
Pursues special interests with enthusiasm and vigor

SOURCE: Copyrighted material from the National Association for Gifted Children (NAGC). This material may not be reprinted without permission of NAGC, Washington, DC, (202) 785-4268, www.nagc.org.

INSIGHTS

Myths and Truths About Gifted Students

Common Myths About Gifted Students

- Gifted students are a homogeneous group, all high achievers.
- Gifted students do not need help. If they are really gifted, they can manage on their own.
- Gifted students have fewer problems than others because their intelligence and abilities somehow exempt them from the hassles of daily life.
- The future of a gifted student is assured; a world of opportunities lies before the student.
- Gifted students are self-directed; they know where they are heading.
- The social and emotional development of the gifted student is at the same level as his or her intellectual development.
- Gifted students are nerds and social isolates.
- The primary value of the gifted student lies in his or her brain power.
- The gifted student's family always prizes his or her abilities.
- Gifted students need to serve as examples to others, and they should always assume extra responsibility.
- Gifted students make everyone else smarter.
- Gifted students can accomplish anything they put their minds to; all they have to do is apply themselves.
- Gifted students are naturally creative and do not need encouragement.
- Gifted children are easy to raise and a welcome addition to any classroom.

Truths About Gifted Students

- Gifted students are often perfectionistic and idealistic. They may equate achievement and grades with self-esteem and self-worth, which sometimes leads to fear of failure and interferes with achievement.
- Gifted students may experience heightened sensitivity to their own expectations and those of others, resulting in guilt over achievements or grades perceived to be low.
- Gifted students are asynchronous. Their chronological age [and] social, physical, emotional, and intellectual development may all be at different levels. For example, a 5-year-old may be able to read and comprehend a third-grade book but may not be able to write legibly.
- Some gifted children are "mappers" (sequential learners), while others are "leapers" (spatial learners). Leapers may not know how they got a "right answer." Mappers may get lost in the steps leading to the right answer.
- Gifted students may be so far ahead of their chronological age mates that they know more than half the curriculum before the school year begins! Their boredom can result in low achievement and grades.
- Gifted children are problem solvers. They benefit from working on open-ended, interdisciplinary problems—for example, how to solve a shortage of community resources. Gifted students often refuse to work for grades alone.
- Gifted students often think abstractly and with such complexity that they may need help with concrete study and test-taking skills. They may not be able to select one answer in a multiple choice question because they see how all the answers might be correct.
- Gifted students who do well in school may define success as getting an "A" and failure as any grade less than an "A." By early adolescence they may be unwilling to try anything where they are not certain of guaranteed success.

SOURCE: ERIC Clearinghouse on Disabilities and Gifted Education. Retrieved November 18, 2013, from http://eric.hoagiesgifted.org/fact/myths.html

Original source material: S. Berger, *College Planning for Gifted Students*, 2nd ed. (Reston, VA: Council for Exceptional Children, 1998), p. 16.

Educators use a variety of instructional strategies to serve pupils who are gifted and talented. This eclectic approach reflects a contemporary trend of not endorsing any one model of instructional delivery (Gibson & Efinger, 2001), but rather providing instruction that best meets the needs of the individual learner. Here we review several different instructional strategies that can benefit pupils who are gifted and talented.

Differentiation

All children are not expected to wear the same size shoes because they are in the same grade. Likewise, parents and educators should expect tremendous differences in interests, needs, and abilities among children and youth of the same age. Differentiation of the curriculum is necessary in order to accommodate these differences and to provide a learning environment in which all children, including children who are gifted and talented, can thrive. "In differentiated classrooms, teachers begin where students are, not the front of a curriculum guide. They accept and build upon the premise that learners differ in important ways" (Tomlinson, 1999, p. 2).

"Each child deserves to make continuous progress, making at least a month's achievement gain for a month in school. Differentiation makes continuous progress possible" (Roberts & Boggess, 2011, p. 86). For children with gifts and talents, it is important to remove the learning ceiling. Children need to learn challenging content and to develop cognitive skills throughout their school careers. Students who do not learn to tackle challenging learning tasks may never learn to do so. See the Suggestions for the Classroom feature (page 558) for an explanation of differentiated programming.

In order to make progress possible, the teacher must preassess what a pupil already knows and is able to do. Preassessment is the key to ascertaining appropriate levels of instruction in each content area so that new learning can occur. Preassessment is the linchpin for defensible differentiation (Roberts, 2010). In order to know what content and skills to preassess, the teacher must first have a well-planned unit of study, including content and skills recommended by local and state guidelines as well as by the national standards. Preassessment will then allow the teacher to differentiate learning experiences and keep the unit challenging for all students in the class. Without preassessing the students' knowledge and skills, teachers will assume that how well students do on the end-of-unit assessment is the result of their teaching; with preassessment, teachers will know what students knew as they began the unit.

Instructional Strategies

Curriculum Compacting

Curriculum compacting is a differentiation strategy that is often used in the general education classroom (Reis & Renzulli, 2005). Simply stated, curriculum compacting is an instructional procedure whereby the time spent on academic subjects is telescoped or reduced so as to allow the student(s) to make continuous progress. The first phase is to determine the goals and objectives of the regular curriculum. The second step is to assess what the student or students already know before teaching a unit of study. If the preassessment indicates that one or more pupils have already mastered the content or a major portion thereof, this student or cluster of students will have time to delve into the content at a more complex level and to develop different and perhaps more sophisticated products. Curriculum compacting is a strategy that responds well to the characteristics of children who are gifted and talented intellectually, in specific academic areas, or in the visual and performing arts. Language arts and mathematics are two content areas where curriculum compacting has been shown to be effective (Reis et al., 2003). See the accompanying First Person feature for teaching suggestions from an award-winning educator (page 560).

Higher-Level Thinking and Problem Solving

Leaders of business and industry have told educators for decades that it is very important for students to develop higher-level thinking and problem-solving skills. When

differentiation: A modification of the curriculum that enables students who are gifted to learn at a level appropriate to their ability.

preassessment: An assessment of a pupil's previously acquired knowledge; allows teacher to provide differentiated learning experiences.

curriculum compacting: An instructional technique whereby the time spent on academic subjects is reduced so as to allow for enrichment activities; typically used with students who are gifted or talented.

SUGGESTIONS FOR THE CLASSROOM

Differentiated Programming: What It Is and What It Isn't

Differentiated programming and *differentiated instruction* are terms for what is really a simple educational concept—providing instruction that meets the differing needs of all students. Although the concept is simple, making it a reality in the classroom is complex. For the student who is gifted, it means the opportunity to advance as far as possible. For a slower learner, it means offering support for advancement at a pace that allows for mastery. Other students have varying abilities, learning styles, interests, and needs, which also must be met. This is what differentiated programming attempts to do.

Differentiated instruction is:

→ Having high expectations for all students.

→ Providing multiple assignments within units that are oriented toward students with different levels of achievement.

→ Allowing students to choose, with teacher direction, ways to learn and how to demonstrate what they have learned.

→ Permitting students to demonstrate mastery of material they already know and progress at their own pace through new material.

→ Structuring class assignments so they require high levels of critical thinking but permit a range of responses.

→ Assigning some activities geared to different learning styles, levels of thinking, levels of interest, and levels of achievement.

→ Providing students with opportunities to have choices about what they learn.

→ Flexible. Teachers may move students in and out of groups after assessing their instructional needs.

Differentiated instruction is not:

→ Individualization. It isn't a different lesson plan for each student each day.

→ Giving all students the same work most of the time.

→ Students spending significant amounts of time teaching material they have mastered to others who have not mastered it.

→ Assigning more work at the same level to high-achieving students.

→ All the time. Often, it is preferable for students to work as a whole class.

→ Grouping students into cooperative learning groups that do not provide for individual accountability or do not focus on work that is new to all students.

→ Using only the differences in student responses to the same class assignment to provide differentiation.

→ Limited to acceleration. Teachers are encouraged to use a variety of strategies.

SOURCE: Susan Allan, unpublished manuscript.

teachers combine higher-level thinking skills with significant content, all children thrive. Children who are gifted and talented will be ready for higher-level thinking and problem solving before many of their age-mates. Services provided by a teacher of gifted pupils can complement the teaching of thinking by the general educator. A gifted resource teacher can provide opportunities for individual and team projects that require higher-level thinking.

Flexible Grouping

The one-room school is a well-known example of flexible grouping. A 9-year-old child could spell with 13-year-olds but do math with 7-year-olds, if those groupings matched his or her level of achievement. Preassessment provides a defensible rationale for grouping and regrouping children to allow for continuous progress. Grouping by interests, needs, or abilities (readiness levels) can be used within a heterogeneous classroom, in a homogeneous classroom, or between classrooms or teams. Flexible grouping is necessary if all children, including those who are gifted and talented, are to thrive in a classroom and make continuous progress.

Educators often use a variety of instructional strategies to meet the unique needs of pupils who are gifted and talented.

Cluster Grouping

Cluster grouping is the practice of placing five or more students who have similar needs and abilities with one teacher. For example, seven fourth-grade students who are gifted in mathematics are placed together in a classroom. The purpose of cluster grouping is twofold. First, from a practical standpoint, a teacher is far more likely to plan instruction to address needs for more advanced content and a faster pace of instruction with a cluster than with a single student. Second, others who have similar needs and interests provide an intellectual peer group as well as age-mates for the students in the cluster.

Cluster grouping has advantages for both students and teachers. For the students who are gifted and talented, the cluster arrangement promotes challenging cognitive and positive social-emotional development. For teachers, the cluster provides a group for which to plan rather than single students sprinkled among all of the teachers.

Grouping students into clusters must be done before the school year begins. Consequently, the decision to cluster group must involve the individual responsible for class scheduling.

Tiered Assignments

This instructional strategy allows the teacher to offer variations of the same lesson to children with differing levels of ability. As an example, if the class is reading *Charlotte's Web,* one group of students (Tier 1) might be working on key information about the plot while Tier 2 might be asked to write a story that makes a change in the plot or in the development of a character. Pupils who are gifted and in Tier 3 might be asked to write their own chapter from the point of view of one of the characters. Tiered assignments allow for matching instruction to level of readiness.

Problem-Based Learning

The application of critical thinking skills and the development of problem-solving abilities along with the acquisition of knowledge are some of the benefits associated with using problem-based learning in the classroom. In this model, students

flexible grouping: The combining or grouping of students according to needs and abilities matched to their level of achievement.

cluster grouping: The practice of placing five or more students who have similar needs and abilities with one teacher; promotes challenging cognitive development and positive social-emotional development.

tiered assignments: An instructional strategy that allows the teacher to offer variations of the same lesson to students with differing levels of ability.

problem-based learning: Instructional approach in which authentic problems having multiple solutions are addressed through the application of critical thinking skills.

FIRST PERSON: PATRICE

One Size Does Not Fit All

How might a classroom involved in the inclusion of gifted students look? Please take a glimpse into my Primary 1 (kindergarten) classroom, Room 21, for a moment, for inclusion is what you will see.

All of the children are working in math centers. Brandy and Alison are using random number generators (dice) to create simple addition sentences. Once they have generated two numbers to write down, they add the numbers together for the sum, and as all good mathematicians do, they double-check their work. At the same time, Lane and Shelby are busy using the random number generators to do double-digit addition. They squeal when they realize that their sum actually took them above 100. Sam and Megan are well above the regular addition process. They have stepped into the world of multiplication. They are using the random number generators and teddy bear counters to create groups representing multiplication. The entire room is a buzz of mathematical vocabulary and a celebration of learning—music to any teacher's ears. My journey to inclusion of the gifted student within my classroom was a result of realizing that I was not meeting the needs of my students.

As a seventeen-year teaching veteran, I have taught Grades K–6. Throughout those years, I have worn many hats. For a two-year period I was the curriculum coordinator for our building. I had the pleasant task of formally assessing students as a part of a verification process of our primary talent pool process. Bright-eyed primary students sat eagerly across from me, amazing me with their high-ability thought processes. Each time a tiny student answered a question that was well above the typical/average level of learning for a primary student, I always asked, "Where did you learn about multiplication/square root/such difficult words to read?" The response was *always* the same: "My mom" or "My dad." I was saddened to never hear, "My teacher." When I returned to the classroom, I became determined to be in on the fun of removing the ceiling of learning for my students. When one of my students amazes everyone by sharing something brilliant, I am hoping she or he will be able to share, "My teacher taught me that!"

As our children walk through the door of our classrooms we must ever be cognizant of the fact that "one size does not fit all." Every classroom, without exception, is a classroom of diverse learners. Through a variety of means, teachers have the ability to orchestrate a classroom so that all needs can and will be met. The most important information a teacher must know before reaching all children includes what *each* of the children knows, what they need to know, how they are able to apply what they have learned, and what kind of connection each child has made to his or her own world.

Before every thematic unit in our kindergarten classroom, the children help prepare a KWL (sometimes a KWHL) chart. *K* stands for "What do we know, or think we know, about this subject?" The *W* represents "What would we like to learn about this subject?" And the *L* is a follow-up for "What have we learned about this subject?" We also have a category for *H,* "How will we find out what we want to know?" The KWL chart is a good way for me to get a pulse of the class's knowledge and interest concerning the content I plan to present. I am able to use the information from the children to divide them into interest groups or to determine if the content needs to be modified in any way for particular students. The KWL is simply one form of preassessment used in our classroom on a regular basis. As the teacher, I simply must know *what* my children know. If a student or group of students is already equipped with the information I want to teach and I "plow ahead" with that unit without adjustments, then I have committed a grave injustice to my students. I have asked them to be patient as I teach the other students. As adults we are outraged when we are asked to sit still and listen to something we already know forward and backward. Our children are the same. When we teach content that a child has mastered, we are asking her or him to run in one spot over and over, much like a cartoon character that never seems to get anywhere.

Children not only come to us at different levels; they learn at different paces. Once you know what the children know individually, you must monitor progress through formative assessments. If a child has mastered a concept, he or she should be able to move on. If a child knows how to do simple addition with 100 percent accuracy, he or she should not be put through the nightmarish experience of extra work in simple addition. That child is ready to move on, not run in place! Math is one area in which I enjoy using the compacting process. For that quick learner, once I find out where he or she is, we move forward. The result of the pretesting is a learning atmosphere such as I described earlier. The overall assessment process is simply described. The pretest is the map for instruction. The formative tests are the detours. The posttesting is the determination of how successful we are in finding the final destination.

Literacy in a classroom should be individualized as much as math. In my classroom each child has his or her own word ring and reading assignments made on a weekly basis. Monitoring the word ring and reading progress at school enables the children to make continuous progress no matter what the reading level of each child may be. I love encouraging the children to go home and "impress" their parents or some other grown-up at home. When discussion of what they are learning is encouraged, the children are more prone to make school-learning connections transfer to home-learning connections. Parents are certainly vital participants in their child's education. But as the teacher, you will be looked upon as the one who should set the pace. We should be ever mindful that the pace for a child means continuous learning.

Textbooks are wonderful resources for teachers, but they are certainly no substitute for allowing children to think for themselves. I love to have the children use questioning—questioning of everything. I especially enjoy setting the stage for learning with a variety of materials centered on certain content and then turning the children loose on creating their own questions. Creativity, problem solving, and real-world learning become the products of such an environment.

Imagine the absolute misery Einstein would feel today sitting in a typical primary classroom. Sitting through simple addition would be torture for him! Every classroom today has the potential of having an Einstein in it. We must make it our duty and responsibility to meet the needs of the Einsteins of the future. ■

–Patrice McCrary
Cumberland Trace Elementary School
Warren County, KY
2003 Kentucky Teacher of the Year
2006 All-USA Teacher Team
2008 Kentucky Teacher Hall of Fame

are confronted with authentic, real-world situations, such as global warming, that are "ill-structured problems." The pupils are asked to solve the problem, which typically has multiple solutions rather than a "right answer." Teachers function as tutors and facilitators as the children work through various solutions and scenarios and evaluate their responses. Sometimes teachers model effective problem-solving strategies by thinking out loud and questioning their own hypotheses and recommendations. Pupils are often highly motivated and very engaged in their own learning (Smith, Polloway, Patton, & Dowdy, 2012).

Pacing Instruction

Individuals who are gifted and talented learn at a faster pace in their area of talent or special interest than their age-mates. This faster pace provides the rationale for differentiation strategies. *Prisoners of Time* (National Education Commission on Time and Learning, 1994) reports, "Some students take three to six times longer than others to learn the same thing. . . . Under today's practices, high-ability students are forced to spend more time than they need on a curriculum developed for students of moderate ability. Many become bored, unmotivated, and frustrated. They become prisoners of time" (p. 15).

Because children who are gifted and talented often complete their work in a fraction of the time that it takes their age-mates, teachers often provide more work to keep them busy. This practice is contrary to the needs of those children who can complete the assignment rapidly. The need for accelerated pacing must be linked with increasingly complex content and challenging learning experiences rather than more work at the same level.

As educators, our goal should be to develop each child's gifts and talents to their fullest degree.

Creativity

Creativity is important for all children. According to Clark (2013), it is "a highly complex human ability that is beyond giftedness and can bring forth that which is new, diverse, advanced, complex, or previously unknown, so that humankind can experience growth in life as fuller, richer, and/or more meaningful" (p. 150). Developing creative thinking skills is an especially important element of services for children who are gifted and talented. E. Paul Torrance (1969) describes four skills that are essential for a creative thinker: originality, fluency, flexibility, and elaboration. Originality is the ability to produce novel ideas. Fluency involves the ability to generate many ideas, and flexibility is the ability to switch categories of ideas. Elaboration is the ability to provide detail to ideas. All teachers should incorporate the teaching of creative thinking skills as an integral part of their curriculum.

Students who are gifted in creativity need opportunities to develop this talent in a risk-free learning environment (Piirto, 2007). They need to interact with creative adults, speculating on possibilities and examining the creative process as well as creative products. Pupils who are gifted thrive when given opportunities to combine their creativity with an interest in a content or talent area.

There is no one "correct" way to teach students who are gifted and talented. Teachers must skillfully match the needs of the pupil with the demands of the curriculum. Effective teaching of learners who are gifted and talented, as with other students, requires planning. It is a matter of constructing a "goodness of fit" between the individual's learning style and the specific content of the curriculum. As educators, our goal should be to develop each pupil's gifts and talents to their fullest degree. The accompanying Effective Instructional Practices feature offers suggestions for teaching students who are gifted (page 565).

Service Delivery Options

Pupils with gifts and talents require exposure to a curriculum that is rigorous and intellectually challenging. These students need instruction that is more complex and abstract than that provided to their typical peers (Burns, Purcell, & Hertberg, 2006). In many instances, this necessitates programming options outside of the general education classroom. The general education classroom, as traditionally organized in terms of curriculum and instruction, is seen as inadequate for meeting the needs of pupils who are gifted and talented (Clark, 2013). Silverman (1995b) believes that too many children who are gifted are "languishing in the regular classroom" (p. 220) because they are exposed to a curriculum that is too simple and was mastered long ago. The general education classroom is, in many cases, an exceedingly restrictive placement for pupils with special talents and gifts, rather than a least restrictive setting (Gallagher, 2003). As a result, many schools provide a range or continuum of service delivery options

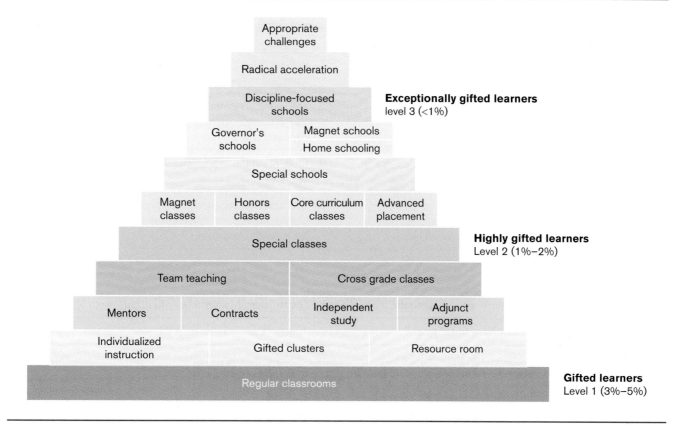

NOTE: All programs for gifted learners, regardless of how they are structured, must provide differentiation, flexible grouping, continuous progress, intellectual peer interaction, continuity, and teachers with specialized education.

SOURCE: Adapted from B. Clark, *Growing Up Gifted,* 8th ed. (Upper Saddle River, NJ: Pearson Education, 2013), p. 289. Reprinted by permission of Pearson Education.

designed to meet the unique needs of students who are gifted. Figure 15.6 portrays an array of programming alternatives appropriate for gifted learners from elementary to high school.

Gifted Resource Services

Children identified in any area of giftedness or talent need some time with others who share their interests and abilities. Working with other children of similar abilities takes away the feeling that many children who are gifted have—that they must hide their abilities in order to "fit in." This service is typically provided through a resource room or pull-out program. Such a program can be the highlight of the students' day or week. It is important that classroom teachers see the time with the gifted resource teacher as an important service but not the only one needed by these children. Children who are gifted and talented are gifted all day, all week; they need ongoing instruction that will remove the learning ceiling and allow for continuous progress. Table 15.4 lists some of the advantages and disadvantages of a resource room model.

Acceleration

The child who is achieving above grade level and is ready to learn at increasingly advanced levels needs **acceleration**. Acceleration matches learning opportunities to

acceleration: An instructional strategy typically used with pupils who are gifted and talented; one approach is placing students in a grade level beyond their chronological age.

AUDIO
Acceleration

■ ■ ■ ■ ■ Table 15.4 **Advantages and Disadvantages: The Resource Room and Pull-Out Models**

Advantages	Disadvantages
1. Pull-out programs are relatively easy to set in motion.	1. Pull-out programs cost more as extra teachers have to be hired and special facilities provided.
2. The teacher in the regular classroom has more time to work with the other students.	2. The regular classroom teacher may get frustrated and feel that students leaving is a disruption to his or her educational plan.
3. Students who are left in the classroom have a chance to shine.	3. Students in the regular classroom may feel resentful.
4. The teacher in the pull-out program can focus on critical and creative thinking because the teacher in the regular classroom focuses on the standard curriculum.	4. The academically talented students might have to make up work in the regular classroom while having more work in the pull-out classroom.
5. The differentiation of curriculum is separated from the classroom flow.	5. Curriculum may have no relationship to curriculum in the regular classroom.
6. Students receive special help in areas of strength.	6. Students are treated differently according to ability.
7. Teachers may feel as if they have "their" kids.	7. Teachers are isolated from the other teachers.
8. Students can have time with other students to discuss intellectual interests that may not be shared by students in the regular classroom.	8. Students may feel different from the rest of the students in their regular classroom.
9. Collaboration with other teachers is encouraged.	9. Students are academically talented all the time and not just during pull-out time.
10. Small groups of students can do special projects that would not be possible in the regular classroom.	10. Small groups of students may receive special privileges other students don't receive (e.g., access to computers, field trips).
11. Teachers of the talented can provide intensive instruction in areas of expertise (e.g., the arts, foreign language).	11. Turf issues with students' regular classroom teacher may arise (e.g., homework, lessons and assemblies missed).

SOURCE: J. Piirto, *Talented Children and Adults,* 3rd ed. (Waco, TX: Prufrock, 2007), p. 87.

the readiness of the student to learn at challenging levels. Researchers have found several beneficial outcomes for acceleration (Colangelo, Assouline, & Gross, 2004; Kulik, 2003). Among these positive outcomes are greater academic achievement, increased interest in school, and enhanced self-concept. Contrary to the worries of some parents and administrators, when properly implemented, acceleration does not contribute to social and emotional problems (Swiatek, 1993).

Acceleration may take several forms. Acceleration may focus on one content area, such as art or mathematics, or it may be a full-year acceleration known as grade skipping. It may also mean starting school at a younger age. Children who are reading when they come to school need to continue to improve their reading skills and to enhance their comprehension. Reading may be accelerated in the class with a cluster of children who are also early readers, or the child/children may join the first grade for the portion of the day devoted to reading. The skipping of a grade will usually be successful if the child wants to do it and if the receiving teacher wants the situation to work well. Acceleration includes taking high school classes while in middle school

REFERENCE

Self-concept

Effective Instructional Practices
Differentiated Instruction

The goal of schools must be to support and encourage lifelong learning. The most likely way to achieve that goal is differentiation, an instructional strategy that is a popular topic for educators to discuss but is less frequently implemented. Because all fourth or eighth graders are not at the same level of achievement in any content area and their interests differ greatly, differentiation is very important. It is the strategy that is most likely to ensure continuous progress of all children, including those who are gifted and talented.

Effective instruction for learners with gifts and talents involves five steps:

Step 1. Preassess.

Once you have planned the unit of study, the starting point in planning differentiation must be to preassess.

Guiding Question: "Who already knows the content and can demonstrate the skills even before the unit of study begins?"

Step 2. Group children for instructional purposes.

Preassessment results provide information to help you decide which students can be clustered for instructional purposes for a particular unit of study. Grouping facilitates learning, providing the vehicle for differentiating learning experiences.

Guiding Question: "Which students are ready to learn the content at the same level and would benefit from being grouped for instruction?"

Step 3. Match learner experiences to the preassessment data (level of achievement, interests).

Differentiation does not just mean providing different learning experiences or offering choice; rather, differentiation is the intentional match of content (basic to complex), process (level of cognitive skill), and product (visual, written, oral, kinesthetic, and technological) (Roberts & Inman, 2009b).

Guiding Question: "How can the learning experiences be shaped to match the preassessment results and to ensure intellectual challenges?"

Step 4. Provide products (ways to demonstrate what has been learned) that will motivate and teach.

A variety of products can be used that will allow students to show what they have learned but in ways that will motivate them to learn.

Guiding Question: "What products will interest students and prepare them to build expertise for current and future use?"

Step 5. Reflect, reflect, reflect.

Learning experiences that remain isolated do not promote lifelong learning. If learning is to be ongoing, it is essential to reflect on what has been learned and what one wants to learn next.

Guiding Question: "What questions will promote reflection and lead to ongoing learning?"

---

or taking College Board Advanced Placement classes throughout high school. It may involve taking advanced courses via distance learning. It may also include early entrance into college.

Besides acceleration, teachers have several other techniques at their disposal for modifying the curriculum in an effort to meet the needs of students with gifts and talents. Examples of these strategies can be found in Table 15.5. A variety of strategies and service options need to be in place in classrooms and schools to address the wide range of gifted learners' needs.

Independent Study

Independent study allows children of all ages to explore topics of interest and provides challenge if appropriate guidelines are established. These guidelines would include use of primary sources and resources that are matched to the child's level of reading and knowledge of the topic. This strategy enables the child to pose questions about topics of interest and to extend learning to related topics if he or she has demonstrated in a

I am still somewhat of a rookie in the field of education. I taught eighth-grade language arts for three years. Although I loved that position and learned so much from it, I recently decided to take on a new challenge—the position of countywide gifted and talented teacher/coordinator. Throughout my career I have attended a wide variety of workshops related to teaching writing, reading across the curriculum, differentiated educational strategies, gender-based instruction, and gifted education. I have served as a model teacher for beginning teachers, and with my new position as gifted teacher/coordinator, I give workshops across the county about the selection process for children who are gifted and talented and strategies for differentiation and acceleration that can be used with all students. I work with four elementary schools and one high school, collaborating with teachers on service plans for students who are gifted and talented. Soon I will be teaching four days a week during which children in Grades 3–8 who are gifted and talented from across the county will come to my classroom and work in a resource room setting.

Strategies for Inclusive Classrooms

Based on my teaching experience, I believe that the key to effective instruction centers on two ingredients—relationships with students and the belief that *every* child has strengths. I set high expectations for all my students. When I plan units, I try to begin with some sort of preassessment to find out what my students already know about the content that I am about to present. Based on the results, I can then adjust my activities to fit the needs of each of my students. Various preassessments that I have used include the following:

- Brainstorming: Students list questions that they have pertaining to that topic.
- KWH Charts: Students chart what they already know, what they want to know about a topic, and how they want to learn it.
- Anticipation Guides: Students are given a list of statements that relate to the concepts that will be covered during the unit. They read each statement, put a check

mark next to the ones with which they agree, engage in discussions about their answers, use the text and other materials for the chapter to either prove or disprove their answers, and finally review the statements and change them as necessary to make them true. The entire class debates the evidence that proves the statements and must come to consensus about each one.

- Most Difficult First: Students are presented with the most difficult vocabulary words from our list, and those who score 80 percent or better on a definition pretest are assigned another activity.

The beauty of each of these strategies is that each one can be used with any content area. Once I have diagnosed the situation, I can then decide which activities my students should complete.

I have found that cluster grouping is a highly effective strategy with students of all ability levels. In my opinion, the most positive outcome of this strategy is that the students who are gifted can excel to their fullest potential when presented with problem-solving activities, yet they don't feel burdened by the lack of motivation sometimes evidenced by their classmates. Additionally, those students who may lack academic confidence gain confidence in their abilities because they find that without someone else to carry the load, they can do it—and they usually do! It's a win-win situation for everyone.

Obviously, based on the repeated success of the differentiated projects, I would highly recommend them to all teachers at any grade level and ability level. In planning for these types of projects, I first reflect on the particular learning styles that exist in my classroom, choose a project type to fit each one, and then develop scoring criteria for each project choice. For example, for visual learners I might choose to include a poster option; for bodily-kinesthetic learners, I might choose a role-play; for those who are verbally gifted, I might choose a newspaper article; and for those who are more intrapersonal in nature, I might choose creation of a webpage that requires individual work. Of course, with each new unit, I adjust the project choices accordingly because I don't want my students to become bored or accustomed to the same types of choices. I have never had a student complain about doing the projects—honestly! They much prefer them to tests, and so do I. In my opinion, these types of projects are true assessments of what students have learned because they tend to gravitate toward the choices that favor their own particular learning style, and consequently, they do well

preassessment that he or she has mastered the core content. Independent study is a positive option for children, including those who are gifted and talented, only if they are taught to work independently. That children are gifted does not mean that they have had the experiences that prepare them to take responsibility for their own learning. The

because they can show me what they know in the way that they know best. I have found that the products my students present to me provide me with an effective tool for building relationships with them because they have the freedom to demonstrate their understanding in a way that is completely unique to them.

Finally, my experience with independent studies has proven to be successful. I have found that allowing students to choose their topic to demonstrate a particular skill is very beneficial because they have the freedom to study something that is meaningful to them. Also, the types of products that they create will be specific to their own particular ability levels.

Successful Collaboration

My teaching experience has taught me one very important lesson: Collaboration is crucial! Due to scheduling problems with planning time, our school cannot plan units by cross-curricular teams (including math, science, language arts, and social studies). However, during my first three years of teaching, I was fortunate enough to work very closely with another language arts teacher who had the same philosophy about teaching and learning that I did. We both believed that all students can learn, and we both were passionate about offering them challenges that expanded their minds and were enjoyable and fostered creativity in the process. We collaborated daily and often fed off one another in our planning of units. Once we were comfortable with one another, we decided to approach the eighth-grade social studies teacher and plan some activities that extended the students' learning of social studies concepts while in language arts class. Perhaps our most successful language arts–social studies collaboration resulted when we planned to read the Revolutionary War novel *My Brother Sam Is Dead* as the students were studying the Revolutionary War. The students loved it, and so did we! As we read the novel, I actually called upon the students to clarify some questions I had periodically, based on what they had learned previously about the war. It's a very gratifying experience to see students begin to make connections from one subject to another. When they master this skill, they are truly demonstrating higher-level thinking skills. My heart smiled as I listened to both my students who are gifted or talented and those with lower ability rattle off war facts without even blinking. Again, setting high expectations for everyone in the room paid huge dividends because students of varying levels gained confidence in their academic abilities.

Working With Parents and Families

While collaboration with other teachers has been beneficial for me, close contact with parents and families is also important. In fact, in some cases, it has saved me. I have had several students who were obviously gifted, yet they were unmotivated and were underperforming academically. When I realized that these students were underachieving, my first inclination was to contact the parents to ask for suggestions concerning tapping into their child's interests. I realized that if I could tweak assignments to cater to the children's areas of interest, they would be much more likely to get involved and have an appropriate learning experience. The line of communication was beneficial both ways, however. Making parents aware of the situation also gave them the chance to ask me for suggestions about ways to inspire their children at home. Although I have had many students who rose to every occasion and performed to the absolute best of their ability, I have had just as many who were less than excited about school because of sheer boredom and complacency. Those individuals definitely require more work, but inspiring them is worth all of the effort—for the student, the parent, and the teacher.

Advice for Making Inclusion and Collaboration Work

When students who are gifted or talented are involved, open-mindedness and flexibility are critical in making inclusion and collaboration work. I believe that the key to success in these situations is to appreciate each student for what he or she can offer the class. It is the teacher's responsibility to know each student's strengths and needs and to continuously assess his or her progress in order to promote academic growth. Modifying activities to fit students' needs, regardless of their ability level, is critical in providing appropriate learning experiences. Although I have always respected my students with gifts and talents, I have tried very hard to let all of my other pupils know that I value them just as much and to convey the message that everyone can learn something from someone else. I believe this philosophy creates an atmosphere of community, and when everyone cares about and helps everyone else, it's a truly productive, magical learning environment.

–Erin DeHaven
Breckinridge County Middle School
Breckinridge, KY
Gifted and Talented Teacher/Gifted Coordinator

skills needed to conduct primary research and to work independently must be taught. Once the young person refines these skills, independent study can provide alternative learning experiences that will allow the student to tap an area of interest and pursue it in depth.

Table 15.5 Strategies for Addressing the Needs of Advanced Learners

Types	Focus of Opportunities	Examples
Enrichment	Opportunities to learn above and beyond what is usually provided at a particular grade level	• In-depth study • Junior Great Books • Competitions • Problem-solving programs • Interdisciplinary seminars • Project-based learning
Acceleration	Opportunities to learn at a pace that matches achievement and interest	• Subject acceleration • Early entrance (kindergarten or college) • Grade acceleration
Differentiation	Opportunities to have curriculum matched to levels of interest and achievement	• Tiered assignments based on content, process, and product
Grouping	Opportunities to learn with others at the same levels of interest and/or achievement	• Cluster grouping • Homogeneous classes (either pull-out or full time) • Magnet schools with a focus on math, science, or the arts

Honors and Advanced Placement Courses

Honors and Advanced Placement classes are appropriate for young people who are ready to learn at advanced levels. Honors courses are offered to middle and high school students who are ready to work hard on advanced content. College Board Advanced Placement (AP) classes are available in approximately thirty different academic areas. Although the AP class is taken at the high school, a score of 3 or higher on the AP exam will earn three or more college credits at most institutions. Only local school policy restricts the grade at which a student is eligible to take AP classes.

Mentorships

"Most mentorships involving the gifted and talented are one-on-one, the relationship most supportive for providing specialized, individual attention to a protégé's development" (Clasen & Clasen, 2003, p. 255). The **mentor** and young person share an interest, making the relationship important to both parties. A mentor may be an older student or an adult with similar interests, a professional, or an artist.

Mentorships are important for young people when pursuing passionate interests and exploring careers. Working with a mentor can open doors to opportunities. Some mentors will communicate via technology. Some may be in a university, a laboratory, or an office. Mentorships may be formal or informal. They may be set up for a specific period of time, or they may be ongoing. Successful mentorships allow serious learners opportunities to pursue ideas in depth.

Self-Contained Classes and Special Schools

Learning with others who share their interests and have similar abilities is essential for children and youth who are gifted and talented. A self-contained class of students who are intellectually gifted provides a learning environment in which many of them will thrive. Special schools are found in many urban school districts. These magnet programs for middle and high school students typically focus on math and science or

mentor: The role fulfilled by an older individual who is an expert in a particular field and who works with and guides a student in an area of mutual interest.

Summer Programming

After much counting down, the long awaited end of the school year is finally here. The anxiously awaited three months of relaxation have arrived. For most gifted kids, this is a time for complete shutdown and withdrawal. They could spend hours sitting in the mind-numbing aura of a television or sleep for twelve hours a day. For some gifted kids, summer is recuperation from the harsh school year they just survived. But for others, myself included, summer is when the long anticipated summer camp takes place. Instead of shutting down and withdrawing, we are stimulated and placed in an environment where gifted kids have no problem "socializing." New information is absorbed, and the brain is kept awake and active. Things some gifted kids miss out on in the school year are presented in large quantities. Things like a caring mentor, an inspiring role model, or just a decent learning environment. Self-esteem skyrockets, and gifted kids begin to understand themselves more, by being around others like them. For me, summer programs were life changing. I gained assertiveness, self-confidence, and self-respect. I learned that I was not alone in the world. I learned that there were many other kids going through the same things I did each school day. I found out that I did, in fact, have the potential to do many things that I never knew I could, such as be popular among my peers, be accepted as who I am, and be known as something more than just "the smart kid." ■

–**Graham Oliver**
Paducah, KY
Ninth Grade

the visual and performing arts. Several states sponsor residential high schools that are academies for mathematics and science and/or the visual and performing arts.

Summer and Saturday Programs

Summer and Saturday programs should challenge young people to learn at high levels and provide opportunities to get to know others who share their interests and have similar abilities. Such programs are offered at colleges and universities as well as by some school districts. The academic content should take students beyond age-level learning experiences. National and state associations for gifted education can be a good source of information on summer and Saturday programs. The accompanying First Person feature offers one adolescent's perspective on a summer camp experience.

Competitions

Competitions do not constitute gifted education, but they do provide motivation and challenge for some young people who are gifted and talented. Just as athletes have both individual and team sports, some competitions are for individuals, others for pairs of children, and still others for teams. Information about a few competitions can be obtained from the websites listed at the end of the chapter, but there are many other competitions targeting a variety of interests and academic areas. *Competitions for Talented Kids* (Karnes & Riley, 2005) provides important information about competitions.

Services for Young Children Who Are Gifted and Talented

The educational needs of young children with special gifts and talents have largely been overlooked (Piirto, 2007). Among the reasons are a lack of federal legislation

1. They are precocious, regardless of the talent area. Some may demonstrate precocious behaviors in several talent areas.

    a. Verbally talented children acquire vocabulary and speak in sentences earlier than age-mates. They can break letter codes and make abstract verbal connections.

    b. Mathematically talented children acquire numeration and number concepts sooner than age-mates.

    c. Musically talented children may often sing on key, demonstrate an interest in the piano or other musical instruments, and stop what they are doing to listen to music.

    d. Children talented in visual arts demonstrate artwork that is similar to that of older children.

    e. Kinesthetically or psychomotor-talented children demonstrate advanced motor ability.

    f. Spatially talented children may want to take things apart to see how they work, and demonstrate an understanding of mechanics that is advanced for their age.

    g. Children talented in the inter- and intrapersonal areas will demonstrate advanced understanding of social relationships, and demonstrate emotion about such things that age-mates will not perceive.

2. They have excellent memories.

3. They concentrate intensely on what interests them, for longer periods of time than age-mates.

4. Dyssynchrony [uneven development] is obvious, especially in high-IQ children.

5. Affective precocity may lead to the assumption of leadership roles and to preferring older companions for play.

SOURCE: J. Piirto, *Talented Children and Adults*, 3rd ed. (Waco, TX: Prufrock Press, 2007), p. 225.

guaranteeing these children an education, difficulties in identifying this unique population of learners, problems in constructing developmentally appropriate educational experiences, and an inconsistent commitment to serving the nation's brightest and most advanced preschoolers.

Early identification is essential to meeting the needs of these youngsters. Parents and other adult caregivers are especially astute at recognizing talents and gifts. More often than not, when parents suspect that their son or daughter is gifted, follow-up assessments support the parents' beliefs (Robinson, Shore, & Enersen, 2007). Table 15.6 lists some of the characteristics typical of young children who are talented.

Despite the early evidence of gifts and talents, children are frequently not identified as gifted and talented until the third or fourth grade. In fact, professionals disagree about the appropriateness of early identification of young children with gifts and talents. Critics of early programming argue that young children are rushed through their childhood. Supporters feel that there is a moral imperative to identify these youngsters and offer them challenging and stimulating opportunities to develop their unique abilities and gifts (Smutny, Walker, & Meckstroth, 2007). One common proposal is early admission to kindergarten or first grade. Howley, Howley, and Pendarvis (1995) consider this suggestion to be pedagogically sound and essential to the development of the child's gifts. When making such a decision, however, parents and educators need to carefully consider the individual's physical and emotional maturity so that an appropriate educational experience can be designed. Preschoolers who evidence gifts in one area, such as artistic talent, may be quite average in their verbal skills and social ability. Parents and professionals must be sensitive to this variability and be careful not to develop unrealistic expectations of advanced ability in all areas of development.

Early school experiences for academically talented pupils must be both enriching and accelerated. The primary concern, however, should always be the child, with his or her special abilities second (Piirto, 2007). Play, which is the "work" of a child, must be a critical component of any curriculum. The curriculum must be balanced and address all areas of development while reflecting the interests of the child. Finger painting and block building are just as important as counting and matching rhyming words.

Adolescents and Adults Who Are Gifted and Talented

Adolescence is a time of awkwardness for most young people, and adolescents who are gifted and talented are no exception. At a time in life when differences can be a liability, adolescents with gifts and talents need opportunities to be with others who share their interests and have similar abilities in order

Early identification is crucial for meeting the needs of young children who are gifted and talented.

to know that their needs, interests, passions, and characteristics are "normal" for them. Csikszentmihalyi, Rathunde, and Whalen (1997) conducted a longitudinal study of 200 talented teenagers. They found some definite differences between talented teenagers and other adolescents. They describe the talented teens as having "personality attributes well suited to the difficult struggle of establishing their mastery over a domain: a desire to achieve, persistence, and a curiosity and openness to experience" (p. 82). Although we know that stereotyping adolescents who are gifted as misfits is not supported by research, "it must be understood that there are unique stresses and dynamic issues associated with a person's giftedness" (Robinson et al., 2007, p. 15).

Early adolescence is a challenging time for all young people, and middle school students who are gifted often feel pressure to "fit in." Middle schoolers who are gifted in any of the categories need challenging opportunities to make continuous progress in their talent areas and to share high-level learning experiences with others who are equally interested in this area. In reality, a lack of appropriately challenging instruction frequently leads to apathy and disengagement from the teaching and learning process (Tomlinson, 1994). Girls of middle school age frequently learn to compete "with boys" or "for boys"; these choices can profoundly affect their later choices. By the time young people enter high school, they set their course of study by the choices they make, selecting or avoiding the most rigorous courses. They also begin to consider and make career choices. Early adolescence is often a particularly complicated and difficult time for students with gifts and talents.

One of the key questions confronting professionals is how best to meet the educational needs of young people who are gifted and talented. Educators disagree as to which pedagogical strategy is best. Among the instructional options available to adolescents and young adults are enrolling in AP classes, International Baccalaureate (IB) classes, high school honors classes, or Saturday programs; seeking early admission to college; and attending a **magnet high school** (a secondary school with a particular focus such as science, mathematics, or the performing arts). Despite the general availability of these services, a fairly large portion of high school dropouts (estimated between 18% and 25%) are gifted (Davis, Rimm, & Siegle, 2011). We can

magnet high school: A school with a strong instructional emphasis on a particular theme, such as performing arts or math and science; an option for secondary pupils who are gifted and talented.

VIDEO

Future Goals

Table 15.7 Characteristics of Families of Children Who Are Gifted

Few children in family
Gifted child oldest or only child
Early stimulation and enrichment given to children, including reading to them, encouraging language development, and exposure to a variety of experiences (e.g., museums, exhibits, and visual and performing arts)
Parents older and better educated than typical parents
Parents show high energy and love of learning
Strong work ethic and valuing of achievement modeled by parents
Parents set clear standards that are flexible and fairly administered
Parents respect the rights and dignity of children
All members of the family are encouraged to develop to the highest level of their ability as individuals
Family relationships and parent-child interactions are healthy
Parents and children share work, learning, and play
Parents involved in school-related activities

SOURCE: B. Clark, *Growing Up Gifted*, 6th ed. (Upper Saddle River, NJ: Prentice Hall, 2002), p. 152. Reprinted by permission.

only speculate that these students are unfulfilled and not academically challenged. Perhaps the lack of support services, the absence of a caring mentor, and the need to be accepted by peers interact to contribute to this phenomenon. For those individuals with gifts and talents who pursue postsecondary education, many colleges and universities offer a variety of honors classes and other opportunities for accelerated and in-depth study and investigation.

One well-known outlet for adults who are gifted is Mensa. Primarily a social organization, this international group consists of individuals who have an IQ in the top 2 percent of the general population. Mensa has approximately 57,000 U.S. members who come from all walks of life but share one common trait—high intelligence (Mensa, 2013).

Family Issues

A synthesis of research evidence paints a picture of some of the characteristics of families who have children who are gifted (see Table 15.7). Families exert a powerful influence on any child, but especially on a child who is gifted (Subotnik, Kassan, Summers, & Wasser, 1993). If parents believe, Clark (2013) writes, that their "child has special ability, [they] will hold different expectations [and] allow more opportunities for the child to develop his or her ability" (p. 38). Family support is vital if ability is to translate into achievement and accomplishment.

Parents play a critical role in their son's or daughter's classroom performance. In a classic study of 12,000 high school students over a four-year period, Steinberg (1996) found that parents and peers exerted the greatest influence on the young person's academic performance, greater than the teacher or the student's IQ score. Steinberg emphasizes the importance of parents setting academic excellence as a priority.

Providing opportunities beyond school to develop talents or to further study in areas of interest can be expensive but critical to the student's future. Parents must

AUDIO
Adolescence
and Giftedness

VIDEO
Family

understand how important it is for their children to find intellectual peers. It is well worth the time and resources that it takes to have the child who is interested in the violin play with a youth orchestra or to have the young person who is interested in any number of academic pursuits drive to the nearest university to participate in a Saturday program. These experiences are often turning points that validate the need to work hard in order to achieve at high levels.

Parents may benefit from reading about children who are gifted and their needs. Parents can also benefit from joining state and national associations that advocate gifted education. They need to know their legal rights and the regulations affecting gifted education in their state and local school system (Karnes, Stephens, & McHard, 2008). Parents need information about due process procedures if they believe that their child is not being provided with appropriate services and is not being challenged to learn at appropriately high levels.

Issues of Diversity

Children who are gifted and talented come from all socioeconomic, racial, and ethnic groups. A concern among educators is to be certain that children from all backgrounds are afforded quality educational opportunities that allow for gifts and talents to emerge and to ensure that students from diverse backgrounds receive appropriate services to develop their talents to optimal levels. A challenge to teachers is to become talent developers so that all pupils are able to demonstrate their special talents and gifts. Despite the best efforts of professionals, three particular dimensions of diversity remain issues today: (1) gifted and talented students with disabilities, (2) girls who are gifted and talented, and (3) the assessment and identification of gifts and talents in pupils from culturally and linguistically diverse populations.

Students With Gifts and Talents and Disabilities

Only recently have educators devoted attention to individuals with gifts and talents who also have a disability. All too often, the gifts and talents of these students are overlooked, and services are focused on the disability. It is tragic that people with disabilities are seldom thought of as possessing gifts and talents (Davis et al., 2011)—most likely because of biases, prejudices, and stereotypic expectations that prevent us from seeing their strengths. Yet think, for example, of the following eminent individuals who, although disabled, are truly gifted and talented in their respective fields of endeavor: Stephen Hawking, theoretical physicist (amyotrophic lateral sclerosis [ALS], also known as Lou Gehrig's disease); Franklin D. Roosevelt, U.S. President (polio); Helen Keller, author and social activist (dual sensory impaired); and Ray Charles, musician (visually impaired). In each of these instances, the individual's accomplishments overshadow his or her disability. Children who are gifted and disabled require programming aimed at remediating the deficit(s) caused by the disability and accommodations that minimize its impact, as well as opportunities that nurture and develop their gifts and talents to the fullest potential (Clark, 2013).

A student may have two (or more) disabilities. These **twice-exceptional** learners constitute a group of children that is frequently misunderstood. A child who is identified as gifted may also have a learning disability, a behavior disorder, a sensory impairment, a physical disability, or attention deficit hyperactivity disorder (ADHD). The challenge confronting professionals is to make a diagnosis that is appropriate. This can be a difficult task because one exceptionality may mask another, or the characteristics of the two exceptionalities may be similar. For example, the pupil who has

twice-exceptional: Students who are gifted and talented but also have a disability.

REFERENCE

Twice Exceptional Students

a learning disability but is intellectually gifted will likely perform at an average level, thereby camouflaging the need for gifted services as well as the need for services due to a learning disability. Another frequent problem is thinking that a child has ADHD when in actuality the child is gifted and exhibiting high energy and intense curiosity. "Gifted children with ADHD are usually labeled as underachieving or lazy long before they are ever labeled as [having] ADHD" (Flint, 2001, p. 65). Knowing the characteristics of children who are gifted and talented in any category is the key to recognizing behaviors that reveal gifts and talents in children with and without other exceptionalities.

In many cases, students who are twice-exceptional are not receiving the services that would allow for the full expression of their potential. In too many instances, their disability masks their gifts and talents, or their giftedness allows them to compensate and achieve at or near grade level so their disability goes undetected; either way, these unique learners are not being appropriately served. Robinson et al. (2007) and King (2005) argue persuasively that these pupils require intervention specially tailored to their needs.

Children who are twice-exceptional are sometimes referred to as *paradoxical learners*. Gifted students who are learning disabled, for instance, exhibit characteristics such as distractibility, inattentiveness, and inefficient learning strategies while, at the same time, presenting patterns typical of students who are gifted. How can teachers best meet the needs of these children? Do we teach to their learning disability, their giftedness, or both? According to Weinfeld, Barnes-Robinson, Jeweler, and Shevitz (2005), students who have both gifts and learning disabilities require an intervention program that nurtures their gifts and talents while accommodating for learning needs. Baum, Rizza, and Renzulli (2006) also recommend teaching to the gifts while providing strategies that compensate for the disability. Effective instructional programming for these pupils thus requires a blending of instructional practices, such as cognitive training coupled with differentiated programming or curriculum compacting.

Nielsen and Higgins (2005) identify four key elements that must be present for successful programming of students who are twice-exceptional. According to these experts, these learners require

- a continuum of service delivery options ranging from the general education classroom to a self-contained classroom supported by related service professionals;
- a complex, integrated, and interdisciplinary curriculum because of their unique learning profiles;
- services and programs that address their social, emotional, and behavioral needs; and
- instruction that targets their gifts and talents while simultaneously providing individualized special education supports.

Girls Who Are Gifted and Talented

Although it may seem a bit unusual to include females who are gifted in a section devoted to diversity, there is ample evidence that girls who are gifted are an underrepresented population and an untapped national resource. This inequity appears to be embedded in a complex and interwoven web of educational, social, and personal barriers, including sex-role stereotyping, unequal educational opportunities, and personal as well as parental expectations (Reis, 2006; Rimm, 2002). Collectively, these barriers frequently become obstacles to achievement and advancement. Some of the characteristics of gifted females are presented in Table 15.8.

◼◼◼◼ ◼ Table 15.8 **A Profile of Gifted Females**

Age Range	Attributes
Younger Gifted Girls	• Many gifted girls are superior physically, have more social knowledge, and are better adjusted than are average girls, although more highly gifted girls are not as likely to seem well adjusted. • Highly gifted girls are often second-born females. • Highly gifted girls have high academic achievement. • In their interests, gifted girls are more like gifted boys than they are like average girls. • Gifted girls are confident in their opinions and willing to argue for their point of view. • Gifted girls by age 10 express wishes and needs for self-esteem and are interested in fulfilling needs for self-esteem through school and club achievements, although highly gifted girls are often loners without much need for recognition. • Gifted girls are more strongly influenced by their mothers than are gifted boys. • Actual occupations of parents do not affect gifted girls' eventual career choices. • Gifted girls have high career goals, although highly gifted girls aspire to careers having moderate rather than high status.
Adolescent Females	• Gifted girls' IQ scores drop in adolescence, perhaps as they begin to perceive their own giftedness as undesirable. • Gifted girls are likely to continue to have higher academic achievement as measured by grade point average. • Gifted girls take less rigorous courses than gifted boys in high school. • Gifted girls maintain a high involvement in extracurricular and social activities during adolescence. • Highly gifted girls do very well academically in high school; however, they often do not receive recognition for their achievements. • Highly gifted girls attend less prestigious colleges than highly gifted boys, a choice that leads to lower-status careers.

SOURCE: Adapted from B. Kerr, *Smart Girls Two,* Rev. ed. (Scottsdale, AZ: Gifted Psychology Press, Inc., 1997).

The education of girls with gifts and talents cannot be neglected. Giftedness in females must be nurtured. Reis (2006) offers the following recommendations for developing this talent pool in both girls and boys:

- Provide equal treatment in a non-stereotyped environment and, in particular, provide encouragement for advanced coursework.
- Reduce sexism and stereotyping in classrooms and establish equity in classroom interactions.
- Help gifted adolescents understand healthy competition.
- Group gifted students homogeneously in separate classes or in clusters within heterogeneous classrooms.
- Expose gifted adolescents to other gifted adults who can act as role models through direct and curricular experiences—field trips, guest speakers, seminars, books, videotapes, articles, and movies.
- Provide educational interventions compatible with cognitive development and styles of learning (independent study projects, small group learning opportunities, etc.).
- Use a variety of authentic assessment tools such as projects and learning centers in addition to tests. (pp. 104–105)

Silverman (1995a) suggests that to preserve giftedness in girls, schools should offer them intellectually challenging courses and assistance in selecting career paths

Table 15.9 Recommendations for Developing the Gifts and Talents of Female Students

Gifted and Talented Girls Should	Teachers Should	Parents, Teachers, and Counselors Should
• Have exposure to or personal contact with female role models and mentors who have successfully balanced career and family. • Participate in discussion groups and attend panel discussions in which gifted and talented girls and women discuss the external barriers they have encountered. • Pursue involvement in leadership roles and extracurricular activities. • Participate in sports, athletics, and multiple extracurricular activities in areas in which they have an interest. • Discuss issues related to gender and success, such as family issues, in supportive settings with other talented girls. • Participate in career counseling at an early age and be exposed to a wide variety of career options and talented women who pursue challenging careers in all areas.	• Provide equitable treatment in a nonstereotyped environment and, in particular, provide encouragement. • Reduce sexism in classrooms and create an avenue for girls to report and discuss examples of stereotyping in schools. • Help creative, talented females appreciate and understand healthy competition. • Group gifted females homogeneously in math/science or within cluster groups of high-ability students in heterogeneous groups. • Encourage creativity in girls. • Use problem solving in assignments and reduce the use of timed tests and timed assignments within class periods; rather, provide options for untimed work within a reasonable time frame. • Expose girls to other creative, gifted females through direct and curricular experiences—field trips, guest speakers, seminars, role models, books, videotapes, articles, movies. • Provide educational interventions compatible with cognitive development and styles of learning (i.e., independent study projects, small-group learning opportunities, and so forth) and use a variety of authentic assessment tools such as projects and learning centers instead of just using tests. • Establish equity in classroom interactions. • Provide multiple opportunities for creative expression in multiple modalities.	• Form forces to advocate programming and equal opportunities and to investigate opportunities for talented, creative girls. • Spotlight achievements of talented females in a variety of different areas; encourage girls and young women to become involved in as many different types of activities, travel opportunities, and clubs as possible. • Encourage girls to take advanced courses in all areas, as well as courses in the arts, and reinforce successes in these and all areas of endeavor; ensure equal representation of girls in advanced classes. • Encourage relationships with other creative girls who want to achieve. • Maintain options for talented, creative girls in specific groups, such as self-contained classes, groups of girls within heterogeneous classes and in separate classes for gifted girls, science and math clubs, or support groups. • Consistently point out options for careers and encourage future choices but help girls focus on specific interests and planning for future academic choices, interests, and careers.

SOURCE: Adapted from S. Reis, "External Barriers Experienced by Gifted and Talented Girls and Women," *Gifted Child Today, 24*(4), 2001, pp. 33–34.

commensurate with their abilities. Additionally, girls who are gifted may require supplementary educational experiences in order to reach their potential (Noble, Subotnik, & Arnold, 1999). Instruction may be necessary to develop assertiveness, instill confidence, and enhance self-esteem. Exposure to female mentors who can offer girls personal and professional advice along with work experience is another common recommendation for fostering the talents and gifts of girls (Robinson et al., 2007). Table 15.9 offers additional suggestions and strategies for developing the gifts and talents of female students.

Identifying and Serving Children From Diverse Backgrounds

One contemporary challenge in the field of gifted education, as in other areas of exceptionality, is that of identifying and serving children from culturally diverse backgrounds and from all socioeconomic groups. There is ample evidence that culturally diverse students are under-represented in the pool of individuals identified as gifted (Clark, 2013; Davis et al., 2011; Ford, Harris, Tyson, & Trotman, 2002). African American pupils, for example, constitute approximately 16 percent of public school enrollment, but only about 8 percent of those in programs for the gifted and talented (Ford, 1998). The Javits legislation mentioned earlier in this chapter emphasizes that

Students from culturally diverse backgrounds are significantly underrepresented in programs for children who are gifted and talented.

children with special gifts and talents can be found throughout society; our job as teachers is to find and provide services for these children. "Culturally diverse children," Plummer (1995) writes, "have much talent, creativity, and intelligence. Manifestations of these characteristics may be different and thus require not only different tools for measuring these strengths, but also different eyes from which to see them" (p. 290).

In a classic investigation, Frasier and her colleagues (1995) identified ten core attributes of giftedness in African American, Native American, and Hispanic children:

- Communication skills
- Humor
- Imagination/creativity
- Inquiry
- Insight
- Interests
- Memory
- Motivation
- Problem solving
- Reasoning

The process of identifying gifted children from culturally diverse backgrounds is sometimes described as finding "the light under the bushel basket" (Gallagher & Gallagher, 1994, p. 410). According to Gallagher and Gallagher (1994), intellectual giftedness often resides within the individual; however, adverse environmental factors, such as poverty or language differences, can mask that gift—like placing a basket over a light. The task of educators is to find strategies that remove the basket and let the light shine forth.

Several factors are thought to contribute to the underrepresentation of culturally diverse learners in programs for gifted and talented pupils. Commonly mentioned variables include the deleterious consequences of poverty, test bias, faulty identification policies, conflicting cultural values, teacher attitudes and expectations, and rigid definitions

REFERENCE

Gifted Minority Students

of giftedness (Davis et al., 2011; Ford, 1998; Robinson et al., 2007). To combat these forces, recommendations have included the following:

- Culturally sensitive identification practices
- Establishing support services (career counseling, mentors, role models)
- Greater community and family involvement
- Multimodal assessment practices, including alternative (nontraditional) strategies (such as peer ratings, portfolios, teacher nominations, and checklists)
- Early identification

Portfolio assessment was thought to be one way of tapping into diverse talent areas. Its alignment with Gardner's concept of multiple intelligences makes it an especially attractive option for assessing giftedness. Unfortunately, this strategy, as well as other proposed solutions, has not solved the problem of underrepresentation.

Appropriate educational opportunities must be in place to develop the talents of children from low-income backgrounds; otherwise, millions of high-ability children from challenging socioeconomic backgrounds will fail to stay in the upper quartile of achievement (Wyner, Bridgeland, & Diiulio, 2007). Special care must be taken to nurture their talents, encourage them to achieve at high levels, and pursue higher education opportunities. Wyner et al. (2007) are optimistic because a large number of children who fall in the upper quartile are from low-income backgrounds; however, it is discouraging that

> there are far fewer lower-income students achieving at the highest levels than there should be, they disproportionately fall out of the high-achieving group during elementary and high school, they rarely rise into the ranks of high achievers during these periods, and perhaps most disturbingly, far too few ever graduate from college or go on to graduate school. (p. i)

Two recent reports highlight the need to be vigilant in looking for potential and ensuring that strategies are in place to develop talents to their highest levels. *Unlocking Emergent Talent* (Olszewski-Kubilius & Clarenbach, 2012) focused attention on the need to implement programming that will permit children from lower socioeconomic groups to thrive in school. Plucker, Burroughs, and Song (2010) offer data in their report, *Mind the (Other) Gap*, which reveal that too few students from gap groups (minority and lower socioeconomic groups) score at the advanced levels on the National Assessment of Educational Progress.

The challenge for educators in today's schools is to create learning environments that are intellectually stimulating and nurture the gifts and talents of all students so that it is just as attractive to be an outstanding student as it is to play on a championship team. See Table 15.10 for instructional suggestions designed to meet the unique needs of traditionally underrepresented groups of learners who are gifted and talented.

Technology and Individuals Who Are Gifted and Talented

Technology is an increasingly important educational tool for children identified as gifted and talented, including students who are twice-exceptional. These pupils may benefit from the different types of assistive technology discussed in Chapter 5 (for example, text-to-speech, word prediction). Technology can also enhance the teaching and learning of students who are gifted and talented (Bouck & Hunley, in press), with the Internet being just one example. Students who are gifted and talented can use the Internet to

Table 15.10 **Suggestions for Teaching Culturally Diverse Students Who Are Gifted**

Cultural Background	Suggestions
African American Gifted Children	• Use small groups for instruction, building trust, and belonging. • Provide structure by use of contracting, clear goals, and individualization. • Provide mentors and role models. • Emphasize use of oral language, providing many opportunities for debate, discussion, and oral presentations. • Provide for visual learning experiences, manipulative materials, and active real-life experiences in learning.
Native American Gifted Children	• Use storytelling, metaphor, and myths as media for delivering information. • Develop personal and group goals relevant to those of the tribal community as well as the student. • Provide visual and spatial experience. • Teach from whole to details. • Explore and honor belief in collective tribal self as an alternative worldview. • Use intuitive ability in learning experiences.
Hispanic Gifted Children	• Use cooperative intellectual peer groups for learning and encouraging independent production. • Provide visual and kinesthetic learning experiences. • Provide extensive experience with both English and Spanish. • Use successful Hispanic Americans as mentors. • Include the family as part of the educational team.

SOURCE: Adapted from B. Clark, *Growing Up Gifted,* 8th ed. (Upper Saddle River, NJ: Pearson Education, 2013), pp. 218–221.

be producers of information rather than just consumers, such as authoring their own e-books (Siegle, 2012). The Internet can also be used to provide online education; online education is often an appropriate option for individuals who are gifted and talented as it allows them to receive advanced content that is individually paced and student-centered (Thomson, 2010). Online learning creates enrichment opportunities for students who are gifted and talented outside of the typical K–12 curriculum. Lastly, social media is having a tremendous impact on the world of gifted education, connecting not only students but also scholars, parents, educators, and even professional organizations (Mersino, 2011).

Trends, Issues, and Controversies

A plethora of issues and controversies confronts educators and other professionals concerned about the education of children and youth who are gifted and talented. We hope to shed some light on a few of these contemporary topics.

Striving for World-Class Standards

In *National Excellence* (Ross, 1993), Secretary of Education Richard W. Riley states that the United States is facing a "quiet crisis in how we educate top students. Youngsters with gifts and talents that range from mathematical to musical are still not challenged to work to their full potential. Our neglect of these students makes it impossible for Americans to compete in a global economy demanding their skills" (p. iii). Two decades later, that "quiet crisis" continues.

PL 103–227, the Goals 2000: Educate America Act, predicted that students in the United States would be first in the world in mathematics and science by the year 2000.

REFERENCE
Online Gifted Education

This goal of international eminence has not been attained. The need to focus on high standards and opportunities for children to learn at challenging levels continues. Top students are not served well when they score at the 99th percentile on standardized tests and earn all As on their report cards without being challenged. The situation is regrettable when a student scores at the 95th percentile in the United States on a standardized test but is at the 50th percentile in Japan (Ross, 1993).

Data from the recent Trends in International Mathematics and Science Study (National Center for Education Statistics, 2012c) sounds another alarm. This survey compared the mathematics and science knowledge skills of fourth and eighth graders in the United States with those of their peers from over fifty other countries. Findings from this survey indicate that only 13 percent of fourth graders and 7 percent of eighth graders performed at the advanced level in mathematics. Likewise, only 15 percent of fourth graders and 10 percent of eighth graders achieved at the highest level in science. These results raise serious concerns about the need for more rigorous curriculum and increasingly challenging learning opportunities.

Assumptions are often made that children who are gifted and talented will learn in spite of their circumstances. On the contrary, students who are gifted are less likely to make a year's achievement gain than are other students (Sanders, 1998). The No Child Left Behind legislation provides little incentive for teachers to gear instruction to individuals who have already achieved proficiency (Neal & Schanzenbach, 2007). Because of the emphasis on proficiency, students who have already achieved proficiency or who are way beyond this level of accomplishment are not receiving the opportunities that allow them to make continuous progress. Unfortunately, the minimum competency requirements of No Child Left Behind have taken the instructional focus off of guiding our most talented students in recognizing, developing, and enriching their gifts. Because the student who is gifted can easily achieve minimum competency standards for grade level, it is imperative that educators look at these children in terms of a growth model. Every pupil, in every classroom, should be experiencing gains; whether those gains are toward minimum proficiency or talent development is irrelevant (S. Burkhardt, personal communication, February 16, 2007).

The goal of education for all students, including children who are gifted and talented, is to make continuous progress. Consequently, it is unacceptable for "proficiency" to place a lid on learning for any child who is already at proficiency or beyond. Academic growth is important for all children.

Equity and Excellence

The issue of equity and excellence has often been distorted into a question of equity versus excellence. Equity allows each child to have his or her needs addressed; it is not doing the same thing for all students on the same time schedule. Each child deserves quality educational opportunities that will allow for continuous progress in academic and talent areas. Excellence involves the pursuit of personal excellence. High standards are critical for all children; however, all children will not be served well unless each is challenged. What will be challenging for individual students depends on what each one already knows and is able to do. All children need to be accepted for who they are and must be genuinely challenged if they are to reach their personal goals.

The "Lake Wobegon phenomenon" describes a situation in which every child is above average. Such a situation denies some children the opportunity to reach a level of personal excellence. It is often said that we need to see that all children achieve at the same high levels. The same comment would never be made about athletics. All students need opportunities to develop their gifts and talents, just as athletes are encouraged to do, but they will achieve different levels of personal excellence when afforded the same opportunities. Equity and excellence are equally important in a society that values moving forward in all fields of endeavor.

Full Inclusion

The general education classroom has become the "ideal" setting in the minds of many educators. For some students with exceptionalities, the general education classroom offers the best alternative; however, for children who are gifted and talented, the idea of full inclusion is often very restrictive. Results of a study by the National Research Center on the Gifted and Talented indicate that third- and fourth-grade teachers typically make only minor modifications in the regular curriculum to address the needs of students who are gifted (Archambault et al., 1993; Westburg & Daoust, 2003). Full inclusion offers challenges to teachers who understand that the needs of children who are gifted and talented cannot be met without differentiating the curriculum. For example, a fifth-grade teacher, in a class with a full range of learners, might have students reading from the first- to the twelfth-grade level. Such a classroom can present an overwhelming challenge to the educator who desires that each pupil make continuous progress.

For young people who are gifted and talented, the least restrictive alternative is often a self-contained class or magnet school. Fifteen states have established residential high schools for mathematics and science and/or the performing arts (Roberts, 2013). Urban school districts across the country have magnet schools with a focus on math and science, the health sciences, and/or the performing arts. Children who are gifted and talented need to be with others who think as they do and who are ready to accept and embrace the intellectual challenge. They also need teachers who are prepared to implement challenging curricula and who recognize the need to challenge even the most exceptional students.

Services for Gifted Students
Instead of the Gifted Program

The trend to move to services for children who are gifted rather than "the" gifted program is in tune with methods of identification that emphasize multiple measures. Children with gifts and talents in science need challenging instruction to allow for the continuous development of their scientific knowledge, skills, and interests. Likewise, children who are gifted in leadership need appropriate opportunities to develop their leadership skills to a higher level, and artistically gifted children need instruction that will provide for the honing of their artistic talents—talents that may differentiate them from other children in their age bracket.

A gifted program is limited in its potential for addressing student needs. Matching services to need (for gifted students, the need is created by a strength) is key to developing children's talents. One service may be similar to classes that have been known as the gifted program; however, it is only one service. Such a service offers advantages because the teacher has expertise and experience with students who have special talents, and the pupils benefit by associating with others who share their interests and have similar abilities. These classes offer opportunities to address the cognitive as well as the social-emotional needs of children who are gifted and talented.

Teachers who are specialists in specific content areas can offer other services. Who better to offer services to develop talent in mathematics than a teacher of math or in art than a teacher of art? The goal of each service is to focus on continuous progress, a concept that will allow children to be challenged beyond grade level. For all children, the learning ceiling must be removed, allowing them to learn what they are ready to learn, at a pace that will encourage them to maintain interest.

SOURCE: Used with permission of J. L. Roberts. Copyright © 2008.

Talent Development

Children who are gifted and talented represent a relatively small part of a school's population, yet they constitute a group with special needs—needs created by their strengths. In spite of the fact that students who are gifted and talented do not appear needy, their needs are intense and must be addressed if they are to reach their potential.

The development of top talent is essential if our communities, states, nation, and world are to thrive. Talent does not develop in a vacuum (see Figure 15.7). Schools that develop top talent establish talent development and continuous progress as school-wide goals. First, students need opportunities to discover interests or passions that can develop into top-level talents. Educators must provide children with numerous quality opportunities to develop these talents. They need opportunities to work with teachers and mentors in their talent areas in addition to opportunities to refine their skills and expand their content knowledge. Finally, young people need opportunities to produce knowledge through research and publications and to perform in competitions, contests, recitals, and exhibitions. Celebrating a wide range of accomplishments and talents is important throughout the talent development process. Examples of talent development opportunities are presented in Table 15.11.

Opportunities are not really opportunities until a person knows about them. The focus of schools must be on developing the gifts and talents of students from all socioeconomic levels and all racial and ethnic backgrounds, as well as students with a range of gifts and talents, including pupils with disabilities. Schools need to celebrate artistic and academic talents in the same ways that they celebrate athletic talent. As Madame Morrible says in the musical *Wicked*, "Never apologize for talent! Talent is a gift! And that is my special talent, encouraging talent" (Cote, 2005, p. 56). Students need individuals to encourage the development of their talents. Children who are gifted and talented need teachers and mentors in the home, school, and community who will provide opportunities that will ensure that they enjoy learning on an ongoing basis and that they make continuous progress in their talent area. Children with gifts and talents will not make it on their own.

AUDIO

Chapter 15 Summary

■■■■ ■ Table 15.11 **Essential Components of a Plan for Talent Development Schools**

Opportunities	Examples
Celebrate a wide range of accomplishments/talents	• Announcements and newsletter articles • Assemblies • Banners, trophies, Hall of Fame • Press releases
Explore and find interests/passions	• Resources—books, people, and Internet • Field trips to museums, labs, science centers, concert halls, universities • Experts to talk about or demonstrate a talent area • Classes in Saturday or summer programs, specialized camps
Learn basic skills and foundational knowledge in artistic, academic, and athletic areas	• Special classes • Visits to talk with and observe experts • Equipment (e.g., labs, instruments, computer programs) • Resources that interest and challenge • Lessons
Refine skills in talent areas as advanced content is learned	• Access to scientists, artists, and other mentors • Specialized equipment • Time with others who share interests and are equally advanced • Instruction with specific feedback • Independent study with mentor
Create/produce in talent area	• Competitions, contents, recitals, exhibits • Mentors focused on scholarly or artistic production • Time devoted to talent area • Performance for peers in talent area • Publications

SOURCE: Used with permission of J. L. Roberts. Copyright © 2008.

CHAPTER IN REVIEW

Defining Giftedness: Refining the Meaning

- Two national reports provide definitions of children who are gifted and talented; however, each state is responsible for establishing its own definition of giftedness. Generally speaking, definitions include high intellectual ability along with giftedness in specific academic areas, creativity, leadership, and/or the visual and performing arts.

Assessing Giftedness and Talent

- The assessment of gifts and talents necessitates multifactorial assessment of the student's strengths, using both formal and informal measures.

Prevalence of Giftedness and Talent

- Educators believe that approximately 3–5 percent of the school-age population is gifted. Some professionals estimate that 10–15 percent of school-age youth are gifted and talented.

Etiology of Giftedness and Talent

- The etiology or causes of giftedness are both genetic and environmental. The complex interaction of genetic patterns and environmental stimulation produces an individual with the capacity to learn or perform at exceptionally high levels in one or more areas of accomplishment.

Characteristics of Individuals Who Are Gifted and Talented

- The characteristics of children who are gifted and talented vary tremendously across the many dimensions of giftedness.
- The degree and intensity of characteristics are often the keys to understanding gifted behavior. Seldom, if ever, do children who are gifted and talented exhibit all of the cognitive and social-emotional characteristics associated with this exceptionality.

Educational Considerations

- The educational needs of pupils with gifts and talents are often best fulfilled via a variety of instructional strategies. Interventions must be planned to allow pupils to make continuous progress, even in areas in which they are advanced.
- Strategies to remove the learning ceiling include differentiating the curriculum and curriculum compacting.
- The curriculum must include learning experiences that combine complex content, high-level thinking and problem solving, and opportunities to think creatively. Other important accommodations addressing the needs of children who are gifted are cluster grouping, cooperative learning activities with academic peers, and problem-based learning.
- A continuum of services is vital to ensure the development of talent to high levels.

- Acceleration is an appropriate option for many gifted children. Independent study, mentors, honors classes, Advanced Placement courses, and International Baccalaureate programs provide challenging learning experiences.
- Self-contained classrooms and special schools provide other venues for delivering services to gifted young people.
- Summer and Saturday programs are important options but should not be in lieu of services within the school setting.

Adolescents and Adults Who Are Gifted and Talented

- Adolescence can be an especially difficult time for students who are gifted and talented. Choosing between making continuous progress in their talent areas and remaining popular with their peers is one area of potential conflict.

Issues of Diversity

- Children who are gifted and talented come from all socioeconomic, racial, and ethnic groups.
- Professionals encounter three unique challenges when confronting issues of diversity: serving students with gifts and talents and a disability, meeting the needs of girls who are gifted and talented, and appropriately identifying and serving children with gifts and talents who happen to be culturally diverse.

STUDY QUESTIONS

1. How are children with gifts and talents identified in your area? Elsewhere?

2. In what ways is the assessment of giftedness an important yet difficult process?

3. How have society's view and understanding of children with gifts and talents changed over time?

4. The etiology of giftedness is seen as the commingling or interaction of what variables?

5. Identify five characteristics typically associated with individuals considered gifted and talented. What implications do these characteristics have for the individuals' teachers?

6. Describe the various delivery models that are frequently used to meet the cognitive and social-emotional needs of children who are gifted and talented.

7. Define the following terms: *curriculum differentiation, preassessment, curriculum compacting, flexible grouping, cluster grouping,* and *pacing.*

8. Distinguish between the concepts of acceleration and enrichment. How can they be used together?

9. List five early indicators of gifts and talents.

10. What challenges do families of children who are gifted and talented frequently encounter?

11. Why are some groups of children underrepresented in programs for students who are gifted and talented? What can be done to remedy this situation?

12. How can technology be used to enhance learning opportunities for students with gifts and talents?

13. Why do some educators believe that full inclusion is not the best option for students who are gifted and talented?

LEARNING ACTIVITIES

1. Write a statement about your philosophy of learning that could guide your teaching of students with gifts and talents.

2. Volunteer to assist with an academic competition, a Saturday program, or a summer program for children and youth who are gifted and talented. Keep a journal of your experiences. How do the children compare with their typical age-mates? What strengths did you observe among the participants? How do the children relate to and interact with their coaches and teachers? What are the advantages and benefits of these activities?

3. Interview two individuals of similar chronological age who are considered gifted and talented. Ask these persons to define what it means to be gifted. Have them describe their educational experiences, career goals, likes and dislikes, social relationships (including family members), and other topics of interest to you. What similarities and differences did you observe between the two individuals? How do these persons differ from their typical age-mates?

4. Visit schools in your area that serve students with gifts and talents. What services are available for pupils who are gifted and talented? What differences did you observe between elementary and secondary programs? What instructional techniques did teachers use that were effective with students who are gifted and talented? How did the other pupils interact with their classmates who are gifted? What was your overall impression of the services—what specific features stood out? How are the individual needs of the students being addressed or ignored? Would you like to be a teacher of children who are gifted and talented? Why or why not?

5. What is the definition of children who are gifted and talented in your state? How does it compare with the definitions presented in this chapter?

6. Locate information about the advocacy organization in your state. What professional development opportunities does it offer? What information does it provide to teachers?

ORGANIZATIONS CONCERNED WITH GIFTEDNESS

The Association for the Gifted (CEC-TAG), Council for Exceptional Children

www.cectag.org

National Association for Gifted Children (NAGC)

www.nagc.org

Supporting Emotional Needs of the Gifted (SENG)

www.sengifted.org

World Council for Gifted and Talented Children

www.world-gifted.org

REFLECTING ON STANDARDS

The following exercises are designed to help you learn to apply the Council for Exceptional Children (CEC) standards to your teaching practice. Each of the reflection exercises below correlates with knowledge or a skill within the CEC standards. For the full text of each of the related CEC standards, please refer to the standards integration grid located in Appendix B.

Focus on Curricular Content Knowledge (*CEC Initial Preparation Standard 3.2*)

Reflect on what you have learned about students who are gifted and talented. If you had an individual who was gifted and talented in math, and well above the rest of your class, how might you use differentiated instruction to keep him or her

challenged while still addressing the needs of the remainder of your pupils? What are some other instructional strategies you could incorporate in your class to meet his or her needs?

Focus on Learning Environments (*CEC Initial Preparation Standard 2.1*)

Reflect on what you have learned about the social-emotional needs of students who are gifted and talented. If you were to have a pupil in your class who was gifted and talented and often received instruction outside your classroom at a higher grade level, what difficulties might this individual have in developing social skills with his or her peers? How might you help encourage or facilitate social interactions when the student is in your classroom during the day?

STUDENT STUDY SITE

Sharpen your skills with SAGE edge at **edge.sagepub.com/gargiulo5e. SAGE edge for students** provides a personalized approach to help you accomplish your coursework goals in an easy-to-use learning environment.

Postscript

You may recall that in Chapter 1 you were introduced to some of the students in Daniel Thompson's fifth-grade class. Mr. Thompson's classroom was like most classrooms in the United States: The majority of the students were typical learners, but five individuals were thought to have special learning needs.

- Victoria, age 11, is a very popular student with a great personality who has been blind since birth.
- Miguel is very shy and timid and interacts minimally with his classmates. Miguel only recently moved into the community from his home in Mexico.
- Jerome is particularly disliked by his peers. He is verbally abusive, often has temper tantrums, and frequently fights with other children. Mr. Thompson suspects that he might be a member of a local gang.
- Stephanie endures friendly teasing from her classmates, who secretly admire her intellectual gifts and talents.
- Robert is an outstanding athlete. In the classroom, however, he asks silly questions, has difficulty following class rules, and occasionally makes animal noises, much to the displeasure of his classmates. Robert has cognitive delays as a result of an automobile accident.

Mr. Thompson wondered why these students were in his class and how he could help them. Hopefully, after studying the preceding chapters, listening to your instructor's presentations, and completing course assignments, along with critically reflecting on the content, you are now in a position to respond to the six questions originally posed in Chapter 1:

1. Why are these pupils in a general education classroom?

2. Will I have students like this in my class?

3. Are these children called disabled, exceptional, or handicapped?

4. What does *special education* mean?

5. How will I know if some of my students have special learning needs?

6. How can I help these pupils?

Teaching children and young adults with exceptionalities is a very challenging yet richly rewarding career. When you stand before your class as a dedicated, committed, and caring professional, you possess the power to make a difference in the lives of all your students. I congratulate you on choosing to become a member of a dynamic profession—teaching.

Good luck!

Federal Definitions of Disabilities

Autism means a developmental disability significantly affecting verbal and nonverbal communication and social interaction, generally evident before age 3, that adversely affects a child's educational performance. Other characteristics often associated with autism are engagement in repetitive activities and stereotyped movements, resistance to environmental change or change in daily routines, and unusual responses to sensory experiences. The term does not apply if a child's educational performance is adversely affected primarily because the child has an emotional disturbance as defined below.

A child who manifests the characteristics of autism after age 3 could be diagnosed as having autism if the criteria in the preceding paragraph are satisfied.

Deaf-blindness means concomitant hearing and visual impairments, the combination of which causes such severe communication and other developmental and educational needs that they cannot be accommodated in special education programs solely for children with deafness or children with blindness.

Deafness means a hearing impairment that is so severe that the child is impaired in processing linguistic information through hearing, with or without amplification, that adversely affects a child's educational performance.

Emotional disturbance is defined as follows:

i. The term means a condition exhibiting one or more of the following characteristics over a long period of time and to a marked degree that adversely affects a child's educational performance:

   A. An inability to learn that cannot be explained by intellectual, sensory, or health factors.
   B. An inability to build or maintain satisfactory interpersonal relationships with peers and teachers.
   C. Inappropriate types of behavior or feelings under normal circumstances.
   D. A general pervasive mood of unhappiness or depression.
   E. A tendency to develop physical symptoms or fears associated with personal or school problems.

ii. The term includes schizophrenia. The term does not apply to children who are socially maladjusted, unless it is determined that they have an emotional disturbance.

Hearing impairment means an impairment in hearing, whether permanent or fluctuating, that adversely affects a child's educational performance but that is not included under the definition of deafness in this section.

Intellectual disability means significantly subaverage general intellectual functioning, existing concurrently with deficits in adaptive behavior and manifested during the developmental period, that adversely affects a child's educational performance.

Multiple disabilities means concomitant impairments (such as intellectual disability–blindness, intellectual disability–orthopedic impairment), the combination of which causes such severe educational needs that they cannot be accommodated in special education programs solely for one of the impairments. The term does not include deaf-blindness.

Orthopedic impairment means a severe orthopedic impairment that adversely affects a child's educational performance. The term includes impairments caused by congenital anomaly (e.g., clubfoot, absence of some member), impairments caused by disease (e.g., poliomyelitis, bone tuberculosis), and impairments from other causes (e.g., cerebral palsy, amputations, and fractures or burns that cause contractures).

Other health impairment means having limited strength, vitality, or alertness, including a heightened alertness to environmental stimuli, that results in limited alertness with respect to the educational environment, that

    i. is due to chronic or acute health problems such as asthma, attention deficit disorder or attention deficit hyperactivity disorder, diabetes, epilepsy, a heart condition, hemophilia, lead poisoning, leukemia, nephritis, rheumatic fever, sickle cell anemia, and Tourette syndrome; and

    ii. adversely affects a child's educational performance.

Specific learning disability is defined as follows:

    i. *General.* The term means a disorder in one or more of the basic psychological processes involved in understanding or in using language, spoken or written, that may manifest itself in an imperfect ability to listen, think, speak, read, write, spell, or do mathematical calculations, including conditions such as perceptual disabilities, brain injury, minimal brain dysfunction, dyslexia, and developmental aphasia.

    ii. *Disorders not included.* The term does not include learning problems that are primarily the result of visual, hearing, or motor disabilities, of intellectual disability, of emotional disturbance, or of environmental, cultural, or economic disadvantage.

Speech or language impairment means a communication disorder, such as stuttering, impaired articulation, a language impairment, or a voice impairment, that adversely affects a child's educational performance.

Traumatic brain injury means an acquired injury to the brain caused by an external physical force, resulting in total or partial functional disability or psychosocial impairment or both, that adversely affects a child's educational performance. The term applies to open or closed head injuries resulting in impairments in one or more areas, such as cognition; language; memory; attention; reasoning; abstract thinking; judgment; problem-solving; sensory, perceptual, and motor abilities; psychosocial behavior; physical functions; information processing; and speech. The term does not apply to brain injuries that are congenital or degenerative, or to brain injuries induced by birth trauma.

Visual impairment including blindness means an impairment in vision that, even with correction, adversely affects a child's educational performance. The term includes both partial sight and blindness.

SOURCE: Individuals with Disabilities Education Improvement Act, 34 C.F.R. Part 300 § 300.8 (C). August 14, 2006.

Council for Exceptional Children

Initial Level Special Educator Preparation Standards

Standard 1. Learner Development and Individual Learning Differences:

Beginning special education professionals understand how exceptionalities may interact with development and learning and use this knowledge to provide meaningful and challenging learning experiences for individuals with exceptionalities.

		Chapter														
		1	2	3	4	5	6	7	8	9	10	11	12	13	14	15
1.1	Beginning special education professionals understanding how language, culture, and family background influence the learning of individuals with exceptionalities.	•		•	•		•	•	•	•	•	•	•	•	•	•
1.2	Beginning special education professionals use understanding of development and individual differences to respond to the needs of individuals with exceptionalities.		•			•	•	•	•	•	•	•	•	•	•	•

Standard 2. Learning Environments

Beginning special education professionals create safe, inclusive, culturally responsive learning environments so that individuals with exceptionalities become active and effective learners and develop emotional well-being, positive social interactions, and self-determination.

		Chapter														
		1	2	3	4	5	6	7	8	9	10	11	12	13	14	15
2.1	Beginning special education professionals through collaboration with general educators and other colleagues create safe, inclusive, culturally responsive learning environments to engage individuals with exceptionalities in meaningful learning activities and social interactions.	•	•	•			•	•	•	•	•	•	•	•	•	•
2.2	Beginning special education professionals use motivational and instructional interventions to teach individuals with exceptionalities how to adapt to different environments.						•	•	•	•	•	•	•	•	•	•
2.3	Beginning special education professionals know how to intervene safely and appropriately with individuals with exceptionalities in crisis.									•						

(Continued)

(Continued)

Standard 3. Curricular Content Knowledge

Beginning special education professionals use knowledge of general and specialized curricula to individualize learning for individuals with exceptionalities.

		Chapter														
		1	2	3	4	5	6	7	8	9	10	11	12	13	14	15
3.1	Beginning special education professionals understand the central concepts, structures of the discipline, and tools of inquiry of the content areas they teach, and can organize this knowledge, integrate cross-disciplinary skills, and develop meaningful learning progressions for individuals with exceptionalities.					•	•	•	•	•	•	•	•	•	•	•
3.2	Beginning special education professionals understand and use general and specialized content knowledge for teaching across curricular content areas to individualize learning for individuals with exceptionalities.	•	•			•	•	•	•	•	•	•	•	•	•	•
3.3	Beginning special education professionals modify general and specialized curricula to make them accessible to individuals with exceptionalities.	•				•	•	•	•	•	•	•	•	•	•	•

Standard 4. Assessment

Beginning special education professionals use multiple methods of assessment and data-sources in making educational decisions.

			Chapter														
		1	2	3	4	5	6	7	8	9	10	11	12	13	14	15
4.1	Beginning special education professionals select and use technically sound formal and informal assessment that minimize bias.		•	•			•	•	•	•	•	•	•	•	•	•
4.2	Beginning special education professionals use knowledge of measurement principles and practices to interpret assessment results and guide educational decisions for individuals with exceptionalities.		•	•			•	•	•	•	•	•	•	•	•	•
4.3	Beginning special education professionals in collaboration with colleagues and families use multiple types of assessment information in making decisions about individuals with exceptionalities.	•	•	•			•	•	•	•	•	•	•	•	•	•
4.4	Beginning special education professionals engage individuals with exceptionalities to work toward quality learning and performance and provide feedback to guide them.						•	•	•	•	•	•	•	•	•	•

(Continued)

Standard 5. Instructional Planning and Strategies

Beginning special education professionals select, adapt, and use a repertoire of evidence-based instructional strategies to advance learning of individuals with exceptionalities.

		Chapter														
		1	2	3	4	5	6	7	8	9	10	11	12	13	14	15
5.1	Beginning special education professionals consider an individual's abilities, interests, learning environments, and cultural and linguistic factors in the selection, development, and adaptation of learning experiences for individuals with exceptionalities.	•	•	•			•	•	•	•	•	•	•	•	•	•
5.2	Beginning special education professionals use technologies to support instructional assessment, planning, and delivery for individuals with exceptionalities.					•	•	•	•	•	•	•	•	•	•	•
5.3	Beginning special education professionals are familiar with augmentative and alternative communication systems and a variety of assistive technologies to support the communication and learning of individuals with exceptionalities.					•					•	•	•		•	
5.4	Beginning special education professionals use strategies to enhance language development and communication skills of individuals with exceptionalities.			•								•			•	
5.5	Beginning special education professionals develop and implement a variety of education and transition plans for individuals with exceptionalities across a wide range of settings and different learning experiences in collaboration with individuals, families, and teams.	•	•				•	•	•	•	•	•	•	•	•	•

	Chapter														
	1	2	3	4	5	6	7	8	9	10	11	12	13	14	15
5.6 Beginning special education professionals teach to mastery and promote generalization of learning.															
5.7 Beginning special education professionals teach cross-disciplinary knowledge and skills such as critical thinking and problem solving to individuals with exceptionalities.															•

Standard 6. Professional Learning and Ethical Practice

Beginning special education professionals use foundational knowledge of the field and their professional Ethical Principles and Practice Standards to inform special education practice, to engage in lifelong learning, and to advance the profession.

	Chapter														
	1	2	3	4	5	6	7	8	9	10	11	12	13	14	15
6.1 Beginning special education professionals use professional Ethical Practices and Professional Practice Standards to guide their practice.	•	•													
6.2 Beginning special education professionals understand how foundational knowledge and current issues influence professional practice.	•	•	•	•	•	•	•	•	•	•	•	•	•	•	•
6.3 Beginning special education professionals understand that diversity is a part of families, cultures, and schools, and that complex human issues can interact with the delivery of special education services.		•	•	•		•	•	•	•	•	•	•	•	•	•
6.4 Beginning special education professionals understand the significance of lifelong learning and participate in professional activities and learning communities.															

(Continued)

(Continued)

		Chapter														
		1	2	3	4	5	6	7	8	9	10	11	12	13	14	15
6.5	Beginning special education professionals advance the profession by engaging in activities such as advocacy and mentoring.															
6.6	Beginning special education professionals provide guidance and direction to paraeducators, tutors, and volunteers.															

Standard 7. Collaboration

Beginning special education professionals collaborate with families, other educators, related service providers, individuals with exceptionalities, and personnel from community agencies in culturally responsive ways to address the needs of individuals with exceptionalities across a range of learning environments.

		Chapter														
		1	2	3	4	5	6	7	8	9	10	11	12	13	14	15
7.1	Beginning special education professionals use the theory and elements of effective collaboration.	•	•		•											
7.2	Beginning special education professionals serve as a collaborative resource to colleagues.	•	•													
7.3	Beginning special education professionals use collaboration to promote the well-being of individuals with exceptionalities across a wide range of settings and collaborators.	•	•	•												

SOURCE: Adapted from the *CEC Initial and Advanced Preparation Standards*. Available at http//www.cec.sped.org/Standards/Special-Educator-Professional-Preparation/CEC-Initial-and-Advanced-Preparation-Standards

NOTE: Standards are effective spring 2015.

PRAXIS™ Series of Professional Assessment for Beginning Teachers

Topics covered by the Praxis II® test, *Education of Exceptional Students: Core Content Knowledge* (0353), are shown here.

Descriptions of each of the content areas covered by the test are provided below. For each content area, the approximate percentage of examination questions pertaining to that area is shown. Not every subtopic in a given content area appears on any one form of the test, but every form of the test contains questions on a broad range of subtopics.

I. Understanding Exceptionalities (25%–30% of test questions)

A. Human development and behavior as related to students with disabilities, including
1. social and emotional development and behavior
2. language development and behavior
3. cognition
4. physical development, including motor and sensory
B. Characteristics of students with disabilities, including the influence of
1. cognitive factors
2. affective and social-adaptive factors, including cultural, linguistic, gender, and socioeconomic factors
3. genetic, medical, motor, sensory, and chronological age factors
C. Basic concepts in special education, including
1. definitions of all major categories and specific disabilities, as well as the incidence and prevalence of various types of disabilities
2. the causation and prevention of disability
3. the nature of behaviors, including frequency, duration, intensity, and degrees of severity
4. the classification of students with disabilities; labeling of students; ADHD; the implications of the classification process for the persons classified, etc.
5. the influence of level of severity and presence of multiple exceptionalities on students with disabilities
D. The influence of (an) exceptional condition(s) throughout an individual's life span

II. Legal and Societal Issues (15%–20% of test questions)

A. Federal laws and legal issues related to special education, including
1. IDEA 2004
2. Section 504
3. Americans with Disabilities Act (ADA)
4. Important legal issues, such as those raised by the following cases: *Rowley* re: program appropriateness, *Tatro* re: related services, *Honig* re: discipline, *Oberti* re: inclusion
B. The school's connections with the families, prospective and actual employers, and communities of students with disabilities; for example:
1. teacher advocacy for students and families, developing student self-advocacy
2. parent partnerships and roles
3. public attitudes toward individuals with disabilities
4. cultural and community influences on public attitudes toward individuals with disabilities
5. interagency agreements
6. cooperative nature of the transition planning process
C. Historical movements/trends affecting the connections between special education and the larger society; for example:
1. deinstitutionalization and community-based placements
2. inclusion
3. application of technology
4. transition

5. advocacy
6. accountability and meeting educational standards

III. Delivery of Services to Students With Disabilities (50%–60% of test questions)

A. Background knowledge, including
1. conceptual approaches underlying service delivery to students with disabilities, including cognitive, constructivist, psychodynamic, behavioral, sociological, ecological, therapeutic (speech/language, physical, and occupational), and medical approaches
2. placement and program issues, such as early intervention; least restrictive environment; inclusion; role of Individualized Education Program (IEP) team; due process guidelines; categorical, noncategorical, and cross-categorical programs; continuum of educational and related services; related services and their integration into the classroom, including roles of other professionals; accommodations, including access to assistive technology; transition of students into and within special education placements; community-based training; postschool transitions
3. integrating best practices from multidisciplinary research and professional literature into the educational setting

B. Curriculum and instruction and their implementation across the continuum of educational placements, including
1. the Individualized Family Service Plan (IFSP)/Individualized Education Program (IEP) process
2. Instructional development and implementation; for example: instructional activities, curricular materials and resources, working with classroom and support personnel, tutoring options
3. teaching strategies and methods; for example: modification of materials and equipment, learning centers, facilitated groups, study skills groups, self-management, cooperative learning, diagnostic-prescriptive method, modeling, skill drill, guided practice, concept generalization, learning strategy instruction, and Direct Instruction
4. instructional format and components; for example: small and large group instruction, facilitated group strategies, functional academics, general academics with focus on special education, ESL and limited English proficiency, language and literacy acquisition, self-care and daily living skills, prevocational and vocational skills
5. career development and transition issues as related to curriculum design and implementation for students with disabilities according to the criteria of ultimate functioning
6. technology for teaching and learning in special education settings; for example: integrating assistive technology into the classroom; computer-assisted instruction; augmentative and alternative communication; adaptive access for microcomputers; positioning and power mobility for students with physical disabilities; accessing and using information technology; use of productivity tools; technology for sensory disabilities; and voice-activated, speech synthesis, speech-recognition, and word-prediction software

C. Assessment, including
1. use of assessment for screening, diagnosis, placement, and the making of instructional decisions; for example: how to select and conduct nondiscriminatory and appropriate assessments; how to interpret standardized and specialized assessment results; how to use evaluation results effectively in development of an Individualized Family Service Plan (IFSP)/Individualized Education Program (IEP); how to prepare written reports and communicate findings
2. procedures and test materials, both formal and informal, typically used for prereferral, referral, eligibility, placement, and ongoing program monitoring
3. how to select, construct, conduct, and modify nondiscriminatory, developmentally, and chronologically age-appropriate informal assessments, including teacher-made tests, curriculum-based assessment, and alternatives to norm-referenced testing (including observation, anecdotal records, error analysis, miscue analysis, self-evaluation questionnaires and interviews, journals and learning logs, portfolio assessment)

D. Structuring and managing the learning environment, including
   1. structuring the learning environment; for example: the physical-social environment for learning (expectations, rules, consequences, consistency, attitudes, lighting, acoustic characteristics, seating, access, safety provisions, and strategies for positive interactions); transitions between lessons and activities; grouping of students; integration of related services (occupational therapy, physical therapy, speech and language therapy)
   2. classroom management techniques; for example: behavioral analysis (identification and definition of antecedents, target behavior, and consequent events); behavioral interventions; functional analysis; data gathering procedures (such as anecdotal data, frequency methods, and interval methods); self-management strategies and reinforcement; cognitive-behavioral interventions; social skills training; behavior management strategies
E. Professional roles, including
   1. specific roles and responsibilities of teachers; for example: teacher as a collaborator with other teachers, teacher educators, parents, community groups, and outside agencies; teacher as a multidisciplinary team member; maintaining effective and efficient documentation; selecting appropriate environments and services for students; critical evaluation and use of professional literature and organizations; reflecting on one's own teaching; teacher's role in a variety of teaching settings (self-contained classroom, resource room, itinerant, co-teacher in inclusion setting, etc.); and maintaining student confidentiality
   2. influence of teacher attitudes, values, and behaviors on the learning of exceptional students
   3. communicating with parents, guardians, and appropriate community collaborators; for example: directing parents and guardians to parent-educators or to other groups and resources; writing reports directly to parents; meeting with parents to discuss student concerns, progress, and IEPs; encouraging parent participation; reciprocal communication and training with other service providers

---

SOURCE: PRAXIS materials from *The Praxis Series: Test at a Glance—Education of Exceptional Students: Core Content Knowledge.* Reprinted by permission of Educational Testing Service, the copyright owner.

NOTE: Permission to reprint PRAXIS materials does not constitute review or endorsement by Educational Testing Service of this publication as a whole or of any other testing information it may contain.

Glossary

abandonment When an individual stops using an assistive technology device.

absence seizure A type of epileptic seizure lasting for a brief period of time whereby the individual loses consciousness and stops moving, formerly known as a petit mal seizure.

acceleration An instructional strategy typically used with pupils who are gifted and talented; one approach is placing students in a grade level beyond their chronological age.

acoustic immittance A technical term for measurements of middle ear function.

acquired immune deficiency syndrome (AIDS) An infectious disease caused by HIV (human immunodeficiency virus) that destroys the immune system, leaving the person open to serious, life-threatening diseases.

active listening A type of listening in which a person is attentive to the feelings as well as the verbal message that is being communicated.

adaptability The ability of an individual or family to change in response to a crisis or stressful event.

adaptive behavior The ability of an individual to meet the standards of personal independence as well as social responsibility appropriate for his or her chronological age and cultural group.

additions An articulation disorder wherein the speaker inserts extra sounds in spoken words.

adventitious (acquired) hearing loss Hearing loss that is acquired after birth, not inherited.

air-conduction audiometry A procedure for measuring hearing sensitivity at certain frequencies using pure tones presented to the listener through earphones or speakers.

albinism A hereditary condition with partial or total absence of pigment in the eye.

amniocentesis A diagnostic medical procedure performed to detect chromosomal and genetic abnormalities in a fetus.

anencephaly Cranial malformation; large part of the brain fails to develop.

anoxia Loss of or inadequate supply of oxygen associated with birth process and frequently resulting in brain damage.

aphakic Absence of the lens, causing light sensitivity and loss of visual acuity.

aphasia Loss or impairment of language functions.

applied behavior analysis (ABA) Application of learning principles derived from operant conditioning; used to increase or decrease specific behaviors.

apraxia of speech Speech and language disorder comprising both a speech disorder, caused by oral-motor difficulty, and a language disorder, characterized by the resultant limitations of expression.

articulation disorders Errors in the formation of individual sounds of speech.

Asperger syndrome A pervasive developmental disorder with severe and sustained impairments in social interaction and the development of restricted, repetitive patterns of behavior, interests, and activities. Disorder causes clinically significant impairments in other important areas of functioning.

assessment The process of gathering information and identifying a student's strengths and needs through a variety of instruments and products; data used in making decisions.

assistive listening devices Devices such as FM or sound field systems that improve the clarity of what is heard by an individual with hearing impairments by reducing background noise levels.

assistive technology device Any item, piece of equipment, or product system that increases, maintains, or improves functional capabilities of individuals with disabilities.

assistive technology service Any service that directly assists an individual in the selection, acquisition, or use of an assistive technology device.

assistive technology specialist A person trained to provide assistive technology services to individuals with disabilities.

asthma A lung disease with acute attacks of shortness of breath and wheezing.

astigmatism A condition in which or more surfaces of the cornea or lens are cylindrical, not spherical, resulting in distorted vision.

ataxic cerebral palsy (ataxia) A type of cerebral palsy that is characterized by poor balance and equilibrium in addition to uncoordinated voluntary movement.

athetoid cerebral palsy A type of cerebral palsy in which movements are contorted, abnormal, and purposeless.

atresia The absence or closure of the ear canal; can be congenital or acquired from injury or disease.

at risk An infant or child who has a high probability of exhibiting delays in development or developing a disability.

attention deficit hyperactivity disorder (ADHD) A disorder characterized by symptoms of inattention, hyperactivity, and/or impulsivity. Frequently observed in individuals with learning disabilities.

audiogram A graphic representation of audiometric findings showing hearing thresholds as a function of frequency.

audiologist A professional who studies the science of hearing, including anatomy, function, and disorders, and provides education and treatment for those with hearing loss.

auditory evoked potentials Neural impulses produced from within the auditory system in response to stimulation of the auditory pathway and recorded as bioelectric events using a special computer.

auditory trainer Type of amplification system used by children with hearing impairments in place of their hearing aids in educational settings.

augmentative and alternative communication (AAC) Symbols, aids, strategies, and techniques used as a supplement or alternative to oral language.

authentic assessment An evaluation of a student's ability by means of various work products, typically classroom assignments and other activities.

autism spectrum disorder A developmental disorder characterized by abnormal or impaired development in social interaction and communication and a markedly restricted repertoire of activity and interests.

autistic savant An individual with autism who possesses special skills in areas such as mathematical calculations, memory feats, artistic and musical abilities, or reading.

autosomal dominant A genetic form of inheritance involving the non–sex-linked chromosomes in which the individual has one normal and one abnormal gene in a gene pair.

autosomal recessive A genetic form of inheritance involving the non–sex-linked chromosomes in which both genes of a gene pair must be affected for the trait to be expressed.

behavioral inhibition A characteristic common in persons with ADHD; impacts executive functions. Typically affects the ability to (1) withhold a planned response; (2) interrupt an ongoing response; and (3) protect an ongoing response from distractions.

behavioral intervention plan A plan required by Public Law 105–17 for students with disabilities who exhibit problematic behavior; a proactive intervention approach that includes a functional behavioral assessment and the use of positive behavioral supports.

bilingual education An educational approach whereby students whose first language is not English are instructed primarily through their native language while developing competency and proficiency in English.

bilingual special education Strategy whereby a pupil's home language and culture are used along with English in an individually designed program of special instruction.

biologically at risk Young children with a history of pre-, peri-, or postnatal conditions and developmental events that heighten the potential for later atypical development.

birth trauma Difficulties associated with the delivery of the fetus.

bone-conduction audiometry A procedure for measuring hearing sensitivity at certain frequencies using pure tones presented through an oscillator placed on the forehead or mastoid bone of the listener. Sound is conducted to the inner ear through the bones of the skull.

Braille A communication system utilizing raised representation of written materials for tactual interpretation.

breech presentation Fetus exits the birth canal buttocks first rather than typical headfirst presentation.

cataracts Lenses that are opaque or cloudy due to trauma or age.

category Label assigned to individuals who share common characteristics and features.

central auditory nervous system Part of the hearing mechanism connecting the ear to the brain.

central auditory processing disorder (CAPD) A problem in the processing of sound not attributed to hearing loss or intellectual capacity, involving cognitive and linguistic functions that directly affect receptive communication skills.

central hearing disorder Difficulty in the reception and interpretation of auditory information in the absence of a hearing loss.

cerebral palsy Several nonprogressive disorders of voluntary movement or posture that are caused by damage to the developing brain.

CHARGE association A rare genetic disorder resulting in deaf-blindness, a syndrome representing a cluster of physical anomalies present at birth.

child-find A function of each state, mandated by federal law, to locate and refer individuals who might require special education.

child maltreatment The neglect and/or physical, emotional, or sexual abuse of a child.

chorionic villus sampling (CVS) A diagnostic medical procedure used to detect a variety of chromosomal abnormalities, usually conducted in the first trimester of pregnancy.

classroom arrangement The physical layout of the classroom and its décor; a proactive intervention technique designed to minimize disruptions while increasing pupil engagement.

cleft lip/cleft palate A congenital defect in which the upper lip is split or there is an opening in the roof of the mouth. Can often be surgically corrected. Hypernasality is common.

clinically derived classification system A system frequently used by mental health professionals to describe childhood, adolescent, and adult mental disorders.

cluster grouping The practice of placing five or more students who have similar needs and abilities with one teacher; promotes challenging cognitive development and positive social-emotional development.

cluttering Type of fluency disorder involving cognitive, linguistic, pragmatic, speech, and motor abilities.

cochlea Shell- or spiral-shaped structure in the inner ear that is responsible for hearing.

cochlear implant A surgically implanted device that allows individuals who are deaf to hear environmental sounds and understand speech.

cohesion Within a family, the degree of freedom and independence experienced by each member.

collaboration How individuals work together; a style of interaction among professionals.

coloboma A congenital condition that results in a teardrop shape of the pupil, iris, lens, retina, choroids, or optic nerve; may involve loss of field vision as well as problems with glare and depth perception.

communication The sharing or exchange of ideas, information, thoughts, and feelings. Does not necessarily require speech or language.

communication breakdown Misunderstanding as to what is being communicated, especially as it relates to individuals who are using some form of augmentative communication.

community-based instruction A strategy for teaching functional skills in the environment in which they would naturally occur rather than in simulated settings.

comorbidity The simultaneous existence of two or more conditions within the same person.

complementary and alternative medicine (CAM) Treatment strategies and interventions for individuals with autism spectrum disorders that lack empirical support.

complex partial seizure A type of epileptic seizure whereby the person exhibits purposeless motor activity for a brief period of time; consciousness is impaired.

computer-assisted instruction (CAI) The application of computer technology to deliver instruction.

conduct disorder A common psychiatric disorder among children and youth characterized by disruptive and aggressive behavior as well as other actions that violate societal rules.

conductive hearing loss The loss of sound sensitivity produced by abnormalities of the outer ear and/or middle ear.

cone cells Light-sensitive cells located mainly in the central area of the retina that define color.

conflict resolution Program designed to teach problem-solving skills along with strategies for negotiation and mediation.

consultation A focused problem-solving process in which one individual offers support and expertise to another person.

content enhancements Instructional aids designed to assist pupils in understanding major concepts, ideas, and vocabulary in a way that aids the acquisition, organization, and recall of material.

contractures Shortened muscles that result in the inability to fully extend a joint.

cooperative learning Instructional process whereby heterogeneous groups of students work together on an assignment.

cooperative teaching An instructional approach in which a special education teacher and a general educator teach together in a general education classroom to a heterogeneous group of students.

cornea The transparent outer portion of the eyeball that transmits light to the retina.

creativity A term with multiple meanings, generally referring to the production of novel or original ideas or products.

crisis prevention and management programs Techniques taught to teachers on how to effectively and proactively deal with students' violent, aggressive, and/or self-injurious behaviors; a proactive preventative approach.

criterion-referenced assessment An assessment procedure in which a student's performance is compared to a particular level of mastery.

cultural pluralism The practice of appreciating and respecting ethnic and cultural differences.

cultural sensitivity A perspective adopted by professionals when working with families in which there is an awareness of and respect for the values, customs, and traditions of individuals and families.

culture The attitudes, values, belief systems, norms, and traditions shared by a particular group of people that collectively form their heritage.

curriculum-based measurement (CBM) A formative assessment procedure for monitoring student progress in core academic subjects that reflect the local school curriculum.

curriculum compacting An instructional technique whereby the time spent on academic subjects is reduced so as to allow for enrichment activities; typically used with students who are gifted or talented.

cytomegalovirus (CMV) A common virus that is part of the herpes group; if initial exposure occurs during pregnancy, severe damage to the fetus often results.

deaf Limited or absent hearing for ordinary purposes of daily living.

deaf-blindness Concomitant hearing and visual impairments.

Deaf culture Refers to individuals who are deaf who share similar values, attitudes, and practices; view American Sign Language as their natural language.

decibel (dB) A unit of measure expressing the magnitude of a sound relative to the softest sound to which the normal human ear can respond.

deinstitutionalization A movement whereby persons with intellectual disabilities are relocated from large institutions into smaller, community-based, group living settings.

developmental delay A term defined by individual states referring to children ages 3 to 9 who perform significantly below developmental norms.

developmental language delay Slowness in the development of adequate vocabulary and grammar, or when a child's language age does not correspond to the child's chronological age.

differentiation A modification of the curriculum that enables students who are gifted to learn at a level appropriate to their ability.

diplegia Paralysis (or spasticity) of the legs and partly the arms.

Direct Instruction (DI) A teacher-directed instructional technique used to produce gains in specific academic skills; emphasizes drill and practice along with immediate feedback and reward.

disability An inability or incapacity to perform a task or activity in a normative fashion.

discrepancy In regard to learning disabilities, the difference between the student's actual academic performance and his or her estimated ability.

distortions Articulation disorder in which a sound is said inaccurately but resembles the intended sound (e.g., *shlip* for *sip*).

doctor's office effect The absence of symptoms of ADHD when the individual is evaluated in a structured environment such as a physician's office.

Down syndrome A chromosomal abnormality frequently resulting in intellectual disability with accompanying distinctive physical features.

Duchenne muscular dystrophy An inherited disease that is characterized by progressive muscle weakness from the degeneration of the muscle fiber.

dyslexia A severe reading disability; difficulty in understanding the relationship between sounds and letters.

early childhood special education Provision of customized services uniquely crafted to meet the individual needs of youngsters with disabilities ages 3 to 5.

early intervention The delivery of a coordinated and comprehensive package of specialized services to infants and toddlers with developmental delays or at-risk conditions and their families.

educable mentally retarded (EMR) Classification of a person with mild intellectual disability who typically develops functional academic skills at a third- or fourth-grade level; IQ range generally between 50–55 and 70–75.

educational technology Technology used for educational purposes such as teaching and learning.

emotional disturbance A term often used when referring to individuals with emotional or behavioral disorders.

emotional or behavioral disorder A chronic condition characterized by behaviors that significantly differ from age norms and community standards to such a degree that educational performance is adversely affected.

encephalitis An inflammation of the brain; may cause damage to the central nervous system.

English learners (ELs) Students whose primary language is not English and who have yet to achieve proficiency in English.

environmental control unit (ECU) A device that allows the user to control electric appliances, telephones, and other items that use electric outlets from a distance.

environmentally at risk Youngsters who are biologically typical yet encounter life experiences or environmental circumstances that are so limiting that there is the possibility of future delayed development.

epilepsy A chronic condition in which the person has recurring seizures.

established risk Youngsters with a diagnosed medical disorder of known etiology and predictable prognosis or outcome.

e-text An electronic presentation of a text, also known as a digital text, that can be read on a computer.

ethnocentrism A perspective whereby a person views his or her cultural practices as correct and those of other groups as inferior, peculiar, or deviant.

etiology A term frequently used when describing the cause of a disability.

eugenics movement A campaign that sought to improve the quality of humankind through carefully controlled selective breeding.

evoked otoacoustic emissions Sounds produced by the inner ear in response to auditory stimulation and measured in the ear canal.

exceptional children Children who deviate from the norm to such an extent that special educational services are required.

exclusionary clause In regard to learning disabilities, the elimination of possible etiological factors to explain a pupil's difficulty in learning.

executive functions Internal regulation of one's behavior through control of emotions, inner speech, working memory, arousal levels, and motivation.

Considered impaired in individuals with attention deficit hyperactivity disorder.

expressive language The formation and production of language, verbal and nonverbal, that is understood by and meaningful to others.

external locus of control The belief that the consequences or outcomes of a person's actions are the result of circumstances and situations beyond one's control rather than a result of one's own efforts.

externalizing disorders A behavior disorder characterized by aggressive, disruptive, acting-out behavior.

familiality study A method for assessing the degree to which a particular characteristic is inherited; the tendency for certain conditions to occur in a single family.

family-centered early intervention A philosophy of working with families that stresses family strengths and capabilities, the enhancement of skills, and the development of mutual partnerships between service providers and families.

family characteristics One dimension of a family systems model; aspects include family size and form, cultural background, and socioeconomic status, as well as the type and severity of the disability.

family-directed assessment A form of assessment, useful for infants, toddlers, and preschool-age youngsters, that focuses on information that families choose to provide regarding needs, concerns, resources, and priorities.

family functions Interrelated activities found within a family systems model; functions range from affection to economics to socialization, among other variables.

family interactions One aspect of a family systems model; refers to the relationships and interactions occurring among and between various family subsystems.

family life cycle Developmental changes occurring within a family over time.

family systems model A model that considers a family as an interrelated social system with unique characteristics and needs.

fetal alcohol effect (FAE) A less severe and more subtle form of fetal alcohol syndrome; caused by drinking alcohol while pregnant.

fetal alcohol syndrome (FAS) Results from mother's consumption of alcohol while pregnant; mild to moderate intellectual disability is common, along with physical deformities. A leading cause of intellectual disability, although completely preventable.

field dependent/sensitive Students who approach learning intuitively rather than analytically and logically. These students tend to find success in cooperative learning situations and group work.

field independent Learners who are detail oriented and analytically inclined. These students tend to thrive in competitive settings.

field loss A restriction to the visual field within the quadrant regions to the right, left, up, and down while gazing straight ahead.

fingerspelling A form of manual communication; different positions or movements of the fingers indicate letters of the alphabet.

flexible grouping The combining or grouping of students according to needs and abilities matched to their level of achievement.

fluency disorders Disorders that involve the flow of speech, influencing the rate and smoothness of an individual's speech.

FM system A wireless system that allows the transmission of a signal from the teacher wearing a microphone to the student wearing a receiver, increasing the volume of the teacher's voice over the volume level of classroom noise.

formal supports Assistance provided by government social programs, habilitation services, or advocacy groups.

fragile X syndrome A chromosomal abnormality leading to intellectual disability along with physical anomalies; believed to be the most common form of inherited intellectual disability.

frequency The number of vibrations per second of a given sound wave; typically measured as cycles per second (cps) or hertz (Hz).

full inclusion An interpretation of the principle of least restrictive environment advocating that all pupils with disabilities are to be educated in the general education classroom.

functional Etiologies of speech and language disorders that have no obvious physical basis (such as environmental stress).

functional academics The application of life skills as a means of teaching academic tasks; core of many instructional programs for students with mild or moderate intellectual disability.

functional behavioral assessment A behavioral strategy that seeks to determine the purpose or function that a particular behavior serves—what is occasioning and maintaining the behavior.

functional curriculum A curriculum that emphasizes practical life skills rather than academic skills.

functional vision How well students use the vision they have to complete a specific task.

functionally blind An educational description when the primary channel of learning is through tactile and auditory means.

galactosemia An inborn error of metabolism that makes infants unable to process galactose, resulting in a variety of physical problems in addition to intellectual disability; dietary intervention reduces potential for problems.

generalizing The ability to transfer previously learned knowledge or skills acquired in one setting to another set of circumstances or situation.

gifted and talented Persons who possess abilities and talents that can be demonstrated, or have the potential for being developed, at exceptionally high levels.

glaucoma A disease caused by increased pressure inside the aqueous portion of the eye with loss in the visual field.

Grade 1 Braille A beginning level of Braille in which a word is spelled out with a Braille letter corresponding to each printed letter.

Grade 2 Braille A more complex level of Braille in which contractions are used to represent parts of words or whole words.

handicap Difficulties imposed by the environment on a person with a disability.

handicapism The unequal and differential treatment accorded individuals with a disability.

hard of hearing Refers to a person who has a hearing loss but uses the auditory channel as the primary avenue for oral communication, with or without a hearing aid.

hearing impairment Less than normal hearing (either sensitivity or speech understanding) resulting from auditory disorder(s).

hearing sensitivity loss Poorer than normal auditory sensitivity for sounds; usually measured in decibels (dB) using pure tones.

hemiplegia Paralysis (or spasticity) on the left or right side of the body.

heritability studies A method for assessing the degree to which a specific condition is inherited; a comparison of the prevalence of a characteristic in fraternal versus identical twins.

hertz (Hz) A unit of measurement for sound frequency, expressed as cycles per second (cps).

high-risk register A list of factors placing infants at increased risk for hearing impairment, including, but not limited to, low birth weight, congenital perinatal infections, a family history of childhood hearing impairment, severe asphyxia, and bacterial meningitis.

hydrocephalus A condition in which the head is unusually large due to accumulation of excessive cerebrospinal fluid; brain damage often minimized by surgically implanting a shunt to remove excess fluid.

hyperactive child syndrome A historical term commonly used to describe youngsters who exhibit impulsivity, inattention, and/or hyperactivity.

hypernasality Disorder of voice resonance, frequently observed as a result of cleft palate, in which too much air passes through the nasal cavities during the production of sounds, giving the speaker a distinctive nasal quality or "twang."

hyperopia Change in the shape of the eye, which shortens the light ray path and causes farsightedness.

hyponasality Disorder of voice resonance in which there is a restricted flow of air through the nostrils, often resulting in the speaker's sounding as if his or her nose is being held.

hypoxia Insufficient amount of oxygen to the brain; can result in brain damage.

incidence A rate of inception; number of new cases appearing in the population within a specific time period.

incus The second of the three middle ear bones for conducting sound to the inner ear, located between the malleus and the stapes; also called the anvil.

individualized education program (IEP) A written detailed plan developed by a team for each pupil ages 3–21 who receives a special education; a management tool.

individualized family service plan (IFSP) A written plan developed by a team that coordinates services for infants and toddlers and their families.

individualized transition plan (ITP) An individualized plan with identified goals and objectives used to prepare the student in making the transition from high school to work (or college).

infant stimulation Programs for infants with disabilities or those experiencing delays; emphasis usually on achieving developmental or cognitive milestones.

information technology Databases and computer-based information sources.

inner ear The snail-shaped part of the ear (cochlea) containing the organs of hearing and balance.

instructional technology Any apparatus or device that supports the teaching-learning process, such as computers or televisions; a tool for the delivery of instruction.

interdisciplinary team A group of professionals from different disciplines who function as a team but work independently; recommendations, however, are the result of sharing information and joint planning.

interindividual differences Differences between two or more persons in a particular area.

internalizing disorders Behavior disorders characterized by anxiety, withdrawal, fearfulness, and other conditions reflecting an individual's internal state.

interpersonal problem solving Teaching pupils the cognitive skills needed to avoid and resolve interpersonal conflicts, peer pressure, and ways of coping with stress and their own feelings.

interpreter A professional who signs, gestures, and/or fingerspells a speaker's message as it is spoken to enable individuals with hearing impairments to understand spoken language.

intervener A person with specialized training and skills in deaf-blindness who provides individualized assistance to students.

intraindividual differences Differences within the individual; unique patterns of strengths and weaknesses.

iris The colored, circular part of the eye in front of the lens that controls the size of the pupil.

job coach An individual who supervises a person with a disability for all or part of the day to provide training, assistance, or support to maintain a job.

joint attention A social communication deficit common in individuals with autism spectrum disorders, the failure to respond to a gaze or pointing by another person.

juvenile ideopathic arthritis (JIA) A chronic arthritic condition affecting the joints that occurs before 16 years of age.

language A code used to communicate ideas via a conventional system of arbitrary signals.

language sample An observational evaluation that includes observing the speech and language characteristics of a child actively communicating.

lead poisoning An environmental toxin used at one time in the manufacture of gasoline and paint; ingestion of lead can cause seizures, brain damage, and impaired central nervous system functioning.

learned helplessness A lack of persistence at tasks that can be mastered; a tendency to expect failure.

learning disability A disability in which there is a discrepancy between a person's ability and academic achievement; individual possesses average intelligence.

learning media The materials and methods a student uses in conjunction with the sensory channels in the process of learning.

learning strategies Instructional methodologies focusing on teaching students how to learn; designed to assist pupils in becoming more actively engaged and involved in their own learning.

least restrictive environment (LRE) A relative concept individually determined for each student; principle that each pupil should be educated, to the maximum extent appropriate, with classmates who are typical.

legally blind A visual acuity of 20/200 or less in the better eye with correction or a visual field that is no greater than 20 degrees.

lens The transparent disc in the middle of the eye behind the pupil that brings rays of light into focus on the retina.

level of support A classification scheme for individuals with intellectual disability that is based on the type and extent of assistance required to function in various areas.

limb deficiency Any number of skeletal abnormalities in which an arm(s) and/or leg(s) is partially or totally missing.

literacy medium The student's preferred method of reading and writing.

low birth weight A term frequently used to describe babies who are born weighing less than 2,500 grams (5 lbs., 8 oz.).

low-incidence disability A special education category representative of students with disabilities that occur relatively infrequently.

low vision A visual impairment that interferes with the ability to perform daily activities and in which the primary channel of learning is through the use of prescription and nonprescription devices.

macroculture The shared or national culture of a society.

macula The area of best central vision.

macular degeneration A common eye disease in adults, which may also occur in young people, involving damage to the central part of the retina cones, affecting central vision, light sensitivity, and color.

magnet high school A school with a strong instructional emphasis on a particular theme, such as performing arts or math and science; an option for secondary pupils who are gifted and talented.

mainstreaming An early term for the practice of integrating students with special needs into a general education classroom for all or part of the school day.

malleus The first and largest of the three middle ear bones for conducting sound to the inner ear. Also called the hammer, it is attached to the tympanic membrane.

manual communication Communication methods that utilize fingerspelling, signs, and gestures.

melting pot A metaphor describing the United States in the early decades of the twentieth century.

meningitis A viral or bacterial infection of the membranes covering the brain and spinal cord; associated with hearing loss and intellectual disability.

mentally ill A generic term often used by professionals outside of the field of special education to refer to individuals with emotional or behavioral disorders.

mentor The role fulfilled by an older individual who is an expert in a particular field and who works with and guides a student in an area of mutual interest.

metacognition The ability to evaluate and monitor one's own performance.

microcephaly A condition in which the head is unusually small, leading to inadequate development of the brain and resulting in intellectual disability.

microcultures Distinct subcultures within a larger culture; these groups maintain their own distinct values, norms, folkways, and identification.

middle ear The air-filled space behind the eardrum that contains three tiny bones (ossicles) that carry sound to the inner ear.

minimal brain injury A once popular term referring to individuals who exhibit behavioral signs of brain injury (such as distractibility or impulsivity) but with no neurological evidence.

mixed cerebral palsy Cerebral palsy that consists of combinations of different types. A person who has both spastic and athetoid cerebral palsy would be considered to have mixed cerebral palsy.

mixed hearing loss Hearing losses resulting from both conductive and sensorineural hearing impairments.

mnemonic strategy A cognitive approach used to assist pupils in remembering material; the use of rhymes, pictures, acronyms, and similar aids to help in recall.

morphological disorder Difficulty learning and using morphological rules of language.

morphology Dictates how the smallest meaningful units of our language (morphemes) are combined to form words.

multicultural education An ambiguous concept that deals with issues of race, language, social class, and culture as well as disability and gender. Also viewed as an educational strategy wherein the cultural heritage of each pupil is valued.

multiculturalism Referring to more than one culture; acknowledges basic commonalities among groups of people while appreciating their differences.

multidisciplinary team A group of professionals from different disciplines who function as a team but perform their roles independent of one another.

multimodal interventions The use of concurrent treatment approaches with students who exhibit attention deficit hyperactivity disorder.

multiple disabilities Concomitant impairments that result in such severe educational needs that a student cannot be accommodated in a special education program solely on the basis of one of the impairments.

multiple intelligences An alternative perspective on intelligence suggesting that there are many different kinds of intelligence.

myopia Elongation of the eye that causes extreme nearsightedness and decreased visual acuity.

natural supports Assistance rendered by family members, friends, teachers, and coworkers.

neuromotor impairments Several types of impairments involving abnormality of, or damage to, the brain, spinal cord, or nerves that send impulses to the muscles of the body.

noncategorical Programs developed based on student needs and common instructional requirements rather than on disability.

nondiscriminatory testing Federal mandate that assessments be conducted in a culturally responsive fashion.

normalization A principle advocating that individuals with disabilities should be integrated, to the maximum extent possible, into all aspects of everyday living.

norm-referenced assessments Refers to standardized tests on which a pupil's performance is compared to that of his or her peers.

off-level testing The use of assessment instruments designed for older students when evaluating the academic ability of a child thought to be gifted.

omissions Articulation disorder that occurs when a sound is not pronounced in a word (e.g., *han* for *hand*).

optic nerve The nerve at the posterior of the eye that carries messages from the retina to the brain.

optic nerve atrophy Degeneration of the optic nerve, which may be congenital or hereditary, causing loss of central vision, color vision, and reduced visual acuity.

oral approaches Methods of instruction for children with hearing impairments that emphasize spoken language skills.

Methodology attempts to use the child's residual hearing and employs auditory training and speechreading.

oral interpreter A professional who silently repeats a speaker's message as it is spoken so that a hearing-impaired person can lipread the message.

orbit A protective cone-shaped cavity in the skull, sometimes called the socket.

organ of Corti Organ of hearing found within the cochlea.

organic Etiologies of speech and language disorders that can be linked to a physiological deficit (such as cleft palate).

orientation and mobility Systematic techniques to plan routes and move from place to place for persons with visual impairments.

orthopedic impairment A physical disability that occurs from congenital anomalies, diseases, or other causes that adversely affect a child's educational performance.

orthotics Various braces or splints that are used to help maintain alignment and decrease the development of contractures.

ossicular chain Three bones in the middle ear (malleus, incus, and stapes) that connect the eardrum to the inner ear and help to amplify sounds.

other health impairment A chronic or acute health problem that results in limited strength, vitality, or alertness and adversely affects educational performance.

otitis media Infection of the middle ear space, causing conductive hearing loss.

outer-directedness A condition characterized by a loss of confidence in one's own capabilities and a reliance on others for cues and guidance.

outer ear The most visible (external) part of the ear, useful in funneling sound to the ear canal and in localizing the source of sound.

oval window The link between the inner ear and the middle ear.

overrepresentation A situation in which a greater number of students from minority groups are placed in special education programs than would be expected based on the proportion of pupils in the general school population.

paraplegia Paralysis (or spasticity) of the legs.

perinatal Events occurring at or immediately after birth.

person-centered planning Useful when developing a student's individualized education program; creates a vision for pupil's future based on an analysis of his or her strengths, needs, and preferences.

phenylketonuria (PKU) An inherited metabolic disorder resulting from the inability of the body to convert phenylalanine to tyrosine; can be detected at birth and controlled by diet; left untreated, consequences are often severe.

phonation Includes speech factors of pitch, loudness, and quality.

phoneme Smallest unit of sound found in spoken language.

phonemic awareness The ability to recognize that words consist of different sounds or phonemes.

phonological awareness Possible explanation for the reading problems of some students with learning disabilities; difficulty in recognizing the correspondence between specific sounds and certain letters that make up words.

phonological disorder Abnormal organization of phonological system resulting in a significant deficit in speech production or perception.

phonology The sound system of a language, including the use of sounds to create meaningful syllables and words.

photophobic Sensitive to light.

physical restraint The restriction of a student's freedom of movement, physical activity, or access to his or her body.

play audiometry A method for measuring hearing sensitivity in young children by rewarding correct responses; turning the evaluation situation into a game in order to maintain interest and cooperation.

portfolio assessment A type of authentic assessment; samples of different work products gathered over time and across curriculum areas are evaluated.

positive behavioral support An alternative approach to punishment; a schoolwide, proactive way of addressing problematic behaviors.

postlingual Referring to the period of time after a child has developed language.

postnatal Events occurring after birth.

pragmatic difficulties Problems in understanding and using language in different social contexts.

pragmatics A sociolinguistic system involving the use of communication skills in social contexts.

preassessment An assessment of a pupil's previously acquired knowledge; allows teacher to provide differentiated learning experiences.

precipitous birth Birth that occurs in less than two hours.

prelingual Referring to the period of time prior to a child's development of language.

prelinguistic Communicative behaviors used by children before the formation of formal speech and language characteristics.

premature births Babies born prior to 37 weeks of gestation age.

prenatal Events occurring before birth.

prereferral intervention Instructional or behavioral strategies introduced by a general educator to assist students experiencing difficulty; designed to minimize inappropriate referrals for special education.

prevalence The total number of individuals in a given category during a particular period of time.

primary literacy medium An individual's most frequently used method of reading and writing.

primary prevention Activities aimed at eliminating a problem or condition prior to its onset; may also refer to reducing the number of new instances of problematic behavior.

print disabilities A disability that prevents an individual from gaining information from printed material;

requires the use of alternative methods to access the material.

problem-based learning Instructional approach in which authentic problems having multiple solutions are addressed through the application of critical thinking skills.

progress monitoring The frequent and systematic assessment of a pupil's academic progress.

proximity and movement management A classroom management strategy focusing on the effective use of classroom space and the arrangement of the physical environment as a means of minimizing disruptive behavior.

psychogenic theories Freudian perspective that if basic psychological bonds are not established between the parent and the child, the child will not be able to establish relationships with others and will fail to progress. Individual psychotherapy recommended as the treatment of choice.

psychostimulants Medications typically prescribed for persons with ADHD. These drugs activate or enhance specific aspects of neurological functioning that in turn affect executive functions.

pupil The circular opening at the center of the iris that controls the amount of light allowed into the eye.

pure-tone audiometry A procedure for measuring hearing sensitivity at certain frequencies using tones that are presented at various intensities.

quadriplegia Paralysis (or spasticity) of both legs and both arms.

rebound effect The behavioral deterioration sometimes observed in persons with ADHD as the effect of psychostimulant medication gradually wears off.

receptive language The ability to understand what is meant by spoken communication.

referral A formal request by a teacher or parent that a student be evaluated for special education services.

regular education initiative (REI) An approach that advocates that general educators assume greater responsibility for the education of students with disabilities.

related services Services defined by federal law whose purpose is to assist a student with exceptionalities in deriving benefit from a special education.

reliable means of response A consistent, reliable way of answering questions.

residual vision An individual's usable vision.

resonance Sound quality of speech.

respite care Temporary or occasional care of an individual with disabilities by nonfamily members.

response to intervention (RTI) A strategy used for determining whether a pupil has a learning disability. Student is exposed to increasing levels of validated instructional intervention; responsiveness to the instruction is assessed; a lack of adequate progress typically leads to a referral for possible special education services.

retina The inner layer of the eye containing light-sensitive cells that connect with the brain through the optic nerve.

retinitis pigmentosa Pigmentation of the retina that can result in night blindness, photophobia, and eventual loss of vision in various parts of the periphery.

retinopathy of prematurity (ROP) An interruption in the vascular system of the eye, due to premature birth, in which veins and arteries begin to grow in an unorganized manner and cause bundles that pull together and detach the retina, resulting in loss of peripheral vision or total blindness.

Rh incompatibility A condition that results when a woman who is Rh negative carries an Rh positive fetus. Mother's body will produce antibodies that can affect babies resulting from future pregnancies; often leads to intellectual disability and other impairments if mother does not receive an injection of Rho immune globulin.

rod cells Light-sensitive cells located mainly in the peripheral areas of the retina that are responsible for shape and motion, function best in reduced illumination, and are not responsive to color.

rubella A viral disease also known as German measles; contact in first trimester of pregnancy often results in a variety of significant impairments.

scaffolding A cognitive teaching strategy in which teacher provides temporary support to student who is learning a new task; supports are gradually removed as pupil becomes increasingly competent with the activity.

seclusion The involuntary confinement of a student to a room or area from which he or she is physically prevented from leaving.

secondary prevention Efforts focusing on minimizing or eliminating potential risk factors in regard to persons with emotional or behavioral disorders; refers to minimizing the possibility that maladaptive or inappropriate behaviors will occur.

seizure A sudden, temporary change in the normal functioning of the brain's electrical system due to excessive, uncontrolled electrical activity in the brain.

self-advocacy Speaking out for one's personal preferences; protecting one's own interests.

self-contained A separate classroom for children with disabilities, usually found in a public school.

self-determination Self-advocacy efforts by an individual with a disability; expression of desire to live one's life according to one's own wishes; assuming personal control over one's life.

self-instruction A cognitive strategy for changing behavior; pupils initially talk to themselves out loud while performing a task and verbally reward themselves for success.

self-monitoring strategies A behavioral self-control strategy; pupils compare their performance to a criterion, record their efforts, and obtain reinforcement if appropriate.

self-regulation The ability of an individual to manage or govern his or her own behavior.

semantic disorder Language difficulty associated with poor vocabulary development, inappropriate use of word meanings, and/or inability to comprehend word meanings.

semantics A psycholinguistic system that involves word meanings and word relationships and their use in communication.

sensorineural hearing loss The loss of sound sensitivity produced by abnormalities of the inner ear or nerve pathways beyond the inner ear to the brain.

sheltered workshop A structured work environment for persons with disabilities in which vocational and social skills are often the focus of attention; may be a temporary or permanent placement.

short-term memory The recall of information after a brief period of time.

Snellen chart An eye chart of clinical measurement of the true amount of distance vision an individual has under certain conditions.

social skills training Using direct instruction to teach students appropriate social behaviors; goal is to increase individual's social competency and acceptance.

socially maladjusted Individuals whose social behaviors are atypical; often regarded as chronic social offenders.

sound field system A system to assist students with hearing impairments in which the teacher wears a microphone that transmits a signal to a speaker strategically placed in the classroom rather than to a body-worn receiver.

spastic cerebral palsy A type of cerebral palsy in which the person has very tight muscles occurring in one or more muscle groups, resulting in stiff, uncoordinated movements.

special education Specially designed instruction to meet the unique needs of an individual recognized as exceptional.

specialized instructional strategies Teaching techniques specifically designed for a particular special education population to assist with learning specific material.

speech The expression of language via sounds; the oral modality for language.

speech audiometry A set of procedures for measuring auditory perception of speech, including syllables, words, and sentences.

speech-generating device (SGD) A high-tech augmentative or alternative communication device capable of generating speech.

speech recognition threshold (SRT) A measure of threshold sensitivity for speech. The SRT represents the softest sound level at which a listener can identify the stimuli 50 percent of the time.

spina bifida Failure of the neural tube to completely close during fetal development. In its most severe form, the baby is born with a sac on his or her back containing part of the spinal cord.

spread The practice of spreading inferences to other unrelated aspects of a disability, often resulting in stereotyping.

stage theory A hypothesized pattern of parents' reaction to the news that their child has a disability.

standard deviation (SD) A descriptive statistic that expresses the variability and distribution of a set of scores relative to the mean.

stapes The third of the middle ear bones for conducting sound to the inner ear. It resembles a stirrup in shape and is sometimes called the stirrup. It is the smallest bone in the body.

statistically derived classification system A system developed to analyze patterns of behaviors based on statistical procedures that characterize children and youth with emotional or behavioral disorders.

stigmatization To experience undesired negative attention due to using assistive technology.

Strauss syndrome A historical term applied to individuals with intellectual disability who exhibit high levels of distractibility and hyperactivity.

strength-based assessment An assessment model that looks at an individual's strengths, abilities, and accomplishments rather than focusing on his or her deficits.

stuttering Type of fluency disorder in which word sounds are repeated.

substitutions Articulation disorder that occurs when one sound is substituted for another in the pronunciation of a word (e.g., *wabbit* for *rabbit*).

summary of performance (SOP) Required by federal regulation for each student who exits secondary school, a summary of the individual's academic achievement and functional performance with recommendations for supports and services aimed at assisting the adolescent in achieving his or her transition goals.

supported competitive employment At a work site for typical workers, individuals with disabilities are employed and work alongside their typical peers but receive ongoing assistance from a job coach.

supported e-text An e-text that allows for content to be presented in multiple modalities while providing additional supports.

syntactical deficits Difficulty in acquiring the rules that control word order and other aspects of grammar.

syntax A series of linguistic rules that determine word order and combinations to form sentences and how such word order is used in the communication process.

syphilis A venereal disease; infection of the mother in the last trimester of pregnancy can cause intellectual disability in the child.

task analysis An instructional methodology whereby complex tasks are analyzed and broken down into sequential component parts; each part is taught separately and then as a whole.

technology productivity tools Computer software, hardware, and related systems designed to help people work effectively.

telecommunication device for the deaf (TDD) An instrument for sending typewritten messages over telephone lines to be received by a person who is deaf or severely hearing impaired as a printed message. Sometimes called TT, TTY, or TTD.

teratogen Infections, drugs, chemicals, or environmental agents that can produce fetal abnormalities.

tertiary prevention Efforts that attempt to limit the adverse consequences of an existing problem while maximizing a person's potential; in regard to persons with emotional or behavioral disorders, refers to an intense level of intervention using strategies and supports designed for individuals with chronic and intense behavior problems.

theory of mind A hypothesis that attempts to explain the inability of the individual with autism to realize that other people have their own unique point of view about the world—different thoughts, plans, and perspectives from their own.

therapeutic abortion Elective termination of a pregnancy due to the presence of a birth defect.

tiered assignments An instructional strategy that allows the teacher to offer variations of the same lesson to students with differing levels of ability.

time management A proactive intervention strategy that attempts to maximize student engagement time and appropriately schedule class activities in addition to instruction in time management skills.

tonic-clonic seizure A convulsive seizure whereby the individual loses consciousness, falls, and begins making rhythmic jerking motions, formerly known as a grand mal seizure.

total communication A method of communication for students with hearing impairments, designed to provide equal emphasis on oral and signing skills to facilitate communication ability.

Tourette syndrome A neurological disorder characterized by motor tics and uncontrollable verbal outbursts.

toxoplasmosis A maternal infection resulting from contact with parasites; especially devastating if exposure occurs during third trimester of pregnancy.

trainable mentally retarded (TMR) Classification of a person with moderate intellectual disability who is capable of learning self-care and social skills; IQ range generally between 35–40 and 50–55.

transdisciplinary team A group of professionals from different disciplines who function as a team but work

independently; however, they share roles, and a peer is identified as the primary interventionist.

transition A broad term used to describe the movement of an individual from one educational environment to another, from one class to another, or from one phase of life (high school) to another (independent adulthood).

transition management The regulating of students as they move from one assignment to another or from one activity to another; a proactive behavioral intervention strategy.

transition plan *See* individualized transition plan.

transition services Individualized and coordinated services that assist the adolescent with a disability to successfully move from school to postschool activities.

transliteration Altering an interpreted message to facilitate understanding by a person who is hearing impaired.

traumatic brain injury An acquired injury to the brain caused by an external force that results in a disability or psychosocial impairment that adversely affects educational performance.

twice-exceptional Students who are gifted and talented but also have a disability.

tympanic membrane A thin, membranous tissue between the ear canal and the middle ear that vibrates when struck by sound waves; also called the eardrum.

underrepresentation A situation in which fewer children from minority groups are placed in special education programs than would be expected based on the proportion of pupils in the general school population.

universal design for learning The design of curriculum materials, instructional activities, and evaluation procedures that can meet the needs of learners with widely varying abilities and backgrounds.

Usher syndrome An inherited disorder resulting in deaf-blindness, deafness present at birth accompanied by progressive vision loss, sometimes associated with intellectual disability.

visual acuity The ability to visually perceive details of near or distant objects.

visual efficiency How well an individual uses remaining visual acuity at a distance or close up.

visual field The amount of vision in the quadrant regions to the right, left, up, and down while gazing straight ahead.

visual impairment An impairment in vision that, even with correction, adversely affects an individual's educational performance. The term includes both partial sight and blindness.

vitreous humor A colorless mass of soft, gelatinlike material that fills the eyeball behind the lens.

voice disorders May result from disorders of the larynx or disorders in phonation.

voice output communication aid (VOCA) Device that can be programmed to produce speech.

walker A mobility aid for individuals requiring support when walking.

word prediction program A software program that provides a list of potential words that correspond to the letters the user is typing so that the user does not have to type out the entire word.

working memory The ability to retain information while also engaging in another cognitive activity.

wraparound plan A coordinated interagency effort at providing supports and services to a student and his or her family in the natural environment—school, home, or community.

X-linked A pattern of inheritance involving the X chromosome, one of an individual's two sex chromosomes.

References

Chapter 1

Ballard, J., Ramirez, B., & Weintraub, F. (1982). *Special education in America: Its legal and governmental foundations.* Reston, VA: Council for Exceptional Children.

Bicard, S., & Heward, W. (2010). Educational equality for students with disabilities. In J. Banks & C. Banks (Eds.), *Multicultural education* (7th ed., pp. 315–341). Hoboken, NJ: Wiley.

Bogdan, R., & Biklen, D. (1977). Handicapism. *Social Policy, 7*(5), 14–19.

Brown, L., Albright, K., Rogan, P., York, J., Solnar, A., Johnson, F., . . . Loomis, R. (1988). An integrated curriculum model for transition. In B. Ludlow, A. Turnbull, & R. Luckasson (Eds.), *Transitions to adult life for people with mental retardation: Principles and practices* (pp. 67–84). Baltimore, MD: Paul H. Brookes.

Bruder, M. (1994). Working with members of other disciplines: Collaboration for success. In M. Wolery & J. Wilbers (Eds.), *Including children with special needs in early childhood programs* (pp. 45–70). Washington, DC: National Association for the Education of Young Children.

Bruder, M. (2010). Early childhood intervention: A promise to children and families for their future. *Exceptional Children, 76*(3), 339–355.

Clark, G., & Knowlton, H. (1988). A closer look at transition issues for the 1990s: A response to Rusch and Menchetti. *Exceptional Children, 54*(4), 365–367.

Cook, B. (2001). A comparison of teachers' attitudes toward their included students with mild and severe disabilities. *Journal of Special Education, 34*(4), 203–213.

Crutchfield, M. (1997, August). Who's teaching our children with disabilities? *National Information Center for Children and Youth with Disabilities News Digest, 27,* 1–23.

Dunn, L. (1973). *Exceptional children in the schools* (2nd ed.). New York, NY: Holt, Rinehart, & Winston.

Friend, M., & Cook, L. (2013). *Interactions: Collaboration skills for school professionals* (7th ed.). Needham Heights, MA: Allyn & Bacon.

Gargiulo, R., & Kilgo, J. (2014). *An introduction to young children with special needs* (4th ed.). Belmont, CA: Wadsworth/Cengage Learning.

Gargiulo, R., & Metcalf, D. (2013). *Teaching in today's inclusive classrooms* (2nd ed.). Belmont, CA: Wadsworth/Cengage Learning.

Giangreco, M., York, J., & Rainforth, B. (1989). Providing related services to learners with severe handicaps in educational settings: Pursuing the least restrictive option. *Pediatric Physical Therapy, 1*(2), 55–63.

Goodlad, J. (1984). *A place called school.* New York, NY: McGraw-Hill.

Halpern, A. (1985). Transition: A look at the foundations. *Exceptional Children, 51*(6), 479–486.

Halpern, A. (1992). Transition: Old wine in new bottles. *Exceptional Children, 58*(3), 202–211.

Harry, B., & Klingner, J. (2007). Discarding the deficit model. *Educational Leadership, 64*(5), 16–21.

Hartman, M. (2009). Step by step: Creating a community-based transition program for students with intellectual disabilities. *Teaching Exceptional Children, 41*(6), 6–11.

Hitchcock, C., Meyer, A., Rose, D., & Jackson, R. (2002). Providing new access to the general curriculum: Universal design for learning. *Teaching Exceptional Children, 35*(2), 8–17.

Hobbs, N. (1975). *The futures of children.* San Francisco, CA: Jossey-Bass.

Hobbs, T., & Westling, D. (1998). Promoting successful inclusion. *Teaching Exceptional Children, 31*(1), 10–14.

Hourcade, J., & Bauwens, J. (2003). *Cooperative teaching: Rebuilding and sharing the schoolhouse* (2nd ed.). Austin, TX: Pro-Ed.

Keefe, E., Moore, V., & Duff, F. (2004). The four "knows" of collaborative teaching. *Teaching Exceptional Children, 36*(5), 36–41.

Kessler Foundation/National Organization on Disability. (2010). *The ADA, 20 years later.* Retrieved March 14, 2013, from http://www.2010disabilitysurveys.org/pdfs/surveyresults.pdf

Kitchin, R. (1998). "Out of place," "knowing one's place": Space, power and the exclusion of disabled people. *Disability and Society, 13,* 343–356.

Kliewer, C., & Biklen, D. (1996). Labeling: Who wants to be called retarded? In W. Stainback & S. Stainback (Eds.), *Controversial issues confronting special education: Divergent perspectives* (pp. 83–95). Boston, MA: Allyn & Bacon.

Koppelman, J. (1986). Reagan signs bills expanding services to handicapped preschoolers. *Report to Preschool Programs, 18,* 3–4.

Lane, H. (1979). *The wild boy of Aveyron.* Cambridge, MA: Harvard University Press.

McCormick, L. (2003). Policies and practices. In L. McCormick, D. Loeb, & R. Schiefelbusch (Eds.), *Supporting children with communication difficulties in inclusive settings* (2nd ed., pp. 155–187). Boston, MA: Allyn & Bacon.

McDonnell, J., Hardman, M., & McDonnell, A. (2003). *Introduction to persons with moderate and severe disabilities* (2nd ed.). Needham Heights, MA: Allyn & Bacon.

McLean, M., Wolery, M., & Bailey, D. (2004). *Assessing infants and preschoolers with special needs* (3rd ed.). Upper Saddle River, NJ: Pearson Education.

Meisels, S., & Shonkoff, J. (2000). Early childhood intervention: A continuing evolution. In J. Shonkoff & S. Meisels (Eds.), *Handbook of early childhood intervention* (2nd ed., pp. 3–31). Cambridge, England: Cambridge University Press.

Murawski, W. (2012). 10 tips for using co-planning time more efficiently. *Teaching Exceptional Children, 44*(4), 8–15.

Murawski, W., & Dieker, L. (2004). Tips and strategies for co-teaching at the secondary level. *Teaching Exceptional Children, 36*(5), 52–58.

National Center for Education Statistics. (2011). *Digest of education statistics 2010*. Washington, DC: U.S. Government Printing Office.

National Commission on Excellence in Education. (1983). *A nation at risk: The imperative for educational reform*. Washington, DC: Author.

National Longitudinal Transition Study 2. (2009). *The post-high school outcomes of youth with disabilities up to 4 years after high school*. Retrieved March 11, 2013, from http://www.nlts2.org/reports/2009_04/nlts2_report_2009_04_complete.pdf

Ohio State University Partnership Grant. (2013). *Fast facts for faculty: Universal design for learning*. Retrieved March 15, 2013, from http://ada.osu.edu/resources/fastfacts/Universal_Design.htm

Orkwis, R., & McLane, K. (1998). *A curriculum every student can use: Design principles for student access* (ED 423 654). Reston, VA: ERIC Clearinghouse on Disabilities and Gifted Education.

Pisha, B., & Coyne, P. (2001). Smart from the start: The promise of universal design for learning. *Remedial and Special Education, 22*(4), 197–203.

Potts, E., & Howard, L. (2011). *How to co-teach*. Baltimore, MD: Paul H. Brookes.

Pugach, M., & Johnson, L. (2002). *Collaborative practitioners, collaborative schools* (2nd ed.). Denver, CO: Love.

Reinhiller, N. (1996). Co-teaching: New variations on a not-so-new practice. *Teacher Education and Special Education, 19*(1), 34–48.

Reynolds, M., Wang, M., & Walberg, J. (1987). The necessary restructuring of special and regular education. *Exceptional Children, 53*(5), 391–398.

Rice, N., Drame, E., Owens, L., & Frattura, E. (2007). Co-instructing at the secondary level. *Teaching Exceptional Children, 39*(6), 12–18.

Sandall, S., Hemmeter, L., McLean, M., & Smith, B. (2005). *DEC recommended practices: A comprehensive guide for practical application in early intervention/early childhood special education*. Longmont, CO: Sopris West.

Scott, S., McGuire, J., & Shaw, S. (2003). Universal design for instruction: A new paradigm for adult instruction in secondary education. *Remedial and Special Education, 24,* 369–379.

Scruggs, T., Mastropieri, M., & McDuffie, K. (2007). Co-teaching in inclusive classrooms: A metasynthesis of qualitative research. *Exceptional Children, 73*(4), 392–416.

Sileo, J. (2011). Co-teaching: getting to know your partner. *Teaching Exceptional Children, 43*(5), 32–38.

Smith, T., Polloway, E., Patton, J., & Dowdy, C. (2012). *Teaching students with special needs in inclusive settings* (6th ed.). Upper Saddle River, NJ: Pearson Education.

U.S. Department of Education. (1992). *Fourteenth annual report to Congress on the implementation of the Individuals with Disabilities Education Act*. Washington, DC: U.S. Government Printing Office.

U.S. Department of Education. (2011). *Thirtieth annual report to Congress on the implementation of the Individuals with Disabilities Education Act, 2008*. Washington, DC: U.S. Government Printing Office.

U.S. Department of Education. (2013). *Historical state-level IDEA data files*. Retrieved November 13, 2013, from http://tadnet.public.tadnet.org/pages/712

Walther-Thomas, C., Korinek, L., McLaughlin, V., & Williams, B. (2000). *Collaboration for inclusive education*. Needham Heights, MA: Allyn & Bacon.

Wehmeyer, M., Lance, D., & Bashinski, S. (2002). Promoting access to the general curriculum for students with mental retardation. *Education and Training in Mental Retardation and Developmental Disabilities, 37*(3), 223–234.

Will, M. (1984). *OSERS programming for the transition of youth with disabilities: Bridges from school to working life*. Washington, DC: Office of Special Education and Rehabilitative Services.

Ysseldyke, J., Algozzine, B., & Thurlow, M. (1992). *Critical issues in special and remedial education* (2nd ed.). Boston, MA: Houghton Mifflin.

Zigler, E. (2000). Foreword. In J. Shonkoff & S. Meisels (Eds.), *Handbook of early childhood intervention* (2nd ed., pp. xi–xv). Cambridge, England: Cambridge University Press.

Chapter 2

Bateman, B., & Linden, M. (2012). *Better IEPs* (5th ed.). Verona, WI: Attainment.

Bennett, T., DeLuca, D., & Bruns, D. (1997). Putting inclusion into practice: Perspectives of teachers and parents. *Exceptional Children, 64*(1), 115–131.

Buck, G., Polloway, E., Smith-Thomas, A., & Cook, K. (2003). Prereferral intervention process: A survey of state practices. *Exceptional Children, 69*(3), 349–360.

Common Core State Standards Initiative. (2012). *Implementing the Common Core State Standards*. Retrieved March 19, 2013, from http://www.corestandards.org/

Constable, S., Grossi, B., Moniz, A., & Ryan, L. (2013). Meeting the Common Core State Standards for students with autism. *Teaching Exceptional Children, 45*(3), 6–13.

Council for Exceptional Children. (1994). *CEC policies for delivering services to exceptional children*. Reston, VA: Author.

Council for Exceptional Children. (1997). What every teacher needs to know: A comparison of Section 504, ADA, and IDEA. *CEC Today, 4*(4), 1, 5, 15.

Council for Exceptional Children. (2003). *No Child Left Behind Act of 2001: Reauthorization of the Elementary and Secondary Education Act* (technical assistance resource). Arlington, VA: Author.

Deno, E. (1970). Special education as developmental capital. *Exceptional Children, 37*(3), 229–237.

Diliberto, J., & Brewer, D. (2012). Six steps for successful IEP meetings. *Teaching Exceptional Children, 44*(4), 30–37.

Downing, J. (2008). *Including students with severe and multiple disabilities in typical classrooms* (3rd ed.). Baltimore, MD: Paul H. Brookes.

Dunn, L. (1968). Special education for the mildly retarded: Is much of it justifiable? *Exceptional Children, 35*(1), 5–22.

Fox, N., & Ysseldyke, J. (1997). Implementing inclusion at the middle school level: Lessons from a negative example. *Exceptional Children, 64*(1), 81–98.

Gargiulo, R., & Kilgo, J. (2014). *An introduction to young children with special needs* (4th ed.). Belmont, CA: Wadsworth/Cengage Learning.

Gargiulo, R., & Metcalf, D. (2013). *Teaching in today's inclusive classrooms* (2nd ed.). Belmont, CA: Wadsworth/Cengage Learning.

Henry, N., & Flynt, E. (1990). Rethinking special education referral: A procedural model. *Intervention in School and Clinic, 26*(1), 22–24.

Kauffman, J. (1995). Why we must celebrate a diversity of restrictive environments. *Learning Disabilities Research & Practice, 10*(4), 225–232.

Kennedy, C., & Horn, E. (Eds.). (2004). *Including students with severe disabilities.* Boston, MA: Allyn & Bacon.

Lipkin, P., & Schertz, M. (2008). Early intervention and its efficacy. In P. Accardo (Ed.), *Capute & Accardo's neurodevelopmental disabilities in infancy and childhood* (3rd ed., Vol. 1, pp. 519–551). Baltimore, MD: Paul H. Brookes.

Meyen, E. (1995). Legislative and programmatic foundations of special education. In E. Meyen & T. Skrtic (Eds.), *Special education and student disability* (4th ed., pp. 35–95). Denver, CO: Love.

Nolet, V., & McLaughlin, M. (2005). *Accessing the general curriculum* (2nd ed.). Thousand Oaks, CA: Corwin.

Noonan, M., & McCormick, L. (2006). *Young children with disabilities in natural environments.* Baltimore, MD: Paul H. Brookes.

Osborne, A. (1996). *Legal issues in special education.* Needham Heights, MA: Allyn & Bacon.

Peterson, J., & Hittie, M. (2010). *Inclusive teaching: The journey towards effective schools for all learners* (2nd ed.). Upper Saddle River NJ: Pearson Education.

Polloway, E., Patton, J., Serna, L., & Bailey, J. (2013). *Strategies for teaching learners with special needs*

(10th ed.). Upper Saddle River, NJ: Pearson Education.

Pretti-Frontczak, K., & Bricker, D. (2004). *An activity-based approach to early intervention* (3rd ed.). Baltimore, MD: Paul H. Brookes.

Reynolds, M. (1962). A framework for considering some issues in special education. *Exceptional Children, 28*(7), 367–370.

Salend, S. (2011). *Creating inclusive classrooms* (7th ed.). Upper Saddle River, NJ: Pearson Education.

Skrtic, T. (1995). The special education knowledge tradition: Crisis and opportunity. In E. Meyen & T. Skrtic (Eds.), *Special education and student disability* (4th ed., pp. 609–672). Denver, CO: Love.

Smith, T. (2002). Section 504: What teachers need to know. *Intervention in School and Clinic, 37*(5), 259–266.

Smith, T., & Patton, J. (2007). *Section 504 and public schools: A practical guide* (2nd ed.) Austin, TX: Pro-Ed.

Turnbull, A., Turnbull, H., Erwin, E., & Soodak, L. (2006). *Families, professionals, and exceptionality* (5th ed.). Upper Saddle River, NJ: Pearson Education.

Turnbull, A., Turnbull, H., Erwin, E., Soodak, L., & Shogren, K. (2011). *Families, professionals, and exceptionality* (6th ed.). Upper Saddle River, NJ: Pearson Education.

Turnbull, H. (1993). *Free appropriate public education: The law and children with disabilities* (4th ed.). Denver, CO: Love.

U.S. Equal Employment Opportunity Commission. (2013). *Notice concerning the Americans with Disabilities Act (ADA) Amendments Act of 2008.* Retrieved March 17, 2013, from http://www.eeoc.gov/ada/amendments_notice.html

Will, M. (1986a). Educating children with learning problems: A shared responsibility. *Exceptional Children, 52*(5), 411–415.

Will, M. (1986b). *Educating students with learning problems: A shared responsibility.* Washington, DC: U.S. Department of Education, Office of Special Education and Rehabilitative Services.

Yell, M. (2012). *The law and special education* (3rd ed.). Upper Saddle River, NJ: Pearson Education.

Ysseldyke, J. (2001). Reflections on a research career: Generalization from

25 years of research on assessment and instructional decision making. *Exceptional Children, 67*(3), 295–309.

Zigmond, N., & Kloo, A. (2011). General and special education are (and should be) different. In J. Kauffman & D. Hallahan (Eds.), *Handbook of special education* (pp. 160–172). New York, NY: Routledge.

Zirkel, P. (2009). What does the law say? New Section 504 student eligibility standards. *Teaching Exceptional Children, 41*(4), 68–71.

Chapter 3

Amos, J. (2008). *Dropouts, diplomas, and dollars.* Washington, DC: Alliance for Excellent Education.

Artiles, A., & Bal, A. (2008). The next generation of disproportionality research: Toward a comparative model in the study of equity in ability differences. *Journal of Special Education, 42*(1), 4–14.

Artiles, A., Kozleski, E., Trent, S., Osher, D., & Ortiz, A. (2010). Justifying and explaining disproportionality, 1968–2008: A critique of underlying views of culture. *Exceptional Children, 76*(3), 279–299.

Artiles, A., & Zamora-Durán, G. (1997). Disproportionate representation: A contentious and unresolved predicament. In A. Artiles & G. Zamora-Durán (Eds.), *Reducing disproportionate representation of culturally diverse students in special and gifted education* (pp. 1–6). Reston, VA: Council for Exceptional Children.

Baca, L., & Baca, E. (2004a). Bilingualism and bilingual education. In L. Baca & H. Cervantes (Eds.), *The bilingual special education interface* (4th ed., pp. 24–45). Upper Saddle River, NJ: Pearson Education.

Baca, L., & Baca, E. (2004b). Bilingual special education: A judicial perspective. In L. Baca & H. Cervantes (Eds.), *The bilingual special education interface* (4th ed., pp. 76–99). Upper Saddle River, NJ: Pearson Education.

Baca, L., Baca, E., & de Valenzuela, J. (2004). Background and rationale for bilingual special education. In L. Baca & H. Cervantes (Eds.), *The bilingual special education interface* (4th ed., pp. 1–23). Upper Saddle River, NJ: Pearson Education.

Banks, J. (2013). Multicultural education: Characteristics and goals. In J. Banks & C. Banks (Eds.), *Multicultural education issues and perspectives* (8th ed., pp. 3–23). Hoboken, NJ: Wiley.

Benner, S. (1998). *Special education issues within the context of American society.* Belmont, CA: Wadsworth.

Bicard, S., & Heward, W. (2013). Educational equity for students with disabilities. In J. Banks & C. Banks (Eds.), *Multicultural education: Issues and perspectives* (8th ed., pp. 245–266). Hoboken, NJ: Wiley.

Boyer, L., & Mainzer, R. (2003). Who's teaching students with disabilities? *Teaching Exceptional Children, 35*(6), 8–11.

Camarota, S. (2007). *100 million more: Projecting the impact of immigration on the U.S. population, 2007 to 2060.* Center for Immigration Studies. Retrieved January 14, 2010, from www.cis.org/impact_on_population.html

Children's Defense Fund. (2012). *The state of America's children handbook.* Retrieved March 31, 2013, from http://www.childrensdefense.org/

Clark, B. (2013). *Growing up gifted: Developing the potential of children at home and at school* (8th ed.). Upper Saddle River, NJ: Pearson Education.

Council for Exceptional Children. (1997). Making assessments of diverse students meaningful. *CEC Today, 4(4),* 8–9..

Council for Exceptional Children. (2013). *New strategies to help diverse students.* Retrieved March 27, 2013, from http://oldsite.cec.sped.org/AM/Template.cfm?Section=Cultural_and_Linguistic_Diversity&template=/CM/Contentdisplay.cfm&ContentID=16130

Coutinho, M., & Oswald, D. (2000). Disproportionate representation in special education: A synthesis and recommendations. *Journal of Child and Family Studies, 9*(2), 135–156.

de Valenzuela, J., & Baca, L. (2004). Issues and theoretical considerations in the assessment of bilingual children. In L. Baca & H. Cervantes (Eds.), *The bilingual special education interface* (4th ed., pp. 162–183). Upper Saddle River, NJ: Pearson Education.

Donovan, S., & Cross, C. (Eds.). (2002). *Minority students in special and gifted education.* Washington, DC: National Research Council.

Figueroa, R. (1989). Psychological testing of linguistic-minority students: Knowledge gaps and regulations. *Exceptional Children, 56*(2), 145–152.

Ford, D. (1998). The underrepresentation of minority students in gifted education. *Journal of Special Education, 32*(1), 4–14.

Ford, D. (2012). Culturally different students in special education: Looking backward to move forward. *Exceptional Children, 78*(4), 391–405.

Ford, D., Grantham, T., & Whiting, G. (2008). Culturally and linguistically diverse students in gifted education: Recruitment and retention issues. *Exceptional Children, 74*(3), 289–306.

Friend, M., & Bursuck, W. (2012). *Including students with special needs* (6th ed.). Boston, MA: Pearson Education.

Garcia, S., & Ortiz, A. (2006). Preventing disproportionate representation: Culturally and linguistically responsive prereferral interventions. *Teaching Exceptional Children, 38*(4), 64–68.

Gardner, H. (2011). *Frames of mind: The theory of multiple intelligence.* New York, NY: Basic Books. (Original work published in 1983)

Gardner, H. (1993). *Multiple intelligences: The theory in practice.* New York, NY: Wiley.

Gardner, H. (2006). *Multiple intelligences: New horizons.* New York, NY: Basic Books.

Gargiulo, R., & Kilgo, J. (2014). *An introduction to young children with special needs* (4th ed.). Belmont, CA: Wadsworth/Cengage Learning.

Gargiulo, R., & Metcalf, D. (2013). *Teaching in today's inclusive classrooms* (2nd ed.) Belmont, CA: Wadsworth/Cengage Learning.

Gollnick, D., & Chinn, P. (2006). *Multicultural education in a pluralistic society* (7th ed.). Upper Saddle River, NJ: Pearson Education.

Gollnick, D., & Chinn, P. (2013). *Multicultural education in a pluralistic society* (9th ed.). Upper Saddle River, NJ: Pearson Education.

Harry, B. (1992). *Cultural diversity, families, and the special education system: Communication and empowerment.* New York, NY: Teachers College Press.

Harry, B. (2008). The disproportionate placement of ethnic minorities in special education. In L. Florian (Ed.), *Sage handbook of special education* (pp. 69–84). London, England: Sage.

Harry, B., & Klinger, J. (2006). *Why are so many minority students in special education?* New York, NY: Teachers College Press.

Harry, B., & Klinger, J. (2007). Discarding the deficit model. *Educational Leadership, 64*(5), 16–21.

Hoover, J., & Collier, C. (2004). Methods and materials for bilingual special education. In L. Baca & H. Cervantes (Eds.), *The bilingual special education interface* (4th ed., pp. 274–297). Upper Saddle River, NJ: Pearson Education.

Hoover, J., Klinger, J., Baca, L., & Patton, J. (2008). *Methods for teaching culturally and linguistically diverse exceptional learners.* Upper Saddle River, NJ: Pearson Education.

Hoover, J., & Patton, J. (2005). *Curriculum adaptation for students with learning and behavior problems: Principles and procedures* (3rd ed.). Austin, TX: Pro-Ed.

Janzen, R. (1994). Melting pot or mosaic? *Educational Leadership, 51*(8), 9–11.

Jasper, A., & Bouck, E. (2013). Disproportionality among African American students at the secondary level: Examining the MID disability category. *Education and Training in Autism and Developmental Disabilities, 48*(1), 31–40.

Kaufman, A., & Kaufman, N. (2004). *Kaufman Assessment Battery for Children II.* Circle Pines, MN: American Guidance Service.

Ladson-Billings, G. (1994). What we can learn from multicultural education research. *Educational Leadership, 51*(8), 22–26.

Linn, R., Miller, M., & Gronlund, N. (2013). *Measurement and assessment in teaching* (11th ed.). Upper Saddle River, NJ: Pearson Education.

Lustig, M., & Koester, J. (2013). *Intercultural competence: Interpersonal communication across cultures* (7th ed.). Upper Saddle River NJ: Pearson Education.

MacMillan, D., & Reschly, D. (1998). Overrepresentation of minority students: The case for greater specificity or reconsideration of the variables examined. *Journal of Special Education, 32*(1), 15–24.

McLoughlin, J., & Lewis, R. (2008). *Assessing students with special needs* (7th ed.). Upper Saddle River, NJ: Pearson Education.

Meyer, L., Bevan-Brown, J., Park, H., & Savage, C. (2013). School inclusion and multicultural issues in special education. In J. Banks & C. Banks (Eds.), *Multicultural education: Issues and perspectives* (8th ed., pp. 269–289). Hoboken, NJ: Wiley.

National Center for Education Statistics. (2010). *Status and trends in the education of racial and ethnic minorities.* Washington, DC: U.S. Department of Education.

National Center for Education Statistics. (2011). *The condition of education 2011.* Washington, DC: U.S. Government Printing Office.

National Center for Education Statistics. (2012). *The condition of education 2012.* Washington, DC: U.S. Department of Education.

National Collaborative on Diversity in the Teaching Force. (2004). *Assessment of diversity in America's teaching force.* Washington, DC: Author.

National Education Association. (2013). *NEA and teacher recruitment: An overview.* Retrieved March 28, 2013, from http://www.nea.org/home/29031.htm

Quality Education for Minorities Project. (1990). *Education that works: An action plan for the education of minorities.* Cambridge, MA: Massachusetts Institute of Technology.

Ryan, F. (1993). The perils of multiculturalism: Schooling for the group. *Educational Horizons, 71,* 134–138.

Salend, S., & Salinas, A. (2003). Language differences or learning difficulties. *Teaching Exceptional Children, 35*(4), 36–43.

Shealey, M., & Callins, T. (2007). Creating culturally responsive literacy programs in inclusive classrooms. *Intervention in School and Clinic, 42*(4), 195–197.

Siccone, F. (1995). *Celebrating diversity: Building self-esteem in today's multicultural classrooms.* Boston, MA: Allyn & Bacon.

Skiba, R., Simmons, A., Ritter, S., Rausch, M., Cuadrado, J., & Chung, C. (2008). Achieving equity in special education: History, status, and current challenges. *Exceptional Children, 74*(3), 244–288.

Sleeter, C., & Grant, C. (2009). *Making choices for multicultural education* (6th ed.). Hoboken, NJ: Wiley.

Smith, D., Smith-Davis, J., Clarke, C., & Mims, V. (2000). Technical assistance makes a difference: The Alliance 2000 story. *Teacher Education and Special Education, 23*(4), 302–310.

Sullivan, A. (2011). Disproportionality in special education identification and placement of English language learners. *Exceptional Children, 77*(3), 317–334.

Tiedt, P., & Tiedt, I. (2010). *Multicultural teaching: A handbook of activities and resources* (8th ed.). Needham Heights, MA: Allyn & Bacon.

U.S. Census Bureau. (2011). *Intercensal estimates of resident population by sex, race, and Hispanic origin for the United States.* Retrieved March 21, 2013, from http://www.census.gov/popest/data/intercensal/national/tables/US-EST00INT-02.xls

U.S. Census Bureau. (2012a). *Statistical abstract of the United States: 2012* (131st ed.). Washington, DC: Author.

U.S. Census Bureau. (2012b). *U.S. population projections, Table 6: Percent of U. S. population by race and Hispanic origin. 2015–2060.* Retrieved March 21, 2013, from www.census.gov/population/projections/files/summary/NP2012-T6.xls

U.S. Department of Education. (1997). *Nineteenth annual report to Congress on the implementation of the Individuals with Disabilities Education Act.* Washington, DC: U.S. Government Printing Office.

U.S. Department of Education. (2009). *Twenty-eighth annual report to Congress on the implementation of the Individuals with Disabilities Education Act, 2006* (Vol. 1). Washington, DC: U.S. Government Printing Office.

U.S. English. (2014). *About U.S. English.* Retrieved January 13, 2014, from http://www.us-english.org/view/13

Utley, C., & Obiakor, F. (2001). Learning problems or learning disabilities of multicultural learners: Contemporary perspectives. In C. Utley & F. Obiakor (Eds.), *Special education, multicultural education, and school reform: Components of quality education for learners with mild disabilities* (pp. 90–117). Springfield, IL: Charles C. Thomas.

Voltz, D. (1998). Cultural diversity and special education teacher preparation: Critical issues confronting the field. *Teacher Education and Special Education, 21*(1), 63–70.

Voltz, D., Sims, M., Nelson, B., & Bivens, C. (2005). M² ECCA: A framework for inclusion in the context of standards-based reform. *Teaching Exceptional Children, 37*(5), 14–19.

Waitoller, F., Artiles, A., & Cheney, D. (2010). The miner's canary: A review of overrepresentation research. *Journal of Special Education, 44*(1), 29–49.

Winzer, M., & Mazurek, K. (1998). *Special education in multicultural contexts.* Upper Saddle River, NJ: Prentice Hall.

Chapter 4

Banks, M. (2003). Disability in the family: A life span perspective. *Cultural Diversity and Ethnic Minority Psychology, 9*(4), 367–384.

Berry, J., & Hardman, M. (1998). *Lifespan perspectives on the family and disability.* Needham Heights, MA: Allyn & Bacon.

Bettelheim, B. (1950). *Love is not enough.* Glencoe, NY: Free Press.

Bettelheim, B. (1967). *The empty fortress: Infantile autism and the birth of the self.* London, England: Collier-Macmillan.

Blacher, J. (1984). Sequential stages of parental adjustment to the birth of a child with handicaps: Fact or artifact? *Mental Retardation, 22*(2), 55–68.

Blasco, P., Johnson, C., & Palomo-Gonzalez, S. (2008). Support for families of children with disabilities. In P. Accardo (Ed.), *Capute & Accardo's neurodevelopmental disabilities in infancy and childhood* (Vol. 1, 3rd ed., pp. 775–801). Baltimore, MD: Paul H. Brookes.

Blue-Banning, M., Summers, J., Frankland, H., Nelson, L., & Beegle, G. (2004). Dimensions of family and professional partnerships: Constructive guidelines for collaboration. *Exceptional Children, 70*(2), 167–184.

Bronfenbrenner, U. (1977). Toward an experimental ecology of human development. *American Psychologist, 32*(7), 513–531.

Bronfenbrenner, U. (1979). *The ecology of human development: Experiments by nature and design.* Cambridge, MA: Harvard University Press.

Cook, R., Klein, M., & Tessier, A. (2013). *Adapting early childhood curricula for children in inclusive settings* (8th ed.). Upper Saddle River, NJ: Pearson Education.

D'Asaro, A. (1998). Caring for yourself is caring for your family: Methods of coping with the everyday stresses of care giving. *Exceptional Parent, 28*(6), 38–40.

Family Support Bulletin. (1991, Spring). Washington, DC: United Cerebral Palsy Association.

Flynn, L., & Wilson, P. (1998). Partnerships with family members: What about fathers? *Young Exceptional Children, 2*(1), 21–28.

Gallagher, J., Beckman, P., & Cross, A. (1983). Families of handicapped children: Sources of stress and its amolioration. *Exceptional Children, 50*(1), 10–19.

Gallagher, P., Powell, T., & Rhodes, C. (2006). *Brothers and sisters: A special part of exceptional families* (3rd ed.). Baltimore, MD: Paul H. Brookes.

Gannotti, M., Handwerker, W., Groce, N., & Cruz, C. (2001). Sociocultural influences on disability status in Puerto Rican children. *Physical Therapy, 81*(9), 1512–1523.

Gargiulo, R. (1985). *Working with parents of exceptional children.* Boston, MA: Houghton Mifflin.

Gargiulo, R., & Graves, S. (1991). Parental feelings: The forgotten component when working with parents of handicapped preschool children. *Childhood Education, 67,* 176–178.

Gargiulo, R., & Kilgo, J. (2014). *An introduction to young children with special needs* (4th ed.). Belmont, CA: Wadsworth/Cengage Learning.

Gargiulo, R., & Metcalf, D. (2013). *Teaching in today's inclusive classrooms* (2nd ed.). Belmont, CA: Wadsworth/ Cengage Learning.

Gearheart, B., Mullen, R., & Gearheart, C. (1993). *Exceptional individuals.* Pacific Grove, CA: Brooks/Cole.

Glidden, L., & Floyd, F. (1997). Disaggregating parental depression and family stress in assessing families of children with developmental delays: A multisample analysis. *American Journal on Mental Retardation, 102*(3), 250–266.

Gollnick, D., & Chinn, P. (2013). *Multicultural education in a pluralistic society* (9th ed.). Upper Saddle River, NJ: Pearson Education.

Graves, S., Gargiulo, R., & Sluder, L. (1996). *Young children: An introduction to early childhood education.* St. Paul, MN: West.

Grossman, F. (1972). *Brothers and sisters of retarded children.* Syracuse, NY: Syracuse University Press.

Hanson, M. (2004a). Ethnic, cultural, and language diversity in service settings. In E. Lynch & M. Hanson (Eds.), *Developing cross cultural competence* (3rd ed., pp. 3–18). Baltimore, MD: Paul H. Brookes.

Hanson, M. (2004b). Families with Anglo-European roots. In E. Lynch & M. Hanson (Eds.), *Developing cross cultural competence* (3rd ed., pp. 81–104). Baltimore, MD: Paul H. Brookes.

Harry, B. (1992). *Cultural diversity, families, and the special education system: Communication and empowerment.* New York, NY: Teachers College Press.

Harry, B. (1995). African American families. In B. Ford, F. Obiakor, & J. Patton (Eds.), *Effective education of African American exceptional learners* (pp. 211–233). Austin, TX: Pro-Ed.

Harry, B. (2002). Trends and issues in serving culturally diverse families of children with disabilities. *Journal of Special Education, 36*(3), 131–138.

Harry, B., & Klinger, J. (2007). Discarding the deficit model. *Educational Leadership, 64*(5), 16–21.

Hayden, V. (1974). The other children. *Exceptional Parent, 4*(2), 26–29.

Hill-Patterson, T. (2011, March). The road to acceptance. *Birmingham Parent,* pp. 28–29.

Hodapp, R., & Krasner, D. (1995). Families of children with disabilities: Findings from a national sample of eighth-grade students. *Exceptionality, 5*(2), 71–81.

Hutton, A., & Caron, S. (2005). Experience of families with children with autism in rural New England. *Focus on Autism and Other Developmental Disabilities, 20*(3), 180–189.

Johnson, C. (2011, March). Coping with your child's special needs diagnosis. *Birmingham Parent,* pp. 25–27.

Kubler-Ross, E. (1969). *On death and dying.* New York, NY: Macmillan.

Lamb, M., & Meyer, D. (1991). Fathers of children with special needs. In M. Seligman (Ed.), *The family with a handicapped child* (2nd ed., pp. 151–179). Boston, MA: Allyn & Bacon.

Lambie, R. (2008). *Family systems within educational and community contexts* (3rd ed.). Denver, CO: Love.

Lerner, J., & Johns, B. (2012). *Learning disabilities and related mild disabilities* (12th ed.). Belmont, CA: Wadsworth/Cengage Learning.

Linan-Thompson, S., & Jean, R. (1997). Completing the parent participation puzzle: Accepting diversity. *Teaching Exceptional Children, 30*(2), 46–50.

Lo, L. (2012). Demystifying the IEP process for diverse parents of children with disabilities. *Teaching Exceptional Children, 44*(3), 14–20.

Lovern, L. (2008). Native American worldview and the discourse of disability. *Essays in Philosophy, 9*(1). Retrieved April 11, 2013, from http://sorrel. humboldt.edu/~essays/lovern.html

Lustig, M., & Koester, J. (2013). *Intercultural competence: Interpersonal communication across cultures* (7th ed.). Boston, MA: Allyn & Bacon.

Lynch, E., & Hanson, M. (Eds.). (2004). *Developing cross cultural competence* (3rd ed.). Baltimore, MD: Paul H. Brookes.

Matuszny, R., Banda, D., & Coleman, T. (2007). A progressive plan for building collaborative relationships with parents from diverse backgrounds. *Teaching Exceptional Children, 39*(4), 24–33.

McHugh, M. (2003). *Special siblings: Growing up with someone with a disability.* Baltimore, MD: Paul H. Brookes.

Meyer, D. (2009). *Thicker than water.* Bethesda, MD: Woodbine House.

Meyer, D., & Vadasy, P. (2008). *Sibshops: Workshops for siblings of children with special needs.* Baltimore, MD: Paul H. Brookes.

Meyer, L., Bevan-Brown, J., Park, H., & Savage, C. (2013). School inclusion and multicultural issues in special education. In J. Banks & C. Banks (Eds.), *Multicultural education: Issues and perspectives* (8th ed., pp. 269–289). Hoboken, NJ: Wiley.

Misra, A. (1994). Partnerships with families. In S. Alper, P. Schloss, & C. Schloss (Eds.), *Families of students with disabilities* (pp. 143–179). Boston, MA: Allyn & Bacon.

Olson, D. (1988). Family types, family stress, and family satisfaction: A family developmental perspective. In C. Folicov (Ed.), *Family transitions: Continuity and change over the life cycle* (pp. 55–79). New York, NY: Guilford Press.

Olsson, M., & Hwang, C. (2001). Depression in mothers and fathers of children with intellectual disability. *Journal* of *Intellectual Disability Research, 45*(6), 535–543.

Parette, H., & Petch-Hogan, B. (2000). Approaching families: Facilitating culturally/linguistically diverse family involvement. *Teaching Exceptional Children, 33*(2), 4–10.

Perl, J. (1995). Improving relationship skills for parent conferences. *Teaching Exceptional Children, 28*(1), 29–31.

Power, P., & Dell Orto, A. (2004). *Families living with chronic illness and disability.* New York, NY: Springer.

Roos, P. (1978). Parents of mentally retarded children: Misunderstood and mistreated. In A. Turnbull & H. Turnbull (Eds.), *Parents speak out* (pp. 12–27). Columbus, OH: Charles Merrill.

Rump, M. (2002). Involving fathers of young children with special needs. *Young Children, 57*(6), 18–20.

Russell, C., Russell, C., & Russell, M. (2003). We're here too! *Exceptional Parent, 33*(6), 36–39.

Salend, S., & Taylor, L. (1993). Working with families: A cross cultural perspective. *Remedial and Special Education, 14*(5), 25–32, 39.

Santelli, B., Turnbull, A., Marquis, J., & Lerner, J. (1997). Parent-to-parent programs: A resource for parents and professionals. *Journal of Early Intervention, 21*(1), 73–83.

Scorgie, K., & Sobsey, D. (2000). Transformational outcomes associated with parenting children who have disabilities. *Mental Retardation, 38*(3), 195–206.

Scorgie, K., Wilgosh, L., & McDonald, L. (1998). Stress and coping in families of children with disabilities: An examination of recent literature. *Developmental Disabilities Bulletin, 26*(1), 22–42.

Seligman, M., & Darling, R. (2007). *Ordinary families, special children* (3rd ed.). New York, NY: Guilford Press.

Seligman, M., Goodwin, G., Paschal, K., Applegate, A., & Lehman, A. (1997). Grandparents of children with disabilities: Perceived levels of support. *Education and Training in Mental Retardation and Developmental Disabilities, 32*(4), 293–303.

Simpson, R., & Mundschenk, N. (2010). *Working with parents and families of exceptional children and youth* (4th ed.). Austin, TX: Pro-Ed.

Singer, G. (2002). Suggestion for a pragmatic program of research on families and disability. *Journal of Special Education, 36*(3), 148–154.

Trachtenburg, S., Batshaw, K., & Batshaw, M. (2007). Caring and coping. In M. Batshaw, L. Pellegrino, & N. Roizen (Eds.), *Children with disabilities* (6th ed.). Baltimore, MD: Paul H. Brookes.

Turnbull, A., Turnbull, R., Erwin, E., & Soodak, L. (2006). *Families, professionals, and exceptionality* (5th ed.). Upper Saddle River, NJ: Pearson Education.

Turnbull, A., Turnbull, R., Erwin, E., Soodak, L., & Shrogren, K. (2011). *Families, professionals, and exceptionality* (6th ed.). Upper Saddle River, NJ: Pearson Education.

Voltz, D. (1998). Cultural diversity and special education teacher preparation: Critical issues confronting the field. *Teacher Education and Special Education, 21*(1), 63–70.

Zajicek-Farber, M. (2013). Caring and coping: Helping the family of a child with a disability. In M. Batshaw, N. Roizen, & G. Lotrecchiano (Eds.), *Children with disabilities* (7th ed., pp. 657–672). Baltimore, MD: Paul H. Brookes.

Ziskin, L. (1978). The story of Jennie. In A. Turnbull & H. Turnbull (Eds.), *Parents speak out* (pp. 70–80). Columbus, OH: Charles Merrill.

Chapter 5

Anderson-Inman, L., & Horney, M. (2007). Supported eText: Assistive technology through text transformations. *Reading Research Quarterly, 42*(1), 153–160.

Apple. (2013). *Mac basics: Dictation.* Retrieved September 17, 2013, from http://support.apple.com/kb/HT5449

Applied Human Factors. (2013). *SoothSayer* [Computer software]. Retrieved September 17, 2013, from http://newsite.ahf-net.com/soothsayer/

Ayres, K., Mechling, L., & Sansosti, F. (2013). The use of mobile technologies to assist with life skills/independence of students with moderate/severe intellectual disability and/or autism spectrum disorders: Considerations for the future of school

psychology. *Psychology in the Schools, 50*(3), 259–271.

Banks, D. (2008, December 3). *Disney survey shows technology trends for kids.* Retrieved September 17, 2013, from http://www.wired.com/geek-dad/2008/12/disney-survey-s/

Bausch, M., & Ault, M. (2008). Assistive technology implementation plan: A tool for improving outcomes. *Teaching Exceptional Children, 41*(1), 6–14.

Bausch, M., Ault, M., Evmenova, A., & Behrmann, M. (2008). Going beyond AT devices: Are AT services being considered? *Journal of Special Education Technology, 23*(2), 1–16.

Bausch, M., Ault, M., & Hasselbring, T. (2006). *Assistive technology planner: From IEP consideration to classroom implementation.* Lexington, KY: National Assistive Technology Research Institute.

Beard, L., Carpenter, L., & Johnston, L. (2011). *Assistive technology: Access for all students* (2nd ed.). Boston, MA: Pearson Education.

Behrmann, M., & Jerome, M. (2002). Assistive technology for students with mild disabilities: Update 2002. *ERIC Digest.* Retrieved September 17, 2013, from http://www.ericdigests.org/2003-1/assistive.htm

Behrmann, M., & Schaff, J. (2001). Assisting educators with assistive technology: Enabling children to achieve independence in living and learning. *Children and Families, 42*(3), 24–28.

Belson, S. (2003). *Technology for exceptional learners.* Boston, MA: Houghton-Mifflin.

Blackhurst, A. (1997). Perspectives on technology in special education. *Teaching Exceptional Children, 29*(5), 41–48.

Blackhurst, A. (2005a). Historical perspectives about technology applications for people with disabilities. In D. Edyburn, K. Higgins, & R. Boone (Eds.), *Handbook of special education technology research and practice* (pp. 3–30). Whitefish Bay, WI: Knowledge by Design.

Blackhurst, A. (2005b). Perspectives on applications of technology in the field of learning disabilities. *Learning Disability Quarterly, 28*(2), 175–178.

Bolkan, J. (2012, December 19). Research: IT predictions for 2013. *THE Journal.* Retrieved September 17,

2013, from http://thejournal.com/articles/2012/12/19/research-it-predictions-for-2013.aspx?admgarea=News1

Bouck, E., & Flanagan, S. (2009). Assistive technology and mathematics: What is there and where can we go in special education. *Journal of Special Education Technology, 24*(2), 17–30.

Bouck, E., & Flanagan, S. (2010). Virtual manipulatives: What they are and how teachers can use them. *Intervention in School and Clinic, 45*(3), 186–191.

Bouck, E., Flanagan, S., Miller, B., & Bassette, L. (2012). Rethinking everyday technology as assistive technology to meet students' IEP goals. *Journal of Special Education Technology, 27*(4), 47–57.

Bouck, E., Shurr, J., Tom, K., Jasper, A., Bassette, L., Miller, B., & Flanagan, S. (2012). Fix it with TAPE: Repurposing technology to be assistive technology for students with high incidence disabilities. *Preventing School Failure, 56*(2), 121–128.

Bryant, D., & Bryant, B. (2003). *Assistive technology for people with disabilities.* Boston, MA: Allyn & Bacon.

Calhoon, M., Emerson, R., Flores, M., & Houchins, D. (2007). Computational fluency performance profile of high school students with mathematics disabilities. *Remedial and Special Education, 28*(5), 292–303.

Cannon, L., Dorward, J., Duffin, J., & Heal, B. (2004). National Library of Virtual Manipulatives. *The Mathematics Teacher, 97*(2), 158–159.

Cass, M., Cates, D., Smith, M., & Jackson, C. (2003). Effects of manipulative instruction on solving area and perimeter problems by students with learning disabilities. *Learning Disabilities Research and Practice, 18*(2), 112–120.

Center for Applied Special Technology. (2009). *Science Writer.* Retrieved September 17, 2013, from http://sciencewriter.cast.org

Chen, C. (n.d.). *CLiCk, Speak* (Version 1.6.17) [Firefox extension]. Retrieved September 18, 2013, from https://addons.mozilla.org/en-us/firefox/addon/clc-click-speakjs/?src=search

Coldewey, D. (2010, March 17). *Generation I: Middle children of the information age.* Retrieved September 17, 2013, from http://techcrunch.com/2010/03/17/generation-i-the-middle-children-of-the-information-age/

DeskShare. (2012). *Dictation Pro* (Version 0.91) [Computer software]. Retrieved September 18, 2013, from http://download.cnet.com/windows/deskshare/3260-20_4-

Devereux, F. (1933). *The educational talking picture.* Chicago, IL: University of Chicago Press.

Don Johnston. (n.d.). *Co:Writer* (Version 7) [Computer software]. Retrieved January 20, 2014, from http://donjohnston.com/cowriter/

Edyburn, D. (2004). Rethinking assistive technology. *Special Education Technology Practice, 5*(4), 16–23.

Edyburn, D. (2005). Assistive technology and students with mild disabilities: From consideration to outcome measurement. In D. Edyburn, K. Higgins, & R. Boone (Eds.), *Handbook of special education technology research and practice* (pp. 239–270). Whitefish Bay, WI: Knowledge by Design.

Englert, C., Zhao, Y., Dunsmore, K., Collings, N., & Wolbers, K. (2007). Scaffolding the writing of students with disabilities through procedural facilitation: Using an Internet-based technology to improve performance. *Learning Disability Quarterly, 30*(1), 9–29.

eType. (2012). *eType* [Computer software]. Retrieved September 18, 2013, from http://www.etype.com/

Flower, L., & Hayes, J. (1981). A cognitive process theory of writing. *College Composition and Communication, 32,* 365–387.

Gierach, J. (Ed.). (2009). *Assessing students' needs for assistive technology (ASNAT): A resource manual for school district teams* (5th ed.). Retrieved September 17, 2013, from http://www.wati.org/?pageLoad=content/supports/free/index.php

Ginger Software. (n.d.). *Ginger* [Computer software] Retrieved September 17, 2013, from http://www.gingersoftware.com/

goQ. (2011). *wordQ+speakQ* [Computer software]. Retrieved September 18, 2013, from http://www.goqsoftware.com/products/

Hasselbring, T., & Bausch, M. (2005). Assistive technologies for reading. *Educational Leadership, 63*(4), 72–75.

Higgins, E., & Raskind, M. (2005). The compensatory effectiveness of the Quicktionary Reading Pen II on the reading comprehension of students with learning disabilities. *Journal of Special Education Technology, 20*(1), 31–40.

Inspiration Software. (2012a). *Inspiration* (Version 9.1) [Computer software]. Retrieved September 17, 2013, from http://www.inspiration.com/

Inspiration Software. (2012b). *Kidspiration* (Version 3.0) [Computer software]. Retrieved September 17, 2013, from http://www.inspiration.com/Kidspiration

Institute for Human & Machine Cognition. (n.d.). *CmapTools* (Version 5.05.0) [Computer software]. Retrieved September 17, 2013, from http://cmap.ihmc.us/

Johnson, L., Beard, L., & Carpenter, L. (2007). *Assistive technology: Access for all students.* Upper Saddle River, NJ: Pearson Education.

Jordan, L., Miller, D., & Mercer, C. (1998). The effects of concrete to semi concrete to abstract instruction in the acquisition and retention of fraction concepts and skills. *Learning Disabilities: A Multidisciplinary Journal, 9,* 115–122.

Kereluik, K., Mishra, P., & Koehler, M. (2010). Reconsidering the T and C in TPACK: Repurposing technologies for interdisciplinary knowledge. In D. Gibson & B. Dodge (Eds.), *Proceedings of Society for Information Technology & Teacher Education International Conference 2010* (pp. 3892–3899). Chesapeake, VA: Association for the Advancement of Computing in Education. Retrieved September 17, 2013, from http://www.editlib.org/p/33987

Kereluik, K., Mishra, P., & Koehler, M. (2011). On learning to subvert signs: Literacy, technology, and the TPACK framework. *The California Reader, 44*(2), 12–18.

King-Sears, M., Swanson, C., & Mainzer, L. (2011). TECHnology and literacy for adolescents with disabilities. *Journal of Adolescent and Adult Literacy, 54*(8), 569–578.

Kolb, L. (2008). *Toys to tools: Connecting student cell phones to education.* Washington, DC: International Society for Technology in Education.

Lahm, E., Bell, J., Blackhurst, A., Abner, G., Bausch, M., Case, D., . . . Zabala, J.

(2002). *Toolkit overview*. University of Kentucky Assistive Technology Project. Retrieved September 17, 2013, from http://edsrc.coe.uky.edu/www/ukatii/

Larson, L. (2010). Digital readers: The next chapter in e-book reading and response. *The Reading Teacher, 64*(1), 15–22.

Lee, H., & Templeton, R. (2008). Ensuring equal access to technology: Providing assistive technology for students with disabilities. *Theory Into Practice, 47*(3), 212–219.

Lewis, P. (1988, August 7). Ex machina; the computer revolution revised. *The New York Times*. Retrieved September 18, 2013, from http://query.nytimes.com/gst/fullpage.html?res=940D-E4DF1F38F934A3575BC0A96E948260&sec=&spon=&pagewanted=1

MacArthur, C. (2009). Reflections on research on writing and technology for struggling writers. *Learning Disabilities Research and Practice, 24*(2), 93–103.

Maccini, P., & Gagnon, J. (2000). Best practices for teaching mathematics to secondary students with special needs. *Focus on Exceptional Children, 32*(5), 1–22.

Maccini, P., & Gagnon, J. (2005). Mathematics and technology-based interventions. In D. Edyburn, K. Higgins, & R. Boone (Eds.), *Handbook of special education research and practice* (pp. 599–622). Whitefish Bay, WI: Knowledge by Design.

Maccini, P., & Gagnon, J. (2006). Mathematics instructional practice and assessment accommodations by secondary special and general educators. *Exceptional Children, 72*(2), 217–234.

Maccini, P., & Hughes, C. (2000). Effects of a problem solving strategy on the introductory algebra performance of secondary students with learning disabilities. *Learning Disabilities Research & Practice, 15*(1), 10–21.

Maccini, P., & Ruhl, K. (2000). Effects of graduated instruction sequence on the algebraic subtraction of integers by secondary students with learning disabilities. *Education and Treatment of Children, 23*(4), 465–489.

Madden, M., Lenhart, A., Duggan, M., Cortesi, S., & Gasser, W. (2013). *Teens and technology 2012*. Washington, DC: Pew Research Center. Retrieved September 17, 2013, from http://www.pewinternet.org/Reports/2013/Teens-and-Tech.aspx

Marino, M., Marino, E., & Shaw, S. (2006). Making informed assistive technology decisions for students with high incidence disabilities. *Teaching Exceptional Children, 38*(6), 18–25.

Mariage, T., & Bouck, E. (2004). Scaffolding literacy learning for students with mild needs. In A. Rodgers & E. Rodgers (Eds.), *Scaffolding literacy instruction: Strategies for K–4 classrooms* (pp. 36–74). Portsmouth, NH: Heinemann.

Mariage, T., Englert, C., & Garmon, M. (2000). The teacher as "more knowledgeable other" in assisting literacy learning with special needs students. *Reading and Writing Quarterly, 16*(4), 299–336.

Mason, L., Harris, K., & Graham, S. (2011). Self-regulated strategy development for students with writing difficulties. *Theory Into Practice, 50*(1), 20–27.

McMullen, R., Shippen, M., & Dangel, H. (2007). Middle school teachers' expectations of organizational behaviors of students with learning disabilities. *Journal of Instructional Psychology, 34*(2), 75–82.

Mechling, L. (2007). Assistive technology as a self-management tool for prompting students with intellectual disabilities to initiate and complete daily tasks: A literature review. *Education and Training in Developmental Disabilities, 42*(3), 252–269.

Microsoft Windows. (2011). *Windows Speech Recognition* [Computer software]. Retrieved September 17, 2013, from http://windows.microsoft.com/en-US/windows7/Set-up-Speech-Recognition

Mishra, P., & Koehler, M. (2007). Technological Pedagogical Content Knowledge (TPCK): Confronting the wicked problems of teaching with technology. In R. Carlsen, K. McFerrin, J. Rice, R. Weber, & D. Willis (Eds.), *Society for Information Technology & Teacher Education, Proceedings of the 18th International Conference* (pp. 2214–2226). Chesapeake, VA: Association for the Advancement of Computing in Education.

Mishra, P., & Koehler, M. (2009). Too cool for school? No way! Using the TPACK framework: You can have your hot tools and teach with them, too. *Learning and Leading with Technology, 36*(7), 14–18.

Mishra, P., Koehler, M., & Kereluik, K. (2009). The song remains the same: Looking back to the future of educational technology. *TechTrends, 53*(5), 48–53.

National Center for Education Statistics. (2012a). *The nation's report card: Mathematics 2011*. Washington, DC: U.S. Department of Education.

National Center for Education Statistics. (2012b). *The nation's report card: Reading 2011*. Washington, DC: U.S. Department of Education.

National Center for Education Statistics. (2012c). *The nation's report card: Writing 2011*. Washington, DC: U.S. Department of Education.

National Center on Accessible Instructional Materials. (2011). *What is the National Instructional Materials Accessibility Standard (NIMAS)?* Retrieved September 18, 2013, from http://aim.cast.org/learn/policy/federal/what_is_nimas

National Commission on Writing for America's Families, Schools, and Colleges. (2005). *Writing: A powerful message from state government*. Retrieved September 18, 2013, from http://www.nwp.oeg/cs/public/print/resource/2541

National Council of Teachers of Mathematics. (n.d.). *Illuminations*. Retrieved September 18, 2013, from http://illuminations.nctm.org/ActivitySearch.aspx

National Reading Panel. (2000). *Teaching children to read: An evidence-based assessment of the scientific research literature on reading and its implications for reading instruction: Report of the subgroups*. Bethesda, MD: Author.

NaturalSoft Limited. (2013). *NaturalReader* (Version 11.0) [Computer software]. Retrieved September 18, 2013, from http://www.naturalreaders.com/

Nazzaro, J. (1977). *Exceptional timetables: Historic events affecting the handicapped and gifted*. Reston, VA: Council for Exceptional Children.

NEO Direct. (2013). *Dana*. Retrieved September 17, 2013, from http://www.neo-direct.com/Dana/default.aspx

Netherton, D., & Deal, W. (2006). Assistive technology in the classroom. *The Technology Teacher, 66*(1), 10–15.

Newby, T., Stepich, D., Lehman, J., & Russell, J. (2000). *Educational technology for teaching and learning*

(4th ed.). Upper Saddle River, NJ: Pearson Education.

Nuance Communications. (2013). *Dragon Dictation* (Version 2.0.25) [Mobile application software]. Retrieved September 17, 2013, from http://www.itunes.apple.com

Petrov, T. (2013). *SpeakIt!* (Version 0.2.6) [Mobile application software]. Retrieved September 17, 2013, from https://chrome.google.com/webstore/

Parette, P., Peterson-Karlan, G., & Wojcik, B. (2005). The state of assistive technology services nationally and implications for future development. *Assistive Technology Outcomes and Benefits, 2*(1), 13–24.

Parette, P., & Scherer, M. (2004). Assistive technology use and stigma. *Education and Training in Developmental Disabilities, 39*(3), 217–226.

Quinn, B., Behrmann, M., Mastropieri, M., Bausch, M., Ault, M., & Chung, Y. (2009). Who is using assistive technology in schools? *Journal of Special Education Technology, 24*(1), 1–13.

Raskind, M., & Bryant, B. (2002). *Functional evaluation for assistive technology.* Austin, TX: Psycho-Educational Services.

Rideout, V., Foehr, U., & Roberts, D. (2010). *Generation M²: Media in the lives of 8- to 18-year-olds.* Menlo Park, CA: Henry J. Kaiser Family Foundation.

Rosen, L. D. (2011). Teaching the iGeneration. *Educational Leadership, 68*(5), 10–15.

Scherer, M., & Craddock, G. (2002). Matching Person & Technology (MPT) assessment process. *Technology & Disability, 14*(3), 125–131.

Scruggs, T., Mastropieri, M., & Okolo, C. (2008). Science and social studies for students with disabilities. *Focus on Exceptional Children, 4*(2), 1–24.

SecondGuess ApS. (2013). *Typ-O* (Version 2.21) [Computer software and mobile app]. Retrieved September 17, 2013, from https://itunes.apple.com/us/app/typ-o-writing-is-for-everybody/id412194836?mt=12&ignmpt=uo%3D4

Shodor Education Foundation. (n.d.). *Interactivate.* Retrieved September 17, 2013, from http://www.shodor.org/interactivate/activities/

Shurr, J., & Taber-Doughty, T. (2012). Increasing comprehension for middle school students with moderate intellectual disability on age-appropriate texts. *Education and Training in Autism and Developmental Disabilities, 47*(3), 359–372.

Smith, S., & Jones, E. (1999). The obligation to provide assistive technology: Enhancing general curriculum access. *Journal of Law & Education, 28*(2), 247–265.

Soft Grup Construct. (2012). *Turbo Type* (Version 1.39.003) [Computer software]. Retrieved September 18, 2013, from http://www.easytousetools.com/turbo_type/

Strangman, N., & Dalton, B. (2005). Using technology to support struggling readers: A review of research. In D. Edyburn, K. Higgins, & R. Boone (Eds.), *Handbook of special education technology, research, and practice* (pp. 545–569). Whitefish Bay, WI: Knowledge by Design.

Terry, L., Mishra, P., Henriksen, D., Wolf, L., & Kereluik, K. (2013). Making it meaningful: The reciprocal relationship between technology and psychology. *TechTrends, 57*(3), 34–39.

Texthelp. (2012). *Read&Write Gold* [Computer software]. Retrieved September 17, 2013, from http://www.texthelp.com/North-America/our-products/readwrite

Tufts University. (2008). *Visual Understanding Environment* (Version 3.1.2) [Computer software]. Retrieved September 18, 2013, from http://vue.tufts.edu/

Vanderheiden, G. (1984). High and light technology approaches in the development of communication systems for the severely physically handicapped person. *Exceptional Education Quarterly, 4*(4), 40–56.

WatchMinder. (2011). Retrieved September 17, 2013, from http://www.watchminder.com/

WizcomTech. (2012). *Quicktionary2.* Retrieved September 17, 2013, from http://www.wizcomtech.com/eng/catalog/platforms/01/default.asp?p-cat=1&platformid=1

WizcomTech. (2013). *ReadingPen2.* Retrieved January 17, 2014, from http://www.wizcomtech.com/eng/catalog/platforms/01/default.asp?p-Cat=3&PlatformID=9

Zabala, J. (1995). *The SETT framework: Critical areas to consider when making informed assistive technology decisions* (ERIC Document Reproduction Service No. ED381962).

Houston, TX: Region IV Education Service Center.

Zirkel, P. (2007). The new IDEA. *Learning Disability Quarterly, 30*(1), 5–7.

Chapter 6

Alberto, P., & Troutman, A. (2013). *Applied behavior analysis for teachers* (9th ed.). Upper Saddle River, NJ: Pearson Education.

Alevriadou, A., & Grouios, G. (2007). Distractor interference effects and identification of safe and dangerous road-crossing sites by children with and without mental retardation. In E. Heinz (Ed.), *Mental retardation research advances* (pp. 75–87). New York, NY: Nova Science.

American Association on Intellectual and Developmental Disabilities. (2010). *FAQ on intellectual disability.* Retrieved January 17, 2010, from http://www.aamr.org/content_104.cfm

American Association on Intellectual and Developmental Disabilities. (2013). *Diagnostic Adaptive Behavior Scale.* Retrieved April 12, 2013, from http://www.aamr.org/content_106.cfm?navID=23

Ayres, K., Mechling, L., & Sansosti, F. (2013). The use of mobile technologies to assist with life skills/independence of students with moderate/severe intellectual disability and/or autism spectrum disorders: Considerations for the future of school psychology. *Psychology in the Schools, 50*(3), 259–271.

Batshaw, M., Gropman, A., & Lanpher, B. (2013). Genetics and developmental disabilities. In M. Batshaw, N. Roizen, & G. Lotrecchiano (Eds.), *Children with disabilities* (7th ed., pp. 3–24). Baltimore, MD: Paul H. Brookes.

Batshaw, M., & Lanpher, B. (2013). Inborn errors of metabolism. In M. Batshaw, N. Roizen, & G. Lotrecchiano (Eds.), *Children with disabilities* (7th ed., pp. 319–332). Baltimore, MD: Paul H. Brookes.

Beirne-Smith, M., Patton, J., & Kim, S. (2006). *Mental retardation* (7th ed.). Upper Saddle River, NJ: Pearson Education.

Blatt, B., & Kaplan, F. (1966). *Christmas in purgatory.* Boston, MA: Allyn & Bacon.

Browder, D., & Snell, M. (2000). Teaching functional academics. In M. Snell &

F. Brown (Eds.), *Instruction of students with severe disabilities* (5th ed., pp. 493–542). Upper Saddle River, NJ: Pearson Education.

Bybee, J., & Zigler, E. (1998). Outer-directedness in individuals with and without mental retardation: A review. In J. Burack, R. Hodapp, & E. Zigler (Eds.), *Handbook of mental retardation and development* (pp. 434–460). Cambridge, England: Cambridge University Press.

Davidson, P., & Myers, G. (2007). Environmental toxins. In M. Batshaw, L. Pellegrino, & N. Roizen (Eds.), *Children with disabilities* (6th ed., pp. 61–70). Baltimore, MD: Paul H. Brookes.

Drew, C., & Hardman, M. (2007). *Intellectual disabilities across the lifespan* (9th ed.). Upper Saddle River, NJ: Pearson Education.

Edgar, E. (1988). Employment as an outcome for mildly handicapped students: Current status and future directions. *Focus on Exceptional Children, 2*(1), 1–8.

Fiscus, R., Schuster, J., Morse, T., & Collins, B. (2002). Teaching elementary students with cognitive disabilities food preparation skills while embedding instructive feedback in prompt and consequent events. *Education and Training in Mental Retardation and Developmental Disabilities, 37*(1), 55–69.

Friend, M., & Bursuck, W. (2012). *Including students with special needs* (6th ed.). Upper Saddle River, NJ: Pearson Education.

Gargiulo, R. (1985). *Working with parents of exceptional children.* Boston, MA: Houghton Mifflin.

Gargiulo, R., & Kilgo, J. (2014). *An introduction to young children with special needs* (4th ed.). Belmont, CA: Wadsworth/Cengage Learning.

Gleason, J., & Ratner, N. (2013). *The development of language* (8th ed.). Boston, MA: Allyn & Bacon.

Grossman, H. (1973). *Manual on terminology and classification in mental retardation.* Washington, DC: American Association on Mental Deficiency.

Grossman, H. (1983). *Classification in mental retardation.* Washington, DC: American Association on Mental Deficiency.

Hartman, M. (2009). Step by step: Creating a community-based transition program for students with intellectual disabilities. *Teaching Exceptional Children, 41*(6), 6–11.

Heber, R. (1961). A manual on terminology and classification in mental retardation (Rev. ed.). *Monograph Supplement to the American Journal of Mental Deficiency, 64.*

Hendricks, D., & Wehman, P. (2009). Transition from school to adulthood for youth with autism spectrum disorders. *Focus on Autism and Other Developmental Disabilities, 24*(2), 77–88.

Hickson, L., Blackman, L., & Reis, E. (1995). *Mental retardation: Foundations of educational programming.* Boston, MA: Allyn & Bacon.

Hoover, J., & Patton, J. (2004). Differentiating standards-based education for students with diverse needs. *Remedial and Special Education, 25*(2), 74–78.

Hughes, C., Washington, B., & Brown, G. (2008). Supporting students in the transition from school to adult life. In F. Rusch (Ed.), *Beyond high school* (2nd ed., pp. 266–287). Upper Saddle River, NJ: Pearson Education.

Jared, J., Frantino, E., & Sturmey, P. (2007). The effects of errorless learning and backward chaining on the acquisition of Internet skills in adults with developmental disabilities. *Journal of Applied Behavior Analysis, 40*(1), 185–189.

Jarrold, C., & Brock, J. (2012). Short-term and working memory in mental retardation. In J. Burack, R. Hodapp, G. Iarocci, & E. Zigler (Eds.), *The Oxford handbook of intellectual disability and development* (pp. 109–124). New York, NY: Oxford University Press.

Johnson, L. (2005). First, do no harm: An argument against mandatory high-stakes testing for students with intellectual disabilities. *Mental Retardation, 43*(4), 292–298.

Johnson, D., Johnson, R., & Holubec, E. (1998). *Cooperation in the classroom* (7th ed.). Edina, MN: Interaction Book.

Johnson, D., Johnson, R., & Holubec, E. (2002). *Circles of learning.* Edina, MN: Interaction Book.

Jones, K., Smith, D., Ulleland, C., & Streissguth, A. (1973). Pattern of malformation in offspring of chronic alcoholic mothers. *Lancet, 1*(7815), 1267–1271.

Katims, D. (2000). Literacy instruction for people with mental retardation: Historical highlights and contemporary analysis. *Education and Training in Mental Retardation and Developmental Disabilities, 35*(1), 3–15.

Kaufman, A., & Kaufman, N. (2004). *Kaufman Assessment Battery for Children—Second Edition.* Circle Pines, MN: American Guidance Service.

Kessler Foundation/National Organization on Disability. (2010). *The ADA, 20 years later.* Retrieved April 24, 2013, from http://www.2010disabilitysurveys.org/pdfs/surveyresults.pdf

Lejune, J., Gautier, M., & Turpin, R. (1959). Études des chromosomes somatiques de neuf enfants mongoliers. *Academie de Science, 248,* 1721–1722.

Lewis, R., & Doorlag, D. (2011). *Teaching students with special needs in general education classrooms* (8th ed.). Upper Saddle River, NJ: Pearson Education.

Lindman, F., & McIntyre, K. (1961). *The mentally disabled and the law.* Chicago, IL: University of Chicago Press.

Luckasson, R., Borthwick-Duffy, S., Buntinx, W., Coulter, D., Craig, E., Reeve, A., . . . Tassé, M. (2002). *Mental retardation: Definition, support, and systems of supports* (10th ed.). Washington, DC: American Association on Mental Retardation.

Luckasson, R., Coulter, D., Polloway, E., Reiss, S., Schalock, R., Snell, M., . . . Stark, J. (1992). *Mental retardation: Definition, classification, and systems of support* (9th ed.). Washington, DC: American Association on Mental Retardation.

Mank, D., Cioffi, A., & Yovanoff, P. (2003). Supported employment outcomes across a decade: Is there evidence of improvement in the quality of implementation? *Mental Retardation, 41*(3), 188–197.

March of Dimes. (2008). *Public health education information sheet: Drinking alcohol during pregnancy.* White Plains, NY: Author.

March of Dimes. (2013a). *Down syndrome.* Retrieved April 20, 2013, from http://www.marchofdimes.com/baby/birthdefects_downsyndrome.html

March of Dimes. (2013b). *Fragile X.* Retrieved April 20, 2013, from http://www.marchofdimes.com/baby/birthdefects_fragilex.html

March of Dimes. (2013c). *Maternal PKU.* Retrieved April 20, 2013, from http://www.marchofdimes.com/pregnancy/complications_maternalPKU.html

McDonnell, J., & Copeland, S. (2011). Teaching academic skills. In M. Snell & F. Brown (Eds.), *Instruction of students with severe disabilities* (7th ed., pp. 492–528). Upper Saddle River, NJ: Pearson Education.

McDonnell, J., Hardman, M., & McDonnell, A. (2003). *An introduction to persons with moderate and severe disabilities* (2nd ed.). Boston, MA: Allyn & Bacon.

Mechling, L. (2007). Assistive technology as a self-management tool for prompting students with intellectual disabilities to initiate and complete daily tasks: A literature review. *Education and Training in Developmental Disabilities, 42*(3), 252–269.

Meyer, G. (2007). X-linked syndromes causing intellectual disability. In M. Batshaw, L. Pellegrino, & N. Roizen (Eds.), *Children with disabilities* (6th ed., pp. 275–283). Baltimore, MD: Paul H. Brookes.

Migliore, A., Mank, D., Grossi, T., & Rogan, P. (2007). Integrated employment or sheltered workshops: Preferences of adults with intellectual disabilities, their families and staff. *Journal of Vocational Rehabilitation, 26*(1), 5–19.

Morrison, G., & Polloway, E. (1995). Mental retardation. In E. Meyen & T. Skritic (Eds.), *Special education and student disability* (4th ed., pp. 213–269). Denver, CO: Love.

Murphy, S., Rogan, P., Handley, M., Kincaid, C., & Royce-Davis, J. (2002). People's situations and perspectives eight years after workshop conversion. *Mental Retardation, 40*(1), 30–40.

National Center for Education Statistics. (2012). *The condition of education 2012.* Washington, DC: U.S. Department of Education.

National Down Syndrome Society. (2013). *Alzheimer's disease and Down syndrome.* Retrieved April 15, 2013, from http://www.ndss.org

National Longitudinal Transition Study 2. (2009). *The post-high school outcomes of youth with disabilities up to 4 years after high school.* Retrieved April 21, 2013, from http://www.nlts2.org/reports/2009_04/nlts2_report_2009_04_complete.pdf

Nirje, B. (1969). The normalization principle and its human management implications. In R. Kugel & W. Wolfensberger (Eds.), *Changing* patterns in residential services for the mentally retarded (pp. 179–195). Washington, DC: President's Committee on Mental Retardation.

Owens, R. (2009). Mental retardation/intellectual disabilities. In D. Bernstein & E. Tiegerman-Farber (Eds.), *Language and communication disorders in children* (6th ed., pp. 246–313). Boston, MA: Pearson Education.

Owens, R. (2014). *Language disorders* (6th ed.). Boston, MA: Pearson Education.

Paulson, J. (2013). Environmental toxicants and neurocognitive development. In M. Batshaw, N. Roizen, & G. Lotrecchiano (Eds.), *Children with disabilities* (7th ed., pp. 37–46). Baltimore, MD: Paul H. Brookes.

Pellegrino, J. (2013). Newborn screening: Opportunities for prevention of developmental disabilities. In M. Batshaw, N. Roizen, & G. Lotrecchiano (Eds.), *Children with disabilities* (7th ed., pp. 61–72). Baltimore, MD: Paul H. Brookes.

Polloway, E., Patton, J., Serna, L., & Bailey, J. (2013). *Strategies for teaching learners with special needs* (10th ed.). Upper Saddle River, NJ: Pearson Education.

Roid, G. (2003). *Stanford-Binet Intelligence Scale–Fifth Edition.* Itasca, IL: Riverside.

Roizen, N. (2013). Down syndrome. In M. Batshaw, N. Roizen, & G. Lotrecchiano (Eds.), *Children with disabilities* (7th ed., pp. 307–318). Baltimore, MD: Paul H. Brookes.

Schalock, R. (2013). *Bob Schalock interview.* Retrieved April 12, 2013, from http://www.aaidd.org/shalock-transcript.cfm

Schalock, R., Borthwick-Duffy, S., Bradley, V., Buntinx, W., Coulter, D., Craig, E., . . . Yeager, M. (2010). *Intellectual disability: Definition, classification, and systems of supports* (11th ed.). Washington, DC: American Association on Intellectual and Developmental Disabilities.

Scheerenberger, R. (1983). *A history of mental retardation.* Baltimore, MD: Paul H. Brookes.

Scheerenberger, R. (1987). *A history of mental retardation: A quarter century of concern.* Baltimore, MD: Paul H. Brookes.

Schilit, J., & Caldwell, M. (1980). A word list of essential career/vocational words for mentally retarded students. *Education and Training of the Mentally Retarded, 15*(2), 113–117.

Schonberg, R. (2013). Birth defects and prenatal diagnosis. In M. Batshaw, N. Roizen, & G. Lotrecchiano (Eds.), *Children with disabilities* (7th ed., pp. 47–60). Baltimore, MD: Paul H. Brookes.

Shogren, K., Bovaird, J., Palmer, S., & Wehmeyer, M. (2010). Examining the development of locus of control orientation in students with intellectual disability, learning disabilities, and no disabilities: A latent growth curve analysis. *Research and Practice for Persons with Severe Disabilities, 35*(3–4), 80–92.

Simmons, J., & Flexer, R. (2013). Transition to employment. In R. Flexer, R. Baer, P. Luft, & T. Simmons (Eds.), *Transition planning for secondary students with disabilities* (4th ed., pp. 279–327). Upper Saddle River, NJ: Pearson Education.

Sitlington, P., Neubert, D., & Clark, G. (2010). *Transition education and services for students with disabilities* (5th ed.). Needham Heights, MA: Allyn & Bacon.

Smith, T., Polloway, E., Patton, J., & Dowdy, C. (2008). *Teaching students with special needs in inclusive settings* (5th ed.). Needham Heights, MA: Allyn & Bacon.

Smith, T., Polloway, E., Patton, J., & Dowdy, C. (2012). *Teaching students with special needs in inclusive settings* (6th ed.). Needham Heights, MA: Allyn & Bacon.

Taylor, P., Collins, B., Schuster, J., & Kleinert, H. (2002). Teaching laundry skills to high school students with disabilities: Generalization of targeted skills and nontargeted information. *Education and Training in Mental Retardation and Developmental Disabilities, 37*(2), 172–183.

Taylor, R., Brady, M., & Richards, S. (2005). *Mental retardation.* Boston, MA: Allyn & Bacon.

Test, D., Carver, T., Evers, L., Haddad, J., & Person, J. (2000). Longitudinal job satisfaction of persons in supported employment. *Education and Training in Mental Retardation and Developmental Disabilities, 35*(4), 365–373.

Thoma, C. (1999). Supporting student voice in transition planning. *Teaching Exceptional Children, 31*(5), 4–9.

Thoma, C., Bartholomew, C., & Scott, L. (2009). *Universal design for transition.* Baltimore, MD: Paul H. Brookes.

Turnbull, A., Turnbull, R., Erwin, E., Soodak, L., & Shogren, K. (2011). *Families, professionals, and exceptionality* (6th ed.). Upper Saddle River, NJ: Pearson Education.

U.S. Department of Education. (2012). *IDEA data*. Retrieved April 22, 2013, from http://www.ideadata.org/PartB ChildCount.asp

U.S. Department of Education. (2013). *Historical state-level IDEA data files*. Retrieved November 14, 2013, from http://tadnet.public.tadnet.org/ pages/712

Vaughn, S., & Bos, C. (2012). *Strategies for teaching students with learning and behavior problems* (8th ed.). Upper Saddle River, NJ: Pearson Education.

Vaughn, S., Bos, C., & Schumm, J. (2014). *Teaching students who are exceptional, diverse, and at risk* (6th ed.). Upper Saddle River, NJ: Pearson Education.

Walker, A., Uphold, D., Richter, S., & Test, D. (2010). Review of the literature on community-based instruction across grade levels. *Education and Training in Autism and Developmental Disabilities, 45*(2), 242–267.

Wechsler, D. (2003). *Wechsler Intelligence Scale for Children–Fourth Edition.* San Antonio, TX: Psychological Corp.

Wehman, P., & Scott, L. (2013). Applications for youth with intellectual disabilities. In P. Wehman (Ed.), *Life beyond the classroom* (5th ed., pp. 379–400). Baltimore, MD: Paul H. Brookes.

Wehmeyer, M. (2003). Defining mental retardation and ensuring access to the general curriculum. *Education and Training in Developmental Disabilities, 38*(3), 271–282.

Wehmeyer, M., Palmer, S., Smith, S., Davies, D., & Stock, S. (2008). The efficacy of technology use by people with intellectual disability: A single-subject design meta-analysis. *Journal of Special Education Technology, 23*(3), 21–30.

Wolfensberger, W. (1972). *Normalization: The principle of normalization in human services.* Toronto, ON: National Institute on Mental Retardation.

Xin, J., & Holmdal, P. (2003). Snacks and skills: Teaching children functional counting skills. *Teaching Exceptional Children, 35*(5), 46–51.

Chapter 7

Aiken, L., & Groth-Marnat, G. (2006). *Psychological testing and assessment* (12th ed.). Boston, MA: Allyn & Bacon.

Alley, G., & Deshler, D. (1979). *Teaching the learning disabled adolescent: Strategies and methods.* Denver, CO: Love.

American Psychiatric Association. (2013). *Diagnostic and statistical manual of mental disorders* (5th ed.). Arlington, VA: Author.

Arnold, L., Christopher, J., Huestis, R., & Smeltzer, D. (1978). Megavitamins for minimal brain dysfunction: A placebo controlled study. *Journal of the American Medical Association, 240,* 2642–2643.

Association for Children with Learning Disabilities. (1986, September–October). ACLD definition: Specific learning disabilities. *ACLD Newsbrief,* pp. 15–16.

Austin, K., & Wittig, K. (2013). Individualized transition planning. In P. Wehman (Ed.), *Life beyond the classroom* (5th ed., pp. 95–119). Baltimore, MD: Paul H. Brookes.

Bender, W. (2008). *Learning disabilities: Characteristics, identification, and teaching strategies* (6th ed.). Needham Heights, MA: Allyn & Bacon.

Bereiter, C., & Engelmann, S. (1966). *Teaching disadvantaged children in the preschool.* Englewood Cliffs, NJ: Prentice Hall.

Berkley, S., Bender, W., Peaster, L., & Saunders, L. (2009). Implementation of response to intervention: A snapshot of progress. *Journal of Learning Disabilities, 42*(1), 85–95.

Bryant, D., & Bryant, B. (2003). *Assistive technology for people with disabilities.* Boston, MA: Allyn & Bacon.

Cavalier, A., Ferretti, R., & Okolo, C. (1994). Technology and individual differences. *Journal of Special Education Technology, 12*(3), 175–181.

Cohen, L., & Spenciner, L. (2011). *Assessment of children and youth with special needs* (4th ed.) Upper Saddle River, NJ: Pearson Education.

Cohen Kadosh, R., & Walsh, V. (2007). Dyscalculia. *Current Biology, 17*(22), R946–R947.

Cortiella, C. (2011). *The state of learning disabilities.* New York, NY: National Center for Learning Disabilities.

Cott, A. (1972). Megavitamins: The orthomolecular approach to behavioral disorders and learning disabilities. *Academic Therapy, 7*(3), 245–258.

Council for Exceptional Children. (2003). Strategies + technology = solutions for reading challenges. *CEC Today, 10*(1), 1, 5, 13, 15.

Council for Learning Disabilities. (1986). Use of discrepancy formulas in the identification of learning disabled individuals. *Learning Disabilities Quarterly, 9,* 245.

Courtad, C., & Bouck, E. (2013). Assistive technology for students with learning disabilities. In J. Bakken, F. Obiakor, & A. Rotatori (Eds.), *Learning disabilities: Practice concerns and students with LD* (pp. 153–172). Bingley, UK: Emerald.

Cruickshank, W. (1972). Some issues facing the field of learning disabilities. *Journal of Learning Disabilities, 5*(5), 380–388.

Deiner, P. (1993). *Resources for teaching children with diverse abilities.* Fort Worth, TX: Harcourt Brace Jovanovich.

Deshler, D., Ellis, E., & Lenz, B. (1996). *Teaching adolescents with learning disabilities* (2nd ed.). Denver, CO: Love.

Dyson, L. (1996). The experiences of families of children with learning disabilities: Parental stress, family functioning and sibling self-concept. *Journal of Learning Disabilities, 29*(3), 280–286.

Edyburn, D. (2006). Cognitive prostheses for students with mild disabilities: Is this what assistive technology looks like? *Journal of Special Education Technology, 21*(4), 62–65.

Engelmann, S. (1977). Sequencing cognitive and academic tasks. In R. Kneedler & S. Tarver (Eds.), *Changing perspectives in special education* (pp. 46–61). Columbus, OH: Merrill.

Feingold, B. (1975). Hyperkinesis and learning disabilities linked to artificial food flavors and colors. *American Journal of Nursing, 75,* 797–803.

Feingold, B. (1976). Hyperkinesis and learning disabilities linked to ingestion of artificial food colors and flavorings. *Journal of Learning Disabilities, 9*(9), 551–559.

Fletcher, J., & Vaughn, S. (2009). Response to intervention: Preventing and remediating academic difficulties.

Child Development Perspectives, 3(1), 30–37.

Friend, M., & Bursuck, W. (2012). *Including students with special needs* (6th ed.). Upper Saddle River, NJ: Pearson Education.

Fuchs, D., & Fuchs, L. (2009). Creating opportunities for intensive intervention for students with learning disabilities. *Teaching Exceptional Children, 42*(2), 60–62.

Fuchs, D., Fuchs, L., & Compton, D. (2012). Smart RTI: A next-generation approach to multilevel prevention. *Exceptional Children, 78*(3), 263–279.

Fuchs, D., Mock, D., Morgan, P., & Young, C. (2003). Responsiveness-to-intervention: Definitions, evidence, and implication for the learning disabilities construct. *Learning Disabilities Research and Practice, 18*(3), 157–171.

Gabrieli, J. (2009). Dyslexia: A new synergy between education and neuroscience. *Science, 325* (5938), 280–283.

Galaburda, A. (2005). Neurology of learning disabilities: What will the future bring? The answer comes from the successes of the recent past. *Learning Disabilities Quarterly, 28*(2), 107–110.

Gargiulo, R., & Kilgo, J. (2014). *An introduction to young children with special needs* (4th ed.). Belmont, CA: Wadsworth/Cengage Learning.

Gargiulo, R., & Metcalf, D. (2013). *Teaching in today's inclusive classrooms* (2nd ed.). Belmont, CA: Wadsworth/Cengage Learning.

Gersten, R., Carnine, D., & Woodward, J. (1987). Direct instruction research: The third decade. *Remedial and Special Education, 8*(6), 48–56.

Gollnick, D., & Chinn, P. (2013). *Multicultural education in a pluralistic society* (9th ed.). Upper Saddle River, NJ: Pearson Education.

Gonzalez, R., Rosenthal, D., & Kim, J. (2011). Predicting vocational rehabilitation outcomes for young adults with specific learning disabilities: Transitioning from school to work. *Journal of Vocational Rehabilitation, 34*(3), 163–172.

Hallahan, D., Kauffman, J., & Lloyd, J. (1999). *Introduction to learning disabilities* (2nd ed.). Needham Heights, MA: Allyn & Bacon.

Hallahan, D., Lloyd, J., Kauffman, J., Weiss, M., & Martinez, E. (2005). *Learning disabilities: Foundations, characteristics, and effective teaching* (3rd ed.). Boston, MA: Allyn & Bacon.

Hallahan, D., & Mercer, C. (2002). Learning disabilities: Historical perspectives. In R. Bradley, L. Danielson, & D. Hallahan (Eds.), *Identification of learning disabilities: Research to practice* (pp. 1–67). Mahwah, NJ: Erlbaum.

Isles, A., & Humby, T. (2006). Modes of imprinted gene action in learning disabilities. *Journal of Intellectual Disability Research, 50*(5), 318–325.

Jennings, J., Caldwell, J., & Lerner, J. (2010). *Reading problems: Assessment and teaching strategies* (6th ed.). Needham Heights, MA: Allyn & Bacon.

Kame'enui, E. (2007). A new paradigm: Responsiveness to intervention. *Teaching Exceptional Children, 39*(5), 6–7.

Kavale, K., & Forness, S. (1983). Hyperactivity and diet treatment: A meta-analysis of the Feingold hypothesis. *Journal of Learning Disabilities, 16*(6), 324–330.

Kirk, S. (1962). *Educating exceptional children.* Boston, MA: Houghton Mifflin.

Lenz, B., & Deshler, D. (2004). *Teaching content to all.* Boston, MA: Allyn & Bacon.

Lenz, B., Ellis, E., & Scanlon, D. (1996). *Teaching learning strategies to adolescents and adults with learning disabilities.* Austin, TX: Pro-Ed.

Lerner, J. (2003). *Learning disabilities* (9th ed.). Boston, MA: Houghton Mifflin.

Lerner, J., & Johns, B. (2009). *Learning disabilities and related mild disabilities* (11th ed.). Belmont, CA: Wadsworth/Cengage Learning.

Lerner, J., & Johns, B. (2012). *Learning disabilities and related mild disabilities* (12th ed.). Belmont, CA: Wadsworth/Cengage Learning.

Lewis, M., Shapiro, B., & Church, R. (2013). Specific learning disabilities. In M. Batshaw, N. Roizen, & G. Lotrecchiano (Eds.), *Children with disabilities* (7th ed., pp. 403–422). Baltimore, MD: Paul H. Brookes.

Lyon, G., Fletcher, J., Shaywitz, S., Shaywitz, B., Torgesen, J., Wood, F., . . . Olson, R. (2001). Rethinking learning disabilities. In C. Finn, A. Rotherham, & C. Hokanson (Eds.), *Rethinking special education for a new century* (pp. 259–287). Washington, DC: Thomas B. Fordham Foundation and Progressive Policy Institute.

Lyon, G., Shaywitz, S., & Shaywitz, B. (2003). Defining dyslexia. *Annals of Dyslexia, 53,* 1–14.

Marchand-Martella, N., Slocum, T., & Martella, R. (Eds.). (2004). *Introduction to direct instruction.* Boston, MA: Allyn & Bacon.

Martin, E. (2002). Response to "Learning disabilities: Historical perspectives." In R. Bradley, L. Danielson, & D. Hallahan (Eds.), *Identification of learning disabilities: Research to practice* (pp. 81–87). Mahwah, NJ: Erlbaum.

Manning, M., Bear, G., & Minke, K. (2006). Self-concept and self-esteem. In G. Bear & K. Minke (Eds.), *Children's needs III: Development, prevention, and intervention* (pp. 341–356). Bethesda, MD: National Association of School Psychologists.

McLeskey, J., Hoppey, D., Williamson, P., & Rentz, T. (2004). Is inclusion an illusion? An examination of national and state trends toward the education of students with learning disabilities in the general education classroom. *Learning Disabilities Research and Practice, 19*(2), 109–115.

McLeskey, J., Landers, E., Hoppey, D., & Williamson, P. (2011). Learning disabilities and the LRE mandate: An examination of national and state trends. *Learning Disabilities Research and Practice, 26*(2), 60–66.

McLeskey, J., & Waldron, N. (2011). Educational programs for elementary students with learning disabilities: Can they be both effective and inclusive? *Learning Disabilities Research & Practice, 26*(1), 48–57.

Meichenbaum, D. (1977). *Cognitive behavior modification.* New York, NY: Plenum.

Meichenbaum, D., & Goodman, J. (1971). Training impulsive children to talk to themselves: A means of developing self-control. *Journal of Abnormal Psychology, 77,* 115–126.

Meltzer, L., & Krishnan, K. (2007). Executive function difficulties and learning disabilities: Understanding and misunderstandings. In L. Meltzer (Ed.), *Executive function in education* (pp. 77–105). New York, NY: Guilford.

Mercer, C., & Pullen, P. (2009). *Students with learning disabilities* (7th ed.). Upper Saddle River, NJ: Pearson Education.

National Center for Education Statistics. (2012). *Digest of education statistics 2011*. Washington, DC: U.S. Department of Education.

National Joint Committee on Learning Disabilities. (2006). *Learning disabilities and young children*. Retrieved May 18, 2013, from http://www.ldonline.org/article/11511/

Newman, L., Wagner, M., Cameto, R., & Knokey, A. (2009). *The post-high school outcomes of youth with disabilities up to four years after high school: A report of findings from the National Longitudinal Transition Study-2*. Menlo Park, CA: SRI International.

O'Connor, R., & Sanchez, V. (2011). Responsive to intervention models for reducing reading difficulties and identifying learning disability. In J. Kauffman & D. Hallahan (Eds.), *Handbook of special education* (pp. 123–133). New York, NY: Routledge.

Paulson, F., Paulson, P., & Meyer, C. (1991). What makes a portfolio a portfolio? *Educational Leadership, 48*(5), 60–63.

Pearl, R., & Donahue, M. (2004). Peer relationships and learning disabilities. In B. Wong (Ed.), *Learning about learning disabilities* (3rd ed., pp. 133–165). San Diego, CA: Elsevier/Academic Press.

Peterson, J., & Hittie, M. (2010). *Inclusive teaching* (2nd ed.). Boston, MA: Allyn & Bacon.

Polloway, E., Patton, J., Serna, L., & Bailey, J. (2013). *Strategies for teaching learners with special needs* (10th ed.). Upper Saddle River, NJ: Pearson Education.

Raskind, W. (2001). Current understanding of the genetic basis of reading and spelling disability. *Learning Disability Quarterly, 24*(2), 141–157.

Reynolds, C. (1992). Two key concepts in the diagnosis of learning disabilities and the habilitation of learning. *Learning Disability Quarterly, 15*, 2–12.

Rourke, B. (2005). Neuropsychology of learning disabilities: Past and present. *Learning Disabilities Quarterly, 28*(2), 111–114.

Sailor, W., & Rogers, B. (2005). Rethinking inclusion: Schoolwide applications. *Phi Delta Kappan, 86*(7), 503–509.

Salend, S. (1998). Using portfolios to assess student performance. *Teaching Exceptional Children, 31*(2), 26–43.

Scanlon, D., Patton, J., & Raskind, M. (2011). Transition to daily living for persons with high incidence disabilities. In J. Kauffman & D. Hallahan (Eds.), *Handbook of special education* (pp. 594–607). New York, NY: Routledge.

Shapiro, B., Church, R., & Lewis, M. (2007). Specific learning disabilities. In M. Batshaw, L. Pellegrino, & N. Roizen (Eds.), *Children with disabilities* (6th ed., pp. 367–385). Baltimore, MD: Paul H. Brookes.

Shalev, R. (2004). Developmental dyscalculia. *Journal of Child Neurology, 19*(10), 765–771.

Sileo, J. (2011). Co-teaching: Getting to know your partner. *Teaching Exceptional Children, 43*(5), 32–38.

Simmons, D., Kame'enui, E., Coyne, M., Chard, D., & Hairrell, A. (2011). Effective strategies for teaching beginning reading. In M. Coyne, E. Kame'enui, & D. Carnine (Eds.), *Effective teaching strategies that accommodate diverse learners* (4th ed., pp. 51–84). Upper Saddle River, NJ: Pearson Education.

Smith, T., Polloway, E., Patton, J., & Dowdy, C. (2012). *Teaching children with special needs in inclusive settings* (6th ed.). Needham Heights, MA: Allyn & Bacon.

Specht, J. (2013). School inclusion. *Education Canada, 53*(2), 16–19.

Spence-Cochran, K., Pearl, C., & Walker, Z. (2013). Full inclusion into schools. In P. Wehman (Ed.), *Life beyond the classroom* (5th ed., pp. 175–195). Baltimore, MD: Paul H. Brookes.

Stasi, G., & Tall, L. (2010). Learning disorders in children and adolescents. In J. Donders & S. Hunter (Eds.), *Principles and practice of lifespan developmental neuropsychology* (pp. 127–142). New York, NY: Cambridge University Press.

Stecker, P. (2007). Tertiary intervention: Using progress monitoring with intensive services. *Teaching Exceptional Children, 39*(5), 50–57.

Sturomski, N. (1997, July). Teaching students with learning disabilities to use learning strategies. *NICHY News Digest, 25*, 2–12.

Swanson, H., Cooney, J., & McNamara, J. (2004). Learning disabilities and memory. In B. Wong (Ed.), *Learning about learning disabilities* (3rd ed., pp. 41–92). San Diego, CA: Elsevier/Academic Press.

Swanson, H., & Jerman, O. (2007). The influence of working memory on reading growth in subgroups of children with reading difficulties. *Journal of Experimental Child Psychology, 96*(4), 249–283.

Swanson, H., Zheng, X., & Jerman, O. (2009). Working memory, short-term memory, and reading disabilities: A selective meta-analysis of the literature. *Journal of Learning Disabilities, 42*(3), 260–287.

Tymchuk, A., Lakin, K., & Luckasson, R. (2001). *The forgotten generation*. Baltimore, MD: Paul H. Brookes.

U.S. Department of Education. (2012). *Thirty-first annual report to Congress on the implementation of the Individuals with Disabilities Education Act, 2009*. Washington, DC: U.S. Government Printing Office.

U.S. Department of Education. (2013). *Historical state-level IDEA data files*. Retrieved November 14, 2013, from http://tadnet.public.tadnet.org/pages/712

U.S. Office of Education. (1977, December 29). Assistance to states for education of handicapped children: Procedures for evaluating specific learning disabilities. *Federal Register, 42*(250), 65082–65085.

Vaughn S., & Bos, C. (2012). *Strategies for teaching students with learning and behavior problems* (8th ed.). Upper Saddle River, NJ: Pearson Education.

Vaughn, S., Bos, C., & Schumm, J. (2014). *Teaching students who are exceptional, diverse, and at risk* (6th ed.). Upper Saddle River NJ: Pearson Education.

Vaughn, S., & Fuchs, L. (2003). Redefining learning disabilities as inadequate response to instruction: The promise and potential problems. *Learning Disabilities Research and Practice, 18*(3), 137–146.

Vaughn, S., & Linan-Thompson, S. (2003). What is special about special education for students with learning disabilities? *Journal of Special Education, 37*(3), 140–147.

Wadsworth, S., & DeFries, J. (2005). Genetic etiology of reading difficulties in boys and girls. *Twin Research and Human Genetics, 8*(6), 594–601.

Walker, B., Shippen, M., Alberto, P., Houchins, D., & Cihak, D. (2005). Using the expressive writing program to improve the writing skills of high school students with learning disabilities. *Learning Disabilities Research and Practice, 20*(3), 175–183.

Wiener, J. (2004). Do peer relationships foster behavioral adjustment in children with learning disabilities? *Learning Disability Quarterly, 27*(1), 21–30.

Wiener, J., & Timmermanis, V. (2012). Social relationships: The 4th R. In B. Wong & D. Butler (Eds.), *Learning about learning disabilities* (4th ed., pp. 89–140). San Diego, CA: Elsevier/Academic Press.

Witte, R., Philips, L., & Kakela, M. (1998). Job satisfaction of college graduates with learning disabilities. *Journal of Learning Disabilities, 31*(3), 259–265.

Wood, F., & Grigorenko, E. (2001). Emerging issues in the genetics of dyslexia: A methodological preview. *Journal of Learning Disabilities, 34*(6), 503–511.

Zigmond, N. (2003). Where should students with disabilities receive special education services? *Journal of Special Education, 37*(3), 193–199.

Zigmond, N., & Baker, J. (1996). Full inclusion for students with learning disabilities: Too much of a good thing? *Theory Into Practice, 35*(1), 26–34.

Zigmond, N., & Kloo, A. (2011). General and special education are (and should be) different. In J. Kauffman & D. Hallahan (Eds.), *Handbook of special education* (pp. 160–172). New York, NY: Routledge.

Zirkel, P., & Thomas. L. (2010a). State laws and guidelines for implementing for RTI. *Teaching Exceptional Children, 43*(1), 60–73.

Zirkel, P., & Thomas. L. (2010b). State laws for RTI: An updated snapshot. *Teaching Exceptional Children, 42*(3), 56–63.

Chapter 8

Alberto, P., & Troutman, A. (2006). *Applied behavior analysis for teachers* (7th ed.). Upper Saddle River, NJ: Pearson Education.

Alberto, P., & Troutman, A. (2013). *Applied behavior analysis for teachers* (9th ed.). Upper Saddle River, NJ: Pearson Education.

American Academy of Pediatrics. (2011). Clinical practice guideline: ADHD: Clinical practice guideline for the diagnosis, evaluation, and treatment of attention-deficit/hyperactivity disorder in children and adolescents. *Pediatrics, 128*(5), 1007–1022.

American Psychiatric Association. (2013). *Diagnostic and statistical manual of mental disorders* (5th ed.). Arlington, VA: Author.

Arnsten, A., Berridge, C., & McCracken, J. (2009). The neurological basis of attention-deficit/hyperactivity disorder. *Primary Psychiatry, 16*(7), 47–54.

Atkins, M., & Mariñez-Lora, A. (2008). Attention-deficit/hyperactivity disorder and psychiatric comorbidity. In P. Accardo (Ed.), *Capute & Accardo's neurodevelopmental disabilities in infancy and childhood* (3rd ed., Vol. 2, pp. 693–703). Baltimore, MD: Paul H. Brookes.

Aune, B., Burt, B., & Gennaro, P. (2010). *Behavior solutions for the inclusive classroom.* Arlington, TX: Future Horizons.

Barbaresi, W., Katusic, S., Colligan, R., Weaver, A., Leibson, C., & Jacobsen, S. (2006). Long term stimulant medication treatment of ADHD: Results from a population based study. *Journal of Developmental & Behavioral Pediatrics, 27*(1), 1–10.

Barkley, R. (1998). *Attention deficit hyperactivity disorder* (2nd ed.). New York, NY: Guilford Press.

Barkley, R. (2000). *Taking charge of ADHD: The complete authoritative guide for parents* (Rev. ed.). New York, NY: Guilford Press.

Barkley, R. (2006). *Attention deficit hyperactivity disorder* (3rd ed.). New York, NY: Guilford Press.

Barkley, R. (2010). *Attention deficit hyperactivity disorder in adults.* Burlington, MA: Jones & Bartlett Learning.

Barkley, R., Fischer, M., Smallish, L., & Fletcher, K. (2006). Young adult outcome of hyperactive children: Adaptive functioning in major life activities. *Journal of the American Academy of Child & Adolescent Psychiatry, 45*(2), 192–202.

Bender, W. (2008). *Learning disabilities: Characteristics, identification, and teaching strategies* (6th ed.). Needham Heights, MA: Allyn & Bacon.

Bos, C., Nahmias, M., & Urban, M. (1999). Targeting home–school collaboration for students with ADHD. *Teaching Exceptional Children, 31*(6), 4–11.

Bradley, W. (1937). The behavior of children receiving Benzedrine. *American Journal of Psychiatry, 94*, 577–585.

Brown, T. (2006). New understandings of AD/HD. In C. Dendy (Ed.), *CHADD educator's manual on attention-deficit/hyperactivity disorder* (pp. 3–12). Landover, MD: CHADD.

Cantwell, D. (1979). The "hyperactive child." *Hospital Practice, 14*, 65–73.

Castellanos, F. (1997). Toward a pathophysiology of attention-deficit/hyperactivity disorder. *Clinical Pediatrics 36*, 381–393.

Centers for Disease Control and Prevention. (2013a). *Attention deficit hyperactivity disorder: Data & statistics.* Retrieved May 26, 2013, from http://www.cdc.gov/ncbddd/adhd/data.html

Centers for Disease Control and Prevention. (2013b). *State-based prevalence data of ADHD diagnosis.* Retrieved May 26, 2013, from http://www.cdc.gov/ncbddd/adhd/prevalence.html

Cohen, D. (2006). Critiques of the "ADHD" enterprise. In G. Lloyd, J. Snead, & D. Cohen (Eds.), *Critical new perspectives on ADHD* (pp. 12–33). London, UK: Routledge.

Conners, C. (2009). *Conners 3.* San Antonio, TX: Pearson/PsychCorp.

Cruickshank, W., Bentzen, F., Ratzeburg, F., & Tannhauser, M. (1961). *A teaching method for brain-injured and hyperactive children.* Syracuse, NY: Syracuse University Press.

Cruickshank, W., Bice, H., & Wallen, N. (1957). *Perception and cerebral palsy.* Syracuse, NY: Syracuse University Press.

Denton, L., & Silver, M. (2012). Listening and understanding: Language and learning disabilities. In L. Barclay (Ed.), *Learning to listen/listening to learn* (pp. 372–453). New York, NY: American Foundation for the Blind.

Dodson, W. (2002). Attention deficit-hyperactivity disorder (AD/HD): The basics and the controversies. *Understanding Our Gifted, 14*(4), 17–21.

Dopheide, J., & Pliszka, S. (2009). Attention-deficit-hyperactivity disorder: An update. *Pharmacotherapy, 29*(6), 656–679.

DuPaul, G., & Kern, L. (2011). *Young children with ADHD.* Washington, DC: American Psychological Association.

DuPaul, G., Power, T., Anastopoulos, A., & Reid, R. (1998). *ADHD Rating Scale–IV: Checklists, norms, and clinical interpretation*. New York, NY: Guilford Press.

DuPaul, G., & Weyandt, L. (2006). School-based interventions for children and adolescents with attention-deficit/hyperactivity disorder: Enhancing academic and behavioral outcomes. *Education and Treatment of Children, 29*(2), 341–358.

Ficks, C., & Waldman, I. (2009). Gene-environment interactions in attention-deficit/hyperactivity disorder. *Current Psychiatry Reports, 11*(5), 387–392.

Floet, A., Scheiner, C., & Grossman, L. (2010). Attention-deficit/hyperactivity disorder. *Pediatrics in Review, 31*(2), 56–69.

Friend, M., & Bursuck, W. (2009). *Including students with special needs* (5th ed.). Upper Saddle River, NJ: Pearson Education

Friend, M., & Bursuck, W. (2012). *Including students with special needs* (6th ed.). Upper Saddle River, NJ: Pearson Education.

Glanzman, M., & Blum, N. (2007). Attention deficit and hyperactivity. In M. Batshaw, L. Pellegrino, & N. Roizen (Eds.), *Children with disabilities* (6th ed., pp. 345–365). Baltimore, MD: Paul H. Brookes.

Glanzman, M., & Blum, N. (2008). Genetics, imaging, and neurochemistry in attention-deficit/hyperactivity disorder. In P. Accardo (Ed.), *Capute & Accardo's neurodevelopmental disabilities in infancy and childhood* (3rd ed., Vol. 2, pp. 617–637). Baltimore, MD: Paul H. Brookes.

Glanzman, M., & Sell, N. (2013). Attention deficit and hyperactivity. In M. Batshaw, N. Roizen, & G. Lotrecchiano (Eds.), *Children with disabilities* (7th ed., pp. 369–402). Baltimore, MD: Paul H. Brookes.

Goldstein, S. (2011). Attention-deficit/hyperactivity disorder. In S. Goldstein & C. Reynolds (Eds.), *Handbook of neurodevelopmental and genetic disorders in children* (2nd ed., pp. 131–150). New York, NY: Guilford Press.

Glynn, E., Thomas, J., & Shee, S. (1973). Behavioral self-control of on-task behavior in an elementary classroom. *Journal of Applied Behavior Analysis, 6*(1), 105–113.

Graham-Day, K., Gardner, R., & Hsin, Y. (2010). Increasing on-task behaviors of high school students with attention deficit hyperactivity disorder. *Education and Treatment of Children, 33*(2), 205–221.

Hallahan, D., Lloyd, J., Kauffman, J., Weiss, M., & Martinez, E. (2005). *Learning disabilities: Foundations, characteristics, and effective teaching* (3rd ed.). Boston, MA: Pearson Education.

Hammerness, P. (2009). *ADHD*. Westport, CT: Greenwood Press.

Harris, K., Friedlander, B., Saddler, B., Frizzelle, R., & Graham, S. (2005). Self-monitoring of attention versus self-monitoring of academic performance: Effects among students with ADHD in general education classroom. *Journal of Special Education, 39*(3), 145–156.

Honos-Webb, L. (2005). *The gift of ADHD*. Oakland, CA: New Harbinger.

Johnson, L., & Johnson, C. (1999). Teaching students to regulate their own behavior. *Teaching Exceptional Children, 31*(4), 6–10.

Jones, C., & Teach, J. (2006). Impact of AD/HD on elementary students. In C. Dendy (Ed.), *CHADD educator's manual on attention-deficit/hyperactivity disorder* (pp. 61–72). Landover, MD: CHADD.

Katusic, S., Barbaresi, W., Colligan, R., Weaver, A., Leibson, C., & Jacobsen, S. (2005). Psychostimulant treatment and risk for substance abuse among young adults with a history of attention-deficit/hyperactivity disorder: A population-based, birth cohort study. *Journal of Child and Adolescent Psychopharmacology, 15*(5), 764–776.

Kauffman, J., & Landrum, T. (2013). *Characteristics of emotional and behavioral disorders of children and youth* (10th ed.). Boston, MA: Pearson Education.

Lerner, J., & Johns, B. (2012). *Learning disabilities and related mild disabilities* (12th ed.). Belmont, CA: Wadsworth/Cengage Learning.

Lerner, J., & Lowenthal, B. (1993). Attention deficit disorders: New responsibilities for the special educator. *Learning Disabilities: A Multidisciplinary Journal, 4*(1), 1–8.

Makris, N., Biederman, J., Monuteaux, M., & Seidman, L. (2009). Towards conceptualizing a neural-systems based anatomy of attention-deficit/hyperactivity disorder. *Developmental Neuroscience, 31*(1–2), 36–49.

Martin, N., Levy, F., Pieka, J., & Hay, D. (2006). A genetic study of attention deficit hyperactivity disorder, conduct disorder, oppositional defiant disorder and reading disability: Aetiological overlaps and implications. *International Journal of Disability, Development and Education, 53*, 21–34.

McKinley, L., & Stormont, M. (2008). The school supports checklist: Identifying support needs and barriers for children with ADHD. *Teaching Exceptional Children, 41*(2), 14–19.

Mercer, C., & Pullen, P. (2009). *Students with learning disabilities* (7th ed.). Upper Saddle River, NJ: Pearson Education.

Mill, J., Caspi, A., Williams, B., Craig, I., Taylor, A., Polo-Tomas, M., . . . Moffit, T. (2006). Prediction of heterogeneity in intelligence and adult prognosis by genetic polymorphisms in the dopamine system among children with attention-deficit/hyperactivity disorder. *Archives of General Psychiatry, 63*, 462–469.

MTA Cooperative Group. (2004). National Institute of Mental Health multimodal treatment study of ADHD follow up: 24-month outcomes of treatment strategies for attention-deficit/hyperactivity disorder. *Pediatrics 113*(4), 754–761.

Murphy, K., Barkley, R., & Bush, T. (2002). Young adults with attention deficit hyperactivity disorder: Subtype differences in educational and clinical history. *Journal of Nervous and Mental Disorders, 19*, 147–157.

National Center for Health Statistics. (2010). *Summary health statistics for U.S. children: National health interview survey, 2009*. Hyattsville, MD: Author.

National Dissemination Center for Children with Disabilities. (2012). *Fact Sheet No. 19: Attention deficit/hyperactivity disorder*. Washington, DC: Author.

National Institute of Mental Health. (2008). *Attention deficit hyperactivity disorder*. Bethesda, MD: Author.

Nikolas, M., & Burt, S. (2010). Genetic and environmental influences on ADHD symptom dimensions of inattention and hyperactivity: A meta-analysis. *Journal of Abnormal Psychology, 119*(1), 1–17.

Scheffler, R., Brown, T., Fulton, B., Hinshaw, S., Levine, P., & Stone, S. (2009). Positive association between attention-deficit/hyperactivity disorder medication use and academic achievement during elementary school. *Pediatrics, 123*(5), 1273–1279.

Shaw, P., & Rubin, C. (2009). New insights into attention-deficit/hyperactivity disorder using structural neuroimaging. *Current Psychiatry Reports, 11*(5), 393–398.

Silver, L. (1990). Attention deficit hyperactivity disorder: Is it a learning disability or a related disorder? *Journal of Learning Disabilities, 23,* 394–397.

Smith, T., Polloway, E., Patton, J., & Dowdy, C. (2008). *Teaching children with special needs in inclusive settings* (5th ed.). Needham Heights, MA: Allyn & Bacon.

Smith, T., Polloway, E., Patton, J., & Dowdy, C. (2012). *Teaching children with special needs in inclusive settings* (6th ed.). Needham Heights, MA: Allyn & Bacon.

Snider, V., Busch, T., & Arrowood, L. (2003). Teacher knowledge of stimulant medication. *Remedial and Special Education, 24*(1), 46–56.

Stein, M., & Shin, D. (2008). Disorders of attention: Diagnosis. In P. Accardo (Ed.), *Capute & Accardo's neurodevelopmental disabilities in infancy and childhood* (3rd ed., Vol. 2, pp. 639–656). Baltimore, MD: Paul H. Brookes.

Still, G. (1902). Some abnormal psychical conditions in children. *Lancet, 1,* 1008–1012, 1077–1082, 1163–1168.

Strauss, A., & Werner, H. (1942). Disorders of conceptual thinking in the brain-injured child. *Journal of Nervous and Mental Disease, 98,* 153–172.

Szwed, K., & Bouck, E. (2013). Clicking away: Using a student response system to self-monitor behavior in a general education classroom. *Journal of Special Education Technology, 28*(2), 1–12.

U.S. Department of Education. (2005). *Twenty-fifth annual report to Congress on the implementation of the Individuals with Disabilities Education Act* (Vol. 2). Washington, DC: U.S. Government Printing Office.

U.S. Department of Education. (2008a). *Identifying and treating attention deficit hyperactivity disorders: A resource for school and home.* Washington, DC: Author.

U.S. Department of Education. (2008b). *Teaching children with attention deficit hyperactivity disorders: Instructional strategies and practices.* Washington, DC: Author.

U.S. Department of Education. (2013). *IDEA data.* Retrieved May 26, 2013, from https://www.ideadata.org/PartBData.asp

Vaidya, C., & Stollstorff, M. (2008). Cognitive neuroscience of attention deficit hyperactivity disorder: Current status and working hypotheses. *Developmental Disabilities Research Reviews, 14*(4), 261–267.

Vaughn, S., Bos, C., & Schumm, J. (2014). *Teaching exceptional, diverse, and at-risk students in the general education classroom* (6th ed.). Upper Saddle River, NJ: Pearson Education.

Volkow, N., Wang, G., Kollins, S., Wigal, T., Newcorn, J., Telang, F., . . . Swanson, J. (2009). Evaluating dopamine reward pathway in ADHD: Clinical implications. *Journal of the American Medical Association, 302*(10), 1084.

Volkow, N., Wang, G., Newcorn, J., Telang, E., Solanto, M., Fowler, J., . . . Swanson, J. (2007). Depressed dopamine activity in caudate and preliminary evidence of limbic involvement in adults with attention-deficit/hyperactivity disorder. *Archives of General Psychiatry, 64*(8), 932–940.

Weiss, S., & Illes, T. (2006). Advanced strategies for challenging behaviors. In C. Dendy (Ed.), *CHADD educator's manual on attention-deficit/hyperactivity disorder* (pp. 73–79). Landover, MD: CHADD.

Werner, H., & Strauss, A. (1941). Pathology of figure–background relation in the child. *Journal of Abnormal and Social Psychology, 36,* 236–248.

Weyandt, L. (2007). *An ADHD primer* (2nd ed.). Mahwah, NJ: Erlbaum.

Weyandt, L. (2009). Executive functions and attention deficit hyperactivity disorder. *The ADHD Report, 17*(6), 1–7.

Wicks-Nelson, R., & Israel, A. (2013). *Abnormal child and adolescent psychology* (8th ed.). Boston, MA: Pearson Education.

Wilens, T., Faraone, S., Biederman, J., & Gunawardene, S. (2003). Does stimulant therapy of attention deficit/hyperactivity disorder beget later substance abuse? *Pediatrics, 111*(1), 179–185.

Chapter 9

Abelev, M. (2009). Advancing out of poverty: Social class worldview and its relation to resiliency. *Journal of Adolescent Research, 24*(1), 114–141.

Alberto, P., & Troutman, A. (2013). *Applied behavior analysis for teachers* (9th ed.). Upper Saddle River, NJ: Pearson Education.

Allen-DeBoer, R., Malmgren, K., & Glass, M. (2006). Reading instruction for youth with emotional and behavioral disorders in a juvenile correctional facility. *Behavioral Disorders, 32*(1), 18–28.

Amato-Zech, N., Hoff, K., & Dorepke, K. (2006). Increasing on-task behavior in the classroom extension of self-monitoring strategies. *Psychology in the Schools, 43*(2), 211–221.

American Psychiatric Association. (2013). *Diagnostic and statistical manual of mental disorders* (5th ed.). Washington, DC: Author.

Austin, K., & Wittig, K. (2013). Individualized transition planning. In P. Wehman (Ed.), *Life beyond the classroom* (5th ed., pp. 97–141). Baltimore, MD: Paul H. Brookes.

Barton-Arwood, S., Wehby, J., & Falk, K. (2005). Reading instruction for elementary-age students with emotional and behavioral disorders: Academic and behavioral outcomes. *Exceptional Children, 72*(1), 7–27.

Beard, K., & Sugai, G. (2004). First step to success: An early intervention for elementary children at risk for antisocial behavior. *Behavioral Disorders, 29*(4), 396–398.

Blood, E., Johnson, J., Ridenour, L., Simmons, K., & Crouch, S. (2011). Using an iPod Touch to teach social and self-management skills to an elementary student with emotional/behavioral disorders. *Education and Treatment of Children, 34*(3), 299–322.

Bower, E. (1960). *Early identification of emotionally disturbed children in school.* Springfield, IL: Charles C. Thomas.

Bower, E. (1981). *Early identification of emotionally handicapped children in school* (3rd ed.). Springfield, IL: Charles C. Thomas.

Bower, E. (1982). Defining emotional disturbance: Public policy and research. *Psychology in the Schools, 19,* 55–60.

Bradshaw, C., Mitchell, M., & Leaf, P. (2010). Examining the effects of schoolwide positive behavioral interventions and supports on student outcomes. *Journal of Positive Behavior Interventions, 12*(3), 133–148.

Cagnon, J., & Barber, B. (2010). Characteristics of and services provided to youth in secure care facilities. *Behavioral Disorders, 36*(1), 7–19.

Chandler, L., & Dahlquist, C. (2010). *Functional assessment: Strategies to prevent and remediate challenging behavior in school settings* (3rd ed.). Upper Saddle River, NJ: Pearson Education.

Children's Defense Fund. (2012). *The state of America's children.* Washington, DC: Author.

Chitiyo, M., & Wheeler, J. (2009). Challenges faced by school teachers in implementing positive behavioral supports in their school systems. *Remedial and Special Education, 30*(1), 6–14.

Cooper, J., Heron, T., & Heward, W. (2007). *Applied behavior analysis* (2nd ed.). Upper Saddle River, NJ: Pearson Education.

Council for Children with Behavioral Disorders. (1990). Position paper on the provision of service to children with conduct disorders. *Behavioral Disorders, 15*(3), 180–189.

Council for Children with Behavioral Disorders. (2000, October). *Draft position paper on terminology and definition of emotional or behavioral disorders.* Reston, VA: Author.

Council for Children with Behavioral Disorders. (2009a, July). *Position summary: The use of physical restraint procedures in school settings.* Reston, VA: Council for Exceptional Children.

Council for Children with Behavioral Disorders. (2009b, July). *Position summary: The use of seclusion in school settings.* Reston, VA: Council for Exceptional Children.

Courtad, C., & Bouck, E. (2012). Technology and students with emotional and behavioural disorders. In J. Bakken, F. Obiakor, & A. Rotatori (Eds.), *Advances in special education—Behavioral disorders: Practice concerns and students with EBD* (Vol. 23, pp. 179–205). Bingley, UK: Emerald Group.

Crundwell, R., & Killu, K. (2007). Understanding and accommodating students with depression in the classroom. *Teaching Exceptional Children, 40*(1), 48–54.

Cullinan, D. (2007). *Students with emotional and behavioral disorders* (2nd ed.). Upper Saddle River, NJ: Pearson Education.

Cullinan, D., Evans, C., Epstein, M., & Ryser, G. (2003). Characteristics of emotional disturbance of elementary school students. *Behavioral Disorders, 28*(2), 94–110.

Despert, J. (1965). *The emotionally disturbed child: Then and now.* New York, NY: Brunner.

DeValenzuela, J., Copeland, S., Qi, C., & Park, M. (2006). Examining educational equity: Revising the disproportionate representation of minority students in special education. *Exceptional Children, 72*(4), 425–441.

Donovan, S., & Nickerson, A. (2007). Strength-based versus traditional social-emotional reports: Impact on multidisciplinary team members' perceptions. *Behavioral Disorders, 32*(4), 228–237.

Dunlap, G., Strain, P., Fox, L., Carta, J., Conroy, M., Smith, B., . . . Sowell, C. (2006). Prevention and intervention with young children's challenging behavior: Perspectives regarding current knowledge. *Behavioral Disorders, 32*(1), 29–45.

Eber, L., Breen, K., Rose, J., Unizycki, R., & London, T. (2008). Wraparound: A tertiary level intervention for students with emotional/behavioral needs. *Teaching Exceptional Children, 40*(6), 16–22.

Eber, L., Sugai, G., Smith, C., & Scott, T. (2002). Wraparound and positive behavioral interventions and supports in the schools. *Journal of Emotional and Behavioral Disorders, 10*(3), 171–180.

Epstein, J., Willis, M., Conners, K., & Johnson, D. (2001). Use of a technological prompting device to aid a student with attention deficit hyperactivity disorder to initiate and complete daily tasks: An exploratory study. *Journal of Special Education Technology, 16*(1), 19–28.

Epstein, M. (2002). *Behavioral and Emotional Rating Scale* (2nd ed.). Austin, TX: Pro-Ed.

Erickson, M., Stage, S., & Nelson, J. (2006). Naturalistic study of the behavior of students with EBD referred for functional behavioral assessment. *Journal of Emotional and Behavioral Disorders, 14*(1), 31–40.

Fairbanks, S., Sugai, G., Guardino, D., & Lathrop, M. (2007). Response to intervention: Examining classroom behavior support in second grade. *Exceptional Children, 73*(3), 288–310.

Fitzpatrick, M., & Knowlton, E. (2009). Bringing evidence-based self-directed intervention practices to the trenches for students with emotional and behavior disorders. *Preventing School Failure, 53*(4), 253–266.

Forgan, J., & Gonzalez-DeHass, A. (2004). How to infuse social skills training into literacy instruction. *Teaching Exceptional Children, 36*(6), 24–30.

Forness, S., & Kavale, K. (2000). Emotional or behavioral disorders: Background and current status of E/BD terminology and definition. *Behavioral Disorders, 25*(3), 264–269.

Friend, M., & Bursuck, W. (2012). *Including students with special needs* (6th ed.). Upper Saddle River, NJ: Pearson Education.

Gargiulo, R., & Kilgo, J. (2014). *An introduction to young children with special needs* (4th ed.). Belmont, CA: Wadsworth/Cengage Learning.

Gollnick, D., & Chinn, P. (2013). *Multicultural education in a pluralistic society* (9th ed.). Upper Saddle River, NJ: Pearson Education.

Griffith, A., Trout, A., Hagaman, J., & Harper, J. (2008). Interventions to improve the literacy functioning of adolescents with emotional and/or behavior disorders: A review of the literature between 1965 and 2005. *Behavioral Disorders, 33*(3), 124–140.

Gulchak, D. (2008). Using a mobile handheld computer to teach a student with an emotional and behavioral disorder to self-monitor attention. *Education & Treatment of Children, 31*(4), 567–581.

Gumpel, T., & David, S. (2000). Exploring the efficacy of self-regulatory training as a possible alternative to social skills training. *Behavioral Disorders, 25*(2), 131–146.

Gunter, P., Shores, R., Jack, S., Rasmussen, S., & Flowers, J. (1995). Teacher/student proximity: A strategy for classroom control through teacher movement. *Teaching Exceptional Children, 28*(1), 12–14.

Harniss, M., & Epstein, M. (2005). Strength-based assessment in children's mental health. In M. Epstein, K. Kurash, & A. Duchnowski (Eds.), *Outcomes for children and youth with emotional and behavioral disorders and their families* (2nd ed., pp. 125–141). Austin, TX: Pro-Ed.

Hayman, M. (1939). The interrelations between mental defect and mental disorder. *Journal of Mental Science, 85*, 1183–1193.

Janas, M. (2002). Twenty ways to build resiliency. *Intervention in School and Clinic, 38*(2), 117–121.

Janney, R., & Snell, M. (2008). *Behavioral support* (2nd ed.). Baltimore, MD: Paul H. Brookes.

Jensen, M. (2005). *Introduction to emotional and behavioral disorders.* Upper Saddle River, NJ: Pearson Education.

Kauffman, J. (1981). *Characteristics of children's behavioral disorders* (2nd ed.). Columbus, OH: Merrill.

Kauffman, J. (2010). Commentary: Current status of the field and future directions. *Behavioral Disorders, 35*(2), 180–184.

Kauffman J., Bruce, A., & Lloyd, J. (2012). Response to intervention (RTI) and students with emotional and behavioral disorders. In J. Bakken, F. Obiakor, & A. Rotatori (Eds.), *Advances in special education–Behavioral disorders: Practice concerns and students with EBD* (Vol. 23, pp. 107–128). Bingley, UK: Emerald Group.

Kauffman, J., & Brigham, F. (2009). *Working with troubled children.* Verona, WI: Attainment.

Kauffman, J., & Landrum, T. (2013). *Characteristics of emotional and behavioral disorders of children and youth* (10th ed.). Upper Saddle River, NJ: Pearson Education.

Kauffman, J., Nelson, C., Simpson, R., & Mock, D. (2001). Contemporary issues. In J. Kauffman & D. Hallahan (Eds.), *Handbook of special education* (pp. 15–26). New York, NY: Routledge.

Kendziora, K. (2004). Early intervention for emotional and behavioral disorders. In R. Rutherford, M. Quinn, &

S. Mathur (Eds.), *Handbook of research in emotional and behavioral disorders* (pp. 327–351). New York, NY: Guilford Press.

Kerr, M., & Nelson, C. (2010). *Strategies for managing behavior problems in the classroom* (6th ed.). Upper Saddle River, NJ: Pearson Education.

Landrum, T. (2011). Emotional and behavioral disorders. In J. Kauffman & D. Hallahan (Eds.), *Handbook of special education* (pp. 209–220). New York, NY: Routledge.

Landrum, T., Katsiyannis, A., & Archwamety, T. (2004). An analysis of placement and exit patterns of students with emotional or behavioral disorders. *Behavioral Disorders, 29*(2), 140–153.

Lane, K. (2003). Identifying young students at risk for antisocial behavior: The utility of "teachers as tests." *Behavioral Disorders, 28*(4), 360–369.

Lane K., Carter, E., Pierson, M., & Glaeser, B. (2006). Academic, social, and behavioral characteristics of high school students with emotional disturbances and learning disabilities. *Journal of Emotional and Behavioral Disorders, 14*(2), 108–117.

Lane, K., Kalberg, J., & Edwards, C. (2008). An examination of school-wide interventions with primary level efforts conducted in elementary schools: Implications for school psychologists. In D. Molina (Ed.), *School psychology: 21st century issues and challenges* (pp. 253–278). New York, NY: Nova Science.

Lane, K., Little, M., Redding-Rhodes, J., Phillips, A., & Welsh, M. (2007). Outcomes of a teacher-led reading intervention for elementary students at risk for behavioral disorders. *Exceptional Children, 74*(1), 47–70.

Lane, K., & Menzies, H. (2010). Reading and writing interventions for students with and at risk for emotional and behavioral disorders: An introduction. *Behavioral Disorders, 35*(2), 82–85.

Lane, K., Robertson, E., & Graham-Bailey, M. (2006). An examination of school-wide interventions with primary level efforts conducted in secondary schools: Methodological considerations. In T. Scruggs & M. Mastropieri (Eds.), *Applications of research methodology* (Vol. 19, pp. 157–199). Oxford, UK: Elsevier/JAI Press.

Lane, K., Wehby, J., & Barton-Atwood, S. (2005). Students with and at risk for emotional and behavioral disorders: Meeting their social and academic needs. *Preventing School Failure, 49*(2), 6–9.

Lane, K., Weisenbach, J., Phillips, A., & Wehby, J. (2007). Designing, implementing, and evaluating function-based interventions using a systematic, feasible approach. *Behavioral Disorders, 32*(2), 122–139.

Larrivee, B. (2009). *Authentic classroom management.* Upper Saddle River, NJ: Pearson Education.

Lee, S., Palmer, S., & Wehmeyer, M. (2009). Goal setting and self-monitoring for students with disabilities: Practical tips and ideas for teachers. *Intervention in School and Clinic, 44*(3), 139–145.

Lerner, J., & Johns, B. (2012). *Learning disabilities and related mild disabilities* (12th ed.). Belmont, CA: Wadsworth/Cengage Learning.

Lewis, C. (1974). Introduction: Landmarks. In J. Kauffman & C. Lewis (Eds.), *Teaching exceptional children with behavior disorders: Personal perspectives* (pp. 2–23). Columbus, OH: Merrill.

Maag, J. (2006). Social skills training for students with emotional and behavioral disorders: A review of reviews. *Behavioral Disorders, 32*(1), 5–17.

McIntyre, T., & Forness, S. (1996). Is there a new definition yet or are our kids still seriously emotionally disturbed? *Beyond Behavior, 7*(3), 4–9.

Mihalas, S., Morse, W., Allsopp, D., & McHatton, P. (2009). Cultivating caring relationships between teachers and secondary students with emotional and behavioral disorders: Implications for research and practice. *Remedial and Special Education, 30*(2), 108–125.

Miller, M., Lane, K., & Wehby, J. (2005). Social skills instruction for students with high incidence disabilities: A school-based intervention to address acquisition deficits. *Preventing School Failure, 49*(2), 27–29.

Milstein, M., & Henry, D. (2000). *Spreading resiliency: Making it happen for schools and communities.* Thousand Oaks, CA: Corwin Press.

National Institute of Mental Health. (2010). *Depression in children and adolescents.* Retrieved March 1, 2010, from http://www.nimh.nih.gov/

health/topics/depression/depres sion-in-children-and-adolescents .shtml

National Institute of Mental Health. (2013). *The numbers count: Mental disorders in America.* Retrieved June 12, 2013, from http://www.nimh.nih. gov/health/publications/the-numbers-count-mental-disorders-in-america/ index.shtml

Nelson, J., Benner, G., & Cheney, D. (2005). An investigation of the language skills of students with emotional disturbance served in public schools. *Journal of Special Education, 39*(2), 97–105.

Nelson, J., Benner, G., Lane, K., & Smith, B. (2004). An investigation of the academic achievement of K–12 students with emotional and behavioral disorders in public school settings. *Exceptional Children, 71*(1), 59–73.

Nelson, J., Benner, G., Neill, S., & Stage, S. (2006). Interrelationships among language skills, externalizing behavior and academic fluency and their impact on the academic skills of students with ED. *Journal of Emotional and Behavioral Disorders, 14*(4), 209–216.

Nelson, J., Benner, G., & Rogers-Adkinson, D. (2003). An investigation of the characteristics of K–12 students with comorbid emotional disturbance and significant language deficits in public school settings. *Behavioral Disorders, 29*(1), 25–33.

Newcomer, P. (2011). *Understanding and teaching emotionally disturbed children and adolescents* (4th ed.). Austin, TX: Pro-Ed.

Oswald, D. (2003). Response to Forness: Parting reflections on education of children with emotional or behavioral disorders. *Behavioral Disorders, 28*(3), 202–204.

Polloway, E., Patton, J., Serna, L., & Bailey, J. (2012). *Strategies for teaching learners with special needs* (10th ed.). Upper Saddle River, NJ: Pearson Education.

Quay, H., & Peterson, D. (1996). *Manual for the Revised Behavior Problem Checklist.* Lutz, FL: Psychological Assessment Resources.

Quinn, M., Rutherford, R., Leone, P., Osher, D., & Poirer, J. (2005). Youth with disabilities in juvenile corrections: A national survey. *Exceptional Children, 71*(3), 339–345.

Rie, H. (1971). Historical perspectives of concepts of child psychopathology. In H. Rie (Ed.), *Perspectives in child psychopathology* (pp. 3–50). New York, NY: Aldine-Atherton.

Rodgers-Adkinson, D. (2003). Language processing in children with emotional disorders. *Behavioral Disorders, 29*(1), 43–47.

Rosenberg, M., Wilson, R., Maheady, L., & Sindelar, P. (2004). *Educating students with behavior disorders* (3rd ed.). Needham Heights, MA: Allyn & Bacon.

Rosenblum, K., Dayton, C., & Muzik, M. (2009). Infant social and emotional development. In C. Zeanah, Jr. (Ed.), *Handbook of infant mental health* (3rd ed., pp. 80–103). New York, NY: Guilford Press.

Rubin, R., & Balow, B. (1971). Learning and behavior disorders: A longitudinal study. *Exceptional Children, 38*(4), 293–299.

Rutter, M. (2006). *Genes and behavior: Nature-nurture interplay explained.* Malden, MA: Blackwell.

Sabornie, E., & deBettencourt, L. (2009). *Teaching students with mild disabilities at the secondary level* (3rd ed.). Upper Saddle River, NJ: Pearson Education.

Safford, P., & Safford, E. (1996). *A history of childhood and disability.* New York, NY: Teachers College Press.

Salend, S. (2011). *Creating inclusive classrooms* (7th ed.). Upper Saddle River, NJ: Pearson Education.

Satcher, D. (1999). *Mental health: A report of the surgeon general.* Washington, DC: U.S. Department of Public Health Services.

Savage, T. (1999). *Teaching self-control through management and discipline* (2nd ed.). Needham Heights, MA: Allyn & Bacon.

Scheuermann, B., & Hall, J. (2012). *Positive behavioral supports for the classroom* (2nd ed.). Upper Saddle River, NJ: Pearson Education.

Scruggs, T., & Mastropieri, M. (2000). Mnemonic strategies for students with behavior disorders: Memory for learning and behavior. *Beyond Behavior, 10*(1), 13–17.

Shaw, D., Gilliom, M., & Giovannelli, J. (2005). Aggressive behavior disorders. In C. Zeanah, Jr. (Ed.), *Handbook of infant mental health* (2nd ed., pp. 397–411). New York, NY: Guilford Press.

Simonsen, B., Britton, L., & Young, D. (2010). School-wide positive behavior support in an alternative school setting: A case study. *Journal of Positive Behavior Interventions, 12*(3), 180–191.

Simonsen, B., Eber, L., Black, A., Sugai, G., Lewandowski, H., Sims, B., . . . Myers, D. (2012). Illinois statewide positive behavioral interventions and supports: Evolution and impact on student outcomes across years. *Journal of Positive Behavior Interventions, 14*(1), 5–15.

Singer, G., Maul, C., Wang, M., & Ethridge, B. (2011). Resilience in families of children with disabilities. In J. Kauffman & D. Hallahan (Eds.), *Handbook of special education* (pp. 654–667). New York, NY: Routledge.

Smith, T., Polloway, E., Patton, J., & Dowdy, C. (2012). *Teaching students with special needs in inclusive settings* (6th ed.). Upper Saddle River, NJ: Pearson Education.

Sprague, J., & Walker, H. (2000). Early identification and intervention for youth with antisocial and violent behavior. *Exceptional Children, 66*(3), 367–379.

Stichter, J., Conroy, M., & Kauffman, J. (2008). *An introduction to students with high-incidence disabilities.* Upper Saddle River, NJ: Pearson Education.

Sugai, G., Simonsen, B., & Horner, R. (2008). Schoolwide positive behavior supports. *Teaching Exceptional Children, 40*(6), 5–6.

Szwed, K., & Bouck, E. (2013). Clicking away: Using a student response system to self-monitor behavior in a general education classroom. *Journal of Special Education Technology, 28*(2), 1–12.

Taylor-Richardson, K., Helflinger, C., & Brown, T. (2006). Experience of strain among of caregivers responsible for children with serious emotional and behavioral disorders. *Journal of Emotional and Behavioral Disorders, 14*(3), 157–168.

Turnbull, A., Turnbull, R., Erwin, E., Soodak, L., & Shrogren, K. (2011). *Families, professionals, and exceptionality* (6th ed.). Upper Saddle River, NJ: Pearson Education.

U.S. Department of Education. (1980). *Second annual report to Congress on the implementation of Public Law 94-142.* Washington, DC: Author.

U.S. Department of Education. (2000). *Safeguarding our children: An action guide*. Washington, DC: Author.

U.S. Department of Education. (2012). *Thirty-first annual report to Congress on the implementation of the Individuals with Disabilities Education Act, 2009*. Washington, DC: U.S. Government Printing Office.

U.S. Department of Education. (2013). *Historical state-level IDEA data files*. Retrieved November 14, 2013, from http://tadnet.public.tadnet.org/pages/712

Vaughn, S., & Bos, C. (2012). *Strategies for teaching students with learning and behavior problems* (8th ed.). Upper Saddle River, NJ: Pearson Education.

Vaughn, S., Bos, C., & Schumm, J. (2014). *Teaching exceptional, diverse, and at-risk students in the general education classroom* (6th ed.). Upper Saddle River, NJ: Pearson Education.

Vaughn, S., & Lancelotta, G. (1990). Teaching interpersonal social skills to low accepted students: Peer-pairing versus no peer-pairing. *Journal of School Psychology, 28*(3), 181–188.

Wagner, M., & Davis, M. (2006). How are we preparing students with emotional disturbance in the transition to young adulthood? Findings from the National Longitudinal Transition Study-2. *Journal of Emotional and Behavioral Disorders, 14*(2), 86–98.

Wagner, M., Kutash, K., Duchnowski, A., Epstein, M., & Sumi, W. (2005). The children and youth we serve: A national picture of the characteristics of students with emotional disturbances receiving special education. *Journal of Emotional and Behavioral Disorders, 13*(2), 79–96.

Wakschlag, L., & Danis, B. (2009). Characterizing early childhood disruptive behavior. In C. Zeanah, Jr. (Ed.), *Handbook of infant mental health* (3rd ed., pp. 392–408). New York, NY: Guilford Press.

Walker, H., Kavanagh, K., Stiller, B., Golly, A., Severson, H., & Feil, E. (1997). *First Step to Success: An early intervention program for antisocial kindergartners*. Longmont, CO: Sopris West.

Walker, H., Severson, H., Seeley, J., Small, J., Golly, A., Frey, A., . . . Forness, S. (2012). The evidence base of the First Step to Success early intervention for preventing emerging antisocial behavior patterns. Retrieved June 26, 2013, from http://www.firststeptosuccess.org/

Webber, J., & Plotts, C. (2008). *Emotional and behavioral disorders: Theory and practice* (5th ed.). Boston, MA: Allyn & Bacon.

Wehby, J., Falk, K., Barton-Arwood, S., Lane, K., & Cooley, C. (2003). The impact of comprehensive reading instruction on the academic and social behavior of students with emotional and behavioral disorders. *Journal of Emotional and Behavioral Disorders, 11*(4), 225–238.

Wehman, P., Sutherland, K., & Achola, E. (2013). Applications for youth with emotional and behavior disorders. In P. Wehman (Ed.), *Life beyond the classroom* (5th ed., pp. 419–445). Baltimore, MD: Paul H. Brookes.

White, C., Palmer, K., & Huffman, L. (2003). Technology instruction for students with emotional and behavioral disorders attending a therapeutic day school. *Beyond Behavior, 13*(1), 23–27.

Whitted, S. (2011). Understanding how social and emotional skill deficits contribute to school failure. *Preventing School Failure, 55*(1), 10–16.

Wicks-Nelson, R., & Israel, A. (2013). *Abnormal child and adolescent psychology* (8th ed.). Upper Saddle River, NJ: Pearson Education.

Young, E., Sabbah, H., Young, B., Reiser, M., & Richardson, M. (2010). Gender differences and similarities in a screening process for emotional and behavioral risks in secondary schools. *Journal of Emotional and Behavioral Disorders, 18*(4), 225–235.

Zigmond, N. (2006). Twenty-four months after high school: Paths taken by youth diagnosed with severe emotional and behavioral disorders. *Journal of Emotional and Behavioral Disorders, 14*(2), 91–107.

Chapter 10

American Psychiatric Association. (2013). *Diagnostic and statistical manual of mental disorders* (5th ed.). Arlington, VA: Author.

Astington, J., & Barricult, T. (2001). Children's theory of mind: How young children come to understand that people have thoughts and feelings. *Infants and Young Children, 13*(1), 1–12.

Autism Society of America. (2013a). *About autism*. Retrieved July 6, 2013, from http://www.autism-society.org/about-autism/

Autism Society of America. (2013b). *Living with autism*. Retrieved August 8, 2013, from http://www.autism-society.org/living-with-autism/lifespan/school-age/educational-planning.html

Ayres, K., Mechling, L., & Sansosti, F. (2013). The use of mobile technologies to assist with life skills/independence of students with moderate/severe intellectual disability and/or autism spectrum disorders: Considerations for the future of school psychology. *Psychology in the Schools, 50*(3), 259–271.

Ball, L., Bilyeu, D., Prentice, C., & Beukelman, D. (2005). Augmentative and alternative communication: Infusing communication in an academic setting. In D. Edyburn, K. Higgins, & R. Boone (Eds.), *Handbook of special education technology: Research and practice* (pp. 423–451). Whitefish Bay, WI: Knowledge by Design.

Bettleheim, B. (1967). *The empty fortress: Infantile autism and the birth of self*. New York, NY: Free Press.

Bondy, A. (2012). The unusual suspects: Myths and misconceptions associated with PECS. *The Psychological Record, 62*(4), 789–816.

Boucher, J. (2012). Putting theory of mind in its place: Psychological explanations of the socio-emotional-communicative impairments in autistic spectrum disorders. *Autism, 16*(3), 226–246.

Bouck, E., Satsangi, R., Doughty, T., & Courtney, W. (2013). Virtual and concrete manipulatives: A comparison of approaches for solving mathematics problems for students with autism spectrum disorder. *Journal of Autism and Developmental Disorders*. doi:10.1007/s10803-013-1863-2

Boutot, E., & Myles, B. (2011). *Autism spectrum disorders*. Upper Saddle River, NJ: Pearson Education.

Brobst, J., Clopton, J., & Hendrick, S. (2009). Parenting children with autism spectrum disorders. *Focus on Autism and Other Developmental Disabilities, 24*(1), 38–49.

Centers for Disease Control and Prevention. (2012). Prevalence of autism spectrum disorders: Autism and Developmental Disabilities Monitoring Network, 14 sites, United States, 2008. *Morbidity and Mortality Weekly Report, 61*(3), 1–19.

Control and Prevention. (2013). *Autism spectrum disorders (ASDs).* Retrieved July 10, 2013, from http://www.cdc.gov/ncbddd/autism/index.html

Challman, T., Voigt, R., & Myers, S. (2008). Nonstandard therapies in developmental disabilities. In P. Accardo (Ed.), *Capute & Accardo's neurodevelopmental disabilities in infancy and childhood* (3rd ed., Vol. 2, pp. 721–741). Baltimore, MD: Paul H. Brookes.

Dahle, K. (2003a). Services to include young children with autism in the general classroom. *Early Childhood Education Journal, 31*(1), 65–70.

Dahle, K. (2003b). The clinical and educational systems: Differences and similarities. *Focus on Autism and Other Developmental Disabilities, 18*(4), 238–246, 256.

Dahle, K., & Gargiulo, R. (2003). Understanding Asperger disorder: A primer for early childhood educators. *Early Childhood Education Journal, 32*(3), 199–203.

Dougherty, J., Maloney, S., Wozniak, D., Rieger, M., Sonnenblick, L., Coppola, G., . . . Heintz, N. (2013). The disruption of *Celf6*, a gene identified by translational profiling of serotonergic neurons, results in autism-related behaviors. *Journal of Neuroscience, 33*(7), 2732–2753.

Edelson, M. (2006). Are the majority of children with autism mentally retarded? *Focus on Autism and Other Developmental Disabilities, 21*(2), 66–83.

Edelson, S. (2000). *Autistic savant.* Salem, OR: Center for the Study of Autism.

Ehlers, S., Gillberg, C., & Wing, L. (1999). A screening questionnaire for Asperger's syndrome and other high-functioning autism spectrum disorders in school-age children. *Journal of Autism and Developmental Disorders, 29*(2), 129–141.

Ekas, N., & Whitman, T. (2011). Adaptation to daily stress among mothers of children with an autism spectrum disorder: The role of daily positive affect. *Journal of Autism and Developmental Disorders, 41*(9), 1202–1213.

Freeman, B. (1999). *Diagnosis of the syndrome of autism: Questions parents ask.* Bethesda, MD: Autism Society of America.

Gabriels, R. (2011). Adolescent transition to adulthood and vocational issues. In D. Amaral, G. Dawson, & D. Geschwind (Eds.), *Autism spectrum disorders* (pp. 1167–1181). New York, NY: Oxford University Press.

Gallagher, P., Powell, T., & Rhodes, C. (2006). *Brothers & sisters* (3rd ed.). Baltimore, MD: Paul H. Brookes.

Gargiulo, R., & Kilgo, J. (2014). *An introduction to young children with special needs* (4th ed.). Belmont, CA: Wadsworth/Cengage Learning.

Gerhardt, P., & Holmes, D. (2005). Employment: Options and issues for adolescents and adults with autism spectrum disorders. In F. Volkmar, R. Paul, A. Klin, & D. Cohen (Eds.), *Handbook of autism and pervasive developmental disorders* (3rd ed., Vol. 2, pp. 1087–1101). Hoboken, NJ: Wiley.

Gerhardt, P., & Lainer, J. (2011). Addressing the needs of adolescents and adults with autism: A crisis on the horizon. *Journal of Contemporary Psychotherapy, 41*(1), 37–45.

Gong, L., Yan, Y., Xie, J., Liu, H., & Sun, X. (2012). Prediction of autism susceptibility genes based on association rules. *Journal of Neuroscience Research, 90*(6), 1119–1125.

Hall, L. (2013). *Autism spectrum disorders* (2nd ed.). Upper Saddle River, NJ: Pearson Education.

Handleman, J., & Harris, S. (Eds.). (2008). *Preschool education programs for children with autism* (3rd ed.). Austin, TX: Pro-Ed.

Heflin, L., & Alaimo, D. (2007). *Students with autism spectrum disorders.* Upper Saddle River, NJ: Pearson Education.

Hendricks, D., & Wehman, P. (2009). Transition from school to adulthood for youth with autism spectrum disorders. *Focus on Autism and Other Developmental Disabilities, 24*(2), 77–88.

Howlin, P., Goode, S., Hutton, J., & Rutter, M. (2004). Adult outcome for children with autism. *Journal of Child Psychology and Psychiatry, 45*(2), 212–229.

Hyman, S., & Levy, S. (2011). Dietary, complementary, and alternative therapies. In D. Amaral, G. Dawson, & D. Geschwind (Eds.), *Autism spectrum disorders* (pp. 1225–1238). New York, NY: Oxford University Press.

Hyman, S., & Levy, S. (2013). Autism spectrum disorders. In M. Batshaw, N. Roizen, & G. Lotrecchiano (Eds.), *Children with disabilities* (7th ed., pp. 345–367). Baltimore, MD: Paul H. Brookes.

Institute of Medicine. (2004). *Immunization safety review: Vaccines and autism.* Washington, DC: National Academies Press.

Institute of Medicine. (2011). *Adverse effects of vaccines: Evidence and causality.* Washington, DC: National Academies Press.

Johnson, C., & Myers, S. (2007). Identification and evaluation of children with autism spectrum disorders. *Pediatrics, 120*(5), 1183–1215.

Kanner, L. (1985). Autistic disturbance of affective contact. In A. Donnellan (Ed.), *Classic readings in autism* (pp. 11–50). New York, NY: Teachers College Press. (Original work published in 1943)

Klinger, L., O'Kelley, S., & Mussey, J. (2009). Assessment of intellectual functioning in autism spectrum disorders. In S. Goldstein, J. Naglieri, & S. Ozonoff (Eds.), *Assessment of autism spectrum disorders* (pp. 209–250). New York, NY: Guilford.

Kogan, M., Blumberg, S., Schieve, L., Boyle, C., Perrin, J., Ghandour, R., . . . van Dyck, P. (2009). Prevalence of parent-reported diagnosis of autism spectrum disorder among children in the US, 2007. *Pediatrics, 124*(5), 1395–1403.

LaVigna, G. (1985). Commentary on positive reinforcement and behavioral deficits of autistic children by C. Fester. In A. Donnellan (Ed.), *Classic readings in autism* (pp. 53–73). New York, NY: Teachers College Press.

Levy, S., Hyman, S., & Pinto-Martin, J. (2008). Autism spectrum disorders: Overview and diagnosis. In P. Accardo (Ed.), *Capute & Accardo's neurodevelopmental disabilities in infancy and childhood* (3rd ed., Vol. 2, pp. 495–511). Baltimore, MD: Paul H. Brookes.

Levy, S., Kim, A., & Olive, M. (2006). Interventions for young children with autism: A synthesis of the literature. *Focus on Autism and Other Developmental Disabilities, 21*(1), 55–62.

Levy, S., Kruger, H., & Hyman, S. (2008). Treatments for children with autism spectrum disorders. In P. Accardo (Ed.), *Capute & Accardo's neurodevelopmental disabilities in infancy and childhood* (3rd ed., Vol. 2, pp. 523–543). Baltimore, MD: Paul H. Brookes.

Lipkin, P., & Schertz, M. (2008). Early intervention and its efficacy. In P. Accardo (Ed.), *Capute & Accardo's neurodevelopmental disabilities in infancy and childhood* (3rd ed., Vol. 1, pp. 519–551). Baltimore, MD: Paul H. Brookes.

Lord, C., Rutter, M., DiLavore, P., Risi, S., Gotham, K., & Bishop, S. (2012). *Autism Diagnostic Observation Schedule* (2nd ed.). Torrance, CA: Western Psychological Services.

Lovaas, I. (1987). Behavioral treatment and normal educational and intellectual functioning in young autistic children. *Journal of Consulting and Clinical Psychology, 55*(1), 3–9.

Lovaas, I. (1993). The development of a treatment-research project for developmentally disabled and autistic children. *Journal of Applied Behavior Analysis, 26*(4), 617–630.

Marcus, L., Kunce, L., & Schopler, E. (2005). Working with families. In F. Volkmar, R. Paul, A. Klin, & D. Cohen (Eds.), *Handbook of autism and pervasive developmental disorders* (3rd ed., Vol. 2, pp. 1055–1086). Hoboken, NJ: Wiley.

Meadan, H., Stoner, J., & Angell, M. (2010). Review of literature related to the social, emotional, and behavioral adjustment of siblings of individuals with autism spectrum disorders. *Journal of Developmental and Physical Disabilities, 22*(1), 83–100.

Mechling, L., Gast, D., & Seid, N. (2010). Evaluation of a personal digital assistant as a self-prompting device for increasing multi-step task completion by students with moderate intellectual disabilities. *Education and Training in Autism and Developmental Disabilities, 45*(3), 422–439.

Minshew, N., Scherf, K., Behrmann, M., & Humphreys, K. (2011). Autism as a developmental neurological disorder: New insights from functional neuroimaging. In D. Amaral, G. Dawson, &

D. Geschwind (Eds.), *Autism spectrum disorders* (pp. 632–650). New York, NY: Oxford University Press.

Muller, R. (2007). The study of autism as a distributed disorder. *Mental Retardation and Developmental Disabilities Research Reviews, 13*(1), 85–95.

Myers, S., & Johnson, C. (2007). Management of children with autism spectrum disorders. *Pediatrics, 120*(5), 1162–1182.

Myles, B., & Simpson, R. (2002). Asperger syndrome: An overview of characteristics. *Focus on Autism and Other Developmental Disabilities, 17*(3), 132–137.

National Autism Center. (2009). *National standards report.* Randolph, MA: Author.

National Education Association. (2006). *The puzzle of autism.* Washington, DC: Author.

National Institute of Mental Health. (2013). *What is autism spectrum disorder?* Retrieved July 13, 2013, from http://www.nimh.nih.gov/health/topics/autism-spectrum-disorders-pervasive-developmental-disorders/index.shtml

Owens, R. (2014). *Language disorders* (6th ed.). Boston, MA: Pearson Education.

Pennington, R. (2010). Computer assisted instruction for teaching academic skills to students with autism spectrum disorders: A review of the literature. *Focus on Autism and Other Developmental Disabilities, 25*(4), 239–248.

Rank, B. (1949). Adaptation of the psychoanalytic technique for the treatment of young children with atypical development. *American Journal of Orthopsychiatry, 19,* 130–139.

Rapin, I. (2008). Etiologies of autism spectrum disorders. In P. Accardo (Ed.), *Capute & Accardo's neurodevelopmental disabilities in infancy and childhood* (3rd ed., Vol. 2, pp. 513–521). Baltimore, MD: Paul H. Brookes.

Rutter, M. (1978). Diagnosis and definition. In M. Rutter & E. Schopler (Eds.), *Autism: A reappraisal of concepts and treatment* (pp. 1–25). New York, NY: Plenum.

Rutter, M., Le Couteur, A., & Lord, C. (2003). *Autism Diagnostic Interview–Revised.* Torrance, CA: Western Psychological Services.

Ryan, J., Hughes, E., Katsiyannis, A., McDaniel, M., & Sprinkle, C. (2011). Researched-based educational practices for students with autism spectrum disorders. *Teaching Exceptional Children, 43*(3), 56–64.

Saracino, J., Noseworthy, J., Steiman, M., Reisinger, L., & Frombonne, E. (2010). Diagnostic and assessment issues in autism surveillance and prevalence. *Journal of Developmental and Physical Disabilities, 22*(4), 317–330.

Schall, C., Targett, P., & Wehman, P. (2013). Applications for youth with autism spectrum disorders. In P. Wehman (Ed.), *Life beyond the classroom* (5th ed., pp. 447–471). Baltimore, MD: Paul H. Brookes.

Schechter, R., & Grether, J. (2008). Continuing increases in autism reported to California's developmental services system: Mercury in retrograde. *Archives of General Psychiatry, 65*(1), 19–24.

Seligman, M., & Darling, R. (2007). *Ordinary families, special children* (3rd ed.). New York, NY: Guilford.

Seltzer, M., Greenberg, J., Lounds, J., Smith, L., Orsmond, G., Esbensen, A., . . . Hong, J. (2011). Adolescents and adults with autism spectrum disorders. In D. Amaral, G. Dawson, & D. Geschwind (Eds.), *Autism spectrum disorders* (pp. 241–252). New York, NY: Oxford University Press.

Sennott, S., & Bowker, A. (2009). Autism, AAC, and Proloquo2Go. *Perspectives on Augmentative and Alternative Communication, 18*(4), 137–145.

Smith, B., Spooner, F., & Wood, C. (2013). Using embedded computer-assisted explicit instruction to teach science to students with autism spectrum disorder. *Research in Autism Spectrum Disorders, 7*(3), 433–443.

Smith, T., Polloway, E., Patton, J., & Dowdy, C. (2012). *Teaching students with special needs in inclusive settings* (6th ed.). Upper Saddle River, NJ: Pearson Education.

Tiegerman-Farber, E. (2009). ASD: Learning to communicate. In D. Bernstein & E. Tiegerman-Farber (Eds.), *Language and communication disorders in children* (6th ed., pp. 314–369). Boston, MA: Allyn & Bacon.

Toma, C., Hervás, A., Balmaña, N., Salgado, M., Maristany, M., Vilella, E., . . . Cormand, B. (2013). Neurotransmitter systems and neurotrophic factors

in autism: Association study of 37 genes suggests involvement of DDC. *World Journal of Biological Psychiatry, 14*(7), 516–527. doi:10.3109/15 622975.2011.602719

Treffert, D. (2013). *Savant syndrome 2013– Myths and realities.* Retrieved July 8, 2013, from http://www.wisconsinmedi calsociety.org/professional/savant-syn drome/resources/articles/savant-syn drome-2013-myths-and-realities

U.S. Department of Education. (2000). *Twenty-second annual report to Congress on the implementation of the Individuals with Disabilities Education Act.* Washington, DC: U.S. Government Printing Office.

U.S. Department of Education. (2013). *Historical state-level IDEA data files.* Retrieved November 14, 2013, from http://tadnet.public.tadnet.org/pages/712

Volkmar, F., & Nelson, D. (1990). Seizure disorders in autism. *Journal of the American Academy of Child Psychiatry, 29,* 127–129.

Volkmar, F., & Pauls, D. (2003). Autism. *Lancet, 362*(9390), 1133–1141.

Volkmar, F., & Wiesner, L. (2009). *A practical guide to autism.* Hoboken, NJ: Wiley.

Warren, Z., & Stone, W. (2011). Best practices: Early diagnosis and psychological assessment. In D. Amaral, G. Dawson, & D. Geschwind (Eds.), *Autism spectrum disorders* (pp. 1271–1282). New York, NY: Oxford University Press.

Wicks-Nelson, R., & Israel, A. (2013). *Abnormal child and adolescent psychology* (8th ed.). Upper Saddle River, NJ: Pearson Education.

Williams, D. (2010). Theory of mind in autism: Evidence of a specific deficit in self-awareness? *Autism, 14*(5), 474–494.

Williams, B., & Williams, R. (2011). *Effective programs for treating autism spectrum disorders.* New York, NY: Routledge.

Williams, J., Scott, F., Stott, C., Allison, C., Bolton, P., Baron-Cohen, S., . . . Brayne, C. (2005). Childhood Asperger Syndrome Test. *Autism, 9*(1), 45–68.

Wing, L. (1981). Asperger syndrome: A clinical account. *Psychological Medicine, 11*(1), 115–129.

Xin, J., & Sutman, F. (2011). Using the smart board to teach social stories to students with autism. *Teaching Exceptional Children, 43*(4), 18–24.

Zimmer, M. (2013). Complementary and alternative therapies. In M. Batshaw, N. Roizen, & G. Lotrecchiano (Eds.), *Children with disabilities* (7th ed., pp. 673–679). Baltimore, MD: Paul H. Brookes.

Chapter 11

American Speech-Language-Hearing Association. (n.d.). *Communication services and supports for individuals with severe disabilities.* Retrieved August 30, 2013, from http://www.asha.org/NJC/faqs-aac-basics.htm

American Speech-Language-Hearing Association. (1993). Definitions of communication disorders and variations. *ASHA, 35*(Suppl. 10), 40–41.

American Speech-Language-Hearing Association. (2008). *Roles and responsibilities of speech-language pathologists in early intervention: Guidelines.* Retrieved August 27, 2013, from http://www.asha.org/policy

American Speech-Language-Hearing Association. (2013). *Cleft lip and cleft palate.* Retrieved August 23, 2013, from http://www.asha.org/public/speech/disorders/CleftLip.htm

Bell, M. (2007). Infections and the fetus. In M. Batshaw, L. Pellegrino, & N. Roizen (Eds.), *Children with disabilities* (6th ed., pp. 71–82). Baltimore, MD: Paul H. Brookes.

Bernthal, J., Bankson, N., & Flipsen, P. (2013). *Articulation and phonological disorders* (7th ed.). Boston, MA: Allyn & Bacon.

Bondy, A. (2012). The unusual suspects: Myths and misconceptions associated with PECS. *The Psychological Record, 62*(4), 789–816.

Brigance, A. (2013). *BRIGANCE® Inventory of Early Development–III.* North Billerica, MA: Curriculum Associates.

Bryant, D., Smith, D., & Bryant, B. (2008). *Teaching students with special needs.* Boston, MA: Pearson Education.

Bunce, B. (2003). Children with culturally diverse backgrounds. In L. McCormick, D. Loeb, & R. Schiefelbusch (Eds.), *Supporting children with communication difficulties in inclusive settings* (2nd ed., pp. 367–407). Boston, MA: Allyn & Bacon.

Clarke, M., Newton, C., Petrides, K., Griffiths, T., Lysley, A., & Price, K. (2012). An examination of relations between participation, communication and age in children with complex communication needs. *Augmentative and Alternative Communication, 28*(1), 44–51.

Cohen, L., & Spenciner, L. (2011). *Assessment of children and youth with special needs* (4th ed.). Upper Saddle River, NJ: Pearson Education.

Friend, M., & Bursuck, W. (2012). *Including students with special needs: A practical guide for classroom teachers* (6th ed.). Upper Saddle River, NJ: Pearson Education.

Gargiulo, R., & Kilgo, J. (2014). *An introduction to young children with special needs* (4th ed.). Belmont, CA: Wadsworth/Cengage Learning.

Goldman, R., & Fristoe, M. (2000). *Goldman-Fristoe Test of Articulation-2.* Circle Pines, MN: American Guidance Service.

Guiberson, M., & Atkins, J. (2012). Speech-language pathologists' preparation, practices, and perspectives on serving culturally and linguistically children. *Communication Disorders Quarterly, 33*(3), 169–180.

Guralnick, M. (2011). Why early intervention works: A systems perspective. *Infants & Young Children, 24*(1), 6–28.

Hoff, E. (2014). *Language development* (5th ed.). Belmont, CA: Wadsworth/Cengage Learning.

Johnson, J., & Wong, M. (2002). Cultural differences in beliefs and practices concerning talk to children. *Journal of Speech, Language, and Hearing Research, 45,* 916–927.

Lipkin, P., & Schertz, M. (2008). Early intervention and its efficacy. In P. Accardo (Ed.), *Capute and Accardo's neurodevelopmental disabilities in infancy and childhood* (3rd ed., Vol. 1, pp. 519–551). Baltimore, MD: Paul H. Brookes.

Luterman, D. (2008). *Counseling persons with communication disorders and their families* (5th ed.). Austin, TX: Pro-Ed.

March of Dimes. (2013). *Cleft lip and cleft palate.* Retrieved August 23, 2013, from http://www.marchofdimes.com/baby/birthdefects_cleftpalate.html

McCormick, L. (2003a). Introduction to language acquisition. In L. McCormick, D. F. Loeb, & R. L. Schiefelbusch (Eds.), *Supporting children with communication difficulties in inclusive settings* (2nd ed., pp. 1–42). Boston, MA: Allyn & Bacon.

McCormick, L. (2003b). Language intervention in the inclusive preschool. In L. McCormick, D. F. Loeb, & R. L. Schiefelbusch (Eds.), *Supporting children with communication difficulties in inclusive settings* (2nd ed., pp. 333–366). Boston, MA: Allyn & Bacon.

National Center for Education Statistics. (2013). *The condition of education 2013.* Washington, DC: U.S. Department of Education.

Owens, R. (2012). *Language development: An introduction* (8th ed.). Boston, MA: Pearson Education.

Owens, R. (2014). *Language disorders* (6th ed.). Boston, MA: Pearson Education.

Owens, R., Metz, D., & Farinella, K. (2011). *Introduction to communication disorders: A lifespan evidence-based perspective* (4th ed.). Boston, MA: Allyn & Bacon.

Paul, D., & Roth, F. (2011). Guiding principles and clinical applications for speech-language pathology practice in early intervention. *Language, Speech, and Hearing Services in Schools, 42*(3), 320–330.

Piaget, J. (1952). *The origins of intelligence in children* (M. Cook, trans.). New York, NY: International Universities Press.

Plante, E., & Beeson, P. (2013). *Communication and communication disorders: A clinical introduction* (4th ed.). Boston, MA: Allyn & Bacon.

Ramig, P., & Pollard, R. (2011). Stuttering and other disorders of fluency. In N. Anderson & G. Shames (Eds.), *Human communication disorders: An introduction* (8th ed., pp. 164–201). Upper Saddle River, NJ: Pearson Education.

Ratner, N. (2013). Atypical language development. In J. Gleason & N. Ratner (Eds.), *The development of language* (8th ed., pp. 266–328). Boston, MA: Pearson Education.

Sennott, S., & Bowker, A. (2009). Autism, AAC, and Proloquo2Go. *Perspectives on Augmentative and Alternative Communication, 18*(4), 137–145.

Smith, T., Polloway, E., Patton, J., & Dowdy, C. (2012). *Teaching students with special needs in inclusive settings* (6th ed.). Upper Saddle River, NJ: Pearson Education.

Turner, J. (2008). Assessment of speech and language disorders in children. In P. Accardo (Ed.), *Capute and Accardo's neurodevelopmental disabilities in infancy and childhood* (3rd ed., Vol. 2, pp. 425–455). Baltimore, MD: Paul H. Brookes.

Urban Institute. (2013). *Immigrants.* Retrieved August 28, 2013, from http://www.urban.org/immigrants/index.cfm

U.S. Department of Education. (2013). *Historical state-level IDEA data files.* Retrieved November 14, 2013, from http://tadnet.public.tadnet.org/pages/712

Van Hattum, R. (1969). *Clinical speech in the schools.* Springfield, IL: Charles C. Thomas.

Van Riper, C., & Emerick, L. (1996). *Speech correction: An introduction to speech pathology and audiology* (9th ed.). Boston, MA: Allyn & Bacon.

Vaughn, S., & Bos, C. (2012). *Strategies for teaching students with learning and behavioral problems* (8th ed.). Upper Saddle River, NJ: Pearson Education.

Vaughn, S., Bos, C., & Schumm, J. (2014). *Teaching students who are exceptional, diverse, and at risk* (6th ed.). Upper Saddle River, NJ: Pearson Education.

Wasem, K. (2013, March). *U.S. immigration policy: Chart book of key trends.* Washington, DC: Congressional Research Service.

Chapter 12

Allen, K., & Cowdery, G. (2012). *The exceptional child: Inclusion in early childhood special education* (7th ed.). Belmont, CA: Wadsworth/Cengage Learning.

American Speech-Language-Hearing Association. (2002). *Guidelines for audiology service provision in and for schools* [Guidelines]. Retrieved November 22, 2013, from http://www.asha.org/policy/GL2002-00005

American Speech-Language-Hearing Association. (2010). *Hearing assessment.* Retrieved January 26, 2010, from http://www.asha.org/public/hearing/testing/assess.htm

American Speech-Language-Hearing Association. (2013a). *Cochlear implant quick facts.* Retrieved December 1, 2013, from http://www.asha.org/public/hearing/Cochlea-Implant-Quick-Facts/

American Speech-Language-Hearing Association. (2013b). *Facts about pediatric hearing loss.* Retrieved November 25, 2013, from http://asha.org/aud/Facts-about-Pediatric-Hearing-Loss

American Speech-Language-Hearing Association. (2013c). *IDEA issue brief: Cochlear implants.* Retrieved November 29, 2013, from http://www.asha.org/uploadedFiles/advocacy/federal/idea/CochlearImplantsBrief.pdf

American Speech-Language-Hearing Association. (2013d). *The prevalence and incidence of hearing loss in children.* Retrieved November 26, 2013, from http://www.asha.org/public/hearing/disorders/children.htm

Berg, A., Ip, S., Hurst, M., & Herb, A. (2007). Cochlear implants in young children: Informed consent as a process and current practices. *American Journal of Audiology, 16*(1), 13–28.

Berk, L. (2013). *Child development* (9th ed.). Boston, MA: Allyn & Bacon.

Bess, F., & Humes, L. (2008). *Audiology: The fundamentals* (4th ed.). Baltimore, MD: Williams & Wilkins.

Buethe, P., Vohr, B., & Herer, G. (2013). Hearing and deafness. In M. Batshaw, N. Roizen, & G. Lotrecchiano (Eds.), *Children with disabilities* (7th ed., pp. 141–168). Baltimore, MD: Paul H. Brookes.

Chin, S., Tsai, P., & Gao, S. (2003). Connected speech intelligibility of children with cochlear implants and children with normal hearing. *American Journal of Speech-Language Pathology, 12*(4), 440–451.

Chute, P. (2004). Cochlear implants: An evolving journey. *ASHA Leader, 9,* 7.

Clark, J., & Martin, F. (1994). *Effective counseling in audiology: Perspectives and practice.* Englewood Cliffs, NJ: Prentice Hall.

Easterbrooks, S., & Baker, S. (2001). Enter the matrix! Considering the communication needs of students who are deaf or hard of hearing. *Teaching Exceptional Children, 33*(3), 70–76.

Gallagher, P., Easterbrooks, S., Malone, D. (2006). Universal newborn hearing screening and intervention. *Infants & Young Children: An Interdisciplinary Journal of Special Care Practices, 19*(1), 59–71.

Gallaudet Research Institute. (2003). *Literacy & deaf students.* Retrieved

January 26, 2010, from http://gri.gallaudet.edu/Literacy/

Gallaudet Research Institute. (2011). *Regional and national summary report of data from the 2009–2010 annual survey of deaf and hard of hearing children and youth.* Washington, DC: Gallaudet University.

Gargiulo, R., & Kilgo, J. (2014). *Young children with special needs* (4th ed.). Belmont, CA: Wadsworth/Cengage Learning.

Hunt, N., & Marshall, K. (2013). *Exceptional children and youth* (5th ed.). Belmont, CA: Wadsworth/Cengage Learning.

Johnson, C., & Seaton, J. (2012). *Educational audiology handbook* (2nd ed.). Clifton Park, NY: Delmar/Cengage Learning.

Johnson, R. (2003, Fall). High stakes testing conference held at Gallaudet. *Research at Gallaudet,* pp. 1–12.

Katz, L., & Schery, T. (2006). Including children with hearing loss in early childhood programs. *Young Children, 61*(1), 86–95.

Kaufman, A., & Kaufman, N. (2004). *Kaufman Assessment Battery for Children–Second Edition.* Circles Pines, MN: American Guidance Service.

King, S., De Caro, J., Karchmer, M., & Cole K. (2001). *College and career programs for deaf students* (11th ed.). Washington, DC: Gallaudet Research Institute.

Kochkin, S. (2013). *The prevalence of hearing loss in the U.S.* Retrieved November 26, 2013, from http://my.clevelandclinic.org/head-neck/departments-centers/audiology/hearing-loss-prevalence.aspx

Kuder, S. (2013). *Teaching students with language and communication disabilities* (4th ed.). Boston, MA: Allyn & Bacon.

Luckner, J., & Bowen, S. (2006). Assessment practices of professionals serving students who are deaf or hard of hearing: An initial investigation. *American Annals of the Deaf, 15*(4), 410–417.

Luckner, J., Slike, S., & Johnson, H. (2012). Helping students who are deaf or hard of hearing succeed. *Teaching Exceptional Children, 44*(4), 58–67.

Luterman, D. (2008). *Counseling persons with communication disorders and their families* (5th ed.). Austin, TX: Pro-Ed.

Marschark, M. (2006). Intellectual functioning of deaf adults and children: Answers and questions. *European Journal of Cognitive Psychology, 18*(1), 70–89.

Marschark, M. (2007). *Raising and educating a deaf child* (2nd ed.). New York, NY: Oxford University Press.

McLean, M., Wolery, M., & Bailey, D. (2004). *Assessing infants and preschoolers with special needs* (3rd ed.). Upper Saddle River, NJ: Pearson Education.

Moores, D. (2001). *Educating the deaf: Psychology, principles, and practices* (5th ed.). Boston, MA: Houghton Mifflin.

Moores, D. (2005). The No Child Left Behind Act and the Individuals with Disabilities Education Acts: The uneven impact of partially funded mandates on education of deaf and hard of hearing students. *American Annals of the Deaf, 150*(2), 75–80.

National Association of the Deaf. (2013). *About us.* Retrieved November 28, 2013, from nad.org/

National Institute on Deafness and Other Communication Disorders. (2013). *Cochlear implants.* Retrieved December 1, 2013, from http://www.nidcd.nih.gov/health/hearing/pages/coch.aspx

Pearson Assessment. (2008). *Stanford Achievement Test* (10th ed.). San Antonio, TX: Author.

Petersen, M., & Willems, P. (2006). Non-syndromic, autosomal-recessive deafness. *Clinical Genetics, 69*(5), 371–392.

Picard, M. (2004). Children with permanent hearing loss and associated disabilities: Revisiting current epidemiological data and causes of deafness. *Volta Review, 104*(4), 221–236.

Roizen, N. (2008). Hearing loss. In P. Accardo (Ed.), *Capute & Accardo's neurodevelopmental disabilities in infancy and childhood* (3rd ed., Vol. 2, pp. 457–470). Baltimore, MD: Paul H. Brookes.

Salvia, J., Ysseldyke, J., & Bolt, S. (2013). *Assessment in special and inclusive education* (12th ed.). Belmont, CA: Wadsworth/Cengage Learning.

Sattler, J., & Hoge, R. (2006). *Assessment of children: Behavioral, social, and clinical foundations* (5th ed.). La Mesa, CA: Sattler.

Scheetz, N. (2012). *Deaf education in the 21st century.* Upper Saddle River, NJ: Pearson Education.

Schum, R. (2004). Psychological assessment of children with multiple handicaps who have hearing loss. *Volta Review, 104*(4), 237–255.

Shaver, D., Newman, L., Huang, T., Yu, J., & Knokey, A. (2011). *Facts from NLTS2: The secondary school experiences and academic performance of students with hearing impairments.* Washington, DC: U.S. Department of Education.

Simeonsson, R., & Rosenthal, S. (Eds.). (2001). *Psychological and developmental assessment: Children with disabilities and chronic conditions.* New York, NY: Guilford Press.

Stach, B. (2010). *Clinical audiology: An introduction* (2nd ed.). Clifton Park, NY: Delmar/Cengage Learning.

Strong, M., & Prinz, P. (1997). A study of the relationship between American Sign Language and English literacy. *Journal of Deaf Studies and Deaf Education, 2*(1), 37–46.

Swanwick, R., & Marschark, M. (2010). Enhancing education for deaf children: Research into practice and back again. *Deafness & Education International, 12*(4), 217–235.

Toriello, H., & Smith, S. (2013). *Hereditary hearing loss and its syndromes* (3rd ed.). New York, NY: Oxford University Press.

Traxler, C. (2000). The Stanford Achievement Test, 9th Edition: National norming and performance standards for deaf and hard-of-hearing students. *Journal of Deaf Studies and Deaf Education, 5*(4), 337–348.

Trezek, B., Wang, Y., & Paul, P. (2010). *Reading and deafness.* Clifton Park, NY: Delmar/Cengage Learning.

U.S. Department of Education. (2013). *Historical state-level IDEA data files.* Retrieved November 26, 2013, from http://tadnet.public.tadnet.org/pages/712

U.S. Department of Health and Human Services. (2013). *Science capsule: Cochlear implants.* Retrieved November 23, 2013, from http://www.nidcd.nih.gov/about/plans/2012-2016/Pages/Science-Capsule-Cochlear-Implants.aspx

Van Hasselt, V., Strain, P., & Hersen, M. (1988). *Handbook of developmental and physical disabilities.* New York, NY: Pergamon Press.

Wechsler, D. (2003). *Wechsler Intelligence Scale for Children* (4th ed.). San Antonio, TX: Psychological Corporation.

Williams, C., & Finnegan, M. (2003). From myth to reality: Sound information for teachers about students who are deaf. *Teaching Exceptional Children, 35*(3), 40–45.

Chapter 13

American Foundation for the Blind. (2010). *Accommodations and modifications at a glance.* Retrieved February 9, 2010, from http://www.familyconnect.org/parebtsite.asp?SectionID=72TopicID=347&DocumentID=3820

American Foundation for the Blind. (2013a). *Learning media assessment.* Retrieved October 9, 2013, from http://www.familyconnect.org/parentsite.asp?SectionID=72&TopicID=369&DocumentID=4068

American Foundation for the Blind. (2013b). *The expanded core curriculum.* Retrieved October 12, 2013, from http://www.familyconnect.org/parentsite.asp?SectionID=72&TopicID=382

American Foundation for the Blind. (2013c). *Transition happens, ready or not!* Retrieved October 15, 2013, from http://www.afb.org/Section.asp?SectionID=7&TopicID=269&DocumentID=3535

Apple. (2013). *iOS: A wide range of features for a wide range of needs.* Retrieved November 7, 2013, from http://www.apple.com/accessibility/ios/#vision

Barraga, N. (1973). Utilization of sensory-perceptual abilities. In B. Lowenfeld (Ed.), *The visually handicapped children in school* (pp. 117–151). New York, NY: John Day.

Best, H. (1919). *The blind.* New York, NY: Macmillan.

Bishop, V. (2004). *Teaching visually impaired children* (3rd ed.). Springfield, IL: Charles C Thomas.

Bouck, E., & Meyer, N. (2012). eText, mathematics and students with visual impairments: What teachers need to know. *Teaching Exceptional Children, 45*(2), 42–49.

Chen, D., & Downing, J. (2006). *Tactile strategies for children who have visual impairments and multiple disabilities.* New York, NY: American Foundation for the Blind.

Diderot, D. (1749). *Lettre sur les aveugles à l'usage de ceux qui voient.* London, UK.

Erin, J. (2000). Students with visual impairments and additional disabilities. In A. Koenig & M. Holbrook (Eds.), *Foundations of education: Instructional strategies for teaching children and youths with visual impairments* (2nd ed., Vol. 2, pp. 730–752). New York, NY: American Foundation for the Blind.

Ferrell, K. (2007). *Issues in the field of blindness and low vision.* National Center on Severe and Sensory Disabilities. Retrieved October 24, 2013, from http://www.unco.edu/ncssd/resources/issues_bvi.shtml

Gargiulo, R., & Metcalf, D. (2013). *Teaching in today's inclusive classrooms* (2nd ed.). Belmont, CA: Wadsworth/Cengage Learning.

Geddie, B., Bina, M., & Miller, M. (2013). Vision and visual impairments. In M. Batshaw, N. Roizen, & G. Lotrecchiano (Eds.), *Children with disabilities* (7th ed., pp. 169–188). Baltimore, MD: Paul H. Brookes.

gh, LLC. (2006). *MathSpeak.* Retrieved November 7, 2013, from http://www.gh-mathspeak.com/

Griffin, H., Williams, S., Davis, M., & Engleman, M. (2002). Using technology to enhance cues for children with low vision. *Teaching Exceptional Children, 35*(2), 36–42.

Huebner, K., Merk-Adam, B., Stryker, D., & Wolffe, K. (2004). *The national agenda for the education of children and youths with visual impairments, including those with multiple disabilities-revised.* New York, NY: American Foundation for the Blind.

Isaacson, M., Schleppenbach, D., & Lloyd, L. (2010/2011). Increasing STEM accessibility in students with print disabilities through MathSpeak. *Journal of Science Education for Students with Disabilities, 14*(1), 25–32.

Johnson, J. (2003). Expanded core curriculum: Technology. In S. Goodman & S. Wittenstein (Eds.), *Collaborative assessment* (pp. 237–263). New York, NY: American Foundation for the Blind.

Lang, M. (1992). Creating inclusive, non-stereotyping environments: The child with a disability. In R. Swallow & M. J. Sanspree (Eds.), *Project video.* Los Angeles: California State University at Los Angeles.

Lash, J. (1980). *Helen and teacher: The story of Helen Keller and Anne Sullivan Macy.* New York, NY: Delacorte Press.

Liefert, F. (2003). Introduction to visual impairment. In S. Goodman & S. Wittenstein (Eds.), *Collaborative assessment* (pp. 1–12). New York, NY: American Foundation for the Blind.

Mittler, J. (2007). Assistive technology and IDEA. In C. Warger (Ed.), *Technology integration: Improving access to the curriculum for students with disabilities.* Reston, VA: Technology and Media Division of the Council for Exceptional Children.

National Eye Institute. (2013). *Impairment in children and adolescents.* Retrieved October 15, 2013, from http://www.nei.nih.gov/healthyvision/objective/children.asp

National Braille Press. (2013). *The need for Braille?* Retrieved November 10, 2013, from http://www.nbp.org/ic/nbp/braille/needforbraille.html

Optometric Center of Los Angeles. (2013). *Visual efficiency evaluation.* Retrieved October 31, 2013, from http://eyecarela.com/visiontherapy/index.html

Paths to Literacy. (2013). *Overview of learning media assessment.* Retrieved October 29, 2013, from http://www.pathstoliteracy.org/learning-media-assessment#whatislma

Pogrund, R., & Fazzi, D. (Eds.). (2007). *Early focus: Working with young blind and visually impaired children and their families* (3rd ed.). New York, NY: American Foundation for the Blind.

Prevent Blindness America. (2013a). *Quick facts: Children's eye problems.* Retrieved October 15, 2013, from http://www.sites/default/files/national/documents/fact_sheets/MK03_QuickFactsChildren.pdf

Prevent Blindness America. (2013b). *Eye safety.* Retrieved October 15, 2013, from http://www.preventblindness.org/safety

Pugh, G., & Erin, J. (Eds.). (1999). *Blind and visually impaired students: Educational service guidelines.* Watertown, MA: Perkins School for the Blind.

Scholl, G., Mulholland, M., & Lonergan, A. (1986). Education of the visually handicapped: A selective timeline. In G. Scholl (Ed.), *Foundations of education for blind and visually handicapped children and youth: Theory and practice* (Inside cover charts). New York, NY: American Foundation for the Blind.

Texas School for the Blind. (2007). *Selected anomalies and diseases of the eye*. Retrieved October 12, 2013, from http://www.tsbvi.edu/Education/anomalies/index.htm

U.S. Department of Education. (2013). *Historical state-level IDEA data files*. Retrieved October 29, 2013, from http://tadnet.public.tadnet.org/pages/712

Zimmerman, G., & Zebehazy, K. (2011). Blindness and low vision. In J. Kauffman & D. Hallahan (Eds.), *Handbook of special education* (pp. 247–261). New York, NY: Routledge.

Chapter 14

Alabama Institute for Deaf and Blind. (2013). *Info: Deafblindness*. Retrieved October 3, 2013, from http://www.aidb.org/reference-desk/info-deafblindness

Alsop, L., Berg, C., Hartman, V., Knapp, M., Lauger, K., Levasseur, C., . . . Prouty, S. (2012). *A family's guide to interveners*. Logan, UT: SKI-HI Institute.

Alsop, L., Blaha, R., & Kloos, E. (2000). *The intervener in early intervention and educational settings for children and youth with deafblindness*. Monmouth, OR: National Technical Assistance Consortium for Children and Young Adults Who Are Deaf-Blind.

American Lung Association. (2012a). *Asthma & children fact sheet*. Retrieved October 3, 2013, from http://www.lung.org/

American Lung Association. (2012b). *Trends in asthma morbidity and mortality*. Retrieved October 3, 2013, from http://www.lung.org/

Barnes-Powell, L. (2007). Infants of diabetic mothers: The effects of hyperglycemia on the fetus and neonate. *Neonatal Network, 26*, 283–290.

Beattie v. Board of Education, 169 Wis. 231, 233, 172 N.W. 153, 154 (1919).

Best, S., & Heller, K. (2009a). Acquired infections and AIDS. In K. Heller, P. Forney, P. Alberto, S. Best, & M. Schwartzman (Eds.), *Understanding physical, health, and multiple disabilities* (2nd ed., pp. 368–386). Upper Saddle River, NJ: Pearson Education.

Best, S., & Heller, K. (2009b). Congenital infections. In K. Heller, P. Forney, P. Alberto, S. Best, & M. Schwartzman (Eds.), *Understanding physical, health, and multiple disabilities* (2nd ed., pp. 387–398). Upper Saddle River, NJ: Pearson Education.

Best, S., Reed, P., & Bigge, J. (2010). Assistive technology. In S. Best, K. Heller, & J. Bigge (Eds.), *Teaching individuals with physical or multiple disabilities* (6th ed., pp. 175–220). Upper Saddle River, NJ: Pearson Education.

Beukelman, D., & Mirenda, P. (2013). *Augmentative and alternative communication* (4th ed.). Baltimore, MD: Paul H. Brookes.

Blackhurst, A. (2005). Perspectives on applications of technology in the field of learning disabilities. *Learning Disability Quarterly, 28*(2), 175–178.

Braine, M., & Smith, J. (2013). Traumatic brain injury in children part 1–initial assessment and management. *British Journal of School Nursing, 8*, 175–179.

Caraballo, R., Darra, F., Fontana, E., Garcia, R., Monese, E., & Bernardina, B. (2011). Absence seizures in the first 3 years of life: An electroclinical study of 46 cases. *Epilepsia, 52*(2), 393–400.

Centers for Disease Control and Prevention. (2009). *AIDS surveillance–general epidemiology*. Retrieved October 3, 2013, from http://www.cdc.gov/hiv/topics/surveillance/resources/slides/epidemiology/

Centers for Disease Control and Prevention. (2013). *How many people have TBI?* Retrieved October 3, 2013, from http://www.cdc.gov/traumaticbraininjury/statistics.html

CHARGE Syndrome Foundation. (2013). *About CHARGE*. Retrieved October 3, 2013, from http://www.chargesyndrome.org/about-charge.asp

Clark, G., Bigge, J., & Best, S. (2010). Self-determination and education for transition. In S. Best, K. Heller, & J. Bigge (Eds.), *Teaching individuals with physical or multiple disabilities* (6th ed., pp. 343–372). Upper Saddle River, NJ: Pearson Education.

Crowe, L., Catroppa, C., Babi, F., & Anderson, V. (2013). Executive function outcomes of children with traumatic brain injury sustained before three years. *Child Neuropsychology, 19*(2), 113–126.

Davis, A., & Dean, R. (2010). Assessing sensory-motor deficits in pediatric traumatic brain injury. *Applied Neuropsychology, 17*(2), 104–109.

Dias, M. (2013). *Hydrocephalus and shunts*. Retrieved September 29, 2013, from http://www.spinabifidaassociation.org/site/c.evKRI7OXIoJ8H/b.8277089/

Downing, J., & Eichinger, J. (2011). Instructional strategies for learners with dual sensory impairments in integrated settings. *Research & Practice for Persons With Severe Disabilities, 36*(3/4), 150–157.

DPHD Critical Issues and Leadership Committee. (2013). *Position statement on specialized health care procedures*. Retrieved September 16, 2013, from http://web.utk.edu/~dphmd/DPHD_position_health.pdf

Eberle, L. (1922, August). The maimed, the halt and the race. *Hospital Social Service, 5*, 59–63. Reprinted in R. Bremner (Ed.). (1971). *Children and youth in America* (vol. ii, pp. 1026–1028). Cambridge, MA: Harvard University Press.

Effgen, S. (2012). *Meeting the physical therapy needs of children* (2nd ed.). Philadelphia, PA: F. A. Davis.

Epilepsy Foundation of America. (2013). *Prevalence and incidence*. Retrieved October 3, 2013, from www.epilepsyfoundation.org/aboutepilepsy/whatisepilepsy/statistics.cfm

Fadiman, A. (1997). *The spirit catches you and you fall down*. New York, NY: Farrar, Straus & Giroux.

Gargiulo, R. (1985). *Working with parents of exceptional children*. Boston, MA: Houghton Mifflin.

Geenen, S., Powers, L., & Lopez-Vasquez, A. (2001). Multicultural aspects of involvement in transition planning. *Exceptional Children, 67*(2), 265–282.

Heller, K. (2009a). Learning and behavioral characteristics of students with physical, health, or multiple impairments. In K. Heller, P. Forney, P. Alberto, S. Best, & M. Schwartzman (Eds.), *Understanding physical, health, and multiple disabilities* (2nd ed., pp. 18–34). Upper Saddle River, NJ: Pearson Education.

Heller, K. (2009b). Monitoring health impairments and individualized healthcare plans. In K. Heller, P. Forney, P. Alberto, S. Best, & M. Schwartzman (Eds.), *Understanding physical, health, and multiple disabilities* (2nd ed., pp. 349–366). Upper Saddle River, NJ: Pearson Education.

Heller, K. (2009c). Traumatic spinal cord injury and spina bifida. In K. Heller,

P. Forney, P. Alberto, S. Best, & M. Schwartzman (Eds.), *Understanding physical, health, and multiple disabilities* (2nd ed., pp. 94–117). Upper Saddle River, NJ: Pearson Education.

Heller, K. (2010). Mathematics instruction and adaptations. In S. Best, K. Heller, & J. Bigge (Eds.), *Teaching individuals with physical or multiple disabilities* (6th ed., pp. 457–493). Upper Saddle River, NJ: Pearson Education.

Heller, K., & Alberto, P. (2010). Reading instruction and adaptations. In S. Best, K. Heller, & J. Bigge (Eds.), *Teaching individuals with physical or multiple disabilities* (6th ed., pp. 375–406). Upper Saddle River, NJ: Pearson Education.

Heller, K., & Avant, M. (2011). Health care procedure considerations and individualized health care plans. *Physical Disabilities: Education and Related Services, 30,* 6–29.

Heller, K., & Bigge, J. (2010). Augmentative and alternative communication. In S. Best, K. Heller, & J. Bigge (Eds.), *Teaching individuals with physical or multiple disabilities* (6th ed., pp. 221–254). Upper Saddle River, NJ: Pearson Education.

Heller, K., Mezei, P., & Schwartzman, M. (2009). Muscular dystrophies. In K. Heller, P. Forney, P. Alberto, S. Best, & M. Schwartzman (Eds.), *Understanding physical, health, and multiple disabilities* (2nd ed., pp. 232–248). Upper Saddle River, NJ: Pearson Education.

Heller, K., & Tumlin-Garrett, J. (2009). Cerebral palsy. In K. Heller, P. Forney, P. Alberto, S. Best, & M. Schwartzman (Eds.), *Understanding physical, health, and multiple disabilities* (2nd ed., pp. 72–93). Upper Saddle River, NJ: Pearson Education.

Herring, J. (2007). *Tachdjian's pediatric orthopaedics* (4th ed.). Philadelphia, PA: W. B. Saunders.

Hille, E., Weisglas-Kuperus, N., van Goudoever, J., Jacobusse, G., Ens-Dokkum, M., de Groot, L., . . . Verloove-Vanhorick, S. (2007). Functional outcomes and participation in young adulthood for very preterm and very low birth weight infants: The Dutch Project on preterm and small for gestational age infants at 19 years of age. *Pediatrics, 120*(3), e587–595.

Holck, P., Nettelbladt, U., & Sandberg, A. (2009). Children with cerebral palsy, spina bifida and pragmatic language impairment: Differences and similarities in pragmatic ability. *Research in Developmental Disabilities, 30*(5), 942–951.

Iddon, J., Morgan, D., Loveday, C., Sahakian, B., & Pickard, J. (2004). Neuropsychological profile of young adults with spina bifida with or without hydrocephalus. *Journal of Neurology, Neurosurgery & Psychiatry, 75*(8), 1112–1118.

Kaiser, A., & Grim, J. (2006). Teaching functional communication skills. In M. Snell & F. Brown (Eds.), *Instruction of students with severe disabilities* (6th ed., pp. 447–488). Upper Saddle River, NJ: Pearson Education.

Katz-Leurer, M., Rotem, H., Keren, O., & Meyer, S. (2009). Balance difficulties and gait characteristics in posttraumatic brain injury, cerebral palsy, and typically developing children. *Developmental Neurorehabilitation, 12*(2), 100–105.

Killoran, J. (2007). *The national deaf-blind child count: 1998–2005 in review.* Retrieved October 5, 2013, from http://www.nationaldb.org/documents/products/Childcountreview-0607Final.pdf

Kirshbaum, M. (2000). A disability culture perspective on early intervention with parents with physical or cognitive disabilities and their infants. *Infants and Young Children, 13*(2), 9–10.

Kliegman, R., Stanton, B., St. Geme, J., Schor, N., & Behrman, R. (2011). *Nelson textbook of pediatrics* (19th ed.). Philadelphia, PA: Elsevier.

La Vor, M. (1976). Federal legislation for exceptional persons: A history. In F. Weintraub, A. Aberson, J. Ballard, & M. La Vor (Eds.), *Public policy and the education of exceptional children* (pp. 96–111). Reston, VA: Council for Exceptional Children.

Lin, S. (2000). Coping and adaptation in families of children with cerebral palsy. *Exceptional Children, 66*(2), 201–218.

Lindsey, L. (2008). *Technology and exceptional individuals* (4th ed.). Austin, TX: Pro-Ed.

Macmillan, D., & Hendrick, I. (1993). Evolution and legacy. In J. Goodlad & T. Lovitt (Eds.), *Integrating general and special education* (pp. 23–48). New York, NY: Merrill.

Majkowska-Zwolińska, B., Zwoliński, P., Roszkowski, M., & Drabik, K. (2012). Long-term results of vagus nerve stimulation in children and adolescents with drug-resistant epilepsy. *Childs Nervous System, 28,* 621–628.

Management of Myelomeningocele Study. (2010). *Overview of management of myelomeningocele.* Retrieved January 6, 2010, from http://www.spinabifidamoms.com/English/overview.html

Merrick, J., Merrick, E., Morad, M., & Kandel, I. (2006). Fetal alcohol syndrome and its long-term effects. *Minerva Pediatrica, 58,* 211–218.

McIntyre, S., Taitz, D., Keogh, J., Goldsmith, S., Badawi, N. & Blair, E. (2013). A systematic review of risk factors for cerebral palsy in children born at term in developed countries. *Developmental Medicine & Child Neurology, 55*(6), 499–508.

Malloy, P. (2010, June). Authentic assessment. *National Consortium on Deaf-Blindness Practice Perspectives, 6,* 1–4.

Miles, B. (2013). *Overview on deaf-blindness.* Retrieved October 3, 2013, from http://www.nationaldb.org/NCDBProducts.php?prodID=38

Murphy, N., Christian, B., Caplin, D., & Young, P. (2007). The health of caregivers for children with disabilities: Caregiver perspectives, *Child: Care, Health and Development, 33*(2), 180–187.

National Consortium on Deaf-Blindness. (2007). *The national deaf-blind child count.* Retrieved January 10, 2007, from http://www.tr.wou.edu/ntac/index.cfm?path=publications/publications_census.html

National Consortium on Deaf-Blindness. (2009). *The 2008 national child count of children and youth who are deaf-blind.* Retrieved October 3, 2013, from http://www.nationaldb.org/documents/products/2008-Census-Tables.pdf

National Consortium on Deaf-Blindness. (2013). *Primary etiologies of deaf-blindness—alphabetically.* Retrieved October 3, 2013, from http://www.nationaldb.org/ISSelectedTopics.php?topicID=989&topicCatID=24

Ostring, G., & Singh-Grewal, D. (2013). Juvenile idiopathic arthritis in the new world of biologics. *Journal of Paediatrics and Child Health, 49*(9), e405–412.

Porter, R. (2011). *The Merck manual* (19th ed.). West Point, PA: Merck & Co.

Rennie, J., Hagmann, C., & Robertson, N. (2007). Outcome after intrapartum hypoxic ischaemia at term. *Seminars in Fetal and Neonatal Medicine, 12*, 398–407.

Rowland, C. (2009). *Assessing communication and learning in young children who are deafblind or who have multiple disabilities.* Portland, OR: Design to Learn Projects, Oregon Health and Science University.

Saxena, V., & Nadkarni, V. (2011). Non-pharmacological treatment of epilepsy. *Annals of Indian Academy of Neurology, 14*(3), 148–152.

Sevcik, R., & Romski, M. (2010). *AAC: More than three decades of growth and development.* Retrieved January 7, 2010, from http://www.asha.org/public/speech/disorders/ACCThreeDecades.htm

Silberman, R., Bruce, S., & Nelson, C. (2004). Children with sensory impairments. In F. Orelove, D. Sobsey, & R. Silberman (Eds.), *Educating children with multiple disabilities* (4th ed., pp. 425–527). Baltimore, MD: Paul H. Brookes.

Simpson, R. (2013). *Computer access for people with disabilities: A human factors approach.* Boca Raton, FL: CRC Press.

Sitlington, P., Neubert, D., & Clark, G. (2011). *Transition education and services for students with disabilities* (5th ed.). Needham Heights, MA: Allyn & Bacon.

Spina Bifida Association of America. (2013). *What is spina bifida.* Retrieved October 3, 2013, from http://www.spinabifidaassociation.org

Temkin, O. (1971). *The falling sickness: A history of epilepsy from the Greeks to the beginning of modern neurology* (2nd ed.). Baltimore, MD: Johns Hopkins University Press.

Tsai, J., Floyd, L., Green, P., & Boyle, C. (2007). Patterns and average volume of alcohol use among women of childbearing age. *Maternal and Child Health Journal, 11*(5), 437–445.

Turnbull, A., Turnbull, R., Erwin, E., Soodak, L., & Shogren, K. (2011). *Families, professionals, and exceptionality* (6th ed.). Upper Saddle River, NJ: Pearson Education.

United Cerebral Palsy. (2013). *CP fact sheet.* Retrieved October 3, 2013, from http://www.ucp.org/wp-content/uploads/2013/02/cp-fact-sheet.pdf

U.S. Department of Education. (2013). *Historical state-level IDEA data files.* Retrieved November 13, 3013, from http://tadnet.public.tadnet.org/pages/712

Valcamonico, A., Accorsi, P., Sanzeni, C., Martelli, P., La Boria, P., & Frusca, T. (2007). Mid- and long-term outcome of extremely low birth weight (ELBW) infants: An analysis of prognostic factors. *The Journal of Maternal-Fetal and Neonatal Medicine, 20*(6), 465–471.

Wehman, P. (2012). *Life beyond the classroom* (5th ed.). Baltimore, MD: Paul H. Brookes.

Williams, P., & Fletcher, S. (2010). Health effects of prenatal radiation exposure. *American Family Physician, 82*(5), 488–493.

Wolf-Schein, E., & Schein, J. (2009). *AIM: Assessment Intervention Matrix.* Coconut Creek, FL: Three Bridge.

Wood, R., & Thomas, R. (2013). Impulsive and episodic disorders of aggressive behavior following traumatic brain injury. *Brain Injury, 27*(3), 253–261.

Ysseldyke, J., & Algozzine, B. (1982). *Critical issues in special and remedial education.* Boston, MA: Houghton Mifflin.

Chapter 15

Archambault, F., Jr., Westberg, K., Brown, S., Hallmark, B., Zhang, W., & Emmons, C. (1993). Classroom practices used with gifted third and fourth grade students. *Journal for the Education of the Gifted, 16*(2), 103–119.

Baum, S., Rizza, M., & Renzulli, S. (2006). Twice-exceptional adolescents: Who are they? What do they need? In F. Dixon & S. Moon (Eds.), *The handbook of secondary gifted education* (pp. 137–164). Waco, TX: Prufrock Press.

Blackbourn, J., Patton, J., & Trainor, A. (2004). *Exceptional individuals in focus* (7th ed.). Upper Saddle River, NJ: Pearson Education.

Bouck, E., & Hunley, M. (in press). Technology and giftedness. In J. Bakken (Ed.), *Giftedness: Current perspectives and issues.* Bingley, UK: Emerald Group.

Burns, D., Purcell, J., & Hertberg, H. (2006). Curriculum for gifted education students. In J. Purcell & R. Eckert (Eds.), *Designing services and programs for high-ability learners* (pp. 87–111). Thousand Oaks, CA: Corwin Press.

Clark, B. (2013). *Growing up gifted: Developing the potential of children at home and at school* (8th ed.). Upper Saddle River, NJ: Pearson Education.

Clark, B. (2008). *Growing up gifted: Developing the potential of children at home and at school* (7th ed.). Upper Saddle River, NJ: Pearson Education.

Clasen, D., & Clasen, R. (2003). Mentoring the gifted and talented. In N. Colangelo & G. Davis (Eds.), *Handbook of gifted education* (3rd ed., pp. 254–267). Needham Heights, MA: Allyn & Bacon.

Colangelo, N., Assouline, S., & Gross, M. U. A. (2004). *A nation deceived: How schools hold back America's brightest students.* Iowa City: University of Iowa.

Cote, D. (2005). *Wicked: The grimmerie.* New York, NY: Hyperion.

Csikszentmihalyi, M., Rathunde, K., & Whalen, S. (1997). *Talented teenagers: The roots of success and failure.* Cambridge, UK: Cambridge University Press.

Davis, G., Rimm, S., & Siegle, D. (2011). *Education of the gifted and talented* (6th ed.). Upper Saddle River, NJ: Pearson Education.

Evans, M. (2001). *Developing and testing an innovation component configuration map for gifted education in the elementary school.* Unpublished dissertation, University of Louisville and Western Kentucky University.

Flint, L. (2001). Challenges of identifying and serving gifted children with ADHD. *Teaching Exceptional Children, 33*(4), 62–69.

Ford, D. (1998). The underrepresentation of minority students in gifted education: Problems and promises in recruitment and retention. *Journal of Special Education, 32*(1), 4–14.

Ford, D., Harris, J., Tyson, C., & Trotman, M. (2002). Beyond deficit thinking: Providing access for gifted African American students. *Roeper Review, 24*, 52–58.

Frasier, M., Hunsaker, S., Lee, J., Mitchell, S., Cramond, B., Krisel, S., . . . Finley, V. (1995). *Core attributes of giftedness: A foundation for recognizing the gifted potential of minority and economically disadvantaged students.* National Research Center on the Gifted and Talented. Storrs: University of Connecticut.

Gallagher, J. (2003). Issues and challenges in the education of gifted students. In N. Colangelo & G. Davis (Eds.), *Handbook of gifted education* (3rd ed., pp. 11–23). Boston, MA: Allyn & Bacon.

Gallagher, J., & Gallagher, S. (1994). *Teaching the gifted child* (4th ed.). Boston, MA: Allyn & Bacon.

Gardner, H. (1983). *Frames of mind: The theory of multiple intelligences.* New York, NY: Basic Books.

Gardner, H. (1993). *Multiple intelligences: The theory in practice.* New York, NY: Basic Books.

Gibson, S., & Efinger, J. (2001). Revisiting the schoolwide enrichment model: An approach to gifted programming. *Teaching Exceptional Children, 33*(4), 48–53.

Gubbins, E. J. (2006). Constructing identification procedures. In J. Purcell & R. Eckert (Eds.), *Designing services and programs for high-ability learners* (pp. 49–61). Thousand Oaks, CA: Corwin Press.

Guilford, J. P. (1967). *The nature of human intelligence.* New York, NY: McGraw-Hill.

Hollingworth, L. (1926). *Gifted children: Their nature and nurture.* New York, NY: Macmillan.

Howley, C., Howley, A., & Pendarvis, E. (1995). *Out of our minds: Anti-intellectualism and talent development for American schooling.* New York, NY: Teachers College Press.

Johnsen, S. (2011). *Identifying gifted students: A practical guide* (2nd ed.). Waco, TX: Prufrock Press.

Karnes, F., & Riley, T. (2005). *Competitions for talented kids.* Waco, TX: Prufrock Press.

Karnes, F., Stephens, K., & McHard, E. (2008). Legal issues in gifted education. In F. Karnes & K. Stephens (Eds.), *Achieving excellence: Educating the gifted and talented* (pp. 18–35). Upper Saddle River, NJ: Pearson Education.

King, E. (2005). Addressing the social and emotional needs of twice-exceptional students. *Teaching Exceptional Children, 38*(1), 16–20.

Kulik, J. (2003). Grouping and tracking. In N. Colangelo & G. Davis (Eds.), *Handbook of gifted education* (3rd ed., pp. 268–281). Boston, MA: Allyn & Bacon.

Landrum, M., Callahan, C., & Shaklee, B. (Eds.). (2001). *Aiming for excellence.* Waco, TX: Prufrock Press.

Landrum, M., & Shaklee, B. (Eds.). (1998). *Pre-K–grade 12 gifted program standards.* Washington, DC: National Association for Gifted Children.

Marland, S. (1972). *Education of the gifted and the talented: Report to the Congress of the United States by the U.S. Commissioner of Education.* Washington, DC: U.S. Government Printing Office.

Mensa. (2013). *American Mensa.* Retrieved November 18, 2013, from http://www.usmensa.org/

Mersino, D. (2011). *10 ways social media and the web are moving gifted education forward.* Retrieved November 18, 2013, from http://www.ingeniosus.net/archives/10-ways-social-media-and-the-web-are-moving-gifted-education-forward

National Association for Gifted Children. (2010). *Pre-K–Grade 12 gifted programming standards.* Retrieved November 14, 2013, from http://www.nagc.org/giftededucationstandards.aspx

National Association for Gifted Children. (2013). *Frequently asked questions.* Retrieved November 16, 2013, from http://www.nagc.org/index.aspx?id=548

National Center for Education Statistics. (2012a). *Digest of education statistics 2011.* Washington, DC: U.S. Department of Education.

National Center for Education Statistics. (2012b). *Highlights from the TIMSS 2011: Mathematics and science achievement of U.S. fourth- and eighth-grade students in an international context.* Washington, DC: U.S. Department of Education.

National Commission on Excellence in Education. (1983). *A nation at risk: The imperative for school reform.* Washington, DC: U.S. Government Printing Office.

National Education Commission on Time and Learning. (1994). *Prisoners of time.* Washington, DC: U.S. Government Printing Office.

National Governors Association Center for Best Practices. (2010). *Common Core State Standards initiative.* Retrieved February 20, 2010, from http://www.corestandards.org/

Neal, D., & Schanzenbach, D. (2007, August). *Left behind by design: Proficiency counts and test-based accountability* (NBER Working Paper No. W13293). Retrieved November 19, 2013, from http://ssrn.com/abstract=1005606

Nielsen, M., & Higgins, L. (2005). The eye of the storm: Services and programs for twice-exceptional learners. *Teaching Exceptional Children, 38*(1), 8–15.

Noble, K., Subotnik, R., & Arnold, K. (1999). To thine own self be true: A new model of female talent development. *Gifted Child Quarterly, 43,* 140–149.

Olszewski-Kubilius, P., & Clarenbach, J. (2012). *Unlocking emergent talent.* Washington, DC: National Association for Gifted Children.

Pfeiffer, S., & Jarosewich, T. (2003). *Pfeiffer-Jarosewich Gifted Rating Scales.* San Antonio, TX: Psychological Corporation.

Piirto, J. (2007). *Talented children and adults: Their development and education* (3rd ed.). Waco, TX: Prufrock Press.

Plucker, J., Burroughs, N., & Song, R. (2010). *Mind the (other) gap!* Bloomington, IN: Center for Evaluation & Education Policy.

Plummer, D. (1995). Serving the needs of gifted children from a multicultural perspective. In J. Genshaft, M. Birely, & C. Hollinger (Eds.), *Serving gifted and talented students* (pp. 285–300). Austin, TX: Pro-Ed.

Reis, S. (2006). Gender, adolescence, and giftedness. In F. Dixon & S. Moon (Eds.), *The handbook of secondary gifted education* (pp. 87–111). Waco, TX: Prufrock Press.

Reis, S., Gubbins, E., Briggs, C., Schreiber, F., Richards, S., Jacobs, J., . . . Alexander, M. (2003). *Reading instruction for talented readers: Case studies documenting few opportunities for continuous progress* (Research Monograph No. 03184). Storrs, CT: National Research Center on the Gifted and Talented, University of Connecticut.

Reis, S., & Renzulli, J. (2005). *Curriculum compacting: An easy start to differentiating for high-potential students.* Waco, TX: Prufrock Press.

Renzulli, J. (1978). What makes giftedness? Reexamining a definition. *Phi Delta Kappan, 60,* 180–184, 261.

Renzulli, J. (1998). A rising tide lifts all ships: Developing the gifts and talents of all students. *Phi Delta Kappan, 80,* 104–111.

Renzulli, J., & Reis, S. (2003). The schoolwide enrichment model: Developing creative and productive giftedness. In N. Colangelo & G. Davis (Eds.), *Handbook of gifted education* (3rd ed., pp. 184–203). Boston, MA: Allyn & Bacon.

Rimm, S. (2002). *How Jane won.* New York, NY: Crown.

Roberts, J. (2013). The Gatton Academy: A case study of a state residential high school with a focus on mathematics and science. *Gifted Child Today, 36*(3), 193–200.

Roberts, J. (2010, Winter). Preassessment: The linchpin for defensible differentiation. *The Challenge, 24,* 10, 12.

Roberts, J., & Boggess, J. (2011). *Teacher's survival guide: Gifted education.* Waco, TX: Prufrock Press.

Roberts, J., & Inman, T. (2009a). *Assessing differentiated student products: A protocol for development and assessment.* Waco, TX: Prufrock Press.

Roberts, J., & Inman, T. (2009b). *Strategies for differentiation instruction* (2nd ed.). Waco, TX: Prufrock Press.

Robinson, A., Shore, B., & Enersen, D. (2007). *Best practices in gifted education.* Waco, TX: Prufrock Press.

Roid, G. (2003). *Stanford-Binet Intelligence Test–Fifth Edition.* Itasca, IL: Riverside.

Ross, P. (Ed.). (1993). *National excellence: A case for developing America's talent.* Washington, DC: U.S. Department of Educational Research and Improvement.

Sanders, W. (1998). Value-added assessment. *School Administrator, 55,* 24–27.

Siegle, D. (2012). Embracing e-books: Increasing students' motivation to read and write. *Gifted Child Today, 35*(2), 137–143.

Silverman, L. (1995a). Gifted and talented students. In E. Meyen & T. Skrtic (Eds.), *Special education and student disability* (4th ed., pp. 379–413). Denver, CO: Love.

Silverman, L. (1995b). Highly gifted children. In J. Genshaft, M. Bireley, & C. Hollinger (Eds.), *Serving gifted and talented students: A resource for school personnel* (pp. 217–240). Austin, TX: Pro-Ed.

Smith, T., Polloway, E., Patton, J., & Dowdy, C. (2012). *Teaching students with special needs* (6th ed.). Upper Saddle River, NJ: Pearson Education.

Smutny, J., Walker, S., & Meckstroth, E. (2007). *Acceleration for gifted learners, K–5.* Thousand Oaks, CA: Corwin.

Steinberg, L. (1996). *Beyond the classroom: Why school reform has failed and what parents need to do.* New York, NY: Simon & Schuster.

Sternberg, R. (1985). *Beyond IQ: A triarchic theory of intelligence.* New York, NY: Cambridge University Press.

Subotnik, R., Kassan, L., Summers, E., & Wasser, A. (1993). *Genius revisited: High IQ children grow up.* Norwood, NJ: Ablex.

Swiatek, M. (1993). A decade of longitudinal research on academic acceleration through the study of mathematically precocious youth. *Roeper Review, 15*(3), 120–123.

Terman, L. (1925). *Mental and physical traits of a thousand gifted children: Vol. 1, Genetic studies of genius.* Stanford, CA: Stanford University Press.

Thomson, D. (2010). Beyond the classroom walls: Teacher's and students' perspectives on how online learning can meet the needs of gifted students. *Journal of Advanced Academics, 21*(4), 662–712.

Tomlinson, C. (1994). Gifted learners: The boomerang kids of middle school? *Roeper Review, 16*(3), 177–181.

Tomlinson, C. (1999). *The differentiated classroom: Responding to the needs of all learners.* Alexandria, VA: Association for Supervision and Curriculum Development.

Torrance, E. (1966, 1998). *Torrance Tests of Creative Thinking: Norms and technical manual.* Bensenville, IL: Scholastic Testing Service.

Torrance, E. (1969). Creative positives of disadvantaged children and youth. *Gifted Child Quarterly, 13,* 71–81.

Ward, V. (1961). *Educating the gifted: An axiomatic approach.* Columbus, OH: Charles Merrill.

Wechsler, D. (2003). *Wechsler Intelligence Scale for Children–Fourth Edition.* San Antonio, TX: Psychological Corporation.

Weinfeld, R., Barnes-Robinson, L., Jeweler, S., & Shevitz, B. (2005). What we learned: Experiences in providing adaptations and accommodations for gifted and talented students with learning disabilities. *Teaching Exceptional Children, 38*(1), 48–53.

Westberg, K., Archambault, F., Jr., Dobyns, S., & Salvin, T. (1993). The classroom practices observation study. *Journal for the Education of the Gifted, 16*(2), 120–146.

Westberg, K., & Daoust, M. (2003, Fall). The results of the replication of the classroom practices survey replication in two states. *The National Research Center on the Gifted and Talented Newsletter,* pp. 3–8.

Williams, F. (1993). *Creativity assessment packet.* Austin, TX: Pro-Ed.

Woodcock, R., McGrew, K., & Mather, N. (2001). *Woodcock-Johnson III Tests of Achievement.* Itasca, IL: Riverside.

Wyner, J., Bridgeland, J., & Diiulio, J. (2007). *Achievement trap: How America is failing millions of high-achieving students from lower-income families.* Retrieved November 17, 2013, from http://www.jkcf.org/news-knowledge/

Photo Credits

Name Index

Subject Index

Note: Boxes, figures, and tables are marked as *b, f, and t,* respectively.

DABS (Diagnostic Adaptive Behavior
   Scale), 164
*Daniel R.R. v. State Board of
   Education,* 44t
Davis, Catherine, 420–421b
Deaf culture, 431–432, 438
"Deaf Donald" (Silverstein), 414f
Deaf-blindness, 488–489, 489t, 493b,
   507–508, 509, 518–520
Deafness
   sibling's perspective of, 121b
   student's perspective on, 427b
   term usage, 401
   See also Hearing impairments
Deal, Drexel, 153
DeHaven, Erin, 566–567b
Deinstitutionalization, 169
Developing and Assessing Products
   (DAP) Tool, 547
Developmental, Individual-Difference,
   Relationship-Based Model (DIR®/
   Floortime), 344t
Developmental delay, 6–8, 170
Developmental language delay, 379
Dexedrine, 271t
Diagnostic Adaptive Behavior Scale
   (DABS), 164
*Diagnostic and Statistical Manual
   of Mental Disorders* (American
   Psychiatric Association), 222, 251,
   289, 331–332, 332t
Diana v. State Board of Education, 43t
Diderot, D., 450
Differentiated instruction,
   557, 558b, 565b
Digital texts, 140–141, 148
Direct Instruction (DI), 231–232
Disability
   definition of, 5
   government legislation on, 45, 50–55
   labeling of, 11–12, 55–56
   prevalence rates, 12–14
   vs. handicap, 6
   See also specific disabilities
Discrete Trial Training (DTT), 344t
Discrimination
   in assessments, 96–97
   college and university accommodation
      requirements, 239
   labeling, effects of, 12
   participatory, 6
Diversity. *See* Cultural diversity; Minority
   students
Dix, Dorothea Lynde, 17t
Doctor's office effect, 260
Down, John Langdon, 170
Down syndrome
   chorionic villus sampling (CVS),
      171–172
   description of, 170–171
   hearing loss and, 411t
   intellectual disability, levels of, 172

life expectancies, 172
physical characteristics, 172
   See also Intellectual disabilities
Drop-out rates, 236, 315
Duchenne muscular dystrophy, 499
Dyslexia, 217, 237b

Early childhood special education,
   32, 146, 569–571, 570t
   See also Early intervention
Early intervention, 32, 65–66
   behavioral or emotional disorders,
      314–315
   hearing impairments, 423–424, 426
   intellectual disabilities, 189–193
   learning disabilities, 233–235
   physical or health disabilities,
      520–521
   speech or language impairments,
      387–390
   visual impairments, 468–469
Educable mentally retarded
   (EMR), 166
Educating the Gifted (Ward), 550
Education for All Handicapped Children
   Act, 208, 550
Education of the Handicapped Act
   Amendments of 1986, 31
Educational reform. *See* Standards-
   based education and reform
Educational rights. *See* Legislation and
   litigation, role in special education
Educational settings/options
   ADHD and, 262–263
   behavioral or emotional disorders and,
      303–304, 304f
   challenges/controversies about, 69–70
   continuum of services model,
      68–69, 69f
   historical timeline of, 72f
   intelligence disabilities and,
      180–182, 182f
   learning disabilities and,
      227–228, 228f
   least restrictive environment (LRE)
      principle, 67–69, 71
   mainstreaming, 70–71
   regular education initiative (REI),
      71–72
   types of, 67t, 68f
   See also Classroom settings;
      Curriculum, educational;
      Inclusion/integration
Educational teams, 22–24, 22f
Educational technology, definition of,
   131–132
   See also Assistive technology
Elementary and Secondary Education
   Act. *See* No Child Left Behind Act
   of 2001
Emotional disorders. *See* Behavioral or
   emotional disorders

*The Emotionally Disturbed Child in the
   Classroom* (Hewett), 293t
Employment
   ADHD and, 276
   autism spectrum disorders and,
      351–352
   learning disabilities and, 239–240
   supported competitive
      employment, 522
   See also Vocational training
The Empty Fortress (Bettelheim), 334
Encephalitis, 176
Engelmann, S., 231
English as a second language, 29
English learners (ELs), 85–89, 88b, 89b
Environmental conditions, effect of,
   175–177, 216, 256
Environmental control unit (ECU), 528
Epilepsy, 504
Epilepsy Foundation of America, 491
E-text or digital text, 140–141
Ethnicity and race. *See* Cultural diversity;
   Minority students
Ethnocentrism, 84
Etiology. *See specific disabilities*
Eugenics movement, 106–107
Exceptional children, definition of, 4–5
Executive functions, 255
External locus of control, 178
Eye functioning, 448–449, 449t,
   450f, 453–455
   See also Visual impairments

Familiality studies, 215
Family involvement
   ADHD and home–school
      collaboration, 266, 267b,
      271–272, 275b
   autism spectrum disorders and,
      349b, 352–353
   behavioral or emotional disorders and,
      317–318
   culturally/linguistically diverse families,
      working with, 122–125
   educational teaming models and,
      23–24
   family systems model,
      109–112, 110f
   family-centered early intervention,
      192–193, 317–318
   family-directed assessment, 384
   with gifted and talented students,
      572–573, 572t
   grandparents, effects on, 119–120
   hearing impairments and, 430–431
   historical context of, 105–109,
      107f, 108t
   information sharing, importance of,
      191b, 235b
   intellectual disability and, 196, 197b
   learning disability and, 240
   marital relationships, effect on, 117

About the Contributors

Carol Allison

Carol Allison is a former instructor in the Program for the Visually Impaired, Department of Curriculum and Instruction, University of Alabama at Birmingham (UAB). She also served as the project coordinator for the Alabama Deafblind Project and as a consultant to local and state education agencies as well as families of children with visual impairments. She received her MA from UAB and completed her postgraduate certification in the area of deaf-blind/multihandicapped. She served as an adjunct faculty member at UAB from 1979 until she became a full-time faculty member in 1999.

Ms. Allison is a native of Louisiana, where she earned her undergraduate degree and worked with children with hearing impairments and emotional disabilities. She has worked in both the public and private sectors of general and special education for the past forty years.

Ms. Allison's special interests focused on the development of a statewide program for creating and promoting arts programs for individuals with disabilities. She was also instrumental in establishing distance education teacher training programs in the field of visual impairments. Additionally, she has been involved in the development and implementation of a program providing vision services to individuals living in poverty in Alabama.

Ms. Allison has made numerous professional presentations to local, state, and international conferences and has served on advisory boards for many educational and civic organizations.

Emily Bouck

Emily Bouck is an Associate Professor of Special Education in the Department of Counseling, Educational Psychology, and Special Education at Michigan State University. She received her doctorate in special education from Michigan State University. Dr. Bouck is the author of numerous peer-reviewed journal articles and chapters relating to her two main areas of research: mathematics education for students with disabilities and functional life-skills education for students with disabilities with a central theme of assistive technology throughout both areas. Dr. Bouck is a Past President of the Division on Autism and Developmental Disabilities of the Council for Exceptional Children and has also been active in the Technology and Media Division of the Council for Exceptional Children. Dr. Bouck taught courses on assistive technology; social, legal, and ethical issues in special education; special education methods; and doctoral seminars. She has experience working with a range of students with disabilities in school-settings from preschool through age 26.

Kathryn Wolff Heller

Kathryn Wolff Heller is a professor of special education at Georgia State University, where she coordinates a master's program in physical and health disabilities.

She also advises and teaches students who are working toward their doctorate with a concentration in the area of physical and health disabilities. In addition, she directs several projects, including a statewide grant that provides technical assistance to school personnel and families in the area of deaf-blindness.

Dr. Heller, a registered nurse with experience in pediatric medicine, worked for five years in intensive care units and then went on to obtain master's and doctoral degrees in special education. She has worked as a classroom teacher of students with orthopedic impairments, intellectual disability, traumatic brain injury, and visual impairments. She has coauthored several books as well as numerous book chapters and journal articles. She chairs and participates on several advisory boards and committees, and she makes frequent presentations. One of her primary interests is in providing effective educational instruction and health care for students with physical, sensory, and health impairments.

Betty Nelson

Betty Nelson, PhD, is an associate professor in the Department of Curriculum and Instruction at the University of Alabama at Birmingham. Dr. Nelson has taught undergraduate and graduate students in special education and has teaching experience in programs serving children with disabilities ranging from early intervention to postsecondary education. Her experience includes working with children in all areas of disabilities within public schools, private institutions, home-based settings, and hospital-based settings. Assistive and instructional technology is the main focus of her teaching, research, and service activities.

Dr. Nelson has authored several books, monographs, teacher training modules, and multimedia resources. She has given numerous presentations to local, state, national, and international conferences. She also served as the president of the Technology and Media (TAM) Division of the Council for Exceptional Children. In addition, she has been the president of the Special Education Technology and Special Interest Group (SETSIG) of the International Society for Technology in Education (ISTE).

Julia Link Roberts

Julia Link Roberts, EdD, is the Mahurin Professor of Gifted Studies at Western Kentucky University. She is also executive director of the Center for Gifted Studies and the Carol Martin Gatton Academy of Mathematics and Science in Kentucky. She was honored in 2001 as the first recipient of the National Association for Gifted Children David W. Belin Advocacy Award. Dr. Roberts serves on the boards of the Kentucky Association for Gifted Education and the Association for the Gifted, an affiliate of the Council for Exceptional Children, and she is a member of the Executive Committee of the World Council for Gifted and Talented Children. She has published several books, chapters, and journal articles and is a frequent speaker at state, national, and international meetings. *Strategies for Differentiating Instruction: Best Practices for the Classroom,* coauthored with Tracy Inman, received the Legacy Book Award for the 2009 outstanding book for educators in gifted education, awarded by the Texas Association for the Gifted and Talented. As the founding director of the Center for Gifted Studies, Dr. Roberts has initiated and implemented many programs and services for children and adolescents who are gifted and talented as well as for educators and parents. She earned a BA at the University of Missouri and an EdD at Oklahoma State University.

Mary Jean Sanspree

Mary Jean Sanspree, PhD, was previously on the faculty of the School of Optometry at the University of Alabama at Birmingham (UAB). Dr. Sanspree was a research professor in the School of Education at UAB and an associate scientist in the UAB Vision Science Research Center. She served as president of the Division on Visual Impairments, Council for Exceptional Children, and is a member of the National Institutes of Health National Eye Institute Public Liaison Program Committee. Dr. Sanspree also chaired the Alabama Early Intervention Interagency Coordinating Personnel Preparation Committee among other service responsibilities. She has conducted research on rural eye care and access to eye care for persons with diabetes and glaucoma.

Dr. Sanspree has trained teachers in the field of visual impairments in developing countries and has published extensively on the topics of Braille literacy, distance education, multiple disabilities, and dual sensory impairment as well as low vision habilitation. She serves on the Helen Keller Birthplace Foundation board of directors and has been associated with the Helen Keller Art Show of Alabama and the Helen Keller International Art Show since its inception in 1984.

About the Author

I have always wanted to be a teacher. I guess I am a rarity in that I never changed my undergraduate major or left the field of education. Teaching must be in my blood. I grew up in Staten Island, New York, in the shadows of Willowbrook State School, a very large residential facility serving individuals with developmental disabilities. As I recall, my initial exposure to people with disabilities occurred when I was about 10 or 12 years of age and encountered some of the residents from Willowbrook enjoying the park that was adjacent to their campus. This experience made a huge impression on me and, in some unknown way, most likely instilled within me a desire to work with people with disabilities.

I left New York City in 1965 and headed west—all the way to western Nebraska where I began my undergraduate education at Hiram Scott College in Scottsbluff. Three years later I was teaching fourth graders in the Milwaukee public schools while working toward my master's degree in intellectual disability at the University of Wisconsin–Milwaukee. At the conclusion of my first year of teaching I was asked to teach a class of young children with intellectual disability. I jumped at the opportunity and for the next three years essentially became an early childhood special educator. It was at this point in my career that I decided to earn my doctorate. I resigned my teaching position and moved to Madison, where I pursued a PhD in the areas of human learning, child development, and behavioral disabilities. Upon receiving my degree I accepted a faculty position in the Department of Special Education at Bowling Green State University (Ohio), where for the next eight years I was a teacher educator. In 1982 I moved to Birmingham, Alabama, and joined the faculty of the University of Alabama at Birmingham (UAB), where I currently serve as a professor in the Department of Curriculum and Instruction.

I have enjoyed a rich and rewarding professional career spanning more than four decades. During the course of this journey I have had the privilege of twice serving as president of the Alabama Federation, Council for Exceptional Children; serving as president of the Division of International Special Education and Services (DISES), Council for Exceptional Children; and, most recently, serving as president of the Division on Autism and Developmental Disabilities (DADD), Council for Exceptional Children. I have lectured abroad extensively and was a Fulbright Scholar to the Czech Republic in 1991. In 2007 I was invited to serve as a Distinguished Visiting Professor, Charles University, Prague, Czech Republic.

I mentioned earlier that teaching has always been my passion. In 1999 I was fortunate to receive UAB's President's Award for Excellence in Teaching. In 2007 I received the Jasper Harvey Award from the Alabama Federation of the Council for Exceptional Children in recognition of being named an outstanding teacher educator in the state.

Because of my background in both educational psychology and special education, my research has appeared in a wide variety of professional journals including *Child Development, Journal of Educational Research, Journal of Learning Disabilities, American Journal of Mental Deficiency, Childhood Education, Journal of Visual Impairment and Blindness, British Journal of Developmental Psychology, Journal of Special Education, Early Childhood Education Journal, International Journal of Clinical Neuropsychology,* and *International Journal of Special Education,* among many others.

In addition to the present text, I have authored or coauthored ten books, ranging in topics from counseling parents of children with disabilities to child abuse, early childhood education, early childhood special education, and, most recently, teaching in inclusive classrooms.